Prentice Hall
LITERATURE
Timeless Voices, Timeless Themes

WORLD LITERATURE

Prentice
Hall

Upper Saddle River, New Jersey
Needham, Massachusetts
Glenview, Illinois

ISBN 0-13-050836-5
4 5 6 7 8 9 10   04 03 02 01

ACKNOWLEDGMENTS

Grateful acknowledgment is made to the following for permission to reprint copyrighted material:

Isabel Allende "Writing as an Act of Hope" by Isabel Allende from *Paths of Resistance* (anthology). Copyright © 1989 by Isabel Allende. Used by permission of the author.

Agencia Literaria Carmen Balcells S.A. "El lago Titicaca" ("Lake Titicaca") by Miguel Angel Asturias, from *America, fabula de fabulas*. © 1972. "Usos y abusos del paraguas" ("Uses and Abuses of the Umbrella") by Gabriel García Márquez, from Obra periodística, vol. 2. Copyright © 1982 by Gabriel García Márquez. Used by permission.

Athlore Press "Mirabeau Bridge" by Guillaume Apollinaire, translated by William Meredith from *Alcools: Poems 1898–1913*. Translation copyright © 1963, 1964 by William Meredith.

Nguyen Ngoc Bich "Thoughts of Hanoi" by Nguyen Thi Vinh from *A Thousand Years of Vietnamese Poetry*, edited by Nguyen Ngoc Bich. © 1962, 1967, 1968, 1969, 1970, 1971, 1974 by The Asia Society and Nguyen Ngoc Bich. Used by permission.

Chana Bloch "Pride" from *The Window* by Dahlia Ravikovitch, translated by Chana Bloch and Ariel Bloch, Sheep Meadow Press, 1989. Copyright © 1989. Reprinted by permission.

Robert Bly "Cristobal Miranda" by Pablo Neruda, from *Neruda and Vallejo: Selected Poems,* edited by Robert Bly, Beacon Press, Boston, 1971, 1993. Copyright © 1993 by Robert Bly. "It Was the Grape's Autumn/Era el otoño de las uvas" by Pablo Neruda, translated by James Wright and Robert Bly, and "To My Brother Miguel/A mi hermano Miguel" by César Vallejo, translated by John Knoepfle and James Wright from *Neruda and Vallejo: Selected Poems,* edited by Robert Bly. Copyright © 1971 by Robert Bly. Used by permission of Robert Bly.

Georges Borchardt, Inc. "Claude Monet or The World Upside Down" by Michael Butor, translated from the French by Joan Templeton and Richard Howard, originally appeared in *Antaeus* 21–22, Spring/Summer 1976. Copyright © 1976 by Michael Butor. Used by permission.

(Acknowledgments continue on p.1145)

Prentice Hall
LITERATURE
Timeless Voices, Timeless Themes

Copper

Bronze

Silver

Gold

Platinum

World Literature

The American Experience

The British Tradition

Introduction to World Literature

Themes in World Literature

Suspense

Striving for Success

Themes in World Literature

Conflicts

Themes in World Literature

Turning Points

Unit 5

Themes in World Literature

Expanding Horizons

Literary Forms in World Literature

Unit 6

Short Stories

Unit 7

Literary Forms in World Literature

Nonfiction

Drama

Unit
9

Literary Forms in World Literature

Poetry

Literary Forms in World Literature

Epics and Legends

Additional Readings and Resources

ANALYZING REAL-WORLD TEXTS

LITERATURE IN TRANSLATION: PAIRED READINGS IN ENGLISH AND SPANISH

Complete Contents by Genre

SHORT STORIES, FABLES, AND PARABLES

POETRY

Complete Contents by Genre

POETRY (CONTINUED)

Complete Contents by Genre

DRAMA

NONFICTION

Complete Contents by Genre

Complete Contents by Theme

Complete Contents by Theme

Complete Contents by Theme

Complete Contents by Theme

Complete Contents by Region

Complete Contents by Region

Complete Contents by Region

Complete Contents by Chronology

Complete Contents by Chronology

Complete Contents by Chronology

Walking Lions in Relief (detail), Babylon, The Metropolitan Museum of Art

Introduction to World Literature

For hundreds of thousands of years, people have been building, fighting, striving, praying, and dreaming. In times before recorded history, they spoke of their dreams, prayers, and ambitions in tales they told around campfires. However, only in the last five thousand years or so, with the invention of writing, have people made a more permanent record of their deepest thoughts and feelings. This inspired record—in the form of poems, dramas, epics, legends, myths, and stories—is world literature. It is an account of the human spirit.

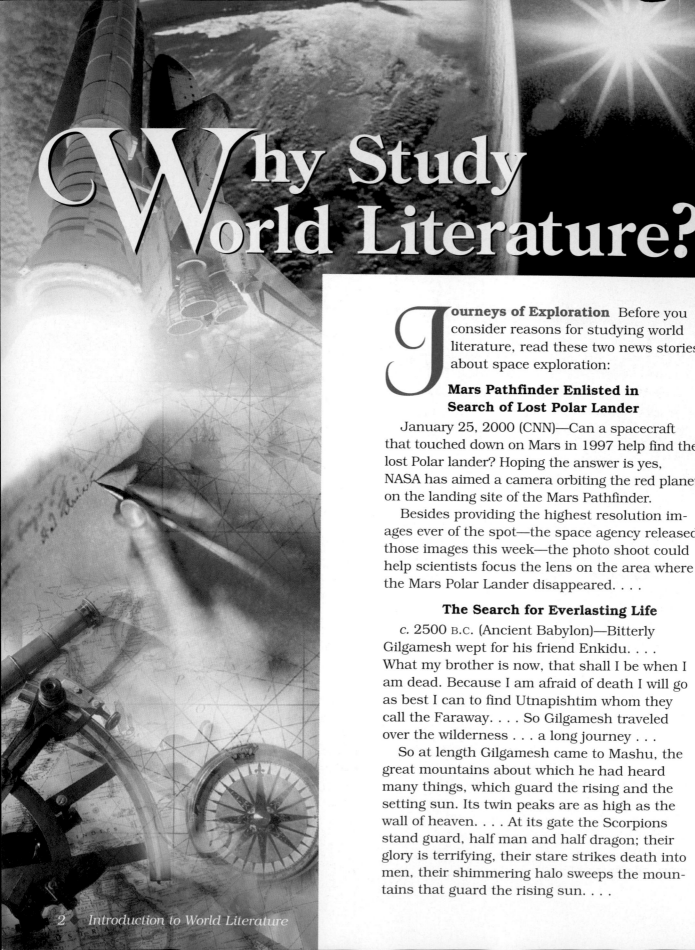

Why Study World Literature?

Journeys of Exploration Before you consider reasons for studying world literature, read these two news stories about space exploration:

Mars Pathfinder Enlisted in Search of Lost Polar Lander

January 25, 2000 (CNN)—Can a spacecraft that touched down on Mars in 1997 help find the lost Polar lander? Hoping the answer is yes, NASA has aimed a camera orbiting the red planet on the landing site of the Mars Pathfinder.

Besides providing the highest resolution images ever of the spot—the space agency released those images this week—the photo shoot could help scientists focus the lens on the area where the Mars Polar Lander disappeared. . . .

The Search for Everlasting Life

c. 2500 B.C. (Ancient Babylon)—Bitterly Gilgamesh wept for his friend Enkidu. . . . What my brother is now, that shall I be when I am dead. Because I am afraid of death I will go as best I can to find Utnapishtim whom they call the Faraway. . . . So Gilgamesh traveled over the wilderness . . . a long journey . . .

So at length Gilgamesh came to Mashu, the great mountains about which he had heard many things, which guard the rising and the setting sun. Its twin peaks are as high as the wall of heaven. . . . At its gate the Scorpions stand guard, half man and half dragon; their glory is terrifying, their stare strikes death into men, their shimmering halo sweeps the mountains that guard the rising sun. . . .

Both of these stories, which are separated by a gap of some 4,500 years, give "news" of explorations. The first describes a recent episode in our exploration of outer space, often called the "last frontier." The second account, from the epic of Gilgamesh, a classic of world literature, tells of an ancient Sumerian king and his search. This king travels beyond the bounds of the world he knows to find the secret of eternal life. He, too, is a space explorer.

"News That Stays News" A comparison of these two accounts demonstrates an important reason for studying world literature—it is, in the words of poet Ezra Pound, "news that stays news." It never gets stale because it is never more information. On the contrary, world literature represents what writers of different times and places *made* of the information available to them. It is information that a writer transformed into delight and wisdom.

For example, *Gilgamesh* is thousands of years old, yet it is as fresh as today's headlines. You know that the Middle East has long been mapped out, and you would not expect to find a mountain there that is guarded by "Scorpions." However, you also know that today, just as in the ancient Middle East, there are regions of our universe that are still unexplored—the planets, the solar system, and the distant stars.

Even more important, you know that we still face the same problems that King Gilgamesh did: how to win respect and recognition, how to mourn the death of our loved ones, and how to

come to terms with our own human limitations. The regions we want to explore are not only in the vast darkness of outer space, but also in the vastness of inner space: our hearts and our minds.

For such journeys of exploration, the authors of world literature are perfect guides. Coming from many different eras and cultures, they have all thought about and felt deeply what it is to be human.

Learning About Different Cultures By taking these authors as guides, you will learn not only what you have in common with them, but also how their values, customs, and beliefs differ from yours.

However, don't be put off by the apparent strangeness of the different ways they describe. Take the differences you find as an opportunity, experiencing through literature what it was like to be a teenager in ancient Egypt or a persecuted noble in eighteenth-century France.

The Focus on Culture section in every unit will help you learn more about the world of ancient Greece and Rome, Japan, Africa, China, Latin America, and many other places and cultures. With this knowledge, and with the Background for Understanding that accompanies each selection or group of selections, you will better understand literary works from many different places and times.

You will also understand how differences among cultures cannot hide a common humanity.

Translators: Helping You Get the "News" In addition, you will gain an appreciation for the work of those unsung heroes and heroines of world literature, the translators. Most of the works you will be reading were first written in other languages—Chinese, Japanese, French, German, ancient Babylonian, and more.

By rendering these works in English—*translation* means literally "to carry across from one language to another"—translators make it possible for you to get the "news" from world literature.

To learn more about translation, read the Comparing Translations feature, p. 14, and Beyond Literature feature on translations of the Bible, p. 70. Also, look at the section called Literature in Translation on p. 1074. It contains original works in Spanish presented alongside English translations. Even if you cannot read the originals, seeing them will give you a sense of another culture.

Simple Curiosity Apart from any lofty reasons for studying world literature, you will enjoy reading it just to satisfy your curiosity about different times, places, and events. Dramas, stories, essays, and poems from other cultures will help you answer questions like these:

- Why did medieval Japanese nobles give official titles to their pets?
  —See *The Pillow Book*, p. 23.

- What happened in "the most terrible and destructive fire" that ancient Rome experienced?
  —See "The Burning of Rome," p. 246.

- How did a New Zealander and a Nepalese Sherpa climb Mt. Everest?
  —See "The Final Assault" and "The Dream Comes True," pp. 142 and 154.

- What was the role of women in nineteenth-century European society?
  —See *A Doll's House*, p. 852.

"The One Great Heart" A final reason for studying world literature is that it takes on greater importance in an era when you can view the Earth from the moon. Photographs taken by astronauts show our cloud-wrapped, blue jewel of a planet alone in outer space. This dramatic new perspective is an immediate and convincing argument for our common humanity.

In world literature of the past and present, that humanity is on display. Alexander Solzhenitsyn, a Nobel Prize–winner from Russia, calls world literature "the one great heart" of our time. He hopes that today's writers, from every corner of the globe, will be a force for truth and justice.

Solzhenitsyn is right to place such hopes in literature. In no other era have writers been needed so much as a heart and conscience for the world. New technologies like the Internet can transmit information from place to place in the blink of an eye. However, information by itself can never replace the wisdom and delight found in literary works.

From France to Colombia, from Senegal to China, poems and stories link up to form a powerful Internet of the imagination. You can gain access to that Net—and explore regions you never dreamed of—by reading world literature.

Voices

from World Literature

In pursuit of learning one knows more every day; in pursuit of the Way one does less every day. One does less and less until one does nothing at all, and when one does nothing at all there is nothing that is undone.

> —**Lao Tzu** (fl. sixth century B.C.)
> *Tao Te Ching*
> **China**

Tell everyone//Now, today, I shall/sing beautifully for/my friends' pleasure.

> —**Sappho** (c. 630 B.C.–570 B.C.)
> **Ancient Greece**

I have written a book that neither the wrath of love, nor fire, nor the sword, nor devouring age shall be able to destroy.

> —**Ovid** (43 B.C.–A.D. 17)
> *Metamorphoses*
> **Ancient Rome**

It is night and one is expecting a visitor. Suddenly one is startled by the sound of raindrops, which the wind blows against the shutters.

> —**Sei Shōnagon** (A.D. tenth–eleventh centuries)
> *The Pillow Book*
> **Japan**

Men of sound intellect and probity,
   weigh with good understanding what lies
      hidden
behind the veil of my strange
   allegory!

> —**Dante Alighieri** (A.D. 1265–1321)
> the *Inferno*
> **Italy**

A great writer is, so to speak, a second government in his country. And for that reason no regime has ever loved great writers, only minor ones.

> —**Alexander Solzhenitsyn** (1918–)
> *The First Circle*
> **Russia**

Nevertheless, in the face of oppression, pillage and abandonment, our reply is life.

> —**Gabriel García Márquez** (1928–)
> *Nobel Address*
> **Colombia**

There is a sense of wovenness, a wholeness in life here; a feeling of how strange and beautiful people can be—just living.

> —**Bessie Head** (1937–1986)
> *Serowe*
> **Botswana**

Guide for Reading

Ovid (43 B.C.–A.D. 17)

The parents of Roman poet Ovid (äv′ id), whose full name was Publius Ovidius Naso, wanted him to be a lawyer or a politician. They sent him from the family estate, which was 90 miles from Rome, Italy, all the way to Athens, Greece, so that he could complete his studies. However, he soon returned to Rome with the idea of becoming a poet and was instantly successful with his first long poem, "Amores" ("Loves").

That Ovid is read today is a tribute to the timelessness of his poetic themes and stories. Indeed, the characters in Ovid's poems are very much like us.

Beginnings and Endings Ovid created several works of poetry and one play, *Medea* (now lost), all written in Latin, his native language.

Late in his life, Ovid said that he tried to write prose, but it always turned out to be poetry.

Metamorphoses, written in A.D. 8, was his greatest achievement. A poem of nearly 12,000 lines, it tells a series of stories beginning with the creation of the world and ending with the death of the Roman ruler Julius Caesar, murdered the year before Ovid was born. In each story, someone or something undergoes a change. The stories are linked by clever transitions, so that the entire work reads as one long, uninterrupted tale.

The excerpt from *Metamorphoses* reprinted here, "Deucalion and Pyrrha," tells of two people who survive a great flood.

Banishment When Ovid was finishing this poem, the Roman emperor Augustus banished him to a remote village on the Black Sea. The reasons for his exile are not entirely clear, but Augustus might have felt that Ovid endangered public morals.

In any case, banishment to a half-civilized place at the far edge of empire was a severe punishment for this worldly poet. Although he kept his property and continued to write, he was never allowed to return to Rome.

◆ Build Vocabulary

GREEK WORD ROOTS: -crypt-

In "Deucalion and Pyrrha," the couple named in the title consult a goddess. They are puzzled, however, by her "cryptic" saying. From their reaction and the meaning of the Greek root *-crypt-,* "secret" or "hidden," you can figure out that *cryptic* means "having hidden meaning."

WORD BANK

scrupulously
desolation
oracles
implore
cryptic

As you read this epic, you will encounter the words in this list. Each word is defined on the page where it first appears. Preview the list before you read.

◆ Build Grammar Skills

KINDS OF SENTENCES

Four different **kinds of sentences,** classified according to their function, are as follows:

- **Declarative** sentences make statements—
  "It was ocean now, a plain of sudden waters."
- **Imperative** sentences express commands or requests—
  "Go from the temple/ . . . and throw/ Your mother's bones behind you!"
- **Interrogative** sentences ask questions—
  "Who would console your grief?"
- **Exclamatory** sentences convey strong emotions and end with an exclamation mark—
  "O my wife,/ The only woman, now, . . . look!"

Notice how the examples from "Deucalion and Pyrrha" show Ovid using all four types of sentences.

◆ *Literature and Your Life*

CONNECT YOUR EXPERIENCE

Change is constant in life, although you may not always notice it. However, suppose your own growth from infancy until now were compressed into a film lasting less than a minute. By speeding up natural processes, this film would make the reality of physical changes seem like dramatic science fiction.

Ovid, the author of *Metamorphoses,* was haunted by the idea of such fantastic changes. The transformation at the end of "Deucalion and Pyrrha" is like a special effect from the latest science-fiction movie.

THEMATIC FOCUS: TURNING POINTS

Changes in your life are like turning points, moments when you shift direction. Ovid's tale is about a turning point in the life of Earth itself.

Journal Writing Write a brief prediction of your next turning point and where it will take you.

◆ Background for Understanding

CULTURE

In his verse tale, Ovid is creating a literary version of a myth, a story that uses the actions of gods and goddesses to explain events in nature. Myths were part of an early oral culture, in which people told—rather than wrote—stories and changed their tales with every telling. (See p. 10 for a description of the gods and goddesses in this tale.)

Ovid, however, was a well-known poet living at the center of a sophisticated world empire. (See the timeline below.) For him, the myths he retold were primitive and it is unlikely that he believed they were literally true. Instead, he used them to suggest life's wonders while amusing and provoking his readers.

Some Dates in the Rise of the Roman Empire

753 B.C.	509 B.C.	275 B.C.	27 B.C.
Founding of Rome	Founding of Roman Republic	Rome defeats all other Italian groups	Roman Empire begins to flower under Augustus

◆ Literary Focus

MOTIF OF TRANSFORMATION

A **motif** (mō tēf) is a repeated incident or device in a literary work, and incidents of **transformation,** dramatic change, are a motif in Ovid's *Metamorphoses.* Writers often use such motifs to organize long narratives, whether in prose or verse.

Miraculous transformations, like that at the end of "Deucalion and Pyrrha," occur repeatedly throughout *Metamorphoses.* (The title of the epic means "changes.") These changes link the many stories. Also, they show the author's taste for the strange and marvelous and his underlying belief that nothing in life disappears: Everything continues by changing.

Reading for Success

Strategies for Reading World Literature

When traveling in foreign countries, you need strategies to cope with different languages, customs, dress, and forms of currency. Reading world literature is like traveling in foreign countries. Translators can help you with your "travels" by creating English versions of selections written in a foreign language. However, you can also help yourself by mastering these strategies.

Use text aids to clarify puzzling words or passages.

When you come to a footnote number in a selection, read the footnote at the bottom of the page. Footnotes explain foreign words or puzzling expressions and often provide a guide to pronunciation. In reading Ovid's "Deucalion and Pyrrha," also refer to the boxed description of gods and goddesses if you are uncertain about a character's identity.

Compare and contrast the selection with other works.

Think about the similarities and differences between the characters, plot, and setting of the work you are reading and those of other works you have read. For example, consider how "Deucalion and Pyrrha" is like and unlike flood stories from other cultures.

Consider the historical and cultural contexts.

The important events of an author's time are the historical context for a work, and the beliefs and customs of an author's society are the cultural context. See the Background for Understanding on the Guide for Reading page to find out how culture and history have influenced these selections.

Consider the literary context.

The literary context of a work refers to its genre (for example, whether it is a drama, a poem, or a novel) and its form (for example, a poem can be a sonnet or a haiku). To understand genre and form in world literature, learn about the literary customs of writers from different lands and times.

Distinguish culture-specific beliefs from universal values.

Some of the beliefs in a work are valid for people living in any culture or time. Others are specific to a particular culture. For example, in Ovid's tale, the love between Deucalion and Pyrrha and their goodness are universal values. However, their belief in certain gods and goddesses is specific to ancient Roman culture. By distinguishing what is universal from what is culture-specific, you can appreciate the elements of a work that still have meaning today.

As you read the following excerpt from Ovid's *Metamorphoses*, look at the notes in the boxes. These notes demonstrate how to apply these strategies to a work of literature.

from Metamorphoses
"Deucalion and Pyrrha"

Ovid Translated by Rolfe Humphries

Jove, angered by the evil deeds of humans, decides to drown the world in a flood. Working with his brother Neptune, he causes floods that sweep away farms and cities alike. Even tall forests are now underwater, and the domain of the wolf and lion is invaded by fish. The few living creatures that have survived are slowly dying of starvation.

Phocis, a fertile land, while there was land,
Marked off Oetean from Boeotian fields.
It was ocean now, a plain of sudden waters.
There Mount Parnassus lifts its twin peaks skyward,
5   High, steep, cloud-piercing. And Deucalion[1] came there
Rowing his wife. There was no other land,
The sea had drowned it all. And here they worshipped
First the Corycian nymphs and native powers,
Then Themis, oracle and fate-revealer.
10   There was no better man than this Deucalion,
No one more fond of right; there was no woman
More <u>scrupulously</u> reverent than Pyrrha.[2]

◆ **Build Vocabulary**

scrupulously (skr oo ′ pyə ləs lē)
adv.: Acting with care to do the
right or proper thing

---

1. **Deucalion** (d oo kāl′ ē ən).
2. **Pyrrha** (pir′ ə).

Compare and contrast the flood in this tale with that in other works.

So, when Jove saw the world was one great ocean,
Only one woman left of all those thousands,
15 And only one man left of all those thousands,
Both innocent and worshipful, he parted
The clouds, turned loose the North-wind, swept them off,
Showed earth to heaven again, and sky to land,
And the sea's anger dwindled, and King Neptune
20 Put down his trident, calmed the waves, and Triton,
Summoned from far down under, with his shoulders
Barnacle-strewn, loomed up above the waters,
The blue-green sea-god, whose resounding horn
Is heard from shore to shore. Wet-bearded, Triton
25 Set lip to that great shell, as Neptune ordered,
Sounding retreat, and all the lands and waters
Heard and obeyed. The sea has shores; the rivers,
Still running high, have channels; the floods dwindle,
Hill-tops are seen again; the trees, long buried,
30 Rise with their leaves still muddy. The world returns.

Deucalion saw that world, all <u>desolation</u>,
All emptiness, all silence, and his tears
Rose as he spoke to Pyrrha: "O my wife,
The only woman, now, on all this earth,
35 My consort and my cousin and my partner
In these immediate dangers, look! Of all the lands
To East or West, we two, we two alone,
Are all the population. Ocean holds
Everything else; our foothold, our assurance,
40 Are small as they can be, the clouds still frightful.
Poor woman—well, we are not all alone—
Suppose you had been, how would you bear your fear?
Who would console your grief? My wife, believe me,

Gods and Goddesses of the Ancient Romans

Apollo (ə päl′ ō): God of the sun, music, poetry, prophecy, and medicine, usually shown with a bow and arrow.

Jove (jōv): King of the gods, who hurls lightning bolts as weapons.

Neptune (nep′ tōōn′): Jove's brother and ruler of the seas, often shown with a three-pronged spear called a trident.

Themis (thē′ mis): Goddess of law and justice.

Triton (trīt′′n): Sea god with the head and upper body of a man and the tail of a fish, usually shown carrying a trumpet made from a large seashell.

◀ **Critical Viewing** Which details of this picture might suggest a world reborn after a great flood? **[Interpret]**

Had the sea taken you, I would have followed.
45 If only I had the power, I would restore
The nations as my father did, bring clay
To life with breathing. As it is, we two
Are all the human race, so Heaven has willed it,
Samples of men, mere specimens."

                    They wept,
50 And prayed together, and having wept and prayed,
Resolved to make petition to the goddess
To seek her aid through <u>oracles</u>. Together
They went to the river-water, the stream Cephisus,
Still far from clear, but flowing down its channel,
55 And they took river-water, sprinkled foreheads,
Sprinkled their garments, and they turned their steps
To the temple of the goddess, where the altars
Stood with the fires gone dead, and ugly moss
Stained pediment and column. At the stairs
60 They both fell prone, kissed the chill stone in prayer:

◆ **Build Vocabulary**

desolation (des´ ə lā´ shən) *n.*: Characterized by loneliness, emptiness, and destruction

oracles (ôr´ ə kəlz) *n.*: Messages or signs from the gods that reveal special instructions or predict the future

from *Metamorphoses, "Deucalion and Pyrrha"* ◆ 11

"If the gods' anger ever listens
To righteous prayers, O Themis, we <u>implore</u> you,
Tell us by what device our wreck and ruin
May be repaired. Bring aid, most gentle goddess,
To sunken circumstance."

What is
universal about
the emotion
Deucalion and
Pyrrha express
in their prayer?
What is **culture-
specific** about
the prayer?

                    And Themis heard them,
And gave this oracle: "Go from the temple,
Cover your heads, loosen your robes, and throw
Your mother's bones behind you!" Dumb, they stood
In blank amazement, a long silence, broken

70 By Pyrrha, finally: she would not do it!
With trembling lips she prays whatever pardon
Her disobedience might merit, but this outrage
She dare not risk, insult her mother's spirit
By throwing her bones around. In utter darkness

75 They voice the <u>cryptic</u> saying over and over,
What can it mean? They wonder. At last Deucalion
Finds the way out: "I might be wrong, but surely
The holy oracles would never counsel
A guilty act. The earth is our great mother,

80 And I suppose those bones the goddess mentions
Are the stones of earth; the order means to throw them,
The stones, behind us."

                  She was still uncertain,
And he by no means sure, and both distrustful
Of that command from Heaven; but what damage,

Recall the
literary context
by telling how
this passage
(lines 85–98)
links the tale to
all the others
Ovid includes
in his epic.

85 What harm, would there be in trying? They descended,
Covered their heads, loosened their garments, threw
The stones behind them as the goddess ordered.
The stones—who would believe it, had we not
The unimpeachable[3] witness of Tradition?—

90 Began to lose their hardness, to soften, slowly,
To take on form, to grow in size, a little,
Become less rough, to look like human beings,
Or anyway as much like human beings
As statues do, when the sculptor is only starting,

95 Images half blocked out. The earthy portion,
Damp with some moisture, turned to flesh, the solid
Was bone, the veins were as they always had been.
The stones the man had thrown turned into men,

---

3. unimpeachable (un´ im pē´ chə bəl) *adj.*: Undoubtable.

The stones the woman threw turned into women,
100 Such being the will of God. Hence we derive
The hardness that we have, and our endurance
Gives proof of what we have come from.

                                        Other forms
Of life came into being, generated
Out of the earth: the sun burnt off the dampness,
105 Heat made the slimy marshes swell; as seed
Swells in a mother's womb to shape and substance,
So new forms came to life. When the Nile river
Floods and recedes and the mud is warmed by sunshine,
Men, turning over the earth, find living things,
110 And some not living, the nearly so, imperfect,
On the verge of life, and often the same substance
Is part alive, part only clay. When moisture
Unites with heat, life is conceived; all things
Come from this union. Fire may fight with water,
115 But heat and moisture generate all things,
Their discord being productive. So when earth,
After that flood, still muddy, took the heat,
Felt the warm fire of sunlight, she conceived,
Brought forth, after their fashion, all the creatures,
120 Some old, some strange and monstrous.

                                        One, for instance,
She bore unwanted, a gigantic serpent,
Python by name, whom the new people dreaded,
A huge bulk on the mountain-side. Apollo,
God of the glittering bow, took a long time
125 To bring him down, with arrow after arrow
He had never used before except in hunting
Deer and the skipping goats. Out of the quiver
Sped arrows by the thousand, till the monster,
Dying, poured poisonous blood on those black wounds.
130 In memory of this, the sacred games,
Called Pythian, were established, and Apollo
Ordained for all young winners in the races,
On foot or chariot, for victorious fighters,
The crown of oak. That was before the laurel,[4]
135 That was before Apollo wreathed his forehead
With garlands from that tree, or any other.

> What does this passage (102–120) reveal about the **historical context** of this work—especially in terms of the history of science?

---

4. laurel (lôr′ əl) *n.*: Tree whose leaves were used to crown the victors in various contests.

◆ **Build Vocabulary**

implore (im plôr′) *v.*: To ask or beg someone to do something

cryptic (krip′ tik) *adj.*: Secret and mysterious

Comparing Translations

There are two good reasons why Ovid's *Metamorphoses*, like many other classics of world literature, exists in different English versions.

First, as the English language itself changes, translators decide to retranslate works like the *Metamorphoses* in order to make them sound more up-to-date. In addition, translators living at the same time may disagree about how to translate a work. As a result, they may each produce their own version of it, letting readers make the decision as to which is better.

Below are two versions of the beginning of the *Metamorphoses,* from translations made in the 1950's. Compare and contrast them with each other, paying attention to their rhythm, word choice, and sentence structure. Remember that both of these translations, despite their differences, are versions of the same passage.

Comparing and Contrasting Translations

1. Compare the two versions, and answer these questions to identify Ovid's main points:
   a) What is the subject of the poem? **b)** Who will help Ovid with the poem? **c)** What will be the time frame of the poem?
2. In what ways does Gregory expand on these ideas to make his passage one line longer than Humphries's?
3. Which translator uses simpler language and sentence structure? Explain.
4. Which version do you prefer and why? Consider such factors as the ease with which you can read the translation and the attractiveness of the sounds and rhythms.
5. How would you use the evidence from these two versions to answer someone who claimed that translation was a mechanical word-by-word process and not an art?

Translated by Rolfe Humphries	Translated by Horace Gregory
My intention is to tell of bodies changed	Now I shall tell of things that change, new being
To different forms; the gods, who made the changes,	Out of old: since you, O gods, created
Will help me—or I hope so—with a poem	Mutable arts and gifts, give me the voice
That runs from the world's beginnings to our own days.	To tell the shifting story of the world
	From its beginning to the present hour.

Guide for Responding

◆ Literature and Your Life

Reader's Response Does the transformation of the stones remind you of anything you've seen in a film? Why or why not?

Thematic Focus In what way is this whole tale a turning point in the history of the Earth? Explain.

Pantomime Using movement and facial expressions only, show the transformation from stone to human.

Questions for Research Suppose you wanted to learn about the influence of Ovid's *Metamorphoses* on later writers. Formulate several questions that would help guide your research.

☑ Check Your Comprehension

1. What qualities of Deucalion and Pyrrha cause Jove to make the floodwaters retreat?
2. For what purpose do Deucalion and Pyrrha seek the aid of Themis?
3. In what way does Deucalion interpret the goddess's message?
4. Briefly describe what happens when Deucalion and Pyrrha obey the goddess.
5. How do creatures other than humans come into existence?

Guide for Responding (continued)

◆ Critical Thinking

INTERPRET

1. What does Deucalion mean when he says that he and his wife are "Samples of men, mere specimens?" **[Interpret]**
2. How do the couple demonstrate their virtue as the tale unfolds? **[Support]**
3. What moral or lesson does this story suggest? Explain. **[Draw Conclusions]**

EVALUATE

4. Is Ovid more interested in teaching a lesson or in entertaining? Explain. **[Assess]**

EXTEND

5. What scientific misconceptions does Ovid express in lines 102–120? **[Science Link]**

◆ Reading for Success

STRATEGIES FOR READING WORLD LITERATURE

Review the reading strategies and the notes showing how to read world literature. Then apply the strategies to answer the following questions.

1. Basing your answer on a text aid, explain why Deucalion and Pyrrha turn to Themis in their need.
2. In lines 50–65, which elements are universal and which are culture-specific? Explain.
3. Compare and contrast the account of creation in "Deucalion and Pyrrha" with that in another creation story you know.

◆ Literary Focus

THE MOTIF OF TRANSFORMATION

A repeated element or recurring theme in a literary work is a **motif,** and Ovid linked the tales in *Metamorphoses* by using the motif of **transformation**—"bodies changed/To different forms," as he says at the start of the epic. In "Deucalion and Pyrrha," Ovid uses vivid details to describe how stones become human.

1. Find two vivid details in the description, and explain how they make the change seem both real and miraculous.
2. Even before this moment of transformation, how does Earth itself change during this tale?

◆ Build Vocabulary

USING THE GREEK ROOT -crypt-

Knowing that the root *-crypt-* means "secret," find the meaning of the italicized words.

1. A puzzling *cryptogram* arrived in the mail from one of our spies.
2. Unable to understand it, we took it to an expert called a *cryptographer.*
3. After several days, the expert sent the results of her *cryptanalysis.*
4. She used a *cryptograph* to decipher the code.

USING THE WORD BANK: Synonyms

Write on your paper the word whose meaning is closest to the meaning of the word from the Word Bank.

1. countenance: (a) face, (b) beard, (c) wings
2. hoary: (a) curly, (b) long, (c) gray
3. scrupulously: (a) quickly, (b) usually, (c) carefully
4. desolation: (a) devastation, (b) desert, (c) mud
5. oracles: (a) predictions, (b) complaints, (c) gifts
6. implore: (a) question, (b) beg, (c) fear
7. cryptic: (a) scary, (b) deadly, (c) mysterious

◆ Build Grammar Skills

KINDS OF SENTENCES

Ovid uses four **kinds of sentences:**
- **declarative,** which makes a statement;
- **imperative,** which expresses a command or request;
- **interrogative,** which asks a question; and
- **exclamatory,** which expresses a strong emotion.

Practice Identify each type of sentence by writing on your paper its number and the word *declarative, imperative, interrogative,* or *exclamatory.*

1. Jove decided to drown the world.
2. He was helped by Neptune.
3. Why were the sacred games called "Pythian"?
4. Do not question what the oracle says.
5. Ovid is cool!

Writing Application Using the four kinds of sentences, write a brief dialogue between Jove and Neptune that occurs as the flood subsides.

*B*uild *Y*our *P*ortfolio

Idea Bank

Writing

1. **Description** In your own words, describe how Jove's flood transforms the Earth.

2. **Film Treatment** Explain how you would adapt for film the transformation described in lines 90–99. Use terms like *cut* ("end a scene quickly"), *fade* ("end a scene gradually"), *close-up* ("shot at close range"), and *long shot* ("shot at far range"). **[Performing Arts Link]**

3. **Response to Criticism** Poet, translator, and critic Horace Gregory declared that Ovid "excelled . . . in the rapid unfolding of a narrative." Using evidence from "Deucalion and Pyrrha," support or refute this statement.

Speaking, Listening, and Viewing

4. **Retelling of a Myth** In your own words, retell Ovid's tale for the class. Keep the story basically the same, but add details to make the transformation of stones into humans even more vivid. **[Performing Arts Link]**

5. **Dramatic Speech** As one of the humans just created from a stone, say something to your benefactors, Deucalion and Pyrrha. **[Performing Arts Link]**

Researching and Representing

6. **Comparision and Contrast** Read "The Story of the Flood" in the epic of Gilgamesh, p. 53. Then compare and contrast that tale with the flood story Ovid tells in "Deucalion and Pyrrha."

7. **Map of Exile** Using a historical atlas, draw a map of the Roman Empire in Ovid's time. On your map, trace the route that Ovid might have taken from Rome to his place of exile—on the site of present-day Constanta in Romania. **[Social Studies Link]**

Online Activity www.phlit.phschool.com

Guided Writing Lesson

Cause-Effect Analysis

Like "Deucalion and Pyrrha," many works of literature deal with transformations. Choose a work in which the transformation is more explainable than it is in Ovid's tale. Also, the change can be one that occurs within a person's mind and heart, rather than a physical change. Write an essay in which you briefly describe the transformation, then analyze what brought it about and what results it had.

Writing Skills Focus: Transitions to Show Cause and Effect

In writing a cause-effect analysis, you need to use **transitions to show cause and effect**—words that show how one thing brings another about or results from it. In lines 116–118 of "Deucalion and Pyrrha," for example, Ovid writes: "*So* when Earth . . . still muddy, took the heat . . . she conceived . . ." The transition *so* indicates that Earth's conceiving resulted from "the heat." Other cause-effect transitions are:
Cause: all things considered, because, since
Result: as a result, consequently, for this reason, obviously, so, therefore

Prewriting Choose a work to write about, identify the central change it describes, and diagram the causes and effects of that change in a flowchart.

Drafting Referring to your diagram, begin by describing the transformation as vividly as possible. Include brief quotations from the work to give your description more flavor. Then, explain the causes and effects of the change, using cause-effect transitions.

Revising Have classmates read your analysis and tell you whether or not they understand what the change was, what brought it about, and what effects it had. If its causes or effects are unclear to them, consider inserting cause-effect transitions to clarify your analysis.

PART 1 *Classics of World Literature*

Wall Painting of a Bird in a Garden, Pompeii, Accademia Italiana, London

Guide for Reading

Lao Tzu *(fl. sixth century B.C.)*

Lao Tzu (lou´ dzu´), which means "Old Master," is the author of the *Tao Te Ching,* or *The Way and Its Power,* one of the basic texts of Taoist philosophy. According to legend, Lao Tzu, unhappy with the political situation of his day, attempted to leave China through a mountain pass in the west. The gatekeeper of the pass recognized him as a wise and learned man, and refused to let him through until he would write down some words of wisdom. Lao Tzu then wrote the *Tao Te Ching* and was allowed to depart.

T'ao Ch'ien *(365–427)*

T'ao Ch'ien (dou´ chen´) was born into a family of government officials in China. When he was thirty-five, he resigned from his government position and settled on a rural farm. There he lived quietly with his family and wrote poetry that expressed his philosophy of living a tranquil life.

Sei Shōnagon *(10th–11th centuries A.D.)*

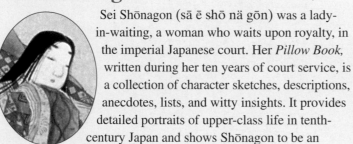

Sei Shōnagon (sā ē shō nä gōn) was a lady-in-waiting, a woman who waits upon royalty, in the imperial Japanese court. Her *Pillow Book,* written during her ten years of court service, is a collection of character sketches, descriptions, anecdotes, lists, and witty insights. It provides detailed portraits of upper-class life in tenth-century Japan and shows Shōnagon to be an intelligent, observant, and quick-witted woman.

Matsuo Bashō *(1644–1694)*

Matsuo Bashō (mä tzōō ō bä shō) was born into a samurai family and began studying poetry at an early age. Eventually, he moved to an isolated hut on the outskirts of Edo (now Tokyo, Japan) and lived the life of a hermit. A master of poetic forms, Bashō traveled the countryside teaching others.

◆ Build Vocabulary

LATIN PREFIXES con-, com-

In the *Tao Te Ching,* Lao Tzu counsels, "Not to honor men of worth will keep people from contention." The word *contention,* which means "the act of dispute, struggle, or quarrel," is derived from the Latin prefix *com-,* meaning "together" and *tendere,* meaning to "stretch." Lao Tzu's message is that if people place less value on social rank and position, they will avoid disputes.

WORD BANK

myriad
manifestations
manifold
contention
calamity
submissive
earnest
chastised
loathsome

As you read these selections, you will encounter the words on this list. Each word is defined on the page where it first appears. Before reading, preview these words from the selections.

◆ Build Grammar Skills

ACTIVE AND PASSIVE VOICE

A verb is in the **active voice** when the subject of the sentence performs the action. A verb is in the **passive voice** when the action is performed on the subject. The passive voice uses a form of the helping verb *be.*

You will see examples of both the active voice and the passive voice in these selections. In some cases, translators have used the passive voice to remain faithful to the spirit of the Chinese or Japanese original.

Active Voice: I *built* my house near where others dwell . . .

Passive Voice: Seven sights *were veiled* in mist.

from the Tao Te Ching ◆ I Built My House Near Where Others Dwell ◆ Haiku ◆ from The Pillow Book

◆ Literature and Your Life

CONNECT YOUR EXPERIENCE

When you consider choosing a career or making any important choice, you may picture yourself at a crossroads. This image of a crossroads, a place where ways divide and you must choose one direction or another, is a common one in Western life and literature.

However, in the *Tao Te Ching,* a Chinese work of philosophy, there is no such thing as a crossroads. There is only the one true Way.

THEMATIC FOCUS: HUMANS AND NATURE

The images in these selections may lead you to ask: Why do these writers and poets frequently focus on nature?

Journal Writing Jot down an image from nature that you might be inspired to write about.

◆ Background for Understanding

CULTURE

The *Tao Te Ching* is the chief work of the Chinese philosophical school of Taoism (dou´ iz´ əm). Founded very early in China's history, Taoism stresses freedom, simplicity, and the contemplation of nature. Taoist philosophy encourages its followers to embrace a simple lifestyle as part of the quest to understand the *Tao,* or "Way," of life. You will see that philosophy reflected in T'ao Chien's poem.

Similarly, Japanese culture stresses a deep appreciation for nature and a preference for simplicity. These values are evident in the Japanese literary form of haiku, in which very few words are used to suggest vivid images from nature. Bashō's poems are excellent examples of this form.

◆ Literary Focus

CULTURAL THEMES IN WORLD LITERATURE

A **theme** is a central idea or insight about life conveyed in a literary work. The theme of a piece of literature often reflects aspects of the culture from which it comes. For example, contemplating nature is a dominant theme in both Chinese and Japanese writing. This theme appears in each of the selections in this grouping.

You will encounter other cultural themes in these selections as well. The Chinese philosophy of Taoism provides the central theme of the *Tao Te Ching.* In Sei Shōnagon's *Pillow Book,* the traditional Japanese themes of the importance of order, rank, and hierarchy are evident.

◆ Reading Strategy

DISTINGUISH UNIVERSAL FROM CULTURE-SPECIFIC THEMES

Some **themes** are universal—they can be understood and appreciated by everyone. Other themes, however, are unique to a particular culture. While everyone can enjoy or value nature, for example, some aspects of the theme of nature are specific to Chinese and Japanese cultures. Both Lao Tzu and T'ao Ch'ien reflect a Chinese perspective: They suggest that, although nature is mysterious, we can begin to understand basic truths about life by observing how nature works.

Sei Shōnagon's writing conveys a specifically Japanese outlook. The desire to protect a battered dog in "The Cat Who Lived in the Palace" represents a fairly universal human emotion. However, giving cats and dogs social ranks reflects uniquely Japanese values.

Use a graphic organizer like the one shown to help you keep track of these distinctions.

Universal Themes	Culture-Specific Themes
Enjoy nature	Observing nature to understand life

from the Tao Te Ching

Lao Tzu

Translated by D. C. Lau

White Clouds Over Xiao and Xiang, Wang Chien,
Freer Gallery of Art, Washington, DC

▲ **Critical Viewing** How does this painting
support Lao Tzu's belief that mystery is a
part of nature? **[Connect]**

I

The way that can be spoken of
Is not the constant way;
The name that can be named
Is not the constant name,
The nameless was the beginning of heaven
    and earth;
5 The named was the mother of the <u>myriad</u>
    creatures.
Hence always rid yourself of desires in order
    to observe its secrets;
But always allow yourself to have desires in
    order to observe its <u>manifestations</u>.
These two are the same
10 But diverge in name as they issue forth.
Being the same they are called mysteries,
Mystery upon mystery—
The gateway of the <u>manifold</u> secrets.

III

Not to honor men of worth will keep the people
from <u>contention</u>; not to value goods which are
hard to come by will keep them from theft; not
to display what is desirable will keep them from
being unsettled of mind.
15   Therefore in governing the people, the sage
empties their minds but fills their bellies,
weakens their wills but strengthens their bones.
He always keeps them innocent of knowledge
and free from desire, and ensures that the
clever never dare to act.
Do that which consists in taking no action,
and order will prevail.

IX

Rather than fill it to the brim by keeping it upright
Better to have stopped in time;[1]
Hammer it to a point

---

1. Rather than . . . in time: These lines refer to a container
that stands in position when empty but overturns when full.

20 And the sharpness cannot be preserved forever;
There may be gold and jade to fill a hall
But there is none who can keep them.
To be overbearing when one has wealth and
   position
Is to bring <u>calamity</u> upon oneself.
25 To retire when the task is accomplished
Is the way of heaven.

XLIII

The most <u>submissive</u> thing in the world can ride
roughshod over the hardest in the world—that
which is without substance entering that which has
no crevices.

   That is why I know the benefit of resorting to
no action. The teaching that uses no words, the
benefit of resorting to no action, these are beyond
the understanding of all but a very few in the world.

I Built My House Near Where Others Dwell
T'ao Ch'ien Translated by William Acker

I built my house near where others dwell,
And yet there is no clamor of carriages and horses.
You ask of me "How can this be so?"
"When the heart is far the place of itself is distant."
5 I pluck chrysanthemums under the eastern hedge,
And gaze afar towards the southern mountains.
The mountain air is fine at evening of the day
And flying birds return together homewards.
Within these things there is a hint of Truth,
10 But when I start to tell it, I cannot find the words.

◆ **Build Vocabulary**

myriad (mir′ ē əd) *adj.*:
Countless

manifestations (man′ ə fes tā′
shənz) *n.*: Forms in which something is shown or experienced

manifold (man′ ə fold′) *adj.*:
Having many forms

contention (kən ten′ shən) *n.*:
Disputing; quarreling

calamity (kə lam′ ə tē) *n.*:
Deep trouble

submissive (sub mis′ iv) *adj.*:
Yielding; giving in

The Monkey Bridge in Koshu Province, Hiroshige Hitsu

▲ **Critical Viewing** What characteristics of
haiku are also evident in this painting?
[Compare and Contrast]

Haiku
Bashō
Translated by Harold G. Henderson (first 3)
and Geoffrey Bownas (last 3)

The sun's way:
Hollyhocks turn toward it
Through all the rain of May.

Poverty's child—
He starts to grind the rice,
And gazes at the moon.

Clouds come from time to time—
And bring to men a chance to rest
From looking at the moon.

The cuckoo—
Its call stretching
Over the water.

Seven sights were veiled
In mist—then I heard
Mii Temple's bell.[1]

Summer grasses—
All that remains
Of soldiers' visions.

---

1. Mii (mē ē′) **Temple's bell:** The bell at Mii Temple is
known for its extremely beautiful sound. The temple is
located near Otsu, a city in southern Japan.

from The Pillow Book

Sei Shōnagon Translated by Ivan Morris

In Spring It Is the Dawn

In spring it is the dawn that is most beautiful. As the light creeps over the hills, their outlines are dyed a faint red and wisps of purplish cloud trail over them.

In summer the nights. Not only when the moon shines, but on dark nights too, as the fire-flies flit to and fro, and even when it rains, how beautiful it is!

In autumn the evenings, when the glittering sun sinks close to the edge of the hills and the crows fly back to their nests in threes and fours and twos; more charming still is a file of wild geese, like specks in the distant sky. When the sun has set, one's heart is moved by the sound of the wind and the hum of the insects.

In winter the early mornings. It is beautiful indeed when snow has fallen during the night, but splendid too when the ground is white with frost; or even when there is no snow or frost, but it is simply very cold and the attendants hurry from room to room stirring up the fires and bringing charcoal, how well this fits the season's mood! But as noon approaches and the cold wears off, no one bothers to keep the braziers[1] alight, and soon nothing remains but piles of white ashes.

The Cat Who Lived in the Palace

The cat who lived in the Palace had been awarded the headdress of nobility and was called Lady Myōbu. She was a very pretty cat, and His Majesty saw to it that she was treated with the greatest care.

One day she wandered onto the veranda, and Lady Uma, the nurse in charge of her, called out, "Oh, you naughty thing! Please come inside at once." But the cat paid no attention and went on basking sleepily in the sun. Intending to give her a scare, the nurse called for the dog, Okinamaro.

"Okinamaro, where are you?" she cried. "Come here and bite Lady Myōbu!" The foolish Okinamaro, believing that the nurse was in earnest, rushed at the cat, who, startled and terrified, ran behind the blind in the Imperial Dining Room, where the Emperor happened to be sitting. Greatly surprised, His Majesty picked up the cat and held her in his arms. He summoned his gentlemen-in-waiting. When Tadataka, the Chamberlain,[2] appeared, His Majesty ordered that Okinamaro be chastised and banished to Dog Island. The attendants all started to chase the dog amid great confusion. His Majesty also reproached Lady Uma. "We shall have to find a new nurse for our cat," he told her. "I no longer feel I can count on you to look after her." Lady Uma bowed; thereafter she no longer appeared in the Emperor's presence.

The Imperial Guards quickly succeeded in catching Okinamaro and drove him out of the Palace grounds. Poor dog! He used to swagger about so happily. Recently, on the third day of the Third Month,[3] when the Controller First Secretary paraded him through the Palace grounds, Okinamaro was adorned with garlands of willow leaves, peach blossoms on his head, and cherry blossoms round his body. How could the dog have imagined that this would be his fate? We all felt sorry for him. "When Her Majesty was having her meals," recalled one of the ladies-in-waiting, "Okinamaro always used to be in attendance and sit opposite us. How I miss him!"

◆ **Build Vocabulary**

earnest (ʉr′ nist) *adj.*: Serious; not joking

chastised (chas′ tīzed′) *v.*: Punished severely

1. **braziers** (brā′ zhərz) *n.*: Metal pans or bowls used to hold burning coals or charcoal.

2. **Chamberlain** (chām′ bər lin) *n.*: A high official in the emperor's court.

3. **the third day of the Third Month:** The day of the Jòmi Festival, an event during which the dogs in the palace were often decorated with flowers.

▲ Critical Viewing The woman depicted in the picture is shown deep in thought as moonlight illuminates her chamber. In what ways does this image help you picture the world portrayed in *The Pillow Book?* **[Connect]**

Triptych of Snow, Moon, and Flower (center panel), Shunsho, Museum of Art, Atami; Japan

a dog. They'll surely kill him. He's being punished for having come back after he was banished. It's Tadataka and Sanefusa who are beating him." Obviously the victim was Okinamaro. I was absolutely wretched and sent a servant to ask the men to stop; but just then the howling finally ceased. "He's dead," one of the servants informed me. "They've thrown his body outside the gate."

That evening, while we were sitting in the Palace bemoaning Okinamaro's fate, a wretched looking dog walked in; he was trembling all over, and his body was fearfully swollen.

"Oh dear," said one of the ladies-in-waiting. "Can this be Okinamaro? We haven't seen any other dog like him recently, have we?"

We called to him by name, but the dog did not respond. Some of us insisted that it was Okinamaro, others that it was not. "Please send for Lady Ukon,"[5] said the Empress, hearing our discussion. "She will certainly be able to tell." We immediately went to Ukon's room and told her she was wanted on an urgent matter.

"Is this Okinamaro?" the Empress asked her, pointing to the dog.

"Well," said Ukon, "it certainly looks like him, but I cannot believe that this <u>loathsome</u> creature is really our Okinamaro. When I called Okinamaro, he always used to come to me, wagging his tail. But this dog does not react at all. No, it cannot be the same one. And besides, wasn't Okinamaro beaten to death and his body thrown away? How could any dog be alive after being flogged by two strong men?" Hearing this, Her Majesty was very unhappy.

When it got dark, we gave the dog something to eat; but he refused it, and we finally decided that this could not be Okinamaro.

On the following morning I went to attend the Empress while her hair was being dressed and she was performing her ablutions.[6] I was holding up the mirror for her when the dog we had seen on the previous evening slunk into the room and crouched next to one of the pillars. "Poor Okinamaro!" I said. "He had such a dreadful beating

It was about noon, a few days after Okinamaro's banishment, that we heard a dog howling fearfully. How could any dog possibly cry so long? All the other dogs rushed out in excitement to see what was happening. Meanwhile a woman who served as a cleaner in the Palace latrines[4] ran up to us. "It's terrible," she said. "Two of the Chamberlains are flogging

---

4. **latrines** (lə trēnz´) *n*.: Lavatories.

5. **Lady Ukon** (o͞o kôn´): One of the ladies in the Palace Attendants' Office, a bureau of female officials who waited on the emperor.
6. **ablutions** (ab lo͞o´ shənz) *n*.: Washings of the body.

yesterday. How sad to think he is dead! I wonder what body he has been born into this time. Oh, how he must have suffered!"

At that moment the dog lying by the pillar started to shake and tremble, and shed a flood of tears. It was astounding. So this really was Okinamaro! On the previous night it was to avoid betraying himself that he had refused to answer to his name. We were immensely moved and pleased. "Well, well, Okinamaro!" I said, putting down the mirror. The dog stretched himself flat on the floor and yelped loudly, so that the Empress beamed with delight. All the ladies gathered round, and Her Majesty summoned Lady Ukon. When the Empress explained what had happened, everyone talked and laughed with great excitement.

The news reached His Majesty, and he too came to the Empress's room. "It's amazing," he said with a smile. "To think that even a dog has such deep feelings!" When the Emperor's ladies-in-waiting heard the story, they too came along in a great crowd. "Okinamaro!" we called, and this time the dog rose and limped about the room with his swollen face. "He must have a meal prepared for him," I said. "Yes," said the Empress, laughing happily, "now that Okinamaro has finally told us who he is."

The Chamberlain, Tadataka, was informed, and he hurried along from the Table Room. "Is it really true?" he asked. "Please let me see for myself." I sent a maid to him with the following reply: "Alas, I am afraid that this is not the same dog after all." "Well," answered Tadataka, "whatever you say, I shall sooner or later have occasion to see the animal. You won't be able to hide him from me indefinitely."

Before long, Okinamaro was granted an Imperial pardon and returned to his former happy state. Yet even now, when I remember how he whimpered and trembled in response to our sympathy, it strikes me as a strange and moving scene; when people talk to me about it, I start crying myself.

◆ **Build Vocabulary**

loathsome (lōth´ səm) *adj*.: Disgusting; detestable

Guide for Responding

◆ *Literature and Your Life*

Reader's Response Which selection did you most enjoy? Explain.

Thematic Focus How might contemplating nature expand your ideas about your own values or your place in the world?

☑ Check Your Comprehension

1. According to Lao Tzu, what is the best way to prevent crime?
2. Does the speaker in "I Built My House Near Where Others Dwell" hear the noises of the town?
3. In Bashō's third haiku, what "... bring[s] to men a chance to rest/From looking at the moon"?
4. In "In Spring It Is the Dawn," Shōnagon reveals what she appreciates about each of the seasons. Choose two seasons and tell what she finds most beautiful about each.

◆ Critical Thinking

INTERPRET

1. In the excerpt from the *Tao Te Ching*, to what do the "nameless" and the "named" refer in section I, lines 5 and 6? **[Interpret]**
2. What conclusion can you draw about T'ao Ch'ien's attitude toward nature from lines 5–8 of "I Built My House Near Where Others Dwell"? **[Draw Conclusions]**
3. How does Bashō's third haiku convey a sense of harmony between humanity and nature? **[Interpret]**
4. How does the first segment of *The Pillow Book* reveal Shōnagon's eye for detail? **[Analyze]**

COMPARE LITERARY WORKS

5. In what ways are Bashō's haiku similar to and different from T'ao Chien's poem? **[Compare and Contrast]**

Guide for Responding (continued)

◆ Reading Strategy

DISTINGUISH UNIVERSAL FROM CULTURE-SPECIFIC THEMES

One **culture-specific theme** evident in the works of both Lao Tzu and T'ao Ch'ien is the idea of contemplating nature as a way to attain greater understanding of fundamental human truths.

1. How do the values Lao Tzu sets forth in section III of the *Tao Te Ching* contrast with widely accepted values of American society?
2. What does the segment "The Cat Who Lived in the Palace" reveal about aristocratic values during Shōnagon's day that are different from those predominant in the western world today?
3. How do the form and content of Bashō's poetry incorporate elements of a traditionally Japanese outlook? In what ways do the haiku differ from traditional western poems you have read?

◆ Build Grammar Skills

ACTIVE AND PASSIVE VOICE

A verb is in the **active voice** when the subject of the sentence performs the action. A verb is in the **passive voice** when the action is performed on the subject. The passive voice uses a form of the helping verb *be.*

Practice In your notebook, indicate whether the verb or verbs in the following sentences are in the active or passive voice.

1. The rice is ground by the boy.
2. He starts to grind the rice, and gazes at the moon.
3. In summer, the rain is beautiful.
4. Sei Shōnagon is moved by all the seasons.
5. Lao Tzu's philosophy refers to a mysterious, unnamable name.

Writing Application In your notebook, rewrite the following sentence, changing the passive voice to the active voice.

The cat who lived in the Palace had been awarded the headdress of nobility and was called Lady Myōbu.

◆ Literary Focus

CULTURAL THEMES IN WORLD LITERATURE

A **theme** is a central idea or insight about life that a writer hopes to convey in a work of literature. In Chinese and Japanese literature, distinct themes reflect particular aspects of each culture.

1. How does T'ao Ch'ien's attitude toward nature in "I Built My House Near Where Others Dwell" incorporate a culture-specific theme regarding a path toward the understanding of life?
2. How do Bashō's haiku reflect the Japanese emphasis on simplicity and suggestiveness?

◆ Build Vocabulary

USING THE LATIN PREFIXES *con-* AND *com-*

Knowing that the Latin prefix *con-,* derived from *com-,* means "together," explain the meanings of the following words. Refer to a dictionary if you need help.

1. connect   3. conflict   5. contain
2. consult   4. confront   6. contest

USING THE WORD BANK: SENTENCE COMPLETIONS

Choose the best word from the Word Bank to complete each sentence. Use each word only once.

1. A tremendous variety, or ____?____, of creatures inhabit the natural landscapes.
2. Their smiles were ____?____ of pure joy.
3. She was overwhelmed by her ____?____ duties.
4. Their disagreement was a sign of ____?____.
5. One who is too proud is sure to bring great misery or ____?____ upon oneself.
6. Sometimes the gentle or ____?____ can triumph over the strong or hard.
7. As she spoke, her grave expression indicated that she was in ____?____.
8. The Emperor ordered that the court dog be ____?____ and banished.
9. The badly bruised dog was so disfigured that the court attendant found him ____?____ to look at.

Build Your Portfolio

 ## Idea Bank

Writing

1. **Journal Entry** Write a journal entry in which you describe the most beautiful time of day in a particular season. Use images that engage as many of the five senses as you can.

2. **Haiku** Write a haiku, following the five-seven-five syllable pattern of most haiku. Use vivid imagery and clear, concise language to relate your own observations of nature.

3. **Review** For a philosophy Home Page on the Internet, write a brief review of the excerpt from the *Tao Te Ching*. Make Web surfers want to read Lao Tzu's work. **[Media Link]**

Speaking, Listening, and Viewing

4. **Oral Interpretation** Choose two of Bashō's haiku, and read them aloud. Change the speed, volume, and tone of your reading to create varied effects. **[Performing Arts Link]**

5. **Debate** With two teams of classmates, debate this statement of Taoist philosophy: "The most submissive thing in the world can ride roughshod over the hardest. . . ." **[Social Studies Link]**

Researching and Representing

6. **Area Map** Create a map of the setting of T'ao Ch'ien's poem, "I Built My House Near Where Others Dwell." Base your map on the details provided in the poem. **[Art Link]**

7. **Japanese Poetry Poster** Create a poster to spark student interest in the Japanese haiku form. Present information about and include examples of haiku. Convey the Japanese appreciation of nature, suggestiveness, and simplicity in your visual presentation. **[Art Link; Social Studies Link]**

Online Activity **www.phlit.phschool.com**

 ## Guided Writing Lesson

Dramatization

Write a dramatization, or dramatic adaptation, of the incident described in "The Cat Who Lived in the Palace" (*The Pillow Book*). Make sure that the way in which your characters act and talk matches the way Shōnagon portrays them.

Writing Skills Focus: Accurate Cultural Details

Including **accurate cultural details** is an important part of writing an effective dramatization. You can't assume, for example, that your audience will be familiar with the importance of hierarchy and social rank in aristocratic Japanese society. In your dramatization, be sure to include dialogue or stage notes that make such cultural details clear.

Prewriting List the events in "The Cat Who Lived in the Palace" and think about how they could be captured through dialogue and stage directions alone. Develop an outline that refers to the characters' titles and social ranks.

Drafting In your draft, make sure that your stage directions are clear and specific and your dialogue seems natural and realistic. Include a vivid description of the setting. Also, make sure that you have included accurate cultural details, such as the relative social ranks of all of the characters, especially Lady Myōbu, the court cat, and the court dog.

Revising Read your draft aloud to a partner who has read the segment from *The Pillow Book*. Ask him or her whether the way your characters act and talk matches the way Shōnagon portrays them. Does your partner feel the details in your dramatization are culturally accurate? Revise your draft based on your partner's suggestions.

Read through your dramatization. Identify sentences written in the passive voice and rewrite them in the active voice. For more on the active and passive voice, see pp. 18 and 26.

Guide for Reading

Dante Alighieri (1265–1321)

Dante Alighieri (dän´ tä al əg yer´ ē) was an Italian poet, philosopher, and political thinker who is most famous for his Christian epic poem *The Divine Comedy*. Today, the best-known portion of Dante's great poem is the *Inferno*, an imaginary journey through Hell.

Early Life Dante was born into a family of the lesser nobility in the northern Italian city of Florence, for which he always felt a patriotic allegiance. Little is known about his mother and father, who died before he was eighteen. However, two men who influenced Dante were Bruno Latini and Guido Cavalcanti. Latini taught Dante to think and speak effectively and to participate in public life. Cavalcanti, a poet, encouraged Dante to write in Italian rather than Latin, which was then the language of scholarship and literature. Soon other writers, following Dante's example, also used Italian.

Political Strife and Exile Dante's Florence was a city torn by political strife. At first, Dante belonged to a group that supported the pope against secular rulers. Later, Dante came to oppose the political and territorial ambitions of a new pope, Boniface VIII. In 1302, while Dante was away from Florence, he was condemned by his political enemies and banished forever from his beloved city.

The Divine Comedy Dante's epic poem is his attempt to make sense of his banishment by placing it in a larger context: the exile of the human soul from God. The poem is an imaginary journey through the three regions of the Christian afterlife: Inferno (or Hell), a deep pit where sinners are forever punished; Purgatory, a "burning mountain" where sinners are cleansed in preparation for entering Paradise; and Paradise itself, where blessed souls live with God.

Dante's Beatrice Dante's guides for this journey are the ancient Roman poet Virgil and a young woman named Beatrice. Dante hardly knew the woman who was the model for Beatrice, but the thought of her purity inspired him to undertake his quest for a union with God.

◆ Build Vocabulary

LATIN WORD ROOTS: *-trem-*

Dante tells how his voice "grew tremulous" when he first learned Virgil's identity. The word *tremulous* is based on the Latin root *-trem-*, meaning "tremble." *Tremulous* means "trembling, in the sense of fearful." Other familiar words with this root are *tremendous*, *tremble*, and *tremor*.

WORD BANK

flounders
gaunt
tremulous
zeal
grotesque
awe
writhes
nimble

As you read the selections from Dante's epic, you will encounter the words on this list. Each word is defined on the page where it first appears. Preview the list before you read.

◆ Build Grammar Skills

VERB TENSES

Verb tenses are forms that verbs take to show that an action or a condition occurs in the past, present, or future. For example, Dante uses *went*, the irregular past tense of *go*, to place his story in the past:

Midway in our life's journey, I went astray . . .

The telling of the story, on the other hand, is taking place in the present, so Dante uses a present-tense form of *give* as he recalls a dark wood:

Its very memory *gives* a shape to fear.

Then, thinking about how he plans to tell the story, he uses the future tense:

I *will recount*/all that I found revealed . . .

Notice how Dante uses these tenses consistently, helping readers orient themselves in time.

from the Inferno, Cantos I, XXXIV

◆ *Literature and Your Life*

CONNECT YOUR EXPERIENCE

Imagine a horror movie that begins like this: The heroine is lost in a dark forest at night. As she looks around, she sees a movement in the underbrush. Suddenly two big jungle cats emerge, baring their fangs. She turns away, only to face a growling wolf.

Though written some 700 years ago, Dante's *Divine Comedy* begins like this scene from a horror movie.

Journal Writing What real or fictional person would make a good guide for a journey that begins in this way? Explain.

THEME: CHOICES AND CONSEQUENCES

In reading these cantos from the *Inferno,* ask yourself this question: In what way does the punishment of each sinner seem appropriate for the sin?

◆ Background for Understanding

CULTURE

Dante uses a symbolism based on the number three in his work. The importance of this number was inspired by the Christian concept of the trinity: Father, Son, and Holy Ghost united as one in God. Following this symbolism, Dante wrote three books—*Inferno, Purgatory,* and *Paradise,* each with 33 sections or cantos (100 cantos in total with the addition of Canto I, the introduction).

◆ Literary Focus

ALLEGORY AND IMAGERY

Dante's imaginary journey is an **allegory,** a story in which characters, events, and settings hint at a meaning that lies outside the story itself. Allegories usually tell stories with spiritual lessons and were popular during the Middle Ages, when religion was often the focus of literature. Allegories would be dry reading, however, if they did not contain **imagery,** language that appeals to the senses. Such language gives the ideas of the allegory a basis in real experience.

Dante's *Divine Comedy,* the most famous allegory of the Middle Ages, tells of a journey through the realms of the Christian afterlife. Through the power of his imagery, he helps readers to experience his adventures. However, in addition to being a stirring tale, Dante's journey is an allegory with a deeper meaning. The poet's encounters show the struggle of the soul to reject sin and approach God.

◆ Reading Strategy

USE TEXT AIDS TO CLARIFY

Allegories, with their hidden meanings, are unfamiliar to many modern readers. That is why it is important to use **text aids,** explanatory prefaces and footnotes, to figure out the ideas and themes hinted at by the story.

Before reading cantos I and XXXIV, the first and last cantos of the *Inferno,* review the biography of Dante, page 28, and the Background for Understanding and Literary Focus on this page.

Also read the translator's preface to each canto. It summarizes what occurs in that canto and explains its allegorical meaning. Then, as you read the poem itself, refer to footnotes that provide information about puzzling words and expressions.

from the Inferno, Canto I

Dante Alighieri, Translated by John Ciardi

The Dark Wood of Error

Midway in his allotted threescore years and ten, Dante comes to himself with a start and realizes that he has strayed from the True Way into the Dark Wood of Error (Worldliness). As soon as he has realized his loss, Dante lifts his eyes and sees the first light of the sunrise (the Sun is the Symbol of Divine Illumination) lighting the shoulders of a little hill (The Mount of Joy). It is the Easter Season, the time of resurrection, and the sun is in its equinoctial rebirth.[1] This juxtaposition of joyous symbols fills Dante with hope and he sets out at once to climb directly up the Mount of Joy, but almost immediately his way is blocked by the Three Beasts of Worldliness: THE LEOPARD OF MALICE AND FRAUD, THE LION OF VIOLENCE AND AMBITION, *and* THE SHE-WOLF OF INCONTINENCE[2] *These beasts, and especially the She-Wolf, drive him back despairing into the darkness of error But just as all seems lost, a figure appears to him. It is the shade of* VIRGIL,[3] *Dante's symbol of* HUMAN REASON.*

*Virgil explains that he has been sent to lead Dante from error. There can, however, be no direct ascent past the beasts: The man who would escape them must go a longer and harder way. First he must descend through Hell (The Recognition of Sin), then he must ascend through Purgatory (The Renunciation of Sin), and only then may he reach the pinnacle of joy and come to the Light of God. Virgil offers to guide Dante, but only as far as Human Reason can go. Another guide (*BEATRICE, *symbol of* DIVINE LOVE*) must take over for the final ascent, for Human Reason is self-limited. Dante submits himself joyously to Virgil's guidance and they move off.*

Midway in our life's journey,[4] I went astray
from the straight road and woke to find myself
alone in a dark wood. How shall I say

what wood that was! I never saw so drear,
5   so rank, so arduous[5] a wilderness!
Its very memory gives a shape to fear.

Death could scarce be more bitter than that place!
But since it came to good, I will recount
all that I found revealed there by God's grace.

10   How I came to it I cannot rightly say,
so drugged and loose with sleep had I become
when I first wandered there from the True Way.

Note: Footnotes adapted from text by John Ciardi.

1. *equinoctial rebirth:* After the vernal equinox, which occurs on about March 21, days become longer than nights.
2. INCONTINENCE: Lack of self-restraint.
3. VIRGIL (vʉr´ jəl): A great Roman poet (70–19 B.C.)
4. Midway in our life's journey: The Biblical life span is threescore years and ten—seventy years. The action opens in Dante's thirty-fifth year, i.e., A.D. 1300.
5. so rank, so arduous: So overgrown, so difficult to cross.

But at the far end of that valley of evil
whose maze had sapped my very heart with fear!
15 I found myself before a little hill

and lifted up my eyes. Its shoulders glowed
already with the sweet rays of that planet[6]
whose virtue leads men straight on every road,

and the shining strengthened me against the fright
20 whose agony had wracked the lake of my heart
through all the terrors of that piteous night.

Just as a swimmer, who with his last breath
flounders ashore from perilous seas, might turn
to memorize the wide water of his death—

25 so did I turn, my soul still fugitive
from death's surviving image, to stare down
that pass that none had ever left alive.

And there I lay to rest from my heart's race
till calm and breath returned to me. Then rose
30 and pushed up that dead slope at such a pace

each footfall rose above the last.[7] And lo!
almost at the beginning of the rise
I faced a spotted Leopard,[8] all tremor and flow

and gaudy pelt. And it would not pass, but stood
35 so blocking my every turn that time and again
I was on the verge of turning back to the wood.

This fell at the first widening of the dawn
as the sun was climbing Aries with those stars
that rode with him to light the new creation.[9]

40 Thus the holy hour and the sweet season
of commemoration did much to arm my fear
of that bright murderous beast with their good omen.

Yet not so much but what I shook with dread
at sight of a great Lion that broke upon me
45 raging with hunger, its enormous head

held high as if to strike a mortal terror
into the very air. And down his track,
a She-Wolf drove upon me, a starved horror

6. that planet: The sun. Medieval astronomers considered it a planet. It is also symbolic of God as He who lights man's way.

7. each footfall . . . last: Dante is saying that he climbed with such zeal and haste that every footfall carried him above the last despite the steepness of the climb. At a slow pace, on the other hand, the rear foot might be brought up only as far as the forward foot.

8. a spotted Leopard: The three beasts that Dante encounters undoubtedly are taken from the Bible, Jeremiah 5:6. They foreshadow the three divisions of Hell (incontinence, violence, and fraud) which Virgil explains at length in Canto XI, 16–111.

9. Aries . . . new creation: The medieval tradition had it that the sun was in the zodiacal sign of Aries at the time of the Creation. It is just before dawn of Good Friday A.D. 1300 when he awakens in the Dark Wood. Thus his new life begins under Aries, the sign of creation, at dawn (rebirth) and in the Easter season (which commemorates the resurrection of Jesus). Dante is obviously constructing poetically the perfect Easter as a symbol of his new awakening.

◆ **Build Vocabulary**

flounders (floun′ dərz) *v.*: Struggles awkwardly when moving, as if stumbling

The Forest, Inferno I, Gustave Doré, New York Public Library

◀ **Critical Viewing**
Which details in this picture capture the mood of fear that Dante creates in this canto? [Connect]

ravening and wasted beyond all belief.
50 She seemed a rack for avarice,[10] gaunt and craving.
Oh many the souls she has brought to endless grief!

She brought such heaviness upon my spirit at sight of
her savagery and desperation
I died from every hope of that high summit.

55 And like a miser—eager in acquisition
but desperate in self-reproach when Fortune's wheel
turns to the hour of his loss—all tears and attrition[11]

10. **a rack for avarice:** An instrument of torture for greed.

11. **attrition:** Weakening; wearing away.

I wavered back; and still the beast pursued,
forcing herself against me bit by bit

60 till I slid back into the sunless wood.

And as I fell to my soul's ruin, a presence
gathered before me on the discolored air,
the figure of one who seemed hoarse from long silence.

At sight of him in that friendless waste I cried:
65 "Have pity on me, whatever thing you are,
whether shade or living man." And it replied:

"Not man, though man I once was, and my blood
was Lombard, both my parents Mantuan.[12]
I was born, though late, *sub Julio*,[13] and bred

70 in Rome under Augustus in the noon
of the false and lying gods.[14] I was a poet
and sang of old Anchises' noble son

who came to Rome after the burning of Troy.[15]
But you—why do *you* return to these distresses
75 instead of climbing that shining Mount of Joy

which is the seat and first cause of man's bliss?"
"And are you then that Virgil and that fountain
of purest speech?" My voice grew <u>tremulous</u>:

"Glory and light of poets! now may that <u>zeal</u>
80 and love's apprenticeship that I poured out
on your heroic verses serve me well!

For you are my true master and first author,
the sole maker from whom I drew the breath
of that sweet style whose measures have brought me honor.

85 See there, immortal sage, the beast I flee.
For my soul's salvation, I beg you, guard me from her,
for she has struck a mortal tremor through me."

And he replied, seeing my soul in tears:
"He must go by another way who would escape
90 this wilderness, for that mad beast that fleers[16]

before you there, suffers no man to pass. She tracks
down all, kills all, and knows no glut,
but, feeding, she grows hungrier than she was.

12. Lombard . . . Mantuan:
Lombardy is a region of
northern Italy; Mantua, the
birthplace of Virgil, is a city in
that region.
13. *sub Julio*: In the reign of
Julius Caesar. It would be
more accurate to say that he
was born during the lifetime
of Caesar (102?–44 B.C.).
Augustus did not begin his
rule as dictator until long after
Virgil's birth, which occurred
in 70 B.C.
**14. under Augustus . . .
lying gods:** Augustus, the
grand-nephew of Julius Caesar, was the emperor of
Rome from 27 B.C. to A.D. 14.
The "lying gods" are the false
gods of classical mythology.
15. and sang . . . Troy:
Virgil's epic poem, the
Aeneid, describes the
destruction of Troy by the
Greeks and the founding of
Roman civilization by the
Trojan Aeneas, son of
Anchises (an k ĭ´ sēz´).
16. fleers (flirz): Laughs
scornfully.

♦ **Build Vocabulary**

gaunt (gônt) *adj.*: Thin and haggard, as
if from great hunger

tremulous (trem´ yo͞o ləs) *adj.*: Trembling; fearful or timid

zeal (zēl) *n.*: Fervor, intense enthusiasm

She mates with any beast, and will mate with more
95 before the Greyhound comes to hunt her down.
He will not feed on lands nor loot, but honor

and love and wisdom will make straight his way.
He will rise between Feltro and Feltro,[17] and in him
shall be the resurrection and new day

100 of that sad Italy for which Nisus died,
and Turnus, and Euryalus, and the maid Camilla.[18]
He shall hunt her through every nation of sick pride

till she is driven back forever to Hell
whence Envy first released her on the world.
105 Therefore, for your own good, I think it well

you follow me and I will be your guide
and lead you forth through an eternal place.
There you shall see the ancient spirits tried

in endless pain, and hear their lamentation
110 as each bemoans the second death[19] of souls.
Next you shall see upon a burning mountain[20]

souls in fire and yet content in fire,
knowing that whensoever it may be
they yet will mount into the blessed choir.

115 To which, if it is still your wish to climb,
a worthier spirit[21] shall be sent to guide you.
With her shall I leave you, for the King of Time,

who reigns on high, forbids me to come there[22]
since, living, I rebelled against his law.
120 He rules the waters and the land and air

and there holds court, his city and his throne.
Oh blessed are they he chooses!" And I to him:
"Poet, by that God to you unknown,

lead me this way. Beyond this present ill
125 and worse to dread, lead me to Peter's gate[23]
and be my guide through the sad halls of Hell."

And he then: "Follow." And he moved ahead
in silence, and I followed where he led.

17. the Greyhound . . . Feltro and Feltro: The Greyhound almost certainly refers to Can Grande della Scala (1290–1329), a great Italian leader born in Verona, which lies between the towns of Feltre and Montefeltro.

18. Nisus . . . Camilla: All were killed in the war between the Trojans and the Latians when, according to legend, Aeneas led the survivors of Troy into Italy. Nisus and Euryalus (*Aeneid* IX) were Trojan comrades-in-arms who died together. Camilla (*Aeneid* XI) was the daughter of the Latian king and one of the warrior women. She was killed in a horse charge against the Trojans after displaying great gallantry. Turnus (*Aeneid* XII) was killed by Aeneas in a duel.

19. the second death: Damnation. "This is the second death, even the lake of fire." (the Bible, Revelation 20:14)

20. a burning mountain: The Mountain of Purgatory, described in the second book of Dante's *Divine Comedy.*

21. a worthier spirit: Beatrice.

22. forbids me to come there: Salvation is only through Christ in Dante's theology. Virgil lived and died before the establishment of Christ's teachings in Rome and cannot, therefore, enter Heaven.

23. Peter's gate: The gate of Purgatory. (See *Purgatorio* IX, 76ff.) The gate is guarded by an angel with a gleaming sword. The angel is Peter's vicar (Peter, the first pope, symbolized all popes; i.e., Christ's vicar on earth) and is entrusted with the two great keys.

from the Inferno, Canto XXXIV

Dante Alighieri, Translated by John Ciardi

Circle Nine: Cocytus[1]—Compound Fraud

Round Four: Judecca, The Treacherous to their Masters, The Center, Satan

"On march the banners of the King," Virgil begins as the Poets face the last depth. He is quoting a medieval hymn, and to it he adds the distortion and perversion of all that lies about him. "On march the banners of the King—of Hell."[2] And there before them, in an infernal parody of Godhead, they see Satan in the distance, his great wings beating like a windmill. It is their beating that is the source of the icy wind of Cocytus, the exhalation of all evil.

All about him in the ice are strewn the sinners of the last round, JUDECCA, *named for Judas Iscariot.[3] These are the* TREACHEROUS TO THEIR MASTERS. *They lie completely sealed in the ice, twisted and distorted into every conceivable posture. It is impossible to speak to them, and the Poets move on to observe Satan.*

He is fixed into the ice at the center to which flow all the rivers of guilt; and as he beats his great wings as if to escape, their icy wind only freezes him more surely into the polluted ice. In a grotesque *parody of the Trinity, he has three faces, each a different color, and in each mouth he clamps a sinner whom he rips eternally with his teeth.* JUDAS ISCARIOT *is in the central mouth;* BRUTUS *and* CASSIUS[4] *in the mouths on either side.*

Having seen all, the Poets now climb through the center, grappling hand over hand down the hairy flank of Satan himself—a last supremely symbolic action—and at last, when they have passed the center of all gravity, they emerge from Hell. A long climb from the earth's center to the Mount of Purgatory awaits them, and they push on without rest, ascending along the sides of the river Lethe, till they emerge once more to see the stars of Heaven, just before dawn on Easter Sunday.

"On march the banners of the King of Hell,"
my Master said. "Toward us. Look straight ahead:
can you make him out at the core of the frozen shell?"

Like a whirling windmill seen afar at twilight,
5   or when a mist has risen from the ground—
just such an engine rose upon my sight

◆ Build Vocabulary

grotesque (grō tesk´) *adj.*: Strangely distorted, absurdly ridiculous

1. **Cocytus:** (kō sī´ təs): This Greek word means "wailing."
2. ***On march the banners of the King—of Hell:*** The hymn was written in the sixth century by Venantius Fortunatus, Bishop of Poitiers. The original celebrates the Holy Cross, and is part of the service for Good Friday to be sung at the moment of uncovering the cross.
3. ***Judas Iscariot*** (is ker´ ē et): The disciple who betrayed Jesus; see the Bible, Matthew 26:14, 48.
4. ***BRUTUS*** and ***CASSIUS*** They took part in a plot against Julius Caesar.

stirring up such a wild and bitter wind
I cowered for shelter at my Master's back,
there being no other windbreak I could find.

10   I stood now where the souls of the last class
(with fear my verses tell it) were covered wholly;
they shone below the ice like straws in glass.

Some lie stretched out; others are fixed in place
upright, some on their heads, some on their soles;
15   another, like a bow, bends foot to face.

When we had gone so far across the ice
that it pleased my Guide to show me the foul creature[5]
which once had worn the grace of Paradise,

he made me stop, and, stepping aside, he said:
20   "Now see the face of Dis![6] This is the place
where you must arm your soul against all dread."

Do not ask, Reader, how my blood ran cold
and my voice choked up with fear. I cannot write it:
this is a terror that cannot be told.

25   I did not die, and yet I lost life's breath:
imagine for yourself what I became,
deprived at once of both my life and death.

The Emperor of the Universe of Pain
jutted his upper chest above the ice;
30   and I am closer in size to the great mountain

the Titans[7] make around the central pit, than they to
his arms. Now, starting from this part,
imagine the whole that corresponds to it!

If he was once as beautiful as now
35   he is hideous, and still turned on his Maker,
well may he be the source of every woe!

With what a sense of <u>awe</u> I saw his head
towering above me! for it had three faces:[8]
one was in front, and it was fiery red;

40   the other two, as weirdly wonderful,
merged with it from the middle of each shoulder
to the point where all converged at the top of the skull;

5. **the foul creature:** Satan.
6. **Dis** (dis): In Greek mythology, the god of the lower world or the lower world itself. Here it stands for Satan.

7. **Titans:** Giant deities who were overthrown by Zeus and the Olympian gods of Greece.
8. **three faces:** Numerous interpretations of these three faces exist. What is essential to all explanation is that they be seen as perversions of the qualities of the Trinity.

◆ **Build Vocabulary**

awe (ô) *n.*: Feelings of reverence, fear, and wonder caused by something impressive

Poets Emerge From Hell, Inferno XXXIV, 139,
Gustave Doré, New York Public Library

◀ Critical Viewing
What does this
picture suggest
about the relation-
ship between Virgil
(on the left) and
Dante? Explain.
[Interpret]

the right was something between white and bile;
the left was about the color that one finds
45   on those who live along the banks of the Nile.

Under each head two wings rose terribly,
their span proportioned to so gross a bird:
I never saw such sails upon the sea.

They were not feathers—their texture and their form
50   were like a bat's wings—and he beat them so
that three winds blew from him in one great storm:

it is these winds that freeze all Cocytus.
He wept from his six eyes, and down three chins
the tears ran mixed with bloody froth and pus.[9]

55   In every mouth he worked a broken sinner
between his rake-like teeth. Thus he kept three
in eternal pain at his eternal dinner.

9. bloody froth and pus:
The gore of the sinners he
chews, which is mixed with
his saliva.

For the one in front the biting seemed to play
no part at all compared to the ripping: at times
60   the whole skin of his back was flayed away.

"That soul that suffers most," explained my Guide,
"is Judas Iscariot, he who kicks his legs
on the fiery chin and has his head inside.

Of the other two, who have their heads thrust forward,
65   the one who dangles down from the black face
is Brutus: note how he <u>writhes</u> without a word.

And there, with the huge and sinewy arms,[10] is the soul
of Cassius.—But the night is coming on[11] and we must
go, for we have seen the whole."

70   Then, as he bade, I clasped his neck, and he,
watching for a moment when the wings were opened
wide, reached over dexterously[12]

and seized the shaggy coat of the king demon;
then grappling matted hair and frozen crusts
75   from one tuft to another, clambered down.

When we had reached the joint where the great thigh
merges into the swelling of the haunch,
my Guide and Master, straining terribly,

turned his head to where his feet had been
80   and began to grip the hair as if he were climbing,[13]
so that I thought we moved toward Hell again.

"Hold fast!" my Guide said, and his breath came shrill[14]
with labor and exhaustion. "There is no way
but by such stairs to rise above such evil."

85   At last he climbed out through an opening
in the central rock, and he seated me on the rim;
then joined me with a <u>nimble</u> backward spring.

I looked up, thinking to see Lucifer
as I had left him, and I saw instead
90   his legs projecting high into the air.

Now let all those whose dull minds are still vexed
by failure to understand what point it was
I had passed through, judge if I was perplexed.

10. huge and sinewy arms:
The Cassius who betrayed
Caesar was more generally
described in terms of Shake-
peare's "lean and hungry
look." Another Cassius is
described by Cicero (*Catiline*
III) as huge and sinewy.
Dante probably confused the
two.
11. he night is coming on:
It is now Saturday evening.
12. dexterously: Skillfully.

13. as if he were climbing:
They have passed the center
of gravity and so must turn
around and start climbing.
14. his breath came shrill:
In Canto XXIII, 85, the fact
that Dante breathes indicates
to the Hypocrites that he is
alive. Virgil's breathing is
certainly a contradiction.

◆ **Build Vocabulary**

writhes (rīt*h*z) *v.*: Twists and turns the
body, as in agony

nimble (nim´ bəl) *adj.*: Able to move or act
quickly, lightly, and easily

"Get up. Up on your feet," my Master said.
95 "The sun already mounts to middle tierce,[15]
and a long road and hard climbing lie ahead."

It was no hall of state we had found there,
but a natural animal pit hollowed from rock
with a broken floor and a close and sunless air.

100 "Before I tear myself from the Abyss,"
I said when I had risen, "O my Master,
explain to me my error in all this:

where is the ice? and Lucifer—how has he
been turned from top to bottom: and how can the sun
105 have gone from night to day so suddenly?"

And he to me: "You imagine you are still
on the other side of the center where I grasped
the shaggy flank of the Great Worm of Evil

which bores through the world—you *were* while I climbed down,
110 but I turned myself about, you passed
the point to which all gravities are drawn.

You are under the other hemisphere where you stand;
the sky above us is the half opposed
to that which canopies the great dry land.

115 Under the midpoint of that other sky
the Man[16] who was born sinless and who lived
beyond all blemish, came to suffer and die.

You have your feet upon a little sphere
which forms the other face of the Judecca.
120 There it is evening when it is morning here.

And this gross Fiend and Image of all Evil
who made a stairway for us with his hide
is pinched and prisoned in the ice-pack still.

On this side he plunged down from heaven's height,
125 and the land that spread here once hid in the sea
and fled North to our hemisphere for fright,[17]

And it may be that moved by that same fear,
the one peak[18] that still rises on this side
fled upward leaving this great cavern[19] here.

15. **middle tierce:** According to the church's division of the day for prayer, tierce is the period from about six to nine a.m. Middle tierce, therefore, is seven-thirty. In going through the center point, they have gone from night to day. They have moved ahead twelve hours.

16. **the Man:** Jesus, who suffered and died in Jerusalem, which was thought to be the middle of the earth.

17. **fled North . . . for fright:** Dante believed that the Northern hemisphere was mostly land and the Southern hemisphere water. Here he explains the reason for this state of affairs.
18. **the one peak:** The Mount of Purgatory.
19. **this great cavern:** The natural animal pit of line 98. It is also "Beelzebub's dim tomb," line 131.

130 Down there, beginning at the further bound
of Beelzebub's[20] dim tomb, there is a space
not known by sight, but only by sound

of a little stream[21] descending through the hollow
it has eroded from the massive stone
135 in its endlessly entwining lazy flow."

My Guide and I crossed over and began
to mount that little known and lightless road
to ascend into the shining world again.

He first, I second, without thought of rest
140 we climbed the dark until we reached the point
where a round opening brought in sight the blest

and beauteous shining of the Heavenly cars.
And we walked out once more beneath the Stars.[22]

20. **Beelzebub's** (bē el′ zə bubz): Beelzebub, which in Hebrew means "god of flies," was another name for Satan.
21. **a little stream:** Lethe (lē′ thē). In classical mythology, the river of forgetfulness, from which souls drank before being born. In Dante's symbolism it flows down from Purgatory, where it has washed away the memory of sin from the souls who are undergoing purification. That memory it delivers to Hell, which draws all sin to itself.
22. **Stars:** As part of his total symbolism, Dante ends each of the three divisions of the *Divine Comedy* with this word. Every conclusion of the upward soul is toward the stars, God's shining symbols of hope and virtue. It is just before dawn on Easter Sunday that the Poets emerge—a further symbolism.

Guide for Responding

◆ Literature and Your Life

Reader's Response As Dante, what emotions would you have felt on climbing out of Hell and seeing the stars?

Thematic Focus How has Dante's journey through Hell been a lesson on the importance of choice?

Questions for Research What key words would you use to research Dante and his epic poem on the Internet? Also, would you have greater confidence in a Dante site sponsored by an individual or by a university? Why?

☑ Check Your Comprehension

1. In what situation does Dante find himself at the beginning of Canto I?
2. In Canto I, what three beasts confront Dante just as he finds his way out?
3. Who offers Dante help in Canto I and what is the plan that this helper proposes?
4. Identify three remarkable details of Satan's appearance in Canto XXXIV?
5. Which three human sinners have it worst in Hell?
6. Summarize the process of Dante's exit from Hell.

◆ Critical Thinking

INTERPRET
1. Find three details that add to the fear in Canto I and explain your choices. **[Support]**
2. Why is Dante's newfound companion a good choice for a guide through the *Inferno*? **[Infer]**
3. What is the link between Dante's journey through Hell and his facing his own sins? **[Connect]**
4. In Canto XXXIV, what might the frozen body of water symbolize? **[Interpret]**
5. To what extent is Satan more like a condemned sinner than the master of his own domain? **[Analyze]**
6. Why is it appropriate that Satan should be found at the center of Hell? **[Draw Conclusions]**

EVALUATE
7. Does Dante present a vivid picture of Hell in his epic? Why or why not? **[Assess]**

APPLY
8. What purpose might Dante have in scaring readers with depictions of the horrors of Hell? **[Speculate]**

COMPARE LITERARY WORKS
9. Compare and contrast the *Inferno*'s setting with a strange and nightmarish setting in another work you have read. **[Compare and Contrast]**

Guide for Responding (continued)

◆ Literary Focus

ALLEGORY AND IMAGERY

Dante's *Inferno* is an **allegory,** a story in which characters, events, and settings hint at a hidden meaning. This diagram can help you visualize the allegorical structure of one episode in the *Inferno* (Canto I):

> **Literal Meaning**
> Leopard bars Dante's way.
>
> ↓
>
> **Allegorical Meaning**
> Soul without restraint can't approach God.

As the diagram suggests, you read the *Inferno* on two different levels at once. On a literal level, the story tells about Dante journeying through Hell and confronting "a spotted Leopard, all tremor and flow/and gaudy pelt." On another level, each of the things Dante sees and experiences has a deeper, allegorical meaning. The leopard that bars his way stands for a sinful lack of restraint that can keep a soul from approaching God.

This same passage indicates the importance of **imagery,** language that appeals to the senses, in giving the literal story the thrill of actuality. Thanks to imagery, Dante's leopard is not merely the symbol of sin. You, the reader, can see the "gaudy" spots splashed across its skin and feel the "tremor and flow" of that skin as it rolls close by like a menacing wave of anger and appetite.

1. Find a memorable passage in either canto and diagram its allegorical structure.
2. Explain how imagery enlivens the literal meaning of this passage.

◆ Reading Strategy

USE TEXT AIDS

By using **text aids,** like introductions and footnotes, you can better understand the hidden meanings of Dante's allegory.

Use text aids to explain the hidden meaning behind these details:

1. Dante is "alone in a dark wood." (Canto I, 1–7)
2. Satan's head has "three faces" rather than one. (Canto XXXIV, 37–45)

◆ Build Vocabulary

USING THE LATIN WORD ROOT *-trem-*

Show how the meaning of the word root *-trem-,* "tremble," contributes to the definition of each italicized word:

1. Dante and Virgil felt several *tremors,* as if an earthquake were about to strike.
2. The pilgrims through Hell heard a *tremendous* outcry from the pit below them.
3. By vibrating the hand holding the strings, the infernal guitarist created a *tremolo* tone.
4. Dante addressed Virgil with a *tremulous* voice.

USING THE WORD BANK: Context

On your paper, use your knowledge of the words in the Word Bank to answer these questions.

1. Why is it better to be described as slim than *gaunt*?
2. Can a sinner show *zeal* and still be evil? Explain.
3. What qualities of Satan might inspire *awe*?
4. What is *grotesque* about Satan in Canto XXXIV?
5. How does Virgil show that he is *nimble*?
6. What is a sinner who *writhes* probably feeling?
7. Is a sinner who *flounders* graceful? Explain.
8. Why is Dante *tremulous* on meeting Virgil?

◆ Build Grammar Skills

VERB TENSES

Writers show that an action or a condition occurs in the past, present, or future by using forms of verbs called **verb tenses.**

Practice Copy these sentences in your notebook. Underline the verbs, and tell whether they indicate past, present, or future tense. (A sentence may contain more than one verb.)

1. I found myself before a little hill.
2. I faced a spotted leopard.
3. He will feed on neither lands nor loot.
4. She tracks down all, kills all.
5. I will be your guide and lead you forth.

Writing Application On your paper, use verb tenses consistently as you summarize the action of Canto XXXIV.

Build Your Portfolio

Idea Bank

Writing

1. **Postcard** As Dante, write a postcard to your family or friends reporting on your tour of Hell. Use imagery to describe how you moved about and what you saw and heard in this strange place.

2. **Travel Feature** As a travel writer for a newspaper or magazine, write a feature piece about Hell in order to attract tourists to the place. Make your description interesting using colorful details and vivid imagery.

3. **Response to Criticism** The critic John Freccero asserts that "The dominant theme [of the *Inferno*] is not mercy but justice . . ." Using examples from the *Inferno* and information from text aids, support or refute his statement.

Speaking, Listening, and Viewing

4. **Interview** With a partner, role-play a television interview with Dante after he has returned from his tour of Hell. Be sure the questions and responses bring out the vivid imagery of the events and their meaning. **[Performing Arts Link]**

5. **Musical Sound Track** With a partner, choose music for Satan's appearance in canto XXXIV. Play the music for the class and read aloud passages that describe Satan. **[Music Link]**

Researching and Representing

6. **Artistic Rendering** Using Dante's description, create a sketch that illustrates a scene or character in one of the cantos. **[Art Link]**

7. **Report on Religion** Use an encyclopedia, a book on religion, or reputable Web sites to research different world religions. Then write a report comparing and contrasting their teachings about the afterlife. **[Social Studies Link]**

Online Activity www.phlit.phschool.com

Guided Writing Lesson

Critique of Selfishness

All of the sinners Dante encounters in the *Inferno* were selfish in one way or another. Using examples from Dante's poem as well as from your own viewing and reading, write a critique of selfishness. Analyze the vice of selfishness by summarizing what it is, describing different varieties of it, and then rating them on a scale of least offensive to most offensive.

Writing Skills Focus: Development by Classification

Develop your thoughts **by classification,** devoting each section of your critique to a different variety of selfishness, as follows:
- Introduction: Nature of selfishness
- Paragraph #1: Description of first type
- Paragraph #2: Description of second type, etc.
- Conclusion: Rating of types

Prewriting Using the *Inferno* and your own viewing and reading, gather examples of different types of selfishness. Collect them in a diagram:

Dante's Satan
out for power

selfishness is. . .

Clyde in *Kaffir Boy,*
selfish about privileges

Drafting Decide what your different examples have in common and include these common elements in a summary. Then, assign a different paragraph to describe each of the types of selfishness you have gathered. Use examples from literature, history, and film to illustrate your descriptions.

Revising Be sure your essay follows the organization shown in the Writing Skills Focus. If a description of a certain type of selfishness is too brief, develop it further with additional examples. Check that you have used verb tenses consistently.

For more on verb tenses, see pp. 28 and 41.

CONNECTIONS TO TODAY'S WORLD

How can Dante Alighieri, who lived more than 700 years ago, be our contemporary? One answer is that Dante deals with the timeless themes of guilt and suffering. Another answer is that Dante is our contemporary because translators continually render his medieval Italian into up-to-date English.

The most recent translation of the *Inferno* into an American idiom is the acclaimed version by Robert Pinsky, the poet laureate of the United States. In order to give the poem a more natural feeling in English, Pinsky had to solve a problem concerning the *Inferno*'s rhyme scheme.

As you know, Dante's poem uses a terza rima structure, in which the pattern of rhymes is as follows: aba bcb cdc . . . This

pattern is easier to achieve in Italian, a language rich in rhymes, than in English, which is comparatively rhyme-poor. Pinsky wanted to avoid straining for rhymes and thereby making his English version seem stiff or artificial.

His solution was to adopt "a more flexible definition of rhyme." He followed Dante's rhyming pattern, but he did it by using many rhymes based on similar consonant sounds, such as "sleep / stop / up," rather than consistently using full rhymes.

As you read his version of the poem's beginning (see below), judge whether or not he was successful in making Dante our contemporary. Be sure you read his lines aloud so you can tell how they sound.

from the Inferno, Canto I
Dante Alighieri, Translated by Robert Pinsky

Midway on our life's journey, I found myself
   In dark woods, the right road lost. To tell
   About those woods is hard—so tangled and
    rough

And savage that thinking of it now, I feel
5   The old fear stirring: death is hardly more
    bitter.
   And yet, to treat the good I found there as
    well

I'll tell what I saw, though how I came to enter
   I cannot well say, being so full of sleep
   Whatever moment it was I began to
    blunder

10 Off the true path. But when I came to stop
   Below a hill that marked one end of the
    valley
   That had pierced my heart with terror,
    I looked up

Toward the crest . . .

1. Find two examples in this passage of the consonantal rhyme that Pinsky used throughout his translation.

2. Compare and contrast Pinsky's version of this passage with Ciardi's on p. 30. Which version sounds more up-to-date and natural? Why?

Focus on Culture

The Ancient Middle East

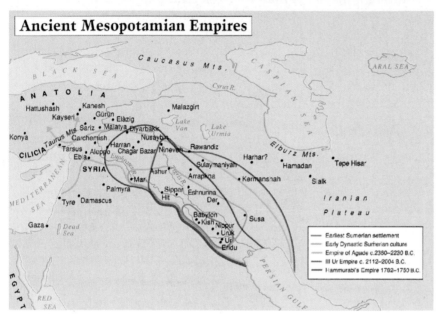

Ancient Mesopotamian Empires

Earliest Sumerian settlement
Early Dynastic Sumerian culture
Empire of Agade c.2360–2230 B.C.
III Ur Empire c. 2112–2004 B.C.
Hammurabi's Empire 1792–1750 B.C.

◀ **Critical Viewing** Based on the map, how did the region known as the Fertile Crescent get its name? **[Interpret]**

"The fellow in charge of punctuality said, 'Why are you late?' Afraid and with pounding heart, I entered before my teacher and made a respectful bow." The student had good reason to be afraid. He knew that offenses such as lateness or sloppy schoolwork might get him a severe punishment.

The student who gave us this vivid description lived a long time ago—in fact, some 5,000 years ago! The account appears on an ancient clay tablet found in the ruins of a Sumerian city in the Middle East. He goes on to describe his school day and his heavy workload: "I recited my tablet, ate my lunch, prepared my new tablet, wrote it, finished it. . . and in the afternoon my exercise tablets were brought to me." That night, at home, the student's father checks his schoolwork: "[I] recited my tablet to him, and he was delighted."

Accounts like this one are like a doorway to the ancient Middle East. They help us imagine what it was like to live in humanity's oldest civilization.

GEOGRAPHIC SETTING

What is the Middle East? The term is a modern one, invented by Europeans to describe the region that lies between Europe and the eastern parts of Asia. In fact, the Middle East is located in southwestern Asia. (See the map on this page.)

"Crossroads of the World" The Middle East stands at the crossroads of three continents: Africa, Asia, and Europe. Since ancient times, it has connected major trade routes, both overland and on the seas. Caravans from India and China brought goods to the busy markets of the Middle East. From there, traders carried the goods across the Mediterranean into Europe or across the Red Sea to East Africa. Today, the region plays a key role in the world's economy because of its strategic location and vital oil supplies.

The Fertile Crescent The hub of the ancient Middle East was a region known as Mesopotamia (mes´ ə pə tā mē ə), or "the land between the rivers." Located in what is now Iraq,

Mesopotamia lay between two rivers, the Tigris (tī´ gris) and the Euphrates (yoo frāt´ ēz). Overflows from the two rivers made the land fertile. As a result, the land also became known as the Fertile Crescent. Yet the rivers could be a curse as well as a blessing. The region was subject to devastating floods that washed away topsoil and destroyed mud-brick villages.

It was here, on the plains of southeastern Mesopotamia, some 5,000 years ago, that the world's oldest civilization began to emerge. The center of this civilization was in the city-states of ancient Sumer.

HISTORY

The beginnings of Sumerian civilization are cloaked in mystery. Modern archaeologists and historians are not even sure where the first Sumerians came from. The Sumerian language is not related to any other known language on Earth.

The Rise of Sumer Still, it seems certain that some time before 4000 B.C., the fertile soil and bountiful water supply of Mesopotamia attracted Stone Age farmers from neighboring lands. As they settled into farming communities, they raised abundant supplies of grain and dates to support a growing population. Farmers also had to cooperate in building irrigation canals to raise crops and dikes to control flood waters. To organize such massive projects, a strong system of government emerged.

By about 3500 B.C., the most successful farming settlements had grown into powerful city-states. Each Sumerian city-state had its own king, government bureaucracy, and local god. Rival city-states such as Erech and Ur often went to war against each other.

The ancient Sumerians have many "firsts" to their credit. They invented the earliest known system of writing, the wedge-shaped characters known as cuneiform (kyoo nē´ ə fôrm). They

Group of votive statuettes, Tell Asmar, ca. 2900–2600 B.C., The Oriental Institute, University of Chicago

▲ **Critical Viewing** This grouping represents a Sumerian god along with priests and worshipers. Which of these figures do you think represents the god? Why? **[Draw Conclusions]**

were the first people known to have used wheeled vehicles. They used their knowledge of astronomy to create an accurate calendar, invented the plow and the sail, and developed a number system based on 60. Our 60-second minute, 60-minute hour, and 360-degree circle come to us from the Sumerians.

A Mix of Peoples In the centuries that followed, a succession of powerful empires conquered and ruled the Fertile Crescent. By 1750 B.C., Sumerian civilization had ceased to exist. Still, these later civilizations—including the Babylonians, the Assyrians, and the Persians—built on Sumerian achievements. They also developed many of their own, such as the Babylonian legal code of the emperor Hammurabi (hä´ moo rä´ bē).

Amidst these powerful empires, a number of smaller groups made important contributions. The Hittites developed skills in ironworking. The Lydians introduced the use of coined money. The Phoenicians (fi nish´ ənz) developed an alphabet that was the basis of the one we use today. And the ancient Israelites, or Hebrews, had a profound effect on modern religions.

▲ **Critical Viewing** Why do you think many religious structures, such as this ziggurat, are built so high? **[Speculate]**

The Ancient Israelites The Israelites recorded their history in the sacred text we now call the Hebrew Bible. Around 2000 B.C., the Israelites migrated from Mesopotamia to the land of Canaan (kā′ nən), along the Red Sea. Eventually, leaders such as David and Solomon founded the kingdom of Israel, with its great capital city of Jerusalem.

After Solomon's death, the kingdom of Israel was divided by civil war and later conquered by powerful neighbors. The Israelites were forced out of their land. (During this period of exile, they became known as the Jews.) Still, the long-term influence of the ancient Israelites on the world would be immense.

SOCIETY AND CULTURE

Archaeologists have found thousands of cuneiform tablets that preserve a good record of Mesopotamian civilizations. These clay tablets record laws, prayers, treaties, medical knowledge, and other information. One tablet contains the description of life in a Sumerian school that you read earlier. Such schools were vital to Sumerian society. Each city-state depended on educated writers, called scribes, to keep important records and run the government bureaucracy.

Sumerian Religion Like many other ancient civilizations, the Sumerians were polytheistic, believing in many gods and goddesses. Each city state worshiped its own special deity. Sumerians thought of the gods as all-powerful beings with very human emotions. They could be quarrelsome, petty, childish, jealous—and, if angered, they would send disasters such as floods or diseases to Earth. As a result of this belief, Sumerian priests gained great influence. Only the priests knew the prayers, hymns, and rituals that would keep the gods happy. Most later peoples of the ancient Middle East, such as the Babylonians and Assyrians, also believed in many gods.

Belief in One God By contrast, the Israelites were unique in the ancient world. They were monotheistic, worshiping a single, all-powerful God. The Israelites believed that God had made a covenant, or solemn agreement, to protect them in return for their faithfulness and obedience. The belief that they were God's "chosen people" sustained the Jewish people through centuries of exile, hardship, and persecution.

The Israelites also developed a strong code of ethics, or moral behavior. This code was most clearly expressed in the Ten Commandments, the laws which the Israelites believed God had given to Moses. The First Commandment expresses the Israelites' sense of their unique relationship with God: "I am the LORD your God, who brought you out of the land of Egypt, out of the house of bondage. You shall have no other gods beside Me." Other Commandments prescribe moral behavior in the family and society, including "Honor your father and mother," "You shall not kill," and "You shall not steal."

The faith of the Israelites eventually developed into modern Judaism. It also helped shape two later religions that arose in the Middle East: Christianity and Islam.

ARTS AND LITERATURE

Most of the surviving artwork of Mesopotamia serves one of two functions: to glorify the gods or to glorify the ruler. Archaeologists have found the remains of fine statues and other artifacts in the ruins of Sumerian temples.

Sumerian Art and Architecture One famous group of marble statues (see p. 45) depicts Abu, the Sumerian god of vegetation, along with a mother goddess and smaller figures representing priests and worshipers. With their wide, staring eyes and their hands clasped in prayer, the statues give a impression of solemnity and awe.

Even more notable is the Sumerians' contribution to architecture. At the center of each city stood a towering building called a ziggurat (zig′ o͞o rat). Each ziggurat was dedicated to the city's chief god or goddess. Wide staircases allowed the gods to come down from heaven. (See the picture on page 46.)

The Epic of Gilgamesh Sumerian art influenced later peoples of the Fertile Crescent. So did the rich Sumerian literary tradition. Clay tablets record religious myths, fables, hymns, proverbs, and tales of great heroes. However, the most lasting contribution of Sumer to literature was the epic of Gilgamesh. This long poem recounts the adventures of a legendary king who seeks the secret of eternal life. His search for immortality fails, and Gilgamesh finally accepts the truth that everyone must die. (See an excerpt from this epic on p. 50.)

Gilgamesh was first passed down orally by the Sumerians. Later peoples added to it.

Babylonian Globe, c. 500 B.C., British Museum, London

◀ **Critical Viewing** This map of the world was created by the ancient Babylonians. What skill shown here did the Babylonians learn from the Sumerians? **[Apply]**

The Bible The literary tradition of the Israelites is found in the sacred writings of the Hebrew Bible (called the Old Testament by Christians). Beginning with an account of the creation of the world, the Bible traces the relationship between the Israelites and their God. Among its most beautiful passages are the Psalms. In rich, poetic language, these sacred songs tell of the Israelites' suffering and triumphs and their abiding faith in God. The Hebrew Bible also contains history, law, proverbs, stories of holy men and women, and discussions of theology. (See excerpts from Genesis and the Psalms on pp. 62 and 67, respectively.)

ACTIVITY
Writing a Museum Guide

Much of what we know about the ancient Middle East has come from the work of archaeologists such as Kathleen Kenyon, Austin Layard, and Charles Leonard Woolley. Use library or Internet resources to research archaeological discoveries in the Middle East. Choose three objects found at one site. For each object, write a brief paragraph to be included in a museum guide. Describe what the object is, where it was found, and what it tells us about that culture. Include illustrations if possible. 🎨

Guide for Reading

The Epic of Gilgamesh
(Second Millennium B.C.)

The epic of Gilgamesh is a long narrative poem about a king named Gilgamesh who lived between 2700 and 2500 B.C. in ancient Sumeria. One of the earliest civilizations, Sumeria was located on the Tigris and Euphrates rivers in what is now Iraq.

Timeless Themes Although this poem is one of the oldest works of literature in existence, its concerns are timeless and universal: how to become known and respected, how to cope with the loss of a dear friend, and how to accept one's own inevitable death.

How It Was Written Stories about King Gilgamesh were told by Sumerians for hundreds of years after his death. By the twenty-first century B.C., these tales existed in written form. When the Babylonians conquered the Sumerians soon afterward, they inherited the Sumerian cultural tradition. A Babylonian author, borrowing from some of the Gilgamesh tales, created a unified epic about this legendary king. Other Babylonian writers modified the epic, and, in the seventh century B.C., it was included in the library of the Assyrian King Ashurbanipal.

An Epic Lost and Found *Gilgamesh* was an international favorite of its era. However, the written version of it was lost during ancient times, and it was not recovered until archaeologists excavated Ashurbanipal's library during the nineteenth century. There they found the poem written on clay tablets in cuneiform (kyo͞o nē´ ə fôrm´), the wedge-shaped writing used by the Babylonians. Scholars were especially excited by the portion of the epic describing a great flood (see pp. 53–57), an account remarkably similar to the story of Noah in the Bible.

N. K. Sandars, the translator responsible for this English version of *Gilgamesh,* did not go back to the original cuneiform but relied on previous scholarly translations of the epic into modern languages.

◆ Build Vocabulary

LATIN PREFIXES: *sub-*

The epic of Gilgamesh tells how a storm that caused a terrible flood finally "subsided." The word *subsided*, meaning "became less intense or sank to a lower level," is made up of *side* from the Latin word *sidere* ("to settle") and the prefix *sub-* ("under or down"). You will find this prefix in many familiar words, including *submarine* and *submerge*.

immolation
succor
teemed
babel
ballast
subsided
transgressor

WORD BANK

In reading this epic, you will encounter the words on this list. Each word is defined on the page where it first appears. Preview the list before you read.

◆ Build Grammar Skills

COMMONLY CONFUSED WORDS: *in* and *into*

In the epic of Gilgamesh, the translator correctly uses both *in* and *into*—two prepositions that are commonly confused. As the following examples from the epic indicate, *in* refers to place or position and *into* suggests motion.

Place or Position: "O Gilgamesh, remember now your boasts *in* Uruk."

Motion: "O my lord, you may go on if you choose *into* this land, but I will go back to the city."

In reading *Gilgamesh,* note the translator's correct use of these prepositions and imitate it in your own writing.

from The Epic of Gilgamesh

◆ *Literature and Your Life*

CONNECT YOUR EXPERIENCE

You have probably imagined what it would be like to live forever. The advantages are obvious. However, the disadvantages would include forever saying goodbye to friends who are mortal.

The hero of *Gilgamesh* is not thinking of the disadvantages of eternal life. He is desperate to find the one man who has avoided death and ask him his secret.

THEMATIC FOCUS: STRIVING FOR SUCCESS

In reading this ancient epic, ask yourself this question: Is the search for immortality a theme that can also be found in today's books and films? Why or why not?

Journal Writing Suppose you could live forever. List three ways in which this fact would change how you live.

◆ Background for Understanding

CULTURE

In the epic of Gilgamesh, you will encounter these ancient Sumerian and Babylonian gods, goddesses, and heroes:

Adad (ā dad): god of storms and weather

Annunaki (ä noō nä′ kē): Anu's sons, gods of the underworld

Anu (ä′ noō): father of gods; god of the heavens

Ea (ā′ ä), also **Enki** (eŋ′ kē): god of waters and wisdom

Enkidu (eŋ′ kē doō): Gilgamesh's friend, who dies

Enlil (en lil′): god of wind and agriculture; with Anu, a senior god.

Ishtar (Ish′ tär): goddess of love and war

Shamash (shä′ mäsh): the sun god; also a lawgiver

Utnapishtim (oōt nə pēsh′ təm): survivor of a great flood

◆ Literary Focus

ARCHETYPAL THEME: THE HERO'S QUEST

An **archetypal theme** is a pattern or idea that occurs in literature from many different cultures because it has significance for all humans. An example is the theme of the **hero's quest,** the effort of an extraordinary person to find or do something of great value.

Gilgamesh is one of the oldest quest stories in literature and involves one of humankind's oldest goals: finding a "cure" for death. Consider whether or not Utnapishtim's story of the flood indicates that Gilgamesh will succeed in his quest.

◆ Reading Strategy

UNDERSTAND THE CULTURAL CONTEXT

Reading epics and legends involves mental travel to far-away places and ancient times. Prepare for this travel by learning about the **cultural context** of such tales—the names, beliefs, and customs of the characters. Also, identify details of the cultural context as you read.

Before reading *Gilgamesh,* review the description of the epic on the previous page and the Background for Understanding on this page. If you encounter an unfamiliar name or place in the epic, refer back to the information on these pages.

In addition, create a chart like the one below and fill in the right column as you read. (You can also add more items in the left column.)

Cultural Detail	What I Learned
writing materials	
construction of cities	
agriculture	
strength or weakness of gods	

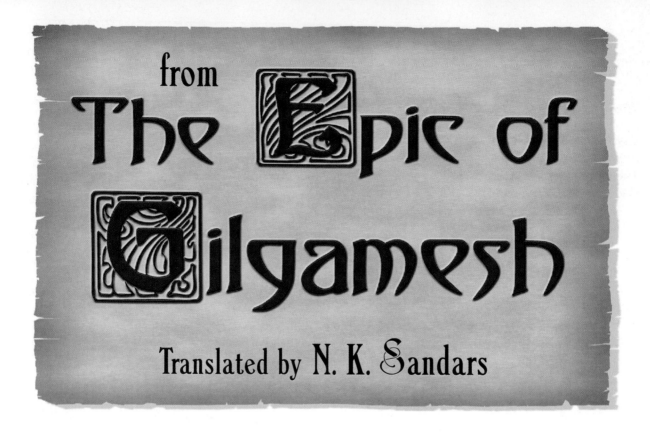

from The Epic of Gilgamesh

Translated by N. K. Sandars

Prologue

I will proclaim to the world the deeds of Gilgamesh. This was the man to whom all things were known; this was the king who knew the countries of the world. He was wise, he saw mysteries and knew secret things, he brought us a tale of the days before the flood. He went on a long journey, was weary, worn out with labor, returning he rested, he engraved on a stone the whole story.

When the gods created Gilgamesh they gave him a perfect body. Shamash the glorious sun endowed him with beauty, Adad the god of the storm endowed him with courage, the great gods made his beauty perfect, surpassing all others, terrifying like a great wild bull. Two thirds they made him god and one third man.

In Uruk he built walls, a great rampart, and the temple of blessed Eanna[1] for the god of the firmament[2] Anu, and for Ishtar the goddess of love. Look at it still today: the outer wall where the cornice runs, it shines with the brilliance of copper; and the inner wall, it has no equal. Touch the threshold, it is ancient. Approach Eanna the dwelling of Ishtar, our lady of love and war, the like of which no latter-day king, no man alive can equal. Climb upon the wall of Uruk; walk along it, I say; regard the foundation terrace and examine the masonry: is it not burnt brick and good? The seven sages[3] laid the foundations.

---

1. In Uruk . . . Eanna: Uruk was an important city in southern Babylonia, with temples to the gods Anu and Ishtar. Eanna was the temple site where these gods were worshiped.
2. firmament (fǔrm´ ə mənt): The sky, viewed poetically as a solid arch.
3. seven sages: Legendary wise men who civilized Mesopotamia's seven oldest cities.

The Battle With Humbaba

When the people of Uruk complain about Gilgamesh's arrogance, the goddess Aruru creates Enkidu to contend with the king and absorb his energies. At first, Enkidu lives like a wild animal and has no contact with other humans. Later, he enters Uruk, loses a wrestling match to Gilgamesh, and becomes his faithful friend. Then the two set off to destroy Humbaba, the giant who guards the cedar forest. As Gilgamesh prepares for battle, Enkidu expresses his fears.

Then Enkidu, the faithful companion, pleaded, answering him, "O my lord, you do not know this monster and that is the reason you are not afraid. I who know him, I am terrified. His teeth are dragon's fangs, his countenance is like a lion, his charge is the rushing of the flood, with his look he crushes alike the trees of the forest and reeds in the swamp. O my lord, you may go on if you choose into this land, but I will go back to the city. I will tell the lady your mother all your glorious deeds till she shouts for joy: and then I will tell the death that followed till she weeps for bitterness." But Gilgamesh said, "Immolation and sacrifice are not yet for me, the boat of the dead⁴ shall not go down, nor the three-ply cloth be cut for my shrouding. Not yet will my people be desolate, nor the pyre be lit in my house and my dwelling burnt on the fire. Today, give me your aid and you shall have mine: what then can go amiss with us two? All living creatures born of the flesh shall sit at last in the boat of the West, and when it sinks, when the boat of Magilum sinks, they

▲ **Critical Viewing** Do you think this ancient bronze head captures the way Gilgamesh looked? Why or why not? **[Assess]**

are gone; but we shall go forward and fix our eyes on this monster. If your heart is fearful throw away fear; if there is terror in it throw away terror. Take your ax in your hand and attack. He who leaves the fight unfinished is not at peace."

Humbaba came out from his strong house of cedar. Then Enkidu called out, "O Gilgamesh, remember now your boasts in Uruk. Forward, attack, son of Uruk, there is nothing to fear." When he heard these words his courage rallied; he answered, "Make haste, close in, if the watchman is there do not let him escape to the woods where he will vanish. He has put on the first of his seven splendors but not yet the other six, let us trap him before he is armed." Like a raging wild bull he snuffed the ground; the watchman of the woods turned full of threatenings, he cried out. Humbaba came from his strong house of cedar. He nodded his head and shook it, menacing Gilgamesh; and on him he fastened his eye, the eye of death. Then Gilgamesh called to Shamash and his tears were flowing, "O glorious Shamash, I have followed the road you commanded but now if you send no succor how shall I escape?" Glorious Shamash heard his prayer and he summoned the great wind, the north wind, the whirlwind, the storm and the icy wind, the tempest and the scorching wind;

> ◆ **Literary Focus**
> Does Gilgamesh's reaction to Humbaba suggest that Gilgamesh is not all-powerful? Explain.

◆ **Build Vocabulary**

immolation (im´ ə lā´ shən) *n*.: Offering of a victim as a sacrifice to the gods

succor (suk´ ər) *n*.: Aid or help in time of distress

---

4. **boat of the dead:** A ceremonial boat on which the dead were placed.

Front of Lyre From Tomb of Queen Pu-Abi, British Museum, London

▲ **Critical Viewing** This picture shows the front of a lyre, an ancient stringed instrument. Music from such a lyre may have accompanied recitations of *Gilgamesh*. What modern instruments would you use to accompany a recitation of this epic? Explain. **[Make a Judgment]**

◆ **Reading Strategy** What do the repeated references to cedar trees suggest about their value in the ancient Middle East?

they came like dragons, like a scorching fire, like a serpent that freezes the heart, a destroying flood and the lightning's fork. The eight winds rose up against Humbaba, they beat against his eyes; he was gripped, unable to go forward or back. Gilgamesh shouted, "By the life of Ninsun my mother and divine Lugulbanda my father, in the Country of the Living, in this Land I have discovered your dwelling; my weak arms and my small weapons I have brought to this Land against you, and now I will enter your house."

So he felled the first cedar and they cut the branches and laid them at the foot of the mountain. At the first stroke Humbaba blazed out, but still they advanced. They felled seven cedars and cut and bound the branches and laid them at the foot of the mountain, and seven times Humbaba loosed his glory on them. As the seventh blaze died out they reached his lair. He slapped his thigh in scorn. He approached like a noble wild bull roped on the mountain, a warrior whose elbows are bound together. The tears started to his eyes and he was pale, "Gilgamesh, let me speak. I have never known a mother, no, nor a father who reared me. I was born of the mountain, he reared me, and Enlil made me the keeper of this forest. Let me go free, Gilgamesh, and I will be your servant, you shall be my lord; all the trees of the forest that I tended on the mountain shall be yours. I will cut them down and build you a palace." He took him by the hand and led him to his house, so that the heart of Gilgamesh was moved with compassion. He swore by the heavenly life, by the earthly life, by the underworld itself: "O Enkidu, should not the snared bird return to its nest and the captive man return to his mother's arms?" Enkidu answered, "The strongest of men will fall to fate if he has no judgment. Namtar, the evil fate that knows no distinction between men, will devour him. If the snared bird returns to its nest, if the captive man returns to his mother's arms, then you my friend will never return to the city where the mother is waiting who gave you birth. He will bar the mountain road against you, and make the pathways impassable."

Humbaba said, "Enkidu, what you have spoken is evil: you, a hireling, dependent for your bread! In envy and for fear of a rival you have spoken evil words." Enkidu said, "Do not listen, Gilgamesh: this Humbaba must die. Kill Humbaba first and his servants after." But Gilgamesh said, "If we touch him the blaze and the glory of light will be put out in confusion, the glory and glamour will vanish, its rays will be quenched." Enkidu said to Gilgamesh, "Not so, my friend. First entrap the bird, and where shall the chicks run then? Afterwards we can search out the glory and the glamour, when the chicks run distracted through the grass."

Gilgamesh listened to the word of his companion, he took the ax in his hand, he drew the sword from his belt, and he struck Humbaba with a thrust of the sword to the neck, and Enkidu his comrade struck the second blow. At the third blow Humbaba fell. Then there followed confusion for this was the guardian of the forest whom they had felled to the ground. For as far as two leagues the cedars shivered when Enkidu felled the watcher of the forest, he at whose voice Hermon and Lebanon used to tremble. Now the mountains were moved and all the hills, for the guardian of the forest was killed. They attacked the cedars, the seven splendors of Humbaba were extinguished. So they pressed on into the forest bearing the sword of eight talents.[5] They uncovered the sacred dwellings of the Anunnaki[6] and while Gilgamesh felled the first of the trees of the forest Enkidu cleared their roots as far as the banks of Euphrates.[7] They set Humbaba before the gods, before Enlil; they kissed the ground and dropped the shroud and set the head before him. When he saw the head of Humbaba, Enlil raged at them. "Why did you do this thing? From henceforth may the fire be on your faces, may it eat the bread that you eat, may it drink where you drink." Then Enlil took again the blaze and the seven splendors that had been Humbaba's: he gave the first to the river, and he gave to the lion, to the stone of execration[8] to the mountain and to the dreaded daughter of the Queen of Hell.

O Gilgamesh, king and conqueror of the dreadful blaze; wild bull who plunders the mountain, who crosses the sea, glory to him, and from the brave the greater glory is Enki's![9]

The Story of the Flood

Enkidu dies, and greatly saddened by his death, Gilgamesh goes on a quest for immortality. He journeys through the mysterious mountain of Manshu, encounters the sun-god Shamash and the goddess Siduri, and travels across the Ocean to Utnapishtim, whose name means "He Who Saw Life." Utnapishtim and his family are the only humans who have been granted immortality. When Gilgamesh asks him how he has defeated death, Utnapishtim tells the following story.

"You know the city Shurrupak, it stands on the banks of Euphrates? That city grew old and the gods that were in it were old. There was Anu, lord of the firmament, their father, and warrior Enlil their counselor, Ninurta the helper, and Ennugi watcher over canals; and with them also was Ea. In those days the world <u>teemed</u>, the people multiplied, the world bellowed like a wild bull, and the great god was aroused by the clamor. Enlil heard the clamor and he said to the gods in council, 'The uproar of mankind is intolerable and sleep is no longer possible by reason of the <u>babel</u>.' So the gods agreed to exterminate mankind. Enlil did this, but Ea because of his oath warned me in a dream. He whispered their words to my house of reeds, 'Reed-house, reed-house! Wall, O wall, harken reed-house, wall reflect: O man of Shurrupak, son of Ubara-Tutu; tear down your house and build a boat, abandon possessions and look for life, despise worldly goods and save your soul alive. Tear down your house, I say, and build a boat. These are the measurements of the barque as you shall build her: let her beam equal her length, let her deck be roofed like the vault that covers the abyss;[10] then take up into the boat the seed of all living creatures.'

"When I had understood I said to my lord, 'Behold, what you have commanded I will honor and perform, but how shall I answer the people, the city, the elders?' Then Ea opened his mouth and said to me, his servant, 'Tell

◆ **Reading Strategy**
Ea whispers to the house so that he can claim he never directly warned Utnapishtim. What does Ea's cunning suggest about the value that Babylonians placed on this kind of slyness?

---

5. **talents:** Large units of weight and money used in the ancient world.
6. **Anunnaki:** Gods of the underworld.
7. **Euphrates:** (yōō frāt′ ēz): A river flowing from Turkey generally southward through Syria and Iraq, joining the Tigris River.
8. **execration** (ek′ si krā′ shən) *n.*: Cursing, denunciation.
9. **Enki's:** Belonging to Enki, god of wisdom and one of the creators of human beings.

10. **like . . . abyss:** Like the firmament or heaven that covers the depths.

◆ **Build Vocabulary**
teemed (tēmd) *v.*: Produced a great many people
babel (bā bəl) *n.*: Confusion of voices or sounds

them this: I have learnt that Enlil is wrathful against me, I dare no longer walk in his land nor live in his city; I will go down to the Gulf[11] to dwell with Ea my lord. But on you he will rain down abundance, rare fish and shy wild-fowl, a rich harvest-tide. In the evening the rider of the storm will bring you wheat in torrents.'

"In the first light of dawn all my household gathered round me, the children brought pitch and the men whatever was necessary. On the fifth day I laid the keel and the ribs, then I made fast the planking. The ground-space was one acre, each side of the deck measured one hundred and twenty cubits,[12] making a square. I built six decks below, seven in all, I divided them into nine sections with bulkheads between. I drove in wedges where needed, I saw to the punt-poles,[13] and laid in supplies. The carriers brought oil in baskets, I poured pitch into the furnace and asphalt and oil; more oil was consumed in caulking[14] and more again the master of the boat took into his stores. I slaughtered bullocks for the people and every day I killed sheep. I gave the shipwrights wine to drink as though it were river water, raw wine and red wine and oil and white wine. There was feasting then as there is at the time of the New Year's festival; I myself anointed my head. On the seventh day the boat was complete.

"Then was the launching full of difficulty; there was shifting of <u>ballast</u> above and below till two thirds was submerged. I loaded into her all that I had of gold and of living things, my family, my kin, the beasts of the field both wild and tame, and all the craftsmen. I sent them on board, for the time that Shamash had ordained was already fulfilled when he said, 'In the evening, when the rider of the storm sends down the destroying rain, enter the boat and batten her down.' The time was fulfilled, the evening came, the rider of the storm sent down the rain. I looked out at the weather and it was terrible, so I too boarded the boat and battened her down. All was now complete, the battening and the caulking; so I handed the tiller to Puzur-Amurri the steersman, with the navigation and the care of the whole boat.

"With the first light of dawn a black cloud came from the horizon; it thundered within where Adad, lord of the storm, was riding. In front over hill and plain Shullat and Hanish, heralds of the storm, led on. Then the gods of the abyss rose up; Nergal pulled out the dams of the nether[15] waters, Ninurta the war-lord threw down the dykes, and the seven judges of hell, the Anunnaki, raised their torches, lighting the land with their livid flame. A stupor of despair went up to heaven when the god of the storm turned daylight to darkness, when he smashed the land like a cup. One whole day the tempest raged, gathering fury as it went, it poured over the people like the tides of battle; a man could not see his brother nor the people be seen from heaven. Even the gods were terrified at the flood, they fled to the highest heaven, the firmament of Anu; they crouched against the walls, cowering like curs. Then Ishtar the sweet-voiced Queen of Heaven cried out like a woman in travail: 'Alas the days of old are turned to dust because I commanded evil; why did I command this evil in the council of all the gods? I commanded wars to destroy the people, but are they not my people, for I brought them forth? Now like the spawn of fish they float in the ocean.' The great gods of heaven and of hell wept, they covered their mouths.

"For six days and six nights the winds blew, torrent and tempest and flood overwhelmed the world, tempest and flood raged together like warring hosts. When the seventh day dawned the storm from the south <u>subsided</u>, the sea grew calm, the flood was stilled; I looked at the face of the world and there was silence, all mankind was turned to clay. The surface of the sea stretched as flat as a rooftop; I opened a

◆ **Reading Strategy**
Does the reaction of the gods to the flood suggest that they were all-powerful? Why or why not?

---

11. Gulf: The abyss, the great depths of the waters, where Ea, also called Enki, was supposed to dwell.
12. cubits: Ancient units of linear measure, about 18–22 inches each (originally, the distance from the elbow to the tip of the middle finger).
13. punt-poles: Poles that are pushed against the bottom of a shallow river or lake in order to propel a boat.
14. caulking (kôk´ iŋ) v.: Stopping up cracks or seams with a sealant.

15. nether (neth´ ər) adj.: Below the earth's surface; lower.

The Legend of the Fish, Gordon Laite, New York Public Library

▶ **Critical Viewing**
Which descriptions of the flood in the epic of Gilgamesh does this picture best illustrate? Why? [Connect]

hatch and the light fell on my face. Then I bowed low, I sat down and I wept, the tears streamed down my face, for on every side was the waste of water. I looked for land in vain, but fourteen leagues[16] distant there appeared a mountain, and there the boat grounded; on the mountain of Nisir the boat held fast, she held fast and did not budge. One day she held, and a second day on the mountain of Nisir she held fast and did not budge. A third day, and a fourth day she held fast on the mountain and did not budge; a fifth day and a sixth day she held fast on the mountain. When the seventh day dawned I loosed a dove and let her go. She flew away, but finding no resting-place she returned. Then I loosed a swallow, and she flew away but finding no resting-place she returned.

I loosed a raven, she saw that the waters had retreated, she ate, she flew around, she cawed, and she did not come back. Then I threw everything open to the four winds, I made a sacrifice and poured out a libation[17] on the mountain top. Seven and again seven cauldrons I set up on their stands, I heaped up wood and cane and cedar and myrtle. When the gods smelled the sweet savor, they gathered like flies over the sacrifice. Then, at last, Ishtar also came, she lifted her necklace with the jewels of

---

16. **leagues:** Units of linear measure, varying in different times and countries; usually a league is about three miles.

17. **libation** (lī bā′ shən) *n*.: A liquid poured out as a sacrifice to a god.

◆ **Build Vocabulary**

ballast (bal′ əst) *n*.: Anything heavy carried in a ship to make it more stable

subsided (səb sīd′ əd) *v*.: Became less intense or sank to a lower level

▶ **Critical Viewing**
How closely do the boats in this ancient relief resemble Utnapishtim's boat? **[Speculate]**

Transporting Timber by Sea, Louvre, Paris

heaven that once Anu had made to please her. 'O you gods here present, by the lapis lazuli[18] round my neck I shall remember these days as I remember the jewels of my throat: these last days I shall not forget. Let all the gods gather round the sacrifice, except Enlil. He shall not approach this offering, for without reflection he brought the flood; he consigned my people to destruction.'

"When Enlil had come, when he saw the boat, he was wroth and swelled with anger at the gods, the host of heaven, 'Has any of these mortals escaped? Not one was to have survived the destruction.' Then the god of the wells and canals Ninurta opened his mouth and said to the warrior Enlil, 'Who is there of the gods that can devise without Ea? It is Ea alone who knows all things.' Then Ea opened his mouth and spoke to warrior Enlil, 'Wisest of gods, hero Enlil, how could you so senselessly bring down the flood?

Lay upon the sinner his sin,
Lay upon the <u>transgressor</u> his transgression,
Punish him a little when he breaks loose,
Do not drive him too hard or he perishes;
Would that a lion had ravaged mankind
Rather than the flood,
Would that a wolf had ravaged mankind
Rather than the flood,
Would that famine had wasted the world
Rather than the flood,
Would that pestilence had wasted
* mankind*
Rather than the flood.

It was not I that revealed the secret of the gods; the wise man learned it in a dream. Now take your counsel what shall be done with him.'

"Then Enlil went up into the boat, he took me by the hand and my wife and made us enter the boat and kneel down on either side, he standing between us. He touched our foreheads to bless us saying. 'In time past Utnapishtim was a mortal man; henceforth he and his wife

---

18. lapis lazuli (lap′ is laz′ yōō lĭ) *n.*: A sky-blue gemstone.

shall live in the distance at the mouth of the rivers.' Thus it was that the gods took me and placed me here to live in the distance, at the mouth of the rivers."

After hearing Utnapishtim's story, Gilgamesh tries to resist sleeping for six days and seven nights to prove that he, too, can attain immorality. He is unsuccessful. Nevertheless, before returning to Uruk with the ferryman Urshanabi, Gilgamesh learns from Utnapishtim *of an underwater plant that magically restores youth. Gilgamesh dives for this plant and finds some to take back to Uruk for his people. On the journey home, however, a serpent steals this sweet flower. Gilgamesh is bitterly disappointed, but there is nothing he can do. When the travelers reach Uruk, Gilgamesh shows Urshanabi the famous walls of the city.*

◆ **Literary Focus**

Gilgamesh is on a quest for immortality. Does Utnapishtim's story suggest that Gilgamesh will succeed? Why or why not?

◆ **Build Vocabulary**

transgressor (trans gres´ sər) *n.*: Person who breaks a law or commandment

Guide for Responding

◆ Literature and Your Life

Reader's Response Is Gilgamesh the kind of hero that you admire? Why or why not?

Thematic Focus What kinds of quests, if any, do people go on today? Explain.

Reader's Journal List some movies that you could show in a film festival about characters engaged in a quest.

Questions for Research What kinds of sources would you consult to learn more about the rediscovery of the epic of Gilgamesh in the nineteenth century? Explain.

☑ Check Your Comprehension

1. What are three achievements credited to Gilgamesh in the opening section of the epic?
2. Briefly describe how Gilgamesh and Enkidu overcome Humbaba.
3. What disaster occurs in the story that Utnapishtim tells Gilgamesh?
4. How do gods help Utnapishtim survive this disaster and win a special privilege?
5. What happens to Gilgamesh as he journeys back to Uruk?

◆ Critical Thinking

INTERPRET

1. How does Gilgamesh contribute to both the physical well-being and the wisdom of his people? **[Analyze]**
2. Is Gilgamesh a hero without faults in the battle with Humbaba? Why or why not? **[Interpret]**
3. Explain whether Utnapishtim is a hero in the same sense as Gilgamesh is. **[Compare and Contrast]**
4. In what way is this epic a story about striving for goals and admitting limitations? **[Synthesize]**

EVALUATE

5. What explains the survival of this epic over a period of about 4,000 years? **[Assess]**

APPLY

6. In what ways would you change this epic to make it into a modern science-fiction tale or film? **[Modify]**

COMPARE LITERARY WORKS

7. Find a hero from literature who, like Gilgamesh, has a companion. Compare and contrast Enkidu with this companion. **[Compare and Contrast]**

from *The Epic of Gilgamesh* ◆ 57

Guide for Responding (continued)

◆ Reading Strategy

UNDERSTAND CULTURAL CONTEXT

As a reader of *Gilgamesh,* you too must engage in a quest—to understand the **cultural context,** the beliefs and customs, of an ancient and faraway world. You can find clues to this context in descriptions, as well as in characters' words and actions.

1. What does the Prologue indicate about the gods worshipped in Uruk and how they were worshipped?
2. Does the flood story show that ancient Sumerian gods cooperated with one another? Explain.
3. Find three clues indicating that Sumeria was a highly organized society, and explain your choices.

◆ Build Vocabulary

USING THE LATIN PREFIX *sub-*

Explain how the Latin prefix *sub-,* which means "under or below," contributes to the meaning of each of the italicized words:

Captain Utnapishtim wondered whether the floodwaters had *subsided.* Then he noticed that less of his ship seemed to be *submerged.* His son-in-law, whose performance in this flood emergency had been *substandard,* was tossing ballast overboard. "Hey," he shouted, "you're my *subordinate;* you take orders from me! I'm going to *subtract* a bullock from your wages."

USING THE WORD BANK: Sentence Completions

On your paper, complete each analogy using the best word from the Word Bank.

1. *Fire* is to *extinguished* as ___?___ is to *quieted.*
2. *Solution* is to *puzzle* as ___?___ is to *desperation.*
3. *Overflowed* is to *glass* as ___?___ is to *city.*
4. *Paperweight* is to *papers* as ___?___ is to *ship.*
5. *Flood* is to *riverbank* as ___?___ is to *law.*
6. *Rebellious* is to *defiant* as ___?___ is to *sacrifice.*
7. *Loosen* is to *clutch* as ___?___ is to *intensified.*

◆ Literary Focus

ARCHETYPAL THEME: THE HERO'S QUEST

The **quest,** or search, of Gilgamesh for immortality is an **archetypal theme** with meaning for readers of many different cultures. All humans must face the fact that they will die. However, few are as determined as Gilgamesh is in trying to get beyond that human limitation.

The search takes Gilgamesh past the boundaries of the known world, to the only man and woman granted eternal life. The man, Utnapishtim, then tells the king a story that takes him backward in time, past the limits of recorded history. When Gilgamesh finally returns to Uruk he brings not the secret of eternal life but this tale.

1. What part might the king's nature—"two-thirds a god, one-third a man"—play in motivating his quest?
2. How is the flood story both a valuable gift to Gilgamesh and a hint that he cannot avoid death?
3. Why does Gilgamesh's need to sleep prove that he must die?
4. Is the quest a complete failure? Why or why not?

◆ Build Grammar Skills

COMMONLY CONFUSED WORDS: *in* and *into*

The preposition *in* refers to place or position, while the preposition *into* suggests motion.

Practice Copy these sentences in your notebook, choosing the correct preposition (*in* or *into*) for each.

1. (Into/In) Uruk he built walls, a great rampart.
2. I would not go (in/into) Humbaba's land if I were you.
3. The god Ea warned me (in/into) a dream.
4. I no longer dare to live (into/in) Enlil's city.
5. We don't know what readers will think of Gilgamesh (into/in) the future.

Writing Application Using both *in* and *into,* write a one-paragraph sequel to the epic. Tell what Gilgamesh did after he returned to Uruk.

Build Your Portfolio

 ## Idea Bank

Writing

1. **Diary Entry** As Gilgamesh, write an entry in your diary on the day you return to Uruk from your quest.

2. **Museum Plaque** Utnapishtim's ship is on display at a museum. Write a plaque that will be placed on the wall beside the ship. Using details from the epic but your own words, describe its dimensions and its history.

3. **Response to Criticism** N. K. Sandars, the translator, wrote, "The gods, who do not die, cannot be tragic. If Gilgamesh is not the first human hero, he is the first tragic hero . . ." Explain why you do or do not agree that Gilgamesh is a tragic hero.

Speaking, Listening, and Viewing

4. **Movie Pitch** In a brief presentation, convince a producer to fund a movie based on *Gilgamesh*. **[Performing Arts Link; Media Link]**

5. **Press Conference** With several classmates, stage a press conference at which the returning Gilgamesh answers questions about his quest. **[Performing Arts Link; Social Studies Link]**

Researching and Representing

6. **Model of Uruk** Using the epic itself and books about ancient Mesopotamia, create a model of the ancient Sumerian city of Uruk. Materials that might be helpful include wood, cardboard, and papier-mâché. **[Art Link; Social Studies Link]**

7. **Choreography of a Quest** Choreograph a brief dance that portrays Gilgamesh's search for immortality. Then have classmates help you perform the dance. **[Performing Arts Link]**

Online Activity www.phlit.phschool.com

 ## Guided Writing Lesson

Comparison and Contrast

Gilgamesh is a hero on a quest for eternal life. Think of a modern-day hero—from the movies, television, or fiction—who also searches for something. Write an essay comparing and contrasting Gilgamesh with this modern hero. Consider the nature of the goal, the obstacles that must be overcome, any help the hero receives, and the hero's success or failure.

Writing Skills Focus: Logical Organization for Comparison/Contrast

Help the reader follow your thinking by using a **logical organization for comparison / contrast**—for example, include points about the heroes in the same paragraph or in different paragraphs, as follows:

Point of Comparison: The Nature of the Goal

Organization I	Organization II
paragraph	paragraph #1
How goals of A and B are same	Nature of A's goals
How goals of A and B differ	paragraph #2
	Nature of B's goals and how they are the same and different from A's

Prewriting Brainstorm for similarities and differences between the two heroes with regard to these points: the goal, obstacles, help, and success or failure.

Drafting Choose one of the methods of organization diagrammed above (or an equally logical method), and follow it consistently.

Revising Be sure that you have included both similarities and differences, and that you have followed the same organization throughout. Also, be sure you have used *in* and *into* correctly.

Guide for Reading

The Hebrew Bible

The most important example of ancient Hebrew literature is the Bible (called by Christians the Old Testament in contrast to the New Testament). Translated into many languages, it has influenced three major religions: Judaism, Christianity, and Islam.

What Is the Bible? The word *Bible* came from the Greek *biblia,* meaning "a collection of writings." The Bible is "a collection" because it contains many books, divided into three sections. The first section is the Torah, from the Hebrew *tora,* meaning "law." It contains the first five books of the Bible. Together with the book of Joshua, these books tell how the Jews established a nation in Canaan (kā nən), present-day Israel and Lebanon.

Another section, the "Prophets," tells what happened to the Jews in Canaan. It also contains the writings of the prophets, those who in God's name summoned the Jews to the path of justice and faith. Still another section, the "Writings," contains a variety of works, including the poems called psalms.

What Are the Bible's Themes? Despite its diversity, the Bible has a few constant themes: the power, goodness, and mercy of the one God (most other peoples of that era worshipped many gods); the covenant, or solemn agreement, into which God enters with the Hebrew people; the tendency of people to stray from the right path; and the forgiveness that they win from God.

The Bible's Influence For Jews, the Bible was a "Temple of Words," sustaining Jewish culture and beliefs when the actual Temple in Jerusalem was destroyed in 586 B.C. and again in A.D. 70. The Bible has also influenced Muslims and Christians, who, like Jews, worship a single God. Muslims have a central book of their own, the Koran. However, they believe that Biblical figures like Moses are forerunners of the last and greatest prophet, Muhammad.

◆ Build Vocabulary

ANGLO-SAXON SUFFIXES: *-ful*

In Genesis, God tells living creatures to "Be fruitful ... " Because the Anglo-Saxon suffix *-ful* often means "full of," he is literally saying, "be full of fruit." He actually means "have many offspring." The suffix *-ful* can also mean "having the qualities, ability, or tendency to," as in *helpful* and *forgetful.*

WORD BANK

void
fruitful
replenish
subdue
enmity
testimony
meditation

In reading the selections from the Bible, you will encounter the words on this list. Each word is defined on the page where it first appears. Preview the list before you read.

◆ Build Grammar Skills

QUOTATION MARKS

In Genesis 1–3, **quotation marks** indicate a speaker's exact words:

> And God blessed them saying, "Be fruitful and multiply, and fill the waters in the seas, and let fowl multiply in the earth."

When a quotation is introduced by a form of the verb *say,* as shown above, a comma follows the verb and precedes the quotation. Commas and periods at the end of a quotation go inside the closing quotation mark, as also shown above.

A question mark or exclamation mark goes inside the closing quotation mark if the end mark is part of the quotation; if it is not part of the quotation, it goes outside the closing quotation mark. Colons and semicolons fall outside the closing quotation mark unless they are part of the quotation.

◆ *Literature and Your Life*

CONNECT YOUR EXPERIENCE

Numbers seem to be precise and all-powerful on drivers' licenses, social security cards, and bank accounts. However, imagine going for a day, or even an hour, without using words to express feelings, thoughts, requests, secrets, or jokes.

The ancient Hebrews believed so strongly in words that, in Genesis, they envisioned God creating the universe through speech.

Journal Writing Jot down other examples of numbers being used as a source of identification in our society.

THEMATIC FOCUS: CHOICES AND CONSEQUENCES

In reading the account of creation and beginnings in Genesis, answer this question: What is the most important choice that anyone makes in this narrative and what results from it?

◆ Reading Strategy

EVALUATE CHARACTERS' DECISIONS

In most narratives, characters make decisions that affect their own and others' lives. You can **evaluate characters' decisions** by analyzing what motivates these choices, identifying their results, and then concluding whether or not they were wise.

The choices that Adam and Eve make in this biblical narrative affect not only their own lives, but those of every other human. In evaluating their decisions, consider the far-reaching effects of what they do. Also consider what may have prompted them to act.

◆ Literary Focus

ARCHETYPAL SETTING AND PARALLELISM

An **archetypal setting** is a place or feature of a landscape that has a similar symbolic meaning for many peoples. For example, a variety of cultures conceived of an ideal setting—called Eden in Genesis—where people lived without strife and fear. Another element in Genesis that is common to different cultures is a great tree that connects the realms of heaven and earth.

Tradition says that the 150 poems and hymns called Psalms (the Greek *psalmas* means "song") were composed by King David (reigned *c.* 1000 B.C.–962 B.C.). They express fear, gratitude, joy, and despair in relation to God. They do so using a verse pattern called **parallelism,** in which they state an idea, and then repeat, negate, or complete it.

◆ Background for Understanding

HISTORY

As the following timeline indicates, the Hebrews began as a nomadic tribe, became a nation, and eventually lost that nation (creating it again, nearly 2,000 years later, in 1948):

c. 2000–1600 B.C. Origin of Hebrews in what is now Iraq | 2000

Arrival of Hebrews in the Promised Land of Canaan (now Israel and Lebanon) | 1600

pre-1200's B.C. Migration of Hebrews to Egypt in order to escape famine; later, enslavement by Egyptians | 1200

c. 1200's B.C. Under leadership of Moses, liberation of Hebrews from enslavement in Egypt and return to Canaan

Hebrews receive the Ten Commandments

c. 1100's B.C. Philistines arrive in Canaan and battle with Hebrews | 1100

c. 1020 B.C. Saul made first king of Hebrews to fight Philistines and other threatening groups

c. 1000 B.C. Monarchy established by King David as a permanent institution in capital city of Jerusalem

587/586 B.C. Southern half of Israel, Judah, conquered by Babylonia, Temple destroyed, and many Jews sent to exile in Babylonia | 500

515 B.C. Temple rebuilt in Jerusalem | 400

A.D. 70 Second Temple destroyed by Romans, leading to the existence of Judaism in communities scattered among different nations | A.D. 70

Genesis 1-3

The Creation and the Fall

King James Version

CHAPTER 1

1 In the beginning God created the heaven and the earth.

2 And the earth was without form, and <u>void</u>; and darkness was upon the face of the deep. And the Spirit of God moved upon the face of the waters.

3 And God said, "Let there be light": and there was light.

4 And God saw the light, that it was good: and God divided the light from the darkness.

5 And God called the light Day, and the darkness he called Night. And the evening and the morning were the first day.

6 And God said, "Let there be a firmament[1] in the midst of the waters, and let it divide the waters from the waters."

7 And God made the firmament, and divided the waters which were under the firmament from the waters which were above the firmament: and it was so.

8 And God called the firmament Heaven. And the evening and the morning were the second day.

9 And God said, "Let the waters under the heaven be gathered together unto one place, and let the dry land appear": and it was so.

10 And God called the dry land Earth; and the gathering together of the waters called he Seas: and God saw that it was good.

11 And God said, "Let the earth bring forth grass, the herb yielding seed, and the fruit tree yielding fruit after his kind, whose seed is in itself, upon the earth": and it was so.

12 And the earth brought forth grass, and herb yielding seed after his kind, and the tree yielding fruit, whose seed was in itself, after his kind: and God saw that it was good.

13 And the evening and the morning were the third day.

14 And God said, "Let there be lights in the firmament of the heaven to divide the day from the night; and let them be for signs, and for seasons, and for days, and years:

15 "And let them be for lights in the firmament of the heaven to give light upon the earth": and it was so.

16 And God made two great lights; the greater light to rule the day, and the lesser light to rule the night: he made the stars also.

17 And God set them in the firmament of the heaven to give light upon the earth,

18 And to rule over the day and over the night, and to divide the light from the darkness: and God saw that it was good.

19 And the evening and the morning were the fourth day.

---

1. **firmament:** (fʉrm´ ə mənt) *n.*: The sky, viewed poetically as a solid arch or vault.

20 And God said, "Let the waters bring forth abundantly the moving creature that hath life, and fowl that may fly above the earth in the open firmament of heaven."

21 And God created great whales, and every living creature that moveth, which the waters brought forth abundantly, after their kind, and every winged fowl after his kind: and God saw that it was good.

22 And God blessed them, saying, "Be fruitful, and multiply, and fill the waters in the seas, and let fowl multiply in the earth."

23 And the evening and the morning were the fifth day.

24 And God said, "Let the earth bring forth the living creature after his kind, cattle, and creeping thing, and beast of the earth after his kind": and it was so.

25 And God made the beast of the earth after his kind, and cattle after their kind, and every thing that creepeth upon the earth after his kind: and God saw that it was good.

26 And God said, "Let us make man in our image, after our likeness: and let them have dominion[2] over the fish of the sea, and over the fowl of the air, and over the cattle, and over all the earth, and over every creeping thing that creepeth upon the earth."

27 So God created man in his own image, in the image of God created he him; male and female created he them.

28 And God blessed them, and God said unto them, "Be fruitful, and multiply, and replenish the earth, and subdue it: and have dominion over the fish of the sea, and over the fowl of the air, and over every living thing that moveth upon the earth."

29 And God said, "Behold, I have given you every herb bearing seed, which is upon the face of all the earth, and every tree, in the which is the fruit of a tree yielding seed; to you it shall be for meat."

30 "And to every beast of the earth, and to every fowl of the air, and to every thing that creepeth upon the earth, wherein there is life, I have given every green herb for meat": and it was so.

31 And God saw every thing that he had made, and, behold, it was very good. And the evening and the morning were the sixth day.

CHAPTER 2

1 Thus the heavens and the earth were finished, and all the host of them.

2 And on the seventh day God ended his work which he had made; and he rested on the seventh day from all his work which he had made.

3 And God blessed the seventh day, and sanctified it: because that in it he had rested from all his work which God created and made.

4 These are the generations of the heavens and of the earth when they were created, in the day that the Lord God made the earth and the heavens,

5 And every plant of the field before it was in the earth, and every herb of the field before it grew: for the Lord God had not caused it to rain upon the earth, and there was not a man to till the ground.

6 But there went up a mist from the earth, and watered the whole face of the ground.

7 And the Lord God formed man of the dust of the ground,[3] and breathed into his nostrils the breath of life; and man became a living soul.

8 And the Lord God planted a garden eastward in Eden; and there he put the man whom he had formed.

9 And out of the ground made the Lord God to grow every tree that is pleasant to the sight, and good for food; the tree of life also in the midst of the garden, and the tree of knowledge of good and evil.

◆ **Literary Focus**
Why do you think that the Bible suggests "a garden" is the ideal setting for humans?

---

3. **And the Lord God . . . ground:** The name Adam is said to come from the Hebrew word 'adhāmāh, meaning "earth."

◆ **Build Vocabulary**
void (void) adj.: Vacant or empty
fruitful (frōōt´ fəl) adj.: Producing much, productive
replenish (ri plen´ ish) v.: Make full or complete again
subdue (səb dōō´) v.: Conquer or master

---

2. **dominion** (də min´ yən) n.: Rule or power to rule.

10 And a river went out of Eden to water the garden; and from thence it was parted, and became into four heads.

11 The name of the first is Pison: that is it which compasseth the whole land of Havilah, where there is gold;

12 And the gold of that land is good: there is bdellium[4] and onyx stone.

13 And the name of the second river is Gihon: the same is it that compasseth the whole land of Ethiopia.

14 And the name of the third river is Hiddekel: that is it which goeth toward the east of Assyria. And the fourth river is Euphrates.[5]

15 And the Lord God took the man, and put him into the garden of Eden to dress it and to keep it.

16 And the Lord God commanded the man, saying, "Of every tree of the garden thou mayest freely eat:"

17 "But of the tree of knowledge of good and evil, thou shalt not eat of it: for in the day that thou eatest thereof thou shalt surely die."

◆ **Reading Strategy**
In Genesis 2:17, God gives a command. What decision will Adam have to make concerning this command?

18 And the Lord God said, "It is not good that the man should be alone; I will make him an help meet for him."

19 And out of the ground the Lord God formed every beast of the field, and every fowl of the air; and brought them unto Adam to see what he would call them: and whatsoever Adam called every living creature, that was the name thereof.

20 And Adam gave names to all cattle, and to the fowl of the air, and to every beast of the field; but for Adam there was not found an help meet for him.

21 And the Lord God caused a deep sleep to fall upon Adam, and he slept: and he took one of his ribs, and closed up the flesh instead thereof;

22 And the rib, which the Lord God had taken from man, made he a woman, and brought her unto the man.

23 And Adam said, "This is now bone of my bones, and flesh of my flesh: she shall be called Woman, because she was taken out of Man."

24 Therefore shall a man leave his father and his mother, and shall cleave unto his wife: and they shall be one flesh.

25 And they were both naked, the man and his wife, and were not ashamed.

CHAPTER 3

1 Now the serpent was more subtil[6] than any beast of the field which the Lord God had made. And he said unto the woman, "Yea, hath God said, 'Ye shall not eat of every tree of the garden'?"

2 And the woman said unto the serpent, "We may eat of the fruit of the trees of the garden:

3 "But of the fruit of the tree which is in the midst of the garden, God hath said, 'Ye shall not eat of it, neither shall ye touch it, lest ye die.'"

4 And the serpent said unto the woman, "Ye shall not surely die:"

5 "For God doth know that in the day ye eat thereof, then your eyes shall be opened and ye shall be as gods, knowing good and evil."

6 And when the woman saw that the tree was good for food, and that it was pleasant to the eyes, and a tree to be desired to make one wise, she took of the fruit thereof, and did eat, and gave also unto her husband with her; and he did eat.

7 And the eyes of them both were opened, and they knew that they were naked; and they sewed fig leaves together, and made themselves aprons.

8 And they heard the voice of the Lord God walking in the garden in the cool of the day: and Adam and his wife hid themselves from the

---

4. **bdellium:** (del´ ē əm): A deep-red gem.
5. **Assyria . . . Euphrates** (yo͞o frāt´ ēz): Assyria was an ancient empire in southwestern Asia; the Euphrates River flows from East Central Turkey generally southward through Syria and Iraq.

---

6. **subtil,** old-fashioned spelling for **subtle** (sut´ 'l) *adj.*: Crafty, sly, and clever.

Expulsion From Paradise, Accademia, Florence, Italy

▲ **Critical Viewing** This picture shows Adam and Eve leaving Eden. What do their faces suggest they are feeling? **[Interpret]**

presence of the Lord God amongst the trees of the garden.

9 And the Lord God called unto Adam, and said unto him, "Where art thou?"

10 And he said, "I heard thy voice in the garden, and I was afraid, because I was naked; and I hid myself."

11 And he said, "Who told thee that thou wast naked? Hast thou eaten of the tree, whereof I

commanded thee that thou shouldest not eat?"

12 And the man said, "The woman whom thou gavest to be with me, she gave me of the tree, and I did eat."

13 And the Lord God said unto the woman, "What is this that thou hast done?" And the woman said, "The serpent beguiled[7] me, and I did eat."

14 And the Lord God said unto the serpent, "Because thou hast done this, thou art cursed above all cattle and above every beast of the

---

7. beguiled (bē gīld') v.: Tricked, deceived.

field; upon thy belly shalt thou go, and dust shalt thou eat all the days of thy life:

15 "And I will put <u>enmity</u> between thee and the woman, and between thy seed[8] and her seed; it shall bruise thy head, and thou shalt bruise his heel."

16 Unto the woman he said, "I will greatly multiply thy sorrow and thy conception; in sorrow thou shalt bring forth children; and thy desire shall be to thy husband, and he shall rule over thee."

17 And unto Adam he said, "Because thou hast hearkened unto the voice of thy wife, and hast eaten of the tree, of which I commanded thee, saying 'Thou shalt not eat of it': cursed is the ground for thy sake; in sorrow shalt thou eat of it all the days of thy life;

18 "Thorns also and thistles shall it bring forth to thee; and thou shalt eat the herb of the field;

19 "In the sweat of thy face shalt thou eat bread, till thou return unto the ground; for out of it wast thou taken: for dust thou art, and unto dust shalt thou return."

20 And Adam called his wife's name Eve; be-cause she was the mother of all living.[9]

21 Unto Adam also and to his wife did the Lord God make coats of skins, and clothed them.

22 And the Lord God said, "Behold, the man is become as one of us, to know good and evil: and now, lest he put forth his hand, and take also of the tree of life, and eat, and live for ever":

23 Therefore the Lord God sent him forth from the garden of Eden, to till the ground from whence he was taken.

24 So he drove out the man; and he placed at the east of the garden of Eden Cherubims[10] and a flaming sword which turned every way, to keep the way of the tree of life.

---

9. **Mother . . . living:** *Hawwāh*, the Hebrew word trans-lated as Eve, is derived from another Hebrew word mean-ing "alive" or "a living thing."

10. **Cherubims** (cher′ ə bimz): Winged heavenly beings that support the throne of God or act as guardian spirits.

◆ **Build Vocabulary**

enmity (en′ mə tē) *n*.: Hostility, the bitter attitude of an enemy

---

8. **seed:** Descendants.

Guide for Responding

◆ *Literature and Your Life*

Reader's Response Which chapters of Genesis did you find most interesting? Why?

Thematic Focus In what way is this narrative about freedom of choice?

☑ **Check Your Comprehension**

1. What does God create on the first day?
2. According to Chapter 1, on what day does God create man and woman?
3. Describe the place where the first man and woman live.
4. Briefly tell how the first man and woman violate God's commandment.
5. What happens to Adam and Eve as a result of their disobedience?

◆ **Critical Thinking**

INTERPRET
1. What relationship do humans have to God and to the rest of creation? **[Interpret]**
2. How are the Adam and Eve of Chapter 2 different from ordinary humans? **[Compare and Contrast]**
3. How do the events of Chapter 3 take Adam and Eve farther from God and closer to humanity? **[Support]**

APPLY
4. How does this narrative explain some basic problems that humans face in everyday life? **[Connect]**

David Composing the Psalms,
Bibliothèque Nationale de France

◄ **Critical Viewing**
What does this picture indicate about the music used to accompany the psalms? **[Interpret]**

Psalm 8
King James Version

1 O Lord our Lord, how excellent is thy name in all the earth! who hast set thy glory above the heavens.

2 Out of the mouth of babes and sucklings hast thou ordained[1] strength because of thine enemies, that thou mightest still the enemy and the avenger.

3 When I consider thy heavens, the work of thy fingers, the moon and the stars, which thou hast ordained;

4 What is man, that thou art mindful of him? and the son of man, that thou visitest him?

5 For thou hast made him a little lower than the angels, and hast crowned him with glory and honor.

6 Thou madest him to have dominion over the works of thy hands; thou has put all things under his feet;

7 All sheep and oxen, yea, and the beasts of the field;

8 The fowl of the air, and the fish of the sea, and whatsoever passeth through the paths of the seas.

9 O Lord our Lord, how excellent is thy name in all the earth!

1. ordained (ôr dānd´) *v.*: Decreed; ordered; established.

from the *Bible* ◆ 67

Psalm 19

King James Version

1 The heavens declare the glory of God; and the firmament showeth his handywork.

2 Day unto day uttereth speech, and night unto night showeth knowledge.

3 There is no speech nor language, where their voice is not heard.

4 Their line[1] is gone out through all the earth, and their words to the end of the world. In them hath he set a tabernacle[2] for the sun,

5 Which is as a bridegroom coming out of his chamber, and rejoiceth as a strong man to run a race.

6 His going forth is from the end of the heaven, and his circuit unto the ends of it: and there is nothing hid from the heat thereof.

7 The law of the Lord is perfect, converting the soul: the testimony of the Lord is sure, making wise the simple.

8 The statutes of the Lord are right, rejoicing the heart: the commandment of the Lord is pure, enlightening the eyes.

9 The fear of the Lord is clean, enduring for ever: the judgments of the Lord are true and righteous altogether.

10 More to be desired are they than gold, yea, than much fine gold: sweeter also than honey and the honeycomb.

11 Moreover by them is thy servant warned: and in keeping of them there is great reward.

12 Who can understand his errors? cleanse thou me from secret faults.

13 Keep back thy servant also from presumptuous sins; let them not have dominion over me: then shall I be upright, and I shall be innocent from the great transgression.[3]

14 Let the words of my mouth, and the meditation of my heart, be acceptable in thy sight, O Lord, my strength, and my redeemer.

▲ Critical Viewing In what way does this sculpture relate to the images in Psalm 23:1–4? [Connect]

---

1. **Their line:** Their call.
2. **tabernacle** (tab´ ər nak´ al): Temporary shelter for a shrine; place of worship.
3. **transgression** (trans gresh´ ən): Sin.

◆ Build Vocabulary

testimony (tes´ tə mō´ nē) *n.:* Statement, word, or declaration

meditation (med´ ə tā´ shən) *n.:* Deep, continued thought

Psalm 23

King James Version

1 The Lord is my shepherd; I shall not want.

2 He maketh me to lie down in green pastures: he leadeth me beside the still waters.

3 He restoreth my soul: he leadeth me in the paths of righteousness for his name's sake.

4 Yea, though I walk through the valley of the shadow of death, I will fear no evil: for thou art with me; thy rod and thy staff they comfort me.

5 Thou preparest a table before me in the presence of mine enemies: thou anointest my head with oil;[1] my cup runneth over.

6 Surely goodness and mercy shall follow me all the days of my life: and I will dwell in the house of the Lord forever.

___

1. **anointest . . . oil:** To put oil on in a ceremony of blessing.

Guide for Responding

◆ Literature and Your Life

Reader's Response Which of the these psalms would be most comforting in a time of crisis? Why?

Thematic Focus In what way do the authors of these psalms choose to relate to God?

Question for Research Jot down what else you would like to learn about the psalms. Also, indicate some sources that might give you this information.

☑ Check Your Comprehension

1. What does Psalm 8 say about "man" in verses 5 and 6?
2. In Psalm 19, what do the heavens do?
3. How does Psalm 19 describe God's "law" and "statutes"?
4. To what does Psalm 23 compare God and the believer?

◆ Critical Thinking

INTERPRET

1. For the author of Psalm 8, what role do humans play in the universe? **[Interpret]**
2. Scholars suggest that Psalm 19 combines two different poems (1–6 and 7–14). How do these poems differ in what they praise? **[Compare and Contrast]**
3. What is the author trying to convey about the relationship between God and humans in verses 1–4 of Psalm 23? **[Draw Conclusions]**

EXTEND

4. Which of these psalms would work best with a musical setting? Why? **[Music Link]**

COMPARE LITERARY WORKS

5. Compare and contrast Genesis 1:26–30 with Psalm 8: 4–8. **[Compare and Contrast]**

Beyond Literature

History Connection

Translations of the Bible The Bible, a collection of books developed over a period of more than 1,200 years, consists of two main parts: the Old Testament and the New Testament. The Old Testament was originally written in Hebrew; the New Testament, in Greek. In the fourth century A.D., St. Jerome began translating the Bible into Latin. This translation, the Vulgate, remained the standard Bible of the West for centuries.

John Wycliffe produced the first English translation from Latin in the late 1300's. However, not until the birth of Protestantism in the 1500's was there a strong demand for a Bible in English. That demand was prompted by two factors: the Protestant emphasis on the authority of the Bible and Gutenberg's invention of movable type, which made it possible for common people—who usually could not read Latin—to own a Bible.

To meet this demand, the Protestant chaplain William Tyndale decided to prepare a new English translation of the Bible. Faced with clerical opposition at home, Tyndale fled to what is now Germany and there published his English translation of the New Testament. However, he was still working on his translation of the Old Testament when he was arrested for heresy and executed near Brussels, Belgium, in 1536.

Tyndale's efforts would not be in vain. Two years earlier, in 1534, Henry VIII had severed ties with the Catholic Church and established the Church of England. As England became more Protestant, the nation began to view Tyndale not as a heretic but as a hero.

By the time King James I ascended the English throne in 1603, there were several competing translations of the Bible. People wanted an English version that everyone would use. In 1604, the king responded by commissioning fifty-four scholars and clergymen to compare all texts of the Bible and come up with a definitive English edition. They consulted other English translations, but they followed most closely the magnificent diction and rhythms of Tyndale's translation.

The King James or Authorized Version of the Bible was published in 1611. It was a culmination of the long efforts to bring the Bible to the common people, as well as a monumental achievement in literature. The King James Bible has been called "the only classic ever created by a committee," and its influence on the English language continues today.

Activity Compare and contrast a passage from the King James Bible with the same passage in several other English translations of the Bible. Note and describe the differences among the versions.

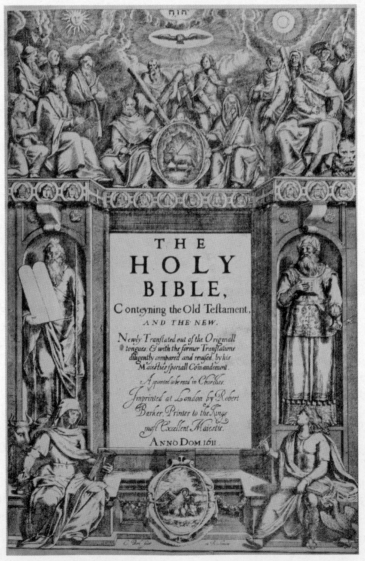

THE
HOLY
BIBLE,
Conteyning the Old Testament,
AND THE NEW.
Newly Translated out of the Originall
tongues, & with the former Translations
diligently compared and reuised, by his
Maiesties speciall Comandement.
Appointed to be read in Churches.
Imprinted at London by Robert
Barker, Printer to the Kings
most Excellent Maiestie.
ANNO DOM. 1611.

Guide for Responding (continued)

◆ Literary Focus

ARCHETYPAL SETTING AND PARALLELISM

An **archetypal setting** is a place or a feature of landscape with a similar meaning for many different peoples. Archetypes in the setting of Genesis 1–3 include Eden itself, a garden safe from the changes of time, and the trees of knowledge and life that grow there. Eden is somewhat similar to the Elysian fields of classical mythology, a place where heroes lived at ease forever.

Parallelism is a system by which biblical writers state an idea in the first half of a verse and then repeat, negate, complete, or otherwise elaborate on it in the second half. For example, in verse 5 of Psalm 19, the second half uses a different comparison to elaborate on the meaning of the first half:

> Which is as a bridegroom coming out of his chamber and rejoiceth as a strong man to run a race.

1. How do the archetypal trees in Genesis provide possible links between humans and the divine?
2. In Psalm 8: 4–7, which numbered verse is not an example of parallelism? Why?
3. Explain the parallelism in Psalm 19:10.

◆ Build Vocabulary

USING THE ANGLO-SAXON SUFFIX -ful

Add the Anglo-Saxon suffix -ful ("full of or having the qualities, ability, or tendency to") to each numbered word, define the new word, and use it in a sentence. (You may have to replace a *y* with an *i*.)

1. fruit   3. forget
2. suspense   4. mercy

USING THE WORD BANK: Synonyms

On your paper, write the word that is the best synonym of the word from the Word Bank.

1. replenish: (a) redo, (b) replete, (c) restock
2. testimony: (a) rules, (b) statement, (c) guilt
3. enmity: (a) hostility, (b) amity, (c) parity
4. fruitful: (a) tasty, (b) helpful, (c) productive
5. subdue: (a) fill, (b) vanquish, (c) undermine
6. void: (a) empty, (b) vast, (c) dark
7. meditation: (a) daydream, (b) repetition, (c) thought

◆ Reading Strategy

EVALUATE CHARACTERS' DECISIONS

You can **evaluate characters' decisions** by analyzing what causes them, determining their results, and then deciding whether or not they were good choices. A chart like this one will help you judge the decisions that Adam and Eve make. (Some entries have been filled in for you.)

Character	Motives	Decision and Results
Serpent		
Eve	• snake convinces her she won't die	• she eats apple and must leave garden
Adam		• he eats apple and must leave garden

1. On your paper, fill in the chart by speculating about the serpent's and Adam's motives, adding motives for Eve, and listing more results of the decisions.
2. Use the chart to evaluate the wisdom of the choices.

◆ Build Grammar Skills

QUOTATION MARKS

A speaker's exact words are placed within opening (") and closing (") **quotation marks.** When the quotation is introduced by a form of the verb *say* or a synonym of it, a comma precedes the quotation.

Commas and periods at the end of a quotation go inside the closing quotation mark. A question mark or exclamation mark goes inside the closing mark if the end mark is part of the closing quotation; if it is not, it falls outside the closing quotation mark. Colons and semicolons fall outside the closing quotation mark unless part of the quotation.

Practice On your paper, correctly insert quotation marks in each sentence.

1. The woman said, The serpent beguiled me.
2. I have given you every herb-bearing seed, God said.
3. He said, Who told thee that thou wast naked?
4. God said, Let . . . the dry land appear: and it was so.
5. The Bible says, And the gold of that land is good: there is bdellium and onyx stone.

Build Your Portfolio

Idea Bank

Writing

1. **Comparison and Contrast** Tell what is similar and different about Adam and Eve. Consider the ways in which God created them, their personalities, and their actions.

2. **Cause-Effect Analysis** Write a cause-effect analysis of the actions in Genesis 3. Show how one action brings about another until Adam and Eve must leave the garden.

3. **Critique** Evaluate the effectiveness of repetition in Genesis 1–3. Consider its role in stressing ideas, showing the stately progress of creation, and reassuring readers that order is coming out of chaos. As an alternative, evaluate the effectiveness of parallelism in one of the psalms.

Speaking, Listening, and Viewing

4. **Choral Reading** With a group, read Genesis 1 or a psalm aloud. Decide which passages will be read by the group and which by individuals. Express the lofty tone and measured pace of the work you choose. **[Performing Arts Link]**

5. **Debate** With a small group of classmates, divide into teams and debate this resolution: The disobedience of Adam and Eve was not primarily their fault. **[Performing Arts Link; Social Studies Link]**

Researching and Representing

6. **Picture of Paradise** Using details from Genesis 2: 8–17 and your own imagination, draw a picture of the Garden of Eden. **[Art Link]**

7. **Report on an Archetype** Describe an archetype from Genesis as it appears in a story from another culture. For example, describe the world-tree Yggdrasill in Norse mythology. **[Social Studies Link]**

Online Activity www.phlit.phschool.com

Guided Writing Lesson

Extended Definition of Paradise

Suppose you had to define the meanings of paradise for someone unfamiliar with this archetype. Using the descriptions of Eden in Genesis 2 and 3, write an extended definition of paradise. Identify and describe all the qualities that make Eden an enchanted place, protected and apart from the world.

Writing Skills Focus:
Illustrate by Using Specific Examples

Your definition will be more complete if you illustrate each quality of paradise with one or more **specific examples:** quotations or descriptions that help readers understand the definition. For instance, you might say that an important quality of paradise is the easy availability of food. Then, as an example to illustrate this quality, you might use Genesis 2:16:

> And the Lord God commanded the man saying, "Of every tree of the garden thou mayest freely eat."

Prewriting To formulate your definition, create a sunburst diagram like this one, with a brief general definition in the center and qualities that you will illustrate at the end of each "sunray":

no death
see 3:19

paradise is a protected place apart . . .

humans can talk with animals
see 3:1–2

Drafting Referring to your diagram, begin with your general definition. Then create an extended definition by describing the qualities you have diagrammed and by using specific examples to illustrate each one.

Revising Have classmates read your definition and tell you whether they understand it. Also, where you have used quotations as examples, check that you have included correct punctuation. For more on quotation marks, see pp. 60 and 71.

PART 2 Modern and Contemporary World Literature

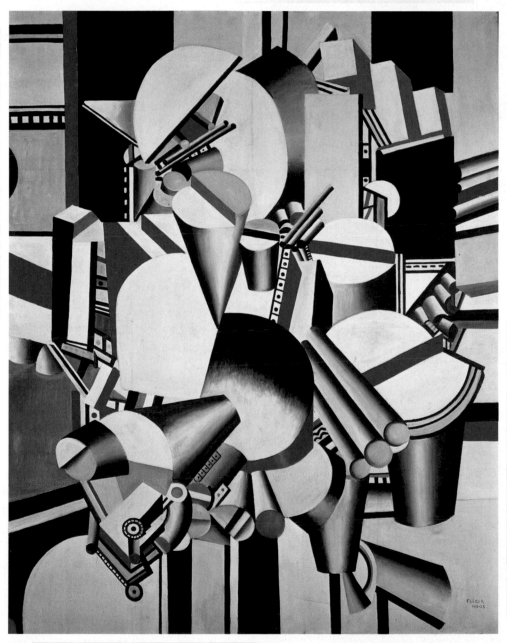

Mechanical Elements, Fernand Léger, Kunstmuseum, Basle, Switzerland

Guide for Reading

Franz Kafka *(1883–1924)*

Franz Kafka (fränts käf´ kə) was born in Prague, then part of the Austro-Hungarian empire and not the capital of Czechoslovakia. Today that once-mighty empire no longer exists, while the once-obscure Kafka is world-famous for his tales and novels that blend realistic and fantastic details.

Problematic Childhood

Kafka grew up as the only son in a family of six. His father was a successful and domineering self-made businessman, and Kafka spent a good part of his life alternately longing for his father's approval and resenting his strictness. Kafka lived in this unhappy family situation until he was thirty-two.

Writer and Bureaucrat
Despite his interest in literature, he studied law at the University of Prague. Eventually, he found employment with an insurance company and pursued a career there until 1922. His office life served as a model for the strange and baffling bureaucracies that appear in his fiction.

An Outsider
Though reasonably successful, Kafka always felt like an outsider. Not only was he at odds with his father, but he was a Jew in an environment that was often anti-Jewish. Also, as a German speaker and writer, he was again an outsider when Prague became the capital of the new country of Czechoslovakia after World War I.

Enduring Work
Yet his feelings that he didn't fit in helped him write for a world in which everyone was becoming an outsider. Although he died of tuberculosis at an early age, Kafka's friend Max Brod preserved his writings. Brod arranged for the publication of Kafka's unfinished novels, *The Trial, The Castle,* and *Amerika,* together with other works. Soon, though too late for him, this outsider was recognized as one of the great authors of the twentieth century.

Gabriela Mistral *(1889–1957)*

Gabriela Mistral (gä brē ā´ lä mēs träl´), worked as a schoolteacher in her native Chile and later served in Chile's foreign service. In 1945, she became the first woman poet and first Latin American to receive the Nobel Prize for Literature.

◆ Build Vocabulary

LATIN PREFIXES: *ir-*

In "The Bucket Rider," the narrator says that he must prove "irrefutably" his dire need for coal. The Latin prefix *ir-,* which is part of this word, often means "no, not, or without." Added to *refutably,* "in a way that can be refuted or proven wrong," this prefix creates a word meaning "in a way that cannot be proven wrong."

rime
irrefutably
dregs
mode
ewe

WORD BANK

As you read these selections, you will encounter the words on this list. Each word is defined on the page where it first appears.

◆ Build Grammar Skills

CORRECT USE OF *who, which,* AND *that*

The translators of Kafka's story correctly use the relative pronouns *who, which,* and *that* when referring to nouns. *Who* refers only to people, *which* refers only to things, and *that* refers to people or things. Following are examples from the story:

I must approach like a beggar, *who* . . . (*who* modifies a person, "beggar")

. . . it must be . . . a very old customer, *that* . . . (*that* refers to a person, "customer")

My bucket has all the virtues . . . except powers of resistance, *which* it has not. (*which* refers to a thing, "powers")

The Bucket Rider ◆ Small White Clothes

◆ Literature and Your Life

CONNECT YOUR EXPERIENCE

When you dream at night, you enter a world in which the ordinary and the fantastic meet and mingle. For example, you might dream of walking out your front door and discovering a vast desert.

The world of "The Bucket Rider" also strangely combines the usual and the impossible. As you read it, you may feel that you are dreaming with your eyes wide open.

Journal Writing Jot down why you think nighttime dreams do or do not serve a specific purpose.

THEME: STRIVING FOR SUCCESS

In reading, ask yourself this question: How is striving for success in Kafka's dreamlike world different from striving for success in the real world?

◆ Background for Understanding

HISTORY

You cannot appreciate how Kafka combines the commonplace and the fantastic until you understand his everyday reality. For example, from the early 1800's to the early 1900's, coal was the main source of energy for all industrial countries. In Austria-Hungary, where Kafka lived, as in many other northern countries, coal was essential for heating homes in the winter.

Kafka lived through a coal shortage in Austria-Hungary during the winter of 1916–1917. The memory of that actual shortage is preserved in the strange story "The Bucket Rider," which Kafka's friend Max Brod called "the sole thing of beauty that came out of the coal shortage."

◆ Literary Focus

THE FANTASTIC

Literature of the **fantastic** combines ordinary with impossible events to express a writer's deepest thoughts and feelings. Such literature differs from simple daydreams and fantasies because it displays a writer's inner realities.

Kafka produced some of the twentieth century's greatest tales of the fantastic. When reading "The Bucket Rider," notice how realistic details are all tangled up with impossible events. Also, decide what inner truth about himself Kafka is expressing with his dreamlike narrative.

◆ Reading Strategy

COMPARE AND CONTRAST WITH OTHER WORKS

You can better understand an unusual work of literature if you **compare and contrast** it with other works, seeing how it is similar and different from them. In comparing works, consider such items as plot, setting, characters, and theme.

Use this technique by comparing and contrasting "The Bucket Rider" with fairy tales, folk tales, and adventure stories you know. Insert your comparisons in a chart like this one (a comparison has been filled in for you):

Other Works	Similarities to Kafka's	Differences from Kafka's
Superman adventure	• Like Superman, Bucket Rider has magic powers	• Unlike Superman, Bucket Rider fails in his quest

The Bucket Rider

Franz Kafka
Translated by Willa and Edwin Muir

Coal all spent; the bucket empty; the shovel useless; the stove breathing out cold; the room freezing; the trees outside the window rigid, covered with <u>rime</u>; the sky a silver shield against anyone who looks for help from it. I must have coal; I cannot freeze to death; behind me is the pitiless stove, before me the pitiless sky, so I must ride out between them and on my journey seek aid from the coaldealer. But he has already grown deaf to ordinary appeals; I must prove <u>irrefutably</u> to him that I have not a single grain of coal left, and that he means to me the very sun in the firmament.[1] I must approach like a beggar, who, with the death rattle already in his throat, insists on dying on the doorstep, and to whom the cook accordingly decides to give the <u>dregs</u> of the coffeepot; just so must the coaldealer, filled with rage, but acknowledging the command "Thou shalt not kill," fling a shovelful of coal into my bucket.

My <u>mode</u> of arrival must decide the matter; so I ride off on the bucket. Seated on the bucket, my hands on the handle, the simplest kind of bridle, I propel myself with difficulty down the stairs; but once downstairs my bucket ascends, superbly, superbly; camels humbly squatting on the ground do not rise with more dignity, shaking themselves under the sticks of their drivers. Through the hard-frozen streets we go at a regular canter; often I am upraised as high as the first story of a house; never do I sink as low as the house doors. And at last I float at an extraordinary height above the vaulted cellar of the dealer, whom I see far below crouching over his table, where he is writing; he has opened the door to let out the excessive heat.

"Coaldealer!" I cry in a voice burned hollow by the frost and muffled in the cloud made by my breath, "please, coaldealer, give me a little coal. My bucket is so light that I can ride on it. Be kind. When I can I'll pay you."

---

1. **firmament** (fʉrmʹ ə ment) *n*.: The sky, viewed poetically as a solid arch.

◆ Literary Focus
Are there any fantastic details in this opening description? Explain.

◆ Build Vocabulary
rime (rīm) *n*.: Icy crystals that form on a freezing surface as moist air contacts it; frost

irrefutably (ir refʹ yo͞o tə blē) *adv*.: In a way that cannot be disproved

dregs (dregz) *n*.: Particles of solid matter that settle at the bottom of a liquid

mode (mōd) *n*.: Method; the manner in which one does something

Untitled, 1983, Georg Baselitz, The Metropolitan Museum of Art

▲ **Critical Viewing** The artist, Georg Baselitz, meant the figure in the picture to be upside down. In what ways does the picture, like Kafka's story, blend realistic and fantastic details? **[Connect]**

The dealer puts his hand to his ear. "Do I hear right?" he throws the question over his shoulder to his wife. "Do I hear right? A customer."

"I hear nothing," says his wife, breathing in and out peacefully while she knits on, her back pleasantly warmed by the heat.

"Oh yes, you must hear," I cry. "It's me; an old customer; faithful and true; only without means at the moment."

"Wife," says the dealer, "it's someone, it must be; my ears can't have deceived me so much as that; it must be an old, a very old customer, that can move me so deeply."

"What ails you, man?" says his wife, ceasing from her work for a moment and pressing her knitting to her bosom. "It's nobody, the street is empty, all our customers are provided for; we could close down the shop for several days and take a rest."

"But I'm sitting up here on the bucket," I cry, and numb, frozen tears dim my eyes, "please look up here, just once; you'll see me directly; I beg you, just a shovelful; and if you give me more it'll make me so happy that I won't know what to do. All the other customers are provided for. Oh, if I could only hear the coal clattering into the bucket!"

"I'm coming," says the coaldealer, and on his short legs he makes to climb the steps of the cellar, but his wife is already beside him, holds him back by the arm and says: "You stay here; seeing you persist in your fancies I'll go myself. Think of the bad fit of coughing you had during the night. But for a piece of business, even if it's one you've only fancied in your head, you're prepared to forget your wife and child and sacrifice your lungs. I'll go."

"Then be sure to tell him all the kinds of coal we have in stock! I'll shout out the prices after you."

"Right," says his wife, climbing up to the street. Naturally she sees me at once. "Frau Coaldealer," I cry, "my humblest greetings; just one shovelful of coal; here in my bucket; I'll carry it home myself. One shovelful of the worst you have. I'll pay you in full for it, of course, but not just now, not just now." What a knell-like sound the words "not just now" have, and how bewilderingly they mingle with the evening chimes that fall from the church steeple nearby!

"Well, what does he want?" shouts the dealer. "Nothing," his wife shouts back, "there's nothing here; I see nothing, I hear nothing; only six striking, and now we must shut up the shop. The cold is terrible; tomorrow we'll likely have lots to do again."

She sees nothing and hears nothing; but all the same she loosens her apron strings and waves her apron to waft me away. She succeeds, unluckily. My bucket has all the virtues of a good steed except powers of resistance, which it has not; it is too light; a woman's apron can make it fly through the air.

"You bad woman!" I shout back, while she, turning into the shop, half-contemptuous, half-reassured, flourishes her fist in the air. "You bad woman! I begged you for a shovelful of the worst coal and you would not give it me." And with that I ascend into the regions of the ice mountains and am lost forever.

> ◆ **Reading Strategy**
> Can you think of a story or film in which a hero with magical powers is defeated as easily as the narrator of this story? Explain.

Small White Clothes

Gabriela Mistral

Translated by
Christine Jacox Kyle

I knit tiny booties, I cut the soft
diapers; I want to make everything by
hand. They'll come from my depths,
they'll remember my perfume.

5   Soft fleece of the <u>ewe</u>: this summer
they sheared you for him. For eight
months your soft wool swelled like a
sponge, bleached by January's moon. It
doesn't have any small thistle needles or
10   blackberry thorns. The soft wool of my
own flesh, where he has slept, is just
like this.

Small white clothes! He looks at
them through my eyes and smiles,
15   imagining them to be the softest . . .

♦ **Build Vocabulary**

ewe (yōō) *n*.: Female sheep

Guide for Responding

♦ *Literature and Your Life*

Reader's Response What did you find most incredible about the Kafka story? Explain.

Thematic Focus How would the bucket rider define success? Explain.

Reader's Journal Copy the first and last sentences of the story. Then, jot down words that express the emotional effect of these sentences.

✓ Check Your Comprehension

1. In the story, what does the narrator need?
2. How does the narrator of "The Bucket Rider" travel to get what he needs?
3. How do the man and the wife in "The Bucket Rider" respond to the narrator in different ways?
4. What happens to the narrator at the end of "The Bucket Rider"?
5. What is the speaker in "Small White Clothes" doing?

♦ Critical Thinking

INTERPRET

1. In what ways is Kafka's narrator both powerful and powerless? **[Support]**
2. The narrator claims that the coaldealer's wife sees him, yet she says, "I see nothing." What accounts for this difference? **[Analyze]**
3. What might the coal in Kafka's story symbolize? **[Draw Conclusions]**
4. In "Small White Clothes," what do the speaker's thoughts suggest about her skills as a parent? **[Draw Conclusions]**

APPLY

5. Jot down the dialogue that the coaldealer in Kafka's story might have with his wife after the narrator vanishes. **[Speculate]**

COMPARE LITERARY WORKS

6. Compare and contrast the coaldealer's wife in Kafka's story with the speaker in "Small White Clothes." **[Compare and Contrast]**

Guide for Responding (continued)

◆ Literary Focus

THE FANTASTIC

Kafka's "The Bucket Rider" is an example of the **fantastic** because it uses realistic and unrealistic events to express the author's inner realities. The coal shortage in the story was based on a shortage that actually occurred. What is strangely unreal, however, is the narrator's use of his empty coal bucket as a magical means of transportation.

Typical of Kafka, however, is his realistic approach to the most unrealistic elements in his story. He could have just said that he traveled on his bucket. Instead, he gives a detailed, almost matter-of-fact description of this unusual method of travel: "Seated on the bucket, my hands on the handle, the simplest kind of bridle . . ."

Most important, Kafka uses such realistic and unrealistic details to express deep feelings of weakness and need. Also, he colors his portrayal of need with what one critic calls "quietly sad gaiety."

1. Identify another realistic and unrealistic detail.
2. Find another passage in which Kafka describes something unreal in a matter-of-fact way. Explain.
3. Show how the realistic and unrealistic details in a passage contribute to the tale's "sad gaiety."

◆ Reading Strategy

COMPARE AND CONTRAST WITH OTHER WORKS

By **comparing and contrasting** "The Bucket Rider" with other works you have read, you can better understand this unusual story. For example, like the youngest sons or daughters in fairy tales, the narrator in Kafka's story uses magical powers. However, unlike these fairy-tale heroes and heroines, the narrator does not achieve success.

1. In what other way is the narrator unlike a fairy-tale hero or heroine?
2. How is the narrator like and unlike another fictional character who searches for something valuable?
3. Compare and contrast the dialogue in this tale with that in a realistic story you know.

◆ Build Vocabulary

USING THE LATIN PREFIX *ir-*

Explain how the prefix *ir-*, which can mean "no, not, or without," contributes to the meaning of each of these words:

1. irrational
2. irregular
3. irresponsible
4. irreligious
5. irresistible

USING THE WORD BANK: True or False?

Copy the following sentences in your notebook. Next to each, write *true* or *false*.

1. You are less likely to see *rime* in summer than in winter.
2. *Dregs* of coffee cannot be seen or tasted.
3. A bucket is a usual *mode* of transportation.
4. You are more likely to see a *ewe* in the city than in the country.
5. It is impossible to disprove *irrefutable* statements.

◆ Build Grammar Skills

CORRECT USE OF *who, which,* AND *that*

The translators of "The Bucket Rider" correctly use the relative pronouns **who, which,** and **that:**
- *Who* refers only to people;
- *Which* refers only to things; and
- *That* refers to people and things.

Practice Identify the relative pronoun in each sentence. Then, on your paper, write the noun it refers to and tell whether that noun is a person or thing.

1. Kafka was a writer who delved into the fantastic.
2. In the fantastic, which is a special kind of literature, impossible events occur.
3. Seriousness of purpose is an element that separates the fantastic from mere fantasy.
4. Kafka's bucket rider, who is nameless, visits a coaldealer.
5. The person that ignores him is the coaldealer's wife.

Writing Application Using each of these three relative pronouns at least once, write a brief summary of "The Bucket Rider."

Build Your Portfolio

Idea Bank

Writing

1. **Instruction Manual** Write a brief instruction manual explaining how to ride a bucket. Include realistic and fantastic details.

2. **Dialogue** Write a brief dialogue that might occur between the narrator of "The Bucket Rider" and the speaker in "Small White Clothes."

3. **Response to Criticism** Novelist John Updike says that Kafka conveys "a sense of an infinite difficulty . . . impeding every step." Using examples from "The Bucket Rider," support or attack this statement.

Speaking, Listening, and Viewing

4. **Monologue** Improvise a monologue for the narrator as he ascends "into the regions of the ice mountains." Have him speak as he does in the story. **[Performing Arts Link]**

5. **Song** Write and perform a song that the narrator of "The Bucket Rider" might sing. Have the song express the "quietly sad gaiety" of the tale. **[Music Link; Performing Arts Link]**

Researching and Representing

6. **Jews in Austria-Hungary** Using biographies of Kafka and books on Jewish history, research the status of Jews in Austria-Hungary. Tell the class what you have learned. Then discuss with them how Kafka's status as an Austro-Hungarian Jew might be reflected in his tale. **[Social Studies Link]**

7. **Comparsion and Contrast** Read another of Kafka's tales, like "Before the Law," p. 486. Then compare and contrast the blending of realistic and unrealistic details in the two stories.

Online Activity www.phlit.phschool.com

Guided Writing Lesson

Literary Interpretation

Puzzling works of literature, like "The Bucket Rider," require an interpretation, an explanation of what they mean. Choose Kafka's tale or another piece of literature and write an interpretation of it. Show how certain actions, statements, or descriptions in the work suggest a wider meaning.

Writing Skills Focus:
Use of Synonyms for Coherence

To give your interpretation a stronger sense of **coherence,** the smooth connection of ideas, repeat key ideas using **synonyms,** different words with a similar meaning.

Prewriting Identify actions, statements, or descriptions that seem to have a deeper meaning. In his first sentence, for example, Kafka uses the words *spent, empty, useless, freezing*. He seems to be describing a condition of life rather than a situation.

Drafting As you explore the meaning of your chosen passages, you may write certain words that seem important. For example, the word *need* may emerge from a discussion of Kafka's first sentence. Consult a thesaurus to find synonyms for *need* that you can weave throughout your interpretation.

Revising Circle the synonyms you have used to express key ideas in your interpretation. Be sure that the circled synonyms appear throughout. If not, add synonyms where they seem to be missing. Also, check to see that you have correctly used the relative pronouns *who, which,* and *that.* (See pp. 74 and 80.)

The Bucket Rider/Small White Clothes ◆ *81*

Guide for Reading

Albert Camus (1913–1960)

A Search for Meaning In novels, plays, stories, and essays, Albert Camus (al ber´ ka moo´) captured the despair and emptiness that overcame a French generation caught up in World War II. However, his writings also burn with a profound determination not to give in to despair. The courageous humanity of his characters in the face of life's absurdity gave his readers a ray of hope. Camus became the voice of his generation in his search for something to believe in.

An Outsider Born in Algeria, Camus was the son of a French colonist. However, he never knew his father, who died in World War I. Camus grew up in a poor, working-class district of Algiers, raised by his mother, who worked as a cleaning woman, and his grandmother. His background shaped his political and literary perspectives: He was always the outsider who didn't fit comfortably anywhere. Later, during the struggle for Algerian independence, he would be criticized for refusing to give complete support to either side.

Overnight Success As a student at the University of Algiers, Camus wrote, directed, and acted in plays. At the outset of World War II, he moved to France and began writing for the underground, anti-Nazi newspaper *Combat*. The publication of his novel *The Stranger* (1942) during the Nazi Occupation of France brought him immediate acclaim.

He was a prolific writer, turning out plays, essays, articles, stories, and two more novels: *The Plague* (1947) and *The Fall* (1956). He also wrote, but did not publish in his lifetime, the novel *The First Man*. In 1957, Camus was awarded the Nobel Prize for Literature.

The awarding of the Nobel was prompted by the publication of his short-story collection *Exile and the Kingdom*. From that collection comes "The Guest," the story of a man, who, like Camus, occupies an awkward niche in Algerian society.

◆ Build Vocabulary

ANGLO-SAXON PREFIXES: *fore-*

In "The Guest," Camus describes an unexpected snowfall that arrives without a *foretaste* of rain. The Anglo-Saxon prefix *fore-* means "before in time, place, order, or rank." Thus, a *foretaste* is "a slight experience or hint of something that is still to come."

plateau
foretaste
contemplation
spite
disconcerted
denounce
furtive

WORD BANK

In reading this story, you will encounter the words on this list. Each word is defined on the page where it first appears. Preview the list before you read.

◆ Build Grammar Skills

PREPOSITIONAL PHRASES AS ADJECTIVES AND ADVERBS

A **prepositional phrase** is a group of words that begins with a preposition and includes its object. Writers often use prepositional phrases as modifiers. When a prepositional phrase modifies a noun or pronoun, it is called an **adjective phrase;** when it modifies a verb, adjective, or adverb, it is called an **adverb phrase.** For example, Camus writes:

> He stepped out onto the terrace in front of the schoolhouse.

Onto the terrace is an adverb phrase. It modifies the adverb *out. In front of the schoolhouse* is an adjective phrase, modifying the noun *terrace.*

As you read "The Guest," you will see that Camus uses many prepositional phrases as modifiers, allowing the reader to visualize what he is describing.

The Guest

◆ Literature and Your Life

CONNECT YOUR EXPERIENCE

Have you ever chosen to do what you believed was right, even though you knew your actions wouldn't make any difference? The ability to make such choices, Camus would say, is what makes us human. In "The Guest," the main character, Daru, asserts his humanity by making a bold choice. The outcome may leave you wondering whether our choices give us any control at all over our lives.

THEMATIC FOCUS: CHOOSING SIDES

Use the experience of the story's central character to help answer this question: Is it possible to choose neither side in a conflict?

Journal Writing Write about a time when you were forced to choose between two sides in a conflict. Explain your choice.

◆ Background for Understanding

HISTORY

In 1954, a war for independence began in Algeria, which had been a colony of France since 1848. More than a century of colonialism had created a deeply divided society with a wealthy European elite, a small European working class, and a large Muslim majority that was mostly poor.

The independence struggle began with terrorist attacks on police posts by a radical Muslim group, the National Liberation Front (FLN). As the revolt spread, the French military retaliated with severe reprisals. The early stages of the rebellion provide the historical context for "The Guest."

◆ Literary Focus

SETTING AND THEME

The **setting** of a story is the time and place of the action. In many stories, the setting serves merely as a context for the characters' words and actions, much like a painted backdrop on a stage. Sometimes, however, an author creates a setting of such power that it takes on a life of its own.

Camus has created just such a setting in "The Guest." Its stark, windswept vistas seem to both embody and mirror the story's theme. The **theme** is the central message or insight into life that is communicated through the story. As you read "The Guest," think about how the setting and theme are intertwined.

◆ Reading Strategy

MAKE INFERENCES

Reading a story can be like solving a mystery. This is because very few writers simply state outright what they want you to know. Instead, they give you details about characters and what they think, say, and do. When you put these clues together with what you already know, you are able to **make inferences,** or logical assumptions, about the story.

In "The Guest," for example, Camus describes the horror of a drought that had lasted for eight months. "The sheep had died then by thousands and even a few men, here and there, sometimes without anyone's knowing." From this detail—"sometimes without anyone's knowing"— you can infer that the region is sparsely populated and its people isolated.

As you continue reading, you might even put this inference together with other evidence to draw larger conclusions about the story's setting, theme, and characters.

The Guest

Albert Camus
Translated by Justin O'Brien

The schoolmaster was watching the two men climb toward him. One was on horseback, the other on foot. They had not yet tackled the abrupt rise leading to the schoolhouse built on the hillside. They were toiling onward, making slow progress in the snow, among the stones, on the vast expanse of the high, deserted <u>plateau</u>. From time to time the horse stumbled. Without hearing anything yet, he could see the breath issuing from the horse's nostrils. One of the men, at least, knew the region. They were following the trail although it had disappeared days ago under a layer of dirty white snow. The schoolmaster calculated that it would take them half an hour to get onto the hill. It was cold; he went back into the school to get a sweater.

He crossed the empty, frigid classroom. On the blackboard the four rivers of France, drawn with four different colored chalks, had been flowing toward their estuaries for the past three days. Snow had suddenly fallen in mid-October after eight months of drought without the transition of rain, and the twenty pupils, more or less, who lived in the villages scattered over the plateau had stopped coming. With fair weather they would return. Daru now heated only the single room that was his lodging, adjoining the classroom and giving also onto the plateau to the east. Like the class windows, his window looked to the south too. On that side the school

was a few kilometers[1] from the point where the plateau began to slope toward the south. In clear weather could be seen the purple mass of the mountain range where the gap opened onto the desert.

Somewhat warmed, Daru returned to the window from which he had first seen the two men. They were no longer visible. Hence they must have tackled the rise. The sky was not so dark, for the snow had stopped falling during the night. The morning had opened with a dirty light which had scarcely become brighter as the ceiling of clouds lifted. At two in the afternoon it seemed as if the day were merely beginning. But still this was better than those three days when the thick snow was falling amidst unbroken darkness with little gusts of wind that rattled the double door of the classroom. Then Daru had spent long hours in his room, leaving it only to go to the shed and feed the chickens or get some coal. Fortunately the delivery truck from Tadjid,[2] the nearest village to the north, had brought his supplies two days before the blizzard. It would return in forty-eight hours.

Besides, he had enough to resist a siege, for the little room was cluttered with bags of wheat

---

1. **kilometers** (kiľ ə mēt′ ərz) *n.*: Measures of distance, each of which is equal to 1,000 meters, or about five-eighths of a mile.
2. **Tadjid** (tä jēd′)

Album de voyage: Spain, Morocco, Algeria, 1834, Chantilly, Eugène Delacroix, Musee Conde, Chantilly, France

▲ **Critical Viewing** In what ways does this picture capture the isolation and emptiness of the setting Camus describes? **[Connect]**

that the administration left as a stock to distribute to those of his pupils whose families had suffered from the drought. Actually they had all been victims because they were all poor. Every day Daru would distribute a ration to the children. They had missed it, he knew, during these bad days. Possibly one of the fathers or big brothers would come this afternoon and he could supply them with grain. It was just a matter of carrying them over to the next harvest. Now shiploads of wheat were arriving from France and the worst was over. But it would be hard to forget that poverty, that army of ragged ghosts wandering in the sunlight, the plateaus burned to a cinder month after month, the earth shriveled up little by little, literally scorched, every stone bursting into

◆ **Literary Focus**
What is the setting of the story?

dust under one's foot. The sheep had died then by thousands and even a few men, here and there, sometimes without anyone's knowing.

In contrast with such poverty, he who lived almost like a monk in his remote schoolhouse, nonetheless satisfied with the little he had and with the rough life, had felt like a lord with his white-washed walls, his narrow couch, his unpainted shelves, his well, and his weekly provision of water and food. And suddenly this snow, without warning, without the <u>foretaste</u> of rain. This is the way the region was, cruel to live in, even without men—who didn't help

◆ **Build Vocabulary**

plateau (pla tō´) *n.*: Elevated tract of relatively level land

foretaste (fôr´ tāst´) *n.*: Slight experience or hint of something that is still to come

The Guest ◆ 85

▲ **Critical Viewing** How is this dwelling similar to or different from your image of Daru's schoolhouse? **[Compare and Contrast]**

matters either. But Daru had been born here. Everywhere else, he felt exiled.

He stepped out onto the terrace in front of the schoolhouse. The two men were now halfway up the slope. He recognized the horseman as Balducci, the old gendarme[3] he had known for a long time. Balducci was holding on the end of a rope an Arab who was walking behind him with hands bound and head lowered. The gendarme waved a greeting to which Daru did not reply, lost as he was in <u>contemplation</u> of the Arab dressed in a faded blue jellaba,[4] his feet in sandals but covered with socks of heavy

raw wool, his head surmounted by a narrow, short *chèche*.[5] They were approaching. Balducci was holding back his horse in order not to hurt the Arab, and the group was advancing slowly.

Within earshot, Balducci shouted: "One hour to do the three kilometers from El Ameur!"[6] Daru did not answer. Short and square in his thick sweater, he watched them climb. Not once had the Arab raised his head. "Hello," said Daru when they got up onto the terrace. "Come in and warm up." Balducci painfully got down from his horse without letting go the rope. From under his bristling mustache he smiled

---

3. **gendarme** (zhän därm´) *n.*: French police officer.
4. **jellaba** (jə lä´ bə) *n.*: Roomy, capelike outer garment worn in the Middle East

5. ***chèche*** (shesh) *n.*: Cloth wrap worn as headware, common in rural Algeria.
6. **El Ameur** (el äm yōōr´)

at the schoolmaster. His little dark eyes, deep-set under a tanned forehead, and his mouth surrounded with wrinkles made him look attentive and studious. Daru took the bridle, led the horse to the shed, and came back to the two men, who were now waiting for him in the school. He led them into his room. "I am going to heat up the classroom," he said. "We'll be more comfortable there." When he entered the room again, Balducci was on the couch. He had undone the rope tying him to the Arab, who had squatted near the stove. His hands still bound, the *chèche* pushed back on his head, he was looking toward the window. At first Daru noticed only his huge lips, fat, smooth . . . yet his nose was straight, his eyes were dark and full of fever. The *chèche* revealed an obstinate forehead and, under the weathered skin now rather discolored by the cold, the whole face had a restless and rebellious look that struck Daru when the Arab, turning his face toward him, looked him straight in the eyes. "Go into the other room," said the schoolmaster, "and I'll make you some mint tea." "Thanks," Balducci said. "What a chore! How I long for retirement." And addressing his prisoner in Arabic: "Come on, you." The Arab got up and, slowly, holding his bound wrists in front of him, went into the classroom.

With the tea, Daru brought a chair. But Balducci was already enthroned on the nearest pupil's desk and the Arab had squatted against the teacher's platform facing the stove, which stood between the desk and the window. When he held out the glass of tea to the prisoner, Daru hesitated at the sight of his bound hands. "He might perhaps be untied." "Sure," said Balducci. "That was for the trip." He started to get to his feet. But Daru, setting the glass on the floor, had knelt beside the Arab. Without saying anything, the Arab watched him with his feverish eyes. Once his hands were free, he rubbed his swollen wrists against each other, took the glass of tea, and sucked up the burn-

ing liquid in swift little sips.

"Good," said Daru. "And where are you headed?"

Balducci withdrew his mustache from the tea. "Here, son."

"Odd pupils! And you're spending the night?"

"No. I'm going back to El Ameur. And you will deliver this fellow to Tinguit.[7] He is expected at police headquarters."

Balducci was looking at Daru with a friendly little smile.

"What's this story?" asked the schoolmaster. "Are you pulling my leg?"

"No, son. Those are the orders."

"The orders? I'm not . . ." Daru hesitated, not wanting to hurt the old Corsican.[8] "I mean, that's not my job."

"What! What's the meaning of that? In wartime people do all kinds of jobs."

"Then I'll wait for the declaration of war!" Balducci nodded.

"O.K. But the orders exist and they concern you too. Things are brewing, it appears. There is talk of a forthcoming revolt. We are mobilized, in a way."

Daru still had his obstinate look.

"Listen, son," Balducci said. "I like you and you must understand. There's only a dozen of us at El Ameur to patrol throughout the whole territory of a small department[9] and I must get back in a hurry. I was told to hand this guy over to you and return without delay. He couldn't be kept there. His village was beginning to stir; they wanted to take him back. You must take him to Tinguit tomorrow before the day is over. Twenty kilometers shouldn't faze a husky fellow like you. After that, all will be over. You'll come back to your pupils and your comfortable life."

◆ **Reading Strategy**
What can you infer about Daru and Balducci from this dialogue?

Behind the wall the horse could be heard snorting and pawing the earth. Daru was looking out the window. Decidedly, the weather was

◆ **Build Vocabulary**

contemplation (kän′ təm plā′ shən) *n*.: Thoughtful inspection or study

7. **Tinguit** (ting′ wēt)
8. **Corsican** (kôr′ si kən) Native of Corsica, a Mediterranean island.
9. **department**: Administrative district in France and certain other countries, similar to a state.

clearing and the light was increasing over the snowy plateau. When all the snow was melted, the sun would take over again and once more would burn the fields of stone. For days, still, the unchanging sky would shed its dry light on the solitary expanse where nothing had any connection with man.

"After all," he said, turning around toward Balducci, "what did he do?" And, before the gendarme had opened his mouth, he asked: "Does he speak French?"

"No, not a word. We had been looking for him for a month, but they were hiding him. He killed his cousin."

"Is he against us?"

"I don't think so. But you can never be sure."

"Why did he kill?"

"A family squabble, I think. One owed the other grain, it seems. It's not at all clear. In short, he killed his cousin with a billhook.[10] You know, like a sheep, *kreezk!*"

Balducci made the gesture of drawing a blade across his throat and the Arab, his attention attracted, watched him with a sort of anxiety. Daru felt a sudden wrath against the man, against all men with their rotten <u>spite</u>, their tireless hates, their blood lust.

But the kettle was singing on the stove. He served Balducci more tea, hesitated, then served the Arab again, who, a second time, drank avidly. His raised arms made the jellaba fall open and the schoolmaster saw his thin, muscular chest.

"Thanks, kid," Balducci said. "And now, I'm off."

He got up and went toward the Arab, taking a small rope from his pocket.

"What are you doing?" Daru asked dryly.

Balducci, <u>disconcerted</u>, showed him the rope.

"Don't bother."

The old gendarme hesitated. "It's up to you. Of course, you are armed?"

"I have my shotgun."

"Where?"

"In the trunk."

---

10. **billhook:** Tool with a carved or hooked blade, used for pruning or cutting.

"You ought to have it near your bed."

"Why? I have nothing to fear."

"You're crazy, son. If there's an uprising, no one is safe, we're all in the same boat."

"I'll defend myself. I'll have time to see them coming."

Balducci began to laugh, then suddenly the mustache covered the white teeth.

"You'll have time? O.K. That's just what I was saying. You have always been a little cracked. That's why I like you, my son was like that."

At the same time he took out his revolver and put it on the desk.

"Keep it; I don't need two weapons from here to El Ameur."

The revolver shone against the black paint of the table. When the gendarme turned toward him, the schoolmaster caught the smell of leather and horseflesh.

"Listen, Balducci," Daru said suddenly, "every bit of this disgusts me, and first of all your fellow here. But I won't hand him over. Fight, yes, if I have to. But not that."

The old gendarme stood in front of him and looked at him severely.

"You're being a fool," he said slowly. "I don't like it either. You don't get used to putting a rope on a man even after years of it, and you're even ashamed—yes, ashamed. But you can't let them have their way."

"I won't hand him over," Daru said again.

"It's an order, son, and I repeat it."

"That's right. Repeat to them what I've said to you: I won't hand him over."

Balducci made a visible effort to reflect. He looked at the Arab and at Daru. At last he decided.

"No, I won't tell them anything. If you want to drop us, go ahead; I'll not <u>denounce</u> you. I have an order to deliver the prisoner and I'm doing so. And now you'll just sign this paper for me."

"There's no need. I'll not deny that you left

♦ Literature and Your Life
Does Daru's standing his ground against his friend remind you of any situation you've experienced?

him with me."

"Don't be mean with me. I know you'll tell the truth. You're from hereabouts and you are a man. But you must sign, that's the rule."

Daru opened his drawer, took out a little square bottle of purple ink, the red wooden penholder with the "sergeant-major" pen he used for making models of penmanship, and signed. The gendarme carefully folded the paper and put it into his wallet. Then he moved toward the door.

"I'll see you off," Daru said.

"No," said Balducci. "There's no use being polite. You insulted me."

He looked at the Arab, motionless in the same spot, sniffed peevishly, and turned away toward the door. "Good-by, son," he said. The door shut behind him. Balducci appeared suddenly outside the window and then disappeared. His footsteps were muffled by the snow. The horse stirred on the other side of the wall and several chickens fluttered in fright. A moment later Balducci reappeared outside the window leading the horse by the bridle. He walked toward the little rise without turning around and disappeared from sight with the horse following him. A big stone could be heard bouncing down. Daru walked back toward the prisoner, who, without stirring, never took his eyes off him. "Wait," the schoolmaster said in Arabic and went toward the bedroom. As he was going through the door, he had a second thought, went to the desk, took the revolver, and stuck it in his pocket. Then, without looking back, he went into his room.

For some time he lay on his couch watching the sky gradually close over, listening to the silence. It was this silence that had seemed painful to him during the first days here, after the war. He had requested a post in the little town at the base of the foothills separating the

Album Afrique 1835–1845," Arab of Constantine (detail), Auguste Raffet, Musee Conde, Chantilly, France

▲ **Critical Viewing** Imagine this Arab is Daru's prisoner. What might he be thinking? **[Speculate]**

upper plateaus from the desert. There, rocky walls, green and black to the north, pink and lavender to the south, marked the frontier of eternal summer. He had been named to a post farther north, on the plateau itself. In the beginning, the solitude and the silence had been hard for him on these wastelands peopled only by stones. Occasionally, furrows suggested cultivation, but they had been dug to uncover a certain kind of stone good for building. The only plowing here was to harvest rocks. Elsewhere a thin layer of soil accumulated in the hollows would be scraped out to enrich paltry village gardens. This is the way it was: bare rock covered three quarters of the region. Towns sprang up, flourished, then disappeared; men came by, loved one another or fought bitterly, then died. No one in this desert, neither he nor his guest, mattered. And yet, outside this desert neither of them, Daru knew, could have really lived.

When he got up, no noise came from the classroom. He was amazed at the unmixed joy he derived from the mere thought that the Arab might have fled and that he would be alone with no decision to make. But the prisoner was there. He had merely stretched out between the stove and the desk. With eyes open, he was staring at the ceiling. In that position, his thick lips were particularly noticeable, giving him a pouting look. "Come," said Daru. The Arab got up and followed him. In the bedroom, the schoolmaster pointed to a chair near the table under the window. The Arab sat down without taking his eyes off Daru.

"Are you hungry?"

"Yes," the prisoner said.

Daru set the table for two. He took flour and oil, shaped a cake in a frying pan, and lighted the little stove that functioned on bottled gas. While the cake was cooking, he went out to the shed to get cheese, eggs, dates, and condensed milk. When the cake was done he set it on the window sill to cool, heated some condensed milk diluted with water, and beat up the eggs into an omelette. In one of his motions he knocked against the revolver stuck in his right pocket. He set the bowl down, went into the classroom, and put the revolver in his desk drawer. When he came back to the room, night was falling. He put on the light and served the Arab. "Eat," he said. The Arab took a piece of the cake, lifted it eagerly to his mouth, and

▼ **Critical Viewing** Is this Arab's clothing appropriate for the setting Camus describes? Why or why not? **[Assess]**

Seated Arab, Eugène Delacroix, Louvre, Paris

stopped short.

"And you?" he asked.

"After you. I'll eat too."

The thick lips opened slightly. The Arab hesitated, then bit into the cake determinedly.

The meal over, the Arab looked at the schoolmaster. "Are you the judge?"

"No, I'm simply keeping you until tomorrow."

"Why do you eat with me?"

"I'm hungry."

The Arab fell silent. Daru got up and went out. He brought back a folding bed from the shed, set it up between the table and the stove, perpendicular to his own bed. From a large suitcase which, upright in a corner, served as a shelf for papers, he took two blankets and arranged them on the camp bed. Then he stopped, felt useless, and sat down on his bed. There was nothing more to do or to get ready. He had to look at this man. He looked at him, therefore, trying to imagine his face bursting with rage. He couldn't do so. He could see nothing but the dark yet shining eyes and the animal mouth.

"Why did you kill him?" he asked in a voice whose hostile tone surprised him.

The Arab looked away.

"He ran away. I ran after him."

He raised his eyes to Daru again and they were full of a sort of woeful interrogation. "Now what will they do to me?"

"Are you afraid?"

He stiffened, turning his eyes away.

"Are you sorry?"

The Arab stared at him openmouthed. Obviously he did not understand. Daru's annoyance was growing. At the same time he felt awkward and self-conscious with his big body wedged between the two beds.

"Lie down there," he said impatiently. "That's your bed."

The Arab didn't move. He called to Daru: "Tell me!"

The schoolmaster looked at him.

"Is the gendarme coming back tomorrow?"

"I don't know."

"Are you coming with us?"

"I don't know. Why?"

The prisoner got up and stretched out on top of the blankets, his feet toward the window. The light from the electric bulb shone straight into his eyes and he closed them at once.

"Why?" Daru repeated, standing beside the bed.

The Arab opened his eyes under the blinding light and looked at him, trying not to blink.

"Come with us," he said.

In the middle of the night, Daru was still not asleep. He had gone to bed after undressing completely; he generally slept naked. But when he suddenly realized that he had nothing on, he hesitated. He felt vulnerable and the temptation came to him to put his clothes back on. Then he shrugged his shoulders; after all, he wasn't a child and, if need be, he could break his adversary in two. From his bed he could observe him, lying on his back, still motionless with his eyes closed under the harsh light. When Daru turned out the light, the darkness seemed to coagulate all of a sudden. Little by little, the night came back to life in the window where the starless sky was stirring gently. The schoolmaster soon made out the body lying at his feet. The Arab still did not move, but his eyes seemed open. A faint wind was prowling around the schoolhouse. Perhaps it would drive away the clouds and the sun would reappear.

During the night the wind increased. The hens fluttered a little and then were silent. The Arab turned over on his side with his back to Daru, who thought he heard him moan. Then he listened for his guest's breathing, become heavier and more regular. He listened to that breath so close to him and mused without being able to go to sleep. In this room where he had been sleeping alone for a year, this presence bothered him. But it bothered him also by imposing on him a sort of brotherhood he knew well but refused to accept in the present circumstances. Men who share the same rooms, soldiers or prisoners, develop a strange alliance as if, having cast off their armor with their clothing, they fraternized every

◆ Reading Strategy
Infer the "circumstances" that cause Daru to refuse to accept the "brotherhood" to which the narrator refers.

evening, over and above their differences, in the ancient community of dream and fatigue. But Daru shook himself; he didn't like such musings, and it was essential to sleep.

A little later, however, when the Arab stirred slightly, the schoolmaster was still not asleep. When the prisoner made a second move, he stiffened, on the alert. The Arab was lifting himself slowly on his arms with almost the motion of a sleepwalker. Seated upright in bed, he waited motionless without turning his head toward Daru, as if he were listening attentively. Daru did not stir; it had just occurred to him that the revolver was still in the drawer of his desk. It was better to act at once. Yet he continued to observe the prisoner, who, with the same slithery motion, put his feet on the ground, waited again, then began to stand up slowly. Daru was about to call out to him when the Arab began to walk, in a quite natural but extraordinarily silent way. He was heading toward the door at the end of the room that opened into the shed. He lifted the latch with precaution and went out, pushing the door behind him but without shutting it. Daru had not stirred. "He is running away," he merely thought. "Good riddance!" Yet he listened attentively. The hens were not fluttering; the guest must be on the plateau. A faint sound of water reached him, and he didn't know what it was until the Arab again stood framed in the doorway, closed the door carefully, and came back to bed without a sound. Then Daru turned his back on him and fell asleep. Still later he seemed, from the depths of his sleep, to hear <u>furtive</u> steps around the schoolhouse. "I'm dreaming! I'm dreaming!" he repeated to himself. And he went on sleeping.

When he awoke, the sky was clear; the loose window let in a cold, pure air. The Arab was asleep, hunched up under the blankets now, his mouth open, utterly relaxed. But when Daru shook him, he started dreadfully, staring at Daru with wild eyes as if he had never seen him and such a frightened expression that the schoolmaster stepped back. "Don't be afraid. It's me. You must eat." The Arab nodded his head and said yes. Calm had returned to his face, but his expression was vacant and listless.

The coffee was ready. They drank it seated together on the folding bed as they munched their pieces of the cake. Then Daru led the Arab under the shed and showed him the faucet where he washed. He went back into the room, folded the blankets and the bed, made his own bed and put the room in order. Then he went through the classroom and out onto the terrace. The sun was already rising in the blue sky; a soft, bright light was bathing the deserted plateau. On the ridge the snow was melting in spots. The stones were about to reappear. Crouched on the edge of the plateau, the schoolmaster looked at the deserted expanse. He thought of Balducci. He had hurt him, for he had sent him off in a way as if he didn't want to be associated with him. He could still hear the gendarme's farewell and, without knowing why, he felt strangely empty and vulnerable. At that moment, from the other side of the schoolhouse, the prisoner coughed. Daru listened to him almost despite himself and then, furious, threw a pebble that whistled through the air before sinking into the snow. That man's stupid crime revolted him, but to hand him over was contrary to honor. Merely thinking of it made him smart with humiliation. And he cursed at one and the same time his own people who had sent him this Arab and the Arab too who had dared to kill and not managed to get away. Daru got up, walked in a circle on the terrace, waited motionless, and then went back into the schoolhouse.

The Arab, leaning over the cement floor of the shed, was washing his teeth with two fingers. Daru looked at him and said: "Come." He went back into the room ahead of the prisoner. He slipped a hunting-jacket on over his sweater and put on walking-shoes. Standing, he waited until the Arab had put on his *chèche* and sandals. They went into the classroom and the schoolmaster pointed to the exit, saying: "Go ahead." The fellow didn't budge. "I'm coming," said Daru. The Arab went out. Daru went back into the room and made a package of pieces of

◆ **Build Vocabulary**

furtive (fur′ tiv) *adj.:* Done in a secret or sneaky way

rusk,[11] dates, and sugar. In the classroom, before going out, he hesitated a second in front of his desk, then crossed the threshold and locked the door. "That's the way," he said. He started toward the east, followed by the prisoner. But, a short distance from the schoolhouse, he thought he heard a slight sound behind them. He retraced his steps and examined the surroundings of the house; there was no one there. The Arab watched him without seeming to understand. "Come on," said Daru.

They walked for an hour and rested beside a sharp peak of limestone. The snow was melting faster and faster and the sun was drinking up the puddles at once, rapidly cleaning the plateau, which gradually dried and vibrated like the air itself. When they resumed walking, the ground rang under their feet. From time to time a bird rent the space in front of them with a joyful cry. Daru breathed in deeply the fresh morning light. He felt a sort of rapture before the vast familiar expanse, now almost entirely yellow under its dome of blue sky. They walked an hour more, descending toward the south. They reached a level height made up of crumbly rocks. From there on, the plateau sloped down, eastward, toward a low plain where there were a few spindly trees and, to the south, toward outcroppings of rock that gave the landscape a chaotic look.

◆ Literary Focus
How do the details of the setting in this paragraph reflect a change in Daru's mood?

Daru surveyed the two directions. There was nothing but the sky on the horizon. Not a man could be seen. He turned toward the Arab, who was looking at him blankly. Daru held out the package to him. "Take it," he said. "There are dates, bread, and sugar. You can hold out for two days. Here are a thousand francs[12] too." The Arab took the package and the money but kept his full hands at chest level as if he didn't know what to do with what was being given him. "Now look," the schoolmaster said as he pointed in the direction of the east, "there's the way to Tinguit. You have a two-hour walk. At Tinguit you'll find the administration and the police. They are expecting you." The Arab looked toward the east, still holding the package and the money against his chest. Daru took his elbow and turned him rather roughly toward the south. At the foot of the height on which they stood could be seen a faint path. "That's the trail across the plateau. In a day's walk from here you'll find pasturelands and the first nomads. They'll take you in and shelter you according to their law." The Arab had now turned toward Daru and a sort of panic was visible in his expression. "Listen," he said. Daru shook his head: "No, be quiet. Now I'm leaving you." He turned his back on him, took two long steps in the direction of the school, looked hesitantly at the motionless Arab, and started off again. For a few minutes he heard nothing but his own step resounding on the cold ground and did not turn his head. A moment later, however, he turned around. The Arab was still there on the edge of the hill, his arms hanging now, and he was looking at the schoolmaster. Daru felt something rise in his throat. But he swore with impatience, waved vaguely, and started off again. He had already gone some distance when he again stopped and looked. There was no longer anyone on the hill.

Daru hesitated. The sun was now rather high in the sky and was beginning to beat down on his head. The schoolmaster retraced his steps, at first somewhat uncertainly, then with decision. When he reached the little hill, he was bathed in sweat. He climbed it as fast as he could and stopped, out of breath, at the top. The rock-fields to the south stood out sharply against the blue sky, but on the plain to the east a steamy heat was already rising. And in that slight haze, Daru, with heavy heart, made out the Arab walking slowly on the road to prison.

A little later, standing before the window of the classroom, the schoolmaster was watching the clear light bathing the whole surface of the plateau, but he hardly saw it. Behind him on the blackboard, among the winding French

---

11. rusk (rusk) *n.*: Sweet bread or cake, toasted or baked until crisp.

12. a thousand francs (franks) *n.*: Francs are monetary units of France and certain other countries, 1,000 francs being enough money for a few days' food and travel.

rivers, sprawled the clumsily chalked-up words he had just read: "You handed over our brother. You will pay for this." Daru looked at the sky, the plateau, and, beyond, the invisible lands stretching all the way to the sea. In this vast landscape he had loved so much, he was alone.

▶ **Critical Viewing**
Imagine this man is the Arab walking toward the police station. What might he be thinking as he turns himself in? **[Speculate]**

Beyond Literature

Cultural Connection

Algerian Culture Throughout its history, the North African nation of Algeria, which is the setting for Camus's *The Guest,* has been home to many strikingly different cultural traditions. Algeria's two main ethnic groups are the Berbers and the Arabs.

The Berbers have lived in North Africa since at least 3000 B.C. No one knows exactly where they came from, but many historians think they migrated from Southwest Asia. They settled in the Atlas Mountains and on plains near Algeria's coast. More than 90 percent of Algerians still live near the coast, where the weather is milder than in the Sahara.

Some Berbers live in Algeria's cities. Most, however, live in villages in rural areas and make a living by farming and herding. They get up as soon as it is light. In the middle of the day, when the sun is hottest, the people rest for several hours. Then, they work until dark.

Traditional Berber households include not just a mother, a father, and their children, but an extended family, as well. Each Berber house has an open courtyard in the back. The windows in the house face the courtyard, not the street. Each married couple in a family has its own home, opening onto the family courtyard. This arrangement allows grandparents, parents, sons, daughters, and cousins to live close together.

Family is so important to the Berbers that their village governments are based on it. The head of each family is a member of the village assembly, which makes laws for the village.

Arab culture became influential in Algeria in the A.D. 600's when the Arabs began to conquer North Africa. Arab traditions were like Berber traditions in many ways. For example, both Muslim Arabs and non-Muslim Berbers traditionally lived with extended families. However, whereas Berbers tended to be farmers, Arabs favored a nomadic lifestyle. This was sometimes a source of conflict, but more often a peaceful settlement was achieved. Farmers would usually let the nomads' herds graze on their land in exchange for livestock and goods.

Over the centuries, there have been many conflicts between Arabs and Berbers. France's colonization of the region in the nineteenth century resulted in even more conflicts because the French seized political and economic control. Yet, there have also been long periods during which these different groups have lived peacefully and, through it all, they have learned from each other. The world hopes that a peaceful cultural exchange can continue in this uniquely diverse society.

Activity Does Camus's story offer an accurate picture of Algeria's Berber or Arab culture? Why or why not?

Guide for Responding

◆ Literature and Your Life

Reader's Response What was your reaction to the end of the story?

Thematic Focus Although Daru refused to take sides, he was sucked into the conflict between Arabs and colonial authorities. Tell about a time when you tried to remain neutral in a conflict.

Reader's Journal Suppose you were Daru. What would you say to the people who wrote the message on your blackboard?

☑ Check Your Comprehension

1. Who is Balducci and what is his purpose in visiting Daru?
2. Briefly describe the political situation that makes Balducci's visit necessary.
3. What is Daru's response to Balducci?
4. What does Daru do with his guest?
5. What is the message on the blackboard and who may have written it?

◆ Critical Thinking

INTERPRET
1. How does Daru feel about his guest? Explain. **[Analyze]**
2. What is the link between Daru's refusal to hand the Arab over and his refusal to accompany the Arab beyond the plateau? **[Connect]**
3. When Daru leaves the Arab, there is "a sort of panic visible in [the Arab's] expression." Why is he frightened? **[Interpret]**
4. What do you think Camus is saying by having Daru struggle as he does, only to find the message on the blackboard? **[Draw Conclusions]**

EVALUATE
5. Do you think Daru's actions are ultimately meaningless? Why or why not? **[Evaluate]**

APPLY
6. Which aspect of Camus's philosophy do you prefer: the idea that life is absurd and meaningless; or the idea that by making choices as if they mattered, one can create meaning? Explain. **[Relate]**

Guide for Responding (continued)

◆ Reading Strategy

MAKE INFERENCES

Balducci affectionately calls Daru "son" and "kid," and compares him to his own son. From this you can **infer**—in other words, make a reasonable assumption—that Balducci feels like a father to Daru.

Use these details to make inferences about Daru's attitude toward Balducci:

1. In refusing Balducci's order, Daru chooses his words carefully.
2. Daru feels empty and vulnerable when he remembers the way Balducci left him.

◆ Literary Focus

SETTING AND THEME

A story's **setting** is the time and place of the action. A story's **theme** is its central message or insight about life. In "The Guest," setting and theme are closely intertwined. For example, one aspect of the story's theme is the absurdity or irrationality of human existence. This absurdity means that humans do not fit comfortably in the world. Three reasons for this lack of a neat fit are conflicts between:

• the goals of different individuals or peoples
• what individuals choose and what actually happens
• human goals and the forces of nature

Camus's descriptions of the setting reinforce the theme of absurdity by emphasizing the mismatch between human goals and natural forces. For example, from the very beginning of the story, the landscape seems harsh and inhospitable:

> They had not yet tackled the abrupt rise leading to the schoolhouse built on the hillside. They were toiling onward, making slow progress in the snow, among the stones, on the vast expanse of the high, deserted plateau.

Words like *tackled, toiling,* and *slow progress* help create the feeling of a place that resists humans. In addition, Camus uses a series of prepositional phrases to describe the landscape and stress the difficulty of the trek— "in . . . among . . . on. . . ."

Find two more descriptions of the setting and explain how they support the theme of absurdity.

◆ Build Vocabulary

USING THE ANGLO-SAXON PREFIX *fore-*

Knowing that the Anglo-Saxon prefix *fore-* means "before in time, place, order, or rank," write a definition for each of the following words:

1. foreman   2. forearm
3. forefather   4. forecast

USING THE WORD BANK: Context

On your paper, write the word from the Word Bank that matches each description.

1. motivation to play a dirty trick on someone
2. what you might do to a corrupt politician
3. a relief after hiking uphill for hours
4. a thief's usual manner
5. an activity for students and philosophers
6. something that might or might not whet your appetite
7. how a waiter feels after dropping a tray of dishes

◆ Build Grammar Skills

PREPOSITIONAL PHRASES AS ADJECTIVES AND ADVERBS

Camus uses many **prepositional phrases** as adjectives and adverbs. When a prepositional phrase modifies a noun or pronoun, it is called an **adjective phrase;** when it modifies a verb, adjective, or adverb, it is called an **adverb phrase.**

Practice In your notebook, write the prepositional phrase used in each sentence. Tell how it is used and what word it modifies.

1. The bound prisoner made his way along the trail.
2. Daru studied the man with the blue jellaba.
3. With quick movements, Daru served them tea.
4. Balducci said goodbye in a hurt tone of voice.
5. The Arabs from the village scribbled a message.

Writing Application Rewrite the sentences, adding a prepositional phrase to each one. Underline the phrase, tell how it is used, and tell what word it modifies.

1. Daru entered the classroom.
2. The students were asleep.
3. A fire was still smoldering.
4. Daru put it out and awoke the students.
5. The Arab walked away.

Build Your Portfolio

 ## Idea Bank

Writing

1. **Police Report** As Balducci, write a brief report for your superior officer describing your visit to Daru and its outcome.

2. **Travel Brochure** Create a brochure advertising Daru's region as a destination for travelers who want to get off the beaten path. Use prepositional phrases to make your writing vivid. **[Media Link; Career Link]**

3. **Response to Criticism** Camus received the Nobel Prize for shedding light on "the problems of the human conscience in our time." Explain how "The Guest" does or does not perform this function.

Speaking and Listening

4. **Casting Discussion** You're making a short film of "The Guest." In a group, discuss who should play the roles of Daru, Balducci, and the Arab. Present your casting choices to the rest of the class. **[Media Link]**

5. **Monologue** Write and deliver a monologue in which you, as Daru, defend your actions to the people of the village. **[Performing Arts Link]**

Projects

6. **Landscape Painting** Drawing on descriptive details from the story, paint or draw a landscape that reflects your impressions of the setting. Display your artwork in class. **[Art Link]**

7. **Research Report** Do a research report on an aspect of twentieth century Algerian history or culture that interests you. Present your report to the class. **[Social Studies Link]**

Online Activity www.phlit.phschool.com

 ## Guided Writing Lesson

Prediction

Many first-time readers of "The Guest" make a mental prediction when Balducci leaves the Arab with Daru: They predict that the Arab will attack Daru in the night. He doesn't, of course.

In a **prediction,** you use your knowledge of past and present events to speculate about future ones. Write a prediction that tells what you think will be the consequences of Daru's actions after the story ends.

Writing Skills Focus: Transitions to Show Time

Your prediction will be clearer to readers if you use **transitions to show time,** words and phrases that show the relationship of events in time: *after, afterward, as soon as, before, finally, later, now, not long after, until, when,* and *while.*

Here is an example from "The Guest": *"A little later, however, when* the Arab stirred slightly, the schoolmaster was *still* not asleep. *When* the prisoner made a second move, he stiffened, on the alert."

Prewriting In chart form, list what you know from the story about how people have reacted or may react to Daru's choice and its results:

Arab villagers	Daru	Balducci

Then, decide what you think will happen as events continue.

Drafting As you write your prediction, be sure to use transitions to show time to make the passage of time and order of events clear.

Revising Before you revise, review "The Guest." Then, reread your prediction and ask yourself: Does my prediction ring true? Make any necessary changes. Add time-transition words where necessary to clarify the order of events.

Guide for Reading

Mark Mathabane (1960–)

The phrase "rags to riches" describes the life of Mark Mathabane (mät´ ä bän´ ä). Growing up in poverty in a black township near Johannesburg, South Africa, he overcame incredible hardships to become a tennis star and then a famous author.

Early Hardships Mathabane started writing *Kaffir Boy,* his autobiography, while still a senior in college. He felt a burning need to tell Americans what it was like to grow up in South Africa, whose laws at that time discriminated against the country's nonwhite majority. His father, an unskilled laborer, lacked legal permission to live in his own home with his own wife and children, and frequently had to flee from the police. Without proper documents, he could not work; without a job, he would be imprisoned for being unemployed.

Later Success Mathabane was saved by three determined women. His mother, his sister, and his grandmother encouraged him to get an education. To stay in school, he had to battle gangs, who mocked and beat him, as well as his own father, who viewed education as a waste of time and would burn his textbooks.

With Help from Friends Befriended by a kindly white family who gave him books and an old tennis racket, he taught himself English and learned to play tennis. This excerpt shows his first meeting with that family. Later, as a star athlete, he struck up friendships with top international players, who urged him to apply for scholarships and helped him to attend college in the United States. He and his family were eventually reunited on Oprah Winfrey's television show.

Shu Ting (1952–)

Shu Ting (sho͞o tiŋ) is the pen name of Chinese poet Gong Peiyu. She lives and writes in the seaport city of Hsia-men (shē ä mʉn).

◆ Build Vocabulary

LATIN WORD ROOTS: -ject-

In *Kaffir Boy,* you will encounter the word *abject,* which contains the Latin root *-ject-,* meaning "throw." Since *ab-* means "from or away," *abject* literally means "thrown away" and its definition is "degraded, miserable, or wretched."

Additional words that include this root are *reject, eject, injection, trajectory,* and *projector.* Consider how the meaning of the root, "throw," influences the meaning of each of these words.

mannequins
immaculate
indefatigable
ramshackle
abject
postulated
honing

WORD BANK

As you read *Kaffir Boy,* you will encounter the words on this list. Each word is defined on the page where it appears. Preview the list before you read.

◆ Build Grammar Skills

CORRECT USE OF *their, there,* AND *they're*

In *Kaffir Boy,* Mathabane correctly uses ***their, there,*** and ***they're,*** words that are easily confused:

• *their,* a possessive pronoun, modifies a noun.

. . . men and women on *their* way to the white world to work.

• *there* can appear at the beginning of a sentence, where a subject would normally be, or it can be used as an adverb.

There was even talk that Aunt Bushy would have to leave school (used at beginning of sentence).
Each time I was *there* . . . (used as adverb).

• *they're* is a contraction for *they are.*

They're so big!

from Kaffir Boy ◆ Fairy Tales

◆ Literature and Your Life

CONNECT YOUR EXPERIENCE

You have probably thought about a goal in life. You may want to become an actor or an athlete, to raise children, write books, or build houses. Goals like these can energize your daily life, giving you something for which you can work.

In *Kaffir Boy,* Mark Mathabane recounts his exciting discovery of a goal in life and how to achieve it.

THEMATIC FOCUS: STRIVING FOR SUCCESS

Mathabane's experience of meeting people very different from himself inspires him to work for a goal. As you read, ask yourself: why does this meeting give him a sense of purpose?

Journal Writing Tell briefly about an experience of meeting somebody different from yourself.

◆ Background for Understanding

HISTORY

In 1971, the time of this story, South Africa had an official policy of racial separation and discrimination aimed at nonwhites. It was called apartheid (ə pär´ tāt´), which means "separateness" in Afrikaans, the Dutch-based language of the whites who then controlled South Africa.

Apartheid laws established Bantustans, tribal homelands for blacks, outside of which they could not vote, own land, travel, or work without permission. The system frequently divided families, forcing husbands and wives to live apart.

Apartheid was abolished during the early 1990's, and in 1994, Nelson Mandela became the first black president of South Africa.

◆ Literary Focus

DIALOGUE IN NONFICTION

Both fiction and nonfiction can include **dialogue,** passages representing spoken conversation. In an autobiography, as in a story, dialogue serves mainly to portray the personalities of people in the narrative. It also adds drama to the account, making you feel as if you are hearing a person's words as they are spoken.

In *Kaffir Boy,* Mathabane uses dialogue to portray personality and create drama. His wonder-filled questions when he first sees skyscrapers in a white neighborhood— "What are those?"—show his ignorance of life outside his small world. They also make you feel that you are participating in his dramatic journey of discovery.

◆ Reading Strategy

CONSIDER HISTORICAL CONTEXT

The important events that relate to both the writing of a work and its setting are its **historical context.** Knowing this context, you will better understand the thoughts, decisions, and feelings of the fictional or real-life characters portrayed in the work.

For example, you cannot fully understand *Kaffir Boy* unless you know that it takes place in South Africa during the era of apartheid (see Background for Understanding). At this time, blacks lived separately from whites and often in great poverty. That is why the narrator's visit to a white family is so unusual, dramatic, and important.

To apply the historical context to the narrative, fill in additional items in a chart like this:

Historical Context: Apartheid	Influence on Narrative
Whites and blacks • live apart and blacks are much poorer • attend different schools	• narrator has never seen a white neighborhood

from
Kaffir Boy

Mark Mathabane

The seven o'clock bus for blacks to Johannesburg was jam-packed with men and women on their way to the white world to work. A huge sign above the driver's booth read:

AUTHORIZED TO CARRY ONLY 65 SEATED PASSENGERS, AND 15 STANDING.

But there must have been close to a hundred perspiring people squeezed into the stuffy bus. People sat on top of one another, some were sandwiched in the narrow aisle between the rows of seats, and some crowded on the steps. I sat on Granny's lap, in the middle of the bus, by a large smudged window. As the bus droned past Alexandra's boundaries, I glued my eyes to the window, anticipating my first look at the white world. What I saw made me think I had just made a quantum leap into another galaxy. I couldn't stop asking questions.

"What are those?"

> ◆ **Reading Strategy**
> What does the narrator's reaction to the sights reveal about the lives of blacks in South Africa at the time?

"Skyscrapers."

"Why do they reach all the way to the sky?"

"Because many white people live and work in them."

Seconds later. "Wow! look at all those nice houses, Granny! They're so big! Do many white people live and work there too?"

"No, those are mansions. Each is owned by one family."

"By one family!" I cried in disbelief. Each mansion occupied an area about three times

that of the yard I lived in, yet the latter was home for over twenty families.

"Yes," Granny said matter-of-factly. "Your grandpa, when he first came to Johannesburg, worked for one such family. The family was so rich they owned an airplane."

"Why are there so many cars in the white people's homes?"

"Because they like to have many cars."

"Those people dressed in white, what game are they playing?"

"The men are playing cricket. Master Smith plays that too. The women are playing tennis. Mrs. Smith plays it too, on Tuesday and Thursday."

Suddenly the bus screeched to a halt, and people crashed into each other. I was thrown into the back of the wooden seat in front of me. Smarting, I asked, "Why did the bus suddenly stop? I didn't see any robots [street lights]."

"Look over there," Granny pointed. "White schoolchildren are crossing the road."

I gazed through the window and for the first time in my life saw white schoolchildren. I scrutinized them for any differences from black schoolchildren, aside from color. They were like little <u>mannequins</u>. The boys were neatly dressed in snow-white shirts, blazers with badges, preppy caps with badges, ties matching the badges, shiny black and brown shoes, worsted[1] knee-high socks. The girls wore

---

1. **worsted** (woŏs′ tid) *adj.*: Made of smooth, hard-twisted thread or yarn.

pleated gymdresses with badges, snow-white shirts, caps with badges, blazers with badges, ties matching badges, shining black and brown shoes. A few of the girls had pigtails. On the back of each boy and girl was slung a school-bag; and each frail, milky-white arm had a wristwatch on it. It suddenly struck me that we didn't even own a clock; we had to rely on cocks for time.

The white schoolchildren were filing out of a large, red-brick building with many large windows, in front of which were beds of multi-colored flowers. A tall black man wearing a traffic uniform, a whistle between his thick lips, stood in the middle of the paved road, one hand raised to stop traffic, the other holding a sign that read in English and Afrikaans:[2]

CHILDREN CROSSING
STOP
KINDERS STAP OOR

None of this orderly and safe crossing of the street ever took place at my school; we had to dash across.

The red-brick building stood on a vast tract of land with <u>immaculate</u> lawns, athletic fields, swings, merry-go-rounds, an Olympic-sized swimming pool, tennis courts, and rows of brightly leafed trees. In the driveway leading to the entrance of the building, scores of yellow school buses were parked. Not even the best of tribal

2. **Afrikaans** (af´ ri käns´) *n.*: Language spoken in South Africa that developed from seventeenth-century Dutch.

◆ **Build Vocabulary**

mannequins (man´ i kinz) *n.*: Models of the human body, used by tailors and dressmakers

immaculate (im mak´ yoo lit) *adj.*: Spotlessly clean

◆ **Reading Strategy**

Basing your answer on the narrator's reactions, describe what his school must look like. **[Hypothesize]**

▼ **Critical Viewing** What do you think the narrator might have thought on seeing a sight like this from the bus window? **[Speculate]**

▲ **Critical Viewing** How do you think the narrator felt on learning a house like this was his destination? **[Speculate]**

schools in Alexandra—in the whole of South Africa—came close to having such magnificent facilities. At our school we didn't even have a school bus. Oh, how I envied the white schoolchildren, how I longed to attend schools like theirs.

◆ **Reading Strategy**
Why do you think the authorities allowed the narrator and his friends to dash across the street while carefully supervising the crossing of white children?

Minutes after all the white schoolchildren were safely across, traffic moved. At the next bus stop, we got off, and crossed the street when the robot flashed green. As we walked along the pavement, headed for Granny's workplace, I clutched her long dress, afraid of letting go, lest I be swallowed by the tremendous din of cars zooming up and down and honking in the busy streets. I began feeling dizzy as my eyes darted from one wonder to the next.

There were so many new and fantastic things around me that I walked as if in a dream. As we continued down the road, I became increasingly conscious of the curious looks white people gave us, as if we were a pair of escaped monkeys. Occasionally, Granny and I had to jump off the pavement to make way for madams and their poodles and English toy spaniels. By constantly throwing my eyes sideways, I accidentally bumped into a parking meter.

We went up a side street. "There is Mrs. Smith's house," Granny remarked as she led me up a long driveway of a beautiful villa-type house surrounded by a well-manicured lawn with sev-

eral beds of colorful, sweet-smelling flowers and rosebushes. We went to a steel gate in the back of the yard, where Granny rang a bell.

"I'm here, madam," she shouted through the gate. Immediately a dog started barking from within; I trembled.

Granny calmed me. A door creaked open, and a high-pitched woman's voice called out, "I'm coming, Ellen. Quiet, Buster, you naughty dog, it's Ellen." The barking ceased. Presently the gate clicked open, and there appeared a short, slender white woman with silver hair and slightly drooping shoulders. She wore white slacks, a white sweater, white shoes, and a white visor.

"I was just getting ready to leave for tennis," she said to Granny; she had not yet seen me.

"Madam, guess who I have with me today," Granny said with the widest smile.

I appeared like a Jack-in-the-box. "Oh, my, you finally brought him with you!" Mrs. Smith exclaimed.

Breaking into a wide smile, revealing gleaming teeth, several of which were made of gold,

---

◆ **Literary Focus**
What do Mrs. Smith's words reveal about her?

---

she continued, "My, what a big lad he is! What small ears!"—touching them playfully— "Is he really your grandson, Ellen?" The warmth in her voice somehow reduced my fears of her; her eyes shone with the same gentleness of the Catholic sisters at the clinic.

"Yes, madam," Granny said proudly; "this is the one I've been telling you about. This is the one who'll some day go to university, like Master Clyde, and take care of me."

"I believe you, Ellen," said Mrs. Smith. "He looks like a very smart pickaninny."[3] Turning to me, she asked, "How old are you?"

"Eleven, madam, eleven," I said, with so wide a smile I thought my jaws would lock.

"He's a year younger than Master Clyde," Granny said, "though the master is much bigger."

"A little chubby, you mean," Mrs. Smith said with a smile. "If you knew how much the little master eats, Ellen; I'm afraid he'll soon turn into a piglet. Sometimes I regret not having had another child. With a sibling, Master Clyde might have turned out differently. As it is, he's so spoiled as an only child."

"Pickaninny has one brother and three sisters," Granny said of me, "and the fifth one is on the way."

"My . . . ! What a large family!" Mrs. Smith exclaimed. "What's the pickaninny's name?"

Using pidgin English,[4] I proceeded not only to give my name and surname, but also my grade in school, home address, tribal affiliation, name of school, principal and teacher—all in a feverish attempt to justify Granny's label of me as a "smart one."

Mrs. Smith was astounded. "What a clever, clever pickaninny!" She turned to a tall, lean black man with an expressionless face and slightly stooping shoulders, dressed in housekeeper's livery (khaki shirt and pants), who had just emerged from the house and who led a poodle on a leash, and said, "Did you hear that, Absalom? Bantu [black] children are smart. Soon they'll be running the country." Absalom simply tortured out a grin and took the poodle for a walk, after receiving instructions to bring brandy, whisky, wine, and gin from the bottle store. Granny remarked that I was a "clever pickaninny" because of all the toys, games, and comic books I had received from Master Clyde. Mrs. Smith seemed extremely pleased to hear that.

Before Mrs. Smith left for tennis, she said, "Ellen, your breakfast is near the washing machine in the garage. I'll be back sometime this afternoon. Please see to it that the flowers near the pool are watered, and that the rosebushes near the front of the gate are trimmed."

After a breakfast of coffee and peanut butter-and-jam sandwiches, Granny took out her gardening tools from the shed, and we started

---

3. **pickaninny:** Insulting term for a black child—here used with affection by someone who feels superior.

4. **pidgin** (pij′ in) **English:** Simplified form of English.

working. As the two of us went about the large yard, I raked leaves and watered the flowers; Granny weeded the lawn. Mrs. Smith's neighbor's children kept on casting curious glances over the fence. From the way they looked at me, it seemed they were seeing a black child for the first time in their lives.

◆ **Literary Focus**
What do the narrator's words reveal about his reaction to the Smiths' house and way of life?

At midday, despite a scorching sun, Granny, seemingly <u>indefatigable</u>, went about with impressive skill trimming the rosebushes as we talked about trees and flowers and how to best cultivate them.

"Someday I'll build a house as big and beautiful as Mrs. Smith's," I said to Granny. "And a garden just as big and beautiful."

"Then I'll be your gardener," Granny said with a smile.

Toward early afternoon Mrs. Smith returned. She called me to the car to remove several shopping bags from the backseat. She took her tennis rackets, closed the doors, then sighed, "Phew, what a tiring day. Don't ever play tennis," she said to me, "it's a killer."

"What's tennis, madam?" I asked.

"You don't know tennis?" she exclaimed. "What sports do you play?"

"Soccer, madam."

"Ugh, that dangerous sport. Soccer is too rough. You should try tennis someday. It's a gentlemen's sport. Wouldn't you like to be a gentleman?"

"I would like to be a gentleman, madam," I replied, even though I hadn't the faintest idea what constituted a gentleman.

"Do you have tennis courts in Alexandra?"

"Yes, madam." The stadium where I played soccer was adjacent to four <u>ramshackle</u> sand courts, used primarily by kitchen girls and kitchen boys on their day off.

"Then I'll see if I can find an old racket for you," she said.

As we were talking, a busload of white schoolchildren stopped in front of the house, and a young boy, with a mop of rebellious brown hair, alighted and ran up the driveway toward Mrs. Smith. After giving her a kiss, he turned and demanded, "Who is he, Mother?"

"That's Ellen's grandson. The one you've been giving all those comic books and toys to."

"What is he doing here?"

"He's visiting us."

"What for? I don't want him here."

"Why not, Clyde," Mrs. Smith said, "he's a nice pickaninny. Ellen is always nice to you, isn't she?"—the boy nodded with pursed lips—"now be nice to her grandson. Now run along inside and Absalom will show you the things I bought you today."

"Did you get my new bicycle and roller skates?"

"Yes, they'll be delivered Saturday. Now run in and change, and have something to eat. Then maybe you can play with pickaninny."

"I don't play with Kaffirs,"[5] the white boy declared. "At school they say we shouldn't."

"Watch your filthy mouth, Clyde," Mrs. Smith said, flushing crimson. "I thought I told you a million times to leave all that rubbish about Kaffirs in the classroom. Ellen's people are not Kaffirs, you hear! They're Bantus. Now go in and do as I told you." Turning to Granny, pruning a rosebush nearby, Mrs. Smith said, in a voice of someone fighting a losing battle, "You know, Ellen, I simply don't understand why those . . . uncivilized Boers[6] from Pretoria teach children such things. What future does this country have if this goes on?"

"I agree *makulu*,[7] madam," Granny said, wiping her sweaty brow with her forearm. "All children, black and white, are God's children, madam. The preacher at my church tells us the Bible says so. 'Suffer little children to come unto me, and forbid them not; for of such is the kingdom of heaven,' the Bible says. Is that not so, madam? Do you believe in the words of the Bible, madam?"

---

5. Kaffirs (kaf′ərz) *n.*: Insulting term for black South Africans.

6. Boers (boorz) *n.*: South Africans whose ancestors were Dutch colonists.

7. makulu: Very much.

"I'm afraid you're right, Ellen," Mrs. Smith said, somewhat touched. "Yes, I do believe in the Bible. That's why I cannot accept the laws of this country. We white people are hypocrites. We call ourselves Christians, yet our deeds make the Devil look like a saint. I sometimes wish I hadn't left England."

I was struck by the openness of the discussion between Granny and Mrs. Smith.

"You're not like most white people I've worked for, madam," Granny said. "Master and you are kind toward our people. You treat us like human beings."

Mrs. Smith didn't answer; she hurried back indoors. Shortly thereafter, Clyde emerged in a pair of denims and a T-shirt advertising a South African rock group. He called out to me. "Come here, pickaninny. My mother says I should show you around."

I went.

I followed him around as he showed me all the things his parents regularly bought him: toys, bicycles, go-carts, pinball machines, Ping-Pong tables, electric trains. I only half-listened: my mind was preoccupied with comparing my situation with his. I couldn't understand why he and his people had to have all the luxuries money can buy, while I and my people lived in abject poverty. Was it because they were whites and we were black? Were they better than we? I could not find the answers; yet I felt there was something wrong about white people having everything, and black people nothing.

We finally came to Clyde's playroom. The room was roughly the size of our house, and was elaborately decorated with posters, pennants of various white soccer and cricket teams, rock stars, and photographs of Clyde in various stages of development. But what arrested my attention were the stacks of comic books on the floor, and the shelves and shelves of books. Never had I seen that many books in my life; even our school, with a student population of over two thousand, did not have half as many books. I was dazed.

Sensing that I was in awe of his magnificent library, Clyde said, "Do you have this many books in your playroom?"

"I don't have a playroom."

"You don't have a playroom," he said bug-eyed. "Can you read?" he smiled sinisterly. "Our boy Absalom can't. And he says black children aren't taught much English at school."

"I can read a little English," I said.

"I doubt if you can read any of my books. Here, read," he ordered, pulling one out of the shelves. The book was thick, looked formidable.

I nervously opened a page, toiled through a couple lines, encountering long words I could not pronounce, let alone understand their meaning. Shaking my head in embarrassment, I handed the book back, "I can't read this type of English."

"Then you must be retarded," Clyde laughed. Though he might have meant it in jest, my pride was deeply wounded. "This book is by William Shakespeare," he went on, waving it in my face, "the greatest English writer that ever lived. I could read it from cover to cover when I was half your age. But I don't blame you if you can't. My teachers tell us that Kaffirs can't read, speak, or write English like white people because they have smaller brains, which are already full of tribal things. My teachers say you're not people like us, because you belong to a jungle civilization. That's why you can't live or go to school with us, but can only be our servants."

"Stop saying that rubbish, you naughty boy," Mrs. Smith said angrily as she entered the room just in time to catch the tail end of her son's knowledge of black people's intelligence, as postulated by the doctrine of apartheid.[8]

◆ Build Vocabulary

indefatigable (in´ di fat´ i gə bəl) *adj.*: Untiring; not giving in to fatigue

ramshackle (ram´ shak´ əl) *adj.*: Of poor construction; flimsy and shaky

abject (ab´ jekt´) *adj.*: Of the worst kind; miserable, wretched

postulated (päs´ chə lāt´ id) *v.*: Assumed without proof to be true or necessary

---

8. **apartheid** (ə pär´ tāt´) *n.*: Policy of separating non-whites and whites and discriminating against nonwhites.

"How many times have I told you that what your teachers say about black people is not true?"

"What do you know, Mama?" Clyde retorted impudently, "you're not a teacher. Besides, there are textbooks where it's so written."

"Still it's not true," insisted Mrs. Smith. "Everything that's in your books is not necessarily true, especially your history books about this country." Changing the subject, she said, "Show him your easy books, and then get your things ready so I can drive you over to your friend's birthday party." Clyde quickly ran down his long list of "easy" books: *The Three Musketeers, Treasure Island, David Copperfield,* the Hardy Boys series, the Sherlock Holmes series, *Tom Sawyer, Robinson Crusoe, The Swiss Family Robinson, The Hunchback of Notre Dame, Black Beauty, A Tale of Two Cities,* and so on. Oh, how I envied Clyde's collection of books. I would have given my life to own just a handful of them.

The remark that black people had smaller brains and were thus incapable of reading, speaking or writing English like white people had so wounded my ego that I vowed that, whatever the cost, I would master English, that I would not rest till I could read, write, and speak it just like any white man, if not better. Finally, I had something to aspire to.

Back with Granny, I told her to be on the lookout whenever Mrs. Smith junked any books. At the end of the day, as Granny and I prepared to leave, I was given a small box by Mrs. Smith.

"It's from Clyde," she said. "He's sorry that he treated you badly. He's promised not to do it again. I'll see to it he keeps his promise. Come and help Ellen in the garden whenever you can; that way you'll earn some pocket money."

The box contained a couple of shirts, pants, and jerseys. Underneath the articles of clothing was a copy of *Treasure Island.*

To learn to express my thoughts and feelings effectively in English became my main goal in life. I saw command of the English language as the crucial key with which to unlock doors leading into that wonderful world of books revealed to me through the reading of Robert Louis Stevenson's gripping tale of buried treasure, mutiny on the high seas, one-legged seamen, and the old sea song that I could recite even in my dreams:

> *Fifteen men on a dead man's chest*
> *Yo-ho-ho, and a bottle of rum.*

My heart ached to explore more such worlds, to live them in the imagination in much the same way as I lived the folktales of my mother and grandmother. I reasoned that if I somehow kept improving my English and ingratiated Mrs. Smith by the fact, then possibly she would give me more books like *Treasure Island* each time Granny took me along. Alas, such trips were few and far between. I could not afford to skip school regularly; and besides, each trip did not yield a book. But I clung to my dream.

A million times I wondered why the sparse library at my tribal school did not carry books like *Treasure Island,* why most of the books we read had tribal points of view. I would ask teachers and would be told that under the Bantu Education law black children were supposed to acquire a solid foundation in tribal life, which would prepare them for a productive future in their respective homelands. In this way the dream of Dr. Verwoerd, prime minister of South Africa and the architect of Bantu Education,[9] would be realized, for he insisted that "the native child must be taught subjects which will enable him to work with and among his own people; therefore there is no use misleading him by showing him the green pastures of European society, in which he is not allowed to graze. Bantu Education should not be used to create imitation whites."

---

9. **Dr. Verwoerd** (fər voŏrt′) . . . **architect of Bantu Education:** Henrick Frensch Verwoerd (1901–1966), a white South African leader who believed whites were superior to blacks and who helped create the discriminatory policy of apartheid.

How I cursed Dr. Verwoerd and his law for prescribing how I should feel and think. I started looking toward the Smiths to provide me with the books about a different reality. Each day Granny came back from work around five in the afternoon, I would be the first to meet her at the gate, always with the same question, "Any books for me today?" Many times there weren't any. Unable to read new English books on a regular basis, I reread the ones I had over and over again, till the pages become dog-eared. With each reading each book took on new life, exposed new angles to the story, with the result that I was never bored.

My bleak vocabulary did not diminish my enthusiasm for reading. I constantly borrowed Mr. Brown's pocket-size dictionary to look up meanings of words, and would memorize them like arithmetic tables and write them in a small notebook. Sometimes I would read the dictionary. My pronunciation was appalling, but I had no way of finding out. I was amazed at the number of words in the English language, at the fact that a word could have different shades of meaning, or that certain words looked and sounded alike and yet differed greatly in meaning. Would I ever be able to learn all that?

At the same time I was discovering the richness of the English language I began imitating how white people talked, in the hope of learning proper pronunciation. My efforts were often hilarious, but my determination increased with failure. I set myself the goal of learning at least two new English words a day.

◆ Reading Strategy
Why do you think the blacks are not taught much English at school?

▼ **Critical Viewing** Which details in this photograph reflect the hardships that blacks like the narrator must face? **[Interpret]**

from *Kaffir Boy* ◆ 107

▲ **Critical Viewing** How might these structures resemble Uncle Pietrus's "shack"? Explain. **[Interpret]**

At this time Uncle Pietrus, on my father's side, had moved into our yard. A bachelor with some education, he read the *World* and the black edition of the *Star* every day. Each evening I would go to his shack to borrow the two papers. I often found him through with chores, and the two of us would sit and discuss the mainstay of black news: crime, sports (mainly boxing and soccer), murder stories (the staggering statistics and the gruesome ways through which blacks killed blacks), and the latest police raids and shebeen swoops.

On Mondays and Fridays we filled out Jack-pots (crossword puzzles that paid cash prizes to winners). We never won anything, but my vocabulary benefited from the exercise. I began looking for opportunities to use my improved vocabulary in conversation. But such opportu-nities were rare: all talk, all teaching, all think-ing for that matter, at my school was in Tsonga.[10] The only time I encountered English was during the English period, one of the shortest in school, devoted mainly to honing servanthood Eng-lish. For lack of practice I soon forgot many of the words and had to relearn them, only to for-get them again, only to relearn them. I refused to quit.

◆ **Reading Strategy**
What do you think the narrator means by "servanthood English"?

---

10. **Tsonga:** Language spoken by the Tsonga people of southern Africa.

◆ **Build Vocabulary**

honing (hōn´ iŋ) *v.*: Perfecting a skill as one would sharpen a blade

Fairy Tales

Shu Ting
Translated by Donald Finkel and Jinsheng Yi

You believed in your own story,
then climbed inside it—
a turquoise flower,
You gazed past ailing trees,
5   past crumbling walls and rusty railings.
Your least gesture beckoned a
    constellation
of wild vetch,[1] grasshoppers, and stars
to sweep you into immaculate distances.

The heart may be tiny
10   but the world's enormous.

And the people in turn believe—
in pine trees after rain,
ten thousand tiny suns, a mulberry branch
bent over water like a fishing-rod,
15   a cloud tangled in the tail of a kite.
Shaking off dust, in silver voices
ten thousand memories sing from your
    dream.

The world may be tiny
but the heart's enormous.

---

1. **wild vetch** (vech): Any of a number of leafy climbing or trailing plants.

Guide for Responding

◆ Literature and Your Life

Reader's Response Would you like to know more about Mathabane's struggle to achieve success? Why or why not?

Thematic Focus Mathabane uses his first encounter with the white world to spur himself to further efforts. What inner qualities help him use his encounter in this way?

☑ Check Your Comprehension

1. Summarize what the narrator notices on the bus trip into the city.
2. What do Mrs. Smith and Clyde each say and do on first seeing the narrator?
3. What most impresses the narrator when he visits Clyde's playroom?
4. As a result of his visit, what becomes the narrator's main goal in life?
5. In Shu Ting's "Fairy Tales," what does the person she is writing about believe in?

◆ Critical Thinking

INTERPRET

1. How do you think the narrator feels about his first sight of the white schoolchildren and their school? **[Infer]**
2. (a) What advantages in life does Clyde have that the narrator lacks? (b) What advantages does the narrator have that Clyde lacks? **[Compare and Contrast]**
3. What factors allowed Mathabane to overcome the obstacles created by apartheid? **[Draw Conclusions]**

EVALUATE

4. Is it fair to expect Clyde to criticize the ideas about blacks he learns in school? **[Evaluate]**

APPLY

5. What topics might Clyde and the narrator discuss if they meet as adults? Why? **[Speculate]**

COMPARE LITERARY WORKS

6. In what ways is Mathabane like or unlike the person Shu Ting writes about in "Fairy Tales"? **[Compare and Contrast]**

Guide for Responding (continued)

◆ Reading Strategy

CONSIDER HISTORICAL CONTEXT

The **historical context** of Mathabane's account—the issues and events of the time—help explain the characters' attitudes and decisions. For example, under the apartheid laws that were still in effect during the early 1970's, black South Africans were extremely poor. They were also economically dependent on whites.

These facts explain why Granny is so eager for a wealthy white family, the Smiths, to help her talented grandson get ahead.

1. How does the system of apartheid help explain Clyde Smith's ideas about race relations?
2. Mrs. Smith grew up in England rather than South Africa. How might her English background explain her reactions to Clyde's ideas about race?
3. In what ways is apartheid both a barrier for the narrator and a spur to action?

◆ Literary Focus

DIALOGUE IN NONFICTION

Mathabane uses **dialogue,** characters' speech, in *Kaffir Boy* to portray characters' personalities and dramatize the action.

He excels at using dialogue and descriptions of facial expressions and gestures to help you see and understand peoples' reactions. For example, the following passage dramatizes Clyde's surprise and tells you about his ignorance of economic inequalities.

"You don't have a playroom," he said bug-eyed.

Explain how in each passage of dialogue and description Mathabane portrays personality and adds drama to his account.

1. "No, those are mansions. Each is owned by one family."
   "By one family!" I cried in disbelief. . . . (p. 100)
2. "Watch your filthy mouth, Clyde," Mrs. Smith said, flushing crimson. (p. 104)
3. "What do you know, Mama?" Clyde retorted impudently, "you're not a teacher. . . ." (p. 106)

◆ Build Vocabulary

USING THE LATIN ROOT *-ject-*

The Latin root *-ject-* means "throw or fling." On your paper, match each numbered word that contains the root with the letter of its definition.

1. eject
2. projector
3. objection
4. trajectory
5. injection

  a. device to "throw" images on a screen
  b. path of a "thrown" object
  c. "throw" someone or something out
  d. "throwing" something into the body with a needle
  e. something "thrown" forward in disagreement

USING THE WORD BANK: Synonyms

On your paper, write a synonym from the Word Bank for each numbered word.

1. tireless
2. models
3. sharpening
4. spotless
5. rickety
6. wretched
7. assumed

◆ Build Grammar Skills

CORRECT USE OF *their, there,* AND *they're*

Mathabane correctly uses three words that sound alike: **their,** a personal pronoun; **there,** an expletive at the beginning of a sentence or an adverb; and **they're,** a contraction for *they are.*

Practice On your paper, choose which of these homonyms should go in the blank in each sentence.

1. _____ were a hundred people in the bus.
2. I had to make way for women and _____ poodles.
3. _____ the ones who live in this white suburb.
4. Do many white people work _____ too?
5. Kitchen boys used the court on _____ day off.

Writing Application As Mathabane, write a brief letter of thanks to Clyde for the books he has given you. Correctly use *their, there,* and *they're.*

Build Your Portfolio

 ## Idea Bank

Writing

1. **Diary Entry** Putting yourself in the narrator's place, write the diary entry he might have written after his visit to Mrs. Smith's house.

2. **Problem-Solution Letter** As Mrs. Smith, write a letter to a newspaper about the problem of racial attitudes being taught in South African schools. Propose a solution. **[Social Studies Link]**

3. **Dialogue** Imagine a meeting between Clyde and the narrator after both have grown up. What would they say to each other? Write their dialogue.

Speaking, Listening, and Viewing

4. **Introduction** Mathabane will be speaking at your school. Write and deliver an introduction to his speech that will tell fellow students what they need to know about him. **[Performing Arts Link; Social Studies Link]**

5. **Dramatic Interpretation** With partners, choose a passage from the selection to read aloud to the class. Have one person read the narrator's part and others read the dialogue. **[Performing Arts Link]**

Researching and Representing

6. **Book Report** Read *Kaffir Boy* in its entirety and report on it to the class. Explain what you liked or disliked about the book. Mention Mathabane's use of such literary devices as dialogue, imagery, and conflict.

7. **End of Apartheid** Using the library and the Internet, research the way in which South Africans ended the system of apartheid. Present your results to the class, with the aid of timelines and diagrams. **[Social Studies Link; Art Link]**

Online Activity www.phlit.phschool.com

 ## Guided Writing Lesson

Comparison and Contrast

Kaffir Boy contains several contrasting pairs of characters: the narrator and Clyde, Mrs. Smith and Granny, and Clyde and his mother. Write a comparison and contrast for one of these pairs, showing how the two characters are similar and different.

Organize your essay by devoting one or more paragraphs to each character, then summing up similarities and differences in a conclusion. As an alternative, focus each paragraph on a single likeness or difference and discuss both characters together. Then you can summarize your findings at the end.

Writing Skills Focus: Supporting Details

Your comparison and contrast will be more persuasive if you include **supporting details** to illustrate your points. For example, in *Kaffir Boy*, Mathabane supports the idea that one boy is poor and the other rich by including a powerful detail. The narrator suddenly realizes that Clyde's playroom "was roughly the size of our house"!

Prewriting After choosing the characters you will compare, fill in a chart like this one:

Clyde	Mrs. Smith
• accepts prejudice he learns in school	• rejects prejudiced ideas her son learns in school

Drafting Use your chart as an outline. As you write, refer back to the story for details to use that support the ideas listed on your chart. Pay special attention to dialogue that supports your points.

Revising Be sure your organization is consistent. Provide details from the story wherever you have made a point without support. Finally, check to be sure you have correctly used *their, there,* and *they're*. For more on correctly using these words, see pp. 98 and 110.

Guide for Reading

Isabel Allende *(1942–)*

In her fiction and nonfiction, Chilean author Isabel Allende (ä yen´ dä) deals with terrible events from her country's recent history.

Yet, Allende writes with such imagination and courage that her books are popular throughout the world.

Caught Up in Events Allende comes from a distinguished family of public officials. Because her father and stepfather were Chilean diplomats, she was born in Peru and spent part of her childhood in Bolivia and Lebanon. A cousin of hers, Salvador Allende, was elected president of Chile in 1970.

In 1973, military leaders had Salvador Allende killed and took over the government, beginning a long period of repression and censorship. Isabel Allende fled Chile together with her husband and their two children. She moved to Venezuela, where she lived for several years.

Books About Her Family and Her Country Allende has said, "My life has been determined by two things . . . love and violence." While in Venezuela, Allende learned that her 99-year-old grandfather was dying. She started writing a letter to him that became her first novel, *The House of the Spirits.* Other novels have dealt with the political problems of Chile. In addition, she has written a popular memoir about the death of her daughter, titled *Paula* after her daughter's name.

Her fiction is sometimes called "magical realism" because, like the work of many other Latin American writers, it combines depictions of reality with fantasy.

International Success Although she writes in Spanish, her books are translated into many other languages and have earned Allende a worldwide reputation.

She has lived in California since 1988. When democratic government was reestablished in Chile, Allende returned fifteen years after leaving to visit her mother and receive an important Chilean literary award.

◆ Build Vocabulary

LATIN PREFIXES: *bene-*

In the first paragraph of her essay, Allende speaks of a "benevolent" image that comes to her mind. The Latin prefix *bene-* means "well." The word *benevolent* is derived from the Latin prefix *bene-*, "well," and the Latin root *-volens-*, "wishing." *Benevolent* means "doing good" or "kindly," which is another way of saying "wishing well." The prefix is also found in the noun *benevolence,* an inclination to do good.

benevolent
explicit
candid
subtleties
paternalistic
prerequisite
genocide

WORD BANK

As you read, you will encounter the words on this list. Each word is defined on the page where it first appears. Preview the list before you read.

◆ Build Grammar Skills

COMMONLY CONFUSED WORDS: *among* AND *between*

Among always implies three or more items, while *between* is generally used only with two items.

Notice the correct use of *among* and *between* in these sentences from "Writing as an Act of Hope":

Among those who can read and write, only very few can buy books, and *among* those who can buy books, very few have the habit of reading.

The difference *between* rich and poor is that the rich wear cocktail gowns all the time and the poor have their faces painted black.

Writing as an Act of Hope

◆ *Literature and Your Life*

CONNECT YOUR EXPERIENCE

There can be many reasons to write. You might want to tell an entertaining story, to organize your thoughts about a subject, or to convince somebody that your position regarding an issue is the right one. In this essay, Isabel Allende suggests other important reasons for writing.

Journal Writing List some of the things you have written in the past year. For each one, indicate the reason it was written.

THEMATIC FOCUS: STRUGGLING FOR JUSTICE

As you read, ask yourself: What connection does Allende make between writing and positive change?

◆ Background for Understanding

HISTORY

In 1970, Salvador Allende, Isabel Allende's cousin and a founder of Chile's Socialist Party, was elected president with 37 percent of the vote. His policies included nationalizing several industries.

In 1973, the Chilean military, under General Augusto Pinochet, took over the government by force. Many people believe that the military assassinated Salvador Allende. The new government banned political parties, censored the media, executed thousands of Chileans, and forced many others into exile.

Conditions began to change in 1988, when a vote was permitted on Pinochet's continuing as president. He was defeated. It was during this year of hope that Allende wrote her essay. When a new president took office in 1990, the government began to investigate the human rights abuses of the Pinochet years.

◆ Literary Focus

ESSAY OF JUSTIFICATION

In an **essay of justification,** the author sets out to prove that his or her position is the correct one from a moral or ethical point of view. As part of this defense, the author explains his or her own beliefs and practices. Sometimes, the author presents a plan for doing right that all readers can follow.

In "Writing as an Act of Hope," Allende explains her own practice as a writer. She also sets forth her beliefs about what every writer and every citizen ought to do.

◆ Reading Strategy

IDENTIFY AUTHOR'S PERSPECTIVE

To identify the **author's perspective** is to decide what viewpoint an author brings to a topic. Often, you can learn what the perspective is from direct statements that an author makes. Other times, you can arrive at an author's point of view only by making inferences from his or her words.

In her essay, for example, Allende makes several statements that reveal her perspective directly:

> The first thing we should do is to write clearly.

> All means are valid if we want to communicate . . .

> There is some hope for the spirit.

Elsewhere, she lets you draw your own conclusions. In one passage, she speaks of the reader who discovered in her books the facts about Chile that the government had suppressed. This passage implies that it is good for a writer to provide information that a repressive government tries to hide.

Writing As An Act Of HOPE

Isabel Allende

Now, for whom do I write?

When I face a clean sheet of paper, I don't think of a large audience or of the people who would raise their knives to cut me in pieces. If I did, terror would paralyze me. Instead, when I write, a benevolent image comes to my mind—that of Alexandra Jorquera, a young woman who lives in Chile whom I scarcely know. She has read my books so many times that she can repeat paragraphs by heart. In fact, she knows them better than I do. She quotes me and I don't know she's quoting me. Once she told me that she had discovered in my books the history of Chile that is denied by the official textbooks of the dictatorship—the forbidden and secret history that nevertheless is still alive in the memories of most Chileans.

This is the best compliment my work has ever received. For the sake of this girl I am very demanding with my writing. Sometimes, tempted by the beauty of a sentence, I am about to betray the truth, and then Alexandra comes to my mind and I remember that she, and others like her, don't deserve that. At other times I'm too explicit, too near the pamphlet. But then I step back, thinking she doesn't deserve that either—to be underestimated. And when I feel helpless against brutality and suffering, her candid face brings back my strength. All writers should have a reader like her, waiting for their words. They would never feel lonely, and their work would have a new and shining dimension.

◆ Build Vocabulary

benevolent (bə nev´ ə lənt) *adj*: Doing good; kindly

explicit (eks plis´ it) *adj*: Outspoken; saying what is meant, without disguise

candid (kan´ did) *adj*: Honest; fair

subtleties (sut´ 'l tēz) *n*: Complex and fine distinctions

paternalistic (pə tur´ nə lis´ tik) *adj*: Treating people as a father would treat children

In Latin America today, 50 percent of the population is illiterate. Among those who can read and write, only very few can buy books, and among those who can buy books, very few have the habit of reading. What, then, is the importance of a book in Latin America? None, would be the reasonable answer. But it's not exactly that way. For some strange reason, the written word has a tremendous impact in that illiterate continent. The totalitarian regimes have persecuted, tortured, sent into exile and murdered many writers. This is not an accident, dictators don't make mistakes in these details. They know that a book can be dangerous for them. In our countries most of the press is controlled by private enterprises or by inefficient governments. Eduardo Galcano, the great writer from Uruguay, puts it bluntly: "Almost all mass media promote a colonialistic culture, which justifies the unjust organization of the world as a result of the legitimate victory of the best—that is, the strongest. They lie about the past and about reality. They propose a lifestyle which postulates consumerism as an alternative to communism, which exalts crime as achievement, lack of scruples as virtue, and selfishness as a natural requirement."

◆ Reading Strategy
What does this paragraph reveal about Allende's perspective? Explain.

What can writers do against this persistent and powerful message? The first thing we should try to do is write clearly. Not simply—that only works with soap advertising; we don't have to sacrifice aesthetics for the sake of ethics. On the contrary, only if we are able to say it beautifully can we be convincing. Most readers are perfectly able to appreciate subtleties and poetic twists and symbols and metaphors. We should not write with a paternalistic attitude, as if readers were simple-minded, but we should also beware of elaborate and unnecessary ornamentation, which frequently hides a lack of ideas. It has been said that we Spanish-speaking people have the vice of empty words, that we need six hundred pages to say what would be better told in fifty.

The opportunity to reach a large number of readers is a great responsibility. Unfortunately, it is hard for a book to stand against the message of the mass media; it's an unfair battle. Writers should therefore look for other forms of expressing their thoughts, avoiding the prejudice that only in books can they make literature. All means are legitimate, not only the cultivated language of academia but also the direct language of journalism, the mass language of radio, television and the movies, the poetic language of popular songs and the passionate language of talking face to face with an audience. These are all forms of literature. Let us be clever and use every opportunity to introduce ourselves in the mass media and try to change them from within.

In Venezuela, José Ignacio Cabrujas, a playwright and novelist, one of the most brilliant intellectuals of the country, writes soap operas.

▼ **Critical Viewing** In what way can letter writing, as shown here, be "an act of hope"? **[Connect]**

▲ **Critical Viewing** What do you think this girl might be writing? Why? **[Interpret]**

cocktail gowns all the time and the poor have their faces painted black. They all go blind or become invalids and then they recover. Just like real life!

Many of the most important Latin American writers have been journalists, and they go back to it frequently because they are aware that their words in a newspaper or on the radio reach an audience that their books can never touch. Others write for the theater or the movies, or write lyrics for popular songs. All means are valid if we want to communicate and don't presume to be writing only for an educated elite or for literary prizes.

In Latin America a book is almost a luxury. My hairdresser calls me Dr. Allende because I usually carry a book, and she probably thinks that a doctorate is the minimum <u>prerequisite</u> for such an extravagance. In Chile a novel of three hundred pages can cost the equivalent of a laborer's monthly wages. In some other countries—like Haiti, for example—85 percent of the population is illiterate. Elsewhere in Latin America, nothing is published in the Indian languages of the majority. Many publishers have been ruined by the economic crisis, and the price of books imported from Spain is very high.

However, we should not despair. There is some hope for the spirit. Literature has survived even in the worst conditions. Political prisoners have written stories on cigarette paper. In the wars of Central America, little soldiers, fourteen years old, write poetry in their school notebook. The Pieroa Indians, those who haven't yet been exterminated by the <u>genocide</u> being carried out against the aborigines of the Amazon, have published some legends in their language.

In my continent, writers often have more prestige than they do in any other part of the world. Some writers are considered witch doctors, or prophets, as if they were illuminated by a sort

These shows are the most important cultural phenomenon in Latin America. Some people watch three or four a day, so you can imagine how important that kind of writing is. Cabrujas doesn't elude reality. His soap operas show a world of contrasts. He presents problems such as . . . machismo, poverty and crime. The result is quite different from "Dynasty." But it's also very successful.

I tried to put some of that soap opera stuff in *Eva Luna*,[1] because I'm fascinated by that version of reality. The ladies on TV wear false eyelashes at eleven in the morning. The difference between rich and poor is that the rich wear

---

1. *Eva Luna:* Novel by Isabel Allende.

♦ **Build Vocabulary**

prerequisite (pri rek´ wə zit) *n.*: Something required before something else can happen

genocide (jen´ ə sīd´) *n.*: Systematic killing of a whole national or ethnic group

of natural wisdom. Jorge Amado has to spend part of the year away from Brazil in order to write, because people crowd into his house seeking advice. Mario Vargas-Llosa directs the opposition to Alan Garcia's government in Peru. García Márquez is a frequent middleman for Central American presidents. In Venezuela, Arturo Uslar Pietri is consulted on issues like corruption and oil. These writers have interpreted their reality and told it to the world. Some of them even have the gift of foretelling the future and put in words the hidden thoughts of their people, which of course include social and political problems, because it is impossible to write in a crystal bubble, disregarding the conditions of their continent.

No wonder Latin American novels are so often accused of being political.

For whom do I write, finally? Certainly for myself. But mainly for others, even if there are only a few. For those who have no voice and for those who are kept in silence. For my children and my future grandchildren. For Alexandra Jorquera and others like her. I write for you.

And why do I write? García Márquez once said that he writes so that his friends will love him more. I think I write so that people will love each other more. Working with words is a beautiful craft, and in my continent, where we still have to name all things one by one, it has a rich and profound meaning.

Guide for Responding

◆ *Literature and Your Life*

Reader's Response Allende says she writes "so that people will love each other more." Do you think that writers can accomplish that aim? Why or why not?

Thematic Focus List some of the ways that Allende thinks writing can contribute to the struggle for justice. Do you agree with her?

Reader's Journal Compare *your* listing of reasons for writing with the reasons that Allende gives. Briefly note how your purposes are similar to, or different from, Allende's.

Questions for Research Many Chileans besides Isabel Allende suffered under the Pinochet regime in Chile. Write three questions that you could use to research Chilean history from 1973 to 1990.

☑ Check Your Comprehension

1. According to Allende, how have totalitarian regimes shown that writers are important?
2. What kind of style does Allende say writers should use?
3. What is shown by the fact that "political prisoners have written stories on cigarette paper"?
4. For whom does Allende say she writes?

◆ Critical Thinking

INTERPRET

1. According to Allende, when can "the beauty of a sentence" be a problem in writing? Explain. **[Interpret]**
2. What is the distinction that Allende draws between writing clearly and writing simply? **[Distinguish]**
3. According to Allende, how can writers reach people who cannot afford books or cannot read? **[Connect]**
4. In your own words, state why Allende believes that writing is an act of hope. **[Synthesize]**

EVALUATE

5. Do you agree that a book can be dangerous for a dictator? Why or why not? **[Make a Judgment]**

APPLY

6. Allende mentions Latin American writers who are considered wise and expert in nonliterary fields. Do you know of any performers or other celebrities who are expected to have special knowledge or abilities outside their primary occupations? Explain. **[Connect]**

Guide for Responding (continued)

◆ Reading Strategy

IDENTIFY AUTHOR'S PERSPECTIVE

By carefully reading Allende's essay, you can identify the **author's perspective;** that is, you can decide what her viewpoint is about writing and its influence on human activity.

Sometimes she tells you directly about her perspective on writing. These direct statements often come as answers to her own questions: "For whom do I write, finally? Certainly, for myself. But mainly for others, even if there are only a few."

At other times, you must draw your own conclusions about her perspective. For example, when she says, "In my continent, writers often have more prestige than they do in any other part of the world," you can infer that Allende believes strongly in the importance of what she does.

1. Find a statement in the last paragraph that directly reveals Allende's perspective on writing, and explain your choice.
2. In the third paragraph, Allende says that sometimes a beautiful sentence tempts her "to betray the truth" and other times her writing is "too near the pamphlet." What do these two statements reveal about her perspective on the relationship between beauty and politics in writing?

◆ Literary Focus

ESSAY OF JUSTIFICATION

Allende has written an **essay of justification,** defending something she does—in this case, writing —by explaining why and for whom she does it.

She presents her justification as the answers to a series of related questions: Now, for whom do I write?...What, then, is the importance of a book in Latin America?...What can writers do against this persistent and powerful message?...For whom do I write, finally?... And why do I write?

1. What is effective about this structure of question-and-answer?
2. Find three examples that Allende uses to show that writers can help individuals or societies.
3. Is there anything Allende could have added to strengthen her justification? Why or why not?

◆ Build Vocabulary

USING THE LATIN PREFIX *bene-*

Explain how the Latin prefix *bene-* contributes to the meaning of each of the following words. Use a dictionary if necessary.

1. beneficiary   2. benefactor   3. benefical

USING THE WORD BANK: Synonyms

On your paper, write the definition that best matches each word.

1. benevolent: (a) showing selfishness, (b) doing good, (c) causing problems
2. explicit: (a) clear, (b) wrong, (c) uncomfortable
3. candid: (a) conceited, (b) voting, (c) honest
4. subtleties: (a) broad generalizations, (b) wrong decisions, (c) fine distinctions
5. paternalistic: (a) treating people like children, (b) abusing a population, (c) making dangerous decisions
6. prerequisite: (a) addition, (b) command, (c) requirement
7. genocide: (a) advantage, (b) insult, (c) extermination

◆ Build Grammar Skills

COMMONLY CONFUSED WORDS: *among* AND *between*

Among is used with three or more items, and **between** is used when referring to two items.

Practice On your paper, choose the word that correctly completes each sentence.

1. A writer must choose (among, between) being truthful and writing a beautiful sentence.
2. A writer can choose (among, between) the mass media for opportunities to reach people.
3. (Among, Between) the writers of Latin America, there are many journalists.
4. Allende points out that there is a difference (among, between) writing to communicate and writing to win literary prizes.
5. Critics consider Allende to be (between, among) the best Latin American authors writing today.

Build Your Portfolio

Idea Bank

Writing

1. **Song** Choose a song with words that contain a real message. Write a brief explanation of why the words say something important. **[Music Link]**

2. **Letter** Think of an author whose writing is important to you. Write a letter to the author, explaining what you like about his or her work.

3. **Essay** Write a short essay about one reason that you have found literature to be important.

Speaking, Listening, and Viewing

4. **Songs of South America** Find recordings of the music of Chile or other South American countries to share with other students. You may be able to find songs that refer to Chile's history in the 1970's. **[Music Link]**

5. **Soap Opera** Watch two or three episodes of a soap opera. Report to your class on how well it deals with real life. **[Performing Arts Link]**

Researching and Representing

6. **Reasons for Writing** A number of authors and journalists have discussed their reasons for writing. Find at least three statements by writers in the library or on the Internet. Copy the most important part of each statement. Write a one-page report comparing their statements with Isabel Allende's. **[Literature Link]**

7. **Crisis in Chile** Research political events, economic crises, or human rights issues that played a role in Chile's history from the 1970's to the 1990's. Report on your findings to the class. **[Social Studies Link]**

Online Activity www.phlit.phschool.com

Guided Writing Lesson

Essay of Justification

In her essay about why she writes, Allende explains the importance of writing and how writers can influence the events of the world. Write your own essay of justification. Choose an activity or belief that is important to you, and then explain why it is important—to you and to others.

Writing Skills Focus: Organization by Order of Importance

Your essay will be easier for readers to follow if you organize it by **order of importance:**

- from least important to most important, or
- from most important to least important

Note how Allende begins her essay by referring to one reader. After pointing out many examples of the importance of writing, she concludes by referring to the most significant groups—all her readers and all people in her continent and the world.

Prewriting Choose an activity that is important to you. Then, list details and examples that will justify its importance. Finally, number the examples according to their order of their significance.

Drafting As you write your first draft, present each detail in the order that you have chosen: from most important to least important, or from least important to most important.

Revising Have classmates read your draft, and ask them whether or not you have successfully justified the importance of your topic. Have you consistently followed an organizational plan? Should any details be moved from one place to another?

Before you prepare a final copy, be sure that you have correctly used *among* and *between*. For more on the correct use of these prepositions, see p. 112 and p. 118.

Writing Process Workshop

Tests are one way to measure how successfully you have learned something. A timed-test essay is an essay on a test that you must complete within a certain time limit.

The following skills will help you write an effective test essay when you have time limits.

Writing Skills Focus

▶ **Support your ideas with details.** For instance, if you say "Every citizen over 21 has a responsibility to vote," say *why* as well.

▶ **Show, don't tell,** the features or qualities of your topic. Offer examples, summarize events, or cite facts.

▶ **Be brief and clear.** Since your time is limited, say only what is essential to cover your topic.

The following excerpt, from an essay about the importance of keeping beaches public, shows these skills.

MODEL

① The writer gets to the point in the first paragraph.

② Here, the writer supports his main idea with details and elaboration.

③ This brief, clear paragraph offers another assertion and example.

Beaches—whose waters, sands, dunes, and cliffs constantly change with the tides and the weather—are among our most inspiring landscapes. As such, they should never be private property. ① We are most likely to treasure and preserve them if we know they belong to us all.

As citizens of the planet, everyone should have the right to explore any tidepool, swim in any surf, or run on any sandy shore. Private ownership of beaches denies these rights and pleasures to all but a privileged few. ② This is unfair.

In addition, private beach ownership often results in destructive development of land closest to the sea. ③ Development may cause erosion of dunes or cliffs, pollution, and disturbance or destruction of wildlife habitats.

Prewriting

Know Your Purpose and Your Audience Usually on an essay test, the topic is assigned to you. Make sure that you know exactly what the question requires you to write, so you won't get off track. Unless the instructions say otherwise, assume that you are expected to write in a formal way to an interested and objective audience.

Plan Your Time Imagine that you have twenty minutes to complete your essay. Quickly plan out your time. Allow a few minutes to gather and organize your thoughts, a large block of time to draft your essay, and a few minutes to revise.

Plan the Points You Will Elaborate Make a list of the main ideas you will introduce in your essay. Under each main idea, note the supporting details you will offer to convince your audience that your reasoning is sensible. Arrange your points in a logical sequence. This outline will prevent you from wasting time on irrelevant details and reorganization.

For practice, choose one of the following topics:

Topic Choices

1. In an essay addressed to parents and teachers, describe both sides of a particular issue, such as a school rule that is controversial. Take a stand and defend it.

2. Write an aphorism or a statement that you think communicates a valuable message about success. In a letter to the editor, explain the message and tell how you consider it relevant to a real-life situation.

Drafting

Get Started As soon as you've organized your main ideas and details, begin drafting. Use an objective tone. Present your main idea in the introduction of your essay.

Support Your Points In the body of your essay, state and develop your ideas. Each paragraph should either directly or indirectly support your main idea. Within each paragraph, make sure that each supporting sentence either directly or indirectly supports the topic sentence of the paragraph.

Conclude Finish your essay with a conclusion, in which you restate your main idea or make a general observation about it.

APPLYING LANGUAGE SKILLS: Standard and Informal English

A timed-test essay should be written in standard English. Standard English uses an objective tone and correct usage, contains no slang, avoids contractions, and often uses long sentences with varied structures.

Informal English:
The Japanese are totally crazy about baseball.

Standard English:
Baseball is extremely popular in Japan.

Practice On your paper, rewrite the following passage in standard English.

Some people are grossed out by sushi, but they're crazy! It totally rules.

Writing Application Check your essay to make sure that it is written in standard English and follows the guidelines given above.

Writer's Solution Connection Writing Lab

For more help on writing a timed-test essay, see Drafting a Timed-Test Essay in the Writing Lab tutorial on Practical/Technical Writing.

Applying Language Skills: Placement of Modifiers

Make sure that all of your modifiers—your adjectives, adverbs, and modifying phrases—are in the proper place in each sentence.

Misplaced Modifier:

A red cross on a white field became the symbol of the Red Cross, which was a reversal of the Swiss flag.

Correctly Placed Modifier:

A red cross on a white field, which borrowed the image but reversed the colors of the Swiss flag, became the symbol of the Red Cross.

Practice On your paper, rewrite the following sentence so that the modifying phrase is in the proper place.

Each year, millions of Americans enter blood centers between the ages of 17 and 66 to donate blood.

Writing Application Review your essay, and make sure that all of your modifiers are correctly placed.

Writer's Solution Connection
Language Lab

For more practice with placement of modifiers, complete the Language Lab lesson on Misplaced Modifiers.

Revising

Check Quickly Because time is limited during this type of essay, you'll have only a few moments in which to review and polish your writing. Look through the tips that follow, and use them as a guide to revise your essay.

- ▶ Reread the essay question to make sure you've addressed it.
- ▶ Skim the introduction and conclusion to make sure you haven't drifted from your original topic.
- ▶ Make sure your ideas are logical and well organized. Review the points you've made. Add supporting details where needed. Delete irrelevant information.
- ▶ Make sure that you use standard English in your essay. Take out any slang terms and any unnecessary contractions. Check your spelling and grammar.

REVISION MODEL

The computer industry is extremely important to the

economy of California, our ① *most populous* ② biggest state. ~~I love playing~~

~~Myst on my computer, but I've never been able to figure~~

③ *The companies of "Silicon Valley" alone employ more than 20,000 people.* ~~out how to get past the final stage.~~

① The student made this sentence more accurate.

② The student deleted this irrelevant sentence.

③ The student added this example to back up her assertion in the first sentence.

Publishing

Share Your Paper Because the information in timed-test essays is organized and compact, the essays are good records of what you've learned about effective writing. Here are some ideas for sharing your work.

- ▶ Start a portfolio of essays.
- ▶ Use the essay as the basis for a research paper.
- ▶ Ask your teacher for feedback and ways to improve your writing on future tests.

Student Success Workshop

Real-World Reading Skills

Strategies for Success

"Buy the sneakers worn by pros!" "Elect the candidate who's working for *you!*" "Support a worthy cause: Give generously!" A persuasive message can be delivered in many ways, but its goal is the same: to persuade you to think or to do something. The following guidelines will help you identify persuasive messages and evaluate the techniques they use:

Identify Persuasive Techniques Look for persuasive techniques. Does the text state facts, or does it deceptively state things that only *sound* like facts? Does the text use logical reasoning or evidence to support ideas or opinions, or might its reasoning be faulty? The following techniques, common in persuasive writing, may be used to mislead you:

- ▶ Using enticing slogans or images to get the reader or viewer to buy a product
- ▶ Promising desirable outcomes
- ▶ Seeming to appeal to the reader's intellect or sense of reason, but in fact appealing to his or her emotions

Evaluate the Message and the Technique
Since persuasive texts often promise outcomes and appeal to your emotions, you must evaluate them on the basis of your needs and on what you believe to be the facts.

As you evaluate an advertisement, ask yourself:

- ▶ Does the message make valid statements or misleading claims?
- ▶ Is the message based on logic and facts or on statements of opinion?
- ▶ Is this message one that I am willing to be persuaded by?

Apply the Strategies

Evaluate the ad below:

Did you ever wish you could have hair like your favorite movie star's?

Now you can with **Hair of the Rich and Famous.**

With our shampoo and conditioner, your hair will practically style itself! So come on—join the beautiful people—get **Hair of the Rich and Famous.**

1. What claim is made in this advertisement?
2. How does the ad attempt to influence you?
3. Does the ad support its claims? If so, how?
4. Would you buy this product after evaluating the ad? Explain.

✔ *It's important to evaluate persuasive texts like these:*
- ▶ Advertisements for health or safety products (*e.g.*, smoke alarms, water purifiers, vitamins)
- ▶ Fund-raising letters (for charitable organizations or political campaigns)
- ▶ Advertisements promising a service (*e.g.*, cheapest telephone rates, Internet access, health care)

Speaking, Listening, and Viewing Workshop

Strategies for Success

Just as authors use imagination to resolve conflicts in their works of literature, you can become more imaginative in your resolution of real-life conflicts. Here are some strategies that will help you ease tense situations and work out solutions to problems.

Imagine the Other Person's Needs Always listen carefully to what others say. Analyze their language for clues to their state of mind, their needs, and their goals. For example, when people use emotionally charged phrases like "out to get me," it is a sign that they are in a defensive and angry frame of mind.

Also, be aware of others' tone of voice, facial expressions, and body language. A raised fist is an obvious sign of anger, but an earlier and less noticeable sign of anger might be a slight tightening of the mouth.

State the Problem Once you see early signs of trouble and conflict, do your best to identify the problem and state it in clear, unemotional language. Remember that disagreements sometimes lead to physical fights because those involved in the conflict fail to say what the problem is. Lacking words, they resort to actions.

State the problem in such a way that everyone involved agrees with the wording. By working together on a statement of the problem, people *in conflict* are now *in cooperation*.

Imagine a Solution After you have clearly stated the problem, have everyone involved work on a solution. If the conflict has been building for days and weeks, do not expect the solution to come quickly.

Explore the possibility of bringing in an unbiased person or group to arbitrate the conflict. However, remember that an arbitrator has to be respected by everyone involved.

Challenge everyone involved in the dispute to be as imaginative as possible in devising a solution. Look for new ideas and fresh approaches. Be sure that your plan offers at least some benefit for everyone.

Build in a Monitoring System Work out a way to keep track of progress toward a solution. It might be helpful to have the arbitrator or some other unbiased person keep an eye on such progress.

Be Prepared to Change As you work toward a solution, you may think of better ideas for resolving the dispute. Stay open to such ideas. However, do not change the plan unless everyone involved in the conflict understands the change and has consented to it.

Apply the Strategies

With a partner or small group, use the techniques of conflict resolution to role-play solutions to these conflicts:

1. Suppose you represent groups that want to use the same basketball court for a regularly scheduled game. No other court is available, and both groups feel they need the court at the same time on the same days.

2. One neighbor feels that another neighbor's dog is tearing up her garden. Pretending to be the neighbors, work together to resolve your dispute.

Tips for Resolving Conflicts

√ *Communication skills will help you at every stage of conflict resolution. Here are some tips to remember:*

▶ *Speak slowly, clearly, and calmly.*

▶ *Listen carefully to what others say.*

▶ *Avoid finger-pointing statements, in which you angrily tell someone, "You did this," or "You said that."*

▶ *Avoid threatening gestures or expressions.*

Test Preparation Workshop

Writing Skills | Planning an Answer to an Essay Question

Strategies for Success

When taking a timed essay test, you may feel the urge to skim through the question and begin answering it immediately. However, by carefully analyzing the question, you can improve your performance. Here are some strategies to use:

Read the Question Carefully It helps to read the question carefully and more than once. As you read, note key words, as well as the specific dos and don'ts that often appear at the end of the question. Look at the following example:

> From the novels, short stories, full-length plays, and poems you have read, choose a work and explain how an important character in it is motivated by the desire to acquire wealth or power. Do not use a work of British or American literature.

Key words for this question would include:

- "novels, short stories, full-length plays, and poems" (don't write about nonfiction)
- "important character" (don't write about a minor character)
- "motivated by the desire to acquire wealth or power" (make sure your character fits this description)

An important *don't* in the question is:

- no works "of British or American literature"

Consider the Best Work to Discuss It is worth taking time to consider the work you will use to answer the question. If you choose a work that is inappropriate, you will have trouble later in the test but may not have time to make another choice.

This model shows how a test-taker found a work to answer the question about "acquiring wealth and power":

- Jamaica Kincaid is one of my favorite authors. I have a clear memory of her story "A Walk to the Jetty" and would like to write about it. The main character is leaving home for the first time. However, maybe this character is acquiring freedom, not "power" in the sense that the question seems to mean—power over others.

- Tolstoy's "How Much Land Does a Man Need?" is a better story to use. The main character wants more and more land, which is a form of wealth. Even the title of the story poses an important question about wealth and power.

Apply the Strategies

Read the following sample essay question, and answer the questions below.

> From the novels, short stories, full-length plays, poems, biographies, and autobiographies you have read, choose one work and explain how an important character in it reacts to the gain or loss of power. The work you choose must be from world literature other than British (England, Ireland, Scotland, and Wales) and American (United States) literature. Give the title and, if you remember, the author of the work.

1. What are the key words in this question? Explain.

2. What important dos and don'ts appear at the end of the question?

3. Name a work you would write about, and explain your choice.

Aeneid I, Fol. 62v, Virgil, Biblioteca Riccardiana, Firenze, Italy

Suspense in World Literature

Your heart pounds, your brow perspires, your stomach is in knots— like riding a rollercoaster, reading suspenseful literature from around the world can be nerve-wracking, even frightening, but always exciting. The stories, poems, epic, and essays you are about to read in this unit will take you to the edge—and beyond. You'll witness a power struggle in precolonial Africa, travel to the top of the world, and live in a haunted house. By the end, you'll feel as if you've gone along on the most dangerous but delightfully daring ride of your life!

Guide for Reading

Bessie Head (1937–1986)

A prominent African novelist and journalist, Bessie Head wrote about both her mixed heritage and her experiences as an exile. Her powerful writing brings to life the themes of discrimination, racism, personal freedom, and African history.

A Rich Heritage Head was born of mixed black and white parentage in Pietermaritzburg, South Africa. Trained as an educator, she taught primary school for several years, and then worked as a reporter in the large South African cities of Johannesburg and Cape Town.

Exile in Botswana At the age of 27, Head moved to Botswana to escape the racial policies of the South African government. These policies, called *apartheid* (ə pär´ tāt)—an Afrikaans word for "the state of being separate"—required blacks to live in segregated, poorer areas and limited their ability to acquire a good education and a well-paying job.

In Botswana, she began to write novels: *When Rain Clouds Gather* (1969), *Maru* (1971), and *A Question of Power* (1973). These stories criticize injustice, whether it is perpetrated by whites or blacks. Head views evil as a universal problem and not the characteristic of a particular race or people.

"Dislike Politics" When asked to express her politics for a brief autobiography, she wrote simply "dislike politics." Nevertheless, her novels and historical chronicles reveal her deeply felt opposition to all kinds of political oppression, including racism and the second-class status of women.

The short story "A Power Struggle" reveals her trust in people's inborn sense of justice. It presents a tale from precolonial times, as told from Head's contemporary, post-colonial perspective.

◆ Build Vocabulary

LATIN PREFIXES: *ad-*

In "A Power Struggle," a new leader is greeted with "a chorus of adulation." In the word *adulation* is the Latin prefix *ad-*, which can mean "to," "motion toward," or "near." The word part *-ulation* comes from the Latin word meaning "tail." Originally meaning "to wag the tail," *adulation* now means "flattery or excessive admiration." What does Head's use of this word suggest about the new leader?

lithe
avarice
intrigue
adulation
obeisance

WORD BANK

As you read this story, you will encounter the words on this list. Each word is defined on the page where it first appears. Preview the list before you read.

◆ Build Grammar Skills

CORRECT USE OF *only*

Sometimes choosing the right word isn't enough—you also have to find the correct place in the sentence for that word. Writers like Bessie Head know that they need to place the modifier *only* with care, making sure it is in front of the word it modifies. Head writes:

Only Davhana felt the pain.

The sentence means that no one other than Davhana felt the pain. Suppose Head had written this sentence instead:

Davhana felt *only* the pain.

This sentence means that Davhana felt nothing other than pain.

A Power Struggle

◆ *Literature and Your Life*

CONNECT YOUR EXPERIENCE

You are part of many communities, including your school and your neighborhood. You might also belong to a team, band, or club. Every community follows rules and traditions, some written and some understood. What happens when someone breaks a rule? How does the community respond?

In "A Power Struggle," Bessie Head writes about how a village responds to a conflict between two village leaders.

Journal Writing Name a community you are part of and write down three or four "unwritten" rules. Describe some of the policies that people within this community follow even though no one talks about them.

THEMATIC FOCUS: RIGHT AND WRONG

One of the central characters in this story is the rightful heir to his father's throne. As you read, ask yourself: Does this character respond appropriately when his claim is challenged? Why or why not?

◆ Background for Understanding

CULTURE

In many ways, the village itself is an important character in Bessie Head's "A Power Struggle." The importance she gives to the village reflects the reality that the village, or clan, was the central social unit in precolonial Africa.

Many writers emphasize the unique dynamics of clan politics, in which the actions of the clan as a group are often more vital or relevant than the actions of individuals, regardless of their rank. The social and cultural traditions of a village could act as a safety net to protect the clan against self-centered leaders.

As foreign powers began to control Africa during the colonial era, some of these social structures were damaged or lost. Africans were forced to obey the laws and rules of the governing country, and traditional social systems were changed forever. During and after the era of colonialism, however, the village retained great importance throughout Africa.

◆ Literary Focus

CONFLICT AND CULTURAL STYLE

A story almost always contains a **conflict**—a struggle between opposing forces:

- An **internal conflict** takes place within a character, as he or she struggles with opposing feelings, beliefs, or needs.
- An **external conflict** occurs between two or more characters or between a character and a natural force.

The events of a story build the conflict until it reaches a final **resolution**—the end of the central conflict.

Often in world literature the nature and resolution of conflicts depends on **cultural style**—the beliefs, customs, and values of a particular group.

In "A Power Struggle," Head analyzes the conflict between two individuals and its effect on their clan. She also describes a resolution that she identifies as uniquely African.

Reading for Success

Literal Comprehension Strategies

With any piece of literature—from fiction to poetry—your first goal in reading is to understand what the writer is saying. Some writers have a clear, direct style that is easy to understand, but others may write in a way that is less clear. However, there are strategies you can apply to help you understand even complex writing.

Reread or read ahead.

▶ Reread a sentence or a paragraph to find the connections among the words.

▶ Read ahead—a word or detail you don't understand may become clear further on.

Use context clues.

Context refers to the words, phrases, and sentences that surround a word. Look for clues in the context to help you figure out the meaning of an unknown word. For example, you might be unfamiliar with the word *lithe* in the following sentence from "A Power Struggle":

He was tall and strongly-built with *lithe,* agile movements.

The context clue "agile," which appears to be a synonym of the unfamiliar word *lithe,* suggests that *lithe* means "flexible or limber."

Analyze or break down confusing sentences.

▶ Read sentences in logical sections, not word by word.

▶ Determine the subject of each sentence (what the sentence is about). Then read to see what the rest of the sentence says about the subject.

Restate for understanding.

▶ Paraphrase, or restate a sentence or a paragraph in your own words.

▶ Summarize at appropriate points; review and state the main ideas or points of what has happened. Notice story details that seem to be important. Try to fit them into your picture of what is happening.

As you read the following story by Bessie Head, look at the notes in the boxes. These notes demonstrate how to apply these strategies to a work of literature.

A Power Struggle

Bessie Head

The universe had a more beautiful dream. It was not the law of the jungle or the survival of the fittest but a dream that had often been the priority of saints —the power to make evil irrelevant. All the people of Southern Africa had lived out this dream before the dawn of the colonial era. Time and again it shed its beam of light on their affairs although the same patterns of horror would arise like dark engulfing waves.

It was as though once people had lived in settled communities for any length of time, hostilities of an intolerable nature developed due to power struggles, rivalries and jealousies. Not all the stories were attractive or coherent; they were often so direct and brutal that it was almost like darkness destroying darkness and no rule was untainted by it. It was before these fierce passions for power that people often gave way and it formed the

◄ **Critical Viewing** What does this sculpture of a warrior suggest about the Zulu culture from which it came? **[Interpret]**

base of the tangled story of tribal move-ment and migration. When it was all over only a tree, a river bank, a hill or a mountain lingered in the memory as the dwelling place of a tribe.

There were two brothers of the Tlabina clan, Davhana and Baeli. In more ways than one Davhana was destined to rule. He was the born heir to the throne and in acknowledgement of this, the old chief, their father, had, once his health began to fail him, handed to Davhana the sacred rain-making apparatus—a symbol of his destiny. But Davhana was also a fearfully rich personality with glowing black eyes. There was about him the restless beauty of the earth in motion and he could laugh for so long and so loudly that his laughter was like the sound of the wind rushing across the open plains. He was tall and strongly-built with <u>lithe</u>, agile movements. People humorously accorded to him the formal and often meaningless ti-tles a king held as his due such as "Beautiful One" or "Great Lion" but un-like other kings, Davhana earned them with his living personality. In spite of this his succession was not assured and his destiny took an unpredictable turn.

They were at the burial ceremony for their father when his brother, Baeli, abruptly threw down the first challenge to his succession. It was Davhana's right as his father's successor to turn the first sod in his grave. It was also a confirma-tion before the assembled people that he would rule. Davhana had his digging im-plement raised but his younger brother, Baeli, stepped in ahead of him and turned the first sod. The older brother stepped back instantly, his digging im-plement relaxed at his side. He flung his head back with an impatient gesture and stared at the horizon, his mouth curled down in contempt. The younger brother straightened up quietly. He too looked

Context clues help you understand the meaning of *apparatus*. Davhana's father hands him something used to make rain, so *apparatus* is probably a word used to describe a tool or machine.

into the distance, a smile on his lips and menace in his eyes. The gestures were so unexpected that the assembled people stirred instinctively and stifled gasps of surprise swept through the crowd. There was not anyone present who did not know that the succession was open to dispute.

Immediately, the dispute did not con-cern the people. The real power struggle would take place in the inner circle of relatives and councilors. It was often an impersonal process as far as the mass of the people were concerned—what they respected was not so much a chief in person as the position he occu-pied. And yet, there seemed a contradiction in this. It was real men of passion who fought for that position and should an evil man gain the throne, people would suffer. People had a number of cynical attitudes to cover such events. One of their attitudes was: "We pay hom-age to all the chief's sons, since which one of them will finally become chief is uncertain . . ." If things became too disruptive a large number of men would suddenly remember that they had not branded their cattle or attended to their everyday affairs.

The two young men of passion turned away from the funeral ceremony and walked side by side for some distance; Davhana purposefully keeping pace with his brother.

"Baeli," he asked in his direct way, "Why did you turn the first sod on fa-ther's grave? It was my duty by right! You have shamed me in front of all the people! Why did you do it?"

Read ahead to find out what the people of the village do after they have time to think about Baeli's leadership.

◆ **Build Vocabulary**

lithe (līth) *adj.*: Bending easily; supple; limber
avarice (av′ ə ris) *n.*: Greed

He listened with his whole body for his brother's reply but no reply was forthcoming—only the pacing of their feet walking in unison filled the silence. Davhana looked sideways at his brother's face. Baeli stared straight ahead; the smile still lingered around his mouth and there was an aloofness in his eyes. Had they in such an abrupt manner suddenly recognized that they were total strangers to each other? A day ago they had shared a youth together, hunted together and appeared to laugh at the same jokes. Only Davhana felt the pain. His personality radiated outwards, always reaching towards love and friendship. His brother's personality turned inwards into a whirlpool of darkness.

He felt himself being dragged down into that whirlpool and instinctively he turned and walked off in his own direction.

Which brother walks off in his own direction? **Analyze** the previous sentence to identify that the pronoun "he" refers to Davhana, who feels he is being drawn into his brother's dark "whirlpool."

Davhana walked until he reached a clearing outside the village. Evening was approaching. The night was warm. A full yellow moon arose behind a small hill in the distance. The atmosphere was deeply silent and still. The subdued murmurs of insects in the grass were peaceful and sweet. The young man settled himself on the earth and was soon lost in his own thoughts. Now and then he sighed deeply as though he were reaching a crossroad with himself, as though he were drawing to himself the scattered fragments of his youthful life. He had lived with the reckless generosity of his personality and nothing in his past seemed a high peak. He had lived, danced, eaten and sung in the full enjoyment of the pleasures of the moment. The events of the day cast their dark shadows over him.

Softly approaching footsteps stirred him out of his reverie. The moonlight outlined the form of one of the elders of the tribe. Davhana turned his head with his glowing look, inviting the old man to seat himself. The old man squatted low beside his reclining form and stared for some time in a detached way at the small hill behind which the moon had arisen.

"Do your thoughts trouble you, Beautiful One?" the old man asked at last. "I have stood here for some time and heard you sigh and sigh."

"Oh no, Uncle," the young man said, with a vigorous shake of his head. "Nothing troubles me. If I sigh it may be only for a carefree youth which I am about to lose."

The elder plucked at a few strands of grass and continued to stare at the distant hill.

"Everyone took note today of the awful deed your brother committed," he said. "It was the most awful breach of good manners and some of us are questioning its motive."

The young man curled his mouth in contempt again as though it were beneath him to recognize <u>avarice</u> and ambition.

"Baeli has always had strange tendencies," he said. "Though I have liked him as my brother."

The old man kept silent a while. When he spoke his voice was as sweet and peaceful as the subdued murmurs of the insects in the grass.

"I have come to teach you a few things about life," he said. "People have never been given a gift like you before, Beautiful One, and they look eagerly forward to your rule because they think that a time of prosperity and happiness lies before them. All these years you have lived with the people and your ways were good to them. When a man built his yard you stopped to tie a knot in the rafters and the hunting spoils you shared generously with all your men, never demanding an abundant share for yourself. You spread happiness and laughter wherever you traveled.

▲ **Critical Viewing** What can you deduce about the region of southern Africa shown in this picture? **[Analyze]**

People understand these qualities. They are the natural gifts of a good man. But these very gifts can be a calamity in a ruler. A ruler has to examine the dark side of human life and understand that men belong to that darkness. There are many men born with inadequate gifts and this disturbs them. They have no peace within themselves and once their jealousy is aroused they do terrible things . . ."

The old man hesitated, uncertain of how to communicate his alarms and fears. A ruler could only reach the day of installation without bloodshed provided no other member of his family had declared his ambition publicly. Baeli had publicly declared his ambition and it needed only a little of that poison for all sorts of perverse things to happen. They had some horrible things in their history. They had been ruled by all sorts of lunatics and mental defectives who had mutually poisoned or assassinated each other. His grandfather had been poisoned by a brother who had in turn been assassinated by another brother. Not even Davhana's father's rule was untainted by it—there were several assassinations behind his father's peaceful and lengthy reign.

"You will soon find out the rules of life, Beautiful One," the old man murmured. "You will have to kill or be killed."

The young man said nothing in reply.

◆ Build Vocabulary

intrigue (in trēg´) *v.*: Plot or scheme secretly

The old man sat bathed in moonlight and the subdued murmurs of insects in the grass were peaceful and sweet.

The struggle that unfolded between Davhana and his brother was so subtle that it was difficult to deal with. It took place when men sat deep in council debating the issues of the day. There was always a point at which Baeli could command all the attention to himself and in doing so make his brother, Davhana, irrelevant. Baeli would catch a debate just at the point at which his brother had spoken and while a question or statement trembled in the air awaiting a reply. Baeli would step in and deflect men's thoughts in a completely new direction, thus making the previous point completely invalid. Some men began to enjoy this game and daily, Davhana rapidly lost ground with them. He refused at crucial points to assert his power and allowed dialogues to drift away from him. He indulged in no counter-intrigue when it became evident from the laughter of the men that his brother had begun to <u>intrigue</u> with them.

When they moved into the dark side of the moon, the most fearful massacre took place. Davhana alone escaped with his life and fled into the dark night. He had a wound in his right shoulder where a spear had pierced him as he lay asleep in his hut. He did not know who had stabbed him but in the confusion of the struggle in the dark he broke free of the hands that lunged at him and escaped.

Once, during his flight in the dark, Davhana paused again and took stock of his destiny. It was still scattered and fragmentary but the freshness and beauty of his youth lay on him like a protective mantle. If power was the unfocused demoniacal stare of his brother then he would have none of that world. Nothing had paralyzed, frustrated and enraged him more than that stare.

Paraphrase this paragraph about Davhana's decision: Davhana stopped to think about his future. He was still young and idealistic. His brother's evil stare made him so angry that he decided that he didn't want to be part of his brother's corrupt world.

"He can take all that he desires," Davhana thought. "I shall not go back there. I want to live."

He chose for himself that night the life of one who would take refuge where he could find it and so he continued his flight into the night.

The people of the Tlabina clan awoke the following morning to a new order. They had a murderer as their ruler. Baeli had slain whatever opposition he was likely to encounter and no one was immediately inclined to oppose him. The ritual of installation proceeded along its formal course. When Baeli appeared a chorus of <u>adulation</u> greeted him and everyone present made humble <u>obeisance</u>. The usual speeches were made to the impersonal office of kingship.

After three moons had waxed and waned word traveled back to the people that their ruler, Davhana, was alive and well and had sought refuge with a powerful Pedi clan. The people of the Tlabina clan began to vanish from their true home, sometimes in large groupings, sometimes in small trickles until they had abandoned Baeli. If the wild dogs ate him, who knows?

A power struggle was the great dialogue of those times and many aspects of the dialogue were touched by the grandeur of kings like Davhana. It was hardly impersonal as living men always set the dialogue in motion. They forced people under duress to make elaborate choices between good and evil. This thread of strange philosophical beauty was deeply woven into the history of the land and the story was repeated many times over so that it became the only history people ever knew.

With the dawn of the colonial era this history was subdued. A new order was imposed on life. People's kings rapidly faded from memory and became myths of the past. No choices were left between what was good and what was evil. There was only slavery and exploitation.

◆ **Build Vocabulary**

adulation (a jōō lā´ shən) *n.*: Intense or excessive admiration

obeisance (ō bā´ səns) *n.*: Gesture of respect, such as a bow or curtsy

Guide for Responding

◆ *Literature and Your Life*

Reader's Response Were you surprised by the outcome of this story? Why or why not?

Thematic Focus How does the clan achieve justice in this story?

☑ Check Your Comprehension

1. How does Baeli first challenge Davhana?
2. How does Davhana respond to Baeli's challenge?
3. What advice does the elder give to Davhana?
4. What happens to the Tlabina clan after they have a new king?

◆ Critical Thinking

INTERPRET

1. How are Davhana and Baeli different? **[Compare and Contrast]**
2. Neither Baeli nor Davhana is perfect. Describe Davhana's most important faults. **[Analyze]**
3. How does Head's story illustrate the opening two sentences of "A Power Struggle"? **[Interpret]**

EVALUATE

4. Do you think Davhana made the best decision to resolve his conflict? Why or why not? **[Make a Judgment]**

Guide for Responding *(continued)*

◆ Reading Strategy

LITERAL COMPREHENSION STRATEGIES

Review the reading strategies and the notes showing how to understand what a writer is saying. Then, apply the strategies to answer the following.

1. Reread the first two paragraphs. How does knowing the story and its outcome help you to better understand the story's opening?
2. Paraphrase—retell in your own words—the scene between Davhana and the elder who comes to give him advice.
3. Use context clues to identify the meaning of *refuge* in this sentence:

   He chose for himself that night the life of one who would take refuge where he could find it and so he continued his flight into the night.

◆ Literary Focus

CONFLICT AND CULTURAL STYLE

Fiction writers almost always describe a specific **conflict**—a struggle between opposing forces. The conflict and its **resolution,** or outcome, reflect both the author's attitudes and the **cultural style**—the beliefs and values—of the characters and the society.

In "A Power Struggle," Bessie Head describes how the Tlabina clan responds to the conflict between Davhana and Baeli. Both men want to rule the clan, and each responds differently to this conflict.

Head's narration indicates that she views the story as uniquely African. Its resolution offers insight into a cultural style in which the village unit is more important than the leader.

1. In addition to the external conflict with his brother, what internal conflict does Davhana face? How does he resolve this inner conflict?
2. Baeli becomes king of the Tlabina clan. Does that mean he wins the power struggle mentioned in the story's title? Explain.
3. What key element of precolonial African culture does Head illustrate with this story?
4. Describe a resolution of the conflict that might have been more in tune with a contemporary cultural style. Explain your choice.

◆ Build Vocabulary

USING THE LATIN PREFIX *ad-*

Knowing that the Latin prefix *ad-* means "to," "motion toward," or "near," match each word with its definition. Use a dictionary if necessary.

1. adhere   **a.** something joined to another thing
2. adjunct   **b.** to take into or toward
3. adsorb   **c.** speak to; give information to
4. advise   **d.** stick to

USING THE WORD BANK: Synonyms

On your paper, write the word whose meaning is closest to that of the first word on each line.

1. adulation: (a) scorn, (b) flattery, (c) pride
2. avarice: (a) power, (b) envy, (c) greed
3. intrigue: (a) retaliate, (b) benefit, (c) conspire
4. lithe: (a) ripe, (b) loathsome, (c) flexible
5. obeisance: (a) respect, (b) folly, (c) fear

◆ Build Grammar Skills

CORRECT USE OF *only*

Remember to place **only** in front of the word you want to modify. Consider the different meanings of these sentences:

   Baeli stared *only* straight ahead.
   Only Baeli stared straight ahead.

In the first sentence, Baeli stares in no direction other than straight ahead. In the second, Baeli is the only person staring straight ahead.

Practice In your notebook, add *only* to each sentence. Read the meaning in parentheses to decide where to place the modifier.

1. The elder told Davhana the most important details. (The elder told Davhana nothing but the most important details.)
2. The elder told Davhana the most important details. (No one other than the elder told Davhana the most important details.)
3. The elder told Davhana the most important details. (There was just one elder, who told Davhana the most important details.)
4. When he became king, Baeli felt triumphant. (No one other than Baeli felt triumphant.)
5. When he became king, Baeli felt triumphant. (Baeli felt no other feeling than triumphant.)

Build Your Portfolio

Idea Bank

Writing

1. **Letter** You are Davhana after leaving your clan. Write a letter to your friends explaining why you chose to leave rather than defend yourself.

2. **Guide for Reading** Write an essay to prepare students to read "A Power Struggle." Explain any background information you believe they will need to understand and appreciate the story. **[Social Studies Link]**

3. **Cultural Analysis** Do you think "A Power Struggle" is uniquely African, or could the story be reset in another region? Support your opinion with examples from the story.

Speaking, Listening, and Viewing

4. **Reunion Scene** Imagine that Davhana and Baeli meet again five or ten years after the end of this story. Act out the meeting for the class. **[Performing Arts Link]**

5. **Casting Announcement** What actors would you cast in a film based on "A Power Struggle"? Defend your choices in a class speech. **[Performing Arts Link]**

Researching and Representing

6. **Collaborative Mural** The Tlabina clan in "A Power Struggle" acts as a unit without consulting one another. Follow this model to create a mural to illustrate the story. Take turns adding elements to the mural, but do not consult with your classmates as you work. **[Art Link]**

7. **African Timeline** Create a timeline showing key events in African history from precolonial times to the present. **[Social Studies Link]**

Online Activity www.phlit.phschool.com

Guided Writing Lesson

Letter to a Local Leader

The conflict in "A Power Struggle" was eventually resolved through the silent actions of the village. The complexity of modern life, however, makes silent action an unlikely force for social change. Writing a political letter can help you take action to resolve a conflict in your community. Identify a conflict that directly affects you, and write a letter to a local leader describing your proposed resolution.

Writing Skills Focus: Persuasive Language

The goal of your letter is to persuade a leader that your resolution will be fair and effective. You need to use **persuasive language,** clear and convincing words, to support your ideas and make them compelling.

Prewriting Brainstorm to create a list of local conflicts that affect you. They might involve your school, town, or neighborhood.

Drafting Begin with a polite greeting and a brief description of the conflict. Then, describe your proposed resolution. As you write, remember to use clear language with positive associations and to avoid unnecessary attacks on individuals or groups.

Revising When reviewing your letter, look for language that feels weak or vague. Replace such words with strong, persuasive ones. Also, review your writing for overall clarity. A reader will not be persuaded by ideas he or she cannot follow.

Check that you have used *only* correctly, placing it in front of the word you want to modify. For more on the correct use of *only,* see pp. 128 and 137.

PART 1 *Daring Decisions*

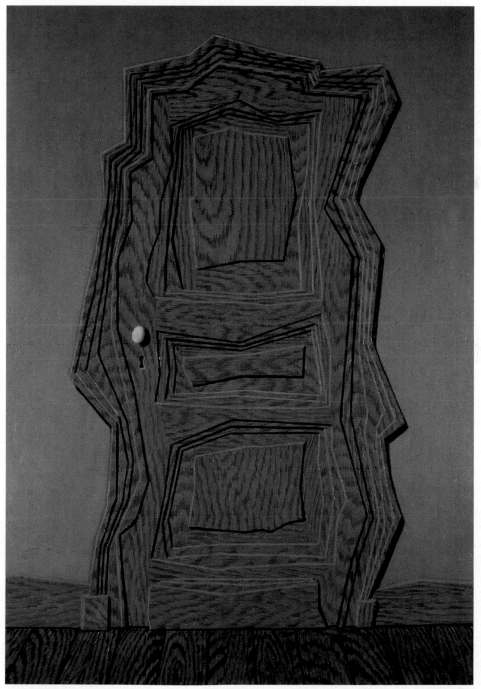

Le Modele Vivant, René Magritte

Guide for Reading

Sir Edmund Hillary *(1919–   )*

Few people can claim they have stood on top of the world—and only one man can claim to have been there first. That person is Sir Edmund Hillary. Although he shares the glory of his achievement with climbing partner Tenzing Norgay, Hillary was the first person to reach the summit of Mount Everest in Nepal, 29,028 feet above sea level—the highest spot on Earth.

Hillary has said of himself, "I've moved from being a child who dreamed a lot and read a lot of books about adventure, to actually getting involved in things like mountaineering, and then becoming a reasonably competent mountaineer. . . ." These are humble words for a man who has climbed the Swiss Alps and conquered eleven different peaks of over 20,000 feet in the Himalayas of Tibet and Nepal.

Tenzing Norgay *(1914–1986)*

At 11:30 on the morning of May 29, 1953, Tenzing Norgay changed the course of his destiny—and began a journey toward international fame. At that moment, he and Edmund Hillary stood on the summit of Mount Everest in Nepal—a place where no man or woman had ever stood before and where few have stood since!

Norgay was born into a family of Sherpa farmers—Nepalese people of Tibetan descent. Norgay started guiding climbers at the age of fourteen. In 1953, he joined a Mount Everest expedition led by Sir John Hunt. Although all the other members of the expedition eventually turned back, Norgay and Hillary struggled on and fulfilled their dream of being the first men ever to reach the summit.

◆ Build Vocabulary

LATIN WORD ROOTS: -voc-

Edmund Hillary recalls that upon reaching the summit of Mount Everest, he felt "a satisfaction less *vociferous* but more powerful than [he] had ever felt on a mountain top before." *Vociferous* contains the Latin word root *-voc-*, which means "speak" or "say." The meaning of the root seems to indicate that something that is *vociferous* speaks out. This meaning is close to the actual definition, which is "loud or noisy in making one's feelings known." It is understandable that Hillary and Norgay would be too tired for a *vociferous* celebration after climbing over 29,000 feet!

precipitous
discernible
belay
encroaching
undulations
vociferous

WORD BANK

Before you read, preview this list of words from the selections.

◆ Build Grammar Skills

COMPOUND PREDICATES

A **compound predicate** consists of two or more verbs or verb phrases (a main verb plus a helping verb) that share the same subject. Compound predicates enable the writer to include a lot of action in a single sentence without having to repeat the subject. In the following example from "The Final Assault," Hillary links two related climbing actions by using a compound predicate to combine them in a single sentence.

S   V   V
I swung my ice axe and started chipping a line of steps upward . . .

As you read "The Final Assault" and "The Dream Comes True," notice the authors' frequent use of compound predicates to describe related or sequential actions.

The Final Assault ◆ The Dream Comes True

◆ *Literature and Your Life*

CONNECT YOUR EXPERIENCE

Whether you are training to improve your race time or studying to get an *A* on your final exam, you may have to convince yourself that your goal is worth the effort required to reach it. When Hillary doubted his ability to reach the top of Everest, he said to himself, "Ed, my boy, this is Everest—you've got to push it a bit harder!"

THEMATIC FOCUS: DARING DECISIONS

As you read these two men's accounts of the dangers they faced in their quest to stand on the highest point on the planet, you may ask yourself, "Where do I find what it takes to reach the top?"

Journal Writing Describe a time when you had to struggle to achieve a goal or complete a task. How did you keep yourself motivated to make the effort required to meet the goal?

◆ Background for Understanding

MATH

The temperature on the day of Hillary and Norgay's historic achievement—twenty degrees *below zero*—was colder than anything you have probably experienced. Read the graph to contrast the temperature with others that may be more familiar to you.

Think about the ways the extreme temperature would make Hillary's and Norgay's climb more difficult.

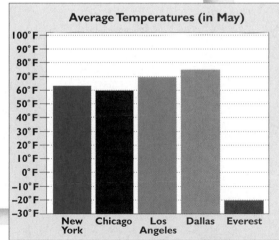

Average Temperatures (in May)

◆ Literary Focus

AUTHOR'S PERSPECTIVE

When you read a novel, a poem, a magazine, or even a newspaper article, you get the point of view of one person: the author. How the author views and interprets the events that he or she sees, hears, or experiences personally is the **author's perspective.** In these two accounts of the ascent of Everest, each man's report is influenced by his own beliefs and assumptions. To identify each author's perspective, pay close attention to the details and events they choose to present and the descriptive words they use.

◆ Reading Strategy

DISTINGUISH FACT FROM OPINION

Many people have died attempting to reach the summit of Everest. That's a **fact**—a statement that can be proved true or false by evidence. Mountain climbing is an exciting sport. That's an **opinion**— a statement that can be *supported* by facts but is not itself a fact.

When you read works of nonfiction, determine whether the author's statements are facts or opinions by asking yourself, "Can this statement be proved true or false by evidence?" If the answer is yes, the statement is a fact; if no, it is an opinion.

By distinguishing fact from opinion, you can form your own opinions and understanding of an event or idea, rather than simply accepting what the author wants you to believe. As you read, use a chart like the one below to separate facts from opinions in these accounts.

Facts	Opinions

142   *Suspense in World Literature*

The Final Assault

from High Adventure
Edmund Hillary

I watched our support party disappear down the ridge and then turned to examine our campsite more closely. It wasn't really much of a place. Above us was a rock cliff—black and craggy, but at least devoid of loose stones to fall on us. From the foot of the cliff a little snow slope ran at an easy angle for eight or nine feet to the top of the steep and exposed South Face of the mountain. This little slope was to be our campsite. It was certainly far from flat and it was going to need a lot of work on it before we could possibly pitch a tent. We carefully moved all the gear to one side and then set to work with our ice axes to remove the surface snow off a reasonably large area. Ten inches down, we struck rock, and after an hour's hard work we had cleared an area about eight feet long and six feet wide. The slope underneath was made up of stones and rubble all firmly glued together with ice. This was much harder going. With the picks on our ice axes we chopped away at the slope, prizing out the separate stones and scraping away the rubble. But our progress was very slow. We weren't using any oxygen at all, but we found we could work very hard indeed for periods of ten minutes or so. Then we'd have to stop and have a short rest. With the debris we chopped out of the slope we tried to build up the platform on the downhill side, but almost invariably saw it collapse and go roaring down over the bluffs below. At times we were buffeted[1] by wind and snow, yet we worked doggedly on, knowing that our tent was our only chance of survival against the rigors of the night.

---

1. **buffeted** (buf´ it əd) *v.*: Beaten back as by repeated blows.

◀ **Critical Viewing** What can you conclude about Hillary based on his desire to conquer mountains like these? **[Draw Conclusions]**

At 6:30 A.M. we crawled slowly out of the tent and stood on our little ledge. Already the upper part of the mountain was bathed in sunlight. It looked warm and inviting, but our ledge was dark and cold. We lifted our oxygen onto our backs and slowly connected up the tubes to our face masks. My thirty-pound load seemed to crush me downward and stifled all enthusiasm, but when I turned on the oxygen and breathed it deeply, the burden seemed to lighten and the old urge to get to grips with the mountain came back. We strapped on our crampons[2] and tied on our nylon rope, grasped our ice axes, and were ready to go.

I looked at the way ahead. From our tent very steep slopes covered with deep powder snow led up to a prominent snow shoulder on the southeast ridge about a hundred feet above our heads. The slopes were in the shade and breaking trail was going to be cold work. Still a little worried about my boots, I asked Tenzing to lead off. Always willing to do his share, and more than his share if necessary, Tenzing scrambled past me and tackled the slope. With powerful thrusts of his legs he forced his way up in

◆ **Literary Focus**
Which details in this paragraph suggest that it is told from Hillary's perspective?

---

2. crampons (kram´ pənz) *n.*: Pair of spiked iron plates fastened on climbers' shoes to prevent slipping.

▼ **Critical Viewing** Why do you think Camps 8 and 9 are so close together compared with Camps 3 and 4? **[Analyze]**

EVEREST
29,028 feet
SUMMIT
SOUTH SUMMIT
CAMP 9
South Column
CAMP 8
LHOTSE
27,890 feet
NUPTSE
25,680 feet
Geneva Spur
CAMP 7
CAMP 6
CAMP 5
Western CWM
CAMP 4
Ice Fall
CAMP 3
CAMP 2
KHUMBU GLACIER
BASE CAMP

The Final Assault

Hillary and Norgay's 1953 expedition to the summit of Mt. Everest

knee-deep snow. I gathered in the rope and followed along behind him.

We were climbing out over the tremendous South Face of the mountain and below us snow chutes and rock ribs plummeted thousands of feet down to the Western Cwm.[3] Starting in the morning straight on to exposed climbing is always trying on the nerves and this was no exception. In imagination I could feel my heavy load dragging me backward down the great slopes below; I seemed clumsy and unstable and my breath was hurried and uneven. But Tenzing was pursuing an irresistible course up the slope and I didn't have time to think too much. My muscles soon warmed up to their work, my nerves relaxed, and I dropped into the old climbing rhythm and followed steadily up his tracks. As we gained a little height we moved into the rays of the sun, and although we could feel no appreciable warmth, we were greatly encouraged by its presence. Taking no rests, Tenzing plowed his way up through the deep snow and led out onto the snow shoulder. We were now at a height of 28,000 feet. Towering directly above our heads was the South Summit—steep and formidable. And to the right were the enormous cornices of the summit ridge. We still had a long way to go.

Ahead of us the ridge was sharp and narrow but rose at an easy angle. I felt warm and strong now, so took over the lead. First I investigated the ridge with my ice ax. On the sharp crest of the ridge and on the right-hand side loose powder snow was lying dangerously over hard ice. Any attempt to climb on this would only produce an unpleasant slide down toward the Kangshung Glacier. But the left-hand slope was better—it was still rather steep, but it had a firm surface of wind-blown powder snow into which our crampons would bite readily.

Taking every care, I moved along onto the left-hand side of the ridge. Everything seemed perfectly safe. With increased confidence I took another step. Next moment I was almost thrown off balance as the wind crust suddenly gave way and I sank through it up to my knee. It took me a little while to regain my breath. Then I gradually pulled my leg out of the hole. I was almost upright again when the wind crust under the other foot gave way and I sank back with both legs enveloped in soft loose snow to the knees. It was the mountaineer's curse—breakable crust. I forced my way along. Sometimes for a few careful steps I was on the surface, but usually the crust would break at the critical moment and I'd be up to my knees again. Though it was tiring and exasperating work, I felt I had plenty of strength in reserve. For half an hour I continued on in this uncomfortable fashion, with the violent balancing movement I was having to make completely destroying rhythm and breath. It was a great relief when the snow condition improved and I was able to stay on the surface. I still kept down on the steep slopes on the left of the ridge, but plunged ahead and climbed steadily upward. I came over a small crest and saw in front of me a tiny hollow on the ridge. And in this hollow lay two oxygen bottles almost completely covered with snow. It was Evans and Bourdillon's[4] dump.

I rushed forward into the hollow and knelt beside them. Wrenching one of the bottles out of its frozen bed, I wiped the snow off its dial—it showed a thousand pounds pressure—it was nearly a third full of oxygen. I checked the other —it was the same. This was great news. It meant that the oxygen we were carrying on our backs only had to get us back to these bottles instead of right down to the South Col. It gave us more than another hour of endurance. I explained this to Tenzing through my oxygen mask. I don't think he understood, but he realized I was pleased about something and nodded enthusiastically.

I led off again. I knew there was plenty of hard work ahead and Tenzing could save his energies for that. The ridge climbed on upward rather more steeply now and then broadened out and

◆ Reading Strategy
Is it a fact or Hillary's opinion that Norgay did not understand Hillary's explanation?

---

3. **Western Cwm** (ko͞om) *n.*: Steep, hollow hole in Everest's mountainside, made by glacial erosion.

4. **Evans and Bourdillon:** Mountain climbers who attempted unsuccessfully to ascend Mount Everest in 1951.

shot up at a sharp angle to the foot of the enormous slope running up to the South Summit. I crossed over onto the right-hand side of the ridge and found the snow was firm there. I started chipping a long line of steps up to the foot of the great slope. Here we stamped out a platform for ourselves and I checked our oxygen. Everything seemed to be going well. I had a little more oxygen left than Tenzing, which meant I was obtaining a slightly lower flow rate from my set, but it wasn't enough to matter and there was nothing I could do about it anyway.

Ahead of us was a really formidable problem and I stood in my steps and looked at it. Rising from our feet was an enormous slope slanting steeply down onto the precipitous East Face of Everest and climbing up with appalling steepness to the South Summit of the mountain 400 feet above us. The left-hand side of the slope was a most unsavory mixture of steep loose rock and snow, which my New Zealand training immediately regarded with grave suspicion, but which in actual fact the rock-climbing Britons, Evans and Bourdillon, had ascended in much trepidation when on the first assault. The only other route was up the snow itself, and still fairly discernible here and there were traces of the track made by the first assault party, who had come down it in preference to their line of ascent up the rocks. The snow route it was for us! There looked to be some tough work ahead, and as Tenzing had been taking it easy for a while I hardheartedly waved him through. With his first six steps I realized that the work was going to be much harder than I had thought. His first two steps were on top of the snow, the third was up to his ankles, and by the sixth he was up to his hips.

But almost lying against the steep slope, he drove himself onward, plowing a track directly upward. Even following in his steps was hard work, for the loose snow refused to pack into safe steps. After a long and valiant spell he was plainly in need of a rest, so I took over.

Immediately I realized that we were on dangerous ground. On this very steep slope the snow was soft and deep with little coherence. My ice ax shaft sank into it without any support and we had no form of a belay. The only factor that made it at all possible to progress was a thin crust of frozen snow which tied the whole slope together. But this crust was a poor support. I was forcing my way upward, plunging deep steps through it, when suddenly with a dull breaking noise an area of crust all around me about six feet in diameter broke off into large sections and slid with me back through three or four steps. And then I stopped; but the crust, gathering speed, slithered on out of sight. It was a nasty shock. My whole training told me that the slope was exceedingly dangerous, but at the same time I was saying to myself, "Ed, my boy, this is Everest—you've got to push it a bit harder!" My solar plexus was tight with

◆ **Build Vocabulary**

precipitous (prē sip´ ə təs) *adj.*: Steep

discernible (di zʉrn´ i bəl´) *adj.*: Recognizable; noticeable

belay (bi lā´) *n.*: Rope support

fear as I plowed on. Halfway up I stopped, exhausted. I could look down 10,000 feet between my legs and I have never felt more insecure. Anxiously I waved Tenzing up to me.

"What do you think of it, Tenzing?" And the immediate response, "Very bad, very danger-ous!" "Do you think we should go on?" and there came the familiar reply that never helped you much but never let you down: "Just as you wish!" I waved him on to take a turn at leading. Changing the lead much more frequently now, we made our unhappy way upward, sometimes sliding back and wiping out half a dozen steps and never feeling confident that at any moment the whole slope might not avalanche. In the hope of some sort of a belay we traversed a little toward the rocks but found no help in their smooth holdless surface. We plunged on upward. And then I noticed that, a little above us, the left-hand rock ridge turned into snow and the snow looked firm and safe. Laboriously and carefully we climbed across some steep rock and I sank my ice ax shaft into the snow of the ridge. It went firm and hard. The pleasure of this safe belay after all the uncertainty below was like a reprieve to a condemned man. Strength flowed into my limbs and I could feel my tense nerves and muscles relaxing. I swung my ice ax at the slope and started chipping a line of steps upward—it was very

steep but seemed so gloriously safe. Tenzing, an inexpert but enthusiastic step cutter, took a turn and chopped a haphazard line of steps up another pitch. We were making fast time now and the slope was starting to ease off. Tenzing gallantly waved me through and with a growing feeling of excitement I cramponed up some firm slopes to the rounded top of the South Summit. It was only 9 A.M.

◆ Literary Focus
How might Hillary's assessment of Nor-gay's climbing skills differ from Norgay's perspective?

With intense interest I looked at the vital ridge leading to the summit—the ridge about which Evans and Bourdillon had made such gloomy forecasts. At first glance it was an exceedingly impressive and indeed a frightening sight. In the narrow crest of this ridge, the basic rock of the mountain had a thin capping of snow and ice—ice that reached out over the East Face in enormous cornices,[5] overhanging and treacherous, and only waiting for the careless foot of the mountaineer to break off and crash 10,000 feet into the Kangshung Glacier. And from the cornices the snow dropped steeply to the left to merge with the enormous rock bluffs which towered 8,000 feet above the Western Cwm. It was

5. **cornices** (kôr´ nis əs) *n.*: Layers of ice and snow projecting over the top of a ridge.

impressive all right! But as I looked, my fears started to lift a little. Surely I could see a route there? For this snow slope on the left, although very steep and exposed, was practically continuous for the first half of the ridge, although in places the great cornices reached hungrily across. If we could make a route along that snow slope we could go quite a distance at least.

With a feeling almost of relief I set to work with my ice ax and cut a platform for myself just down off the top of the South Summit. Tenzing did the same, and then we removed our oxygen sets and sat down. The day was still remarkably fine and we felt no discomfort through our thick layers of clothing from either wind or cold. We had a drink out of Tenzing's water bottle and then I checked our oxygen supplies. Tenzing's bottle was practically exhausted, but mine still had a little in it. As well as this we each had a full bottle. I decided that the difficulties ahead would demand as light a weight on our backs as possible, so determined to use only the full bottles. I removed Tenzing's empty bottle and my nearly empty one and laid them in the snow. With particular care I connected up our last bottles and tested to see that they were working efficiently. The needles on the dials were steady on 3,300 pounds per square inch pressure—they were very full bottles, holding just over 800 liters of oxygen each. At 3 liters a minute we consumed 180 liters an hour, and this meant a total endurance of nearly 4 1/2 hours. This didn't seem much for the problems ahead, but I was determined if necessary to cut down to 2 liters a minute for the homeward trip.

I was greatly encouraged to find how, even at 28,700 feet and with no oxygen, I could work out slowly but clearly the problems of mental arithmetic that the oxygen supply demanded. A correct answer was imperative—any mistake could well mean a trip with no return. But we had no time to waste. I stood up and took a series of photographs in every direction, then thrust my camera back to its warm home inside my clothing. I heaved my now pleasantly light oxygen load onto my back and connected up my tubes. I did the same for Tenzing and we were ready to go. I asked Tenzing to belay me

and then with a growing air of excitement I cut a broad and safe line of steps down to the snow saddle below the South Summit. I wanted an easy route when we came back up here weak and tired. Tenzing came down the steps and joined me and then belayed[6] once again.

I moved along onto the steep snow slope on the left side of the ridge. With the first blow of my ice ax my excitement increased. The snow—to my astonishment—was crystalline and hard. A couple of rhythmical blows of the ice ax produced a step that was big enough even for our oversize high-altitude boots. But best of all, the steps were strong and safe. A little conscious of the great drops beneath me, I chopped a line of steps for the full length of the rope—forty feet—and then forced the shaft of my ice ax firmly into the snow. It made a fine belay and I looped the rope around it. I waved to Tenzing to join me, and as he moved slowly and carefully along the steps I took in the rope as I went on cutting steps. It was exhilarating work—the summit ridge of Everest, the crisp snow, and the smooth, easy blows of the ice ax all combined to make me feel a greater sense of power than I had ever felt at great altitudes before. I went on cutting for rope length after rope length.

We were now approaching a point where one of the great cornices was encroaching onto our slope. We'd have to go down to the rocks to avoid it. I cut a line of steps steeply down the slope to a small ledge on top of the rocks. There wasn't much room, but it made a reasonably safe stance. I waved to Tenzing to join me. As he came down to me I realized there was something wrong with him. I had been so absorbed in the technical problems of the ridge that I hadn't thought much about Tenzing except for a vague feeling that he seemed to move along the steps with unnecessary slowness. But now it was quite obvious that he was not only moving extremely slowly but was breathing quickly and with difficulty and was

◆ Reading Strategy
Is it a fact or an opinion that the ledge is "safe"?

---

6. **belayed** (bi lād´) v.: Supported by a rope.

in considerable distress. I immediately suspected his oxygen set and helped him down onto the ledge so that I could examine it. The first thing I noticed was that from the outlet of his face mask there were hanging some long icicles. I looked at it more closely and found that the outlet tube—about two inches in diameter—was almost completely blocked up with ice. This was preventing Tenzing from exhaling freely and must have made it extremely unpleasant for him. Fortunately the outlet tube was made of rubber, and by manipulating this with my hand I was able to release all of the ice and let it fall out. The valves started operating and Tenzing was given immediate relief. Just as a check I examined my own set and found that it, too, had partly frozen up in the outlet tube, but not sufficiently to have affected me a great deal. I removed the ice out of it without a great deal of trouble. Automatically I looked at our pressure gauges—just over 2,900 pounds (2,900 pounds was just over 700 liters; 180 into 700 was about 4)—we had nearly four hours' endurance left. That meant we weren't going badly.

I looked at the route ahead. This next piece wasn't going to be easy. Our rock ledge was perched right on top of the enormous bluff

▲ **Critical Viewing** What feelings are revealed in the expressions on Hillary's and Norgay's faces? **[Interpret]**

running down into the Western Cwm. In fact, almost under my feet, I could see the dirty patch on the floor of the cwm which I knew was Camp IV. In a sudden urge to escape our isolation I waved and shouted, then as suddenly stopped as I realized my foolishness. Against the vast expanse of Everest, 8,000 feet above them, we'd be quite invisible to the best binoculars. I turned back to the problem ahead. The rock was far too steep to attempt to drop down and go around this pitch. The only thing to do was to try and shuffle along the ledge and cut handholds in the bulging ice that was trying to push me off it. Held on a tight rope by Tenzing, I cut a few handholds and then thrust my ice ax as hard as I could into the solid snow and ice. Using this to take my weight, I moved quickly along the ledge. It proved easier than I had anticipated. A few more handholds, another quick swing across them, and I was able to cut a line of steps up onto a safe slope and chop out a roomy terrace from which to belay Tenzing as he climbed up to me.

We were now fast approaching the most formidable obstacle on the ridge—a great rock step. This step had always been visible in aerial photographs and in 1951 on the Everest Reconnaissance we had seen it quite clearly with glasses from Thyangboche. We had always thought of it as the obstacle on the ridge which could well spell defeat. I cut a line of steps across the last snow slope and then

◆ **Build Vocabulary**

encroaching (en krōch´ iŋ) v.: Trespassing or intruding

▲ **Critical Viewing** What elements in this photograph suggest the dangers of climbing? **[Analyze]**

commenced traversing[7] over a steep rock slab that led to the foot of the great step. The holds were small and hard to see and I brushed my snow glasses away from my eyes. Immediately I was blinded by a bitter wind sweeping across the ridge and laden with particles of ice. I hastily replaced my glasses and blinked away the ice and tears until I could see again. But it made me realize how efficient was our clothing in protecting us from the rigors of even a fine day at 29,000 feet. Still half-blinded, I climbed across the slab and then dropped down into a tiny snow hollow at the foot the step. And here Tenzing slowly joined me.

I looked anxiously up at the rocks. Planted squarely across the ridge in a vertical bluff,

_____

7. **traversing** (trə vʉrs´ iŋ) v.: Crossing.

they looked extremely difficult, and I knew that our strength and ability to climb steep rock at this altitude would be severely limited. I examined the route out to the left. By dropping fifty or a hundred feet over steep slabs, we might be able to get around the bottom of the bluff, but there was no indication that we'd be able to climb back onto the ridge again. And to lose any height now might be fatal. Search as I could, I was unable to see an easy route up to the step or in fact any route at all. Finally, in desperation, I examined the right-hand end of the bluff. Attached to this and overhanging the precipitous East Face was a large cornice. This cornice, in preparation for its inevitable crash down the mountainside, had started to lose its grip on the rock and a long narrow vertical crack had been formed between the rock and the ice. The crack was large enough to take the human frame, and though it offered little security it was at least a route. I quickly made up my mind—Tenzing had an excellent belay and we must be near the top—it was worth a try.

Before attempting the pitch I produced my camera once again. I had no confidence that I would be able to climb this crack and with a surge of competitive pride which unfortunately afflicts even mountaineers I determined to have proof that at least we had reached a good deal higher than the South Summit. I took a few photographs and then made another rapid check of the oxygen—2,500 pounds pressure (2,550 from 3,300 leaves 750; 750 is about 2/9; 2/9 off 800 liters leaves about 600 liters; 600 divided by 180 is nearly 3 1/2. Three and a half hours to go. I examined Tenzing's belay to make sure it was a good one and then slowly crawled inside the crack.

In front of me was the rock wall, vertical but with a few promising holds. Behind me was the ice wall of the cornice, glittering and hard but cracked and there. I took a hold on the rock in front and then jammed one of my crampons hard into the ice behind. Leaning back with my oxygen set on the ice, I slowly levered myself upward. Searching feverishly with my spare boot, I found a tiny ledge on the rock and took some of the weight off my other leg. Leaning back on the cornice, I fought to regain my breath. Constantly at the back of my mind was the fear that the cornice might break off, and my nerves were taut with suspense. But slowly I forced my way up—wriggling and jamming and using every little hold. In one place I managed to force my ice ax into a crack in the ice, and this gave me the necessary purchase to get over a holdless stretch. And then I found a solid foothold in a hollow in the ice and next moment I was reaching over the top of the rock and pulling myself to safety. The rope came tight—its forty feet had been barely enough.

I lay on the little rock ledge panting furiously. Gradually it dawned on me that I was up the step and I felt a glow of pride and determination that completely subdued my temporary feeling of weakness. For the first time on the whole expedition I really knew I was going to get to the top. "It will have to be pretty tough to stop us now" was my thought. But I couldn't entirely ignore the feeling of astonishment and wonder that I'd been able to get up such a difficulty at 29,000 feet even with oxygen.

When I was breathing more evenly I stood and, leaning over the edge, waved to Tenzing to come up. He moved into the crack and I gathered in the rope and took some of his weight. Then he, in turn, commenced to struggle and jam and force his way up until I was able to pull him to safety—gasping for breath. We rested for a moment. Above us the ridge continued on as before—enormous overhanging cornices on the right and steep snow slopes on the left running down to the rock bluffs. But the angle of the snow slopes was easing off. I went on chipping a line of steps, but thought it safe enough for us to move together in order to save time. The ridge rose up in a great series of snakelike <u>undulations</u> which bore away to the right, each one concealing the next. I had no idea where the top was. I'd cut a line of steps around the side of one undulation and another would come into view. We were getting desperately tired now and Tenzing was going very slowly. I'd been cutting steps for almost two hours and my back and arms were starting to tire. I tried cramponing along the slope without cutting steps, but my feet slipped uncomfortably down the slope. I went on cutting. We seemed to have been going for a very long time and my confidence was fast evaporating. Bump followed bump with maddening regularity. A patch of shingle barred our way and I climbed dully up it and started cutting steps around another bump. And then I realized that this

◆ **Literary Focus**
Which details in this paragraph reveal that it is told from Hillary's perspective?

◆ **Build Vocabulary**
undulations (un′ dyo͞o lā′ shənz) *n.*: Waves

was the last bump, for ahead of me the ridge dropped steeply away in a great corniced curve, and out in the distance I could see the pastel shades and fleecy clouds of the highlands of Tibet.

To my right a slender snow ridge climbed up to a snowy dome about forty feet above our heads. But all the way along the ridge the thought had haunted me that the summit might be the crest of a cornice. It was too late to take risks now. I asked Tenzing to belay me strongly and I started cutting a cautious line of steps up the ridge. Peering from side to side and thrusting with my ice ax, I tried to discover a possible cornice, but everything seemed solid and firm. I waved Tenzing up to me. A few more whacks of the ice ax, a few very weary steps, and we were on the summit of Everest.

It was 11:30 A.M. My first sensation was one of relief—relief that the long grind was over; that the summit had been reached before our oxygen supplies had dropped to a critical level; and relief that in the end the mountain had been kind to us in having a pleasantly rounded cone for its summit instead of a fearsome and unapproachable cornice. But mixed with the relief was a vague sense of astonishment that I could have been the lucky one to attain the ambition of so many brave and determined climbers. It seemed difficult at first to grasp that we'd got there. I was too tired and too conscious of the long way down to safety really to feel any great elation. But as the fact of our success thrust itself more clearly into my mind I felt a quiet glow of satisfaction spread through my body—a satisfaction less vociferous but more powerful than I had ever felt on a mountaintop before. I turned and looked at Tenzing. Even beneath his oxygen mask and the icicles hanging from his hair I could see his infectious grin of sheer delight.

◆ Build Vocabulary

vociferous (vō sif´ ər əs) *adj.*: Loud; noisy

Guide for Responding

◆ *Literature and Your Life*

Reader's Response How did you feel when Hillary and Norgay finally reached the summit of Everest? Explain your reaction.

Thematic Focus Norgay and Hillary possessed certain qualities that helped them reach the top. What character traits are needed to face a difficult challenge?

Group Discussion As a group, discuss why people are so interested in conquering mountains, raging rivers, and other wilderness challenges. Also, discuss whether or not you would try to climb to the summit of a mountain and why you would or would not.

☑ Check Your Comprehension

1. Summarize the events leading up to the reaching of the summit on the final day of climbing.
2. What does Hillary find in the snow? Why is it such a helpful discovery?
3. At what time do Hillary and Norgay reach the summit?

◆ Critical Thinking

INTERPRET

1. Why does Hillary continually mention the progress and condition of his partner? **[Infer]**
2. Do you think Norgay's oxygen situation was as critical as Hillary made it seem? Explain your answer. **[Make a Judgment]**

APPLY

3. After reading about the effort and energy required to conquer Everest, why do you think two men from such different backgrounds are able to help each other succeed? **[Speculate]**

In April 1996, writer and climber Jon Krakauer signed on as a client of an Everest expedition to report on the growing commercialization of Everest. As he horrifyingly discovered, climbing in the Himalayas is just as dangerous today as it was in Hillary's and Norgay's day.

from Into Thin Air

Jon Krakauer

Straddling the top of the world, one foot in Tibet and the other in Nepal, I cleared the ice from my oxygen mask, hunched a shoulder against the wind, and stared absently at the vast sweep of earth below. I understood on some dim, detached level that it was a spectacular sight. I'd been fantasizing about this moment, and the release of emotion that would accompany it, for many months. But now that I was finally here, standing on the summit of Mount Everest, I just couldn't summon the energy to care.

It was the afternoon of May 10. I hadn't slept in 57 hours. The only food I'd been able to force down over the preceding three days was a bowl of Ramen soup and a handful of peanut M&M's. Weeks of violent coughing had left me with two separated ribs, making it excruciatingly painful to breathe. Twenty-nine thousand twenty-eight feet up in the troposphere, there was so little oxygen reaching my brain that my mental capacity was that of a slow child. Under the circumstances, I was incapable of feeling anything but cold and tired.

* * *

I snapped four quick photos of Harris and Bourkeev [two guides] striking summit poses, and then turned and started down. My watch read 1:17 P.M. All told, I'd spent less than five minutes on the roof of the world.

After a few steps, I paused to take another photo, this one looking down the Southeast Ridge, the route we had ascended. Training my lens on a pair of climbers approaching the summit, I saw something that until this moment had escaped my attention. To the south, where the sky had been perfectly clear just an hour earlier, a blanket of clouds now hid Pumori, Ama Dablam, and the other lesser peaks surrounding Everest.

Days later—after six bodies had been found, after the search for two others had been abandoned, after surgeons had amputated the gangrenous right hand of my teammate Beck Weathers—people would ask why, if the weather had begun to deteriorate, had climbers on the upper mountain not heeded the signs? Why did veteran Himalayan guides keep moving upward, leading a gaggle of amateurs, each of whom had paid as much as $65,000 to be ushered safely up Everest, into an apparent death trap?

* * *

Climbers, as a species, are simply not distinguished by an excess of common sense. And that holds especially true for Everest climbers: When presented with a chance to reach the planet's highest summit, people are surprisingly quick to abandon prudence altogether.

> Compare and contrast Krakauer's expedition to Hillary and Norgay's.

The Dream Comes True
from The Tiger of the Snows
Tenzing Norgay

**Written in collaboration
with James Ramsey Ullman**

From the south summit we first had to go down a little. Then up, up, up. All the time the danger was that the snow would slip, or that we would get too far out on a cornice that would then break away; so we moved just one at a time, taking turns going ahead, while the second one wrapped the rope around his ax and fixed the ax in the snow as an anchor. The weather was still fine. We were not too tired. But every so often, as had happened all the way, we would have trouble breathing and have to stop and clear away the ice that kept forming in the tubes of our oxygen sets. In regard to this, I must say in all honesty that I do not think Hillary is quite fair in the story he later told, indicating that I had more trouble than he with breathing

▲ **Critical Viewing** Do you think this photo was taken at the beginning or end of the climb? Explain. **[Infer]**

> ◆ **Reading Strategy**
> Is this statement a fact or an opinion?

and that without his help I might have been in serious difficulty. In my opinion our difficulties were the same—and luckily never too great—and we each helped and were helped by the other in equal measure.

Anyhow, after each short stop we kept going, twisting always higher along the ridge between the cornices and the precipices. And at last we came to what might be the last big obstacle below the top. This was a cliff of rock rising straight up out of the ridge and blocking it off, and we had already known about it from aerial photographs and from seeing it through binoculars from Thyangboche.[1] Now it was a question of how to get over or around it, and we could find only one possible way. This was along a steep, narrow gap between one side of the rock and the inner

---

1. **Thyangboche** (tän bō´ chā): Village in Nepal.

▲ **Critical Viewing** What qualities do you think Norgay needed to guide climbers through mountains like these? **[Speculate]**

side of an adjoining cornice, and Hillary, now going first, worked his way up it, slowly and carefully, to a sort of platform above. While climbing, he had to press backwards with his feet against the cornice, and I belayed him from below as strongly as I could, for there was great danger of the ice giving way. Luckily, however, it did not. Hillary got up safely to the top of the rock and then held the rope while I came after.

Here again I must be honest and say that I do not feel his account, as told in *The Conquest of Everest*, is wholly accurate. For one thing, he has written that this gap up

◆ **Literary Focus**
How does Norgay's perspective differ from Hillary's?

the rock wall was about forty feet high, but in my judgment it was little more than fifteen. Also, he gives the impression that it was only he who really climbed it on his own, and that he then practically pulled me, so that I "finally collapsed exhausted at the top, like a giant fish when it has just been hauled from the sea after a terrible struggle." Since then I have heard plenty about that "fish," and I admit I do not like it. For it is the plain truth that no one pulled or hauled me up the gap. I climbed it myself, just as Hillary had done; and if he was protecting me with the rope while I was doing it, this was no more than I had done for him. In speaking of this I must make one thing very plain. Hillary is my friend. He is a fine climber and a fine man, and I am proud to have gone with him to the top of Everest. But I do feel that in his story of our final climb he is not quite fair to me; that all the way through he indicates that when things went well it was

his doing and when things went badly it was mine. For this is simply not true. Nowhere do I make the suggestion that I could have climbed Everest by myself; and I do not think Hillary

▲ **Critical Viewing** Describe how Hillary and Norgay must have felt as they looked ahead and back from this point. **[Infer]**

should suggest that he could have, or that I could not have done it without his help. All the way up and down we helped, and were helped by, each other—and that was the way it should be. But we were not leader and led. We were partners.

◆ *Literature and Your Life*

How would you respond to false accusations or rumors that were being spread about you?

On top of the rock cliff we rested again. Certainly, after the climb up the gap we were both a bit breathless, but after some slow pulls at the oxygen I am feeling fine. I look up; the top is very close now; and my heart thumps with excitement and joy. Then we are on our way again. Climbing again. There are still the cornices on our right and the precipice on our left, but the ridge is now less steep. It is only a row of snowy humps, one beyond the other, one higher than the other. But we are still afraid of the cornices and, instead of following the ridge all the way, cut over to the left, where there is now a long snow slope above the precipice. About a hundred feet below the top we come to the highest bare rocks. There is enough almost level space here for two tents, and I wonder if men will ever camp in this place, so near the summit of the earth. I pick up two small stones and put them in my pocket to bring back to the world below. Then the rocks, too, are beneath us. We are back among the snowy humps. They are curving off to the right, and each time we pass one I wonder, "Is the next the last one? Is the next the last?"

Finally we reach a place where we can see past the humps, and beyond them is the great open sky and brown plains. We are looking down the far side of the mountain upon Tibet. Ahead of us now is only one more hump—the last hump. It is not a pinnacle. The way to it is an easy snow slope, wide enough for two men to go side by side. About thirty feet away we stop for a minute and look up. Then we go on. . . .

I have thought much about what I will say now: of how Hillary and I reached the summit of Everest. Later, when we came down from the mountain, there was much foolish talk about who got there first. Some said it was I, some Hillary. Some that only one of us got there—or neither. Still others that one of us had to drag the other up. All this was nonsense. And in Katmandu,[2] to put a stop to such talk Hillary and I signed a statement in which we said, "we reached the summit almost together." We hoped this would be the end of it. But it was not the end. People kept on asking questions and making up stories. They pointed to the "almost" and said, "What does that mean?" Mountaineers understand that there is no sense to such a question; that when two men are on the same rope they are *together*, and that is all there is to it. But other people did not understand. In India and Nepal, I am sorry to say, there has been great pressure on me to say that I reached the summit before Hillary. And all over the world I am asked, "Who got there first? Who got there first?"

♦ **Literary Focus**
Which details indicate that the account is told from Norgay's perspective?

Again I say: it is a foolish question. The answer means nothing. And yet it is a question that has been asked so often—that has caused so much talk and doubt and misunderstanding—that I feel, after long thought, that the answer must be given. As will be clear, it is not for my own sake that I give it. Nor is it for Hillary's. It is for the sake of Everest—the prestige of Everest—and for the generations who will come after us. "Why," they will say, "should

there be a mystery to this thing? Is there something to be ashamed of? To be hidden? Why can we not know the truth?" . . . Very well: now they will know the truth. Everest is too great, too precious, for anything but the truth.

A little below the summit Hillary and I stopped. We looked up. Then we went on. The rope that joined us was thirty feet long, but I held most of it in loops in my hand, so that there was only about six feet between us. I was not thinking of "first" and "second." I did not say to myself, "There is a golden apple up there. I will push Hillary aside and run for it." We went on slowly, steadily. And then we were there. Hillary stepped on top first. And I stepped up after him.

So there it is: the answer to the "great mystery." And if, after all the talk and argument, the answer seems quiet and simple, I can only say that that is as it should be. Many of my own people, I know, will be disappointed at it. They have given a great and false importance to the idea that it must be I who was "first." These people have been good and wonderful to me, and I owe them much. But I owe more to Everest—and to the truth. If it is a discredit to me that I was a step behind Hillary, then I must live with that discredit. But I do not think it was that. Nor do I think that, in the end, it will bring discredit on me that I tell the story. Over and over again I have asked myself, "What will future generations think of us if we allow the facts of our achievement to stay shrouded in mystery? Will they not feel ashamed of us—two comrades in life and death—who have something to hide from the world?" And each time I asked it the answer was the same: "Only the truth is good enough for the future. Only the truth is good enough for Everest."

Now the truth is told. And I am ready to be judged by it.

We stepped up. We were there. The dream had come true. . . .

What we did first was what all climbers do when they reach the top of their mountain. We shook hands. But this was not enough for Everest. I waved my arms in the air and then

---

2. **Katmandu** (kät′män dōō′): Capital of Nepal.

◀ **Critical Viewing** How does this image reflect the climbers' triumph? **[Connect]**

threw them around Hillary, and we thumped each other on the back until, even with the oxygen, we were almost breathless. Then we looked around. It was eleven-thirty in the morning, the sun was shining, and the sky was the deepest blue I have ever seen. Only a gentle breeze was blowing, coming from the direction of Tibet, and the plume of snow that always blows from Everest's summit was very small. Looking down the far side of the mountain, I could see all the familiar landmarks from the earlier expeditions: the Rongbuk Monastery, the town of Shekar Dzong, the Kharta Valley, the Rongbuk and East Rongbuk Glaciers, the North Col, the place near the northeast ridge where we had made Camp Six in 1938. Then, turning, I looked down the long way we ourselves had come: past the south summit, the long ridge, the South Col; onto the Western Cwm, the icefall, the Khumbu Glacier; all the way down to Thyangboche and on to the valleys and hills of my homeland.

Beyond them, and around us on every side, were the great Himalayas, stretching away through Nepal and Tibet. For the closer peaks—giants like Lhotse, Nuptse and Makalu— you now had to look sharply downward to see their summits. And farther away, the whole sweep of the greatest range on earth—even Kangchen-junga[3] itself—seemed only like little bumps under the

---

3. **Kangchenjunga** (kän´ chən jōon´ gə): Third highest mountain in the world, lies near Mount Everest.

spreading sky. It was such a sight as I had never seen before and would never see again: wild, wonderful and terrible. But terror was not what I felt. I loved the mountains too well for that. I loved Everest too well. At that great moment for which I had waited all my life my mountain did not seem to me a lifeless thing of rock and ice, but warm and friendly and living. She was a mother hen, and the other mountains were chicks under her wings. I too, I felt, had only to spread my own wings to cover and shelter the brood that I loved.

We turned off our oxygen. Even there on top of the world it was possible to live without it, so long as we were not exerting ourselves. We cleared away the ice that had formed on our masks, and I popped a bit of sweet into my mouth. Then we replaced the masks. But we did not turn on the oxygen again until we were ready to leave the top. Hillary took out his camera, which he had been carrying under his clothing to keep it from freezing, and I unwound the four flags from around my ax. They were tied together on a string, which was fastened to the blade of the ax, and now I held the ax up and Hillary took my picture. Actually he took three, and I think it was lucky, in those difficult conditions, that one came out so well. The order of the flags from top to bottom was United Nations, British, Nepalese, Indian; and the same sort of people who have made trouble in other ways have tried to find political meaning in this too. All I can say is that on Everest I was not thinking about politics. If I had been, I suppose I would have put the Indian or Nepalese flag highest—though that in itself would have been a bad problem for me. As it is, I am glad that the U.N. flag was on top. For I like to think that our victory was not only for ourselves—not only for our own nations—but for all men everywhere.

◆ Literature and Your Life

Reader's Response Whose account of climbing Everest was more appealing to you—Hillary's or Norgay's? Why?

Thematic Focus Hillary and Norgay spent many years preparing themselves mentally and physically for the climb of their lives. Discuss ways in which you prepare yourself—mentally and physically—for a challenging task.

Role Play With a partner, take turns role-playing a conversation with Tenzing Norgay. Ask him questions about his preparation and attitude and how they helped him conquer Everest. Also, ask his advice on how you can prepare yourself for challenges you face.

☑ Check Your Comprehension

1. What qualities does Norgay possess that helped contribute to his success?
2. Who does Norgay say reached the summit first?
3. What do Norgay and Hillary do when they reach the top of Everest?

◆ Critical Thinking

INTERPRET

1. Why is Norgay so bothered by the comparison Hillary makes between Norgay and a "giant fish"? **[Connect]**
2. (a) Why do you think Norgay is so concerned with the "prestige of Everest"? (b) What does he mean by "Everest and the truth"? **[Analyze]**

EVALUATE

3. Norgay calls Hillary his friend at the beginning of this excerpt. Do you think that was a sincere compliment? Why or why not? **[Evaluate]**

COMPARE LITERARY WORKS

4. Based on the content of each text, compare and contrast Hillary's and Norgay's purposes for writing. **[Compare and Contrast]**

Guide for Responding (continued)

◆ Reading Strategy

DISTINGUISH FACT FROM OPINION

Norgay and Hillary include many **facts**—statements that can be proven—in their accounts of the climb up Everest. They also include their **opinions**, statements that can be supported but not proved. For instance, Norgay supports his statement that Hillary was not quite fair with examples from Hillary's writing. However, since the statement cannot be proved true or false by evidence, it is an opinion.

1. Identify one fact and one opinion that each climber states about the other.
2. Hillary calls Norgay "an inexpert but enthusiastic step cutter." Explain whether this statement is a fact or an opinion.
3. List two examples of the writers' different opinions about the same events.

◆ Literary Focus

AUTHOR'S PERSPECTIVE

Like most nonfiction works, "The Final Assault" and "The Dream Comes True" are each told from one **author's perspective**—the presentation of events that reflects the author's personal outlook and recollection of the experience. For example, from Hillary's perspective, Norgay often struggled and needed Hillary's help during their ascent of Everest. However, from Norgay's perspective, the climbers helped each other equally.

1. List three details in the account told from Hillary's perspective that are not included in the account told from Norgay's perspective.
2. List two details in the account told from Norgay's perspective that are not included in the account told from Hillary's perspective.
3. Compare the two writers' perspectives on the final moment of the climb—reaching the summit.
4. In what ways might an account of Hillary and Norgay's expedition written by someone who was not involved in the expedition be different from these first-person accounts?

◆ Build Vocabulary

USING THE LATIN ROOT -*voc*-

The Latin root -*voc*- means "speak" or "say." Define each of these words. Explain how the definition of each word is related to "speaking" or "saying."

1. vocal   2. vocabulary   3. vocalist

USING THE WORD BANK: Synonyms

Write the letter of the word that is the best synonym for, or has the closest meaning to, the first word on each line.

1. precipitous: (a) rainy, (b) steep, (c) noisy
2. discernible: (a) visible, (b) agreeable, (c) ornery
3. belay: (a) support, (b) hindrance, (c) alcove
4. encroaching: (a) growing, (b) helping, (c) invading
5. undulations: (a) holes, (b) waves, (c) shivers
6. vociferous: (a) timid, (b) uneventful, (c) loud

◆ Build Grammar Skills

COMPOUND PREDICATES

A **compound predicate** consists of two or more verbs or verb phrases that share the same subject and are joined by a conjunction.

Practice On your paper, copy the following sentences. Then write *S* over each subject and *V* over each verb in the compound predicates.

1. Hillary chipped away at ice, secured his rope support, and hoisted himself up to the next level.
2. Making their way up the mountain, they sometimes slid backward, sometimes changed leads, and always hoped they would conquer Everest.
3. Norgay checked his oxygen level, paused to adjust his backpack, and then trudged on.

Writing Application Combine the following sentences using compound predicates.

1. Hillary and Norgay cleared away ice and rocks. They pitched a tent. They prepared their gear for the following day.
2. Hillary waited for Norgay to catch his breath. He also helped him secure his oxygen mask. Then, Hillary blazed a trail for Norgay to follow.

Build Your Portfolio

 ## Idea Bank

Writing

1. **Book Jacket** Write a summary for the back-cover of either Hillary's or Norgay's book. Highlight a gripping scene or suspenseful moment to entice your readers to read the book.

2. **Article on Everest** Write a newspaper article about the first successful Everest climb based on what you learned from Hillary's and Norgay's accounts. Include an attention-grabbing headline.

3. **Mountain's Eye View** Write a description of what you think the world looks like from the top of Everest based on the accounts you read in the selections.

Speaking, Listening, and Viewing

4. **Advice for Future Climbers** Drawing from the details in one or both of the selections, prepare a brief talk in which you provide advice to aspiring climbers. Present your talk to the class.

5. **Oral Report** Using information in these selections and facts that you gather through research, prepare and present a brief oral report on an aspect of mountain climbing. **[Science Link]**

Researching and Representing

6. **Everest Statistics** Create a chart illustrating some statistics related to Mount Everest. For example, how many people have attempted to climb it, and how many have succeeded? How many have died trying? **[Math Link]**

7. **Video Game Design** Design the graphics for a video game based on this story. Present your ideas in a series of sketches. Show what the game screens will look like, how the players will move, and where the hazards will be. **[Art Link]**

Online Activity www.phlit.phschool.com

 ## Guided Writing Lesson

Hall-of-Fame Placards

Choose your favorite sport—it doesn't have to be mountain climbing—and write **placards** (display cards that briefly describe a player's achievements, statistics, and accomplishments) for your favorite players. The following tip will help you indicate the time-order of events.

Writing Skills Focus: Transitions to Show Time

When writing your placards, use **transitions to show time.** Transitional words that show time include *first, next, finally, before, after, later,* and *at the same time.*

Tenzing Norgay uses transitions to show what happened first and next as he recalls his famous climb:

> From the south summit we *first* had to go down a little. *Then* up, up, up.

As you draft, use transitions to show the order of events and achievements you jotted down in prewriting. Check for clear transitions when you revise.

Prewriting Begin by making individual lists for each athlete, recording his or her statistics, achievements, and any interesting anecdotes you may discover. Choose only the most significant statistics and facts and arrange them in time order.

Drafting As you draft each placard, be sure to write your facts and statistics using transitions to show time. For example, you might start by saying "First ___?___ did ___?___. Then ___?___. Finally ___?___ capped his career off with ___?___."

Revising Have a friend read your placards and see if the time relations are clear. If not, you may need to insert transitions where your readers could get confused.

Guide for Reading

Julio Cortázar *(1914–1984)*

Julio Cortázar (hoó lē ō kôr tä´ zər) was born in Brussels, Belgium, to Argentinian parents. He returned to Argentina while still a small boy and later began a career there as a teacher. After moving to Buenos Aires, he found work as a translator and began to write the fiction that would make him famous. Upon winning a scholarship from the French government, he traveled to Paris, where he worked as a translator for the United Nations—a job he held for the rest of his life.

In addition to his work as a translator, Cortázar continued to write novels and short stories. He is best known for his experimental fiction, which sometimes allows the reader to participate in creating the story. Cortázar once summarized his view of fiction as follows: "The fantastic is something that one must never say goodbye to lightly."

Alexander Pushkin *(1799–1837)*

This father of modern Russian literature is more like an adventurous teenager than a settled "father." Although born into the nobility, he had great sympathy for poor Russian peasants and criticized the absolute power and corruption of the government. His dangerous opinions got him banished to a remote part of Russia and later to his family's estate.

In literature, too, he was a rebel. His poems express his democratic ideas and draw on themes from folklore, the oral literature of the people. "The Bridegroom," for example, is like a literary version of a song passed on by word of mouth.

Pushkin's own death was like an incident from a folk tale or ballad. Resettled in the capital city of St. Petersburg, he was as hotheaded as ever and died after being wounded in a duel.

Portrait of the Poet Pushkin, Orest Adamovich Kiprensky, Tretyakov Gallery, Moscow, Russia

◆ Build Vocabulary

RELATED WORDS: WORDS FOR *right* AND *left*

The word *dexterity,* meaning "skill in using one's hands," appears in Cortázar's story. It comes from the Latin *dexter,* "of or on the right-hand side." The Latin word *sinister,* meaning "of the left-hand side," has associations based on superstitions we no longer believe. It means "unlucky," and the English word that comes from it means "threatening harm."

WORD BANK

Preview the list before you read.

indispensable
replete
dexterity
vestibule
brusquely
foreboding
tumult

◆ Build Grammar Skills

REGULAR AND IRREGULAR VERB FORMS

A verb has four basic forms known as principal parts: the present (also known as the infinitive), the present participle, the past, and the past participle. All verbs form the present participle by adding *-ing* to the present form. **Regular** verbs form their past and past participles by adding *-d* or *-ed* to the present form. Other verbs are **irregular**; they form their past and past participles in some other way.

Regular: We *amused* ourselves sufficiently . . .
Irregular: . . . I *woke* up immediately . . .

It is important to know the irregular forms so that you can use them correctly.

House Taken Over ◆ The Bridegroom

◆ Literature and Your Life

CONNECT YOUR EXPERIENCE

The words *choice*, *will*, and *determination* suggest that you can control events. If you're losing in any situation, the answer is to get determined, figure out the problems, and make some choices.

The characters in this story and poem are faced with choices about their futures. You will soon see how their choices and actions affect their lives.

Journal Writing Describe a situation that you influenced through your own choices.

THEMATIC FOCUS: DARING DECISIONS

As you read this story and poem, think about the extent to which people can control life events.

◆ Background for Understanding

LITERATURE

In literature of the fantastic, writers harness the power of fantasy to challenge, puzzle, unsettle, and entertain readers. Like dreams and daydreams, fantastic stories distort and expand our usual world. They open up passageways into mysterious places.

Just as no dream is totally unrealistic—even the strangest have recognizable characters and actions—no fantastic story is entirely fantastic. In literature of the fantastic, fantasy and reality exist side by side.

As you read "House Taken Over" and "The Bridegroom," look for elements of reality alongside elements of the fantastic.

◆ Literary Focus

FORESHADOWING

Writers determine the outcome of *all* the events in the fictional worlds they create. They keep you interested in what will happen by giving you hints, called **foreshadowing**, of future events. If you find these hints, you will have the fun of almost knowing what the future will bring.

To find the foreshadowing in "House Taken Over," think about the calmness of tone and the references to an unused portion of the house in the first part of the story. Also consider the narrator's reaction when he first hears sounds from the unoccupied part of the house. While reading "The Bridegroom," be alert for clues to future events in Natasha's changing reaction to her suitor.

◆ Reading Strategy

PREDICT OUTCOMES

You can use a writer's hints at future events to **predict outcomes** or to make educated guesses about what will happen in a story or poem. Your predictions will keep you involved in the world the author creates as you read on to see whether you were correct.

In predicting the outcome of "House Taken Over," consider what the title reveals about events to come. To figure out what will happen in "The Bridegroom," think about who is coming to Natasha's wedding. One guest is a clue to her plans.

As you read, jot down predictions in a chart like this one. Note predictions in one column and the actual outcome in the other.

Predictions	Actual Outcome

La Nuit (Night), René Magritte

House Taken Over

Julio Cortázar

Translated by Paul Blackburn

We liked the house because, apart from its being old and spacious (in a day when old houses go down for a profitable auction of their construction materials), it kept the memories of great-grandparents, our paternal grandfather, our parents and the whole of childhood.

Irene and I got used to staying in the house by ourselves, which was crazy, eight people could have lived in that place and not have gotten in each other's way. We rose at seven in the morning and got the cleaning done, and about eleven I left Irene to finish off whatever rooms and went to the kitchen. We lunched at noon precisely; then there was nothing left to do but a few dirty plates. It was pleasant to take lunch and commune with[1] the great hollow, silent house, and it was enough for us just to keep it clean. We ended up thinking, at times, that that was what had kept us from marrying. Irene turned down two suitors for no particular reason, and María Esther went and died on me before we could manage to get engaged. We were easing into our forties with the unvoiced concept that the quiet, simple marriage of sister and brother was the indispensable end to a line established in this house by our grandparents. We would die here someday, obscure and distant cousins would inherit the place, have it torn down, sell the bricks and get rich on the building plot; or more justly and better yet, we would topple it ourselves before it was too late.

Irene never bothered anyone. Once the morning housework was finished, she spent the rest of the day on the sofa in her bedroom, knitting. I couldn't tell you why she knitted so much; I think women knit when they discover that it's a fat excuse to do nothing at all. But Irene was not like that, she always knitted necessities, sweaters for winter, socks for me, handy morning robes and bedjackets for herself. Sometimes she would do a jacket, then

unravel it the next moment because there was something that didn't please her; it was pleasant to see a pile of tangled wool in her knitting basket fighting a losing battle for a few hours to retain its shape. Saturdays I went downtown to buy wool; Irene had faith in my good taste, was pleased with the colors and never a skein[2] had to be returned. I took advantage of these trips to make the rounds of the bookstores, uselessly asking if they had anything new in French literature. Nothing worthwhile had arrived in Argentina since 1939.[3]

But it's the house I want to talk about, the house and Irene, I'm not very important. I wonder what Irene would have done without her knitting. One can reread a book, but once a pullover is finished you can't do it over again, it's some kind of disgrace. One day I found that the drawer at the bottom of the chiffonier, replete with mothballs, was filled with shawls, white, green, lilac. Stacked amid a great smell of camphor—it was like a shop; I didn't have the nerve to ask her what she planned to do with them. We didn't have to earn our living, there was plenty coming in from the farms each month, even piling up. But Irene was only interested in the knitting and showed a wonderful dexterity, and for me the hours slipped away watching her, her hands like silver sea-urchins, needles flashing, and one or two knitting baskets on the floor, the balls of yarn jumping about. It was lovely.

How not to remember the layout of that house. The dining room, a living room with tapestries, the library and three large bedrooms in the

---

2. **skein** (skān) *n.*: A quantity of thread or yarn wound in a coil.

3. **Nothing worthwhile . . . since 1939:** When World War II began in 1939, communications with Europe were disrupted.

◆ **Build Vocabulary**

indispensable (in′ di spen′ sə bəl) *adj.*: Absolutely necessary or required

replete (ri plēt′) *adj.*: Well-filled; stocked

dexterity (deks ter′ ə tē) *n.*: Skillfulness in the use of one's hands

---

1. **commune** (kə myo͞on′) **with:** Be in close rapport or harmony with.

Door, 1969–70, George Tooker, New Britain Museum of American Art, Connecticut

◀ **Critical Viewing** Like the narrator in the story, the man in this picture seems to be trying to hold a door shut. What do you think is behind the door? **[Hypothesize]**

section most recessed, the one that faced toward Rodríguez Peña.[4] Only a corridor with its massive oak door separated that part from the front wing, where there was a bath, the kitchen, our bedrooms and the hall. One entered the house through a vestibule with enameled tiles, and a wrought-iron grated door opened onto the living room. You had to come in through the vestibule and open the gate to go into the living room; the doors to our bedrooms were on either side of this, and opposite it was the corridor leading to the back section; going down the passage, one swung open the oak door beyond which was the other part of the house; or just before the door, one could turn to the left and go down a narrower passageway which led to the kitchen and the bath. When the door was open, you became aware of the size of the house; when it was closed, you had the impression of an apartment, like the ones they build today, with barely enough room to move around in. Irene and I always lived in this part of the house and hardly ever went beyond the oak door except to do the cleaning. Incredible how much dust collected on the furniture. It may be Buenos Aires[5] is a clean city, but she owes it to her population and nothing else. There's too much dust in the air, the slightest breeze and it's back on the marble console tops and in the diamond patterns of the tooled-leather desk set. It's a lot of work to get it off with a feather duster; the motes[6] rise and hang in the air, and settle again a minute later on the pianos and the furniture.

I'll always have a clear memory of it because it happened so simply and without fuss. Irene was knitting in her bedroom, it was eight at

night, and I suddenly decided to put the water up for *mate*.[7] I went down the corridor as far as the oak door, which was ajar, then turned into the hall toward the kitchen, when I heard something in the library or the dining room. The sound came through muted and indistinct, a chair being knocked over onto the carpet or the muffled buzzing of a conversation. At the same time, or a second later, I heard it at the end of the passage which led from those two rooms toward the door. I hurled myself against the door before it was too late and shut it, leaned on it with the weight of my body; luckily, the key was on our side; moreover, I ran the great bolt into place, just to be safe.

◆ **Literary Focus**
How does the initial response of the brother and sister to the noises foreshadow future events?

I went down to the kitchen, heated the kettle, and when I got back with the tray of *mate*, I told Irene:

"I had to shut the door to the passage. They've taken over the back part."

She let her knitting fall and looked at me with her tired, serious eyes.

"You're sure?"

I nodded.

"In that case," she said, picking up her needles again, "we'll have to live on this side."

I sipped at the *mate* very carefully, but she took her time starting her work again. I remember it was a gray vest she was knitting. I liked that vest.

The first few days were painful, since we'd both left so many things in the part that had been taken over. My collection of French literature, for example, was still in the library. Irene had left several folios of stationery and a pair of slippers that she used a lot in the winter. I missed my briar pipe, and Irene, I

---

4. **Rodríguez Peña** (rō drē gəz pā′ nyə): A fashionable street in Buenos Aires.
5. **Buenos Aires** (bwā′ nəs er′ ēz): The capital of Argentina.
6. **motes**: Specks of dust or other tiny particles.

---

7. ***mate*** (mä′ tā′): A beverage made from the dried leaves of a South American evergreen tree.

◆ **Build Vocabulary**
vestibule (ves′ tə byōōl′) *n.*: A small entrance hall

think, regretted the loss of an ancient bottle of Hesperidin.[8] It happened repeatedly (but only in the first few days) that we would close some drawer or cabinet and look at one another sadly.

"It's not here."

One thing more among the many lost on the other side of the house.

But there were advantages, too. The cleaning was so much simplified that, even when we got up late, nine-thirty for instance, by eleven we were sitting around with our arms folded. Irene got into the habit of coming to the kitchen with me to help get lunch. We thought about it and decided on this: while I prepared the lunch, Irene would cook up dishes that could be eaten cold in the evening. We were happy with the arrangement because it was always such a bother to have to leave our bedrooms in the evening and start to cook. Now we made do with the table in Irene's room and platters of cold supper.

Since it left her more time for knitting, Irene was content. I was a little lost without my books, but so as not to inflict myself on my sister, I set about reordering papa's stamp collection; that killed some time. We amused ourselves sufficiently, each with his own thing, almost always getting together in Irene's bedroom, which was the more comfortable. Every once in a while, Irene might say:

"Look at this pattern I just figured out, doesn't it look like clover?"

After a bit it was I, pushing a small square of paper in front of her so that she could see the excellence of some stamp or another from Eupen-et-Malmédy.[9] We were fine, and little by little we stopped thinking. You can live without thinking.

(Whenever Irene talked in her sleep, I woke up immediately and stayed awake. I never could get used to this voice from a statue or a parrot, a voice that came out of the dreams, not from a throat. Irene said that in my sleep I flailed about enormously and shook the blankets off. We had the living room between us, but at night you could hear everything in the house. We heard each other breathing, coughing, could even feel each other reaching for the light switch when, as happened frequently, neither of us could fall asleep.

Aside from our nocturnal rumblings, everything was quiet in the house. During the day there were the household sounds, the metallic click of knitting needles, the rustle of stamp-album pages turning. The oak door was massive, I think I said that. In the kitchen or the bath, which adjoined the part that was taken over, we managed to talk loudly, or Irene sang lullabies. In a kitchen there's always too much noise, the plates and glasses, for there to be interruptions from other sounds. We seldom allowed ourselves silence there, but when we went back to our rooms or to the living room, then the house grew quiet, half-lit, we ended by stepping around more slowly so as not to disturb one another. I think it was because of this that I woke up irremediably[10] and at once when Irene began to talk in her sleep.)

Except for the consequences, it's nearly a matter of repeating the same scene over again. I was thirsty that night, and before we went to sleep, I told Irene that I was going to the kitchen for a glass of water. From the door of the bedroom (she was knitting) I heard the noise in the kitchen; if not the kitchen, then the bath, the passage off at that angle dulled the sound. Irene noticed how brusquely I had paused, and came up beside me without a word. We stood listening to the noises, growing more and more sure that they were on our side of the oak door, if not the kitchen then the bath, or in the hall itself at the turn, almost next to us.

> ◆ Reading Strategy
> What outcome do you predict the narrator's actions will cause? Why?

---

8. Hesperidin (hes per´ i din): A vitamin that comes from the rind of green citrus fruits and is used for various medicinal purposes.

9. Eupen-et-Malmédy (yo͞o pen´ ā mäl mā dē´): Districts in eastern Belgium.

---

10. irremediably (ir´ ri mē´ de ə blē) *adv.*: In a way that cannot be helped or corrected.

We didn't wait to look at one another. I took Irene's arm and forced her to run with me to the wrought-iron door, not waiting to look back. You could hear the noises, still muffled but louder, just behind us. I slammed the grating and we stopped in the vestibule. Now there was nothing to be heard.

"They've taken over our section," Irene said. The knitting had reeled off from her hands and the yarn ran back toward the door and disappeared under it. When she saw that the balls of yarn were on the other side, she dropped the knitting without looking at it.

"Did you have time to bring anything?" I asked hopelessly.

"No, nothing."

We had what we had on. I remembered fifteen thousand pesos[11] in the wardrobe in my bedroom. Too late now.

I still had my wristwatch on and saw that it was 11 P.M. I took Irene around the waist (I think she was crying) and that was how we went into the street. Before we left, I felt terrible; I locked the front door up tight and tossed the key down the sewer. It wouldn't do to have some poor devil decide to go in and rob the house, at that hour and with the house taken over.

---

11. **fifteen thousand pesos:** A large sum of money at that time, equivalent to over a thousand dollars.

◆ **Build Vocabulary**

brusquely (brusk´ lē) *adv.*: In an abrupt manner

Guide for Responding

◆ *Literature and Your Life*

Reader's Response Would you have acted as the narrator did if you were in his place? Explain.

Thematic Focus In what way were the characters' decisions daring or cowardly?

Reader's Journal Have you ever recalled a real-life experience and thought, "It was like something out of a dream"? In your journal, write about such a time, using vivid language to capture the sense of mystery you felt.

Questions for Research "House Taken Over" was written in 1951, when Cortázar was living in Argentina. What questions might you ask to learn whether this story reflects or comments on Argentina's political situation at the time?

☑ Check Your Comprehension

1. Who are the story's characters?
2. What separates the front wing from the back section of the house?
3. What does the brother do when he first hears noises coming from the back section of the house?
4. What happens when the brother and sister hear noises in the front part of the house?
5. Where do the brother and sister go at the story's end?

◆ Critical Thinking

INTERPRET

1. What can you infer about the narrator and his sister on the basis of their daily routines? **[Infer]**
2. The narrator never tells us very much about the invaders of the house. To whom or what do you think he is referring when he says, "They've taken over the back part"? **[Speculate]**
3. Although the narrator and his sister seem unnaturally accepting of the bizarre forces intruding upon them, how does their disturbed sleep reveal their true reaction to the invasion of their house? **[Interpret]**
4. (a) Express the theme, or central meaning, of this story. (b) What details in the story led you to identify this theme? **[Evaluate]**

EVALUATE

5. Would the story have been more effective or less effective if Cortázar had described in detail what was invading the house? **[Assess]**

APPLY

6. Cortázar wrote "House Taken Over" after having a nightmare. In what ways does the story resemble a nightmare? **[Synthesize]**

The Bridegroom

Alexander Pushkin
Translated by D. M. Thomas

For three days Natasha,
The merchant's daughter,
Was missing. The third night,
She ran in, distraught.
5   Her father and mother
Plied her with questions.
She did not hear them,
She could hardly breathe.

Stricken with foreboding
10   They pleaded, got angry,
But still she was silent;
At last they gave up.
Natasha's cheeks regained
Their rosy color.
15   And cheerfully again
She sat with her sisters.

Once at the shingle-gate
She sat with her friends
—And a swift troika[1]
20   Flashed by before them;
A handsome young man
Stood driving the horses;
Snow and mud went flying,
Splashing the girls.

25   He gazed as he flew past,
And Natasha gazed.
He flew on. Natasha froze.

Headlong she ran home.
"It was he! It was he!"
30   She cried. "I know it!
I recognized him! Papa,
Mama, save me from him!"

Full of grief and fear,
They shake their heads, sighing.
35   Her father says: "My child,
Tell me everything.
If someone has harmed you,
Tell us . . . even a hint."
She weeps again and
40   Her lips remain sealed.

The next morning, the old
Matchmaking woman
Unexpectedly calls and
Sings the girl's praises;
45   Says to the father: "You
Have the goods and I
A buyer for them:
A handsome young man.

"He bows low to no one,
50   He lives like a lord
With no debts nor worries;
He's rich and he's generous,

---

1. **troika** (troi´ kə) *n.*: Russian carriage or sleigh drawn by a specially trained team of three horses abreast.

◆ **Build Vocabulary**

foreboding (fôr bōd´ iŋ) *n.*: Feeling that something bad will happen

▲ **Critical Viewing** What might you infer about Natasha's marriage from this painting? [Infer]

The Lights of Marriage (detail), Marc Chagall, Kunsthaus, Zurich

Says he will give his bride,
On their wedding-day,
55 A fox-fur coat, a pearl,
Gold rings, brocaded² dresses.

"Yesterday, out driving,
He saw your Natasha;
Shall we shake hands
60 And get her to church?"
The woman starts to eat
A pie, and talks in riddles,
While the poor girl
Does not know where to look.

65 "Agreed," says her father;
"Go in happiness
To the altar, Natasha;
It's dull for you here;
A swallow should not spend
70 All its time singing,
It's time for you to build
A nest for your children."

Natasha leaned against
The wall and tried
75 To speak—but found herself
Sobbing; she was shuddering
And laughing. The matchmaker
Poured out a cup of water,
Gave her some to drink,
80 Splashed some in her face.

---

2. brocaded (brō kād′ əd) *adj.*: Woven, raised design in a cloth.

Her parents are distressed.
Then Natasha recovered,
And calmly she said:
"Your will be done. Call
85 My bridegroom to the feast,
Bake loaves for the whole world,
Brew sweet mead³ and call
The law to the feast."

"Of course, Natasha, angel!
90 You know we'd give our lives
To make you happy!"
They bake and they brew;
The worthy guests come,
The bride is led to the feast,
95 Her maids sing and weep;
Then horses and a sledge⁴

With the groom—and all sit.
The glasses ring and clatter,
The toasting-cup is passed

100 From hand to hand in tumult,
The guests are drunk.

BRIDEGROOM
"Friends, why is my fair bride
Sad, why is she not
Feasting and serving?"

105 The bride answers the groom:
"I will tell you why
As best I can. My soul
Knows no rest, day and night
I weep; an evil dream
110 Oppresses me." Her father
Says: "My dear child, tell us
What your dream is."

"I dreamed," she says, "that I
Went into a forest,
115 It was late and dark;
The moon was faintly
Shining behind a cloud;
I strayed from the path;

Nothing stirred except
120 The tops of the pine-trees.

"And suddenly, as if
I was awake, I saw
A hut. I approach the hut
And knock at the door
125 —Silence. A prayer on my lips
I open the door and enter.
A candle burns. All
Is silver and gold."

BRIDEGROOM
"What is bad about that?
130 It promises wealth."

BRIDE
"Wait, sir, I've not finished.
Silently I gazed
On the silver and gold,
The cloths, the rugs, the silks,
135 From Novgorod,⁵ and I
Was lost in wonder.

"Then I heard a shout
And a clatter of hoofs . . .
Someone has driven up
140 To the porch. Quickly
I slammed the door and hid
Behind the stove. Now
I hear many voices . . .
Twelve young men come in,

145 "And with them is a girl,
Pure and beautiful.
They've taken no notice
Of the ikons,⁶ they sit
To the table without
150 Praying or taking off
Their hats. At the head,

---

5. Novgorod: City in the northwestern part of Russia.
6. ikons (ī känz′) *n.*: Images of Jesus, Mary, a saint, or another sacred Christian religious figure.

---

3. mead (mēd) *n.*: Drink made of fermented honey and water.
4. sledge *n.*: Sleigh.

◆ **Build Vocabulary**
tumult (tōō′ mult) *n.*: Noisy commotion

The eldest brother,
At his right, the youngest;
At his left, the girl.
155 Shouts, laughs, drunken clamor . . . "

BRIDEGROOM
"That betokens merriment."

BRIDE
"Wait, sir, I've not finished.
The drunken din goes on
And grows louder still.
160 Only the girl is sad.

"She sits silent, neither
Eating nor drinking;
But sheds tears in plenty;
The eldest brother
165 Takes his knife and, whistling,
Sharpens it; seizing her by

The hair he kills her
And cuts off her right hand."

"Why," says the groom, "this
170 Is nonsense! Believe me,
My love, your dream is not evil."
She looks him in the eyes.
"And from whose hand
Does this ring come?"
175 The bride said. The whole throng
Rose in the silence.

With a clatter the ring
Falls, and rolls along
The floor. The groom blanches,
180 Trembles. Confusion . . .
"Seize him!" the law commands.
He's bound, judged, put to death.
Natasha is famous!
Our song at an end.

Guide for Responding

◆ Literature and Your Life

Reader's Response Do you admire Natasha? Why or why not?

Thematic Focus What does the poem suggest about the power of choice versus that of chance or fate?

Questions for Research Name another song or ballad that, like "The Bridegroom," tells a story. Then, write one or more questions you could research about the song or ballad.

☑ Check Your Comprehension

1. What unexplained event occurs at the very beginning of the poem?
2. What upsets Natasha when she's sitting with her friends at the gate?
3. Describe her changing reactions to the marriage.
4. Summarize the events of the wedding.

◆ Critical Thinking

INTERPRET
1. Where was Natasha during the three days she was missing? **[Infer]**
2. Why does she refuse to reveal where she was to her parents? **[Analyze]**
3. What accounts for her changing reactions to the marriage? **[Infer]**
4. Do you think Natasha had the "evil" dream she describes? Explain. **[Interpret]**
5. How does Natasha's behavior at the beginning of the poem contrast with her behavior at the end? **[Compare and Contrast]**
6. Why does Natasha become famous? **[Draw Conclusions]**

EVALUATE
7. Is the title of the poem effective in grabbing your attention and hinting at the poem's story? Explain. **[Criticize]**

COMPARE LITERARY WORKS
8. Compare and contrast the authors' use of fate as a theme in the story and the ballad. **[Compare and Contrast]**

Guide for Responding (continued)

◆ Reading Strategy

PREDICT OUTCOMES

Reading in "The Bridegroom" that Natasha invites "the whole world" and "the law" to her wedding, you may wonder why she singles out someone who enforces the law. This clue helps you **predict the outcome** of the story because it suggests that Natasha plans to capture a criminal.

1. Explain how each of these other details helps you predict the outcome of "The Bridegroom": Natasha's sudden decision to have the wedding; her refusal to eat and drink at the wedding; and her tale of "an evil dream."
2. List two clues from "House Taken Over" that suggest the brother and sister will eventually abandon their house.

◆ Literary Focus

FORESHADOWING

In the story and the poem, hints of future events, called **foreshadowing,** give you glimpses of what will happen that make you want to find out more. Sometimes these hints give a general sense of what will come. Other times, they can be linked to specific occurrences, although you may not understand the connection until much later.

For example, in "House Taken Over," when the brother says "How not to remember the layout of that house," the reader senses that something will happen to destroy the home or that something remarkable will happen within it.

1. What details in the first part of "House Taken Over" foreshadow the strange behavior of the brother and sister?
2. How does the initial reaction of the brother and sister to the noises foreshadow their eventual abandonment of the house?
3. In "The Bridegroom," why is Natasha's first reaction to the "handsome young man" an example of foreshadowing?
4. Natasha invites "the law" to her wedding. What specific later event does this invitation foreshadow?

◆ Build Vocabulary

RELATED WORDS: WORDS FOR *right* AND *left*

Use your knowledge of the Latin words *dexter* and *sinister* to define the italicized words.

1. Irene spends her days knitting, and she possesses great manual *dexterity*.
2. The calm atmosphere, coupled with the unexplained noises, creates an eerie, somewhat *sinister* mood.

USING THE WORD BANK: Synonyms

On your paper, write the word whose meaning is closest to that of the first word on each line:

1. indispensable: (a) useless, (b) essential, (c) offered
2. replete: (a) divided, (b) empty, (c) filled
3. dexterity: (a) skillfulness, (b) strength, (c) clumsiness
4. vestibule: (a) garment, (b) hall, (c) armor
5. brusquely: (a) smoothly, (b) joyfully, (c) abruptly
6. foreboding: (a) forewarning, (b) hindsight, (c) unawareness
7. tumult: (a) boredom, (b) order, (c) commotion

◆ Build Grammar Skills

REGULAR AND IRREGULAR VERBS

Irregular verbs, like the ones in the following chart, form their past and past participles in a variety of ways.

Practice Choose a form of the given irregular verb to complete the sentences.

Present	Past	Past Participle
know	knew	known
see	saw	seen
become	became	become

1. The brother ____?____ that Irene's knitting was important to her. (know)
2. Both brother and sister had ____?____ comfortable with their daily routines. (become)
3. Once she ____?____ the balls of yarn disappear on the other side of the door, Irene dropped her knitting. (see)
4. Natasha ____?____ a sight that terrified her. (see)
5. Natasha's tale revealed what she ____?____. (know)

Build Your Portfolio

Idea Bank

Writing

1. **Newspaper Headlines** For each selection, write two headlines that would entice people to read the sensational story. An example of such a headline might be "Bridegroom in Big Trouble."

2. **Story Continuation** Write a story in which you tell what happens to the narrator, his sister, and the house after "House Taken Over" ends.

3. **Literary Analysis** Write a literary analysis of "The Bridegroom" in which you identify the poem's theme. Use evidence from the poem to support your ideas.

Speaking, Listening, and Viewing

4. **Television Interview** With a partner, role-play an interview between Natasha from "The Bridegroom" and a television reporter. Focus on Natasha's three-day absence and her plans for confronting the criminal. **[Media Link]**

5. **Retelling** As a much older Natasha, retell the story of "The Bridegroom" to your grandchildren. **[Performing Arts Link]**

Researching and Representing

6. **Poster Showing Fortuna** Research Fortuna, the ancient goddess of fortune. Then create a poster illustrating what you've learned about her. **[Social Studies Link; Art Link]**

7. **Blueprint** Create a blueprint, or diagram, of the house that is featured in "House Taken Over." Mark the order in which the brother and sister retreated from various rooms. Display your blueprint for the class. **[Art Link]**

Online Activity www.phlit.phschool.com

Guided Writing Lesson

Yearbook Prediction

The characters in these selections take steps to provide for their futures. The characters in "House Taken Over" try to ensure their future safety by abandoning their house. In "The Bridegroom," Natasha unmasks a murderer to protect her future happiness. Think about what you'd like the future to hold for you, and write a yearbook prediction based on this wish. Use transitions to show the cause-and-effect relationships involved in making your prediction a reality.

Writing Skills Focus: Transitions to Show Cause and Effect

You'll need to use **transitions to show cause and effect**—words and phrases that show how one thing brings about another—when writing a how-to essay, a prediction, or a short story. Such transitions include words like *because*, *as a result*, and *consequently*.

Cortázar uses a transition in this passage to show how a situation influences the narrator's memory:

$$\text{effect} \qquad\qquad \text{transition}$$
"I'll always have a clear memory of it because
$$\text{cause}$$
it happened so simply and without fuss."

Prewriting Make an imaginary timeline showing how today's interests and abilities can lead you step by step to tomorrow's opportunities. In addition, list cause-and-effect transition words you can draw on as you draft and revise your prediction.

Drafting Refer to your cause-and-effect word list as you write, using transitions to show how one event brings about another.

Revising Reread your prediction and add transitions to clarify any vague cause-and-effect relationships.

Circle any irregular verbs in your draft. Then, check to be sure you have used the correct forms. For more on regular and irregular verb forms, see pp. 162 and 174.

Guide for Reading

Jamaica Kincaid (1949–)

Imagine leaving everyone and everything that is familiar to you and moving to a foreign country on your own. That is exactly what this writer did.

At the age of sixteen, Jamaica Kincaid set off into the unknown.

She left her home in Antigua to take a job caring for the children of a family in New York.

A Changing Family Situation

She was born Elaine Potter Richardson on the West Indian island of Antigua. Although she grew up in a home without electricity or running water, Kincaid's early childhood was a happy one because of her deep connection with her mother. As a teen how-ever, she yearned for a life of her own.

She moved to America, held a series of unskilled jobs, and made an unsuccessful attempt to get a college degree. Despite setbacks, she entered the New York publishing world and soon was writing articles for teen magazines. She also adopted the pen name Jamaica Kincaid, a symbol of her new, independent self.

Literary Success

Jamaica Kincaid has won acclaim for her autobiographical novels *Annie John* and *Lucy*. These works focus on the complex relationship between a mother and daughter and how it changes, sometimes painfully.

"A Walk to the Jetty" is the conclusion to *Annie John*. It describes the narrator's last walk through her childhood world, as she prepares to leave her native island.

◆ Build Vocabulary

LATIN WORD ROOTS: *-stup-*

In "A Walk to the Jetty," the main character shakes herself as if waking herself "out of a *stupor*." The word *stupor* contains the Latin root *-stup-*, which means "to be stunned or amazed." Knowing this meaning, you can figure out that *stupor* means "a state in which the mind is stunned."

loomed
apprenticed
raked
stupor

WORD BANK

As you read the excerpt from "A Walk to the Jetty," you will encounter the words on this list. Each word is defined on the page where it first appears. Preview the list before you read.

◆ Build Grammar Skills

CLAUSES

Clauses are groups of words with both a subject and a verb. An **independent clause** can stand by itself as a sentence, and a sentence can contain more than one independent clause. A **subordinate clause** cannot stand alone. It must be linked with an independent clause to form a sentence.

Kincaid uses both types of clauses:

subordinate clause   independent clause

    S   V   S   V

When we were all on board, the launch headed out to sea.

from A Walk to the Jetty

◆ *Literature and Your Life*

CONNECT YOUR EXPERIENCE

One day you might move away from home to go to college, join the military, or live on your own. Preparing to leave, you may be flooded with memories. A little keepsake may recall a store that your family often visited. A battered volleyball may remind you of a field where you played with friends.

The teenage girl in this story is about to leave her island home, and her walk to the harbor is along a road of bittersweet memories.

Journal Writing Jot down some of the things you would miss most if you were leaving home.

THEMATIC FOCUS: DARING DECISIONS

On the verge of being an adult, the young woman in this story leaves her home and says goodbye to her childhood self.

◆ Background for Understanding

HISTORY

Antigua is the island home that Annie John, the main character in this story, is leaving. It is also the place where the author herself grew up. Antigua became a British colony in the seventeenth century and won its independence in 1981. As a result of the long-term British presence on the island, Antiguans speak English, use the British monetary system, and play British games such as cricket.

Early on, the British discovered that the island's tropical climate was ideal for growing sugar cane. Until 1834 when they abolished slavery, the British brought enslaved Africans to work on the island's sugar plantations. Most Antiguans, like Annie John and the author herself, are descendants of these Africans.

◆ Literary Focus

FLASHBACK

A **flashback** is a section of a literary work that interrupts the sequence of events to relate an event from an earlier time. Writers often use flashbacks to show what motivates a character or to reveal something about a character's past in a dramatic way.

In this story, you learn about Annie John's childhood through a series of flashbacks triggered by familiar sights as she walks through town. These flashbacks hint at the reasons for Annie's departure.

◆ Reading Strategy

DRAW INFERENCES

As you read a story, you can **draw inferences**—reach conclusions—about characters based on their speech, thoughts, and actions. These inferences help you better understand who the characters are and why they behave as they do.

In "A Walk to the Jetty," characters' present actions and flashbacks can serve as evidence in the text for inferences you draw. At the beginning of the story, for example, a flashback shows you how proud Annie's mother was when her five-year-old daughter went on an errand alone. From this detail, you can infer that Annie and her mother were very close.

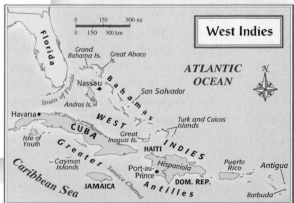

from A Walk to the Jetty

from Annie John

Jamaica Kincaid

My mother had arranged with a stevedore[1] to take my trunk to the jetty ahead of me. At ten o'clock on the dot, I was dressed, and we set off for the jetty. An hour after that, I would board a launch that would take me out to sea, where I then would board the ship. Starting out, as if for old time's sake and without giving it a thought, we lined up in the old way: I walking between my mother and my father. I loomed way above my father and could see the top of his head. We must have made a strange sight: a grown girl all dressed up in the middle of a morning, in the middle of the week, walking in step in the middle between her two parents, for people we didn't know stared at us. It was all of half an hour's walk from our house to the jetty, but I was passing through most of the years of my life. We passed by the house where Miss Dulcie, the seamstress that I had been apprenticed to for a time, lived, and just as I was passing by, a wave of bad feeling for her came over me, because I suddenly remembered that the months I spent with her all she had me do was sweep the floor, which was always full of threads and pins and needles, and I never seemed to sweep it clean enough to please her. Then she would send me to the store to buy buttons or thread, though I was only allowed to do this if I was given a sample of the button or thread, and then she would find fault even though they were an exact match of the samples she had given me. And all the while she said to me, "A girl like you will never learn to sew properly, you know." At the time, I don't suppose I minded it, because it was customary to treat the first-year apprentice with such scorn, but now I placed on the dustheap of my life Miss Dulcie and everything that I had had to do with her.

◆ **Reading Strategy**
How does this first reminiscence of childhood help you infer why Annie might be leaving the island?

◆ **Build Vocabulary**

loomed (lōōmd) v.: Appeared in a large or threatening form

apprenticed (ə pren´ tist) v.: Assigned to work a specified length of time in a craft or trade in return for instruction

---

1. **stevedore** (stē´ və dôr) n.: Person whose job is loading and unloading ships.

San Antonio de Oriente (detail), José Antonio Velásquez. Collection of the Art Museum of the Americas, Organization of American States

▲ **Critical Viewing** In what ways does this picture evoke a small-town feel? **[Interpret]**

We were soon on the road that I had taken to school, to church, to Sunday school, to choir practice, to Brownie meetings, to Girl Guide meetings, to meet a friend. I was five years old when I first walked on this road unaccompanied by someone to hold my hand. My mother had placed three pennies in my little basket, which was a duplicate of her bigger basket, and sent me to the chemist's shop to buy a pennyworth of senna leaves, a pennyworth of eucalyptus leaves, and a pennyworth of camphor.[2] She then instructed me on what side of the road to walk, where to make a turn, where to cross, how to look carefully before I crossed, and if I met anyone that I knew to politely pass greetings and keep on my way. I was wearing a freshly ironed yellow dress that had printed on it scenes of acrobats flying through the air and swinging on a trapeze. I had just had a bath, and after it, instead of powdering me with my baby-smelling talcum powder, my mother had, as a special favor, let me use her own talcum powder, which smelled quite perfumy and came in a can that had painted on it people going out to dinner in nineteenth-century London and was called Mazie. How it pleased me to walk out the door and bend my head down to sniff at myself and see that I smelled just like my mother. I went to the chemist's shop, and he had to come from behind the counter and bend down to hear what it was that I wanted to buy, my voice was so little and timid then. I went back just the way I had come, and when I walked into the yard and presented my basket with its three packages to my mother, her eyes filled with tears and she swooped me up and held me high in the air and said that I was wonderful and good

> ◆ **Literary Focus**
> What details in this flashback help you to picture in your mind Annie's first walk?

and that there would never be anybody better. If I had just conquered Persia, she couldn't have been more proud of me.

We passed by our church—the church in which I had been christened and received[3] and had sung in the junior choir. We passed by a house in which a girl I used to like and was sure I couldn't live without had lived. Once, when she had mumps, I went to visit her against my mother's wishes, and we sat on her bed and ate the cure of roasted, buttered sweet potatoes that had been placed on her swollen jaws, held there by a piece of white cloth. I don't know how, but my mother found out about it, and I don't know how, but she put an end to our friendship. Shortly after, the girl moved with her family across the sea to somewhere else. We passed the doll store, where I would go with my mother when I was little and point out the doll I wanted that year for Christmas. We passed the store where I bought the much-fought-over shoes I wore to church to be received in. We passed the bank. On my sixth birthday, I was given, among other things, the present of a sixpence.[4] My mother and I then went to this bank, and with the sixpence I opened my own savings account. I was given a little gray book with my name in big letters on it, and in the balance column it said "6d." Every Saturday morning after that, I was given a sixpence—later a shilling, and later a two-and-sixpence piece—and I would take it to the bank for deposit. I had never been allowed to withdraw even a farthing from my bank account until just a few weeks before I was to leave; then the whole account was closed out, and I received from the bank the sum of six pounds ten shillings and two and a half pence.

---

2. **chemist's shop . . . camphor** (kam′ fər): The first phrase is a British term for a pharmacy. The items mentioned are small amounts of plant matter to be used in remedies.

3. **received** *v.*: Accepted into the congregation as a mature Christian.

4. **sixpence** *n.*: A monetary unit in the British commonwealth, worth six pennies (not of the same value as the pennies in United States currency). A shilling is worth two sixpence, a two-and-sixpence is two and one-half shillings, that is, two shillings and one sixpence. A pound is worth twenty shillings. A farthing is a "fourthing": one fourth of a penny.

We passed the office of the doctor who told my mother three times that I did not need glasses, that if my eyes were feeling weak a glass of carrot juice a day would make them strong again. This happened when I was eight. And so every day at recess I would run to my school gate and meet my mother, who was waiting for me with a glass of juice from carrots she had just grated and then squeezed, and I would drink it and then run back to meet my chums. I knew there was nothing at all wrong with my eyes, but I had recently read a story in *The Schoolgirl's Own Annual* in which the heroine, a girl a few years older than I was then, cut such a figure to my mind with the way she was always adjusting her small, round, horn-rimmed glasses that I felt I must have a pair exactly like them. When it became clear that I didn't need glasses, I began to complain about the glare of the sun being too much for my eyes, and I walked around with my hands shielding them—especially in my mother's presence. My mother then bought for me a pair of sunglasses with the exact horn-rimmed frames I wanted, and how I enjoyed the gestures of blowing on the lenses, wiping them with the hem of my uniform, adjusting the glasses when they slipped down my nose, and just removing them from their case and putting them on. In three weeks, I grew tired of them and they found a nice resting place in a drawer, along with some other things that at one time or another I couldn't live without.

We passed the store that sold only grooming aids, all imported from England. This store had in it a large porcelain dog—white, with black spots all over and a red ribbon of satin tied around its neck. The dog sat in front of a white porcelain bowl that was always filled with fresh water, and it sat in such a way that it looked as if it had just taken a long drink. When I was a small child, I would ask my mother, if ever we were near this store, to please take me to see the dog, and I would stand in front of it, bent over slightly, my hands resting on my knees, and stare at it and stare at it. I

Port de la Saline, Haiti, Lois Mailou Jones

▲ **Critical Viewing** The people in this painting are setting out on unique adventures. Explain how you can be surrounded by people sharing a similar experience and yet still be alone. **[Analyze]**

thought this dog more beautiful and more real than any actual dog I had ever seen or any actual dog I would ever see. I must have outgrown my interest in the dog, for when it disappeared I never asked what became of it. We passed the library, and if there was anything on this walk that I might have wept over leaving, this most surely would have been the thing. My mother had been a member of the library long before I was born. And since she took me everywhere with her when I was quite little, when she went to the library she took me along there, too. I would sit in her lap very quietly as she read books that she did not want to take home with her. I could not read the words yet, but just the way they looked on the page was interesting to me. Once, a book she was reading had a large picture of a man in it, and when I asked her who he was she told me that he was Louis Pasteur[5] and that the book was about his life. It stuck in my mind, because she said it was because of him that she boiled my milk to purify it before I was allowed to drink it, that it was his idea, and that that was why the process was called pasteurization. One of the things I had put away in my mother's old trunk in which she kept all my childhood things was my library card. At that moment, I owed sevenpence in overdue fees.

◆ **Reading Strategy**
Infer why the library is such an important part of Annie's childhood.

As I passed by all these places, it was as if I were in a dream, for I didn't notice the people coming and going in and out of them, I didn't feel my feet touch ground, I didn't even feel my own body—I just saw these places as if they were hanging in the air, not having top or bottom, and as if I had gone in and out of them all in the same moment. The sun was bright; the sky was blue and just above my head. We then arrived at the jetty.

---

5. **Louis Pasteur** (Pas tʉr´) (1822–1895): The French chemist and bacteriologist who developed the process (pasteurization) for using heat to kill disease-causing bacteria in milk.

My heart now beat fast, and no matter how hard I tried, I couldn't keep my mouth from falling open and my nostrils from spreading to the ends of my face. My old fear of slipping between the boards of the jetty and falling into the dark-green water where the dark-green eels lived came over me. When my father's stomach started to go bad, the doctor had recommended a walk every evening right after he ate his dinner. Sometimes he would take me with him. When he took me with him, we usually went to the jetty, and there he would sit and talk to the night watchman about cricket[6] or some other thing that didn't interest me, because it was not personal; they didn't talk about their wives, or their children, or their parents, or about any of their likes and dislikes. They talked about things in such a strange way, and I didn't see what they found funny, but sometimes they made each other laugh so much that their guffaws would bound out to sea and send back an echo. I was always sorry when we got to the jetty and saw that the night watchman on duty was the one he enjoyed speaking to; it was like being locked up in a book filled with numbers and diagrams and what-ifs. For the thing about not being able to understand and enjoy what they were saying was I had nothing to take my mind off my fear of slipping in between the boards of the jetty.

Now, too, I had nothing to take my mind off what was happening to me. My mother and my father—I was leaving them forever. My home on an island—I was leaving it forever. What to make of everything? I felt a familiar hollow space inside. I felt I was being held down against my will. I felt I was burning up from head to toe. I felt that someone was tearing me up into little pieces and soon I would be able to see all the little pieces as they floated out into nothing in the deep blue sea. I didn't know whether to laugh or cry. I could see that it would be

---

6. **cricket** *n.*: A British game, similar to baseball, but played with a flat bat and eleven players on each team.

better not to think too clearly about any one thing. The launch was being made ready to take me, along with some other passengers, out to the ship that was anchored in the sea. My father paid our fares, and we joined a line of people waiting to board. My mother checked my bag to make sure that I had my passport, the money she had given me, and a sheet of paper placed between some pages in my Bible on which were written the names of the relatives—people I had not known existed—with whom I would live in England. Across from the jetty was a wharf, and some stevedores were loading and unloading barges. I don't know why seeing that struck me so, but suddenly a wave of strong feeling came over me, and my heart swelled with a great gladness as the words "I shall never see this again" spilled out inside me. But then, just as quickly, my heart shriveled up and the words "I shall never see this again" stabbed at me. I don't know what stopped me from falling in a heap at my parents' feet.

When we were all on board, the launch headed out to sea. Away from the jetty, the water became the customary blue, and the launch left a wide path in it that looked like a road. I passed by sounds and smells that were so familiar that I had long ago stopped paying any attention to them. But now here they were, and the ever-present "I shall never see this again" bobbed up and down inside me. There was the sound of the seagull diving down into the water and coming up with something silverish in its mouth. There was the smell of the sea and the sight of small pieces of rubbish floating around in it. There were boats filled with fishermen coming in early. There was the sound of their voices as they shouted greetings to each other. There was the hot sun, there was the blue sea, there was the blue sky. Not very far away, there was the white sand of the shore, with the run-down houses all crowded in next to each other, for in some places only poor people lived near the shore. I was seated in the launch between my parents, and when I realized that I was

gripping their hands tightly I glanced quickly to see if they were looking at me with scorn, for I felt sure that they must have known of my never-see-this-again feelings. But instead my father kissed me on the forehead and my mother kissed me on the mouth, and they both gave over their hands to me, so that I could grip them as much as I wanted. I was on the verge of feeling that it had all been a mistake, but I remembered that I wasn't a child anymore, and that now when I made up my mind about something I had to see it through. At that moment, we came to the ship, and that was that.

The goodbyes had to be quick, the captain said. My mother introduced herself to him and then introduced me. She told him to keep an eye on me, for I had never gone this far away from home on my own. She gave him a letter to pass on to the captain of the next ship that I would board in Barbados.[7] They walked me to my cabin, a small space that I would share with someone else—a woman I did not know. I had never before slept in a room with someone I did not know. My father kissed me goodbye and told me to be good and to write home often. After he said this, he looked at me, then looked at the floor and swung his left foot, then looked at me again. I could see that he wanted to say something else, something that he had never said to me before, but then he just turned and walked away. My mother said, "Well," and then she threw her arms around me. Big tears streamed down her face, and it must have been that—for I could not bear to see my mother cry—which started me crying, too. She then tightened

◆ **Reading Strategy**
What can you infer about Annie's relationship with her mother based on the fact that she cannot breathe because her mother squeezes her so tightly?

7. **Barbados** (bär bā´ dōs): The easternmost island in the West Indies; southeast of Antigua.

her arms around me and held me to her close, so that I felt that I couldn't breathe. With that, my tears dried up and I was suddenly on my guard. "What does she want now?" I said to myself. Still holding me close to her, she said, in a voice that <u>raked</u> across my skin, "It doesn't matter what you do or where you go, I'll always be your mother and this will always be your home."

I dragged myself away from her and backed off a little, and then I shook myself, as if to wake myself out of a <u>stupor</u>. We looked at each other for a long time with smiles on our faces, but I know the opposite of that was in my heart. As if responding to some invisible cue, we both said, at the very same moment, "Well." Then my mother turned around and walked out the cabin door. I stood there for I don't know how long, and then I remembered that it was customary to stand on deck and wave to your relatives who were returning to shore. From the deck, I could not see my father, but I could see my mother facing the ship, her eyes searching to pick me out. I removed from my bag a red cotton handkerchief that she had earlier given me for this purpose, and I waved it wildly in the air. Recognizing me immediately, she waved back just as wildly, and we continued to do this until she became just a dot in the matchbox-size launch swallowed up in the big blue sea.

I went back to my cabin and lay down on my berth. Everything trembled as if it had a spring at its very center. I could hear the small waves lap-lapping around the ship. They made an unexpected sound, as if a vessel filled with liquid had been placed on its side and now was slowly emptying out.

◆ Build Vocabulary

raked (rākd) *v.*: Scratched or scraped, as with a rake

stupor (stōō´ per) *n.*: Mental dullness, as if drugged

Guide for Responding

◆ Literature and Your Life

Reader's Response Do you admire Annie for leaving home? Why or why not?

Thematic Focus There are many quieter ways of showing independence than a dramatic departure from home. Tell about a quiet way in which you have shown greater maturity and independence.

Timeline On a timeline showing the next five years, indicate some of the steps you will take to achieve an important goal.

☑ Check Your Comprehension

1. Identify four of the places that remind Annie of episodes from her childhood.
2. Briefly summarize the memory that each of these places calls up.
3. What are Annie's feelings about leaving home?
4. Describe how her mother and father say goodbye.

Beyond Literature

Geography Connection

The Landscape and Climate of Antigua White sand beaches, spectacular coral reefs, and an average temperature of 80 degrees make Antigua a popular vacation spot. There are 365 beaches on Antigua—one for each day of the year! Antigua is about 14 miles long and 11 miles wide, covering 108 square miles. With an average rainfall of only 40 inches per year, Antigua is one of the sunniest eastern Caribbean islands. While this is welcome news for tourists, for the people who live on Antigua year-round, droughts can be devastating to their property and livelihood. Why do you think islands are such popular tourist spots?

Guide for Responding (continued)

◆ Critical Thinking

INTERPRET
1. In what way is Annie walking through time as well as through space? **[Infer]**
2. Why does Annie reexperience her old fear of falling through the boards of the jetty? **[Infer]**
3. Compare Annie's relationship with her father with the one she has with her mother. **[Compare and Contrast]**
4. Describe Annie's response to leaving the island. **[Interpret]**

APPLY
5. Will Annie be successful in her new life? Why or why not? **[Hypothesize]**

EXTEND
6. Although Annie disliked it, an apprentice situation could have advantages. Name three trades that could be best learned this way. **[Career Link]**

◆ Reading Strategy

DRAW INFERENCES
Annie's mother hugs Annie so tightly that she can hardly breathe. From this painful embrace and Annie's response to it, you can **infer** that Annie sometimes feels trapped by her mother.

From the following text details, draw inferences about Annie's relationship with her father.
1. His conversation with the watchman didn't interest her "because it was not personal."
2. As they part, he wants "to say . . . something he had never said . . . before," but then he walks away.

◆ Literary Focus

FLASHBACK
This story is told mainly through **flashbacks,** journeys back into time. These flashbacks help you understand how Annie developed, but their precise details also make the past come alive.
1. Find two other flashbacks and explain how the author uses precise details to make them vivid.
2. What do the flashbacks suggest about Annie's reasons for leaving home?

◆ Build Vocabulary

USING THE LATIN ROOT *-stup-*
Knowing that *-stup-* means "to be stunned or amazed," choose the letter of the best synonym for each of the numbered words containing *-stup-*.
1. stupefy: (a) entertain, (b) numb, (c) revive
2. stupendous: (a) astonishing, (b) excessive, (c) ridiculous
3. stupefaction: (a) alertness, (b) satisfaction, (c) bewilderment

USING THE WORD BANK: Sentence Completions
On your paper, complete each sentence with the most appropriate word from the Word Bank:
1. Annie had been ____?____ to a rude and stern seamstress.
2. Annie ____?____ above her father and could see the top of his head.
3. Annie complained that her mother's voice ____?____ across her skin.
4. For a moment, staring at her mother, Annie was in a ____?____.

◆ Build Grammar Skills

CLAUSES
A **clause** is a group of words that contains both a subject and a verb. An **independent clause** can stand alone as a sentence, but a **subordinate clause** cannot.

Practice Identify the independent and subordinate clauses in these sentences from the story.
1. If I had just conquered Persia, she couldn't have been more proud of me.
2. We passed the bank.
3. We then arrived at the jetty.
4. My father paid our fares, and we joined a line of people waiting to board.
5. She told him to keep an eye on me, for I had never gone this far away from home on my own.

Writing Application Write a paragraph describing places that are special to you. Include at least three sentences that contain subordinate clauses.

Build Your Portfolio

 ## Idea Bank

Writing

1. **Annie's Packing List** Create a list of items that Annie might have packed for her journey to England.

2. **Letter of Introduction** As Annie John, write a letter of introduction to an English family or business, offering a brief biography and a description of your skills. **[Career Link]**

3. **Description of Antigua for the Internet** Write a description of Antigua for an Internet Home Page. Describe Antigua's attractions so that Internet surfers will want to visit the island. **[Media Link; Social Studies Link]**

Speaking, Listening, and Viewing

4. **Telephone Interview** Like Annie John, you may soon be making a trip on your own. Interview a local travel agent by phone to learn some of the dos and don'ts for the teenage traveler.

5. **Persuasive Speech** One way in which teenagers can travel abroad is to participate in exchange programs. Write a persuasive speech that convinces listeners that your school should participate in such a program. **[Social Studies Link]**

Researching and Representing

6. **The Statistics of a Decision** Create a chart that shows the numbers of high-school graduates who move out of state to pursue education or job opportunities. **[Social Studies Link; Math Link]**

7. **Map of Annie's Walk** Using details from the story and your own imagination, create a map showing Annie's walk to the jetty. Include all the landmarks mentioned in the story. **[Art Link]**

Online Activity www.phlit.phschool.com

 ## Guided Writing Lesson

How-to Manual for New Students

Write a how-to manual for new students in your school. Include tips, advice, and amusing anecdotes. As you cover everything from lunchroom behavior to test taking, be sure to explain clearly any procedures new students must follow.

Writing Skills Focus: Clear Explanation of Procedures

Problem-solution essays and informative speeches also require a clear **explanation of procedures.** Even short stories may contain such explanations, as this example from "A Walk to the Jetty" proves.

Model From the Story

My mother . . . instructed me on what side of the road to walk, where to make a turn, where to cross, how to look carefully before I crossed, and if I met anyone that I knew to politely pass greetings and keep on my way.

Your explanation won't be designed for a five-year-old, but like this one it will contain all the necessary details. Also, you can develop **your explanation** at every stage of the writing process.

Prewriting Brainstorm for items to include in your how-to manual. Then identify the items you will actually include. After identifying the procedures you'll explain, break them down into steps.

Drafting Begin by drafting the most important procedures and explain them as clearly as possible. For example, don't just say, "Join a team." Give the steps involved in trying out for a team.

Revising Have a classmate read your explanations of procedures and determine whether or not they're clear and concise. Where appropriate, add or clarify steps in a procedure to ensure that your manual will be useful to a newcomer.

PART 2 *Dangerous Destinies*

Hidden Treasures, 1969, Consuelo González Amézcua

Guide for Reading

Elie Wiesel *(1928–   )*

Elie Wiesel (el′ ē wi zel′) grew up in the small Rumanian town of Sighet, where his family were members of a devout Jewish community. At the height of World War II, when Germany had overrun the area, he and the rest of Sighet's Jews were shipped off to the Auschwitz concentration camp in Poland. There, Elie was separated from the females in his family; he would never see his mother or youngest sister again.

Remaining with his father, he eventually wound up in the Buchenwald concentration camp in Germany, where his father died of starvation and disease just days before the Americans liberated the camp.

Witness to Horror After the war, Wiesel lived with other Jewish orphans in France. There, he attended school and later found work as a journalist. Although he was convinced that he had survived the Nazi death camps in order to "bear witness" to the horrors, he waited nearly a decade to relate his experiences. "I didn't want to use the wrong words," he recalled. "I was afraid that words might betray it." In 1954, French author Francois Mauriac persuaded Wiesel to tell of the nightmare he had experienced. The result was his internationally famous *Night,* published in English in 1960.

Speaking Out By this time, Wiesel had settled in the United States and was working for a Yiddish-language newspaper. (Yiddish, a language derived from German, is spoken by East European Jews and their descendants in other countries.) He also continued to publish books about the Nazi persecution of Jews and the role of the Jewish faith in the modern world. Yet, Wiesel has never confined his efforts to Jewish issues alone. Over the decades he has spoken out against apartheid in South Africa, the atrocities committed in Cambodia, ethnic cleansing in Bosnia, and any other inhumanity that reminded him of his experiences at the hands of the Nazis. As a result of his humanitarian efforts, Wiesel was awarded the Nobel Peace Prize in 1986.

◆ Build Vocabulary

LATIN WORD ROOTS: *-numer-*

This translation of *Night* includes the word *innumerable,* which contains the Latin root *-numer-,* meaning "number." In *innumerable, -numer-* is combined with the prefix *in-,* meaning "not," and the suffix *-able,* meaning "capable of being." *Innumerable* literally means "not capable of being numbered" or "too many to count."

plaintive
beseeching
livid
spasmodically
liquidated
innumerable
deportees

WORD BANK

As you read the selection, you will encounter the words on this list. Each word is defined on the page where it first appears. Preview the list before you read.

◆ Build Grammar Skills

ABSOLUTE PHRASES

Night uses several **absolute phrases** to provide information concisely. These phrases, which contain a noun or a pronoun usually modified by a participle or a participial phrase, have no grammatical relationship to the rest of the sentence.

In other words, they do not serve as subjects, objects, or complements; they simply add information in a shorthand way. In the following sentence, the absolute phrase is in italics and the participle, which is understood, is in brackets.

My father grew weaker day by day, *his gaze [being] veiled.*

Notice how economically this absolute phrase adds a precise detail to the description of the narrator's father.

from Night

◆ *Literature and Your Life*

CONNECT YOUR EXPERIENCE

Think about the experiences and emotions that you associate with the night. In *Night*, Elie Wiesel describes his experiences in a Nazi concentration camp during World War II.

As you read about his experiences, consider what he implies about his experiences by entitling his story *Night*.

THEMATIC FOCUS: DANGEROUS DESTINIES

As you read, ask yourself: Besides death, what other dangers does Wiesel face in the concentration camp?

◆ Background for Understanding

HISTORY

In *Night* and other writings, Wiesel gives the world a firsthand account of the Holocaust—the systematic persecution and murder of Jews and others by Germany's Nazi party under the leadership of Adolph Hitler.

During World War II (1939–1945), the Nazi leaders devised a plan that called for the destruction of every Jew in the lands Germany had conquered. Special forces rounded up Jews and shot them or shipped them to concentration camps like Auschwitz and Buchenwald, where those not strong enough to work were gassed to death, and then burned in buildings called "crematoriums." Others died of starvation, disease, awful living conditions, or during forced marches through the snow. By the war's end, the Nazis had killed about 6 million Jews—nearly two thirds of Europe's entire Jewish population.

◆ Literary Focus

THEME AND HISTORICAL BACKGROUND

The **theme** of a work is its central meaning, the general comment that it makes about life and values. In *Night*, the theme is strongly tied to its **historical background** and comments on the Holocaust by showing us what it was like for those who suffered through it and those who perished in its grip.

As you read the selection from *Night*, identify the message Weisel is trying to convey. Consider how the theme relates both to the historical context of the piece and to other events in history.

◆ Reading Strategy

USE CONTEXT CLUES

When you comes across an unfamiliar word in your reading, try figuring out its meaning from its **context,** or surroundings. Consider this paragraph from *Night*:

> The officer came up to him and shouted at him to be quiet. But my father did not hear him. He went on calling me. The officer dealt him a violent blow to the head with his *truncheon*.

Truncheon may be an unfamiliar word, but the context indicates that it is something an officer may use to deal a violent blow on the head. From the clues in the context, you can figure out that a truncheon must be something similar to a police officer's nightstick or baton.

As you read the selection from *Night*, list unfamiliar words on a chart like the one below, and use the context clues to figure out their likely meaning.

Unfamiliar Word	Likely Meaning

from *Night*

Elie Wiesel
Translated by Stella Rodway

That same evening, we reached our destination.

It was late at night. The guards came to unload us. The dead were abandoned in the train. Only those who could still stand were able to get out.

Meir Katz stayed in the train. The last day had been the most murderous. A hundred of us had got into the wagon. A dozen of us got out—among them, my father and I.

We had arrived at Buchenwald.[1]

At the gate of the camp, SS[2] officers were waiting for us. They counted us. Then we were directed to the assembly place. Orders were given us through loudspeakers:

"Form fives!" "Form groups of a hundred!" "Five paces forward!"

I held onto my father's hand—the old, familiar fear: not to lose him.

Right next to us the high chimney of the crematory oven[3] rose up. It no longer made any impression on us. It scarcely attracted our attention.

An established inmate of Buchenwald told us that we should have a shower and then we could go into the blocks. The idea of having a hot bath fascinated me. My father was silent. He was breathing heavily beside me.

"Father," I said. "Only another moment more. Soon we can lie down—in a bed. You can rest. . . ."

He did not answer. I was so exhausted myself that his silence left me indifferent. My only wish was to take a bath as quickly as possible and lie down in a bed.

But it was not easy to reach the showers.

---

1. Buchenwald: (boook´ 'n wôld´): Village in Germany that was the site of a Nazi concentration camp and extermination center.
2. SS: Quasi-military unit of the Nazi party, used as a special police.

3. crematory oven: Large oven in which the corpses of Holocaust victims were burned. In some cases, victims were burned while still alive.

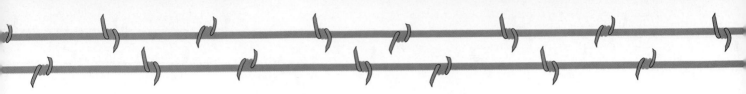

Hundreds of prisoners were crowding there. The guards were unable to keep any order. They struck out right and left with no apparent result. Others, without the strength to push or even to stand up, had sat down in the snow. My father wanted to do the same. He groaned.

"I can't go on. . . . This is the end. . . . I'm going to die here. . . ."

He dragged me toward a hillock of snow from which emerged human shapes and ragged pieces of blanket.

"Leave me," he said to me. "I can't go on. . . . Have mercy on me. . . . I'll wait here until we can get into the baths. . . . You can come and find me."

I could have wept with rage. Having lived through so much, suffered so much, could I leave my father to die now? Now, when we could have a good hot bath and lie down?

"Father!" I screamed. "Father! Get up from here! Immediately! You're killing yourself. . . ."

I seized him by the arm. He continued to groan.

"Don't shout, son. . . . Take pity on your old father. . . . Leave me to rest here. . . . Just for a bit, I'm so tired . . . at the end of my strength. . . ."

▲ **Critical Viewing** The band on this boy's arm reads "Buchenwald," the name of the concentration camp that Wiesel describes. Are you surprised that such a young boy would be sent there? Why or why not? **[Relate]**

He had become like a child, weak, timid, vulnerable.

"Father," I said. "You can't stay here."

I showed him the corpses all around him; they too had wanted to rest here.

"I can see them, son. I can see them all right. Let them sleep. It's so long since they closed their eyes. . . . They are exhausted . . . exhausted. . . ."

His voice was tender.

I yelled against the wind:

"They'll never wake again! Never! Don't you understand?"

For a long time this argument went on. I felt that I was not arguing with him, but with death itself, with the death that he had already chosen.

The sirens began to wail. An alert. The lights went out throughout the camp. The guards drove us toward the blocks. In a flash, there was no one left on the assembly place. We were only too glad not to have had to stay outside longer in the icy wind. We let ourselves sink down onto the planks. The beds were in several tiers. The cauldrons of soup at the entrance attracted no one. To sleep, that was all that mattered.

It was daytime when I awoke. And then I remembered that I had a father. Since the alert, I had followed the crowd without troubling about

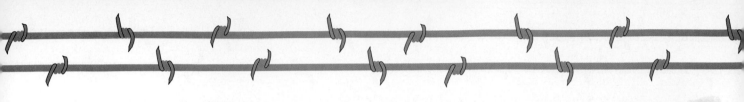

▶ Critical
Viewing
What does
this photo-
graph reveal
about the
conditions
under which
Wiesel and
others lived
while interned
in concentra-
tion camps?
[Analyze]

him. I had known that he was at the end, on the brink of death, and yet I had abandoned him.

I went to look for him.

But at the same moment this thought came into my mind: "Don't let me find him! If only I could get rid of this dead weight, so that I could use all my strength to struggle for my own survival, and only worry about myself." Immediately I felt ashamed of myself, ashamed forever.

I walked for hours without finding him. Then I came to the block where they were giving out black "coffee." The men were lining up and fighting.

A <u>plaintive</u>, <u>beseeching</u> voice caught me in the spine:

"Eliezer . . . my son . . . bring me . . . a drop of coffee. . . ."

I ran to him.

"Father! I've been looking for you for so long. . . . Where were you? Did you sleep? . . . How do you feel?"

He was burning with fever. Like a wild beast, I cleared a way for myself to the coffee cauldron. And I managed to carry back a cupful. I had a sip. The rest was for him. I can't forget the light of thankfulness in his eyes while he gulped it down—an animal gratitude. With those few gulps of hot water, I probably brought him more satisfaction than I had done during my whole childhood.

He was lying on a plank, <u>livid</u>, his lips pale and

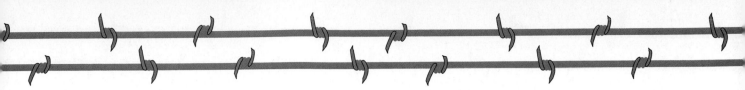

dried up, shaken by tremors. I could not stay by him for long. Orders had been given to clear the place for cleaning. Only the sick could stay.

We stayed outside for five hours. Soup was given out. As soon as we were allowed to go back to the blocks, I ran to my father.

"Have you had anything to eat?"

"No."

"Why not?"

"They didn't give us anything . . . they said that if we were ill we should die soon anyway and it would be a pity to waste the food. I can't go on any more. . . ."

I gave him what was left of my soup. But it was with a heavy heart. I felt that I was giving it up to him against my will. No better than Rabbi Eliahou's son had I withstood the test.

He grew weaker day by day, his gaze veiled, his face the color of dead leaves. On the third day after our arrival at Buchenwald, everyone had to go to the showers. Even the sick, who had to go through last.

On the way back from the baths, we had to wait outside for a long time. They had not yet finished cleaning the blocks.

Seeing my father in the distance, I ran to meet him. He went by me like a ghost, passed me without stopping, without looking at me. I called to him. He did not come back. I ran after him:

"Father, where are you running to?"

He looked at me for a moment, and his gaze was distant, visionary; it was the face of someone else. A moment only and on he ran again.

Struck down with dysentery,[4] my father lay in his bunk, five other invalids with him. I sat by his side, watching him, not daring to believe that he could escape death again. Nevertheless, I did all I could to give him hope.

Suddenly, he raised himself on his bunk and put his feverish lips to my ear:

"Eliezer . . . I must tell you where to find the gold and the money I buried . . . in the cellar. . . . You know. . . ."

He began to talk faster and faster, as though he were afraid he would not have time to tell me. I tried to explain to him that this was not the end, that we would go back to the house together, but he would not listen to me. He could no longer listen to me. He was exhausted. A trickle of saliva, mingled with blood, was running from between his lips. He had closed his eyes. His breath was coming in gasps.

For a ration of bread, I managed to change beds with a prisoner in my father's bunk. In the afternoon the doctor came. I went and told him that my father was very ill.

"Bring him here!"

I explained that he could not stand up. But the doctor refused to listen to anything. Somehow, I brought my father to him. He stared at him, then questioned him in a clipped voice:

"What do you want?"

"My father's ill," I answered for him. "Dysentery . . ."

"Dysentery? That's not my business. I'm a surgeon. Go on! Make room for the others."

Protests did no good.

"I can't go on, son. . . . Take me back to my bunk. . . ."

I took him back and helped him to lie down. He was shivering.

"Try and sleep a bit, father. Try to go to sleep. . . ."

His breathing was labored, thick. He kept his eyes shut. Yet I was convinced that he could see everything, that now he could see the truth in all things.

Another doctor came to the block. But my father would not get up. He knew that it was useless.

Besides, this doctor had only come to finish off the sick. I could hear him shouting at them that they were lazy and just wanted to stay in

---

4. **dysentery:** (dis´ ən ter´ ē) *n.*: Disease of the intestines.

◆ **Build Vocabulary**

plaintive (plān´ tiv) *adj.*: Sad; mournful

beseeching (bē sēch´ ing) *adj.*: Pleading

livid (liv´ id) *adj.*: Bruised; grayish blue or pale

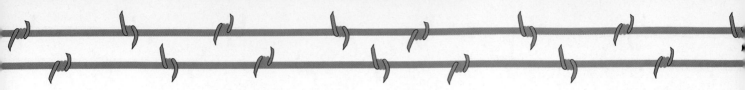

bed. I felt like leaping at his throat, strangling him. But I no longer had the courage or the strength. I was riveted to my father's deathbed. My hands hurt, I was clenching them so hard. Oh, to strangle the doctor and the others! To burn the whole world! My father's murderers! But the cry stayed in my throat.

When I came back from the bread distribution, I found my father weeping like a child.

"Son, they keep hitting me!"

"Who?"

I thought he was delirious.

"Him, the Frenchman . . . and the Pole . . . they were hitting me."

Another wound to the heart, another hate, another reason for living lost.

"Eliezer . . . Eliezer . . . tell them not to hit me. . . . I haven't done anything. . . . Why do they keep hitting me?"

I began to abuse his neighbors. They laughed at me. I promised them bread, soup. They laughed. Then they got angry; they could not stand my father any longer, they said, because he was now unable to drag himself outside to relieve himself.

The following day he complained that they had taken his ration of bread.

"While you were asleep?"

"No. I wasn't asleep. They jumped on top of me. They snatched my bread . . . and they hit me . . . again. . . . I can't stand any more, son . . . a drop of water. . . ."

I knew that he must not drink. But he pleaded with me for so long that I gave in. Water was the worst poison he could have, but what else could I do for him? With water, without water, it would all be over soon anyway. . . .

"You, at least, have some mercy on me. . . ."

Have mercy on him! I, his only son!

A week went by like this.

"This is your father, isn't it?" asked the head of the block.

"Yes."

"He's very ill."

"The doctor won't do anything for him."

"The doctor *can't* do anything for him, now. And neither can you."

He put his great hairy hand on my shoulder and added:

"Listen to me, boy. Don't forget that you're in a concentration camp. Here, every man has to fight for himself and not think of anyone else. Even of his father. Here, there are no fathers, no brothers, no friends. Everyone lives and dies for himself alone. I'll give you a sound piece of advice—don't give your ration of bread and soup to your old father. There's nothing you can do for him. And you're killing yourself. Instead, you ought to be having his ration."

I listened to him without interrupting. He was right, I thought in the most secret region of my heart, but I dared not admit it. It's too late to save your old father, I said to myself. You ought to be having two rations of bread, two rations of soup. . . .

Only a fraction of a second, but I felt guilty. I ran to find a little soup to give my father. But he did not want it. All he wanted was water.

"Don't drink water . . . have some soup. . . ."

"I'm burning . . . why are you being so unkind to me, my son? Some water. . . ."

I brought him some water. Then I left the block for roll call. But I turned around and came back again. I lay down on the top bunk. Invalids were allowed to stay in the block. So I would be an invalid myself. I would not leave my father.

There was silence all round now, broken only by groans. In front of the block, the SS were giving orders. An officer passed by the beds. My father begged me:

"My son, some water. . . . I'm burning. . . . My stomach. . . ."

"Quiet, over there!" yelled the officer.

"Eliezer," went on my father, "some water. . . ."

The officer came up to him and shouted at him to be quiet. But my father did not hear him. He went on calling me. The officer dealt him a violent blow on the head with his truncheon.

I did not move. I was afraid. My body was

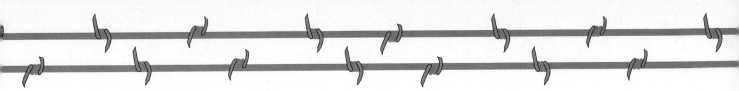

afraid of also receiving a blow.

Then my father made a rattling noise and it was my name: "Eliezer."

I could see that he was still breathing—spasmodically.

I did not move.

When I got down after roll call, I could see his lips trembling as he murmured something. Bending over him, I stayed gazing at him for over an hour, engraving into myself the picture of his blood-stained face, his shattered skull.

Then I had to go to bed. I climbed into my bunk, above my father, who was still alive. It was January 28, 1945.

I awoke on January 29 at dawn. In my father's place lay another invalid. They must have taken him away before dawn and carried him to the crematory. He may still have been breathing.

There were no prayers at his grave. No candles were lit to his memory. His last word was my name. A summons, to which I did not respond.

I did not weep, and it pained me that I could not weep. But I had no more tears. And, in the depths of my being, in the recesses of my weakened conscience, could I have searched it, I might perhaps have found something like—free at last!

I had to stay at Buchenwald until April eleventh. I have nothing to say of my life during this period. It no longer mattered. After my father's death, nothing could touch me any more.

I was transferred to the children's block, where there were six hundred of us.

The front was drawing nearer.

I spent my days in a state of total idleness. And I had but one desire—to eat. I no longer thought of my father or of my mother.

From time to time I would dream of a drop of soup, of an extra ration of soup. . . .

On April fifth, the wheel of history turned.

It was late in the afternoon. We were standing in the block, waiting for an SS man to come and count us. He was late in coming. Such a delay was unknown till then in the history of Buchenwald. Something must have happened.

Two hours later the loudspeakers sent out an order from the head of the camp: all the Jews must come to the assembly place.

This was the end! Hitler was going to keep his promise.

The children in our block went toward the place. There was nothing else we could do. Gustav, the head of the block, made this clear to us with his truncheon. But on the way we met some prisoners who whispered to us:

"Go back to your block. The Germans are going to shoot you. Go back to your block, and don't move."

We went back to our block. We learned on the way that the camp resistance organization had decided not to abandon the Jews and was going to prevent their being liquidated.

As it was late and there was great upheaval—innumerable Jews had passed themselves off as non-Jews—the head of the camp decided that a general roll call would take place the following day. Everybody would have to be present.

The roll call took place. The head of the camp announced that Buchenwald was to be liquidated. Ten blocks of deportees would be evacuated each day. From this moment, there would be no further distribution of bread and soup. And the evacuation began. Every day, several thousand prisoners went through the camp gate and never came back.

On April tenth, there were still about twenty thousand of us in the camp, including several hundred children. They decided to evacuate us all at once, right on until the evening. Afterward, they were going to blow up the camp.

◆ Build Vocabulary

spasmodically (spaz mäd´ ik lē) *adv.*: In spasms; intermittently; irregularly

liquidated (lik´ wi dāt´ id) *adj.*: Disposed of; killed

innumerable (in no͞o´ mer ə bəl) *adj.*: Countless; many

deportees (dē´ pôr tēz´) *n.*: People who are officially ordered to leave a place

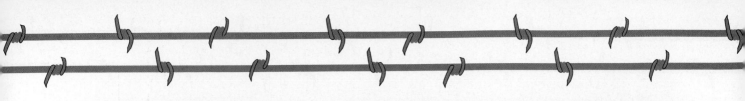

▲ **Critical Viewing** Compare and contrast the faces of these young concentration camp inmates with those of the adults on p.192 **[Compare and Contrast]**

So were massed in the huge assembly square, in rows of five, waiting to see the gate open. Suddenly, the sirens began to wail. An alert! We went back to the blocks. It was too late to evacuate us that evening. The evacuation was postponed again to the following day.

We were tormented with hunger. We had eaten nothing for six days, except a bit of grass or some potato peelings found near the kitchens.

At ten o'clock in the morning the SS scattered through the camp, moving the last victims toward the assembly places.

Then the resistance movement decided to act. Armed men suddenly rose up everywhere. Bursts of firing. Grenades exploding. We children stayed flat on the ground in the block.

The battle did not last long. Toward noon everything was quiet again. The SS had fled and the resistance had taken charge of the running of the camp.

At about six o'clock in the evening, the first American tank stood at the gates of Buchenwald.

Beyond Literature

History Connection

Remembering the Holocaust Elie Wiesel headed the United States Holocaust Memorial Council from 1980 to 1986 and was instrumental in creating the United States Holocaust Memorial Museum. The museum opened in Washington, D.C., in April 1993, honoring victims, survivors, liberators, and rescuers. In his dedication speech, Wiesel stressed the importance of remembering those who died, saying "Memory is not only a victory over time, it is also a triumph over injustice." **Question** Do you think that learning about the Holocaust by viewing displays in this museum would be more powerful than reading a survivor's account? Explain.

Guide for Responding

◆ Literature and Your Life

Reader's Response What were your feelings when Elie was liberated at the end?

Thematic Focus What dangers—physical and otherwise—do Wiesel and the other concentration camp victims face?

Questions for Research *Night* offers a grim picture of Nazi concentration camps during the Holocaust. Write one or more questions that you could research to learn more about this dark episode in human history.

☑ Check Your Comprehension

1. When the train arrives at Buchenwald, in what condition is Elie Wiesel's father?
2. What does Wiesel do for his father, and what do the others advise him to do?
3. What finally happens to Wiesel's father?
4. On April 5, what do the Jews initially think will happen, and what actually happens?

◆ Critical Thinking

INTERPRET

1. (a) In what ways does Wiesel change during his time in the camp? (b) What causes these changes? **[Interpret]**
2. What internal conflict does Wiesel experience relating to his father? **[Analyze]**
3. (a) What causes some of the other prisoners to turn on Wiesel's father? (b) What does the behavior of the prisoners reveal about human instincts? **[Draw Conclusions]**
4. In addition to sorrow, what does Wiesel feel about his father's death? How do you know? **[Draw Conclusions]**

EXTEND

5. What details does the selection provide about the daily routine in Nazi concentration camps and the specific treatment that many camp prisoners had to endure? **[Social Studies Link]**

Guide for Responding (continued)

◆ Reading Strategy

USE CONTEXT CLUES
Give the meaning of the italicized word and explain what **context clues** helped you determine its meaning.
1. The guards drove us toward the blocks. . . . The *cauldrons* of soup at the entrance attracted no one.
2. The head of the camp announced that Buchenwald was to be liquidated. Ten blocks of deportees would be *evacuated* each day. From this moment, there would be no further distribution of bread and soup. And the evacuation began. Every day, several thousand prisoners went through the camp gate and never came back.

◆ Build Grammar Skills

ABSOLUTE PHRASES
An **absolute phrase** has no grammatical relationship to the rest of the sentence. It usually contains a noun or a pronoun modified by a participle or a participial phrase.

Practice On a separate paper, identify the absolute phrase or phrases in each sentence. If a sentence has no absolute phrase, write *none*.
1. We left the train, the many dead remaining behind.
2. We followed orders, everyone forming fives.
3. His face livid, my father sighed, breathing in gasps.
4. He begged for water, his eyes closed, his voice weak.
5. He died one night, and they carried him away.

Writing Application On a separate paper, expand each sentence by adding at least one absolute phrase.
1. Buchenwald was an awful place.
2. The guards were cruel.
3. Disease was common.
4. The end of the war drew near.
5. The Americans arrived at last.

◆ Literary Focus

THEME AND HISTORICAL CONTEXT
Weisel's firsthand account of the Holocaust conveys an important message about human behavior and the consequences of certain behaviors. This message, or **theme,** is closely tied to the account's historical context.
1. What is Wiesel trying to show about the Holocaust?
2. How does his theme relate to human societies in general, and to the future as well as the past?
3. What message does Wiesel convey through his descriptions of the behavior of both the prisoners and their captors?
4. What events in recent history can you think of that are in some ways similar to those that Weisel describes? Explain your answer.
5. Why is it important to read an account such as Weisel's?

◆ Build Vocabulary

USING THE LATIN WORD ROOT *-numer-*
Explain how the Latin root *-numer-*, meaning "number," figures into the meanings of these words:

1. numerical   2. numerous   3. enumerate

USING THE WORD BANK: Antonyms
On your paper, write the letter of the word that is the *antonym*—opposite in meaning—to the first word.
1. spasmodically: (a) regularly, (b) harshly, (c) loudly
2. liquidated: (a) created, (b) destroyed, (c) drank
3. deportee: (a) teacher, (b) immigrant, (c) promise
4. innumerable: (a) many, (b) few, (c) mathematical
5. plaintive: (a) defensive, (b) fancy, (c) happy
6. livid: (a) pale, (b) wounded, (c) unblemished
7. beseeching: (a) refusing, (b) asking, (c) wondering

Build Your Portfolio

 ## Idea Bank

Writing

1. **Diary Entry** Write the diary entry that Wiesel might have written on the day his father died or on the day of his liberation.

2. **Letter** Imagine yourself as one of the American soldiers liberating the camp where Wiesel had been imprisoned. Describe your experiences and emotions in a letter to a friend or loved one back home.

3. **Eulogy** Write the eulogy, or funeral speech, that might have been given for Wiesel's father if funerals had been allowed at Buchenwald. Provide details that pay tribute to Wiesel's father and the suffering he endured.

Speaking, Listening, and Viewing

4. **Interview** Imagine Elie Wiesel is being interviewed by an American official after Buchenwald is liberated. Perform this interview with a classmate. **[Performing Arts Link]**

5. **War Crimes Trial** With a group of classmates, conduct a mock war crimes trial in which a high-ranking Nazi is held accountable for what happened in the concentration camps. One of the witnesses is Elie Wiesel. **[Performing Arts Link]**

Researching and Representing

6. **Mural** Working alone or with a classmate, create a mural mourning the loss of so many millions in the Holocaust. **[Art Link]**

7. **Research Paper** Do research to learn more about Auschwitz or Buchenwald, two of the concentration camps in which Wiesel was imprisoned. Where was the camp located? When was it built? What was it like? How many perished there? Answer these questions in a brief written report. **[Social Studies Link]**

Online Activity www.phlit.phschool.com

 ## Guided Writing Lesson

Description of a Setting

Write a brief description of the concentration camp in which the events of the selection take place.

> #### Writing Skills Focus: Transitions to Show Place
> Your setting description will be easier for readers to picture if you use **transitions that show place** or position—connecting words that help readers orient themselves in space. Here are some examples.
>
> - beside
> - alongside
> - next to
> - near
> - above
> - under
> - farther away
> - in the distance
> - on the left
> - on the right
> - in the middle
> - behind
> - in front of
> - in back of
> - at the top
> - at the bottom
> - outside
> - inside

Prewriting Go through the selection, and list the details it provides about the concentration camp. Decide on the overall impression to which most of the details point. Then, jot down words and phrases that might help you convey that impression.

Drafting Begin your description with a general statement in which you identify the setting and state the overall impression it conveys.

Then, provide details that support your statement. Use adjectives, adverbs, prepositional phrases, and absolute phrases to help convey the impression you have of the setting.

Revising Be sure that you have provided enough details about the setting, and enough descriptive language to convey your overall impression of that setting. Make sure that you have used clear transitions to show the placement or position of details in the camp.

If you need to add more descriptive details, try including them in absolute phrases. For more on absolute phrases, see pp. 188 and 198.

Guide for Reading

Gabriela Mistral *(1889–1957)*

Most fifteen-year-olds do not have full-time jobs, but at fifteen, Gabriela Mistral (gä brē ā´ lä mē sträl´) was a full-time grade-school teacher in her native Chile. When Mistral (whose real name is Lucila Godoy Alcayaga) began publishing her poetry, she tried a variety of pen names, eventually settling on Gabriela Mistral.

In 1945, Mistral became the first woman poet and the first Latin American to receive the Nobel Prize for Literature.

Octavio Paz *(1914–1998)*

The wide-ranging travel of the Mexican poet Octavio Paz (ok täv´ yō päs) was matched by the freedom of his imagination. Paz's poetry has universal appeal, and in 1990 he received the Nobel Prize for Literature. For all the acclaim he won and the places he traveled, however, Paz remained deeply committed to his Mexican heritage.

Pablo Neruda *(1904–1973)*

The Chilean poet Pablo Neruda (pä´ blô ne rōō´ thä) changed his name from Neftali Ricardo Reyes when, as a young man, he began to publish poetry. He did so for fear that his father would be offended if the poems appeared under his real name. Surely his father would not have been offended if he had known that Pablo Neruda would one day receive the Nobel Prize for Literature!

When Neruda was twenty, the Chilean government recognized his talent and appointed him to diplomatic positions so that he could travel to other countries. In his travels, he developed great sympathy for the plight of working people. This sympathy is apparent in many of Neruda's poems, including "Cristobal Miranda," which expresses great respect for those who labor under hard conditions.

◆ Build Vocabulary

GREEK PREFIXES: *ec-/ex-*

In "Cristobal Miranda," you will encounter the word *ecstatic*. This word combines the Greek prefix *ec-*, a form of *ex-*, which means "out of," and the Greek root *-stat-*, meaning "place or position." Although *ecstatic* literally means "put out of place," its common meaning is "overpowered by emotion, usually joy." If you don't see the connection between these two meanings, consider the phrase "beside oneself with joy."

WORD BANK

As you read the poems, you will encounter the words on this list. Each word is defined on the page where it first appears. Preview the list before you read.

ecstatic
nimbleness
memento

◆ Build Grammar Skills

PRONOUNS AND ANTECEDENTS

A pronoun's **antecedent** is the noun or pronoun to which it refers. An antecedent can come before or after the pronoun, can be in another sentence, and might be more than one word. In poetry, an antecedent may be on a different line, as in the following example from "The street":

antecedent
Someone behind me also stepping on

                              pronoun
stones, leaves:/if I slow down, *he* slows

As you read "Fear," however, you'll notice that the pronoun *them* has no antecedent. Think about why the poet leaves it out.

◆ *Literature and Your Life*

CONNECT YOUR EXPERIENCE

As you grow older, you face new and sometimes difficult experiences. You may have to overcome your shyness to make a presentation to the class, or you may have to sacrifice time with friends to work at an after-school job. Without experiences like these, however, you'd remain the same person throughout your life—never changing, never growing.

Like you, the subjects in these poems must face difficult and frightening challenges.

THEMATIC FOCUS: DANGEROUS DESTINIES

These selections about challenges and change raise the question "What kind of courage does it take to live in an uncertain world?"

Journal Writing In the center of a sunburst diagram like the one shown, note a challenge you are facing. Along the rays projecting from it, briefly describe the rewards and difficulties associated with this challenge.

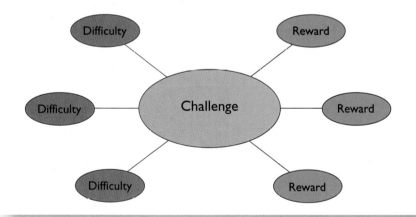

◆ Background for Understanding

LITERATURE

Translators face an especially difficult challenge; they must carry the meaning of a poem or story from one language to another. This job is difficult because a word in one language can often be translated by several possible words in another.

For example, the word *niña* in the Spanish original of Mistral's poem "Fear" could be translated as "child" or "little girl." Those translating "Fear" must make many such choices. As a result, different translators may write different versions of a poem or story.

◆ Literary Focus

IMAGERY

No matter what language they speak, people can all understand the language of the senses. For that reason, the element of a poem that is often easiest to appreciate is its **imagery,** the descriptive language that re-creates sensory experiences.

You can begin to enter the world each poem describes by identifying its imagery. In reading "Cristobal Miranda," for example, notice the sensory language the poet uses to describe the bargemen and the work they are doing.

◆ Reading Strategy

RESTATE FOR UNDERSTANDING

Reading a poem is like having a conversation. Often in conversation, you have to **restate** in your own words what the other person has said in order to understand its meaning. Similarly, restating lines of a poem can help you make sense of difficult passages.

In "Cristobal Miranda," for example, the poet uses a lot of figurative language. When you encounter a phrase like "blind stomach of the ships," try restating it in your own words so that you can first understand the phrase on a literal level. Then, reread the passage to grasp the underlying meaning.

Fear

Gabriela Mistral
Translated by **Doris Dana**

Woman with Child, Pablo Picasso, Museo Picasso, Barcelona, Spain

I don't want them to turn
my little girl into a swallow.
She would fly far away into the sky
and never fly again to my straw bed,
5   or she would nest in the eaves[1]
where I could not comb her hair.
I don't want them to turn
my little girl into a swallow.

I don't want them to make
10   my little girl a princess.
In tiny golden slippers
how could she play on the meadow?
And when night came, no longer
would she sleep at my side.
15   I don't want them to make
my little girl a princess.

And even less do I want them
one day to make her queen.
They would put her on a throne
20   where I could not go to see her.
And when nighttime came
I could never rock her . . .
I don't want them to make
my little girl a queen!

▲ **Critical Viewing** What might the mother in this painting
fear? Explain your answer. **[Draw Conclusions]**

---

1. eaves (ēvz) *n.*: The lower edge or edges of a
roof, usually projecting beyond the sides of a
building.

The street

Octavio Paz
Translated by **Muriel Rukeyser**

A long and silent street.
I walk in blackness and I stumble and fall
and rise, and I walk blind, my feet
stepping on silent stones and dry leaves.
5   Someone behind me also stepping on
     stones, leaves:
if I slow down, he slows;
if I run, he runs, I turn: nobody.

Everything dark and doorless.
Turning and turning among these corners
10 which lead forever to the street
where nobody waits for, nobody follows me,
where I pursue a man who stumbles
and rises and says when he sees me: nobody.

Guide for Responding

◆ Literature and Your Life

Reader's Response Did you want to comfort the speakers in these poems? Why or why not?

Thematic Focus Briefly describe the challenges that each speaker faces.

☑ Check Your Comprehension

1. Who is the speaker in "Fear"?
2. Describe three fears the speaker has.
3. What happens in the first stanza of "The street"? The second?

◆ Critical Thinking

INTERPRET

1. Find three details that give "Fear" the quality of a fairy tale and explain your choices. **[Support]**
2. In "Fear" what is the common element in each of the fears the speaker expresses? **[Draw Conclusions]**
3. Show how there are two speakers in "The street" and explain who they are. **[Interpret]**
4. In what ways does "The street" resemble a nightmare? **[Compare and Contrast]**
5. Compare and contrast the fears of the speaker in "Fear" with the fears expressed in "The street." **[Compare and Contrast]**

APPLY

6. Describe a situation that could lead up to the speech in "Fear." For example, how might the mother's speech be a response to fairy tales she has just told her daughter? **[Hypothesize]**

EXTEND

7. Mistral begins the first two stanzas of "Fear" with the words "I don't want." Imagine that you are Mistral. Name two other things you don't want. **[Relate]**

CRISTOBAL MIRANDA

(Shoveler at Tocopilla)

Pablo Neruda
Translated by Robert Bly

I met you on the broad barges
in the bay, Cristobal, while the sodium nitrate[1]
was coming down, wrapped in a burning
November day, to the sea.
5   I remember the <u>ecstatic</u> <u>nimbleness</u>,
the hills of metal, the motionless water.
And only the bargemen, soaked
with sweat, moving snow.
Snow of the nitrates, poured
10   over painful shoulders, dropping
into the blind stomach of the ships.
Shovelers there, heroes of a sunrise
eaten away by acids, and bound
to the destinies of death, standing firm,
15   taking in the floods of nitrate.
Cristobal, this <u>memento</u> is for you,
for the others shoveling with you,
whose chests are penetrated by the acids
and the lethal gases,
20   making the heart swell up
like crushed eagles, until the man drops,
rolls toward the streets of town,
toward the broken crosses out in the field.
Enough of that, Cristobal, today
25   this bit of paper remembers you, each of you,
the bargemen of the bay, the man
turned black in the boats, my eyes
are moving with yours in this daily work
and my soul is a shovel which lifts
30   loading and unloading blood and snow
next to you, creatures of the desert.

---

1. **sodium nitrate:** Clear, odorless, crystalline salt used in manufacturing explosives, fertilizers, and other chemical compounds.

◆ Build Vocabulary

ecstatic (ek stat´ ik) *adj.*: Overpowered by emotion, usually joy

nimbleness (nim´ bəl nes) *n.*: The quality of being quick and agile

memento (mə men´ tō) *n.*: Something serving as a reminder or warning

◀ Critical Viewing These workers are breaking up boulders of nitrate. How do the working conditions shown here compare to those described in the poem? **[Compare and Contrast]**

Guide for Responding

◆ Literature and Your Life

Reader's Response How do you feel about the bargemen after reading this poem? Explain why you feel this way.

Thematic Focus In what way do the bargemen face a dangerous destiny?

Reader's Journal Write a short journal entry describing a time when you had to perform a dangerous task.

Questions for Research Formulate several questions that would help you learn more about the history and people of Chile.

☑ Check Your Comprehension

1. What is the "snow" that the workers are shoveling?
2. For whom has the speaker written "this memento"?
3. To what does the speaker compare his own soul at the end of the poem?

◆ Critical Thinking

INTERPRET

1. Explain what is meant when the speaker says the men are "bound to the destinies of death." **[Interpret]**
2. Why do you think the speaker wants to make the poem a "memento"? **[Draw Conclusions]**

EVALUATE

3. How accurately do you think the speaker describes the workers? Explain. **[Assess]**

COMPARE AND CONTRAST

4. Compare and contrast the challenges faced by the speakers in "Fear" and "The street" with those faced by the workers in "Cristobal Miranda." **[Compare and Contrast]**

Guide for Responding (continued)

◆ Reading Strategy

RESTATE FOR UNDERSTANDING

If you **restate** a difficult passage—say it again in your own words—in order to grasp its literal meaning, you will also be able to understand its figurative meaning more easily.

1. Give a one-sentence summary of each of the three stanzas in "Fear."
2. Restate in your own words the first four lines of "The street."
3. On your paper, rewrite lines 9–11 of "Cristobal Miranda" without the use of figurative language.

◆ Build Vocabulary

USING THE GREEK PREFIXES *ec-/ex-*

Knowing that the Greek prefixes *ec-* and *ex-* mean "out of," use one of the words provided to complete each of the following sentences. Use each word only once, and write the complete sentences in your notebook.

a. eccentric   **c.** exclude
b. excerpt   **d.** export

1. A small portion of text taken from a larger text is an ___?___ .
2. To leave something out is to ___?___ it.
3. To ship something out of the country is to ___?___ it.
4. If someone's manner is "off-center" or unconventional, he or she is ___?___ .

USING THE WORD BANK: Analogies

On your paper, write the word from the Word Bank that will make the relationship between the second pair of words similar to the relationship between the first pair. Use each word only once.

1. Tortoise is to sluggishness as cheetah is to ___?___ .
2. Warmth is to sweater as memory is to ___?___ .
3. Angry is to furious as happy is to ___?___ .

◆ Literary Focus

IMAGERY

These poets use **imagery**—language that describes sensory experiences—to enhance your appreciation of the dangers and difficulties they describe. In "Cristobal Miranda," for example, words that appeal to the sense of touch—"burning"; "soaked/with sweat"—stress the hard conditions under which the men are working.

1. (a) Find a passage in "Cristobal Miranda" that describes experiences of both touch and sight. (b) Explain how this passage helps you appreciate the challenges faced by the workers.
2. Explain how two sensory descriptions in "Fear" help you understand the speaker's anxiety about losing her daughter.
3. Which sensory description in these poems creates the most vivid image of a struggle? Explain.

◆ Build Grammar Skills

PRONOUNS AND ANTECEDENTS

An **antecedent** is a noun or pronoun to which a pronoun refers. In "Fear" the speaker refers several times to *them*, a pronoun without an antecedent. By leaving out the antecedent, the poet creates a sense of mystery about *them*.

On the other hand, the pronoun *you* is used frequently in "Cristobal Miranda," but there is no doubt as to its antecedent. In your own writing, you will want every pronoun to refer clearly to an antecedent.

Practice Copy these lines from the poems. Find the underlined pronoun's antecedent in the poem and then write it next to the line you've copied.

1. for the others shoveling with <u>you</u> ("Cristobal Miranda," l. 17)
2. if I slow down, <u>he</u> slows ("The street," l. 7)
3. and rises and says when <u>he</u> sees me: nobody. ("The street," l. 13)
4. <u>She</u> would fly far away into the sky ("Fear," l. 3)
5. And even less do I want them/one day to make <u>her</u> a queen. ("Fear," ll. 17–18)

Build Your Portfolio

 ## Idea Bank

Writing

1. **Letter to a Poet** Respond to one of the poems by writing a letter to the poet. Tell how the poem made you feel and which images helped you share the experience the poet describes.

2. **Poem** Write your own poem about a struggle or challenge using imagery that will help your readers share the experience.

3. **Short Story Based on a Poem** Turn one of these poems into a short story. Expand on the situation in the poem by showing, for example, why the man in "The street" is running or how the speaker in "Fear" brings up her daughter.

Speaking, Listening, and Viewing

4. **Oral Interpretation** Practice reading one of these poems aloud. Experiment with using your tone of voice, reading speed, and word emphasis to express your interpretation. Then, read the poem for the class. **[Performing Arts Link]**

5. **Speech** Write a speech in which you defend the rights of those who labor under hazardous conditions, like the men Neruda describes. Then, deliver your speech to the class. **[Performing Arts Link]**

Researching and Representing

6. **Profile of a Country** In "Cristobal Miranda," the speaker describes a scene at a port in Chile. Conduct research to learn about this South American country. Then, create a chart that provides an overview of its vital information, including its climate, exports, and culture. **[Social Studies Link]**

7. **Dance** Create a two-person dance that communicates the action and mood of "The street." With a partner, practice and perform your dance for the class. **[Performing Arts Link]**

Online Activity www.phlit.phschool.com

 ## Guided Writing Lesson

Anecdote About a Challenge

Draw on your own experience to tell an **anecdote**—an interesting or amusing story— about a challenge. The following tip will help you clarify the cause-and-effect relationships in your anecdote.

Writing Skills Focus: Cause-and-Effect Relationships

Whether you're writing an anecdote, a remembrance, or a problem-and-solution essay, you must show how one event or condition (the **cause**) brings about another (the **effect**). Even a poem like "The street" describes cause-and-effect relationships:

> **Cause**: Dark street
>
> **Effect**: Speaker stumbles
>
> **Cause**: Speaker stumbles
>
> **Effect**: Speaker falls

In planning, writing, and revising your anecdote, show the cause-and-effect relationships among events.

Prewriting To find a topic for an anecdote, think about a mistake you have made, like showing up at the wrong time for an appointment. Jot down some amusing consequences that resulted from the error.

Drafting You can create humor in your account by showing how silly causes lead to ridiculous effects at an ever-quickening pace.

Revising In reviewing your draft, clarify any cause-and-effect relationships that are unclear by using words like *as a result, consequently,* and *because.*

Also, be sure that each pronoun you use has an easily identifiable antecedent. For more on pronouns and antecedents, see Build Grammar Skills on pp. 200 and 206.

Guide for Reading

Guy de Maupassant (1850–1893)

Many authors have earned lasting fame with the publication of their first novel, but few have done so with the publication of their first short story. The French author Guy de Maupassant (gē də mō pä sän´) is one who did. His story "Ball of Fat," which he published in 1880, made him an instant celebrity and earned him the respect of some of the greatest French writers of the day. Since then, his stories have been enjoyed by generations of readers and have influenced a number of twentieth-century writers.

Early Influences Born in 1850 to an aristocratic and educated family, Maupassant spent his youth in Normandy. After graduating from high school, he joined the French armed forces and fought in the Franco-Prussian War (1870–1871). His experiences in the armed service had a strong influence on his literary works, including "Two Friends."

After his service in the army, Maupassant settled in Paris. There he began developing his skills as a writer, guided by the famous French author Gustave Flaubert, (flō ber´) who was a personal friend of Maupassant's mother. He also joined a circle of writers led by the French novelist Émile Zola (zō´ lä´). With Zola's encouragement and support, Maupassant published his first story. That was all the help he would need.

Success in Abundance The overwhelming success of "Ball of Fat" allowed Maupassant to devote himself exclusively to literary activities, and he went on to establish himself as a productive and extremely popular writer. He also received critical acclaim for his realistic depictions of life's bitter ironies.

Then, as he might have described in one of his own stories, his weaknesses caught up with him. Troubled by health problems, he died in his early forties. Yet he left a "fortune" to every future reader: 300 short stories.

◆ Build Vocabulary

SPECIALIZED WORDS: WORDS FOR SEASONS

Because English borrows from many other languages, it has a rich vocabulary. For example, it offers both simple Anglo-Saxon words and fancy Latin terms to describe the seasons. The word *vernal* from "Two Friends" comes from the Latin *vernalis*, meaning "the season spring," and is a fancy alternative to the Anglo-Saxon word *spring*. Other Anglo-Saxon and Latin word pairs for the seasons are hibernal-winter, estival-summer, and autumnal-fall.

ardent
vernal
jauntiness

WORD BANK

As you read "Two Friends," you will encounter these words. Each word is defined on the page where it first appears. Preview the list before you read.

◆ Build Grammar Skills

APPOSITIVES

Maupassant gives details about characters by using **appositives**—nouns or noun phrases that are placed near another noun or pronoun to explain it:

...M. Morissot, *watchmaker by trade but local militiaman for the time being*, stopped short ...

The italicized appositive quickly explains both Morissot's usual trade and his military duties during the war. If Maupassant had provided these details in a separate sentence, he would have slowed down the pace of his story. Instead, he includes the appositive, separating it by commas because it is not essential to the meaning.

Two Friends

◆ Literature and Your Life

CONNECT YOUR EXPERIENCE

Mathematics says that if you share something with another person, you each have less than the total amount. Friendship proves this statement wrong. If you share a dream, a joke, or a story with a friend, it increases in value—and you both get to keep it.

"Two Friends" shows the value of friendship. It also shows how life can test friendship.

Journal Writing Jot down some of the qualities that you look for in a friend. Then tell why each of these qualities is important to you.

THEMATIC FOCUS: DANGEROUS DESTINIES

As the tension mounts in this story, ask yourself: Will friendship—and the friends—survive?

◆ Background for Understanding

LITERATURE

Realism was a literary movement that emerged in mid-nineteenth-century France as a reaction to Romanticism. Unlike the Romantics, Realists confronted many of the harsh realities of the nineteenth-century world. Naturalism grew out of the Realist movement and moved even further away from the optimistic vision of the Romantics. Naturalists frequently depicted characters whose lives were shaped by forces of nature or society they could not understand or control.

Guy de Maupassant had personal ties to some of the leading Realist and Naturalist writers in France. Although Maupassant resisted any labels being put on his writing, the influence of both Realism and Naturalism is apparent in "Two Friends."

◆ Literary Focus

CLIMAX

The **climax** of a story is the point at which the tension is the greatest. It is also the point at which the outcome is about to be revealed. In some stories, the tension increases gradually, leading to a climax that you know is coming. In other stories, the climax arrives suddenly and unexpectedly.

"Two Friends" shows one way of building towards a climax. As you read the story, decide whether the moment of greatest tension is expected or unexpected.

◆ Reading Strategy

SIGNIFICANT DETAILS

Significant details in a story often hint at how events may turn out. Sometimes these details describe character traits—human qualities that help to determine the outcome of events. Other times, these details are events in the world that surround the characters.

As you read "Two Friends," jot down details about the characters themselves; then, ask yourself how these details might influence what happens. Notice significant details in the surroundings, as well, even if they seem to be off in the distance. Then consider how things that were distant may suddenly become all too close.

Use a graphic organizer like the one below to keep track of details and their eventual consequences. As you read, jot down significant setting and character details in the first column. Fill in the second column when the consequences of those details are revealed.

Detail	Consequence

Two Friends

Guy de Maupassant
Translated by Gordon R. Silber

The following story is set during the Franco-Prussian War. Beginning on July 19, 1870, the war had resulted from the Prussian prime minister Otto von Bismarck's belief that a war with France would strengthen the bond between the German states, along with French emperor Napoleon III's feeling that a successful conflict with Prussia would help him to gain support among the French people. As it turned out, the French army was no match for the German forces. After a series of victories, one of which ended in the capture of Napoleon III, the German army established a blockade around Paris on September 19, 1870. Led by a provisional government, Paris managed to hold out until January 28, 1871, though the city's inhabitants were plagued by famine and a sense of hopelessness. As Maupassant's story begins, the city is on the verge of surrender.

Paris was blockaded, starved, in its death agony. Sparrows were becoming scarcer and scarcer on the rooftops and the sewers were being depopulated. One ate whatever one could get.

As he was strolling sadly along the outer boulevard one bright January morning, his hands in his trousers pockets and his stomach empty, M.[1] Morissot, watchmaker by trade but local militiaman for the time being, stopped short before a fellow militiaman whom he recognized as a friend. It was M. Sauvage, a riverside acquaintance.

Every Sunday, before the war, Morissot left at dawn, a bamboo pole in his hand, a tin box on his back. He would take the Argenteuil railroad, get off at Colombes, and walk to Marante Island. As soon as he arrived at this ideal spot he would start to fish; he fished until nightfall.

Every Sunday he would meet a stout, jovial little man, M. Sauvage, a haberdasher[2] in Rue Notre-Dame-de-Lorette, another <u>ardent</u> fisherman. Often they spent half a day side by side, line in hand and feet dangling above the current. Inevitably they had struck up a friendship.

Some days they did not speak. Sometimes they did; but they understood one another admirably without saying anything because they had similar tastes and responded to their surroundings in exactly the same way.

On a spring morning, toward ten o'clock, when the young sun was drawing up from the tranquil stream wisps of haze which floated off in the direction of the current and was pouring down its <u>vernal</u> warmth on the backs of the two fanatical anglers,[3] Morissot would sometimes say to

◆ Build Vocabulary

ardent (ärd´ ənt) *adj.*: Intensely enthusiastic or devoted

vernal (vʉrn´ əl) *adj.*: Springlike

---

1. **M.:** Abbreviation for *Monsieur* (mə syö´), or "Mister" or "Sir" (French).
2. **haberdasher** (hab´ ər dash´ ər) *n.*: Person who is in the business of selling men's clothing.
3. **anglers** (an´ glərz) *n.*: People who fish.

The Anglers, Georges Seurat, Musée National d'Art Moderne, Troyes, France

his neighbor, "Nice, isn't it?" and M. Sauvage would answer, "There's nothing like it." And that was enough for them to understand and appreciate each other.

▲ **Critical Viewing** Compare this painting with the description in the story of an autumn afternoon. [Compare and Contrast]

◆ *Literature and Your Life*

Does their friendship remind you of one of your own friendships?

On an autumn afternoon, when the sky, reddened by the setting sun, cast reflections of its scarlet clouds on the water, made the whole river crimson, lighted up the horizon, made the two friends look as ruddy as fire, and gilded the trees which were already brown and beginning to tremble with a wintery shiver, M. Sauvage would look at Morissot with a smile and say, "Fine sight!" And Morissot, awed, would answer, "It's better than the city, isn't it?" without taking his eyes from his float.

As soon as they recognized one another they shook hands energetically, touched at meeting under such changed circumstances. M. Sauvage, with a sigh, grumbled, "What goings-on!" Morissot groaned dismally, "And

what weather! This is the first fine day of the year."

The sky was, in fact, blue and brilliant.

They started to walk side by side, absent-minded and sad. Morissot went on, "And fishing! Ah! Nothing but a pleasant memory."

"When'll we get back to it?" asked M. Sauvage.

They went into a little café and had an absinthe,[4] then resumed their stroll along the sidewalks.

Morissot stopped suddenly, "How about another, eh?" M. Sauvage agreed, "If you want." And they entered another wine shop.

On leaving they felt giddy, muddled, as one does after drinking on an empty stomach. It was mild. A caressing breeze touched their faces.

---

4. **absinthe** (ab´ sinth) *n.*: Type of liqueur.

The Cabassud Houses in the Town of Avray, Jean Baptiste Camille Corot, Louvre, Paris

The warm air completed what the absinthe had begun. M. Sauvage stopped. "Suppose we went?"

"Went where?"

"Fishing, of course."

"But where?"

"Why, on our island. The French outposts are near Colombes. I know Colonel Dumoulin; they'll let us pass without any trouble."

Morissot trembled with eagerness: "Done! I'm with you." And they went off to get their tackle.

An hour later they were walking side by side on the highway. They reached the villa which the Colonel occupied. He smiled at their request and gave his consent to their whim. They started off again, armed with a pass.

Soon they passed the outposts, went through the abandoned village of Colombes, and reached the edge of the little vineyards

▲ **Critical Viewing** This painting does not suggest the horror or hardships of war. What aspects of this story does it illustrate? **[Draw Conclusions]**

which slope toward the Seine. It was about eleven.

Opposite, the village of Argenteuil seemed dead. The heights of Orgemont and Sannois dominated the whole countryside. The broad plain which stretches as far as Nanterre was empty, absolutely empty, with its bare cherry trees and its colorless fields.

◆ **Reading Strategy**
What significant details suggest the possible danger of this setting?

Pointing up to the heights, M. Sauvage murmured, "The Prussians are up there!"

◆ **Build Vocabulary**

jauntiness (jônt' ē nis) *n.*: Carefree attitude

And a feeling of uneasiness paralyzed the two friends as they faced this deserted region.

"The Prussians!" They had never seen any, but for months they had felt their presence—around Paris, ruining France, pillaging, massacring, starving the country, invisible and all-powerful. And a kind of superstitious terror was superimposed on the hatred which they felt for this unknown and victorious people.

Morissot stammered, "Say, suppose we met some of them?"

His Parisian jauntiness coming to the surface in spite of everything, M. Sauvage answered, "We'll offer them some fish."

But they hesitated to venture into the country, frightened by the silence all about them.

Finally M. Sauvage pulled himself together: "Come on! On our way! But let's go carefully." And they climbed over into a vineyard, bent double, crawling, taking advantage of the vines to conceal themselves, watching, listening.

A stretch of bare ground had to be crossed to reach the edge of the river. They began to run, and when they reached the bank they plunged down among the dry reeds.

Morissot glued his ear to the ground and listened for sounds of anyone walking in the vicinity. He heard nothing. They were indeed alone, all alone.

Reassured, they started to fish.

Opposite them Marante Island, deserted, hid them from the other bank. The little building which had housed a restaurant was shut up and looked as if it had been abandoned for years.

M. Sauvage caught the first gudgeon.[5] Morissot got the second, and from then on they pulled in their lines every minute or two with a silvery little fish squirming on the end, a truly miraculous draught.

Skillfully they slipped the fish into a sack made of fine net which they had hung in the water at their feet. And happiness pervaded their whole being, the happiness which seizes upon you when you regain a cherished pleasure of which you have long been deprived.

The good sun was pouring down its warmth on their backs. They heard nothing more; they no longer thought about anything at all; they forgot about the rest of the world—they were fishing!

But suddenly a dull sound which seemed to come from under ground made the earth tremble. The cannon were beginning.

Morissot turned and saw, over the bank to the left, the great silhouette of Mount Valérien wearing a white plume on its brow, powdersmoke which it had just spit out.

And almost at once a second puff of smoke rolled from the summit, and a few seconds after the roar still another explosion was heard.

Then more followed, and time after time the mountain belched forth death-dealing breath, breathed out milky-white vapor which rose slowly in the calm sky and formed a cloud above the summit.

◆ **Reading Strategy**
Which details about the mountain may be significant, and why?

M. Sauvage shrugged his shoulders. "There they go again," he said.

As he sat anxiously watching his float bob up and down, Morissot was suddenly seized by the wrath which a peace-loving man will feel toward madmen who fight, and grumbled, "Folks sure are stupid to kill one another like that."

M. Sauvage answered, "They're worse than animals."

And Morissot, who had just pulled in a bleak, went on, "And to think that it will always be like this as long as there are governments."

M. Sauvage stopped him: "The Republic[6] wouldn't have declared war—"

Morissot interrupted: "Under kings you

---

5. **gudgeon** (guj´ ən) *n.*: Small European freshwater fish.

6. **The Republic:** The provisional republican government that assumed control when Napoleon III was captured by the Prussians.

have war abroad; under the Republic you have war at home."

And they started a leisurely discussion, unraveling great political problems with the sane reasonableness of easygoing, limited individuals, and found themselves in agreement on the point that men would never be free. And Mount Valérien thundered unceasingly, demolishing French homes with its cannon, crushing out lives, putting an end to the dreams which many had dreamt, the joys which many had been waiting for, the happiness which many had hoped for, planting in wives' hearts, in maidens' hearts, in mothers' hearts, over there, in other lands, sufferings which would never end.

"That's life for you," opined M. Sauvage.

"You'd better say 'That's death for you,'" laughed Morissot.

But they shuddered in terror when they realized that someone had just come up behind them, and looking around they saw four men standing almost at their elbows, four tall men, armed and bearded, dressed like liveried[7] servants, with flat caps on their heads, pointing rifles at them.

The two fish lines dropped from their hands and floated off down stream.

In a few seconds they were seized, trussed up, carried off, thrown into a rowboat and taken over to the island.

And behind the building which they had thought deserted they saw a score of German soldiers.

A kind of hairy giant who was seated astride a chair smoking a porcelain pipe asked them in excellent French: "Well, gentlemen, have you had good fishing?"

Then a soldier put down at the officer's feet the sack full of fish which he had carefully brought along. The Prussian smiled: "Aha! I see that it didn't go badly. But we have to talk about another little matter. Listen to me and don't get excited.

"As far as I am concerned, you are two spies sent to keep an eye on me. I catch you and I shoot you. You were pretending to fish in order to conceal your business. You have fallen into my hands, so much the worse for you. War is like that.

"But—since you came out past the outposts you have, of course, the password to return. Tell me that password and I will pardon you."

The two friends, side by side, pale, kept silent. A slight nervous trembling shook their hands.

The officer went on: "No one will ever know. You will go back placidly. The secret will disappear with you. If you refuse, it is immediate death. Choose."

They stood motionless, mouths shut.

The Prussian quietly went on, stretching out his hand toward the stream: "Remember that within five minutes you will be at the bottom of that river. Within five minutes! You have relatives, of course?"

> ◆ Literary Focus
> How does the officer's calm manner add to the tension?

Mount Valérien kept thundering.

The two fishermen stood silent. The German gave orders in his own language. Then he moved his chair so as not to be near the prisoners and twelve men took their places, twenty paces distant, rifles grounded.

The officer went on: "I give you one minute, not two seconds more."

Then he rose suddenly, approached the two Frenchmen, took Morissot by the arm, dragged him aside, whispered to him, "Quick, the password? Your friend won't know. I'll pretend to relent."

Morissot answered not a word.

The Prussian drew M. Sauvage aside and put the same question.

M. Sauvage did not answer.

They stood side by side again.

And the officer began to give commands. The soldiers raised their rifles.

Then Morissot's glance happened to fall on the sack full of gudgeons which was lying on the grass a few steps away.

---

7. **liveried** (liv′ ər ēd) *adj.*: Uniformed.

A ray of sunshine made the little heap of still squirming fish gleam. And he almost weakened. In spite of his efforts his eyes filled with tears.

He stammered, "Farewell, Monsieur Sauvage."

M. Sauvage answered, "Farewell, Monsieur Morissot."

They shook hands, trembling from head to foot with a shudder which they could not control.

The officer shouted, "Fire!"

The twelve shots rang out together.

M. Sauvage fell straight forward, like a log. Morissot, who was taller, tottered, half turned, and fell crosswise on top of his comrade, face up, as the blood spurted from his torn shirt.

The German gave more orders.

His men scattered, then returned with rope and stones which they tied to the dead men's feet. Then they carried them to the bank.

Mount Valérien continued to roar, its summit hidden now in a mountainous cloud of smoke.

Two soldiers took Morissot by the head and the feet, two others seized M. Sauvage. They swung the bodies for a moment then let go. They described an arc and plunged into the river feet first, for the weights made them seem to be standing upright.

There was a splash, the water trembled, then grew calm, while tiny wavelets spread to both shores.

A little blood remained on the surface.

The officer, still calm, said in a low voice: "Now the fish will have their turn."

And he went back to the house.

And all at once he caught sight of the sack of gudgeons in the grass. He picked it up, looked at it, smiled, shouted, "Wilhelm!"

A soldier in a white apron ran out. And the Prussian threw him the catch of the two and said: "Fry these little animals right away while they are still alive. They will be delicious."

Then he lighted his pipe again.

Guide for Responding

◆ Literature and Your Life

Reader's Response Were you shocked by the outcome of the story? Why or why not?

Thematic Focus In this story, is it friendship itself that leads the two men into danger and finally to death? Explain.

Farewell Note As Morissot or Sauvage, write a brief farewell note to your family before you are executed.

☑ Check Your Comprehension

1. How does the wartime situation in Paris affect the Sunday habits of Morissot and Sauvage?
2. How do they succeed for a while in defying the war?
3. What surprise do they encounter?
4. How does a final choice they have to make lead to the end of the story?

◆ Critical Thinking

INTERPRET
1. What causes the two friends to try fishing again? **[Infer]**
2. (a) Find two details of the men's journey to the island that might give readers an uneasy feeling. (b) Explain your choices. **[Infer]**
3. What message does Maupassant convey by showing how war breaks in on the peacefulness of fishing? **[Synthesize]**

EVALUATE
4. Is it effective to end the story with the Prussian officer's order to cook the fish? Explain. In answering, consider what this detail does or does not add to the central idea of the story. **[Assess]**

APPLY
5. What does this story suggest about the effects of modern warfare on everyday life? **[Generalize]**

Guide for Responding (continued)

◆ Reading Strategy

SIGNIFICANT DETAILS

Paying close attention to the **significant details** in this story helps you guess the fate of the two characters. The strange "silence all about" Morissot and Sauvage near the river suggests that there is danger lurking, and the way the two men talk about the war as though it does not affect them suggests that they will soon be affected by it.

1. In "Two Friends," what is significant about the "powdersmoke" that Morissot and Sauvage see on the mountain?
2. What details about the two men in "Two Friends" might lead you to believe that they will not betray each other?
3. How is the initial mention of Marante Island a significant detail?
4. Explain the ultimate significance of Sauvage's remark, "We'll offer them some fish."

◆ Build Vocabulary

USING WORDS FOR SEASONS

The words *hibernate, autumnal, vernal,* and *estivate* are derived from the Latin words for the seasons. On your paper, complete the following sentences with these words. Use each word only once.

1. Some animals ___?___ in winter, while others ___?___ in summer.
2. In the Northern Hemisphere, the ___?___ equinox occurs in September and the ___?___ equinox occurs in March.

USING THE WORD BANK: Antonyms

On your paper, write the letter of the word that is the antonym—opposite in meaning—of the first word:

1. ardent: (a) indifferent, (b) confident, (c) intent
2. vernal: (a) mild, (b) angry, (c) wintry
3. jauntiness: (a) seriousness, (b) lightheartedness, (c) reluctance

◆ Literary Focus

CLIMAX

Some stories build up to a **climax**—the moment of greatest tension—like an imaginary drumroll that gets louder and louder. In "Two Friends," however, the climax comes unexpectedly. The drumming of cannon seems part of the background, a noise in a faraway war that does not concern the friends. Suddenly, the distant war comes close, in the form of a Prussian officer with the power of life and death.

1. What is the climax in "Two Friends"? Give reasons for your answer.
2. In "Two Friends," Maupassant hints at the climax even though it arrives with a shocking suddenness. Find three of these hints; then tell why a reader might overlook them.
3. Do you think the story would have been more powerful if the clues leading up to its climax had been more obvious? Explain.

◆ Build Grammar Skills

APPOSITIVES

Appositives are nouns or noun phrases placed near another noun or pronoun to explain it. By including information in appositives, authors avoid putting each new fact in a separate sentence.

Practice Identify the appositives in the following sentences.

1. It was M. Sauvage, a riverside acquaintance.
2. Morissot, a shy man, grew bolder as he drank absinthe.
3. The Prussian officer, a man of honor, insisted on executing the friends.

Writing Application Combine each pair of sentences by using appositives.

1. He saw M. Sauvage while strolling along the outer boulevard. M. Sauvage was an old friend.
2. The Colonel was careless to have let the men pass. The Colonel was an otherwise responsible person.
3. Morissot stopped short before a fellow militiaman. Morissot was a watchmaker by trade but local militiaman for the time being.

Build Your Portfolio

Idea Bank

Writing

1. **Epitaph for Morissot and Sauvage** Write a few words to be carved into a stone that will stand above the graves of Morissot and Sauvage. **[Art Link]**

2. **Yearbook Profiles** Write yearbook profiles for yourself and a good friend. Include information about your accomplishments and preferences.

3. **Report of the Prussian Officer** As the Prussian officer in "Two Friends," write a report for your superior on the execution of Morissot and Sauvage. Include such details as where you discovered them, what they were doing, and why you had them shot. **[Social Studies Link]**

Speaking, Listening, and Viewing

4. **Role Play** With a partner, role-play a conversation between the two friends in Maupassant's story, discussing whether or not you should give away the password. **[Performing Arts Link]**

5. **Humorous Monologue** Write and deliver a funny speech about a friend. Purposely exaggerate your friend's ordinary experiences, pretending that they're dangerous adventures. **[Performing Arts Link]**

Researching and Representing

6. **Friendship Collage** Create a collage of pictures from magazines, ticket stubs, photographs, and other items that "illustrate" an adventure you've had with a friend. **[Art Link]**

7. **Brochure for a Friendship Film Festival** Choose three movies about friendship to be included in a brochure for a "Friendship Film Festival." Create a brochure describing why each film is included in the festival. **[Media Link]**

Online Activity www.phlit.phschool.com

Guided Writing Lesson

Extended Definition of Friendship

Use your own ideas and feelings as well as events in "Two Friends" to write an extended definition of friendship. Unlike a dry dictionary definition, your extended definition will illustrate your ideas with concrete examples of friends and their behavior from your own experience, literature, the movies, and television.

Writing Skills Focus: Concrete Examples

Use **concrete examples** to support your ideas when writing an extended definition, a problem-and-solution essay, or an editorial. Such examples even help to make a short story more vivid. Maupassant, for example, begins "Two Friends" with a general statement and then brings it to life with two concrete examples:

Model From the Story

Paris was blockaded, starved, in its death agony. *Sparrows were becoming scarcer and scarcer on the rooftops* and *the sewers were being depopulated.*

Jot down concrete examples of friendship as you plan your extended definition, and refer to them as you draft and revise it.

Prewriting Start with a two-column chart. In the left column, write general ideas about friendship. In the right column, describe a concrete example that supports each idea.

Drafting Use the left column of your chart to write a general definition of friendship. Then choose the best examples from the right column to make that definition more vivid.

Revising Illustrate each general point you make about friendship with a concrete example. Where necessary, describe the actions that show what friends do for each other and how they express their devotion.

Focus on Culture

Ancient Greece and Rome

▲ **Critical Viewing** In what way is the Roman Colosseum (above) similar to modern structures? **[Connect]**

The wailing of mourners filled the air as Pericles (per´ i klēz´), the leader of Athens, rose to speak. The Greek city-state was engaged in a bitter war. Now, in 431 B.C., Athenians had gathered to bury their fallen soldiers.

His voice ringing, Pericles reminded the crowd of the greatness of their city: "Our constitution is called a democracy because power is in the hands not of a minority but of the whole people." Only in Athens, he said, did citizens consider it a duty to take part in public life. "Our city is an education to Greece," he declared. "Future ages will wonder at us."

The war would drag on for 27 years and eventually destroy Athenian greatness. Yet the prediction Pericles made in his famous Funeral Oration came true. Later ages have admired the remarkable achievements of Athens, especially its democracy. The later empire of ancient Rome has also had a lasting influence.

GEOGRAPHIC SETTING

Greece and Rome are located in southern Europe. They formed part of the ancient Mediterranean world that also included the Middle East and North Africa.

Greece The Greek mainland is a mountainous peninsula. Rugged terrain made transportation and communication difficult. As a result, the Greeks developed small, separate communities. In time, these communities grew into city-states that fiercely defended their individuality.

The coastline of Greece has many fine harbors, while hundreds of islands dot the Aegean and Mediterranean seas. Early on, Greeks took to the sea. They sailed to Egypt and Mesopotamia, bringing home goods and ideas from these older civilizations.

The Italian Peninsula West of Greece lies the boot-shaped Italian peninsula. Italy is centrally located in the Mediterranean, and the city of Rome is located on the Tiber River in central Italy. Location helped the Romans as they expanded, first through Italy, and then around the Mediterranean.

Unlike Greece, Italy is not broken up into small, isolated valleys. In addition, the Appenine Mountains, which run down the length of the Italian peninsula, are less rugged than the mountains of Greece. As a result, Italy was much easier to unify.

HISTORY

From 1400 B.C. to 1200 B.C., the seagoing Mycenaeans (mī´ sə nē´ ənz) dominated the Aegean world. These early Greeks are best known for the war they fought against the city of Troy.

For centuries, the Trojan War was viewed as merely a legend. The only record came from the *Iliad* and *Odyssey*. These two epic poems are attributed to the Greek poet Homer, who probably lived around 750 B.C. Then, in the 1870's, an amateur German archaeologist dug up the ruins of Troy in Turkey. Though the details are still lost, most historians today agree that the Trojan War was an actual event.

The Greek City-States By the sixth century B.C., a number of city-states had emerged on the mainland. The most powerful were Athens and Sparta. As you have read, Athens developed an early form of democracy. Sparta, by contrast, resembled a military dictatorship.

In 490 B.C., Athens and Sparta joined forces to ward off a threat from the Persian empire. After the Persian Wars, Athens became the dominant city-state. Under Pericles, it enjoyed a golden age of culture. However, the other city-states resented Athenian power. From 431 B.C. to 404 B.C., the Peloponnesian (pel´ ə pə nē´ zhən) War engulfed all of Greece.

Alexander the Great In the next century, King Philip of Macedon brought all of Greece under his control. His son Alexander went on to conquer a huge empire that stretched from Greece and Egypt eastward to the edge of India.

Rome Builds an Empire By 264 B.C., Roman legions had conquered all of Italy. They then won lands in North Africa, Spain, and Greece.

At first, Rome was a republic. As a result of social and economic problems, though, Rome turned to a brilliant military leader, Julius Caesar. Under Caesar, Rome won new lands in Europe and around the Mediterranean.

Afraid of Caesar's growing power, a group of senators assassinated him in 44 B.C. Caesar's death marked the end of the republic. In 27 B.C., his adopted son declared himself emperor, taking the title Augustus Caesar.

Some of Augustus' successors were weak or even downright evil. The cruel emperor Nero, for example, is blamed for setting a great fire that destroyed much of Rome. Still, for the first 200 years, the Roman Empire enjoyed relative peace and prosperity. This period is known as the "Pax Romana," or Roman peace. Romans carried their ideas and the Latin language to diverse lands, from Spain in the west to the Euphrates River in the east.

Rise of Christianity Among the lands under Roman rule was Palestine. There, Jesus was born around 4 B.C. When he was 30, Jesus

▲ **Critical Viewing** The Parthenon was dedicated to the Greek goddess Athena. How does the design convey a sense of harmony? **[Analyze]**

began preaching about the goodness and mercy of God. He attracted many disciples. Some declared that he was the Messiah, the savior God promised to the Jewish people. Concerned about his growing popularity, Roman officials had Jesus put to death.

Followers of Jesus spread the new religion of Christianity, teaching that Jesus was the son of God. At first, the Roman Empire persecuted Christians. As Christianity gained strength, though, the emperor Constantine tolerated the new religion and converted on his deathbed. Finally, in A.D. 395, Christianity became the official religion of the empire.

Decline of Rome By Constantine's time, Rome was already in a slow decline. Several factors contributed to the decline of the empire. As leaders competed for the throne, civil war became frequent. Fighting disrupted trade and

weakened the economy. At the same time, outside invaders attacked the empire. Finally, in the fifth century A.D., the western Roman Empire collapsed.

SOCIETY AND CULTURE

Greece and Rome are the classical civilizations of Europe. The Greco-Roman tradition formed the basis for western culture.

Greek Society The two leading Greek city-states, Athens and Sparta, developed vastly different ways of life. At the age of seven, Spartan boys began training for a lifetime in the military. They endured rigid discipline and brutal punishment. Girls, too, were trained to exercise in order to produce healthy sons for the army. Spartans looked down on trade, forbade their own citizens to travel, and had little use for new ideas or the arts.

By contrast, Athenian society was much freer. Citizens gathered in the open air to discuss important religious and political events. Athenian boys attended school if their families could afford it. In addition to learning to read and write, they studied music and memorized poetry. They also studied *rhetoric* (ret´ ər ik)—the art of skillful speaking—because, as citizens in a democracy, they would have to voice their views. The Athenian course of study became the basis for what we now call the humanities.

Roman Society In the early years of the Roman republic, the most powerful class were patricians, or wealthy landowners. The plebeians, or common people, had little real voice. Gradually, the plebeians gained more rights, including the right to participate in the senate. As in Athens, women and slaves had no political rights.

Still, both girls and boys learned to read and write. Even many lower-class Romans were taught to read. By the late days of the republic, many wealthy Romans hired private tutors, often

Greek slaves, for their children. Like Athenians, Romans learned rhetoric in order to participate in government.

During the Pax Romana, Romans gathered to watch chariot races at the Circus Maximus or gladiator contests at the Coliseum. (See the picture on p. 218.) The government also provided free grain to the poor. This policy of "bread and circuses" was seen as a way to control the city's restless mobs.

Perhaps Rome's greatest legacy was its commitment to the rule of law. Under the Roman system of justice, everyone was to be treated as equal before the law. The Romans introduced the idea that an accused person is innocent until proven guilty. They also allowed the use of evidence in court and set up procedures to ensure a fair trial. Such ideas still influence our society today.

ARTS AND LITERATURE

Greek philosophers like Plato (plāt´ ō) and Aristotle (ar´ is tät´´l) emphasized reason, balance, and the search for perfect truth and beauty. Such values also shaped classical Greco-Roman arts.

Ideals of Perfection Greek sculptors carved statues that were based on an ideal notion of the human form. More than 1,500 years later, European artists continued to use Greek examples as models for their work.

Greek architects sought to convey a sense of perfect balance to reflect the harmony of the universe. The most famous Greek building, the Parthenon, is a simple rectangular temple, with tall columns supporting a gently sloping roof. (See the picture on p. 220.) Later, Roman architects modeled their buildings on Greek designs but introduced their own improvements, such as the use of domes.

The Greek Theater Western drama has its roots in ancient Greece. The first Greek plays evolved out of religious festivals. Plays were performed in large outdoor arenas with little or no scenery. Actors wore elaborate costumes and stylized masks. A chorus sang or chanted comments on the action.

The Greeks developed two types of drama, comedy and tragedy. Comedies made fun of people, ideas, and social customs. Tragedies told stories of human suffering that usually ended in disaster. In the tragedy *Antigone*, by the playwright Sophocles, a young woman is condemned when she decides to bury her brother in defiance of the king. (See p. 814.)

Greco-Roman Literature As you have read, Greek literature began with the Homeric epics. (See p. 228 for an excerpt from the *Iliad*.) They strongly influenced later writers, such as the Roman poet Virgil. In the *Aeneid*, Virgil told of the founding of Rome by Aeneas, a Trojan soldier who survived the destruction of Troy.

Other Greek and Roman poets wrote about the joys and sorrows of their own times. Sappho sang of love and of the beauty of her Greek island home. (See p. 919.) Pindar wrote odes celebrating competitors in the Olympic games. The Roman writers Horace and Juvenal wrote blistering satires on Roman life.

Greeks and Romans also pioneered the writing of history. The Greek historians Herodotus (hə räd´ ə təs) and Thucydides (thoo sid´ i dēz´) presented the history of Greek wars, not as the deeds of gods, but as the study of human actions. The Roman historian Tactitus (tas´ i təs) wrote bitterly about Augustus and his successors, who he felt had destroyed Roman liberty. (See p. 246.)

ACTIVITY
Writing a Biographical Sketch

Use Internet or library resources to find out about a notable political leader, philosopher, or writer of ancient Greece or Rome. Write a brief biographical sketch of that person for a classroom *Who's Who of the Classical World*. 🦋

Guide for Reading

About "Damon and Pythias"

For writers and artists, the myths and legends of ancient Greece are more than stories: They are part of the tool kit of the imagination, a store of images and ideas that an artist can use to create new visions. "Damon and Pythias" is part of this tool kit, remembered for its dramatic definition of friendship. It inspired a sixteenth-century play by Richard Edwards (1523?–1566) and a 1962 Hollywood movie.

Unlike many myths, the tale is set in historical times. Syracuse is a real city; a real Dionysus ruled there. Instead of telling of supernatural wonders, the story tells of the human wonder of friendship.

Homer *(c. 800–750 B.C.)*

At the dawn of Western literature stands a figure nearly lost in shadow: Homer, the blind ancient Greek poet. It was to him that the ancient Greeks credited their two great epic poems, the *Iliad* and the *Odyssey*. Little is known about his life (some even doubt his existence). His works, though, shine as a beacon guiding writers down to the present. And his image—the blind bard singing the myths of his people—is a striking symbol for the beginning of literature.

In the *Iliad* and the *Odyssey,* Homer first set down in writing legends that had been recited by generations of poets before him. The two epics retell stories of the heroes and gods who fought in the war between Greece and Troy.

Homer probably lived in Asia Minor (modern Turkey) or on an island in the eastern Mediterranean. It is also thought, based on descriptions of poetic performance in the *Odyssey,* that he was a wandering poet who recited his poems at royal courts in exchange for food and lodging.

Homer's epics were recited at Panhellenic festivals, occasions when people gathered from around the Greek world for athletic and musical competitions. Generations of poets after him strove to match his language. They basked in Homer's light and labored in his shadow.

◆ Build Vocabulary

LATIN WORD ROOTS: -ped-

The Latin word root *-ped-* is derived from the Latin word for "foot." Using this fact, you might be able to deduce that the meaning of *impediment* is "hindrance." An impediment was originally a shackle placed on the *foot* to make it impossible for a prisoner to walk away.

WORD BANK

impediments
hindrances
annals
reproach
unremittingly
beguilement
avenger
implored

As you read, you will encounter the following words. Each word is defined on the page where it first appears. Preview the list before you read.

◆ Build Grammar Skills

RESTRICTIVE AND NONRESTRICTIVE APPOSITIVES

Authors give details about characters by using **appositives,** nouns or noun phrases placed near another noun or pronoun to explain it. A **restrictive appositive** adds essential information about the noun or pronoun it explains. It is not set off by commas. In the following example, the appositive *Damon and Pythias* is restrictive. It is essential because it identifies which faithful friends are meant:

The faithful friends *Damon and Pythias* won over the tyrant.

A **nonrestrictive appositive** is not essential. It is set off by commas, as in the following example:

No, they ran for the life of Hektor, *breaker of horses.*

Damon and Pythias
◆ *from* The Death of Hektor ◆

◆ *Literature and Your Life*

CONNECT YOUR EXPERIENCE

You don't have to be facing an armed warrior or a mighty king to need courage. It takes courage to stand up against a bully. It takes courage to speak out in defense of a friend. In these selections, you will read of heroes whose deeds show the real meaning of friendship and honor.

Journal Writing Describe a situation in which you had to weigh your own interests against those of others.

THEMATIC FOCUS: DANGEROUS DESTINIES

As you read these selections, ask yourself: How do the choices made by heroes take them into and out of danger?

◆ Background for Understanding

PLOT OF THE *ILIAD*

The *Iliad* recounts an episode in the war the Greeks (also known as Achaians or Argives) waged against the city of Troy. The Greeks fought for the return of Helen, wife of the Greek Menelaus, who was taken to Troy by Paris, son of King Priam of Troy. Stalemated by the Trojans, the Greeks spent ten years laying siege to the city.

Set in the tenth year of the war, the *Iliad* tells the story of the wrath of Achilleus, the foremost Greek warrior. Humiliated when King Agamemnon takes back a war prize, Achilleus vows not to fight until the Trojans set fire to the Greek ships. Without his help, the Greeks suffer tremendous losses. When Achilleus' best friend, Patroklos, enters battle, he is killed by the Trojan warrior Hektor, who then sets fire to the Greek fleet. In Book XXII, the climax of the epic, Achilleus sets out to avenge Patroklos' death.

◆ Reading Strategy

ANALYZE CONFUSING SENTENCES

Homer wove lines dense with images and other details. To **analyze confusing sentences,** read them in logical sections, not word by word. First, determine the main subject(s) (what the sentence is about) and the main verb(s) (what each main subject does). Once you understand the main action of the sentence, read to see what the rest of the sentence tells you about the main action.

Use a chart like the one shown to help you separate the essential from the nonessential elements of a sentence.

◆ Literary Focus

MYTH AND EPIC POETRY

A **myth** is a story about gods and heroes passed down by tradition. Myths answer basic questions about the world and the heart: Why do we have fire? What is the meaning of friendship? Often, myths provide material for epic poetry.

An **epic poem** glorifies the deeds of a hero from a people's mythical past and sums up their key values. Homeric epics share a number of characteristics:

- a beginning that states the subject of the poem and calls on the help of the Muses—goddesses governing the arts
- a plot that starts *in medias res* ("in the middle of matters"); an audience familiar with the traditional tales did not need background
- the use of **stock epithets,** phrases used repeatedly to refer to a thing or person, such as *wine-dark sea* or *swift-footed Achilleus*
- a standard line made up of six "feet" (groups of long and short syllables)

Main Action: Main Subject + Main Verb	Other Information About the Main Action

Damon and Pythias

Retold by William F. Russell, Ed.D.

Damon and Pythias were two noble young men who lived on the island of Sicily in a city called Syracuse. They were such close companions and were so devoted to each other that all the people of the city admired them as the highest examples of true friendship. Each trusted the other so completely that nobody could ever have persuaded one that the other had been unfaithful or dishonest, even if that had been the case.

◆ **Reading Strategy**
In a shorter sentence, restate the main idea of this sentence. Then, add another sentence to provide the necessary additional information.

Now it happened that Syracuse was, at that time, ruled by a famous tyrant named Dionysius, who had gained the throne for himself through treachery, and who from then on flaunted his power by behaving cruelly to his own subjects and to all strangers and enemies who were so unfortunate as to fall into his clutches. This tyrant, Dionysius, was so unjustly cruel that once, when he awoke from a restless sleep during which he dreamt that a certain man in the town had attempted to kill him, he immediately had that man put to death.

It happened that Pythias had, quite unjustly, been accused by Dionysius of trying to overthrow him, and for this supposed crime of treason Pythias was sentenced by the king to die. Try as he might, Pythias could not prove his innocence to the king's satisfaction, and so, all hope now lost, the noble youth asked only for a few days' freedom so that he could settle his business affairs and see to it that his relatives would be cared for after he was executed. Dionysius, the hardhearted tyrant, however, would not believe Pythias's promise to return and would not allow him to leave unless he left behind him a hostage, someone who would be put to death in his place if he should fail to return within the stated time.

Pythias immediately thought of his friend Damon, and he unhesitatingly sent for him in this hour of dire necessity, never thinking for a moment that his trusty companion would refuse his request. Nor did he, for Damon hastened straightaway to the palace—much to the amazement of King

▶ **Critical Viewing** What does this picture reveal about the characters of Damon and Pythias? **[Infer]**

Damon and Pythias

Dionysius—and gladly offered to be held hostage for his friend, in spite of the dangerous condition that had been attached to this favor. Therefore, Pythias was permitted to settle his earthly affairs before departing to the Land of the Shades,[1] while Damon remained behind in the dungeon, the captive of the tyrant Dionysius.

After Pythias had been released, Dionysius asked Damon if he did not feel afraid, for Pythias might very well take advantage of the opportunity he had been given and simply not return at all, and then he, Damon, would be executed in his place. But Damon replied at once with a willing smile: "There is no need for me to feel afraid, O King, since I have perfect faith in the word of my true friend, and I know that he will certainly return before the appointed time—unless, of course, he dies or is held captive by some evil force. Even so, even should the noble Pythias be captured and held against his will, it would be an honor for me to die in his place."

Such devotion and perfect faith as this was unheard of to the friendless tyrant; still, though he could not help admiring the true nobility of his captive, he nevertheless determined that Damon should certainly be put to death should Pythias not return by the appointed time.

◆ **Literary Focus**
How do these details add to the tension of the climax?

And, as the Fates would have it, by a strange turn of events, Pythias was detained far longer in his task than he had imagined. Though he never for a single minute intended to evade the sentence of death to which he had been so unjustly committed, Pythias met with several accidents and un-

avoidable delays. Now his time was running out and he had yet to overcome the many impediments that had been placed in his path. At last he succeeded in clearing away all the hindrances, and he sped back the many miles to the palace of the king, his heart almost bursting with grief and fear that he might arrive too late.

Meanwhile, when the last day of the allotted time arrived, Dionysius commanded that the place of execution should be readied at once, since he was still ruthlessly determined that if one of his victims escaped him, the other should not. And so, entering the chamber in which Damon was confined, he began to utter words of sarcastic pity for the "foolish faith," as he termed it, that the young man of Syracuse had in his friend.

In reply, however, Damon merely smiled, since, in spite of the fact that the eleventh hour had already arrived, he still believed that his lifelong companion would not fail him. Even when, a short time later, he was actually led out to the site of his execution, his serenity remained the same.

Great excitement stirred the crowd that had gathered to witness the execution, for all the people had heard of the bargain that had been struck between the two friends. There was much sobbing and cries of sympathy were heard all around as the captive was brought out, though he himself somehow retained complete composure even at this moment of darkest danger.

---

1. **Land of the Shades:** Mythical place where people go when they die.

◆ **Build Vocabulary**

impediments (im pēd′ ə məntz) *n*.: Things standing in the way of something else

hindrances (hin′ drəns əz) *n*.: People or things in the way; obstacles

annals (an′ əlz) *n*.: Historical records or chronicles; history

Presently the excitement grew more intense still as a swift runner could be seen approaching the palace courtyard at an astonishing speed, and wild shrieks of relief and joy went up as Pythias, breathless and exhausted, rushed headlong through the crowd and flung himself into the arms of his beloved friend, sobbing with relief that he had, by the grace of the gods, arrived in time to save Damon's life.

This final exhibition of devoted love and faithfulness was more than even the stony heart of Dionysius, the tyrant, could resist. As the throng of spectators melted into tears at the companions' embrace, the king approached the pair and declared that Pythias was hereby pardoned and his death sentence canceled. In addition, he begged the pair to allow him to become their friend, to try to be as much a friend to them both as they had shown each other to be.

Thus did the two friends of Syracuse, by the faithful love they bore to each other, conquer the hard heart of a tyrant king, and in the annals of true friendship there are no more honored names than those of Damon and Pythias—for no person can do more than be willing to lay down his life for the sake of his friend.

◆ *Literature and Your Life*

When have you observed that friendship can be contagious?

Guide for Responding

◆ *Literature and Your Life*

Reader's Response At what point in the story were you most nervous about the return of Pythias? Explain.

Thematic Focus You may not have risked your life for a friend, as Damon does in this tale. However, you have probably helped friends who were in danger of failing a test, not making a team, or doing the wrong thing in a social situation. Choose one such incident and tell how you came through for your friend.

☑ Check Your Comprehension

1. As the story begins, what reputations do Damon, Pythias, and Dionysius have in Syracuse?
2. What are the events leading up to the execution scene at the end?
3. How does the outcome of the story affect the king?

◆ Critical Thinking

INTERPRET

1. Give two examples of how Damon and Pythias are "noble" in ways other than their birth. **[Infer]**
2. Compare and contrast Dionysius's behavior at the beginning and end of the story. **[Compare and Contrast]**
3. Why isn't Damon afraid as he waits for Pythias? **[Infer]**
4. What universal message does this myth teach? **[Interpret]**

EVALUATE

5. Remembering what you know about tyrants—both ancient and modern—decide whether the king's change of heart is realistic. **[Evaluate]**

APPLY

6. Could a friendship like the one between Damon and Pythias exist in our own times? Why or why not? **[Relate]**

from the
Iliad,
from Book XXII

The Death
Of Hektor

Homer

Translated by Richmond Lattimore

At the climax of the Iliad, *Hektor, greatest of the Trojan warriors, has slain Patroklos, best friend of Achilleus. Filled with rage, Achilleus, greatest of the Greek warriors, returns to battle to avenge his friend's death. Aided by the god Apollo, all of the Trojans but Hektor flee to safety within the city walls. Hektor must make a decision whether to stay and fight Achilleus.*

Deeply troubled he [Hektor] spoke to his own great-hearted spirit:
"Ah me! If I go now inside the wall and the gateway,
Poulydamas[1] will be first to put a <u>reproach</u> upon me,
since he tried to make me lead the Trojans inside the city
5 on that accursed night when brilliant Achilleus rose up,
and I would not obey him, but that would have been far better.
Now, since by my own recklessness I have ruined my people,
I feel shame before the Trojans and the Trojan women with trailing
robes, that someone who is less of a man than I will say of me:
10 'Hektor believed in his own strength and ruined his people.'
Thus they will speak; and as for me, it would be much better
at that time, to go against Achilleus, and slay him, and come back,
or else be killed by him in glory in front of the city.
Or if again I set down my shield massive in the middle
15 and my ponderous helm, and lean my spear up against the rampart
and go out as I am to meet Achilleus the blameless
and promise to give back Helen, and with her all her possessions,
all those things that once in the hollow ships Alexandros
brought back to Troy, and these were the beginning of the quarrel;
20 to give these to Atreus' sons to take away, and for the Achaians
also to divide up all that is hidden within the city,
and take an oath thereafter for the Trojans in conclave[2]
not to hide anything away, but distribute all of it,
as much as the lovely citadel keeps guarded within it;
25 yet still, why does the heart within me debate on these things?
I might go up to him, and he take no pity upon me
nor respect my position, but kill me naked so, as if I were
a woman, once I stripped my armor from me. There is no
way any more from a tree or a rock to talk to him gently
30 whispering like a young man and a young girl, in the way
a young man and a young maiden whisper together.
Better to bring on the fight with him as soon as it may be.
We shall see to which one the Olympian grants the glory."
    So he pondered, waiting, but Achilleus was closing upon him
35 in the likeness of the lord of battles, the helm-shining warrior,
and shaking from above his shoulder the dangerous Pelian[3]
ash spear, while the bronze that closed about him was shining

1. **Poulydamas** (pôl′ ə däm′ əs): Fighter and seer who frequently opposed his brother Hektor's reckless strategy.

◆ **Build Vocabulary**
reproach (ri prōch′) *n*.: An expression of blame

2. **conclave** (kän′ klāv′): *n*.: Private or secret meeting.

3. **Pelian** (Pel′ ē ən) *adj*.: Belonging to Peleus, Achilleus' father.

Achilles Defeating Hector, Peter Paul Rubens, Musée des Beaux-Arts, Pau, France

▲ **Critical Viewing** Do you think this depiction of the battle between Hektor and Achilleus by Peter Paul Rubens (1577–1640) is historically accurate? Why or why not? **[Make a Judgment]**

---

like the flare of blazing fire or the sun in its rising.
And the shivers took hold of Hektor when he saw him, and he
    could no longer
stand his ground there, but left the gates behind, and fled,
40   frightened,
and Peleus' son went after him in the confidence of his quick feet.
As when a hawk in the mountains who moves lightest of things
    flying
makes his effortless swoop for a trembling dove, but she slips away
from beneath and flies and he shrill screaming close after her
45   plunges for her again and again, heart furious to take her;
so Achilleus went straight for him in fury, but Hektor
fled away under the Trojan wall and moved his knees rapidly.
They raced along by the watching point and the windy fig tree

always away from under the wall and along the wagon-way
and came to the two sweet-running well springs. There there are

50   double
springs of water that jet up, the springs of whirling Skamandros.
One of these runs hot water and the steam on all sides
of it rises as if from a fire that was burning inside it.
But the other in the summer-time runs water that is like hail

55   or chill snow or ice that forms from water. Beside these
in this place, and close to them, are the washing-hollows
of stone, and magnificent, where the wives of the Trojans and their
       lovely
daughters washed the clothes to shining, in the old days
when there was peace, before the coming of the sons of the
       Achaians.

60   They ran beside these, one escaping, the other after him.
It was a great man who fled, but far better he who pursued him
rapidly, since here was no festal[4] beast, no ox-hide
they strove for, for these are prizes that are given men for their
       running.
No, they ran for the life of Hektor, breaker of horses.

65   As when about the turnposts racing single-foot horses
run at full speed, when a great prize is laid up for their winning,
a tripod or a woman, in games for a man's funeral,
so these two swept whirling about the city of Priam
in the speed of their feet, while all the gods were looking upon them.

70   First to speak among them was the father of gods and mortals;
"Ah me, this a man beloved whom now my eyes watch
being chased around the wall; my heart is mourning for Hektor
who has burned in my honor many thigh pieces of oxen
on the peaks of Ida[5] with all her folds, or again on the uttermost

75   part of the citadel, but now the brilliant Achilleus
drives him in speed of his feet around the city of Priam.
Come then, you immortals, take thought and take counsel, whether
to rescue this man or whether to make him, for all his valor,
go down under the hands of Achilleus, the son of Peleus."

80   Then in answer the goddess gray-eyed Athene spoke to him:
"Father of the shining bolt, dark misted, what is this you said?
Do you wish to bring back a man who is mortal, one long since
doomed by his destiny, from ill-sounding death and release him?
Do it, then; but not all the rest of us gods shall approve you."

85   Then Zeus the gatherer of the clouds spoke to her in answer:
"Tritogeneia,[6] dear daughter, do not lose heart; for I say this
not in outright anger, and my meaning toward you is kindly.
Act as your purpose would have you do, and hold back no longer."
       So he spoke, and stirred on Athene, who was eager before this,

90   and she went in a flash of speed down the pinnacles of Olympos.
But swift Achilleus kept <u>unremittingly</u> after Hektor,
chasing him, as a dog in the mountains who has flushed from his
       covert[7]

4. **festal** (fes′ təl) *adj.*: Of a joyous celebration.

5. **Ida** (ī′ də) *n.*: Mountain near the site of Troy.

6. **Tritogeneia** (trī tō jen′ ē ə): Another name for Athene, who was born near Lake Tritonis in a part of Africa.

7. **covert** (kuv′ ərt) *n.*: A hiding place.

◆ **Build Vocabulary**

unremittingly (un′ ri mit′ iŋ lē) *adv.*: Persistently

a deer's fawn follows him through the folding ways and the valleys,
and though the fawn crouched down under a bush and be hidden
95 he keeps running and noses him out until he comes on him;
so Hektor could not lose himself from swift-footed Peleion.
If ever he made a dash right on for the gates of Dardanos
to get quickly under the strong-built bastion, endeavoring
that they from above with missiles thrown might somehow defend
    him,
100 each time Achilleus would get in front and force him to turn back
into the plain, and himself kept his flying course next the city.
As in a dream a man is not able to follow one who runs
from him, nor can the runner escape, nor the other pursue him,
so he could not run him down in his speed, nor the other get clear.
105 How then could Hektor have escaped the death spirits, had not
Apollo, for this last and uttermost time, stood by him
close, and driven strength into him, and made his knees light?
But brilliant Achilleus kept shaking his head at his own people
and would not let them throw their bitter projectiles[8] at Hektor
110 for fear the thrower might win the glory, and himself come second.
But when for the fourth time they had come around to the well
    springs
then the Father balanced his golden scales, and in them
he set two fateful portions of death, which lays men prostrate;[9]
one for Achilleus, and one for Hektor, breaker of horses,
115 and balanced it by the middle; and Hektor's death-day was heavier
and dragged downward toward death, and Phoibos Apollo
    forsook[10] him.
But the goddess gray-eyed Athene came now to Peleion
and stood close beside him and addressed him in winged words:
    "Beloved
of Zeus, shining Achilleus, I am hopeful now that you and I
120 will take back great glory to the ships of the Achaians, after
we have killed Hektor, for all his slakeless[11] fury for battle.
Now there is no way for him to get clear away from us,
not though Apollo who strikes from afar should be willing to
    undergo
much, and wallow[12] before our father Zeus of the aegis.
125 Stand you here then and get your wind again, while I go
to this man and persuade him to stand up to you in combat."
    So spoke Athene, and he was glad at heart, and obeyed her,
and stopped, and stood leaning on his bronze-barbed ash spear.
    Meanwhile
Athene left him there, and caught up with brilliant Hektor,
130 and likened herself in form and weariless voice to Deïphobos.[13]
She came now and stood close to him and addressed him in
    winged words:
"Dear brother, indeed swift-footed Achilleus is using you roughly
and chasing you on swift feet around the city of Priam.

8. **projectiles** (prō jek´ təlz) *n.*: Objects designed to be thrown forward.

9. **prostrate** (präs´ trāt) *adj.*: Flat; face downward; completely overcome.

10. **forsook** (fôr sŏŏk´) *v.*: Abandoned.

11. **slakeless** (slāk´ ləs) *adj.*: Unable to be satisfied or lessened.

12. **wallow** (wäl´ ō) *v.*: Move heavily and clumsily.

13. **Deïphobos** (dā´ i fō´ bōs): Son of Priam; powerful Trojan fighter.

Come on, then; let us stand fast against him and beat him back
    from us."
135   Then tall Hektor of the shining helm answered her: "Deïphobos,
before now you were dearest to me by far of my brothers,
of all those who were sons of Priam and Hekabe, and now
I am minded all the more within my heart to honor you,
you who dared for my sake, when your eyes saw me, to come forth
140 from the fortifications, while the others stand fast inside them."
     Then in turn the goddess gray-eyed Athene answered him:
"My brother, it is true our father and the lady our mother, taking
my knees in turn, and my companions about me, entreated
that I stay within, such was the terror upon all of them.
145 But the heart within me was worn away by hard sorrow for you.
But now let us go straight on the fight hard, let there be no
    sparing
of our spears, so that we can find out whether Achilleus
will kill us both and carry our bloody war spoils back
to the hollow ships, or will himself go down under your spear."
150   So Athene spoke and led him on by beguilement.
Now as the two in their advance were come close together,
first of the two to speak was tall helm-glittering Hektor:
"Son of Peleus, I will no longer run from you, as before this
I fled three times around the great city of Priam, and dared not
155 stand to your onfall. But now my spirit in turn has driven me
to stand and face you. I must take you now, or I must be taken.
Come then, shall we swear before the gods? For these are the
    highest
who shall be witnesses and watch over our agreements.
Brutal as you are I will not defile you, if Zeus grants
160 to me that I can wear you out, and take the life from you.
But after I have stripped your glorious armor, Achilleus,
I will give your corpse back to the Achaians. Do you do likewise."
     Then looking darkly at him swift-footed Achilleus answered:
"Hektor, argue me no agreements. I cannot forgive you.
165 As there are no trustworthy oaths between men and lions,
nor wolves and lambs have spirit that can be brought to agreement
but forever these hold feelings of hate for each other,
so there can be no love between you and me, nor shall there be
oaths between us, but one or the other must fall before then
to glut with his blood Ares the god who fights under the
170   shield's guard.
Remember every valor of yours, for now the need comes
hardest upon you to be a spearman and a bold warrior.
There shall be no more escape for you, but Pallas Athene
will kill you soon by my spear. You will pay in a lump for all those
175 sorrows of my companions you killed in your spear's fury."
     So he spoke, and balanced the spear far shadowed, and threw it;
but glorious Hektor kept his eyes on him, and avoided it,

◆ **Literary Focus**
Find a stock epithet
in lines 163 to 170.

◆ **Build Vocabulary**
beguilement (bē gīl′
mənt) *n.*: Trickery; deceit

▲ **Critical Viewing** Which of the figures in this tapestry is Hektor? Why? **[Interpret]**

Hector and Andromache From the Destruction of Troy, from the *Trojan War* series, workshop of Pasquier Grenier(?), Tournai, France, The Metropolitan Museum of Art

for he dropped, watchful, to his knee, and the bronze spear flew
over his shoulder
and stuck in the ground, but Pallas Athene snatched it, and
    gave it
180 back to Achilleus, unseen by Hektor shepherd of the people.
But now Hektor spoke out to the blameless son of Peleus:
"You missed; and it was not, o Achilleus like the immortals,
from Zeus that you knew my destiny; but you thought so;
    or rather
you are someone clever in speech and spoke to swindle me,
185 to make me afraid of you and forget my valor and war strength.
You will not stick your spear in my back as I run away from you
but drive it into my chest as I storm straight in against you;
if the god gives you that; and now look out for my brazen
spear. I wish it might be taken full length in your body.
190 And indeed the war would be a lighter thing for the Trojans
if you were dead, seeing that you are their greatest affliction."
    So he spoke, and balanced the spear far shadowed, and threw it,
and struck the middle of Peleïdes' shield, nor missed it,
but the spear was driven far back from the shield, and Hektor was
    angered
because his swift weapon had been loosed from his hand in a vain[14]
195   cast.
He stood discouraged, and had no other ash spear; but lifting
his voice he called aloud on Deïphobos of the pale shield,
and asked him for a long spear, but Deïphobos was not near him.
And Hektor knew the truth inside his heart, and spoke aloud:
200 "No use. Here at last the gods have summoned me deathward.
I thought Deïphobos the hero was here close beside me,
but he is behind the wall and it was Athene cheating me,
and now evil death is close to me, and no longer far away,
and there is no way out. So it must long since have been pleasing
to Zeus, and Zeus' son who strikes from afar, this way; though
205   before this
they defended me gladly. But now my death is upon me.
Let me at least not die without a struggle, inglorious,
but do some big thing first, that men to come shall know of it."
    So he spoke, and pulling out the sharp sword that was slung
210 at the hollow of his side, huge and heavy, and gathering
himself together, he made his swoop, like a high-flown eagle
who launches himself out of the murk of the clouds on the flat
    land
to catch away a tender lamb or a shivering hare; so
Hektor made his swoop, swinging his sharp sword, and Achilleus
215 charged, the heart within him loaded with savage fury.
In front of his chest the beautiful elaborate great shield
covered him, and with the glittering helm with four horns
he nodded; the lovely golden fringes were shaken about it

14. vain (vān) *adj.*: Ineffective; fruitless; unprofitable.

which Hephaistos had driven close along the horn of the helmet.
220 And as a star moves among stars in the night's darkening,
Hesper, who is the fairest star who stands in the sky, such
was the shining from the pointed spear Achilleus was shaking
in his right hand with evil intention toward brilliant Hektor.
He was eyeing Hektor's splendid body, to see where it might best
225 give way, but all the rest of the skin was held in the armor,
    brazen and splendid, he stripped when he cut down the strength of
      Patroklos;
    yet showed where the collar-bones hold the neck from the
      shoulders,
    the throat, where death of the soul comes most swiftly; in this
      place
    brilliant Achilleus drove the spear as he came on in fury,
    and clean through the soft part of the neck the spearpoint was
230   driven.
Yet the ash spear heavy with bronze did not sever the windpipe,
so that Hektor could still make exchange of words spoken.
But he dropped in the dust, and brilliant Achilleus vaunted above
    him:
"Hektor, surely you thought as you killed Patroklos you would be
235 safe, and since I was far away you thought nothing of me,
o fool, for an <u>avenger</u> was left, far greater than he was,
behind him and away by the hollow ships. And it was I;
and I have broken your strength; on you the dogs and the vultures
shall feed and foully rip you; the Achaians will bury Patroklos."
240   In his weakness Hektor of the shining helm spoke to him:
"I entreat you, by your life, by your knees, by your parents,
do not let the dogs feed on me by the ships of the Achaians,
but take yourself the bronze and gold that are there in abundance,
those gifts that my father and the lady my mother will give you,
245 and give my body to be taken home again, so that the Trojans
and the wives of the Trojans may give me in death my rite of
      burning."[15]
    But looking darkly at him swift-footed Achilleus answered:
"No more entreating of me, you dog, by knees or parents.
I wish only that my spirit and fury would drive me
250 to hack your meat away and eat it raw for the things that
you have done to me. So there is no one who can hold the dogs
    off
from your head, not if they bring here and set before me ten times
and twenty times the ransom, and promise more in addition,
not if Priam son of Dardanos should offer to weigh out
255 your bulk in gold; not even so shall the lady your mother
who herself bore you lay you on the death-bed and mourn you:
no, but the dogs and the birds will have you all for their feasting."
    Then, dying, Hektor of the shining helmet spoke to him:
"I know you well as I look upon you, I know that I could not

◆ **Reading Strategy**
Write a sentence summing up the main action in the sentence in lines 220 to 223.

15. **rite of burning:** Proper funeral ritual of burning the dead body.

◆ **Build Vocabulary**
avenger (ə ven´ jər) *n.*: One who takes revenge, especially on behalf of another

260 persuade you, since indeed in your breast is a heart of iron.
Be careful now; for I might be made into the gods' curse
upon you, on that day when Paris and Phoibos Apollo
destroy you in the Skaian gates, for all your valor."
    He spoke, and as he spoke the end of death closed in upon him,
and the soul fluttering free of the limbs went down into Death's
265   house
mourning her destiny, leaving youth and manhood behind her.
Now though he was a dead man brilliant Achilleus spoke to him:
"Die: and I will take my own death at whatever time
Zeus and the rest of the immortals choose to accomplish it."
270   He spoke, and pulled the brazen spear from the body, and laid it
on one side, and stripped away from the shoulders the bloody
armor. And the other sons of the Achaians came running about
    him,
and gazed upon the stature and on the imposing beauty
of Hektor; and none stood beside him who did not stab him;
and thus they would speak one to another, each looking at his
275   neighbor:
"See now, Hektor is much softer to handle than he was
when he set the ships ablaze with the burning firebrand."
    So as they stood beside him they would speak, and stab him.
But now, when he had despoiled[16] the body, swift-footed brilliant
Achilleus stood among the Achaians and addressed them in winged
280   words:
"Friends, who are leaders of the Argives and keep their counsel:
since the gods have granted me the killing of this man
who has done us much damage, such as not all the others together
have done, come, let us go in armor about the city
285 to see if we can find out what purpose is in the Trojans,
whether they will abandon their high city, now that this man
has fallen, or are minded to stay, though Hektor lives no longer.
Yet still, why does the heart within me debate on these things?
There is a dead man who lies by the ships, unwept, unburied:
290 Patroklos: and I will not forget him, never so long as
I remain among the living and my knees have their spring beneath me.
And though the dead forget the dead in the house of Hades,
even there I shall still remember my beloved companion.
But now, you young men of the Achaians, let us go back, singing
295 a victory song, to our hollow ships; and take this with us.
We have won ourselves enormous fame; we have killed the great
    Hektor
whom the Trojans glorified as if he were a god in their city."
    He spoke, and now thought of shameful treatment for glorious
    Hektor.
In both of his feet at the back he made holes by the tendons
in the space between ankle and heel, and drew thongs of ox-hide
300   through them,

16. **despoiled** (dē spoild') v.:
Deprived of value and honor.

and fastened them to the chariot so as to let the head drag,
and mounted the chariot, and lifted the glorious armor inside it,
then whipped the horses to a run, and they winged their way
    unreluctant.
A cloud of dust rose where Hektor was dragged, his dark hair was
    falling
about him, and all that head that was once so handsome was
305   tumbled
in the dust; since by this time Zeus had given him over
to his enemies, to be defiled in the land of his fathers.
    So all his head was dragged in the dust; and now his mother
tore out her hair, and threw the shining veil far from her
310 and raised a great wail as she looked upon her son; and his father
beloved groaned pitifully, and all his people about him
were taken with wailing and lamentation all through the city.
It was most like what would have happened, if all lowering
Ilion had been burning top to bottom in fire.
315 His people could scarcely keep the old man in his impatience
from storming out of the Dardanian gates; he <u>implored</u> them
all, and wallowed in the muck before them calling on each man
and naming him by his name: "Give way, dear friends,
and let me alone though you care for me, leave me to go out
320 from the city and make my way to the ships of the Achaians.
I must be suppliant to this man, who is harsh and violent,
and he might have respect for my age and take pity upon it
since I am old, and his father also is old, as I am,
Peleus, who begot and reared him to be an affliction
325 on the Trojans. He has given us most sorrow, beyond all others,
such is the number of my flowering sons he has cut down.
But for all of these I mourn not so much, in spite of my sorrow,
as for one, Hektor, and the sharp grief for him will carry me
    downward
into Death's house. I wish he had died in my arms, for that way
330 we two, I myself and his mother who bore him unhappy,
might so have glutted[17] ourselves with weeping for him and
    mourning."
    So he spoke, in tears, and beside him mourned the citizens.
But for the women of Troy Hekabe led out the thronging
chant of sorrow: "Child, I am wretched. What shall my life be
335 in my sorrows, now you are dead, who by day and in the night
were my glory in the town, and to all of the Trojans
and the women of Troy a blessing throughout their city. They
    adored you
as if you were a god, since in truth you were their high honor
while you lived. Now death and fate have closed in upon you."
340   So she spoke in tears but the wife of Hektor had not yet
heard: for no sure messenger had come to her and told her
how her husband had held his ground there outside the gates;

◆ **Literature
and Your Life**
Describe a time
when someone you
know took a vic-
tory "too far."
Compare the per-
son's actions to
those of Achilleus.
**[Compare
and Contrast]**

17. glutted (glut′ əd) v.:
Filled; stated.

◆ **Build Vocabulary**
implored (im plord′) v.:
Asked or begged
earnestly

Hephaestus Making Armor for Achilles (detail),
The Dutuit Painter, Museum of Fine Arts, Boston

◀ **Critical Viewing** This vase painting shows the blacksmith god Hephaistos making a shield for Achilleus. Why do you think the quality of a shield was important? Cite a passage from the text to support your answer. **[Speculate]**

but she was weaving a web in the inner room of the high house,
a red folding robe, and inworking[18] elaborate figures.

345   She called out through the house to her lovely-haired handmaidens
to set a great cauldron over the fire, so that there would be
hot water for Hektor's bath as he came back out of the fighting;
poor innocent, nor knew how, far from waters for bathing,
Pallas Athene had cut him down at the hands of Achilleus.
She heard from the great bastion the noise of mourning and

350   sorrow.
Her limbs spun, and the shuttle dropped from her hand to the
     ground.
Then she called aloud to her lovely-haired handmaidens: "Come
     here.
Two of you come with me, so I can see what has happened.

355   I heard the voice of Hektor's honored mother; within me

18. inworking (in´ wər´ kiŋ)
v.: Sewing into fabric.

from the Iliad, *from* Book XXII, *"The Death of Hektor"* ◆ *239*

my own heart rising beats in my mouth, my limbs under me
are frozen. Surely some evil is near for the children of Priam.
May what I say come never close to my ear; yet dreadfully
I fear that great Achilleus might have cut off bold Hektor

360 alone, away from the city, and be driving him into the flat land,
might put an end to that bitter pride of courage, that always
was on him, since he would never stay back where the men were in
   numbers
but break far out in front, and give way in his fury to no man."
   So she spoke, and ran out of the house like a raving woman

365 with pulsing heart, and her two handmaidens went along with her.
But when she came to the bastion and where the men were
   gathered
she stopped, staring, on the wall; and she saw him
being dragged in front of the city, and the running horses
dragged him at random toward the hollow ships of the Achaians.

370 The darkness of night misted over the eyes of Andromache.
She fell backward, and gasped the life breath from her, and far off
threw from her head the shining gear that ordered her headdress,
the diadem[19] and the cap, and the holding-band woven together,
and the circlet,[20] which Aphrodite the golden once had given her

375 on that day when Hektor of the shining helmet led her forth
from the house of Eëtion, and gave numberless gifts to win her.
And about her stood thronging her husband's sisters and the wives
   of his brothers
and these, in her despair for death, held her up among them.
But she, when she breathed again and the life was gathered back
   into her,

380 lifted her voice among the women of Troy in mourning:
"Hektor, I grieve for you. You and I were born to a single
destiny, you in Troy in the house of Priam, and I
in Thebe, underneath the timbered[21] mountain of Plakos
in the house of Eëtion, who cared for me when I was little,

385 ill-fated he, I ill-starred. I wish he had never begotten me.
Now you go down to the house of Death in the secret places
of the earth, and left me here behind in the sorrow of mourning,
a widow in your house, and the boy is only a baby
who was born to you and me, the unfortunate. You cannot help
   him,

390 Hektor, any more, since you are dead. Nor can he help you.
Though he escape the attack of the Achaians with all its sorrows,
yet all his days for your sake there will be hard work for him
and sorrows, for others will take his lands away from him. The day
of bereavement leaves a child with no agemates to befriend him.

395 He bows his head before every man, his cheeks are bewept,[22] he
goes, needy, a boy among his father's companions,
and tugs at this man by the mantle, that man by the tunic,
and they pity him, and one gives him a tiny drink from a goblet,

19. diadem (dī ə dem´) *n.*:
A decorated cloth headband
worn as a crown.

20. circlet (sʉr´ klit) *n.*: A
ring or circular band worn
on the head.

21. timbered (tim´ bərd)
adj.: Covered with trees.

22. bewept (bē wept´)
adj.: Wet with tears.

enough to moisten his lips, not enough to moisten his palate.

400 But one whose parents are living beats him out of the banquet
hitting him with his fists and in words also abuses him:
'Get out, you! Your father is not dining among us.'
And the boy goes away in tears to his widowed mother,
Astyanax, who in days before on the knees of his father

405 would eat only the marrow or the flesh of sheep that was fattest.
And when sleep would come upon him and he was done with his
    playing,
he would go to sleep in a bed, in the arms of his nurse, in a soft
bed, with his heart given all its fill of luxury.
Now, with his dear father gone, he has much to suffer:

410 he, whom the Trojans have called Astyanax, lord of the city,
since it was you alone who defended the gates and the long walls.
But now, beside the curving ships, far away from your parents,
the writhing worms will feed, when the dogs have had enough of
    you,
on your naked corpse, though in your house there is clothing laid up

415 that is fine-textured and pleasant, wrought by the hands of women.
But all of these I will burn up in the fire's blazing,
no use to you, since you will never be laid away in them;
but in your honor, from the men of Troy and the Trojan women."
    So she spoke, in tears; and the women joined in her mourning.

Guide for Responding

◆ Literature and Your Life

Reader's Response Do you think that Hektor chose wisely or foolishly in deciding to face Achilleus alone?

Thematic Focus How do Hektor's choices affect the fate of his city? How do Achilleus' choices affect the fate of others?

☑ Check Your Comprehension

1. What decision does Hektor make in the opening scene?
2. What does Hektor ask of Achilleus before they fight?
3. What role does Athene play in Hektor's defeat?
4. How does Achilleus treat the corpse of slain Hektor?
5. How does Hektor's wife react to his death? How does Priam react?

◆ Critical Thinking

INTERPRET
1. Give three motives that affect Hektor's decision to fight Achilleus. **[Analyze]**
2. What does Achilleus mean when he says that there can be "no trustworthy oaths between men and lions"? **[Interpret]**
3. What does Achilleus' treatment of Hektor's corpse show about Achilleus? **[Infer]**
4. Is Homer's world a world of "good guys" and "bad guys," or are his characters more rounded? Support your answer with details from the selection. **[Draw Conclusions]**

COMPARE LITERARY WORKS
5. Compare the results of friendship in "Damon and Pythias" and in the *Iliad*. Explain what factors besides friendship distinguish the two situations. **[Compare and Contrast]**

Guide for Responding (continued)

◆ Reading Strategy

ANALYZE CONFUSING SENTENCES

You can **analyze confusing sentences** in literature by first identifying the essential actions or conditions they describe. Then, you can relate additional phrases to those actions to appreciate the full impact of the sentences.

For instance, in the following sentence from "Damon and Pythias," you can identify two main actions: "It happened that *Pythias had,* quite unjustly, *been accused* by Dionysius of trying to overthrow him, and for this supposed crime of treason *Pythias was sentenced* by the king *to die.*" The other words in the sentence fill out the picture of these main actions.

Identify the main action(s) in each of the following sentences. Then, write a short sentence explaining another detail the sentence gives about the main action.

1. The paragraph beginning "Presently the excitement grew more intense still" in "Damon and Pythias," p. 227.
2. Lines 209 to 215 of "The Death of Hektor."
3. Lines 345 to 349 of "The Death of Hektor."

◆ Build Vocabulary

USING THE LATIN ROOT -ped-

Knowing that the Latin root *-ped-* means "foot," write a definition for the following words:

1. pedestrian   2. pedal   3. pedicure

USING THE WORD BANK: Antonyms

On your paper, write the letter of the word that is closest to being the antonym—the word opposite in meaning—of the first word:

1. impediments: (a) footwear, (b) obstacles, (c) aids
2. hindrances: (a) fronts, (b) conveniences, (c) lances
3. reproach: (a) praise, (b) recook, (c) fault
4. implored: (a) prayed, (b) commanded, (c) wept
5. avenger: (a) victim, (b) detective, (c) vindicator
6. unremittingly: (a) nonstop, (b) occasionally, (c) constantly
7. beguilement: (a) disenchantment, (b) innocence, (c) craftiness
8. annals: (a) records, (b) myths, (c) newspapers

◆ Literary Focus

MYTH AND EPIC

A **myth** is a story about gods and heroes that has been passed down by tradition. It answers basic questions about the world and human values. An **epic poem,** drawing on a people's mythological traditions, glorifies the deeds of a hero from the mythical past.

1. Describe one way in which "Damon and Pythias" resembles other myths and one way in which it does not.
2. Find three examples of repeated epithets (adjective-noun phrases) used by Homer.
3. The *Iliad* celebrates warrior values, such as glory and fierceness in battle. (a) Explain how Hektor's and Achilleus' actions illustrate these values. (b) Explain how Homer uses their story to show the high price of holding to these values.

◆ Build Grammar Skills

RESTRICTIVE AND NONRESTRICTIVE APPOSITIVES

An **appositive** is a noun or noun phrase placed near another noun or pronoun to explain it. A **restrictive appositive** adds essential information about the noun or pronoun and is not set off by commas. A **nonrestrictive appositive** does not add essential information and is set off by commas.

Practice Identify the appositive phrase in each sentence as *restrictive* or *nonrestrictive,* and indicate whether commas are needed to set it off.

1. Dionysius the hard-hearted tyrant, however, would not believe Pythias' promise to return. . . .
2. But the goddess gray-eyed Athene came now to Peleion and stood close beside him. . . .
3. But now, you young men of the Achaians, let us go back, singing a victory song, to our hollow ships. . . .

Writing Application Combine these pairs of sentences using appositive phrases.

1. Damon and Pythias are a model of friendship. Damon and Pythias were two noble young men from Syracuse.
2. Hektor had slain Achilleus' best friend. Patroklos was Achilleus' friend.

Build Your Portfolio

 ## Idea Bank

Writing

1. **Hero** Write a definition of a hero in today's world. Give examples from movies, contemporary events, or sports. Then, explain which heroes, Achilleus, Hektor, or Damon and Pythias, best fit your definition.

2. **Editorial** Write two brief editorials, one for the *Achaian Examiner* and one for the *Trojan Times,* commenting on whether or not Achilleus' treatment of Hektor was heroic. Adopt a point of view appropriate to your intended, ancient-times audience.

3. **Everyday Epic** Take an event from your daily life and write an epic version of it. Use Homeric techniques to make your character and events larger than life. Include epithets, extended comparisons, and repetitions.

Speaking, Listening, and Viewing

4. **Skit** Write a brief skit adapting the story of Damon and Pythias to modern circumstances. Present it to the class. **[Performing Arts Link]**

5. **Movie Preview** Write the narration for a preview of a film version of "The Death of Hektor." Perform your preview for the class. **[Performing Arts Link]**

Researching and Representing

6. **Memorial Marker** Research *stelae* (Greek grave markers), and then draw a *stele* for Damon and Pythias, complete with an epitaph summing up their lives. **[Art Link; Social Studies Link]**

7. **Multimedia Map** Create a multimedia map of Homer's Troy. Link sites on the map to photographs, sound recordings, and references to the *Iliad.* **[Social Studies Link]**

Online Activity www.phlit.phschool.com

 ## Guided Writing Lesson

Code of Conduct

When Achilleus drags Hektor's body around the battlefield, you might think he is violating an unwritten rule: Victors should be merciful. Unofficial rules govern our behavior in a few areas of life, such as sports. Write an essay in which you create a code of conduct for a particular team sport.

Writing Skills Focus: Classification

Classification is the art of sorting a group of items into categories (general classes). Your essay will be better organized if you first identify several types of situations in which rules are needed. For instance, you might discuss some rules under "How to Act When Your Team Wins."

Prewriting Choose a team sport. Then, use a classification chart like the following to organize your ideas.

TYPE OF CONDUCT	Acceptable Behavior	Unacceptable Behavior
Treatment of opponents	polite acknowledgment	yelling insults
Player's reaction to his or her own achievement		

Drafting As you draft, explain each rule thoroughly, giving examples of acceptable and unacceptable conduct.

Revising Ask a partner to read your draft and comment on the organization and clarity of your exposition. Use his or her comments to help guide your revision.

Be sure that you have correctly used restrictive and nonrestrictive appositives. For more on these two types of appositives, see pages 222 and 242.

Guide for Reading

Publius Cornelius Tacitus

(A.D. 56–d.c. 120)

Publius Cornelius Tacitus (tas´ i təs) lived in the early decades of the Roman Empire, when the more liberal rule of the Roman Republic had been replaced by the rule of one man. Tacitus survived the oppressive regimes of a few depraved and tyrannical emperors, mainly by keeping silent.

Breaking Silence When the vicious emperor Domitian died, though, in A.D. 96, the long period of censorship in Rome ended. At last it was possible to tell the truth. Tacitus turned to writing history. Looking back on the days of oppression, he observes, "We should have lost memory as well as voice, had it been as easy to forget as to keep silence." Tacitus' portrayal of the early emperors, especially Nero, broke that silence, and ensured that the history of their abuses would be remembered for millennia.

The Works Tacitus was a master of several kinds of prose writing on a variety of subjects. His major works, the *Annals* and the *Histories,* give a year-by-year account of the first eighty years of the Roman Empire. The *Annals* begins with the death of Augustus Caesar in A.D. 14 and end with the death of Nero in A.D. 68. The *Histories* continue the story of the empire down to the assassination of Domitian in A.D. 96.

In all his works, Tacitus shows a gift for drama, as well as a genius for concise, convincing psychological portraits. The results in the *Annals* are an unforgettable condemnation of the abuse of power and a powerful argument in favor of truth and virtue.

Statesman, Soldier, Orator, Historian
Domitian's death also opened the way for Tacitus' success in public life. Well schooled in the arts of oratory and persuasion, he performed brilliantly as a trial lawyer and judge. His long silence over, the words with which he broke it were eloquent and powerful.

◆ Build Vocabulary

LATIN SUFFIXES: *-tion*

In the *Annals,* you will encounter the word *conflagration,* derived from the Latin verb *conflagrare,* which means "to burn." The suffix *-tion* means "the act, state, or quality of." *Conflagration* means "a great state of burning, or a disastrous fire."

conflagration
unhampered
destitute
antiquity
precipitous
demarcation
munificence

WORD BANK

Preview this list of words from the selection before you read. Each is defined on the page where it first appears.

◆ Build Grammar Skills

COMMONLY CONFUSED WORDS: *less* and *fewer*

Less is used with qualities or quantities that cannot be counted. It modifies a singular noun and answers the question "How much?"

It takes *less* time to start a conflagration than it takes to extinguish it.

Fewer is used with objects that can be counted. It modifies a plural noun and answers the question "How many?"

Here there were *fewer* casualties; but the destruction of temples and pleasure arcades was even worse.

from the Annals:
from The Burning of Rome

◆ Literature and Your Life

CONNECT YOUR EXPERIENCE

If a bus you are riding breaks down, the easy rhythm of the day is interrupted, replaced by a confused babble of questions: "What happened? How long will it take to fix?"

When Rome caught on fire in A.D. 64, the rhythms of life were interrupted in ways more serious than a bus breakdown. Tacitus shows that, as questions poured in, the emperor's answers were not always reassuring.

THEMATIC FOCUS: HUMANS AND NATURE

As you read, notice the ways in which natural forces interrupt the orderly rhythms of life, and the ways in which people respond.

Journal Writing Note what you would do if a natural force, such as a fire or flood, interrupted your daily routines.

◆ Background for Understanding

CULTURE

In 31 B.C., after a century of civil war, the Roman Republic died and the Empire was born. The outward show of a republic survived: a senate, a popular assembly, and presiding magistrates. These institutions, however, merely rubber-stamped imperial decisions. Any resemblance to democracy was an illusion.

The first emperor, Augustus, was a responsible ruler, but those who came after were tyrants who governed badly. Tacitus presents Nero to us as a terrifying example of the dangers of this kind of absolute power.

◆ Literary Focus

ANNALS

In historical writing, **annals** are histories that present events year by year, using simple chronological sequence (*annus* is Latin for "year").

Annals-writing has the virtue of a clear, straightforward organization. It may lack, though, in explanations, interpretations, and descriptive color. The earliest Roman annals were the Great Annals, a record of the year's most important events posted by a high priest. Beginning in the late third century B.C., Roman historians began to fill in chronological presentations of events with dialogue, narrative, description, and explanation. Tacitus, with his narrative skills and insight into characters and causes, brought new depth to this form of historical writing.

◆ Reading Strategy

REREAD OR READ AHEAD

Don't get stuck on a word or detail that you don't understand. Use the strategies of reading ahead and rereading. When you **read ahead,** you may find help understanding an unfamiliar word or new detail further on.

For example, when you read that Nero punished Christians "with every refinement," you may wonder what *refinement* has to do with *punishment.* If you read ahead, you will see that Tacitus means the punishments were elaborate, cruel spectacles.

Some sentences or paragraphs are confusing because they contain unfamiliar ideas or references. In such cases, **reread** the sentence or paragraph to find the connections between details.

For example, by rereading the first paragraph of "The Burning of Rome," you can understand the connections among the Circus, the Palatine hills, and the Caelian hills, even if the names are unfamiliar to you: The hills lie near the Circus, which is a flat area.

The Burning of Rome, Hubert Robert, Musée des Beaux-Arts Andre Malraux, Le Havre, France

▲ **Critical Viewing** Basing your answer on this painting, how serious was the fire that Tacitus describes? [Analyze]

FROM THE ANNALS
FROM THE BURNING OF ROME
TACITUS　　TRANSLATED BY MICHAEL GRANT

Now started the most terrible and destructive fire which Rome had ever experienced. It began in the Circus,[1] where it adjoins the Palatine and Caelian hills.[2] Breaking out in shops selling inflammable goods, and fanned by the wind, the <u>conflagration</u> instantly grew and swept the whole length of the Circus. There were no walled mansions or temples, or any other obstructions, which could arrest it. First, the fire swept violently over the level spaces. Then it climbed the hills—but returned to ravage the lower ground again. It outstripped every counter-measure. The ancient city's narrow winding streets and irregular blocks encouraged its progress.

Terrified, shrieking women, helpless old and young, people intent on their own safety, people unselfishly supporting invalids or waiting for them, fugitives and lingerers alike—all heightened the confusion. When people looked back, menacing flames sprang up before them or outflanked them. When they escaped to a neighboring quarter, the fire followed—even districts believed remote proved to be involved. Finally, with no idea where or what to flee they crowded onto the country roads or lay in the fields. Some who had lost everything—even their food for the day—could have escaped, but preferred to die. So did others, who had failed to rescue their loved ones. Nobody dared fight the flames. Attempts to do so were prevented by menacing gangs. Torches, too, were openly thrown in, by men crying that they acted under orders. Perhaps they had received orders. Or they may just have wanted to plunder <u>unhampered</u>.

Nero was at Antium.[3] He only returned to

---

3. **Antium** (an´ tē əm) *n*.: Town in central Italy where Nero was born.

---

1. **Circus** (sur´ kəs) *n*.: In ancient Rome, games and chariot races were held in the Circus, an oval arena surrounded by tiers of seats.
2. **Palatine and Caelian** (pal´ ə tīn´ and kē´ lē ən) **hills**: Where Nero's imperial palaces were located.

◆ Build Vocabulary

conflagration (kän´ flə grā´ shən) *n*.: A large fire
unhampered (un ham´ pərd) *adv*.: Not hindered or impeded; free of burdens or other constraints

the city when the fire was approaching the mansion he had built to link the Gardens of Maecenas to the Palatine. The flames could not be prevented from overwhelming the whole of the Palatine, including his palace. Nevertheless, for the relief of the homeless, fugitive masses he threw open the Field of Mars, including Agrippa's public buildings, and even his own Gardens. Nero also constructed emergency accommodation for the destitute multitude. Food was brought from Ostia[4] and neighboring towns, and the price of corn was cut to less than ¼ sesterce[5] a pound. Yet these measures, for all their popular character, earned no gratitude. For a rumor had spread that, while the city was burning, Nero had gone on his private stage and, comparing modern calamities with ancient, had sung of the destruction of Troy.

◆ **Literary Focus**
What characteristic of annals does this paragraph illustrate?

By the sixth day enormous demolitions had confronted the raging flames with bare ground and open sky, and the fire was finally stamped out at the foot of the Esquiline Hill. But before panic had subsided, or hope revived, flames broke out again in the more open regions of the city. Here there were fewer casualties; but the destruction of temples and pleasure arcades was even worse. This new conflagration caused additional ill-feeling because it started on Tigellinus' estate[6] in the Aemilian district. For people believed that Nero was ambitious to found a new city to be called after himself.

---

4. **Ostia** (äs′ tē ə) *n*.: Roman port at the mouth of the Tiber River.
5. **sesterce** (ses′ tərs) *n*.: Roman coin, equal in value to two and a half cents.
6. **Tigellinus' estate** (ti jel ē′ nəs): Land belonging to Tigellinus, second to Nero in power.

Of Rome's fourteen districts only four remained intact. Three were leveled to the ground. The other seven were reduced to a few scorched and mangled ruins. To count the mansions, blocks, and temples destroyed would be difficult. They included shrines of remote antiquity, such as Servius Tullius' temple of the Moon, the Great Altar and holy place dedicated by Evander to Hercules, the temple vowed by Romulus to Jupiter the Stayer, Numa's sacred residence, and Vesta's shrine containing Rome's household gods. Among the losses, too, were the precious spoils of countless victories, Greek artistic masterpieces, and authentic records of old Roman genius. All the splendor of the rebuilt city did not prevent the older generation from remembering these irreplaceable objects. It was noted that the fire had started on July 19th, the day on which the Senonian Gauls[7] had captured and burnt the city. Others elaborately calculated that the two fires were separated by the same number of years, months, and days.[8]

---

7. **Senonian Gauls** (sə nō′ nē ən gôlz): Barbarians from Gaul, an ancient region in western Europe; they burned Rome in 390 B.C.
8. **the same number of years, months, and days:** 418 years, months, and days.

◆ **Build Vocabulary**

destitute (des′ tə tōōt′) *adj*.: Not having; lacking; poor

antiquity (an tik′ wə tē) *n*.: The early period of history

precipitous (prē sip′ ə təs) *adj*.: Steep

demarcation (dē′ mär kā′ shən) *n*.: Boundary

But Nero profited by his country's ruin to build a new palace. Its wonders were not so much customary and commonplace luxuries like gold and jewels, but lawns and lakes and faked rusticity—woods here, open spaces and views there. With their cunning, impudent[9] artificialities, Nero's architects and engineers, Severus and Celer, did not balk at effects which Nature herself had ruled out as impossible.

They also fooled away an emperor's riches. For they promised to dig a navigable canal from Lake Avernus to the Tiber estuary,[10] over the stony shore and mountain barriers. The only water to feed the canal was in the Pontine marshes. Elsewhere, all was <u>precipitous</u> or waterless. Moreover, even if a passage could have been forced, the labor would have been unendurable and unjustified. But Nero was eager to perform the incredible; so he attempted to excavate the hills adjoining Lake Avernus. Traces of his frustrated hopes are visible today.

In parts of Rome unfilled by Nero's palace, construction was not—as after the burning by the Gauls without plan or <u>demarcation</u>. Street-fronts were of regulated alignment, streets were broad, and houses built round courtyards. Their height was restricted, and their frontages protected by colonnades. Nero undertook to erect these at his own expense, and also to clear debris from building-sites before transferring them to their owners. He announced bonuses, in proportion to rank and resources, for the completion of houses and blocks before a given date. Rubbish was to be dumped in the Ostian marshes by cornships returning down the Tiber.

A fixed proportion of every building had to be massive, unlimbered stone from Gabii[11] or Alba[12] (these stones being fireproof). Furthermore, guards were to ensure a more abundant and extensive public water supply, hitherto diminished by irregular private enterprise. Householders were obliged to keep firefighting apparatus in an accessible place; and semidetached houses were forbidden—they must have their own

◆ **Reading Strategy**
Read ahead in this sentence to determine the meaning of the word *semi-detached*.

walls. These measures were welcomed for their practicality, and they beautified the new city. Some, however, believed that the old town's configuration had been healthier, since its narrow streets and high houses had provided protection against the burning sun, whereas now the shadowless open spaces radiated a fiercer heat.

So much for human precautions. Next came attempts to appease heaven. After consultation of the Sibylline Books,[13] prayers were addressed to Vulcan, Ceres, and Proserpina. Juno, too, was propitiated.[14] Women who had been married were responsible for the rites—first on the Capitol, then at the nearest sea-board, where water was taken to sprinkle her temple and statue. Women with husbands living also celebrated ritual banquets and vigils.

---

9. impudent (im´ pyoo dənt) *adj.*: Shamelessly bold and disrespectful; saucy.

10. Tiber estuary (tī´ bər es´ choo wer´ ē): The wide mouth of the Tiber, a river in central Italy that flows south through Rome.

11. Gabii (gäb´ ē ē) *n.*: Ancient Roman town where Romulus, legendary founder of Rome, was reared. Gabii supposedly resisted a siege and was an important city until it was overshadowed by Rome.

12. Alba (äl´ bə) *n.*: Alba Longa, a powerful ancient Roman city; legendary birthplace of Romulus and Remus.

13. Sibylline (sib´ əl in) **Books:** Books of prophecies by Sibyl, Apollo's priestess at Cumae, a city in southwest Italy near Naples.

14. propitiated (prō pish´ ē āt´ əd) *v.*: Appeased.

But neither human resources, nor imperial munificence, nor appeasement of the gods, eliminated sinister suspicions that the fire had been instigated. To suppress this rumor, Nero fabricated scapegoats—and punished with every refinement the notoriously depraved Christians (as they were popularly called). Their originator, Christ, had been executed in Tiberius' reign[15] by the governor of Judaea,[16] Pontius Pilatus. But in spite of this temporary setback the deadly superstition had broken out afresh, not only in Judaea (where the mischief had started) but even in Rome. All degraded and shameful practices collect and flourish in the capital.

First, Nero had self-acknowledged Christians arrested. Then, on their information, large numbers of others were condemned—not so much for incendiarism[17] as for their antisocial tendencies. Their deaths were made farcical. Dressed in wild animals' skins, they were torn to pieces by dogs, or crucified, or made into torches to be ignited after dark as substitutes for daylight. Nero provided his Gardens for the spectacle, and exhibited displays in the Circus, at which he mingled with the crowd—or stood in a chariot, dressed as a charioteer. Despite their guilt as Christians, and the ruthless punishment it deserved, the victims were pitied. For it was felt that they were being sacrificed to one man's brutality rather than to the national interest.

Meanwhile Italy was ransacked for funds, and the provinces were ruined—unprivileged and privileged communities alike. Even the gods were included in the looting. Temples at Rome were robbed, and emptied of the gold dedicated for the triumphs and vows, the ambitions and fears, of generations of Romans. Plunder from Asia and Greece included not only offerings but actual statues of the gods. Two agents were sent to these provinces. One, Acratus, was an ex-slave, capable of any depravity. The other, Secundus Carrinas, professed Greek culture, but no virtue from it percolated to his heart.

Seneca,[18] rumor went, sought to avoid the odium of this sacrilege by asking leave to retire to a distant country retreat, and then—permission being refused—feigning a muscular complaint and keeping to his bedroom. According to some accounts one of his former slaves, Cleonicus by name, acting on Nero's orders intended to poison Seneca but he escaped—either because the man confessed or because Seneca's own fears caused him to live very simply on plain fruit, quenching his thirst with running water.

At this juncture there was an attempted breakout by gladiators at Praeneste.[19] Their army guards overpowered them. But the Roman public, as always terrified (or fascinated) by revolution, were already talking of ancient calamities such as the rising of Spartacus.[20] Soon afterwards a naval disaster occurred. This was not on active service; never had there been such profound peace. But Nero had ordered the fleet to return to Campania by a fixed date regardless of

> ◆ **Literary Focus**
> Explain how, in this paragraph, Tacitus goes beyond the information strictly required by annals-writing.

---

15. Tiberius' (tī bir´ ē əs) **reign:** Tiberius was emperor of Rome A.D. 14–37.
16. Judaea (jōō dē´ ə) *n.*: Ancient region of South Palestine.
17. incendiarism (in sen´ dē ə riz'm) *n.*: Willful destruction of property by fire.

18. Seneca (sen´ ə kə) *n.*: Philosopher and minister of Nero.
19. Praeneste (prī nest´): A town in central Italy.
20. Spartacus (spärt´ ə kəs) *n.*: Ancient Thracian slave and gladiator who led a slave revolt.

weather. So, despite heavy seas the steersmen started from Formiae. But when they tried to round Cape Misenum a southwesterly gale drove them ashore near Cumae and destroyed numerous warships and smaller craft.

As the year ended omens of impending misfortune were widely rumored—unprecedentedly frequent lightning; a comet (atoned for by Nero, as usual, by aristocratic blood); two-headed offspring of men and beasts, thrown into the streets or discovered among the offerings to those deities to whom pregnant victims are sacrificed. Near Placentia a calf was born beside the road with its head fastened to one of its legs. Soothsayers deduced that a new head was being prepared for the world—but that it would be neither powerful nor secret since it had been deformed in the womb and given birth by the roadside.

◆ Build Vocabulary

munificence (myoō nif′ ə səns) *n.*: Generosity

Guide for Responding

◆ *Literature and Your Life*

Reader's Response Compare news reports of catastrophic events in our time with Tacitus' reporting in the *Annals*. What qualities do they have in common? Where do they differ?

Thematic Focus Compare three ways in which Romans responded to the interruption of their lives by the fire. Explain whether you find any inappropriate, and why.

☑ Check Your Comprehension

1. Cite three possible explanations Tacitus gives for the fire.
2. What were the consequences of the rumor that Nero sang poetry while Rome burned?
3. What positive measures did Nero take to relieve the distress caused by the fire?
4. Name three precautions taken against fire when the city was rebuilt.
5. Cite two details from the conclusion of the excerpt suggesting that Nero's reign was troubled at the end.

◆ Critical Thinking

INTERPRET

1. Tacitus reports the story of Nero's singing while Rome burned as rumor, not fact. What effect does this qualification have on the reader's attitude toward Tacitus' account? **[Draw Conclusions]**
2. Give two details in Tacitus' account that present Nero in an unfavorable light and two that present him in a favorable light. **[Analyze]**
3. (a) Give two examples in which public opinion called Nero's actions into question. (b) Consider where Tacitus places these references in relation to reports of Nero's accomplishments. What impression does this placement create? **[Analyze]**
4. Explain how Tacitus uses the stories of the slave revolt and of the loss of the fleet to indirectly criticize Nero through comparisons with the Roman past. **[Connect]**
5. What general picture of Nero does a reader form from Tacitus' account? **[Draw Conclusions]**

EVALUATE

6. Was Tacitus' account of the fire without bias, or did he have a hidden agenda? Cite examples to support your evaluation. **[Assess]**

Guide for Responding (continued)

◆ Reading Strategy

REREAD OR READ AHEAD

It is often useful to **read ahead** in a work or to **reread** it until the connections of all its parts— paragraphs to paragraphs, sentences to sentences, and words to words—are clear.

1. Note one detail in the second paragraph that is explained in more detail later in the selection. Also, note the passage that explains it.
2. Reread the paragraph beginning "But neither human resources, nor imperial munificence . . ." (p. 250). Then, sum up the attitude of the Romans of the time toward Christians and Christianity.

◆ Build Vocabulary

USING THE LATIN SUFFIX -*tion*

The Latin suffix -*tion* means "state, act, or quality of."

Use the meaning of the suffix to define each of the words shown. Use a dictionary if necessary.

1. destruction
2. demolition
3. accommodation
4. completion
5. configuration
6. consultation
7. revolution

USING THE WORD BANK: Synonyms

On your paper, write the letter of the word or phrase that is the best synonym for, or is closest in meaning to, the first word.

1. conflagration: (a) fire, (b) tsunami, (c) flood
2. unhampered: (a) unlaundered, (b) free, (c) careless
3. destitute: (a) immoral, (b) official, (c) poor
4. antiquity: (a) days of old, (b) nearby things, (c) valuable things
5. precipitous: (a) rainy, (b) steep, (c) preposterous
6. demarcation: (a) border, (b) writing, (c) hill
7. munificence: (a) generosity, (b) awkwardness, (c) miserliness

◆ Literary Focus

ANNALS

Annals are records that tell of events in chronological order, year by year. The annals-writing style emphasizes straightforward reporting using strict chronological order. However, writers of annals such as Tacitus expanded on the form by choosing to amplify on—or add drama to—certain events.

1. Write a list outlining the sequence of events described in "The Burning of Rome." Does Tacitus' narrative follow strict chronological order?
2. Tacitus interrupts the story of the suspicions that Nero had started the fire. (a) How does Tacitus' organization of information lead him to interrupt this story? (b) What limitations of annals-writing does this interruption suggest?
3. Cite an instance in which Tacitus expands on an event for dramatic purposes.

◆ Build Grammar Skills

COMMONLY CONFUSED WORDS: *less* AND *fewer*

The adjective **less** is used with qualities or quantities that cannot be counted. It answers the question "How much?" The adjective **fewer** is used with objects that can be counted. It answers the question "How many?"

Practice In the following sentences, choose the proper modifier, *less* or *fewer*.

1. The fire caused ____?____ damage on the seventh day than it had on the fifth.
2. There were ____?____ buildings standing after the great fire than were left standing after the invasion of the Gauls.
3. There was ____?____ wealth in the provinces after Nero's agents had visited and plundered them.

Writing Application In your notebook, write three sentences using *less* and *fewer* to describe the new building laws Rome enacted after the fire.

*B*uild *Y*our *P*ortfolio

 ## Idea Bank

Writing

1. **Annals** Keep a chronological record of the most significant events in a week of your life. Write them up as an "annal" of your week.

2. **Column Reporting a Disaster** Research and write a short column about a catastrophic disaster in modern times, such as the Great Chicago Fire or the eruption of Mount St. Helens.

3. **Biography of Nero** Using details from Tacitus, write a brief biography of Nero. Instead of following chronological order, arrange details for maximum dramatic impact.

Speaking, Listening, and Viewing

4. **Debate** With a group, debate this resolution: The burning of Rome was instigated by Nero. **[Social Studies Link]**

5. **Roman Gossip Skit** Present a brief skit in which a group of Romans gossip about the fire and about events during Nero's reign. **[Social Studies Link]**

Researching and Representing

6. **Illustrated Timeline** Construct a timeline of Roman history from Augustus to Domitian. Include a portrait of each emperor and illustrations for each event. **[Social Studies Link]**

7. **Multimedia Presentation** In a group, prepare a multimedia presentation contrasting the Roman Republic and the Roman Empire. **[Media Link; Social Studies Link]**

Online Activity www.phlit.phschool.com

 ## Guided Writing Lesson

Eyewitness Account

People enjoy reading reports of events by those who witnessed them. Such eyewitness accounts often contain details and convey an excitement that may be missing from other sources. Write an eyewitness account of an event that you have witnessed. (You may retell an event that is not of general interest, as long as you present it in the style of "real news.") To keep the sequence of events in your report clear, use transitional words.

Writing Skills Focus: Transitions to Show Time

Use **transitions**—words that show connections—to indicate clearly the sequence in which events occur. Such words include: *after, because, before, during, first, meanwhile, next, then,* and *while.* Tacitus uses a transition to show time in the following passage.

Model From the Story

First, Nero had self-acknowledged Christians arrested. *Then*, on their information, large numbers of others were condemned. . .

Prewriting Freewrite to gather all the details that you can remember about the event you have chosen. Review what you have written. Then, arrange your facts in chronological order.

Drafting In your draft, begin with an introduction creating the proper mood and giving the reader necessary background information for your report. Then, tell the story of the event you are reporting, expanding on the details you have listed.

Revising Reread your draft. Add transitions where necessary to clarify the sequence of events. Eliminate details that detract from the telling of the story.

Comparison-and-Contrast Essay

Writing Process Workshop

In the selections in this section, you probably saw similarities and differences in the ways in which writers view the subject matter they presented.

A **comparison-and-contrast essay** is a brief written exploration of the similarities and differences between two (or more) things. Using the skills listed below write a comparison-and-contrast essay on a topic that interests you.

Writing Skills Focus

▶ **Choose a logical method of organization.** Decide whether your subject is best suited for point-by-point organization or subject-by-subject organization.

▶ **Use sensory language.** Words and phrases that appeal to one of the five senses help your readers vividly experience what you're comparing and contrasting.

▶ **Use transitions** such as *likewise, similarly, nevertheless,* and *in contrast* to indicate the relationships between ideas.

In the following excerpt, author Rachel Carson uses these skills to compare the shore under two different tides.

① Carson first describes the conditions at low tide; then she describes the conditions at high tide.

② The writer includes sensory details of *heat, cold, wind, rain,* and *drying sun.*

③ The transition *yet* indicates the contrast between the lack of life one would expect in this harsh environment and the abundance of life forms that exists there.

MODEL FROM LITERATURE

from *The Marginal World* by Rachel Carson

The shore has a dual nature, changing with the swing of the tides, belonging now to the land, now to the sea. ① On the ebb tide it knows the harsh extremes of the land world, being exposed to the heat and cold, to wind, to rain, and drying sun. ② On the flood tide it is a water world, returning briefly to the stability of the open sea.

Only the most hardy and adaptable can survive in a region so mutable, ③ *yet* the area between the tides is crowded with plants and animals.

Prewriting

Brainstorm to Find a Topic With a small group of class-mates, brainstorm to come up with possible topics. Consider topics such as actors, musicians, athletes, cities, television programs, and so on. List the ideas your group offers, then choose the topic that you find most interesting.

Decide on Your Purpose After choosing a topic, decide on the reason for your comparison. It might be one of the following reasons:

▶ **To inform** readers about your two subjects
▶ **To persuade** readers to accept a specific point of view related to the two subjects
▶ **To entertain** your audience by making an unlikely or unusual comparison

Once you've decided on your purpose, gather details that will help you achieve your purpose.

Keep Your Audience in Mind Identify your audience. Then, keep the answers to questions such as these in mind as you gather details and write your essay:

▶ How old are my readers?
▶ What type of language will appeal to them?
▶ What might they already know about my topic?
▶ What might they not know that I should explain?

Organize Your Details Before you begin writing, use a Venn diagram like the one below to help organize your details. Write similarities in the space where the circles overlap, and note the differences in the outer sections of the circles.

Venn Diagram

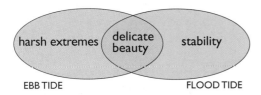

EBB TIDE   FLOOD TIDE

Drafting

Use Comparison-and-Contrast Organization There are two basic types of comparison-and-contrast organization: point-by-point and subject-by-subject. In point-by-point organization, each aspect of your subject is discussed in turn. For example, you might compare and contrast tape players and CD players in terms of cost, availability, and convenience of use.

In a subject-by-subject comparison, you would discuss all the features of one kind of player first and then discuss the features of the second kind.

APPLYING LANGUAGE SKILLS: Commas

Use **commas** correctly in your essay. Too few commas cause confusion, while too many make writing choppy and slow. The following are some common uses of commas:

To Separate Items in a Series:
ghost crabs, herons, starfish . . .

To Set Off Interrupting Words:
The shore, however, . . .

To Separate Clauses in a Compound Sentence:
The tide is low, and I can reach the cave.

Practice On your paper, place commas correctly in the following sentences:

1. Parrot-fish struggle to survive in the competitive environment of the coral reef but their strong jaws give them an advantage.
2. There are many life forms within the coral reef, including starfish coral sea squirts fronds and Tubularia.

Writing Application Review your use of commas in your essay. Revise when necessary.

Writer's Solution Connection
Language Lab

For help organizing your essay, use the Organizing and Ordering Details section of the Exposition tutorial in the Writing Lab.

APPLYING LANGUAGE SKILLS: Forms of Comparison

Make sure you use the proper **forms of comparison** for adjectives and adverbs. Use the basic, or positive, form to modify another word, the comparative form to compare two things, and the superlative form to compare more than two things.

Positive Form:
slow, sunny, humid, bad

Comparative Form:
slower, sunnier, more humid, worse

Superlative Form:
slowest, sunniest, most humid, worst

Practice On your paper, correct the forms of comparison in the following sentences.

1. Of the two cars, Jack's was fastest.
2. Of all the cars, mine was the more colorful.

Writing Application Review your essay, checking that you have used the proper forms of comparison for all modifiers.

Writer's Solution Connection Writing Lab

For more practice with comparisons, complete the Language Lab lesson on Forms of Comparison.

Give Specific Examples Be specific about the ways in which your subjects are alike and different. For example, if you are comparing and contrasting life in a desert region and life in a polar region, offer details showing how the climate specifically affects things such as shelter, diet, and general health. Also, include similarities and differences in the sensory details.

Revising

Use a Checklist Refer to the Writing Skills Focus on p. 254, and use the items as a checklist to evaluate and revise your comparison-and-contrast essay. Ask yourself the following questions, and make revisions as necessary:

▶ Have I used transitions to show comparisons?
▶ Have I organized my points logically?
▶ Have I used sensory language?

REVISION MODEL

When you're choosing whether to buy cassettes or CDs ① , you

should consider several factors. Cassette tapes are

cheap ② er est. Time and use, however, deteriorate the tape.

③ on the other hand,
CDs, will not deteriorate in quality.

① The writer adds a comma to make the sentence clear.
② The writer corrects this comparison.
③ The writer adds this transitional phrase to make the essay flow smoothly.

Publishing

Post Your Writing Electronically You can reach a large audience by posting your writing on the Internet for users interested in your subject. Consult with an experienced Internet user, or visit Prentice Hall on the World Wide Web at **http://www.phschool.com.**

Give an Oral Presentation Arrange with a teacher or librarian for a time and place to give an oral reading of your paper. Then, post a notice on a bulletin board, inviting people to attend the reading. In the notice, make the subject of your paper clear. During the reading, speak clearly and maintain eye contact with the audience. Leave time at the end to answer questions.

Student Success Workshop

Real-World Reading Skills

Using Text Organizers to Find Information

Strategies for Success

Your social studies homework requires you to answer questions about cities of the Indus Valley. You have your social studies book; now you just have to find the specific information you need to answer the questions. Use the strategies that follow to find specific information in a textbook or other reference.

Use the Table of Contents and the Index
The table of contents may list a topic that is broader than your specific needs, but it will get you close. For example, information about the Indus Valley might be listed in the chapter entitled "Early Civilizations in India and China." An index lists very specific topics. For example, if you know the names of one of the cities, you could look it up in the index and find the exact page on which information about that city appears.

Scan Subheads and Key Words Scan the pages for subheads or key words that refer, or are related to, your topic. For example, if you want to find the location of the Indus Valley, scan the subheads until you find one that refers to geography or neighboring countries.

Apply the Strategies

Scan the information in the sample textbook page to the left to answer these questions.

1. Where is the Indus Valley located? Which words helped you find this information?

2. Describe the three major zones of the Indian subcontinent. Which words helped you find the section with this information?

3. Describe how the monsoon affects Indian life. How did you find this information?

4. In which section of this chapter would you begin looking for information about rulers of northern China in 1027 B.C.?

Early Civilizations in India and China

Chapter Outline
1. Cities of the Indus Valley
2. Kingdoms of the Ganges
3. Early Civilization in China

Cities of the Indus Valley

In 1922, archaeologists made a startling discovery. While digging in the Indus River valley, they unearthed bricks, small statues, and other artifacts. They soon realized that they had uncovered a "lost civilization." They had found the cities of the Indus Valley.

Geography:
The Indian Subcontinent

The Indus Valley is located in the region known as South Asia or the subcontinent of India. The Indian subcontinent is a huge, wedge-shaped peninsula extending into the Indian Ocean. Towering snow-covered mountain ranges arc across the northern border of the subcontinent.

Three regions. The Indian subcontinent is divided into three major zones. They are the well-watered northern plain, the dry triangular Deccan plateau, and the coastal plains on either side of the Deccan.

The monsoons. Today, as in the past, a defining feature of Indian life is the monsoon. In late May or early June, the wet summer monsoon blows from the southwest. These winds pick up moisture over the Indian Ocean and then drench the land with daily downpours. Each year, people welcome the rain that is desperately needed to water the crops. If the rains are late, famine and starvation may occur.

✔ *You may also read for specific information:*
- ▶ Newspapers and magazines
- ▶ Almanacs
- ▶ Encyclopedias

Speaking, Listening, and Viewing Workshop

No one else has had all the same experiences as you. Because every reader has a unique perspective, readers often have different interpretations of the same literary work. Your interpretation might give your listeners a new way of understanding a text. The following strategies will help you present a literary interpretation:

Choose a Topic First, you'll need a topic. Avoid one that's too broad, such as the themes of Shakespeare's plays, or one that's too narrow, such as the significance of one line spoken by a minor character. Select an idea about the literary work which may not be obvious to every reader, such as that the tone of the poem is melancholy or that the novel's main character is modeled on the author or that the essay's humor is expressed through figurative language.

Use Supporting Evidence The main ideas of a valid interpretation are supported with evidence and examples from the text. For example, suppose that you have chosen to interpret Gerard Manley Hopkins's use of personification in "The Wreck of the *Deutschland,*" a poem about an 1875 shipwreck. Among other lines, you might focus on these:

> Hope had grown gray hairs,
> Hope had mourning on. . . .

You might point out that instead of simply stating that the situation was hopeless, the poet invites the reader to imagine the *feeling* of hopelessness—by personifying hope as an aging person, grieving. However, a valid interpretation could not argue that the poet has personified hope as an aging woman, because there is no evidence to support that idea in the text.

Organize Whether you read directly from a written essay or refer to notes or an outline, your interpretation should be presented in an organized, logical way. Practicing your presentation beforehand will help you feel confident.

Plan Consider where you'll present your literary interpretation, how much time you'll have, and who your audience will be. Will you have ten minutes to speak to a small group of classmates sitting in a circle? You may also want to prepare beforehand for any questions from your audience.

Present To hold your audience's attention, show enthusiasm for your topic from the start. Make eye contact with your audience and speak clearly. Visual aids, such as transparencies or photocopies that you hand out, may also help to keep your listeners interested.

Apply the Strategies

Present a valid literary interpretation. The text you choose to interpret can be from this unit.

1. Choose a short story with a strong main character. Present an interpretation of what motivated the main character's actions.
2. Select a biographical text. Present your interpretation of how events in the person's life prepared him or her to achieve a major accomplishment.

Test Preparation Workshop

Writing Skills

Strategies for Success

Answering an essay question can be similar to interviewing for a job or auditioning for a dramatic role. In your written answer, you have to establish from the beginning that you are confident and knowledgeable, just as you would in an interview or audition. These strategies will help you impress those who evaluate your response:

Use Good Writing Strategies On other writing assignments, you allot enough time for the three main stages of writing: prewriting, drafting, and revising. Make the same time allowances for your test essay. In your haste to draft an answer, do not skip the prewriting and revising stages. By planning and correcting your essay, you will create a logical, coherent response that will satisfy evaluators.

Use the Question to Formulate a Thesis Evaluators will have greater confidence in your answer if your thesis statement is responsive to the question. Create such a thesis statement by using language from the question. Suppose, for example, that you must answer a question like this:

From the novels, short stories, full-length plays, poems, biographies, and autobiographies you have read, choose one work and identify the dominant mood. Using specific references from the work, explain how the setting and details are used to establish and illustrate the mood, the effect of the mood on the characters, and the importance of the mood to the overall work. . . .

You might use the language of the question to formulate a thesis like this one (words from the question have been italicized):

In the *story* "The Bucket Rider" by Franz Kafka, the *dominant mood* is a strange mixture of sad gaiety. Kafka *establishes that mood* by combining realistic *details* of a coal shortage with fantastic *details* from dreams. The sad gaiety of the story has an important *effect* on the behavior of the main *character.* It is also a clue to the author's theme that even magical powers will not allow us to meet our needs.

Be as Accurate as Possible In referring to a work's title and author, and in citing passages from the work to support your thesis, be as accurate as possible. Inaccuracies will cause evaluators to lose confidence in your answer.

Apply the Strategies

Read the following sample essay question, and answer the questions below it.

From the novels, short stories, full-length plays, poems, biographies, and autobiographies you have read, choose one work and explain how a character or a society reacts to cultural change, what the consequences are to the character or the society, and the effect of the change on the overall work.

1. Assuming you had an hour to answer this question, how much time would you allot for prewriting, for drafting, and for revising? Explain.

2. Accurately name the title and author of a work about which you would write.

3. Formulate a thesis for your answer.

4. Holding to your planned time allotment and using your thesis statement, write an answer to the essay question.

5. Have a classmate evaluate your answer, determining whether it is accurate, coherent, and responsive to the question.

Marco Polo Entering Peking, 14th-century miniature from the Livre de Merveilles

Striving for Success in World Literature

Y ou will strive to reach many goals in life— getting your driver's license, graduating from high school, establishing a successful career, starting a family—and along the way you may have to over- come many obstacles. Let these poems, stories, and essays inspire you to strive for success and accom- plish your goals. Share the determination and fear, the disappointment and hope of people from a wide variety of times and places.

Guide for Reading

Naguib Mahfouz *(1911–   )*

Egyptian writer Naguib Mahfouz is widely acknowledged as one of the foremost writers of modern Arabic literature. He was born in 1911 in an old quarter of Cairo—the setting for many of his works. He has written dozens of novels and collections of short stories that examine the social and political aspects of Egyptian life. In 1988, Mahfouz was awarded the Nobel Prize for Literature, becoming the first Arab writer to be so distinguished.

A Literary Innovator Mahfouz is acclaimed for his brilliant writing in the novel form. He adapted the Western novel genre and made it "Egyptian." While doing so, he modernized the literary language of his country, preferring to use the Arabic of the streets in his writing rather than the traditional classical Arabic. By using the language of the people, he gives voice to the disillusions and dreams of the average Egyptian.

Avoiding Censorship Mahfouz began his career as a novelist in the repressive atmosphere of Egyptian

political unrest. Because people who opposed the government's policies were harshly punished, Mahfouz used his narrative method to imply criticism of contemporary Egyptian society without jeopardizing his career. In the 1940's Mahfouz wrote three historical novels set in ancient Egypt. Mixing history with symbolism, Mahfouz's tales of tyrannical rule and the expulsion of foreign invaders strongly paralleled what was currently happening in Egypt. Using ancient history to make his points allowed Mahfouz to avoid being censored.

Later Life and Works The Egyptian Revolution of 1952 caused Mahfouz to withdraw from writing until 1959. His novels of the 1960's reflect the changing nature of Egyptian society after the revolution. His more recent work reflects the uneasiness of current life in Egypt. Now, almost deaf and partially blind, Mahfouz claims to live only to write; he has said, "If the urge should ever leave me, I want that day to be my last."

◆ Build Vocabulary

WORDS DESCRIBING CROWDS

The word *throngs*, used in "Half a Day" is just one word that means "crowd." Several words in English can be used to refer to a crowd, but they have different connotations, or associations. For example, a *horde* calls up a negative association of an unruly crowd, and an *assembly* calls up a positive association of a refined and orderly group of people.

WORD BANK

unmarred
intimacy
intricate
presumed
throngs
avail
hastened

As you read "Half a Day," you will encounter the words on this list. Each word is defined on the page where it first appears. Preview this list before you begin reading.

◆ Build Grammar Skills

SUBJECT-AND-VERB AGREEMENT IN INVERTED SENTENCES

Subjects and verbs must agree in number, even if the subject follows the verb. When a subject follows the verb, the sentence is said to be inverted. Sentences that begin with the words *here* and *there* are almost always inverted. The following example of an inverted sentence appears in "Half a Day."

verb   subject

Then there <u>was</u> a <u>band</u> announcing the opening of a circus, with clowns and weight lifters walking in front.

The singular verb *was* agrees with the singular subject subject *band,* which follows the verb.

Half a Day

◆ *Literature and Your Life*

CONNECT YOUR EXPERIENCE

"Where has the time gone?" Perhaps you've made that observation as you pause to take in the changes that you and the world have experienced over the years. In this story, Naguib Mahfouz examines the quickness with which time elapses and the changes it brings.

THEMATIC FOCUS: STRIVING FOR SUCCESS

As you read, ask yourself: How might a person who strives for success view the passage of time?

Journal Writing Write about a period in your life when time seemed to move extremely fast.

◆ Background for Understanding

CULTURE

"Half a Day" is set in Cairo, Egypt, the city in which Naguib Mahfouz grew up. Just as the story explores the mysteries of passing time, Cairo itself embodies those mysteries. It is an ancient city with views of nearby pyramids *and* a bustling modern city with modern buildings, as the picture on this page indicates.

Narrow twisting streets that had been the domain of camels, horses, and pedestrians, are now choked with vehicular traffic. Western influences, too, can be seen in people's clothing, fast-food restaurants, and even language.

As you read this story, look for details that describe the changes that both the setting and the story's narrator have undergone.

◆ Literary Focus

SURREALISM

Surrealism, which means "beyond realism," is an artistic and literary movement in which realistic people, objects, and events are portrayed in an unreal or dreamlike environment. Writers who use surrealistic techniques go beyond the boundaries of logic to arrive at basic truths.

In the following passage from "Half a Day," Mahfouz combines realistic details with a surreal, dreamlike situation:

> I proceeded a few steps, then came to a startled halt. . . . Where was the street lined with gardens? Where had it disappeared to?

As you read "Half a Day," look for other details and imagery that contribute to its surrealistic, dreamlike quality. You may want to fill out a chart like this one to keep track of the types of details you encounter while reading.

Realistic Details	Surrealistic Details

Reading for Success

Interactive Reading Strategies

You wouldn't stand in front of a video game and just watch it like a movie, would you? Of course not! Video games are interactive—your choices affect the way the game turns out. Like a video game, reading is also interactive. It's a process by which you get involved with the ideas, images, events, and information presented in the text. The more involved you are, the richer your understanding is.

Apply the following strategies to interact with what you read:

Establish a purpose for reading.

Decide why you are reading a piece. You may read for enjoyment, for information, or to discover new ideas. For example, Mahfouz's story "Half a Day" can give you a new perspective on the passage of time.

Use your prior background knowledge.

Keep in mind what you already know—in this case, your experience of time moving on and the changing nature of the world. Use that knowledge to make connections with what the author is saying. You may find details in the text that confirm opinions you already have, as well as details that change your opinions.

Question.

Don't accept everything you read as true. Ask yourself questions about why certain information is included or how a fact or idea fits in with what you have already read. Then, look for answers to your questions as you continue to read. Questioning will help you recognize the relationships between ideas and form your own opinion about the work.

Clarify details and information.

Make an effort to understand or clear up any parts of the work you find confusing. The best way to do this is to read ahead for more information or read back to review what you have already learned. Another technique is to represent information visually. For instance, you can clarify the story's setting by making a cluster diagram in which you jot down key details from the story that describe it.

Summarize.

Periodically pause to review and state the main points of the author. Take note of the details that seem important, and fit them into your picture of what the author is saying.

As you read "Half a Day," look at the notes in the boxes. These notes demonstrate how to apply the above strategies to a work of literature.

Half A Day

Naguib Mahfouz
Translated by Denys Johnson-Davies

I proceeded alongside my father, clutching his right hand, running to keep up with the long strides he was taking. All my clothes were new: the black shoes, the green school uniform, and the red tarboosh.[1] My delight in my new clothes, however, was not altogether unmarred, for this was no feast day but the day on which I was to be cast into school for the first time.

My mother stood at the window watching our progress, and I would turn toward her from time to time, as though appealing for

> **Establish a purpose** for reading this story.

---

1. **tarboosh** (tär boosh´) *n.*: Brimless cap of felt or other cloth shaped like a truncated cone.

▲ **Critical Viewing** Compare and contrast the clothing of this Egyptian boy with that of young Americans. **[Compare and Contrast]**

---

help. We walked along a street lined with gardens; on both sides were extensive fields planted with crops, prickly pears, henna trees, and a few date palms.

"Why school?" I challenged my father openly. "I shall never do anything to annoy you."

"I'm not punishing you," he said, laughing. "School's not a punishment. It's the factory

◆ **Build Vocabulary**

unmarred (un märd´) *adj.*: Unspoiled; unimpaired

that makes useful men out of boys. Don't you want to be like your father and brothers?"

I was not convinced. I did not believe there was really any good to be had in tearing me away from the <u>intimacy</u> of my home and throwing me into this building that stood at the end of the road like some huge, high-walled fortress, exceedingly stern and grim.

When we arrived at the gate we could see the courtyard, vast and crammed full of boys and girls. "Go in by yourself," said my father, "and join them. Put a smile on your face and be a good example to others."

I hesitated and clung to his hand, but he gently pushed me from him. "Be a man," he said. "Today you truly begin life. You will find me waiting for you when it's time to leave."

Use your **prior knowledge** to better understand the narrator's feelings about the first day of school

I took a few steps, then stopped and looked but saw nothing. Then the faces of boys and girls came into view. I did not know a single one of them, and none of them knew me. I felt I was a stranger who had lost his way. But glances of curiosity were directed toward me, and one boy approached and asked, "Who brought you?"

"My father," I whispered.

"My father's dead," he said quite simply.

I did not know what to say. The gate was closed, letting out a pitiable screech. Some of the children burst into tears. The bell rang. A lady came along, followed by a group of men. The men began sorting us into ranks. We were formed into an <u>intricate</u> pattern in the great courtyard surrounded on three sides by high buildings of several floors; from each floor we were overlooked by a long balcony roofed in wood.

"This is your new home," said the woman. "Here too there are mothers and fathers. Here there is everything that is enjoyable and beneficial to knowledge and religion. Dry your tears and face life joyfully."

We submitted to the facts, and this submission brought a sort of contentment. Living beings were drawn to other living beings, and from the first moments my heart made friends with such boys as were to be my friends and fell in love with such girls as I was to be in love with, so that it seemed my misgivings had had no basis. I had never imagined school would have this rich variety. We played all sorts of different games: swings, the vaulting horse, ball games. In the music room we chanted our first songs. We also had our first introduction to language. We saw a globe of the Earth, which revolved and showed the various continents and countries. We started learning the numbers. The story of the Creator of the universe was read to us, we were told of His present world and of His Hereafter, and we heard examples of what He said. We ate delicious food, took a little nap, and woke up to go on with friendship and love, play and learning.

As our path revealed itself to us, however, we did not find it as totally sweet and un-clouded as we had <u>presumed</u>. Dust-laden winds and unexpected accidents came about suddenly, so we had to be watchful, at the ready, and very patient. It was not all a matter of playing and fooling around. Rivalries could bring about pain and hatred or give rise to fighting. And while the lady would sometimes smile, she would often scowl and scold. Even more frequently she would resort to physical punishment.

In addition, the time for changing one's mind was over and gone and there was no question of ever returning to the paradise of home. Nothing lay ahead of us but exertion, struggle, and perseverance. Those who were able took advantage of the opportunities for

◆ **Build Vocabulary**

intimacy (in′ tə mə sē) *n*.: Familiarity; closeness

intricate (in′ tri kit) *adj*.: Complicated; elaborate

presumed (prē zoomd′) *v*.: Taken for granted

throngs (thrôŋz) *n*.: Crowds

avail (ə vāl′) *n*.: Benefit; use

▲ **Critical Viewing** In what way does the story chart a course between the boy shown on p. 265 and the older man shown here? **[Connect]**

success and happiness that presented themselves amid the worries.

The bell rang announcing the passing of the day and the end of work. The <u>throngs</u> of children rushed toward the gate, which was opened again. I bade farewell to friends and sweethearts and passed through the gate. I peered around but found no trace of my father, who had promised to be there. I stepped aside to wait.

When I had waited for a long time without <u>avail</u>, I decided to return home on my own. After I had taken a few steps, a middle-aged man passed by, and I realized at once that I knew him. He came toward me, smiling, and shook me by the hand, saying "It's a long time since we last met—how are you?"

With a nod of my head, I agreed with him and in turn asked, "And you, how are you?"

"As you can see, not all that good, the Almighty be praised!"

Again he shook me by the hand and went off. I proceeded a few steps, then came to a startled halt. . . . Where was the street lined with gardens? Where had it disappeared to? When did all these vehicles invade it? And when did all these hordes of humanity come to rest upon its surface? How did these hills of refuse come to cover its sides? And where were the fields that bordered it? High buildings had taken over, the street surged with children, and disturbing noises shook the air. At various points stood conjurers showing off their tricks and making snakes appear from baskets. Then there was a band announcing the opening of a circus, with clowns and weight lifters walking in front. A line of trucks carrying central security troops crawled majestically by. The siren of a fire engine shrieked, and it was not clear how the vehicle would cleave its way to reach the blazing fire. A battle raged between a taxi driver and his passenger, while the passenger's wife called out for help and no one answered. . . . I was in a daze. My head spun. I almost went crazy. How could all this have happened in half a day between early morning and sunset? I would find the answer at home with my father. But where was my home? I could see only tall buildings and hordes of people. I <u>hastened</u> on to the crossroads between the gardens and Abu Khoda. I had to cross Abu Khoda to reach my house, but the stream of cars would not let up. The fire engine's siren was shrieking at full pitch as it moved at a snail's pace, and I said to myself, "Let the fire take its pleasure in what it consumes." Extremely irritated, I wondered when I would be able to cross. I stood there a long time, until the young lad employed at the ironing shop on the corner came up to me. He stretched out his arm and said gallantly, "Grandpa, let me take you across."

> Summarize what has happened in the story.

◆ **Build Vocabulary**

hastened (hās′ ənd) v.: Hurried; moved swiftly

Guide for Responding

◆ Literature and Your Life

Reader's Response Do you feel sympathy for the narrator? Why or why not?

Thematic Focus Is the author optimistic about people's ability to achieve success? Explain.

Journal Writing Write a brief news article that describes the narrator's remarkable "half a day."

Questions for Research "Half a Day" takes place in Cairo, Egypt. What three questions does this story raise in your mind about modern life in Egypt? How would you go about finding answers to those questions?

☑ Check Your Comprehension

1. Where does the father take the narrator?
2. Who does the narrator meet outside the school gates?
3. What changes does the narrator notice outside the school gates?
4. Where is the narrator trying to go after school? What prevents him from going?
5. What does the lad from the ironing shop call the narrator at the story's end?

Guide for Responding (continued)

◆ Critical Thinking

INTERPRET

1. What type of relationship does the boy have with his father? **[Infer]**
2. What does Mahfouz mean by the line, "[T]he time for changing one's mind was over and gone and there was no question of ever returning to the paradise of home." **[Interpret]**
3. At what point in the story do you realize that its time frame is accelerated? **[Analyze]**
4. What is the theme, or central message, of "Half a Day"?

APPLY

5. In what ways is the story's theme applicable to your life? **[Relate]**

◆ Reading Strategy

INTERACTIVE READING STRATEGIES

1. How does your prior knowledge help you to understand the narrator's situation?
2. List one question you asked yourself while reading. Then, explain how you answered it.
3. (a) Summarize what happens to the narrator in the course of the story. (b) In what ways does your summary help you to understand the story's theme, or central message?

◆ Literary Focus

SURREALISM

Surrealism is the deliberate use of unreal or dreamlike details in art or literature in order to reveal truths. As you read "Half a Day," you encountered dreamlike details and images that contributed to its surrealistic style. The following passage from the story is strange and unusual, but it reveals a truth—that the students and learning experiences within a school make up a world of their own.

"This is your new home," said the woman. "Here too there are mothers and fathers. Here there is everything that is enjoyable and beneficial to knowledge and religion."

1. At what point in "Half a Day" does it become clear that the people and events are surreal? Explain.
2. (a) Identify two examples of surrealistic description in the story. (b) Explain how those examples help convey the author's points.

◆ Build Vocabulary

WORDS DESCRIBING CROWDS

In your notebook, explain the differences among the definitions of the following words that describe crowds:

1. throngs
2. hordes
3. assemblies
4. swarms
5. masses

USING THE WORD BANK: Context

In your notebook, write your answers to the following questions:

1. Is an *unmarred* piece of furniture likely to cost more than a marred piece? Explain.
2. Would you feel "on guard" in an atmosphere of *intimacy*? Why or why not?
3. Is an *intricate* dance step easy to learn? Explain.
4. If someone is *presumed* innocent, is he or she free to go? Explain.
5. Would you be likely to see *throngs* on a desert island? Why or why not?
6. If a method is of no *avail*, would you be likely to try it again? Explain.
7. If a person *hastened* to your side, would you have to wait a long time? Explain.

◆ Build Grammar Skills

SUBJECT-AND-VERB AGREEMENT IN INVERTED SENTENCES

In inverted sentences—when the subject follows the verb—writers must be especially careful to ensure that the **subject and verb agree** in number.

Practice Number your paper 1 through 5. Read each of the following sentences, and locate the subject and verb in each. If the subject and verb agree, write *correct* on your paper. If the subject and verb do not agree, rewrite the sentence to correct it.

1. There was many moments when the boy enjoyed school.
2. Here was many students who became his friends.
3. There were lessons in geography, science, and language.
4. There were the boy's father, outside the school.
5. There was loud noise in the boy's neighborhood.

Build Your Portfolio

Idea Bank

Writing

1. **Letter Writing** Write a letter to the narrator, advising him on how to deal with the difficulties he has encountered in school.

2. **Description** In a brief essay, describe what it is like when "time flies." Cite personal experiences as well as examples from film and literature.

3. **Critical Response** Michael Beard writes that Mahfouz is "read abroad for local color, for his crowded canvasses, and the closely observed social detail." Support or refute this comment.

Speaking, Listening, and Viewing

4. **Monologue** Use details from the story to write a monologue in which the narrator voices his emotions as he leaves the school. Rehearse your monologue and perform it for the class.

5. **Discussion Panel** With a small group, form a panel and discuss the nature of change and progress as it relates to your experience. Appoint one group member to take notes on the group's ideas, and to summarize its conclusions. **[Social Studies Link]**

Researching and Representing

6. **Multimedia Presentation** Mahfouz's story is set in Cairo, Egypt. Prepare and present a multimedia presentation on Egyptian culture, including special traditions, art, photographs, maps, and music. **[Technology Link]**

7. **Sketch** Based on details in "Half a Day," sketch a scene from the story that captures the essence of the narrator and the setting. Share your finished sketch with the class. **[Art Link]**

Online Activity www.phlit.phschool.com

Guided Writing Lesson

Surrealistic Description

In "Half a Day," Mahfouz uses surrealistic imagery: He describes ordinary objects and events in an unusual and dreamlike way. Think about an object or event that interests you, and describe it in surrealistic terms. In your description, provide a balance of details that are realistic and surrealistic.

> ### Writing Skills Focus: Balancing Realistic and Surrealistic Details
> When writing in the surrealistic style, it is important to include a **balance** of realistic and surrealistic details. If you use too many surrealistic details, your readers won't be able to understand what you have to say; if you choose too few surrealistic details, they will appear to be errors that are out of place in the story.

Prewriting Once you have selected the topic of your description, brainstorm for details you would like to use. You may want to make a T-chart, listing realistic details on the left and surrealistic ones on the right. Then, decide on the most effective way to begin and end your description.

Drafting As you draft your description, refer to your prewriting notes to be sure you have left nothing out. While writing, concentrate on seamlessly combining the descriptive details to create a unified whole.

Revising Reread your description, checking to see if you maintained a balance between realistic and surrealistic details. To ensure that an audience will be able to understand what you're writing about, read your description to a classmate and get his or her response.

Skim your draft. Whenever you begin a sentence with *here* or *there,* check to be sure that its subject and verb agree in number. For more information on subject-verb agreement, see pp. 262 and 269.

PART 1 *Overcoming Obstacles*

Pilgrimage, Shraga Weil

*G*uide for Reading

Leo Tolstoy *(1828–1910)*

Leo Tolstoy is remembered almost as much for his unusual lifestyle as he is for his literary achievements.

Tolstoy's life reads like a Cinderella story in reverse. He was born rich and died poor.

After inheriting the wealth and power of his family's estate at the age of nineteen, he opened a school for peasant children and tried somewhat unsuccessfully to improve the lives of the serfs who were bound to the estate.

One Wife, Two Masterpieces, Thirteen Children

When he was thirty-four, Tolstoy married an intelligent, headstrong woman named Sonya Baers. She energetically supported his writing, copying by hand his long, nearly indecipherable manuscript for the mammoth novel *War and Peace* nine times, by candlelight, so that it could be sent to publishers. At the same time, she found time to manage Tolstoy's estate and raise thirteen children.

Tolstoy's other masterpiece is *Anna Karenina*, a tragic love story. While working on the novel, Tolstoy began to question the meaning of life and the inevitability of death.

A Personal Crisis

After *Anna Karenina* was published in installments from 1875 to 1877, Tolstoy suffered a spiritual crisis. He created his own religion, took up shoemaking, became a vegetarian, and stopped drinking and smoking. He handed over the copyrights to all of his works produced before 1881 to his wife and attempted to be as self-sufficient as possible. He often wore peasant's clothes and worked in the fields. His actions placed a great strain on his marriage and eventually forced him to leave home.

◆ Build Vocabulary

WORDS IN CONTEXT: TECHNICAL AND MULTIPLE-MEANING WORDS

As the title of Tolstoy's story suggests, many of the words you will encounter in this story are farming terms. Some of these words, such as *fallow*, which means "not cultivated," can be used in other contexts as well. *Fallow* can refer to land left uncultivated or, for example, to a mind that is inactive.

WORD BANK

piqued
disparaged
forbore
aggrieved
sheaf
arable
fallow

As you read you will encounter the words on this list. Each word is defined on the page where it first appears. Preview the list before you read, and look for more farming terms, such as *sowed*, that can have other implications in other contexts.

◆ Build Grammar Skills

POSSESSIVE NOUNS

In this story about owning land, you will see many **possessive nouns**—nouns that show ownership, belonging, or another close relationship. The chart shows how to form possessive nouns.

Rules for Possessive Forms of Nouns	Examples
To form the possessive of singular nouns, add an apostrophe and s.	• Pahom's field • sun's rays
To form the possessive of plural nouns that end in s, just add an apostrophe.	• peasants' complaints • three days' work
To form the possessive of plural nouns that do not end in s, add an apostrophe and s.	• women's conversation • people's land

Notice other examples of these possessive forms of nouns in Tolstoy's story.

How Much Land Does a Man Need?

◆ *Literature and Your Life*

CONNECT YOUR EXPERIENCE

Just one more... just a little longer... just a little farther—almost everyone has used one of these phrases at one time or another. For instance, you yourself have probably felt that you could have done better on that last test if you had had just a little longer!

The events in this Russian tale illustrate the universal truth that "a little more" is *never* enough.

THEMATIC FOCUS: OVERCOMING OBSTACLES

Tolstoy's story illustrates the old proverb, "The more you have, the more you want." As you read this story, ask yourself, How much is enough?

◆ Background for Understanding

HISTORY

From the sixteenth century to the mid-nineteenth century, Russian peasants were bound by law to work land they could rent but not own. They grew food they couldn't eat, cultivated crops they couldn't sell, and worked to exhaustion to make a profit for the landowner. Peasants could be bought and sold with the land they lived on. This story is set after the laws had been changed to allow ordinary people to own land. Because of the old laws, however, land is more than just property. Land ownership represents the ability to control one's own destiny.

It is not a coincidence that Tolstoy uses land to explore the question "How much is enough?" He uses an image that was close to the heart of every Russian.

◆ Literary Focus

PARABLE

Tolstoy's story is not simply a tale about land. It is a **parable**, a simple, brief narrative that teaches a lesson by using characters and events to stand for abstract ideas or moral principles.

This parable focuses on Pahom, a Russian peasant who feels that all his problems would be solved if he had enough land. Through Pahom's actions, the story explores the question "How much land is enough land?" Think about the lesson that this parable teaches, a lesson concerning the difference between *need* and *greed*.

◆ Reading Strategy

PREDICT BASED ON CHARACTER TRAITS

When you read stories that teach a lesson, you can usually **predict** the outcome before you actually read what happens. In such stories, casual remarks and small details are filled with meaning and hint at future events. Clouds on the horizon can foretell a thunderstorm; a minor dispute between neighbors can fore-shadow a bitter feud.

In "How Much Land Does a Man Need?" the peasant Pahom's wife says to her wealthier sister, "Though you often earn more than you need, you're very likely to lose all you have." This statement hints at the lesson to come. Pahom's response to the conversation between the two women reveals character traits that will help you predict how he will act in the story.

How Much *Land* Does a Man Need?

Leo Tolstoy

Translated by Louise and Aylmer Maude

Rest During the Harvest, Alexander Morosov, Tretyakov Gallery, Moscow, Russia

▲ **Critical Viewing** Why do you think people like the peasants in this picture place great importance on owning land? **[Speculate]**

1

An elder sister came to visit her younger sister in the country. The elder was married to a shopkeeper in town, the younger to a peasant in the village. As the sisters sat over their tea talking, the elder began to boast of the advantages of town life, saying how comfortably they lived there, how well they dressed, what fine clothes her children wore, what good things they ate and drank, and how she went to the theater, promenades,[1] and entertainments.

The younger sister was piqued, and in turn disparaged the life of a shopkeeper, and stood up for that of a peasant.

"I wouldn't change my way of life for yours," said she. "We may live roughly, but at least we're free from worry. You live in better style than we do, but though you often earn more than you need, you're very likely to lose all you have. You know the proverb, 'Loss and gain are brothers twain.'[2] It often happens that people who're wealthy one day are begging their bread the next. Our way is safer. Though a peasant's life is not a rich one, it's long. We'll never grow rich, but we'll always have enough to eat."

The elder sister said sneeringly:

"Enough? Yes, if you like to share with the pigs and the calves! What do you know of elegance or manners! However much your good man may slave, you'll die as you live—in a dung heap—and your children the same."

"Well, what of that?" replied the younger sister. "Of course our work is rough and hard. But on the other hand, it's sure, and we need not bow to anyone. But you, in your towns, are surrounded by temptations; today all may be right, but tomorrow the Evil One may tempt your husband with cards, wine, or women, and all will go to ruin. Don't such things happen often enough?"

Pahom, the master of the house, was lying on the top of the stove and he listened to the women's chatter.

"It is perfectly true," thought he. "Busy as we are from childhood tilling mother earth, we peasants have no time to let any nonsense settle in our heads. Our only trouble is that we haven't land enough. If I had plenty of land, I shouldn't fear the Devil himself!"

The women finished their tea, chatted a while about dress, and then cleared away the tea things and lay down to sleep.

But the Devil had been sitting behind the stove and had heard all that had been said. He was pleased that the peasant's wife had led her husband into boasting and that he had said that if he had plenty of land he would not fear the Devil himself.

"All right," thought the Devil. "We'll have a tussle. I'll give you land enough;

---

1. **promenades** (präm´ ə nädz) *n.*: Balls or formal dances.
2. **twain** (twān) *n.*: Two.

♦ **Build Vocabulary**

piqued (pēkt) *v.*: Offended

disparaged (di spar´ ijd) *v.*: Spoke slightly of; belittled

and by means of the land I'll get you into my power."

2

Close to the village there lived a lady, a small landowner who had an estate of about three hundred acres. She had always lived on good terms with the peasants until she engaged as her manager an old soldier, who took to burdening the people with fines. However careful Pahom tried to be, it happened again and again that now a horse of his got among the lady's oats, now a cow strayed into her garden, now his calves found their way into her meadows—and he always had to pay a fine.

Pahom paid up, but grumbled, and, going home in a temper, was rough with his family. All through that summer Pahom had much trouble because of this manager, and he was actually glad when winter came and the cattle had to be stabled. Though he grudged the fodder when they could no longer graze on the pasture land, at least he was free from anxiety about them.

In the winter the news got about that the lady was going to sell her land and that the keeper of the inn on the high road was bargaining for it. When the peasants heard this they were very much alarmed.

"Well," thought they, "if the innkeeper gets the land, he'll worry us with fines worse than the lady's manager. We all depend on that estate."

So the peasants went on behalf of their village council and asked the lady not to sell the land to the innkeeper, offering her a better price for it themselves. The lady agreed to let them have it. Then the peasants tried to arrange for the village council to buy the whole estate, so that it might be held by them all in common. They met twice to discuss it, but could not settle the matter; the Evil One sowed discord among them and they could not agree. So they decided to buy the land individually, each according to his means; and the lady agreed to this plan as she had to the other.

Presently Pahom heard that a neighbor of his was buying fifty acres, and that the lady had consented to accept one half in cash and to wait a year for the other half. Pahom felt envious.

"Look at that," thought he, "the land is all being sold, and I'll get none of it." So he spoke to his wife.

"Other people are buying," said he, "and we must also buy twenty acres or so. Life is becoming impossible. That manager is simply crushing us with his fines."

So they put their heads together and considered how they could manage to buy it. They had one hundred rubles[3] laid by. They sold a colt and one half of their bees, hired out one of their sons as a farmhand and took his wages in advance, borrowed the rest from a brother-in-law, and so scraped together half the purchase money.

Having done this, Pahom chose a farm of forty acres, some of it wooded, and went to the lady to bargain for it. They came to an agreement, and he shook hands with her upon it and paid her a deposit in advance.

◆ **Reading Strategy**
Based on what you know about Pahom's character, predict whether he will be happy now.

Then they went to town and signed the deeds, he paying half the price down, and undertaking to pay the remainder within two years.

So now Pahom had land of his own. He borrowed seed and sowed it on the land he had bought. The harvest was a good one, and within a year he had managed to pay off his debts both to the lady and to his brother-in-law. So he became a landowner, plowing and sowing his own

---

3. **rubles** (roo′ bəlz) *n.*: Russian money.

land, making hay on his own land, cutting his own trees, and feeding his cattle on his own pasture. When he went out to plow his fields, or to look at his growing corn, or at his grass meadows, his heart would fill with joy. The grass that grew and the flowers that bloomed there seemed to him unlike any that grew elsewhere. Formerly, when he had passed by that land, it had appeared the same as any other land, but now it seemed quite different.

3

So Pahom was well contented, and everything would have been right if the neighboring peasants would only not have trespassed on his wheatfields and meadows. He appealed to them most civilly, but they still went on: now the herdsmen would let the village cows stray into his meadows, then horses from the night pasture would get among his corn. Pahom turned them out again and again, and forgave their owners, and for a long time he forbore to prosecute anyone. But at last he lost patience and complained to the District Court. He knew it was the peasants' want of land, and no evil intent on their part, that caused the trouble, but he thought:

"I can't go on overlooking it, or they'll destroy all I have. They must be taught a lesson."

So he had them up, gave them one lesson, and then another, and two or three of the peasants were fined. After a time Pahom's neighbors began to bear him a grudge for this, and would now and then let their cattle onto his land on purpose. One peasant even got into Pahom's wood at night and cut down five young lime trees for their bark. Pahom, passing through the wood one day, noticed something white. He came nearer and saw the stripped trunks lying on the ground, and close by stood the stumps where the trees had been. Pahom was furious.

"If he'd only cut one here and there it would have been bad enough," thought Pahom, "but the rascal has actually cut down a whole clump. If I could only find out who did this, I'd get even with him."

He racked his brains as to who it could be. Finally he decided: "It must be Simon—no one else could have done it." So he went to Simon's homestead to have a look around, but he found nothing and only had an angry scene. However, he now felt more certain than ever that Simon had done it, and he lodged a complaint. Simon was summoned. The case was tried, and retried, and at the end of it all Simon was acquitted, there being no evidence against him. Pahom felt still more aggrieved, and let his anger loose upon the Elders and the Judges.

"You let thieves grease your palms," said he. "If you were honest folk yourselves you wouldn't let a thief go free."

So Pahom quarreled with the judges and with his neighbors. Threats to burn his hut began to be uttered. So though Pahom had more land, his place in the community was much worse than before.

About this time a rumor got about that many people were moving to new parts.

◆ **Literary Focus**
How do Pahom's experiences begin to teach a lesson about greed?

"There's no need for me to leave my land," thought Pahom. "But some of the others may leave our village and then there'd be more room for us. I'd take over their land myself and make my estates somewhat bigger. I could then live more at ease. As it is, I'm still too cramped to be comfortable."

◆ **Build Vocabulary**
forbore (tôr bôr´) v.: Refrained from
aggrieved (ə grēvd´) v.: Wronged

One day Pahom was sitting at home when a peasant, passing through the village, happened to drop in. He was allowed to stay the night, and supper was given him. Pahom had a talk with this peasant and asked him where he came from. The stranger answered that he came from beyond the Volga,[4] where he had been working. One word led to another, and the man went on to say that many people were settling in those parts. He told how some people from his village had settled there. They had joined the community there and had had twenty-five acres per man granted them. The land was so good, he said, that the rye sown on it grew as high as a horse, and so thick that five cuts of a sickle made a sheaf. One peasant, he said, had brought nothing with him but his bare hands, and now he had six horses and two cows of his own.

Pahom's heart kindled with desire.

"Why should I suffer in this narrow hole, if one can live so well elsewhere?" he thought. "I'll sell my land and my homestead here, and with the money I'll start afresh over there and get everything new. In this crowded place one is always having trouble. But I must first go and find out all about it myself."

Toward summer he got ready and started out. He went down the Volga on a steamer to Samara,[5] then walked another three hundred miles on foot, and at last reached the place. It was just as the stranger had said. The peasants had plenty of land: every man had twenty-five acres of communal land given him for his use, and anyone who had money could buy, besides, at a ruble and a half an acre, as much good freehold land[6] as he wanted.

Having found out all he wished to know, Pahom returned home as autumn came on, and began selling off his belongings. He sold his land at a profit, sold his homestead and all his cattle, and withdrew from membership in the village. He only waited till the spring, and then started with his family for the new settlement.

4

As soon as Pahom and his family reached their new abode, he applied for admission into the council of a large village. He stood treat to the Elders and obtained the necessary documents. Five shares of communal land were given him for his own and his sons' use: that is to say—125 acres (not all together, but in different fields) besides the use of the communal pasture. Pahom put up the buildings he needed and bought cattle. Of the communal land alone he had three times as much as at his former home, and the land was good wheat land. He was ten times better off than he had been. He had plenty of arable land and pasturage, and could keep as many head of cattle as he liked.

At first, in the bustle of building and settling down, Pahom was pleased with it all, but when he got used to it he began to think that even here he hadn't enough land. The first year he sowed wheat on his share of the communal land and had a good crop. He wanted to go on sowing wheat, but had not enough communal land for the purpose, and what he had already used was not available, for in

♦ *Literature and Your Life*

How do you react when you feel you're missing out on a good thing?

---

4. **Volga** (väl´ gə): The major river in western Russia.
5. **Samara** (Sə ma´ rə): City in eastern Russia.

---

6. **freehold land:** Privately owned land that the owner can lease to others for a fee.

Cornfield at Ewell, c. 1846 (detail), William Holman Hunt, Tate Gallery, London

those parts wheat is sown only on virgin soil or on fallow land. It is sown for one or two years, and then the land lies fallow till it is again overgrown with steppe grass. There were many who wanted such land, and there was not enough for all, so that people quarreled about it. Those who were better off wanted it for growing wheat, and those who were poor wanted it to let to dealers, so that they might raise money to pay their taxes. Pahom wanted to sow more wheat, so he

◆ **Build Vocabulary**

sheaf (shēf) *n.*: Bundle of grain

arable (ar´ ə bəl) *adj.*: Suitable for growing crops

fallow (fal´ ō) *adj.*: Plowed, but not planted

▲ **Critical Viewing** What might be going through the mind of the person tending to this land? **[Speculate]**

rented land from a dealer for a year. He sowed much wheat and had a fine crop, but the land was too far from the village —the wheat had to be carted more than ten miles. After a time Pahom noticed that some peasant dealers were living on separate farms and were growing wealthy, and he thought:

"If I were to buy some freehold land and have a homestead on it, it would be a different thing altogether. Then it would all be fine and close together."

The question of buying freehold land recurred to him again and again.

He went on in the same way for three years, renting land and sowing wheat. The seasons turned out well and the crops were good, so that he began to lay by money. He might have gone on living contentedly, but he grew tired of having to rent other people's land every year and having to scramble for it. Wherever there was good land to be had, the peasants would rush for it and it was taken up at once, so that unless you were sharp about it, you got none. It happened in the third year that he and a dealer together rented a piece of pasture land from some peasants, and they had already plowed it up, when there was some dispute and the peasants went to law about it, and things fell out so that the labor was all lost.

◆ Reading Strategy
What can you predict about Pahom's future decisions?

"If it were my own land," thought Pahom, "I should be independent, and there wouldn't be all this unpleasantness."

So Pahom began looking out for land which he could buy, and he came across a peasant who had bought thirteen hundred acres, but having got into difficulties was willing to sell again cheap. Pahom bargained and haggled with him, and at last they settled the price at fifteen hundred rubles, part in cash and part to be paid later. They had all but clinched the matter when a passing dealer happened to stop at Pahom's one day to get feed for his horses. He drank tea with Pahom, and they had a talk. The dealer said that he was just returning from the land of the Bashkirs,[7] far away, where he had bought thirteen thousand acres of land, all for a thousand rubles.

Pahom questioned him further, and the dealer said:

"All one has to do is to make friends with the chiefs. I gave away about one hundred rubles' worth of silk robes and carpets, besides a case of tea, and I gave wine to those who would drink it; and I got the land for less than three kopecks[8] an acre." And he showed Pahom the title deed, saying:

"The land lies near a river, and the whole steppe is virgin soil."

Pahom plied him with questions, and the dealer said:

"There's more land there than you could cover if you walked a year, and it all belongs to the Bashkirs. They're as simple as sheep, and land can be got almost for nothing."

"There, now," thought Pahom, "with my one thousand rubles, why should I get only thirteen hundred acres, and saddle myself with a debt besides? If I take it out there, I can get more than ten times as much for my money."

5

Pahom inquired how to get to the place, and as soon as the grain dealer had left him, he prepared to go there himself. He left his wife to look after the homestead, and started on his journey, taking his hired man with him. They stopped at a town on their way and bought a case of tea, some wine, and other presents, as the grain dealer had advised.

On and on they went until they had gone more than three hundred miles, and on the seventh day they came to a place where the Bashkirs had pitched their round tents. It was all just as the dealer had said. The people lived on the

---

7. **Bashkirs** (bash kirz´): Nomadic people who live in the plains of southwestern Russia.

8. **kopecks** (kō´ peks) n.: Russian money, equal to one hundredth of a ruble.

The Hay Harvest, (detail), Boris Kustodiev, St. Petersburg, Russia

▲ **Critical Viewing** Based on this painting, what do you learn about the responsibility of owning a lot of land? **[Interpret]**

steppe,[9] by a river, in felt-covered tents. They neither tilled the ground nor ate bread. Their cattle and horses grazed in herds on the steppe. The colts were tethered behind the tents, and the mares were driven to them twice a day. The mares were milked, and from the milk kumiss[10] was made. It was the women who prepared the kumiss, and they also made cheese. As far as the men were concerned, drinking kumiss and tea, eating mutton, and playing on their pipes was all they cared about. They were all stout and merry, and all the summer long they never thought of doing any work. They were quite ignorant, and knew no Russian, but were good-natured enough.

As soon as they saw Pahom, they came out of their tents and gathered around the visitor. An interpreter was found, and Pahom told them he had come about some land. The Bashkirs seemed very glad; they took Pahom and led him into one of the best tents, where they made him sit on some down cushions placed on a carpet, while they sat around him. They gave him some tea and

---

9. **steppe** (step) *n.*: High grassland of central Asia.
10. **kumiss** (ko͞o´ mis) *n.*: Mare's milk that has been fermented and is used as a drink.

kumiss, and had a sheep killed, and gave him mutton to eat. Pahom took presents out of his cart and distributed them among the Bashkirs, and divided the tea amongst them. The Bashkirs were delighted. They talked a great deal among themselves and then told the interpreter what to say.

"They wish to tell you," said the interpreter, "that they like you and that it's our custom to do all we can to please a guest and to repay him for his gifts. You have given us presents, now tell us which of the things we possess please you best, that we may present them to you."

"What pleases me best here," answered Pahom, "is your land. Our land is crowded and the soil is worn out, but you have plenty of land, and it is good land. I never saw the likes of it."

The interpreter told the Bashkirs what Pahom had said. They talked among themselves for a while. Pahom could not understand what they were saying, but saw that they were much amused and heard them shout and laugh. Then they were silent and looked at Pahom while the interpreter said:

"They wish me to tell you that in return for your presents they will gladly give you as much land as you want. You have only to point it out with your hand and it is yours."

The Bashkirs talked again for a while and began to dispute. Pahom asked what they were disputing about, and the interpreter told him that some of them thought they ought to ask their chief about the land and not act in his absence, while others thought there was no need to wait for his return.

6

While the Bashkirs were disputing, a man in a large fox-fur cap appeared on the scene. They all became silent and rose to their feet. The interpreter said: "This is our chief himself."

Pahom immediately fetched the best dressing gown and five pounds of tea, and offered these to the chief. The chief accepted them and seated himself in the place of honor. The Bashkirs at once began telling him something. The chief listened for a while, then made a sign with his head for them to be silent, and addressing himself to Pahom, said in Russian:

"Well, so be it. Choose whatever piece of land you like; we have plenty of it."

"How can I take as much as I like?" thought Pahom. "I must get a deed to make it secure, or else they may say: 'It is yours,' and afterward may take it away again."

"Thank you for your kind words," he said aloud. "You have much land, and I only want a little. But I should like to be sure which portion is mine. Could it not be measured and made over to me? Life and death are in God's hands. You good people give it to me, but your children might wish to take it back again."

"You are quite right," said the chief. "We will make it over to you."

"I heard that a dealer had been here," continued Pahom, "and that you gave him a little land, too, and signed title deeds to that effect. I should like to have it done in the same way."

The chief understood.

"Yes," replied, he, "that can be done quite easily. We have a scribe, and we will go to town with you and have the deed properly sealed."

"And what will be the price?" asked Pahom.

"Our price is always the same: one thousand rubles a day."

Pahom did not understand.

"A day? What measure is that? How many acres would that be?"

"We do not know how to reckon it out," said the chief. "We sell it by the day. As much as you can go around on your feet in a day is yours, and the price is one thousand rubles a day."

Pahom was surprised.

"But in a day you can get around a large tract of land," he said.

The chief laughed.

"It will all be yours!" said he. "But there is one condition: If you don't return on the same day to the spot whence you started, your money is lost."

"But how am I to mark the way that I have gone?"

"Why, we shall go to any spot you like and stay there. You must start from that spot and make your round, taking a spade with you. Wherever you think necessary, make a mark. At every turning, dig a hole and pile up the turf; then afterward we will go around with a plow from hole to hole. You may make as large a circuit as you please, but before the sun sets you must return to the place you started from. All the land you cover will be yours."

Pahom was delighted. It was decided to start early next morning. They talked a while, and after drinking some more kumiss and eating some more mutton, they had tea again, and then the night came on. They gave Pahom a featherbed to sleep on, and the Bashkirs dispersed for the night, promising to assemble the next morning at daybreak and ride out before sunrise to the appointed spot.

7

Pahom lay on the featherbed, but could not sleep. He kept thinking about the land.

"What a large tract I'll mark off!" thought he, "I can easily do thirty-five miles in a day. The days are long now, and within a circuit of thirty-five miles what a lot of land there will be! I'll sell the poorer land or let it to peasants, but

I'll pick out the best and farm it myself. I'll buy two ox teams and hire two more laborers. About a hundred and fifty acres shall be plowland, and I'll pasture cattle on the rest."

Pahom lay awake all night and dozed off only just before dawn. Hardly were his eyes closed when he had a dream. He thought he was lying in that same tent and heard somebody chuckling outside. He wondered who it could be, and rose and went out, and he saw the Bashkir chief sitting in front of the tent holding his sides and rolling about with laughter. Going nearer to the chief, Pahom asked: "What are you laughing at?" But he saw that it was no longer the chief but the grain dealer who had recently stopped at his house and had told him about the land. Just as Pahom was going to ask: "Have you been here long?" he saw that it was not the dealer, but the peasant who had come up from the Volga long ago, to Pahom's old home. Then he saw that it was not the peasant either, but the Devil himself with hoofs and horns, sitting there and chuckling, and before him lay a man, prostrate on the ground, barefooted, with only trousers and a shirt on. And Pahom dreamed that he looked more attentively to see what sort of man it was lying there, and he saw that the man was dead, and that it was himself. Horror-struck, he awoke.

◆ Reading Strategy
How does this dream help you predict what will happen?

"What things one dreams about!" thought he.

Looking around he saw through the open door that the dawn was breaking.

"It's time to wake them up," thought he. "We ought to be starting."

He got up, roused his man (who was sleeping in his cart), bade him harness, and went to call the Bashkirs.

▲ **Critical Viewing** How does the setting in this picture relate to the theme of this parable? **[Connect]**

"It's time to go to the steppe to measure the land," he said.

The Bashkirs rose and assembled, and the chief came, too. Then they began drinking kumiss again, and offered Pahom some tea, but he would not wait.

"If we are to go, let's go. It's high time," said he.

8

The Bashkirs got ready and they all started; some mounted on horses and some in carts. Pahom drove in his own small cart with his servant and took a spade with him. When they reached the steppe, the red dawn was beginning to kindle. They ascended a hillock (called by the Bashkirs a shikhan) and, dismounting from their carts and their horses, gathered in one spot. The chief came up to Pahom and, stretching out his arm toward the plain:

"See," said he, "all this, as far as your eye can reach, is ours. You may have any part of it you like."

Pahom's eyes glistened: it was all virgin soil, as flat as the palm of your hand, as black as the seed of a poppy, and in the hollows different

◆ *Literature and Your Life*
How do you feel when someone offers you as much as you want of something?

kinds of grasses grew breast-high.

The chief took off his fox-fur cap, placed it on the ground, and said:

"This will be the mark. Start from here, and return here again. All the land you go around shall be yours."

Pahom took out his money and put it on the cap. Then he took off his outer coat, remaining in his sleeveless undercoat. He unfastened his girdle[11] and tied it tight below his stomach, put a little bag of bread into the breast of his coat, and, tying a flask of water to his girdle, he drew up the tops of his boots, took the spade from his man, and stood ready to start. He considered for some moments which way he had better go—it was tempting everywhere.

"No matter," he concluded, "I'll go toward the rising sun."

He turned his face to the east, stretched himself, and waited for the sun to appear above the rim.

"I must lose no time," he thought, "and it's easier walking while it's still cool."

The sun's rays had hardly flashed above the horizon when Pahom, carrying the spade over his shoulder, went down into the steppe.

Pahom started walking neither slowly nor quickly. After having gone a thousand yards he stopped, dug a hole, and placed pieces of turf one on another to make it more visible. Then he went on; and now that he had walked off his stiffness he quickened his pace. After a while he dug another hole.

Pahom looked back. The hillock could be distinctly seen in the sunlight, with the people on it, and the glittering iron rims of the cartwheels. At a rough guess Pahom concluded that he had walked three miles. It was growing warmer; he took off his undercoat, slung it across

his shoulder, and went on again. It had grown quite warm now; he looked at the sun—it was time to think of breakfast.

"The first shift is done, but there are four in a day, and it's too soon yet to turn. But I'll just take off my boots," said he to himself.

He sat down, took off his boots, stuck them into his girdle, and went on. It was easy walking now.

"I'll go on for another three miles," thought he, "and then turn to the left. This spot is so fine that it would be a pity to lose it. The further one goes, the better the land seems."

He went straight on for a while, and when he looked around, the hillock was scarcely visible and the people on it looked like black ants, and he could just see something glistening there in the sun.

"Ah," thought Pahom, "I have gone far enough in this direction; it's time to turn. Besides, I'm in a regular sweat, and very thirsty."

He stopped, dug a large hole, and heaped up pieces of turf. Next he untied his flask, had a drink, and then turned sharply to the left. He went on and on; the grass was high, and it was very hot.

Pahom began to grow tired: he looked at the sun and saw that it was noon.

"Well," he thought, "I must have a rest."

He sat down, and ate some bread and drank some water; but he did not lie down, thinking that if he did he might fall asleep. After sitting a little while, he went on again. At first he walked easily; the food had strengthened him; but it had become terribly hot and he felt sleepy. Still he went on, thinking: "An hour to suffer, a lifetime to live."

He went a long way in this direction also, and was about to turn to the left again, when he perceived a damp hollow:

"It would be a pity to leave that out,"

---

11. girdle (gurd´ əl) *n*.: Belt or sash.

he thought. "Flax would do well there." So he went on past the hollow and dug a hole on the other side of it before he made a sharp turn. Pahom looked toward the hillock. The heat made the air hazy: it seemed to be quivering, and through the haze the people on the hillock could scarcely be seen.

"Ah," thought Pahom, "I have made the sides too long; I must make this one shorter." And he went along the third side, stepping faster. He looked at the sun: it was nearly halfway to the horizon, and he had not yet done two miles of the third side of the square. He was still ten miles from the goal.

"No," he thought, "though it will make my land lopsided, I must hurry back in a straight line now. I might go too far, and as it is I have a great deal of land."

So Pahom hurriedly dug a hole and turned straight toward the hillock.

9

Pahom went straight toward the hillock, but he now walked with difficulty. He was exhausted from the heat, his bare feet were cut and bruised, and his legs began to fail. He longed to rest, but it was impossible if he meant to get back before sunset. The sun waits for no man, and it was sinking lower and lower.

"Oh, Lord," he thought, "if only I have not blundered trying for too much! What if I am too late?"

He looked toward the hillock and at the sun. He was still far from his goal, and the sun was already near the rim of the sky.

Pahom walked on and on; it was very hard walking, but he went quicker and quicker. He pressed on, but was still far from the place. He began running, threw away his coat, his boots, his flask, and

his cap, and kept only the spade which he used as a support.

"What am I to do?" he thought again. "I've grasped too much and ruined the whole affair. I can't get there before the sun sets."

And this fear made him still more breathless. Pahom kept on running; his trousers stuck to him, and his mouth was parched. His breast was working like a blacksmith's bellows, his heart was beating like a hammer, and his legs were giving way as if they did not belong to him. Pahom was seized with terror lest he should die of the strain.

Though afraid of death, he could not stop.

"After having run all that way they will call me a fool if I stop now," thought he.

And he ran on and on, and drew near and heard the Bashkirs yelling and shouting to him, and their cries inflamed his heart still more. He gathered his last strength and ran on.

The sun was close to the rim of the sky and, cloaked in mist, looked large, and red as blood. Now, yes, now, it was about to set! The sun was quite low, but he was also quite near his goal. Pahom could already see the people on the hillock waving their arms to make him hurry. He could see the fox-fur cap on the ground and the money in it, and the chief sitting on the ground holding his sides. And Pahom remembered his dream.

"There's plenty of land," thought he, "but will God let me live on it? I have lost my life, I have lost my life! Never will I reach that spot!"

Pahom looked at the sun, which had reached the earth: one side of it had already disappeared. With all his remaining strength he rushed on, bending his body forward so that his legs could hardly follow fast enough to keep him from falling. Just as he reached the hillock it suddenly grew dark. He looked up—the sun had already set!

He gave a cry: "All my labor has been in vain," thought he, and was about to stop, but he heard the Bashkirs still shouting and remembered that though to him, from below, the sun seemed to have set, they on the hillock could still see it. He took a long breath and ran up the hillock. It was still light there. He reached the top and saw the cap. Before it sat the chief, laughing and holding his sides. Again Pahom remembered his dream, and he uttered a cry: his legs gave way beneath him, he fell forward and reached the cap with his hands.

"Ah, that's a fine fellow!" exclaimed the chief. "He has gained much land!"

Pahom's servant came running up and tried to raise him, but he saw that blood was flowing from his mouth. Pahom was dead.

The Bashkirs clicked their tongues to show their pity.

His servant picked up the spade and dug a grave long enough for Pahom to lie in, and buried him in it.

Six feet from his head to his toes was all he needed.

◆ **Literary Focus**
What lesson do you learn from Pahom's experiences?

Guide for Responding

◆ Literature and Your Life

Reader's Response Do you sympathize with Pahom? Why or why not?

Thematic Focus Ultimately, Pahom pays for "success" with his life. What price are you willing to pay for success?

Questions for Research Like Pahom, many people find themselves always wanting something *more* to make them happy. With a group of classmates, write a questionnaire that could be used to interview people about happiness.

☑ Check Your Comprehension

1. What does Pahom believe is the only trouble that peasants face?
2. How does Pahom come to buy his first parcel of land?
3. List three problems Pahom experiences as he increases his land holdings.
4. How do the Bashkirs determine how much land a man can own?
5. Briefly summarize what happens on the last day of Pahom's life.

Beyond Literature

History Connection

Russia in the Twentieth Century In 1922, Russia became part of the newly established Union of Soviet Socialist Republics (USSR), better known as the Soviet Union. The Soviet Union initially consisted of four republics, with the Russian Republic being the strongest and most influential one. The Soviet Union gained further territory after World War II, under Joseph Stalin's rule. Increasing disillusionment with communism and demands for greater freedoms led to the eventual defeat of Communist party rule and the dissolution of the Soviet Union in 1991. Throughout the Soviet era and the years that followed, Russia has remained a highly agricultural society, like the one depicted in the story. Conduct research to find out how Russia is adapting to a changing economic climate in an increasingly industrial and technological world.

Guide for Responding (continued)

◆ Critical Thinking

INTERPRET

1. How and why does Pahom's attitude toward his first plot of land change? **[Analyze]**
2. How do Pahom's and the Bashkirs' attitudes toward landownership differ? **[Compare and Contrast]**
3. How does the last sentence in the story reflect the message that answers the title question? **[Connect]**

EVALUATE

4. Explain whether you think that most people would behave as Pahom does if they were put in his situation. **[Make a Judgment]**

EXTEND

5. (a) Name one other character you know from literature who, like Pahom, is never satisfied with what he or she has. (b) What happens to this character? **[Literature Link]**

◆ Reading Strategy

PREDICT BASED ON CHARACTER TRAITS

Based on Pahom's greed, you were probably able to **predict**—make an educated guess—that he would try to wrestle a large parcel of land from the Bashkirs.

1. Identify two things Pahom said or did that helped you predict he would try to take more land than he should have taken from the Bashkirs.
2. Did you predict the story's ending? Did you find it satisfying? Surprising? Explain.

◆ Literary Focus

PARABLE

Tolstoy's story of ownership and greed is classified as a **parable,** a type of short story that teaches a lesson.

1. What is the lesson that Tolstoy's parable teaches?
2. Parables are often used as a means of moral instruction. How might "How Much Land Does a Man Need?" be used for this purpose?

◆ Build Vocabulary

USING WORDS IN CONTEXT

Words that have very specific meanings in one context often have a broader meaning in a broader context. For instance, in the context of land cultivation, *sheaf* refers to a bundle of grain stalks. In a broader context, *sheaf* is also used to describe any collection of things gathered together—such as a *sheaf* of paper.

Choose a word from the Word Bank to complete each sentence.

1. The landowner stormed into the house, holding a   ?   of bills in his hand.
2. His mind has gone   ?   ; he hasn't read a book in a month.

USING THE WORD BANK: Sentence Completion

Choose the word from the Word Bank that best fits each sentence. Write the complete sentence in your notebook.

1. Although the area used to be a desert, irrigation made the land   ?   .
2. Pahom's sister-in-law   ?   the country ways.
3. The   ?   peasants complained to the landowner.
4. Pahom was   ?   by his neighbor's inconsiderate behavior.

◆ Build Grammar Skills

POSSESSIVE NOUNS

The **possessive** form of a noun or pronoun shows ownership, belonging, or another close relationship.

Practice Copy the following sentences in your notebook, using the possessive form of the noun in parentheses.

1. (Pahom) heart kindled with desire.
2. He gave away about one hundred (rubles) worth of silk robes and carpets.
3. It was the (Bashkirs) custom to sell land by the day.
4. The (chief) real identity is revealed at the end of the story.

Build Your Portfolio

 Idea Bank

Writing

1. **Newspaper Article** Write a news article that reports the events leading up to Pahom's death. You may include quotations from other characters who knew or met Pahom. **[Career Link]**

2. **Land Advertisement** Write an advertisement for a piece of property or a building near your home. Focus on good points, such as beautiful views or access to schools. **[Career Link]**

3. **Parable** Using "How Much Land Does a Man Need?" as a model, write a contemporary parable. Choose a lesson you think would help people today. Teach your lesson by focusing on the actions of one or two main characters.

Speaking, Listening, and Viewing

4. **Update the Story** With a small group, improvise a scene from an updated version of this story. Perform your scene for the class. **[Performing Arts Link]**

5. **Eulogy** Prepare a eulogy—a speech about a person who has died—for Pahom. Look back at the story to recall some facts about his life. Deliver your eulogy to the class.

Researching and Representing

6. **Map of Russia** Make a map of modern Russia. On the map, label the various geographic regions and the peoples—including the Bashkirs—who live in each region. **[Social Studies Link]**

7. **Scale Diagram of Pahom's Field** Create a scale diagram that shows the dimensions of Pahom's field. Use one-half inch to represent a mile. You may need to convert some measurements from the story into miles before you create your diagram. **[Math Link]**

Online Activity www.phlit.phschool.com

 Guided Writing Lesson

Video Script

Have you ever read a story and thought, "That would make a great movie"? Now's your chance to try your hand at making one. Choose any of parts one through nine from "How Much Land Does a Man Need?" and write a **video script** for that part. The following tip will ensure that your video turns out as you envision it.

Writing Skills Focus: Clear Explanation of Procedure

A good video script gives a **clear explanation** of everything that will be seen and heard. If you want the camera to show a scene moving from left to right, state those directions clearly. Explain how you see settings, action, sounds, music, and spoken words working together. The following technical terms will help you explain your ideas clearly.

long shot: view from a distance, showing one or more people and the background
close-up: shot of a single person or object
pan: move the camera across the scene
zoom: adjust from a long shot to a close-up using a single lens
cut: move directly from one shot to another
audio dub: sound added to the video
voice-over: comment or narration by an unseen person

Prewriting Create a storyboard—a rough sketch of each scene in your video. Then decide how you will make the visual transition from one image to another.

Drafting Describe what will be heard as well as what will be seen. Use technical terms to explain clearly how the parts of the video script work together.

Revising Compare your draft with your storyboards. If your script does not have a clear explanation of each shot you mapped out, add the necessary instructions.

Guide for Reading

Egyptian Pastoral Poetry of the New Kingdom

(c. 1539–1075 B.C.)

"I Think I'll Go Home and Lie Very Still," "My Heart Remembers How I Once Loved You," and "I Love a Girl, but She Lives Over There" are examples of ancient Egyptian pastoral poems.

Although the term *pastoral* comes from the Latin word *shepherd,* meaning "pastor," pastoral poetry is not simply about shepherds and shepherdesses.

> **Such poetry may celebrate, for instance, the pleasures of simple rural life or revolve around the longings and desires of simple people.**

A pastoral poem is meant to help readers "escape" from the demands of daily life and, for a moment or two, indulge in simple pleasures and romantic love.

A Complex Simplicity Although the names of the poets who wrote these poems have been lost over the centuries, it is probable that the poets were very cultured members of society. In each, the poet assumes a much simpler identity through the poem's speaker. By doing so, the poets can explore emotions associated with romantic love that are pure, free of complexity and sophistication.

Although these poems are thousands of years old, they express timeless emotions. In many ways the voices in these poems are even more moving because they call to readers across the expanse of so many centuries.

◆ Build Vocabulary

LATIN WORD ROOTS: *-term-*

In "I Think I'll Go Home and Lie Very Still," the speaker says he will pretend to have a *terminal* illness. The Latin root *-term-* means "end." A terminal illness, therefore, usually refers to a final, or fatal, illness.

terminal
troop
intricate

WORD BANK

As you read these ancient Egyptian poems, you will encounter the words on this list. Each word is defined on the page where it first appears. Preview the list before you read.

◆ Build Grammar Skills

COMPOUND NOUNS

A noun is a word that names a person, place, thing, or idea. A **compound noun** is a noun that is made up of more than one word. Some compound nouns, such as *spellbound* and *hairdo,* are written as one word; others, such as *brother-in-law,* are written with a hyphen between words; and still others, such as *sign language,* are written as separate words.

As you read these Egyptian poems, look for compound nouns and take note of how they are written.

◆ *Literature and Your Life*

CONNECT YOUR EXPERIENCE

Most people appreciate things more if they have to work to get them. For example, would you be prouder of a *B* in science that you had to work for or an *A* in French that came easily? For the speakers in the poems that follow, attaining true love does not come easily; they must overcome obstacles that are strewn on their path to happiness.

THEMATIC FOCUS: OVERCOMING OBSTACLES

As Shakespeare so wisely observed, "The course of true love never did run smooth." As you read the poems that follow, identify the obstacles that each speaker faces while in pursuit of romantic love.

Journal Writing Jot down the title of your favorite poem, story, play, or movie dealing with romantic love and the obstacles faced by its characters. Then briefly explain why you find the story worthwhile.

◆ Background for Understanding

CULTURE

The New Kingdom (c. 1539–1075 B.C.) in Egypt was a highly sophisticated period marked by the flowering of ancient Egyptian culture. It was a time of expansion abroad—the Egyptian empire reached to the Euphrates River—and increased opportunity at home. Women enjoyed a greater prestige in New Kingdom society than they did in perhaps any other ancient culture. With a legal status equal to that of men, they could will property and initiate lawsuits.

It is not surprising that people in such an advanced culture might want to enjoy some simplicity in their leisure time. Pastoral poetry—like the three love poems in this group—was one way to pursue such relaxation.

◆ Literary Focus

THE SPEAKER IN A POEM

Whenever you read a poem, you should identify its **speaker**—the voice assumed by the poet. A poem's speaker may be the poet him- or herself, a fictional character, an object such as a rock or tree, or an animal character. As you read each of these poems, use clues within the text to identify the speaker and his or her unique situation and personality.

◆ Reading Strategy

INFERRING THE DRAMATIC CONTEXT

You make **inferences,** educated guesses, about people and situations you encounter every day. Someone's words and actions, for instance, may help you make an inference about his or her attitude or occupation.

Similarly, looking at clues within a poem can help you **infer its dramatic context**—to identify and understand the speaker's situation. The speaker may, for example, give hints that reveal his or her attitude toward a situation or allude to events that have previously taken place.

As you read, use a diagram like the one below to infer the dramatic situation behind each poem.

Detail	What It Suggests About the Dramatic Context

I Think I'll Go Home and Lie Very Still

Translated by John L. Foster

I think I'll go home and lie very still,
       feigning[1] terminal illness.
Then the neighbors will all troop over to stare,
       my love, perhaps, among them.
How she'll smile while
       the specialists snarl in their teeth!—

       she perfectly well knows what ails me.

---

1. **feigning** (fān´iŋ) *v.*: Pretending.

◆ **Build Vocabulary**

terminal (tʉr´ mə nəl) *adj.*: Final or fatal

troop (tro͞op) *v.*: To gather or go together in a group; to walk or go

intricate (in´ tri kit) *adj.*: Complex; full of elaborate detail

Critical Viewing ▶
In what ways do the gestures of these young Egyptian women capture the spirit of these poems? [**Connect**]

Ladies Offering a Lemon and a Mandragora Root to Another Lady During a Banquet
Detail of a wall-painting in the tomb of Nakht, Luxor, Thebes, Egypt

Critical Viewing Do you think the young Egyptian woman shown in this sculpture could be the speaker in the poem on this page? Why or why not? [Connect]

Lid of a Canopic Jar, Representing a Royal Woman of the Amarna Period,
The Metropolitan Museum of Art, New York

My Heart Remembers How I Once Loved You
Translated by John L. Foster

My heart remembers how I once loved you,
　　as I sit with my hair half done.
And I'm out running, looking for you,
　　searching for you with my hair down!

If I ever get back, I'll weave
　　an <u>intricate</u> hairdo down to my toes.
Love, there's so much time now to finish . . .

I Love a Girl, but She Lives Over There

Translated by John L. Foster

I love a girl, but she lives over there
       on the too far side of the River.
A whole Nile at floodstage[1] rages between,
       and a crocodile hunched on the sand
Keeps motionless guard at the crossing.
       Still I go down to the water,
Stride out into the waves—
       how is it
5 Desire can soar in the wrench of this current,
       rough water be tame as my fields?
Why she loves me!   she loves me!   hers is the love
       anchors the shifting toeholds;
My charming girl whispered water magic
       (crocodile sits spellbound)—   O my love,
Where are you, whose hand
       is so small yet has mastered the River?
—There, over there! already waiting,
       right in the path of my burning eyes!
10 The only one dear to my heart,
       and she crowns the shore like a queen!

---

1. Nile at floodstage: The Nile river, which flows through
Egypt, floods once every year.

The romantic spirit that inspired writers of ancient love poems such as "I Love a Girl, but She Lives Over There" is still alive in Egypt today. Egyptian pop superstar Amr Diab (ä mir´ dē äb´), has won the hearts of millions by singing similar songs of devotion.

This is an English translation of part of a song he has made famous.

"Habibi Ya Nour El Ain"
("My Darling, You Are the Glow in My Eyes")
Lyrics by Ahmed Shatta

My darling, you are the glow in my eyes.
You live in my imagination.
I adored you for years. No one else is in my mind.

My darling, my darling, my darling
Glow in my eyes, aah.
My darling, my darling, my darling glow in my eyes.
You live in my imagination.

The most beautiful eyes I ever saw in this universe.
God be with you . . . what magic eyes.
Your eyes are with me . . .

1. How is the description of the woman in this song similar to that in "I Love a Girl, but She Lives Over There"?
2. Would the poem "I Love a Girl, but She Lives Over There" work well as the lyrics for a pop song? Why or why not?

Guide for Responding

◆ Literature and Your Life

Reader's Response With which poem's speaker did you most closely sympathize? Why?

Thematic Focus If the obstacles that keep the speaker from his or her love were removed from any of these poems, in what way would the poem be different? Explain.

Reader's Journal Rewrite one of these poems from the point of view of the person being addressed.

☑ Check Your Comprehension

1. What will the speaker pretend to do in "I Think I'll Go Home and Lie Very Still"?
2. What will the speaker's love do when she sees him lying "very still"?
3. In "My Heart Remembers How I Once Loved You," what will the speaker do if she ever gets back?
4. In "I Love a Girl, but She Lives Over There," what lies between the speaker and his beloved?
5. What keeps guard at the river crossing?

◆ Critical Thinking

INTERPRET
1. In "I Think I'll Go Home and Lie Very Still," why will the speaker's love smile when she sees him lying "very still"? **[Interpret]**
2. What role does irony—the difference between appearance and reality—play in "I Think I'll Go Home and Lie Very Still"? **[Analyze]**
3. What do the words "there's so much time now to finish" suggest may have happened to the speaker's beloved in "My Heart Remembers How I Once Loved You"? **[Draw Conclusions]**
4. In "I Love a Girl, but She Lives Over There," why is the speaker crossing the Nile? **[Infer]**
5. Explain what effect the use of repetition in lines 6 and 9 has on the poem's meaning. **[Interpret]**

EVALUATE
6. Is the speaker's solution in "I Think I'll Go Home and Lie Very Still" one you would recommend? Why or why not? **[Make a Judgment]**

Guide for Responding (continued)

◆ Reading Strategy

INFERRING THE DRAMATIC CONTEXT

As you read poetry, look for clues to make educated guesses about what is taking place within a poem. When you do this, you **infer a poem's dramatic context**—you identify what has been happening to whom. For example, in "I Think I'll Go Home and Lie Very Still," clues within the poem suggest that the speaker is a young boy who is experiencing his first rejection in love.

1. (a) What clues in "My Heart Remembers How I Once Loved You" suggest that the speaker is a woman? (b) In the poem, what is the speaker doing, and why?
2. If you were to capture the essence of "I Love a Girl, but She Lives Over There" in a painting, what details would you depict? Describe at least four details from the poem that you would feature in the painting.

◆ Literary Focus

THE SPEAKER IN A POEM

The voice "speaking" a poem is not necessarily that of the poet, although it can be. In each of these poems, the **speakers** are simpler, and perhaps younger, characters than the very sophisticated poets themselves. For example, in "I Think I'll Go Home and Lie Very Still," the speaker seems to be a young boy who is experiencing a case of puppy love.

1. If you were to choose an actor to portray the speaker in "I Think I'll Go Home and Lie Very Still," whom would you choose? Why?
2. Name some details that help you identify the speaker in "My Heart Remembers How I Once Loved You."
3. (a) What is the attitude of the speaker in "I Love a Girl, but She Lives Over There"? (b) What clues in the poem led you to your answer? **[Explain]**

◆ Build Vocabulary

USING THE LATIN ROOT *-term-*

Knowing that the Latin root *-term-* means "end," answer the following questions in your notebook.

1. When do you hand in a *term* paper?
2. How would you *terminate* a conversation?
3. Why does the speaker in "I Think I'll Go Home and Lie Very Still" plan to feign a *terminal* illness?

USING THE WORD BANK: Synonyms

On your paper, write the word whose meaning is closest to the meaning of the word from the Word Bank.

1. terminal: (a) proud, (b) fatal, (c) foolish
2. troop: (a) scatter, (b) play, (c) gather
3. intricate: (a) detailed, (b) simple, (c) visual

◆ Build Grammar Skills

COMPOUND NOUNS

"I Love a Girl, but She Lives Over There" contains some **compound nouns,** nouns that consist of two or more words. Examples of compound nouns in this poem include *toeholds* and *water magic.* Compound nouns are written in several ways: They may be hyphenated, combined, or written as two or more words.

Practice Copy the following sentences into your notebook. Underline each compound noun.

1. In "I Love a Girl," the speaker says the Nile is at floodstage.
2. The speaker in "I Love a Girl" may be a young nobleman.
3. The doctors in "I Think I'll Go Home" make a house-call on the speaker.
4. The speaker in "I Think I'll Go Home" resembles a character in a soap opera.
5. In fact, the poem's love interest has an understanding of exactly what is going on.

Build Your Portfolio

 Idea Bank

Writing

1. **Diagnosis** The speaker in "I Think I'll Go Home and Lie Very Still" plans to pretend to be ill. Imagine that you are a doctor, one of the "specialists" referred to in the poem. Write a brief diagnosis, describing the speaker's illness.

2. **Letter to a Poet** Choose one of the poems in this group. Write a letter to the poet, responding to the attitude of the poem's speaker. Explain whether you find the speaker's attitude reasonable, and why.

3. **Analysis of a Poem** Choose one of the ancient Egyptian poems and write an analysis of it. In your analysis, examine the poet's use of words and the overall message conveyed by the piece.

Speaking, Listening, and Viewing

4. **Dramatic Reading** In a dramatic reading of "I Love a Girl but She Lives Over There," capture the speaker's emotions using vocal inflections and gestures. **[Performing Arts Link]**

5. **Panel Discussion** Role-play a panel discussion that might take place among the three speakers in these poems. Have one group member act as a moderator who leads a discussion about overcoming obstacles in love. **[Performing Arts Link]**

Researching and Representing

6. **Music of the New Kingdom** Research the music that might have accompanied these pastoral love poems and prepare a presentation for the class. If possible, play recordings of ancient Egyptian music. **[Music Link]**

7. **Oral Report** Research Egyptian life during the New Kingdom period. Present your report to the class, using drawings, maps, and charts. **[Social Studies Link; Art Link]**

Online Activity www.phlit.phschool.com

Guided Writing Lesson

Advice Column

An advice column provides readers with suggestions for solving problems or improving their lives. You can find examples of advice columns in many newspapers and magazines. Write your own advice column in response to one of the speakers in these poems. As you do so, take into consideration the speaker's dramatic situation.

Writing Skills Focus: Know the Dramatic Context

When you respond to a poem's speaker, it is important to **know the dramatic context,** especially if you plan to give that speaker advice. Look for clues within the poem to help you understand the dramatic situation—what is happening to whom—and the speaker's emotional state. When you fully understand what the dramatic context is, you can respond appropriately.

Prewriting Choose the poem whose speaker you want to advise. Then, reread the poem and jot down clues to the dramatic context, such as the speaker's actions and attitude toward his or her situation.

Drafting Begin your advice column by rephrasing the situation that the speaker finds himself or herself in. Then, develop and support your advice based on what you know about the speaker and the dramatic context.

When possible, use compound nouns, such as *love potion*, instead of longer descriptions, such as "a magic drink supposed to induce feelings of love in the drinker."

Revising As you revise, look for ways to make your advice more closely respond to the dramatic context presented in the poem. Also, check to make sure you have clearly and effectively supported the reasons for your advice.

Guide for Reading

Jorge Luis Borges (1899–1986)

Can a person be two people at once? In a prose poem entitled "Borges and I," Argentinian Jorge Luis Borges (hôr´ hā loo´ ēs bôr´ hās) writes of the "other Borges," the writer whose mail he gets and whose name appears listed with those of other professors. As he teasingly separates Borges the living person from Borges the noted author, Borges displays the playful, paradoxical style that won him an international audience.

An International Background

Growing up in Buenos Aires, Borges knew English as well as Spanish, since his wealthy family included an English grandmother. From childhood, he had access to an international array of great literature. "If I were asked to name the chief event in my life," he once observed, "I should say my father's library." In 1914, his family moved to Switzerland, where he learned German and French. In Spain, after World War I (1914–1918), he mingled with a group of writers whose experimental style influenced his own work. Returning to Argentina in 1921, he contributed fiction and poetry to several magazines.

The Fiction of Ideas

In 1938, the year of his father's death, Borges himself nearly died from a serious head injury. Shaken, he began to doubt his own artistic abilities; yet the prose he produced around this time is considered some of his finest.

These short works emphasize ideas over story elements such as plot and character. In them, Borges tests concepts such as identity, memory, and time, pushing them to the breaking point. Many of these fictions are collected in such landmark volumes as *The Garden of Forking Paths* (1941), *Fictions* (1944), and *The Aleph* (1949).

Borges was first named national librarian in 1938, but he lost the post during the regime of dictator Juan Perón, whose rule he opposed. After Perón fell from power in 1955, the position was given back to him. By the time of his death in 1986, Borges had won international recognition for his work.

◆ Build Vocabulary

LATIN PREFIXES: *ab-*

The Latin prefix *ab-* (or *a-* or *abs-*) means "away" or "from." Before a *c* or a *t*, it is usually spelled *abs-*. In the word *abstract,* which appears in the essay, *abs-* comes before the Latin root *-tract-,* which means "to draw or pull." A thought, painting, or other thing is *abstract* if it is "pulled away" from the material world and deals purely with general ideas or forms. The word *abstract* means "that which is general, apart from things that can be perceived by the senses."

concrete
abstract
besieging
dissonances

WORD BANK

Each of these words from the selections is defined on the page where it first appears. Preview the list before you read.

◆ Build Grammar Skills

CORRECT STYLE WITH PARENTHESES

In his essay, Borges puts interrupting details and comments in **parentheses.** Parenthetical remarks such as these can be tricky to capitalize and punctuate.

- If the remark is a complete sentence, capitalize the first letter, and put the final punctuation inside the closing parenthesis.

  Jorge Luis Borges is one of Argentina's greatest writers. *(Another is Julio Cortázar.)*

- If the remark is not a complete sentence, do not capitalize the first letter or include any final punctuation inside the closing parenthesis.

  The blind live in . . . an undefined world from which certain colors emerge: for me, yellow, blue *(except that the blue may be green),* and green *(except that the green may be blue).*

from Blindness

◆ *Literature and Your Life*

CONNECT YOUR EXPERIENCE
There are about as many versions of the world as there are people in it. In this essay, Borges invites you to cross into the world of the blind. Along the way, you will learn something about the world of a writer.

Journal Writing Imagine that you have to give up the ability to see just one color. Which would you give up, and why? Jot down your thoughts in a paragraph or two.

THEMATIC FOCUS: OVERCOMING OBSTACLES
As you read, consider the obstacles that blindness presents to Borges and how it affects his writing.

◆ Background for Understanding

LITERATURE
An avid reader since childhood, Jorge Luis Borges was familiar with literary works from many different cultures and often drew on them in his own work. In his essay, he mentions these four famous authors:

- William Shakespeare (1564–1616): English poet and playwright that many consider the greatest writer in the English language.
- Fray Luis de Léon (loo´es də lā´ on) (1521–1591): Spanish monk famous for his religious writings and lyrical poetry.
- Edgar Allan Poe (1809–1849): American poet and storyteller known for his eerie tales and for inventing the modern detective story.
- Johann Wolfgang von Goethe (yō´ hän vôlf´ gän fôn gö´ tə) (1749–1832): Influential German poet and playwright.

◆ Literary Focus

QUOTATIONS AS ALLUSIONS
An **allusion** is a brief reference within a work to something famous outside the work, such as a well-known person, character, place, event, work of art, or work of literature. Many of the allusions in the essay are quotations from the writings of famous authors.

As you read the essay, consider why Borges includes these quotations. What light do they help throw on his subject? Which of his ideas do they help support? What effect might such references to familiar works have on knowledgeable readers?

◆ Reading Strategy

ESTABLISH A PURPOSE
When you read nonfiction, it is especially useful to **establish a purpose,** or decide why you are reading the work. Is it for enjoyment? for information? to compare one work with another? Your purpose should determine the details that you focus on as you read.

As you read the essay, complete a chart like the one below. Add at least one more purpose that you might have for reading. Then, list details from the essay that are most relevant for each particular purpose.

Purpose	Relevant Ideas and Details
to learn more about Borges	
to learn more about blindness	

from
Blindness

Jorge Luis Borges

Translated by Eliot Weinberger

In the course of the many lectures—too many lectures—I have given, I've observed that people tend to prefer the personal to the general, the <u>concrete</u> to the <u>abstract</u>. I will begin, then, by referring to my own modest blindness. Modest, because it is total blindness in one eye, but only partial in the other. I can still make out certain colors; I can still see blue and green. And yellow, in particular, has remained faithful to me. I remember when I was young I used to linger in front of certain cages in the Palermo zoo: the cages of the tigers and leopards. I lingered before the tigers' gold and black. Yellow is still with me, even now. I have written a poem entitled "The Gold of the Tigers," in which I refer to this friendship.

People generally imagine the blind as enclosed in a black world. There is, for example, Shakespeare's line: "Looking on darkness which the blind do see." If we understand *darkness* as *blackness*, then Shakespeare is wrong.

One of the colors that the blind—or at least this blind man—do *not* see is black; another is red. *Le rouge et le noir*[1] are the colors denied us. I, who was accustomed to sleeping in total darkness, was bothered for a long time at having to sleep in this world of mist, in the greenish or bluish mist, vaguely luminous, which is the world of the blind. I wanted to lie down in darkness. The world of the blind is not the night that people imagine. (I should say that I am speaking for myself, and for my father and

my grandmother, who both died blind—blind, laughing, and brave, as I also hope to die. They inherited many things—blindness, for example—but one does not inherit courage. I know that they were brave.)

The blind live in a world that is inconvenient, an undefined world from which certain colors emerge: for me, yellow, blue (except that the blue may be green), and green (except that the green may be blue). White has disappeared, or is confused with gray. As for red, it has vanished completely. But I hope some day—I am following a treatment—to improve and to be able to see that great color, that color which shines in poetry, and which has so many beautiful names in many languages. Think of *scharlach* in German, *scarlet* in English, *escarlata* in Spanish, *écarlate* in French. Words that are worthy of that great color. In contrast, *amarillo*, yellow, sounds weak in Spanish, in English it seems more like yellow. I think that in Old Spanish it was *amariello*.

◆ **Reading Strategy**
What do you want to learn by reading this essay?

I live in that world of colors, and if I speak of my own modest blindness, I do so, first, because it is not that perfect blindness which people imagine, and second, because it deals with me. My case is not especially dramatic. What is dramatic are those who suddenly lose their sight. In my case, that slow nightfall, that slow loss of sight, began when I began to see. It has continued since 1899 without dramatic moments, a slow nightfall that has lasted more

---

1. *Le rouge et le noir:* (lə rōozh´ ā lə nwär´): French for red and black.

than three quarters of a century. In 1955 the pathetic moment came when I knew I had lost my sight, my reader's and writer's sight.

. . .

I have said that blindness is a way of life, a way of life that is not entirely unfortunate. Let us recall those lines of the greatest Spanish poet, Fray Luis de León:

Vivir quiero conmigo,
gozar quiero del bien que debo
        al cielo,
a solas sin testigo,
libre de amor, de celo,
de odio, de esperanza,
        de recelo.

[I want to live with myself,
I want to enjoy the good that I
        owe to heaven,
alone, without witnesses,
free of love, of jealousy,
of hate, of hope, of fear.]

Edgar Allan Poe knew this stanza by heart. For me, to live without hate is easy, for I have never felt hate. To live without love I think is impossible, happily impossible for each one of us. But the first part—"I want to live with myself,/I want to enjoy the good that I owe to heaven"—if we accept that in the good of heaven there can also be darkness, then who lives more with themselves? Who can explore

Homage to the Square, Josef Albers, Galleria Naziona d'Arte Moderna, Rome

▲ **Critical Viewing** Which colors in this abstract painting could Borges have seen? Explain. **[Connect]**

themselves more? Who can know more of themselves? According to the Socratic phrase,[2] who can know himself more than the blind man?

A writer lives. The task of being a poet is not completed at a fixed schedule. No one is a poet from eight to twelve and from two to six. Whoever is a poet is one always, and continually assaulted by poetry. I suppose a painter feels that colors and shapes are <u>besieging</u> him. Or a musician feels that the strange world of sounds—the strangest world of art—is always seeking him out, that there are melodies and <u>dissonances</u> looking for him. For the task of an artist, blindness is not a total misfortune. It may be an instrument. Fray Luis de León dedicated one of his most beautiful odes to Francisco Salinas, a blind musician.

A writer, or any man, must believe that what-

◆ **Build Vocabulary**

concrete (kän krēt´) *n.*: That which is specific, particular, or material; things that can perceived by the senses

abstract (ab strakt´) *n.*: That which concerns general qualities, considered apart from particular things; things that cannot be perceived by the senses

besieging (bē sēj´ iŋ) *v.*: Surrounding with attacking forces; crowding in on

dissonances (dis´ ə nəns´ iz) *n.*: Sounds that are not harmonious; discords

2. **Socratic:** (sə krat´ ik) **phrase:** "Know thyself" was the famous decree of the ancient Greek philosopher Socrates (säk´ rə tēz´) (469?–399 B.C.)

ever happens to him is an instrument; everything has been given for an end. This is even stronger in the case of the artist. Everything that happens, including humiliations, embarrassments, misfortunes, all has been given like clay, like material for one's art. One must accept it. For this reason I speak in a poem of the ancient food of heroes: humiliation, unhappiness, discord. Those things are given to us to transform, so that we may make from the miserable circumstances of our lives things that are eternal, or aspire to be so.

If a blind man thinks this way, he is saved. Blindness is a gift. I have exhausted you with the gifts it has given me. It gave me Anglo-Saxon,[3] it gave me some Scandinavian, it gave me knowledge of Medieval literature I had ignored, it gave me the writing of various books, good or bad, but which justified the moment in which they were written. Moreover, blindness has made me feel surrounded by the kindness of others. People

always feel good will toward the blind.

I want to end with a line of Goethe: *"Alles Nahe werde fern,"* everything near becomes distant. Goethe was referring to evening twilight. Everything near becomes distant. It is true. At nightfall, the things closest to us seem to move away from our eyes. So the visible world has moved away from my eyes, perhaps forever.

Goethe could be referring not only to twilight but to life. All things go off, leaving us. Old age is probably the supreme solitude—except that the supreme solitude is death. And "everything near becomes distant" also refers to the slow process of blindness, of which I hoped to show, speaking tonight, that it is not a complete misfortune. It is one more instrument among the many—all of them so strange—that fate or chance provide.

◆ **Literary Focus**
How does the quotation from Goethe relate to the subject of the essay?

---

3. **Anglo-Saxon:** Old English, the most ancient form of our language, which evolved from the language of the Germanic peoples who invaded England long ago.

Guide for Responding

◆ *Literature and Your Life*

Reader's Response Would you like to have known Borges personally? Why or why not?

Thematic Focus How has Borges dealt with the obstacle of his blindness? What relationship does he see between writing and blindness?

☑ Check Your Comprehension

1. (a) What sorts of things can Borges see, and what can he not see? (b) What color does he miss most?
2. In what basic way is the world of the blind different from what sighted people imagine?
3. What relatives' experiences provided examples to Borges of how to face his disease?
4. How, according to Borges, must a writer view anything that happens to him or her?
5. List five gifts Borges says blindness has given him.

◆ Critical Thinking

INTERPRET

1. What adjectives would you use to describe Borges's attitude toward his blindness? **[Infer]**
2. Why might the blind "live more with themselves" than others do? **[Interpret]**
3. Why might Borges say that one "must believe that whatever happens to [one] is an instrument"? **[Interpret]**
4. (a) What is "the ancient food of heroes"? (b) What does this metaphor suggest about the task of writers? **[Interpret]**
5. (a) Explain how Borges applies Goethe's line to his blindness. (b) Do you think writers are "near" life or "distant" from it? Explain. **[Draw Conclusions]**

EVALUATE

6. Evaluate Borges's attitude toward his blindness. **[Evaluate]**

Guide for Responding (continued)

◆ Reading Strategy

ESTABLISH A PURPOSE

Knowing your **purpose** for reading a particular work helps you focus on the ideas and details that will help fulfill that purpose.

For example, if you were reading the essay to learn what it is like to be blind, you would focus on passages in which Borges describes what he can and cannot see. If you were reading to learn more about Borges's thoughts about life, you would focus on his discussion of his attitude toward blindness.

1. Which details would you focus on if your purpose were to learn more about the different writers who influenced Borges? Explain.
2. Which details would you focus on if your purpose were to learn about the way some blind people perceive color? Explain.

◆ Build Vocabulary

USING THE LATIN PREFIX *ab-*

Explain how the Latin prefix *ab-* (or *abs-*), meaning "away" or "from," contributes to the meanings of these words. Use a dictionary if necessary.

1. abnormal
2. abscond
3. absent
4. absorb

USING THE WORD BANK: Multiple Choice

On your paper, write the letter of the example that best illustrates each word.

1. concrete: (a) beauty, (b) lily, (c) hope
2. abstract: (a) pebble, (b) hand, (c) patriotism
3. besieging: (a) crowding around a celebrity, (b) making a speech, (c) stamping a foot
4. dissonances: (a) pleasant melodies, (b) calm waters, (c) noises on city streets

◆ Literary Focus

QUOTATIONS AS ALLUSIONS

In his essay, Borges makes several **allusions,** or brief references, to something famous outside his work. For example, to compare his progressive blindness to twilight and aging, he includes a quotation by the German poet Johann Wolfgang von Goethe, "Everything near becomes distant."

1. (a) What allusion to Shakespeare does Borges make in the form of a quotation? (b) For what purpose does Borges include this quotation?
2. What point does Borges make when citing the quotation by the Spanish poet Fray Luis de Léon?
3. Explain why concluding with a quotation from Goethe makes the essay more memorable than an ending that uses only Borges's own ideas.

◆ Build Grammar Skills

CORRECT STYLE WITH PARENTHESES

Full sentences within **parentheses** are capitalized and punctuated as sentences, but other phrases or clauses in parentheses are not.

Practice On your paper, rewrite these sentences, correcting any errors in capitalization or punctuation. If the sentence is correct as is, write correct.

1. In the course of the many lectures (Too many lectures) I have given, I have observed many things.
2. People imagine that the blind live in a black world. (consider the famous Shakespeare quotation.)
3. I began going blind when I was born (Like my father and grandmother before me.)
4. My father and grandmother faced their blindness bravely (As I hope to do.)
5. I still see some (but not all) colors. (I really miss red).

Build Your Portfolio

Idea Bank

Writing

1. **Interview Questions** Imagine that you are a magazine reporter about to interview Borges. List at least ten questions based on his essay, including some on his family, his literary interests, and his blindness. **[Career Link]**

2. **Essay with Allusions** Write a brief essay about an obstacle that you or someone you know has overcome. Include at least four allusions in the form of quotations from literature (you may consult a dictionary of quotations).

3. **Poem** Write a version of the poem "The Gold of the Tigers" mentioned by Borges. Consider what Borges remembers about tigers and how they appear to him now that he is nearly blind.

Speaking, Listening, and Viewing

4. **Role Play** With a classmate, take on the roles of Borges and his wife on a walk. Borges should discuss what he can and cannot see; the wife should further clarify the scene. **[Performing Arts Link]**

5. **Class Discussion** Do research to find out more about special programs that offer literature to the blind. Share your results in a class discussion. **[Career Link]**

Researching and Representing

6. **Colorblindness Chart** Investigate the phenomenon of colorblindness. Create a chart showing the different forms of colorblindness and a diagram explaining the workings of color vision. **[Science Link]**

7. **Book of Quotations** With a group of classmates, create a book of interesting, amusing, or profound quotations. Gather your quotations from the news, literature, reference works, and other reliable sources. Organize them by theme, and be sure to make the author and source clear.

Online Activity www.phlit.phschool.com

Guided Writing lesson

Literary Analysis of a Persona

When an author presents himself or herself in writing, the writer uses words to create a sense of himself or herself as friendly, serious, sly, straightforward, and so on. The writer projects a personality, or **persona.** Write a brief essay in which you analyze the persona that Borges conveys in this essay. What sort of person does he seem to be? Which details point to that personality? Answer these questions in your analysis.

Writing Skills Focus: Use of Quotations for Support

Your analysis will require you to **use quotations** from the essay to support the general statements you make about the persona that Borges projects. In using such quotations, remember to

- choose quotations that clearly support the points you are making.
- copy the quotation accurately.
- use quotation marks around shorter quotations.
- indent and set off quotations of four or more lines.

Prewriting Reread the essay, jotting down qualities or attitudes that seem to be part of Borges's persona. For each, note lines in the essay that illustrate it.

Drafting Begin with a general statement of your essay's main idea. Then, do a point-by-point analysis of Borges's persona, supporting each point by providing quotations or other details from the essay.

Revising Be sure that you have supported general statements with enough examples. Also, check to make sure your quotations are accurate and correctly punctuated.

If you have used parentheses, be sure you have used them correctly. For more on their correct use, see pp. 298 and 303.

PART 2 *Reaching a Goal*

Three Jumping Carp, Yi Dynasty, Brooklyn Museum, New York

Guide for Reading

Patricia Grace *(1937–)*

Some writers pride themselves on the uniqueness of their vision. In contrast, Patricia Grace proudly bases her work on the ancient traditions of New Zealand's native people, the Maori. Born in Wellington, New Zealand, Grace is one of the most successful Maori writers in English today. Her narratives *Mutuwhenua: The Moon Sleeps* (1978), *The Dream Sleepers and Other Stories* (1980), and *Potiki* (1986) preserve, in writing, the Maori way of life.

Maori Subject and Style Although she usually writes in English, Grace's topics and style are very much in the Maori tradition. "And So I Go" is a good example of how she presents Maori language patterns, culture, and traditions without using the Maori language itself. Her work has been translated into many other languages, including Finnish, German, French, Dutch, and Samoan.

Okot p'Bitek *(1931–1982)*

In an interview shortly before his death, Okot p'Bitek (ō´ kät pē bē tak´) said that "an artist should tease people" and stick "needles into everybody so that they don't go to sleep and think everything is fine." This desire to raise awareness and stir up controversy is nowhere more evident than in p'Bitek's popular book *Song of Lawino* (1966), a sequence of poems about the clash between African and Western values.

A Contrast of Cultures Born in Uganda, p'Bitek embodied the contrast of cultures in that country. Though educated in English-speaking schools, he never lost touch with traditional African values. His *Song of Lawino*, which has been called the "first important poem in English to emerge from Eastern Africa," draws on the oral techniques of traditional Ugandan poetry.

◆ Build Vocabulary

RELATED WORDS: WORDS RELATED TO "HUMORS"

In the excerpt from *Song of Lawino*, you will encounter the word *bile,* "a bodily fluid associated with anger." In the Middle Ages, doctors believed that bile was one of four *humors* (fluids in the body) controlling bodily functions and temperament. It was believed that an excess of yellow bile made people quick-tempered and that too much black bile made them gloomy and sad.

baptizing
plaiting
mottled
anoint
extensively
impenetrable
corrosive
perished
bile

WORD BANK

As you read the story, you will encounter the words on this list. Each word is defined on the page where it first appears. Preview the list before you read.

◆ Build Grammar Skills

INVERTED WORD ORDER

"Dark it is and very damp," a line from *Song of Lawino,* may sound a little odd to you. Its unusual sound is due to the **inverted word order**—the sentence is turned around.

Usually, English sentences follow the pattern *subject-verb-complement.* In the line from Okot p'Bitek's poem, the complement, *dark,* precedes the subject and verb, *it is.* The poet intentionally uses inverted word order to give emphasis to the word *dark,* thus underscoring the sorrow felt by the speaker.

If you are confused by inverted word order in a sentence, mentally rearrange the parts of the sentence in normal order to find the meaning. You would rearrange p'Bitek's line as follows: "It is dark and very damp."

◆ *Literature and Your Life*

CONNECT YOUR EXPERIENCE

Without shared experiences, even close friends may become strangers. In these selections, characters pursue new experiences, experiences they cannot share with those they know. The selections examine the price people pay as they strive for new goals.

THEMATIC FOCUS: REACHING A GOAL

As you read, notice what the characters may lose or have already lost in the pursuit of a goal.

Journal Writing Briefly describe a goal you have. Then, describe the losses and gains associated with this goal.

◆ Background for Understanding

CULTURE

The Maori (mä´ or rē) are the Polynesian natives of New Zealand, making up about 9 percent of the population of that country. Nearly all of today's Maori have some European ancestry, a result of the European colonization of that land in the 1800's.

An important part of Maori culture involves the performance of oral literature on the *marae* (tribal meeting place). Maori poetry is often paired with music, and includes laments, songs of love and courtship, and gossip songs. "And So I Go" has many of the qualities of the *karanga,* which is something between a song and a chant. A karanga is usually performed by women welcoming or saying goodbye to visitors on the marae.

◆ Literary Focus

DEVELOPMENT BY DIALOGUE AND MONOLOGUE

A **dialogue** is a conversation between characters. Just as your own conversations show much about you, dialogue can show much about the characters who are speaking. Writers use dialogue to reveal character, to present events, and to add variety to a story.

A **monologue** is a speech by one character in a play, story, or poem. A monologue may be addressed to another character or to the audience, or it may be a *soliloquy*—a speech that presents the character's thoughts as though the character were overheard when alone.

As you read, notice how these writers use a dialogue or a monologue to reveal characters' thoughts and feelings.

◆ Reading Strategy

QUESTION

It is rare for a writer to spell out the significance of each detail or action in a work. Instead, the reader must ask questions and look for answers. **Question** as you read, asking yourself about the meaning of events, characters' actions, and key details. Why does a character act the way he or she does? Does a specific detail of the setting have an underlying meaning?

Keep your questions in mind as you continue reading. Piece together details that will enable you to answer them. For example, to answer a question about a character's actions, you might gather information about his or her attitude. To help you record and answer your question, fill out a chart like this one as you read.

Question	Details	Answer

AND SO I GO

PATRICIA GRACE

Our son, brother, grandchild, you say you are going away from this place you love, where you are loved. Don't go. We warm you. We give you strength, we give you love.
These people are yours.
These hills, this soil, this wide stretch of sea.
This quiet place.

This land is mine, this sea, these people. Here I give love and am loved but I must go, this is in me. I go to learn new ways and to make a way for those who follow because I love.

My elders, brothers and sisters, children of this place, we must go on. This place we love cannot hold us always. The world is large. Not forever can we stay here warm and quiet to turn the soil and reap the sea and live our lives. This I've always known. And so I go ahead for those who come. To stand mid-stream and hold a hand to either side. It is in me. Am I not at once dark and fair, fair and dark. A mingling. Since our blue-eyed father held our dark-eyed mother's hand and let her lead him here.

But, our brother, he came, and now his ways are hers out of choice because of love.

◆ **Reading Strategy**
What question does the line "And I go because of love" suggest? Where is your question answered?

And I go because of love. For our mother and her people and for our father. For you and for our children whose mingling will be greater than our own. I make a way. Learn new ways. So I can take up that which is our father's and hold it to the light. Then the people of our mother may come to me and say, 'How is this?' And I will hold the new thing to the light for them to see. Then take up that which is our mother's and say to those of our father, 'You see? See there, that is why.'

And brother, what of us. Must we do this too? Must we leave this quiet place at the edge of hills, at the edge of sea and follow you? For the sake of our mother's people who are our own. And for our father and because we love?

◆ **Build Vocabulary**

baptizing (bap′ tīz′ iŋ) *n.*: Immersion of an individual in water or sprinkling of an individual with water as a sign of purification; a ritual often associated with admission into Christianity or a specific Christian church

plaiting (plāt′ iŋ) *v.*: Braiding or interweaving

▲ **Critical Viewing** This picture shows a food storehouse in a Maori village like the one in this story. What materials and tools do you think the villagers used to build it? Explain. **[Speculate]**

You must choose but if you do not feel it in you, stay here in warmth. Let me do this and do not weep for my going. I have this power in me. I am full. I ache for this.

Often I have climbed these hills and run about as free as rain. Stood on the highest place and looked down on great long waves looping on to sand. Where we played, grew strong, learned our body skills. And learned the ways of summers, storms, and tides. From where we stepped into the spreading sea to bathe or gather food. I have watched and felt this ache in me.

I have watched the people. Seen myself there with them living too. Our mother and our blue-eyed father who came here to this gentle place that gives us life and strength. Watched them work and play, laugh and cry, and love.

Seen our uncle sleeping. Brother of our mother. Under a tree bright and heavy with sunned fruit. And beside our uncle, his newest baby daughter sleeping too. And his body sweat ran down and over her head in a new <u>baptizing</u>. I was filled with strength.

And old Granny Roka sits on her step combing her granddaughter's hair, patiently grooming. <u>Plaiting</u> and tying the heavy tangled kelp which is her pride. Or walk together on the mark of tide, old Granny and the child, collecting sun-white sticks for the fire. Tying the sticks into bundles and carrying them on their backs to the little house. Together.

And seen the women walk out over rocks when the tide is low, submerging by a hole of rock with clothes ballooning. Surfacing with wine-red crayfish, snapping tails and clawing air on a still day. And on a special day the river stones fired for cooking by our father, our cousins, and our uncles who laugh and sing. Working all as one.

Our little brother's horse walks home with our little one asleep. Resting a head on his pony's neck, breathing in the warm horse stink, knees locked into its sides. Fast asleep on the tired flesh of horse. And I ache. But not forever this. And so I go.

◆ **Literary Focus**
Explain how the italicized parts of the dialogue help the work to flow.

And when you go our brother as you say you must will you be warm? Will you know love? Will an old woman kiss your face and cry warm tears because of who you are? Will children take your hands and say your name? In your new life our brother will you sing?

The warmth and love I take from here with me and return for their renewal when I can. It is not a place of loving where I go, not the same as love that we have known.

> No love fire there to warm one's self
>   beside
> No love warmth
> Blood warmth
> Wood and tree warmth
> Skin on skin warmth
> Tear warmth
> Rain warmth
> Earth warmth
> Breath warmth
> Child warmth
> Warmth of sunned stones
> Warmth of sunned water
> Sunned sand
> Sand ripple
> Water ripple
> Ripple sky
> (Sky Earth
> Earth Sky
> And our beginning)

▲ **Critical Viewing** This is the carving of a seated man on a Maori canoe. What mood does this figure convey? Explain. **[Interpret]**

And you ask me shall I sing. I tell you this. The singing will be here within myself. Inside this body. Fluting through these bones. Ringing in the skies of being. Ribboning in the course of blood to soothe swelled limbs and ache bruised heart.

You say to us our brother you will sing. But will the songs within be songs of joy? Will they ring? Out in the skies of being as you say? Pipe through bone, caress flesh wounding? Or will the songs within be ones of sorrow?

> *Of warmth dreams*
> *Love dreams*
> *Of aching*
> *And flesh bruising.*
> *If you listen will it be weeping that you hear?*
> *Lament of people*
> *Earth moan*
> *Water sigh*
> *Morepork[1] cry of death?*

My sisters, brothers, loved ones, I cannot tell. But there will be gladness for me in what I do. I ask no more. Some songs will be of joy and others hold the moan and sigh, the owl cry and throb of loneliness.

What will you do then our brother when the singing dirges through your veins, pressing and swelling in your throat and breast, pricking at your mind with its aching needles of sound?

What should I do but deny its needling and stealing into mind. Its pressing into throat and breast. I will not put a hand of comfort over . . . finger blistered veins in soothing. The wail, the lament shall not have my ear. I will pay the lonely body ache no mind. Thus I go.

I stand before my dark-eyed mother, blue-eyed father, brothers, sisters. My aunts and uncles and their children and these old ones. All the dark-eyed, light-eyed minglings of this place.

We gather. We sing and dance together for my going. We laugh and cry. We touch. We mingle tears as blood.

I give you my farewell.

Now I stand on a tide wet rock to farewell you sea. I listen and hear your great heart thud. I hear you cry. Do you too weep for me? Do you reach out with <u>mottled</u> hands to touch my brow and <u>anoint</u> my tear wet face with tears of salt? Do not weep but keep them well. Your great heart beats I know for such as these. Give them sea, your great sea love. Hold them gently. Already they are baptized in your name.

---

1. **Morepork:** Bird found in New Zealand.

▲ **Critical Viewing** This face appears on a Maori sculptured pillar. What do you think its purpose is? Why? **[Interpret]**

◆ **Build Vocabulary**

mottled (mät´ 'ld) *adj.*: Marked with spots and streaks

anoint (ə nɔint´) *v.*: To put oil or some other substance on in a ceremony of blessing

As am I
And take your renewal where I go
And your love
Take your strength
And deep heart thud
Your salt kiss
Your caring.

Now on a crest of hill in sweeping wind. Where I have climbed and run. And loved and walked about. With life brimming full in me as though I could die of living.

Guardian hill you do not clutch my hand, you do not weep. You know that I must go and give me blessing. You guard with love this quiet place rocking at the edge of sea . . .

And now at the highest place I stand. And feel a power grip me. And a lung-bursting strength. A trembling in my legs and arms. A heavy ache weighting down my groin.

And I lie on soil in all my heaviness and trembling. Stretch out my arms on wide Earth Mother and lay my face on hers. Then call out my love and speak my vow.

And feel release in giving to you earth, and to you sea, to these people.

So I go. And behind me the sea-moan and earth-cry, the sweet lament of people. Towards the goddess as she sleeps I go. On with light upon my face.

Guide for Responding

◆ Literature and Your Life

Reader's Response Would you encourage the speaker to leave, or are you moved by the words of those who want the speaker to stay? Why?

Thematic Focus What qualities does the speaker have that will enable him to reach a goal?

Reader's Journal Jot down a goal you recently reached, and record the feelings you had as you worked toward it. Compare these feelings with those described in the chant.

☑ Check Your Comprehension

1. Who are the speakers in this chant?
2. What does the individual speaker want?
3. What do those who speak as a group want?
4. Briefly describe the everyday activities of Granny Roka.
5. Describe the kind of life the group leads.

◆ Critical Thinking

INTERPRET

1. Why do the chanters in "And So I Go" urge the individual speaker not to leave? **[Interpret]**
2. What does the individual speaker in "And So I Go" hope to accomplish by leaving? **[Infer]**
3. Citing passages from the chant, explain whether the speaker's decision is a matter of reason, of feeling, or of both. **[Analyze]**
4. The speaker expects to retain a connection with the spirit of the group in at least two ways. Explain. **[Support]**
5. Do you think the speaker will be successful in maintaining a connection with the past? Why or why not? **[Speculate]**

EXTEND

6. Explain the good and the bad consequences of introducing modern Western ways among traditional peoples. **[Social Studies Link]**

from Song of Lawino[1]

Okot p'Bitek

from My Husband's House Is a Dark Forest of Books

Translated by the author

Listen, my clansmen,
I cry over my husband
Whose head is lost.
Ocol has lost his head
5   In the forest of books.

When my husband
Was still wooing me
His eyes were still alive,
His ears were still unblocked,
10   Ocol had not yet become a fool
My friend was a man then!

He had not yet become a woman,
He was still a free man,
His heart was still his chief.

15   My husband was still a Black man
The son of the Bull
The son of Agik[2]
The woman from Okol[3]
Was still a man,
20   An Acoli[4]

My husband has read much.
He has read <u>extensively</u> and deeply, . . .
And he is clever like white men

And the reading
25   Has killed my man,
In the ways of his people
He has become
A stump.

He abuses all things Acoli,
30   He says
The ways of black people
Are black
Because his eyeballs have exploded,
And he wears dark glasses,
35   My husband's house
Is a dark forest of books.
Some stand there
Tall and huge
Like the *tido* tree . . .

40   The papers on my husband's desk
Coil threateningly
Like the giant forest climbers,
Like the *kituba* tree
That squeezes other trees to death;
45   Some stand up,
Others lie on their backs,
They are interlocked
Like the legs of youths
At the *orak*[5] dance,

---

1. **Lawino** (lă weˈ nō): The speaker, a woman.
2. **The son of the Bull . . . Agik** (ä jēkˈ): References to the ancestors of the speaker's husband.
3. **Okol** (ô kōlˈ): A town in northern Uganda.
4. **Acoli** (ä chōlˈ ē): A people of northern Uganda, sharing a cultural, linguistic, and geographic heritage.

5. ***orak*** (ô rakˈ) *n.*: A traditional dance; an inner circle of young women and an outer circle of young men dance intricate steps until the two circles are intertwined.

◆ **Build Vocabulary**

extensively (ek stenˈ siv lē) *adv.*: Widely

Ubi Girl from Tai Region, Lois Mailou Jones, The Hayden Collection, Museum of Fine Arts, Boston

◀ **Critical Viewing**
What does the woman shown in the upper right portion of this picture have in common with the speaker in this poem? **[Connect]**

50 Like the legs of the planks
    Of the *goggo* fence,
    They are tightly interlocked
    Like the legs of the giant forest climbers
    In the <u>impenetrable</u> forest.

55 My husband's house
    Is a mighty forest of books,
    Dark it is and very damp,
    The steam rising from the ground
    Hot, thick and poisonous
60 Mingles with the <u>corrosive</u> dew
    And the rain drops
    That have collected in the leaves. . . .

◆ **Build Vocabulary**

impenetrable (im pen´ i trə bəl) *adj.*: Impossible to get through

corrosive (kə rōs´ iv) *adj.*: Eating or wearing away, by rust or chemical action

perished (per´ isht) *v.*: Died a violent or untimely death

bile (bīl) *n.*: Bodily fluid associated with bitterness or anger

O, my clansmen,
Let us all cry together!
65 Come,
Let us mourn the death of my husband,
The death of a Prince
The Ash that was produced
By a great Fire!
70 O, this homestead is utterly dead,
Close the gates
With *lacari*[6] thorns,
For the Prince
The heir to the Stool[7] is lost!
75 And all the young men
Have perished in the wilderness!
And the fame of this homestead
That once blazed like a wild fire
In a moonless night

80 Is now like the last breaths
Of a dying old man!

There is not one single true son left,
The entire village
Has fallen into the hands
85 Of war captives and slaves!
Perhaps one of our boys
Escaped with his life!
Perhaps he is hiding in the bush
Waiting for the sun to set!

90 But will he come
Before the next mourning?
Will he arrive in time?

Bile burns my inside!
I feel like vomiting!

95 For all our young men
Were finished in the forest,
Their manhood was finished
In the class-rooms, . . .

---

6. *lacari* n.: Large thorns, some as long as three inches. The branches of the *lacari* tree are woven together to make a natural barbed wire that is used to protect homes and livestock.
7. **heir to the Stool:** Determined by birth to be a chief.

Guide for Responding

◆ Literature and Your Life

Reader's Response Do you feel more sympathetic to Lawino or to her husband? Why?

Thematic Focus Contrast one of Lawino's goals with a probable goal of her husband's.

Reader's Journal As Lawino's husband, explain how you feel about her attitude toward what you have accomplished.

Questions for Research Okot p'Bitek is from Uganda. Jot down two questions you could research about the impact of Western influences on this country.

☑ Check Your Comprehension

1. To whom is Lawino speaking?
2. According to Lawino, what qualities has her husband, Ocol, lost?
3. What does she claim Ocol has become?
4. Name a particular thing Ocol does that alienates him from his people.
5. What is Lawino's fear for the future of her people?

◆ Critical Thinking

INTERPRET

1. What is the basic conflict between Lawino and her husband? **[Interpret]**
2. By calling Ocol a woman, what is Lawino implying about his position in Acoli society? **[Infer]**
3. (a) Name two things to which Lawino compares Ocol's papers and books. (b) To what does she compare his influence on the village? **[Analyze]**
4. Explain why the writer chose these particular comparisons to express Lawino's views. **[Infer]**
5. How reasonable are Lawino's fears for the future of her people? Explain. **[Draw Conclusions]**

EVALUATE

6. Do you think Lawino is being fair in her assessment of Ocol's life and values? Explain. **[Make a Judgment]**

COMPARE LITERARY WORKS

7. Explain how the person who is leaving in "And So I Go" would react to Lawino's criticism of her husband in "Song of Lawino." **[Speculate]**

Guide for Responding (continued)

◆ Reading Strategy

QUESTION

As you read a literary work, **question** details to determine what they tell you about characters and events. After reading, answer unresolved questions by going back to the text to piece together details.

1. (a) What is the main question you had about the character who is leaving in "And So I Go"? (b) How would you answer that question?
2. (a) What is the main question that came to mind about the speaker in *Song of Lawino?* (b) After reading, how would you answer that question?

◆ Build Vocabulary

WORDS RELATED TO "HUMORS"

Bile, meaning "a bodily fluid associated with anger" is a word linked with the old-fashioned theory of bodily humors—fluids that supposedly influence a person's emotions and disposition. Other words deriving from this outmoded theory are *sanguine* (confident), *choleric* (angry), *melancholy* (sad), and *phlegmatic* (slow and dull). Use one of these four words to fill in the blank in each of the following sentences.

1. Though the situation seemed desperate, Phil remained quite ____?____ .
2. Anyone else would have started yelling at the clerk, but Bonnie is too ____?____ to react even to the rudest behavior.
3. Make sure that you are by an open door when you tell him you broke his watch: Stan is on the ____?____ side.
4. Don't even bother trying to cheer her up; her ____?____ is perpetual.

USING THE WORD BANK: Synonyms

On your paper, write the word or phrase that is closest in meaning to that of the first word.

1. baptizing: (a) cleansing, (b) blessing, (c) drowning
2. plaiting: (a) playing, (b) polishing, (c) braiding
3. mottled: (a) canned, (b) spotted, (c) bright
4. anoint: (a) bless, (b) name, (c) irritate
5. extensively: (a) widely, (b) joyfully, (c) frequently
6. impenetrable: (a) blank, (b) solid, (c) free
7. corrosive: (a) generous, (b) right, (c) destructive
8. perished: (a) lost, (b) split, (c) died
9. bile: (a) recklessness, (b) bitterness, (c) hopelessness

◆ Literary Focus

DEVELOPMENT BY DIALOGUE AND MONOLOGUE

The use of **dialogue**—an interchange between two or more people—in "And So I Go" reveals the relationship between the individual who is leaving and the group that wants him to stay.

In *Song of Lawino,* the speaker delivers a **monologue** revealing her feelings and attitudes. The effect is especially powerful because it seems as if the speaker is revealing her character by speaking for herself, without the help of the writer.

1. Explain how "And So I Go" can be considered a dialogue.
2. In "And So I Go," what is the effect of reading the speakers' words, but not having the author's description of the speakers?
3. Basing your answer on what you have learned about Maori culture, explain why a dialogue is a more effective form for "And So I Go" than a monologue would have been.
4. Evaluate how successfully the monologue in *Song of Lawino* reveals the speaker's character. Support your answer with specific references to the poem.

◆ Build Grammar Skills

INVERTED WORD ORDER

A sentence with **inverted word order** does not follow the usual pattern of *subject-verb-complement.*

Practice Identify each sentence with inverted word order. Write out these sentences in normal word order.

1. This I've always known.
2. I have watched the people.
3. Towards the goddess as she sleeps I go.
4. His heart was still his chief.
5. Your words I will answer.

Writing Application Write four sentences based on the selections. Use normal word order. Then, rewrite them, using inverted word order. For each, explain which is the most effective version.

Build Your Portfolio

Idea Bank

Writing

1. **Letter** Write a letter that the person leaving in "And So I Go" might have written to the people back home six months later.

2. **Diary Entry** Write a diary entry that the husband in *Song of Lawino* might have written the day his wife made this speech to her clansmen.

3. **Personal Credo** These selections express two different attitudes toward changing ways of life. Write an essay explaining your attitude toward changes in your life. Discuss your own plans for the future.

Speaking, Listening, and Viewing

4. **Dialogue** With a partner, write and perform a dialogue between the wife and the husband in *Song of Lawino.* **[Performing Arts Link]**

5. **Choral Reading** With a group, prepare and perform a choral reading of "And So I Go." Have several people read in unison the villager's words and one person read the departing person's words. **[Social Studies Link]**

Researching and Representing

6. **Multimedia Presentation [Cooperative Learning]** Work with a group to create a presentation on Uganda. Research the peoples of the country, colonial times, and modern times. Also, obtain such audiovisual aids as maps, charts, and music. **[Social Studies Link; Art Link]**

7. **Conflict-Resolution Activities** Create an activity that might help people like Lawino and her husband resolve their differences. Role-play the activity with a group of classmates. **[Social Studies Link]**

Online Activity www.phlit.phschool.com

Guided Writing Lesson

Narrative About Reaching a Goal

When you write a narrative, you tell a story. The story can be real or invented, but it must involve a plot (a series of linked events) that centers on a conflict (a struggle). A narrative has one or more characters who participate in the plot; it also has a setting, the time and place of the story.

Write a narrative about reaching a goal, based on your own life, someone else's life, or the life of a fictional character. Include dialogue to help bring your characters to life.

Writing Skills Focus: Effective Dialogue

When writing a narrative, it often helps to include **effective dialogue,** realistic conversation between two or among several people. Effective dialogue

- sounds like speech that characters of the given type and in the given situation would actually use.
- reveals or is consistent with their personalities.
- moves the plot along by telling parts of the story or by bringing the speakers into conflict.

Prewriting Decide on the plot, setting, and characters of your narrative. Jot down specific quotations that reveal the personality or the speaking style of each character. List other words and phrases that each character might use.

Drafting As you write your narrative, include dialogue between the characters. Include the quotations and other phrases from your notes, and make the dialogue as believable as you can.

Revising Read your narrative aloud with a partner. Listen to make sure that the speakers are responding to each other's words. If a sentence or word does not sound like something the character would say, revise it.

Guide for Reading

Thomas Mann (1875–1955)

German writer Thomas Mann (tō′ mäs män′) produced novels and short stories that reflected the political and social issues of his time.

Early Success Mann was born in the German city of Lübeck into a wealthy merchant family. He began writing while studying part time, publishing short stories that earned him some notice. He then traveled to Italy, where he began to work on his first novel, *Buddenbrooks* (1900). Depicting the history of a German merchant family similar to his own, *Buddenbrooks* made him instantly famous.

Concern and Inspiration During the years leading up to World War I, Mann became concerned with society's increasing loss of faith in traditional values. His concerns prompted him to begin writing *The Magic Mountain* in 1912. This novel, which took him twelve years to write, is set in a type of hospital on the eve of World War I and captures the conflicting values that had emerged in European society.

Fighting Nazi and Fascist Regimes In the aftermath of World War I, Mann tried to warn people of the dangers posed by Nazism and fascism. As a result, when the Nazis seized control of Germany in 1933, he was forced into exile in Switzerland. Five years later, he moved to the United States. Throughout World War II, Mann used both his writing and speaking talents to attack the Nazi regime. Two years after the war ended, he published his despairing novel *Doktor Faustus*, which symbolically depicts the rise of Nazism.

Lasting Regard Mann moved back to Switzerland in 1952 and remained there for the last years of his life. As a person, he is primarily remembered as one who never shied away from political or social issues in either his writing or his public life, regardless of the consequences. His lasting fame rests primarily on his novels, but his shorter works, like "The Infant Prodigy," are also widely appreciated.

◆ Build Vocabulary

ANGLO-SAXON SUFFIXES: *-less*

Mann describes the infant prodigy's face as having an "unfinished nose and a guileless mouth." Knowing that the Anglo-Saxon suffix *-less* means "without," you can figure out that *guileless* means "without guile" or "without deceit."

| prodigy |
| countenance |
| guileless |
| objectively |
| abysmal |
| proffered |
| ineffable |

WORD BANK

As you read "The Infant Prodigy," you will encounter the words on this list. Each word is defined on the page where it first appears. Preview the list before you read. Also look for other words with the suffix *-less*, like *breathless, noiselessly,* and *worthlessness.*

◆ Build Grammar Skills

COMPOUND ADJECTIVES

A **compound adjective** is an adjective that is made up of more than one word. Most compound adjectives are hyphenated, but some have the words closed up without a hyphen. This translation of "The Infant Prodigy," contains many compound adjectives, including these examples:

. . . but the wrist was strong and unlike a child's, with *well-developed* bones.

There were even some children, with their legs hanging down demurely from their chairs and their shining eyes staring at their gifted little *white-clad* contemporary.

The Infant Prodigy

◆ *Literature and Your Life*

CONNECT YOUR EXPERIENCE

Chances are, you have been a part of many different audiences. Being part of an audience can create a shared experience, but each person retains unique thoughts and feelings. In "The Infant Prodigy," Mann explores questions about the audience as a group and also as individuals.

THEMATIC FOCUS: REACHING A GOAL

As you read, ask yourself: Does the young musician who performs succeed in pleasing all the members of the audience?

Journal Writing Jot down in your journal your remembrances of a time that you and a friend or family member had different reactions to a movie, television program, or book.

◆ Background for Understanding

CULTURE

A true prodigy is a child who has an innate talent, not a child who is pushed to succeed or who is overtrained by adults. With their accelerated and remarkable accomplishments, child prodigies have always fascinated audiences. Musical prodigies, such as Wolfgang Amadeus Mozart, Franz Schubert, and Felix Mendelssohn, often begin composing works by the age of twelve. In fact, Mozart published his first violin sonatas at the age of eight.

◆ Literary Focus

POINT OF VIEW AND THEME

Point of view refers to the vantage point from which a story is told. "The Infant Prodigy" is told from an omniscient third-person point of view. In other words, the story is recounted by a *narrator* who does not participate in it (third-person) but can see into the minds of all the characters (omniscient). A *limited narrator* is one who cannot see into the minds of all characters. Often, a limited narrator relates the thoughts and feelings of a single character.

Authors select a point of view that will help them communicate a desired **theme,** a work's overall message or insight. As you read "The Infant Prodigy," think about why Mann selected an omniscient third-person narrator for this story. Your answer will help you interpret the story's theme.

◆ Reading Strategy

CLARIFY DETAILS AND INFORMATION

As you read, you may need to **clarify** details that you don't understand. The best way to do this is to read ahead for more information or to read back to review what you have already learned. Footnotes can also provide details that help you understand specific elements.

Another technique is to represent information visually. For instance, you can clarify the descriptions of audience members by completing a chart like the one below that lists the name and a brief description of each character.

Bibi	an infant prodigy; composer; contemptuous
the impresario	
the princess	
the businessman	

The Infant Prodigy

by Thomas Mann

Translated by H. T. Lowe-Porter

The infant prodigy entered. The hall became quiet.

It became quiet and then the audience began to clap, because somewhere at the side a leader of mobs, a born organizer, clapped first. The audience had heard nothing yet, but they applauded; for a mighty publicity organization had heralded the prodigy and people were already hypnotized, whether they knew it or not.

The prodigy came from behind a splendid screen embroidered with Empire[1] garlands and great conventionalized flowers, and climbed nimbly up the steps to the platform, diving into the applause as into a bath; a little chilly and shivering, but yet as though into a friendly element. He advanced to the edge of the platform and smiled as though he were about to be photographed; he made a shy, charming gesture of greeting, like a little girl.

He was dressed entirely in white silk, which the audience found enchanting. The little white jacket was fancifully cut, with a sash underneath it, and even his shoes were made of white silk. But against the white socks his bare little legs stood out quite brown; for he was a Greek boy.

He was called Bibi Saccellaphylaccas.[2] And such indeed was his name. No one knew what Bibi was the pet name for, nobody but the impresario,[3] and he regarded it as a trade secret. Bibi had smooth black hair reaching to his shoulders; it was parted on the side and fastened back from the narrow domed forehead by a little silk bow. His was the most harmless childish countenance in the world, with an unfinished nose and guileless mouth. The area beneath his pitch black mouselike eyes was already a little tired and visibly lined. He looked as though he were nine years old but was really eight and given out for seven. It was hard to tell whether to believe this or not. Probably everybody knew better and still believed it, as happens about so many things. The average man thinks that a little falseness goes with beauty. Where should we get any excitement out of our daily life if we were not willing to pretend a bit? And the average man is quite right, in his average brains!

---

1. **Empire:** The Empire style is a manner of French interior decoration and costume.

---

2. **Bibi Saccellaphylaccas** (bē´ bē sa səl la´ fə la kəs)
3. **impresario** (im´ prə sär´ ē ō): The organizer, director, or manager of an opera or ballet company or concert series.

The Old Burgtheater, 1888–1889 , Gustav Klimt, Historisches Museum der Stadt Wien, Vienna

▲ Critical Viewing How do you think "the infant prodigy" feels performing before an audience like this one? [Relate]

The prodigy kept on bowing until the applause died down, then he went up to the grand piano, and the audience cast a last look at its programs. First came a *Marche solennelle*,[4] then a *Rêverie*,[5] and then *Le Hibou et les moineaux*[6]—all by Bibi Saccellaphylaccas. The whole program was by him, they were all his compositions. He could not score them, of course, but he had them all in his extraordinary little head and they possessed real artistic significance, or so it said, seriously and objectively, in the program. The program sounded as though the impresario had wrested these concessions from his critical nature after a hard struggle.

The prodigy sat down upon the revolving stool and felt with his feet for the pedals, which were raised by means of a clever device so that Bibi could reach them. It was Bibi's own piano; he took it everywhere with him. It rested upon wooden trestles and its polish was somewhat marred by the constant transportation—but all that only made things more interesting.

Bibi put his silk-shod feet on the pedals; then he made an artful little face, looked straight ahead of him, and lifted his right hand. It was a brown, childish little hand; but the wrist was strong and unlike a child's, with well-developed bones.

Bibi made his face for the audience because he was aware that he had to entertain them a little. But he had his own private enjoyment in the thing too, an enjoyment which he could never convey to anybody. It was that prickling delight, that secret shudder of bliss, which ran through him every time he sat at an open piano—it would always be with him. And here was the keyboard again, these seven black and white octaves, among which he had so often lost himself in abysmal and thrilling adventures—and yet it always looked as clean and untouched as a newly washed blackboard. This was the realm of music that lay before him. It

lay spread out like an inviting ocean, where he might plunge in and blissfully swim, where he might let himself be borne and carried away, where he might go under in night and storm, yet keep the mastery: control, ordain—he held his right hand poised in the air.

A breathless stillness reigned in the room— the tense moment before the first note came. . . . How would it begin? It began so. And Bibi, with his index finger, fetched the first note out of the piano, a quite unexpectedly powerful first note in the middle register, like a trumpet blast. Others followed, an introduction developed—the audience relaxed.

The concert was held in the palatial hall of a fashionable first-class hotel. The walls were covered with mirrors framed in gilded arabesques,[7] between frescoes[8] of the rosy and fleshy school. Ornamental columns supported a ceiling that displayed a whole universe of electric bulbs, in clusters darting a brilliance far brighter than day and filling the whole space with thin, vibrating golden light. Not a seat was unoccupied, people were standing in the side aisles and at the back. The front seats cost twelve marks;[9] for the impresario believed that anything worth having was worth paying for. And they were occupied by the best society, for it was in the upper classes, of course, that the greatest enthusiasm was felt. There were even some children, with their legs hanging down demurely[10] from their chairs and their shining eyes staring at their gifted little white-clad contemporary.

---

7. **arabesques** (ar´ ə besks´) *n.*: Complex and elaborate designs of intertwined patterns, painted or carved in low relief.
8. **frescoes** (fres´ kōz) *n.*: Paintings or designs made with watercolors on wet plaster.
9. **marks:** The mark was the German monetary unit prior to World War I.
10. **demurely** (di myoor ´ lē) *adv.*: Modestly; reservedly.

---

4. *Marche solennelle* (märsh sə len el´): "Solemn March" (French).
5. *Rêverie* (rev´ ər ē): "Dreamy thinking"; "musing" (French).
6. *Le Hibou et les moineaux* (lö ē boo´ ā lā mwä nō´): *The Owl and the sparrows* (French).

◆ **Build Vocabulary**

objectively (äb´ jek´ tiv lē) *adv.*: Impartially

abysmal (ə biz´ m'l) *adj.*: Immeasurably bad

proffered (präf´ ərd) *v.*: Offered

Down in front on the left side sat the prodigy's mother, an extremely obese woman with a powdered double chin and a feather on her head. Beside her was the impresario, a man of oriental appearance with large gold buttons on his conspicuous cuffs. The princess was in the middle of the front row—a wrinkled, shriveled little old princess but still a patron of the arts, especially everything full of sensibility. She sat in a deep, velvet-upholstered armchair, and a Persian carpet was spread before her feet. She held her hands folded over her gray striped-silk breast, put her head on one side, and presented a picture of elegant composure as she sat looking up at the performing prodigy. Next to her sat her lady-in-waiting, in a green striped-silk gown. Being only a lady-in-waiting she had to sit up very straight in her chair.

Bibi ended in a grand climax. With what power this wee manikin belabored the keyboard! The audience could scarcely trust its ears. The march theme, an infectious, swinging tune, broke out once more, fully harmonized, bold and showy; with every note Bibi flung himself back from the waist as though he were marching in a triumphal procession. He ended *fortissimo*,[11] bent over, slipped sideways off the stool, and stood with a smile awaiting the applause.

And the applause burst forth, unanimously, enthusiastically; the child made his demure little maidenly curtsy and people in the front seat thought: "Look what slim little hips he has! Clap, clap! Hurrah, bravo, little chap, Saccophylax or whatever your name is! Wait, let me take off my gloves—what a little devil of a chap he is!"

Bibi had to come out three times from behind the screen before they would stop. Some latecomers entered the hall and moved about looking for seats. Then the concert continued. Bibi's *Reverie* murmured its numbers, consisting almost entirely of arpeggios,[12] above which a bar of melody rose now and then, weak-winged. Then came *Le Hibou et les moineaux.* This piece was brilliantly successful, it made a strong impression; it was an effective childhood fantasy, remarkably well envisaged.[13] The bass represented the owl, sitting morosely[14] rolling his filmy eyes; while in the treble the impudent, half-frightened sparrows chirped. Bibi received an ovation when he finished, he was called out four times. A hotel page with shiny buttons carried up three great laurel wreaths onto the stage and <u>proffered</u> them from one side while Bibi nodded and expressed his thanks. Even the princess shared in the applause, daintily and noiselessly pressing her palms together.

Ah, the knowing little creature understood how to make people clap! He stopped behind the screen; they had to wait for him; he lingered a little on the steps of the platform, admired the long streamers on the wreaths—although actually such things bored him stiff by now. He bowed with the utmost charm, he gave the audience plenty of time to rave itself out, because applause is valuable and must not be cut short. "*Le Hibou* is my drawing card," he thought—this expression he had learned from the impresario. "Now I will play the fantasy, it is a lot better than *Le Hibou*, of course, especially the C-sharp passage. But you idiots dote on the *Hibou*, though it is the first and the silliest thing I wrote." He continued to bow and smile.

Next came a *Méditation*[15] and then an *Étude*[16]—the program was quite comprehensive. The *Méditation* was very like the *Rêverie*—which was nothing against it—and the *Étude*[16] displayed all of Bibi's virtuosity, which naturally fell a little short of his inventiveness. And then the *Fantaisie*.[17] This was his favorite; he varied it a little each time, giving himself free rein and sometimes surprising even himself, on good evenings, by his own inventiveness.

---

11. *fortissimo* (fôr tis´ ə mō´): Very loud.
12. arpeggios (är pej´ ōz) n.: Chords in which the notes are played in quick succession rather than simultaneously.

13. envisaged (en viz´ ijd) v.: Visualized; imagined.
14. morosely (mə rōs´ lē) adv.: Gloomily; sullenly.
15. *Méditation* (mā dē ta syōn´): "Meditation" (French).
16. *Étude* (ā´ tōōd): "Study" (French).
17. *Fantaisie* (fan te zē´) n.: "Fancy" (French).

He sat and played, so little, so white and shining, against the great black grand piano, elect and alone, above that confused sea of faces, above the heavy, insensitive mass soul, upon which he was laboring to work with his individual, differentiated soul. His lock of soft black hair with the white silk bow had fallen over his forehead, his trained and bony little wrists pounded away, the muscles stood out visibly on his brown childish cheeks.

Sitting there he sometimes had moments of oblivion and solitude, when the gaze of his strange little mouselike eyes with the big rings beneath them would lose itself and stare through the painted stage into space that was peopled with strange vague life. Then out of the corner of his eye he would give a quick look back into the hall and be once more with his audience.

"Joy and pain, the heights and the depth— that is my *Fantaisie*," he thought lovingly. "Listen, here is the C-sharp passage." He lingered over the approach, wondering if they would notice anything. But no, of course not, how should they? And he cast his eyes up prettily at the ceiling so that at least they might have something to look at.

All these people sat there in their regular rows, looking at the prodigy and thinking all sorts of things in their regular brains. An old gentleman with a white beard, a seal ring on his finger, and a bulbous swelling on his bald spot, a growth if you like, was thinking to himself: "Really, one ought to be ashamed." He had never got any further than "Ah, thou dearest Augustin" on the piano, and here he sat now, a gray old man, looking on while this little hop-o'-my-thumb performed miracles. Yes, yes, it is a gift of God, we must remember that. God grants his gifts, or he withholds them, and there is no shame in being an ordinary man. Like with the Christ child.—Before a child one may kneel without feeling ashamed. Strange that thoughts like these should be so satisfying—he would even say so sweet, if it was not

too silly for a tough old man like him to use the word. That was how he felt, anyhow.

Art . . . the businessman with the parrot-nose was thinking. "Yes, it adds something cheerful to life, a little good white silk and a little tumty-ti-ti-tum. Really he does not play so badly. Fully fifty seats, twelve marks apiece, that makes six hundred marks—and everything else besides. Take off the rent of the hall, the lighting, and the programs, you must have fully a thousand marks profit. That is worthwhile."

"That was Chopin[18] he was just playing," thought the piano teacher, a lady with a pointed nose; she was of an age when the understanding sharpens as the hopes decay. "But not very original—I will say that afterward; it sounds well. And his hand position is entirely amateur. One must be able to lay a coin on the back of the hand—I would use a ruler on him.

Then there was a young girl, at that self-conscious and chlorotic[19] time of life when the most <u>ineffable</u> ideas come into the mind. She was thinking to herself: "What is it he is playing? It is expressive of passion, yet he is a child. If he kissed me it would be as though my little brother kissed me—no kiss at all. Is there such a thing as passion all by itself, without any earthly object, a sort of child's-play of passion? What nonsense! If I were to say such things aloud they would just be at me with some more cod-liver oil. Such is life."

An officer was leaning against a column. He looked on at Bibi's success and thought: "Yes, you are something and I am something, each in his own way." So he clapped his heels together and paid to the prodigy the respect which he felt to be due to all the powers that be.

Then there was a critic, an elderly man in a shiny black coat and turned-up trousers splashed with mud. He sat in his free seat and thought: "Look at him, this young beggar of a Bibi. As an individual he has still to develop,

◆ Build Vocabulary

ineffable (in ef´ ə b'l) *adj*.: Inexpressible

---

18. Chopin (shō´ pan): Frédéric François Chopin (1810–1849), a Polish-born composer and pianist.
19. chlorotic (klə rät´ ik) *adj*.: Having chlorosis, a condition that causes the skin to turn a greenish color.

At the Theatre (detail), Pierre Auguste Renoir, National Gallery, London

▲ **Critical Viewing** If this woman is watching "the
infant prodigy" perform, what might she be thinking?
[Connect]

but as a type he is already quite complete, the artist *par excellence*.[20] He has in himself all the artist's exaltation and his utter worthlessness, his charlatanry[21] and his sacred fire, his burning contempt and his secret raptures. Of course I can't write all that, it is too good. Of course, I should have been an artist myself if I had not seen through the whole business so clearly."

Then the prodigy stopped playing and a perfect storm arose in the hall. He had to come out again and again from behind his screen. The man with the shiny buttons carried up more wreaths: four laurel wreaths, a lyre[22] made of violets, a bouquet of roses. He had not arms enough to convey all these tributes; the impresario himself mounted the stage to help him. He hung a laurel wreath round Bibi's neck, he tenderly stroked the black hair—and suddenly as though overcome he bent down and gave the prodigy a kiss, a resounding kiss, square on the mouth. And then the storm became a hurricane. That kiss ran through the room like an electric shock, it went direct to people's marrow and made them shiver down their backs. They were carried away by a helpless compulsion of sheer noise. Loud shouts mingled with the hysterical clapping of hands. Some of Bibi's commonplace little friends down there waved their handkerchiefs. But the critic thought: "Of course that kiss had to come—it's a good old gag. Yes, good Lord, if only one did not see through everything quite so clearly—"

And so the concert drew to a close. It began at half past seven and finished at half past eight. The platform was laden with wreaths and two little pots of flowers stood on the lamp stands of the piano. Bibi played as his last number his *Rhapsodie grecque*,[23] which turned into the Greek national hymn at the end. His fellow countrymen in the audience would gladly have sung it with him if the company had not been so august. They made up for it with a powerful noise and hullabaloo, a hot-blooded national demonstration. And the aging critic was thinking: "Yes, the hymn had to come too. They have to exploit every vein—publicity cannot afford to neglect any means to its end. I think I'll criticize that as inartistic. But perhaps I am wrong, perhaps that is the most artistic thing of all. What is the artist? A jack-in-the-box. Criticism is on a higher plane. But I can't say that." And away he went in his muddy trousers.

After being called out nine or ten times the prodigy did not come anymore from behind the screen but went to his mother and the impresario down in the hall. The audience stood about among the chairs and applauded and pressed forward to see Bibi close at hand. Some of them wanted to see the princess too. Two dense circles formed, one round the prodigy, the other round the princess, and you could actually not tell which of them was receiving more homage. But the court lady was commanded to go over to Bibi; she smoothed down his silk jacket a bit to make it look suitable for a court function, led him by the arm to the princess, and solemnly indicated to him that he was to kiss the royal hand. "How do you do it, child?" asked the princess. "Does it come into your head of itself when you sit down?" *"Oui, madame,"*[24] answered Bibi. To himself he thought: "Oh, what a stupid old princess!" Then he turned round shyly and uncourtierlike and went back to his family.

Outside in the cloakroom there was a crowd. People held up their numbers and received with open arms furs, shawls, and galoshes. Somewhere among her acquaintances the piano teacher stood making her critique. "He is not very original," she said audibly and looked about her.

In front of one of the great mirrors an elegant young lady was being arrayed in her evening cloak and fur shoes by her brothers,

---

20. *par excellence* (pär ek se läns′): "Beyond comparison" (French).
21. charlatanry (shär′ lə t′n rē) *n*.: Pretense at having expert knowledge or skill that one does not have.
22. lyre (līr) *n*.: A small stringed instrument of the harp family.
23. *Rhapsodie grecque* (räp sə dē′ grek): Greek Rhapsody (French).

---

24. *Oui, madame* (wē mä däm′): "Yes, ma'am" (French).

two lieutenants. She was exquisitely beautiful, with her steel-blue eyes and her clean-cut, well-bred face. A really noble dame. When she was ready she stood waiting for her brothers. "Don't stand so long in front of the glass, Adolf," she said softly to one of them, who could not tear himself away from the sight of his simple, good-looking young features. But Lieutenant Adolf thinks: "What cheek!" He would button his overcoat in front of the glass, just the same. Then they went out on the street where the arc lights gleamed cloudily through the white mist. Lieutenant Adolf struck up a little dance on the frozen snow to keep warm, with his hands in his slanting overcoat pockets and his collar turned up.

A girl with untidy hair and swinging arms, accompanied by a gloomy-faced youth, came out just behind them. "A child!" she thought. "A charming child. But in there he was an awe-inspiring . . ." and aloud in a toneless voice she said: "We are all infant prodigies, we artists."

"Well, bless my soul!" thought the old gentleman who had never got further than "Augustin" on the piano, and whose boil was now concealed by a top hat. "What does all that mean? She sounds very oracular." But the gloomy youth understood. He nodded his head slowly.

Then they were silent and the untidy-haired girl gazed after the brothers and sister. She rather despised them, but she looked after them until they had turned the corner.

Guide for Responding

◆ Literature and Your Life

Reader's Response Would you like to attend a concert by a child prodigy? Why or why not?

Thematic Focus Do you think that the prodigy's performance succeeds in making a group of distinct personalities into a unified audience? Why or why not?

Reader's Journal Suppose that you were going to conduct an interview with a child prodigy. Write down five questions you would like to ask.

Questions for Research "The Infant Prodigy" revolves around a concert given by a gifted young composer and pianist. If you were to write such a story, what questions might you have to research? List those questions in your notebook.

☑ Check Your Comprehension

1. Which two people in the audience does Bibi know?
2. How does the audience as a whole respond to Bibi's performance?
3. Describe four individuals who are listening to Bibi's performance.
4. What is the final image of the story?

◆ Critical Thinking

INTERPRET

1. How is Bibi's attitude toward his music different from his attitude toward his audience? **[Compare and Contrast]**
2. (a) Identify two elements of Bibi's performance that indicate genuine talent, and two elements that reflect clever showmanship. (b) Why do you think Mann includes both types of elements in his story? **[Speculate]**
3. What does Mann's depiction of the audience imply about how well group responses reflect individual feelings? **[Infer]**
4. What does this story suggest about the ability of society to appreciate art? Support your answer. **[Draw Conclusions]**

EVALUATE

5. Is Mann effective in showing the variety of reactions in the audience? Why or why not? **[Evaluate]**

APPLY

6. In what ways might this story be different if it were set in the contemporary United States and focused on a young rock musician? **[Modify]**

Guide for Responding (continued)

◆ Reading Strategy

CLARIFY DETAILS AND INFORMATION

When you become confused by the events or reflections in a story, be sure to **clarify details and information** by rereading, reading ahead, or checking footnotes for clues to meaning.

For example, to clarify the term *palatial hall*, you could read ahead to learn that the hall was "in a fashionable, first-class hotel," its "walls were covered with mirrors framed in gilded arabesques," and it had "ornamental columns." All these clues help you to guess that a palatial hall is a "palacelike room."

1. (a) What do you learn about the character of the princess? (b) How did you clarify that information?
2. (a) What does the title *Le Hibou et les moineaux* mean? (b) How did you find out?

◆ Build Vocabulary

USING THE ANGLO-SAXON SUFFIX *-less*

Knowing that the Anglo-Saxon suffix *-less* means "without," choose the letter of the word that is the best antonym, or opposite, of the first word.

1. worthless: (a) poor, (b) valuable, (c) earnest
2. peerless: (a) common, (b) unique, (c) popular
3. helpless: (a) righteous, (b) inadequate, (c) powerful
4. pitiless: (a) cruel, (b) hopeless, (c) humane

USING THE WORD BANK: Analogies

On your paper, write the word from the Word Bank that will make the relationship between the second pair of words similar to the relationship between the first pair. Use each word only once.

1. *Fierce* is to *meek* as *cunning* is to ___?___ .
2. *Held* is to *gripped* as *offered* is to ___?___ .
3. *Good* is to *excellent* as *bad* is to ___?___ .
4. *Age* is to *youth* as *sage* is to ___?___ .
5. *Placid* is to *calm* as *inexpressible* is to ___?___ .
6. *Swiftly* is to *slowly* as *subjectively* is to ___?___ .
7. *Vision* is to *eyesight* as *expression* is to ___?___ .

◆ Literary Focus

POINT OF VIEW AND THEME

Writers select a specific vantage point—or **point of view**—from which to tell a story. An omniscient narrator can see into the minds of all the characters; a third-person narrator does not participate in the story. Thomas Mann chose an omniscient, third-person narrator for "The Infant Prodigy," enabling him to reveal both the artist's and his audience's inner thoughts. These insights help readers identify the story's **theme,** or central message.

1. How does the story's point of view help suggest that the audience in the story symbolizes, or represents, society as a whole?
2. Why would Mann have had difficulty communicating the story's theme if he had used a limited narrator who conveyed only Bibi's thoughts and feelings?
3. After the concert, a girl with untidy hair comments, "We are all infant prodigies, we artists." What does this remark suggest about the story's central theme?

◆ Build Grammar Skills

COMPOUND ADJECTIVES

An adjective that is made up of more than one word is called a **compound adjective.** Most compound adjectives are hyphenated, although some are joined.

> **Example:** Next to her sat her lady-in-waiting, in a green striped-silk gown.

Practice On your paper, write the compound adjectives in each sentence.

1. The well-dressed patrons filled the old-fashioned auditorium.
2. Bibi's left-handed arpeggio impressed the spellbound audience.
3. The princess sat in her velvet-upholstered armchair.
4. The impresario's farsighted plans led to the audience's sure-fire response.
5. The piano teacher's firsthand experiences made her a self-appointed critic.

Build Your Portfolio

 Idea Bank

Writing

1. **Advertising Flyer** Create a flyer the impresario might have used to promote the infant prodigy's concert tour. **[Career Link]**

2. **Concert Review** Assume the role of the critic in Bibi's audience. Review your reactions to the concert, and write a review for a daily newspaper.

3. **Literary Analysis** Write an analysis in which you discuss how Mann's use of an omniscient narrator contributes to the theme of the story. Support your argument with specific examples.

Speaking, Listening, and Viewing

4. **Film Storyboard** Create a storyboard—a series of pictures showing camera shots—for a film based on "The Infant Prodigy." What film techniques can you use to reflect the point of view in this story? **[Performing Arts Link]**

5. **Musical Comparison** Select two works by a composer who was a child prodigy, like Motzart. Choose one work the composer wrote in youth and one he or she wrote as an adult. Play selections from the works for the class, and lead a discussion comparing and contrasting the two pieces. **[Music Link]**

Researching and Representing

6. **Modern Prodigies** Research a prodigy of today and write a report on his or her accomplishments and plans for the future. Share your completed report with the class.

7. **Award Roster** Thomas Mann received the Nobel Prize for Literature in 1929. Create an annotated list of other winners of this award, briefly describing their accomplishments.

Online Activity www.phlit.phschool.com

Guided Writing Lesson

Radio Advertisement

Impresarios, like the one in "The Infant Prodigy," need to attract audiences for the events they stage. Many events of today, such as concert, theater, and sports events, are promoted with radio advertisements. Act as an impresario, and write the script for a radio ad persuading people to attend an event you are promoting. As you write the ad, choose language that will capture the interest of your audience.

Writing Skills Focus: Use Language for the Ear

When writing for the radio, remember that your advertisement will be read aloud. Choose **language that catches the ear** and is easy to understand. Here are some guidelines you can consider as you write:

- Choose short, powerful words. Long or unfamiliar words can be confusing on the radio.

- Avoid groups of *s* sounds. Too many *s* sounds can create an unpleasant whistling effect.

- Vary sentence length and type. Use questions to intrigue listeners.

Prewriting Identify the group or individual you want to promote. Then, write a list of reasons people might have for attending the concert. These are the points you will want to emphasize in your advertisement.

Drafting Make an immediate appeal to your audience: Give them the facts simply and quickly. Then, make use of repetition to ensure that your main message gets across.

Revising Read your radio advertisement aloud to a partner, and get feedback about its effectiveness. Review your word choice, replacing inappropriate language with language better suited to your audience and purpose.

Check your use of compound adjectives, and select only the most effective to use in your ad. For more on these adjectives, see pages 318 and 328.

Focus on Culture

China

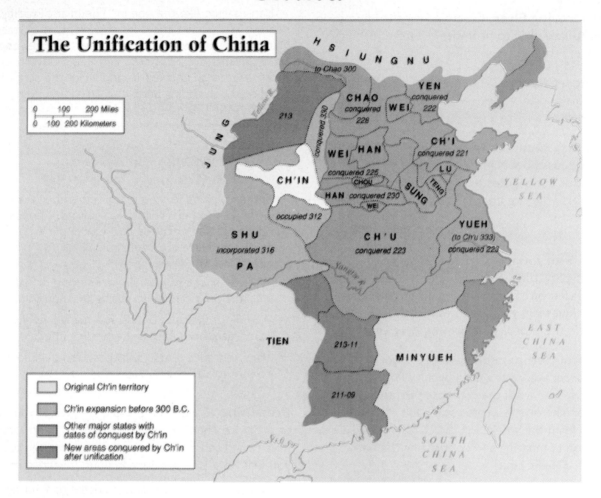

The Unification of China

	Original Ch'in territory
	Ch'in expansion before 300 B.C.
	Other major states with dates of conquest by Ch'in
	New areas conquered by Ch'in after unification

"Beginning with childhood, all of a man's study is centered on one aim alone: to emerge successfully from the three days' examination, and all he has in his mind is what success can bring to him." Thus did one scholar describe China's grueling civil service examinations.

For more than 2,000 years, ambitious scholars endured the agony of the exams. To pass, they had to memorize the writings of China's leading thinkers and compose elegant essays.

In the end, most candidates failed, but those who passed became respected lifetime officials.

▲ **Critical Viewing** Shih Huang-ti was the first emperor to unite most of China. Which area was conquered last? (All the dates on the map are B.C.) **[Analyze]**

GEOGRAPHIC SETTING

China covers an area of 3.7 billion square miles. It is home to 1.25 billion people—more than one fifth of the world's total population.

Location The early Chinese called their land the "Middle Kingdom." They thought they lived at the center of the Earth, in part because of distance and physical barriers. The vast Gobi

330 ◆ *Striving for Success in World Literature*

Desert, the rugged Mongolian and Tibetan plateaus, and the lofty Himalayan Mountains limited China's contact with other civilizations.

Still, China did have some contact with other peoples. Trading caravans trekked long distances to India and the Middle East. Buddhist missionaries from India and Mongol invaders from the west helped spread new ideas. Today, modern transportation and communication closely link China to the world.

"River of Sorrow" The Huang Ho (wäŋ´ huh´), or Yellow River, snakes for thousands of miles across northern China. It gets its name because it carries yellow-brown soil, called *loess* (lō´ es´), from the North China Plain. It was in the fertile Huang He valley that China's first civilization, the Shang, emerged around 1650 B.C.

Early on, the Chinese developed techniques to build dikes and canals. Still, terrible floods have repeatedly devastated the land. In 1931, for example, a flood wiped away China's crops and almost 4 million people died of starvation. Such destruction has earned the Huang Ho the nickname "River of Sorrow."

HISTORY

The Chinese believed that heaven granted each ruler a mandate, or right, to rule. In return for good government, the people owed the ruler complete obedience. However, if the ruler failed to maintain order, the people had the right to rebel. War, floods, and famine were signs that a dynasty, or ruling family, had lost the Mandate of Heaven. During China's long history, many dynasties rose and fell.

Schools of Thought During the C'hou dynasty (1027 B.C.–221 B.C.), three influential schools of thought emerged. China's best-known philosopher, Confucius (kən fyoō´ shəs), placed family and the good of society above the individual. He taught that five relationships governed society: ruler and ruled, father and son, older brother and younger brother, husband and wife, friend and friend. In all but the last, said Confucius,

one person is superior to the other. The duty of the superior is to set a good example for his inferiors. (See the excerpt from Confucius' *Analects* on p. 336.)

While Confucius stressed proper behavior, Lao Tzu (lou´ dzu´) emphasized simplicity and a calm acceptance of nature. Lao Tzu founded the religion of Taoism (dou´ iz´ əm). To Taoists, social rules disturbed the natural order. The best government is the one with the fewest laws. (See the excerpt from Lao Tzu's *Tao Te Ching* on p. 20.)

Legalism also rejected Confucian ideas of behavior. The Legalist thinker Han-fei-tzu taught that people acted out of self-interest and would respond to rewards and punishments, rather than to good examples.

Powerful Empires The Ch'in emperor Shih Huang-ti (sher´ wäŋ´ dē´) was the first Chinese ruler to create a unified empire. (See the map on p. 330.) He used harsh means to centralize power. He banned all books except Legalist works and persecuted Confucian scholars. He imposed a uniform law code and forced peasants to build the 1,500 mile-long Great Wall to protect against invasion.

China enjoyed golden ages of peace and prosperity during the Han (206 B.C.–A.D. 220), T'ang (618–907), and Sung (960–1279) dynasties. Confucian ideas were revived. Rulers introduced the civil service system to select officials based on merit. China also made impressive advances in technology, including paper making, block printing, gunpowder, the mechanical clock, and the magnetic compass.

In 1279, Mongol invaders from Central Asia conquered China. In 1368, the Ming dynasty restored Chinese rule. Under the Ming, the great explorer Cheng Ho (dzuŋ´ heh´) sailed as far as East Africa. However, China's rulers suddenly banned overseas voyages.

China and the West While China pursued isolation, Europe was expanding. In 1793, the Ch'ing emperor refused Britain's request for

The Poet Li Po Admiring a Waterfall, Hokusai, Honolulu Academy of Arts

▲ **Critical Viewing** Here, the T'ang poet Li Po admires a waterfall. How does this painting reflect Taoist values? **[Connect]**

trading rights. He said haughtily that China had no need to trade with "barbarians." In fact, China would pay a heavy price for turning its back on Europe's new industrial technology.

In 1839, modern British warships decimated the out-of-date Chinese fleet. China was forced to sign a series of "unequal treaties" granting concessions to westerners. By 1900, European powers and Japan had carved China into spheres of influence for themselves.

Although a few reformers called for China to modernize, conservatives opposed change. In the Boxer Rebellion of 1900, anti-foreign Chinese forces attacked and killed many foreigners and Chinese Christians. Western powers quickly organized an army to crush the rebels.

In 1911, the Ch'ing dynasty collapsed and China declared itself a republic. However, civil war soon erupted. By 1928, the Nationalist party, led by Chiang Kai-shek, controlled China.

Communist China By the 1930's, Chinese communists led by Mao Tse-tung challenged the Nationalists. During World War II, the two sides joined forces against Japanese aggression. After the war, however, the struggle resumed. In 1949, the triumphant communists marched into the capital of Beijing. Mao declared the birth of the People's Republic of China.

Mao turned China into a communist dictatorship. He divided China into communes where farmers pooled their land and labor. When peasants resisted, food production fell. Flood and drought led to a massive famine.

In 1966, Mao introduced the Cultural Revolution to renew revolutionary spirit. Students and young workers organized the Red Guards, attacking those who did not fully support Mao. Many were forced to confess to imaginary crimes against the communist state. (See Bei Dao's "The Homecoming Stranger," p. 468, and his poem "All," p. 338, which reflect on this period of Chinese history.)

Mao's successors reformed the economy, but kept a tight reign on their authority. In 1989, students gathered in Beijing's Tiananmen (tyen´ än men) Square to seek democratic reform. The army killed or wounded thousands. The government later tortured or executed many pro-democracy leaders.

SOCIETY AND CULTURE

Communist China has officially rejected Confucianism. Still, Confucian ideas shaped Chinese society and culture for centuries.

Social Classes In Confucian society, the gentry held the highest place. These wealthy landowners were educated in the Confucian classics. As a leisure class, they looked down on physical labor. The gentry produced most of the scholars who ran the imperial bureaucracy.

The majority of people were peasants who lived in villages. Some owned their own land and were relatively rich. Peasants paid taxes, but otherwise governed their own affairs with little interference from imperial officials.

Artisans and merchants occupied a low place in Confucian society. Still, many gained great wealth. Sometimes, artisans and merchants— and even peasants—could move up in society by educating their sons to take the civil service examination.

Family Life From birth, children learned to put the family's interests first. Parents expected complete obedience and respect. This ideal of filial piety extended to a family's ancestors.

As you have read, Confucius taught that women were inferior to men. Girls were valued for the work they did and the children they would bear.

Social Change The communists set out to build a classless society. They did away with the landowning class and mocked the scholars who had once ruled. Still, Communist party members enjoy privileges others lack.

The communists also tried to weaken the influence of the family. Despite such attacks, filial piety and other traditions have survived.

ARTS AND LITERATURE

Literature and the arts have a long history in China. As early as the Shang dynasty, Chinese artisans produced richly decorated bronze vessels. *The Book of Songs*, a collection of poems dating to Chou times, offers glimpses into the lives of women and men of all classes.

The Visual Arts By the time of the T'ang dynasty, craftworkers had perfected the art of making porcelain, a hard, smooth, shiny pottery. T'ang artists made lovely figures of warriors, court ladies, servants, musicians, dancers, camels, and horses. The blue-and-white porcelain vases of the Ming dynasty are highly prized today.

Traditionally, painting was an art of the gentry class. They painted fine landscapes in ink on silk or paper scrolls. Chinese landscape paintings reflect Taoist ideas. Rushing rivers and rugged mountains convey the vastness of nature and the harmony of the universe. Tiny human figures suggest that people are merely a small part of the natural order.

Literature Poetry, too, was a highly prized skill among the gentry. Scholars wrote verses that followed strict literary forms. The brilliant T'ang writer Li Po (lē´ pō´) wrote 2,000 poems that celebrate harmony with nature in Taoist fashion or lament the passage of time. (See the picture on p. 332 and Li Po's poem "The Moon at the Fortified Pass" on p. 967.) His contemporary and occasional companion Tu Fu (tōō´ fōō´) was another great Tang poet. His work reflects a gradual loss of faith in the Confucian order. (See Tu Fu's poem "Jade Flower Palace" on p. 966.)

Since 1949, the government has supported writing that glorifies the values of the communist system. However, authors like Bei Dao (bā dou), who now lives in the United States, have written poetry and fiction critical of the government.

ACTIVITY
Using Oral History

Use Internet or library resources to find firsthand accounts of an event in modern Chinese history, such as the Cultural Revolution or the Tiananmen Square protests. Then, with a partner, use these accounts as the basis for a television interview. Conclude by offering a commentary on what you have learned. 🌏

Guide for Reading

Confucius (551?–449? B.C.)

One man's ideas have influenced the pattern of Chinese life for more than two thousand years. That man is Confucius (kən fyoo´ shəs), a scholar from the Shantung province in northeast China.

Confucius lived at a time when corruption and civil strife raged in China. He taught that by following tradition and authority with the proper spirit of reverence, the country's health could be restored.

The words of one who warned of the decline of tradition became a tradition in their own right. Starting in the 100's B.C., under the Han emperors, Confucianism became an official state doctrine and its study was required of all who served in government. Soon his ideas spread to other countries in the region.

While a number of works have been attributed to Confucius, his own words survive only in *The Analects,* a collection of sayings and conversations recorded by his students.

Bei Dao *(1949–   )*

Born two months before the founding of the People's Republic of China in October 1949, Bei Dao seemed destined for a successful government career. However, he dropped out of school and joined the Red Guards, a movement of teenagers seeking to revitalize the Chinese Revolution. When he became disillusioned with the violent tactics of this movement, he turned to writing poetry. Soon his poems, including "All," became rallying cries for those who wanted China to become more democratic. He has lived outside China since 1989, when Chinese leaders ordered the massacre of protesting students in Tiananmen Square.

Shu Ting *(1952–   )*

As a teenager, Shu Ting was forced by political events to leave Beijing and live in a small peasant village. She gained fame as a poet while still in her twenties. She won China's National Poetry Award in 1981 and 1983.

◆ Build Vocabulary

LATIN SUFFIXES: *-ment*

In the excerpt from *The Analects,* you will see the word *chastisements.* The Latin suffix *-ment* can help you figure out that this word is the noun form of the verb *chastise,* which means "punish." *Chastisements,* then, are "punishments."

WORD BANK

Before you read, preview this list of words from the selections. As you read, look for other words—like *treatment* and *improvement*—that end with *-ment.*

| chastisements |
| lamentation |

◆ Build Grammar Skills

INFINITIVES AND INFINITIVE PHRASES

An **infinitive** is the base form of a verb, usually preceded by *to;* it can be used as a noun, an adjective, or an adverb. An **infinitive phrase** is an infinitive with modifiers or complements (words that complete the meaning of the verb), all acting together as a single part of speech.

The following sentence from *The Analects* contains two infinitive phrases. The phrase *To demand much from oneself and little from others* acts as a noun: It is the subject of the sentence. The infinitive phrase *to banish discontent* is an adjective. It answers the question *which one?* about the word *way.*

To demand much from oneself and little from others is the way . . . to banish discontent.

◆ Literature and Your Life

CONNECT YOUR EXPERIENCE

Advice—you can't escape it. You get it from teachers, parents, and friends—even from talk show hosts. People love to tell you what you should do or think. Authors are no different. They want to communicate what they have learned about life.

These writers may not give you the same advice, but that's understandable because they come from different places and eras. Think about what they say and suggest about life's goals.

THEMATIC FOCUS: REACHING A GOAL

Each of these works offers a different answer to the question, "How do we measure the success of a life?"

Journal Writing Make a cluster diagram, like the one at the right, to map out the ingredients of a successful life.

◆ Background for Understanding

CULTURE

As you read *The Analects,* you may be surprised at Confucius' emphasis on traditional rules of conduct. Many Americans are uncomfortable with such rules. "How can I express the 'real me,'" they wonder, "if I have to act or dress according to old ideas?"

For Confucius, tradition—respect for one's elders, the proper fulfillment of rituals—is crucial to the well-being of a person, family, or country. At the same time, he teaches that it is not enough to "go through the motions" of tradition. "[R]itual performed without reverence," he says, is among "the things I cannot bear to see." Confucius' ideal is a *sincere* obedience to tradition. Instead of a conflict between inner feelings and outward forms, Confucius sees them working together.

◆ Literary Focus

APHORISMS

The ideas of Confucius have endured partly because they were expressed as **aphorisms**—brief sayings that express a basic truth. Many cultures pass on truths in the form of aphorisms, like gifts handed from one generation to another.

All the literature selections in this group contain aphorisms. Look for these brief sayings. Then, read them thoughtfully, as if you were slowly unwrapping a gift sent to you across many miles or years.

◆ Reading Strategy

RELATE TO WHAT YOU KNOW

These selections come from China, a country across the globe. They were influenced by circumstances that you have not experienced, yet their themes concern universal human experiences. By **relating,** or connecting, an author's ideas to your own experience, you can better appreciate their universal meaning.

For instance, consider Bei Dao's line "every meeting a first encounter" ("All," l. 8). To relate this line to your own experience, you might think of a movie that you have seen in which a man meets a friend who has forgotten him. You can then better understand Bei Dao's experience of a time of disruption in which "meetings" between friends are like meetings between strangers.

As you read these selections, relate ideas and images to your own prior experiences and knowledge.

from *The Analects*

Confucius

Translated by Arthur Waley

The Master[1] said, To learn and at due times to repeat what one has learnt, is that not after all[2] a pleasure? That friends should come to one from afar, is this not after all delightful? To remain unsoured even though one's merits are unrecognized by others, is that not after all what is expected of a gentleman?

The Master said, A young man's duty is to behave well to his parents at home and to his elders abroad, to be cautious in giving promises and punctual in keeping them, to have kindly feelings towards everyone, but seek the intimacy of the Good. If, when all that is done, he has any energy to spare, then let him study the polite arts.[3]

The Master said, (the good man) does not grieve that other people do not recognize his merits. His only anxiety is lest he should fail to recognize theirs.

The Master said, He who rules by moral force is like the pole-star,[4] which remains in its place while all the lesser stars do homage to it.

The Master said, If out of three hundred Songs[5] I had to take one phrase to cover all my teaching, I would say, "Let there be no evil in your thoughts."

The Master said, Govern the people by regulations, keep order among them by <u>chastisements</u>, and they will flee from you, and lose all self-respect. Govern them by moral force, keep order among them by ritual, and they will keep their self-respect and come to you of their own accord.

▲ Critical Viewing What clues in this picture indicate that Confucius held a respected position in his society? [Deduce]

---

1. **The Master:** Confucius.
2. **after all:** Even though one does not hold public office.
3. **the polite arts:** Such activities as reciting from *The Book of Songs*, practicing archery, and learning proper behavior.

---

4. **pole-star:** Polaris, the North Star.
5. **three hundred Songs:** Poems in *The Book of Songs*.

◆ **Build Vocabulary**

chastisements (chas tīz´ mintz) *n*.: Punishments

Meng Wu Po[6] asked about the treatment of parents. The Master said, Behave in such a way that your father and mother have no anxiety about you, except concerning your health.

The Master said, A gentleman can see a question from all sides without bias. The small man is biased and can see a question only from one side.

The Master said, Yu[7] shall I teach you what knowledge is? When you know a thing, to recognize that you know it, and when you do not know a thing, to recognize that you do not know it. That is knowledge.

The Master said, High office filled by men of narrow views, ritual performed without reverence, the forms of mourning observed without grief—these are things I cannot bear to see!

The Master said, In the presence of a good man, think all the time how you may learn to equal him. In the presence of a bad man, turn your gaze within!

The Master said, In old days a man kept a hold on his words, fearing the disgrace that would ensue should he himself fail to keep pace with them.

The Master said, A gentleman covets the reputation of being slow in word but prompt in deed.

The Master said, In old days men studied for the sake of self-improvement; nowadays men study in order to impress other people.

The Master said, A gentleman is ashamed to let his words outrun his deeds.

The Master said, He who will not worry about what is far off will soon find something worse than worry close at hand.

The Master said, To demand much from oneself and little from others is the way (for a ruler) to banish discontent.

---

6. **Meng Wu Po** (muŋ wōō bō): The son of one of Confucius' disciples.
7. **Yu** (yōō): Tzu-lu, one of Confucius' disciples.

Guide for Responding

◆ *Literature and Your Life*

Reader's Response If you had lived in China during the time of Confucius, do you think you would have been drawn to him and his ideas? Explain.

Thematic Focus According to Confucius, what attributes make a successful leader?

Group Discussion With a group, discuss how well some leaders of today fit Confucius' model of a successful leader.

☑ Check Your Comprehension

1. How does Confucius believe people should behave toward their parents?
2. What does Confucius believe knowledge is?

◆ Critical Thinking

INTERPRET
1. What does Confucius mean when he says that a ruler should govern by "moral force"? **[Interpret]**
2. Give two examples from these passages that show that Confucius attaches great importance to humility. **[Support]**

APPLY
3. Which of Confucius' ideas do you think you could apply to your own life? Explain. **[Apply]**

EXTEND
4. Which of Confucius' ideas do you think today's politicians should practice to gain more respect from voters? **[Social Studies Link]**

All

Bei Dao

Translated by Donald Finkel
and Xueliang Chen

Old Trees by Cold Waterfall, Wen Zhengming (1470–1559), The Los Angeles County Museum of Art

All is fated,
all cloudy,

all an endless beginning,
all a search for what vanishes,

5 all joys grave,
all griefs tearless,

every speech a repetition,
every meeting a first encounter,

all love buried in the heart,
10 all history prisoned in a dream,

all hope hedged with doubt,
all faith drowned in <u>lamentation</u>.

Every explosion heralds an instant of stillness,
every death reverberates forever.

▲ **Critical Viewing** What might these people be hoping to find in this natural setting? **[Speculate]**

◆ **Build Vocabulary**

lamentation (la mən tā´ shən) *n.*: Act of crying out in grief; wailing

Also All

In Answer to Bei Dao's "All"

Shu Ting

Translated by Donald Finkel
and Jinsheng Yi

Not all trees are felled by storms.
Not every seed finds barren soil.
Not all the wings of dream are broken,
nor is all affection doomed
5   to wither in a desolate heart.

No, not all is as you say.

Not all flames consume themselves,
shedding no light on other lives.
Not all stars announce the night
10   and never dawn. Not every song
will drift past every ear and heart.

No, not all is as you say.

Not every cry for help is silenced,
nor every loss beyond recall.
15   Not every chasm spells disaster.
Not only the weak will be brought
    to their knees,
nor every soul be trodden under.

It won't all end in tears and blood.
Today is heavy with tomorrow—
20   the future was planted yesterday.
Hope is a burden all of us shoulder
though we might stumble under the load.

◆ Guide for Responding

◆ Literature and Your Life

Reader's Response If you could ask either of these poets a question, what would you ask? Why?

Thematic Focus Judging from these poems, do you think either of these poets believes in striving to overcome obstacles? Explain.

☑ Check Your Comprehension

1. Summarize what the poet says in "All."
2. Summarize the speaker's view of life in "Also All."

◆ Critical Thinking

INTERPRET

1. What effect does the repetition have on the feeling that "All" calls up? **[Analyze]**
2. Explain how the last two lines of "Also All" suggest the possibility of hope. **[Interpret]**
3. List three details in "Also All" that indicate that Shu Ting's optimism is difficult to maintain. **[Analyze]**

APPLY

4. Bei Dao's poem "All" is a response to political events in China. What events in American news today might inspire someone to write a poem like this? Explain. **[Hypothesize]**
5. Describe a situation in which a person—either someone you know or someone in the news—showed courage and perseverance when all hope seemed lost. **[Relate]**

EXTEND

6. "Also All" was written in response to Bei Dao's poem "All." (a) What is Shu Ting's interpretation of the poem she is answering? (b) Explain how lines 19 and 20 express her disagreement with "All." **[Literature Link]**

Guide for Responding (continued)

◆ Reading Strategy

RELATE TO WHAT YOU KNOW

Relating, or connecting, what these writers say to your own experience and knowledge will help you find meaning in their work. For instance, Confucius says that "A gentleman is ashamed to let his words outrun his deeds." You might recall a time when a friend boasted that he could perform some feat, only to fail in the attempt. Remembering your friend's embarrassment will help you see the meaning of Confucius' words.

1. Confucius describes the ideal ruler as one who "rules by moral force," leading by example. Describe a person in your own life, or in literature, the movies, or history who "rules" this way.
2. Describe an experience in your life in which one of Confucius' principles was illustrated.
3. (a) Give an example you are familiar with that illustrates the feelings expressed in "All." (b) Give an example you are familiar with that illustrates the feelings expressed in "Also All."
4. Explain how one person might be able to experience the feelings expressed in both "All" and "Also All."

◆ Literary Focus

APHORISMS

The authors of these pieces write in **aphorisms**—brief sayings that illustrate an important truth. However, the best aphorisms are not just brief. By using clear, simple images, by repeating key words, and by balancing words against one another, they create a memorable effect. For instance, in "All" Bei Dao balances the contrasting words *griefs* and *joys* in this powerful aphorism of despair: "all joys grave, /all griefs tearless" (ll. 5–6).

1. Identify an aphorism in *The Analects* expressing what you think is a basic truth.
2. Select an aphorism from *The Analects,* and explain how it balances one word against another.
3. Give an example of how Bei Dao repeats words and balances words against one another in "All."
4. Identify one striking image in "Also All." Explain how such an image helps make the poet's meaning clearer than a lengthy explanation might.

◆ Build Vocabulary

USING THE LATIN SUFFIX *-ment*

The Latin suffix *-ment* indicates the noun form of the word to which it is attached. Use the suffix *-ment* to create a noun for each of the following examples:

1. To state your opinion is to make a ___?___.
2. You replace something with a ___?___.
3. A ruler commands with a ___?___.
4. A teacher assigns an ___?___.

USING THE WORD BANK: Antonyms

In your notebook, write the antonym for each word from the Word Bank:
1. lamentation: (a) despair, (b) interest, (c) rejoicing
2. chastisements: (a) rewards, (b) orders, (c) duties

◆ Build Grammar Skills

INFINITIVES AND INFINITIVE PHRASES

Infinitives, which are the base forms of verbs and usually begin with the word *to*, can be used as nouns, adjectives, or adverbs. **Infinitive phrases** include an infinitive with its modifiers and complements (words that complete the meaning of the verb), all acting as a single part of speech.

Writers of aphorisms, like Confucius, often use infinitives to express universal ideas. The infinitive form gives the action being described a timeless flavor.

Practice Copy each sentence in your notebook. Underline the infinitives or the infinitive phrases.
1. To learn and at due times to repeat what one has learnt, is that not after all a pleasure?
2. To remain unsoured even though one's merits are unrecognized by others, is that not after all what is expected of a gentleman?
3. The Master said, A young man's duty is to behave well to his parents at home and to his elders abroad, to be cautious in giving promises and punctual in keeping them, to have kindly feelings towards everyone, but seek the intimacy of the Good.

Build Your Portfolio

 ## Idea Bank

Writing

1. **Letter to an Author** Write a letter to an author from this group. In your letter, explain why you agree or disagree with his or her ideas.

2. **Life Poem** Each writer expresses his or her view of life. Write a poem in which you express your view of life. Use images and examples from your own experience to express your ideas.

3. **Comparing and Contrasting Poems** Shu Ting wrote "Also All" as a rebuttal to Bei Dao's "All." Write a short essay in which you evaluate which poem makes a better case.

Speaking, Listening, and Viewing

4. **Oral Interpretation** Practice reading one of these works aloud. Vary the tone and speed of your voice for emphasis. Perform your reading for the class. **[Performing Arts Link]**

5. **Interview** With a partner, role-play an interview with one of the writers in this group. Develop questions about the author's views and experiences. Base your answers on what you've learned from their works and biographies.

Researching and Representing

6. **Tiananmen Square Presentation** "All" and "Also All" are responses to political events in China during the 1980's. In April 1989, students took over Tiananmen Square. Find out more about this event and give a presentation on it for your class. **[Social Studies Link]**

7. **Collage** Assemble a number of images with words from one of these works at the center. Find images in newspapers, magazines, and personal photos that reflect the ideas expressed. Display your collage in the classroom. **[Art Link]**

Online Activity www.phlit.phschool.com

 ## Guided Writing Lesson

Aphorism Calendar

Aphorisms are meant to be useful in daily life. What better way to make them a part of your daily life than by putting them in a calendar? Create your own aphorism calendar by making up one brief saying for each month of the year. The following tips will help you state your ideas concisely.

> #### Writing Skills Focus: Brevity and Clarity
>
> Like written directions and essays on tests, aphorisms are best when they are **brief and clear.** In the following example, Confucius clearly states a basic principle of conduct in just two sentences:
>
> The Master said, A gentleman can see a question from all sides without bias. The small man is biased and can see a question only from one side.
>
> This aphorism can be easily remembered and understood. As you plan, draft, and revise your calendar, use the fewest words possible to convey your ideas clearly.

Prewriting Brainstorm for single words that name qualities you admire in a person. Then briefly describe examples of each quality in action.

Drafting Refer to your prewriting notes as an inspiration for your twelve aphorisms. For example, you might write, "Courage is ___?___" and then use your description of someone's courageous action to help fill in the blank. Convey as much information as you can in a few words.

Revising Revise each aphorism and eliminate any words that do not add to the meaning. However, ask a classmate to read your abbreviated sayings, and determine whether or not they are clear.

Problem-and-Solution Essay

Writing Process Workshop

Air pollution...information overload...can't concentrate on schoolwork...Everywhere you turn, there are problems! What can you do about it? One thing you can do is write a **problem-and-solution essay.** In a problem-and-solution essay, you identify a problem, then lay out a plan for solving that problem. In the course of the essay, you explain the strategy for solving the problem, as well as the steps required to solve it. For this type of essay to work, it's important that a solution to the problem exist.

The following skills will help you write an effective problem-and-solution essay.

Writing Skills Focus

▶ As you explain your solution, **show the benefits of your proposal.** Few will be willing to accept your proposed solution to the problem if they do not know the benefits of it.

▶ Every problem has both a cause and an effect. Make sure you clearly **show cause-and-effect relationships**—how one event or condition brings about another.

James Thurber puts these skills to humorous use as he explains how his family tried to deal with a troublesome dog.

MODEL FROM LITERATURE

from "The Dog That Bit People" by James Thurber

① Here, the writer reveals his particular problem: The biting dog won't come inside.

② Further details emphasize the importance of the problem.

③ The writer signals that a solution to the problem is coming.

④ The solution to the problem is given here: a thunder machine.

. . . Muggs used to spend practically all of his time outdoors. . . . ① It was hard to get him to come in and as a result the garbage man, the iceman, and the laundry man wouldn't come near the house. ② We had to haul the garbage down to the corner, take the laundry out and bring it back, and meet the iceman a block from home. After this had gone on for some time ③ we hit on an ingenious arrangement for getting the dog in the house. . . . Thunder frightened him out of his senses. . . . So we fixed up a thunder machine [to scare him inside]. ④

Prewriting

Choose an Interesting Topic Choose a problem that interests you and about which you have an opinion. If you're having trouble thinking of one, use a problems-and-solutions chart like the one below to help you.

Problems	Solutions
overdevelopment	zoning restrictions
pollution	recycling
elderly	retirement communities
loneliness	friends
obesity	exercise and a good diet

Focus Decide whether your problem is too broad to explain a solution in the time and space you are given. If your problem has too many parts or aspects to it, decide on just one part to examine. For example, instead of discussing all the problems associated with illiteracy, discuss illiteracy in your community and how your school could do its part in setting up tutoring programs.

Drafting

Show the Benefits of Your Proposed Solution As you draft your proposed solution, show your readers why your suggestions are the most logical or beneficial. Explain how the steps you recommend will lead to a solution of the problem, and emphasize the positive effects of solving the problem.

Show Cause-and-Effect Relationships People are more likely to follow your advice if you show how their actions will bring about these positive effects. Make the cause-and-effect relationships clear in your proposed solution.

> People often ask me how to lose weight. I used to give them detailed explanations about calories and the body's ability to use fuel. Now I give a simple answer—to lose weight, eat less and exercise more.

Here the writer has clearly identified the causes (eating less, exercising more) and the effect (losing weight).

APPLYING LANGUAGE SKILLS: Sentence Fragments

A sentence fragment lacks a subject or a verb or simply does not express a complete thought. Always try to express your ideas in complete sentences, which contain a subject and a verb and express a complete thought.

Sentence Fragment:
While almost everyone likes to eat sweets.

Complete Sentence:
While almost everyone likes to eat sweets, you need to eat healthy foods to stay slim.

Practice On your paper, rewrite the following fragments as complete sentences.

1. Because our rivers are polluted.
2. Exercising on a daily basis.

Writing Application Check your problem-and-solution essay to make sure that all of your sentences are complete.

Writer's Solution Connection Language Lab

For more practice on fixing sentence fragments, complete the Language Lab lesson on Run-on Sentences and Fragments.

Applying LANGUAGE SKILLS: Subordination

Use subordination to vary your sentences. Subordinating conjunctions such as *because, since, while,* and *though* link a subordinate clause (a clause of less importance) to a main clause.

Example: subordinate clause
Because we have an addiction to junk food, many of us find it difficult to lose weight.

Practice On your paper, underline the subordinate clauses in the following sentences.

1. Grapefruits help you to lose weight because they speed up your metabolism and also contain lots of water.

2. Although it may at first be difficult to maintain, a healthy diet has many benefits.

Writing Application Review your essay. Look for places where subordinate clauses would make your sentence structure more interesting.

Writer's Solution Connection Writing Lab

For more tips on how to be a peer reviewer, look at the tips for peer reviewers in the Writing Lab tutorial on Exposition.

Revising

Use a Checklist Make sure that the following are true for your paper.

▶ Your opening sentences lead logically into your topic.
▶ You identify a problem and suggest a solution.
▶ You clearly show the relationships between causes and effects. Your instructions show how the reader's actions can bring about a desired effect.
▶ Your essay grabs and keeps the reader's interest.

Use a Peer Reviewer A classmate can often point out weaknesses that you may have missed. Ask one of your classmates to read your paper and comment on it.

If you are the peer reviewer, make sure that you offer your criticism in a positive way. This will ensure that your comments are put to good use instead of causing resentment.

Negative Comment	**Positive Comment**
This is totally unorganized!	Reorganize your points so that the reader can follow them more easily.

REVISION MODEL

① *Because*
~~W~~e don't think about how our actions affect the future. Many

of us don't do our part to conserve natural resources.
② *If*   *gasoline use and air pollution will be reduced*
People ~~should~~ drive in carpools.

① The writer combines two sentences by making one a subordinate clause. The subordinating conjunction *because* clarifies the cause-and-effect relationship.

② The writer adds details that show the benefits of his suggestion.

Publishing

Publish Your Paper On-Line No matter what your topic is, there's bound to be a site related to it on the World Wide Web. Consult with an experienced Internet user to post your paper on the appropriate Web site.

Student Success Workshop

Research Skills

Locating Information on the Internet

Strategies for Success

Tools like the Internet can make conducting research less time-consuming than it once was. Sometimes, however, finding specific information on the Internet can be difficult. For instance, if you search for information about the 1998 Winter Olympic Games in Nagano, Japan, you might find thousands of pages of information— from biographies of athletes to the history of the Olympics, along with details about individual sports. How do you find exactly what you want?

Rev Up Your Search Engines Search engines such as Yahoo, Lycos, or Excite can help you find your way through the maze of Internet information. They search for Internet "links" to Web pages and deliver them to Internet users. Search engines invite you to use "key words." If you're looking for information about your favorite NFL football team, you might type "Dallas Cowboys" or "NFL Football" into the blank key-word space provided by the search engine.

Narrow Your Topic To save time and reduce the risk of reaching a dead end, be as specific as possible in indicating what you're looking for. Say you want to learn more about a particular musician. The key word *music* might eventually get you to information about that musician, but it could take a long time. Typing in the person's name as the key word—or the kind of music he or she performs—will more quickly lead you to information you want.

Select Reliable Sources Anyone with a computer and Internet access can set up an Internet Web page. To get accurate information, search for sites from individuals or organizations with credentials. For example, if you are planning a trip to New York City, you will most likely find more complete, accurate, and up-to-date information on a Web site produced by an official New York City tourism agency than by a private citizen offering information about his favorite restaurants. You must evaluate the credibility and accuracy of information sources you consult.

Apply the Strategies

Use the Internet to gather information on the history of your home state, a recipe for a favorite meal, the author of a book you enjoyed, or a topic of your own. Then answer these questions:

1. How did you narrow down your search topic? Were your key words too broad, too narrow, or just right?

2. Which search engine did you use? Did one search engine provide more useful information than others? Explain how "links" worked to help you in your search.

3. Describe some characteristics of Web sites you visited. Which were helpful? Which characteristics were unnecessary?

4. Which information sources did you consider most accurate? Why?

✔ *Here are situations in which you may want to locate information on the Internet:*

▶ **Comparing different product brands**
▶ **Researching information about colleges**
▶ **Needing a long-range weather forecast**
▶ **Learning about groups that interest you**
▶ **Researching a city, state, or country**
▶ **Searching for a text in an out-of-town library**

If you haven't done so already, you may soon apply for your first job and go on your first job interview. Whether you're looking for an after-school job, a summer job, or your first full-time job, the impression you make during your job interview will determine whether you are offered the position.

Make a Good Impression First impressions are important. Create a good one by arriving on time and being dressed appropriately. During the interview, be aware of the nonverbal messages you send through body language, eye contact, and gestures. Maintain eye contact with your interviewer; don't look around the room as if you're uninterested or avoiding answering questions. Positive body language, such as a firm handshake and good posture, will suggest that you are self-assured, confident, and capable. Speak clearly and loudly enough, and avoid using slang or clichés.

Throughout, listen attentively to your interviewer. Answer the questions asked, and listen for cues about what is important. You might use these cues to ask follow-up questions.

Apply the Strategies

With a partner, role-play these situations. Using the tips above, make a good impression at the following job interviews:

1. An interview at a local television show to help with teleprompting, set construction, and setting up camera equipment

2. An interview at a doctor's office for administrative work

3. An interview for a position as a baby sitter

Strategies for a Successful Job Interview

✔ *If you want to make a good impression during your interview, remember these strategies:*

▶ Arrive on time and dressed neatly
▶ Speak clearly, confidently, and positively about yourself and what you will bring to your new position
▶ Take your time answering questions, to make sure you answer completely
▶ Ask questions about the position to show your interest in the company

Test Preparation Workshop

Reading Comprehension
Using Context Clues to Determine Word Meanings

Strategies for Success

The reading sections of standardized tests often require you to understand multiple-meaning words and specialized and technical terms. Use these strategies to answer test questions with the help of context clues:

Multiple-Meaning Words The context in which a multiple-meaning word appears can help you determine which definition applies. Find words that suggest the word's part of speech and connotation. Look at the following example:

> Shayla always assumed she would go to Springfield State with Amy, one of her best friends. But her application was denied. Then, Shayla got a letter from a <u>private</u> college in a city 2,000 miles away. The letter informed her that she had been accepted for <u>matriculation</u>. Shayla knew she should jump at the opportunity—it was a noteworthy college in a beautiful location, but she would be far from home.

1 What is the best meaning for *private?*

A soldier in the army   **C** secluded; isolated
B not publicly owned   **D** dreary

Look at the context in which *private* appears. Answer **D** can be eliminated, since she said the location is beautiful. Because the passage has nothing to do with soldiers or the army, and *private* is used as an adjective and not a noun, **A** is wrong. **C** is also incorrect: If the college is in a city, it must not be secluded or isolated. Also consider Shayla's assumption that she would attend a state, or publicly owned, college with her friend. Answer **B** is the correct choice.

Specialized and Technical Terms Context clues can also help you determine the meaning of specialized or technical terms—terms used only in a particular context.

2 Use context to determine which of the following might be the meaning of the word *matriculation*:

A refusal   **C** humiliation
B test   **D** admission; registration

Answer **C** can be eliminated because the context words "opportunity" and "noteworthy" are positive, and Shayla seems honored. The context does not support **B** because the passage implies that Shayla is being offered an opportunity, not a test. Shayla considers attending the private college, so **A** can be eliminated. **D** must be correct.

Apply the Strategies

Read the following sample text, and answer the questions below.

> Before the Articles of Confederation could become law, each state had to <u>ratify</u> them. By 1779, only the state of Maryland had not voted in favor of the articles. During colonial times, seven states had received <u>charters</u> granting them control of western lands. Maryland, one of six states that had not received western territory from Great Britain, wanted all western lands turned over to the federal government.

1 Which word best defines *charters* as it is used in the passage?

A legal documents giving privileges
B letters from the government
C contracts to rent land
D documents creating institutions

2 In the passage, the word *ratify* means

A ignore   **C** approve
B enjoy   **D** reject

Test Preparation Workshop ♦ 347

Krishna's Magic Flute, Unknown Artist, Kangra Valley, New York Public Library

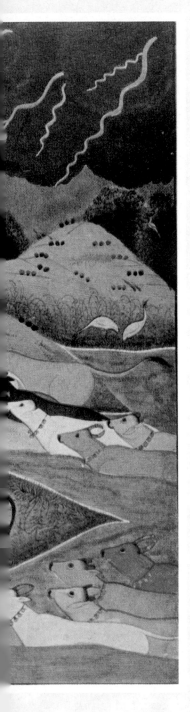

Conflicts in World Literature

There are many conflicts in life—good versus evil, right versus wrong, man versus nature. The stories, poems, and essays you're about to read come from different parts of the globe—India, Iraq, South Africa, and Russia—but they share one common theme: They all deal with the clashing forces that we encounter in life. Turn the page to see how real people and fictional characters respond to—and often overcome—obstacles and injustices.

Guide for Reading

Doris Lessing (1919–)

Some writers shy away from controversy; Doris Lessing, however, seems to invite it. When her novel *The Golden Notebook* appeared in 1962, she was accused of being a "man-hater" because of the resentment and anger toward men that some of her female characters expressed. Lessing has also written about the conflicts between cultures, focusing especially on the conflicts between Europeans and Africans.

Growing up in Africa

Doris May Taylor was born on October 22, 1919, in Persia (now Iran). In 1924, enticed by the prospect of getting rich by farming maize, her father moved the family to the colony of Rhodesia (now Zimbabwe) in southern Africa. There, Lessing began to observe how, under colonialism, Europeans displaced Africans from their land and ignored their traditions.

From Outcast to Hero

In 1950, Lessing published her first novel, *The Grass Is Singing*. In this and her later novels, Lessing highlights the injustices suffered by black Africans at the hands of white colonials. Her strong views provoked a strong reaction.

> *In 1956, Lessing was declared a "prohibited alien" by the governments of Southern Rhodesia and South Africa.*

Ironically, when apartheid ended in South Africa in 1994, she was welcomed back as a hero—for writing about the very topics for which she was banished earlier.

A Different Kind of Conflict

In this story, Lessing doesn't write about the conflicts between men and women or between cultures. Instead, she describes the struggle going on in the mind of a boy.

◆ Build Vocabulary

LATIN WORD ROOTS: -lum-

In this story, you will encounter the word *luminous*. The word root *-lum-* comes from the Latin *lumen*, meaning "light." Knowing this root can help you figure out that words that contain the root *-lum-* are related to light. *Luminous* means "giving off light."

WORD BANK

contrition
promontories
luminous
supplication
frond
convulsive
gout

As you read this story, you will encounter the words on this list. Each word is defined on the page where it first appears. Preview the list before you read.

◆ Build Grammar Skills

PARTICIPIAL PHRASES

"Going to the shore on the first morning of the vacation, the young English boy stopped at a turning of the path ..." So begins "Through the Tunnel"—with a participial phrase. A **participial phrase** consists of a participle (a verb form ending in *-ing*, *-ed*, or an irregular ending) plus any other words that go with it. Participial phrases function as adjectives.

The participial phrase "Going to the shore on the first morning of the vacation," beginning with the present participle *going*, acts as an adjective modifying "boy." Lessing varies her sentence structure and creates vivid pictures of the characters and setting in this story by using participial phrases.

Through the Tunnel

◆ *Literature and Your Life*

CONNECT YOUR EXPERIENCE

When you set personal goals, you challenge yourself, push yourself to see just how far you can go. Whether or not you succeed, you learn something about yourself. The boy in Lessing's story gives himself a physical challenge that requires all his courage to meet.

Journal Writing Write about a challenge you have successfully met—either physical, emotional, or intellectual. List the steps you took to accomplish your goal.

THEMATIC FOCUS: CLASHING FORCES

In this story, a boy chooses to take on an underwater challenge despite his inner fear of failure. How do you think success or failure to meet a challenge changes a person?

◆ Background for Understanding

SCIENCE

Oxygen, which your body needs on a regular basis, is an important, but relatively small, part of the air you breathe. Depriving the brain of oxygen can quickly cause dizziness and, if prolonged, brain damage. However, you don't usually have to think about breathing. Special cells, called chemoreceptors, sense the oxygen and carbon dioxide levels in your blood. These cells then send out signals that quicken or slow the rate of breathing as necessary.

Jerry, the young boy in this story, deprives his body of oxygen, pushing the limit of how long he can hold his breath. His self-testing makes for interesting reading, but it is not something you should imitate.

◆ Literary Focus

INTERNAL CONFLICT

The personal challenge that Jerry, the main character in "Through the Tunnel," sets for himself involves an **internal conflict**—a struggle within a character over opposing feelings, beliefs, or needs. Jerry's struggle with his opposing feelings about this enormous and frightening challenge he faces results in a gripping story.

Use a graphic organizer like the one shown to identify Jerry's conflicting feelings.

Jerry's Feelings

Wants to go to bay → ← Doesn't want to hurt mother's feelings

→ ←

→ ←

How much oxygen is in the air you breathe?

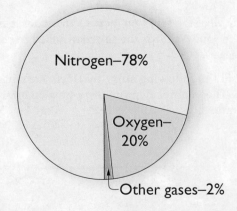

Nitrogen—78%

Oxygen—20%

Other gases—2%

Reading for Success

Interactive Reading Strategies

Reading is interactive. When you interact with the words on each page, you can really feel the sights and sounds of new worlds. Otherwise, if you just sit back and passively look at the words, it's like going on a field trip and never getting off the bus!

When you read, apply the following strategies to help you interact with the text:

Predict.

What do you think will happen? Why? Look for hints in the story that seem to suggest a certain outcome. As you read on, you will see whether your predictions are correct.

Use your prior background knowledge.

No matter how different a character, subject matter, opinion, or situation is from what you are familiar with, chances are you will be able to relate to certain aspects of the character or experience. If a character goes to the beach, think about a trip to the beach you may have taken. This technique will give you a mental picture of what is happening and help you relate to the character better.

Question.

What questions come to mind as you are reading? For example, why do the characters act as they do? What causes events to happen? Why does the writer include certain information? Look for answers to your questions as you read.

Form mental images.

Use details from the selection you are reading to create pictures in your mind. As you read along, change your picture as the story unfolds and your understanding grows. If you find yourself confused, try to state your confusion. Use your visualization to clarify whatever hasn't been clear to you.

Respond.

Think about what the selection means. What does it say to you? What feelings does it evoke in you? What has the selection added to your understanding of people and of life in general?

As you read the following story by Doris Lessing, look at the notes along the margins. These notes demonstrate how to apply these strategies to a work of literature.

...Through the Tunnel

Doris Lessing

▲ **Critical Viewing** How does the use of shadows and light affect the mood of this photograph? **[Analyze]**

Going to the shore on the first morning of the vacation, the young English boy stopped at a turning of the path and looked down at a wild and rocky bay, and then over to the crowded beach he knew so well from other years. His mother walked on in front of him, carrying a bright striped bag in one hand. Her other arm, swinging loose, was very white in the sun. The boy watched that white, naked arm, and turned his eyes, which had a frown behind them, toward the bay and back again to his mother. When she felt he was not with her, she swung around. "Oh, there you are, Jerry!" she said. She looked impatient, then smiled. "Why, darling, would you rather not come with me? Would you rather—" She frowned, conscientiously worrying over what amusements he might secretly be longing for, which she had been too busy or too careless to imagine. He was very familiar with that anxious, apologetic smile. <u>Contrition</u> sent him running after her. And yet, as he ran, he looked back over his shoulder at the

> This detail helps you **predict** that something will happen at the bay.

◆ Build Vocabulary

contrition (kən trish´ ən) *n.*: Feeling of remorse for having done something wrong

Through the Tunnel ◆ 353

wild bay; and all morning, as he played on the safe beach, he was thinking of it.

Next morning, when it was time for the routine of swimming and sunbathing, his mother said, "Are you tired of the usual beach, Jerry? Would you like to go somewhere else?"

"Oh, no!" he said quickly, smiling at her out of that unfailing impulse of contrition—a sort of chivalry. Yet, walking down the path with her, he blurted out, "I'd like to go and have a look at those rocks down there."

She gave the idea her attention. It was a wild-looking place, and there was no one there; but she said, "Of course, Jerry. When you've had enough, come to the big beach. Or just go straight back to the villa, if you like." She walked away, that bare arm, now slightly reddened from yesterday's sun, swinging. And he almost ran after her again, feeling it unbearable that she should go by herself, but he did not.

She was thinking. Of course he's old enough to be safe without me. Have I been keeping him too close? He mustn't feel he ought to be with me. I must be careful.

He was an only child, eleven years old. She was a widow. She was determined to be neither possessive nor lacking in devotion. She went worrying off to her beach.

As for Jerry, once he saw that his mother had gained her beach, he began the steep descent to the bay. From where he was, high up among red-brown rocks, it was a scoop of moving bluish green fringed with white. As he went lower, he saw that it spread among small <u>promontories</u> and inlets of rough, sharp rock, and the crisping, lapping surface showed stains of purple and darker blue. Finally, as he ran sliding and scraping down the last few yards, he saw an edge of white surf and the shallow, <u>luminous</u> movement of water over

▲ **Critical Viewing** Compare the details of this painting with the way you envisioned the "big beach" in the story. [**Compare and Contrast**]

white sand, and, beyond that, a solid, heavy blue.

He ran straight into the water and began swimming. He was a good swimmer. He went out fast over the gleaming sand, over a middle region where rocks lay like discolored monsters under the surface, and then he was in the real sea—a warm sea where irregular cold currents from the deep water shocked his limbs.

When he was so far out that he could look back not only on the little bay but past the promontory that was between it and the big beach, he floated on the buoyant surface and looked for his mother. There she was, a speck of yellow under an umbrella that looked like a slice of orange peel. He swam back to shore, relieved at being sure she was there, but all at once very lonely.

The Beach Treat (detail), Suzanne Nagler

On the edge of a small cape that marked the side of the bay away from the promontory was a loose scatter of rocks. Above them, some boys were stripping off their clothes. They came running, naked, down to the rocks. The English boy swam toward them, but kept his distance at a stone's throw. They were of that coast; all of them were burned smooth dark brown and speaking a language he did not understand. To be with them, of them, was a craving that filled his whole body. He swam a little closer; they turned and watched him with narrowed, alert dark eyes. Then one smiled and waved. It was enough. In a minute, he had swum in and was on the rocks beside them, smiling with a desperate, nervous <u>supplication</u>. They shouted cheerful greetings at him; and then, as he preserved his nervous, uncomprehending smile, they understood that he was a foreigner strayed from his own beach, and they proceeded to forget him. But he was happy. He was with them.

They began diving again and again from a high point into a well of blue sea between rough, pointed rocks. After they had dived and come up, they swam around, hauled themselves up, and waited their turn to dive again. They were big boys—men, to Jerry. He dived, and they watched him; and when he swam around to take his place, they made way for him. He felt he was accepted and he dived again, carefully, proud of himself.

Soon the biggest of the boys poised himself, shot down into the water, and did not come up. The others stood about, watching. Jerry, after waiting for the sleek brown head to appear, let out a yell of warning; they looked at him idly and turned their eyes back toward the water. After a long time, the boy came up on the other side of a big dark rock, letting the air out of his lungs in a sputtering gasp and a shout of triumph. Immediately the rest of them dived in. One moment, the morning seemed full of chattering boys; the next, the air and the surface of the water were empty. But through the heavy blue, dark shapes could be seen moving and groping.

Jerry dived, shot past the school of underwater swimmers, saw a black wall of rock looming at him, touched it, and bobbed up at once to the surface, where the wall was a low barrier he could see across. There was no one visible; under him, in the water, the dim shapes of the swimmers had disappeared. Then one, and then another of the boys came up on the far side of the barrier of rock, and he understood that they had swum through some gap or hole in it. He plunged down again. He could see nothing through the stinging salt water but the blank rock. When he came up the boys were all on the diving rock, preparing

◆ Build Vocabulary

promontories (präm´ ən tôr´ ēz) *n.*: High places extending out over a body of water

luminous (lōō´ mə nəs) *adj.*: Giving off light

supplication (sup´ lə kā´ shən) *n.*: The act of asking humbly and earnestly

to attempt the feat again. And now, in a panic of failure, he yelled up, in English, "Look at me! Look!" and he began splashing and kicking in the water like a foolish dog.

They looked down gravely, frowning. He knew the frown. At moments of failure, when

Question why Jerry might be acting this way. Is he trying to get attention?

he clowned to claim his mother's attention, it was with just this grave, embarrassed inspection that she rewarded him.

Through his hot shame, feeling the pleading grin on his face like a scar that he could never remove, he looked up at the group of big brown boys on the rock and shouted, *"Bonjour! Merci! Au revoir! Monsieur, monsieur!"*[1] while he hooked his fingers round his ears and waggled them.

Water surged into his mouth; he choked, sank, came up. The rock, lately weighted with boys, seemed to rear up out of the water as their weight was removed. They were flying down past him, now, into the water; the air was full of falling bodies. Then the rock was empty in the hot sunlight. He counted one, two, three. . . .

At fifty, he was terrified. They must all be drowning beneath him, in the watery caves of the rock! At a hundred, he stared around him at the empty hillside, wondering if he should yell for help. He counted faster, faster, to hurry them up, to bring them to the surface quickly, to drown them quickly—anything rather than the terror of counting on and on into the blue emptiness of the morning. And then, at a hundred and sixty, the water beyond the rock was full of boys blowing like brown whales. They swam back to the shore without a look at him.

He climbed back to the diving rock and sat down, feeling the hot roughness of it under his thighs. The boys were gathering up their bits of

Think about how you would **respond** to this situation.

clothing and running off along the shore to another promontory. They were

leaving to get away from him. He cried openly, fists in his eyes. There was no one to see him, and he cried himself out.

It seemed to him that a long time had passed, and he swam out to where he could see his mother. Yes, she was still there, a yellow spot under an orange umbrella. He swam back to the big rock, climbed up, and dived into the

Use these sensory details to **form a mental image** of how difficult it is to swim in this place.

blue pool among the fanged and angry boulders. Down he went, until he touched the wall of rock again. But the salt was so painful in his eyes that he could not see.

He came to the surface, swam to shore and went back to the villa to wait for his mother. Soon she walked slowly up the path, swinging her striped bag, the flushed, naked arm dangling beside her. "I want some swimming goggles," he panted, defiant and beseeching.

She gave him a patient, inquisitive look as she said casually, "Well, of course, darling."

But now, now, now! He must have them this minute, and no other time. He nagged and pestered until she went with him to a shop. As soon as she had bought the goggles, he grabbed them from her hand as if she were going to claim them for herself, and was off, running down the steep path to the bay.

Jerry swam out to the big barrier rock, adjusted the goggles, and dived. The impact of the water broke the rubber-enclosed vacuum, and the goggles came loose. He understood that he must swim down to the base of the rock from the surface of the water. He fixed the goggles tight and firm, filled his lungs, and floated, face down, on the water. Now he could see. It was as if he had eyes of a different kind—fish eyes that showed everything clear and delicate and wavering in the bright water.

Under him, six or seven feet down, was a floor of perfectly clean, shining white sand, rippled firm and hard by the tides. Two grayish shapes steered there, like long, rounded pieces of wood or slate. They were fish. He saw them nose toward each other, poise motionless, make a dart forward, swerve off, and come

---

1. *Bonjour! . . . monsieur!* (bōn zhōōr . . . mə syö´): Babbling of commonly known French words: "Hello! Thank you! Goodbye! Sir, sir!"

The Diver, Dennis Angel

▲ **Critical Viewing** How do you think this diver feels? **[Speculate]**

around again. It was like a water dance. A few inches above them the water sparkled as if sequins were dropping through it. Fish again—myriads of minute fish, the length of his fingernail, were drifting through the water, and in a moment he could feel the innumerable tiny touches of them against his limbs. It was like swimming in flaked silver. The great rock the big boys had swum through rose sheer out of the white sand—black, tufted lightly with greenish weed. He could see no gap in it. He swam down to its base.

> This discovery will help you **predict** that upcoming plot events will be related to the tunnel.

Again and again he rose, took a big chestful of air, and went down. Again and again he groped over the surface of the rock, feeling it, almost hugging it in the desperate need to find the entrance. And then, once, while he was clinging to the black wall, his knees came up and he shot his feet out forward and they met no obstacle. He had found the hole.

He gained the surface, clambered about the stones that littered the barrier rock until he found a big one, and, with this in his arms, let himself down over the side of the rock. He dropped, with the weight, straight to the sandy floor. Clinging tight to the anchor of stone, he lay on his side and looked in under the dark shelf at the place where his feet had gone. He could see the hole. It was an irregular, dark gap; but he could not see deep into it. He let go of his anchor, clung with his hands to the edges of the hole, and tried to push himself in.

He got his head in, found his shoulders jammed, moved them in sidewise, and was inside as far as his waist. He could see nothing ahead. Something soft and clammy touched his mouth; he saw a dark <u>frond</u> moving against the grayish rock, and panic filled him. He thought of octopuses, of clinging weed. He pushed himself out backward and caught a glimpse, as he retreated, of a harmless tentacle of seaweed drifting in the mouth of the tunnel. But it was enough. He reached the sunlight, swam to shore, and lay on the diving rock. He looked down into the blue well of water. He knew he must find his way through that cave, or hole, or tunnel, and out the other side.

First, he thought, he must learn to control his breathing. He let himself down into the water with another big stone in his arms, so that he could lie effortlessly on the bottom of the sea. He counted. One, two, three. He counted steadily. He could hear the movement of blood in his chest. Fifty-one, fifty-two. . . . His chest was hurting. He let go of the rock and went up into the air. He saw that the sun was low. He rushed to the villa and found his mother at her supper. She said only "Did you enjoy yourself?" and he said "Yes."

All night the boy dreamed of the water-filled cave in the rock, and as soon as breakfast was

◆ **Build Vocabulary**

frond (fränd) *n.*: Leaflike shoot of seaweed

over he went to the bay.

That night, his nose bled badly. For hours he had been underwater, learning to hold his breath, and now he felt weak and dizzy. His mother said, "I shouldn't overdo things, darling, if I were you."

That day and the next, Jerry exercised his lungs as if everything, the whole of his life, all that he would become, depended upon it. Again his nose bled at night, and his mother insisted on his coming with her the next day. It was a torment to him to waste a day of his careful self-training, but he stayed with her on that other beach, which now seemed a place for small children, a place where his mother might lie safe in the sun. It was not his beach.

He did not ask for permission, on the following day, to go to his beach. He went, before his mother could consider the complicated rights and wrongs of the matter. A day's rest, he discovered, had improved his count by ten. The big boys had made the passage while he counted a hundred and sixty. He had been counting fast, in his fright. Probably now, if he tried, he could get through that long tunnel, but he was not going to try yet. A curious, most unchildlike persistence, a controlled impatience, made him wait. In the meantime, he lay underwater on the white sand, littered now by stones he had brought down from the upper air, and studied the entrance to the tunnel. He knew every jut and corner of it, as far as it was possible to see. It was as if he already felt its sharpness about his shoulders.

He sat by the clock in the villa, when his mother was not near, and checked his time. He was incredulous and then proud to find he could hold his breath without strain for two minutes. The words "two minutes," authorized by the clock, brought close the adventure that was so necessary to him.

In another four days, his mother said casually one morning, they must go home. On the day before they left, he would do it. He would do it if it killed him, he said defiantly to himself. But two days before they were to leave—a day of triumph when he increased his count by fifteen—his nose bled so badly that he turned dizzy and had to lie limply over the big rock like a bit of seaweed, watching the thick red blood flow onto the rock and trickle slowly down to the sea.

The next paragraph provides the answer to the **question** of whether or not Jerry will go through the tunnel.

He was frightened. Supposing he turned dizzy in the tunnel? Supposing he died there, trapped? Supposing—his head went around, in the hot sun, and he almost gave up. He thought he would return to the house and lie down, and next summer, perhaps, when he had another year's growth in him—*then* he would go through the hole.

But even after he had made the decision, or thought he had, he found himself sitting up on the rock and looking down into the water; and he knew that now, this moment, when his nose had only just stopped bleeding, when his head was still sore and throbbing—this was the moment when he would try. If he did not do it now, he never would. He was trembling with fear that he would not go; and he was trembling with horror at that long, long tunnel under the rock, under the sea. Even in the open sunlight, the barrier rock seemed very wide and very heavy; tons of rock pressed down on where he would go. If he died there, he would lie until one day—perhaps not before next year—those big boys would swim into it and find it blocked.

He put on his goggles, fitted them tight, tested the vacuum. His hands were shaking. Then he chose the biggest stone he could carry and slipped over the edge of the rock until half of him was in the cool, enclosing water and half in the hot sun. He looked up once at the empty sky, filled his lungs once, twice, and then sank fast to the bottom with the stone. He let it go and began to count. He took the edges of the hole in his hands and drew himself into it, wriggling his shoulders in sidewise as he remembered he must, kicking himself along with his feet.

Soon he was clear inside. He was in a small rockbound hole filled with yellowish-gray water. The water was pushing him up against the roof. The roof was sharp and pained his back.

He pulled himself along with his hands—fast, fast—and used his legs as levers. His head knocked against something; a sharp pain dizzied him. Fifty, fifty-one, fifty-two. . . . He was without light, and the water seemed to press upon him with the weight of rock. Seventy-one, seventy-two. . . . There was no strain on his lungs. He felt like an inflated balloon, his lungs were so light and easy, but his head was pulsing.

He was being continually pressed against the sharp roof, which felt slimy as well as sharp. Again he thought of octopuses, and wondered if the tunnel might be filled with weed that could tangle him. He gave himself a panicky, <u>convulsive</u> kick forward, ducked his head, and swam. His feet and hands moved freely, as if in open water. The hole must have widened out. He thought he must be swimming fast, and he was frightened of banging his head if the tunnel narrowed.

A hundred, a hundred and one. . . . The water paled. Victory filled him. His lungs were beginning to hurt. A few more strokes and he would be out. He was counting wildly; he said a hundred and fifteen, and then, a long time later, a hundred and fifteen again. The water was a clear jewel-green all around him. Then he saw, above his head, a crack running up through the rock. Sunlight was falling through it, showing the clean, dark rock of the tunnel, a single mussel shell, and darkness ahead.

He was at the end of what he could do. He looked up at the crack as if it were filled with air and not water, as if he could put his mouth to it to draw in air. A hundred and fifteen, he heard himself say inside his head—but he had

Coast Scene, Isles of Shoals, 1901, Childe Hassam, The Metropolitan Museum of Art

▲ **Critical Viewing** Does this picture make you think of Jerry's beach or his mother's? Explain. **[Compare and Contrast]**

said that long ago. He must go on into the blackness ahead, or he would drown. His head was swelling, his lungs cracking. A hundred and fifteen, a hundred and fifteen pounded through his head, and he feebly clutched at rocks in the dark, pulling himself forward, leaving the brief space of sunlit water behind. He felt he was dying. He was no longer quite conscious. He struggled on in the darkness between lapses into unconsciousness. An immense, swelling pain filled his head, and then the darkness cracked with an explosion of green light. His hands, groping forward, met nothing; and his feet, kicking back, propelled him out into the open sea.

He drifted to the surface, his face turned up

◆ **Build Vocabulary**

convulsive (kən vul′ siv) *adj.*: Marked by an involuntary muscular contraction

to the air. He was gasping like a fish. He felt he would sink now and drown; he could not swim the few feet back to the rock. Then he was clutching it and pulling himself up on to it. He lay face down, gasping. He could see nothing but a red-veined, clotted dark. His eyes must have burst, he thought; they were full of blood. He tore off his goggles and a <u>gout</u> of blood went into the sea. His nose was bleeding, and the blood had filled the goggles.

He scooped up handfuls of water from the cool, salty sea, to splash on his face, and did not know whether it was blood or salt water he tasted. After a time, his heart quieted, his eyes cleared, and he sat up. He could see the local boys diving and playing half a mile away. He did not want them. He wanted nothing but to get back home and lie down.

In a short while, Jerry swam to shore and climbed slowly up the path to the villa. He flung himself on his bed and slept, waking at the sound of feet on the path outside. His mother was coming back. He rushed to the bathroom, thinking she must not see his face with bloodstains, or tearstains, on it. He came out of the bathroom and met her as she walked into the villa, smiling, her eyes lighting up.

"Have a nice morning?" she asked, laying her hand on his warm brown shoulder a moment.

"Oh, yes, thank you," he said.

"You look a bit pale." And then, sharp and anxious, "How did you bang your head?"

"Oh, just banged it," he told her.

She looked at him closely. He was strained; his eyes were glazed-looking. She was worried. And then she said to herself, Oh, don't fuss! Nothing can happen. He can swim like a fish.

They sat down to lunch together.

"Mummy," he said, "I can stay under water for two minutes—three minutes, at least." It came bursting out of him.

"Can you, darling?" she said. "Well, I shouldn't overdo it. I don't think you ought to swim any more today."

She was ready for a battle of wills, but he gave in at once. It was no longer of the least importance to go to the bay.

◆ **Build Vocabulary**

gout (gout) *n.*: Spurt; splash; glob

Guide for Responding

◆ *Literature and Your Life*

Reader's Response Do you think Jerry's victory is worth the pain and risks entailed? Why or why not?

Thematic Focus How has Jerry changed as a result of his success?

Questions for Research Select a sport (such as scuba diving) and make a list of questions about the sport that could be researched. Discuss what resources you could use to research each question.

☑ Check Your Comprehension

1. What concerns does Jerry's mother have about raising him?
2. (a) Describe Jerry's encounter with the local boys. (b) What effect does it have on him?
3. How does Jerry prepare for his task?
4. Briefly summarize how Jerry finally swims through the tunnel.
5. What happens after Jerry passes the test he sets for himself?

*G*uide for Responding *(continued)*

◆ Critical Thinking

INTERPRET

1. (a) Describe Jerry's relationship with his mother at the beginning of the story. (b) How does it change by the story's end? Support your answer with examples. **[Analyze]**
2. What must Jerry prove to himself by swimming through the tunnel? **[Infer]**
3. At the end of the story, why is going to the bay "no longer of the least importance" to Jerry? **[Draw Conclusions]**

APPLY

4. Why do many young people set up situations in which they test themselves, as Jerry does? Give examples. **[Speculate]**

EXTEND

5. What jobs require people to meet physical challenges on a regular basis? What are the rewards of some of these jobs? **[Career Link]**

◆ Reading for Success

INTERACTIVE READING STRATEGIES

Review the reading strategies and notes showing how to read interactively. Then apply those strategies to answer the following questions.

1. What hints enable you to predict when Jerry will make his attempt?
2. What words help you form a mental image of Jerry's passage through the tunnel?
3. What does Jerry's experience with the tunnel tell you about the nature of growing up?

◆ Literary Focus

INTERNAL CONFLICT

A conflict involves a struggle between opposing forces. An **internal conflict** involves a character in conflict with himself. Jerry's internal conflict begins as he experiences "a craving that filled his whole body" to be one of the local boys who swim through the tunnel.

1. What are the two opposing forces in the internal conflict?
2. How does the physical challenge make the internal conflict more exciting?

◆ Build Vocabulary

USING THE LATIN ROOT *-lum-*

Knowing that the Latin root *-lum-* means light, define the *-lum-* words that appear in the following sentences.

1. The astronomer observed the *luminous* planet.
2. The torches *illuminate* the cave passage.
3. The scientist studied the *luminosity* of the star.
4. The great scientist is considered a *luminary* of our time.

USING THE WORD BANK: Synonyms

On your paper, write the word from the Word Bank that is the best synonym for each of the following words.

1. spurt
2. shining
3. ridges
4. remorse
5. leaf
6. begging
7. shaking violently

◆ Build Grammar Skills

PARTICIPIAL PHRASES

A **participial phrase** consists of a present or past participle (a verb form ending in *-ing*, *-ed*, or an irregular ending) and any other words that go with it. Participles function as adjectives.

Doris Lessing uses a variety of sentence elements to keep "Through the Tunnel" moving as swiftly as Jerry through the underwater cave. One element she uses frequently is the participial phrase.

Practice Copy the following sentences in your notebook. Underline each participial phrase and circle the noun it modifies. Each participial phrase begins with a present participle.

1. His mother walked on in front of him, carrying a bright striped bag.
2. Her other arm, swinging loose, was very white in the sun.
3. The boy came up, letting the air out of his lungs.
4. Walking down the path with her, he blurted out, "I'd like to go and have a look at those rocks."

*B*uild *Y*our *P*ortfolio

 ## Idea Bank

Writing

1. **Water Safety Rules** Jerry is lucky to have survived the dangers of his underwater challenge. Write a list of water safety rules that wiser swimmers should follow. **[Physical Education Link]**

2. **Letter** As Jerry, write a letter to one of your friends at home, describing your accomplishment. Describe your thoughts and feelings before, during, and after your swim.

3. **Observation** Jerry first wants to swim through the tunnel in order to win acceptance from the local boys. Using your own experience, write an observation showing how peer pressure affects people's actions and decisions.

Speaking, Listening, and Viewing

4. **Account of an Outdoor Adventure** Give an oral presentation about an outdoor adventure you have had or would like to experience. Use visuals or props to enliven your presentation.

5. **Dialogue** Imagine that another boy has discovered Jerry's plan and wants to talk him out of it. Role-play the dialogue that might take place between the two boys. **[Performing Arts Link]**

Researching and Representing

6. **Collage** Doris Lessing uses vivid words to describe the setting of this story. Create your own vivid image of the setting in the form of a collage. Incorporate a variety of artistic media and found objects, such as sand, fabric, and shells. **[Art Link]**

7. **Movie Score** Use songs you know to create a musical score for a film version of this story. Choose different songs for different scenes. Play your choices for the class. **[Music Link]**

Online Activity www.phlit.phschool.com

 ## Guided Writing Lesson

Travel Brochure

Choose a vacation place that you have visited or would like to visit and write a travel brochure about it. Packing a lot of information into a small space, use descriptions and colorful images to attract tourists. Provide specific details about things to do and sights to see. The following tip will help you convince readers that your destination is a worthwhile place to visit.

Writing Skills Focus: Persuasive Tone

Persuasive essays use a **persuasive tone**—they take a positive attitude toward the ideas and actions they want readers to accept. Here's how you can achieve a persuasive tone:

- Use words that appeal to readers' senses: *soft, tropical breezes.*
- Convey your own enthusiasm for activities: *a fun-filled afternoon of shopping.*
- Stress the benefits of a place or a plan: *For only a few dollars more, you can . . .*

Prewriting Consider what your readers may desire in a travel destination. Depending on the place you choose, you may want to highlight physical beauty, comfort, historical interest, or activities.

Drafting As you write, introduce your main points with phrases that create appealing images ("Leave the world behind . . .") or compelling reasons ("It's worth an extra day just to . . ."). Don't expect your readers to accept your claims at face value. Support each point you make with details and examples.

Revising Ask a partner to read your brochure to see if he or she would like to visit the place you describe. If not, add descriptions or details that would help persuade your partner to visit the place.

PART 1 *Personal Challenges*

Indian Miniature of Akbar Period, Art Resource, N.Y.

Focus on Culture

India

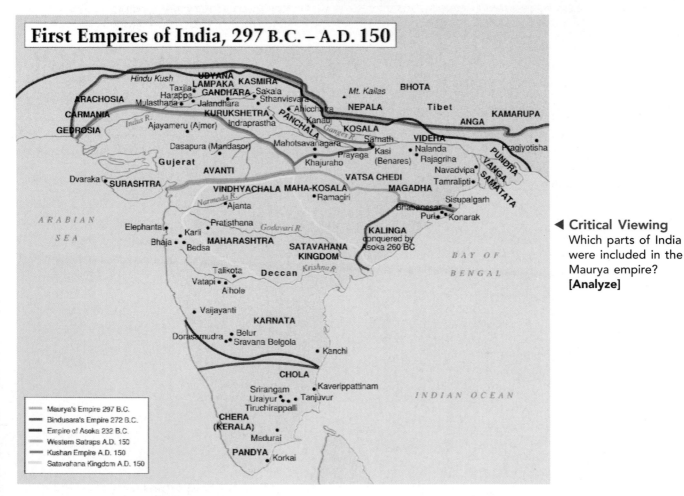

First Empires of India, 297 B.C. – A.D. 150

Maurya's Empire 297 B.C.
Bindusara's Empire 272 B.C.
Empire of Asoka 232 B.C.
Western Satraps A.D. 150
Kushan Empire A.D. 150
Satavahana Kingdom A.D. 150

◀ **Critical Viewing**
Which parts of India were included in the Maurya empire? **[Analyze]**

Every year, crowds gather in a town in the south of India. A reporter described visitors lining up at the beach overlooking the Indian Ocean: "They were dressed with surprising formality, many of the men wearing ties and the women fine [garments] which streamed and snapped in the wind." The people had come to see a long-awaited annual event: The first signs of the summer rains, or monsoons.

At last, their vigil was rewarded. "Thunder boomed. Lightning went zapping into the sea. . . . 'The rains!' everybody sang. The wind struck us with a force that made our line bend and waver. Everyone shrieked and grabbed at each other. . . . The deluge began."

India is home to one of the world's oldest cultures. The region has seen revolutionary changes. Yet today, as in the past, the coming of the monsoon rains holds special significance.

GEOGRAPHIC SETTING

The modern nation of India has existed since 1947. Through most of history, though, the term India has been used to describe the entire subcontinent that is also called South Asia.

A Vast Subcontinent South Asia is a triangular peninsula jutting southward from Asia. The region is bounded on the north by the towering Himalaya and Hindu Kush mountains. The rest of the subcontinent is surrounded by the Arabian Sea to the west, the Indian Ocean to the south, and the Bay of Bengal to the east. These bodies of water set South Asia apart from other regions, but they have also served as highways linking India to other parts of the world.

Today, eight independent nations occupy South Asia. India is by far the largest. The region also includes Pakistan, Bangladesh, Nepal, Bhutan, and the island nations of Sri Lanka and the Maldives. Culturally, South Asia is highly diverse. India alone has more than 700 languages and regional dialects.

Climate The climate of South Asia is dominated by the monsoon, a seasonal wind. In late May or early June, the wet monsoon of summer brings moist air from the sea to the land. In October, the dry monsoon winds of winter blow back toward the sea.

HISTORY

The earliest Indian civilization arose about 2500 B.C. in the fertile valley of the Indus River. Archaeological evidence points to a highly organized government. The ruins of the cities of Harappa and Mohenjo-Daro show signs of well-planned streets, a uniform building code, and an extensive public water supply system.

Vishnu Seated on the Snake Shesha Surrounded by Dieties, The Granger Collection, New York

▲ Critical Viewing This painting shows the god Vishnu surrounded by a symbolic flame. Why does religious art often use symbolism? **[Analyze]**

By 1500 B.C., the Indus civilization had vanished. Around that time, Aryan invaders swept into India through passes in the Hindu Kush mountains. Gradually, these nomads settled the northern plains. Over time, Aryan religious beliefs developed into Hinduism.

Two Religions Unlike most major world religions, Hinduism has no founder or formal church. Its chief gods are Brahma, the creator; Vishnu, the preserver (see the picture above); and Siva, the destroyer. The idea of reincarnation, the rebirth of the soul in various forms, is central to Hinduism. It is linked to karma, the belief that each deed performed in this life will affect a soul's fate in a future life.

In the sixth century, B.C., a second major religion, Buddhism, also emerged in India. The Hindu reformer Siddhartha Gautama (sid där´ tə gout´ ə mə)—known as the *Buddha*, or "Enlightened One"—taught that desire was the root of all human suffering. Although Buddhism eventually died out in India, it became the chief religion of most of Southeast and East Asia.

Powerful Empires Over many centuries, a series of powerful empires rose and fell in India. (See the map on p. 364). The first was the Maurya (mō´ ʉr yə) dynasty, which ruled much of the subcontinent from about 321 B.C. to 185 B.C.

India enjoyed a golden age during the Gupta empire (A.D. 320–535). Under the Guptas, trade expanded and the arts flourished. Gupta mathematicians developed the decimal system and the concept of zero.

In 1526, a Mongol army invaded India. Its leader, Babur (bä´ bʉr), founded the Mughal empire, which ruled India for more than 300 years. Under the Mughals, Islamic civilization reached its height in India. Its greatest monument is the Taj Mahal (täzh mə häl), the fabulous tomb of a Mughal ruler's wife. (See the picture on p. 367.) At the same time, clashes arose between the ruling Muslims and India's Hindu majority. Although the brilliant Mughal emperor Akbar promoted religious toleration, his successors followed harsher policies.

British Rule In 1498, the Portuguese explorer Vasco da Gama reached India by sailing around Africa. It was a turning point in Indian history. As the Mughal empire declined, European powers began to compete for power and influence. Slowly, Britain came to dominate most of India. In 1858, the British government declared India a colony.

The British considered India the "jewel in the crown"—the richest part of their global empire. A growing number of Indians, however, resented British rule. In 1885, the Indian National Congress (INC) was formed. Ironically, its members were mostly Hindus who had been educated by the British to help rule the empire. Another group, the Muslim League, also emerged to protest British rule.

Independence By the 1920's, the INC was calling for complete independence. Nationalist leader Mohandas Gandhi promoted civil disobedience, or nonviolent resistance, to British rule. He supported strikes and called on all Indians to boycott British-made goods. Although Gandhi was arrested many times, he continued to gain support.

Finally, in 1947, Britain granted India its independence. At the same time, widespread distrust led to violence between Hindus and Muslims. As a result, Britain partitioned the subcontinent into two separate nations: Hindu India and Muslim Pakistan. (East Pakistan later broke away from Pakistan and became Bangladesh.)

SOCIETY AND CULTURE

Today, as in the past, Hinduism continues to shape Indian life. They are closely linked to the caste system, a strict social order.

The Caste System Since ancient times, Indians believed that every person was born into a certain caste and remained a member of that caste for life. Over time, thousands of castes and sub-castes developed, each with its own jobs, duties, and rules of behavior. At the top stood the Brahmans, who were considered the purest members of society. At the very bottom were the untouchables, who were considered so impure they could not even draw water from the village well.

Through most of history, Indians at all levels accepted the caste system. In modern times, leaders such as Gandhi have condemned the harsh treatment of the lower castes. Recent laws have tried to weaken caste restrictions. Still, such laws have little effect on deeply rooted attitudes.

Village and Family Traditionally, Indians identified first with their family, then with their village. The traditional family was patriarchal, with authority residing in the oldest male. The head of the family arranged marriages to benefit or protect the family. Often, families arranged marriages for children at an early age.

Each village was generally self-sufficient, producing most of what it needed. A variety of castes performed all jobs necessary for daily life. Today, most villages continue to follow traditional ways. Only about half have electricity and few have running water. Many farmers still plant crops by hand and use ox-drawn plows.

Modern Life Still, rapid modernization and urbanization have weakened many Indian traditions. Millions of people have left villages to look for work in huge cities like Calcutta and Bombay. There, many live in shocking poverty in crowded urban slums.

Among upper-class city dwellers, parents continue to arrange most marriages. Young couples, though, often meet before the wedding. They may even have the freedom to reject their parents' choice.

ARTS AND LITERATURE

Across India, both Hindus and Buddhists carved huge temples into hillsides. At Ellora, Hindu workers built an immense temple 96 feet high by chiseling from the top of a hill down to its base.

Sculpture Sculptors decorated temples with rich carvings. Through these carvings, people learned Hindu stories and traditions.

Many sculptures depict Hindu gods in traditional poses. The god Siva, for example, is often shown with four hands. One hand holds a drum representing creation. Another holds fire, a symbol of destruction. A third hand is raised to carry the message "Fear not." With the fourth, Siva points to an evil demon that he is crushing underfoot. (Symbolic poses and movements like these also influenced the development of Indian classical dance.)

Classical Literature The classical epics of Indian literature also contain many Hindu ideas. In some 100,000 verses, the *Mahabharata* (mə hä´ bä´ rä tə) tells the story of a long battle between two branches of a royal family. The *Ramayana* (rä mä´ yə nə) is about the efforts of the prince Rama to recover his kidnapped wife Sita. (See page 1036.) Though thousands of years old, these epics continue to be popular, even in television reenactments.

Later classics include the *Panchatantra*, a collection of stories, many of them humorous fables featuring animal characters. (See page 378.)

Modern Literature India's most respected modern writer was Rabindranath Tagore (rə bēn´ drə nät´ tə gôr´). He wrote poems, short stories, essays, fables, and plays in both English and Bengali. (See page 386.) In 1913, Tagore became the first Asian writer to win the Nobel Prize for Literature.

Many Indian writers give realistic pictures of contemporary life. The novels of R. K. Narayan often deal with the clash of traditional and modern ways in a fictional village. (See page 398.)

ACTIVITY
GIVING A NEWS REPORT

Search the Internet for a current newspaper from India. Find an article or editorial that interests you. Then, use the article as the basis for a television news report. Include a commentary on what the article shows about life in India today. 🖎

▲ **Critical Viewing** The Taj Mahal shows the influence of Muslim art in Mughal India. Why do you think the Taj Mahal is one of the most admired buildings in the world? **[Connect]**

Guide for Reading

The Panchatantra

People today write all sorts of "how-to" books that instruct readers on how to learn, build, or repair all kinds of things. Ancient India also had a famous "how-to" book, a collection of tales that taught young princes how to rule a kingdom and conduct their lives.

No one can date this collection with any certainty. Oral versions of some of its tales may date back as far as the fifth century B.C., but they were not collected until much later. According to legend, twelve books of tales were gathered, but seven were lost. The remaining five are called the *Panchatantra* (pän´ chə tän´ trə), which in the Sanskrit language of ancient India means "Five Books."

A Much-Traveled Work The earliest Sanskrit manuscripts of the *Panchatantra* have not survived. In the sixth century A.D., a physician visiting India discovered the five books and had them translated into his native Pahlavi, a language of ancient Iran. This famous translation is also lost, but it inspired other translations throughout the Middle East, which are among the world's oldest-surviving manuscripts. From the Middle East, the tales entered Greece and eventually the rest of Europe, some of them traveling all the way to Iceland. The stories also traveled in the other direction, influencing Asian literature as far east as the Pacific island of Java.

A Mysterious Storyteller Although no single person composed the tales of the *Panchatantra*, some surviving versions attribute the collection to a Bidpai, or Pilpay, a name that simply means "king's favorite." Another early manuscript identifies the storyteller as a Brahman named Vishnusharman, a name that indicates devotion to the Hindu god Vishnu. It is this version, one of the oldest surviving Sanskrit versions, that Arthur W. Ryder turned to when making his famous translation.

Arthur W. Ryder *(1877–1938)*

"Ten men like him would make a civilization." Such was the praise a colleague gave to the brilliant Sanskrit scholar Arthur W. Ryder. The first professor of Sanskrit at the University of California at Berkeley, Ryder completed his translation of the *Panchatantra* in 1924.

◆ Build Vocabulary

LATIN SUFFIXES: *-ance*

In one tale in the *Panchatantra*, elephants seek "a means of deliverance" from a deadly trap. *Deliverance* is formed by adding the suffix *-ance*, meaning "the action of," to *deliver*, which can mean "to rescue." *Deliverance* means "the action of rescuing."

A noun-forming suffix, *-ance* can also mean "a thing that." For example, the Word Bank also contains *hindrance*, "a thing that blocks; an obstruction."

retinue
lumbering
deliverance
fettered
acute
hindrance
hubbub

WORD BANK

As you read the tales from the *Panchatantra*, you will encounter these words. Each word is defined on the page where it appears. Preview the list before you read.

◆ Build Grammar Skills

ADJECTIVE CLAUSES

Ryder's translation of the *Panchatantra* uses many **adjective clauses**—groups of words that contain a subject and a verb, modify a noun or a pronoun, and usually begin with *who, whom, whose, that,* or *which*.

In the following sentence, Ryder adds more information about the mice by using the adjective clause *who were old settlers there:*

So the mice, who were old settlers there, occupied the chinks in the floors . . .

Look for other adjective clauses as you read the two stories from the *Panchatantra*. Notice how the adjective clauses add information about nouns or pronouns.

from the Panchatantra

◆ Literature and Your Life

CONNECT YOUR EXPERIENCE

Do you remember the tale of the bored farm boy who kept crying "Wolf!" when there was no wolf? Then, when a hungry wolf actually did appear, no one believed his warning. The *Panchatantra* collects simple stories like that, stories designed to teach you important lessons about life.

Journal Writing Think of childhood stories you heard or read that were designed to guide your behavior. Then, sum up one such tale and the lesson it tried to teach.

THEMATIC FOCUS: PERSONAL CHALLENGES

As you read these tales, ask yourself: What challenges do the characters face?

◆ Background for Understanding

LITERATURE

In the opening of the *Panchatantra,* we learn that the king of a certain southern city is dissatisfied with his three sons. He wants them to know "the wise conduct of life," but instead he considers them "blockheads."

One of his counselors advises him to entrust the princes to Vishnusharman, a Brahman "with a reputation for competence in numerous sciences." The king agrees. Vishnusharman then proceeds to teach the boys the stories of the *Panchatantra,* or Five Books.

◆ Literary Focus

INDIAN FABLES

A **fable** is a brief, simple tale that teaches a lesson about human conduct. Fables often feature animal characters. Whether the characters are human or not, they *behave* like human beings, and their experiences in the fable point to a lesson about human behavior called a **moral.** The moral may be stated directly or merely implied.

As you will see from these tales, the characters in the *Panchatantra* include all sorts of animals found in India—elephants, tigers, jackals, mongooses, and so on—as well as human characters and sometimes supernatural ones, like ghosts and monsters.

As you read, consider the moral each fable teaches. How would you state that moral in a sentence?

◆ Reading Strategy

PREDICT

You will often appreciate a story more if you try to **predict,** or make educated guesses, about what will happen later in the work. Making predictions will help focus your interest: Once you make a prediction, you will want to keep reading to see if that prediction turns out to be correct.

As you read the two stories from the *Panchatantra,* look for hints in each story that seem to suggest a certain outcome. Ask yourself, "What will probably happen next?" and "What will probably happen in the end?"

Jot down your predictions on a chart like the one below. Then keep reading to see if your predictions come true.

"The Mice That Set Elephants Free"	
Prediction	Actual Outcome

"The Brahman, the Thief, and the Ghost"	
Prediction	Actual Outcome

from the Panchatantra

The Mice That Set Elephants Free

Vishnusharman
Translated by Arthur W. Ryder

There once was a region where people, houses, and temples had fallen into decay. So the mice, who were old settlers there, occupied the chinks in the floors of stately dwellings with sons, grandsons (both in the male and female line), and further descendants as they were born, until their holes formed a dense tangle. They found uncommon happiness in a variety of festivals, dramatic performances (with plots of their own invention), wedding-feasts, eating-parties, drinking-bouts, and similar diversions. And so the time passed.

But into this scene burst an elephant-king, whose <u>retinue</u> numbered thousands. He, with his herd, had started for the lake upon information that there was water there. As he marched through the mouse community, he crushed faces, eyes, heads, and necks of such mice as he encountered.

Then the survivors held a convention. "We are being killed," they said, "by these <u>lumbering</u> elephants —curse them! If they come this way again, there will not be mice enough for seed.[1] Besides:

> An elephant will kill you, if
> He touch; a serpent if he sniff;
> King's laughter has a deadly sting;
> A rascal kills by honoring.

Therefore let us devise a remedy effective in this crisis."

When they had done so, a certain number went to the lake, bowed before the elephant-king, and said respectfully: "O king, not far from here is our community, inherited from a long line of ancestors. There we have prospered through a long succession of sons and grandsons. Now you gentlemen, while coming here to water, have destroyed us by the thousand. Furthermore, if you travel that way again, there will not be enough of us for seed. If then you feel compassion toward us, pray travel another path. Consider the fact that even creatures of our size will some day prove of some service."

And the elephant-king turned over in his mind what he had heard, decided that the statement of the mice was entirely logical, and granted their request.

---

1. **seed:** Descendants; posterity.

Akbar Inspecting the Wild Elephant Captured From the Herd Near Malwa,
From the "Akbarnama," Victoria and Albert Museum

◀ **Critical Viewing**
What does this picture
suggest about the way
in which elephants were
trapped or restrained?
[Connect]

Now in the course of time a certain king commanded his elephant-trappers to trap elephants. And they constructed a so-called water-trap, caught the king with his herd, three days later dragged him out with a great tackle made of ropes and things, and tied him to stout trees in that very bit of forest.

When the trappers had gone, the elephant-king reflected thus: "In what manner, or through whose assistance, shall I be delivered?" Then it occurred to him: "We have no means of <u>deliverance</u> except those mice."

So the king sent the mice an exact description of his disastrous position in the trap through one of his personal retinue, an elephant-cow[2] who had not ventured into the trap, and who had previous information of the mouse community.

When the mice learned the matter, they gathered by the thousand, eager to return the favor shown them, and visited the elephant herd. And seeing king and herd <u>fettered</u>, they gnawed the guy-ropes[3] where they stood, then swarmed up the branches, and by cutting the ropes aloft, set their friends free.

---

2. elephant-cow: Female adult elephant.
3. guy-ropes: Ropes used to steady, secure, or guide something.

from the *Panchatantra* ◆ *371*

from the Panchatantra

The Brahman, the Thief, and the Ghost

Vishnusharman
Translated by Arthur W. Ryder

There was once a poor Brahman[1] in a certain place. He lived on presents, and always did without such luxuries as fine clothes and ointments and perfumes and garlands and gems and betel-gum.[2] His beard and his nails were long, and so was the hair that covered his head and his body. Heat, cold, rain, and the like had dried him up.

Then someone pitied him and gave him two calves. And the Brahman began when they were little and fed them on butter and oil and fodder[3] and other things that he begged. So he made them very plump.

Then a thief saw them and the idea came to him at once: "I will steal these two cows from this Brahman." So he took a rope and set out at night. But on the way he met a fellow with a row of sharp teeth set far apart, with a high-bridged nose and uneven eyes, with limbs covered with knotty muscles, with hollow cheeks, with beard and body as yellow as a fire with much butter in it.

◆ **Reading Strategy**
Do you think the thief will succeed? Why or why not?

And when the thief saw him, he started with <u>acute</u> fear and said: "Who are you, sir?"

The other said: "I am a ghost named Truthful. It is now your turn to explain yourself."

The thief said: "I am a thief, and my acts are cruel. I am on my way to steal two cows from a poor Brahman."

---

1. **Brahman** (brä´ mən) *n.*: In Hindu culture, a member of the highest caste, or class—that of priests—though not necessarily a member of the highest economic class.
2. **betel-gum** (bēt´l gum) *n.*: Reddish chewing gum made from the nuts and leaves of betel palm trees. This gum is chewed by many people in Asian and Pacific cultures for pleasure, and as a digestive aid.
3. **fodder** (fäd´ ər) *n.*: Coarse food, such as cornstalks and hay, used to feed cows and other livestock.

Then the ghost felt relieved and said: "My dear sir, I take one meal every three days. So I will just eat this Brahman today. It is delightful that you and I are on the same errand."

So together they went there and hid, waiting for the proper moment. And when the Brahman went to sleep, the ghost started forward to eat him. But the thief saw him and said: "My dear sir, this is not right. You are not to eat the Brahman until I have stolen his two cows."

The ghost said: "The racket would most likely wake the Brahman. In that case all my trouble would be in vain."

"But, on the other hand," said the thief, "if any hindrance arises when you start to eat him, then I cannot steal the two cows either. First I will steal the two cows, then you may eat the Brahman."

So they disputed, each crying "Me first! Me first!" And when they became heated, the hubbub waked the Brahman. Then the thief said: "Brahman, this is a ghost who wishes to eat you." And the ghost said: "Brahman, this is a thief who wishes to steal your two cows."

When the Brahman heard this, he stood up and took a good look. And by remembering a prayer to his favorite god, he saved his life from the ghost, then lifted a club and saved his two cows from the thief.

◆ **Build Vocabulary**
acute (ə kyo͞ot´) *adj.:* Sharp
hindrance (hin´drəns) *n.:* An obstacle
hubbub (hu´ bub) *n.:* Noise; commotion

Guide for Responding

◆ Literature and Your Life

Reader's Response What did you think of the endings of these tales? Why?

Thematic Focus What different challenges do the mice and the elephants face in "The Mice That Set Elephants Free"?

Questions for Research The stories in the *Panchatantra* supposedly aim to teach proper behavior to Indian princes. Write one or more questions you could research to learn more about how ancient India was governed.

✓ Check Your Comprehension

1. In "The Mice That Set Elephants Free," what favor did the mice ask of the elephants?
2. What do the mice do to return the favor?
3. In "The Brahman, the Thief, and the Ghost," what do the thief and the ghost each intend to do?
4. How does the Brahman escape harm?

◆ Critical Thinking

INTERPRET
1. What lessons about life do the mice and the elephants learn in "The Mice That Set Elephants Free"? **[Interpret]**
2. In "The Brahman, the Thief, and the Ghost," how is the Brahman different from the other two characters? **[Compare and Contrast]**

EVALUATE
3. In "The Mice That Set Elephants Free," do you think the elephants meant to harm the mice in the first place? Explain your opinion. **[Assess]**

APPLY
4. What kinds of human beings might the mice and the elephants represent today? **[Generalize]**

COMPARE LITERARY WORKS
5. Compare this fable to others you know, such as the fables of Aesop. What is similar and different about the characters and the lessons that the fables teach? **[Compare and Contrast]**

from the *Panchatantra* ◆ 373

Guide for Responding (continued)

◆ Reading Strategy

PREDICT

In asking the elephants to travel a different path, the mice in the first fable tell the elephants: "Consider the fact that even creatures of our size will some day prove of some service." This comment is a clue that can help you **predict**, or make an educated guess, about what will happen later in the tale.

1. Identify at least one more clue that points to the outcome of "The Mice That Set Elephants Free," and explain how it helps you predict the outcome.
2. Were you able to predict the outcome of "The Brahman, the Thief, and the Ghost"? If so, which details helped you predict the ending? Why?

◆ Literary Focus

INDIAN FABLES

The stories from the *Panchatantra* are examples of **fables**—brief, simple tales that each teach a lesson about human behavior. Supposedly aimed at teaching proper conduct to young Indian princes, the fables in the *Panchatantra* convey their lessons to anyone who reads or hears them. The lesson about human conduct that a fable conveys is called a **moral.**

In some fables, the moral is stated in a single sentence at the end. In others—including the two you just read from the *Panchatantra*—the morals are not stated but instead are implied, or suggested, by the story details.

Consider these details in "The Mice That Set Elephants Free": A group of elephants kindly agree to stop trampling on some mice. In return, when the elephants are trapped and their own lives are in danger, the mice save them. The general message from these details suggests the following moral: It often pays to be kind to those who seem weak and insignificant.

1. How would you state the moral of "The Brahman, the Thief, and the Ghost"? Explain how the details of the fable point to this moral.
2. Consider the lessons of both fables. How, in particular, might they be helpful to princes or other political leaders?

◆ Build Vocabulary

USING THE LATIN SUFFIX -ance

Knowing that the suffix *-ance* can mean "the action of" or "a thing that," write definitions for these words:

1. continuance   2. performance   3. utterance

USING THE WORD BANK: Antonyms

On your paper, write the letter of the word that is the antonym—opposite in meaning—to the first word:

1. acute: (a) hideous, (b) clever, (c) dull
2. deliverance: (a) joy, (b) suffering, (c) message
3. fettered: (a) unchained, (b) unnoticed, (c) unclean
4. hindrance: (a) help, (b) blunder, (c) cause
5. hubbub: (a) quiet, (b) clatter, (c) interior
6. lumbering: (a) enjoying, (b) cutting, (c) tiptoeing
7. retinue: (a) attendant, (b) leader, (c) cornea

◆ Build Grammar Skills

ADJECTIVE CLAUSES

An **adjective clause** is a group of words that contains a subject and a verb, modifies a noun or a pronoun, and usually begins with the word *who, whom, whose, that,* or *which.*

In the following sentence, the adjective clause *that mice set free,* which contains the subject *mice* and the verb *set,* modifies the noun *elephants.*

The fable tells about elephants *that mice set free.*

Practice Identify the adjective clauses in the following sentences, the subject and verb in each clause, and the noun or pronoun that each clause modifies.

1. Into the scene burst the king, whose retinue numbered thousands.
2. The king sent the mice information through someone who had not ventured into the trap.
3. The Brahman fed the calves on butter and oil and fodder and other things that he begged.
4. The thief said, "Brahman, this is a ghost who will eat you."
5. When the Brahman heard that, he spoke a prayer that saved his life.

Build Your Portfolio

Idea Bank

Writing

1. **Five Morals** Write five statements about human behavior that you think would be able to serve as the morals of five different fables.

2. **Police Report** Imagine that you are the police officer called to the scene at the end of "The Brahman, the Thief, and the Ghost." Write a brief police report providing details about the attempted crime and its outcome. **[Career Link]**

3. **Fable Update** Rewrite either fable for an audience of modern American children. Keep the basic plot and teach the same moral, but change the details to suit a contemporary American audience.

Speaking, Listening, and Viewing

4. **Group Discussion** With a group of classmates, discuss the best theme under which to classify each tale. Examples of themes in the *Panchatantra*: Loss of Friends, Winning of Friends, War and Peace, Loss of Gains, and Ill-Considered Action.

5. **Oral Retelling** Pretend that you are Vishnusharman telling one of the fables to the three young sons of the king. Retell the story aloud as you might tell it to an audience of youngsters. **[Performing Arts Link]**

Researching and Representing

6. **Cover Illustration** Create a cover illustration for a new edition of the *Panchatantra*. Incorporate details from both fables into your cover art. **[Art Link]**

7. **Research and Summary** Using library resources or the Internet, obtain and read at least two more fables from the *Panchatantra*. Sum up each fable, and indicate its moral. **[Media Link]**

Online Activity www.phlit.phschool.com

Guided Writing Lesson

Animal Fable

Basing your work on what you have learned about fables, write a brief fable of your own. In it, use animal characters to teach a lesson about human behavior. Spell that lesson out at the end of the fable by including a moral that flows logically from the events you narrate.

**Writing Skills Focus:
Clear Purpose and Moral**

Your main purpose in telling a fable is to convey a particular **moral** or lesson about human behavior. Here is a checklist for conveying your moral effectively:

- Are my characters related to the qualities treated in my moral? For example, if my moral is about greed, is at least one of my characters greedy?

- Does the outcome of my fable illustrate my moral? For example, if my moral says that greed is bad, does the greedy behavior in my fable have a bad outcome?

- If the moral is stated within my fable, is the statement brief and clear?

Prewriting Make a list of proverbs or sayings that offer rules or observations about human behavior. Then, choose one as a moral of your fable. Jot down ideas for animal characters and a plot related to your moral.

Drafting Write a fable based on your rough outline. Keep your moral in mind as you write, and try to choose details that help point to it.

Revising Reread your fable to make sure that the details point to the moral and that you have enough details to make the moral clear. Use adjective clauses to add more details. For more on adjective clauses, see pp. 368 and 374.

Guide for Reading

Rabindranath Tagore
(1861–1941)

Rabindranath Tagore spent his life fighting for India's independence—but his weapon was a pen, not a sword or a gun. Six years after his death, Tagore's dream came true: India won its independence.

A Man of Many Talents

Tagore was a very diverse man. He was a poet, short-story writer, novelist, playwright, philosopher, and an accomplished painter and composer. He composed more than 2,000 songs, including India's national anthem.

A Man of Principles
Tagore was deeply disturbed by the poverty and other hardships faced by millions of Indians. He was also troubled by the British army's use of force to suppress any type of protest by the Indian people. (Britain ruled India at the time.) He took action in response to the problems he saw.

Tagore turned down a knighthood as a protest against the injustices of British rule in India.

Although Tagore died in 1941 at the age of 80, his work continues to grow in popularity throughout the world. In honor of his work as a writer, Tagore received the Nobel Prize for Literature in 1913. He was the first Indian to win this award.

◆ Build Vocabulary

LATIN WORD ROOTS: -jud-
In this selection, you will encounter the word *judicious*. The Latin word root *-jud-*, which means "judge," gives you a clue that *judicious* means "showing good judgment," or "common sense."

precarious
impending
judicious
euphemism
imploring
fettered
sordid
pervaded

WORD BANK
As you read "The Cabuliwallah," you will encounter the words on this list. Each word is defined on the page where it first appears. Preview the list before you read. With a partner, explain the meanings of any words you think you already know.

◆ Build Grammar Skills

PRONOUN AND ANTECEDENT AGREEMENT
Pronouns help writers avoid repeating the same nouns over and over. For a pronoun to make sense, however, it must **agree** with its **antecedent** (the noun or pronoun it replaces) in **number** (singular or plural) and **gender** (masculine, feminine, or neuter).

Notice the pronouns in these examples:

. . . the two *friends* so far apart in age would subside into *their* old language and *their* old jokes . . .

(The plural pronoun *their* refers to the plural antecedent *friends*.)

I cannot tell what my *daughter's* feelings were at the sight of this *man*, but *she* began to call *him* loudly.

(The singular feminine pronoun *she* refers to the singular feminine noun *daughter*; the singular masculine pronoun *him* refers to the singular masculine noun *man*.)

The Cabuliwallah

◆ *Literature and Your Life*

CONNECT YOUR EXPERIENCE

Your memory records people from your past like snapshots in a scrapbook. When you don't see or hear from someone for a long time, that person becomes "frozen" on the film of your memory. A childhood friend who moved away remains five years old in your mind, although he or she would be attending high school now.

The main character in this story experiences a conflict created by such a "time freeze."

Journal Writing Describe someone you used to know who is "frozen" on the film of your memory. What do you think that person is like now?

THEMATIC FOCUS: STRUGGLING FOR JUSTICE

In this story, clashing forces send a man to prison, separating him from his family and friends for eight years. You may find yourself questioning whether his punishment fits his crime.

◆ Background for Understanding

CULTURE

The Cabuliwallah in this story is a kind of traveling salesman. The Indian word *wallah* means "salesman"; the *Cabuli*wallah is the "salesman from Cabul" (Kabul, the capital of Afghanistan).

People travel from their homes to live and work temporarily in other countries for a variety of reasons. Frequently, these "guest workers" come to a country with greater economic opportunities, working hard and living poorly so they can send money to loved ones at home. The Cabuliwallah travels from Afghanistan to India, returning home once a year to visit his wife and daughter.

◆ Literary Focus

RELATIONSHIPS BETWEEN CHARACTERS

You can learn a lot about a person by the company he or she keeps. Similarly, in a short story you can learn a lot by examining the **relationships between characters**—the interactions and feelings that pass between the people in the story. For instance, in "The Cabuliwallah" a little girl grows up and grows away from her childhood friend who has been gone for eight years. The changes in the way she responds to him reveal important changes in her character.

◆ Reading Strategy

ENGAGE YOUR SENSES

People say "a picture is worth a thousand words," but pictures show you only how something looks. You can't *hear* a picture of a bell or *taste* a picture of an orange. When you read a short story, **engage your senses**—use the details of sight, sound, taste, smell, and touch to fully experience the richness of the characters and the setting. For example, when Tagore describes the sound of his daughter's laughter and the feel of sunshine on his face, draw on your own memories to try to experience these sensations yourself.

Use a sensory details chart to record the variety of sensory details that bring this story to life.

Sight	Sound	Touch	Taste	Smell
	Daughter's laughter	Sunshine on his face		

The Cabuliwallah

Rabindranath Tagore

Translated From the Bengali Language

Mini, my five-year-old daughter, cannot live without chattering. I really believe that in all her life she has not wasted one minute in silence. Her mother is often vexed at this and would stop her prattle, but I do not. To see Mini quiet is unnatural, and I cannot bear it for long. Because of this, our conversations are always lively.

One morning, for instance, when I was in the midst of the seventeenth chapter of my new novel, Mini stole into the room and, putting her hand into mine, said: "Father! Ramdayal the doorkeeper calls a crow a krow! He doesn't know anything, does he?"

Before I could explain the language differences in this country, she was on the trace of another subject. "What do you think, Father? Shola says there is an elephant in the clouds, blowing water out of his trunk, and that is why it rains!"

The child had seated herself at my feet near the table and was playing softly, drumming on her knees. I was hard at work on my seventeenth chapter, where Pratap Singh, the hero, had just caught Kanchanlata, the heroine, in his arms and was about to escape with her by the third-story window of the castle, when all of a sudden Mini left her play and ran to the window, crying "A Cabuliwallah! a Cabuliwallah!" Sure enough, in the street below was a Cabuliwallah passing slowly along. He wore the loose, soiled clothing of his people, and a tall turban; there was a bag on his back, and he carried boxes of grapes in his hand.

I cannot tell what my daughter's feelings were at the sight of this man, but she began to call him loudly. Ah, I thought, he will come in, and my seventeenth chapter will never be finished!

Critical Viewing How does this market scene reflect the mood at ▶ the beginning of "The Cabuliwallah"? **[Connect]**

At this exact moment the Cabuliwallah turned and looked up at the child. When she saw this, she was overcome by terror, fled to her mother's protection, and disappeared. She had a blind belief that inside the bag which the big man carried were two or three children like herself. Meanwhile, the peddler entered my doorway and greeted me with a smiling face.

So precarious was the position of my hero and my heroine that my first impulse was to stop and buy something, especially since Mini had called to the man. I made some small purchases, and a conversation began about Abdurrahman, the Russians, the English, and the frontier policy.[1]

As he was about to leave, he asked: "And where is the little girl, sir?"

I, thinking that Mini must get rid of her false fear, had her brought out. She stood by my chair, watching the Cabuliwallah and his bag. He offered her nuts and raisins, but she would not be tempted and only clung closer to me, with all her doubts increased. This was their first meeting.

One morning, however, not many days later, as I was leaving the house, I was startled to find Mini seated on a bench by the door, laughing and talking with the great Cabuliwallah at her feet. In all her life, it appeared, my small daughter had never found so patient a listener, except for her father. Already the corner of her little sari[2] was stuffed with almonds and raisins, gifts from her visitor. "Why did you give her those?" I said and, taking out an eight-anna piece,[3] handed it to him. The man accepted the money without delay, and slipped it into his pocket.

Alas, on my return an hour later, I found the unfortunate coin had made twice its own worth of trouble. The Cabuliwallah had given it to

Mini, and her mother, seeing the bright round object, had pounced on the child with: "Where did you get that eight-anna piece?"

"The Cabuliwallah gave it to me," said Mini cheerfully.

"The Cabuliwallah gave it to you!" cried her mother much shocked. "O Mini! how could you take it from him?"

Entering at this moment, I saved her from impending disaster and proceeded to make my own inquiries. I found that it was not the first or the second time the two had met. The Cabuliwallah had overcome the child's first terror by a judicious bribery of nuts and almonds, and the two were now great friends.

They had many quaint jokes which afforded them a great deal of amusement. Seated in front of him, and looking with all her tiny dignity on his gigantic frame, Mini would ripple her face with laughter and begin "O Cabuliwallah! Cabuliwallah! what have you got in your bag?"

He would reply in the nasal accents of a mountaineer: "An elephant!" Not much cause for merriment, perhaps, but how they both enjoyed their joke! And for me, this child's talk with a grown-up man always had in it something strangely fascinating.

Then the Cabuliwallah, not to be caught behind, would take his turn with: "Well, little one, and when are you going to the father-in-law's house?"[4]

Now most small Bengali[5] maidens have heard long ago about the father-in-law's house, but we, being a little modern, had kept these things from our child, and at this question Mini must have been a trifle bewildered. But she would not show it and with instant composure replied: "Are you going there?"

Among men of the Cabuliwallah's class, however, it is well-known that the words "father-in-law's house" have a double meaning. It is a euphemism for jail, the place where we are well cared for at no expense. The sturdy peddler

---

1. **Abdurrahman . . . policy:** Political issues between Great Britain and Afghanistan at the time of the story.
2. **sari** (sä´ rē) *n.*: Garment worn by a Hindu woman, which consists of a long piece of cloth worn wrapped around the body, with one end forming an ankle-length skirt and the other end draped over one shoulder and, sometimes, around the head.
3. **eight-anna piece:** Coin formerly used in India.

---

4. **father-in-law's house:** An expression meaning "getting married."
5. **Bengali:** Of or from Bengal, a region of eastern India and, now, Bangladesh.

would take my daughter's question in this sense. "Ah," he would say, shaking his fist at an invisible policeman, "I will thrash my father-in-law!" Hearing this, and picturing the poor, uncomfortable relative, Mini would go into peals of laughter, joined by her formidable friend.

These were autumn mornings, the time of

◆ **Reading Strategy**
To which sense or senses does this paragraph appeal?

year when kings of old went forth to conquest; and I, never stirring from my corner in Calcutta,[6] would let my mind wander over the whole world. At the very name of another country, my heart would go out to it, and at the sight of a foreigner in the streets, I would fall to weaving a network of dreams: the mountains, the glens,[7] the forests of his distant homeland with a cottage in its setting, and the free and independent life of faraway wilds. Perhaps these scenes of travel pass in my imagination all the more vividly because I lead a vegetable existence such that a call to travel would fall upon me like a thunderbolt. In the presence of this Cabuliwallah I was immediately transported to the foot of mountains, with narrow defiles[8] twisting in and out amongst their towering, arid peaks. I could see the string of camels bearing merchandise, and the company of turbaned merchants carrying queer old firearms, and some of their spears down toward the plains. I could see—but at this point Mini's mother would intervene, imploring me to "beware of that man."

Unfortunately Mini's mother is a very timid lady. Whenever she hears a noise in the street or sees people coming toward the house, she always jumps to the conclusion that they are either thieves, drunkards, snakes, tigers, malaria, cockroaches, caterpillars, or an English sailor. Even after all these years of experience, she is not able to overcome her terror. Thus she was full of doubts about the Cabuliwallah and used to beg me to keep a watchful eye on him.

I tried to gently laugh her fear away, but then she would turn on me seriously and ask solemn questions.

Were children never kidnapped?

Was it, then, not true that there was slavery in Cabul?

Was it so very absurd that this big man should be able to carry off a tiny child?

I told her that, though not impossible, it was highly improbable. But this was not enough, and her dread persisted. As her suspicion was unfounded, however, it did not seem right to forbid the man to come to the house, and his familiarity went unchecked.

Once a year, in the middle of January, Rahmun the Cabuliwallah was in the habit of returning to his country, and as the time approached, he would be very busy going from house to house collecting his debts. This year, however, he always found time to come and see Mini. It would have seemed to an outsider that there was some conspiracy between them, for when he could not come in the morning, he would appear in the evening.

Even to me it was a little startling now and then, to suddenly surprise this tall, loose-garmented man of bags in the corner of a dark room; but when Mini would run in, smiling, with her "O Cabuliwallah! Cabuliwallah!" and the two friends so far apart in age would subside into their old language and their old jokes, I felt reassured.

◆ **Literary Focus**
What does this sentence suggest about the father's feelings toward the Cabuliwallah?

One morning, a few days before he had made up his

---

6. **Calcutta:** Large city in eastern India.
7. **glens** (glenz) n.: Valleys.
8. **defiles** (de fīls´) n.: Deep, narrow mountain passes.

◆ **Build Vocabulary**

precarious (prē ker´ ē əs) adj.: Dangerously lacking in security or stability

impending (im pen´ diŋ) adj.: About to happen

judicious (jōō dish´ əs) adj.: Exhibiting sound judgment or common sense

euphemism (yōō´ fə miz´ əm) n.: Word or phrase substituted for a more offensive word or phrase

imploring (im plôr´ iŋ) v.: Asking or begging

The Cabuliwallah and Mini's father both discover that the passage of time changes relationships. This theme of changing relationships is common in songs as well as in literature. The song "Yesterday" by The Beatles deals with this theme.

The Beatles—George Harrison, John Lennon, Paul McCartney, and Ringo Starr—burst onto the American music scene in 1962 with their hit "Love Me Do." Although their early musical style was influenced by such American rock artists as Chuck Berry, Buddy Holly, and the Everly Brothers, the Beatles gave a new direction to rock-and-roll in the middle and late sixties. Earlier rock music was based mostly on rhythm—a strong beat—but The Beatles emphasized melody, complex chord progressions, and imaginative and meaningful lyrics. The Beatles also incorporated Indian instruments into some of their music. This ballad, from their later years, is one of their most popular.

YESTERDAY
Paul McCartney and John Lennon

Yesterday, all my troubles seemed so far away
Now it looks as though they're here to stay
Oh, I believe in yesterday

Suddenly, I'm not half the man I used to be
There's a shadow hanging over me
Oh, yesterday came suddenly

Why she had to go, I don't know, she wouldn't say
I said something wrong, now I long for yesterday

Yesterday, love was such an easy game to play
Now I need a place to hide away
Oh, I believe in yesterday

Why she had to go, I don't know, she wouldn't say
I said something wrong, now I long for yesterday

Yesterday, love was such an easy game to play
Now I need a place to hide away
Oh, I believe in yesterday.

1. If this song were sung by a character in "The Cabuliwallah," who would sing it? Explain.
2. How does the mood of the song compare and contrast with the mood of the story?

---

mind to go, I was correcting my proof sheets[9] in my study. It was chilly weather. Through the window the rays of the sun touched my feet, and the slight warmth was very welcome. It was almost eight o'clock, and the early pedestrians were returning home with their heads covered. All at once I heard an uproar in the street and, looking out, saw Rahmun bound and being led away between two policemen, followed by a crowd of curious boys. There were bloodstains on the clothes of the Cabuliwallah, and one of the policemen carried a knife. Hurrying out, I stopped them and inquired what it all meant. Partly from one, partly from another, I gathered that a certain neighbor had owed the peddler something for

---

9. **proof sheets:** Copies of a typeset manuscript on which changes or corrections are made by the author or an editor.

◆ **Build Vocabulary**

fettered (fet´ ərd) *adj.*: Restrained, as with a chain

sordid (sôr´ did) *adj.*: Filthy or dirty

pervaded (pər vād´ id) *v.*: Spread throughout; filled

a Rampuri shawl[10] but had falsely denied having bought it, and that in the course of the quarrel Rahmun had struck him. Now, in the heat of his excitement, the prisoner began calling his enemy all sorts of names. Suddenly, from a verandah of my house my little Mini appeared, with her usual exclamation: "O Cabuliwallah! Cabuliwallah!" Rahmun's face lighted up as he turned to her. He had no bag under his arm today, so she could not discuss the elephant with him. She at once therefore proceeded to the next question: "Are you going to the father-in-law's house?" Rahmun laughed and said: "Just where I am going, little one!" Then seeing that the reply did not amuse the child, he held up his fettered hands. "Ah," he said, "I would have thrashed that old father-in-law, but my hands are bound!"

On a charge of murderous assault, Rahmun was sentenced to many years of imprisonment.

Time passed, and he was forgotten. The accustomed work in the accustomed place was ours, and the thought of the once free mountaineer spending his years in prison seldom occurred to us. Even my lighthearted Mini, I am ashamed to say, forgot her old friend. New companions filled her life. As she grew older, she spent more of her time with girls, so much in fact that she came no more to her father's room. I was scarcely on speaking terms with her.

Many years passed. It was autumn once again, and we had made arrangements for Mini's marriage; it was to take place during the Puja holidays.[11] With the goddess Durga returning to her seasonal home in Mount Kailas, the light of our home was also to depart, leaving our house in shadows.

10. **Rampuri shawl:** Shawl from Rampur, India. Such shawls are the finest in India because of the quality of the fabric.
11. **Puja holidays:** Great Hindu festival (also called Durgapuja) that honors Durga, a war goddess. It is a time for family reunions and other gatherings, as well as religious ceremonies.

▶ **Critical Viewing** What details of this man's appearance do you think five-year-old Mini would notice? **[Speculate]**

The morning was bright. After the rains, there was a sense of cleanness in the air, and the rays of the sun looked like pure gold; so bright that they radiated even to the sordid brick walls of our Calcutta lanes. Since early dawn, the wedding pipes had been sounding, and at each beat my own heart throbbed. The wailing tune, Bhairavi,[12] seemed to intensify my pain at the approaching separation. My Mini was to be married tonight.

From early morning, noise and bustle pervaded the house. In the courtyard the canopy had to be slung on its bamboo poles; the tinkling chandeliers should be hung in each room and verandah; there was great

12. **Bhairavi** (bī΄ rə vē): The name of a particular tune. It is a happy piece of music and is associated with joyous events.

hurry and excitement. I was sitting in my study, looking through the accounts, when someone entered, saluting respectfully, and stood before me. It was Rahmun the Cabuliwallah, and at first I did not recognize him. He had no bag, nor the long hair, nor the same vigor that he used to have. But he smiled, and I knew him again.

"When did you come, Rahmun?" I asked him.

"Last evening," he said, "I was released from jail."

The words struck harsh upon my ears. I had never talked with anyone who had wounded his fellowman, and my heart shrank when I realized this, for I felt that the day would have been better omened if he had not turned up.

"There are ceremonies going on," I said, "and I am busy. Could you perhaps come another day?"

At once he turned to go; but as he reached the door, he hesitated and said: "May I not see the little one, sir, for a moment?" It was his belief that Mini was still the same. He had pictured her running to him as she used to do, calling "O Cabuliwallah! Cabuliwallah!" He had imagined that they would laugh and talk together, just as in the past. In fact, in memory of those former days he had brought, carefully wrapped up in paper, a few almonds and raisins and grapes, somehow obtained from a countryman—his own little fund was gone.

I said again: "There is a ceremony in the house, and you will not be able to see anyone today."

The man's face fell. He looked wistfully at me for a moment, said "Good morning," and went out.

I felt a little sorry, and would have called him back, but saw that he was returning of his own accord. He came close up to me, holding out his offerings, and said: "I brought these few things, sir, for the little one. Will you give them to her?"

I took them and was going to pay him, but he caught my hand and said: "You are very kind, sir! Keep me in your recollection; do not offer me money! You have a little girl; I too have one like her in my own home. I thought of my

own and brought fruits to your child, not to make a profit for myself."

Saying this, he put his hand inside his big loose robe and brought out a small dirty piece of paper. With great care he unfolded this and smoothed it out with both hands on my table. It bore the impression of a little hand, not a photograph, not a drawing. The impression of an ink-smeared hand laid flat on the paper. This touch of his own little daughter had been always on his heart, as he had come year after year to Calcutta to sell his wares in the streets.

Tears came to my eyes. I forgot that he was a poor Cabuli fruit seller, while I was—but no, was I more than he? He was also a father.

That impression of the hand of his little Parbati in her distant mountain home reminded me of my own little Mini, and I immediately sent for her from the inner apartment. Many excuses were raised, but I would not listen. Clad in the red silk of her wedding day, with the sandal paste[13] on her forehead, and adorned as a young bride, Mini came and stood bashfully before me.

The Cabuliwallah was staggered at the sight of her. There was no hope of reviving their old friendship. At last he smiled and said: "Little one, are you going to your father-in-law's house?"

◆ Literature and Your Life

Discuss a time when you saw someone after many years who did not look as you remembered.

But Mini now understood the meaning of the word "father-in-law," and she could not reply to him as in the past. She flushed at the question and stood before him with her bride's face looking down.

I remembered the day when the Cabuliwallah and my Mini first met, and I felt sad. When she had gone, Rahmun heaved a deep sigh and sat down on the floor. The idea had suddenly come to him that his daughter also must have grown up during this long time, and that he would

---

13. **sandal paste:** Paste made from sandalwood sawdust mixed with water and used as a liquid makeup that gives the skin a paler appearance.

have to make friends with her all over again. Surely he would not find her as he used to know her; besides, what might have happened to her in these eight years?

The marriage pipes sounded, and the mild autumn sun streamed around us. But Rahmun sat in the little Calcutta lane and saw before him the barren mountains of Afghanistan.

I took out a bank note and gave it to him, saying: "Go back to your own daughter, Rahmun, in your own country, and may the happiness of your meeting bring good fortune to my child!"

After giving this gift, I had to eliminate some of the festivities. I could not have the electric lights, nor the military band, and the ladies of the house were saddened. But to me the wedding feast was brighter because of the thought that in a distant land a long-lost father met again with his only child.

Beyond Literature

Social Studies Connection

India and Its People India is the second largest country in the world in population. In fact, nearly one out of every six people in the world lives in India! A country of vast differences, India's land includes a desert, jungles, broad plains, the tallest mountain system in the world, and one of the world's rainiest areas. The map shows the diversity of physical features in India. The people of India belong to many different ethnic groups, religions, and caste systems—or social classes. They speak sixteen major languages and more than 1,000 minor languages and dialects.

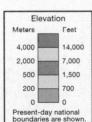

Elevation	
Meters	Feet
4,000	14,000
2,000	7,000
500	1,500
200	700
0	0

Present-day national boundaries are shown.

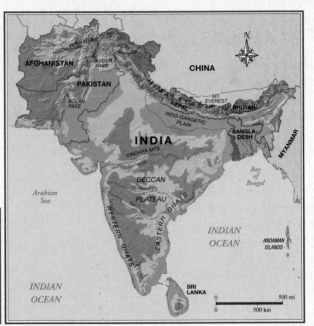

Guide for Responding

◆ *Literature and Your Life*

Reader's Response With which character do you identify most? Why?

Thematic Focus The Cabuliwallah loses eight years of his life and eight years of his daughter's life. His experiences may have led you to question the justice of his situation.

☑ Check Your Comprehension

1. What is Mini's relationship with her mother? With her father?
2. Why is Mini afraid of the Cabuliwallah at first?
3. What are the two meanings of "the father-in-law's house"?
4. What is Mini's father's final act of kindness and justice to Rahmun the Cabuliwallah?

Guide for Responding (continued)

◆ Critical Thinking

INTERPRET

1. (a) Why do Mini and the Cabuliwallah develop such a close relationship? (b) What does each gain from the other? **[Infer]**
2. In what ways do you think Mini has changed in the eight years of the Cabuliwallah's absence? **[Speculate]**
3. Why do you think Mini acts so reserved with the Cabuliwallah when she sees him again? **[Hypothesize]**

APPLY

4. Why is it sometimes awkward to see someone you haven't seen in a long time? **[Relate]**

EVALUATE

5. Do you believe Mini's father acted appropriately toward the Cabuliwallah at the end of the story? Why or why not? **[Make a Judgment]**

◆ Reading Strategy

ENGAGE YOUR SENSES

Tagore provides many details to help you **engage your senses** to fully experience his characters and setting.

1. What are two sounds associated with Mini as a young girl?
2. Identify three sensory details that helped you imagine the Cabuliwallah.

◆ Literary Focus

RELATIONSHIPS BETWEEN CHARACTERS

Important changes in the characters of Mini and her father are revealed in their **relationships** to each other and to the Cabuliwallah.

1. (a) Describe Mini's relationship with the Cabuliwallah before he is arrested. (b) Describe her reaction to him when he returns on her wedding day.
2. Explain how Mini's relationship with her father has changed.
3. Why does Mini's father feel such a close relationship to the Cabuliwallah at the end of the story?

◆ Build Vocabulary

USING THE LATIN ROOT *-jud-*

Knowing that the Latin word root *-jud-* means "judge," match the word in Column A with its definition in Column B.

Column A	Column B
1. judicial	a. a judgment or opinion formed before the facts are known
2. prejudice	b. showing sound judgment
3. judicious	c. belonging to or related to judges and law courts

USING THE WORD BANK: Antonyms

In your notebook, match each numbered word from the Word Bank to the letter of its antonym, the word most opposite in meaning.

1. sordid	a. safe
2. imploring	b. distant
3. precarious	c. clean
4. impending	d. blunt statement
5. euphemism	e. refusing
6. fettered	f. free
7. pervaded	g. emptied

◆ Build Grammar Skills

PRONOUN AND ANTECEDENT AGREEMENT

A **pronoun** must agree with its **antecedent** in number (singular or plural) and gender (masculine, feminine, or neuter).

Practice In your notebook, copy the following sentences from the story. Circle each pronoun and draw an arrow to its antecedent. Then, label each pronoun as masculine, feminine, or neuter and as singular or plural.

1. Mini, my five-year-old daughter, cannot live without chattering. I really believe that in all her life she has not wasted one minute in silence.
2. The man accepted the money without delay, and slipped it into his pocket.
3. Whenever Mini's mother sees people in the street, she thinks they are thieves.

Build Your Portfolio

 ## Idea Bank

Writing

1. **Description** Describe a place that could be the setting for a short story about an episode from your childhood. Include sensory details that will help your readers experience the setting.

2. **Character's Journal Entry** Write a journal entry as the Cabuliwallah, expressing your thoughts and feelings about the events of the wedding day.

3. **Letter to the Embassy** Write a letter to the Indian embassy requesting information about the history and culture of the country. Use a business-letter format. **[Social Studies Link]**

Speaking, Listening, and Viewing

4. **Courtroom Speech** As the Cabuliwallah's lawyer, give a speech recommending that the Cabuliwallah be given a light sentence for his crime. In your speech, refer to the circumstances of his life and the character traits you have discovered in the story.

5. **Oral Interpretation** Find a story from Indian mythology. Practice reading the story aloud, using an expressive voice. Then read the story to the class. **[Performing Arts Link]**

Researching and Representing

6. **Timeline** Create a timeline that shows key events in India's fight for independence. Illustrate your timeline with copies of photos from magazines, newspapers, or books. **[Social Studies Link; Media Link]**

7. **Sketch** Using any medium (pencil, ink, or paint), draw what you think the Cabuliwallah looks like at the beginning of the story. **[Art Link]**

Online Activity www.phlit.phschool.com

 ## Guided Writing Lesson

Firsthand Biography

Tagore describes his characters so well that readers almost feel as if they've met them in person! Write a firsthand biography of someone you do know. A **firsthand biography** tells about the life of a person with whom the writer is personally acquainted. This close relationship allows for personal insights that are not found in biographies based solely on research. The following tips will help you create a biography that reads smoothly and carries the reader along from idea to idea.

Writing Skills Focus: Logical Organization

Your firsthand biography should have a logical, consistent overall **order.** Chronological order (time order) and order of importance are both good choices for a firsthand biography.

If you want to tell the events in the order in which they happened, use chronological order. Begin with events from the subject's childhood, and work your way up to the present day.

If you want to stress what you think are the person's most important qualities, arrange the details you include around each important quality you want to illustrate. Present the details in order of importance.

Prewriting Talk with the subject of your biography. Ask him or her to identify some significant events. Take careful notes during your discussion. Then arrange your notes into an outline.

Drafting Add details to the bare bones of your biography. Where you include the details depends on the kind of organization you choose.

Revising Compare your draft with your outline to ensure that you've used a consistent organization. In addition, look for places where you can add transitions to make the organization more clear.

Guide for Reading

R. K. Narayan *(1906–   )*

If the Indian writer R. K. Narayan lived in your city or town, he might turn it on its head to create an imaginary place full of characters that would make you smile in recognition.

Narayan's own town, Mysore, probably served as the basis for his fictional town of Malgudi, a place full of eccentric characters who find themselves in peculiar situations.

Imaginary Town Writers sometimes devise special settings for the cast of characters that pass through their books, and Narayan has done this with Malgudi. "Malgudi was an earth-shaking discovery for me, because I had no mind for facts and things like that, which would be necessary in writing about . . . any real place." Narayan's fictional south Indian town of Malgudi has seen so many changes and human dramas that it almost seems like a character itself.

Narayan's Languages R. K. Narayan, whose initials stand for Rasipuram Kirshnaswamy, speaks both the Indian language Tamii and English—but he writes all his fiction in English. As a child, he was also taught traditional Indian melodies and prayers in Sanskrit. As an adult, Narayan went on to translate from Sanskrit the ancient Indian epic *Mahabharata*, a poem consisting of more than 90,000 pairs of rhyming lines!

Literary Forms R. K. Narayan has written extensively in several forms: novels, short stories, essays, and travel books among them.

If you want to find out more about the life of R. K. Narayan, you might be interested in reading his memoir, *My Days*. His best-known novels include *Swami and Friends* (1935), *The English Teacher* (1945), and *The Painter of Signs* (1976).

◆ Build Vocabulary

LATIN WORD ROOTS: *-gratis-*

In "Like the Sun," you will learn that Sekhar's boss behaves in an ingratiating way. Knowing that the word root *-gratis-* comes from a Latin word meaning "pleasing" or "a favor," you can figure out that being *ingratiating* means "trying to please."

essence
tempering
shirked
incessantly
ingratiating
stupefied
scrutinized

WORD BANK

As you read "Like the Sun," you will encounter the words on this list. Each word is defined on the page where it first appears. Preview the list before you read, and identify any words that are already familiar to you. In your notebook, write what you think they mean.

◆ Build Grammar Skills

COMPARATIVE AND SUPERLATIVE FORMS

When writers compare two things, they use the **comparative form** of an adjective. To compare more than two things, they use the **superlative form.**

Comparative Form: No judge delivering a sentence felt *more pained* and *hopeless*.

In comparing a story character with one other person, the author uses the comparative form of the adjectives *pained* and *hopeless*. The comparative of these adjectives is formed by using *more* with them.

Superlative Form: Sekhar felt the *greatest* pity for him.

The author implies that of all the pity there is to feel, the character Sekhar feels the most. Therefore, the author uses *greatest,* the superlative form of the adjective *great.*

Like the Sun

◆ *Literature and Your Life*

CONNECT YOUR EXPERIENCE
Your closest friend just gave a less-than-impressive performance in the class play and asks for your honest response. Do you reveal your true opinion or do you spare your friend's feelings?

You're not alone with this dilemma. The matter of whether to tell the whole, unvarnished truth has troubled people throughout the ages. Follow Sekhar, the main character in this story, as he decides how to deal with the truth—at least for a day.

Journal Writing Briefly note what might happen if everyone told the truth all the time.

THEMATIC FOCUS: PERSONAL CHALLENGES
Narayan's story poses this challenging question: Is it better to tell the absolute truth or to modify it for the sake of getting along with others?

◆ Background for Understanding

MUSIC
"Like the Sun" features the performance of a song, and this is not surprising, because song is at the root of south Indian music. The headmaster in the story sings an *alapana*—the introductory section of a piece of music—and then goes on to sing a song written by Thyagaraja (1767–1847), a composer who strongly influenced the music of south India. The region's biggest music festival, in fact, is named after Thyagaraja.

You'll notice, too, that the headmaster sings to the accompaniment of a drum and a violin. The violin is widely used in southern Indian music, and percussion instruments include the double-headed drum known as *mridangam* and the *ghatam*, a clay pot that the player may sometimes toss into the air.

◆ Literary Focus

IRONY
Irony is the literary technique that involves surprising, interesting, or amusing contradictions at work. These differences can result from clashes between what a character believes and what is actually the case. Irony might also result from clashes between what a character expects to happen and what actually happens.

By focusing on the clash between the main character's ideals and the real situation, you'll understand the irony of this tale.

◆ Reading Strategy

ANALYZE CAUSES AND EFFECTS
In life, you must experience directly the **effects** of your actions—the results of what you do. The advantage of reading a story, however, is that you can sit safe and sound in a chair and analyze the causes and effects in someone else's experience.

"Like the Sun" is a perfect story with which to analyze the relationship between causes and effects. Sekhar makes an important decision right off, a decision that just seems to invite consequences. Filling out a graphic organizer like the following will help you connect Sekhar's actions and their results.

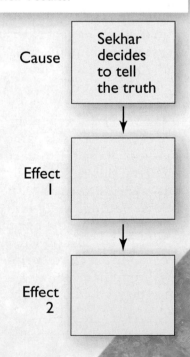

Cause — Sekhar decides to tell the truth

Effect 1

Effect 2

Like the Sun

R. K. Narayan

Truth, Sekhar reflected, is like the sun. I suppose no human being can ever look it straight in the face without blinking or being dazed. He realized that, morning till night, the essence of human relationships consisted in tempering truth so that it might not shock. This day he set apart as a unique day—at least one day in the year we must give and take absolute Truth whatever may happen. Otherwise life is not worth living. The day ahead seemed to him full of possibilities. He told no one of his experiment. It was a quiet resolve, a secret pact between him and eternity.

The very first test came while his wife served

◆ **Reading Strategy**
What is the first consequence of Sekhar's "pact" with "eternity"?

him his morning meal. He showed hesitation over a tit-bit, which she had thought was her culinary[1] masterpiece. She asked, "Why, isn't it good?" At other times he would have said, considering her feelings in the matter, "I feel full up, that's all." But today he said, "It isn't good. I'm unable to swallow it." He saw her wince and said to himself, Can't be helped. Truth is like the sun.

His next trial was in the common room when one of his colleagues came up and said, "Did you hear of the death of so-and-so? Don't you think it a pity?" "No," Sekhar answered. "He was such a fine man—" the other began. But Sekhar cut him short with: "Far from it. He always struck me as a mean and selfish brute."

During the last period when he was teaching geography for Third Form A, Sekhar received a note from the headmaster: "Please see me before you go home." Sekhar said to himself: It

must be about these horrible test papers. A hundred papers in the boys' scrawls; he had shirked this work for weeks, feeling all the time as if a sword were hanging over his head.

The bell rang, and the boys burst out of the class.

Sekhar paused for a moment outside the headmaster's room to button up his coat; that was another subject the headmaster always sermonized about.

He stepped in with a very polite "Good evening, sir."

The headmaster looked up at him in a very friendly manner and asked, "Are you free this evening?"

Sekhar replied, "Just some outing which I have promised the children at home—"

"Well, you can take them out another day. Come home with me now."

"Oh . . . yes, sir, certainly . . ." And then he added timidly, "anything special, sir?"

"Yes," replied the headmaster, smiling to himself . . . "You didn't know my weakness for music?"

"Oh, yes, sir . . ."

"I've been learning and practicing secretly, and now I want you to hear me this evening. I've engaged a drummer and a violinist to accompany me—this is the first time I'm doing it full-dress,[2] and I want your opinion. I know it will be valuable."

Sekhar's taste in music was well known. He was one of the most dreaded music critics in the town. But he never anticipated his musical inclinations would lead him to this trial. . . . "Rather a surprise for you, isn't it?" asked the

---

1. **culinary** (kyōō′ lə ner′ ē) *adj.*: Having to do with cooking or the kitchen.

2. **full-dress:** Complete in every respect.

Face in Sun, Hal Lose

▲ **Critical Viewing** Describe the personality the artist has given the sun. [Interpret]

and then gave him hope; how his ambition in life was to forget himself in music.

At home the headmaster proved very <u>ingratiating</u>. He sat Sekhar on a red silk carpet, set before him several dishes of delicacies, and fussed over him as if he were a son-in-law of the house. He even said, "Well, you must listen with a free mind. Don't worry about these test papers." He added half humorously, "I will give you a week's time."

"Make it ten days, sir," Sekhar pleaded.

"All right, granted," the headmaster said generously. Sekhar felt really relieved now—he would attack them at the rate of ten a day and get rid of the nuisance.

The headmaster lighted incense sticks. "Just to create the right atmosphere," he explained. A drummer and a violinist, already seated on a Rangoon mat, were waiting for him. The headmaster sat down between them like a professional at a concert, cleared his throat and began an alapana,[3] and paused to ask, "Isn't it good Kalyani?"[4] Sekhar pretended not to have heard the question. The headmaster went on to sing a full song composed by Thyagaraja and followed it with two more. All the time the headmaster was singing, Sekhar went on commenting within himself. He croaks like a dozen frogs. He is bellowing like a buffalo. Now he sounds like loose window shutters in a storm.

The incense sticks burnt low. Sekhar's head throbbed with the medley of sounds that had assailed his eardrums for a couple of hours now. He felt half <u>stupefied</u>. The headmaster had gone nearly hoarse, when he paused to ask, "Shall I go on?" Sekhar replied, "Please don't, sir; I think this will do. . . ." The headmaster looked stunned. His face was beaded with perspiration. Sekhar felt the greatest pity for him. But he felt he could not help it. No judge delivering a sentence felt more pained and helpless. Sekhar noticed that the headmaster's wife peeped in

headmaster. "I've spent a fortune on it behind closed doors. . . ." They started for the headmaster's house. "God hasn't given me a child, but at least let him not deny me the consolation of music," the head-master said, pathetically, as they walked. He <u>incessantly</u> chattered about music: how he began one day out of sheer boredom; how his teacher at first laughed at him

◆ **Build Vocabulary**

essence (es´ əns) *n.*: The crucial element or basis
tempering (tem´ pə riŋ) *adj.*: Modifying or adjusting
shirked (shûrkt) *v.*: Neglected or avoided
incessantly (in ses´ ənt lē) *adv.*: Endlessly; constantly
ingratiating (in grā´ shē āt´ iŋ) *adj.*: Bringing into favor
stupefied (stoo´ pə fīd´) *adj.*: Dazed; stunned

---

3. **alapana:** Improvisational Indian music in the classical style.
4. **Kalyani:** Traditional Indian folk songs.

from the kitchen, with eager curiosity. The drummer and the violinist put away their burdens with an air of relief. The headmaster removed his spectacles, mopped his brow, and asked, "Now, come out with your opinion."

"Can't I give it tomorrow, sir?" Sekhar asked tentatively.

"No. I want it immediately—your frank opinion. Was it good?"

"No, sir . . ." Sekhar replied.

"Oh! . . . Is there any use continuing my lessons?"

"Absolutely none, sir . . ." Sekhar said with his voice trembling. He felt very unhappy that he could not speak more soothingly. Truth, he reflected, required as much strength to give as to receive.

All the way home he felt worried. He felt that his official life was not going to be smooth sailing hereafter. There were questions of increment and confirmation[5] and so on, all depending upon the headmaster's goodwill. All kinds of worries seemed to be in store for him. . . . Did not Harischandra[6] lose his throne, wife, child, because he would speak nothing less than the absolute Truth whatever happened?

At home his wife served him with a sullen face. He knew she was still angry with him for his remark of the morning. Two casualties for today, Sekhar said to himself. If I practice it for a week, I don't think I shall have a single friend left.

He received a call from the headmaster in his classroom next day. He went up apprehensively.

"Your suggestion was useful. I have paid off the music master. No one would tell me the truth about my music all these days. Why such antics at my age! Thank you. By the way, what about those test papers?"

"You gave me ten days, sir, for correcting them."

"Oh, I've reconsidered it. I must positively have them here tomorrow. . . ." A hundred papers in a day! That meant all night's sitting up! "Give me a couple of days, sir . . ."

"No. I must have them tomorrow morning. And remember, every paper must be thoroughly scrutinized."

"Yes, sir," Sekhar said, feeling that sitting up all night with a hundred test papers was a small price to pay for the luxury of practicing Truth.

---

5. **increment and confirmation:** Salary increase and job security.
6. **Harishchandra** (hə rish chən′ drə): Legendary Hindu king who was the subject of many Indian stories. His name has come to symbolize truth and integrity.

◆ **Build Vocabulary**

scrutinized (skr$\overline{oo}$t′ ən īzd′) v.: Looked at carefully; examined closely

---

Guide for Responding

◆ Literature and Your Life

Reader's Response Would you find telling the truth all day, as Sekhar does in this story, to be pleasurable? Why or why not?

Thematic Focus Give a reason why a person might set himself or herself the personal challenge of telling the absolute truth for one day.

☑ Check Your Comprehension

1. What experiment did Sekhar set for himself at the beginning of the story?
2. For what reason did the headmaster want to meet with Sekhar?
3. What was Sekhar's response to having to grade 100 test papers in a day?

Guide for Responding (continued)

◆ Critical Thinking

INTERPRET

1. What effect does the headmaster's remark that he has spent a fortune on his music have on the story? **[Analyze]**
2. The phrase "luxury of practicing Truth" appears at the end of the story. How can truth be a luxury? **[Interpret]**

EVALUATE

3. Was Sekhar brave or foolish to tell the truth all day? Why? **[Make a Judgment]**

APPLY

4. Describe a situation in which you might "temper the truth." **[Interpret]**

◆ Reading Strategy

ANALYZE CAUSES AND EFFECTS

This story is somewhat unusual in that all its key events are so clearly the **effects** of a single decision: Sekhar's vow to tell the truth all day.

1. Identify two consequences that follow as a result of Sekhar's truthfulness about the headmaster's performance.
2. In describing the effects of his vow, Sekhar calls them "casualties." Why?
3. Is Sekhar right in predicting that if he keeps telling the truth, he won't have a single friend left? Why or why not?

◆ Literary Focus

IRONY

The central **irony** in this story is the clash between Sekhar's idealistic expectations and what actually occurs. For example, telling the absolute truth, as Sekhar vows to do, seems to be a noble goal. However, this vow leads to bad feelings. At breakfast, Sekhar's wife winces when he criticizes her cooking. The contrast between noble intention and disappointing effect is what creates irony.

1. What do you think Sekhar believes might happen as a result of his poor review of the headmaster's performance?
2. What is ironic about the headmaster's actual reaction to the criticism?

◆ Build Vocabulary

USING THE LATIN ROOT -*gratis*-

Use your knowledge of the root -*gratis*-, which means "pleasing" or "a favor," to define these words.

1. grateful
2. gratitude
3. ingrate
4. gratis
5. gratuitous

USING THE WORD BANK: Sentence Completions

Write the paragraph on your paper and fill in the blanks with words from the Word Bank. Use each word just once.

The ___?___ of Sekhar's vow was to tell the truth. This one day at least, he was not in favor of ___?___ truth to protect people's feelings. ___?___ throughout the day, he ___?___ no opportunity of telling his wife and colleagues exactly what he thought. As they ___?___ Sekhar's behavior, many of his colleagues were ___?___. They expected Sekhar to be more ___?___.

◆ Build Grammar Skills

COMPARATIVE AND SUPERLATIVE FORMS

Almost all one-syllable adjectives and some two-syllable adjectives use -*er* to form the **comparative** and -*est* to form the **superlative.** Many adjectives of two or more syllables use the words *more* or *most*, respectively, for comparative and superlative forms.

Practice In your notebook, write the correct form of the adjective from the choices given in parentheses.

1. Sekhar didn't say whether he liked one of the headmaster's songs (better, best) than the other.
2. If Sekhar had told the headmaster his music was the (more fine, most fine, finer, finest) he'd ever heard, the story would have had a different ending.
3. Sekhar would have told a (more temperate, most temperate, temperater, temperatest) truth the next day.

Writing Application Write a paragraph in which you compare Sekhar and the headmaster. Use at least two each of the comparative and the superlative forms of adjectives.

Build Your Portfolio

Idea Bank

Writing

1. **Advice Column** Write an advice column response to tenth-grader Dara. Should Dara tell her friend, who can't carry a tune, not to try out for the school musical? Give reasons for your answer.

2. **Guidelines** You and your classmates will be exchanging ideas and editing one another's papers throughout the year. Write a set of guidelines for telling the truth in a useful, constructive way.

3. **Fairy Tale** Write a fairy tale about a teenager who must tell the truth in every situation. Set your fairy tale in ancient or modern times.

Speaking, Listening, and Viewing

4. **Oral Argument** Suppose that Sekhar was fired for telling the truth. As his attorney, prepare and deliver an oral argument summing up why he has been unfairly treated and why he should be rehired. **[Social Studies Link]**

5. **Debate** With a small group, debate the question of whether it is better to reveal the truth fully in social interactions or to soften it in some way. **[Social Studies Link; Performing Arts Link]**

Researching and Representing

6. **Research Songs** The term *Kalyani* refers to traditional Indian folk songs. Using text and musical resources at the library or via the Internet, find out more about Kalyani and present your findings to the class. If possible, play a recording of Kalyani. **[Music Link]**

7. **Map** Draw a map of southern India that shows Madras, where Narayan was born, and Mysore, which served as the basis for Narayan's fictional Malgudi. **[Social Studies Link]**

Online Activity www.phlit.phschool.com

Guided Writing Lesson

Review of a Song

Sekhar had to give an oral review of his headmaster's song. In writing, a **review** is an article giving a critical evaluation of a work of art. Use your knowledge of music to write a review of a song. Address your review to readers of a popular music magazine and win their confidence by clearly supporting your opinions with reasons.

Writing Skills Focus: Supporting Details

When writing a review, a research paper, or an editorial, use **supporting details**—facts, statistics, examples, or reasons—to persuade readers that your assertions are true.

Suppose, for example, that you write this topic sentence: "The lyrics of the song have particular meaning for teenagers living in the city." Your readers are going to ask themselves why this is the case. To answer that question, you can provide a supporting detail: "The lyrics of the song focus on what it feels like to be alone on a crowded city street."

Prewriting Create an outline for your review. For each paragraph, come up with a topic sentence and at least two supporting details to back it up.

    I. Paragraph topic sentence

        A. Supporting detail

        B. Supporting detail

Drafting Your details should support the point in your topic sentence by clarifying, explaining, or giving an example.

Revising Show your review to a friend or writing partner. Ask whether your supporting details fit with their topic sentences. If any supporting details seem unclear, rewrite them to establish a clear connection to the main idea of your paragraph.

PART 2

Right and Wrong

The Torment of the Poet, Giorgio de Chirico, Yale University Art Gallery

Guide for Reading

The Thousand and One Nights

If you ever heard of Sindbad the Sailor, Ali Baba and his secret password "Open Sesame," or Aladdin and his magic lamp, then you are already familiar with some of the tales in *The Thousand and One Nights.*

The world-famous story collection, sometimes called *The Arabian Nights,* has existed in Arabic since about A.D. 850 and was translated from an earlier work in Persian (the language of present-day Iran). Over the centuries, additional stories from Egypt, India, Greece, and other neighboring cultures were incorporated into it.

Frame Story The tales in *The Thousand and One Nights* are loosely pieced together into one long narrative. The connecting framework tells of a King Shahriyar, whose wife's betrayal has made him hate all women. Each day he weds another wife, only to have her killed the next morning before marrying a new one.

Then, a young woman named Scheherazade (shə her´ ə zä´ də) devises a scheme to avoid execution. On the night after she weds the king, she tells a spellbinding story, but withholds the ending, promising to finish the tale the next night. Shahriyar lets her live to finish the tale, but when she does, she immediately starts another.

Scheherazade keeps this up for a thousand and one nights—hence the title of the story collection—until finally the king falls in love with her and decides not to have her killed. "The Fisherman and the Jinnee" (jē´ nē) is one of the 1,001 stories that helped keep her alive.

N. J. Dawood *(1927–   )*

Born in Baghdad, Iraq, Nessim Joseph Dawood won a scholarship to attend the University of London and, after completing his studies, remained in England as a publishing executive and Middle East consultant. His translation of *The Thousand and One Nights* first appeared in 1954.

◆ Build Vocabulary

LATIN WORD ROOTS: -vert-

In the selection from *The Thousand and One Nights,* the jinnee's huge nostrils are described as "two *inverted* bowls." The word inverted contains the Latin root -vert-, which means "turn." *Inverted* means "turned upside down."

inverted
blasphemous
adjured
indignantly
resolutely
enraptured
munificence
ominous

WORD BANK

As you read the story, you will encounter these words. Each word is defined on the page where it first appears. Preview the list before you read.

◆ Build Grammar Skills

ACTION AND LINKING VERBS

Action verbs express physical or mental action. **Linking verbs** express a state of being, showing what the subject is by linking it to a word that further identifies or describes it.

Action: Scheherazade *told* fabulous stories.
Linking: Scheherazade *was* a fabulous storyteller.

There are all sorts of action verbs. However, linking verbs include only forms of the verb *be* (like *am, is, are, was,* and *were*) and a handful of other verbs (such as *seem, become, remain, stay, appear, look, smell, taste, sound, feel,* and *grow*) when they are used with a meaning similar to *be.* As you read the selection, identify action verbs and linking verbs.

The Fisherman and the Jinnee
from The Thousand and One Nights

◆ *Literature and Your Life*

CONNECT YOUR EXPERIENCE

Suppose you had a powerful magical helper who, at the slightest command, would fulfill your wishes. Snapping your fingers, you could call on this creature to improve your grades or win you a place on a school team. In "The Fisherman and the Jinnee," a poor fisherman finds a bottle with such a magical helper inside.

Journal Writing Jot down some problems that might result from having a powerful magical helper.

THEMATIC FOCUS: STRUGGLING FOR JUSTICE

Justice plays a role in all three interlocking tales in "The Fisherman and the Jinnee." As you read, ask yourself: Which characters behave justly, and which behave unjustly?

◆ Background for Understanding

CULTURE

Most of the tales in *The Thousand and One Nights* are set in Arabic-speaking areas like Egypt and Baghdad (now the capital of Iraq) or in adjoining lands like Persia (now Iran) where the Muslim religion is also dominant. Of the three interlocking tales in "The Fisherman and the Jinnee," two are set in Persia, and all feature characters who are Muslim.

◆ Literary Focus

FOLK TALES

Folk tales are stories that simple, everyday people composed and handed down orally long before they were written down. As a product of common folk, not professional writers, they have these characteristics:

- characters display just a few traits
- good and evil are clearly indicated
- plots have supernatural elements
- trickery enables the seemingly weak and powerless—with whom the common folk identify—to outsmart the strong

As you read "The Fisherman and the Jinnee," look for supernatural elements and trickery that are part of the plot. Also decide which traits the characters display.

◆ Reading Strategy

FORM MENTAL IMAGES

When you read a story, you'll often be able to follow it better if you use the details that the author provides to **form mental images,** or create pictures in your mind. Concentrate on the opening details, and use them to form your first mental image. Then, change that image as the story unfolds and your understanding grows.

For example, as you read "The Fisherman and the Jinnee," the first thing you might try to picture is the poor fisherman trying to draw in his overburdened fishing net. As you continue reading, your next mental image might be the bottle that the fisherman finds, and your next might be the jinnee that comes out of the bottle. To help you visualize each image, make a sketch like the one below.

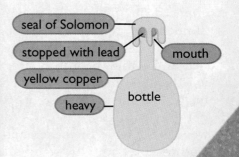

from The Thousand and One Nights

The Fisherman and the Jinnee

translated
by N. J. Dawood

Once upon a time there was a poor fisherman who had a wife and three children to support.

He used to cast his net four times a day. It chanced that one day he went down to the sea at noon and, reaching the shore, set down his basket, rolled up his shirt sleeves, and cast his net far out into the water. After he had waited for it to sink, he pulled on the cords with all his might; but the net was so heavy that he could not draw it in. So he tied the rope ends to a wooden stake on the beach and, putting off his clothes, dived into the water and set to work to bring it up. When he had carried it ashore, however, he found in it a dead donkey.

"By Allah,[1] this is a strange catch!" cried the

1. **Allah** (al' lə): The Arabic word for God.

▲ **Critical Viewing** How would you feel if you were suddenly confronted with a magical creature like this one? **[Respond]**

fisherman, disgusted at the sight. After he had freed the net and wrung it out, he waded into the water and cast it again, invoking Allah's help. But when he tried to draw it in he found it even heavier than before. Thinking that he had caught some enormous fish, he fastened the ropes to the stake and, diving in again, brought up the net. This time he found a large earthen vessel filled with mud and sand.

Angrily the fisherman threw away the vessel, cleaned his net, and cast it for the third time. He waited patiently, and when he felt the net grow heavy he hauled it in, only to find it filled with bones and broken glass. In despair, he lifted his eyes to heaven and cried: "Allah knows that I cast my net only four times a day. I have already cast it for the third time and caught no fish at all. Surely He will not fail me again!"

With this the fisherman hurled his net far out into the sea and waited for it to sink to the bottom. When at length he brought it to land he found in it a bottle made of yellow copper. The mouth was stopped with lead and bore the seal of our master Solomon, son of David.[2] The fisherman rejoiced and said: "I will sell this in the market of the coppersmiths. It must be worth ten pieces of gold." He shook the bottle and, finding it heavy, thought to himself: "I will first break the seal and find out what is inside."

The fisherman removed the lead with his knife and again shook the bottle; but scarcely had he done so when there burst from it a great column of smoke which spread along the shore and rose so high that it almost touched the heavens. Taking shape, the smoke resolved itself into a jinnee of such prodigious[3] stature that his head reached the clouds, while his feet were planted on the sand. His head was a huge dome and his mouth as wide as a cavern, with teeth ragged like broken rocks. His legs towered like the masts of a ship, his nostrils were two inverted bowls, and his eyes, blazing like torches, made his aspect fierce and menacing.

The sight of this jinnee struck terror to the fisherman's heart; his limbs quivered, his teeth chattered together, and he stood rooted to the ground with parched tongue and staring eyes.

"There is no god but Allah and Solomon is His Prophet!" cried the jinnee. Then, addressing himself to the fisherman, he said: "I pray you, mighty Prophet, do not kill me! I swear never again to defy your will or violate your laws!"

"Blasphemous giant," cried the fisherman, "do you presume to call Solomon the Prophet of Allah? Solomon has been dead these eighteen hundred years, and we are now approaching the end of time. But what is your history, pray, and how came you to be imprisoned in this bottle?"

On hearing these words the jinnee replied sarcastically: "Well, then; there is no god but Allah! Fisherman, I bring you good news."

"What news?" asked the old man.

"News of your death, horrible and prompt!" replied the jinnee.

"Then may heaven's wrath be upon you, ungrateful wretch!" cried the fisherman. "Why do you wish my death, and what have I done to deserve it? Have I not brought you up from the depths of the sea and released you from your imprisonment?"

But the jinnee answered: "Choose the manner of your death and the way that I shall kill you. Come, waste no time!"

"But what crime have I committed?" cried the fisherman.

"Listen to my story, and you shall know," replied the jinnee.

"Be brief, then, I pray you," said the fisherman, "for you have wrung my soul with terror."

"Know," began the giant, "that I am one of the rebel jinn who, together with Sakhr the Jinnee, mutinied against Solomon, son of David. Solomon sent against me his vizier,[4] Asaf ben Berakhya, who vanquished me despite my supernatural power and led me captive before his master. Invoking the name of Allah, Solomon adjured me to embrace his faith and pledge him absolute obedience. I refused, and he imprisoned me in this bottle, upon which he set a seal of lead bearing the Name of the Most High. Then he sent for several of his faithful jinn, who carried me away and cast me into the middle of the sea. In the ocean depths I vowed: 'I will bestow eternal riches on him who sets me free!' But a hundred years

> ◆ **Literary Focus**
> What supernatural elements does this folk tale contain?

---

4. vizier (vi zir´): A high officer in the government; a minister.

◆ **Build Vocabulary**

inverted (in vurt´ id) *adj.*: Upside down

blasphemous (blas´fə məs) *adj.*: Showing lack of respect for God or religious teachings

adjured (a joord´) *v.*: Commanded; ordered

---

2. Solomon . . . David: In the Old Testament, David and his son Solomon are both Kings of Israel and are considered prophets by Muslims.

3. prodigious (prə dij´ əs) *n.*: Wonderful; amazing.

passed away and no one freed me. In the second hundred years of my imprisonment I said: 'For him who frees me I will open up the buried treasures of the earth!' And yet no one freed me. Whereupon I flew into a rage and swore: 'I will kill the man who sets me free, allowing him only to choose the manner of his death!' Now it was you who set me free; therefore prepare to die and choose the way that I shall kill you."

"O wretched luck, that it should have fallen on my lot to free you!" exclaimed the fisherman. "Spare me, mighty jinnee, and Allah will spare you; kill me, and so shall Allah destroy you!"

"You have freed me," repeated the jinnee. "Therefore you must die."

"Chief of the jinn," cried the fisherman, "will you thus requite[5] good with evil?"

"Enough of this talk!" roared the jinnee. "Kill you I must."

At this point the fisherman thought to himself: "Though I am but a man and he is a jinnee, my cunning may yet overreach his malice." Then, turning to his adversary, he said: "Before you kill me, I beg you in the Name of the Most High engraved on Solomon's seal to answer me one question truthfully."

The jinnee trembled at the mention of the Name, and, when he had promised to answer truthfully, the fisherman asked: "How could this bottle, which is scarcely large enough to hold your hand or foot, ever contain your entire body?"

"Do you dare doubt that?" roared the jinnee indignantly.

"I will never believe it," replied the fisherman, "until I see you enter this bottle with my own eyes!"

Upon this the jinnee trembled from head to foot and dissolved into a column of smoke, which gradually wound itself into the bottle and disappeared inside. At once the fisherman snatched up the leaden stopper and thrust it into the mouth of the bottle. Then he called out to the jinnee: "Choose the manner of your death and the way that I shall kill you! By Allah, I will throw you back into the sea, and keep watch on this shore to warn all men of your treachery!"

When he heard the fisherman's words, the jinnee struggled desperately to escape from the bottle, but was prevented by the magic seal. He now altered his tone and, assuming a submissive air, assured the fisherman that he had been jesting with him and implored him to let him out. But the fisherman paid no heed to the jinnee's entreaties[6] and resolutely carried the bottle down to the sea. "What are you doing with me?" whimpered the jinnee helplessly.

"I am going to throw you back into the sea!" replied the fisherman. "You have lain in the depths eighteen hundred years, and there you shall remain till the Last Judgment![7] Did I not beg you to spare me so that Allah might spare you? But you took no pity on me, and He has now delivered you into my hands."

"Let me out," cried the jinnee in despair, "and I will give you fabulous riches!"

"Perfidious[8] jinnee," retorted the fisherman, "you justly deserve the fate of the king in the tale of Yunan and the doctor."

"What tale is that?" asked the jinnee.

The Tale of King Yunan and Duban The Doctor

It is related (began the fisherman) that once upon a time there reigned in the land of Persia a rich and mighty king called Yunan. He commanded great armies and had a numerous retinue of followers and courtiers. But he was afflicted with a leprosy[9] which baffled his physicians and defied all cures.

One day a venerable[10] old doctor named Duban came to the king's capital. He had studied books written in Greek, Persian, Latin, Arabic, and Syriac, and was deeply versed in the wisdom of the ancients. He was master of many sciences, knew the properties of plants and herbs, and was above all skilled in astrology and medicine. When this physician heard of the leprosy with which Allah had plagued the

---

5. **requite** (ri kwīt') v.: To make return or repayment for.

6. **entreaties** (en trēt' ēz) n.: Earnest requests.
7. **Last Judgment:** The final judgment of humankind at the end of the world.
8. **perfidious** (pər fid' ē əs) adj.: Treacherous.
9. **leprosy** (lep' rə sē) n.: A chronic infectious disease that attacks the skin, flesh, and nerves.
10. **venerable** (ven' ər ə b'l) adj.: Worthy of respect by reason of age and dignity or character.

king and of his doctors' vain endeavors to cure him, he put on his finest robes and betook himself to the royal palace. After he had kissed the ground before the king and called down blessings upon him, he told him who he was and said: "Great king, I have heard about the illness with which you are afflicted and have come to heal you. Yet will I give you no potion to drink, nor any ointment to rub upon your body."

The king was astonished at the doctor's words and asked: "How will you do that? By Allah, if you cure me I will heap riches upon you, and your children's children after you. Anything you wish for shall be yours and you shall be my companion and my friend."

Then the king gave him a robe of honor and other presents and asked: "Is it really true that you can heal me without draft or ointment? When is it to be? What day, what hour?"

"Tomorrow, if the king wishes," he replied.

The doctor took leave of the king, and hastening to the center of the town rented for himself a house, to which he carried his books, his drugs, and his other medicaments. Then he distilled balsams and elixirs,[11] and these he poured into a hollow polo stick.

Next morning he went to the royal palace and, kissing the ground before the king, requested him to ride to the field and play a game of polo with his friends. The king rode out with his viziers and his chamberlains,[12] and when he had entered the playing field the doctor handed him the hollow club and said: "Take this and grasp it firmly. Strike the ball with all your might until the palm of your hand and the rest of your body begin to perspire. The cure will penetrate your palm and course through the veins and arteries of your body. When it has done its work, return to the palace, wash yourself, and go to sleep. Thus shall you be cured; and peace be with you."

The king took hold of the club and, gripping it firmly, struck the ball and galloped after it with the other players. Harder and harder he struck the ball as he dashed up and down the field, until his palm and all his body perspired. When the doctor saw that the cure had begun its work, he ordered the king to return to the palace.

◆ **Reading Strategy**
A knowledge of what sport might help you envision this scene? Explain.

The slaves hastened to make ready the royal bath and hurried to prepare the linens and the towels. The king bathed, put on his nightclothes, and went to sleep.

Next morning the physician went to the palace. When he was admitted to the king's presence he kissed the ground before him and wished him peace. The king hastily rose to receive him; he threw his arms around his neck and seated him by his side.

For when the king left the bath the previous evening, he looked upon his body and rejoiced to find no trace of the leprosy. His skin had become as pure as virgin silver.

The king regaled the physician sumptuously all day. He bestowed on him robes of honor and other gifts, and when evening came gave him two thousand pieces of gold and mounted him on his own favorite horse. And so enraptured was the king by the consummate skill of his doctor that he kept repeating to himself: "This wise physician has cured me without draft or ointment. By Allah, I will load him with honors and he shall henceforth be my companion and trusted friend." And that night the king lay down to sleep in perfect bliss, knowing that he was clean in body and rid at last of his disease.

Next morning, as soon as the king sat down upon his throne, with the officers of his court standing before him and his lieutenants and viziers seated on his right and left, he called for the physician, who went up to him and kissed the ground before him. The king rose and seated the doctor by his side. He feasted him all day, gave him a thousand pieces of gold and

---

11. **balsams** (bôl′ səmz) **and elixirs** (i lik′ sərz): Two potions with supposed healing powers.
12. **chamberlains** (chām′ bər linz) *n*.: High officials in the king's court.

◆ **Build Vocabulary**

indignantly (in dig′nənt lē) *adv*.: In an angry or scornful manner

resolutely (rez′ ə lōōt′ lē) *adv*.: In a determined manner; without hesitation

enraptured (en rap′ chərd) *adj*.: Completely delighted

more robes of honor, and conversed with him till nightfall.

Now among the king's viziers there was a man of repellent aspect, an envious, black-souled villain, full of spite and cunning. When this vizier saw that the king had made the physician his friend and lavished on him high dignities and favors, he became jealous and began to plot the doctor's downfall. Does not the proverb say: "All men envy, the strong openly, the weak in secret?"

So, on the following day, when the king entered the council chamber and was about to call for the physician, the vizier kissed the ground before him and said: "My bounteous master, whose <u>munificence</u> extends to all men, my duty prompts me to forewarn you against an evil which threatens your life; nor would I be anything but a base-born wretch were I to conceal it from you."

Perturbed at these <u>ominous</u> words, the king ordered him to explain his meaning.

"Your majesty," resumed the vizier, "there is an old proverb which says: 'He who does not weigh the consequences of his acts shall never prosper.' Now I have seen the king bestow favors and shower honors upon his enemy, on an assassin who cunningly seeks to destroy him. I fear for the king's safety."

"Who is this man whom you suppose to be my enemy?" asked the king, turning pale.

"If you are asleep, your majesty," replied the vizier, "I beg you to awake. I speak of Duban, the doctor."

"He is my friend," replied the king angrily, "dearer to me than all my courtiers; for he has cured me of my leprosy, an evil which my physicians had failed to remove. Surely there is no other physician like him in the whole world, from East to West. How can you say these monstrous things of him? From this day I will appoint him my personal physician and give him every month a thousand pieces of gold. Were I to bestow on him the half of my kingdom, it would be but a small reward for his service. Your counsel, my vizier, is the prompting of jealousy and envy. Would you have me kill my benefactor and repent of my rashness, as King Sindbad repented after he had killed his falcon?"

The Tale of King Sindbad and the Falcon

Once upon a time (went on King Yunan) there was a Persian king who was a great lover of riding and hunting. He had a falcon which he himself had trained with loving care and which never left his side for a moment; for even at nighttime he carried it perched upon his fist, and when he went hunting took it with him. Hanging from the bird's neck was a little bowl of gold from which it drank. One day the king ordered his men to make ready for a hunting expedition and, taking with him his falcon, rode out with his courtiers. At length they came to a valley where they laid the hunting nets. Presently a gazelle fell into the snare, and the king said: "I will kill the man who lets her escape!"

They drew the nets closer and closer round the beast. On seeing the king the gazelle stood on her haunches and raised her forelegs to her head as if she wished to salute him. But as he bent forward to lay hold of her, she leaped over his head and fled across the field. Looking round, the king saw his courtiers winking at one another.

"Why are they winking?" he asked his vizier.

"Perhaps because you let the beast escape," ventured the other, smiling.

"On my life," cried the king, "I will chase the gazelle and bring her back!"

At once he galloped off in pursuit of the fleeing animal, and when he had caught up with her, his falcon swooped upon the gazelle, blinding her with his beak, and the king struck her down with a blow of his sword. Then dismounting he flayed the animal and hung the carcass on his saddle-bow.

It was a hot day and the king, who by this time had become faint with thirst, went to search for water. Presently, however, he saw a huge tree, down the trunk of which water was

◆ Build Vocabulary

munificence (myo͞o nif´ ə sens) *n.*: Great generosity

ominous (äm´ ə nəs) *adj.*: Hinting at bad things to come

trickling in great drops. He took the little bowl from the falcon's neck and, filling it with this water, placed it before the bird. But the falcon knocked the bowl with its beak and toppled it over. The king once again filled the bowl and placed it before the falcon, but the bird knocked it over a second time. Upon this the king became very angry and, filling the bowl a third time, set it down before his horse. But the falcon sprang forward and knocked it over with its wings.

"Allah curse you for a bird of ill omen!" cried the king. "You have prevented yourself from drinking and the horse also."

So saying, he struck the falcon with his sword and cut off both its wings. But the bird lifted its head as if to say: "Look into the tree!" The king raised his eyes and saw in the tree an enormous serpent spitting its venom down the trunk.

The king was deeply grieved at what he had done and, mounting his horse, hurried back to the palace. He threw his kill to the cook, and no sooner had he sat down, with the falcon still perched on his fist, than the bird gave a convulsive gasp and dropped down dead.

The king was stricken with sorrow and remorse for having so rashly killed the bird which had saved his life.

When the vizier heard the tale of King Yunan, he said: "I assure your majesty that my counsel is prompted by no other motive than my devotion to you and my concern for your safety. I

Charge of the Faramourz Cavaliers, Musée Reza Abbasi, Teheran

▲ **Critical Viewing** Which one of these figures is most likely to be King Yunan or King Sindbad? Why? **[Infer]**

beg leave to warn you that, if you put your trust in this physician, it is certain that he will destroy you. Has he not cured you by a device held in the hand? And might he not cause your death by another such device?"

"You have spoken wisely, my faithful vizier," replied the king. "Indeed, it is quite probable that this physician has come to my court as a spy to destroy me. And since he cured my illness by a thing held in the hand, he might as

The Fisherman and the Jinnee ◆ 403

cunningly poison me with the scent of a perfume. What should I do, my vizier?"

"Send for him at once," replied the other, "and when he comes, strike off his head. Only thus shall you be secure from his perfidy."

Thereupon the king sent for the doctor, who hastened to the palace with a joyful heart, not knowing what lay in store for him.

"Do you know why I have sent for you?" asked the king.

"Allah alone knows the unspoken thoughts of men," replied the physician.

"I have brought you here to kill you," said the king.

The physician was thunderstruck at these words and cried: "But why should you wish to kill me? What crime have I committed?"

"It has come to my knowledge," replied the king, "that you are a spy sent here to cause my death. But you shall be the first to die."

Then he called out to the executioner, saying: "Strike off the head of this traitor! "

"Spare me, and Allah will spare you!" cried the unfortunate doctor. "Kill me, and so shall Allah kill me!"

But the king gave no heed to his entreaties. "Never will I have peace again," he cried, "until I see you dead. For if you cured me by a thing held in the hand, you will doubtless kill me by the scent of a perfume or by some other foul device."

"Is it thus that you repay me?" asked the doctor. "Will you thus requite good with evil?"

But the king said: "You must die; nothing can now save you."

When he saw that the king was determined to put him to death, the physician wept and bitterly repented the service he had done him. Then the executioner came forward, blindfolded the doctor and, drawing his sword, held it in readiness for the king's signal. But the doctor continued to wail, crying: "Spare me, and Allah will spare you! Kill me, and so shall Allah kill you!"

Moved by the old man's lamentations, one of the courtiers interceded for him with the king, saying: "Spare the life of this man, I pray you. He has committed no crime against you, but rather has he cured you of an illness which

your physicians have failed to remedy."

"If I spare this doctor," replied the king, "he will use his devilish art to kill me. Therefore he must die."

Again the doctor cried: "Spare me, and Allah will spare you! Kill me, and so shall Allah kill you!" But when at last he saw that the king was fixed in his resolve, he said: "Your majesty, if you needs must kill me, I beg you to grant me a day's delay, so that I may go to my house and wind up my affairs. I wish to say farewell to my family and my neighbors and instruct them to arrange for my burial. I must also give away my books of medicine, of which there is one, a work of unparalleled virtue, which I would offer to you as a parting gift, that you may preserve it among the treasures of your kingdom."

"What may this book be?" asked the king.

"It holds secrets and devices without number, the least of them being this: that if, after you have struck off my head, you turn over three leaves of this book and read the first three lines upon the left-hand page, my severed head will speak and answer any questions you may ask it."

The king was astonished to hear this and at once ordered his guards to escort the physician to his house. That day the doctor put his affairs in order and next morning returned to the king's palace. There had already assembled the viziers, the chamberlains, the nabobs,[13] and all the chief officers of the realm, so that with their colored robes the court seemed like a garden full of flowers.

The doctor bowed low before the king; in one hand he had an ancient book and in the other a little bowl filled with a strange powder. Then he sat down and said: "Bring me a platter!" A platter was instantly brought in, and the doctor sprinkled the powder on it, smoothing it over with his fingers. After that he handed the book to the king and said: "Take this book and set it down before you. When my head has been cut off, place it upon the powder to stanch the bleeding. Then open the book."

---

13. **nabobs** (nāʹ bäbz) *n.*: Very rich or important people; aristocrats.

The king ordered the executioner to behead the physician. He did so. Then the king opened the book, and, finding the pages stuck together, put his finger to his mouth and turned over the first leaf. After much difficulty he turned over the second and the third, moistening his finger with his spittle at every page, and tried to read. But he could find no writing there.

"There is nothing written in this book," cried the king.

"Go on turning," replied the severed head.

The king had not turned six pages when the venom (for the leaves of the book were poisoned) began to work in his body. He fell backward in an agony of pain, crying: "Poisoned! Poisoned!" and in a few moments breathed his last.

"Now, treacherous jinnee," continued the fisherman, "had the king spared the physician, he in turn would have been spared by Allah. But he refused, and Allah brought about the king's destruction. And as for you, if you had been willing to spare me, Allah would have been merciful to you, and I would have spared your life. But you sought to kill me; therefore I will throw you back into the sea and leave you to perish in this bottle!"

Guide for Responding

◆ Literature and Your Life

Reader's Response Did you enjoy the technique of telling stories within stories? Explain.
Thematic Focus What role does justice play in the fates of both the jinnee and Yunan?

☑ Check Your Comprehension

1. How does the fisherman trick the jinnee and render him harmless?
2. What does the fisherman do to illustrate the fate that he feels the jinnee deserves?
3. What is King Yunan's reaction when the vizier first denounces Duban the Doctor?
4. In the story that Yunan tells, how does the falcon save King Sindbad's life?
5. After King Yunan changes his attitude toward Duban, what does Duban do to get even?
6. What conclusion does the fisherman draw from the story of King Yunan?

◆ Critical Thinking

INTERPRET

1. What character trait in the jinnee allows the fisherman to defeat him? Explain. **[Analyze]**
2. What kinds of rulers do Yunan and Sindbad seem to be? Cite details to support your answer. **[Infer]**
3. What do the behavior of the jinnee, Yunan, and Sindbad all have in common? **[Compare and Contrast]**
4. What do the outcomes of the three stories suggest about the way human beings should treat one another? **[Draw Conclusions]**

EVALUATE

5. Which characters do you think are treated the most unfairly? Explain your assessment. **[Assess]**

COMPARE LITERARY WORKS

6. In what ways is this tale like or unlike other folk tales you know? **[Compare and Contrast]**

Guide for Responding (continued)

◆ Reading Strategy

FORM MENTAL IMAGES

The details in a story help you **form mental images** of the people, objects, scenes, and events that the story contains.

For example, a jinnee is an unfamiliar creature, but the fifth paragraph of "The Fisherman and the Jinnee" tells you that the jinnee had "prodigious stature," a head that "reached the clouds" and was "a huge dome," a mouth "wide as a cavern" with "teeth ragged like broken rocks," legs that "towered like the masts of a ship," nostrils that were "two inverted bowls," and eyes "blazing like torches." These details help you form a mental image of a jinnee.

1. In "The Tale of King Yunan and Duban the Doctor," which details help you picture the polo game? Why?
2. What are some of the mental images you form in "The Tale of King Sindbad and the Falcon"?

◆ Literary Focus

FOLK TALE

"The Fisherman and the Jinnee" and the two other stories it contains are all examples of **folk tales,** stories that were originally composed and transmitted orally among the common people. Folk tales often contain one-dimensional characters, a clear division between good and evil, supernatural elements, and trickery by which weak characters outsmart the strong.

In "The Fisherman and the Jinnee," the jinnee is an evil supernatural creature whose chief traits are arrogance and cruelty. The good fisherman seems much weaker, yet he manages to trick the jinnee back into the bottle, where his powers are lost and the fisherman can toss him back to the oblivion from which he came.

1. What would you say is the fisherman's chief trait?
2. What supernatural elements appear in "The Tale of King Yunan and Duban the Doctor" and "The Tale of King Sindbad and the Falcon"?
3. Where in those two stories does a seemingly weak character use trickery to win the day?
4. Which characters in those stories seem entirely good or evil, and which seem to be something in between? Why?

◆ Build Vocabulary

USING THE LATIN WORD ROOT *-vert-*

Explain how the root *-vert-,* meaning "turn," figures into the meanings of the italicized words:
1. a *convert* to a religion
2. *revert* to an older way of behaving
3. *vertigo,* dizziness

USING THE WORD BANK: Sentence Completion

On a separate sheet, write the word from the word bank that best completes each statement. Use each word only once.
1. Thunder is often a(n) ____?____ sign.
2. A person showing determination acts ____?____.
3. It is ____?____ to show lack of respect for religion.
4. Children are often ____?____ by fireworks.
5. The letter W resembles a(n) ____?____ letter M.
6. The jinnee ____?____ the fisherman to release him.
7. A person who feels insulted may bristle ____?____.
8. The head of a charity thanks donors for their ____?____.

◆ Build Grammar Skills

ACTION AND LINKING VERBS

Action verbs express physical or mental action. **Linking verbs** express state of being and tell what the subject is by linking it to a word that further identifies or describes it. Many linking verbs can also be used as action verbs. If you can replace the verb with a form of *be* and the sentence still expresses a similar meaning, the verb is a linking verb.

Action: The fisherman *looked* in the bottle.
Linking: The jinnee *looked* monstrous.

Practice Identify the verb in each sentence, and state whether it is an action or a linking verb.
1. The bottle felt heavy.
2. The fisherman broke the seal.
3. The jinnee from inside seemed like a powerful giant.
4. The fisherman felt a great fear.
5. The fisherman tricked the jinnee in the end.

Writing Application On your paper, write a summary of this folk tale. Use at least two sentences with linking verbs and two with action verbs.

Build Your Portfolio

Idea Bank

Writing

1. **Justification** As the fisherman, write a justification of your treatment of the jinnee. Explain what the jinnee has done to deserve your actions.

2. **Story Outline** How would you update "The Fisherman and the Jinnee" if you were setting it in modern times? Outline your updated version, providing plot summaries and character descriptions.

3. **Sports Article** Imagine that you are a sports reporter in Persia of old. Write an article reporting on Yunan's polo game or Sindbad's hunting expedition. Use precise, interesting action verbs. **[Career Link]**

Speaking, Listening, and Viewing

4. **Oral Retelling** As Scheherazade, tell the king the story of "The Fisherman and the Jinnee." Stop at a suspenseful moment to make the king want to hear more the next day. **[Performing Arts Link]**

5. **Musical Review** Obtain the famous musical work *Scheherazade* by Russian composer Nikolai Rimsky-Korsakov. Play passages for the class. Then, in a review, discuss how well the music captures the mood of *The Thousand and One Nights*. **[Music Link]**

Researching and Representing

6. **Painting or Drawing** Choose a mental image that you formed as you read the tale, and turn it into a painting or drawing. **[Art Link]**

7. *The Arabian Nights* Using the Internet, encyclopedias, and other reference books, find out more about *The Arabian Nights* and its influence. Report your findings to the class.

Online Activity www.phlit.phschool.com

Guided Writing Lesson

Critique of a Work

The three interlocking stories that make up "The Fisherman and the Jinnee" have been told and retold for many centuries. Write a brief critique that tries to account for the enduring popularity of these tales. Include a critical analysis of the work that reveals the elements contributing to its continued appeal.

> **Writing Skills Focus: Relate to Universal Human Experience**
>
> In your critique, show how aspects of the three stories move beyond the era that produced them and have **universal appeal** for readers in different cultures at different times. For each of the three tales, ask yourself these questions:
>
> - What events or experiences in the story still seem relevant today?
> - What does the story say about human nature that still seems relevant today?
> - What aspects of the plot would today's audiences find interesting or amusing?
> - What else makes the story relevant or appealing?

Prewriting Divide a chart into three sections, one for each of the three stories that make up "The Fisherman and the Jinnee." Then, in the appropriate section, list the examples, reasons, and other details that you will use to support your opinion.

Drafting Begin your evaluation with a statement about the enduring appeal of "The Fisherman and the Jinnee." Then, provide details to explain the appeal. You might organize your explanation into three sections, each focusing on a different one of the interlocking stories.

Revising Make sure that you have provided enough examples to support your opinions and that you have used cause-effect transitions like *consequently* and *as a result* to make your reasoning clear.

Guide for Reading

Alan Paton (1903–1988)

In the middle of the last century, many people around the world first learned of South Africa's harsh racial policies through a bestseller called *Cry, the Beloved Country.* That novel was written by Alan Paton (pāt′ 'n), a white South African who spent most of his life fighting racial injustice in his native land.

Early Career As a young man, Paton taught physics and math to privileged white students in South Africa's racially segregated schools. A bout of illness prompted him to reevaluate his life, and he took a job as principal of Diepkloff Reformatory, a school for delinquent black African boys.

Certain that most of the boys' bad behavior stemmed more from social injustice than from their criminal natures, he replaced barbed wire with geraniums and harsh discipline with fatherly concern, transforming the school into a humane institution.

Working for Reform In 1948, the National Party came to power and established South Africa's apartheid (ə pär′ tāt′) laws (apartheid means "apartness") discriminating against nonwhites. Paton left his post at the reformatory and embarked on a study of overseas prisons. (For more on apartheid, see the Background for Understanding, p. 409.)

Political Activist It was during this trip to Europe and America that he wrote his landmark first novel, *Cry, the Beloved Country.* Returning to his homeland in the early 1950's, he helped found South Africa's Liberal Party, which championed social reform and argued against imprisonment of black activists like Nelson Mandela.

He also penned several more works of fiction and nonfiction, including a 1961 story collection based on his reformatory experiences, called *Tales from a Troubled Land.* "Ha'penny" comes from this collection.

Paton did not live to see the end of his long struggle. He died of cancer in 1988, just a few years before the repeal of the apartheid laws and the election of Nelson Mandela as South Africa's first black president.

◆ Build Vocabulary

LATIN WORD ROOTS: -manu-/-mani-

The narrator of "Ha'penny," a principal at a boys' reformatory, tries "to *manifest* a fatherly care" for the boys in his charge. The word *manifest* contains the Latin root -*mani-,* which means "hand." To *manifest* is "to show that something is right at hand"—in other words, "to show plainly."

WORD BANK

obliquely
estrangement
pilfering
apprehension
manifest
enjoined
prodigal

As you read the story, you will encounter these words. Each word is defined on the page where it first appears. Preview the list before you read.

◆ Build Grammar Skills

SUBJECT-VERB AGREEMENT

A **verb must agree with its subject** in number (singular or plural). In these sentences adapted from "Ha'penny," notice how the singular subject, *boy,* takes a singular verb, *turns,* while the plural subject, *boys,* takes a plural verb, *turn:*

A small *boy turns* instinctively towards affection.

Small *boys turn* instinctively towards affection.

Subject-verb agreement is mainly a problem in the present tense. In the past tense, most verbs have the same form with singular and plural subjects. An exception is the verb *be,* which in the past tense is *was* with singular subjects and *were* with plural subjects.

Ha'penny

◆ Literature and Your Life

CONNECT YOUR EXPERIENCE

Think of the teachers and principals you have admired. What are the qualities and behaviors that make them good leaders?

The story "Ha'penny" is told by a school principal who seems to be very concerned with his students.

Journal Writing If you were a school principal, how would you treat the students? Jot down your thoughts in a paragraph or two, and explain why you think your approach would work.

THEMATIC FOCUS: STRUGGLING FOR JUSTICE

"Ha'penny" takes place at a time of severe racial injustice in South Africa. As you read, ask yourself: How might the African boys' troubles relate to the injustice they face?

◆ Background for Understanding

HISTORY

Never more than a fifth of the population, white South Africans nevertheless controlled the nation for centuries. In the 1930's, when "Ha'penny" takes place, South Africa's races were strictly segregated. "Colored" South Africans of mixed ancestry (part black and part white), like Mrs. Maarman in the story, had limited rights and privileges. Black Africans like Ha'penny had almost none.

Then, in 1948, the National Party came to power and over the next two years codified the nation's racial practices into the laws of apartheid ("apartness"). The situation grew increasingly repressive. It was not until 1990 that the government began to repeal the apartheid laws.

◆ Literary Focus

CHARACTERIZATION

Characterization refers to the means by which a writer develops a character. Sometimes a writer uses **direct characterization,** directly stating information about a character's personality. At other times, a writer uses **indirect characterization,** revealing personality traits through the character's appearance, speech, thoughts, and actions.

In "Ha'penny," Paton uses both kinds of characterization:

Direct: "Ha'penny was a clever boy."

Indirect: When we see Ha'penny in action and hear the elaborate story he weaves, we recognize that he is clever.

◆ Reading Strategy

RESPOND

You **respond** to literature when you react to it both emotionally and intellectually. You focus on what the story makes you think and feel, allowing yourself to sympathize with some characters and be critical of others. When you respond to the work in this personal way, you are bound to appreciate it more fully.

As you read "Ha'penny," respond fully to the story. Ask yourself, "What do characters and situations say to me about people or life in general?" and "What feelings do they evoke in me?" You might keep track of your responses on a diagram like this one.

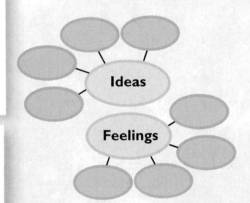

Ha'penny

Alan Paton

Of the six hundred boys at the reformatory, about one hundred were from ten to fourteen years of age. My Department had from time to time expressed the intention of taking them away, and of establishing a special institution for them, more like an industrial school than a reformatory. This would have been a good thing, for their offenses were very trivial, and they would have been better by themselves. Had such a school been established, I should have liked to have been Principal of it myself, for it would have been an easier job; small boys turn instinctively towards affection, and one controls them by it, naturally and easily.

Some of them, if I came near them, either on parade or in school or at football, would observe me watchfully, not directly or fully, but obliquely and secretly; sometimes I would surprise them at it, and make some small sign of recognition, which would satisfy them so that they would cease to observe me, and would give their full attention to the event of the moment. But I knew that my authority was thus confirmed and strengthened.

These secret relations with them were a source of continuous pleasure to me. Had they been my own children I would no doubt have given a greater expression to it. But often I would move through the silent and orderly parade, and stand by one of them. He would look straight in front of him with a little frown of concentration that expressed both childish awareness of and manly indifference to my nearness. Sometimes I would tweak his ear, and he would give me a brief smile of acknowledgment, or frown with still greater concentration. It was natural I suppose to confine these outward expressions to the very smallest, but they were taken as symbolic, and some older boys would observe them and take themselves to be included. It was a relief, when the reformatory was passing through times of turbulence and trouble, and when there was danger of estrangement between authority and boys, to make these simple and natural gestures, which were reassurances both to me and them that nothing important had changed.

On Sunday afternoons when I was on duty, I would take my car to the reformatory and watch the free boys being signed out at the gate. This simple operation was also watched by many boys not free, who would tell each other "in so many weeks I'll be signed out myself." Amongst the watchers were always some of the small boys, and these I would take by turns in the car. We would go out to the Potchefstroom Road with its ceaseless stream of traffic, and to the Baragwanath crossroads, and come back by the Van Wyksrus road to the reformatory. I would talk to them about their families, their parents, their sisters and brothers, and I would pretend to know nothing of Durban, Port Elizabeth, Potchefstroom, and Clocolan, and ask them if these places were bigger than Johannesburg.

One of the small boys was Ha'penny,[1] and he was about twelve years old. He came from Bloemfontein and was the biggest talker of them all. His mother worked in a white person's house, and he had two brothers and two sisters. His brothers were Richard and Dickie and his sisters Anna and Mina.

"Richard and Dickie?" I asked.

"Yes, *meneer*."[2]

"In English," I said, "Richard and Dickie are the same name."

When we returned to the reformatory, I sent for Ha'penny's papers; there it was plainly set down, Ha'penny was a waif, with no relatives at all. He had been taken in from one home to another, but he was naughty and uncontrollable, and eventually had taken to pilfering at the market.

I then sent for the Letter Book, and found that Ha'penny wrote regularly, or rather that others wrote for him till he could write himself, to Mrs. Betty Maarman, of 48 Vlak Street, Bloemfontein. But Mrs. Maarman had never once replied to him. When questioned, he had said, perhaps she is sick. I sat down and wrote at once to the Social Welfare Officer at Bloemfontein, asking him to investigate.

The next time I had Ha'penny out in the car, I questioned him again about his family. And he told me the same as before, his mother,

◆ Build Vocabulary

obliquely (o blēk´ lē) *adv.*: At an angle; indirectly

estrangement (e stranj´mənt) *n.*: The act or process of becoming hostile or indifferent

pilfering (pil´fə r iŋ) *n.*: The theft of a small sum or of items of little value

---

1. **Ha'penny** (hā´ pen´ē): A half-penny coin of small size and worth; used here as a nickname.
2. *meneer* (mə nēr´) *n.*: Dutch for "sir."

▲ **Critical Viewing** Suppose this boy is Ha'penny. What might he be thinking? [**Respond**]

Richard and Dickie, Anna and Mina. But he softened the "D" of "Dickie," so that it sounded now like Tickie.

"I thought you said Dickie," I said.

"I said Tickie," he said.

He watched me with concealed <u>apprehension</u>, and I came to the conclusion that this waif of Bloemfontein was a clever boy, who had told me a story that was all imagination, and had changed one single letter of it to make it safe

from any question. And I thought I understood it all too, that he was ashamed of being without a family, and had invented them all, so that no one might discover that he was fatherless and motherless, and that no one in the world cared whether he was alive or dead. This gave me a strong feeling for him, and I went out of my way to <u>manifest</u> towards him that fatherly care that the State, though not in those words,

had <u>enjoined</u> upon me by giving me this job.

Then the letter came from the Social Welfare Officer in Bloemfontein, saying that Mrs. Betty Maarman of 48 Vlak Street was a real person, and that she had four children, Richard and Dickie, Anna and Mina, but that Ha'penny was no child of hers, and she knew him only as a derelict of the streets. She had never answered his letters, because he wrote to her as *mother,* and she was no mother of his, nor did she wish to play any such role. She was a decent woman, a faithful member of the church, and she had no thought of corrupting her family by letting them have anything to do with such a child.

But Ha'penny seemed to me anything but the usual delinquent, his desire to have a family was so strong, and his reformatory record was so blameless, and his anxiety to please and obey so great, that I began to feel a great duty towards him. Therefore I asked him about his "mother."

He could not speak enough of her, nor with too high praise. She was loving, honest, and

▲ **Critical Viewing** Do you think Ha'penny would have liked to live with a family like this one? Why or why not? **[Connect]**

strict. Her home was clean. She had affection for all her children. It was clear that the homeless child, even as he had attached himself to me, would have attached himself to her; he had observed her even as he had observed me, but did not know the secret of how to open her heart, so that she would take him in, and save him from the lonely life that he led.

"Why did you steal when you had such a mother?" I asked.

He could not answer that; not all his brains nor his courage could find an answer to such a question, for he knew that with such a mother he would not have stolen at all.

"The boy's name is Dickie," I said, "not Tickie."

◆ **Build Vocabulary**

apprehension (ap′rē hen′shən) *n.*: Nervous fear; anxiety

manifest (man′ ə fest) *v.*: To make evident or plain

enjoined (en join′) *v.*: Forced by law, custom, or circumstance; imposed

And then he knew the deception was revealed. Another boy might have said, "I told you it was Dickie," but he was too intelligent for that; he knew that if I had established that the boy's name was *Dickie*, I must have established other things too. I was shocked by the immediate and visible effect of my action. His whole brave assurance died within him, and he stood there exposed, not as a liar, but as a homeless child who had surrounded himself with mother, brothers, and sisters, who did not exist. I had shattered the very foundation of his pride, and his sense of human significance.

He fell sick at once, and the doctor said it was tuberculosis.[3] I wrote at once to Mrs. Maarman, telling her the whole story, of how this small boy had observed her, and had decided that she was the person he desired for his mother. But she wrote back saying that she could take no responsibility for him. For

---

3. **tuberculosis** (too bur′ kyoo lō′ sis) *n.*: Deadly, wasting disease, most often of the lungs.

▲ **Critical Viewing** Port Elizabeth, shown in this painting, is one of the cities the narrator mentions on p. 411. What impression of Port Elizabeth does this image convey? Explain. **[Interpret]**

Port Elizabeth, Old Town, 1940, Robert Broadley, South African National Gallery, Cape Town, South Africa

one thing, Ha'penny was a Mosuto,[4] and she was a colored woman; for another, she had never had a child in trouble, and how could she take such a boy?

Tuberculosis is a strange thing; sometimes it manifests itself suddenly in the most unlikely host, and swiftly sweeps to the end. Ha'penny withdrew himself from the world, from all Principals and mothers, and the doctor said there was little hope. In desperation I sent money for Mrs. Maarman to come.

---

4. **Mosuto** (ma sōō′ tō): A member of the black South African people called the Basotho, or Basuto. Mosuto is now usually spelled Mosotho.

She was a decent homely woman, and seeing that the situation was serious, she, without fuss or embarrassment, adopted Ha'penny for her own. The whole reformatory accepted her as his mother. She sat the whole day with him, and talked to him of Richard and Dickie, Anna and Mina, and how they were all waiting for him to come home. She poured out her affection on him, and had no fear of his sickness, nor did she allow it to prevent her from satisfying his hunger to be owned. She talked to him of what they would do when he came back, and how he would go to the school, and what they would buy for Guy Fawkes night.[5]

He in his turn gave his whole attention to her, and when I visited him he was grateful, but I had passed out of his world. I felt judged in that I had sensed only the existence and not the measure of his desire. I wished I had done something sooner, more wise, more prodigal.

We buried him on the reformatory farm, and Mrs. Maarman said to me, "when you put up the cross, put he was my son."

"I'm ashamed," she said, "that I wouldn't take him."

---

5. **Guy Fawkes night:** English holiday celebrated on the fifth of November with bonfires and fireworks.

"The sickness," I said, "the sickness would have come."

"No," she said, shaking her head with certainty. "It wouldn't have come. And if it had come at home, it would have been different."

So she left for Bloemfontein, after her strange visit to a reformatory. And I was left too, with the resolve to be more prodigal in the task that the State, though not in so many words, had enjoined on me.

◆ **Reading Strategy**
What is your response to Mrs. Maarman's observation?

◆ **Build Vocabulary**

prodigal (präd´ i gəl) *adj.*: Extremely generous; lavish

Guide for Responding

◆ Literature and Your Life

Readers Response How did you react to the outcome of Ha'penny's story? Explain.

Thematic Focus What role do you think racial injustice played in determining Ha'penny's fate?

Reader's Journal In a paragraph or two, express your own hopes for other boys like Ha'penny. What do you wish for them and why?

Questions for Research "Ha'penny" is based on Alan Paton's own experiences as the principal of Diepkloff Reformatory. Write one or more questions you could research to learn more about Paton's experiences at this school.

☑ Check Your Comprehension

1. What does Ha'penny say about his family, and what is the actual situation?
2. What reasons does Mrs. Maarman give for refusing to acknowledge Ha'penny?
3. What happens to Ha'penny after the narrator exposes the false nature of the boy's story?

◆ Critical Thinking

INTERPRET

1. What does the narrator mean when he says that on learning of Ha'penny's lie, he developed "a strong feeling for him"? **[Interpret]**
2. Why do you think Mrs. Maarman changes her mind about acknowledging Ha'penny? **[Infer]**
3. What does the narrator seem to take away from his experience with Ha'penny? **[Synthesize]**

EVALUATE

4. Do you blame the narrator or Mrs. Maarman for what happened to Ha'penny? Explain. **[Evaluate]**

APPLY

5. What changes can the narrator make so that tragedies like Ha'penny's can be avoided in the future? **[Speculate]**

COMPARE LITERARY WORKS

6. Compare this story to other works about race relations that you have read. What is similar and what is different about the situations and outcomes? **[Compare and Contrast]**

Guide for Responding (continued)

◆ Reading Strategy

RESPOND

When you **respond** to "Ha'penny," you focus on what the characters and situations make you feel and think.

For example, you might feel sympathy for Ha'penny's plight and sorrow for his early death. You also might think about the broader ideas that his experiences convey about racial injustice, family ties, juvenile delinquency, and social responsibility.

1. How do you respond to the narrator of the story? Discuss your emotional response as well as the broader ideas his experiences help convey.
2. How do you respond to the situation at the reform school? For example, what seems wrong with it, and does anything about it seem right?

◆ Literary Focus

CHARACTERIZATION

In "Ha'penny," you learn about the characters' personalities through a combination of **direct** and **indirect characterization:** directly, from what the narrator says about them; indirectly, from the way they speak and behave.

For example, the narrator directly states that Ha'penny leads a "lonely life." However, you also see Ha'penny's loneliness indirectly through his action of adopting Mrs. Maarman's family as his own.

1. What qualities besides loneliness does Ha'penny display?
2. Give details from the story that show the author conveying Ha'penny's qualities through direct characterization and suggesting them through indirect characterization.
3. Show how Paton uses a combination of direct and indirect characterization to convey Mrs. Maarman's personality.
4. Demonstrate how something you know about the narrator himself comes from direct characterization, indirect characterization, or both.

◆ Build Vocabulary

USING THE LATIN WORD ROOT *-manu-/mani-*

Explain how the Latin root *-manu-*, meaning "hand," contributes to the meanings of these words:

1. manuscript 2. manufacture 3. manual (adjective)

USING THE WORD BANK: True or False

Copy the following statements in your notebook, and indicate if each statement is true or false.

1. People sometimes *manifest* sleepiness by yawning.
2. Stealing nuclear weapons is an example of *pilfering*.
3. A stingy person is *prodigal* in his or her spending.
4. Students often face tests with some *apprehension*.
5. A judge is *enjoined* to hear a case fairly.
6. In an *estrangement*, two people grow more friendly.
7. If light slants down at an angle, it shines *obliquely*.

◆ Build Grammar Skills

SUBJECT-VERB AGREEMENT

A **subject and verb must agree** in number (singular or plural), even if the subject follows the verb. (*There* at the beginning of a sentence is never the subject.)

At the reformatory *are* six hundred *boys*.

There *is* one *boy* with the nickname Ha'penny.

Remember that the subject of a sentence is never part of a prepositional phrase.

One of the boys *gets* tuberculosis.

Diseases of this sort *cause* problems among the poor.

Practice For each sentence, identify the subject and indicate which verb in parentheses agrees with it.

1. One of the students (invents, invent) a family.
2. From his stories (comes, come) a picture of happy family life.
3. There (is, are) some odd details in the boy's story.
4. The information in the school records (tells, tell) a different story.
5. In the boy's file (is, are) the true facts about him.

Build Your Portfolio

 Idea Bank

Writing

1. **School Records** Write the entry that the Social Welfare Officer in Bloemfontein might have made in Ha'penny's school records at the time the officer investigated Mrs. Maarman. **[Career Link]**

2. **Diary Entry** How do you think the narrator felt about Ha'penny and his own treatment of the boy? Express those feelings in a diary entry that the narrator might have written soon after Ha'penny's death.

3. **Letters** Write the series of letters from Ha'penny to Mrs. Maarman that the narrator might have found in the Letter Book.

Speaking, Listening, and Viewing

4. **Role Play** What do you think Mrs. Maarman told Richard, Dickie, Anna, and Mina when she returned to Bloemfontein after Ha'penny died? With a group of students, role-play the scene. **[Performing Arts Link]**

5. **Research and Speech** Pretending that you are a health department official, provide information about tuberculosis in a speech to students. **[Science Link]**

Researching and Representing

6. **Mural** Create a mural that the students at Ha'penny's school might have created to express their feelings about his untimely death. **[Art Link]**

7. **Research Paper** How has the education of black South Africans improved? What problems still exist? Answer these questions in a short research paper. **[Social Studies Link]**

Online Activity www.phlit.phschool.com

 Guided Writing Lesson

Evaluation

Paton's story takes place in the racially segregated South Africa of the 1930's. Using what you know or research, write an evaluation in which you assess how well the story reflects its time and place. Consider descriptions of the setting as well as people's attitudes, behavior, and speech.

Writing Skills Focus: Transitions to Show Examples

In your evaluation, you will need to make general statements about South Africa or the story and then support them with examples. Here are some **transitions to show examples:**

- for example
- a few of these are
- in particular
- especially

Prewriting Review the author biography and Background for Understanding on pp. 408 and 409. (If you like, you can also research South Africa in the 1930's and 1940's.) Then, jot down aspects of the time or culture that you think are or are not accurately reflected in the story.

Drafting Begin your evaluation with a statement of how effectively Paton captures the time and culture in which his story is set. Then, support the statement by citing details from the story. Use transitiions to show examples.

Revising Make sure that you have provided enough examples to support your opinions and that you have used transitions to make your examples clear.

Also, check your sentences for subject-verb agreement. For more on subject-verb agreement, see pp. 408 and 416.

Guide for Reading

Maxim Gorky *(1868–1936)*

Maxim Gorky (gôr´kē) lived a life of startling contradictions that reflected those of his homeland, Russia.

> *Throughout the most turbulent years of Russian history, he championed the poor and fought for justice. Yet Gorky's dreams of revolution ended in a nightmarish reality.*

A Brutal Childhood Gorky's real name was Alexis Peshkov. He was born into poverty, began working at age eight, and became an orphan at age nine. He spent years wandering the countryside as a vagrant. Angry at the suffering he saw all across Russia, he became a revolutionary, determined to overthrow an unjust social system.

An Overnight Success When he began writing his observations, at age twenty-four, he changed his name to Maxim Gorky. This pen name means "Maxim the Bitter One." As a journalist, playwright, and short-story writer, Gorky was an overnight success. He soon became a wealthy, world-famous celebrity, adored by working-class people for his play *The Lower Depths*, a passionate appeal for the rights of the oppressed.

A Reluctant Revolutionary For a time, Gorky joined ranks with the Bolsheviks (bōl´ shə viks´), the radicals who seized power during the Russian Revolution of 1917. However, Gorky opposed the Bolsheviks' seizure of power and came to believe that the Bolshevik leader, Lenin, was really a cruel dictator.

Exile and Return Disillusioned with the Revolution, Gorky escaped from the newly formed Soviet Union to Italy in 1921, and lived there until 1928. Receiving a hero's welcome upon his return, he spent the rest of his life working in the Soviet Union to moderate the harsh rule of a new Soviet tyrant, Joseph Stalin. Gorky died a bitter, disheartened man in 1936.

◆ Build Vocabulary

LATIN WORD ROOTS: -numer-

In "The Gardener" Maxim Gorky describes the "innumerable" regiments of soldiers he sees returning from battle during the Russian Revolution. *Innumerable* contains the Latin root -*numer*-, which means "to count." Combining the root -*numer*- with the prefix in-, meaning "not," *innumerable* means "countless" or "too many to be counted."

WORD BANK

bristle
engrossed
innumerable
agog
shriveled

As you read, you will encounter the words on this list. Each word is defined on the page where it first appears. Preview the list before you read.

◆ Build Grammar Skills

ADVERB CLAUSES

An **adverb clause** is a subordinate clause—a group of words that contains a subject and a verb, but cannot stand by itself as a complete sentence—that modifies a verb, an adjective, or an adverb.

Adverb clauses clarify information in other clauses by telling *where, when, why, how, to what extent,* or *under what conditions* actions occur. Such clauses are introduced by subordinating conjunctions like *when, whenever, where, although, because, since, if, as,* and *while.*

In this example from "The Gardener," the adverb clause clarifies *when* the gardener scolds the onlookers and soldiers.

As he walks along, he scolds both onlookers and soldiers . . .

◆ *Literature and Your Life*

CONNECT YOUR EXPERIENCE

A famous poem by Rudyard Kipling, "If—" declares "If you can keep your head when all about you / Are losing theirs . . . you'll be a Man, my son." However, as you read Gorky's journal entries about the Russian Revolution, you may wonder about Kipling's advice. When is it important to "keep your head" and go about your own work, and when is it important to be part of the events of your time?

THEMATIC FOCUS: RIGHT AND WRONG

As you read Gorky's descriptions of a gardener's conflicts with soldiers, ask yourself: Were the soldiers wrong to do what they did? Why or why not?

Journal Writing Write a brief description of a flower garden that you have seen.

◆ Background for Understanding

HISTORY

These events form the backdrop for Gorky's observations:

1547–1917 Russia is ruled by emperors called "Czars."

Early twentieth century Peasants travel to St. Petersburg and take low-paying factory jobs. Political rebels begin organizing the urban poor.

1914 Russia enters World War I on the side of Britain and France.

1914–1917 Russia suffers serious casualties in the war.

February-March 1917 Food shortages and poor morale among the troops lead to riots in Petrograd, today's St. Petersburg.

March 1917 Czar Nicholas is forced to step down.

July 1917 Bolsheviks, under Lenin, stage a military uprising that fails.

November 1917 Second uprising by Bolsheviks succeeds.

◆ Literary Focus

JOURNAL

In a **journal**, a writer records his or her observations, thoughts, and feelings about the daily events of life. Some journals are strictly personal records of the writer's own individual experiences. Other journals record, in addition to private experiences, observations of political and social events of the time.

Maxim Gorky's journals contain political and social observations that he made during the Russian Revolution. His daily notes enable you to peek through the keyhole of history and see what it was like to live during this dramatic era. Look for details in his account that reveal the conflicts people experienced.

◆ Reading Strategy

USE PRIOR KNOWLEDGE

Whether you are reading a short story or a nonfiction account of historic events, you can use your own **prior knowledge** about what you already know to help you understand what you are reading.

Before you read Gorky's journal, recall what you already know about the Russian Revolution. Reread Gorky's biography on p. 418, and the Background for Understanding, on this page. Then, copy the chart below, and fill in what you already know about the events of 1917. As you read Gorky's journal, add details and insights that Gorky provides about the events.

Dates	Feb 1917	Mar 1917	Nov 1917
What Gorky Adds			
What I Know			

The Gardener

Maxim Gorky

Translated by Moura Budberg

February 1917

Motor-cars, splashing mud against the walls and smothering passers-by, tear rumbling and hooting down the street. They are crowded to overflowing with soldiers and sailors, and <u>bristle</u> with the steel quills of bayonets,[1] like huge hedgehogs running amok. Every now and then there is the crack of a rifle. Revolution! The Russian nation is scurrying about, bewildered with its newly-acquired freedom; it is trying to grasp it, but finds it somewhat elusive.

In the Alexander Park a gardener is <u>engrossed</u> in his solitary work; a thick-set man in the fifties. Clumsily and quietly he sweeps away last year's fallen leaves and the litter from paths and flower-beds, and brushes off the freshly fallen snow. He takes not the slightest interest in the bustle that is going on around him, and remains deaf to the screeching of klaxons,[2] the shouts and songs and shots. He does not even see the red flags. I watched him to see if he would look up presently and notice the people running about, the trucks glittering with bayonets. But he bent down over his work and went on with it as stubbornly as a mole. Apparently he is as blind as one also.

---

1. **bayonets** (bā′ ə nets′) n.: Daggerlike blades attached to the ends of rifles.

2. **klaxons** (klaks′ ənz) n.: Electric horns with a loud, shrill sound.

◆ Build Vocabulary

bristle (bris′ əl) v. Become stiff, like bristles

engrossed (en grōst′) adj. Completely involved

Cossacks, 1910–11, Wassily Kandinsky, Tate Gallery, London

▲ **Critical Viewing** Gorky wrote his journal entries during the Russian Revolution of 1917. Which details in this painting capture the feeling of a revolution? Why? **[Support]**

March 1917

Along the streets, along the paths in the park, in the direction of the Narodni Dom, hundreds, thousands of soldiers in grey are moving slowly, some of them dragging machine-guns behind them like small iron pigs tied to a string. This is one of the <u>innumerable</u> machine-gun regiments that has just arrived from Oranienbaum. They say that there are more than ten thousand men in it. They do not know what to do with themselves, and ever since they arrived this morning they have been wandering about the town, looking for lodgings. The passers-by step aside when they meet them, for these men are war-weary, hungry and fierce. Some of them, I noticed, had squatted down by a large, round flower-bed and had scattered their rifles and haversacks[3] over it.

◆ **Literary Focus**
Which details indicate that Gorky's journal has more of a social than a personal focus? Explain

Presently, not hurrying himself in the least, the gardener came up with his broom. He surveyed them angrily:

"What sort of a camping ground do you think you've got here? This is a flower-bed—flowers are going to grow here. You know what flowers are, don't you? Are you all blind? This is the children's playground. Come off it, I say. D'you hear me?"

And the fierce, armed men meekly crawled away from the flower-bed.

6 July 1917

Soldiers in steel helmets, just recalled from the front, are surrounding the Peter and Paul Fortress. They are marching leisurely along the pavements and through the park, dragging their machine-guns behind them, their rifles carelessly dangling from their shoulders. Occasionally one of them calls out good-naturedly to a passer-by:

"Hurry up; there's going to be some shooting!"

The inhabitants are all <u>agog</u> to see the battle and are following the soldiers silently, with fox-like movements, dodging from tree to tree and straining their necks, looking eagerly ahead.

In the Alexander Park flowers are growing at the sides of the paths; the gardener is busying himself among them. He has a clean apron on and carries a spade in his hand. As he walks along he scolds both onlookers and soldiers as though they were a flock of sheep.

"Where are you walking, there? Is that grass made for you to trample on? Isn't there enough room for you on the path?"

A bearded, iron-headed peasant in soldier's uniform, his rifle under his arm, says to the gardener:

"You look out yourself, old boy, or we'll shoot you straight away."

"Oh, will you? You just try! Fine shot, you are. . . ."

"Don't you know there's a war on? There's going to be some fighting."

"Oh, is there? Well, get on with your fighting, and I'll get on with my job."

"I'm with you there. Have you got a cigarette?"

Pulling out his pouch from his pocket the gardener grumbled: "Trampling about where you're not allowed to . . ."

"It's war."

"What's that got to do with me? Fighting's all very well for them that likes it, and you've got plenty of others to help you; but I'm all alone in this job. You'd better clean that rifle of yours a bit; it's all rusty . . ."

There is a whistle and the soldier, unable to light the cigarette in his lips, puts it hastily in his pocket and runs off between the trees.

---

3. haversacks (hav´ ər saks´) *n.*: Canvas bags for carrying supplies, usually worn over the shoulder.

The gardener spits after him in disgust and shouts angrily:

"What the devil are you running over the grass for? Isn't there any other road you can go by?"

Autumn, 1917

The gardener walks leisurely along the path, a ladder on his shoulder and a pair of shears in his hand. Every now and then he stops to cut off the dead branches by the side of the path. He has grown thinner—seems almost <u>shriveled</u>; his clothes hang on him like a sail on a mast on a windless day. The shears snip angrily and creakily as he cuts down the barren wood.

Watching him, I could not help thinking that neither an earthquake nor a flood would prevent him from going on with his work. And if the trumpets of the archangels announcing the day of judgment were not shining brilliantly enough, I am quite certain that he would scold the archangels in precisely the same voice as he scolded the soldier.

"You'd better clean those trumpets of yours a bit, they're all dirty . . ."

◆ Build Vocabulary

innumerable (in noo′ mer ə bəl) *adj.*: Too many to be counted

agog (ə gäg′) *adj.*: In a state of eager anticipation

shriveled (shriv′ əld) *adj.*: Shrunken and made wrinkled and withered

Guide for Responding

◆ *Literature and Your Life*

Reader's Response Do you admire the gardener? Why or why not?

Thematic Focus Was the gardener wrong to ignore the conflicts of the Russian revolution? Why or why not?

☑ Check Your Comprehension

1. What is the gardener doing as soldiers first begin rumbling into town?
2. Briefly describe what happens when soldiers drop their belongings on the gardener's flower bed.
3. In July, what do many people in the city do when they hear there's going to be a battle nearby?
4. What does the gardener say when he hears about the battle?
5. By autumn, how has the gardener changed, and how is he still the same?

◆ Critical Thinking

INTERPRET

1. In the February entry, why does Gorky describe the gardener as being "blind"? **[Infer]**
2. In the March entry, why does the gardener accuse the soldiers of being "blind"? **[Infer]**
3. Why do you think the soldiers crawl away "meekly" when the gardener scolds them? **[Analyze]**
4. How does Gorky seem to feel about the gardener's fearlessness in confronting the soldiers? **[Interpret]**
5. How and why do you think Gorky's attitude toward the gardener changes during the year? **[Synthesize]**

EVALUATE

6. Is the gardener foolish or wise to confront the soldiers? Explain. **[Make a Judgment]**

Guide for Responding (continued)

◆ Reading Strategy

USE PRIOR KNOWLEDGE

Your **prior knowledge**—what you already knew about the Russian Revolution before reading Gorky's journal—should have helped you to understand many of the details in Gorky's journal entries.

For example, the Background for Understanding on p. 419 indicates that in February 1917 food shortages and poor morale among troops caused riots in Petrograd. Knowing these facts, you can recognize evidence of those riots in Gorky's diary entry for February 1917: Truckloads of soldiers and sailors "tear rumbling and hooting down the street." Occasionally a shot is fired by one of these dissatisfied fighters.

1. Find evidence in Gorky's March diary entry that connects with the timeline in the Background For Understanding. Explain.
2. In July, Gorky describes citizens following the soldiers "all agog to see the battle." What background information helped you understand what was going on?
3. In his autumn entry, Gorky describes the gardener as "thinner . . . almost shriveled." Basing your answer on your prior knowledge, tell why the gardener might have changed in this way.

◆ Literary Focus

JOURNAL

Gorky's journal—his recording of his own personal observations over a period of time—offers valuable insights about what it was like to live through the events of the Russian Revolution.

The entries provide actual conversations overheard on the street. Such conversations would not be part of most standard histories of this time. However, they give clues to the way ordinary people were acting and reacting.

1. Choose one passage of dialogue and show how it gives a human dimension to historical events.
2. Identify three other descriptive details in the journal that could only have been provided by an eyewitness to the Revolution. Explain your choices.
3. Why do you think Gorky keeps recording his impressions of the gardener as the months go by?

◆ Build Vocabulary

USING THE LATIN ROOT -numer-

Knowing that the Latin root -numer- means "to count," match each -numer- word in Column A with its definition in Column B.

Column A	Column B
1. numeral	a. many
2. enumerate	b. figure used to represent a number
3. numerous	c. the top number in a fraction
4. numerator	d. to count

USING THE WORD BANK: Sentence Completion

Write this paragraph on your paper and fill in the blanks with words from the Word Bank. Use each word just once.

The gardener is so _____?_____ in his work that he can ignore _____?_____ distractions. He stays quietly focused while everyone else is _____?_____ with excitement about the Revolution. As the soldiers' bayonets _____?_____, the gardener keeps working. Even when his flowers have _____?_____ in the cold, he continues to work.

◆ Build Grammar Skills

ADVERB CLAUSES

An **adverb clause** is a subordinate clause—a group of words that contains a subject and a verb, but cannot stand by itself as a complete sentence—that modifies a verb, an adjective, or an adverb.

Practice Copy the following sentences into your notebook. Underline the adverb clause and circle the word it modifies.

1. Most citizens step aside when they see the war-weary soldiers.
2. The gardener is angry because the soldiers are trampling his flower beds.
3. When he scolds the soldiers, they meekly leave.
4. After they leave, the gardener continues his work.
5. He goes on working although people are fighting.

Writing Application On your paper, add an adverb clause to make each sentence more specific.

1. The gardener walked across the street.
2. The soldier lifted his rifle.

Build Your Portfolio

Idea Bank

Writing

1. **Letter to a Friend** As Gorky, write a letter to a friend in the year 1917. In your letter describe conditions in your city and how you feel about what is going on.

2. **Journal Entry** Rewrite one of Gorky's journal entries from the gardener's point of view. As the gardener, describe the events of the day and your thoughts and feelings about them.

3. **Editorial** Imagine that you are the editor of a Russian newspaper during the Revolution. Write an editorial explaining why you support or oppose the actions of the Bolsheviks and soldiers fighting to take over the government. **[Social Studies Link]**

Speaking, Listening, and Viewing

4. **Role-Play** With a partner, role-play a conversation that might have taken place between Maxim Gorky and the gardener during one of the months of 1917.

5. **Debate** With a small group, debate the following proposition: "It is morally wrong to ignore the important social conflicts taking place during your lifetime." **[Social Studies Link]**

Researching and Representing

6. **Multimedia Presentation** Using film clips, diary entries, recordings, pictures, and quotations, report on the life of Maxim Gorky. **[Media Link]**

7. **Timeline** Create a timeline that shows key events during the Russian Revolution and the civil war that followed it. Illustrate your timeline with photos of people who were important leaders during this period. **[Social Studies Link; Art Link]**

Online Activity www.phlit.phschool.com

Guided Writing Lesson

Newspaper Story

Imagine that you are a reporter who witnessed one of the events Gorky describes. Rewrite Gorky's journal entry as a newspaper story. Use the details Gorky provides and, if you need further details, make up ones consistent with Gorky's.

Writing Skills Focus: Key Questions in a Newspaper Story

Your newspaper story should answer six key **questions** about the events you describe: *Who? What? Where? When? Why?* and *How?*

Summarize your answers and grab readers' attention in the opening paragraph, called the lead. Here is a sample lead for a story based on Gorky's July entry.

Model

July 6, 1917: Thousands of Bolshevik troops thronged the Peter and Paul Fortress in Petrograd today, preparing to battle troops loyal to the government.

Prewriting Choose a date for your newspaper story. Then reread Gorky's journal for that date, as well as the Background. Take notes on facts that answer the questions *Who? What? Where? When? Why?* and *How?*

Drafting Draft an attention-getting lead. Then, use details from your notes to flesh out the story. Follow good news-writing practice by including less important facts at the end of the story.

Revising Be sure that you have answered all the key questions. Also, confirm that the sequence of events is clear, complete, and accurate.

Note whether you have correctly used adverb clauses to clarify information in other clauses. For more on adverb clauses, see pp. 418 and 424.

Position Paper

Writing Process Workshop

If you had a strong opinion about a controversial issue, you would want to let others know about it. One way to do this is to write a **position paper**. In a position paper, the writer attempts to persuade the reader to accept his or her viewpoint on a controversial issue. In many cases, position papers are written for an audience, such as a town council, with the power to shape policy related to the issue.

Write a position paper on an issue that's important to you. The following skills will help you write a persuasive position paper.

Writing Skills Focus

▶ **Elaborate** with details, examples, and facts to support your claims. The more specific and factual your argument is, the more compelling it will be.

▶ **Use a logical organization** for your paper. Order of importance, cause and effect, pro and con, and comparison and contrast are all good methods of organization.

▶ **Be accurate.** Use care in expressing your ideas—avoid words like *all* and *never* unless you know they are true.

The following excerpt uses these skills to argue a point persuasively: Youths need more training to drive safely.

MODEL

① The writer uses statistics to support her position.

② The writer cites a reliable source of information to back up her example.

New drivers under the age of twenty-one should be required to take at least thirty hours of formal driver training. ① Drivers age twenty-one and under make up less than 10 percent of the driving population, yet they represent nearly 20 percent of Americans killed in auto accidents.

A study by the University of North Carolina's Highway Safety Research Center ② suggests that a major reason so many young people are involved in accidents is that they are inadequately prepared . . .

Prewriting

Choose Your Topic You'll find many ideas for a position paper in newspapers and magazines. Scan the contents of a newspaper or magazine. Do any issues or current events especially engage your interests or emotions? What issues make you want to write to a government official or other leader? Jot down your reactions to various stories or photographs. Then review your notes and choose a topic. Write your topic as a statement of your position.

Know Your Audience Knowing the identity of the audience you're trying to persuade is essential. Use the following questions to help identify your audience.

▶ Who is your audience? Your peers? Teachers? Experts on the topic?

▶ How old are the people in your audience? Are they younger than, older than, or the same age as you?

▶ What is your audience's view on the position you'll argue? If it's an opposing view, what counterarguments can you devise?

▶ What parts of your subject might especially interest your audience? How can you make these parts stand out?

As you draft your position paper, you can make your points address the concerns of the audience you've identified.

Drafting

Distinguish Fact From Opinion Facts are statements that can be proven true by research or direct observation. Opinions are statements of belief that can be supported, but not proven, with facts. As you draft, use facts from your research to support your opinions. Notice how the following facts support opinions:

Opinions	Facts
This is a responsible newspaper.	This newspaper won a Pulitzer Prize.
Americans eat too much fat.	The average American diet is 40 percent fat.
We need more pet shelters.	Last year, more than 600 stray animals were destroyed because shelters had no room for them.

Writer's Solution Connection Writing Lab

To help you choose a topic, refer to the Inspirations for Persuasion in the Writing Lab tutorial on Persuasion.

APPLYING LANGUAGE SKILLS: Appositives

An **appositive** is a noun or pronoun placed near another noun or pronoun to identify or provide more information about it.

My main mode of transportation, my car, is not very reliable.

Here, *my car* identifies the writer's main mode of transportation.

Use appositives to add details and specifics to your position paper. For example, don't just say "drivers under twenty-one," say "drivers under twenty-one, *the majority of drivers in our state,* account for . . ."

Practice On your paper, identify the appositives in the following sentences.

1. My friend Mahmoud was born in Cairo.
2. Head-on collisions, the most dangerous accidents, are on the rise.

Writing Application Review your position paper, adding appositives where they would strengthen your writing.

Writer's Solution Connection
Language Lab

For more practice with appositives, complete the Language Lab lesson on Varying Sentence Structure.

Revising

Use a Self-Evaluation Checklist Review your draft and answer the following questions about it.

▶ Do you elaborate on assertions with facts and statistics? *Add facts where necessary to make your argument more compelling.*

▶ Are your researched facts and statistics accurate? *Check with at least two sources to make sure that the integrity of your information cannot be challenged.*

▶ Is your organization coherent? *Make sure that your paragraphs and sentences within each paragraph follow a logical and easy-to-understand organizational plan.*

▶ Have you checked your spelling and grammar?

REVISION MODEL

① In countries where formal driver education is mandated, teen driver fatalities are significantly lower.
For any driver under 21, formal driver education should

be required. In addition, there should be a lower limit of

the number of points, from the current ②12 10, a driver is

allowed to collect before his or her license is suspended.

① The writer strengthens her argument with a fact that supports her position.
② The writer changes this inaccurate information.

Publishing

Deliver a Persuasive Speech One way to publish your position paper is by presenting it as a speech. Use these tips to guide you as you present your speech:

▶ Practice several times on your own.
▶ Mark places that you want to emphasize.
▶ Speak slowly and clearly.
▶ Allow your voice to rise and fall naturally.
▶ Speak loudly enough to be heard.
▶ Look directly at your audience or the camera.

Student Success Workshop

Real-World Reading Skills

Strategies for Success

Reading without a purpose is like starting a car trip without knowing your destination—you might get lost if you don't know where you want to go. If you can read with a purpose, you are more likely to get what you want from a text, and you might even save time. Even if you just want to relax and read a novel, you still need to know your purpose—to enjoy what you're reading.

Establish Your Purpose Ask yourself whether your purpose for reading is to enjoy, to discover, to interpret, to analyze, to evaluate, to compare and contrast, to do research, or to do something else. If you decide what aspect of a work most interests you, it will be easier to stay focused as you read. For example, your purpose for reading an article on African lions could be to learn about how lions hunt. But if you haven't decided your purpose for reading the article, you might get lost in the author's wide-ranging information and conclusions.

You Can Have More Than One Often, you'll have more than one purpose for reading. For example, you may want to read a particular poet's works for the sheer enjoyment you experience when you read them; you may also want to read them in order to analyze the poet's use of imagery so you can write about it in a paper.

> ✔ Here are some situations in which it's helpful to establish a purpose for reading:
> ▶ Looking through a travel guide
> ▶ Searching the Internet
> ▶ Reading a cookbook

Apply the Strategies

Write a sentence explaining what purpose (or purposes) you might have for reading each of the following texts:

1. Computer software manual
2. Newspaper article about new recycling laws
3. Poem entitled "Electric Blue Skies"
4. Science-fiction novel *Foundation's Edge* by Isaac Asimov
5. Biography of Rabindranath Tagore
6. Movie review entitled "*Underwater Voyage Sinks Off the Screen*"
7. Article about black holes in an astronomy magazine
8. Latest *Garfield* comic strip
9. Henrik Ibsen's play *A Doll's House*
10. Encyclopedia article on the Nile River

You are not always going to agree with other people's opinions and suggestions, but it is up to you to decide when to express your disagreement. Sometimes, expressing disagreement can cause tension between you and the person with whom you are disagreeing. It's important to learn how to express disagreement constructively and in a way that will not alienate others.

Present Your Case If you disagree with a person's comments, opinions, or actions, express your disagreement in a way that makes your position known without offending or upsetting others. Suppose your friends think that the legal driving age should be changed from sixteen or seventeen to fourteen. You feel, however, that fourteen-year-olds lack the maturity needed for such an awesome responsibility, and furthermore, you know plenty of sixteen- and seventeen-year-olds who aren't mature enough to drive. In expressing your disagreement, present your position in a calm, clear voice. Arguing with people will only cause them to defend their own position more firmly, and they will fail to see your point.

Express Disagreement Successfully To express your disagreement in an intelligent and effective way, follow these strategies:

- ▶ Think about how you look and sound. Use a clear, respectful tone, while remaining assertive. Do not raise your voice or get upset when expressing disagreement. Doing so will only cause tension between you and the person with whom you are disagreeing.
- ▶ Present specific reasons why you disagree.
- ▶ Offer evidence, if available, to support your position. For example, if you believe the legal driving age should be raised, you could cite the statistic that drivers age twenty-one and under make up less than 10 percent of the driving population, yet they represent nearly 20 percent of Americans killed in auto accidents.

Apply the Strategies

With a partner, role-play these situations. Express your disagreement clearly and constructively:

1. You and your best friend disagree over what movie to see. How would you express your disagreement?

2. Your sister borrows your clothes without asking you first and sees nothing wrong with doing so. What would you say to her to express your disagreement with her actions?

3. One person in your science lab makes decisions and plans projects without consulting the rest of the group. What would you say to this person to get him or her to listen to input from the rest of the group?

Test Preparation Workshop

Reading Comprehension

Strategies for Success

The reading sections of standardized tests often require you to read a passage to understand a stated or implied main idea. The following strategies can help:

Identify the Stated Main Idea Look for a topic sentence that states what the passage is about. Recognizing supporting details will help you identify the stated main idea. For example, suppose you were asked to find a stated main idea in this passage:

Minerals are essential to good health. They control the body's water balance and act as parts of hormones, enzymes, and vitamins. Eating a variety of foods will help ensure that the body receives enough minerals.

An overabundance of certain minerals, however, can lead to serious health problems. Most people get more sodium than they need. An adult's body requires only 500 milligrams of sodium a day.

What is the stated main idea of the second paragraph?

A We need 500 milligrams of sodium a day.
B Too much of certain minerals can be harmful.
C Too much sodium can be harmful.
D Minerals are essential to good health.

Answer **A** is a supporting detail. Answer **C** is a detail not stated in the paragraph. Answer **D** is an idea from the first paragraph. Answer **B**, which summarizes the main idea, is correct.

Identify the Implied Main Idea An implied main idea is one that is not stated directly in the text. Summarizing the author's points can help you identify an implied main idea. For example, in the passage about minerals, what is the implied main idea of the first paragraph?

A The body needs minerals.
B Minerals control the body's water balance.
C Although the body needs minerals, too much of certain minerals can be harmful.
D Eating many different foods will give the body the minerals it needs to stay healthy.

Answer **A** is only part of the main idea. Answer **B** is a supporting detail. Answer **C** is a detail from the second paragraph. Answer **D**, which combines and summarizes the ideas in the first paragraph, is the correct answer.

Apply the Strategies

Read the following passage from a newspaper editorial, and answer the questions that follow.

The critics of the proposed recycling initiative are concerned that recycling plastic and aluminum containers will create more work for citizens who already recycle glass and newspaper. While this notion is true, it misses a more important point.

By recycling plastic and aluminum we will reduce the waste in our landfill. Most important, the initiative will better the planet. Isn't that worth the extra time?

I What is the stated main idea of the first paragraph?

A Recycling plastic and aluminum containers will create more work for citizens.
B The critics miss a more important point.
C The initiative will improve our lives.
D Citizens already recycle glass and paper.

2 What is the implied main idea of the passage?

A Citizens can extend the life of the landfill.
B A compromise must be found.
C Recycling plastic and aluminum containers is worth the time it takes.
D Plastic and aluminum harm our planet.

Spring Returns to the Streets, Pham Luan

Turning Points in World Literature

Turning points can be exciting and frightening. Windows of opportunity open briefly and life-changing decisions must be made. Stories, poems, and essays from around the world can show you how some people approach these fateful moments. Share the anticipation and anxiety of the writers and characters in this unit as they deal with the chances and challenges that change their lives.

Guide for Reading

Vladimir Nabokov (1899–1977)

Besides being a novelist, a poet, and a translator, Russian-born Vladimir Nabokov was a passionate butterfly collector. Some critics have said that Nabokov, who wrote in both Russian and English, treated words like butterflies: each a rare, colorful specimen pinned to the page.

Early Success Nabokov was born into an upper-class but politically liberal Russian family from St. Petersburg. He quickly became, in his own words, "a perfectly normal trilingual child." His languages were Russian, French, and English. By the time he was fifteen years old, he had published his first volume of Russian verse.

Early Tragedy The Russian Revolution of 1917 drove the Nabokovs into exile, and Vladimir finished his education at an English university. There, in 1922, he learned the tragic news that his father had been assassinated while shielding another man at a political gathering. Nabokov's great affection for his father and equally great feeling of loss are evident in his autobiography.

From Exile to Citizenship Nabokov spent years in Europe, living away from his native Russia. In 1940, he had to flee Hitler's Germany. He moved his wife and young son to the United States, where he taught at various universities. In 1945, he became a citizen of this country.

Literary Achievements From his early teens until his death, Nabokov was a committed writer. His carefully constructed and playful novels include *Bend Sinister* (1947), *Pnin* (1957), and *Ada* (1969). He also won acclaim for his autobiography, *Speak, Memory* (1967), whose title shows the importance of memory for this writer. Not only words but memories were the rare, fluttering specimens of this literary butterfly collector.

◆ Build Vocabulary

LATIN PREFIXES: *pro-*

In this personal narrative, you will encounter the word *procession*. Knowing that the Latin prefix *pro-* often means "before in place or time" or "moving forward," you can figure out the part that it plays in the word *procession,* which means "a number of persons or things moving forward."

procession
proficiency
laborious
portentously
limpid

WORD BANK

As you read this excerpt from *Speak, Memory,* you will encounter the words on this list. Work together with a group of classmates to write sentences containing as many of the words as you can. If necessary, use a dictionary to help you.

◆ Build Grammar Skills

DASHES

Throughout this selection, Nabokov uses **dashes**—punctuation marks that create longer pauses than commas do. Used in pairs, dashes separate material that would interrupt the flow of the thought:

The kind of Russian family to which I belonged—a kind now extinct—had, among other virtues . . .

Used singly, dashes can announce an example or definition or can signal an abrupt change of mood:

Summer *soomerki*—the lovely Russian word for dusk.

For Nabokov, dashes—and the information they set off—are like little notes with further background.

from Speak, Memory

◆ *Literature and Your Life*

CONNECT YOUR EXPERIENCE

Just think, no two people have read the exact same books, articles, and stories in their lifetime. The special combination of books you have read contributes uniquely to your personality.

In this section of his autobiography, Nabokov fondly recalls his first reading experiences—he learned to read English before Russian, his native language!

Journal Writing Jot down some impressions of your first reading experiences.

THEMATIC FOCUS: TURNING POINTS

Learning to read is a turning point in most people's lives. This narrative asks (and gives one answer to) the question: How does what you read affect your life?

◆ Background for Understanding

THE STORY BEHIND THE STORY

People write in order to preserve what might otherwise be lost. Nabokov's autobiography preserves the upper-class life with loving parents that was snatched from him by the Russian Revolution of 1917. (In this picture, you see Vladimir, age seven, with his beloved father.)

Nabokov was a teenager when his family was forced to leave Russia. From the graced life of his childhood, he took a few belongings and countless vivid memories—some of which he shares in this excerpt from his autobiography. The life he lost became the life he could never forget.

◆ Literary Focus

PERSONAL NARRATIVE

This episode from a larger autobiography of Vladimir Nabokov's life is a **personal narrative**—a true story about a memorable person, event, or situation in the writer's life. Writers tell such narratives from the first-person point of view. They also hint at or state directly the meaning of this chapter in their lives. In his narrative, Nabokov captures memories of childhood reading just as he netted butterflies. He closes in on some fluttering early impressions, traps them, pins them down, and examines them in a clear light.

Use a graphic organizer like the one shown to jot down details that help you share Nabokov's memories.

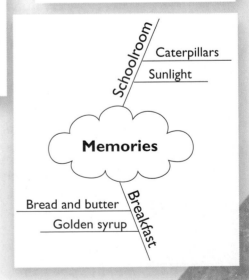

Reading for Success

Strategies for Reading Critically

When you read a work that presents an individual's perspective or ideas on a subject, it is a good idea to read the work critically. Examine and question the writer's ideas. Evaluate the information the writer includes (or doesn't include) as support, and form a judgment about the content and quality of the work. Here are specific strategies to help you read critically:

Recognize the author's purpose.

The author's purpose is his or her reason for writing, such as to inform or to persuade. An author might have more than one purpose. In a personal narrative, for example, an author might want to inform *and* entertain.

Writers sometimes express a particular bias—a point of view influenced by their experience. It's important to be aware of any factors that might bias a writer's opinion. For example, Nabokov's aristocratic background certainly influenced his attitude toward the Russian Revolution.

Distinguish fact from opinion.

A fact is information that can be proved true or false. An opinion cannot be proved true or false. Nabokov's statement that he "learned to read English before . . . Russian" is a fact. However, when he describes children's book characters as "wan-faced, big-limbed, silent nitwits," he's expressing an opinion.

Some forms of literature, including personal narratives, contain both fact and opinion. However, it's always important to be able to tell the two apart.

Evaluate the writer's credibility.

Evaluating credibility involves making a critical judgment about an author's trustworthiness as a source of information. Ask questions like these:
- ▶ Does the writer present facts that are true or seem to be true?
- ▶ Does the writer support opinions with sound reasons?
- ▶ Does the writer's background or experience qualify him or her to make such a statement?
- ▶ How might the writer's motivation, or reason for writing, affect his or her credibility?

Judge the writer's work.

As you judge the work in its totality, ask yourself questions like these:
- ▶ Do the statements follow logically?
- ▶ Is the material clearly organized?
- ▶ Are the writer's points interesting and well supported?

As you read this excerpt from *Speak, Memory* by Vladimir Nabokov, look at the notes in the boxes. These notes demonstrate how to apply these strategies to a work of literature.

from

Speak, Memory

Vladimir Nabokov

1

The kind of Russian family to which I belonged—a kind now extinct—had, among other virtues, a traditional leaning toward the comfortable products of Anglo-Saxon civilization. Pears' Soap, tar-black when dry, topaz-like when held to the light between wet fingers, took care of one's morning bath. Pleasant was the decreasing weight of the English collapsible tub when it was made to protrude a rubber underlip and disgorge its frothy contents into the slop pail. "We could not improve the cream, so we improved the tube," said the English toothpaste. At breakfast, Golden Syrup imported from London would entwist with its glowing coils the revolving spoon from which enough of it had

> These details show that Nabokov came from an aristocratic background, which helps explain his **bias** about the characters in his books.

slithered onto a piece of Russian bread and butter. All sorts of snug, mellow things came in a steady <u>procession</u> from the English Shop on Nevski Avenue: fruitcakes, smelling salts, playing cards, picture puzzles, striped blazers, talcum-white tennis balls.

I learned to read English before I could read Russian. My first English friends were four simple souls in my grammar—Ben, Dan, Sam and Ned. There used to be a great deal of fuss about their identities and whereabouts— "Who is Ben?" "He is Dan," "Sam is in bed," and so on. Although it all remained rather stiff and patchy (the compiler was handicapped by having to employ—for the initial lessons, at least—words of not more than three letters), my imagination somehow managed to obtain the necessary data. Wan-faced, big-limbed, silent nitwits, proud in the possession of certain tools ("Ben has an axe"), they now drift with a slow-motioned slouch across the remotest backdrop of memory; and, akin to the mad alphabet of an optician's chart, the grammar-book lettering looms again before me.

> It is a **fact** that Nabokov learned to read English before he could read Russian, but it was Nabokov's **opinion** that the text of his grammar book was "stiff and patchy."

◆ Build Vocabulary

procession (prō sesh´ ən) *n.*: Number of persons or things moving forward in an orderly or formal way

MODEL

The schoolroom was drenched with sunlight. In a sweating glass jar, several spiny caterpillars were feeding on nettle[1] leaves (and ejecting interesting, barrel-shaped pellets of olive-green grass). The oilcloth that covered the round table smelled of glue. Miss Clayton smelled of Miss Clayton.

---

1. **nettle** (net´ əl) *n.*: Any of various other stinging or spiny plants.

▲ **Critical Viewing** What details in this picture reflect the feelings Nabokov associates with reading? **[Connect]**

Fantastically, gloriously, the blood-colored alcohol of the outside thermometer had risen to 24° Réaumur (86° Fahrenheit) in the shade. Through the window one could see kerchiefed peasant girls weeding a garden path on their hands and knees or gently raking the sun-mottled sand. (The happy days when they would be cleaning streets and digging canals for the State were still beyond the horizon.) Golden orioles in the greenery emitted their four brilliant notes: dee-del-dee-O!

Ned lumbered past the window in a fair impersonation of the gardener's mate Ivan

Here, the **author's purpose** is to emphasize the profound effect learning to read had on him as a child and how it has continued with him throughout adulthood.

(who was to become in 1918 a member of the local Soviet). On later pages longer words appeared; and at the very end of the brown, inkstained volume, a real, sensible story unfolded its adult sentences ("One day Ted said to Ann: Let us—"), the little reader's ultimate triumph and reward. I was thrilled by the thought that some day I might attain such <u>proficiency</u>. The magic has endured, and whenever a grammar book comes my way, I instantly turn to the last page to enjoy a forbidden glimpse of the <u>laborious</u> student's future, of that promised land where, at last, words are meant to mean what they mean.

2

Summer *soomerki*—the lovely Russian word for dusk. Time: a dim point in the first decade of this unpopular century. Place: latitude[2] 59° north from your equator, longitude[3] 100° east from my writing hand. The day would take hours to fade, and everything—sky, tall flowers, still water—would be kept in a state of infinite vesperal[4] suspense, deepened rather than resolved by the doleful moo of a cow in a distant meadow or by the still more moving cry that came from some bird beyond the lower course of the river, where the vast expanse of a misty-blue sphagnum[5] bog, because of its mystery and remoteness, the Rukavishnikov children had baptized America.

In the drawing room of our country house, before going to bed, I would often be read to in English by my mother. As she came to a particularly dramatic passage, where the hero was about to encounter some strange, perhaps fatal danger, her voice would slow down, her words would be spaced <u>portentously</u>, and before turning the page she would place upon it her hand, with its familiar pigeon-blood ruby and diamond ring (within the <u>limpid</u> facets of which, had I been a better crystal-gazer, I might have seen a room, people, lights, trees in the rain—a whole period of émigré life for which that ring was to pay).

Evaluate Nabokov's description of and feelings about the "lovely" summer dusk: His supporting details create a soft, warm, and satisfying time of day that ended with his mother reading to him.

There were tales about knights whose terrific but wonderfully aseptic[6] wounds were bathed by damsels in grottoes.[7] From a windswept clifftop, a medieval maiden with flying hair and a youth in hose gazed at the round Isles of the Blessed. In "Misunderstood," the fate of Humphrey used to bring a more specialized lump to one's throat than anything in Dickens or Daudet[8] (great devisers of lumps), while a shamelessly allegorical story, "Beyond the Blue Mountains," dealing with two pairs of little travelers—good Clover and Cowslip, bad Buttercup and Daisy—contained enough exciting details to make one forget its "message."

Nabokov expresses the **opinion** that stories about knights were better than the works he read by Dickens or Daudet.

---

2. **latitude** (lat´ ə tōod) *n.*: Angular distance, measured in degrees, north or south from the equator.
3. **longitude** (län´ jə tōod) *n.*: Distance east or west on the Earth's surface, measured as an arc of the equator.
4. **vesperal** (ves´ pər əl) *adj.*: Eveninglike.
5. **sphagnum** (sfag´ nəm) *n.*: Highly absorbent, spongelike, grayish peat mosses found in bogs.

6. **aseptic** (ā sep´ tik) *adj.*: Free from, or keeping away, disease-producing microorganisms.
7. **grottoes** (grät´ ōz) *n.*: Caves.
8. **Dickens** (dik´ ənz) **or Daudet** (dō dā´): Charles Dickens and Alphonse Daudet, nineteenth-century novelists who sympathized with common people.

There were also those large, flat, glossy picture books. I particularly liked the blue-coated, red-trousered, coal-black Golliwogg, with underclothes buttons for eyes, and his meager harem of five wooden dolls. By the illegal method of cutting themselves frocks out of the American flag (Peg taking the motherly stripes, Sarah Jane the pretty stars) two of the dolls acquired a certain soft femininity, once their neutral articulations had been clothed. The Twins (Meg and Weg) and the Midget remained stark naked and, consequently, sexless.

We see them in the dead of night stealing out of doors to sling snowballs at one another until the chimes of a remote clock ("But Hark!" comments the rhymed text) send them back to their toybox in the nursery. A rude jack-in-the-box shoots out, frightening my lovely Sarah, and that picture I heartily disliked because it reminded me of children's parties at which this or that graceful little girl, who had bewitched me, happened to pinch her finger or hurt her knee, and would forthwith expand into a purple-faced goblin, all wrinkles and bawling mouth. Another time

they went on a bicycle journey and were captured by cannibals; our unsuspecting travelers had been quenching their thirst at a palm-fringed pool when the tom-toms sounded. Over the shoulder of my past I admire again the crucial picture: the Golliwogg, still on his knees by the pool but no longer drinking; his hair stands on end and the normal black of his face has changed to a weird ashen hue. There was also the motorcar book (Sarah Jane, always my favorite, sporting a long green veil), with the usual sequel—crutches and bandaged heads.

And, yes—the airship. Yards and yards of yellow silk went to make it, and an additional tiny balloon was provided for the sole use of the fortunate Midget. At the immense altitude to which the ship reached, the aeronauts huddled together for warmth while the lost little soloist, still the object of my intense envy notwithstanding his plight, drifted into an abyss of frost and stars—alone.

> **Judge** whether Nabokov has successfully presented the pleasure and satisfaction of his learning to read.

Guide for Responding

◆ *Literature and Your Life*

Reader's Response Compare the earliest books and stories you read with those that Nabokov read as a boy.

Thematic Focus Explain why learning to read might be considered a turning point.

Questions for Research Suppose that you are conducting a survey to research people's earliest reading experiences. What questions will you ask?

☑ Check Your Comprehension

1. Who were the author's "first English friends," and where did they come from?
2. What were the author's impressions of his first English friends?
3. Why does the author now always turn to the last page of a "grammar" (student's first reader)?
4. Summarize the author's impressions of the "Golliwog and his harem."

Guide for Responding (continued)

◆ Critical Thinking

INTERPRET

1. Why does Nabokov say the kind of family to which he belonged is "now extinct"? **[Speculate]**
2. What does Nabokov intend for you to know about his mother's ruby and diamond ring? **[Draw Conclusions]**
3. Nabokov was strongly affected by the books of his childhood. Support this statement with evidence from the selection. **[Support]**
4. What was the author's purpose in writing these particular impressions of his childhood? **[Infer]**

APPLY

5. Recommend a book or story that you think Nabokov would have liked. Give reasons for your recommendation. **[Apply]**

EXTEND

6. What are some reasons that people would use products imported from another country, as the Nabokovs did? **[Social Studies Link]**

◆ Reading For Success

STRATEGIES FOR READING CRITICALLY

Apply the strategies and the notes showing how to read critically to answer the following questions.

1. Give an example of an opinion from this essay and explain how you know it's an opinion.
2. Explain how Nabokov's first sentence reflects the bias of an upper-class Russian.
3. What do you think was the author's purpose in recording these impressions of his early reading?

◆ Literary Focus

PERSONAL NARRATIVE

Nabokov's essay is a **personal narrative**—a true story drawn from his own life and told in the first person.

1. How does the first sentence indicate that this work is a personal narrative?
2. Find two details that help you see the characters Ben, Dan, Sam, and Ned.
3. Show how Nabokov appeals to every sense except taste in his description of the schoolroom.

◆ Build Vocabulary

USING THE LATIN PREFIX *pro-*

In the following words, the Latin prefix *pro-* means "before in place or time" or "moving forward." Match each *pro-* word with the correct definition.

1. proceed   **a.** drive forward
2. projection   **b.** something read before a drama
3. prologue   **c.** go forward
4. propel   **d.** a look ahead

USING THE WORD BANK: Sentence Completions

On your paper, fill in the blanks with words from the Word Bank. Use each word only once.

Nabokov offers a ___?___ of sensory details, rendered with ___?___. The author is accurate without being ___?___. You can almost see the ___?___ facets of his mother's jewels and hear how she ___?___ lowers her voice.

◆ Build Grammar Skills

DASHES

As Nabokov introduces you to his childhood world, he uses **dashes** to set off interrupting or clarifying phrases, to show an unfinished thought, and to introduce a final word that changes or emphasizes a thought.

Practice In your notebook, write the following sentences, adding two dashes where necessary to set off interrupting phrases or sentences, or one dash to signal a clarification or shift in thought.

1. A biography of Nabokov the first major one in years shows the relationship between his life and work.
2. You can read about Nabokov his life, work, and travels in reference sources on world authors.
3. Nabokov spent many years in France and Germany impoverished.
4. Everyone knows Nabokov's favorite hobby butterfly collecting.
5. Nabokov not popular with all readers is greatly respected by those who call themselves his fans.

Build Your Portfolio

 ## Idea Bank

Writing

1. **On-line Message** Write a message about this excerpt from Nabokov's *Speak, Memory* to send to an on-line reader's circle. Tell why you liked or disliked it. Support your opinion.

2. **Children's Story** Make up characters like Nabokov's Golliwog and friends and write a story about them that children would enjoy reading.

3. **The Author's World** Write a description of the world Nabokov lost when he left Russia as a teenager. Use details from *Speak, Memory*, as well as from an encyclopedia and books on early twentieth-century Russia. **[Social Studies Link]**

Speaking, Listening, and Viewing

4. **Memory Exchange** In a small group, exchange stories about some of your most important achievements as young children—for example, learning to read, swim, or travel by yourself. Record your stories on tape or tell them to the class. **[Performing Arts Link]**

5. **Oral Presentation** Give a presentation to your class on a children's book that meant a great deal to you. Following Nabokov's example, describe the characters and events of the book so that your listeners will "see" them. **[Art Link]**

Researching and Representing

6. **Multimedia Presentation** Using film clips, recordings, pictures from books, and quotations from authors, research and report on the Russian Revolution of 1917. **[Social Studies Link]**

7. **Illustration** Choose one of Nabokov's detailed descriptions and illustrate it with a drawing or painting. **[Art Link]**

Online Activity www.phlit.phschool.com

 ## Guided Writing Lesson

Memory of a Milestone

Nabokov describes how he learned to read English. Choose a milestone (significant event) from your life and write a **narrative** about your memory of it. You might describe learning to swim, moving to a new home, or graduating from school. Tell readers not only what happened, but why it was important. Help them understand its importance by using sensory details to make events come alive.

Writing Skills Focus: Sensory Details

Sensory details—details that appeal to the senses—are important in stories, personal narratives, and descriptions of all kinds. Nabokov begins his personal narrative with details that appeal both to the eye and to the sense of touch:

> Pears' Soap, tar-black when dry, topaz-like when held to the light between wet fingers, took care of one's morning bath.

The sensory details help you experience this long-lost bath as he did himself. Even before you draft your narrative, begin gathering sensory details you can use.

Prewriting In gathering sensory details, pay special attention to the often neglected senses of smell, touch, and taste.

Drafting Sometimes you can suggest how important a milestone was by showing someone else's reaction to it. For example, you might show how catching your first fish won you the respect of your brothers and sisters.

Revising Ask a classmate whether it's clear why the event was a milestone. If not, add sensory details to make the description more vivid, or include a statement explaining the importance of what happened.

PART 1 *Working It Out*

The Astronomer, Jan Vermeer van Delft, Louvre, Paris

*G*uide for Reading

Gabriel García Márquez
(1928–)

The Colombian author Gabriel García Márquez (gä´ vrē el´ gär sē´ ä mär´ kes) is known as a master of magical realism, a literary style that combines fantastical characters, events, and details with realistic ones.

García Márquez was born on March 6, 1928 in Aracataca, a town in northern Colombia. Because his parents were poor and struggling at the time, he was taken in and raised by his maternal grandparents.

Early Influences He loved listening to the mysterious and strange tales he heard from his grandmother and the stories of military adventures he heard from his grandfather. Later, as a mature author, he adapted for his own work some of the stirring tales he had heard as a young boy.

His more formal experiences with literature date from the time he studied law and journalism at the National University in Bogotá and the University of Cartagena. There he read classical and modern authors.

Two modern authors who made a strong impression on him were Franz Kafka and William Faulkner. In Kafka's story "The Metamorphosis," he discovered a boldness of imagination that surprised and pleased him. In Faulkner's work, he discovered a fictional Mississippi county that inspired him to invent his own fictional town of Macondo. Based on García Márquez's home town of Aracataca, Macondo is the setting for much of his fiction.

The Writer In 1955, García Márquez published *Leaf Storm*, the collection of short stories that first introduced Macondo. His later masterpiece, *One Hundred Years of Solitude* (1967), chronicles a century of life in this imaginary town. This novel, one of the finest examples of magical realism, earned worldwide recognition for the author. In 1982, he was awarded the Nobel Prize for literature.

The story you will read, "A Very Old Man With Enormous Wings," is from *Leaf Storm*. As the title of the story suggests, it combines the everyday ("a very old man") and the miraculous ("with enormous wings").

◆ Build Vocabulary

LATIN PREFIXES: *magna-/magni-*

In this short story, García Márquez uses the word *magnanimous* to describe a couple's action in the story. The word *magnanimous* contains the Latin prefix *magna-* ("great"), sometimes spelled *magni-*, added to the root *animus* ("intention"). Therefore, the word *magnanimous* means "having great intentions" or "noble-minded."

WORD BANK

celestial
magnanimous
impertinences
terrestrial
prudence
proliferated
providential

As you read, you will encounter the words on this list. Each word is defined on the page where it first appears. Preview the list before you read.

◆ Build Grammar Skills

SUBORDINATION

Subordination is the process by which writers connect two unequal but related ideas. The subordinate (less important) idea cannot stand alone, but it limits, develops, describes, or adds meaning to the main idea.

For example, in the following sentence from the story, the italicized subordinate clause further describes the main clause.

The chicken coop was the only thing *that didn't receive any attention.*

The less important idea is introduced with the relative pronoun *that.* Other words that indicate the relationship between a main clause and a subordinate clause include the subordinating conjunctions *after, because, while, unless, when, if,* and *than,* as well as the relative pronouns *who, which,* and *that.*

A Very Old Man With Enormous Wings

◆ Literature and Your Life

CONNECT YOUR EXPERIENCE

You hear a knock at the door and when you go to answer it, there is no one there. You pick up a ringing phone, only to hear a dial tone at the other end. These events are baffling because you are unable to explain what has happened.

In García Márquez's story, "A Very Old Man With Enormous Wings," characters are faced with the same problem: trying to explain an event that cannot be explained.

Journal Writing From books, television, or your own experience, list a few events that seem unexplainable.

THEMATIC FOCUS: PERSONAL CHALLENGES

As you read, ask yourself: In what ways do different characters meet the challenge of the unexplainable?

◆ Background for Understanding

LITERATURE

For Colombian García Márquez, the work of the Eastern European writer Franz Kafka was the key that opened the door to his own writing. As a young man, García Márquez read Kafka's long story "The Metamorphosis." The story tells, in a plain, businesslike way, how a man who has become a cockroach tries to conduct his normal life.

It was the strange combination of fantastic and realistic details in the tale that most impressed García Márquez. Kafka's way of telling a story reminded him of his grandmother's: "...the wildest things with a completely natural tone of voice."

◆ Literary Focus

SYMBOLISM AND THEME

A **symbol** in literature is a setting, an event, an action, a character, or any detail that stands for or represents something else. A **theme** is the central message or insight into life revealed through a literary work. The symbols in a story can suggest its theme. For example, a story may tell about two birds, one caged and the other free. The birds may symbolize captivity and freedom, and their different fates may reveal an insight into life.

In "A Very Old Man With Enormous Wings," the appearance of a strange old man in a village disrupts everyday life. The old man is a symbol that reveals the main theme of the story. As you read, think about what the old man stands for and what theme is implied by people's reactions to him.

◆ Reading Strategy

QUESTION

In literature that uses symbolism, an author does not necessarily tell you which details are symbolic or what they represent. It is up to you to **question** as you read, asking and answering questions about significant details and their possible meaning.

As you read "A Very Old Man," use a chart like the one below to record your questions, the clues that help you answer them, and the answers you formulate. By asking questions about even the smallest details, you will better understand the story's symbolism.

Questions	Clues/Answers

A Very Old Man With Enormous Wings

A Tale for Children

Gabriel García Márquez
Translated by Gregory Rabassa

On the third day of rain they had killed so many crabs inside the house that Pelayo had to cross his drenched courtyard and throw them into the sea, because the newborn child had a temperature all night and they thought it was due to the stench. The world had been sad since Tuesday. Sea and sky were a single ash-gray thing and the sands of the beach, which on March nights glimmered like powdered light, had become a stew of mud and rotten shellfish. The light was so weak at noon that when Pelayo was coming back to the house after throwing away the crabs, it was hard for him to see what it was that was moving and groaning in the rear of the courtyard. He had to go very close to see that it was an old man, a very old man, lying face down in the mud, who, in spite of his tremendous efforts couldn't get up, impeded by his enormous wings.

Salvador Dali, *Landscape of Port Lligat,* (1950) Oil on canvas, 23 x 31 inches, Collection of the Salvador Dali Museum, St. Petersburg, Florida. © 2000 Salvador Dali Museum, Inc.

▲ **Critical Viewing** Using the title and this painting, predict what the story will be about. **[Hypothesize]**

Frightened by that nightmare, Pelayo ran to get Elisenda, his wife, who was putting compresses on the sick child, and he took her to the rear of the courtyard. They both looked at the fallen body with mute stupor. He was dressed like a ragpicker. There were only a few faded hairs left on his bald skull and very few teeth in his mouth, and his pitiful condition of a drenched great-grandfather had taken away any sense of grandeur he might have had. His huge buzzard wings, dirty and half-plucked, were forever entangled in the mud. They looked at him so long and so closely that Pelayo and Elisenda very soon overcame their surprise and in the end found him familiar. Then they dared speak to him, and he answered in an incomprehensible dialect with a strong sailor's voice. That was how they skipped over the inconvenience of the wings and quite intelligently concluded that he was a lonely castaway from some foreign ship wrecked by the storm. And yet, they called in a neighbor woman who knew everything about life and death to see him, and all she needed was one look to show them their mistake.

"He's an angel," she told them. "He must have been coming for the child, but the poor fellow is so old that the rain knocked him down."

On the following day everyone knew that a flesh-and-blood angel was held captive in Pelayo's house. Against the judgment of the wise neighbor woman, for whom angels in those times were the fugitive survivors of a celestial conspiracy, they did not have the heart to club him to death. Pelayo watched over him all afternoon from the kitchen, armed with his bailiff's club, and before going to bed he dragged him out of the mud and locked him up with the hens in the wire chicken coop. In the middle of the night, when the rain stopped, Pelayo and Elisenda were still killing crabs. A short time afterward the child woke up without a fever and with a desire to eat. Then they felt magnanimous and decided to put the angel on

a raft with fresh water and provisions for three days and leave him to his fate on the high seas. But when they went out into the courtyard with the first light of dawn, they found the whole neighborhood in front of the chicken coop having fun with the angel, without the slightest reverence, tossing him things to eat through the openings in the wire as if he weren't a supernatural creature but a circus animal.

Father Gonzaga arrived before seven o'clock, alarmed at the strange news. By that time onlookers less frivolous than those at dawn had already arrived and they were making all kinds of conjectures concerning the captive's future. The simplest among them thought that he should be named mayor of the world. Others of sterner mind felt that he should be promoted to the rank of five-star general in order to win all wars. Some visionaries[1] hoped that he could be put to stud in order to implant on earth a race of winged wise men who could take charge of the universe. But Father Gonzaga, before becoming a priest, had been a robust woodcutter. Standing by the wire, he reviewed his catchism[2] in an instant and asked them to open the door so that he could take a close look at that pitiful man who looked more like a huge decrepit hen among the fascinated chickens. He was lying in a corner drying his open wings in the sunlight among the fruit peels and breakfast leftovers that the early risers had thrown him. Alien to the impertinences of the world, he only lifted his antiquarian[3] eyes and murmured something in his dialect when Father Gonzaga went into the chicken coop and said good morning to him in Latin. The parish priest had his first suspicion of an impostor

---

1. **visionaries** (vizh′ ən er′ ēz) *n.*: People whose ideas and plans are impractical, too idealistic, or fantastic; dreamers.
2. **catechism** (kat′ ə kiz′ əm) *n.*: A handbook of questions and answers for teaching the principles of a religion.
3. **antiquarian** (an′ ti kwer′ ē ən) *adj.*: Old-fashioned; outdated.

when he saw that he did not understand the language of God or know how to greet His ministers. Then he noticed that seen close up he was much too human: he had an unbearable smell of the outdoors, the back side of his wings was strewn with parasites and his main feathers had been mistreated by <u>terrestrial</u> winds, and nothing about him measured up to the proud dignity of angels. Then he came out of the chicken coop and in a brief sermon warned the curious against the risks of being ingenuous. He reminded them that the devil had the bad habit of making use of carnival tricks in order to confuse the unwary. He argued that if wings were not the essential element in determining the difference between a hawk and an airplane, they were even less so in the recognition of angels. Nevertheless, he promised to write a letter to his bishop so that the latter would write to his primate so that the latter would write to the Supreme Pontiff in order to get the final verdict from the highest courts.

His <u>prudence</u> fell on sterile hearts. The news of the captive angel spread with such rapidity that after a few hours the courtyard had the bustle of a marketplace and they had to call in troops with fixed bayonets to disperse the mob that was about to knock the house down. Elisenda, her spine all twisted from

◆ **Literary Focus**

What does people's treatment of the old man reveal about them?

Vieillard aile barbu (Old Man with Wings and Beard), 1895, Odilon Redon, Louvre, Paris

▲ **Critical Viewing** Imagine that this is the old man being held captive in Pelayo's house. What do you think he is feeling? Why? **[Infer]**

sweeping up so much marketplace trash, then got the idea of fencing in the yard and charging five cents admission to see the angel.

The curious came from far away. A traveling carnival arrived with a flying acrobat who buzzed over the crowd several times, but no one paid any attention to him because his wings were not those of an angel but, rather, those of a sidereal bat. The most unfortunate invalids on earth came in search of health: a poor woman who since childhood had been

◆ **Build Vocabulary**

celestial (sə les′ chəl) *adj.*: Of heaven; divine

magnanimous (mag nan′ ə məs) *adj.*: Noble in mind; generous in spirit, especially in overlooking injury or insult

impertinences (im pʉrt′n əns əs) *n.*: Examples of insolence or lack of respect

terrestrial (tə res′ trē əl) *adj.*: Of this world; earthly

prudence (prood′ 'ns) *n.*: Practical, sound judgment

A Very Old Man With Enormous Wings ◆ 449

Odilon Redon, *The Accused,* 1886. Charcoal on paper, 21 x 14 5/8" (53.3 x 37.2 cm.). The Museum of Modern Art, New York, acquired through the Lillie P. Bliss Bequest. Photograph ©2000 The Museum of Modern Art

▲ **Critical Viewing** If this is the old man in the chicken coop, what do you think is the source of his seemingly supernatural patience? **[Speculate]**

counting her heartbeats and had run out of numbers; a Portuguese man who couldn't sleep because the noise of the stars disturbed him; a sleepwalker who got up at night to undo the things he had done while awake; and many

◆ **Build Vocabulary**

proliferated (prō lif´ ər āt´ id) *v.*: Grew rapidly

providential (präv´ ə den´ shəl) *adj.*: As if decreed by God

others with less serious ailments. In the midst of that shipwreck disorder that made the earth tremble, Pelayo and Elisenda were happy with fatigue, for in less than a week they had crammed their rooms with money and the line of pilgrims waiting their turn to enter still reached beyond the horizon.

The angel was the only one who took no part in his own act. He spent his time trying to get comfortable in his borrowed nest, befuddled by the hellish heat of the oil lamps and sacramental candles that had been placed along the wire. At first they tried to make him eat some mothballs, which, according to the wisdom of the wise neighbor woman, were the food prescribed for angels. But he turned them down, just as he turned down the papal[4] lunches that the penitents[5] brought him, and they never found out whether it was because he was an angel or because he was an old man that in the end he ate nothing but eggplant mush. His only supernatural virtue seemed to be patience. Especially during the first days, when the hens pecked at him, searching for stellar parasites that <u>proliferated</u> in his wings, and the cripples pulled out feathers to touch their defective parts with, and even the most merciful threw stones at him, trying to get him to rise so they could see him standing. The only time they succeeded in arousing him was when they burned his side with an iron for branding steers, for he had been motionless for so many hours that they thought he was dead. He awoke with a start, ranting in his hermetic[6] language and with tears in his eyes, and he flapped his wings a couple of times, which brought on a whirlwind of chicken dung and lunar dust and a gale of

4. **papal** (pā´ pəl) *adj.*: Appropriate for the pope or the papacy.
5. **penitents** (pen´ i tənts) *n.*: People receiving or intending to receive the sacrament of penance, which involves the confession and repentance of sin or wrongdoing.
6. **hermetic** (hər met´ ik) *adj.*: Obscure; hard to understand.

panic that did not seem to be of this world. Although many thought that his reaction had been one not of rage but of pain, from then on they were careful not to annoy him, because the majority understood that his passivity was not that of a hero taking his ease but that of a cataclysm[7] in repose.

Father Gonzaga held back the crowd's frivolity with formulas of maidservant inspiration while awaiting the arrival of a final judgment on the nature of the captive. But the mail from Rome showed no sense of urgency. They spent their time finding out if the prisoner had a navel, if his dialect had any connection with Aramaic,[8] how many times he could fit on the head of a pin, or whether he wasn't just a Norwegian with wings. Those meager letters might have come and gone until the end of time if a <u>providential</u> event had not put an end to the priest's tribulations.

It so happened that during those days, among so many other carnival attractions, there arrived in town the traveling show of the woman who had been changed into a spider for having disobeyed her parents. The admission to see her was not only less than the admission to see the angel, but people were permitted to ask her all manner of questions about her absurd state and to examine her up and down so that no one would ever doubt the truth of her horror. She was a frightful tarantula the size of a ram and with the head of a sad maiden. What was most heartrending, however, was not her outlandish shape but the sincere affliction with which she recounted the details of her misfortune. While still practically a child she had sneaked out of her parents' house to go to a

◆ **Reading Strategy**
What is the relationship, if any, between the girl's situation and the old man's? Explain.

dance, and while she was coming back through the woods after having danced all night without permission, a fearful thunderclap rent the sky in two and through the crack came the lightning bolt of brimstone that changed her into a spider. Her only nourishment came from the meatballs that charitable souls chose to toss into her mouth. A spectacle like that, full of so much human truth and with such a fearful lesson, was bound to defeat without even trying that of a haughty angel who scarcely deigned to look at mortals. Besides, the few miracles attributed to the angel showed a certain mental disorder, like the blind man who didn't recover his sight but grew three new teeth, or the paralytic[9] who didn't get to walk but almost won the lottery, and the leper whose sores sprouted sunflowers. Those consolation miracles, which were more like mocking fun, had already ruined the angel's reputation when the woman who had been changed into a spider finally crushed him completely. That was how Father Gonzaga was cured forever of his insomnia[10] and Pelayo's courtyard went back to being as empty as during the time it had rained for three days and crabs walked through the bedrooms.

The owners of the house had no reason to lament. With the money they saved they built a two-story mansion with balconies and gardens and high netting so that crabs wouldn't get in during the winter, and with iron bars on the windows so that angels wouldn't get in. Pelayo also set up a rabbit warren close to town and gave up his job as bailiff for good, and Elisenda bought some satin pumps with high heels and many dresses of iridescent silk, the kind worn on Sunday by the most desirable women in those times. The chicken coop was the only thing that didn't receive any attention. If they washed it down with creolin[11] and burned

7. **cataclysm** (kat′ ə kliz′ əm) *n.*: A violent upheaval.
8. **Aramaic** (ar′ ə mā′ ik) *n.*: A Semitic language that was common throughout the Near East from *ca.* 300 B.C. to *ca.* A.D. 650; one of its dialects was spoken by Jesus and his disciples.

9. **paralytic** (par′ ə lit′ ik) *n.*: A person who is paralyzed.
10. **insomnia** (in säm′ nē ə) *n.*: Chronic inability to sleep.
11. **creolin** (krē′ ə lin) *n.*: Possibly an antiseptic.

tears of myrrh[12] inside it every so often, it was not in homage[13] to the angel but to drive away the dungheap stench that still hung everywhere like a ghost and was turning the new house into an old one. At first, when the child learned to walk, they were careful that he not get too close to the chicken coop. But then they began to lose their fears and got used to the smell, and before the child got his second teeth he'd gone inside the chicken coop to play, where the wires were falling apart. The angel was no less standoffish with him than with other mortals, but he tolerated the most ingenious infamies with the patience of a dog who had no illusions. They both came down with chicken pox at the same time. The doctor who took care of the child couldn't resist the temptation to listen to the angel's heart, and he found so much whistling in the heart and so many sounds in his kidneys that it seemed impossible for him to be alive. What surprised him most, however, was the logic of his wings. They seemed so natural on that completely human organism that he couldn't understand why other men didn't have them too.

When the child began school it had been some time since the sun and rain had caused the collapse of the chicken coop. The angel went dragging himself about here and there like a stray dying man. They would drive him out of the bedroom with a broom and a moment later find him in the kitchen. He seemed to be in so many places at the same time that they grew to think that he'd been duplicated, that he was reproducing himself all through the house, and the exasperated and unhinged Elisenda shouted that it was awful living in that hell full of angels. He could scarcely eat and his antiquarian eyes had also become so foggy that he went about bumping into posts. All he had left were the bare cannulae[14] of his last feathers. Pelayo threw a blanket over him

Rodolphe Bresdin, Odilon Redon, Louvre, Paris

▲ **Critical Viewing** In what way is this figure, like the angel, mysterious? **[Connect]**

and extended him the charity of letting him sleep in the shed, and only then did they notice that he had a temperature at night, and was delirious with the tongue twisters of an old Norwegian. That was one of the few times they became alarmed, for they thought he was going to die and not even the wise neighbor woman had been able to tell them what to do with dead angels.

And yet he not only survived his worst winter, but seemed improved with the first sunny days. He remained motionless for several days in the farthest corner of the courtyard, where no one would see him, and at the beginning of Decem-

---

12. myrrh (mŭr) *n.*: A fragrant, bitter-tasting perfume.
13. homage (hăm´ ij) *n.*: Anything done to show reverence, honor, or respect.

14. cannulae (kan´ yōō lē) *n.*: Tubes that are inserted into the body.

ber some large, stiff feathers began to grow on his wings, the feathers of a scarecrow, which looked more like another misfortune of decrepitude. But he must have known the reason for those changes, for he was quite careful that no one should notice them, that no one should hear the sea chanteys that he sometimes sang under the stars. One morning Elisenda was cutting some bunches of onions for lunch when a wind that seemed to come from the high seas blew into the kitchen. Then she went to the window and caught the angel in his first attempts at flight. They were so clumsy that his fingernails opened a furrow in the vegetable patch and he was on the point of knocking the shed down with the ungainly flapping that slipped on the light and couldn't get a grip on the air. But he did manage to gain altitude. Elisenda let out a sigh of relief, for herself and for him, when she saw him pass over the last houses, holding himself up in some way with the risky flapping of a senile vulture. She kept watching him even when she was through cutting the onions and she kept on watching until it was no longer possible for her to see him, because then he was no longer an annoyance in her life but an imaginary dot on the horizon of the sea.

Guide for Responding

◆ *Literature and Your Life*

Reader's Response Is the old man with enormous wings treated fairly? Why or why not?

Thematic Focus Why does the unknown—the identity of the mysterious old man, for example—represent a challenge for people?

Questions for Research Generate several research questions that could help you learn more about García Márquez's style of writing, magical realism.

☑ Check Your Comprehension

1. Describe the old man and tell how he is first discovered.
2. According to the wise neighbor woman, why has the old man come to Pelayo and Elisenda's house?
3. For what two reasons does Father Gonzaga suspect the old man is not an angel?
4. What do Pelayo and Elisenda do with the old man when they realize that people are eager to see him?
5. Briefly summarize the events leading to the old man's departure.

◆ Critical Thinking

INTERPRET

1. Compare and contrast the reactions of the following characters to the old man: Pelayo and Elisenda, the wise neighbor woman, and Father Gonzaga. **[Compare and Contrast]**
2. Does García Márquez regard his characters with a humorous eye? Why or why not? **[Interpret]**
3. To whom in the story is the old man not a carnival attraction, a suspicious character, or an annoyance? Explain. **[Analyze]**
4. García Márquez calls this story "A Tale for Children." Is he serious about this and, if so, what makes children a more appropriate audience for the story than adults? Explain. **[Draw Conclusions]**

EVALUATE

5. Is García Márquez right not to explain who the old man is? Why or why not? **[Make a Judgment]**

APPLY

6. What would have happened to the old man if he had not flown away? Explain. **[Speculate]**

COMPARE LITERARY WORKS

7. Think of another story with an unusual character. Compare and contrast this character with the old man in this tale. **[Compare and Contrast]**

Guide for Responding (continued)

◆ Reading Strategy

QUESTION

By **asking questions** about the details in this story, you better understood their symbolism or larger meaning. For example, you might have asked, What do the spider-woman and the old man with enormous wings have in common?

One possible answer is that people regard them as carnival attractions. Going further, you might also conclude that these two characters reveal people's limitations. Both the woman and the old man appeal to people's superstitious beliefs without really inspiring a true sense of wonder.

Write three questions you asked yourself while reading this work. Then, jot down your answers to these questions and explain how these answers helped you understand the story.

◆ Literary Focus

SYMBOLISM AND THEME

A **symbol**—a detail, character, or situation in a story that stands for more than itself—can often reveal the story's **theme,** its central message. For example, in García Márquez's story, the old man serves as a symbol rather than as a fully developed character. You never learn who he is, why he has wings, or from what mysterious place he has come.

However, this lack of information inspires the other characters to make up things about him. Their stories, explanations, and behavior reveal more about themselves than they do about the old man.

For example, even though people believe he is an angel, they are willing to treat him quite badly. Some even throw stones at him to get him to rise.

1. In what way does Pelayo and Elisenda's first conclusion about the old man show a lack of logic?
2. What does the people's sudden loss of interest in the angel reveal about them?
3. What central message does this story convey about the way people deal with the unknown?

◆ Build Vocabulary

USING THE LATIN PREFIX *magna-/magni-*

Knowing the meaning of the Latin prefix *magna-/magni-* (great or big), match each word with its definition. Use a dictionary to correct your answers.

1. magnate   a. beautiful in a great or dignified way
2. magnificent   b. a great man
3. magnify   c. greatness in size, importance, or influence
4. magnitude   d. to make greater in size

USING THE WORD BANK: Antonyms

On your paper, match each word with the word or phrase most nearly opposite in meaning.

1. celestial   a. courtesies
2. magnanimous   b. decreased
3. impertinences   c. earthly
4. terrestrial   d. petty
5. prudence   e. random
6. proliferated   f. heavenly
7. providential   g. carelessness

◆ Build Grammar Skills

SUBORDINATION

Subordination is the process by which writers connect two related but unequal ideas. The less important idea is introduced by a subordinating conjunction (examples: *although, as, because, since, when*) or by a relative pronoun (*who, which,* or *that*), and this idea, by itself, is not a complete thought.

Practice On your paper, identify the subordinate clause in each sentence.

1. When Pelayo came back to the house, he could not see what was moving and groaning in the courtyard.
2. They called in a neighbor who knew everything.
3. Although Father Gonzaga was a priest, he had been a robust woodcutter.
4. Because the spider-woman came to town, people lost interest in the old man.
5. She was cutting onions when she felt a breeze.

Build Your Portfolio

Idea Bank

Writing

1. **Advertisement** Write an advertisement that Pelayo and Elisenda might have written to entice people to see the old man with wings. **[Career Link]**

2. **Character History** In García Márquez's story, you never find out who the old man is or why he has wings. Write a character sketch describing how the old man got his wings and the events leading up to his appearance in the couple's home.

3. **Response to Criticism** A critic wrote that García Márquez's stories are "a wondrous mixture of realism and truth-stretching, with humor the glue that holds the two together." Basing your response on this story, support or refute this statement.

Speaking, Listening, and Viewing

4. **Television News Story** Prepare and deliver a news story about the old man with enormous wings. Include in your report interviews with various characters. **[Media Link; Performing Arts Link]**

5. **Group Discussion** With a small group, imagine that you have discovered the old man in the story. Hold a discussion to determine what course of action you will take. **[Performing Arts Link]**

Researching and Representing

6. **Illustration** Illustrate a memorable scene from the story, such as Pelayo's discovery of the old man or the old man's flight into the horizon at the end of the story. Write a caption describing the theme suggested by your picture. **[Art Link]**

7. **Research Project** Another story involving a winged hero is the Greek myth of Icarus. Research this myth, noting similarities and differences between Icarus and the old man in this story. Share your findings with the class.

Online Activity www.phlit.phschool.com

Guided Writing Lesson

Writing From Another Perspective

In "A Very Old Man With Enormous Wings," García Márquez describes the old man's appearance and the villagers' reactions to him. However, we learn little about the old man's personality, thoughts, and feelings. Imagine that you are the old man in the story and rewrite the story from his point of view.

Writing Skills Focus: Consistency of Perspective

To keep your story clear and to give your readers a true understanding of the old man, maintain a **consistent perspective**—use the pronoun "I" and include only what the old man sees, thinks, and feels. Everything you write should flow from his experiences.

Prewriting Briefly list the characteristics of the story's setting, characters, and main events. This will help you to determine what the old man experiences and does. Then, decide on a voice for the old man. Does he speak formally, or casually? What expressions does he use?

Drafting As you write, the old man's voice will become more recognizable, especially if you maintain a consistent perspective. Use your list of the main events and the details of the story's scenes to guide your writing.

Revising Have a partner evaluate the effectiveness of your portrayal. Do you use the pronoun "I" and consistently write from the old man's perspective? Do the old man's impressions seem convincing? Are they consistent with the character created by García Márquez?

If your sentences are choppy, combine sentences by using subordination. For more on subordination, see pp. 444 and 454.

Guide for Reading

Leopold Staff *(1878–1957)*

Leopold Staff loved the quiet moments of life: marveling at the beauty of nature or musing on the glories of long-past civilizations. The miracle of Staff's poetry is that he kept true to those concerns despite the times in which he lived. Poland was a major battleground during both World War I and World War II, yet during that same period Staff and a group of other poets revitalized Polish literature.

Rainer Maria Rilke *(1875–1926)*

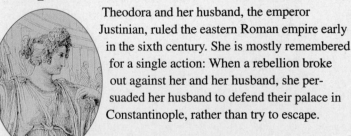

Rainer Maria Rilke (rī′ nər mä rē′ ä ril′ kə) is considered to be one of the most important poets of the twentieth century. He was born and largely schooled in Prague, which was part of the Austro-Hungarian Empire at that time.

He traveled widely throughout Europe, acquiring material for his writing, and lived in Russia, France, and Switzerland. Like many of Rilke's poems, "The Last Evening" explores the effect that a threatening environment has on people's lives.

Anna Akhmatova *(1889–1966)*

Anna Akhmatova published her first poetry at the age of eighteen. She survived the most tumultuous events of modern times: two world wars, the Russian Revolution of 1917, and the "reign of terror" of dictator Joseph Stalin. Through it all, Akhmatova's poetry celebrated the personal heroism she prized above everything else.

Empress Theodora *(c. 497–548)*

Theodora and her husband, the emperor Justinian, ruled the eastern Roman empire early in the sixth century. She is mostly remembered for a single action: When a rebellion broke out against her and her husband, she persuaded her husband to defend their palace in Constantinople, rather than try to escape.

◆ **Build Vocabulary**

LATIN WORD ROOTS: -dom-
The time: A.D. 532. The place: Rome, the emperor's palace. The main character: the *indomitable* Empress Theodora. The word *indomitable* contains the Latin root *-dom-*, which means "to rule." Add the prefix *in-*, meaning "not," and you might guess that the meaning of *indomitable* is "unrulable," which is close to the actual meaning—"not easily defeated."

WORD BANK
Before you read, preview this list of words from the selections.

seductive
distracted
timorous
indomitable

◆ **Build Grammar Skills**

NEGATIVES AND DOUBLE NEGATIVES
The Roman empress Theodora cries out in her speech, "... may I never see the day when those who meet me do not call me empress." In this dramatic request, she uses two **negatives**—words or word parts that deny or mean "no." In former times, two negatives may have been used to make a point emphatically, but today it is incorrect to use a **double negative**—two negatives that express the same "no." For instance, it would be incorrect to say "... may I *not never* see the day ..."

The Bridge ◆ The Last Evening
◆ I Am Not One of Those Who Left the Land ◆
Speech During the Invasion of Constantinople

◆ *Literature and Your Life*

CONNECT YOUR EXPERIENCE

Life is filled with situations in which we're forced to make tough decisions. It might involve something as simple as deciding to try out for the school play despite having terrible stage fright. In the following selections, however, you'll encounter characters who show the courage to make decisions that could be a matter of life or death.

Journal Writing Jot down your memories about the toughest decision you've faced. What was the outcome?

THEMATIC FOCUS: WORKING IT OUT

These selections may set you thinking about decisions you've made or fears you've overcome.

◆ Background for Understanding

HISTORY

In 532, citizens of the eastern Roman empire rebelled against Emperor Justinian and Empress Theodora. When rebels stormed the castle, Theodora encouraged her husband to face their attackers rather than flee. As it turned out, Justinian and Theodora survived.

Fourteen centuries later, in the early 1900's, Russia was torn by civil war. Many Russians emigrated to Germany and France. The poet Anna Akhmatova, however, refused to go, even after her husband was executed and her son put in jail.

◆ Literary Focus

DRAMATIC SITUATION

The life-and-death conditions under which Empress Theodora makes her speech create a gripping backdrop for her impassioned words. This **dramatic situation**—the circumstances and conflicts that form the focal point of a literary work—provides a context that helps you understand the full significance of Theodora's words.

The dramatic situation of Akhmatova's poem arises from the circumstances of the civil war in Russia. Due to food shortages, riots, strikes, and political oppression, many of Akhmatova's friends and neighbors fled the country. The dramatic situation gives you a framework in which you can appreciate the courage of her decision.

◆ Reading Strategy

AUTHOR'S PERSPECTIVE

If you've just lost a game, the account you give will be very different from the story told by the winner. The details that are included in a piece of literature depend on the **author's perspective**—his or her outlook on the subject.

Often, writers hint at or directly reveal their perspective. For example, Akhmatova indicates her perspective in the opening lines of her poem:

> I am not one of those
> who left the land/to the
> mercy of its enemies.

In other cases, however, it is left up to the reader to determine the author's perspective by looking closely at the use of words to see what attitude the words convey. To fully understand an author's perspective, it is sometimes necessary to go beyond the text and gather information about the historical or social context in which the work was written.

THE BRIDGE

Leopold Staff
Translated by Czeslaw Milosz

I didn't believe,
Standing on the bank of a river
Which was wide and swift,
That I would cross that bridge
5   Plaited[1] from thin, fragile reeds
Fastened with bast.[2]
I walked delicately as a butterfly
And heavily as an elephant,
I walked surely as a dancer
10   And wavered like a blind man.
I didn't believe that I would cross that bridge,
And now that I am standing on the other side,
I don't believe I crossed it.

---

1. **plaited** (plāt´ ed) *adj.*: Braided; woven.
2. **bast** (bast) *n.*: Inner bark of trees.

The Last Evening

Rainer Maria Rilke

Translated by Stephen Mitchell
(By permission of Frau Nonna)

And night and distant rumbling; now the army's
carrier-train was moving out, to war.
He looked up from the harpsichord,[1] and as
he went on playing, he looked across at her

5   almost as one might gaze into a mirror:
so deeply was her every feature filled
with his young features, which bore his pain and were
more beautiful and <u>seductive</u> with each sound.

Then, suddenly, the image broke apart.
10   She stood, as though <u>distracted</u>, near the window
and felt the violent drum-beats of her heart.

His playing stopped. From outside, a fresh wind blew.
And strangely alien on the mirror-table
stood the black shako[2] with its ivory skull.

---

1. **harpsichord:** Stringed musical instrument, resembling the piano, that was popular in Europe from the sixteenth to the eighteenth century.
2. **shako** (shak´ ō) *n.*: Stiff, cylindrical military headdress, usually with a flat top and plume. They were typically worn by grenadiers, or soldiers trained to hurl grenades.

◆ **Build Vocabulary**

seductive (si duk´ tiv) *adj.*: Tempting; enticing
distracted (dis trakt´ əd) *adj.*: Having one's attention diverted

I Am Not One of Those Who Left the Land

Anna Akhmatova
Translated by Stanley Kunitz

I am not one of those who left the land
to the mercy of its enemies.
Their flattery leaves me cold,
my songs are not for them to praise.

5   But I pity the exile's lot.
Like a felon, like a man half-dead,
dark is your path, wanderer;
wormwood infects your foreign bread.

But here, in the murk of conflagration,[1]
10   where scarcely a friend is left to know,
we, the survivors, do not flinch
from anything, not from a single blow.

Surely the reckoning will be made
after the passing of this cloud.
15   We are the people without tears,
straighter than you . . . more proud . . .

---

1. **conflagration** (kän′ flə grā′ shən) n.: Destructive fire.

▼ **Critical Viewing** Why do you think these people are on this train? [**Speculate**]

Speech During the Invasion of Constantinople

Empress Theodora

In his collection of historical speeches, Lend Me Your Ears, William Safire wrote the following introduction to Empress Theodora's inspirational words.

⚜

Roman Emperor Justinian, on January 18 of the year 532, was certain he was about to be overthrown by rebel leader Hypatius and killed. A fast galley waited at the palace's private harbor to take him and Empress Theodora to safety in Thrace. His <u>timorous</u> advisers persuaded him that the rebellion could not be stopped and that the way out for the imperial couple was flight. As the panicky leader made for the door, the <u>indomitable</u> empress rose from her throne and delivered a brief speech that kept her husband in Rome and led to the slaughter of the rebels.

▲ **Critical Viewing** This picture shows a strong, triumphant Theodora. Identify details in the speech that reflect these qualities. **[Connect]**

◆ **Build Vocabulary**

timorous (tim´ ər es) *adj.*: Full of fear; timid

indomitable (in däm´ it ə bəl) *adj.*: Not easily defeated

My lords, the present occasion is too serious to allow me to follow the convention that a woman should not speak in a man's council. Those whose interests are threatened by extreme danger should think only of the wisest course of action, not of conventions.

In my opinion, flight is not the right course, even if it should bring us to safety. It is impossible for a person, having been born into this world, not to die; but for one who has reigned it is intolerable to be a fugitive. May I never be deprived of this purple robe, and may I never see the day when those who meet me do not call me empress.

If you wish to save yourself, my lord, there is no difficulty. We are rich; over there is the sea, and yonder are the ships. Yet reflect for a moment whether, when you have once escaped to a place of security, you would not gladly exchange such safety for death. As for me, I agree with the adage that the royal purple is the noblest shroud.

Beyond Literature

Social Studies Connection

Byzantine Empire At the height of its power in the fifth century A.D., the Byzantine empire (also known as the East Roman empire) included parts of southern and eastern Europe, as well as parts of northern Africa and the Middle East. Christianity, Greek culture, and Roman customs flourished in the empire, which served as a link between ancient and modern European civilization. From A.D. 527 to 565, the Byzantine empire was ruled by Emperor Justinian.

Activity Use an encyclopedia to find the extent of Justinian's empire. On a copy of a contemporary world map, indicate the areas he ruled.

Guide for Responding

◆ Literature and Your Life

Reader's Response What personal experiences do these works call to mind?

Thematic Focus Why is courage required at turning points?

☑ Check Your Comprehension

1. What surprises the speaker in "The Bridge"?
2. In "The Last Evening," what item stands on the mirror-table?
3. In "I Am Not One of Those . . . ," what is the speaker's attitude toward those who fled Russia?
4. How does the Empress Theodora feel about dying?

◆ Critical Thinking

INTERPRET

1. Why doesn't the speaker in "The Bridge" think he can cross the bridge? [Speculate]
2. In relation to war, what do the "violent drumbeats" of the woman's heart in "The Last Evening" represent? [Infer]

EVALUATE

3. Do you think it is more courageous to face the dangers of traveling across a continent and an ocean or to stay and live in difficult and dangerous circumstances? [Apply]

COMPARE LITERARY WORKS

4. Compare and contrast the advice you think the speaker of each poem would give to you and your friends. [Compare and Contrast]

Guide for Responding (continued)

◆ Reading Strategy

AUTHOR'S PERSPECTIVE

Understanding the historical context of Anna Akhmatova's poem "I Am Not One of Those Who Left the Land" helps you identify the **author's perspective**—the viewpoint from which the poem is written. An author's perspective affects the details that are included in the work, as well as the way an event or idea is presented.

For instance, Akhmatova's reference to the wormwood in foreign bread reflects her deep love for her country as well as her disapproval of those who would leave.

1. Leopold Staff lived through some of the most devastating events in history. What details in Staff's poem indicate that he has lived through dangerous times?
2. Empress Theodora's speech is made from the perspective of royalty. What details are included that might not be included in a speech by one of the common people during the invasion?
3. Identify two details in Akhmatova's poem that indicate she opposes the rulers of her country.

◆ Literary Focus

DRAMATIC SITUATION

The **dramatic situation**—the circumstances and events that provide the context of a work of literature—of Akhmatova's poem is the turmoil of civil war in Russia. For Empress Theodora's speech, the dramatic situation is the rebellion that threatens the lives of the empress and her husband.

1. Theodora makes her speech just as she and Justinian are about to board a ship and sail to Thrace. How does this detail add to the drama of her remarks?
2. Akhmatova stayed in Russia in the "murk of conflagration" while others fled. How do the circumstances surrounding her decision make her situation more dramatic?
3. Leopold Staff's poem was written in the aftermath of the tremendous devastation that Poland suffered during World War II. How does knowing this affect your understanding of the poem?

◆ Build Vocabulary

USING THE LATIN ROOT -dom-

Fill in the blanks to complete the meanings of these words that include the Latin root -dom-, meaning "to rule."

1. domineer: ____?____ in a harsh or arrogant way
2. domain: the area that is ____?____
3. dominant: ____?____ over another

USING THE WORD BANK: Analogies

On your paper, complete the following word pairs with words from the Word Bank.

1. Courageous is to hero as ____?____ is to ruler.
2. Wide is to narrow as ____?____ is to repulsive.
3. Enraged is to joyful as ____?____ is to brave.
4. Scolded is to praised as ____?____ is to focused.

◆ Build Grammar Skills

NEGATIVES AND DOUBLE NEGATIVES

Negatives are words or word parts that deny or mean "no." Some examples of negatives include *no, not* (and contractions with *n't*), *never, none, nobody, no one, nothing, nowhere, neither, barely, scarcely,* and *hardly.* Using a **double negative**—two negative words where only one is needed—is incorrect.

Practice Identify which of the following sentences use double negatives and which use negatives correctly. Correct the double negatives you identify.

1. Although Empress Theodora did not leave, she was not killed during the rebellion.
2. Staff's poem tells of a man who didn't believe he could never get across a bridge.
3. Hardly none of Akhmatova's friends remained in Russia.
4. Rilke's characters could not hardly bear the pain of separation.

Writing Application In your notebook, rewrite each of these sentences using only one negative.

1. Those who meet me don't never call me empress.
2. Scarcely no friends are left to know.
3. We do not flinch from nothing.
4. I didn't believe in nothing.
5. She wasn't scared of no one.

Build Your Portfolio

Idea Bank

Writing

1. Summaries Write a summary of each of these works that captures the key details.

2. News Commentary Write a commentary that a newscaster might give following Empress Theodora's speech. Summarize what she said and discuss the impact that the speech may have.

3. Comparison-and-Contrast Essay Write an essay in which you compare and contrast Anna Akhmatova's poem with Empress Theodora's speech. Look at similarities and differences in the attitudes of the speakers, the situations they face, and the character traits they exhibit.

Speaking, Listening, and Viewing

4. Speech Give a short speech in which you answer Empress Theodora and try to persuade Emperor Justinian and his aides that the wiser course of action is to board the ship and sail to safety in Thrace. Deliver your speech to the class. **[Performing Arts Link]**

5. Role Play Role-play a conversation between Akhmatova and someone who chose to leave Russia. Use what you learned from the poem and from the background on p. 457 as the basis for the discussion.

Researching and Representing

6. Timeline Several of these works are written in response to specific historical events. Using information gathered through research, create a timeline that captures the events surrounding one of these works. **[Social Studies Link]**

7. Collage Create a collage of visual images, quotations, and found objects that captures the ideas expressed in one of these works. **[Art Link]**

Online Activity www.phlit.phschool.com

Guided Writing Lesson

Poem About a Turning Point

Each of these works captures the thoughts of a person making a choice—facing a turning point. Write a **poem** about a turning point in your own life. You might write about a social or political issue that affects your life (as Akhmatova does), or you might write about a personal choice. Use the following tip to help you communicate your ideas.

Writing Skills Focus: Figurative Language

Words such as *happy* or *sad* and other abstract language—language that refers to things that cannot be experienced with the senses—can mean something different to every person. By connecting abstract words to concrete images, however, you can help readers identify with what you're describing. The best way to do this is to use **figurative language**—writing not meant to be interpreted literally. For example, Leopold Staff uses figurative language when he describes a period of life as a fragile bridge. The specific type of figurative language that Staff uses is a **metaphor**—a comparison in which one thing is described as another. You can also use **similes**—comparisons between dissimilar things using the word *like* or *as*.

Prewriting Choose the experience on which you will focus. Then, brainstorm for a list of images you can use to help capture your feelings associated with the experience.

Drafting Don't overload your poem with a wide variety of images. Choose a small number that are related, and use them as the focus of your poem.

Revising Read your poem to a friend. Get feedback about how you can improve the wording or strengthen the images in your poem.

PART 2 *Fateful Moments*

They Did Not Expect Him, Ilya Efimovich Repin, Tretyakov Gallery, Moscow, Russia

Guide for Reading

Bei Dao *(1949–   )*

Bei Dao (bā dou), which means "Northern Island," is the pen name of one of China's most important contemporary authors. This author's given name is Zhao Zhenkai. He was born in Beijing, just two months before communists, under Mao Tse-tung, gained control of China.

Member of the Red Guard Bei Dao attended one of China's best schools and seemed destined for a successful career in the communist government. Instead, in the mid-1960's he—like millions of other Chinese youths—dropped out of school and joined the Red Guard, a paramilitary group.

This group of idealistic teenagers sought to revitalize the Chinese Revolution by criticizing people they felt were enjoying unfair privileges. However, idealism turned to hatred when the Red Guard began persecuting artists, teachers, and other intellectuals.

Government Protestor Soon disillusioned with the violent tactics of the Red Guard, Bei Dao began expressing his views in poems and stories. He developed into a leading writer and intellectual in the pro-democracy movement, which sought greater political freedom in China. In 1976, his poem "Answer" became a rallying cry for that movement.

The Chinese regime was angered by Bei Dao's open support for human rights. As punishment for his "antigovernment" writings, Bei Dao was sent to the countryside, where he became a construction worker.

Political Exile In June 1989, students were killed by government forces during a protest for democracy in Beijing's Tiananmen Square. Bei Dao was traveling abroad at the time, and the period of repression that followed the massacre made it impossible for him to return. He now lives in Davis, California.

In "The Homecoming Stranger," he writes about the Cultural Revolution with an insider's knowledge.

◆ Build Vocabulary

ANGLO-SAXON SUFFIXES: *–ness*

A character in "The Homecoming Stranger" attributes the vice of *slovenliness* to ducklings. *Slovenliness* ends in the Anglo-Saxon suffix *-ness,* meaning "the state or quality of." When added to the adjective *slovenly,* meaning "untidy, or careless in appearance or work," *-ness* forms the noun *slovenliness*—"the quality of being untidy or careless in work or appearance."

WORD BANK

rehabilitation
spasm
elusive
slovenliness
knead
compunction
imploring

As you read "The Homecoming Stranger," you will encounter the words on this list. Each word is defined on the page where it first appears. Before you read, preview the list.

◆ Build Grammar Skills

PAST PARTICIPIAL PHRASES

In "The Homecoming Stranger," Bei Dao adds information to some of his sentences by using past participles. A past participle is a past form of a verb that is acting as an adjective. It usually ends in *-ed,* but it may also have an irregular ending, such as *-t* or *-en.*

A **past participial phrase** consists of a past participle and its modifiers and complements, and it functions as an adjective. In this sentence from the story, the italicized participial phrase modifies the noun *boats.*

> On the cement platform in front of us, several old wooden boats, *corroded by wind and rain*, were lying upside down, dirt and dry leaves forming a layer over them.

The Homecoming Stranger

◆ Literature and Your Life

CONNECT YOUR EXPERIENCE

After summer vacation, you may feel awkward when you first meet friends again. Now, imagine what it would be like to meet those friends after an absence of twenty years!

In "The Homecoming Stranger," Lanlan finds herself struggling to accept her father when he returns after a long absence.

Journal Writing List several ways to overcome awkwardness when meeting friends or relatives after a separation.

THEMATIC FOCUS: FATEFUL MOMENTS

As you read, ask yourself: What is Lanlan's state of mind leading up to and following her reunion with her father?

◆ Background for Understanding

HISTORY

In 1966, Communist Party chairman Mao Tse-tung, who had led China for nearly twenty years, attacked the system that he himself had established. He started the Cultural Revolution because he feared that, like the Soviet Union, China was becoming too comfortably traditional. He closed China's schools and directed young people, organized into Red Guard units, to publicly criticize artists, intellectuals, and teachers.

Mao's revolution continued for ten years—until his death. It brought untold confusion and suffering. "The Homecoming Stranger" uses one family as a kind of test case for examining the effects of this difficult time.

◆ Literary Focus

CONFLICT AND RESOLUTION

Stories usually involve **conflict**, a struggle between opposing forces. An **internal conflict** takes place within a character, as he or she struggles with opposing feelings, beliefs, or needs. An **external conflict** occurs between characters or between a character and an external force. The **resolution** of a conflict is the way it is solved.

"The Homecoming Stranger" contains both internal and external conflicts. The overall story suggests the external social conflicts of the Cultural Revolution. Within the story, the return of Lanlan's father provokes a conflict between him and his daughter. In addition, his return prompts a conflict within Lanlan.

◆ Reading Strategy

EVALUATE CREDIBILITY

When you read a story, you instinctively **evaluate the credibility**, or believability, of its characters, setting, and plot. You make judgments by asking and answering questions like these: Do characters have good reasons to act as they do? Are descriptions of settings and historical details accurate? Does one event flow naturally and logically from another?

As you read "The Homecoming Stranger," use what you know about the Cultural Revolution and also what you know about human nature to evaluate the believability of Lanlan's responses as she adjusts to her father's return. Use a chart like the one below to help you evaluate the credibility of characters and events in "The Homecoming Stranger."

Character, Setting, or Plot Detail	Question	Answer/ Evaluation

The Homecoming
Stranger
Bei Dao

Translated by Susette Ternent Cooke with the assistance of Bonnie S. McDougall

1

Papa was back.

After exactly twenty years of reform through labor, which took him from the Northeast to Shanxi,[1] and then from Shanxi to Gansu,[2] he was just like a sailor swept overboard by a wave, struggling blindly against the undertow until miraculously he is tossed by another wave back onto the same deck.

◆ **Literary Focus**
What external conflict do the opening paragraphs suggest? Explain.

The verdict was: it was entirely a misjudgment, and he has been granted complete rehabilitation. That day, when the leaders of the Theater Association honored our humble home to announce the decision, I almost jumped up: when did you become so clever? Didn't the announcement that he was an offender against the people come out of your mouths too? It was Mama's eyes, those calm yet suffering eyes, that stopped me.

Next came the dress rehearsal for the celebration: we moved from a tiny pigeon loft into a three-bedroom apartment in a big building: sofas, bookcases, desks, and chrome folding chairs appeared as if by magic (I kept saying half-jokingly to Mama that these were the troupe's props); relatives and friends came running in and out all day, until the lacquer doorknob was rubbed shiny by their hands, and even those uncles and aunts who hadn't shown up all those years rushed to offer congratulations . . . all right, cheer, sing, but what does all this have to do with me? My Papa died a long time ago, he died twenty years ago, just when a little four- or five-year-old girl needed a father's love—that's what Mama, the school, kind-hearted souls, and the whole social upbringing that starts at birth told me. Not only this, you even wanted me to hate him, curse him. It's even possible you'd have given me a whip so I could lash him viciously! Now it's the other way round, you're wearing a different face. What do you want me to do? Cry or laugh?

Yesterday at dinner time, Mama was even more considerate than usual, endlessly filling my bowl with food. After the meal, she drew a telegram from the drawer and handed it to me, showing not the slightest sign of any emotion.

"Him?"

"He arrives tomorrow, at 4:50 in the afternoon."

I crumbled the telegram, staring numbly into Mama's eyes.

"Go and meet him, Lanlan." She avoided my gaze.

"I have a class tomorrow afternoon."

◆ **Build Vocabulary**
rehabilitation (rē´ hə bil´ ə tā´ shən) *n.*: Restoration of rank, privileges, and property

spasm (spaz´ əm) *n.*: Sudden, involuntary muscular contraction

1. **Shanxi** (shän´shē´): Province of northeast China.
2. **Gansu** (gän´sü´): Province of northwest China.

▲ **Critical Viewing** This illustration shows political prisoners of the Cultural Revolution, some wearing cone or "dunce" hats, being driven through the streets. Why do you think Cultural Revolutionists treated prisoners like Lanlan's father in this way? **[Draw Conclusions]**

Untitled (People Arrested During the Cultural Revolution), James McMullan

"Get someone to take it for you."

I turned toward my room. "I won't go."

"Lanlan." Mama raised her voice. "He is your father, after all!"

"Father?" I muttered, turning away fiercely, as if overcome with fear at the meaning of this word. From an irregular <u>spasm</u> in my heart, I realized it was stitches from the old wound splitting open one by one.

I closed the composition book spread in front of me: Zhang Xiaoxia,[3] 2nd Class, 5th Year. A

spirited girl, her head always slightly to one side in a challenging way, just like me as a child. Oh yes, childhood. For all of us life begins with those pale blue copybooks, with those words, sentences, and punctuation marks smudged by erasers; or, to put it more precisely, it begins with a certain degree of deception. The teachers delineated life with halos, but which of them does not turn into a smoke ring or an iron hoop?

Shadows flowed in from the long old-fashioned windows, dulling the bright light on the glass desktop. The entire staff-room was steeped in

---

3. **Zhang Xiaoxia** (jöŋ shou´shä´)

drowsy tranquillity. I sighed, tidied my things, locked the door and crossing the deserted school grounds walked toward home.

The apartment block with its glittering lights was like a huge television screen, the unlit windows composing an elusive image. After a little while some of the windows lit up, and some went dark again. But the three windows on the seventh floor remained as they were: one bright, two dark. I paced up and down for a long time in the vacant lot piled with white line and fir poles. On a crooked, broken signboard were the words: "Safety First."

Strange, why is it that in all the world's languages, this particular meaning comes out as the same sound: Papa. Fathers of different colors, temperaments, and status all derive the same satisfaction from this sound. Yet I still can't say it. What do I know about him? Except for a few surviving old photographs retaining a childhood dream (perhaps every little girl would have such dreams): him, sitting on an elephant like an Arab sheik, a white cloth wound round his head, a resplendent mat on the elephant's back, golden tassels dangling to the ground . . . there were only some plays that once created a sensation and a thick book on dramatic theory which I happened to see at the wastepaper salvage station. What else was there? Yes, add those unlucky letters, as punctual and drab as a clock; stuck in those brown paper envelopes with their red frames, they were just like death notices, suffocating me. I never wrote back, and afterward, I threw them into the fire without even looking at them. Once, a dear little duckling was printed on a snow-white envelope, but when I tore it open and looked, I was utterly crushed. I was so upset I cursed all ugly ducklings, counting up their vices one by one: greed, pettiness, slovenliness . . . because they hadn't brought me good luck. But what luck did I deserve?

The elevator had already closed for the day, and I had to climb all the way up. I stopped outside the door to our place and listened, holding my breath. From inside came the sounds of the television hum and the clichés of an old film. God, give me courage!

As soon as I opened the door, I heard my younger brother's gruff voice: "Sis's back." He rushed up as if making an assault on the enemy, helping me take off my coat. He was almost twenty, but still full of a childish attachment to me, probably because I had given him the maternal love which had seemed too heavy a burden for Mama in those years.

The corridor was very dark and the light from the kitchen split the darkness in two. He was standing in the doorway of the room opposite, standing in the other half of darkness, and next to him was Mama. The reflection from the television screen flickered behind their shoulders.

A moment of dead silence.

Finally, he walked over, across the river of light. The light, the deathly white light, slipped swiftly over his wrinkled and mottled neck and face. I was struck dumb: was this shriveled little old man him? Father. I leaned weakly against the door.

He hesitated a moment and put out his hand. My small hand disappeared in his stiff, big-jointed hand. These hands didn't match his body at all.

"Lanlan." His voice was very low, and trembled a little.

Silence.

"Lanlan," he said again, his voice becoming a little more positive, as if he were waiting eagerly for something.

But what could I say?

"You're back very late. Have you had dinner?" said Mama.

"Mm." My voice was so weak.

"Why is everyone standing? Come inside," said Mama.

He took me by the hand. I followed obediently. Mama turned on the light and switched off the television with a click. We sat down on the sofa. He was still clutching my hand tightly, staring at me intently. I evaded his eyes and let my gaze fall on the blowup plastic doll on the windowsill.

◆ **Reading Strategy**
Is Lanlan's younger brother's greeting of his sister believable? Why or why not?

An unbearable silence.

"Lanlan," he called once again.

I was really afraid the doll might explode, sending brightly colored fragments flying all over the room.

"Have you had your dinner?"

I nodded vigorously.

"Is it cold outside?"

"No." Everything was so normal, the doll wouldn't burst. Perhaps it would fly away suddenly like a hydrogen balloon, out the window, above the houses full of voices, light, and warmth, and go off to search for the stars and moon.

"Lanlan." His voice was full of compassion and pleading.

All of a sudden, my just-established confidence swiftly collapsed. I felt a spasm of alarm. Blood pounded at my temples. Fiercely I pulled back my hand, rushed out the door into my own room, and flung myself headfirst onto the bed. I really felt like bursting into tears.

The door opened softly; it was Mama. She came up to the bed, sat down in the darkness and stroked my head, neck, and shoulders. Involuntarily, my whole body began to tremble as if with cold.

"Don't cry, Lanlan."

Cry? Mama, if I could still cry the tears would surely be red, they'd be blood.

She patted me on the back. "Go to sleep, Lanlan, everything will pass."

Mama left.

Everything will pass. Huh, it's so easily said, but can twenty years be written off at one stroke? People are not reeds, or leeches, but oysters, and the sands of memory will flow with time to change into a part of the body itself, teardrops will never run dry.

. . . a basement. Mosquitoes thudded against the searing light bulb. An old man covered with cuts and bruises was tied up on the pommel horse, his head bowed, moaning hoarsely. I lay in the corner sobbing. My knees were cut to ribbons by the broken glass; blood and mud mixed together . . .

I was then only about twelve years old. One night, when Mama couldn't sleep, she suddenly hugged me and told me that Papa was a good man who had been wrongly accused. At these words hope flared up in the child's heart: for the first time she might be able to enjoy the same rights as other children. So I ran all around, to the school, the Theater Association, the neighborhood committee, and the Red Guard[4] headquarters, to prove Papa's innocence to them. Disaster was upon us, and those louts took me home savagely for investigation. I didn't know what was wrong with Mama, but she repudiated all her words in front of her daughter. All the blame fell on my small shoulders. Mama repented, begged, wished herself dead, but what was the use? I was struggled against, given heavy labor, and punished by being made to kneel on broken glass.

. . . the old man raised his bloody face: "Give me some water, water, water!" Staring with frightened eyes, I forgot the pain, huddling tightly into the corner. When dawn came and the old man breathed his last, I fainted with fright too. The blood congealed on my knees . . .

Can I blame Mama for this?

2

The sky was so blue it dazzled the eyes. Its intense reflections shining on the ground. My hair tied up in a ribbon, I was holding a small empty bamboo basket and standing amidst the dense waist-high grass. Suddenly, from the jungle opposite appeared an elephant, the

---

◆ Build Vocabulary

elusive (ē loo′ siv) adj.: Hard to grasp mentally; puzzling

slovenliness (sluv′ ən lē nes) n.: Lack of care for one's appearance; untidiness

---

4. **Red Guard** Groups of young students that, during the Cultural Revolution, formed a fanatical arm of the Communist party. They reported and arrested people believed to be "suspect" in their support of the Revolution.

◀ **Critical Viewing**
Do you find the mood expressed by the woman in the painting similar to that of Lanlan when she thinks of her father? Why or why not? **[Compare and Contrast]**

tassels of the mat on its back dangling to the ground; Papa sat proudly on top, a white turban on his head. The elephant's trunk waved to and fro, and with a snort it curled round me and placed me up in front of Papa. We marched forward, across the coconut grove streaked with leaping sunlight, across the hills and gullies gurgling with springs. I suddenly turned my head and cried out in alarm. A little old man was sitting behind me, his face blurred with blood; he was wearing convict clothes and on his chest were printed the words "Reform Through Labor." He was moaning hoarsely, "Give me some water, water, water . . ."

I woke up in fright.

It was five o'clock, and outside it was still dark. I stretched out my hand and pulled out the drawer of the bedside cupboard, fumbled for cigarettes, and lit one. I drew back fiercely

and felt more relaxed. The white cloud of smoke spread through the darkness and finally floated out through the small open-shuttered window. The glow from the cigarette alternately brightened and dimmed as I strained to see clearly into the depths of my heart, but other than the ubiquitous silence, the relaxation induced by the cigarette, and the vague emptiness left by the nightmare, there was nothing.

I switched on the desk lamp, put on my clothes, and opened the door quietly. There was a light on in the kitchen and a rustling noise. Who was up so early? Who?

Under the light, wearing a black cotton-padded vest, he was crouching over the wastepaper basket with his back toward me, meticulously picking through everything; spread out beside him were such spoils as vegetable leaves, trimmings, and fish heads.

I coughed.

He jumped and looked round in alarm, his face deathly white, gazing in panic toward me.

The fluorescent light hummed.

He stood up slowly, one hand behind his back, making an effort to smile. "Lanlan, I woke you up."

"What are you doing?"

"Oh, nothing, nothing." He was flustered and kept wiping his trousers with his free hand.

I put out my hand. "Let me see."

After some hesitation he handed the thing over. It was just an ordinary cigarette pack, with nothing odd about it except that it was soiled in one corner.

◆ Reading Strategy

Basing your answer on what you know about the Cultural Revolution, are Lanlan's father's actions believable? Explain.

I lifted my head, staring at him in bewilderment.

"Oh, Lanlan," beads of sweat started from his balding head, "yesterday I forgot to examine this cigarette pack when I threw it away, just in case I wrote something on it; it would be terrible if the team leader saw it."

"Team leader?" I was even more baffled. "Who's the team leader?"

"The people who oversee us prisoners are called team leaders." He fished out a handkerchief and wiped the sweat away. "Of course, I know, it's beyond their reach, but better to find it just in case . . ."

My head began to buzz. "All right, that's enough."

He closed his mouth tightly, as if he had even bitten out his tongue. I really hadn't expected our conversation would begin like this. For the first time I looked carefully at him. He seemed even older and paler than yesterday, with a short grayish stubble over his sunken cheeks, wrinkles that seemed to have been carved by a knife around his lackluster eyes, and an ugly sarcoma[5] on the tip of his right ear. I could not help feeling some compassion for him.

"Was it very hard there?"

"It was all right, you get used to it."

Get used to it! A cold shiver passed through me. Dignity. Wire netting. Guns. Hurried footsteps. Dejected ranks. Death. I crumpled up the cigarette pack and tossed it into the wastepaper basket. "Go back to sleep, it's still early."

"I've had enough sleep, reveille's[6] at 5:30." He turned to tidy up the scattered rubbish.

Back in my room, I pressed my face against the ice-cold wall. It was quite unbearable to begin like this, what should I do next? Wasn't he a man of great integrity before? Ah, Hand of Time, you're so cruel and indifferent, to knead a man like putty, you destroyed him before his daughter could remember her father's real face clearly . . . eventually I calmed down, packed my things into my bag, and put on my overcoat.

Passing through the kitchen, I came to a standstill. He was at the sink, scrubbing his big hands with a small brush, the green soap froth dripping down like sap.

"I'm going to work."

"So early?" He was so absorbed he did not even raise his head.

"I'm used to it."

I did not turn on the light, going down along the darkness, along each flight of stairs.

3

For several days in a row I came home very late. When Mama asked why, I always offered the excuse that I was busy at school. As soon as I got home, I would dodge into the kitchen and hurriedly rake up a few leftovers, then bore straight into my own little nest. I seldom ran into him, and even when we did meet I

---

5. **sarcoma** (sär kō′mə) n.: Malignant tumor that develops in the skin.

6. **reveille** (rev′ə lē) n.: Signal to waken soldiers.

would hardly say a word. Yet it seemed his silence contained enormous compunction, as if to apologize for that morning, for his unexpected arrival, for my unhappy childhood, these twenty years and my whole life.

My brother was always running in like a spy to report on the situation, saying things like: "He's planted a pot of peculiar dried-up herbs." "All afternoon he stared at the fish in the tank." "He's burned a note again" . . . I would listen without any reaction. As far as I was concerned, it was all just a continuation of that morning, not worth making a fuss about. What was strange was my brother, talking about such things so flatly, not tinged by any emotion at all, not feeling any heavy burden on his mind. It was no wonder; since the day he was born Papa had already flown far away, and besides, in those years he was brought up in his Grandma's home, and with Mama's wings and mine in turn hanging over Grandma's little window as well, he never saw the ominous sky.

One evening, as I was lying on the bed smoking, someone knocked at the door. I hurriedly stuffed the cigarette butt in a small tin box as Mama came in.

"Smoking again, Lanlan?"

As if nothing had happened I turned over the pages of a novel beside my pillow.

"The place smells of smoke, open a window."

Thank heavens, she hadn't come to nag. But then I realized that there was something strange in her manner. She sat down beside the small desk, absently picked up the ceramic camel pen-rack and examined it for a moment before returning it to its original place. How would one put it in diplomatic language? Talks, yes, formal talks . . .

"Lanlan, you're not a child anymore," Mama was weighing her words.

It had started; I listened with respectful attention.

"I know you've resented me since you were little, and you've also resented him and resented everyone else in the world, because you've had

◆ Build Vocabulary

compunction (kəm puŋk´shən) *n.:* Sense of guilt or regret

enough suffering . . . but Lanlan, it isn't only you who's suffered."

"Yes, Mama."

"When you marry Jianping,[7] and have children, you'll understand a mother's suffering . . ."

"We don't want children if we can't be responsible for their future."

"You're blaming us, Lanlan," Mama said painfully.

"No, not blaming. I'm grateful to you, Mama, it wasn't easy for you in those years . . ."

"Do you think it was easy for him?"

"Him?" I paused. "I don't know, and I don't want to know either. As a person, I respect his past . . ."

"Don't you respect his present? You should realize, Lanlan, his staying alive required great courage!"

"That's not the problem, Mama. You say this because you lived together for many years, but I, I can't make a false display of affection . . ."

"What are you saying!" Mama grew angry and raised her voice. "At least one should fulfill one's own duties and obligations!"

"Duties? Obligations?" I started to laugh, but it was more painful than crying. "I heard a lot about them during those years. I don't want to lose any more, Mama."

"But what have you gained?"

"The truth."

"It's a cold and unfeeling truth!"

"I can't help it," I spread out my hands, "that's how life is."

"You're too selfish!" Mama struck the desk with her hand and got up, the loose flesh on her face trembling. She stared furiously at me for a moment, then left, shutting the door heavily.

Selfish, I admit it. In those years selfishness was a kind of instinct, a means of self-defense. What could I rely on except this? Perhaps I shouldn't have provoked Mama's anger, perhaps I should really be a good girl and love Papa, Mama, my brother, life, and myself.

◆ Literary Focus
What internal conflict does Lanlan's description of her "selfishness" suggest?

7. **Jianping** (jen´piŋ´)

4

During the break between classes, I went into the reception office and rang Jianping.

"Hello, Jianping, come over this evening."

"What's up? Lanlan?" He was shouting, over the clatter of the machines his voice sounding hoarse and weary.

"He's back."

"Who? Your father?"

"Clever one, come over and help; it's an absolutely awful situation."

He started to laugh.

"Huh, if you laugh, just watch out!" I clenched my fists and banged down the receiver.

It's true, Jianping has the ability to head off disaster. The year when the production brigade chief withheld the grain ration from us educated youth,[8] it was he who led the whole bunch of us to snatch it all back. Although I normally appear to be quite sharp-witted, I always have to hide behind his broad shoulders whenever there's a crisis.

That afternoon I had no classes and hurried home early. Mama had left a note on the table, saying that she and Papa had gone to call on some old friends and would eat when they returned. I kneaded some dough, minced the meat fillings, and got everything ready to wrap the dumplings.

Jianping arrived. He brought with him a breath of freshness and cold, his cheeks flushed red, brimming with healthy vitality. I snuggled up against him at once, my cheek pressed against the cold buttons on his chest, like a child who feels wronged but has nowhere to pour out her woes. I didn't say anything, what could I say?

We kissed and hugged for a while, then sat down and wrapped dumplings, talking and joking as we worked. From gratitude, relaxation, and the vast sleepiness that follows affection, I was almost on the verge of tears.

When my brother returned, he threw off his work clothes, drank a mouthful of water, and flew off like a whirlwind.

It was nearly eight when they got home. As they came in, it gave them quite a shock to see us. Mama could not then conceal a conciliatory and motherly smile of victory; Papa's expression was much more complicated. Apart from the apologetic look of the last few days, he also seemed to feel an irrepressible pleasure at this surprise, as well as a precautionary fear.

"This is Jianping, this is . . ." My face was suffocated with red.

"This is Lanlan's father," Mama filled in.

Jianping held out his hand and boomed, "How do you do, Uncle!"

Papa grasped Jianping's hand, his lips trembling for a long time. "So you're, so you're Jianping, fine, fine . . ."

Delivering the appropriate courtesies, Jianping gave the old man such happiness he was at a loss what to do. It was quite clear to me that his happiness had nothing to do with these remarks, but was because he felt that at last he'd found a bridge between him and me, a strong and reliable bridge.

At dinner, everyone seemed to be on very friendly terms, or at least that's how it appeared on the surface. Several awkward silences were covered over by Jianping's jokes. His conversation was so witty and lively that it even took me by surprise.

After dinner, Papa took out his Zhonghua[9] cigarettes from a tin cigarette case to offer to Jianping. This set them talking about the English method of drying tobacco and moving on to soil salinization,[10] insect pests among peanuts and vine-grafting. I sat bolt upright beside them, smiling like a mannequin in a shop window.

Suddenly, my smile began to vanish. Surely this was a scene from a play? Jianping was the protagonist—a clever son-in-law, while I, I was the meek and mild new bride. For reasons only the devil could tell, everyone was acting to the

---

8. educated youth: During the Cultural Revolution, educated people (young and old) were distrusted and persecuted.

9. Zhonghua (jʊ̄ŋ´hwä´): A trademark of one of the best-known brands of cigarettes in China.
10. soil salinization (sal´ə nə zā´shən) *n.*: Process of contaminating soil with salts.

hilt, striving to forget something in this scene. Acting happiness, acting calmness, acting glossed-over suffering. I suddenly felt that Jianping was an outsider to the fragmented, shattered suffering of this family.

I began to consider Jianping in a different light. His tone, his gestures, even his appearance, all had an unfamiliar flavor. This wasn't real, this wasn't the old him. Could strangeness be contagious? How frightening.

Jianping hastily threw me an inquiring glance, as if expecting me to repay the role he was playing with a commending smile. This made me feel even more disgusted. I was disgusted with him, and with myself, disgusted with everything the world is made of, happiness and sorrow, reality and sham, good and evil.

Guessing this, he wound up the conversation. He looked at his watch, said a few thoroughly polite bits of nonsense, and got to his feet.

As usual, I accompanied him to the bus stop. But along the way, I said not a single word, keeping a fair distance from him. He dejectedly thrust his hands in his pockets, kicking a stone.

An apartment block ahead hid the night. I felt alone. I longed to know how human beings survive behind these countless containers of suffering, broken families. Yet in these containers, memory is too frightening. It can only deepen the suffering and divide every family until everything turns to powder.

When we reached the bus stop, he stood with his back to me, gazing at the distant lights. "Lanlan, do I still need to explain?"

"There's no need."

He leaped onto the bus. Its red taillights flickering, it disappeared round the corner.

5

Today there was a sports meet at the school, but I didn't feel like it at all. Yesterday afternoon, Zhang Xiaoxia kept pestering me to come and watch her in the 100 meter race.

I just smiled, without promising anything. She pursed her little mouth and, fanning her cheeks, which were streaming with sweat, with her handkerchief, stared out the window in a huff. I put my hands on her shoulders and turned her round. "I'll go then, all right?" Her face broadening into dimples, she struggled free of me in embarrassment and ran off. How easy it is to deceive a child.

I stretched, and started to get dressed. The winter sunlight seeped through the fogged-up window, making everything seem dim and quiet, like an extension of sleep and dreams. When I came out of my room, it was quiet and still; evidently everyone had gone out. I washed my hair and put my washing to soak, dashing busily to and fro. When everything was done, I sat down to eat breakfast. Suddenly I sensed that someone was standing behind me, and when I looked round it was Papa, standing stiffly in the kitchen doorway and staring at me blankly.

"Didn't you go out?" I asked.

"Oh, no, no, I was on the balcony. You're not going to school today?"

"No. What is it?"

"I thought," he hesitated, "we might go for a walk in the park, what do you think?" There was an <u>imploring</u> note in his voice.

"All right." Although I didn't turn round, I could feel that his eyes had brightened.

It was a warm day, but the morning mist had still not faded altogether, lingering around eaves and treetops. Along the way, we said almost nothing. But when we entered the park, he pointed at the tall white poplars[11] by the side of the road. "The last time I brought you here, they'd just been planted." But I didn't remember it at all.

After walking along the avenue for a while, we sat down on a bench beside the lake. On the cement platform in front of us, several old wooden boats, corroded by wind and rain, were lying upside down, dirt and dry leaves forming a layer over them. The ice on the surface of the water crackled from time to time.

He lit a cigarette.

---

11. **poplars** (päp´lərz) *n.*: Trees of the willow family.

Rise With Force and Spirit, James Bama, The Greenwich Workshop, Inc.

▲ **Critical Viewing** Does the mood of the man in this picture correspond to that of Lanlan's father at the story's end? Why or why not? **[Analyze]**

"Those same boats," he said pensively.
"Oh?"

"They're still the same boats. You used to like sitting in the stern, splashing with your bare feet and shouting, 'Motorboat! Motorboat!'" The shred of a smile of memory appeared on his face. "Everyone said you were like a boy . . ."

"Really?"

"You liked swords and guns; whenever you went into a toy shop you'd always want to come out with a whole array of weapons."

"Because I didn't know what they were used for."

All at once a shadow covered his face and his eyes darkened. "You were still a child then . . ."

Silence, a long silence. The boats lying on the bank were turned upside down here. They were covering a little girl's silly cries, a father's carefree smile, soft-drink bottletops, a blue satin ribbon, children's books and toy guns, the taste of earth in the four seasons, the passage of twenty years . . .

◆ **Build Vocabulary**

imploring (im plôr´ iŋ) *adj.*: As if begging or asking

"Lanlan," he said suddenly, his voice very low and trembling. "I, I beg your pardon."

My whole body began to quiver.

"When your mother spoke of your life in these years, it was as if my heart was cut with a knife. What is a child guilty of?" His hand clutched at the air and came to rest against his chest.

"Don't talk about these things," I said quietly.

"To tell you the truth, it was for you that I lived in those years. I thought if I paid for my crime myself, perhaps life would be a bit better for my child, but . . ." he choked with sobs, "you can blame me, Lanlan, I didn't have the ability to protect you. I'm not worthy to be your father . . ."

"No, don't don't . . ." I was trembling, my whole body went weak, all I could do was wave my hands. How selfish I was! I thought only of myself, immersed myself only in my own sufferings, even making suffering a kind of pleasure and a wall of defense against others. But how did he live? For you, for your selfishness, for your heartlessness! Can the call of blood be so feeble? Can what is called human nature have completely died out in my heart?

". . . twenty years ago, the day I left the house, it was a Sunday. I took an afternoon train, but I left at dawn; I didn't want you to remember this scene. Standing by your little bed, the tears streaming down, I thought to myself: 'Little Lanlan, shall we ever meet again?' You were sleeping so soundly and sweetly, with your little round dimples . . . the evening before as you were going to bed, you hugged my neck and said in a soft voice, 'Papa, will you take me out tomorrow?' 'Papa's busy tomorrow.' You went into a sulk and pouted unhappily. I had to promise. Then you asked again, 'Can we go rowing?' 'Yes, we'll go rowing.' And so you went to sleep quite satisfied. But I deceived you, Lanlan, when you woke up the next day, what could you think . . ."

"Papa!" I blurted out, flinging myself on his shoulder and crying bitterly.

With trembling hands he stroked my head. "Lanlan, my child."

"Forgive me, Papa," I said, choked with sobs. "I'm still your little Lanlan, always . . ."

"My little Lanlan, always."

A bird whose name I don't know hovered over the lake, crying strangely, adding an even deeper layer of desolation to this bleak winter scene.

I lay crying against Papa's shoulder for a long time. My tears seeped drop by drop into the coarse wool of his overcoat. I seemed to smell the pungent scent of tobacco mingling with the smell of mud and sweat. I seemed to see him in the breaks between heavy labor, leaning wearily against the pile of dirt and rolling a cigarette staring into the distance through the fork between the guard's legs. He was pulling a cart, struggling forward on the miry road, the cartwheels screeching, churning up black mud sods. The guard's legs. He was digging the earth shovelful after shovelful, straining himself to fling it toward the pit side. The guard's legs. He was carrying his bowl, greedily draining the last mouthful of vegetable soup. The guard's legs . . . I dared not think anymore, I dared not. My powers of imagining suffering were limited after all. But he actually lived in a place beyond the powers of human imagination. Minute after minute, day after day, oh God, a full twenty years . . . no, amidst suffering, people should be in communication with one another, suffering can link people's souls even more than happiness, even if the soul is already numb, already exhausted . . .

"Lanlan, look," he drew a beautiful necklace from his pocket. "I made this just before I left there from old toothbrush handles. I wanted to give you a kind of present, but then I was afraid you wouldn't want this crude toy . . ."

"No, I like it." I took the necklace, moving the beads lightly to and fro with my finger, each of these wounded hearts . . .

On the way back, Papa suddenly bent over and picked up a piece of paper, turning it over and over in his hand. Impulsively I pulled up his arm and laid my head on his shoulder. In my heart I understood that this was because of a new strangeness, and an attempt to resist this strangeness.

Here on this avenue, I seemed to see a scene from twenty years earlier. A little girl with a blue ribbon in her hair, both fists outstretched, totters along the edge of the concrete road. Beside her walks a middle-aged man relaxed and at ease. A row of little newly planted poplars separates them. And these little trees, as they swiftly swell and spread, change into a row of huge insurmountable bars. Symbolizing this are twenty years of irregular growth rings.

"Papa, let's go."
He tossed away the

piece of paper and wiped his hand carefully on his handkerchief. We walked on again.

Suddenly I thought of Zhang Xiaoxia. At this moment, she'll actually be in the race. Behind rises a puff of white smoke from the starting gun, and amid countless faces and shrill cries falling away behind her, she dashes against the white finishing tape.

◆ **Literary Focus**
How has the conflict between Lanlan and her father been resolved?

Guide for Responding

◆ *Literature and Your Life*

Reader's Response Were Lanlan's feelings indeed "selfish," or were her reactions natural and understandable?

Thematic Focus What is the most significant moment in this story about Lanlan's reactions to her father's homecoming? Explain.

Reader's Journal Assume Lanlan's character for a few moments, and write a journal entry describing an important moment in the story.

Questions for Research In this story, Bei Dao examines the psychological scars of the victims and survivors of the Cultural Revolution. Write down two or three aspects of the Cultural Revolution about which you would like to know more.

☑ Check Your Comprehension

1. Where has Lanlan's father been for twenty years?
2. Briefly describe the scene when father and daughter are reunited.
3. What does Lanlan see her father doing the next morning?
4. Briefly describe the dinner at which Jianping joins Lanlan's family.
5. Summarize what occurs between Lanlan and her father in the park.

◆ Critical Thinking

INTERPRET
1. Why does Lanlan have difficulty saying the word *Papa*? **[Interpret]**
2. Why is Lanlan grateful to Jianping at first and then resentful of him? **[Analyze]**
3. What accounts for the differences in Lanlan's attitude toward her father at the beginning and the end of the story? **[Synthesize]**
4. What has Lanlan learned by the end of the story? **[Draw Conclusions]**
5. Explain the meaning of the story's title and its final image. **[Interpret]**

EVALUATE
6. Would this story have been more effective or less effective if Bei Dao had included a detailed description of the Cultural Revolution? Explain. **[Make a Judgment]**

EXTEND
7. What insight did this story give you into how the Cultural Revolution affected people's lives? **[Social Studies Link]**

COMPARE LITERARY WORKS
8. Compare and contrast the reconciliation between Lanlan and her father with a family reconciliation in another story. **[Compare and Contrast]**

Guide for Responding *(continued)*

◆ Reading Strategy

EVALUATE CREDIBILITY

Rely on what you know about historical events and human nature to **evaluate the credibility** of the events and characters presented in "The Homecoming Stranger."

For example, what you learned about the Cultural Revolution can help you evaluate the credibility of Lanlan's memories on p. 471. She remembers an "old man" with a "bloody face" begging for water. This man may have been one of the intellectuals humiliated and physically attacked by the Red Guard. The historical facts, therefore, give credibility to the memory.

1. Explain how your knowledge of the Cultural Revolution helps you evaluate the credibility of the opening paragraphs of the story.
2. From what you know of human nature, is Lanlan's first reaction to her father's homecoming believable? Why or why not?
3. Is Lanlan's change of heart toward her father believable? Explain.

◆ Literary Focus

CONFLICT AND RESOLUTION

The conflicts in "The Homecoming Stranger" are both **internal**—within a character—and **external** —between a character and another character or between a character and an external force. The **resolution,** which is the solution of the conflicts, occurs at the story's end. However, not all the conflicts may be solved.

Lanlan has an external conflict with the social forces that have shattered her family. She also experiences an internal conflict involving anger at her father and love for him. This inner conflict spills over into an external conflict with her father as she avoids him and cannot express her emotions.

Find a passage that illustrates each of the following conflicts, and explain your choice. Tell how each conflict is resolved or unresolved as the story ends.

1. Conflict between Lanlan and society
2. Conflict within Lanlan
3. Conflict between Lanlan and her father

◆ Build Vocabulary

USING THE ANGLO-SAXON SUFFIX: -ness

Knowing that a word ending in -ness means the "state or quality of something," define the following words in your notebook:

1. narrowness   3. uneasiness
2. seriousness   4. completeness

USING THE WORD BANK: Synonyms

On your paper, identify the lettered word that is the synonym for each numbered word.

1. rehabilitation: (a) action, (b) restoration, (c) installation
2. spasm: (a) contraction, (b) easiness, (c) fight
3. elusive: (a) solid, (b) puzzling, (c) starving
4. slovenliness: (a) business, (b) untidiness, (c) restlessness
5. knead: (a) want, (b) care, (c) form
6. compunction: (a) punctuation, (b) regret, (c) hope
7. imploring: (a) begging, (b) abandoning, (c) forcing

◆ Build Grammar Skills

PAST PARTICIPIAL PHRASES

A **past participial phrase** contains a past participle and its modifers and complements, and it functions as an adjective. Past participial phrases add descriptive details to sentences.

Practice Copy the following sentences into your notebook. Underline each past participial phrase and circle the noun it modifies.

1. Judged to be completely rehabilitated, Lanlan's father returned home after a twenty-year absence.
2. Her family, forced to suffer for so many years, adjusted to the father's homecoming.
3. Punished for talking about her father's innocence, Lanlan felt frightened and confused.
4. Burdened by her childhood memories, Lanlan avoided her father.
5. After listening to her father talk about his emotions and experiences, Lanlan, shocked by her own selfishness, forgives and accepts him.

Build Your Portfolio

Idea Bank

Writing

1. **Letter** Imagine that you are Lanlan as a teenager, and write a letter to a friend about the effects of your father's imprisonment on your family.

2. **Story Sequel** Write a continuation of this story, using what you know about human nature to show Lanlan's increasing acceptance of herself and her family.

3. **Response to Criticism** Critic and translator Bonnie S. McDougall says that Bei Dao's stories "are not so much concerned with exposing the past as exploring the problems of the present." Using this story as evidence, support or refute her statement.

Speaking, Listening, and Viewing

4. **Role Play** With a partner, role-play the scene in which Lanlan and her father walk together in the park. Use tone of voice, posture, and body language appropriate to your character. **[Performing Arts Link]**

5. **Radio Interview** With a partner, role-play a radio interview in which Lanlan's father describes his experiences while he was away from his family. Use details from the story to give credibility to your interview. **[Performing Arts Link; Social Studies Link]**

Researching and Representing

6. **Map** Draw a map of contemporary China. Label places mentioned in the story, such as Beijing, Shanxi, and Sansu. **[Art Link; Social Studies Link]**

7. **Pro-Democracy Poster** Research China's pro-democracy movement, in which Bei Dao participated. Then, design a poster expressing the ideals of this movement. **[Art Link; Social Studies Link]**

Online Activity www.phlit.phschool.com

Guided Writing Lesson

Review of a Story

In "The Homecoming Stranger," Bei Dao tries to show how social forces affect one particular Chinese family. Write a review of the story in which you evaluate how effectively he accomplishes his goal. As part of your review, evaluate the believability of characters' motives and historical details. Also, explain whether or not the conflicts and their resolution contribute to the author's purpose.

Writing Skills Focus: Elaborate to Make Writing Personal

Tell readers what the story meant to you by elaborating to make your writing personal. As you make your evaluation, include your own opinions, insights, and reactions. By doing so, you have a better chance of engaging readers and convincing them of your sincerity.

Prewriting List story details that you think are believable or not believable. Also, jot down notes on the story's conflicts, and how they reveal the effects of social forces. Finally, note details in the story to which you had a strong response.

Drafting In your introduction, mention the author and title, explain the author's purpose, and briefly evaluate the author's success in achieving his purpose. As you write the review, refer to your prewriting notes for details that support your evaluation. Engage readers by including your own personal reactions to the story.

Revising Have a partner evaluate your writing on many levels: its overall organization, paragraph unity, sentence variety, and word choice. Also discuss with your partner ways in which to make your review more personal.

Where necessary, add details to sentences by using past participial phrases. For more on past participial phrases, see pp. 466 and 480.

Guide for Reading

Dahlia Ravikovitch *(1936–)*

The intensely personal poems of this Israeli author also use images of history, religion, and mythology. A native of Tel Aviv, Dahlia Ravikovitch is known for her translations of children's literature as well as the works of William Butler Yeats, Edgar Allan Poe, and T. S. Eliot. In turn, two of her books, *Dress of Fire* and *The Window*, have been translated into English.

Francis Ponge *(1899–1988)*

Francis Ponge (frän sēs´ pônzh) was almost unknown in the French literary community until he was in his early forties. The beginnings of his fame date from the publication of his remarkable book *Siding With Things* (1942). Ponge "sides" with things in this book by eliminating all preconceived ideas about them. Instead, he describes such items as a candle, a crate, blackberries, or an orange in new and surprising ways.

His descriptions are in the form of prose poems that do without rhyme, meter, and stanzas and look like little essays with ordinary paragraphs. It is as if Ponge is "siding with things" by stripping his poems of all fancy extras and thereby making them more like ordinary "things."

In "The Butterfly," which comes from *Siding With Things,* Ponge captures the flittering strangeness of this creature.

Franz Kafka *(1883–1924)*

In his will, the Czech writer Franz Kafka asked that all his unpublished literary works be burned and all others be allowed to go out of print. Fortunately, his wishes were ignored, and much of Kafka's major work was published after his death.

Kafka's writing reflects the anxiety and alienation that pervaded much of twentieth-century society. "Before the Law" is a parable—a narrative in which the actions of characters represent abstract ideas and moral principles.

◆ Build Vocabulary

LATIN WORD ROOTS: -sat-

Have you ever wanted something so badly that you kept asking and asking for it? You might say that your desire was *insatiable*. *Insatiable* has as its root -sat- and comes from the Latin *satiare* meaning "to fill entirely." An *insatiable* desire, therefore, is one that cannot be filled.

WORD BANK

Before you read, preview this list of words from the selections.

elaborated
torsos
emaciated
importunity
contemplation
insatiable

◆ Build Grammar Skills

SIMPLE, COMPOUND, AND COMPLEX SENTENCES

Authors create sentence variety by using different sentence structures. Following are definitions of these structures with examples of each from Kafka's "Before the Law":

Simple sentence—a single independent clause.

Example "Now he has not very long to live."

Compound sentence—two or more independent clauses joined by a comma and a coordinating conjunction or by a semicolon.

Example "He forgets the other doorkeepers, and this man seems to him the sole obstacle preventing access to the Law."

Complex sentence—one independent clause and one or more subordinate clauses.

Example "He waves him nearer, since he can no longer raise his stiffening body."

Pride ◆ The Butterfly ◆ Before the Law

◆ *Literature and Your Life*

CONNECT YOUR EXPERIENCE

If you could control all the events that affect your life, you'd win every game and pass every test. Sometimes, however, life throws a curve ball: Your team forfeits the game, or the science test includes questions you weren't expecting. These selections show how people and other living creatures respond to circumstances that are (or seem to be) beyond their control.

THEMATIC FOCUS: FATEFUL MOMENTS

These selections show how specific events become fateful moments that change a life forever. The different ways with which these events are dealt may lead you to examine how you respond to events that seem to be out of your control.

Journal Writing Jot down ideas for adjusting to circumstances you cannot change, taking action on circumstances you can change, and knowing the difference between the two.

◆ Background for Understanding

CULTURE

To appreciate Kafka's parable "Before the Law," you must appreciate his complex relationship to Judaism, the religion into which he was born.

Kafka did not worship as a Jew. However, living in Prague, he had direct experience of persecution directed at Jews. Also, he strongly identified as a Jew in a cultural sense, and his work focuses on such Jewish themes as exile, sin, and forgiveness.

In a way, Kafka was a man exiled from his own religion because he could not observe it in a simple and sincere way. However, he still believed in the Law that Judaism sets forth. His parable captures this paradox of believing in something in which you cannot participate.

◆ Literary Focus

STATED AND IMPLIED THEME

The **theme** of a work is its central message, the comment its writer is making about human life and values. In some literary works, the theme is **stated directly.** In others, it is **implied** or suggested, and you must figure it out by analyzing the resolution of conflicts, characters' actions, and other details.

For example, "Pride" implies the theme that a hidden wound can eventually cause a person to "break," just as a hidden crack can eventually cause a rock to crumble.

◆ Reading Strategy

EVALUATE A WRITER'S MESSAGE

You walk out of a movie theater discussing the movie you just saw with your friends. As you evaluate it, you consider a variety of questions. Did the movie have a point? Did the plot make sense? You can examine literature in a similar way. You **evaluate a writer's message** by first identifying the message and then judging whether the message is valid—that is, whether it makes sense and is well supported. You can evaluate a message without necessarily agreeing or disagreeing with it.

In the poem "Pride," Dahlia Ravikovitch communicates a message about how difficulties and troubles affect people. Your evaluation of her message will rate how well you think she communicates and supports her message. Identify the message in each of the other selections. Then use a graphic organizer like the one shown to help you evaluate the message.

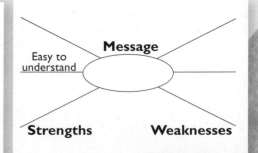

Pride

Dahlia Ravikovitch
Translated by Chana Bloch and Ariel Bloch

I tell you, even rocks crack,
and not because of age.
For years they lie on their backs
in the heat and the cold,
5   so many years,
it almost seems peaceful.
They don't move, so the cracks stay hidden.
A kind of pride.
Years pass over them, waiting.
10 Whoever is going to shatter them
hasn't come yet.
And so the moss flourishes, the seaweed
whips around,
the sea pushes through and rolls back—
15 the rocks seem motionless.
Till a little seal comes to rub against them,
comes and goes away.
And suddenly the rock has an open wound.
I told you, when rocks break, it happens by surprise.
20 And people, too.

The Butterfly

Francis Ponge
Translated by C. K. Williams

When the sugar <u>elaborated</u> in the stems gushes up in the bottom of flowers so that they look like badly washed cups, a great struggle breaks out on the ground, from which butterflies suddenly take flight.

5 But as the caterpillars all had their heads blinded and blackened, their <u>torsos</u> <u>emaciated</u> by the veritable explosion from which their symmetrical wings blazed up,

The erratic butterfly now only alights, or at least so it seems, haphazardly.

10 A flying match whose flame's not contagious. Beside, it arrives too late, after the flowers have already bloomed. Never mind: like a maintenance man it checks their oil one after the other. It sets the shrunken rag of a body it still carries with it on their summits, and avenges its protracted, shapeless humiliation as a caterpillar at their
15 feet.

Tiny sailing ship of the air, which the wind buffets about like a superfluous petal, it vagabonds in the garden.

◀ **Critical Viewing**
What details in the picture on this page indicate a sense of isolation? **[Analyze]**

Enigma of the Hour, 1912, Giorgio de Chirico, Coll. Mattioli, Milan, Italy

Before the Law

Franz Kafka
Translated by Willa and Edwin Muir

Before the Law stands a doorkeeper. To this doorkeeper there comes a man from the country and prays for admittance to the Law. But the doorkeeper says that he cannot grant admittance at the moment. The man thinks it over and then asks if he will be allowed in later. "It is possible," says the doorkeeper, "but not at the moment." Since the gate stands open, as usual, and the doorkeeper steps to one side, the man stoops to peer through the gateway into the interior. Observing that, the doorkeeper laughs and says: "If you are so drawn to it, just try to go in despite my veto.[1] But take note: I am powerful. And I am only the least of the doorkeepers. From hall to hall there is one doorkeeper after another, each more powerful than the last. The third doorkeeper is already so terrible that even I cannot bear to look at him." These are difficulties the man from the country has not expected; the Law, he thinks, should surely be accessible at all times and to everyone, but as he now takes a closer look at the doorkeeper in his fur coat, with his big sharp nose and long, thin, black Tartar[2] beard, he decides that it is better to wait until he gets permission to enter. The doorkeeper gives him a stool and lets him sit

---

1. veto (vē´ tō) *n.*: An order prohibiting some proposed or intended act.

2. Tartar (tär´ tər): Member of a Turkic people living in a region of European Russia.

down at one side of the door. There he sits for days and years. He makes many attempts to be admitted, and wearies the doorkeeper by his <u>importunity</u>. The doorkeeper frequently has little interviews with him, asking him questions about his home and many other things, but the questions are put indifferently, as great lords put them, and always finish with the statement that he cannot be let in yet. The man, who has furnished himself with many things for his journey, sacrifices all he has, however valuable, to bribe the doorkeeper. The doorkeeper accepts everything, but always with the remark: "I am only taking it to keep you from thinking you have omitted anything." During these many years the man fixes his attention almost continuously on the doorkeeper. He forgets the other doorkeepers, and this one seems to him the sole obstacle preventing access to the Law. He curses his bad luck, in his early years boldly and loudly; later, as he grows old, he only grumbles to himself. He becomes child-ish, and since in his yearlong <u>contemplation</u> of the doorkeeper he has come to know even the fleas in his fur collar, he begs the fleas as well to help him and to change the doorkeeper's mind. At length his eyesight begins to fail, and he does not know whether the world is really darker or whether his eyes are only deceiving him. Yet in his darkness he is now aware of a radiance that streams inextinguishable from the gateway of the Law. Now he has not very long to live. Before he dies, all his experiences in these long years gather themselves in his head to one point, a question he has not yet asked the doorkeeper. He waves him nearer, since he can no longer raise his stiffening body. The doorkeeper has to bend low toward him, for the difference in height between them has altered much to the man's disadvantage. "What do you want to know now?" asks the doorkeeper; "you are <u>insatiable</u>." "Everyone strives to reach the Law," says the man, "so how does it happen that for all these many years no one but myself has ever begged for admittance?" The doorkeeper recognizes that the man has reached his end, and, to let his failing senses catch the words, roars in his ear: "No one else could ever be admitted here, since this gate was made only for you. I am now going to shut it."

◆ **Build Vocabulary**

importunity (im′ pôr tōōn′ i tē) *n.*: Persistence in requesting or demanding

contemplation (kän′ tem plā′ shən) *n.*: Thoughtful inspection; study

insatiable (in sā′ shə bəl) *adj.*: Cannot be satisfied; constantly wanting more

Guide for Responding

◆ *Literature and Your Life*

Reader's Response Suggest another title that you think would fit one of these selections.

Thematic Focus What do these works say about turning points?

☑ Check Your Comprehension

1. In "Pride," what causes the rocks to crack?
2. In Ponge's poem, what is the "flying match whose flame's not contagious"?
3. Why has no one else begged admittance to the Law in "Before the Law"?

◆ Critical Thinking

INTERPRET
1. What does the seal represent in "Pride"? **[Apply]**

APPLY
2. Would Ponge's "The Butterfly" have a different effect if it were written in verse? Explain. **[Modify]**

COMPARE LITERARY WORKS
3. Compare these works to other stories or poems you have read that treat the theme of love, pride, or justice. **[Compare and Contrast]**

Guide for Responding (continued)

◆ Reading Strategy

EVALUATE A WRITER'S MESSAGE

You **evaluate a writer's message,** by first identifying the message, and then deciding whether you agree or disagree with it.

For example, in "The Butterfly" the details and images provided by Ponge offer clues that the message of the work may concern both the renewal of life and its fragility.

1. (a) How clearly does Ponge communicate his message? (b) Do you agree or disagree with the message? Give reasons for your opinion.
2. On the basis of your own experience, explain whether you think the message of "Pride" is valid.
3. Identify and evaluate the message in "Before the Law."

◆ Literary Focus

STATED AND IMPLIED THEME

The **theme** of a work is its central message, the insight into life that the author is offering. This theme can be **directly stated,** or it may be **implied**—suggested through the work's imagery, action, or events.

1. Explain how Ravikovitch conveys the theme of "Pride" in the last line without fully stating it.
2. What images does Ponge use to communicate his theme in "The Butterfly"? Explain.
3. Choose a word that describes the feeling you get from reading "Before the Law." How does this feeling give you a clue to Kafka's theme?

Beyond Literature

Science Connection

The Life Cycle of a Butterfly Ponge's poem describes the four-stage transformation of a caterpillar into a butterfly. After hatching from its egg, the caterpillar enters the larval stage when it eats leaves and grows to full size. Then, the caterpillar becomes a pupa, usually in the winter, by spinning or creating a cocoon around itself, in which it hibernates. Finally, in the spring a newly formed butterfly emerges. **Activity** Find information on one type of butterfly.

◆ Build Vocabulary

USING THE LATIN ROOT -sat-

On your paper, complete the meanings of these words that include the Latin root -sat- ("to fill").
1. satisfy: _____?_____ one's needs or expectations
2. satiate: to completely _____?_____
3. saturate: to cause to be soaked _____?_____

USING THE WORD BANK: Synonyms

On your paper, match each numbered word from the Word Bank to the letter of its synonym, the word most similar in meaning.

1. elaborated   a. greedy
2. torsos   b. starved
3. emaciated   c. entreaty
4. importunity   d. body parts
5. contemplation   e. changed
6. insatiable   f. examination

◆ Build Grammar Skills

SIMPLE, COMPOUND, AND COMPLEX SENTENCES

In these selections, the authors use **simple sentences** (a single independent clause), **compound sentences** (two or more independent clauses linked by a coordinating conjunction), and **complex sentences** (an independent clause linked to one or more subordinate clauses).

Practice In your notebook, identify each sentence as simple, compound, or complex. Then, explain the reasons for your choice.
1. The sea pushes through, and the sea rolls back.
2. They look like badly washed cups.
3. The doorkeeper has to bow low toward him, for the difference in height between them has altered.
4. The butterfly, which looks like a piece of paper, flitters over the garden.
5. The rock is like a proud person, and its solidity is the symbol of its pride.

Writing Application On your paper, combine each pair of sentences in two ways, by creating a compound sentence and by creating a complex sentence.
1. The man sits at the gate. The man cannot enter.
2. The doorkeeper is sympathetic. The doorkeeper refuses to admit the man.

Build Your Portfolio

Idea Bank

Writing

1. **Prose Poem** Choose an animal or object that is familiar to you, and write a prose poem about it. Help your readers see your subject in a fresh way.

2. **Imagery** Just as Ravikovitch describes pride in terms of a rock, use imagery to describe another human quality or emotion. For example, you might depict serenity by describing a pool of water.

3. **Parable** Write a parable like Kafka's, a tale in which the actions and characters represent ideas or moral principles. However, like Kafka, let your tale be a little mysterious—don't include a simple moral.

Speaking, Listening, and Viewing

4. **Oral Interpretation** Prepare an oral interpretation of "The Butterfly" or "Pride." Decide how you will vary the tone and pitch of your voice to express the poem's theme. **[Performing Arts Link]**

5. **Improvisational Skit** With a partner, perform a skit based on a conversation between the man and the gatekeeper from "Before the Law." Be humorous if you like. Afterwards, explain your reasons for performing the skit as you did. **[Performing Arts Link]**

Researching and Representing

6. **Diagram** Ponge's poem describes a caterpillar changing into a butterfly. Research the butterfly. Then, create a labeled diagram showing the stages of its development. If you prefer, use computer graphics software to create your diagram. **[Science Link; Art Link]**

7. **Report** Research the life of Franz Kafka and prepare a report on it for your class. Include details that will help students better understand "Before the Law." **[Social Studies Link]**

Online Activity www.phlit.phschool.com

Guided Writing Lesson

Letter to the Editor

Characters in Franz Kafka's work are often frustrated by paperwork and troublesome officials. You, too, may have had a frustrating experience in dealing with a requirement or procedure established by a company or a government organization. Choose one such experience and write about it in a letter to the editor of your local newspaper. Explain what happened and offer recommendations for improving the policy or procedure.

Writing Skills Focus: Objective Tone

In order to write an effective letter, maintain an **objective tone,** a tone of voice that sounds reasonable rather than emotional or biased. Achieve such a tone by following these suggestions:

• Avoid words with strong emotional associations.

• Stick to facts where possible, and support opinions with evidence.

Prewriting Jot down the facts and details of your frustrating experience. Then, list some possible solutions for the problem you encountered. Circle any emotionally charged words you have used and be sure to avoid them in your letter.

Drafting Describe your experience and its effects in straightforward, neutral language. Show how your experience might affect others as well. Then, recommend specific, practical ways in which the organization or company can fix the problem.

Revising Replace emotional language with language that is neutral and objective. Also, be sure you have supported your opinions with facts and details.

Determine whether you have used a mixture of simple, compound, and complex sentences. For more on these sentence structures, see pp. 482 and 488.

Focus on Culture

Southeast Asia

A Cambodian folk tale tells the story of a king who comes across a boy sweeping the floors of the palace. The king asks the boy whether he is rich or poor.

"I think that I am as rich as a king," the boy replies. "Your Majesty, I may receive only six *sen* each month, but I eat from one plate and you also eat from one plate. I sleep for one night and you also sleep for one night. We eat and sleep the same. There is no difference." Like many Southeast Asian tales, this story carries a Buddhist message about the unimportance of worldly things.

Buddhist and Hindu beliefs from India played a major role in Southeast Asia. China was also a powerful force in the region. Still, local peoples blended such outside influences to form their own unique cultures.

▲ **Critical Viewing** Why do you think Khmer kings put so much expense and effort into building this temple at Angkor Wat? **[Speculate]**

GEOGRAPHIC SETTING

Southeast Asia is sandwiched between two giants: India to the west and China to the north. The region consists of a giant mainland peninsula and a mass of islands.

Mainland Southeast Asia Mainland Southeast Asia lies between the South China Sea and the Indian Ocean. Today, the peninsula includes five independent nations: Myanmar (mē´ un mär) formerly known as Burma; Thailand (tī´ land´); Laos; Cambodia; and Vietnam.

Island Southeast Asia The islands of Southeast Asia are scattered across thousands of miles of ocean. Two nations, Indonesia and the Philippines, are huge island chains. Indonesia alone includes more than 13,500 separate islands. Island Southeast Asia also includes the nations of Malaysia, Brunei (broo nī′), and Singapore.

Island Southeast Asia is located on the Ring of Fire, a line of volcanoes around the Pacific Ocean. When volcanoes erupt, they often spread ash over nearby lands. Since volcanic ash is rich in minerals, the soil becomes fertile. As a result, many people farm near active volcanoes. However, volcanoes also pose very real dangers to people, crops, and buildings.

HISTORY

Because of its geography, no single ruler could conquer the diverse lands and peoples of Southeast Asia. Instead, most rulers controlled relatively small areas.

Diverse Kingdoms The kingdom of Pagan (pä gän′), arose in what is today Myanmar. According to tradition, King Anawrata brought Buddhism to Pagan in the eleventh century. In 1287, Mongol armies from China conquered Pagan. By the 1400's, however, Pagan had thrown off Chinese rule.

Chinese domination lasted much longer in Vietnam. In A.D. 39, the noble Trung sisters led Vietnamese resistance against invaders from China. In the end, though, these honored heroes were defeated and executed. During more than 1,000 years of Chinese rule, Chinese culture and language, as well as Confucian philosophy, strongly influenced Vietnam.

The Khmer (kə mer′) kingdom controlled the Mekong delta in what is today Cambodia and southern Vietnam. Khmer rulers absorbed Hindu beliefs from Indian traders. In the 1100's, King Suryvraman II built Angkor, a capital city dedicated to the Hindu god Vishnu. Later Khmer rulers converted to Buddhism,

but elements of Hinduism remained strong in Cambodian culture.

Modern Thailand has its roots in several early peoples and kingdoms. In the 1300's, the Tai kingdom of Lan Na began to dominate. In 1782, the Chakkri family set up a new dynasty with Bangkok as their capital. Today, the Thai people still recognize the Chakkris as their royal family.

Rulers of Srivijava (shrē vä jī′ yä) controlled an island empire from their base on Sumatra. Srivijava profited from a thriving spice trade through the Strait of Malacca, a vital waterway connecting the Indian and Pacific oceans.

European Dominance By the 1500's, the spice trade also attracted traders from Europe. Through bargaining and force, Portugal won the right to set up trading posts in Southeast Asia. Other European powers were soon competing for trade and power. In 1521, Ferdinand Magellan claimed the Philippines for Spain.

By the late 1800's, most of Southeast Asia was under western domination. Dutch planters controlled the Indonesian island of Java. The British ruled Malaya and Burma. France carved out an empire known as Indochina (present-day Vietnam, Cambodia, and Laos). Europeans profited from valuable resources such as rubber, tin, and coffee.

Thailand, then known as Siam, was able to retain its independence. Its king, Mongkut, shrewdly made treaties with several European nations. He and his successors also hired European experts to help Siam modernize.

Nationalism and Independence As in India, nationalists in Southeast Asian countries sought an end to European rule. The drive for independence quickened during World War II, even as Japan overran most of Southeast Asia. At first, many welcomed the retreat of the French, British, and Dutch. Soon, though, harsh actions by Japanese troops caused many nationalists to switch sides.

After the defeat of Japan in 1945, some nations achieved independence peacefully, such as Burma. Others, including Indonesia and Malaysia, faced armed struggles as European colonial powers reasserted their dominance.

In 1946, France moved to regain control of Indochina. Vietnamese nationalists, including the communist Ho Chi Minh, waged a guerrilla war. In 1954, after a devastating defeat, France withdrew from both Vietnam and Cambodia.

Vietnam War Vietnam was divided into the communist North and the noncommunist South. For nearly twenty years, civil war raged. The United States sent combat forces to support the South. In 1974, American troops withdrew. A year later, the government of South Vietnam fell. Vietnam became a united nation under communist rule.

Before it ended, the Vietnam War had widened to engulf Laos and Cambodia. In 1975, Cambodia fell under the brutal communist dictatorship of the Khmer Rouge, led by Pol Pot. Executions and famine killed as many as two million Cambodians before the Khmer Rouge was finally ousted.

SOCIETY AND CULTURE

Southeast Asia is home to diverse cultures and religions. Early on, Hinduism from India was a strong influence. Later, Arab traders brought Islam to the region, and European missionaries spread Christianity. Today, Indonesia is the most populous Muslim country in the world, while most Filipinos are Roman Catholic. On the mainland, however, Buddhism remains the dominant religion.

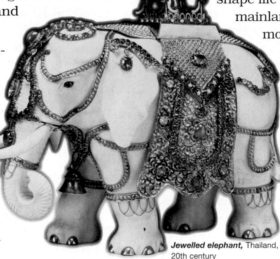

Jewelled elephant, Thailand, 20th century

▲ **Critical Viewing**
What does this jewelled elephant reveal about Thai skill at crafts? **[Hypothesize]**

Buddhism Buddhism is based on the idea that desire is the root of all human suffering. Through meditation, Buddhists try to achieve nirvana, the condition of wanting nothing. Buddhism also stresses "right conduct"— virtues such as kindness, truthfulness, and compassion for all creatures.

Buddhist influences have helped shape life in Southeast Asia. In mainland countries, Buddhist monasteries and temples are centers of village life. Farmers turn to Buddhist monks for advice on daily life and sometimes for political leadership.

Ways of Life In most parts of Southeast Asia, people today make a living as their ancestors did, by fishing or farming. Most people are subsistence farmers, growing enough to live on, although an increasing number sell their surplus food for cash.

The major food crop is rice. In lowland areas, farmers grow "wet rice," soaking the rice fields, or *padis*, with water before planting the seedlings. The padis remain flooded until almost harvest time. Wet-rice farming is hard work, requiring the labor of the entire family. Men plow the padis, operate rice-planting machinery, and harvest the crop. Women plant rice by hand and husk the cut rice.

Women Since early times, women in Southeast Asia have enjoyed many rights. One thirteenth-century visitor to Cambodia noted that many women there were highly educated and held respected government positions. (See the Cambodian folk tale "The Story of Princess Amaradevi," p. 498.)

In Vietnam, the legal code ensured the rights of women to own property and to marry without parental approval. Despite the influence of China and India, where women were seen as inferior to men, Southeast Asian women generally maintained their traditional rights.

Arts and Literature

Indian literature influenced the poetry, plays, and stories of Southeast Asia. At the same time, each culture developed its own folk tales, its own love poems, and its own epics about kings, queens, and heroes.

Literature Vietnam's most famous poem is *The Tale of Kieu*. Written in the early 1800's, the poem blends Confucian and Buddhist ideas in this story of a young woman who sells herself into slavery to save her family. *The Tale of Kieu* is so popular that many Vietnamese can recite passages from memory.

Contemporary writers often examine social issues. Indonesian novelist Yudhistira Ardi Noegraha has used his fiction to criticize the gap between rich and poor. Vietnamese poets like Nguyen Thi Vinh have expressed the sorrows caused by decades of warfare. (See her poem "Thoughts of Hanoi," on p. 496.)

Performing Arts Traditional Southeast Asian music uses a different scale and different instruments than western music. For example, the *gamelan* (gam′ ə lan′), or traditional orchestra of Java, is made up of gongs of various sizes and pitches, drums, brass kettles, and xylophone-like instruments of wood or bronze. Flutes and two-stringed lutes are also part of the group. The leader plays the largest drum.

Gamelan music often accompanies a form of drama known as shadow play. As a narrator tells a story, jointed puppets controlled by rods move behind a screen. The audience sees only the shadows of the puppets. Traditional shadow plays were often based on classical Indian epics. Recent plays also deal with current political events.

Classical dance is also popular throughout Southeast Asia. Dancers use highly symbolic gestures and facial expressions to convey meaning, often of a religious nature. In Cambodia, the Khmer Rouge destroyed traditional dance groups. Since then, the few surviving older dancers have struggled to pass on their ancient art to a new generation.

Architecture and Art Great monuments and temples are scattered across Southeast Asia. In Cambodia, the ruins of the Khmer temple of Angkor Wat reflects Hindu influences in its architecture and its miles of carvings. (See the picture on p. 490.) On the island of Java, the towering temple of Borobudur contains more than 400 images of the Buddha.

Southeast Asian artisans have produced fine handicrafts. Textile makers use a dyeing technique known as batik (bə tēk′) to produce vivid multi-color patterns and scenes. The island of Bali is famous for its beautiful, intricate wood-carvings. Still, industrialization today threatens such traditional arts.

Activity
Creating a Map of the Arts

Use library or Internet resources to create a map of the arts for Southeast Asia. In addition to countries and major cities, include specific works of literature and art forms for each country. On the map, write a brief note about each work or art form. 🌐

*G*uide for Reading

Nguyen Thi Vinh *(1924–   )*

A prominent South Vietnamese poet and fiction writer, Nguyen Thi Vinh (n $\overline{oo}$ ´ yin tī vin) has also worked as an editor and publishing executive. Among her works that are translated into English are *The Poetry of Nguyen Thi Vinh* and her story "Two Sisters," which appears in the anthology *Vietnamese Short Stories.*

Although she lived in Saigon, capital of South Vietnam, Nguyen Thi Vinh writes of the North Vietnamese capital city in "Thoughts of Hanoi." In this poem she describes the human pain of Vietnam's civil war, in which old friends sometimes fought on opposing sides.

She remained in Vietnam after the communist takeover of South Vietnam in 1975 but refused to play any public role. Then, in 1983, she was able to join her family in Norway.

Cambodian Folk Tales

"The Story of Princess Amaradevi" comes from a collection of ancient Cambodian folk tales. These stories support principles derived from Buddhist teachings, such as the values of justice and compassion and the evils of greed and deceit. Buddhism, which was developed in India in the sixth century B.C., became the primary religion in Cambodia about 700 years ago.

Like "The Story of Princess Amaradevi," many of these folk tales show good people foiling plans by greedy nobles. The tales also describe the predicaments that foolish people create for themselves and the consequences of lying and scheming to hurt others.

Muriel Paskin Carrison and the Venerable Kong Chhean

While working with Cambodian refugees in southern California, educator Muriel Paskin Carrison met Kong Chhean, a Buddhist monk and the religious leader of a Cambodian community. (Chhean's position as leader is the source of his title "Venerable," which means "worthy of respect.") Together they created English versions of Cambodian folk tales.

◆ Build Vocabulary

ANGLO-SAXON PREFIXES: *un-*

In the Cambodian folk tale, a princess matches wits with "unscrupulous ministers" who tell lies to destroy her husband. The prefix *un-* in *unscrupulous* means "not." (The prefix can also mean "the lack of or the opposite of.") Knowing that *scrupulous* means "acting according to what is right or correct," you can figure out that *unscrupulous* means "not acting according to what is right or correct."

WORD BANK

As you read these selections, you will encounter the words on this list. Each word is defined on the page where it first appears. Preview this list of words before you read.

| basking |
| obsolete |
| unscrupulous |
| recess |
| restraint |
| perfidy |

◆ Build Grammar Skills

PRESENT PARTICIPIAL PHRASES

In these selections, the authors sometimes add details to a description with a **present participial phrase,** a group of words with a present participle, a verb form ending in *-ing.* A present participial phrase functions as an adjective, modifying a noun or pronoun.

For example, Nguyen Thi Vinh uses a present participial phrase in this passage from "Thoughts of Hanoi":

> village graybeards *strolling to the temple*

The present participial phrase *strolling to the temple* is an adjective that modifies the noun *graybeards.*

◆ Thoughts of Hanoi ◆
The Story of Princess Amaradevi

◆ Literature and Your Life

CONNECT YOUR EXPERIENCE

Suppose you came home from school and learned that you were moving to another state—before the end of the term. Immediately, you would start to miss the people and places that had become familiar to you. A similar separation from loved people or places also confronts the characters in "Thoughts of Hanoi" and "The Story of Princess Amaradevi."

Journal Writing Summarize a recent news story that deals with someone leaving a familiar environment.

THEMATIC FOCUS: FATEFUL MOMENTS

As you read, ask yourself this question: In what ways do the characters meet or fail to meet the challenge of events?

◆ Background for Understanding

HISTORY

This timeline shows how the Vietnam war began:
- **1946** With World War II over, Vietnamese nationalists battle the French, who control the region as a colony.
- **1954** The French suffer a major military defeat. A ceasefire agreement divides the country into South Vietnam and North Vietnam.
- **1956** The ceasefire had called for elections to unify Vietnam. South Vietnam refuses to hold elections, and the United States supports this decision. Fighters called the Viet Cong—helped by North Vietnam, Russia, and China—battle the South Vietnamese government.
- **1964** The United States sends troops to Vietnam.

◆ Literary Focus

UNIVERSAL PATTERNS

A **universal pattern** is a situation or series of events common to stories from many different cultures. The familiarity of such situations or events makes it possible for all readers to recognize and respond to them.

Both "Thoughts of Hanoi" and "The Story of Princess Amaradevi" contain such patterns. Thi Vinh's poem describes the tragic but all-too-common situation of civil war, in which friend must fight against friend. The Cambodian folk tale has a type of plot that occurs in many stories and legends from around the world: It tells of evildoers who scheme against a good person.

◆ Reading Strategy

DISTINGUISH UNIVERSAL FROM CULTURE-SPECIFIC DETAILS

Universal details are values, beliefs, and customs that are common to many different cultures. **Culture-specific details** are values, beliefs, and customs that belong only to one particular culture. To distinguish between these details when reading, decide which apply to humans in general and which to a specific group.

"Thoughts of Hanoi" and "The Story of Princess Amaradevi" contain both universal and culture-specific details. Use a chart like the one below to distinguish these different kinds of details (two items have been filled in for you):

Story/Poem	Universal Details	Culture-Specific Details
"Thoughts of Hanoi"	Speaker's longing for a former home	Description of "raven-bill scarves" of Vietnamese village girls
"The Story of Princess Amaradevi"		

Thoughts of Hanoi

Nguyen Thi Vinh

Translated by Nguyen Ngoc Bich With Burton Raffel and W. S. Merwin

The night is deep and chill
as in early autumn. Pitchblack,
it thickens after each lightning flash.
I dream of Hanoi:
5 Co-ngu[1] Road
ten years of separation
the way back sliced by a frontier of hatred.
I want to bury the past
to burn the future
10 still I yearn
still I fear
those endless nights
waiting for dawn.

Brother,
15 how is Hang Dao[2] now?
How is Ngoc Son[3] temple?
Do the trains still run
each day from Hanoi
to the neighboring towns?
20 To Bac-ninh, Cam-giang, Yen-bai,[4]
the small villages, islands
of brown thatch in a lush green sea?

---

1. **Co-ngu** (cô gōō)
2. **Hang Dao** (häŋ dɔu)
3. **Ngoc Son** (nōk sōn)
4. **Bac-ninh** (bäk nin), **Cam-giang** (cäm giäŋ),
Yen-bai (ēŋ bǐ)

◆ **Build Vocabulary**

basking (bäs´ kiŋ) *v.*: Enjoying a pleasant warmth

obsolete (äb´ sə lēt´) *adj.*: Out of date; no longer in
fashion

Peacefulness, Tran Nguyen Dan, Indochina Arts Project

The girls
    bright eyes
25   ruddy cheeks
    four-piece dresses
      raven-bill scarves
    sowing harvesting
      spinning weaving
30   all year round,
  the boys
    plowing
      transplanting
    in the fields
35   in their shops
    running across
      the meadow at evening
  to fly kites
      and sing alternating songs.

40 Stainless blue sky,
    jubilant voices of children
  stumbling through the alphabet,
    village graybeards strolling to the
        temple,
  grandmothers basking in twilight sun,
45   chewing betel leaves
  while the children run—

Brother,
how is all that now?
Or is it obsolete?
50 Are you like me,
reliving the past,
imagining the future?
Do you count me as a friend
or am I the enemy in your eyes?
55 Brother, I am afraid
that one day I'll be with the March-
      North Army
meeting you on your way to the South.
I might be the one to shoot you then
or you me
60 but please
not with hatred.
For don't you remember how it was,
you and I in school together,
plotting our lives together?
65 Those roots go deep!

Brother, we are men,
conscious of more
than material needs.
How can this happen to us
70 my friend
my foe?

Guide for Responding

◆ Literature and Your Life

Reader's Response Explain a situation in which someone you thought of as a "foe" became a friend.

Thematic Focus What are some turning points that could change friends into enemies or enemies into friends?

☑ Check Your Comprehension

1. What is probably the speaker's hometown?
2. What does the speaker remember the "village graybeards" doing?

◆ Critical Thinking

INTERPRET

1. Why would the speaker wonder if the daily life he describes is now obsolete? **[Analyze]**

EVALUATE

2. Do you think it's possible to shoot someone "not with hatred" in war? Explain. **[Make a Judgment]**

EXTEND

3. How might the situation described in the poem compare with others in history? Explain. **[Social Studies Link]**

The Story of Princess Amaradevi

Retold by Muriel Paskin Carrison
Translated by the Venerable Kong Chhean

In a small kingdom of Kampuchea, there once lived a wealthy princess by the name of Amaradevi who was an educated and talented young woman. Now, there were four old grand ministers of the palace who unfortunately had no appreciation of Amaradevi's many accomplishments, but, being attracted by her riches, they all wished to marry her. Princess Amaradevi kindly rejected their proposals, choosing instead to marry a fine young man whose name was Mahoseth Pandide.

Amaradevi and Mahoseth loved and respected each other. They lived happily together in peace and harmony. But the four grand ministers were very bitter and resentful. Whenever they spoke to Mahoseth, they tried to be as insulting and offensive as possible. They even started vicious rumors throughout the palace, claiming that Mahoseth Pandide was disloyal to the king. Then they began to whisper to the king himself that Mahoseth was dishonest and deceitful. The gentle king, who loved his daughter and her husband, urged the ministers to be more reasonable and cautious in their accusations. But the more the king urged, the more determined the ministers became to destroy Mahoseth.

One day, they decided to tell the king that Mahoseth Pandide was plotting to kill him and take the throne. This time, their arguments and false proofs were so convincing that the king believed them. Without even giving Mahoseth Pandide a chance to defend himself, the angry king ordered him to leave the country immediately and never return.

The four ruthless ministers were satisfied with the result of their schemes. Delighted with their success, they congratulated each other and began plotting their next steps. "Of course," First Grand Minister Senak advised, "we do not know which one of us Amaradevi will wish to marry. We must each ask her, one at a time. Then after she chooses and marries one of us, we will divide her riches equally. But now, she must be mourning for her foolish husband. So let us wait two weeks from today before we talk with her."

Meanwhile, with her husband banished from the kingdom forever, Amaradevi passed the days in sorrow. She blamed herself for not being able to save her husband. She had known that the powerful grand ministers had wanted to marry her for her money. She had known that the ministers had plotted against her beloved husband. So each day as she paced back and forth in her palace rooms, she relived her own stupidity and tried to think of a way to prove to the king that Mahoseth had always been loyal and that the four ministers had been the real evil plotters.

"Oh, you greedy, wretched monsters!" she would cry to herself. "I will find a way to punish you. I will never be your rich puppet-wife. I will find a way to have my Mahoseth returned to me. I will find a way to teach you to respect and honor a woman's mind and heart."

Two weeks after Mahoseth Pandide's banishment, First Grand Minister Senak came to visit Amaradevi with his proposals of love and marriage. Amaradevi listened to him quietly and slowly replied, "Yes, my dear Senak, I am quite lonesome. Perhaps I could love you and marry you. If you wish to visit with me, why not return later this evening, at seven o'clock?"

Silver Pagoda, wall mural, Phnom Penh, Cambodia

▲ **Critical Viewing** What does this wall painting reveal about Cambodian life? **[Interpret]**

First Grand Minister Senak was delighted. He bowed excessively and promised to return at the appointed time.

During the same morning, Amaradevi was surprised by the visits of the other three ministers. It seemed that almost as soon as one left, another appeared. They all praised her beauty, professed their love, and begged her to marry them. Amaradevi was polite to all of them. As they left, she graciously invited each one to visit with her that same evening. The second grand minister, Pakkos, she told to come at eight o'-clock. The third grand minister, Kapindu, she told to come at nine o'clock. And the fourth grand minister, Devin, she told to come at ten. But all that morning, as Amaradevi had been listening quietly to the four <u>unscrupulous</u> ministers, she had been trying to think of a way to entrap them and prove their treachery to the king. Now, Amaradevi had been educated not only in music, painting, and the fine art of poetry but also in government, law, the sciences, and engineering construction. Being so talented, she was quite capable of planning a clever strategy that would ensnare the falsehearted ministers and at the same time legally prove their villainy to the king.

Soon after the last grand minister left, Amaradevi summoned her servants to her palace rooms. First she instructed them on how to dig a huge pit under the floor of her small back parlor, and how to prevent it from caving in. Next, she told them how to make a special mixture of mud, hot water, and sticky rice in a large caldron. The servants then poured this mixture into the pit, filling it halfway. Finally, Amaradevi skillfully taught the servants how to construct a trap door to cover the large hole. The trap door was

◆ **Reading Strategy**
In what way is the description of the princess culture-specific?

◆ **Build Vocabulary**

unscrupulous (un skrōō´ pyə ləs) *adj.*: Not acting according to what is right or correct

The Story of Princess Amaradevi ◆ 499

operated by a rope secretly hidden behind a curtained recess.

When the construction work was finished, Amaradevi dismissed the servants and sent for her personal maid. She ordered her maid to bring all of her precious jewels and pile them carelessly on a table near the trap door in the small back parlor. When that was done, Amaradevi told the maid to expect the visits of the four grand ministers. The maid was to welcome them respectfully and ask them politely to wait for the princess in the small back parlor. The maid bowed obediently, and Amaradevi continued, "When each man arrives and is in the small back parlor, please come to me."

That evening, promptly at seven o'clock, first Grand Minister Senak arrived. The maid graciously greeted him and let him to the small back parlor. Then she walked softly to her mistress's rooms. Amaradevi rose quickly, saying to the maid, "Follow me quietly and do as I tell you."

The maid followed after Amaradevi to the small back parlor. They slipped silently behind the curtained recess, waited, and watched. First Grand Minister Senak was bending over the table of glistening jewels. He put his hand out to touch one. Then he quickly pulled his hand back to his side and stepped back. He paced the room a bit and slowly returned to the table, putting his hand out once more, then down again. The jewels were like magnets, pulling his hands to them. He just must touch one. He looked around the room and through the doorway. Then, quickly reaching out, he grabbed a huge ruby and stuffed it deep into his pocket. At that moment, Amaradevi signaled her maid. Both women pulled hard on the rope. The trap-door opened, throwing First Grand Minister Senak screaming into the large pit of warm mud and sticky rice. Then the heavy trap-door closed neatly and tightly, muffling the wretched man's shouts.

The three other grand ministers arrived at their appointed times. Each in turn was politely greeted by the maid. Each in turn was asked to wait for the princess in the small back parlor. And each in turn became bewitched by the table of shimmering rubies, emeralds, and diamonds. None of them could resist the temptation of stuffing at least one of the jewels into his pocket. As each grand minister stuffed his pocket, the two women pulled the trap-door rope, throwing another wretched man into the deep pit filled with warm mud and sticky rice. As each grand minister fell into the pit, the mud and sticky rice rose higher and higher until the men could barely breathe. As they thrashed about trying to escape, they almost choked on the drying mud and swelling rice.

Amaradevi kept the trap door tightly closed all night. The next morning, she told her servants to take the mud-caked ministers out of the pit, bind their hands, and lead them to the royal court. In solemn dignity, she followed behind them. When they reached the throne room, the princess bowed before her father. With great restraint, she spoke, "Your Majesty, I ask your permission to prove to the royal court the perfidy of these four grand ministers of the palace."

The king nodded, and Amaradevi continued. "The grand ministers all asked for my hand in marriage because they were greedy for my riches. When I refused their proposals and married the good Mahoseth Pandide, they plotted against him, finally convincing the royal court that he was disloyal and dishonest. Now the ministers have come to me again with proposals of love and marriage. But the only thing that they really love is our royal jewels. I trapped them as they were stealing our sacred treasures from my apartments. I will prove this to you. Now you will know who the guilty traitors really are."

Amaradevi signaled her maid. The woman reached into each grand minister's pocket, pulled out a precious royal jewel, and held it up before everyone's eyes.

The king was both saddened and furious. He ordered the palace guards to tie the mud-caked ministers to elephants and drag them through the streets for all the people to see.

Amaradevi bowed to the king and returned to her palace rooms.

◆ Build Vocabulary

recess (rē´ ses) *n*.: Space set back in a wall

restraint (ri strānt´) *n*.: Self-control in matters of emotion and behavior

perfidy (pur´ fə dē) *n*.: Betrayal of trust; treachery

CONNECTIONS TO TODAY'S WORLD

"The Story of Princess Amaradevi" illustrates a remarkable feature of Southeast Asian society: the equality of men and women. Even hundreds of years ago, when most cultures viewed women as mere possessions, women in Southeast Asia were treated with great respect.

This equality is apparent in contemporary Southeast Asian music, as men and women contribute equally to the creation of many new and unique styles of music. The album *White Elephants and Golden Ducks* features various artists, including the well-known female vocalist Daw Yi Yi Thant, from the Southeast Asian country of Myanmar (formerly Burma). The following review of that album offers a glimpse at the exciting new music that is emerging from this country and the important role that women have in creating it.

Review of White Elephants and Golden Ducks
Cliff Furnald

Here is a thoughtful, sometimes clever look at the modern, living traditions of Burma. Burma, now called Myanmar, is a country bordering India, China, Laos, and Thailand. . . .

. . . The performers here are neither classical court musicians, westernized pop artists, or folk revivalists and preservationists. Rather, what we get here is a collection of music by a music scene that has assimilated and co-opted influences and instruments from its neighbors and invaders. . . .

Two tracks point out this amazing ability to conquer the cultural invasion. "Mya Man Giri" is sung by a duo of male and female vocalists, accompanied by small hand cymbals and an electric piano. The effect of the local music on the piano playing is quite stunning, leaving an impression of ancient melodies, but at the same time giving an almost avant garde approach. "Sabe" brings together bamboo flute, tuned drums, and siwa with violin and slide guitar. It's a remarkable tune, gentle and yet challenging to the ear, hinting at Indonesian string music, Thai folk, and even a touch of what could be called blues.

Throughout the record are further proofs of the vitality of the Burmese musical landscape, a reminder that no folk tradition should go untouched . . . , but should be nurtured, revitalized, and given lots of room for growth.

1. What does the presence of women on an experimental album like this suggest about their role in contemporary Southeast Asian music?
2. Do you think that foreign influences are good or bad for a country's musical tradition? Explain.

Guide for Responding

◆ Literature and Your Life

Reader's Response Do you admire the princess's strategy for exposing the ministers? Why or why not?

Thematic Focus What turning point in the story spurs the princess to take action? Explain.

☑ Check Your Comprehension

1. Whom does the princess marry and whose proposals does she reject?
2. At first, how does the princess respond to her husband's banishment?
3. Summarize the plan that the princess uses to trap the ministers.

◆ Critical Thinking

INTERPRET
1. Why does the princess not take immediate action when her husband is banished? **[Infer]**
2. Why does the princess feel she must prove the ministers' guilt instead of just explaining the true situation to her father? **[Draw Conclusions]**

EVALUATE
3. Was the princess right to leave the ministers in the pit overnight? Explain. **[Make a Judgment]**

COMPARE LITERARY WORKS
4. Compare and contrast how the princess and the speaker in "Thoughts of Hanoi" deal with difficult situations. **[Compare and Contrast]**

Guide for Responding (continued)

◆ Reading Strategy

DISTINGUISH UNIVERSAL FROM CULTURE-SPECIFIC DETAILS

You can **distinguish universal from culture-specific details** in a work of literature by noting which customs, beliefs, and values are common to all people, and which belong to a particular culture.

For example, in "Thoughts of Hanoi," the speaker shares details of life in a Vietnamese village. Some details, like the mention of "harvesting," apply to any small farming community. Others, like the chewing of "betel leaves," pertain to Vietnam and perhaps several other cultures.

In "The Story of Princess Amaradevi," Amaradevi at first appears to be a typical folk-tale princess. However, she later demonstrates qualities and abilities that reflect Cambodian culture of the time.

1. List three universal details in "Thoughts of Hanoi."
2. List three culture-specific details in the poem.
3. For "The Story of Princess Amaradevi," give two examples of universal traits and two of culture-specific traits that the princess displays.

◆ Literary Focus

UNIVERSAL PATTERNS

Both "Thoughts of Hanoi" and "The Story of Princess Amaradevi" reveal **universal patterns**—circumstances and events common to works from many different cultures.

The pattern in the poem is that of a conflict in which friend must fight against friend. Readers from different cultures can respond to the terrible feeling called up by this situation. This feeling is heightened when the speaker directly expresses his fear of killing or being killed by his friend (lines 55–65).

1. In what way do lines 60–61 reflect the only way in which the speaker can deal with the situation?
2. How do lines 66–71 summarize the universal pattern found in the poem?
3. What details in the first two paragraphs of the folk tale reveal the universal pattern behind the story? Explain.
4. Is the conclusion of the folk tale a satisfying resolution of its universal pattern? Why or why not?

◆ Build Vocabulary

USING THE ANGLO-SAXON PREFIX *un-*

Knowing that the Anglo-Saxon prefix *un-* means "not, lack of, or the opposite of," write definitions of the following words.

1. unchanged
2. unending
3. unrestrained
4. unconcerned
5. uncover

USING THE WORD BANK: Sentence Completions

Choose the best word from the Word Bank to complete each sentence. Use each word only once.

1. The computer is so old it is ____?____ .
2. The ____?____ thief stole a baby's candy.
3. The cat is ____?____ in the window seat.
4. We put the television in a ____?____ in the wall.
5. The crime is proof of his ____?____ .
6. Her ____?____ kept her from crying.

◆ Build Grammar Skills

PRESENT PARTICIPIAL PHRASES

A **present participial phrase** consists of a present participle, which is a verb form ending in *-ing*, and any words that go with it. The phrase functions as an adjective, modifying a noun or a pronoun.

Practice Copy these sentences. Underline the present participial phrase in each sentence, and circle the word it modifies.

1. I remember the boys running across the meadow at evening.
2. At school, they talked together for hours, plotting their future lives.
3. The princess rejected their proposals, choosing a fine young man instead.
4. The maid, bowing obediently, listened to the princess.
5. Slipping silently behind the curtain, they waited and watched.

Writing Application Combine each pair of sentences by making one of them a present participial phrase.

1. The grandmothers bask in the sun. They chew betel leaves.
2. The heavy trap-door closed tightly. The door muffled the ministers' screams.

Build Your Portfolio

 ## Idea Bank

Writing

1. **Letter** As the speaker of the poem, write a letter to your friend reminding him of the past. Include details from the poem in your letter.

2. **Poem** In lines 17–46 of "Thoughts of Hanoi," the speaker describes his pleasant memories of the villages near Hanoi. Write a poem describing a happy memory of your own. Use images to help readers picture the scene.

3. **Film Treatment** Briefly explain how you would adapt "The Story of Princess Amaradevi" as a film. Discuss where you would set the film and how you would cast it. Also mention a few of the camera shots you might use.

Speaking, Listening, and Viewing

4. **Improvisation** With a partner, improvise a meeting of the poem's speaker and his old friend, either during or after the Vietnam War. **[Performing Arts Link]**

5. **Speech** As the king of Kampuchea in the folk tale, give a speech welcoming Mahoseth Pandide home. Review the story so that your speech is in tune with the king's character. **[Performing Arts Link]**

Researching and Representing

6. **Culture Collage** Create a collage showing similarities and differences between the Vietnamese and Cambodian cultures. Include pictures or descriptions of food, clothing, architecture, and social customs. **[Social Studies Link; Art Link]**

7. **Hanoi Timeline** Create a timeline showing changes in Hanoi from the time of the French occupation of Vietnam to the present day. Use encyclopedia articles as well as newspaper or magazine stories. **[Social Studies Link; Media Link]**

Online Activity www.phlit.phschool.com

Guided Writing Lesson

Literary Analysis

Write a literary analysis of "Thoughts of Hanoi" or "The Story of Princess Amaradevi." In a literary analysis, you explore how elements in a piece of literature work together to create an effect or to support the theme, an insight into life. To convince readers of the points you are making, use specific details and passages from the work.

Writing Skills Focus: Sufficiency of Supporting Details

Be sure that the supporting details you include are **sufficient,** meaning that they relate to your point. Avoid simply listing or repeating details without indicating how they support your argument. In the following paragraph, the writer uses a sufficient detail.

Model

In "Thoughts of Hanoi," Thi Vinh uses images like a series of frames in a film to re-create the untroubled life that is now gone: "the boys / plowing / transplanting / in the fields." These quick images, each only a word or two, seem to vanish as quickly as they appear—just as normal life has vanished.

Prewriting Choose the poem or the folk tale, and jot down its theme or its overall effect on the reader. Then, briefly note how literary elements contribute to the effect or theme.

Drafting Begin by formulating your thesis—a brief statement about the overall effect or theme and the elements that contribute to it. In the body of the paper, support your thesis with sufficient details from the poem or folk tale.

Revising Be sure that you have clearly explained the relationship between details from the selection and the points they support.

To create sentence variety and avoid choppiness, combine sentences using present participial phrases. For more information on present participial phrases, see pp. 494 and 502.

Writing Process Workshop

Much of the pleasure we take in the world around us comes through our senses. We observe the beauties of nature, listen to music, enjoy the feel of comfortable clothing, and taste and smell our favorite foods. **Description** is writing that captures the sensory pleasures in the world using precise details to show the way something looks, tastes, smells, sounds, or feels. Effective description re-creates a scene or an image so that readers can perceive it for themselves.

The following skills will help you write an effective descriptive essay.

Writing Skills Focus

▶ **Use sensory details**—words that appeal to the five senses.

▶ **Use appropriate language** for your purpose.

▶ **Use figurative language** such as metaphors, similes, or personification.

▶ **Make abstract terms concrete.** Connect abstract terms, such as *delicate* or *powerful,* to concrete images, such as a *butterfly* or a *freight train.*

Anne Tyler uses these skills to describe one man's experience with old age.

MODEL FROM LITERATURE

① The author's language is simple and direct, appropriate for a short story.

② *Numbness appeals to the sense of touch.*

③ *The writer connects the abstract term weakness to the concrete images of air and water.*

④ *The words wheezed and creaked appeal to the sense of hearing.*

from "With All Flags Flying" by Anne Tyler

① Weakness was what got him in the end. He had been expecting something more definite—chest pains, a stroke, arthritis—but it was only weakness that put a finish to his living alone. ② A numbness in his head, an airy feeling when he walked. ③ A wateriness in his bones that made it an effort to pick up his coffee cup in the morning. He waited some days for it to go away, but it never did. And meanwhile the dust piled up in the corners; the refrigerator wheezed and creaked ④ for want of defrosting. Weeds grew around his rosebushes.

Prewriting

Choose a Topic Choose a topic that you find interesting enough to describe in detail. Memorable people, remarkable places, unusual events, and intriguing objects or ideas all make great topics for description. Use the following chart to help you choose a topic.

If you're considering...	Then try this ...
A remarkable place	Think about cities, regions, or countries you've visited or would like to visit.
A memorable person	Make a list of five distinct groups of people; for example, Sports Heroes or People From Mythology. Write down people for each category, and choose one.
An idea description	Consider subjects that interest you at school.

Consider Your Purpose How do you want your description to affect the people who read it? Your purpose will shape your tone, word choice, and details. For example, if your purpose is to encourage people to visit a place, you'll want to provide attractive details and use positively charged words and phrases, such as *breathtaking views* or *pleasant climate year-round*. On the other hand, if your purpose is to describe a trip that you didn't enjoy, you will focus on unpleasant details and use words and phrases with negative connotations, such as *dismal, gloomy weather,* or *surly, annoying waiters*.

Drafting

Organize Your Draft Choose the right method of organization for your topic. You may choose **chronological order** and place details in the order in which they happened in time. If you use chronological order, include transitional terms, such as *before, next,* and *a few minutes later.*

If you use **spatial order,** you place details as they appear in some physical relationship to one another. To make spatial order clear, use directional terms, such as *next to, in the center,* or *on the right.*

If you present ideas in **order of importance,** you place details from most important to least important or vice versa.

**Writer's Solution Connection
Writing Lab**

For more examples of topics for descriptive writing, see the Inspirations for Description in the Description tutorial in the Writing Lab.

APPLYING LANGUAGE SKILLS: Precise Nouns

Vague or general nouns will make your description less effective and more difficult for your readers to envision. Use **precise nouns** to give your readers a vivid and accurate picture of what you are describing.

Vague Nouns:
building, food, animal, ballplayer

More Specific Nouns:
library, pasta, reptile, shortstop

Precise Nouns:
Ridgewood Public Library, ziti, crocodile, Derek Jeter

Practice Replace the vague nouns with precise ones in the following sentences.

1. I bought my friend a piece of colored jewelry with an animal on it.
2. A vehicle passed the place where the man stood.

Writing Application Review your description. Replace any vague nouns with precise ones.

Writer's Solution Connection
Language Lab

For more practice with precise nouns, complete the Language Lab lesson on Exact Nouns.

Revising

Have a Peer Review Your Work Team up with a classmate to review each other's work. Ask your peer reviewer to read your description once straight through to get a general impression. Then, he or she should read it a second time and jot down notes indicating what is strong about the description, pointing out areas that need clarification and offering constructive criticism with specific suggestions for improvement. Use the following questions to guide your peer reviewer:

▶ What is the central impression of the description? Does the language contribute to the impression?
▶ Is the description vivid? Where can I add sensory details or precise nouns?
▶ Where can I use figurative language to make comparisons more vivid?
▶ Is the imagery effective? How can I improve these details to make them more vivid or interesting?

REVISION MODEL

I save everything. Nothing ever goes into the garbage without my rapt contemplation over whether or not I am throwing away something meaningful. My drawers ① *overflow* ② *ticket stubs, playbills, old letters, and photographs* ~~are filled to the brim with junk~~ that would be worthless to ③ *packrat, storing up memories like food for the cold winter.* anybody else. I am a ~~saver, a collector of memories.~~

① The writer adds the precise word *overflow.*
② These sensory details clarify the vague term *junk.*
③ The writer adds a metaphor and a simile to compare himself to an image of a creature famous for saving things.

Publishing

▶ **Create a Class Anthology** Working with classmates, gather your writings into a book of descriptions. Include a cover, title, and table of contents. Artistically talented students might also add illustrations.
▶ **Post Your Work On-line** The Internet has many sites where you can post your writing. For a list of sites that publish student work, visit Prentice Hall at **http://www.phlit.phschool.com**.

Student Success Workshop

Real-World Reading Skills

Analyzing Text Structures

Strategies for Success

Every text has a structure. Consider the basic structure of an essay: introduction, elaboration, and conclusion. In nonfiction, the text structure may be organized on a principle of comparison and contrast, cause and effect, or some type of order, such as chronological order. As you analyze a text structure, you may want to create a graphic organizer, such as a chart, diagram, or timeline, to help make sense of the information.

Comparison and Contrast If the author's purpose is to compare and contrast, the structure of the text will point out similarities and differences between things or ideas. For example, an article might compare and contrast two car models. A chart that compares and contrasts the features of each car might be included.

Cause and Effect Nonfiction texts often show cause-and-effect relationships between pieces of information. A magazine article on a space shuttle flight may include a paragraph explaining how bad weather forced the shuttle to land somewhere other than the planned spot and how that change delayed the launching of a communications satellite. You can use a graphic organizer like this chart to list causes and effects:

Cause	Effect
Bad weather	Unplanned landing site
Unplanned landing site	Satellite launch rescheduled

Chronological Order Text is sometimes structured in chronological order, which means the order in which events occurred. To analyze the chronological order of those events, draw up a timeline, listing dates and corresponding events in the order in which they occurred.

Apply the Strategies

Read the text that follows. Then answer the questions.

In 1970, the average commercial fisherman on Cape Island Bay pulled in three tons of fish each week. As more people bought boats and became fishermen, the quantity of cod each person caught began to shrink. By 1990, the average commercial fisherman on Cape Island Bay was catching less than one ton of fish per week. Yet, as boats became more expensive, fishermen fished for longer periods, hoping to catch enough fish to pay for their boats. By 1998, cod stocks had dwindled. Many fishermen have had to sell their boats and seek other types of work.

1. Identify the text structure in the passage above, and explain how it helps you understand the author's information. Create a graphic organizer based on the text structure.

2. Analyze the text structures of a newspaper article and an editorial. Then create graphic organizers to represent the text structure of each.

✔ Here are some situations in which it may be important to analyze text structures with the help of graphic organizers:
▶ Reading a scientific report
▶ Reading about computer technology to find out which products you want or need
▶ Reading a novel or story in which the events are arranged in the order in which a character thinks about them

When a new friend gives you directions to her house over the phone or a teacher gives you instructions before a test, you're getting directions orally. Oral directions are more critical than written ones because you have only one chance to get them right.

Tips for Listening to Oral Directions

✔ *Getting correct directions is the first step in ensuring that you arrive at your destination or achieve your goal. When listening to oral directions, keep these points in mind:*
  ▶ Listen attentively and carefully.
  ▶ Repeat what you have heard.
  ▶ If steps must be followed in a certain order, be sure you understand that order.
  ▶ Ask questions to clarify any part of the oral directions that are confusing or unclear.
  ▶ Take notes as the person gives the directions; do not rely on your memory.
  ▶ If you are getting directions to a place, ask for visual identification markers to locate key points along the way.

Listen The most important thing to remember when receiving oral directions is to listen carefully. Focus on hearing and remembering important details. If you are unclear on any part of the directions, ask for that portion of the directions to be repeated. Otherwise, when you actually carry out the directions, you may find yourself lost or confused.

Repeat What You Hear Repeat the directions to the person who gave them. Doing so will ensure that you have heard the directions correctly.

Apply the Strategies

With a partner, role-play these situations:
1. Take turns giving each other oral directions on how to get from one part of your school to another. After you have followed the directions, discuss with your partner how successful each of you was in both giving and receiving oral directions.
2. Dictate directions to a place that both you and your partner know. Do not identify the place. Have your partner mentally follow your directions and identify the place.

Test Preparation Workshop

Reading Comprehension | Stated and Implied Main Ideas

Strategies for Success

The reading sections of both national and standardized tests require you to read a passage to understand a stated or implied main idea. The following strategies can help:

Identify the Stated Main Idea Look for a topic sentence that states what the passage is about. Recognizing supporting details will help you identify the stated main idea. For example, suppose you were asked to find a stated main idea in this passage:

> Minerals are essential to good health. They control the body's water balance and act as parts of hormones, enzymes, and vitamins. Eating a variety of foods will help ensure that the body receives enough minerals.
>
> An overabundance of certain minerals, however, can lead to serious health problems. Most people get more sodium than they need. An adult's body requires only 500 milligrams of sodium a day.

What is the stated main idea of the second paragraph?

A We need 500 milligrams of sodium a day.
B Too much of certain minerals can be harmful.
C Too much sodium can be harmful.
D Minerals are essential to good health.

Answer **A** is a supporting detail. Answer **C** is a detail not stated in the paragraph. Answer **D** is an idea from the first paragraph. Answer **B**, which summarizes the main idea, is correct.

Identify the Implied Main Idea An implied main idea is one that is not stated directly in the text. Summarizing the author's points can help you identify an implied main idea. For example, in the passage about minerals, what is the implied main idea of the first paragraph?

A The body needs minerals.
B Minerals control the body's water balance.
C Although the body needs minerals, too many of certain minerals can be harmful.
D Eating many different foods will give the body the minerals it needs to stay healthy.

Answer **A** is only part of the main idea. Answer **B** is a supporting detail. Answer **C** is a detail from the second paragraph. Answer **D**, which combines and summarizes the ideas in the first paragraph, is the correct answer.

Apply the Strategies

Read the following passage from a newspaper editorial, and answer the questions that follow.

> The critics of the proposed recycling initiative are concerned that recycling plastic and aluminum containers will create more work for citizens who already recycle glass and newspaper. While this notion is true, it misses a more important point.
>
> By recycling plastic and aluminum we will reduce the waste in our landfill. Most important, the initiative will better the planet. Isn't that worth the extra time?

1 What is the stated main idea of the first paragraph?

A Recycling plastic and aluminum containers will create more work for citizens.
B The critics miss a more important point.
C The initiative will improve our lives.
D Citizens already recycle glass and paper.

2 What is the implied main idea of the passage?

A Citizens can extend the life of the landfill.
B A compromise must be found.
C Recycling plastic and aluminum containers is worth the time it takes.
D Plastic and aluminum harm our planet.

Contemporary African Carvings, Joseph Agbana of the Inisha Workshop

Expanding Horizons in World Literature

New places, new ideas, new friends—every new experience expands your horizons. Your world becomes larger when you consider new ways of seeing and doing. Through the stories, poems, and essays in this unit, you will travel from China to Nigeria, meeting a thoughtful middle-aged man, celebrities, and a band of thieves. Your horizons will expand with a variety of new experiences and interesting people.

Guide for Reading

Lu Hsun *(1881–1936)*

Lu Hsun (loo shun) was born Chou Shu-jen in the Chinese province of Chekiang. His family was a high-ranking one, but suffered severe financial setbacks when he was a boy. Nevertheless, the family scraped together enough money to send him to a private school in the city of Nanking, and then to Japan to study medicine.

A Moment of Insight In 1905, during the Russo-Japanese War, Chou Shu-jen saw a film that showed a Chinese man, accused of spying for the Russians, being executed by the Japanese. The incident made it clear to him that the Chinese nation had deteriorated to such an extent that its citizens were at the mercy of Western countries and Japan.

A Career Change Hoping to affect the direction that modern China was taking, Chou Shu-jen quit medical school and vowed to become a writer so he could use his pen to promote change within China. Under the pen name of Lu Hsun, he began publishing articles and translations in a journal called *New Life*. In 1918 he joined the circle of Chinese writers that came to be known as the New Culture Movement. Encouraged by other members of the group, he soon published his first story, "Diary of a Madman."

Writing Successes Lu Hsun became a highly successful and prolific writer, composing poems and essays as well as short stories. Probably his best-known tale is "The True Story of Ah Q" (1921), a satirical attack on the Chinese society of his day. His most influential essay, published in 1924, gives a brief history of Chinese fiction.

A Lasting Legacy In the final years of his life, Lu Hsun grew convinced that republican government would not work in China. While he never joined the Communist Party, he sympathized with many of its goals. Thus, though he died of tuberculosis in 1936, his works remained popular in China even after the Communists came to power. Today, many scholars in both China and the West consider him the most important Chinese fiction writer of the twentieth century. To learn more about Lu Hsun see page 720.

◆ Build Vocabulary

LATIN ROOTS: *-dign-*

In Lu Hsun's "My Old Home," one character gets very "indignant" because the main character has forgotten who she is. The word *indignant* contains the Latin root *-dign-*, which means "worth" or "worthy." *Indignant* means "angry for being treated in an unworthy way."

WORD BANK

somber
talisman
stealthily
contemptuously
indignantly
gentry
dissipation

As you read "My Old Home," you will encounter these words. Each word is defined on the page where it first appears. Preview the list before you read.

◆ Build Grammar Skills

CORRECT USE OF *than* AND *then*

In "My Old Home" you will come across the similar-sounding words **than** and **then,** which people often confuse. *Than* is used to make comparisons:

I was a bit older *than* Jun-tu.

Then means "at that time" or "next":

I went inside, and *then* spoke with my mother.

As you read this story, be aware of how the translators correctly use *than* and *then*.

My Old Home

◆ *Literature and Your Life*

CONNECT YOUR EXPERIENCE

Think what it might be like to return to a place from which you moved, or to meet people you haven't seen in a long time. What might stay the same? What might have changed? When the narrator of "My Old Home" returns to his village after a long absence, he is surprised at many of the changes that have taken place there—and within himself.

Journal Writing Imagine that you have returned to your town or neighborhood after being away for many years. In your notebook, briefly describe the changes you think will have taken place.

THEMATIC FOCUS: PEOPLE AND STYLES

Although "My Old Home" takes place in China in the early twentieth century, many of the characters' experiences and feelings transcend boundaries of time and space. As you read, ask yourself: In what ways are these characters similar to and different from other characters I have read about or people I have known?

◆ Background for Understanding

HISTORY

The Chinese empire lasted for more than two thousand years, surviving numerous wars, invasions, rebellions, and changes in "dynasty," or ruling family.

The society produced many landmark cultural achievements, and it fostered a deep respect for tradition and ancestors. Yet, Chinese society had sharp class distinctions. The bulk of the population was expected to humbly serve the rich and the well-born. By the dawn of the twentieth century, warfare with Japan and Western efforts to colonize China had taken a heavy toll on political stability.

In 1911–1912, a revolution occurred that replaced rule by an emperor with a republic founded on new political thinking. Unfortunately, the republic itself proved highly inefficient. Factional fighting brought more political instability, poverty continued to plague the country, and many of the old social barriers remained in place.

It is during this turbulent time in Chinese history that the events in "My Old Home" unfold.

◆ Literary Focus

APPRECIATING HISTORICAL CONTEXT

Historical context refers to the events and conditions that exist in a particular setting. When a story is set in the past, knowledge about its historical context can help you better understand the attitudes and actions of the characters.

As you read "My Old Home," use the background on early twentieth-century China provided on this page to help you better understand the characters' situations and actions.

Reading for Success

Strategies for Constructing Meaning

In order to understand a piece of writing fully, you must do more than simply comprehend the writer's words. You have to go a step further and put the words and ideas together in your own mind. Why did the author write it? What idea does he or she want to convey? What does the work mean to you? In looking for answers to questions like these, you construct the meaning that the work has for you.

Use these strategies to help you construct meaning:

Draw inferences.

Writers don't always tell you everything directly. You have to draw inferences to arrive at ideas that writers suggest but don't say. You draw an inference by considering the details that the writer includes or doesn't include. Sometimes it's also helpful to "read between the lines." This means looking beyond the literal meaning of the words to obtain a full understanding of what the author means.

Draw conclusions.

A conclusion is a general statement that you can make and explain by reasons or that you can support with details from the text. A series of inferences can lead you to a conclusion.

Interpret the information.

Interpret, or explain the meaning or significance of, what you read. When you interpret, you also explain the importance of what the author is saying.

Identify relationships in the text.

Identify the various relationships in the story. For example, look for the causes and effects of important actions, keep clear in your mind the sequence of events, and identify which events are of greater or lesser importance. This will help you get the "nuts and bolts" of the story down and let you devote your energy to more challenging tasks, such as finding out the theme.

Compare and contrast the ideas.

Compare and contrast ideas in the work with other ideas in the same work or with ideas that are already familiar to you. For example, you might look for ways in which an experience described in an essay is similar to something you've done or different from anything you've heard of or experienced.

Recognize the writer's purpose.

A writer's purpose will influence the details he or she chooses to present. This factor can affect the meaning that you take from a work.

As you read "My Old Home," look at the notes in the boxes. These notes demonstrate how to apply these strategies to a piece of literature.

My Old Home

Lu Hsun

Translated by Yang Hsien-yi and Gladys Yang

Braving the bitter cold, I traveled more than seven hundred miles back to the old home I had left over twenty years before.

It was late winter. As we drew near my former home the day became overcast and a cold wind blew into the cabin of our boat, while all one could see through the chinks in our bamboo awning were a few desolate villages, void of any sign of life, scattered far and near under the <u>somber</u> yellow sky. I could not help feeling depressed.

Ah! Surely this was not the old home I had remembered for the past twenty years?

The old home I remembered was not in the least like this. My old home was much better. But if you asked me to recall its peculiar charm or describe its beauties, I had no clear impression, no words to describe it. And now it seemed this was all there was to it. Then I rationalized the matter to myself, saying: Home was always like this, and although it has not improved, still it is not so depressing as I imagine; it is only my mood that has changed, because I am coming back to the country this time with no illusions.

This time I had come with the sole object of saying goodbye. The old house our clan had lived in for so many years had already been sold to another family, and was to change hands before the end of the year. I had to hurry there before New Year's Day to say goodbye forever to the familiar old house, and to move my family to another place where I was working, far from my old home town.

> **Draw Inferences** about the reasons for the differences between the narrator's memories of his village and the way it appears to him now.

◆ **Build Vocabulary**
somber (säm´ bər) *adj.*: Dark; gloomy

At dawn on the second day I reached the gateway of my home. Broken stems of withered grass on the roof, trembling in the wind, made very clear the reason why this old house could not avoid changing hands. Several branches of our clan had probably already moved away, so it was unusually quiet. By the time I reached the house my mother was already at the door to welcome me, and my eight-year-old nephew, Hung-erh, rushed out after her.

Though mother was delighted, she was also trying to hide a certain feeling of sadness. She told me to sit down and rest and have some tea, letting the removal wait for the time being. Hung-erh, who had never seen me before, stood watching me at a distance.

But finally we had to talk about the removal. I said that rooms had already been rented elsewhere, and I had bought a little furniture; in addition it would be necessary to sell all the furniture in the house in order to buy more things. Mother agreed, saying that the luggage was nearly all packed, and about half the furniture that could not easily be moved had already been sold. Only it was difficult to get people to pay up.

"You must rest for a day or two, and call on our relatives, and then we can go," said mother.

"Yes."

"Then there is Jun-tu. Each time he comes here he always asks after you, and wants very much to see you again. I told him the probable date of your return home, and he may be coming any time."

At this point a strange picture suddenly flashed into my mind: a golden moon suspended in a deep blue sky and beneath it the seashore, planted as far as the eye could see with jade-green watermelons, while in their midst a boy of eleven or twelve, wearing a silver necklet and grasping a steel pitchfork in his hand, was thrusting with all his might at a *zha*[1] which dodged the blow and escaped between his legs.

This boy was Jun-tu. When I first met him he was just over ten—that was thirty years ago, and at that time my father was still alive and the family well off, so I was really a spoiled child. That year it was our family's turn to take charge of a big ancestral sacrifice, which came round only once in thirty years, and hence was an important one. In the first month the ancestral images were presented and offerings made, and since the sacrificial vessels were very fine and there was such a crowd of worshipers, it was necessary to guard against theft. Our family had only one part-time laborer. (In our district we divide laborers into three classes: those who work all the year for one family are called full-timers; those who are hired by the day are called dailies; and those who farm their own land and only work for one family at New Year, during festivals or when rents are being collected are called part-timers.) And since there was so much to be done, he told my father that he would send for his son Jun-tu to look after the sacrificial vessels.

When my father gave his consent I was overjoyed, because I had long since heard of Jun-tu and knew that he was about my own age, born in the intercalary month,[2] and when his horoscope was told it was found that of the five elements[3] that of earth was lacking, so his father called him Jun-tu (Intercalary Earth). He could set traps and catch small birds.

I looked forward every day to New Year, for New Year would bring Jun-tu. At last, when the end of the year came, one day mother told me that Jun-tu had come, and I flew to see him. He was standing in the kitchen. He had a round, crimson face and wore a small felt cap on his head and a gleaming silver

---

1. *zha* (jä): A badger-like animal.

2. **intercalary month:** Each year in the Chinese lunar calendar consists of 360 days, divided into twelve months of twenty-nine or thirty days. To compensate for the five additional days included in the traditional Western calendar, a thirteenth, or intercalary, month is added to the Chinese calendar every few years.

3. **the five elements:** Metal, water, fire, wood, and earth.

necklet round his neck, showing that his father doted on him and, fearing he might die, had made a pledge with the gods and buddhas,[4]

Identify relationships in the text by figuring out why the narrator was "the only person" who did not frighten Jun-tu.

using the necklet as a talisman. He was very shy, and I was the only person he was not afraid of. When there was no one else there, he would talk with me, so in a few hours we were fast friends.

I don't know what we talked of then, but I remember that Jun-tu was in high spirits, saying that since he had come to town he had seen many new things.

The next day I wanted him to catch birds.

"Can't be done," he said. "It's only possible after a heavy snowfall. On our sands, after it snows, I sweep clear a patch of ground, prop up a big threshing basket with a short stick, and scatter husks of grain beneath. When the birds come there to eat, I tug a string tied to the stick, and the birds are caught in the basket. There are all kinds: wild pheasants, woodcocks, wood-pigeons, 'blue-backs.' . . ."

Accordingly I looked forward very eagerly to snow.

"Just now it is too cold," said Jun-tu another time, "but you must come to our place in summer. In the daytime we'll go to the seashore to look for shells, there are green ones and red ones, besides 'scare-devil' shells and 'buddha's hands.' In the evening when dad and I go to see to the watermelons, you shall come too."

"Is it to look out for thieves?"

"No. If passers-by are thirsty and pick a watermelon, folk down our way don't consider it as stealing. What we have to look out for are badgers, hedgehogs and zha. When under the moonlight you hear the crunching sound made by the zha when it bites the melons, then you take your pitchfork and creep stealthily over. . . ."

I had no idea then what this thing called zha was—and I am not much clearer now for that matter—but somehow I felt it was something like a small dog, and very fierce.

"Don't they bite people?"

"You have a pitchfork. You go across, and when you see it you strike. It's a very cunning creature and will rush toward you and get away between your legs. Its fur is as slippery as oil. . . ."

I had never known that all these strange things existed: at the seashore there were shells all colors of the rainbow; watermelons were exposed to such danger, yet all I had known of them before was that they were sold in the greengrocer's.

"On our shore, when the tide comes in, there are lots of jumping fish, each with two legs like a frog. . . ."

Jun-tu's mind was a treasure-house of such strange lore, all of it outside the ken of my former friends. They were ignorant of all these things and, while Jun-tu lived by the sea, they like me could see only the four corners of the sky above the high courtyard wall.

Unfortunately, a month after New Year Jun-tu had to go home. I burst into tears and he took refuge in the kitchen, crying and refusing to come out, until finally his father carried him off. Later he sent me by his father a packet of shells and a few very beautiful feathers, and I sent him presents once or twice, but we never saw each other again.

Now that my mother mentioned him, this childhood memory sprang into life like a flash of lightning, and I seemed to see my beautiful old home. So I answered:

◆ Build Vocabulary

talisman (tal′ is mən) *n.*: A charm or token; a lucky object

stealthily (stel′ thə lē) *adv.*: In a sneaky manner; secretly

---

4. **buddhas** (bo͞o′ dəz): In the Buddhist religion, buddhas are figures who embody divine wisdom and virtue.

▲ **Critical Viewing** Compare and contrast the mood prompted by this picture with the mood that the story calls up. **[Compare and Contrast]**

Landscape, Zhu Qizhan, Private Collection

"Fine! And he—how is he?"

"He? . . . He's not at all well off either," said mother. And then, looking out of the door: "Here come those people again. They say they want to buy our furniture; but actually they just want to see what they can pick up. I must go and watch them."

Mother stood up and went out. The voices of several women could be heard outside. I called Hung-erh to me and started talking to him, asking him whether he could write, and whether he would be glad to leave.

"Shall we be going by train?"

"Yes, we shall go by train."

"And boat?"

"We shall take a boat first."

"Oh! Like this! With such a long mustache!" A strange shrill voice suddenly rang out.

I looked up with a start, and saw a woman of about fifty with prominent cheekbones and thin lips. With her hands on her hips, not wearing a skirt but with her trousered legs apart, she stood in front of me just like the compass in a box of geometrical instruments.

I was flabbergasted.

"Don't you know me? Why, I have held you in my arms!"

I felt even more flabbergasted. Fortunately my mother came in just then and said:

"He has been away so long, you must excuse him for forgetting. You should remember," she said to me, "this is Mrs. Yang from across the road. . . . She has a beancurd shop."

Then, to be sure, I remembered. When I was a child there was a Mrs. Yang who used to sit nearly all day long in the beancurd shop across the road, and everybody used to call her Beancurd Beauty. She used to powder herself, and her cheekbones were not so prominent then nor her lips so thin; moreover she remained seated all the time, so that I had never noticed this resemblance to a compass. In those days people said that, thanks to her, that beancurd shop did very good business. But, probably on account of my age, she had made no impression on me, so that later I forgot her entirely. However, the Compass was extremely indignant and looked at me most <u>contemptuously</u>, just as one might look at a Frenchman who had never heard of Napoleon or an American who had never heard of Washington, and smiling sarcastically she said:

<table>
<tr><td>How do you interpret the Compass's remark? Does she feel resentment toward the narrator? Explain.</td></tr>
</table>

"You had forgotten? Naturally I am beneath your notice. . . ."

"Certainly not . . . I . . ." I answered nervously, getting to my feet.

"Then you listen to me, Master Hsun. You have grown rich, and they are too heavy to move, so you can't pos-

sibly want these old pieces of furniture anymore. You had better let me take them away. Poor people like us can do with them."

"I haven't grown rich. I must sell these in order to buy. . . ."

"Oh, come now, you have been made the intendant of a circuit,[5] how can you still say you're not rich? You have three concubines now, and whenever you go out it is in a big sedan-chair with eight bearers. Do you still say you're not rich? Hah! You can't hide anything from me."

Knowing there was nothing I could say, I remained silent.

"Come now, really, the more money people have the more miserly they get, and the more miserly they are the more money they get . . ." remarked the Compass, turning <u>indignantly</u> away and walking slowly off, casually picking up a pair of mother's gloves and stuffing them into her pocket as she went out.

After this a number of relatives in the neighborhood came to call. In the intervals between entertaining them I did some packing, and so three or four days passed.

One very cold afternoon, I sat drinking tea after lunch when I was aware of someone coming in, and turned my head to see who it was. At the first glance I gave an involuntary start, hastily stood up and went over to welcome him.

The newcomer was Jun-tu. But although I knew at a glance that this was Jun-tu, it was not the Jun-tu I remembered. He had grown to twice his former size. His round face, once crimson, had become sallow and acquired deep lines and wrinkles; his eyes too had become like his father's, the rims swollen and red, a feature common to most peasants who work by the sea and are exposed all day to the wind from the ocean. He wore a shabby felt cap and just one very thin padded jacket, with the result that he was shivering from head to foot. He carried a paper package and

◆ Build Vocabulary

contemptuously (kən temp′ ch$\overline{oo}$ əs lē) *adv.*: In a rude or dismissive manner; scornfully; disrespectfully

indignantly (in dig′ nənt lē) *adj.*: Insulted or angry because someone has not shown respect

---

5. intendant of a circuit: An official position between the county and provincial levels.

a long pipe, nor was his hand the plump red hand I remembered, but coarse and clumsy and chapped, like the bark of a pine tree.

Delighted as I was, I did not know how to express myself, and could only say:

"Oh! Jun-tu—so it's you? . . ."

After this there were so many things I wanted to talk about, they should have poured out like a string of beads: woodcocks, jumping fish, shells, *zha*. . . . But I was tongue-tied, unable to put all I was thinking into words.

> What do the continual comparisons between past and present relationships suggest about the **author's purpose?**

He stood there, mixed joy and sadness showing on his face. His lips moved, but not a sound did he utter. Finally, assuming a respectful attitude, he said clearly: "Master! . . ."

I felt a shiver run through me; for I knew then what a lamentably thick wall had grown up between us. Yet I could not say anything.

He turned his head to call:

"Shui-sheng, bow to the master." Then he pulled forward a boy who had been hiding behind his back, and this was just the Jun-tu of twenty years before, only a little paler and thinner, and he had no silver necklet.

"This is my fifth," he said. "He's not used to company, so he's shy and awkward."

Mother came downstairs with Hung-erh, probably after hearing our voices.

"I got your letter some time ago, madam," said Jun-tu. "I was really so pleased to know the master was coming back. . . ."

"Now, why are you so polite? Weren't you playmates together in the past?" said mother gaily. "You had better still call him Brother Hsun as before."

"Oh, you are really too. . . . What bad manners that would be. I was a child then and didn't understand." As he was speaking Jun-tu motioned Shui-sheng to come and bow, but the child was shy, and stood stock-still behind his father.

"So he is Shui-sheng? Your fifth?" asked

mother. "We are all strangers, you can't blame him for feeling shy. Hung-erh had better take him out to play."

When Hung-erh heard this he went over to Shui-sheng, and Shui-sheng went out with him, entirely at his ease. Mother asked Jun-tu to sit down, and after a little hesitation he did so; then leaning his long pipe against the table he handed over the paper package, saying:

"In winter there is nothing worth bringing; but these few beans we dried ourselves, if you will excuse the liberty, sir."

When I asked him how things were with him, he just shook his head.

"In a very bad way. Even my sixth can do a little work, but still we haven't enough to eat . . . and then there is no security . . . all sorts of people want money, there is no fixed rule . . . and the harvests are bad. You grow things, and when you take them to sell you always have to pay several taxes and lose money, while if you don't try to sell, the things may go bad. . . ."

He kept shaking his head; yet, although his face was lined with wrinkles, not one of them moved, just as if he were a stone statue. No doubt he felt intensely bitter, but could not express himself. After a pause he took up his pipe and began to smoke in silence.

From her chat with him, mother learned that he was busy at home and had to go back the next day; and since he had had no lunch, she told him to go to the kitchen and fry some rice for himself.

After he had gone out, mother and I both shook our heads over his hard life: many children, famines, taxes, soldiers, bandits, officials and landed gentry, all had squeezed him as dry as a mummy. Mother said that we should offer him all the things we were not going to take away, letting him choose for himself.

That afternoon he picked out a number of things: two long tables, four chairs, an incense burner and candlesticks, and one balance.

He also asked for all the ashes from the stove (in our part we cook over straw, and the ashes can be used to fertilize sandy soil), saying that when we left he would come to take them away by boat.

That night we talked again, but not of anything serious; and the next morning he went away with Shui-sheng.

After another nine days it was time for us to leave. Jun-tu came in the morning. Shui-sheng did not come with him—he had just brought a little girl of five to watch the boat. We were very busy all day, and had no time to talk. We also had quite a number of visitors, some to see us off, some to fetch things, and some to do both. It was nearly evening when we left by boat, and by that time everything in the house, however old or shabby, large or small, fine or coarse, had been cleared away.

As we set off, in the dusk, the green mountains on either side of the river became deep blue, receding toward the stern of the boat.

Hung-erh and I, leaning against the cabin window, were looking out together at the indistinct scene outside, when suddenly he asked:

"Uncle, when shall we go back?"

"Go back? Do you mean that before you've left you want to go back?"

"Well, Shui-sheng has invited me to his home. . . ." He opened wide his black eyes in anxious thought.

Mother and I both felt rather sad, and so Jun-tu's name came up again. Mother said that ever since our family started packing up, Mrs. Yang from the beancurd shop had come over every day, and the day before in the ash-heap she had unearthed a dozen bowls and plates, which after some discussion she insisted must have been buried there by Jun-tu, so that when he came to remove the ashes he could take them home at the same time. After making this discovery Mrs. Yang was very pleased with herself, and flew off taking the dog-teaser with her. (The dog-teaser is used by poultry keepers in our parts. It is a wooden cage inside which food is put, so that hens can stretch their necks in to eat but dogs can only look on furiously.) And it was a marvel, considering the size of her feet, how fast she could run.

I was leaving the old house farther and farther behind, while the hills and rivers of my old home were also receding gradually ever farther in the distance. But I felt no regret. I only felt that all round me was an invisible high wall, cutting me off from my fellows, and this depressed me thoroughly. The vision of that small hero with the silver necklet among the watermelons had formerly been as clear as day, but now it suddenly blurred, adding to my depression.

Mother and Hung-erh fell asleep.

I lay down, listening to the water rippling beneath the boat, and knew that I was going my way. I thought: although there is such a barrier between Jun-tu and myself, the children still have much in common, for wasn't Hung-erh thinking of Shui-sheng just now? I hope they will not be like us, that they will not allow a barrier to grow up between them. But again I would not like them, because they want to be akin, all to have a treadmill existence like mine, nor to suffer like Jun-tu until they become stupefied,[6] nor yet, like others, to devote all their energies to <u>dissipation</u>. They should have a new life, a life we have never experienced.

The access of hope made me suddenly afraid. When Jun-tu asked for the incense burner and candlesticks I had laughed up

♦ **Build Vocabulary**

gentry (jen´ trē) *n*.: Well-born landowning families ranked just below the nobility; gentlemen and gentlewomen

dissipation (dis´ ə pā´ shən *n*.: Wasteful or immoral behavior; overindulgence

6. **stupefied** (stōō´ pə fīd) *v*.: Stunned; made dull or lethargic.

my sleeve at him to think that he still wor-shiped idols and could not put them out of his mind. Yet what I now called hope was no more than an idol I created myself. The only difference was that what he desired was close at hand, while what I desired was less easily realized.

As I dozed, a stretch of jade-green seashore spread itself before my eyes, and above a round golden moon hung in a deep blue sky. I thought: hope cannot be said to exist, nor can it be said not to exist. It is just like roads across the earth. For actu-ally the earth had no roads to begin with, but when many men pass one way, a road is made.

> **Compare and Contrast** this perspective on hope with other ideas about hope that you have heard.

Guide for Responding

◆ Literature and Your Life

Reader's Response Should the narrator have helped Jun-tu? Explain.

Thematic Focus Which of the narrator's experi-ences and discoveries seem to be unique? Which seem to be universal, or shared with others?

Reader's Journal Write a brief character sketch of the narrator. Include details about his background and personality, his behavior toward other charac-ters, and the concerns that he seems to have.

Questions for Research "My Old Home" takes place in the early twentieth century, when the new Chinese republic was experiencing instability. Write one or more questions that you could research to learn more about China as an empire or China as a republic.

☑ Check Your Comprehension

1. Why has the narrator returned to his old home after twenty years?
2. Who is Jun-tu?
3. Why does the narrator look forward to seeing Jun-tu?
4. After learning of Jun-tu's family's situation, what does the narrator do for Jun-tu?
5. What "barrier" does the narrator view hopefully in the end?

◆ Critical Thinking

INTERPRET

1. Why does the narrator become depressed dur-ing his journey back to his old home? **[Interpret]**
2. During the flashback in which the narrator re-calls his experiences with Jun-tu, what is revealed about the ancient superstitions and traditions of the people of rural China? **[Analyze]**
3. How is the actual experience of meeting Jun-tu different from what the narrator expects? **[Compare and Contrast]**
4. (a) What is Mrs. Yang's attitude toward the narra-tor? (b) Why does she have this type of attitude? **[Deduce]**
5. Why does the narrator assume that Jun-tu must feel "intensely bitter"? **[Connect]**
6. At what conclusion does the narrator arrive when he makes a comparison between himself and Jun-tu, Hung-erh, and Shui-sheng? **[Analyze]**

EVALUATE

7. Were the narrator's actions and attitudes to-ward his former neighbors and Jun-tu fair? Explain. **[Make a Judgement]**

EXTEND

8. Do class distinctions, such at those depicted in "My Old Home" exist in any form in the United States today? Explain. **[Social Studies Link]**

Guide for Responding (continued)

◆ Reading Strategy

STRATEGIES FOR CONSTRUCTING MEANING

Review the reading strategies and notes showing how to construct meaning from what you read. Then, apply the strategies to answer these questions.

1. What do you infer about the relationship Hung-erh has begun with Shui-sheng?
2. How do you interpret the story's closing paragraph? To what hope does it refer, and how is that hope like the "roads across the earth"?
3. Based on your interpretations and conclusions, what would you identify as the writer's purpose in telling this story?

◆ Build Vocabulary

USING THE LATIN ROOT *-dign-*

On your paper, explain how the Latin root *-dign-*, meaning "worth" or "worthy," figures into the meanings of these words:

1. dignified 2. dignitary 3. indignation

USING THE WORD BANK: Multiple Choice

On your paper, write the letter of the answer that best answers each question.

1. When would you expect to see a *somber* sky? (a) before a storm (b) on a sunny day (c) at sunrise
2. Where would you most likely find a *talisman?* (a) in a lab (b) in a book (c) on a necklace
3. What would an *indignant* person most probably do? (a) giggle (b) weep (c) snort angrily
4. Which of these people is part of the *gentry?* (a) a landowner (b) a poor servant (c) an emperor
5. Which of these moves *stealthily?* (a) a runaway horse (b) a fox sneaking into a henhouse (c) a fashion model
6. Who displays *dissipation?* (a) a payroll clerk (b) a spendthrift (c) a hard worker
7. Who would probably answer *contemptuously?* (a) a rude person (b) a kind person (c) a frightened person

◆ Literary Focus

APPRECIATING HISTORICAL CONTEXT

Understanding the **historical context** of "My Old Home"—the characters, their circumstances, and the setting—helps readers to better appreciate the social barriers that the characters face and the narrator's reactions to them. For example, knowing that Chinese society had a rigid class system, you would be able to understand and appreciate why the friendship between Jun-tu and the narrator was bound to rupture.

1. Why were so many of the story's characters living in poverty?
2. According to the story, what forces combined to make Jun-tu's life so difficult?

◆ Build Grammar Skills

CORRECT USE OF *than* AND *then*

The often-confused words *than* and *then* are used correctly in the translation of Lu Hsun's "My Old Home." The word *than* is used in comparisons:

I traveled more *than* seven hundred miles back to the old home I had left over twenty years before.

The word *then* is used to show time or sequence:

When . . . you hear the crunching sound . . . *then* you take your pitchfork.

Practice In your notebook, identify the word that correctly completes each sentence.

1. The narrator last saw his home more (than, then) twenty years ago
2. Everyone was younger (than, then).
3. He travels over land and (than, then) takes a boat.
4. The home seems shabbier (than, then) it did before.
5. (Than, Then) the narrator goes inside.

Build Your Portfolio

 ## Idea Bank

Writing

1. Advertisement In the story, the narrator's house and furniture are up for sale. Write an advertisement for them that might have appeared in a local newspaper. **[Career Link]**

2. Letter to the Editor Express the narrator's newfound thoughts about society and class distinctions in a letter that he would send to the editor of a newspaper.

3. Analysis In an essay, explain why Lu Hsun may have chosen not to give the narrator of "My Old Home" a name. Use details from the story to support your ideas.

Speaking, Listening, and Viewing

4. Role Play With a group of classmates, take on the roles of Jun-tu and his family discussing recent events. Describe your experiences and your feelings about the past, the present, and the future. **[Performing Arts Link]**

5. Tableau A tableau is a depiction of a scene for an audience using silent and motionless actors. With a group of classmates, choose a scene from the story that you believe is important or central to its theme. Then, create a tableau to show the class, with each group member assuming a role in the scene. **[Performing Arts Link]**

Researching and Representing

6. Illustration Create an illustration of the narrator's home, the hunting of the *zha,* or another scene that the story brings to mind. If time permits, learn more about Chinese watercolors and do your illustration in that medium. **[Art Link]**

7. Research Paper Do research to learn more about China's dynastic families such as the T'ing and Ming. Share your findings in a brief written report. **[Social Studies Link]**

Online Activity www.phlit.phschool.com

 ## Guided Writing Lesson

Comparison-and-Contrast Essay

In "My Old Home" the narrator compares and contrasts people, things, and ideas of the past with those of the present. Follow the narrator's example, and write a comparison-and-contrast essay exploring such a relationship in "My Old Home." As you write, create smooth links between your ideas by choosing appropriate transitions.

Writing Skills Focus: Transitions to Show Similarities and Differences

As you draft, use **transitions,** words that link ideas, to show similarities and differences between items. You may choose from the following transitions or create your own.

although, also, as well, but, despite, in the same way, either, however, likewise, similarly, in contrast, on the other hand, too

Prewriting Make a two-column chart on which you list the two things you are comparing and contrasting, and the similarities and differences between them. Reread the story carefully to gather as many points of similarity and difference as you can. Then, decide whether you will organize your details subject-by-subject or point-by-point.

Drafting Begin your essay by stating your topic and your main idea about the topic. In the body of your essay, present the details that support your ideas. Weave in transitions as you draft to show the relationships between your ideas. Then, conclude your essay by restating your main idea and summarizing your most important points.

Revising Check to be sure that the details you cite from the story are accurate, and that you have used transitions to make your comparisons and contrasts clear. Also, correct any errors you find in grammar, spelling, and punctuation.

Read through your draft and underline the words *than* and *then.* Review your usage of those words, and correct any errors you find. For more on the correct use of *than* and *then,* see pp. 512 and 523.

PART **1** *People and Styles*

Mingling, Diana Ong

Guide for Reading

Les A. Murray (1938–   )

Raised on a farm in New South Wales, Australia, poet Les A. Murray feels the importance of rooting oneself in the land. In 1975, he bought back part of his family's dairy farm, where he now lives. A number of his works, including *Dog Fox Field* (1990), explore the textures of life in rural Australia.

Murray's experiences are not confined to the outback. He has served as writer-in-residence at universities in England and the United States. He has also attended many international poetry conferences and has sometimes poked fun at such gatherings in affectionately satirical poems. His poetry has won a number of awards, including the 1997 T. S. Eliot Prize.

Murray's love of rural life leads him naturally to "The Dream of Wearing Shorts Forever," in which he celebrates that most casual item of clothing—short pants.

Umberto Eco (1932–   )

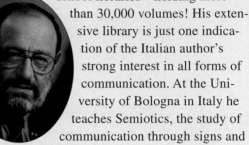

Umberto Eco's personal library is larger than some school libraries—holding more than 30,000 volumes! His extensive library is just one indication of the Italian author's strong interest in all forms of communication. At the University of Bologna in Italy he teaches Semiotics, the study of communication through signs and symbols.

He is also an avid follower of the information revolution taking place on the Internet. Eco achieved an international audience with his 1981 novel, *The Name of the Rose,* a suspenseful tale of murder in a Benedictine monastery.

◆ Build Vocabulary

LATIN PREFIXES: *ex-*

In "How to React to Familiar Faces," Umberto Eco uses the word *expound,* meaning "to explain in detail." The word is formed in part with the Latin prefix *ex-*, meaning "out." When someone expounds on a topic, he or she "sets out" a point-by-point explanation.

WORD BANK

cardinal
paucity
entropy
ambit
expound
syndrome
amiably
protagonist

As you read this poem and story, you will encounter the words on this list. Each word is defined on the page where it first occurs. Preview the list of words before you read.

◆ Build Grammar Skills

PRONOUN AGREEMENT WITH AN INDEFINITE ANTECEDENT

A pronoun's **antecedent** is the noun or pronoun to which the pronoun refers. A pronoun must agree in number (singular or plural) and gender (feminine or masculine) with its antecedent. Sometimes the gender or the number of the antecedent may not be known. For instance, in his essay, Eco says:

. . . we don't speak of *this person* in a loud voice when *he* or *she* can overhear.

Because the antecedent, *this person*, is singular but of unknown gender, Eco use the singular *he* or *she* to refer to the antecedent.

A common mistake is to use the word *they* in this situation; however, *they* is plural, so it does not agree with the singular antecedent.

◆ *Literature and Your Life*

CONNECT YOUR EXPERIENCE

There's more to you than meets the eye—but what meets the eye is part of who you are. That is why you care whether your hair or clothing looks right. At the same time, your image is definitely *not* you, as when someone judges you unfairly by your appearance.

In his essay, Umberto Eco warns that a celebrity's image can take on a life of its own. By contrast, Les A. Murray discovers that when you wear shorts you just might turn invisible!

THEMATIC FOCUS: PEOPLE AND STYLES

As you read these selections, ask yourself: How do media and clothing define the ways in which we see ourselves and others?

Journal Writing Briefly describe a clothing ad you have seen in print or on television. Then, explain the image that it was trying to create.

◆ Background for Understanding

ENTERTAINMENT

Umberto Eco was born in 1932, so the entertainment names he's familiar with may not be familiar to you. Then again, they might be. The following information identifies the people to whom Eco refers in his essay.

The film actor Anthony Quinn was born in Chihuahua, Mexico, in 1916. After years of being stereotyped in such roles as a Mexican bandit and an Indian warrior, Quinn eventually achieved international fame, winning two Academy Awards. Charlton Heston is an American actor. Johnny Carson was the host of *The Tonight Show* for thirty years, until 1992. Oprah Winfrey has been one of the most successful talk-show hosts in history.

◆ Literary Focus

TONE

Each of these literary selections has a distinct **tone**—that is, an attitude toward its readers and its subject matter. A writer's tone may be formal or informal, friendly or distant, personal or impersonal. For example, Eco's tone is lighthearted and amusing. His attitude toward his subject and his readers is good-natured.

◆ Reading Strategy

DRAW INFERENCES

When you see a man wearing a tuxedo, you might **draw inferences** (reach conclusions) about him based on your associations with tuxedos. For instance, you might draw the inference that he is going to a wedding. Like a suit of clothes, a literary work is filled with clues that you can use to increase your understanding.

For example, in "How to React to Familiar Faces," Eco mentions a disagreeable experience celebrities often have in public. Then, he writes "Now, as a rule, when we see someone we don't know personally, we don't stare into his or her face at length . . ." Because celebrities have a "disagreeable experience" and because their experience is probably an exception to the "rule," you can infer that people *do* stare into celebrities' faces.

As you read, draw the inferences you need to fill in your understanding of the work.

Anthony Quinn

The Dream Of Wearing Shorts Forever

Les Murray

To go home and wear shorts forever
in the enormous paddocks,[1] in that warm climate,
adding a sweater when winter soaks the grass,

to camp out along the river bends
5   for good, wearing shorts, with a pocketknife,
a fishing line and matches.

or there where the hills are all down, below the plain,
to sit around in shorts at evening
on the plank verandah[2]—

10   If the <u>cardinal</u> points of costume
are Robes, Tat, Rig and Scunge,[3]
where are shorts in this compass?

They are never Robes
as other bareleg outfits have been:
15   the toga, the kilt, the lava-lava
the Mahatma's cotton dhoti;[4]

---

1. paddocks: In Australia, enclosed pieces of land.
2. verandah (və ran′ də) *n.*: Open porch, usually roofed, along the outside of a building.
3. If the cardinal . . . Scunge: If the main styles of clothing are robes; tat, shabby clothes worn to make a social or political statement; rig, clothes for a specific trade or job, like those of a farmer; and scunge, shabby or everyday clothes, worn unselfconsciously.
4. the toga, the kilt, the lava-lava / the Mahatma's cotton dhoti (dō′ tē): Toga, the loose, one-piece, robelike outer garment worn by people in ancient Rome; kilt, the pleated skirt worn by men in Scotland; lava-lava, the cloth or skirt of printed cloth worn around the hips by men and women on South Pacific islands; dhoti, the cloth worn around the hips by Hindu men, like that worn by Mahatma Gandhi, the founder of modern India.

◆ **Build Vocabulary**

cardinal (kärd′′ nəl) *adj.*: Principal; chief; of main importance

paucity (pô′ sə tē) *n.*: Scarcity; fewness

entropy (en′ trə pē) *n.*: A state of affairs that has the least order

archbishops and field marshals
at their ceremonies never wear shorts.
The very word
20   means underpants in North America.

Shorts can be Tat,
Land-Rovering bush-environmental tat,
socio-political ripped-and-metal-stapled tat,
solidarity-with-the-Third World tat tvam asi,[5]

25   likewise track-and-field shorts worn to parties
and the further humid, modeling negligée
of the Kingdom of Flaunt,
that unchallenged aristocracy.

More plainly climatic, shorts
30   are farmers' rig, leathery with salt and bonemeal,
are sailors' and branch bankers' rig,
the crisp golfing style
of our youngest male National Costume.

Most loosely, they are Scunge,
35   ancient Bengal bloomers[6] or moth-eaten hot pants
worn with a former shirt,
feet, beach sand, hair
and a paucity of signals.

Scunge, which is real negligée
40   housework in a swimsuit, pyjamas worn all day,
is holiday, a freedom from ambition.
Scunge makes you invisible
to the world and yourself.

The entropy of costume,
45   scunge can get you conquered by more vigorous cultures
and help you to notice it less.

To be or to become
is a serious question posed by a work-shorts counter
with its pressed stacks, bulk khaki and blue,
50   reading Yakka or King Gee,[7] crisp with steely warehouse
     odor.

5. solidarity-with-the- . . . asi:
Feeling of unity with less-developed nations that is symbolized by the wearing of shorts. The phrase "tat tvam asi" means "thou art that" in Sanskrit, an ancient Indian language, and expresses the idea that all things are connected.

6. bloomers: Baggy pants gathered at the knee or ankle.

7. Yakka or King Gee: Clothing companies in Australia and New Zealand that specialize in work clothes.

Satisfied ambition, defeat, true unconcern,
the wish and the knack for self-forgetfulness
all fall within the scunge <u>ambit</u>
wearing board shorts or similar;
55 it is a kind of weightlessness.

Unlike public nakedness, which in Westerners
is deeply circumstantial, relaxed as exam time,
artless and equal as the corsetry of a hussar regiment,[8]

shorts and their plain like
60 are an angelic nudity,
spirituality with pockets!
A double updraft as you drop from branch to pool!

Ideal for getting served last
In shops of the temperate zone
65 they are also ideal for going home, into space,
into time, to farm the mind's Sabine acres[9]
for products or subsistence.

Now that everyone who yearned to wear long pants
has essentially achieved them,
70 long pants, which have themselves been underwear
repeatedly, and underground more than once,
it is time perhaps to cherish the culture of shorts,

8. corsetry of a hussar (hŏŏ zär´) **regiment:** Closefitting undergarments worn around the midsection by soldiers in dress uniform; they give all the soldiers the same ideal body shape.

9. to farm . . . Sabine (sā´ bǐn´) **acres:** To think quietly and without distraction, as one can do in a rural setting; a reference to the ancient Roman poet Horace, who retreated to his farm in the Sabine region of Italy in order to escape the bustle of Rome.

to moderate grim vigor
with the knobble of bare knees,
75   to cool bareknuckle feet in inland water,
slapping flies with a book on solar wind
or a patient bare hand, beneath the cadjiput trees,

to be walking meditatively
among green timber, through the grassy forest
80   towards a calm sea
and looking across to more of that great island
and the further topics.

◆ **Build Vocabulary**

ambit (am' bit) *n.*: Limits or range
of a phenomenon

Guide for Responding

◆ *Literature and Your Life*

Reader's Response Murray classifies clothing
into "Robes, Tat, Rig, and Scunge." How might you
divide the clothing in your wardrobe?

Thematic Focus Explain how the possibility of
wearing different kinds of clothing expands your
horizons.

Reader's Journal Jot down several of your favorite clothing fashions. Then, give reasons for your
choices.

☑ Check Your Comprehension

1. Give an example of the kind of shorts that can
be "tat."
2. Give an example of shorts used as "rig."
3. In what circumstances, according to Murray, are
shorts "scunge"?
4. With what attitudes does the author associate
shorts worn as "scunge"?
5. Summarize the scenes with which Murray ends
the poem.

◆ Critical Thinking

1. Using examples from the poem, describe two
ways in which "Scunge / makes you invisible / to
the world and yourself" (ll. 42–43). **[Support]**
2. What two approaches to life does Murray have
in mind when he refers to the question, "To be
or to become" (l. 47)? **[Interpret]**
3. What experiences does Murray think the "culture of shorts" (l. 72) promotes? **[Interpret]**
4. Why does he find these experiences valuable?
[Draw Conclusions]

APPLY

5. Give an example of "scunge" and one of "rig"
from your own life. **[Relate]**

EXTEND

6. Take a side on an issue involving the kinds of
clothes people are expected (or commanded) to
wear. Then, explain what light Murray's thoughts
on "scunge" might shed on the issue. **[Social
Studies Link]**

How to React to Familiar Faces

Umberto Eco
Translated by William Weaver

▲ **Critical Viewing** This photograph is of the movie star Anthony Quinn. What do you think he is reacting to in this picture? **[Hypothesize]**

A few months ago, as I was strolling in New York, I saw, at a distance, a man I knew very well heading in my direction. The trouble was that I couldn't remember his name or where I had met him. This is one of those sensations you encounter especially when, in a foreign city, you run into someone you met back home, or vice versa. A face out of context creates confusion. Still, that face was so familiar that, I felt, I should certainly stop, greet him, converse; perhaps he would immediately respond, "My dear Umberto, how are you?" or "Were you able to do that thing you were telling me about?" And I would be at a total loss. It was too late to flee. He was still looking at the opposite side of the street, but now he was beginning to turn his eyes towards me. I might as well make the first move; I would wave and then, from his voice, his first remarks, I would try to guess his identity.

We were now only a few feet from each other, I was just about to break into a broad, radiant smile, when suddenly I recognized him. It was Anthony Quinn. Naturally, I had never met him in my life, nor he me. In a thousandth of a second I was able to check myself, and I walked past him, my eyes staring into space.

Afterwards, reflecting on this incident, I realized how totally normal it was. Once before, in a restaurant, I had glimpsed Charlton Heston and had felt an impulse to say hello. These faces inhabit our memory; watching the screen, we spend so many hours with them that they are as familiar to us as our relatives', even more so. You can be a student of mass communication, debate the effects of reality, or the confusion between the real and the imagined, and <u>expound</u> the way some people fall permanently into this confusion; but still you are not immune to the <u>syndrome</u>. And there is worse.

I have received confidences from people who, appearing fairly frequently on TV, have been subjected to the mass media over a certain period of time. I'm not talking about Johnny Carson or Oprah Winfrey, but public figures, experts who have participated in panel discussions often enough to become recognizable. All of them complain of the same disagreeable experience. Now, as a rule, when we see someone we don't know personally, we don't stare into his or her face at length, we don't point out the person to the friend at our side, we don't speak of this person in a loud voice when he or she can overhear. Such behavior would be rude, even—if carried too far—aggressive. But the same people who would never point to a customer at a counter and remark to a friend that the man is wearing a smart tie behave quite differently with famous faces.

My guinea pigs insist that, at a newsstand, in the tobacconist's, as they are boarding a train or entering a restaurant toilet, they encounter others who, among themselves, say aloud, "Look there's X." "Are you sure?" "Of course I'm sure. It's X, I tell you." And they continue their conversation amiably, while X hears them, and they don't care if he hears them: it's as if he didn't exist.

Such people are confused by the fact that a protagonist of the mass media's imaginary world should abruptly enter real life, but at the same time they behave in the presence of the real person as if he still belonged to the world of images, as if he were on a screen, or in a weekly picture magazine. As if they were speaking in his absence.

I might as well have grabbed Anthony Quinn by the lapel, dragged him to a phone booth, and called a friend to say, "Talk about coincidence! I've run into Anthony Quinn. And you know something? He seems real!" (After which I would throw Quinn aside and go on about my business.)

The mass media first convinced us that the imaginary was real, and now they are convincing us that the real is imaginary; and the more reality the TV screen shows us, the more cinematic our everyday world becomes.

◆ **Build Vocabulary**

expound (eks pound´) v.: Explain in detail

syndrome (sin´ drōm) n.: Group of signs that occur together and may form a pattern

amiably (ā´ mē ə blē) adv.: In a cheerful, friendly way

protagonist (prō tag´ ə nist´) n.: Main character; person who plays a leading part

Guide for Responding

◆ *Literature and Your Life*

Reader's Response Do you react to celebrities in the way Umberto describes? Explain.

Thematic Focus Which celebrities interest you? Why?

☑ **Check Your Comprehension**

1. What celebrity does the author see in New York?
2. What reaction does Eco say most people have to celebrities?
3. Why does Eco say people react as they do?

◆ **Critical Thinking**

INTERPRET

1. How do you think Eco feels about the way people react to celebrities? **[Interpret]**
2. Explain how the title of the essay relates to its message. **[Connect]**
3. Explain Eco's understanding of the role the media plays in our reaction to and attitude toward famous people. **[Analyze]**

APPLY

4. Based on Eco's observations, do you think you would like to be famous? Why or why not? **[Relate]**

Guide for Responding (continued)

◆ Reading Strategy

DRAW INFERENCES

Authors do not always spell out their meaning. To understand a work fully you need to **draw inferences**—to figure out what is implied by given details. For instance, Murray writes, "...the cardinal points of costume / are Robes, Tat, Rig, and Scunge" (ll. 10–11). You can draw the inference that, just as all directions can be expressed using the four points on a compass, Murray thinks all clothing falls in the categories of Robes, Tat, Rig, or Scunge.

1. In "How to React to Familiar Faces," why does Eco feel compelled to greet the person with the "familiar" face?
2. Based on his descriptions, what is Eco's opinion of those who comment loudly on celebrities when they are present?
3. Murray writes in "The Dream of Wearing Shorts Forever" that scunge expresses: "Satisfied ambition, defeat, true unconcern, / the wish and the knack for self-forgetfulness" (ll. 51–52). What can you infer from this statement about the reasons he believes people wear robes and tat?

◆ Literary Focus

TONE

The **tone** of a literary work is the writer's attitude toward the readers and toward the subject. In his social commentary "How to React to Familiar Faces," Eco's purpose is to explore a common human behavior, and his tone is suitably objective. It is also a bit humorous.

In "The Dream of Wearing Shorts Forever," Murray uses an objective, serious-sounding tone to refer to things often treated as trivial, such as fleeting fashions. This combination creates humor. At the same time, it helps readers see the universal significance of even a lowly pair of shorts.

1. Find two statements in "How to React to Familiar Faces" that reflect a humorous tone.
2. Describe the tone of the last paragraph of Eco's essay.
3. Explain how the reference in Murray's poem to "the Kingdom Flaunt, / that unchallenged aristocracy" (ll. 27–28) creates a mildly sarcastic tone.

◆ Build Vocabulary

USING THE LATIN PREFIX ex–

Explain what the Latin prefix ex- ("out or away from") adds to these words:
1. exit
2. exhaust
3. exhale

USING THE WORD BANK: Context

On your paper, respond to the following items.
1. Name the *cardinal* points on a compass.
2. Explain why you might not like shopping in a store with a *paucity* of goods.
3. If *entropy* is a general principle, what might happen to the universe over the course of time?
4. If a task is within the *ambit* of a person's job, would you expect him or her to take responsibility for it?
5. What kind of person might *expound* on the importance of reading?
6. Name a person to whom you respond *amiably*.
7. Describe the *protagonist* in your favorite movie.
8. Describe a humorous *syndrome* that might affect students early on a Monday morning.

◆ Build Grammar Skills

PRONOUN AGREEMENT WITH AN INDEFINITE ANTECEDENT

Singular pronouns must be used to refer to **indefinite antecedents** such as *someone, anyone,* and *everybody*. If the gender is unknown, it's best to use a combination of two singular personal pronouns such as *he or she,* or *his or her*. Antecedents like *all* or *several* require a plural pronoun.

Practice On your paper, write these sentences and choose the correct pronoun for each.
1. Everyone should be careful of (their, his, her, his or her) behavior.
2. Several celebrities complained to Eco about (their, his, her, his or her) treatment by strangers.
3. Everybody I know likes times when (they, he, she, he or she) can wear scunge.
4. All of my friends think that wearing scunge makes (them, him, her, him or her) feel relaxed.
5. Several of my friends do not care about (their, his, her, his or her) clothes.

Build Your Portfolio

 ## Idea Bank

Writing

1. **Fan Magazine Interview** Write five questions you would ask your favorite celebrity in an interview. Write an answer to one of the questions as if you were the celebrity.

2. **Dialogue** Write a dialogue between the speaker in "The Dream of Wearing Shorts Forever" and a fashion designer. **[Career Link]**

3. **Poem** Write a poem in which you explain the positive effects of wearing formal clothing such as a suit, fancy dress, or a uniform.

Speaking, Listening, and Viewing

4. **Perform and Evaluate** With a group, enact a scene in which several teenagers recognize their favorite music star somewhere near them in public. When you are in the "audience," evaluate how true to life each group's scene is. **[Performing Arts Link]**

5. **Debate** Divide into teams to debate this statement: A person should not have to care about the image he or she creates. **[Social Studies Link]**

Researching and Representing

6. **Drawing** Create a portfolio of drawings or a collage representing clothing from the categories of Robes, Tat, Rig, and Scunge. **[Art Link]**

7. **Celebrity Home Page** Design a home page for one of the celebrities Eco mentions in his nonfiction piece. Choose visuals and suggest topics and links. **[Technology Link]**

Online Activity **www.phlit.phschool.com**

 ## Guided Writing Lesson

Description of a Trend

The popularity of celebrities and of clothing comes and goes in *trends*—general tendencies or patterns in events. Do some research, and write a description of a contemporary trend in clothing, sports, politics, movies, or other field.

Writing Skills Focus: Transitions That Show Emphasis

As you draft, use **transitions that show emphasis,** words that connect ideas and show readers what importance to assign a new idea. For instance, if you start an explanation with the word *basically,* readers will expect a simple, convenient, but possibly incomplete explanation. If you use the transition *in fact,* readers will know that the next idea illustrates the previous one, but that it may be surprising.

Following are transitions to show emphasis:

actually	despite	in reality
basically	essentially	indeed
certainly	in fact	of course

Prewriting Consult contemporary periodicals and other references for facts, figures, and examples concerning the trend you are describing.

Drafting In your introduction, define the trend you will describe using the most striking facts or examples from your research. In the body of your paper, present the events causing or defining the trend in clear, chronological order.

Revising Read your draft aloud to a partner. Ask him or her to identify places in which the order and significance of ideas was most clear and where it was least clear. Revise your draft using your partner's comments for guidance.

Be sure that the pronouns you have used agree with their antecedents. For more on pronoun agreement with indefinite antecedents, see pp. 526 and 534.

Guide for Reading

Hans Magnus Enzensberger (1929–)

Skilled in many writing forms, Hans Magnus Enzensberger (häns mäg´ nəs en´ zens bər´ gər) offers cultural commentary in poetry, prose, drama, journalism, and essays. He has been called one of Germany's greatest living poets, and he is also respected as a thinker.

A Literary Life Enzensberger was born in Bavaria, a section of Germany, in 1929 and grew up in Nuremberg. At the age of seventeen, he began studying English translation. He quickly embraced a life and career revolving around literature and language. In addition to writing, Enzensberger joined Gruppe 47, an influential postwar German writer's collective, and edited an influential literary magazine.

Throughout his career, Enzensberger has experimented with many different writing genres. His publications include *Defense of the Wolves*, a poetry anthology; *Hearings in Havana*, a play; *The Sinking of the Titanic: A Comedy*, an epic poem; *Civil Wars: From L.A. to Bosnia*, a political analysis; and *The Number Devil*, a mathematical fantasy for children.

Common Themes, Diverse Forms In each form of writing, Enzensberger explores themes related to the complexities and contradictions of modern life. He often uses his sharp humor to criticize accepted cultural ideas. He questions the concept of progress, as well as the idea that any system, political or social, can be perfect.

> *"Consistency," Enzensberger writes, "will turn any good cause into a bad one."*

Enzensberger has probably achieved his greatest renown as a cultural essayist and social critic on the subject of progress. "The Future of Luxury" is the final essay in his collection *Zig Zag: The Politics of Culture and Vice Versa* (1999). The essay returns to the subject of a short documentary film he wrote and directed in 1995: *Luxury: What Is It?*

◆ Build Vocabulary

LATIN PREFIXES: *multi-*

In "The Future of Luxury," Enzensberger uses the word "multifarious." The Latin prefix *multi-* means "many," and the word part *-farious* comes from a word meaning "to do or make." The prefix and the word part combine to create an adjective, *multifarious,* meaning "having a great variety."

WORD BANK

conjecture
multifarious
arbitrary
cognitive
precarious
ostentatious
relinquish
parameters

As you read this essay, you will encounter the words on this list. Each word is defined on the page where it first appears. Preview the list before you read.

◆ Build Grammar Skills

SUBJECT AND VERB AGREEMENT

When forming lengthy or complex sentences, writers must ensure that **subjects and verbs agree in number.** For example, Enzensberger's essay includes this sentence:

> *Watching* the melee of money and politics, sports and art, technology, and advertising, *leaves* little attention leftover.

The subject of the sentence is *watching,* a singular gerund. Although the subject is followed by a number of plural nouns, the subject itself remains singular; therefore, the writer correctly chose a singular verb, *leaves.*

As you read this essay, look for subject and verb agreement in long, complex sentences.

from The Future of Luxury

◆ *Literature and Your Life*

CONNECT YOUR EXPERIENCE

You are bombarded with advertising images every day in the form of commercials, product packaging, billboards, magazine advertisements, designer logos and much more. Most of the advertisements sell products that are far from essential—you would probably call many of them pure luxuries.

In this essay, Hans Magnus Enzensberger discusses his ideas about the changing definition of "luxury."

Journal Writing Make a list of five luxury items you would like to buy if you had unlimited funds. Then, jot down your ideas about how you were influenced to make each choice.

THEMATIC FOCUS: PEOPLE AND STYLES

Enzensberger predicts how the luxuries of the future will be different from those of today. As you read, ask yourself: What products or qualities will be so uncommon in the future that they become rare luxuries?

◆ Background for Understanding

SOCIAL SCIENCES

This chart shows how people's idea of "necessities" changed between 1973 and 1991. What items that are luxuries today will be considered necessities in twenty years?

What Is a "Necessity"?

Percentage of People Identifying Each Item as a Necessity

	1973	1991
Television	57	74
Home Air Conditioning	26	47
Automobile	90	85
VCR	N/A	18
Basic Cable Service	N/A	26
Microwave	N/A	44
Home Computer	N/A	11

N/A = This item did not exist, was not widely used, or was not asked about in 1973.

◆ Literary Focus

ESSAY OF PREDICTION

In an **essay of prediction,** a writer uses a brief work of nonfiction to present ideas about the future. The writer might explore the likely future of a nation, a cultural trend, or even an entire planet. The main goal of the essay is usually not to "guess the right future," but to point out basic truths about our own times by indicating the probable effects our way of living will have on future generations.

In "The Future of Luxury," Hans Magnus Enzensberger uses logic, counterlogic, humor, and insight to predict a meaningful change in people's notions about what is valuable.

◆ Reading Strategy

CLARIFY DETAILS AND INFORMATION

Some writers use detailed language that can be confusing initially. When you read difficult passages, pause to **clarify details and information.** Reread to help you locate and review the main idea of a sentence or paragraph. Read ahead to find more information or to make connections among ideas.

For example, you will read in the first paragraph that things such as "quiet" may become luxuries in the future. To clarify this provocative statement, read ahead. You will find a full explanation of quiet as a luxury in item 4, p. 540.

from

The Future
of Luxury

Hans Magnus Enzensberger
Translated by Linda Haverty Rugg

So one must ask if private luxury has any future at all. I hope and fear: yes. For if it is true that the struggle for difference is a part of the mechanism of evolution, and that the desire to squander has its roots in our natural drives, then luxury can never completely disappear, and the question is only which form it will take in its flight from its own shadow.

All we can offer is <u>conjecture</u>. And so I would guess that there will be completely different priorities in our future battles over distribution. Fast cars and gold watches, cases of champagne and perfume are available on every street corner; they are not scarce, rare, expensive or desirable in this age of raging consumerism. Instead, it is the elementary necessities of life that come at a great price: quiet, good water, and enough space.

It is a peculiar reversal of the logic of desire: the luxury of the future will turn away from excess and strive for the necessary; which, it is to be feared, will be available to only a select few. The things that matter will not be sold in any Duty Free Shop:[1]

1. *Time.* This is the most important of all luxury items. Strangely enough it is precisely the elite who have the least say over their own time. This is not primarily a question of quantity, though many members of this class work upward of eighty hours a week; it is much more a matter of the <u>multifarious</u> dependencies that enslave them. They are expected to be on call at all times. Besides that, they are bound to a day-planner that extends years into the future.

   But other professions, too, are bound to regulations that limit their temporal sovereignty to a minimum. Workers are tied to the pace of their machines, housewives (in Europe) to absurd shopping hours, parents to school functions, and almost all commuters have to travel at peak times. Under the circumstances, it is the

---

1. **Duty Free Shop:** Kind of variety store, usually found in airports, in which no taxes are imposed on items sold.

▲ **Critical Viewing** Which details in this picture might convey the idea of an unkown or mysterious future? Why? **[Interpret]**

L'Univers Demasque, René Magritte, Coll. Crik, Brussels, Belgium

person who always has time who lives in luxury; time for what he wants to do, and the power to decide what he does with his time, how much he does, when, and where he does it.

2. *Attention.* This, too is a scarce commodity, with all the media competing bitterly for a piece. Watching the melee of money and politics, sports and art, technology, and advertising, leaves little attention leftover. Only the person who turns his back on these overbearing claims on his attention and turns off the roar of the channels can decide for himself what is worth his attention and what is not. In the barrage of <u>arbitrary</u> information our perceptive and <u>cognitive</u> capabilities decline, they grow

when we limit our attention to those things and only those things that we ourselves want to see, hear, feel and know. In this we can see an occasion for luxury.

3. *Space.* As the day-planner is to the economy of time, congestion is to space. In a sense, everywhere and everything is

◆ Build Vocabulary

conjecture (kən jek´ chər) *n.*: Prediction based on guesswork

multifarious (mul´ tə far´ ē əs) *adj.*: Of great variety; diverse

arbitrary (är´ bə trer´ ē) *adj.*: Random; not based on a system or rules

cognitive (käg´ nit iv) *adj.*: Related to knowing, memory, and judgment

from *The Future of Luxury* ◆ 539

crowded. We have rising rents, housing shortages, and sardine-packed public transport. We feel the press of flesh on sidewalks, public swimming pools, discotheques, and tourist spots. All of this creates a density in living conditions that verges on a robbery of freedom. Anyone who can remove himself from this cagelike existence lives in luxury. But he must be prepared to shovel himself out from under a mountain of consumer items, as well. Usually our already-too-small living space is jammed with furniture, appliances, knick-knacks, and clothes. What is missing is the excess of space that is required for free movement. Today a room seems luxurious when it is empty.

4. *Quiet.* This, too, is a basic requirement that has become harder and harder to satisfy. Anyone who wants to escape the everyday din must be very extravagant. In general, apartments cost more the quieter they are; restaurants that do not pour musical pollution into the ears of their guests demand higher prices of their discerning clientele. The raging traffic, the howling sirens, the clatter of helicopters, the neighbor's droning stereo, the month-long roar of the street fair—the person who can elude all of that enjoys luxury.

5. *The Environment.* That one can breathe the air and drink the water, that it does not smoke and does not stink, is, as everyone knows, not a given but a privilege enjoyed by fewer and fewer. Anyone who does not produce his own food must pay a premium for nontoxic edibles. It is a problem for most to avoid the risk to life and limb in the workplace, in traffic, and in the dangerous bustle of leisure. In this arena, too, the possibility of withdrawal proves ever-more scarce.

6. *Security.* This is perhaps the most precarious of all luxury items. As the state has become less able to guarantee safety, the private demand for it has

grown and driven the prices skyhigh. Bodyguards, security services, alarm systems—anything that promises security now belongs to the realm of privilege, and these businesses can count on further growth in the future. If one takes a look around the wealthier neighborhoods, one can already sense that luxury does not promise unmitigated pleasure. As in the past, it will bring with it not only freedom but obligations. For the person of privilege who wants to remain safe does not just lock others out, he locks himself in.

All in all, these speculations revolve on an about-face that is rich in ironies. If there is anything to them, the luxury of the future will depend not on increase, as it did in the past, but on decrease, not on accumulation but on avoidance. Excess will enter a new stage in which it negates itself. The answer to the paradox of mass exclusivity would then be a further paradox: minimalism and abstinence could prove to be just as rare, expensive, and desirable as <u>ostentatious</u> spending once was.

With that, in any case, luxury would <u>relinquish</u> its role as representation. Its privatization would be complete. It would no longer require viewers, but would exclude them. Its reason for being would be, precisely, to be invisible. But even with that kind of withdrawal from reality, luxury would still be true to its origins; it has always been at odds with the reality principle. Perhaps it has never been more than an attempt to flee life's monotony and misery.

◆Reading Strategy
What does Enzensberger mean when he says luxury "would no longer require viewers . . . Its reason for being would be . . . to be invisible"?

◆ **Build Vocabulary**

precarious (prē ker´ ē əs) *adj.*: Uncertain; dependent on circumstances

ostentatious (äs´ tən tā´ shəs) *adj.*: Done as a showy display

relinquish (ri liŋ´ kwish) *v.*: Give up; abandon

parameters (pə ram´ ə tərz) *n.*: Factors; characteristics

New and bewildering, however, is another question that must be posed in light of future prospects: who will count among the beneficiaries of luxury in the future? The original <u>parameters</u> of social position, income, and fortune will no longer be the deciding factors. A top executive, star athlete, banker, or leading politician will quite simply not be able to afford the items discussed here. Such individuals can buy sufficient space and a certain degree of security. But they have no time and no peace.

On the other hand, the unemployed, the elderly, and refugees, who in the future will make up the majority of the world's population, usually dispose of their time as they like. But it would be sheer mockery to call that a privilege. Crammed into crowded living space, with no money or security, many of them can make little use of their empty time. It is difficult to say how the scarce commodities of the future will be distributed, but one thing is clear: anyone who has only one of them enjoys none of them. There can be as little hope of justice in the future as there was in the past. At least in this respect, luxury will remain what it always was—a stubborn opponent of equality.

Guide for Responding

◆ Literature and Your Life

Reader's Response Which of Enzensberger's five "luxuries" is most important to you? Why?

Thematic Focus What current cultural trend do you believe poses the greatest threat to the future? Why?

Reader's Journal Note in your journal the qualities or possessions that you believe make a person "rich."

Questions for Research Suppose you wanted to survey friends and classmates in order to determin which items they regarded as luxuries and which they regarded as necessities. Jot down some questions you might ask them to learn what their views are on this subject.

☑ Check Your Comprehension

1. What elements of daily life does Enzensberger claim will be considered luxuries in the future?
2. What group of people does the author say have least control of their own time? Why?
3. What examples does Enzensberger provide to show that silence has become a luxury?
4. According to Enzensberger, what failure of the state makes security more "precarious"?

◆ Critical Thinking

INTERPRET

1. Why doesn't Enzensberger identify any products as luxuries of the future? **[Infer]**
2. What does Enzensberger mean when he says "the luxury of the future will depend not on increase, as it did in the past, but on decrease, not on accumulation but on avoidance"? **[Interpret]**
3. What paradox—seeming contradiction that reveals a truth—does Enzensberger identify about the future of luxury? **[Analyze]**
4. Does Enzensberger's essay encourage or discourage increased consumerism? Explain your answer. **[Draw Conclusions]**

EVALUATE

5. Do you agree that luxury will always remain "a stubborn opponent of equality"? Why or why not? **[Evaluate]**

EXTEND

6. Choose a local department store with which you are familiar, and estimate the percentage of items it carries that are necessities and those that are luxuries. Make a chart in which you show the breakdown of items, department by department. **[Math Link]**

Guide for Responding (continued)

◆ Reading Strategy

CLARIFY DETAILS AND INFORMATION

As you read, you can often **clarify details and information** by rereading and reading ahead. For example, Enzensberger refers to "private luxury" in the opening of his essay. This phrase may not be immediately clear, but after reading ahead, you can interpret the phrase to mean "luxury that is possessed by individuals."

1. (a) What are the "multifarious dependencies that enslave" people? (b) How did you clarify this quotation?
2. (a) What point is the author supporting when he says that "a room seems luxurious when it is empty"? (b) How did you clarify that information?
3. Review the section of the essay about the environment. How would you clarify the key point that "the possibility of withdrawal proves ever-more scarce"?

◆ Build Vocabulary

USING THE LATIN PREFIX *multi-*

Knowing that the prefix *multi-* means "many," match each word with its definition.

1. multinational
2. multidwelling
3. multiprocessing
4. multitudinous

a. place of many homes
b. including many individuals
c. relating to more than two nations
d. performing many processes at once

USING THE WORD BANK: Synonyms

On your paper, write the letter of the word that is the best synonym for the first word.

1. arbitrary: (a) planned, (b) random, (c) sturdy
2. cognitive: (a) mechanical, (b) functional, (c) mental
3. conjecture: (a) injection, (b) action, (c) speculation
4. multifarious: (a) diverse, (b) evil, (c) infinite
5. ostentatious: (a) showy, (b) petrified, (c) awkward
6. parameters: (a) solids, (b) distances, (c) limits
7. precarious: (a) valuable, (b) uncertain, (c) curious
8. relinquish: (a) conquer, (b) taste, (c) abandon

◆ Literary Focus

ESSAY OF PREDICTION

An **essay of prediction** identifies how current trends will influence the future. One of the methods Enzensberger uses to envision the future is to exaggerate trends that are apparent today. For example, he notices the increase in the availability of luxury goods such as cars and expensive watches, and he claims that they are now so common that they are not expensive or desirable. This overstated claim emphasizes his point in a humorous way.

1. How is Enzensberger's description of the current environment exaggerated? What is the purpose of this exaggeration?
2. Some essays of prediction are prescriptions for change. By identifying an undesirable future, the author suggests the need for changes that will prevent the predictions from coming true. What changes do you think Enzensberger would recommend to prevent the future he predicts?

◆ Build Grammar Skills

SUBJECT AND VERB AGREEMENT

No matter the length or complexity of a sentence, its **subject and verb must agree** in number. A phrase or clause that interrupts a subject and its verb does not affect subject and verb agreement.

Example: *Our ideas* about the future, with all its complexities and uncertainties, *vary greatly.*

Practice Copy each sentence. Underline each subject and choose the verb in parentheses that agrees with the subject.

1. The luxuries most desired by the average consumer (is, are) quite unnecessary.
2. Commuters in every major city (travel, travels) during peak hours.
3. Our ability to avoid advertising images, cultural symbols, and the endless products of the entertainment industry (decline, declines).
4. Mountains of products from the marketplace (accumulate, accumulates) in our homes, our schools, and our offices.
5. Escaping the deluge of modern conveniences (require, requires) determined resistance.

Build Your Portfolio

Idea Bank

Writing

1. **Advertising Inventory** Compile a list of advertisements for luxury items that you often see. When the list is complete, arrange the ads according to the types of products or services they advertise.

2. **Commercial Script** Consider how entrepreneurs of the future will try to sell one of the luxuries Enzensberger identifies. Then, write the script for a future television or radio commercial advertising one of those luxuries. **[Career Link]**

3. **Essay of Prediction** Write an essay in which you predict how one current cultural trend will affect the future. Explain why you think this trend will be so influential, giving details to support your ideas.

Speaking, Listening, and Viewing

4. **Theatrical Sketch** Work with a team to create a theatrical sketch inspired by "The Future of Luxury." Your sketch might be set in a city of the future and depict the lack of space, quiet, and time. **[Performing Arts Link]**

5. **Radio Review** Write a review of Enzensberger's essay to broadcast on school or local radio. Summarize the subject, present your evaluation, and support your analysis with details from the essay. If possible, tape-record and share your review with others. **[Performing Arts Link]**

Researching and Representing

6. **Timeline of Luxuries** Create an annotated timeline showing popular luxury items for each decade of the twentieth century. At the end of your timeline, include a list of five items that you predict will become luxuries in the next twenty years. **[History Link]**

7. **Student Poll** Conduct a survey to identify the luxury items most desired by students in your school. Analyze your findings, and share them with the class. **[Math Link]**

Online Activity www.phlit.phschool.com

Guided Writing Lesson

Description of a Day in the Future

Enzensberger paints an interesting view of the world of the future. Which of his predictions do you think will come true in one hundred years? Write a description of a day one hundred years from today. As you write, choose pronouns that will help you avoid unnecessary repetition of nouns.

Writing Skills Focus: Use of Pronouns for Coherence

Writers use pronouns to avoid repeating nouns and to create a sense of **coherence,** or unity, by referring back to previous subjects. Pronouns compress writing and add fluidity. However, you need to use pronouns carefully, making sure that each one clearly relates to a specific, stated noun. A sentence with too many pronouns could be confusing or choppy.

Prewriting To help you imagine a day one hundred years in the future, jot down ideas about what a person might do at each hour of the day. For example, do people use alarm clocks, or does some futuristic invention take their place?

Drafting As you draft, arrange the details chronologically, beginning with waking up in the morning. In your description, use vivid words that bring to life what it would be like to "live" in your future world. As a challenge, you may want to include passages of dialogue that indicate the ways in which the English language itself might change.

Revising Reread your description critically. Add descriptive language to make your account more appealing. Also, add pronouns where necessary to avoid repeating subjects. However, be sure each pronoun has a clear antecedent.

Identify the subject and verb of each sentence to ensure that they agree in number. For more on subject-verb agreement, see pp. 536 and 542.

Focus on Culture

Africa

Molapatene grew up among the Batlokwa people of Southern Africa. When he was 12, the older men of his clan led him and the other boys his age away from their village. It was a vital step on the way to becoming an adult member of the community.

For thirty days, the boys received instruction in the ways of their people. "Beliefs and philosophies were transmitted through singing, chanting, and the talking drum," Molapatene recalled. "I was taught respect, honor, praise, veneration, and worship of my ancestors. . . . I must never forget."

Africa is home to diverse peoples and ways of life. Indeed, there is no such thing as a single "African culture." Still, much of the continent shares a common history and common values. While outside influences and modernization have threatened older traditions, Africans vow that they "must never forget" their heritage.

▲ **Critical Viewing** Masks, like the ones shown here, are often used in religious rituals. What emotions do these masks convey to you? **[Relate]**

GEOGRAPHIC SETTING

Africa is the second-largest continent, after Asia. It straddles the Equator, extending for thousands of miles north and south of that line. It also contains more independent nations than any other continent on Earth.

Regions The main regions of Africa are North Africa, West Africa, Central Africa, East Africa, and Southern Africa. Geographic features give each region its own identity, but great variety also exists within each region.

North Africa is dominated by the Sahara, the world's largest desert. Because of its access to the Mediterranean and Red seas, North Africa has always had close contact with the Middle East and Europe. At the same time, it is closely linked to the regions south of the Sahara, often called sub-Saharan Africa.

South of the Sahara, West Africa bulges into the Atlantic Ocean. This region includes Nigeria, the most populous nation in Africa. Central Africa is dominated by the Zaire River and the large nation of Congo. East Africa, along the Indian Ocean coast, includes the nations of Kenya, Uganda, and Tanzania.

The region of Southern Africa stretches from the Indian Ocean to the Atlantic. At its very tip lies the nation of South Africa.

Diversity Africa's varied landforms and climates have contributed to the diversity of its cultures. As people migrated across the continent, they developed five basic types of societies, depending on where they settled: farming, herding, fishing, hunting and food-gathering, or urban.

Today, the majority of Africans live in the savanna, a grassland that covers almost half of the continent. Most of the people are farmers. Those parts of the savanna that are free from the tsetse (tset´ sē) fly also support cattle-herding societies such as the Masai (mä sī´) of East Africa. (See the picture on p. 546.)

Cities have long flourished on the Mediterranean coast of North Africa, in the savanna of West Africa, and on the coast of East Africa. Today, cities are rapidly growing throughout the continent.

HISTORY

Scientists believe that human history began in the Great Rift Valley of East Africa, where archaeologists have found the earliest known human remains. Also, one of the world's oldest and greatest civilizations emerged in North Africa—the Nile kingdom of Egypt.

Kingdoms and Trading States From early times, people traded across a long route that stretched from the Middle East and North Africa to the savanna lands of West Africa. Camel caravans crossed the Sahara, carrying valuable cargoes of gold or salt.

In time, a succession of trading empires rose in West Africa. Ghana flourished from about 500 to 1076. By the 1300's, Mali controlled the gold trade. The Muslim emperor of Mali, Mansa Musa, won widespread fame when he made a religious pilgrimage to the Arabian city of Mecca. In the 1400's, a new empire, Songhai (sôŋ´ hī), rose in the savanna. Its great city of Timbuktu was a center of learning, attracting scholars from all over the Muslim world.

The kingdom of Benin rose in the forests near the Equator. Further inland, the rulers of Great Zimbabwe (zim bä´ bwā) controlled rich gold mines and built walled cities. In East Africa, city-states such as Mogadishu (mō´ gä dē´ shōō), Kilwa, and Mombasa formed part of a prosperous trade route across the Indian Ocean.

Impact of Europe Direct contact between Europeans and West Africans began in the 1400's. Portugal sent sailors to map a sea route around Africa to India. In time, the Portuguese and others built small stations along the coast and traded with the peoples of West Africa.

In the 1500's, European traders began to ship Africans across the Atlantic to work as slaves in the Americas. As in the rest of the world, slavery had existed in Africa since ancient times. The Atlantic slave trade, though, was far more extensive. At its height, up to 60,000 Africans a year were being packed into the holds of slave ships. Western traders relied on local African rulers to capture and supply slaves. New West African states, such as the Asante kingdom, grew rich on the slave trade. The slave trade finally ended in the 1800's.

By the late 1800's, a new threat had risen: imperialism. Eager for raw materials and new markets, Europe's industrial powers carved Africa into colonies. Many Africans, such as the

▲ **Critical Viewing** How can traditional clothing, like the costume of this Masai woman, be a sign of pride? **[Speculate]**

Ibo and Fulani of West Africa, resisted fiercely. In the end, most were unable to withstand Europe's advanced weapons.

Independence and Development During the 1950's and 1960's, demands for freedom led to the birth of many new African nations. Most won independence peacefully. In the Gold Coast, Kwame Nkrumah (kwä´ mē ən kroo´ mə) organized strikes and boycotts to protest British rule. Weakened by World War II, Britain finally gave in. In 1957, the Gold Coast became Ghana—the first black African nation to win independence. (See the map on p. 555.)

In some areas, independence movements led to war. The French waged a long battle to hold on to Algeria. Fighting also broke out against the British in Kenya, the Belgians in the Congo, and the Portuguese in Mozambique and Angola. Eventually, all these nations won their struggles for freedom.

The new nations worked toward building strong, independent economies and stable, democratic governments. They faced many challenges, however. In Nigeria, for example, ethnic tensions flared between the Ibo people of the southeast and the dominant Hausa-Fulani of the north. In 1967, the Ibo seceded to form the Republic of Biafra. After three years of brutal civil war, a defeated Biafra rejoined Nigeria. Since then, Nigeria, like a number of other African nations, has alternated between civilian and military rule.

SOCIETY AND CULTURE

In Africa, as elsewhere around the world, family loyalty was a bond that held a society together. Traditional family patterns varied, however. Members of hunting and gathering societies, for example, usually lived in small groups. The nuclear family, made up of parents and their children, was the norm.

Family Ties In farming or herding societies, extended families were more common. An extended family included parents, unmarried children, married children and their spouses, and other relatives. In villages, extended families often shared a common living area, with separate homes for different family members.

Ties of kinship united people even beyond the extended family. In many societies, a group of distant kin would trace their descent back to a common ancestor. This common lineage created bonds of loyalty and understanding.

Today, urbanization is changing family life. In cities, people tend to live in nuclear rather than extended families. While traditional bonds of lineage are weakening, they remain. Often, the first family member who moves to the city is responsible for helping those that follow.

Religions Today, as in the past, religious beliefs and practices reflect the great variety of cultures in Africa. Most traditional religions included belief in a Supreme Being who created the world. Often, though, people viewed the Supreme Being as a remote figure. Instead, they turned to many lesser gods and spirits. Respect for ancestors and for nature also formed a part of many African religions.

Both Christianity and Judaism reached Africa in ancient times. For centuries, Ethiopia was a Christian kingdom that also boasted a large Jewish community. During the age of imperialism, Christianity took root in much of Africa, spread by western missionaries. Today, many churches blend Christian beliefs with traditional African music and dancing.

In the 600's, Arab armies carried Islam into North Africa. In the centuries that followed, Muslim traders carried Islam into West Africa. Today, North Africa is still predominantly Muslim. Like Christianity, Islam has absorbed many local beliefs and practices.

ARTS AND LITERATURE

In African cultures, as elsewhere, art has served both religious and political purposes. A bronze figure of a king, for example, is a symbol of his divine nature. A carved mask worn by a dancer in a religious ceremony, might represent the power of a nature spirit. (See the picture above.)

Visual Arts African artists are probably best known for their sculpture. In forested areas, artists carved green wood into human figures, masks, and everyday objects. Unfortunately, only a few examples of ancient wood carvings have survived attacks by termites and other insects. In the kingdom of Benin, craftworkers produced fine figures and plaques in bronze.

In the early 1900's, westerners began to study African art styles. The Spanish artist Pablo Picasso admired the unique features of African masks and statues. He applied similar techniques in his own influential paintings.

Oral Literature Africa has a rich heritage of oral literature. In traditional societies, the *griot* (grē´ ō), or storyteller, held a place of honor. The griot spoke the praises of the ruler, retold events from history, challenged listeners with riddles, and

Mask of the Bena Biombo Tribe,
Josef Herman Collection, London

▲ **Critical Viewing** From what material has this mask been carved? **[Infer]**

recited poems and folktales. Many tales contained morals—for example, the lesson that people must respect nature in order to prosper. "If one wants to catch a large fish," states a West African proverb, "one must give something to the stream."

In villages today, people still gather to hear familiar tales and poems. They can also listen to griots on the radio or recordings.

Written Literature In the 1930's, Senegalese poet Léopold Sédare Senghor took the lead in the *négritude*, or blackness, movement. In his poems, Senghor urged Africans to take pride in their heritage and work for unity among African peoples. (See p. 596 for Senghor's poem "Prayer to Masks.") Many later writers, such as David Diop, have echoed similar themes. (See p. 556 for Diop's poem "Africa.")

Modern African writers often depict the conflicts that have beset the continent. In his acclaimed novel *Things Fall Apart*, Nigerian writer Chinua Achebe shows how the arrival of the British disrupted patterns of village life. In his story "Civil Peace," Achebe captures the confusion that followed the Nigerian civil war, when Biafra rejoined Nigeria. (See p. 550.) Okot p'Bitek, Uganda's best-known poet, often stresses the need to preserve traditional cultures and protect them from western influences. (See p. 313 for p'Bitek's "Song of Lawino.")

ACTIVITY
Creating a Database

Choose one modern African nation. Then, use Internet resources to create a database about that nation. Emphasize the connections among society, religion, and literature. Include a map and, if possible, other illustrations, as well as a summary of one recent news story involving that nation.

Guide for Reading

Chinua Achebe *(1930–)*

During civil war in his homeland of Nigeria, Chinua Achebe (chin wä´ ə cheb´ ā) survived the bombing of his house. He fled the town, leaving behind a book in press at the publishing company he had formed with his friend, poet Christopher Okigbo. That book was *How the Leopard Got His Claws,* Achebe's parable about Nigeria. Okigbo died in the war, and when Achebe returned, the Citadel Press was demolished. There remained only one copy of the proofs of the book, which someone had managed to save.

Early Life Born in the Ibo village of Ogibi, Nigeria, Achebe was brought up with both the traditional values of the Ibo people as well as Western values. He believes that stories are a way to preserve the traditional values that are so important to him.

> *"Stories are not just meant to make people smile . . . our life depends on them."*

Achebe has also been influenced by his experiences with war and its aftermath.

Professional Life Achebe has directed a radio station, taught in universities, and involved himself in local Nigerian politics as a diplomat. His greatest success, however, has been as a novelist. His novels, including *Things Fall Apart* (1958) and *Anthills of the Savannah* (1987), convey the tragic history of tribal Africa's encounter with European power.

David Diop *(1927–1960)*

David Diop (dē´ ôp) published only one volume of poetry before his life was tragically cut short in a plane crash. That one book, *Hammerblows*, reflects Diop's rejection of colonialism in Africa.

Diop was born in France, but his roots were in the region that became the West African nation of Senegal. His poem "Africa" captures the power and dignity of a continent struggling against oppression.

◆ Build Vocabulary

LATIN WORD ROOTS: -reput-

In "Civil Peace" you will encounter the word *disreputable*, which means "not respectable." It contains the Latin word root -reput- which refers to "the opinion commonly held about a person or thing."

WORD BANK

As you read these selections, you will encounter the words on this list. Each word is defined on the page where it first appears. Preview this list of words before you read.

inestimable
disreputable
amenable
edifice
destitute
imperious
commiserate
impetuous

◆ Build Grammar Skills

PAST AND PAST PERFECT TENSES

The **past tense** of a verb indicates that an action took place prior to the present.

The **past perfect tense** indicates a past action that was completed before another action that took place in the past. It is formed with *had* and the past participle of a verb (the form ending in -*ed* or an irregular ending such as -*n* or -*t*).

In the following sentence from the story, the past perfect *had started* indicates that the water began running before the other past actions

past   past
...he ...*bought* fresh palm-wine which he *mixed*

past perfect
...with the water which *had* recently *started* running again ...

Notice other places in the story where Achebe uses the past and past perfect tenses to indicate the relationship between past events.

◆ *Literature and Your Life*

CONNECT YOUR EXPERIENCE

Different factors, such as your outlook or your circumstances, influence the way you respond to a loss: If you lose the last five dollars you had for this month, your reaction will probably be stronger than if you lose five dollars the day before you get paid for your after-school job.

The main character in "Civil Peace" faces losses more serious than that of five dollars, yet he tries to keep a positive attitude.

Journal Writing What strategies do you use to keep a positive attitude?

THEMATIC FOCUS: PEOPLE AND STYLES

The changes in the world of the main character broaden his horizons, but they also create difficulty. His experiences may lead you to ask yourself, "How do I deal with the difficulties of change?"

◆ Background for Understanding

HISTORY

In the late 1800's, the British annexed lands in west Africa, eventually setting up the colony of Nigeria. Local rulers resisted British domination, and in 1960, Nigeria finally achieved independence.

Religious, economic, and ethnic divisions flared after independence. The Ibo in the southeast felt that the Muslim Huasa-Fulani of the north dominated Nigeria. The Ibo seceded from Nigeria, setting up the independent Republic of Biafra. A brutal civil war followed, and in 1970, a defeated Biafra rejoined Nigeria. "Civil Peace" takes place in the aftermath of this civil war.

◆ Literary Focus

KEY STATEMENT

Just as a key unlocks a door, **key statements** unlock the meaning of a work. Key statements often go beyond the events of a particular story or poem and point to a general truth about life.

Chinua Achebe uses repetition to emphasize one key statement in "Civil Peace." Such key statements can help you unlock the meaning behind the tale. Use a graphic organizer like the one shown to identify and explore the meaning of key statements in "Civil Peace."

◆ Reading Strategy

PRIOR BACKGROUND KNOWLEDGE

When a story takes you to another country or introduces you to unfamiliar people and places, you may feel the need for a "guide." Your **prior knowledge**—what you already know and can relate to—can guide you in understanding the new experiences and ideas.

In "Civil Peace," Achebe tells about a man in a particular historical situation—a man returning home after the civil war in Nigeria. Even if you have not lived through a war, you can use your prior knowledge of coping with loss and gain to understand the man's experiences.

Key Statement	Possible Meaning
Happy survival!	

Civil Peace

Chinua Achebe

Jonathan Iwegbu counted himself extraordinarily lucky. "Happy survival!" meant so much more to him than just a current fashion of greeting old friends in the first hazy days of peace. It went deep to his heart. He had come out of the war with five inestimable blessings—his head, his wife Maria's head and the heads of three out of their four children. As a bonus he also had his old bicycle—a miracle too but naturally not to be compared to the safety of five human heads.

The bicycle had a little history of its own. One day at the height of the war it was commandeered "for urgent military action." Hard as its loss would have been to him he would still have let it go without a thought had he not had some doubts about the genuineness of the officer. It wasn't his disreputable rags, nor the toes peeping out of one blue and one brown canvas shoe, nor yet the two stars of his rank done obviously in a hurry in biro,[1] that troubled Jonathan; many good and heroic soldiers looked the same or worse. It was rather a certain lack of grip and firmness in his manner. So Jonathan, suspecting he might

---

1. **biro** (bir´ ō) *n*.: Ballpoint pen.

◆ **Build Vocabulary**

inestimable (in es´ tə mə bəl) *adj*.: Priceless; beyond measure

disreputable (dis rep´ yŏŏ tə bəl) *adj*.: Not respectable

amenable (ə mē´ nə bəl) *adj*.: Responsive; open

◀ Critical Viewing
Why would a bicycle
be important to
Jonathan, who lives
in a landscape like
the one shown?
[Infer]

be <u>amenable</u> to influence, rummaged in his raf-
fia bag and produced the two pounds with
which he had been going to buy firewood which
his wife, Maria, retailed to camp officials for extra stock-fish and corn meal, and got his bicycle back. That night he buried it in the little
clearing in the bush where the dead of the
camp, including his own youngest son, were

buried. When he dug it up again a year later after the surrender all it needed was a little palm-
oil greasing. "Nothing puzzles God," he said in
wonder.

He put it to immediate use as a taxi and
accumulated a small pile of Biafran[2] money

2. **Biafran** (bē äf´ rən) *adj.*: From the east part of the
Gulf of Guinea on the west coast of Africa.

ferrying camp officials and their families across the four-mile stretch to the nearest tarred road. His standard charge per trip was six pounds and those who had the money were only glad to be rid of some of it in this way. At the end of a fortnight[3] he had made a small fortune of one hundred and fifteen pounds.

Then he made the journey to Enugu and found another miracle waiting for him. It was unbelievable. He rubbed his eyes and looked again and it was still standing there before him. But, needless to say, even that monumental blessing must be accounted also totally inferior to the five heads in the family. This newest miracle was his little house in Ogui Overside. Indeed nothing puzzles God! Only two houses away a huge concrete <u>edifice</u> some wealthy contractor had put up just before the war was a mountain of rubble. And here was Jonathan's little zinc house of no regrets built with mud blocks quite intact! Of course the doors and windows were missing and five sheets off the roof. But what was that? And anyhow he had returned to Enugu early enough to pick up bits of old zinc and wood and soggy sheets of cardboard lying around the neighborhood before thousands more came out of their forest holes looking for the same things. He got a <u>destitute</u> carpenter with one old hammer, a blunt plane and a few bent and rusty nails in his tool bag to turn this assortment of wood, paper and metal into door and window shutters for five Nigerian shillings or fifty Biafran pounds. He paid the pounds, and moved in with his overjoyed family carrying five heads on their shoulders.

His children picked mangoes near the military cemetery and sold them to soldiers' wives for a few pennies—real pennies this time—and his wife started making breakfast akara balls[4]

---

3. **fortnight** (fôrt´ nīt) *n.*: Two weeks.
4. **akara** (ə kär´ ə) **balls:** Balls made of cooked yams.

◆ Build Vocabulary

edifice (ed´ i fis) *n.*: Building

destitute (des´ tə tōōt´) *adj.*: Poverty stricken; in great need

for neighbors in a hurry to start life again. With his family earnings he took his bicycle to the villages around and bought fresh palm-wine which he mixed generously in his rooms with the water which had recently started running again in the public tap down the road, and opened up a bar for soldiers and other lucky people with good money.

At first he went daily, then every other day and finally once a week, to the offices of the Coal Corporation where he used to be a miner, to find out what was what. The only thing he did find out in the end was that that little house of his was even a greater blessing than he had thought. Some of his fellow ex-miners who had nowhere to return at the end of the day's waiting just slept outside the doors of the offices and cooked what meal they could scrounge together in Bournvita tins. As the weeks lengthened and still nobody could say what was what Jonathan discontinued his weekly visits altogether and faced his palm-wine bar.

But nothing puzzles God. Came the day of the windfall when after five days of endless scuffles in queues[5] and counterqueues in the sun outside the Treasury he had twenty pounds counted into his palms as ex-gratia[6] award for the rebel money he had turned in. It was like Christmas for him and for many others like him when the payments began. They called it (since few could manage its proper official name) egg-rasher.

◆ **Literary Focus**
How does the key statement that begins this paragraph capture the spirit of Jonathan's attitude toward good and bad events?

As soon as the pound notes were placed in his palm Jonathan simply closed it tight over them and buried fist and money inside his trouser pocket. He had to be extra careful because he had seen a man a couple of days earlier collapse into near-madness in an instant before that oceanic crowd because no sooner had he got his twenty pounds than some heartless ruffian picked it off him. Though it was not

---

5. **queues** (kyōōz) *n.*: Lines.
6. **ex-gratia** (eks grä´ shē ə): As a favor.

right that a man in such an extremity of agony should be blamed yet many in the queues that day were able to remark quietly at the victim's carelessness, especially after he pulled out the innards of his pocket and revealed a hole in it big enough to pass a thief's head. But of course he had insisted that the money had been in the other pocket, pulling it out too to show its comparative wholeness. So one had to be careful.

Jonathan soon transferred the money to his left hand and pocket so as to leave his right free for shaking hands should the need arise, though by fixing his gaze at such an elevation as to miss all approaching human faces he made sure that the need did not arise, until he got home.

He was normally a heavy sleeper but that night he heard all the neighborhood noises die down one after another. Even the night watchman who knocked the hour on some metal somewhere in the distance had fallen silent after knocking one o'clock. That must have been the last thought in Jonathan's mind before he was finally carried away himself. He couldn't have been gone for long, though, when he was violently awakened again.

▲ **Critical Viewing** What is the effect of this extreme close-up photo? **[Interpret]**

♦ **Reading Strategy**

How does your prior knowledge of anxiety help you understand Jonathan's experience here?

"Who is knocking?" whispered his wife lying beside him on the floor.

"I don't know," he whispered back breathlessly.

The second time the knocking came it was so

♦ **Build Vocabulary**

imperious (im pir´ ē əs) *adj*.: Commanding; powerful

loud and <u>imperious</u> that the rickety old door could have fallen down.

"Who is knocking?" he asked them, his voice parched and trembling.

"Na tief-man and him people," came the cool reply. "Make you hopen de door."[7] This was followed by the heaviest knocking of all.

Maria was the first to raise the alarm, then he followed and all their children.

7. **"Na tief-man . . . hopen de door":** The man is speaking a dialect of English that includes some word forms and grammar of his own language. He is saying, "I am not a thief with my accomplices. Open the door." As you read the rest of the story, read aloud when characters speak this way and try to figure out what they are saying.

Civil Peace ♦ 553

"Police-o! Thieves-o! Neighbors-o! Police-o! We are lost! We are dead! Neighbors, are you asleep? Wake up! Police-o!"

This went on for a long time and then stopped suddenly. Perhaps they had scared the thief away. There was total silence. But only for a short while.

"You done finish?" asked the voice outside. "Make we help you small. Oya, everybody!"

"Police-o! Tief-man-so! Neighbors-o! we done loss-o! Police-o! . . ."

There were at least five other voices besides the leader's.

Jonathan and his family were now completely paralyzed by terror. Maria and the children sobbed inaudibly like lost souls. Jonathan groaned continuously.

The silence that followed the thieves' alarm vibrated horribly. Jonathan all but begged their leader to speak again and be done with it.

"My frien," said he at long last, "we don try our best for call dem but I tink say dem all done sleep-o . . . So wetin we go do now? Sometaim you wan call soja? Or you wan make we call dem for you? Soja better pass police. No be so?"

"Na so!" replied his men. Jonathan thought he heard even more voices now than before and groaned heavily. His legs were sagging under him and his throat felt like sandpaper.

"My frien, why you no de talk again. I de ask you say you wan make we call soja?"

"No."

"Awrighto. Now make we talk business. We no be bad tief. We no like for make trouble. Trouble done finish. War done finish and all the katakata wey de for inside. No Civil War again. This time na Civil Peace. No be so?"

"Na so!" answered the horrible chorus.

"What do you want from me? I am a poor man. Everything I had went with this war. Why do you come to me? You know people who have money. We . . ."

◆ Build Vocabulary

commiserate (kə miz′ ər āt′) v.: Sympathize; share suffering

"Awright! We know say you no get plenty money. But we sef no get even anini. So derefore make you open dis window and give us one hundred pound and we go commot. Orderwise we de come for inside now to show you guitar-boy like dis . . ."

A volley of automatic fire rang through the sky. Maria and the children began to weep aloud again.

"Ah, missisi de cry again. No need for dat. We done talk say we na good tief. We just take our small money and go nwayorly. No molest. Abi we de molest?"

"At all!" sang the chorus.

"My friends," began Jonathan hoarsely. "I hear what you say and I thank you. If I had one hundred pounds . . ."

"Lookia my frien, no be play we come play for your house. If we make mistake and step for inside you no go like am-o. So derefore . . ."

"To God who made me; if you come inside and find one hundred pounds, take it and shoot me and shoot my wife and children. I swear to God. The only money I have in this life is this twenty-pounds *egg-rasher* they gave me today . . ."

"Ok. Time de go. Make you open dis window and bring the twenty pound. We go manage am like dat."

There were now loud murmurs of dissent among the chorus: "Na lie de man de lie; e get plenty money . . . Make we go inside and search properly well . . . Wetin be twenty pound? . . ."

"Shurrup!" rang the leader's voice like a lone shot in the sky and silenced the murmuring at once. "Are you dere? Bring the money quick!"

"I am coming," said Jonathan fumbling in the darkness with the key of the small wooden box he kept by his side on the mat.

At the first sign of light as neighbors and others assembled to commiserate with him he was already strapping his five-gallon demijohn[8] to his bicycle carrier and his wife, sweating in the open fire, was turning over akara balls in a

---

8. **demijohn** (dem′ i jän′) n.: Large bottle.

wide clay bowl of boiling oil. In the corner his eldest son was rinsing out dregs of yesterday's palm-wine from old beer bottles.

"I count it as nothing," he told his sympathizers, his eyes on the rope he was tying. "What is *egg-rasher*? Did I depend on it last week? Or is it greater than other things that went with the war? I say, let *egg-rasher* perish in the flames! Let it go where everything else has gone. Nothing puzzles God."

Beyond Literature

Cultural Connection

Changing Boundaries in Africa

In 1945, four European powers—Britain, France, Belgium, and Portugal—controlled almost all of Africa. However, a great liberation took place in Africa following World War II. Slowly at first, and then with increasing speed, the peoples of Africa regained their independence.
Activity In the struggle for independence, some nations, like Nigeria, have experienced internal difficulties. Using library or Internet resources, research and compare the cultural changes that have occurred in two or more African nations since they regained independence.

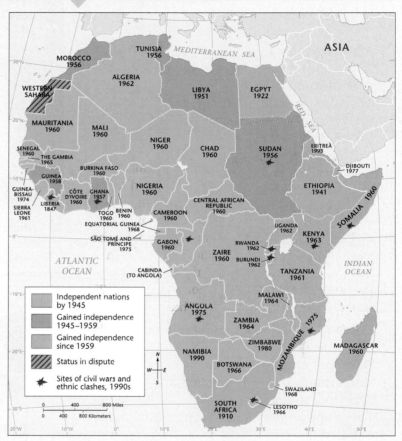

Guide for Responding

◆ Literature and Your Life

Reader's Response In what ways do you identify with Jonathan? Explain.
Thematic Focus Did reading about Jonathan's experiences make you feel more or less connected to people in Nigeria? Explain.

☑ Check Your Comprehension

1. What does Jonathan Iwegbu count as his greatest blessings? For what else is he grateful?
2. How does Jonathan earn money?
3. How do Jonathan and his family behave after their money is stolen?

Africa

David Diop

Translated by Ulli Beier

to my Mother

Africa my Africa
Africa of proud warriors in the ancestral
    savannahs[1]
Africa my grandmother sings of
Beside her distant river
5 I have never seen you
But my gaze is full of your blood
Your black blood spilt over the fields
The blood of your sweat
The sweat of your toil
10 The toil of slavery
The slavery of your children
Africa, tell me Africa,
Are you the back that bends
Lies down under the weight of humbleness?
15 The trembling back striped red
That says yes to the sjambok[2] on the roads
    of noon?
Solemnly a voice answers me
"Impetuous child, that young and sturdy tree
That tree that grows
20 There splendidly alone among white and
    faded flowers
Is Africa, your Africa. It puts forth new
    shoots
With patience and stubbornness puts forth
    new shoots
Slowly its fruits grow to have
The bitter taste of liberty."

---

1. **savannahs** (sə vä´ nəz) *n.*: Tropical grassland containing scattered trees.
2. **sjambok** (jam´ bôk) *n.*: Whip.

◆ **Build Vocabulary**

impetuous (im pech´ o͞o əs) *adj.*: Impulsive; passionate

Traditional Yam Harvest, John Mainga, LAMU, The Gallery of Contemporary African Art

▲ **Critical Viewing** Discuss how this painting reflects the thoughts conveyed in both poems. [Synthesize]

Old Song

t r a d i t i o n a l

Do not seek too much fame,
but do not seek obscurity.
Be proud.
But do not remind the world of your deeds.
5 Excel when you must,
but do not excel the world.
Many heroes are not yet born,
many have already died.
To be alive to hear this song is a victory.

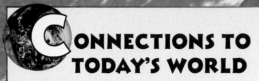

CONNECTIONS TO TODAY'S WORLD

Until the 1990's, the right to vote and equal access to schools and public facilities were denied to South Africa's black majority.

However, mounting international pressure helped bring an end to **apartheid**—South Africa's system of forced segregation. Among the many voices to speak out against apartheid were musicians such as Peter Gabriel, who wrote the following song of tribute to Stephen Biko, a pioneer in the struggle against apartheid. Biko was killed by police in 1977.

1. Like poetry, song lyrics use a variety of sound devices, such as rhyme and repetition, to create a rhythmical effect and emphasize meaning. Explain how Gabriel uses rhyme and repetition in "Biko."
2. Look at lines 17–20. (a) In what way do they resemble an aphorism? (b) Explain what they mean in terms of the struggle for justice.
3. Explain how the last line of Bei Dao's poem— "every death reverberates forever"—is similar in meaning to lines 17–20 of this song.

BIKO
Peter Gabriel

September '77
Port Elizabeth weather fine
It was business as usual
In police room 619
5 Oh Biko, Biko, because Biko
Oh Biko, Biko, because Biko
Yihla Moja, Yihla Moja
—The man is dead

When I try to sleep at night
10 I can only dream in red
The outside world is black and white
With only one colour dead
Oh Biko, Biko, because Biko
Oh Biko, Biko, because Biko
15 Yihla Moja, Yihla Moja
—The man is dead

You can blow out a candle
But you can't blow out a fire
Once the flames begin to catch
20 The wind will blow it higher
Oh Biko, Biko, because Biko
Yihla Moja, Yihla Moja
—The man is dead

And the eyes of the world are
25   watching now
    watching now

Guide for Responding

◆ *Literature and Your Life*

Reader's Response Which poem did you find more powerful? Why?

Thematic Focus These poems suggest that success can rise out of failure. Explain why you agree or disagree.

Reader's Journal How do you define success? Write a short journal entry in which you explain what makes a person successful.

☑ Check Your Comprehension

1. What question does the speaker of "Africa" ask?
2. In what manner does a voice answer the speaker?
3. How does the voice describe liberty?
4. What advice about fame is found in "Old Song"?

Guide for Responding (continued)

◆ Critical Thinking

INTERPRET

1. In "Civil Peace," how did the war affect the lives of people like Jonathan? **[Infer]**
2. Compare and contrast the attitude toward money of the leader of the thieves with that of Jonathan. **[Compare and Contrast]**
3. How would you sum up Jonathan's attitude toward life? **[Interpret]**

EVALUATE

4. Why is "Civil Peace" an appropriate title for this story? Consider the meanings of the word *civil*. **[Assess]**

EXTEND

5. What does Diop's poem "Africa" tell you about the history of the African continent? Explain. **[Social Studies Link]**

◆ Reading Strategy

PRIOR KNOWLEDGE

Although "Civil Peace" takes place after a civil war in another country, your **prior knowledge** about dealing with unexpected events can help you understand the main character's experiences and reactions.

1. Jonathan frequently quotes a proverb as a reaction to events in his life. What proverbs or sayings do you use to respond to events in your life?
2. Jonathan experiences several turns of fortune during this story. Compare and contrast his reactions to his changing luck with the way you respond to life's ups and downs.

◆ Literary Focus

KEY STATEMENTS

Chinua Achebe makes use of a proverb that has been important in Ibo life. This proverb also acts as a **key statement** that throws light on the central meaning of his story.

1. What does the key statement, "Happy survival!" reveal about Jonathan's values?
2. Why do you think the proverb "Nothing puzzles God" is repeated in the story? How does it help reveal the story's message about life?

◆ Build Vocabulary

USING THE LATIN ROOT -reput-

Write the sentences below in your notebook and fill in the blanks with *disreputable, reputation,* or *reputed.*

Jonathan is ___?___ to be a careful man. He also has a ___?___ for honesty. Unfortunately, he was robbed by some ___?___ men.

USING THE WORD BANK: Context

Copy the following book titles in your notebook. Next to each title, write the word from the Word Bank that you would expect to find in the book.

1. *The Architecture of Frank Lloyd Wright*
2. *Kings and Queens of the World*
3. *Sharing Your Pain*
4. *Getting Others to Agree*
5. *The Causes of Poverty*
6. *Jewels and Gemstones*
7. *Criminals I Have Known*
8. *The Life of a Daredevil*

◆ Build Grammar Skills

PAST AND PAST PERFECT TENSES

Past tense indicates an action or condition that began and ended at a given time in the past. **Past perfect tense** (formed with *had* plus a past participle) shows an action or condition that was completed when another past action began.

Practice In your notebook, copy each of these sentences. Circle the past tense verbs and underline the verbs in the past perfect tense.

1. Only two houses away a huge concrete edifice some wealthy contractor had put up before the war was a mountain of rubble.
2. ...he had returned to Enugu early enough ... before thousands more came out of their forest holes ...
3. ...that little house of his was even a greater blessing than he had thought.
4. ...he pulled out the innards of his pocket and revealed a hole in it.... But of course he had insisted that the money had been in the other pocket ...
5. This went on for a long time and then stopped suddenly. Perhaps they had scared the thief away.

Build Your Portfolio

 ## Idea Bank

Writing

1. **News Interview** Create a list of five interview questions a reporter covering the aftermath of the civil war might ask Jonathan. Based on details in the story, write Jonathan's answers to the questions. [Social Studies Link]

2. **Human-Interest Article** Use the events described in the story to write a human-interest article about one family's experiences after the civil war.

3. **Poem** Write a short poem expressing some thoughts or feelings that the story "Civil Peace" evoked in you.

Speaking, Listening, and Viewing

4. **Oral Interpretation** Perform the poems "Africa" and "Old Song" for classmates. Use meaning and punctuation to guide where you pause. [Performing Arts Link]

5. **Multimedia Collage** Create a collage composed of magazine pictures, your own artwork, poems, music or musical lyrics, and words, which shows your interpretation of the proverb "Nothing puzzles God." If possible, create and share your multimedia collage on a computer. [Art Link]

Researching and Representing

6. **Proverbs Presentation** With a panel of "experts," collect some proverbs and sayings. Present the origins and applications of each, and speculate on why the saying has survived the test of time.

7. **Scenic Sketches** Sketch the settings for several scenes of a movie version of "Civil Peace." Possible scenes to include are Jonathan's home, the road to Enugu, and the outside of the Treasury. [Art Link]

Online Activity **www.phlit.phschool.com**

 ## Guided Writing Lesson

Annotated Map of Nigeria

The setting of this story is Nigeria, a country of great diversity and political and social change. Conduct research and create an **annotated map** of Nigeria to instruct readers about significant features of the country's landscape, ethnic diversity, and types of industry. The annotations you write will give essential information about each aspect of Nigeria you decide to include. The following tip will help you in preparing your annotations.

Writing Skills Focus: Brevity and Clarity

When you need to convey a great deal of information in a small space, **brevity and clarity** (being brief and being clear) are especially important. Bulleted lists, numbered sentences, and charts are a few ways you can communicate important information in a small space. Annotations that you write in sentence form should be brief and to the point.

Prewriting Brainstorm for a list of questions you could research to help someone better understand the story. For instance, researching the question *In which regions do different ethnic groups live?* might give insight into the causes and boundaries of the civil war.

Drafting Put numbers on the map to locate the area to which each annotation refers. Then write your annotations. Try to avoid making the map too crowded, but include the facts that will be most helpful to readers.

Revising Look back at the biography of Achebe and the story. See if there is any information that you could present that would further enhance reading. Review each of your annotations to make sure they are not only short but clear.

Guide for Reading

Barbara Kimenye (1940–)

Decades ago, when Barbara Kimenye (ki men´ yā) was raising her sons in Uganda, the boys' grandmother in England would send them children's storybooks. Too often, however, the gulf between English and African experience made it difficult for the boys to relate to the stories.

What Is Snow? Snow, for instance, was completely foreign to them, as were many of the everyday activities of the English characters. Though Africa had a long tradition of fables and folk tales aimed at young audiences, such stories were set in the past. Kimenye realized that her sons would prefer children's fiction about contemporary Africa.

However, such stories were very scarce. To remedy the situation, Kimenye began writing a series of children's books about an African boy named Moses—a series that remains enormously popular in Africa today.

Ugandan Roots Born in the Buganda (bōō gan´ dä) region of Uganda, Kimenye worked as secretary and librarian for Buganda's hereditary ruler, the Kabaka, and also served in his Ministry of Education.

In 1965, she published her first book, *Kalasanda,* a collection of stories set in Buganda. Her first children's book, *The Smugglers,* appeared one year later, along with a sequel to the story collection, *Kalasanda Revisited.* In the 1970's, she won additional fame throughout East Africa as a columnist for the newspaper *Uganda Nation.*

Driven from her homeland in the political turmoil that overtook it, Kimenye eventually joined family members in England. There she found employment as a social worker and also continued her writing. Her most recent publications include several works of children's fiction as well as a modern African cookbook. In "The Winner," Kimenye incorporates the culture of her beloved native Uganda into a gently humorous story.

◆ Build Vocabulary

LATIN WORD ROOTS: -aud-

Pius Ndawula, the main character in Kimenye's story, swallows "audibly" when a reporter asks him a question. The word *audibly* contains the Latin root *-aud-*, which means "hear." *Audibly* means "loudly enough to be heard."

| unpretentious |
| edification |
| garrulous |
| audibly |
| incredulity |
| aplomb |
| formidable |
| impetuous |

WORD BANK

As you read the story, you will encounter these words. Each word is defined on the page where it first appears. Preview the list before you read.

◆ Build Grammar Skills

APPOSITIVE PHRASES

To add information to their stories, writers use **appositive phrases**—noun phrases placed near other nouns or pronouns in order to explain them further.

An appositive phrase is not part of the basic sentence, but adds information to it. Usually, it interrupts the sentence and is set off with commas or other punctuation marks. In the following example from "The Winner," the italicized appositive phrase provides more information about the noun *Ggombolola Headquarters.*

> . . . When it had met at the Ggombolola Headquarters—*the postal address of everyone residing within a radius of fifteen miles*—Musisi had brought it out personally . . .

The Winner

◆ *Literature and Your Life*

CONNECT YOUR EXPERIENCE

Suppose that you won a great deal of money in a lottery or television quiz show. What would you do with it? How do you think it would affect your life?

Pius, the main character in "The Winner," is delighted to learn that he is the winner in a big lottery held in Uganda. However, not everything turns out as he expects.

Journal Writing As the winner of a large sum of money, briefly discuss your plans for spending it.

THEMATIC FOCUS: PEOPLE AND STYLES

"The Winner" takes place in Uganda, yet the characters may not seem all that unfamiliar. As you read, ask yourself: What do the characters have in common with contemporary Americans?

◆ Background for Understanding

CULTURE

Kalasanda, the fictional setting of "The Winner," is a village in the Buganda region of the East African nation of Uganda. Once a British colony, Uganda won independence in 1962, and the story probably takes place a year or two after this. The Buganda region, on the north shore of Lake Victoria, is the traditional homeland of the Ganda people, the largest of Uganda's many ethnic groups.

Because these ethnic groups have different native tongues, English is Uganda's official language. It is used for government and business communications. Not everyone speaks or reads English, however, and even fewer people knew it in the early 1960's. Thus, only a handful of characters can read the English telegram that the character named Pius receives.

◆ Literary Focus

SURPRISE ENDING

Some stories have **surprise endings,** or unexpected twists at the end. Sometimes the author includes details that mislead you about the ending. More often, authors try to make a surprise ending believable by providing some clues that point to it.

As you read "The Winner," consider what is surprising about the ending. Also, consider whether or not the ending seems believable and what clues to the ending the author provided.

◆ Reading Strategy

IDENTIFY RELATIONSHIPS IN THE TEXT

When you read a story, you may be able to anticipate a surprise ending if you identify relationships in the text:

- the sequence of events
- causes and effects of important actions
- distinctions between important and unimportant events

As you read "The Winner," keep track of the sequence of events. Also, figure out how one event causes another by using a diagram like this one:

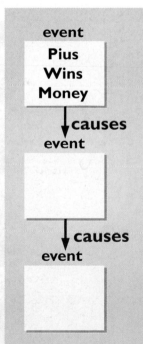

The Winner

Barbara Kimenye

Drinking Water, Rosemary Karuga, Contemporary African Art Gallery, New York City

▲ **Critical Viewing** What does this picture suggest about the setting for the story? **[Speculate]**

When Pius Ndawula won the football pools,[1] overnight he seemed to become the most popular man in Buganda.[2] Hosts of relatives converged upon him from the four corners of the kingdom: cousins and nephews, nieces and uncles, of whose existence he had never before been aware, turned up in Kalasanda by the busload, together with crowds of individuals who, despite their downtrodden appearance, assured Pius that they and they alone were capable of seeing that his money was properly invested—preferably in their own particular businesses! Also lurking around Pius's <u>unpretentious</u> mud hut were newspaper reporters, slick young men weighed down with cameras and sporting loud checked caps or trilbies set at conspicuously jaunty angles, and serious young men from Radio Uganda who were anxious to record Pius's delight at his astonishing luck for the <u>edification</u> of the Uganda listening public.

The rest of Kalasanda were so taken by surprise that they could only call and briefly congratulate Pius before being elbowed out of the way by his more <u>garrulous</u> relations. All, that is to say, except Pius's greatest friend Salongo, the custodian of the Ssabalangira's tomb. He came and planted himself firmly in the house, and nobody attempted to move him. Almost blind, and very lame, he had tottered out with the aid of a stout stick. Just to see him arrive had caused a minor sensation in the village, for he hadn't left the tomb for years. But recognizing at last a chance to house Ssabalangira's remains in a state befitting his former glory, made the slow, tortuous journey worthwhile to Salongo.

1. **football pools:** A kind of lottery based on the performance of soccer teams.
2. **Buganda** (bo͞o gän´ dä): An area of southern Uganda, on the northern shore of Lake Victoria.

Nantondo hung about long enough to have her picture taken with Pius. Or rather, she managed to slip beside him just as the cameras clicked, and so it was that every Uganda newspaper, on the following day, carried a front-page photograph of "Mr. Pius Ndawula and his happy wife," a caption that caused Pius to shake with rage and threaten legal proceedings, but over which Nantondo gloated as she proudly showed it to everybody she visited.

"Tell us, Mr. Ndawula, what do you intend to do with all the money you have won . . . ?"

"Tell us, Mr. Ndawula, how often have you completed pools coupons . . . ?"

"Tell us . . . Tell us . . . Tell us . . ."

Pius's head was reeling under this bombardment of questions, and he was even more confused by Salongo's constant nudging and muttered advice to "Say nothing!" Nor did the relatives make things easier. Their persistent clamoring for his attention, and the way they kept shoving their children under his nose, made it impossible for him to think, let alone talk.

It isn't at all easy, when you have lived for sixty-five years in complete obscurity, to adjust yourself in a matter of hours to the role of a celebrity, and the strain was beginning to tell.

Behind the hut—Pius had no proper kitchen—gallons of tea were being boiled, whilst several of the female cousins were employed in ruthlessly hacking down the bunches of *matoke* from his meager plantains[3] to cook food for everybody. One woman—she had introduced herself as Cousin Sarah—discovered Pius's hidden store of banana beer, and dished it out to all and sundry as though it were her own. Pius had become very wary of Cousin Sarah. He didn't like the way in which she kept loudly remarking that he needed a woman about the place, and he was even more seriously alarmed when suddenly Salongo gave him a painful dig in the ribs and muttered, "You'll have to watch that one—she's a sticker!"

Everybody who came wanted to see the telegram that announced Pius's win. When it had arrived at the Ggombolola Headquarters—

the postal address of everyone residing within a radius of fifteen miles—Musisi had brought it out personally, delighted to be the bearer of such good tidings. At Pius's request he had gone straightaway to tell Salongo, and then back to his office to send an acknowledgment on behalf of Pius to the pools firm, leaving the old man to dream rosy dreams. An extension of his small coffee *shamba*,[4] a new roof on his house—or maybe an entirely new house—concrete blocks this time, with a veranda perhaps. Then there were hens. Salongo and he had always said there was money in hens these days, now that the women ate eggs and chicken; not that either of them agreed with the practice. Say what you liked, women who ate chicken and eggs were fairly asking to be infertile! That woman welfare officer who came around snooping occasionally, tried to say it was all nonsense, that chicken meat and eggs made bigger and better babies. Well, they might look bigger and better, but nobody could deny that they were fewer! Which only goes to show.

But news spreads fast in Africa—perhaps the newspapers have contacts in the pools offices. Anyway, before the telegram had even reached Pius, announcements were appearing in the local newspapers, and Pius was still quietly lost in his private dreams when the first batch of visitors arrived. At first he was at a loss to understand what was happening. People he hadn't seen for years and only recognized with difficulty fell upon him with cries of joy. "Cousin Pius, the family are delighted!" "Cousin Pius, why have you not visited us all this time?"

Pius was pleased to see his nearest and dearest gathered around him. It warmed his old heart once more to find himself in the bosom of his family, and he welcomed them effusively. The second crowd to arrive were no less well received, but there was a marked coolness on the part of their forerunners.

However, as time had gone by and the flood of strange faces had gained momentum, Pius's

> ◆ **Literary Focus**
> What does the number of visitors suggest about the way the story might end?

---

3. **plantains** (plan´ tinz) *n.*: Tropical plants with broad flat leaves. The banana-like fruit, called *matoke,* is served cooked like a vegetable.

4. *shamba* (shäm´ bä) *n.*: A field or garden for a particular crop; a small plantation.

shamba had come to resemble a political meeting. All to be seen from the door of the house was a turbulent sea of white *kanzus* and brilliant *busutis*,[5] and the house itself was full of people and tobacco smoke.

The precious telegram was passed from hand to hand until it was reduced to a limp fragment of paper with the lettering partly obliterated: not that it mattered very much, for only a few members of the company could read English.

"Now, Mr. Ndawula, we are ready to take the recording." The speaker was a slight young man wearing a checked shirt. "I shall ask you a few questions, and you simply answer me in your normal voice." Pius looked at the leather box with its two revolving spools, and licked his lips. "Say nothing!" came a hoarse whisper from Salongo. The young man steadfastly ignored him, and went ahead in his best BBC manner.[6] "Well, Mr. Ndawula, first of all let me congratulate you on your winning the pools. Would you like to tell our listeners what it feels like suddenly to find yourself rich?" There was an uncomfortable pause, during which Pius stared mesmerized at the racing spools and the young man tried frantically to span the gap by asking, "I mean, have you any plans for the future?" Pius swallowed <u>audibly</u>, and opened his mouth to say something, but shut it again when Salongo growled, "Tell him nothing!"

The young man snapped off the machine, shaking his head in exasperation. "Look here, sir, all I want you to do is to say something—I'm not asking you to make a speech! Now, I'll tell you what. I shall ask you again what it feels like suddenly to come into money, and you say something like 'It was a wonderful surprise, and naturally I feel very pleased'—and will you ask your friend not to interrupt! Got it? Okay, off we go!"

The machine was again switched on, and the man brightly put his question, "Now, Mr. Ndawula, what does it feel like to win the pools?" Pius swallowed, then quickly chanted in a voice all off key, "It was a wonderful surprise and naturally I feel very happy and will you ask your

friend not to interrupt!" The young man nearly wept. This happened to be his first assignment as a radio interviewer, and it looked like it would be his last. He switched off the machine and mourned his lusterless future, groaning. At that moment Cousin Sarah caught his eye. "Perhaps I can help you," she said. "I am Mr. Ndawula's cousin." She made this pronouncement in a manner that suggested Pius had no others. The young man brightened considerably. "Well, madam, if you could tell me something about Mr. Ndawula's plans, I would be most grateful." Cousin Sarah folded her arms across her imposing bosom, and when the machine again started up, she was off. Yes, Mr. Ndawula was very happy about the money. No, she didn't think he had any definite plans on how to spend it—with all these people about he didn't have time to think. Yes, Mr. Ndawula lived completely alone, but she was prepared to stay and look after him for as long as he needed her. Here a significant glance passed between the other women in the room, who clicked their teeth and let out long "Eeeeeehs!" of <u>incredulity</u>. Yes, she believed she was Mr. Ndawula's nearest living relative by marriage . . .

Pius listened to her confident <u>aplomb</u> with growing horror, while Salongo frantically nudged him and whispered, "There! What did I tell you! That woman's a sticker!"

Around three in the afternoon, *matoke* and tea were served, the *matoke*, on wide fresh plantain leaves, since Pius owned only three plates, and the tea in anything handy—tin cans, old jars, etc.—because he was short of cups too. Pius ate very little, but he was glad of the tea. He had shaken hands with so many people that his arm ached, and he was tired of the chatter and the comings and goings in his house of all these strangers. Most of all he was tired of Cousin Sarah, who insisted on treating him like an idiot invalid. She kept everybody else at bay, as far as she possibly could, and when one woman plonked a sticky fat baby

---

5. *kanzus* (kän′ zōōz) . . . *busutis* (bōō sōō′ tēz): Long, flowing robes, the first worn by men, the second by women.

6. **BBC manner:** Polite and polished style of the British Broadcasting Corporation's reporters.

◆ **Build Vocabulary**

audibly (ô′ də blē) *adv.*: Loudly enough to be heard
incredulity (in′ krə dyōō′ lə tē) *n.*: Disbelief; astonishment
aplomb (ə pläm′) *n.*: Poise; self-assurance

on his lap, Cousin Sarah dragged the child away as though it were infectious. Naturally, a few cross words were exchanged between Sarah and the fond mother, but by this time Pius was past caring.

Yosefu Mukasa and Kibuka called in the early evening, when some of the relatives were departing with effusive promises to come again tomorrow. They were both alarmed at the weariness they saw on Pius's face. The old man looked utterly worn out, his skin gray and sickly. Also, they were a bit taken aback by the presence of Cousin Sarah, who pressed them to take tea and behaved in every respect as though she were mistress of the house. "I believe my late husband knew you very well, sir," she told Yosefu. "He used to be a Miruka chief in Buyaga County. His name was Kivumbi." "Ah, yes," Yosefu replied, "I remember Kivumbi very well indeed. We often hunted together. I was sorry to hear of his death. He was a good man." Cousin Sarah shrugged her shoulders. "Yes, he was a good man. But what the Lord giveth, He also taketh away." Thus was the late Kivumbi dismissed from the conversation.

Hearing all this enabled Pius to define the exact relationship between himself and Cousin Sarah, and even by Kiganda standards it was virtually nonexistent, for the late Kivumbi had been the stepson of one of Pius's cousins.

"Your stroke of luck seems to have exhausted you, Pius," Kibuka remarked, when he and Yosefu were seated on the rough wooden chairs brought forth by Cousin Sarah.

Salongo glared at the world in general and snarled, "Of course he is exhausted! Who wouldn't be with all these scavengers collected to pick his bones?" Pius hushed him as one would a child. "No, no, Salongo. It is quite natural that my family should gather round me at a time like this. Only I fear I am perhaps a little too old for all this excitement."

Salongo spat expertly through the open doorway, narrowly missing a group of guests who were preparing to bed down, and said, "That woman doesn't think he's too old. She's out to catch him. I've seen her type elsewhere!"

Yosefu's mouth quirked with amusement at the thought that "elsewhere" could only mean the Ssabalangira's tomb, which Salongo had guarded for the better part of his adult life. "Well, she's a fine woman," he remarked. "But

see here, Pius," he went on, "don't be offended by my proposal, but wouldn't it be better if you came and stayed with us at Mutunda for tonight? Miriamu would love to have you, and you look as though you need a good night's rest, which you wouldn't get here—those relatives of yours outside are preparing a fire and are ready to dance the night away!"

"I think that's a wonderful idea!" said Cousin Sarah, bouncing in to remove the tea cups. "You go with Mr. Mukasa, Cousin Pius. The change will do you as much good as the rest. And don't worry about your home—I shall stay here and look after things." Pius hesitated. "Well, I think I shall be all right here—I don't like to give Miriamu any extra work. . . ." Salongo muttered. "Go to Yosefu's. You don't want to be left alone in the house with that woman—there's no knowing what she might get up to . . . !" "I'll pack a few things for you, Pius," announced Cousin Sarah and bustled off before anything more could be said, pausing only long enough to give Salongo a look that was meant to wither him on the spot.

So Pius found himself being driven away to Mutunda in Yosefu's car, enjoying the pleasant sensation of not having to bother about a thing. Sa-longo too had been given a lift to as near the tomb as the car could travel, and his wizened old face was contorted into an irregular smile, for Pius had promised to help him build a new house for the Ssabalangira. For him the day had been well spent, despite Cousin Sarah.

◆ **Reading Strategy**
What has been the common theme in everything Sarah has done so far?

Pius spent an enjoyable evening with the Mukasas. They had a well-cooked supper, followed by a glass of cold beer as they sat back and listened to the local news on the radio. Pius had so far relaxed as to tell the Mukasas modestly that he had been interviewed by Radio Uganda that morning, and when Radio Newsreel was announced they waited breathlessly to hear his voice. But instead of Pius, Cousin Sarah came booming over the air. Until that moment the old man had completely forgotten the incident of the tape recording. In fact, he had almost forgotten Cousin Sarah. Now it all came back to him with a shiver of apprehension. Salongo was right. That woman did mean business! It was a chilling thought. However, it didn't cause him to lose any sleep. He slept like a cherub,[7] as if he hadn't a care in the world.

Because he looked so refreshed in the morning, Miriamu insisted on keeping him at Mutunda for another day. "I know you feel better, but after seeing you yesterday, I think a little holiday with us will do you good. Go home tomorrow, when the excitement has died down a bit," she advised.

Soon after lunch, as Pius was taking a nap in a chair on the veranda, Musisi drove up in the Land Rover, with Cousin Sarah by his side. Miriamu came out to greet them, barely disguising her curiosity about the <u>formidable</u> woman about whom she had heard so much. The two women sized each other up and decided to be friends.

Meanwhile, Musisi approached the old man. "Sit down, son." Pius waved him to a chair at his side. "Miriamu feeds me so well it's all I can do to keep awake."

"I am glad you are having a rest, sir." Musisi fumbled in the pocket of his jacket. "There is another telegram for you. Shall I read it?" The old man sat up expectantly and said, "If you'll be so kind."

Musisi first read the telegram in silence, then he looked at Pius and commented, "Well, sir, I'm afraid it isn't good news."

"Not good news? Has somebody died?"

Musisi smiled. "Well, no. It isn't really as bad as that. The thing is, the pools firm say that owing to an unfortunate oversight they omitted to add, in the first telegram, that the prize money is to be shared among three hundred other people."

Pius was stunned. Eventually he murmured, "Tell me, how much does that mean I shall get?"

"Three hundred into seventeen thousand pounds won't give you much over a thousand shillings."[8]

To Musisi's astonishment, Pius sat back and chuckled. "More than a thousand shillings!" he said. "Why, that's a lot of money!"

"But it's not, when you expected so much more!"

"I agree. And yet, son, what would I have done with all those thousands of pounds? I am getting past the age when I need a lot."

Miriamu brought a mat onto the veranda and she and Cousin Sarah made themselves comfortable near the men. "What a disappointment!" cried Miriamu, but Cousin Sarah sniffed and said, "I agree with Cousin Pius. He wouldn't know what to do with seventeen thousand pounds, and the family would be hanging round his neck forevermore!"

At mention of Pius's family, Musisi frowned. "I should warn you, sir, those relatives of yours have made a terrific mess of your *shamba*—your plantains have been stripped—and Mrs. Kivumbi here," nodding at Sarah, "was only just in time to prevent them digging up your sweet potatoes!"

"Yes, Cousin Pius," added Sarah. "It will take us some time to put the *shamba* back in order. They've trodden down a whole bed of young beans."

"Oh, dear," said Pius weakly. "This is dreadful news."

"Don't worry. They will soon disappear when I tell them there is no money, and then I shall send for a couple of my grandsons to come and help us do some replanting." Pius could not help but admire the way Sarah took things in her stride.

Musisi rose from his chair. "I'm afraid I can't stay any longer, so I will go now and help Cousin Sarah clear the crowd, and see you tomorrow to take you home." He and Sarah climbed back into the Land Rover and Sarah waved energetically until the vehicle was out of sight.

"Your cousin is a fine woman," Miriamu told Pius, before going indoors. Pius merely grunted, but for some odd reason he felt the remark to be a compliment to himself.

All was quiet at Pius's home when Musisi brought him home next day. He saw at once that his *shamba* was well nigh wrecked, but his drooping spirits quickly revived when Sarah placed a mug of steaming tea before him, and sat on a mat at his feet, explaining optimistically how matters could be remedied. Bit by bit he began telling her what he planned to do with the prize money, ending with, "Of course, I shan't be

---

7. **slept like a cherub:** An expression meaning "slept peacefully," using the image of a cherub, or child angel, to convey innocence and freedom from worries.

8. **pounds . . . shillings:** Ugandan currency, distinct from British pounds and shillings.

▲ **Critical Viewing** In ways does this picture reflect the modest but happy life Pius may enjoy with Sarah? **[Connect]**

The Birds, Rosemary Karuga, Contemporary African Art Gallery, New York City

able to do everything now, especially since I promised Salongo something for the tomb."

Sarah poured some more tea and said, "Well, I think the roof should have priority. I noticed last night that there are several leaks. And whilst we're about it, it would be a good idea to build another room on and a small outside kitchen. Mud and wattle[9] is cheap enough, and then the whole place can be plastered. You can still go

◆ **Build Vocabulary**

formidable (fôr′ mə də bəl) _adj._: Inspiring awe; impressive; imposing

impetuous (im pech′ o̅o̅ əs) _adj._: Deciding and acting quickly; impulsive

ahead and extend your coffee. And as for hens, well, I have six good layers at home, as well as a fine cockerel. I'll bring them over!"

Pius looked at her in silence for a long time. She is a fine looking woman, he thought, and that blue _busuti_ suits her. Nobody would ever take her for a grandmother—but why is she so anxious to throw herself at me?

"You sound as if you are planning to come and live here," he said at last, trying hard to sound casual.

Sarah turned to face him and replied, "Cousin Pius, I shall be very frank with you. Six months ago my youngest son got married and brought his wife to live with me. She's a very nice girl, but somehow I can't get used to having another woman in the house. My other son is in Kampala, and although I know I would be welcome there, he too has a wife, and three children, so if I went there I wouldn't be any better off. When I saw that bit about you in the paper, I suddenly remembered—although I don't expect you to—how you were at my wedding and so helpful to everybody. Well, I thought to myself, here is somebody who needs a good housekeeper, who needs somebody to keep the leeches off, now that he has come into money. I came along right away to take a look at you, and I can see I did the right thing. You do need me." She hesitated for a moment, and then said, "Only you might prefer to stay alone . . . I'm so used to having my own way, I never thought about that before."

Pius cleared his throat. "You're a very im-petuous woman," was all he could find to say.

A week later, Pius wandered out to the tomb and found Salongo busily polishing the Ssa-balangira's weapons. "I thought you were dead," growled the custodian, "it is so long since you came here—but then, this tomb thrives on neglect. Nobody cares that one of Buganda's greatest men lies here."

"I have been rather busy," murmured Pius. "But I didn't forget my promise to you. Here! I've brought you a hundred shillings, and I only wish it could have been more. At least it will buy a few cement blocks."

---

9. **wattle** _n._: Sticks woven together and used as a framework to support the grasses and mud used to thatch a roof.

Salongo took the money and looked at it as if it were crawling with lice. Grudgingly he thanked Pius and then remarked, "Of course, you will find life more expensive now that you are keeping a woman in the house."

"I suppose Nantondo told you," Pius smiled sheepishly.

"Does it matter who told me?" the custodian replied. "Anyway, never say I didn't warn you. Next thing she'll want will be a ring marriage!"

Pius gave an uncertain laugh. "As a matter of fact, one of the reasons I came up here was to invite you to a wedding—it's next month."

Salongo carefully laid down the spear he was rubbing upon a piece of clean barkcloth and stared at his friend as if he had suddenly grown another head. "What a fool you are! And all this stems from your scribbling noughts and crosses[10] on a bit of squared paper! I knew it

would bring no good! At your age you ought to have more sense. Well, all I can advise is that you run while you still have the chance!"

For a moment Pius was full of misgivings. Was he, after all, behaving like a fool? Then he thought of Sarah, and the wonders she had worked with his house and his *shamba* in the short time they had been together. He felt reassured. "Well, I'm getting married, and I expect to see you at both the church and the reception, and if you don't appear, I shall want to know the reason why!" He was secretly delighted at the note of authority in his voice, and Salongo's face was the picture of astonishment. "All right," he mumbled, "I shall try and come. Before you go, cut a bunch of bananas to take back to your good lady, and there might be some cabbage ready at the back. I suppose I've got to hand it to her! She's the real winner!"

◆ **Literary Focus**
What, if anything, about the story's ending suprised you? Explain.

---

10. **noughts** (nôts) **and crosses:** Zeros and *X*'s used to mark the spaces on the football-pool card.

Guide for Responding

◆ *Literature and Your Life*

Reader's Response Did you find this story amusing? Why or why not?

Thematic Focus What aspects of the characters' behavior seemed like behavior you might encounter among people you know?

☑ Check Your Comprehension

1. What happens to Pius's home after he wins the football pools?
2. What does Salongo say about Sarah?
3. What does Sarah do for Pius, and what does she reveal about her own situation?
4. What does the second telegram say?
5. What do Pius and Sarah decide in the end?

◆ Critical Thinking

INTERPRET
1. In what ways does Pius react to the changes that his good luck brings? **[Synthesize]**
2. How is Sarah like and unlike the others who show up at Pius's hut? **[Compare and Contrast]**
3. Why is Pius glad to learn that his winnings are less than expected? **[Infer]**
4. Why do you think that Pius decides to marry Sarah? **[Draw Conclusions]**

EVALUATE
5. Do you think Pius makes the right decision about Sarah? Why or why not? **[Assess]**

EXTEND
6. What might Kimenye be suggesting about African traditions and the modern world? **[Social Studies Link]**

Guide for Responding (continued)

◆ Reading Strategy

IDENTIFY RELATIONSHIPS IN THE TEXT

By **identifying relationships** among events in "The Winner," you can determine
- what the sequence of events is.
- how one event causes another.
- why characters react as they do.

For example, the announcement that Pius has won the football pools leads to the arrival of all sorts of relatives and even the media. This crowd of people causes chaos in Pius's life and prompts him to flee his home.

1. Jot down the sequence of events in "The Winner."
2. Which events are important and which are only incidental? Explain.
3. Showing how one event causes another, analyze the chain of events that brings Sarah to Pius's door.

◆ Literary Focus

SURPRISE ENDING

Kimenye provides a **surprise ending** for "The Winner," an unexpected turn of events at the conclusion of the story. Rather than being upset by the telegram informing him that his winnings are less than he originally thought, Pius laughs. Also, Cousin Sarah, who at first horrifies Pius with her boldness, becomes his bride.

However, when you review the story, you can see clues to each of these surprising developments. For example, descriptions of how relatives and reporters invade Pius's house suggest that Pius might be glad not to win so much money.

1. In what way is Pius's reaction to Miriamu's compliment of Sarah a hint of the wedding to come?
2. Find another passage that suggests Pius is developing a more positive opinion of Sarah, and explain your choice.
3. (a) Explain how the surprise ending of the story makes both Pius and Sarah winners. (b) How does the ending suggest that real winning is different from simply gaining wealth?

◆ Build Vocabulary

USING THE LATIN ROOT *-aud-*

Show how the root *-aud-*, meaning "hear," contributes to the meanings of these words:
1. audience 2. auditorium 3. audition 4. inaudible

USING THE WORD BANK: Antonyms

On your paper, write the letter of the word that is the **antonym**—or opposite in meaning—of the first word.
1. aplomb: (a) calm, (b) nervousness, (c) gracefulness
2. impetuous: (a) thoughtful, (b) active, (c) polite
3. audibly: (a) silently, (b) loudly, (c) significantly
4. unpretentious: (a) shy, (b) showy, (c) invisible
5. garrulous: (a) smooth, (b) youthful, (c) quiet
6. edification: (a) education, (b) ignorance, (c) collapse
7. formidable: (a) unimpressive, (b) untrained, (c) large
8. incredulity: (a) foolishness, (b) wonder, (c) certainty

◆ Build Grammar Skills

APPOSITIVE PHRASES

Appositive phrases are noun phrases placed near other nouns or pronouns in order to explain them further.

Practice On your paper, identify the appositive phrase in each sentence and the noun or pronoun it explains. If there is no appositive phrase, write *none*.
1. Pius's closest friend, Salongo, was almost blind.
2. Salongo, the custodian of the Ssabalangira's tomb, hoped Pius would make a donation.
3. Salongo was suspicious of Sarah, who claimed to be Pius's cousin.
4. Sarah, a widow, seemed to take charge of things.
5. To Salongo, Sarah was a "sticker," someone who would not leave.

Writing Application On your paper, use an appositive phrase to combine each pair of sentences into one sentence.
1. Kimenye is a Ugandan. She writes of her homeland.
2. Pius is an older man. He wins the football pools.

Build Your Portfolio

Idea Bank

Writing

1. **Telegrams** Write the two telegram announcements that appear in the story. In the first, announce that Pius has won the football pools. In the second, clarify that he must share the prize with others.

2. **Newspaper Story** Write a story that the newspaper *Uganda Nation* might have run about Pius's winning the football pools. The article should accurately reflect details in the story. **[Career Link]**

3. **Retelling From Another Point of View** Retell an episode from "The Winner" from Sarah's point of view, and have her use the pronoun *I*. Include her thoughts as well as her speech and actions.

Speaking, Listening, and Viewing

4. **Interview** With a small group, perform the complete radio interview described in the story. Have different classmates portray Pius, Sarah, Salongo, and the interviewer. **[Performing Arts Link]**

5. **Role-Play** With a classmate, pretend you are Pius and Sarah retelling the events of the story. Each of you should indicate what events, if any, surprised you. **[Performing Arts Link]**

Researching and Representing

6. **Report on Updating the Story** If the story were set in today's Uganda, would it be different in any way? Use the Internet, encyclopedias, books, and magazine articles to research this question. Present your results to the class. **[Social Studies Link]**

7. **African Children's Literature** Research what Kimenye and other authors have done to create children's literature set in contemporary Africa. Report on your findings to the class.
[Social Studies Link]

Online Activity ▸ **www.phlit.phschool.com**

Guided Writing Lesson

Editorial

What do you think of lotteries like the one in the story? Do they entertain people and bring in needed revenue, or do they encourage gambling and serve as a hidden tax on the poor? Write an editorial on this question for a local newspaper. In it, express your opinion of lotteries, and discuss their benefits and drawbacks.

Writing Skills Focus: Transitions to Show Contrast

In your editorial, you will probably need to contrast the benefits and drawbacks of lotteries. Here are some **transitions** you can use to introduce those contrasts:

- although
- either
- in spite of
- even though
- but
- despite

Prewriting Read editorials in your local newspaper for ideas about format, length, and appropriate language. Then, research facts and statistics about lotteries. On a two-column chart, jot down benefits and drawbacks, including specific examples where possible.

Drafting Begin by stating your overall opinion of lotteries. As you support your opinion, use facts and statistics from your chart. Also, help readers follow your argument by employing transitions to show contrast.

Revising Be sure that you have clearly stated your opinion of lotteries and that you have introduced contrasting arguments with transitions to show the contrast.

Add appositive phrases to clarify terms that need further explanation. For information on appositive phrases, see pp. 560 and 569.

PART 2 *A Larger World*

Above the Trees, Emily Carr, Vancouver Art Gallery

Guide for Reading

Colette (1873–1954)

Sidonie-Gabrielle Colette (kō let´) grew up in the French province of Burgundy but came to Paris at the age of twenty, when she married Henri Gauthier-Villars. A well-known literary figure, Gauthier-Villars often published the writings of others under his own pen name of Willy. Soon his wife became one of his ghost writers, publishing *Claudine at School* in 1900. After the breakup of her first marriage, Colette worked briefly in a music hall before again taking up the pen. Writing simply as Colette, she won lasting fame for fiction and autobiographical works chronicling the lives of early twentieth-century French women. A remarkably independent woman, Colette married twice more and continued to write after she began suffering from crippling arthritis. Among her best-known works is the long story *Gigi* (1944).

Nicolás Guillén (1902–1989)

One of Cuba's most famous poets, Nicolás Guillén (gē yen´) published his masterpiece, *Sóngoro Cosongo*, in 1931. Of mixed African and European background, Guillén drew heavily on the speech, legends, and music of Cubans of African descent. The style of poetry that he pioneered has come to be called Afro-Cuban.

Deeply committed to political change, Guillén devoted much of his verse to attacking racism and exposing the plight of Cuba's poor. In 1936, he traveled to Spain to fight against fascism in the Spanish Civil War. After returning to Cuba, he continued writing and also served as a visiting professor in both Canada and the United States. He was exiled from his homeland for political reasons during the 1950's, but returned after the communist revolution of 1959.

◆ Build Vocabulary

PREFIXES: *en-*

When used to form verbs, the prefix *en-* means "to put or make into." By adding *en-* to the noun *rapture*, which means "a state of great delight," you get the verb *enrapture*, "to put into a state of great delight." In Colette's story, Madame Augelier is *enraptured*, or "greatly delighted," by a blue glass bracelet.

WORD BANK

supple
connoisseur
convalescent
enraptured
iridescent
bangle
congealed
fossilized

As you read the selections, you will encounter these words. Each of these words from the selections is defined on the page where it first appears. Preview the list before you read.

◆ Build Grammar Skills

CORRECT USE OF *set* AND *sit*

People sometimes confuse the verbs **set** and **sit**. *Set* means "to put (something) in a certain place." It is a transitive verb that has as its direct object the thing that is being put down.

dir. obj.
She *set* the bracelet on the dresser.

The principal parts of the verb set are *set, setting, set,* and *(have) set.*

Sit means "to be seated or resting in a particular spot." It is usually intransitive. You cannot "sit" something; you can only "sit" yourself.

The glass beads *sit* on the dresser.
At suppertime, I *sit* myself down at the table.

The principal parts of the verb *sit* are *sit, sitting, sat,* and *(have) sat.*

The Bracelet ◆ Can You?

◆ Literature and Your Life

CONNECT YOUR EXPERIENCE
Owning a pencil is a little different from owning a photograph of an old friend. You might swap your pencil for another one without thinking twice about it. The photo of your friend, though, may sum up a whole period in your life.

The main character in "The Bracelet" owns quite a few valuable things. Still, she searches for a thing that might hold a part of herself.

Journal Writing Briefly describe a treasured childhood possession.

THEMATIC FOCUS: A LARGER WORLD
As you read, ask what the story and the poem each say about the value of things and the meaning of possession.

◆ Background for Understanding

CULTURE
At the turn of the twentieth century, the women's rights movement was still in its infancy. Women were just beginning to enjoy the educational and employment opportunities that western women now take for granted, and marriage was still the best road to economic security.

Like most of Colette's fiction, "The Bracelet" touches on the changing role of women in early twentieth-century France. The main character, Madame Augelier, is married to a wealthy business executive. In a subtle fashion, the story asks: Is the security and predictability of such a marriage enough for happiness?

◆ Literary Focus

UNDERSTANDING EPIPHANY
In Greek mythology, an *epiphany* is an incident in which a concealed god or goddess suddenly reveals his or her identity. Irish writer James Joyce (1882–1941) first used the word as a literary term. In his definition, an **epiphany** is a sudden flash of insight that a character has. Epiphanies in literature do not always reveal a new, positive truth. Often, they are moments of disillusionment, when a character loses an old vision of things.

As you read "The Bracelet," look for the sudden insight or revelation that the main character, Madame Augelier, experiences.

◆ Reading Strategy

DRAW CONCLUSIONS
A short story or a poem is built of layers of meaning. If you understand only the top layer—the meaning that is stated directly—you are missing out on the full significance of the work. To uncover deeper meanings, you need to draw conclusions as you read. A **conclusion** is a general statement that you can explain or support with details from the selection.

In "The Bracelet," for example, the author does not tell us directly that the Augeliers are a wealthy couple. However, the details of the story—the description of Madame Augelier's bedroom and the gifts she receives from her husband—all suggest that the couple is quite well-to-do.

Copy the chart below. Then, list conclusions that you draw as you read "The Bracelet" and "Can You?" In the right column, list the details that help point to your conclusions.

Conclusion	Supporting Details

The Bracelet

Colette
Translated by Matthew Ward

". . . Twenty-seven, twenty-eight, twenty-nine . . . There really are twenty-nine . . ."

Madame Augelier mechanically counted and recounted the little *pavé*[1] diamonds. Twenty-nine square brilliants, set in a bracelet, which slithered between her fingers like a cold and supple snake. Very white, not too big, admirably matched to each other—the pretty bijou[2] of a connoisseur. She fastened it on her wrist, and shook it, throwing off blue sparks under the electric candles; a hundred tiny rainbows, blazing with color, danced on the white tablecloth. But Madame Augelier was looking more closely instead at the other bracelet, the three finely engraved creases encircling her wrist above the glittering snake.

"Poor François . . . what will he give me next year, if we're both still here?"

François Augelier, industrialist, was traveling in Algeria at the time, but, present or absent, his gift marked both the year's end and their wedding anniversary. Twenty-eight jade bowls, last year; twenty-seven old enamel plaques mounted on a belt, the year before . . .

"And the twenty-six little Royal Dresden[3] plates . . . And the twenty-four meters of antique Alençon lace[4] . . ." With a slight effort of memory Madame Augelier could have gone back as far as four modest silver place settings, as far as three pairs of silk stockings . . .

"We weren't rich back then. Poor François, he's always spoiled me so . . ." To herself, secretly, she called him "poor François," because she believed herself guilty of not loving him enough, underestimating the strength of affectionate habits and abiding fidelity.

Madame Augelier raised her hand, tucked her little finger under, extended her wrist to erase the bracelet of wrinkles, and repeated

---

3. **Royal Dresden** (drez´ dən): A fine, decorated porcelain or chinaware made near Dresden, a city in south-central Germany.
4. **Alençon** (ə len´ sən) **lace:** A needlepoint lace with a solid design on a net background.

---

1. *pavé* (pȧ vā´): A setting of jewelry in which the gems are placed close together so that no metal shows.
2. **bijou** (bē´ zhoō) *n.*: A jewel.

◀ **Critical Viewing**
In what ways does
the mood of this
woman reflect that
of Madame Augelier?
[Connect]

Portrait of Madame Mayden, Amedeo Modigliani

intently, "It's so pretty . . . the diamonds are so white . . . I'm so pleased . . ." Then she let her hand fall back down and admitted to herself that she was already tired of her new bracelet.

"But I'm not ungrateful," she said naively with a sigh. Her weary eyes wandered from the flowered tablecloth to the gleaming window. The smell of some Calville apples in a silver bowl made her feel slightly sick and she left the dining room.

In her boudoir[5] she opened the steel case which held her jewels, and adorned her left hand in honor of the new bracelet. Her ring had on it a black onyx band and a blue-tinted brilliant; onto her delicate, pale, and somewhat wrinkled little finger, Madame Augelier slipped a circle of dark sapphires. Her prematurely white hair, which she did not dye, appeared even whiter as she adjusted amid slightly frizzy curls a narrow fillet sprinkled with a dusting of diamonds, which she immediately untied and took off again.

"I don't know what's wrong with me. I'm not feeling all that well. Being fifty is a bore, basically . . ."

She felt restless, both terribly hungry and sick to her stomach, like a convalescent whose appetite the fresh air has yet to restore.

"Really now, is a diamond actually as pretty as all that?"

Madame Augelier craved a visual pleasure which would involve the sense of taste as well; the unexpected sight of a lemon, the unbearable squeaking of the knife cutting it in half, makes the mouth water with desire . . .

"But I don't want a lemon. Yet this nameless pleasure which escapes me does exist, I know it does, I remember it! Yes, the blue glass bracelet . . ."

---

5. **boudoir** (bo͞od′ wär) *n*.: A woman's bedroom, dressing room, or private sitting room.

A shudder made Madame Augelier's slack cheeks tighten. A vision, the duration of which she could not measure, granted her, for a second time, a moment lived forty years earlier, that incomparable moment as she looked, enraptured, at the color of the day, the iridescent, distorted image of objects seen through a blue glass bangle, moved around in a circle, which she had just been given. That piece of perhaps Oriental glass, broken a few hours later, had held in it a new universe, shapes not the inventions of dreams, slow, serpentine animals moving in pairs, lamps, rays of light congealed in an atmosphere of indescribable blue . . .

The vision ended and Madame Augelier fell back, bruised, into the present, into reality.

But the next day she began searching, from antique shops to flea markets, from flea markets to crystal shops, for a glass bracelet, a certain color of blue. She put the passion of a collector, the precaution, the dissimulation[6] of a lunatic into her search. She ventured into what she called "impossible districts," left her car at the corner of strange streets, and in the end, for a few centimes, she found a circle of blue glass which she recognized in the darkness, stammered as she paid for it, and carried it away.

---

6. **dissimulation** (di sim′ yə lā′ shən) *n*.: The hiding of one's feelings or motives by pretense.

◆ **Build Vocabulary**

convalescent (kän′ və les′ ənt) *n*.: Someone who is recovering his or her health

enraptured (en rap′ chʉrd) *adj*.: Filled with great delight; enchanted

iridescent (ir′i des′ ənt) *adj*.: Showing shifting changes in color; rainbowlike

bangle (baŋ′ gəl) *n*.: A decorative bracelet

congealed (kən jēl′d′) *adj*.: Grew more solid, as by cooling; thickened

In the discreet light of her favorite lamp she set the bracelet on the dark field of an old piece of velvet, leaned forward, and waited for the shock . . . But all she saw was a round piece of bluish glass, the trinket of a child or a savage, hastily made and blistered with bubbles; an object whose color and material her memory and reason recognized; but the powerful and sensual genius who creates and nourishes the marvels of childhood, who gradually weakens, then dies mysteriously within us, did not even stir.

Resigned, Madame Augelier thus came to know how old she really was and measured the infinite plain over which there wandered, beyond her reach, a being detached from her forever, a stranger, turned away from her, rebellious and free even from the bidding of memory: a little ten-year-old girl wearing on her wrist a bracelet of blue glass.

> ◆ **Literary Focus**
> What does Madame Augelier learn about herself and about life in this epiphany?

Guide for Responding

◆ Literature and Your Life

Reader's Response Do you sympathize with Madame Augelier? Why or why not?

Thematic Focus (a) For what "larger world" beyond her present existence does Madame Augelier search? (b) Explain how she is limited to defining both her marriage and this larger world through possessions.

Questions for Research "The Bracelet" takes place at the start of the twentieth century, when women's roles were in a state of change in America and France. Write one or more questions that you could investigate to learn more about women at that time.

☑ Check Your Comprehension

1. What anniversary gift has Madame Augelier received from her husband?
2. Where is her husband?
3. What special childhood possession does Madame Augelier recall as she sits in her boudoir?
4. What happens when Madame Augelier purchases the item she has been looking for and takes it home?

◆ Critical Thinking

INTERPRET
1. Why does Madame Augelier feel restless, hungry, and sick to her stomach? **[Infer]**
2. Why is the blue glass bracelet special to Madame Augelier? **[Infer]**
3. Why do you think it has become so important to her at this point in her life? **[Interpret]**
4. (a) What effect does the new blue glass bracelet have on Madame Augelier? (b) What has changed since her childhood? **[Interpret]**
5. What has she realized at the end of the story? **[Interpret]**

APPLY
6. Think of a time when you returned to a place you knew as a child. Did the place live up to your memories of it? Why do you think you had the experience you did? **[Apply]**

EXTEND
7. What does the story suggest about upper-class life in early twentieth-century France? **[Social Studies Link]**

Can You?

Nicolás Guillén
Translated by Robert Márquez

Can you sell me the air that passes through your fingers
and hits your face and undoes your hair?
Maybe you could sell me five dollars' worth of wind,
or more, perhaps sell me a cyclone?
5   Maybe you would sell me
the thin air, the air
(not all of it) that sweeps
into your garden blossom on blossom
into your garden for the birds,
10   ten dollars of pure air.

The air it turns and passes
with butterfly-like spins.
No one owns it, no one.

Can you sell me some sky,
15   the sky that's blue at times,
or gray again at times,
a small part of your sky,
the one you bought—you think—with all the trees
of your orchard, as one who buys the ceiling with the house?
20   Can you sell me a dollar's worth
of sky, two miles
of sky, a fragment of your sky,
whatever piece you can?

The sky is in the clouds.
25   The clouds are high, they pass.
No one owns them, no one.

Can you sell me some rain, the water
that has given you your tears and wets your tongue?
Can you sell me a dollar's worth of water
30   from the spring, a pregnant cloud,
as soft and graceful as a lamb,
or even water fallen on the mountain,
or water gathered in the ponds
abandoned to the dogs,
35   or one league[1] of the sea, a lake perhaps,
a hundred dollars' worth of lake?

1. **league:** Unit of linear measurement used most often in sea travel, and equal to about three miles.

The water falls, it runs.
The water runs, it passes.
No one holds it, no one.

40   Can you sell me some land, the deep night
       of the roots, the teeth of
       dinosaurs and the scattered lime
       of distant skeletons?
       Can you sell me long since buried jungles, birds now extinct,
45   fish <u>fossilized</u>, the sulphur
       of volcanoes, a thousand million years
       rising in spiral? Can you
       sell me some land, can you
       sell me some land, can you?

50   The land that's yours is mine.
       The feet of all walk on it.
       No one owns it, no one.

◆ **Build Vocabulary**

fossilized (fäs´ ə līz'd') *adj.*: Turned into a fossil, the hardened imprint left behind by once-living things

Guide for Responding

◆ *Literature and Your Life*

Reader's Response Which images in the poem appealed the most to your imagination? Why?

Thematic Focus Even though you cannot own the things that Guillén describes, in what ways does his description expand your horizons?

Reader's Journal Write an additional two stanzas, one of ten lines and the other of three, that you think would fit the poem. Match the style of the stanzas currently in the poem. Your two stanzas might come after line 13, 26, 39, or 52.

Questions for Research Formulate some questions that would help you learn more about the life and work of Nicolás Guillén. To which sources would you go to answer them? Why?

☑ Check Your Comprehension

1. What four things does the speaker ask about?
2. What does he conclude about each of the four things?

◆ Critical Thinking

INTERPRET

1. What do the four main things described in the poem have in common? **[Compare and Contrast]**
2. (a) Find two images the speaker uses to suggest the true value of the four things. (b) Explain what your examples show about the value of the things. **[Support]**
3. (a) What does the poem suggest about the idea of possessing things? (b) Why is it significant that the poet concludes by discussing the land? **[Draw Conclusions]**

EVALUATE

4. Do you agree with the general sentiment expressed in this poem? Cite examples from real-world experiences to support your opinion. **[Assess]**

COMPARE LITERARY WORKS

5. What do you think the poem's speaker would say to Madame Augelier about her husband's gifts? About the blue bracelet? **[Connect]**

Guide for Responding (continued)

◆ Reading Strategy

DRAW CONCLUSIONS

The details in a selection can often help you **draw conclusions** about the characters and their situations. In "The Bracelet," for example, the details about what Madame Augelier craved and her search for the glass bracelet suggest that she is not happy and longs for something that she feels is missing in her life.

1. How long have the Augeliers been married? Which details lead you to that conclusion?
2. What conclusions can you draw about Madame Augelier's relationship with her husband? How has it changed over the years? Cite details that point to your conclusions.
3. What conclusion can you draw from ll. 27–28 of "Can You?" about the speaker's idea of the true value of rain?

◆ Build Grammar Skills

CORRECT USE OF *set* AND *sit*

In "The Bracelet," Madame *sets* the bracelet on a piece of velvet while she *sits* in her boudoir. Be careful to distinguish between *set*, a transitive verb meaning "to put (something) in a certain place," and *sit*, usually an intransitive verb, meaning "to be seated or resting in a particular spot." The principal parts of *set* are *set, setting, set,* and *(have) set.* The principal parts of *sit* are *sit, sitting, sat,* and *(have) sat.*

Practice On your paper, identify the correct form of the verb in each sentence.

1. Twenty-nine square stones (set, sat) in the bracelet.
2. Madame Augelier (set, sat) the bracelet in the box.
3. She was (setting, sitting) in her bedroom.
4. She had (set, sat) the box on the dresser.
5. She raced around and finally (set, sat) herself down.

Writing Application Write five sentences about the things you think you could someday own and the things you think you could never own. Correctly use the verb *sit* or *set* in each sentence.

◆ Literary Focus

UNDERSTANDING EPIPHANY

An **epiphany** is a sudden revelation or flash of insight that a person has about himself or herself, another person, a particular situation, or life in general.

For instance, "The Bracelet" ends with an epiphany that Madame Augelier experiences about her situation in life.

1. At the end of the story, what sudden realization does Madame Augelier have about her life?
2. How do you think Madame Augelier will behave after her epiphany?
3. Describe the epiphany that the speaker in "Can You?" might wish to encourage in the reader.

◆ Build Vocabulary

USING THE PREFIX *en-*

Using the fact that the prefix *en-* means "to put or make into," define each of these verbs:

1. encircle   2. endanger   3. enslave   4. entangle

USING THE WORD BANK: Analogy

On your paper, write the letter of the pair of words that expresses a relationship *most like* the relationship of the pair in capital letters.

1. HARD : FOSSILIZED :: (a) dry : watered
   (b) wet : moistened   (c) thick : thinned
2. SUPPLE : BREAKABLE :: (a) stubborn : certain
   (b) awkward : clumsy   (c) smooth : coarse
3. HAPPY : ENRAPTURED :: (a) annoyed : furious
   (b) joyful : sorrowful   (c) silent : quiet
4. IRIDESCENT : DIAMOND :: (a) dark : sun
   (b) transparent : gold   (c) green : grass
5. CONGEALED : MELTED :: (a) lied : deceived
   (b) strengthened : diluted   (c) heated : softened
6. BANGLE : WRIST :: (a) crown : head
   (b) glove : arm   (c) pearl : oyster
7. CONVALESCENT : HEALTH ::
   (a) amnesiac : memory   (b) teacher : education
   (c) sinner : evil
8. CONNOISSEUR : BEAUTY :: (a) fool : knowledge
   (b) gourmet : food   (c) review : critic

Build Your Portfolio

 ## Idea Bank

Writing

1. Inventory Make an inventory of the gifts Madame Augelier received from her husband. Describe each gift and the circumstances in which it was given. Add details to those provided in the story.

2. Character Sketch Write a character sketch of the speaker in "Can You?" Show his personality, values, and likely behavior, based on the details in the poem.

3. Response to Criticism John Weightman faults Colette for "overwrit(ing) and gush(ing)." Evaluate the writing in "The Bracelet." Is the story "over-written," or does it effectively convey experience?

Speaking, Listening, and Viewing

4. Role-Play With a classmate, role-play the conversation that might take place between Madame Augelier and her husband after he returns home. **[Performing Arts Link]**

5. Multimedia Presentation Give a slide show presentation of "Can You?" Pair images illustrating the poem with ones showing consumerism. Lead the class in a discussion of the contrasts between images. **[Technology Link]**

Researching and Representing

6. Recreation of Jewelry Using metal, stones, or any other suitable medium, re-create one of the jewelry items described in "The Bracelet." **[Visual Arts Link]**

7. Research Paper Do research to learn more about the custom of gift giving in different cultures. Present your findings in a brief report. **[Social Studies Link]**

Online Activity www.phlit.phschool.com

 ## Guided Writing Lesson

Literary Analysis

An **image** is a word or phrase that appeals to one or more of the five senses. Write a brief paper in which you analyze how images help to convey meaning in either "The Bracelet" or "Can You?"

Literary Analysis: Transitions to Link Specific Examples to General Points

When you discuss the images in the selection, you need to make clear connections between your general points and your specific examples. Here are some of the **transitions,** words linking ideas, that you might use:

for example   in fact   specifically

for instance   in particular   in this way

Prewriting Carefully go through the story or poem, and list the images that it contains. Then, reread it. Write down in a sentence or two the main theme of the selection (its general message or question). For each image, jot down associations that link it to the meaning or ideas expressed in the selection.

Drafting Begin with a general statement about the theme or main idea of the selection. Then, cite specific examples to show how the images in the selection suggest or develop that theme or main idea.

Revising As you review your draft, add examples of images as needed to illustrate your points. Use transitions to make clear connections between examples and general points.

Check that you use words correctly, including the verbs *set* and *sit*. For more in the correct use of *set* and *sit,* see pages 572 and 580.

Guide for Reading

Josephina Niggli *(1910–1983)*

When Josephina Niggli was just a child, she and her family fled their native Mexico to escape the turmoil of the Mexican Revolution. They settled in San Antonio, Texas, where Niggli grew up.

From Texas to Hollywood

Niggli was educated at home until she reached high school. Her first book of poems was published shortly after her high-school graduation. After college, she began writing and producing plays, and later, movie scripts.

> *Niggli spent two years in Hollywood as a screenwriter.*

Niggli's background in drama served her well in her prose works. Her dialogue is believable, and her skill at describing a setting enables the reader to picture the scene as if it were on stage.

Cultural Influences

Although she left Mexico at a young age, Niggli carried the richness of her Mexican culture with her to the United States. In 1945, she published *Mexican Village,* a collection of ten stories, all set in the Sabinas Valley of northern Mexico. In these stories, she shows a talent for capturing the local color—the details of life in this valley.

Daring Heroes

As a child, she heard exciting stories of the fearless heroes Pancho Villa and Emiliano Zapata, who fought for reform during the Mexican Revolution. Pepe Gonzalez, the main character in "The Street of the Cañon," exhibits the same daring, romantic nature as these historical figures.

◆ Build Vocabulary

ANGLO-SAXON SUFFIXES: *-ly*

The Anglo-Saxon suffix *-ly* is one of the most common in English. Most, but not all, words that end in *-ly* are adverbs. An adverb is a word that modifies a verb, adjective, or another adverb. Josephina Niggli uses adverbs to make her writing more descriptive. When one of her characters *nonchalantly* enters a room, for instance, you can picture the person's walk as he tries to enter the room without being noticed.

WORD BANK

officious
mottled
nonchalantly
audaciously
imperiously
plausibility

As you read "The Street of the Cañon," you will encounter the words on this list. Each word is defined on the page where it first appears. Preview the list before you read.

◆ Build Grammar Skills

COMMAS IN A SERIES

A **comma** can make a big difference in the clarity of your writing. Separating three or more items in a series is one way that commas make writing clear.

> . . . the air was hot with the too-sweet perfume of gardenias, tuberoses, and the pungent scent of close-packed humanity.

In this sentence, commas separate the three details that describe what the room is hot with. Notice that Niggli uses a comma before the coordinating conjunction *and,* which joins the last two items.

If the items in the series are already separated by conjunctions (such as *and* or *or*), commas are not necessary.

> There were yellow cheese *and* white cheese *and* curded cheese from cow's milk.

The Street of the Cañon

◆ Literature and Your Life

CONNECT YOUR EXPERIENCE

Celebrations acknowledge significant occasions. Some celebrations, such as a Fourth of July picnic or a town parade, are public. Others, such as a wedding or birthday party, are personal. In this story, a young woman named Sarita celebrates her birthday. The celebration has elements of a public event, however, as Sarita's father throws a fiesta to which the whole town is invited.

Journal Writing Describe the last celebration you attended, and tell what made it special.

THEMATIC FOCUS: A LARGER WORLD

Celebrations sometimes unite you with other cultural groups who honor the same event or person. How does celebrating with others enlarge your world?

◆ Background for Understanding

CULTURE

Courtship and marriage customs play an important role in this story. In Mexico, there have been different traditional marriage customs, depending on the region. In some regions, a young man seeking to marry must still ask permission of the young woman's family elders. In some regions, the parents still arrange a match. Marriages typically take place within the community. In the town of San Juan Iglesias, the Mexican village in which this story is set, "to walk around the plaza with a girl" is a sign of engagement.

◆ Literary Focus

POINT OF VIEW

Imagine a kind of microscope that allows you to see someone's thoughts and feelings. Actually, writers give you this kind of look into fictional characters' minds. They do it through **point of view** in a story—the vantage point from which the story is told. The point of view determines what you as a reader know.

When a story is told from a **third-person** point of view, it is told by a narrator who is not a story character but who reveals the thoughts and feelings of one main character. If the third-person point of view is all-knowing, or **omniscient,** the narrator knows and reveals the thoughts and feelings of more than one character. This is the point of view of "The Street of the Cañon." Niggli allows us to peek into the minds of several characters, and she reveals some details that even the characters don't know!

◆ Reading Strategy

PREDICT

Your baseball team is up against a team whose best players are injured. You can probably predict that your team will win. You can **predict** story events in much the same way—you make an educated guess based on what the text reveals about the characters and the situation, and based on what you know from experience.

No matter how logical your predictions, however, you may need to revise them as new information is revealed. If the injured players from the other team were suddenly able to play, you might reconsider your prediction. Similarly, new circumstances introduced by the author may lead you to change your predictions about story events.

Use a chart like the one shown to keep track of your predictions and how they change as you read this story.

Question	Clues	Prediction
Who is the stranger?		
What does he have tightly clutched to his side?		
Why is he going to San Juan Iglesias?		
Why would the townspeople turn on him if they recognized him?		

The Street of the Cañon

from Mexican Village

Josephina Niggli

Fandango (detail), Theodore Gentilz, Gift of the Yanaguana Society, Daughters of the Republic of Texas Library

▲ **Critical Viewing** What time period do you think this painting depicts? What details suggest the time period? **[Infer]**

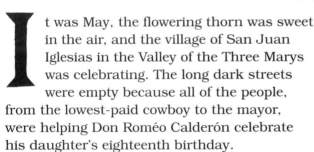

It was May, the flowering thorn was sweet in the air, and the village of San Juan Iglesias in the Valley of the Three Marys was celebrating. The long dark streets were empty because all of the people, from the lowest-paid cowboy to the mayor, were helping Don Roméo Calderón celebrate his daughter's eighteenth birthday.

On the other side of the town, where the Cañon Road led across the mountains to the Sabinas Valley, a tall slender man, a package clutched tightly against his side, slipped from shadow to shadow. Once a dog barked, and the man's black suit merged into the blackness of a wall. But no voice called out, and after a moment he slid into the narrow, dirt-packed street again.

The moonlight touched his shoulder and spilled across his narrow hips. He was young, no more than twenty-five, and his black curly head was bare. He walked swiftly along, heading always for the distant sound of guitar and flute. If he met anyone now, who could say from which direction he had come? He might be a trader from Monterrey, or a buyer of cow's milk from farther north in the Valley of the Three Marys. Who would guess that an Hidalgo[1] man dared to walk alone in the moonlit streets of San Juan Iglesias?

Carefully adjusting his flat package so that it was not too prominent, he squared his shoulders and walked jauntily across the street to the laughter-filled house. Little boys packed in the doorway made way for him, smiling and nodding to him.

1. **Hidalgo** (ē dalˊ gō) *adj.*: Nearby village.

The long, narrow room with the orchestra at one end was filled with whirling dancers. Rigid-backed chaperones were gossiping together, seated in their straight chairs against the plaster walls. Over the scene was the yellow glow of kerosene lanterns, and the air was hot with the too-sweet perfume of gardenias, tuberoses, and the pungent scent of close-packed humanity.

The man in the doorway, while trying to appear at ease, was carefully examining every smiling face. If just one person recognized him, the room would turn on him like a den of snarling mountain cats, but so far all the laughter-dancing eyes were friendly.

Suddenly a plump, <u>officious</u> little man, his round cheeks glistening with perspiration, pushed his way through the crowd. His voice, many times too large for his small body, boomed at the man in the doorway. "Welcome, stranger, welcome to our house." Thrusting his arm through the stranger's, and almost dislodging the package, he started to lead the way through the maze of dancers. "Come and drink a toast to my daughter—to my beautiful Sarita. She is eighteen this night."

In the square patio the gentle breeze ruffled the pink and white oleander bushes. A long table set up on sawhorses held loaves of flaky crusted French bread, stacks of thin, delicate tortillas, plates of barbecued beef, and long red rolls of spicy sausages. But most of all there were cheeses, for the Three Marys was a cheese-eating valley. There were yellow cheese

and white cheese and curded cheese from cow's milk. There was even a flat white cake of goat cheese from distant Linares, a delicacy too expensive for any but feast days.

To set off this feast were bottles of beer floating in ice-filled tin tubs, and another table was covered with bottles of mescal, of tequila, of maguey wine.

Don Roméo Calderón thrust a glass of tequila into the stranger's hand. "Drink, friend, to the prettiest girl in San Juan. As pretty as my fine fighting cocks, she is. On her wedding day she takes to her man, and may she find him soon, the best fighter in my flock. Drink deep, friend. Even the rivers flow with wine."

The Hidalgo man laughed and raised his glass high. "May the earth be always fertile beneath her feet."

Someone called to Don Roméo that more guests were arriving, and with a final delighted pat on the stranger's shoulder, the little man scurried away. As the young fellow smiled after his retreating host, his eyes caught and held another pair of eyes—laughing black eyes set in a young girl's face. The last time he had seen that face it had been white and tense with rage, and the lips clenched tight to prevent an out-gushing stream of angry words. That had been in February, and she had worn a white lace shawl over her hair. Now it was May, and a gardenia was a splash of white in the glossy dark braids. The moonlight had <u>mottled</u> his face that February night, and he knew that she did not recognize him. He grinned impudently back at her, and her eyes widened, then slid sideways to one of the chaperones. The fan in her small hand snapped shut. She tapped its parchment tip against her mouth and slipped away to join the dancing couples in the front room. The gestures of a fan translate into a

◆ **Build Vocabulary**

officious (ə fish´ əs) *adj.*: Overly ready to serve
mottled (mät´ əld) *adj.*: Marked with spots of different shades

The Street of the Cañon ◆ 585

coded language on the frontier. The stranger raised one eyebrow as he interpreted the signal.

But he did not move toward her at once. Instead, he inched slowly back against the table. No one was behind him, and his hands quickly unfastened the package he had been guarding so long. Then he <u>nonchalantly</u> walked into the front room.

The girl was sitting close to a chaperone. As he came up to her he swerved slightly toward the bushy-browed old lady.

"Your servant, señora. I kiss your hands and feet."

The chaperone stared at him in astonishment. Such fine manners were not common to the town of San Juan Iglesias.

"Eh, you're a stranger," she said. "I thought so."

"But a stranger no longer, señora, now that I have met you." He bent over her, so close she could smell the faint fragrance of talcum on his freshly shaven cheek.

"Will you dance the *parada* with me?"

This request startled her eyes into popping open beneath the heavy brows. "So, my young rooster, would you flirt with me, and I old enough to be your grandmother?"

"Can you show me a prettier woman to flirt with in the Valley of the Three Marys?" he asked <u>audaciously</u>.

She grinned at him and turned toward the girl at her side. "This young fool wants to meet you, my child."

The girl blushed to the roots of her hair and shyly lowered her white lids. The old woman laughed aloud.

"Go out and dance, the two of you. A man clever enough to pat the sheep has a right to play with the lamb."

The next moment they had joined the circle of dancers and Sarita was trying to control her laughter.

"She is the worst dragon in San Juan. And how easily you won her!"

"What is a dragon," he asked <u>imperiously</u>, "when I longed to dance with you?"

"Ay," she retorted, "you have a quick tongue. I think you are a dangerous man."

In answer he drew her closer to him, and turned her toward the orchestra. As he reached the chief violinist he called out, "Play the *Virgencita*, 'The Shy Young Maiden.'"

The violinist's mouth opened in soundless surprise. The girl in his arms said sharply, "You heard him, the *Borachita*, 'The Little Drunken Girl.'"

With a relieved grin, the violinist tapped his music stand with his bow, and the music swung into the sad farewell of a man to his sweetheart:

Farewell, my little drunken one,
I must go to the capital
To serve the master
Who makes me weep for my return.

The stranger frowned down at her. "Is this a joke, señorita?" he asked coldly.

"No," she whispered, looking about her quickly to see if the incident had been observed. "But the *Virgencita* is the favorite song of Hidalgo, a village on the other side of the mountains in the next valley. The people of Hidalgo and San Juan Iglesias do not speak."

"That is a stupid thing," said the man from Hidalgo as he swung her around in a large turn. "Is not music free as air? Why should one town own the rights to a song?"

The girl shuddered slightly. "Those people from Hidalgo—they are wicked monsters. Can you guess what they did not six months since?"

The man started to point out that the space of time from February to May was three months, but he thought it better not to appear too wise. "Did these Hidalgo monsters frighten you, señorita? If they did, I personally will kill them all."

She moved closer against him and tilted her face until her mouth was close to his ear. "They

◆ **Reading Strategy**
Make a prediction about the stranger, based on his actions.

attempted to steal the bones of Don Rómolo Balderas."

"Is it possible?" He made his eyes grow round and his lips purse up in disdain. "Surely not that! Why, all the world knows that Don Rómolo Balderas was the greatest historian in the entire Republic. Every school child reads his books. Wise men from Quintana Roo to the Río Bravo bow their heads in admiration to his name. What a wicked thing to do!" He hoped his virtuous tone was not too virtuous for plausibility, but she did not seem to notice.

"It is true! In the night they came. Three devils!"

"Young devils, I hope."

"Young or old, who cares? They were devils. The blacksmith surprised them even as they were opening the grave. He raised such a shout that all of San Juan rushed to his aid, for they were fighting, I can tell you. Especially one of them—their leader."

"And who was he?"

"You have heard of him doubtless. A proper wild one named Pepe Gonzalez."

"And what happened to them?"

"They had horses and got away, but one, I think, was hurt."

◆ Build Vocabulary

nonchalantly (nän´ shə länt´ lē) adv.: Casually; indifferently

audaciously (ô dā´ shəs lē) adv.: In a bold manner

imperiously (im pir´ ē əs lē´) adv.: Arrogantly

plausibility (plô´ zə bil´ ə tē) n.: Believability

▲ **Critical Viewing** How do the style and arrangement of figures in this photograph suggest a celebration? **[Analyze]**

The Hidalgo man twisted his mouth remembering how Rubén the candymaker had ridden across the whitewashed line high on the cañon trail

◆ **Literary Focus**
What clues do the stranger's memories provide about his identity?

that marked the division between the Three Marys' and the Sabinas' sides of the mountains, and then had fallen in a faint from his saddle because his left arm was broken. There was no candy in Hidalgo for six weeks, and the entire Sabinas Valley resented that broken arm as fiercely as did Rubén.

The stranger tightened his arm in reflexed anger about Sarita's waist as she said, "All the world knows that the men of Hidalgo are sons of the mountain witches."

"But even devils are shy of disturbing the honored dead," he said gravely.

"'Don Rómolo was born in our village,' Hidalgo says. 'His bones belong to us.' Well, anyone in the valley can tell you he died in San Juan Iglesias, and here his bones will stay! Is that not proper? Is that not right?"

To keep from answering, he guided her through an intricate dance pattern that led them past the patio door. Over her head he could see two men and a woman staring with amazement at the open package on the table.

His eyes on the patio, he asked blandly, "You say the leader was one Pepe Gonzalez? The name seems to have a familiar sound."

"But naturally. He has a talent." She tossed her head and stepped away from him as the music stopped. It was a dance of two *paradas*.

He slipped his hand through her arm and guided her into place in the large oval of parading couples. Twice around the room and the orchestra would play again.

"A talent?" he prompted.

"For doing the impossible. When all the world says a thing cannot be done, he does it to prove the world wrong. Why, he climbed to the top of the Prow, and not even the long vanished Joaquín Castillo had ever climbed that mountain before. And this same Pepe caught a mountain lion with nothing to aid him but a rope and his two bare hands."

"He doesn't sound such a bad friend," protested the stranger, slipping his arm around her waist as the music began to play the merry song of the soap bubbles:

> *Pretty bubbles of a thousand colors*
> *That ride on the wind*
> *And break as swiftly*
> *As a lover's heart.*

The events in the patio were claiming his attention. Little by little he edged her closer to the door. The group at the table had considerably enlarged. There was a low murmur of excitement from the crowd.

"What has happened?" asked Sarita, attracted by the noise.

"There seems to be something wrong at the table," he answered, while trying to peer over the heads of the people in front of him. Realizing that this might be the last moment of peace he would have that evening, he bent toward her.

"If I come back on Sunday, will you walk around the plaza with me?"

She was startled into exclaiming, "Ay, no!"

"Please. Just once around."

"And you think I'd walk more than once with you, señor, even if you were no stranger? In San Juan Iglesias, to walk around the plaza with a girl means a wedding."

"Ha, and you think that is common to San Juan alone? Even the devils of Hidalgo respect that law." He added hastily at her puzzled

upward glance. "And so they do in all the villages." To cover his lapse he said softly, "I don't even know your name."

A mischievous grin crinkled the corners of her eyes. "Nor do I know yours, señor. Strangers do not often walk the streets of San Juan."

Before he could answer, the chattering in the patio swelled to louder proportions. Don Roméo's voice lay on top, like thick cream on milk. "I tell you it is a jewel of a cheese. Such flavor, such texture, such whiteness. It is a jewel of a cheese."

"What has happened?" Sarita asked of a woman at her elbow.

"A fine goat's cheese appeared as if by magic on the table. No one knows where it came from."

"Probably an extra one from Linares," snorted a fat bald man on the right.

"Linares never made such a cheese as this," said the woman decisively.

"Silence!" roared Don Roméo. "Old Tío[2] Daniel would speak a word to us."

A great hand of silence closed down over the mouths of the people. The girl was standing on tiptoe trying vainly to see what was happening. She was hardly aware of the stranger's whispering voice although she remembered the words that he said. "Sunday night—once around the plaza."

She did not realize that he had moved away, leaving a gap that was quickly filled by the blacksmith.

Old Tío Daniel's voice was a shrill squeak, and his thin, stringy neck jutted forth from his body like a turtle's from its shell. "This is no cheese from Linares," he said with authority, his mouth sucking in over his toothless gums between his sentences. "Years ago, when the great Don Rómolo Balderas was still alive, we had such cheese as this—ay, in those days we had

◆ **Reading Strategy**
Predict why the stranger has left.

---

2. **Tío** (tē´ ō): Spanish for "uncle."

it. But after he died and was buried in our own sainted ground, as was right and proper . . . ."

"Yes, yes," muttered voices in the crowd. He glared at the interruption. As soon as there was silence again, he continued:

"After he died, we had it no more. Shall I tell you why?"

"Tell us, Tío Daniel," said the voices humbly.

"Because it is made in Hidalgo!"

The sound of a waterfall, the sound of a wind in a narrow cañon, and the sound of an angry crowd are much the same. There were no distinct words, but the sound was enough.

"Are you certain, Tío?" boomed Don Roméo.

"As certain as I am that a donkey has long ears. The people of Hidalgo have been famous for generations for making cheese like this—especially that wicked one, that owner of a cheese factory, Timotéo Gonzalez, father to Pepe, the wild one, whom we have good cause to remember."

"We do, we do," came the sigh of assurance.

"But on the whole northern frontier there are no vats like his to produce so fine a product. Ask the people of Chihuahua, of Sonora. Ask the man on the bridge at Laredo, or the man in his boat at Tampico, 'Hola, friend, who makes the finest goat cheese?' And the answer will always be the same, 'Don Timotéo of Hidalgo.' "

It was the blacksmith who asked the great question. "Then where did that cheese come from, and we haters of Hidalgo these ten long years?"

No voice said, "The stranger," but with one fluid movement every head in the patio turned toward the girl in the doorway. She also turned, her eyes wide with something that she realized to her own amazement was more apprehension than anger.

But the stranger was not in the room. When the angry, muttering men pushed through to the street, the stranger was not on the plaza. He was not anywhere in sight. A few of the more religious crossed themselves for fear that the Devil had walked in their midst. "Who was he?" one voice asked another. But Sarita, who was meekly listening to a lecture from Don Roméo on the propriety of dancing with strangers, did not have to ask. She had a strong suspicion that she had danced that night within the circling arm of Pepe Gonzalez.

> ◆ **Literary Focus**
> Why do you think the author reveals the stranger's identity through the thoughts of Sarita?

Guide for Responding

◆ Literature and Your Life

Reader's Response Based on this excerpt, would you like to read more of *Mexican Village*? Why or why not?

Thematic Focus In this story, a family celebration expands a young girl's horizons by showing her that people are not always who they seem to be. How can participating in town and family celebrations expand your horizons?

☑ Check Your Comprehension

1. What kind of welcome does Pepe Gonzalez receive?
2. What two things does Pepe set out to do at the party?
3. What outrageous deed had men from Hidalgo attempted in San Juan Iglesias three months previously?
4. What causes an uproar among the guests?

Guide for Responding *(continued)*

◆ Critical Thinking

INTERPRET

1. What does Pepe Gonzalez's caution in arriving in the village suggest about his motives? **[Draw Conclusions]**
2. Describe Gonzalez's personality. **[Infer]**
3. Give three reasons Pepe Gonzalez might have had for leaving the cheese. **[Infer]**

EVALUATE

4. Do you think Pepe Gonzalez was wise to go to Sarita's party when doing so posed such a great danger to him? Explain. **[Make a Judgment]**

APPLY

5. What do you think will happen now between Pepe and Sarita and between the two villages? Give your reasons for making those predictions. **[Speculate]**

◆ Reading Strategy

PREDICT

Review the story and your process of **making predictions.** Evaluate the reasons you made certain predictions and whether you revised them when new information was revealed.

1. What predictions did you make about the stranger when he first arrived?
2. What details helped you predict his identity?
3. What details led you to revise, or at least reconsider, a prediction?

◆ Literary Focus

POINT OF VIEW

A story told from a **third-person point of view** is told by an outside observer. "The Street of the Cañon" is told in third-person omniscient point of view—the narrator, who is all knowing, allows readers to know the thoughts and feelings of more than one character.

1. What are the stranger's thoughts when Sarita talks about the people of Hidalgo?
2. What is Sarita thinking at the end of the story?
3. Why do you think Niggli wants readers to know the thoughts and feelings of both Sarita and Pepe Gonzalez?

◆ Build Vocabulary

USING THE ANGLO-SAXON SUFFIX *-ly*

Add *-ly* to the following words to make them adverbs. Then, on your paper, complete the following sentences with one of the adverbs you created.

> confident   timid   generous

1. She gave ___?___, keeping hardly any for herself.
2. The nervous men entered the room ___?___.
3. The champ smiled ___?___ at his weaker opponent.

USING THE WORD BANK: Context

In your notebook, write your response to each of the numbered items.

1. Which character from the story behaves *audaciously*?
2. Name an animal whose coat is *mottled*.
3. Describe a situation in which you would try to act *nonchalantly*.
4. What types of details give an advertisement *plausibility*?
5. Would you want to work with an *officious* person? Why or why not?
6. Which character or characters from the story behave *imperiously*?

◆ Build Grammar Skills

COMMAS IN A SERIES

When you list three or more items in a series, separate them with commas to make your meaning clear. A series may be a series of words, a series of phrases, or a series of clauses.

Practice In your notebook, copy the following sentences. Insert commas to separate each of the items in the series.

1. A table held loaves of bread stacks of tortillas and plates of beef.
2. Sarita nodded smiled and turned away.
3. The sound of a waterfall the sound of a wind in a narrow cañon and the sound of an angry crowd are much the same.

Writing Application In a paragraph or two, describe a celebration you've attended. Include at least two series. Punctuate the series.

Build Your Portfolio

 ## Idea Bank

Writing

1. **Postcard** Write a postcard home to your family describing your recent visit to San Juan Iglesias. Use sensory details to help your family envision the town.

2. **Legend** Pepe Gonzalez's feats quickly became legendary among the people of San Juan Iglesias. Write a legend about a person who performed a heroic feat. Base your legend on a news story you read or something impressive done by a friend.

3. **Compare and Contrast** In an essay, compare and contrast Pepe Gonzalez with another hero you know—real or fictional. Present readers with specific examples of the legends and feats surrounding your hero.

Speaking, Listening, and Viewing

4. **Dialogue** With a partner, take turns speaking as Sarita and Pepe when they meet in the plaza now that Sarita is aware of Pepe's identity.

5. **Debate** Break into two teams to debate the question from the story, "Is not music free as air?" Develop your arguments around current issues related to the censorship and rating of music.

Researching and Representing

6. **Sketch** Choose your favorite scene in the story and illustrate it. In your illustration, try to convey the same sense of mystery that Niggli creates in her writing. **[Art Link]**

7. **Photo Essay** Collect photographs of Mexico from travel magazines and brochures. Organize your photos around a theme or a message. Arrange the photos and display them.

Online Activity www.phlit.phschool.com

 ## Guided Writing Lesson

Song for a Moment in the Story

Music is an important part of the celebration in this story. Imagine that you are a playwright who wants to turn this story into a musical. Select a moment in the story and write the **lyrics** to a song that will be sung in your musical.

As you plan and write the song lyrics, keep these points in mind:

Writing Skills Focus: Connotation

All writers, whether consciously or unconsciously, select words to convey a certain message or elicit a particular feeling or emotion. A word's **connotation** is the set of associations that the word calls to mind. For example, most people would prefer a "vintage automobile" to a "used car." A word's connotation can be positive, negative, or neutral.

Prewriting Reread the story, keeping an eye out for scenes that would be suitable for a song. For example, you might identify the opening scene or the scene where Sarita and Pepe dance. After you've selected a scene for your song, think about whether you want your scene to be happy, sad, or funny. Then, jot down words that elicit the specific connotations that you are trying to convey.

Drafting As you write the lyrics to your song, capture the actions and mood of the moment in the story. Include some of the words you jotted down.

Revising Reread your draft. Make sure you've used words with connotations that will stir in your audience the feelings you desire. If necessary, add details that strengthen the song's connection with the actions and mood of the moment in the story.

Guide for Reading

Alexander Solzhenitsyn *(1918–   )*

Born in the Soviet Union, Alexander Solzhenitsyn (sōl´ zhə nēt´ sin) began to write poetry while imprisoned in a labor camp for the crime of criticizing Communist leader Joseph Stalin in 1945. His first book, *One Day in the Life of Ivan Denisovitch*—the story of an inmate in a Soviet labor camp—brought its author instant recognition, but its publication was banned in the Soviet Union. Despite his 1970 Nobel Prize for Literature, Solzhenitsyn was tried for treason and exiled after the publication in Paris of parts of *The Gulag Archipelago*. Only since 1991 has his work been available to the people of his homeland.

Henrik Ibsen *(1828–1906)*

It all started with poetry for Henrik Ibsen. Isolated on a small farm near the port town of Skien, Norway, young Henrik turned for solace to writing poetry. His first successful play, *Brand,* was in fact originally written as a narrative poem. It was his plays, however, that made him famous. His emphasis on character rather than the predictable plots that were popular at the time resulted in realistic plays such as *A Doll's House* and *Hedda Gabler.*

Léopold Sédar Senghor *(1906–   )*

We don't often think of great poets as being world leaders, but Léopold Sédar Senghor (lā ô pōld´ sā dàr´ sä*n* gôr´) is both. Not only is he considered one of the greatest African poets writing in French, but he also served as president of the West African nation of Senegal, from its independence in 1960 until his retirement in 1980.

Though born in Senegal, Senghor attended Paris's Sorbonne—one of the world's most respected universities. There, Senghor and other young black writers launched the influential literary movement known as *negritude* (neg´ rə tōōd´), which promoted traditional African cultural values. (See Background for Understanding, p. 593.)

◆ Build Vocabulary

BORROWED WORDS: LATIN TERMS

When Alexander Solzhenitsyn describes the terror of being caught in a violent thunderstorm while in the mountains, he mentions that, for only a second, he and his companions felt as if they were on *terra firma. Terra firma* (which means "solid earth") is one of many Latin phrases that have found their way unchanged into modern English.

> terra firma
> sultry
> eternity
> despotism
> pitiable
> immobile

WORD BANK

Before you read, preview this list of words from the selections.

◆ Build Grammar Skills

CORRECT USE OF *like* AND *as*

A common usage error is to use *like* when we mean as.

Like, a preposition meaning "similar to" introduces a prepositional phrase —a preposition and a noun or pronoun.

> *Like* the arrows of Sabaoth, the lightning flashes…

As, a subordinating conjunction, introduces a subordinate clause—a group of words that contains a subject and a verb but that cannot stand alone as a sentence.

> … we forgot to be afraid of the lightning, the thunder, and the downpour, just *as* [not *like*] a droplet in the ocean has no fear of a hurricane.

A Storm in the Mountains ◆
In the Orchard ◆ Prayer to Masks

◆ *Literature and Your Life*

CONNECT YOUR EXPERIENCE

You watch the full moon rise, and imagine what it would be like to walk on it. You are alone with your wonder, yet in some ways you are sharing it with people who lived thousands of years ago.

In these selections, the speakers encounter natural forces that fill them with a similar sense of wonder.

THEMATIC FOCUS: A LARGER WORLD

As you read these selections, ask yourself: In what ways do these writers make scenes from life seem larger than life?

Journal Writing Describe the last time you paused to examine something in nature. How did it make you feel?

◆ Background for Understanding

CULTURE

They were black university students in Paris—thousands of miles from their homelands in Africa or the Caribbean. They saw their rich cultural heritage disappearing under the influence of European colonization. They decided to act.

In the 1930's, these gifted students began a literary movement known as *negritude* (neg´ rə tood´), which celebrated their African origins. Their movement was a response to French domination of native cultures in Africa and the West Indies. However, negritude helped revitalize pride in black identity not just in French colonies, but around the world.

One of the movement's products was Senghor's poem "Prayer to Masks," which affirms African cultural values and evokes a respect for tradition that is universal.

◆ Literary Focus

SPEAKER

Each of these selections has a **speaker,** the imaginary voice assumed by the writer of a work. The speaker is the character—the poet, person, animal, or object—who says the work.

These selections present a range of speakers, each with a distinct personality. To enrich your understanding of what is being said, consider who might be speaking in each of these works and what you can tell about each speaker.

◆ Reading Strategy

ENGAGE THE SENSES

To fully appreciate poems with sensory images, you need to **engage your senses** as you read. This means allowing the poem to speak not just to your mind, but to your eyes and nose. For example, when the speaker of "In the Orchard" says "Brothers! there is better music / In the singing of the birds," he is counting on your sense of hearing (and your memory) to re-create the sound of that singing, so you can experience and be moved by the image.

To help you engage your senses as you read, construct a chart of the five senses, like the one below. Fill in as many sensory details as you can.

	"Storm"	"Orchard"	"Masks"
Sight			
Sound			
Smell			
Taste			
Touch			

A Storm in the Mountains

Alexander Solzhenitsyn
Translated by Michael Glenny

It caught us one pitch-black night at the foot of the pass. We crawled out of our tents and ran for shelter as it came towards us over the ridge.

Everything was black—no peaks, no valleys, no horizon to be seen, only the searing flashes of lightning separating darkness from light, and the gigantic peaks of Belaya-Kaya and Djuguturlyuchat[1] looming up out of the night. The huge black pine trees around us seemed as high as the mountains themselves. For a split second we felt ourselves on terra firma; then once more everything would be plunged into darkness and chaos.

The lightning moved on, brilliant light alternating with pitch blackness, flashing white, then pink, then violet, the mountains and pines always springing back in the same place, their hugeness filling us with awe; yet when they disappeared we could not believe that they had ever existed.

The voice of the thunder filled the gorge, drowning the ceaseless roar of the rivers. Like the arrows of Sabaoth,[2] the lightning flashes rained down on the peaks, then split up into serpentine streams as though bursting into spray against the rock face, or striking and then shattering like a living thing.

As for us, we forgot to be afraid of the lightning, the thunder, and the downpour, just as a droplet in the ocean has no fear of a hurricane. Insignificant yet grateful, we became part of this world—a primal world in creation before our eyes.

---

1. **Belaya-Kaya** (bye lǐ´ə kǐ´ə) **and Djuguturlyuchat** (djoo goo toor lyoo´ chət): Russian mountains.
2. **Sabaoth** (sab´ ā äth´): Biblical word for "armies."

◆ **Build Vocabulary**

terra firma (ter´ ə fur´ mə): Latin for "solid earth"

In the Orchard

Henrik Ibsen
Translated by Sir Edmund Gosse

In the sunny orchard closes,[1]
   While the warblers sing and swing,
Care not whether blustering Autumn
   Break the promises of Spring!
5 Rose and white, the apple blossom
   Hides you from the <u>sultry</u> sky—
Let it flutter, blown and scatter'd,
   On the meadows by-and-by!

Will you ask about the fruitage
10   In the season of the flowers?
Will you murmur, will you question,
   Count the run of weary hours?
Will you let the scarecrow clapping
   Drown all happy sounds and words?
15 Brothers! there is better music
   In the singing of the birds.

From your heavy-laden garden
   Will you hunt the mellow thrush;
He will play you for protection

20   With his crown-song's liquid rush.
O but you will win the bargain,
   Though your fruit be spare and late,
For remember Time is flying
   And will shut the garden gate.

25 With my living, with my singing,
   I will tear the hedges down.
Sweep the grass and heap the blossom!
   Let it shrivel, pale and brown!
Swing the wicket![2] Sheep and cattle,
30   Let them graze among the best!
I broke off the flowers; what matter
   Who may revel with the rest?

---

2. **wicket:** Small door or gate.

◆ **Build Vocabulary**

sultry (sul´ trē) *adj.*: Oppressively hot and moist; sweltering

---

▲ **Critical Viewing** Explain how the photograph on this page suggests the speaker's sense of celebration. **[Connect]**

---

1. **closes:** Enclosed place, as a farmyard.

PRAYER TO MASKS

Léopold Sédar Senghor
Translated by Gerald Moore and Ulli Beier

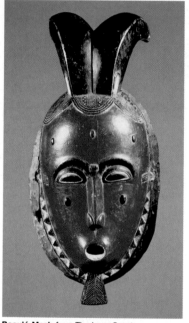

Baoulé Mask from The Ivory Coast

Mask from The Ivory Coast

◀ **Critical Viewing** Why might masks like these fill the speaker in this poem with a sense of wonder? **[Connect]**

Black mask, red mask, you black and white masks,
Rectangular masks through whom the spirit breathes,
I greet you in silence!
And you too, my lionheaded ancestor.
5   You guard this place, that is closed to any feminine laughter, to any
        mortal smile.
You purify the air of <u>eternity</u>, here where I breathe the air of my
        fathers.
Masks of markless faces, free from dimples and wrinkles,
You have composed this image, this my face that bends over the altar
        of white paper.
In the name of your image, listen to me!

10   Now while the Africa of <u>despotism</u> is dying—it is the agony of a
          <u>pitiable</u> princess
      Like that of Europe to whom she is connected through the navel[1]—
      Now fix your <u>immobile</u> eyes upon your children who have been called
      And who sacrifice their lives like the poor man his last garment
      So that hereafter we may cry "here" at the rebirth of the world being
          the leaven[2] that the white flour needs.
15   For who else would teach rhythm to the world that has died of
          machines and cannons?
      For who else should ejaculate the cry of joy, that arouses the dead and
          the wise in a new dawn?
      Say, who else could return the memory of life to men with a torn
          hope?
      They call us cotton heads, and coffee men, and oily men,
      They call us men of death.
20   But we are the men of the dance whose feet only
          gain power when they beat the hard soil.

---

1. navel (nā´ vəl) *n.*: The scar on the abdomen where the umbilical cord, which supplies oxygen and nutrients from the mother, was attached to the fetus in the womb.

2. leaven (lev´ ən): *n.*: A small piece of fermenting dough that is added to a larger batch of dough to make it rise.

◆ **Build Vocabulary**

eternity (ē tʉr´ nə tē) *n.*: Time without end; the endless time after death

despotism (des´ pət iz´ əm) *n.*: Tyranny; rule or domination by a person with unlimited authority

pitiable (pit´ ē ə bəl) *adj.*: Being weak or foolish and therefore inspiring sorrow mixed with contempt or scorn

immobile (im mō´ bəl) *adj.*: Motionless; unmoving

Guide for Responding

◆ *Literature and Your Life*

Reader's Response Which poem most makes you want to share the experience of the speaker? Why?

Thematic Focus How is each speaker's sense of the world broadened by the experience described in each poem?

Journal Entry Write a short journal entry about something that fills you with a sense of wonder.

Questions for Research Formulate several questions that would help you learn more about the role of masks in different cultures.

☑ **Check Your Comprehension**

1. Describe the setting of "A Storm in the Mountains."
2. In which season is "In the Orchard" set? How do you know?
3. In "Prayer to Masks," how does the speaker greet the masks?

◆ **Critical Thinking**

INTERPRET

1. Why does the speaker in "A Storm..." feel on terra firma for only a split second? **[Interpret]**
2. Explain the significance of the scarecrow in the second stanza of "In the Orchard." **[Interpret]**
3. How well does Ibsen's use of sensory images communicate the meaning of "In the Orchard"? **[Assess]**

EVALUATE

4. Senghor and the negritude movement aimed to promote traditional African cultural values. How well do you think "Prayer to Masks" supports this ideal? Explain. **[Make a Judgment]**

APPLY

5. Identify and explain the significance of some objects that are revered in your own culture as the masks are in "Prayer to Masks." **[Relate]**

Guide for Responding (continued)

◆ Reading Strategy

ENGAGE YOUR SENSES

Sensory details in a poem or a description allow you to enter a work completely. **Engaging your senses** as you read helps you to experience the work's sights, sounds, smells, textures, and tastes. For example, language like "The voice of the thunder filled the gorge, drowning the ceaseless roar of the rivers" from "A Storm in the Mountains" appeals to your sense of hearing to help you feel the power of what the speaker witnessed.

1. What two senses do Solzhenitsyn's words "the searing flashes of lightning" call upon?
2. Which image in "In the Orchard" made you most "sense the meaning" of the poem, and why?
3. From your chart, choose a sensory detail from the poem "Prayer to Masks," and explain why it is important to the poem.

◆ Build Vocabulary

USING LATIN TERMS

The following list gives some Latin terms, and their English definitions, that have found their way, unchanged, into English. Fill in the blanks below with the correct Latin term.

ad hoc: for a specific purpose
caveat emptor: let the buyer beware
status quo: the existing state of things
de facto: in reality

1. The school board assembled a(an) ____?____ committee to handle budget issues.
2. A good slogan for those who purchase items from street vendors might be ____?____.
3. Though Kim was editor of the school paper, everyone knew that Ms. Lao was the ____?____ editor.
4. The rest of the group decided it would be easier to maintain the ____?____.

USING THE WORD BANK: Context

On your paper, respond to the numbered sentences using words from the Word Bank.

1. Write a weather forecast using the word *sultry.*
2. Use the word *despotism* to describe the government of a country that is in the news.
3. Use the term *terra firma* in a passage from a travel journal.

◆ Literary Focus

SPEAKER

Even with no conversation, poems can sometimes seem like a dialogue between the **speaker,** or voice telling the poem, and the person (or thing) being addressed. Often a poet chooses to speak directly to you, the reader, but sometimes he or she will speak to a character or object in the poem.

1. Whom is the speaker addressing in "In the Orchard"? Give evidence from the poem to support your answer.
2. Among the following, who is the most likely speaker of "In the Orchard"—a tree, the wind, the poet, or a song? Explain your choice.
3. What is the effect of having the speaker in "Prayer to Masks" address the masks directly?

◆ Build Grammar Skills

CORRECT USE OF *like* AND *as*

Both *like* and *as* can be used in making comparisons. When writing, use *like* as the preposition in a prepositional phrase that compares one thing with another. Do not use *like* as a conjunction to introduce a subordinate clause (a group of words that contains a subject and a verb but cannot stand alone as a sentence).

Practice Write these sentences in your notebook, replacing the blanks with *like* or *as.*

1. It strikes and then shatters ____?____ a living thing.
2. ____?____ a blanket, flowers cover the meadow.
3. He speaks to the masks ____?____ a musician might speak to his instrument.
4. The speaker loves the apple trees ____?____ a child loves its mother.
5. The birds in the orchard sound ____?____ a choir.

Writing Application On your paper, follow the directions to write a sentence for each numbered item. Use the word indicated in parentheses.

1. Compare the way the wind moves with the way the ocean moves. (as)
2. Compare the masks in "Prayer to Masks" to something that symbolizes tradition in your own culture. (like)

Build Your Portfolio

Idea Bank

Writing

1. **Description** From the point of view of a third-person observer, write a description of a tree in a severe storm. Use strong images to engage your readers' senses.

2. **Poem** Using "Prayer to Masks" as a guide, write a brief poem in which the speaker addresses an inanimate object.

3. **Biographical Sketch** Write a biographical sketch on Russian writer Alexander Solzhenitsyn.

Speaking, Listening, and Viewing

4. **Video or Audio** At the library, look up a video or audio recording of or about Solzhenitsyn's life or work. Share it with the class. **[Social Studies Link]**

5. **Interview** With a partner, role-play a television interview with the speaker of "A Storm in the Mountains." **[Performing Arts Link]**

Researching and Representing

6. **Art Exhibit** Create a classroom display of photographs and sketches that contrast nature's power, as depicted in "A Storm in the Mountains," with its serene beauty, as depicted in "In the Orchard." **[Art Link]**

7. **Multimedia Presentation** Give a multimedia presentation on masks from different parts of the world. Use text, photographs, actual masks, recordings, and film clips to explain the roles that masks play in various cultures. **[Social Studies Link; Media Link]**

Online Activity www.phlit.phschool.com

Guided Writing Lesson

Monologue Spoken by a Plant or an Animal

Each poem in this group can be read as a **monologue,** a speech delivered without interruption from others. A monologue may be spoken in the presence of others and may or may not reveal what the speaker really thinks or feels. Open your imagination and write a monologue from the perspective of a plant or an animal.

Writing Skills Focus: Grab Readers' Attention

Don't bury your most stylish line or interesting fact deep within your monologue. Your audience might walk out before you get to it! **Grab their attention** with a strong, controversial statement, a joke, or an exceptionally curious fact. Here's the beginning of a monologue spoken by a queen ant to its worker ants:

> You pay homage to me every hour of your miserable, sniveling lives, but do you think my life is a bed of roses?

This disagreeable speaker immediately raises a question in your mind: Why is her life not a "bed of roses"?

Prewriting Establish a speaker and a situation. After all, your plant or animal must speak *about* something. Decide what the speaker wants to say about the situation, and jot down main points or key phrases.

Drafting In the monologue, your speaker will respond to a situation in its life; it should do so with emotion. Through its emotion, your speaker will communicate its personality and attitude to the audience.

Revising Ask a classmate whether the beginning of your monologue is attention-grabbing, if the "voice" of your speaker is consistent throughout, and if the speaker's emotion is communicated. Be sure you have used *like* and *as* correctly. For more on using these words, see pp. 592 and 598.

Writing Process Workshop

In class, you are frequently asked to think about and discuss a particular sentence or passage in a literary work. Similarly, in an essay test, you may be asked to respond to a question or idea based on a particular literary passage that you've read. The test is designed to assess your writing ability, so be sure you respond fully and directly to the test question. Organize your ideas and supporting details clearly and logically, to make your writing interesting. Stay focused on your purpose for writing so that your sentences all contribute to the whole.

The following skills will help you write an essay responding to literature:

▶ **Give specific examples.** If you say that Chinua Achebe uses dialect in his story "Civil Peace," include a sample of it.

▶ **Elaborate,** or develop details so that the reader can clearly picture what you are saying.

▶ **Give precise details.** Instead of saying, "Our class has helped many people," say "The 150 residents of the local nursing home have enjoyed our weekly concerts."

The following excerpt from an essay about "Mothers & Daughters" demonstrates these skills:

① The writer gives a specific example of a long-lasting mother-and-daughter relationship.

② The writer elaborates on the many types of relationships by describing the variety of emotions and social situations presented.

③ The writer provides a precise detail about one photographer's unique perspective.

WRITING MODEL

Relationships come in all shapes and sizes. It is clear when you read the photo essay "Mothers & Daughters" that these relationships are unique and are not limited to the early years of life. ① Eudora Welty's mother, for example, shared lessons about a love of reading from the time Eudora was two or three until she was an adult. ② The essay includes observations of mothers and daughters who are happy, sullen, wealthy, and poor. ③ One photographer compares the mothers and daughters in the pictures she takes.

Prewriting

Choose a Position In his Nobel lecture, on page 727, Alexander Solzhenitsyn shares his view that "mankind's salvation lies exclusively in everyone's making everything his business. . . ." Write an essay explaining your reaction to this idea.

Reread the selection to understand how Solzhenitsyn supports his belief. Decide whether or not you share his view, and support your position with examples from the selection and from your own experiences. Remember, it was Solzhenitsyn's own personal experiences that led him to share his opinion. In choosing your position, you too should consider your own experiences.

Gather Details After forming your opinion, review Solzhenitsyn's lecture, looking for supporting evidence. Focus on the lecture to gather details. Your essay should refer often and specifically to the selection. If you share Solzhenitsyn's point of view, you'll want to cite examples from his speech. If you disagree with his view, support your opinion with passages from the selection, as well as examples from your own experiences.

Drafting

Engage Your Audience Experienced writers know that they need to grab readers' attention at the beginning. Don't just repeat the test question in your first sentence. Instead, try one of these approaches:

▶ Start with a quotation from Solzhenitsyn's speech that highlights your position.
▶ Begin with a startling example from current events that supports your position.
▶ Cite an example from personal experience to introduce your point of view.

Use Transition Words To strengthen your essay, add transition words to show how your ideas work together. Choose words from the Transition Word Bin below:

Transition Word Bin

Spatial	Cause and Effect	Compare and Contrast
behind	because	identically
at the center	as a result	in the same way
alongside	consequently	different from
within	side effect	more, less, most
on top of	outcome	similarly, equally

APPLYING LANGUAGE SKILLS: Eliminating Unnecessary Words

Needless words weigh down your writing and may confuse your readers. **Eliminate unnecessary words** in your essay.

Wordy: The Sierra 2000 is more or less a pretty decent value in those fun things we love to call cameras. As a matter of fact, I believe that I'll hop right on down to the store and buy one for my little old self.

Streamlined: The Sierra 2000 is such a decent value in camera equipment, I think I'll buy one for myself.

Practice Eliminate unnecessary words in the following:

Past history shows that just when you think that the camera can't possibly be improved or made easier to use by professionals and amateurs alike, some smart inventor comes along and does just that.

Writing Application Make sure that your essay has no unnecessary words.

Writer's Solution Connection Language Lab

For more practice streamlining your sentences, complete the Language Lab lesson on Eliminating Unnecessary Words.

Applying Language Skills: Infinitives and Infinitive Phrases

An **infinitive** is the base form of a verb, usually preceded by *to*; it can be used as a noun, an adjective, or an adverb. An **infinitive phrase** contains an infinitive and all the words that go with it.

Infinitive: <u>To connect</u> is this author's goal.

Infinitive Phrase: <u>To connect with people around the world</u> is this author's goal.

Practice On your paper, change the following sentence into one with an infinitive:

Expressing the common experiences of people around the world is one goal of good literature.

Writing Application Review your essay. Add infinitives where they would make your sentence structure more interesting.

Writer's Solution Connection Writing Lab

To help you revise your essay, see the Revising and Editing screen of the Writing Lab Tutorial for Response to Literature.

Revising

Use a Checklist Use the following checklist to improve your essay:

▶ Did I respond directly to the test question?
▶ What appropriate details and quotations from the literature can I add to strengthen my point of view?
▶ Have I used precise language and correct spelling, grammar, and usage?
▶ Is my organization clear and easy to follow?
▶ Have I elaborated on my points to make them clear to the reader?

REVISION MODEL

The observations in "Mothers & Daughters" show many

① *Tillie Olsen and Julie Olsen Edwards give examples of a wide range of relationships, while Eudora Welty focuses on a single relationship with her own mother.*

viewpoints. The photographs and text work together to

②

explain this unique ~~and amazing~~ relationship. In

understanding this essay, "reading" the photographs is

③ *, as Estelle Jussim points out in her observation,*

crucial   *"it requires a grasp of visual language."*

just as ~~important~~ as reading the text.

---

① The writer adds this detail to specify the types of relationships discussed in the essay.
② The writer eliminates an unnecessary word.
③ The writer changes a word to clarify meaning.
④ The writer elaborates on the last sentence to support it with a detail.

Publishing

Submit Your Essay to Be Scored If you are satisfied with your essay's content, read it through one last time to check for errors. Then, submit it to your teacher.

Student Success Workshop

Research Skills — Evaluating Sources of Information

Strategies for Success

Research is a major part of writing a report. (See the Research Handbook, beginning on p. 1133, for suggestions about sources of information.) As you undertake your research, you may find yourself poring through books, magazines, encyclopedias, and other materials that may have information on your topic. Before you plunge into writing, evaluate your sources of information to determine which resources will provide the best information.

Consider the Source Before choosing a source, investigate the author of the text. Is he or she an expert on the subject? Look in the book for biographical information that tells the author's qualifications.

Consider the Date Check to see when a book was published. (You can usually find the date on the page following the title page.) The information in older works might be outdated, especially if the subjects are science or social studies. For example, if you were researching

information on Germany today and used a book from 1987, it would refer to East Germany and West Germany, but it would not include information about the reunification of Germany since the Berlin Wall came down in 1989. The information would not be current.

Apply the Strategies

You are writing a research paper on the relationship between cats and their owners. Look at the sources available to you as you answer the questions that follow:

> *The World Book Encyclopedia,* Volume C, © 1998
>
> *Cats: Creatures of Wonder,* by Lori Rigby, © 1960 by Roan Publishing
>
> "New Research on Cat–People Connection," *The Washington Post,* February 5, 1998
>
> "Cats Have Feelings Too," *Milford Daily News,* November 8, 1975
>
> *Cat Fancy* by Dr. R. Gonzales, © 1998 by Prentice Hall

1. Which would you prefer to use—the encyclopedia or *The Washington Post* article? Why?
2. Which of the two newspapers would you prefer to use? Why?
3. Which of the two books would you prefer to use? Why?

✔ Here are other situations in which it is helpful to evaluate sources of information:
   ▶ Reading newspaper editorials
   ▶ Investigating a rumor
   ▶ Reading two articles on the same topic

Speaking, Listening, and Viewing Workshop

Visual representations—including photographs, television ads and programs, films, news reports, paintings, book and magazine illustrations, and Internet Web pages—all communicate messages visually. Some combine images and text. If several images and phrases from a TV documentary on Cambodia come to mind when you think of that country, that documentary has influenced your idea of a part of the world. What you see in visual representations often shapes your perception of reality. When you have a chance to produce your own visual representation to express an idea to an audience, the following strategies will help:

Decide on Your Message Before you can decide what type of visual representation to produce, you need to be clear about your reason for producing it. Ask yourself these questions:

▶ What do I want to say?
▶ To what audience do I want to direct my message?

For example, you might want to tell a group of friends what you learned about the architecture of a neighborhood across town.

Decide on Your Medium Think about the variety of media forms you could use to get your message across. Your representation of the architecture across town might be

produced as a video, a poster combining words and images, a three-dimensional model, a series of photographs or drawings with or without captions, or a series of linked Web pages. You decide.

Plan It Out Depending on the form you choose, you will need a plan for creating your product. For example, to produce a video, you might begin by making a list of scenes to include. Next, you might make a storyboard: a series of "thumbnail" drawings showing the sequence of film shots. Then you could use the storyboard as a guide for shooting the video.

Create Your Product The creative process is the most fulfilling—and sometimes the most challenging—part of producing a visual representation. Keep your plan and your message in mind, and follow it!

Be Your Own Best Critic Once you have completed your product, take time to reflect on it critically. Imagine that you are a member of your audience. What does the finished product say to you? Is your product's message the same as the one you intended to communicate? If you find that your product needs revision, you'll need to return to the creative process.

Apply the Strategies

Use what you've learned about producing a visual representation to create one or more of the following media products:

1. Produce a five-minute documentary about a family member or friend.
2. With a partner, create an illustrated children's book.
3. Design an Internet Home Page for yourself or a Web site to promote a service or product.
4. Create a holiday greeting card.
5. Produce a parody of a commercial or a music video.

Test Preparation Workshop

Reading Comprehension

Recognizing Cause and Effect; Predicting Outcomes

Strategies for Success

The reading sections of standardized tests often require you to read a passage to understand cause-and-effect relationships. The test may also require you to predict future actions and outcomes. Use the following strategies to answer test questions on these skills:

Recognize Causes and Effects A *cause* is an event that makes something else happen, and an *effect* is the result that happens. In a passage on a test, you may find words and phrases that hint at cause-and-effect relationships, such as *because* and *as a result*. To recognize cause-and-effect relationships, ask yourself: "What happened? What was the result? What caused this occurrence?"

You might be asked to recognize the cause-and-effect relationships in a passage such as this:

Last month's ski trip was a flop. Only eight of our thirty members came. Some had no transportation. Others had prior holiday commitments. In addition, the cost of the trip was more than most members could pay. We need to work together to address these concerns before scheduling the next trip.

1 What effect did the holidays have on the trip?
   A Some members had no transportation.
   B Some members couldn't afford to go.
   C The trip's organizers had not planned well.
   D Some members had other holiday plans.

Answers **A** and **B** refer to causes of low attendance on the trip. Answer **C** does not explain why the holidays had an effect on who could go on the trip. Answer **D** is correct because it explains how the holidays prevented some people from participating.

Predict Actions and Outcomes Use what you know from the text and your own experience to predict probable future actions and outcomes. Ask yourself, "What might happen next?"

2 What can you predict about the next ski trip?
   A The cost will still be too high for most.
   B The trip will be planned more carefully.
   C The trip will be another failure.
   D The planners will disagree on where to go.

Answers **A, C,** and **D** are incorrect because the passage suggests that the organizers are aware of the problems and want to address them. Answer **B** is the correct answer.

Apply the Strategies

Read the following passage, and answer the questions that follow.

Gina and Phoebe had planned to study together for tomorrow's algebra exam, as they often did. They had agreed to meet at the library at six-thirty. But as Gina was leaving the house, her mother fell and hurt her arm. Gina had to rush her to the hospital. By the time she could call Phoebe, it was past her bedtime. Although it wasn't her fault that she missed their appointment, Gina was worried that Phoebe would be angry with her.

1 Why didn't Gina meet Phoebe at the library?
   A Gina forgot that they had planned to meet.
   B Gina's mother hurt her arm.
   C Gina took her mother to the hospital.
   D It was past closing time at the library.

2 How might Phoebe react to Gina's explanation?
   A She will doubt Gina's story.
   B She will pretend to be understanding, but will actually feel angry or hurt.
   C She will never study with Gina again.
   D She will probably be understanding.

The Village of Andreikovo (detail), Vladimir Stozharov, The Tretyakov Gallery, Moscow

Short Stories in World Literature

As long as people have had language, they have had stories—stories of the hunt, stories of battles, stories of romance, mystery, and adventure. There are no limits to the places short stories can take you. In a realistic short story, you might share the experiences of someone like yourself, while in a fantastic short story, you might travel to a strange, dreamlike world. No matter where you go or whom you meet, however, you can be sure your brief encounter will enrich your life.

Guide for Reading

Manuel Rojas *(1896–1973)*

A man of strength and vigor, Manuel Rojas (mà no͞o el´ rō´ häs) is known for his forceful and moving prose. Of Chilean descent, Rojas was born and raised in Argentina. Having lost his father when he was not yet five, he had to work as a laborer during his early teens.

A Variety of Jobs Rojas moved to Chile at age sixteen. There, he worked as a sailor, housepainter, bargeman, night watchman, typographer, and railroad worker. In 1924, he settled in Santiago, the capital of Chile, and began writing. Two years later, he published his first collection of short stories, *Men of the South,* based on his experiences as a laborer.

In 1931 Rojas was named the director of the University of Chile Press. Over the next thirty years, he produced many works, including *Launches in the Bay* (1932), *The Biretta From Maule* (1943), *Son of a Thief* (1951), and *Better Than Wine* (1958).

Based on Real Life Regarded as Rojas's finest work, the novel *Son of a Thief* tells of the sufferings of a young Argentine boy. After his father is imprisoned for burglary, the boy spends his childhood in poverty. As Rojas did in his own childhood, the boy works as a laborer and goes to Chile in search of a better life. There, he accidentally gets involved in a street riot and is unjustly imprisoned. Rojas's penetrating insight into the inner workings of the boy's mind established this novel as one of the finest ever produced in Latin America.

The Story Behind the Story Despite the success of *Son of a Thief*, Rojas is remembered mainly for his short stories. "The Glass of Milk" is a typical Rojas story. Based on his personal experiences, the story is told in a simple and restrained, yet authoritative and moving, manner.

◆ Build Vocabulary

LATIN SUFFIXES: *-ity*

At one point in the story, the boy's timidity prevents him from doing something. The word *timidity* is built on *timid* with the Latin suffix *-ity*, which means "state, character, condition, or an instance of." The suffix *-ity* makes a noun of the word to which it is added. Knowing this will help you figure out other words with the same suffix, such as *civility*.

WORD BANK

As you read the story, you will encounter the words on this list. Each word is defined on the page where it first appears. Preview the list before you read.

gaudy
timidity
anguished
entrails

◆ Build Grammar Skills

CONJUNCTIVE ADVERBS

A **conjunctive adverb** is an adverb that acts as a conjunction to connect complete ideas. Conjunctive adverbs include: *accordingly, again, also, besides, consequently, finally, furthermore, however, indeed, moreover, nevertheless, otherwise, then, therefore,* and *thus*. This sentence from "The Glass of Milk" includes the conjunctive adverb *then*.

> The lady returned, and placed before him a large glass of milk, and a dish full of vanilla wafers; *then* she went back to her place behind the counter.

As you read, notice how conjunctive adverbs are used to help you clearly follow the order of events.

The Glass of Milk

◆ *Literature and Your Life*

CONNECT YOUR EXPERIENCE

Think about how you feel when you haven't eaten for more than five hours. Imagine how you would feel if you hadn't eaten for a full day. Then, imagine two or even three days without food. This is what the boy in this story faces.

THEMATIC FOCUS: PERSONAL CHALLENGES

As you read, notice how the boy tries to meet the personal challenge of finding food to sustain himself. What other options might he have had?

Journal Writing In your journal, write about the things that you think can be done to address the problem of hunger in the United States and other countries. When you have finished reading, review your entry to see if your thoughts have changed in any way.

◆ Background for Understanding

SOCIAL STUDIES

The setting for the story is a port city north of Punta Arenas in southern Chile. The port city is not named, but it could be any one of the port cities marked on this map. As you'll notice from looking at the map, Chile is a long, narrow country on the Pacific coast of South America. With 2,700 miles of coastline, it is not surprising shipping to plays a key role in Chile's economy. Although the Chilean economy has enjoyed periods of prosperity, it has always had a sizeable population of poor, unskilled laborers like the main character in this story.

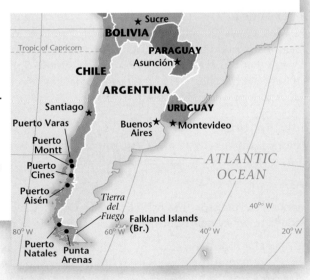

◆ Literary Focus

CONFLICT AND RESOLUTION

The hunger that this story's main character experiences creates rising tension as the story progresses. This type of tension, or struggle between opposing forces, is known as **conflict.** Just about every novel and short story has at least one conflict. The conflict can be internal or external.

- An **internal conflict** takes place within a character, as he or she struggles with opposite feelings, beliefs, or needs.

- An **external conflict** occurs between two or more characters or between a character and a natural force.

- **Resolution** refers to the way in which the conflict is solved.

Reading for Success

Strategies for Reading Fiction

Suppose you could visit a new and exciting place each week—you can if you read works of fiction! Reading fiction allows you to explore unfamiliar places and unusual worlds.

Just as mapping out a strategy for a vacation helps ensure a pleasant trip, applying effective strategies as you read fiction helps you understand and enjoy what you are reading. When you read fiction, use the following strategies:

Predict what will happen or what the author will say.

As you read, ask yourself what might happen. You may base a prediction on your own experience in a similar situation or on information that has been provided in the text. Continue to make predictions as you read.

Identify with a character or the situation.

Identify with a character or the situation in your reading. Put yourself in the place of the character and experience his or her thoughts, feelings, and so on. Ask yourself how you would handle the situation.

Envision the setting and the action.

Use details from the story to create a picture in your mind, as if you were watching the story unfold on the big screen. For example, see the house that your character lives in. Is it big or small? How is it decorated? As you read, envision the action and revise the images in your mind as events unfold.

Draw inferences.

Writers don't always tell you everything directly. You have to make inferences to arrive at ideas that writers suggest but don't state. You make an inference by considering the details that the writer includes or doesn't include. Sometimes it's also helpful to "read between the lines"—to look beyond the literal meaning of the words to obtain a full picture of what the author is saying.

Draw conclusions.

A conclusion is a general statement that you can support with details from the text. A series of inferences can lead you to a conclusion.

Respond.

Think about what the story means. What feelings does it evoke in you? What has the story added to your understanding of people and of life in general?

As you read the following story by Manuel Rojas, look at the notes in the boxes. These notes demonstrate how to apply these strategies to a work of fiction.

The Glass of Milk

Manuel Rojas
Translated by Zoila Nelken

Propped on the starboard[1] rail, the sailor seemed to be waiting for someone. A bundle wrapped in white paper, grease-spotted, was in his left hand; his right tended his pipe.

From behind some freight-cars, a thin youth appeared; he paused a moment, looked out to sea, and then walked on along the edge of the wharf with his hands in his pockets, idling or thinking.

When he passed in front of the ship, the sailor called out to him in English:

"I say, look here!"

The youth raised his head, and without stopping, answered in the same language:

"Hello! What?"

"Are you hungry?"

There was a brief silence during which the youth seemed to be thinking, and took one shorter step as if to stop, but then replied, smiling feebly at the sailor:

"No. I'm not hungry. Thanks, sailor."

"All right."

The sailor took his pipe from his mouth, spat, and replacing it, looked away. The youth, ashamed that he had seemed to need charity, walked a little faster, as if afraid he might change his mind.

A moment later, a gaudy tramp with a long, blond beard and blue eyes, dressed in odd rags and oversized, torn shoes, passed before the sailor, who without greeting called to him:

"Are you hungry?"

He had not yet finished the phrase when the tramp looked with shining eyes at the package

the sailor held in his hand and answered hurriedly:

"Yes, sir; I'm very much hungry!"

The sailor smiled. The package flew through the air and landed in the eager hands. The hungry fellow did not even say "thanks," but sat right down on the ground, opened the still-warm bundle, and happily rubbed his hands as he saw what it contained. A port loafer might not speak English well, but he would never forgive himself if he didn't know enough to ask food from someone who did speak it.

The youth who passed by first had stopped nearby, and had seen what happened.

He was hungry too. He had not eaten for exactly three days, three long days. And more from timidity and shame than from pride, he refused to wait by the gangways at mealtimes, hoping the generosity of the sailors would produce some package of left-overs and bits of meat. He could not do it, he would never be able to do it. And when, as just now, someone did offer him a handout, the boy refused it heroically, though he felt his hunger increase with the refusal.

He had been wandering for six days around the side streets and docks of that port. An English vessel had left him there after bringing him

> **Identify** with the boy and ask yourself—if I were hungry would I ask for help? Why or why not?

◆ **Build Vocabulary**

gaudy (gôd′ ē) adj.: Cheaply bright and showy

timidity (tə mid′ ə tē) n.: Quality of being shy and easily frightened

---

1. **starboard** (stär′ bərd) adj.: On the right-hand side of a ship.

from Punta Arenas,[2] where he had jumped a previous ship on which he had served as captain's mess boy. He had spent a month there helping an Austrian crabber and then had stowed away on the first ship bound north.

He was discovered the day after sailing, and put to work in the boiler room. At the first large port of call, he had been put off, and there he had remained, like a bale without a label, without an acquaintance, without a penny, and without a trade.

As long as the ship was in port, the boy managed to eat, but after that . . . The great city that rose up beyond the back streets with their taverns and cheap inns did not attract him; it seemed a place of slavery: stale, dark, without the grand sweep of the sea; among its high walls and narrow streets people lived and died bewildered by agonizing drudergy.

The boy was gripped by that fascination of the sea which molds the most peaceful and orderly lives as a strong arm a thin rod. Although very young, he had already made several trips along the coast of South America on various ships, doing odd jobs and tasks, tasks and odd jobs which were almost useless on land.

Retrato de un Joven (Portrait of a Youth), Leonor Fini

▲ **Critical Viewing** If this is the boy in the story after the ship has departed, what do you imagine he is thinking? Explain. **[Speculate]**

After the ship left him, the boy walked and walked, hoping to chance upon something that would enable him to live somehow until he could get back to his home grounds; but he found nothing. The port was not very busy, and the few ships that had work would not take him on.

The docks were swarming with confirmed tramps: sailors on the beach, like himself, who had either jumped ship or were fleeing some crime; loafers given to idleness, who kept alive one knows not how, by begging and stealing, spending their days as if they were the beads of some grimy rosary,[3] waiting for who knows what extraordinary events, or not expecting anything; people of the strangest and most exotic races and places, and even some in whose existence one doesn't believe until one sees a living example.

The following day, convinced that he could not hold out much longer, the youth decided to resort to any means to get some food.

Walking along, he found himself in front of a ship that had docked the night before, and was loading

What details from the author's description help you **envision** the port? Explain.

---

2. **Punta Arenas** (pōōn´ tä ä re´ näs): A city in southern Chile.

3. **rosary** (rō´ zər ē) *n.:* A string of beads used to keep count in saying prayers.

wheat. A line of men, heavy sacks on their shoulders, shuttled from the freight-cars, across the gangplank to the hatchways of the ship's hold where the stevedores[4] received the cargo.

He watched for a while, until he dared to speak to the foreman, offering his services. He was accepted, and enthusiastically he took his place in the long line of dock workers.

During the first period of the day he worked well; but later, he began to feel tired and dizzy; he swayed as he crossed the gangplank, the heavy load on his shoulder, on seeing at his feet the opening between the side of the ship and the thick wall of the wharf, at the bottom of which the sea, stained with oil and littered with garbage, lapped quietly.

There was a brief pause at lunch time, and while some of the men went off to nearby eating places, and others ate what they had brought, the boy stretched out on the ground to rest, hiding his hunger.

He finished the day's work completely exhausted, covered with sweat, at the end of his rope. While the laborers were leaving, the boy sat on some sacks, watching for the foreman, and when the last man had gone, approached him; confused and stuttering, he asked, without explaining what was happening to him, if he could be paid immediately, or if it were possible to get an advance on his earnings.

The foreman answered that it was customary to pay at the end of the job, and that it would still be necessary to work the following day in order to finish loading the ship. One more day! On the other hand, they never paid a cent in advance.

"But," he said, "if you need it, I could lend you about forty cents . . . That's all I have."

The boy thanked him for his offer with a <u>anguished</u> smile, and left.

Then the boy was seized by acute despair. He was hungry, hungry, hungry! Hunger doubled him over, like a heavy, broad whiplash. He saw everything through a blue haze, and he staggered like a drunk when he walked. Neverthe-

less, he would not have been able to complain or to shout, for his suffering was deep and exhausting; it was not pain, but anguish, the end! It seemed to him that he was flattened out by a great weight.

Suddenly he felt his <u>entrails</u> on fire, and he stood still. He began to bend down, down, doubling over forcibly like a rod of steel, until he thought that he would drop. At that instant, as if a window opened before him, he saw his home, the view from it, the faces of his mother, brothers and sisters, all that he wanted and loved appeared and disappeared before his eyes shut by fatigue. . . Then, little by little, the giddiness passed and he began to straighten up, while the burning subsided gradually. Finally he straightened up, breathing deeply. One more hour and he would drop unconscious to the ground.

He quickened his step, as if he were fleeing another dizzy spell, and, as he walked, he made up his mind to eat anywhere, without paying, even if they shamed him, beat him, sent him to jail, anything; the main thing was to eat, eat, eat. A hundred times he mentally repeated the word: eat, eat, eat, until it lost its meaning, leaving his head feeling hot and empty.

He did not intend to run away; he would simply say to the owner, "Sir, I was hungry, hungry, hungry, and I can't pay. . . Do what you want."

He came to the outskirts of the city, and on one of the first streets he found a milk bar. It was a small, clean, and airy place, with little tables with marble tops. Behind the counter stood a blonde lady in a very white apron.

> What details help you **predict** that the boy will ask for food?

He chose that place. There were few passersby. He could have eaten at one of the cheap grills near the wharves but they were always full of people who gambled and drank.

---

4. **stevedores** (stē′ və dôrz′) *n.*: People employed at loading and unloading ships.

◆ Build Vocabulary

anguished (aŋ′ gwisht) *adj.*: Showing worry, grief, or pain

entrails (en′ trālz) *n.*: Intestines; guts

There was only one customer in the milk bar. He was a little old man with glasses, who sat reading, his nose stuck between the pages of a newspaper, motionless, as if glued to his chair. On the little table there was a half-empty glass of milk.

While he waited for him to leave, the boy walked up and down the sidewalk; he felt the burning sensation in his stomach returning little by little; and he waited five, ten, up to fifteen minutes. He grew tired, and stood to one side of the door, from where he cast glances like stones at the old man.

What the devil could he be reading with such attention? The boy even imagined the old man was his enemy, who knew his intentions and had decided to frustrate them. He felt like entering and saying something insulting that would force the old man to leave, a rude word or phrase that would show him he had no right to sit there reading for an hour for so small a purchase.

Finally, the client finished what he was reading, or at least, interrupted it. He downed the rest of the milk in one gulp, got up slowly, paid, and walked toward the door. He went out. He was a stoop-shouldered old man, probably a carpenter or varnisher.

Once in the street, the old man put on his glasses, stuck his nose in the newspaper again, and walked slowly away, stopping every ten steps to read more closely.

The youth waited until he was some distance away, and then entered. For a moment the boy stood by the entrance, undecided, not knowing where to sit. Finally, he chose a table and walked toward it, but halfway there he changed his mind, walked backed, tripped over a chair, and finally installed himself in a corner.

The lady came, wiped the table top with a rag, and in a soft voice that had a trace of Castilian[5] accent, asked him,

"What will you have?"

"A glass of milk."

"Large?"

"Yes, large."

"Is that all?"

"Are there any biscuits?"

"No, Vanilla wafers."

"Well, vanilla wafers."

When the lady had turned away, he wiped his hands on his knees, rejoicing, as if he were cold and were about to drink something hot.

The lady returned, and placed before him a large glass of milk, and a dish full of vanilla wafers; then she went back to her place behind the counter.

His first impulse was to drink the milk in one gulp and then eat the vanilla wafers, but he immediately changed his mind. He felt the woman's eyes were watching him with curiosity and attention. He did not dare to look at her; he felt that if he did she would guess his situation and his shameful intentions, and he would have to get up and leave without touching what he had ordered.

Slowly, he took a vanilla wafer and moistening it in the milk, he took a bite; he took a sip of milk and he felt the burning in his stomach diminishing, dying away. But he became aware of the reality of his desperate situation at once, and he felt something tight and hot well up inside, choking him. He realized that he was about to cry, to sob aloud, and although he knew that the lady was looking at him, he could neither hold back nor undo the burning knot of tears that grew tighter and tighter. He fought it, and as he fought he ate hurriedly, as if frightened, afraid that crying would keep him from eating. When he had finished the milk and the wafers, his eyes clouded and something hot rolled down his nose and into the glass. A terrible sob racked his whole body.

He held his head in his hands, and for a long time he cried; cried with rage, cried with shame, crying as he had never cried before.

He was hunched over crying when he felt a hand caress his tired head, and heard a woman's voice with a sweet Castilian accent say to him:

"Cry, son, cry. . . ."

Again his eyes filled with tears and he cried as intensely as before, but this

> Basing your answer on the woman's manner and comment, what **inferences** can you make about her?

---

5. **Castilian** (kas til´ yən): Of Castile, a region in northern and central Spain.

Puerto de Villefranche, Joaquim Torres-Garcia, Christie's, New York

▲ **Critical Viewing** How do details in this picture convey a mood similar to that of the story? **[Connect]**

time, not with pain but with joy; he felt a great refreshing sensation spread inside him, extinguishing the hot something that had nearly strangled him. As he cried, it seemed to him that his life and feelings were cleansed like a glass under a stream of water, recovering the clearness and firmness of former days.

When the crying spell passed, he wiped his eyes and face with his handkerchief, feeling relieved. He raised his head and looked at the lady, but she was no longer looking at him, she was gazing out at the street, at a distant point in space, and her face seemed sad.

On the table before him there was another glass of milk and another dish heaped with vanilla wafers. He ate slowly, without thinking about anything, as if nothing had happened to him, as if he were at home and his mother were

that woman who was standing behind the counter.

When he finished, it had grown dark, and the place was lit by an electric light. He remained seated for a while, wondering what he would say to the lady when he left, without thinking of anything appropriate.

At last he got up and said simply, "Thank you very much, ma'am; goodbye. . ." "Goodbye, son," she answered.

He went out. The wind blowing from the sea refreshed his face, still hot from weeping. He walked about aimlessly for a while, then went down a street that led to the docks. It was a very beautiful night, and large stars gleamed in the summer sky.

He thought about the blonde lady who had treated him so generously, resolving to repay her, to reward her as she deserved, when he got some money. But these thoughts of gratitude vanished with the burning of his face, until not one remained, and the recent event receded and was lost in the recesses of his past life.

Suddenly, he surprised himself humming. He straightened up happily, strode on with assurance and determination.

He came to the edge of the sea, and walked back and forth with a spring in his step; he felt like a new man, as if his inner forces, previously scattered, had reassembled and united solidly.

Then he sat down on a pile of burlap sacks; fatigue, like a tingling sensation, climbed up his legs. He looked at the sea. The lights of the wharf and ships spread over the water in a reddish-gold ripple, trembling softly. He stretched out on his back, looking up at the sky for a long time. He did not feel like thinking, or singing, or talking. He just felt alive, that was all. Then he fell asleep with his face toward the sea.

> **Respond** to the story by asking yourself—Do I think that this boy's life will get better? Why or why not?

Guide for Responding

◆ *Literature and Your Life*

Reader's Response What is your reaction to the young man's plight? Do you feel sympathetic toward him? Why or why not?

Thematic Focus What qualities do you think helped the boy take care of his most pressing problem? What qualities stood in his way?

Reader's Journal Think about a time when you were very hungry, cold, hot, or tired. What happened to change your situation? How did you feel after you had taken care of the problem?

☑ Check Your Comprehension

1. (a) What does the sailor offer the thin youth, and (b) what is the youth's reaction?
2. (a) What is the youth's most pressing problem, and (b) what is the first thing he does to try to solve it?
3. What is the youth's desperate plan?
4. How does the blonde woman help the youth?
5. How does the youth react to the blonde woman's help?

◆ Critical Thinking

INTERPRET

1. Why does the young man choose not to accept the sailor's handout or the foreman's loan? **[Interpret]**
2. Why does the young man lapse into a fit of uncontrollable weeping in the milk bar? **[Infer]**
3. Why do you think the young man's feelings of gratitude vanish so quickly? **[Speculate]**
4. How would you characterize the young man? **[Synthesize]**
5. What do you see as the theme, or central message, of this story? Explain. **[Draw Conclusions]**

APPLY

6. (a) What advice would you give the young man? (b) What reasons would you give to persuade him to take your advice? **[Apply]**

COMPARE LITERARY WORKS

7. Compare the thin youth in "The Glass of Milk" with another literary character who faces serious hardship. Explain how their circumstances and actions are alike and different. **[Literary Link]**

Guide for Responding (continued)

◆ Reading Strategy

STRATEGIES FOR READING FICTION

Strategies for reading fiction include predicting, identifying, envisioning, drawing inferences, drawing conclusions, and responding. Review these strategies and the notes showing how to apply them. Then, apply the strategies to answer the following questions.

1. What predictions did you make about how the boy would solve his problem? Which predictions did you change before you read the end of the story?
2. What inferences can you draw about the boy's upbringing from his behavior? Explain.
3. Relate a scene from the story in which you identified with one of the characters. Explain why.
4. Describe the interior of the milk bar as you envisioned it.
5. What conclusions can you draw about human behavior, based on the events in the story? Explain.
6. How did you respond to the story's message about the workings of self-respect?

◆ Build Vocabulary

USING THE LATIN SUFFIX -ity

Use the meaning of the Latin suffix -ity ("state, character, condition, or an instance of") to define each of these words.

1. purity   6. accessibility
2. continuity   7. activity
3. humanity   8. generality
4. stability   9. curiosity
5. abnormality   10. popularity

USING THE WORD BANK: Context

On your paper, answer the following questions.
1. What might a *gaudy* outfit look like?
2. Describe the manner of a person approaching you with *timidity*.
3. Would an *anguished* person go to a party? Explain.
4. Where would an injury in an animal's *entrails* be?

◆ Literary Focus

CONFLICT AND RESOLUTION

A **conflict** is a struggle between opposing forces that drives the action of a story. A conflict can be either external, between a character and an outside force, or internal, within a character. A story's **resolution** are the events or insights through which the conflict is solved.

1. Describe the story's conflict. What are the forces involved?
2. Explain whether the conflict is internal or external.
3. Describe the resolution of the story's conflict, and explain what it reveals about the youth and about the woman who helps him.
4. How powerful was the story's conflict? Did it make you want to keep reading?
5. How satisfying was the resolution of the conflict?

◆ Build Grammar Skills

CONJUNCTIVE ADVERBS

A **conjunctive adverb** joins *only* independent clauses—not single words, phrases, or subordinate clauses—and acts as a modifier. Conjunctive adverbs include *accordingly, also, besides, consequently, still, furthermore, hence, however, indeed, instead, thus, moreover, nonetheless, otherwise, then,* and *therefore.*

Practice Copy the following sentences. In each blank, write an appropriate conjunctive adverb.
1. The boy had not eaten; ___?___, he was very hungry.
2. He had no skills; ___?___, no one would hire him.
3. He needed to eat; ___?___, he would become ill.
4. He had no money; ___?___, he ordered some milk.

Writing Application Write a brief review in which you tell what you did and did not like about this story. Use at least five conjunctive adverbs in your review. Circle each one you use.

Build Your Portfolio

 ## Idea Bank

Writing

1. **Diary Entry** Write the diary entry that the thin youth in "The Glass of Milk" might have written about what happened in the milk bar and how he reacted.

2. **Character Analysis** Write a brief essay in which you analyze what you learned about the young man's character based on his actions in the story. Support each of your points with details from the story.

3. **Story From a Different Point of View** Retell the story of the events in the milk bar from the waitress's point of view. Include what she might have been thinking when "her face seemed sad."

Speaking, Listening, and Viewing

4. **Dramatization** With a classmate, reenact the scene in the milk bar. Pay close attention not only to the dialogue and how you speak it, but also to your body language. **[Performing Arts Link]**

5. **Interview** Imagine that you can interview Manuel Rojas. With a partner, develop questions and responses based on his life. Perform your interview for the class. **[Performing Arts Link]**

Researching and Representing

6. **Multimedia Presentation** Choose a Latin American country, and find out about life there in the early twentieth century. Present your findings to the class, using photographs, maps, music, charts, and other resources. **[Social Studies Link]**

7. **Hunger Chart** Conduct research to find out how long a person can survive without food, and to identify the effects of a lack of food on the human body. Create a chart in which you present your findings. **[Science Link]**

Online Activity **www.phlit.phschool.com**

 ## Guided Writing Lesson

Study Notes: Summary

When you **summarize,** you condense a long piece of writing into a few sentences or a paragraph. Writing a summary of a work can be a useful method of studying. When writing a summary of a short story, you should include the key events of the story's plot. Plan and write a summary of "The Glass of Milk."

Writing Skills Focus: Transitions to Show Time

When summarizing, it's important to indicate which events happened before others. Show relations between events by including transition words. Transitions to show time order include *first, then, next, afterward, at that time, before, earlier, immediately, in the past, later, now, soon, when,* and so on. These words indicate how one event is related to another in time.

Prewriting Reread "The Glass of Milk." As you read, jot down the key events in the order in which they occur. In addition, keep track of the people involved. You can make your notes in the form of a list, a timeline, or an outline.

Drafting Using your prewriting notes, draft a summary of the story. Develop each key event into a sentence or two. Use transitional words to show readers the relationships between the events as they occurred over time.

Revising Reread your draft. Make sure you captured all the key events and people in your summary. Add any important details you may have forgotten, as well as transitional words and phrases that show time order. If you have used any conjunctive adverbs in your summary, check to make sure you have used them correctly. For more on conjunctive adverbs, see pp. 608 and 617.

PART 1   *Plot, Point of View, and Character*

Diego Martelli, Edgar Degas, The National Gallery of Scotland

*G*uide for Reading

Honoré de Balzac *(1799–1850)*

Honoré de Balzac (ô nô *rā´* də bȧl zȧk´) is generally considered to be the greatest nineteenth-century French novelist. A tireless writer, he produced more than ninety novels and novellas and numerous stories.

From Law to Letters

Balzac was born in Tours, France, to middle-class parents. In 1814, Balzac's family moved back to Paris. When Balzac completed his studies, he went on to earn a law degree. To his parents' disappointment, however, Balzac announced his intention to become a writer.

Slow Rise to Fame By 1822, Balzac had written several novels under pseudonyms, but his work was largely ignored. To make money, Balzac embarked on several business ventures, but they all failed, leaving Balzac with massive debts that plagued him for the rest of his life.

Les Chouans was Balzac's first successful novel published under his own name. Balzac soon began to gain notice as a writer of merit. In 1834, he conceived the notion of weaving together his old novels and adding new ones to create a single work that would portray French society as a whole. He titled the work *La Comédie Humaine* (*The Human Comedy*).

A Larger-Than-Life Figure Balzac was renowned for his larger-than-life personality. He consumed gallons of strong black coffee each day, preferring to write from midnight to until midday. Periodically, Balzac would take breaks from writing to plunge into the social scene of Paris. He would splurge on wildly expensive dinners, clothes, and antiques and run up further debts. To pay off those debts, Balzac would then have to work furiously again, writing more and more novels.

La Comédie Humaine In *La Comédie Humaine,* Balzac created more than two thousand characters, keeping track of them on charts covering three walls in his house in Paris. Through the characters and stories in this work, Balzac provides social commentary on life in France from the French Revolution (1789–1799) to his own time. This use of the novel as a forum for social commentary set a new direction for novelists, pointing them toward realism.

◆ Build Vocabulary

LATIN WORD ROOTS: -*duc*-

In "The Conscript," Madame de Dey serves dinners "conducive" to her guests' comfort. The word root -*duc*- in *conducive* comes from the Latin *ducere,* meaning "to lead." Knowing this root can help you figure out that words containing -*duc*- are related to leading. *Conducive* means "leading or contributing to."

esteem
melancholy
magnanimity
abyss
punctiliously
conducive
fastidious
recluses

WORD BANK

Before you read, preview this list of words from the story. Each word is defined on the page where it first appears.

◆ Build Grammar Skills

CORRELATIVE CONJUNCTIONS

In "The Conscript," you will see examples of **correlative conjunctions**—words that work in pairs to join elements of equal importance in a sentence. In the following sentence, correlative conjunctions join two ideas of equal importance, the dejection and the joy of the countess.

The merchant understood at once *both* the dejection *and* the joy of the countess.

Other correlative conjunctions include *either . . . or, neither . . . nor, not only . . . but also,* and *whether . . . or.* Look for examples of correlative conjunctions throughout the story.

The Conscript

◆ *Literature and Your Life*

CONNECT YOUR EXPERIENCE

Most everyone feels protective toward those who are younger or weaker than themselves. This sense of protectiveness is sometimes fierce, like that of a mother bear for her cubs. The main character in "The Conscript" feels so protective of her beloved son that she takes tremendous personal risks.

THEMATIC FOCUS: DANGEROUS DESTINIES

As you read "The Conscript," ask yourself: Do people choose their own destinies, or does fate lend a hand?

◆ Literary Focus

PLOT STRUCTURE

Plot is the sequence of events that make up a story. Most plots contain an exposition, which introduces the setting, characters, and basic situation. An inciting incident introduces the story's central conflict, or problem. During the rising action, the conflict develops until it reaches a high point of interest called the climax. The events that directly follow the climax are the falling action. In the resolution, the conflict is settled and loose ends are tied up.

Use a plot diagram like the one shown here to record the plot elements of "The Conscript."

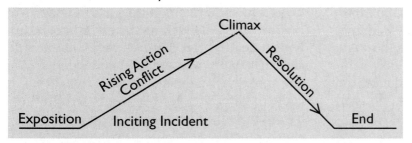

◆ Reading Strategy

PREDICT

To become an involved reader, **predict** story events, based on what the author reveals about the characters and their situations. You may also base predictions on your own experiences or on other stories.

To make predictions, look for clues within the text that foreshadow future events. Also, note each character's personality and how he or she will probably respond to story events.

As you read "The Conscript," pose questions about events in the story, and make predictions.

◆ Background for Understanding

THE FRENCH REVOLUTION

"The Conscript" takes place during the French Revolution, which began in 1789 when the lower and middle classes rebelled against the oppressive nobility. On July 14, 1789, Parisians stormed the Bastille, a prison that to them symbolized oppression, and formed a revolutionary government.

Over the next several years many nobles, called *émigrés,* fled France. Some of them conspired with King Louis XVI to overthrow the new government. In 1793—during which "The Conscript" is set—the revolutionary government started a military draft, or conscription, to provide troops to fight the royalists.

On January 21, 1793, the king was executed. Then, from September, 1793, through July, 1794, a period known as the Reign of Terror, thousands of aristocrats, including France's queen, were sent to the guillotine. The French general Napoleon Bonaparte took over the government in 1799, ending the revolution.

The Conscript

Honoré de Balzac Translated by Sylvia Raphael

One evening in the month of November 1793, the most important people in Carentan were gathered together in the drawing-room of Madame de Dey, who received company every day. Certain circumstances, which would not have attracted attention in a large town but which were bound to arouse curiosity in a small one, gave an unwonted interest to this everyday gathering. Two days earlier, Madame de Dey had closed her doors to visitors, and she had not received any the previous day either, pretending that she was unwell. In normal times these two events would have had the same effect in Carentan as the closing of the theaters has in Paris. On such days existence is, in a way, incomplete. But in 1793 Madame de Dey's behavior could have the most disastrous consequences. At that time if an aristocrat risked the least step, he was nearly always involved in a matter of life and death. To understand properly the eager curiosity and the narrow-minded cunning which, during that evening, were expressed on the faces of all these Norman worthies, but above all to appreciate the secret worries of Madame de Dey, the part she played at Carentan must be explained. As the critical position in which she was placed at that time was, no doubt, that of many people during the Revolution, the sympathies of more than one reader will give an emotional background to this narrative.

Madame de Dey, the widow of a lieutenant-general, a chevalier of several orders,[1] had left the Court at the beginning of the emigration. As she owned a considerable amount of property in the Carentan region, she had taken refuge there, hoping that the influence of the Terror[2] would be little felt in those parts. This calculation, founded on an accurate knowledge of the region, was correct. The Revolution wrought little havoc in Lower Normandy. Although, in the past, when Madame de Dey visited her property in Normandy, she associated only with the noble families of the district, she now made a policy of opening her doors to the principal townspeople and to the new authorities, trying to make them proud of having won her over, without arousing either their hatred or their jealousy. She was charming and kind, and gifted with that indescribable gentleness which enabled her to please without having to lower herself or ask favors. She had succeeded in winning general <u>esteem</u> thanks to her perfect tact which enabled her to keep wisely to a narrow path, satisfying the demands of that mixed society without humiliating the touchy *amour propre* of the parvenus,[3] or upsetting the sensibilities of her old friends.

She was about thirty-eight years old, and she still retained, not the fresh, rounded good looks which distinguish the girls of Lower Normandy, but a slender, as it were aristocratic, type of beauty. Her features were neat and delicate; her figure was graceful and slender. When she spoke, her pale face seemed to light up and come to life. Her large black eyes were full of friendliness, but their calm, religious expression seemed to show that the mainspring of her existence was no longer within herself. In the prime of her youth she had been married to a jealous old soldier, and her false position at a flirtatious court no doubt helped to spread a veil of serious <u>melancholy</u> over a face which must once have shone with the charms and vivacity of love. Since, at an age when a woman still feels rather than reflects, she had always had

---

1. **chevalier** (shə val yā´) **of several orders:** Distinguished member of the French nobility.
2. **the Terror:** The Reign of Terror, a period between 1793 and 1794, when the Revolutionary government executed many members of French royalty and nobility as enemies of France.

---

3. *amour propre* (à mo͞or´ prô´ pr´) **of the parvenus** (pär´ və nyo͞oz´) Self-love of those who have recently acquired wealth.

to repress her instinctive feminine feelings and emotions, passion had remained unawakened in the depths of her heart. And so her principal attraction stemmed from this inner youthfulness which was, at times, revealed in her face and which gave her thoughts an expression of innocent desire. Her appearance commanded respect, but in her bearing and in her voice there was always the expectancy of an unknown future as with a young girl. Soon after meeting her the least susceptible of men would find himself in love with her and yet retain a kind of respectful fear of her, inspired by her courteous, dignified manner. Her soul, naturally great but strengthened by cruel struggles, seemed far removed from ordinary humanity, and men recognized their inferiority. This soul needed a dominating passion. Madame de Dey's affections were thus concentrated in one single feeling, that of maternity. The happiness and the satisfactions of which she had been deprived as a wife, she found instead in the intense love she had for her son. . . . She was unhappy when he was away, and, anxious during his absence, she could never see enough of him and lived only through and for him. To make the reader appreciate the strength of this feeling, it will suffice to add that this son was not only Madame de Dey's only child, but also her last surviving relative, the one being on whom she could fasten the fears, the hopes and the joys of her life. The late Comte de Dey was the last of his family and she was the sole heiress of hers. Material motives and interests thus combined with the noblest needs of the soul to intensify to the countess's heart a feeling which is already so strong in women. It was only by taking the greatest of care that she had managed to bring up her son and this had made him even more dear to her. Twenty times the doctors told her she would lose him, but confident in her own hopes and

◆ Build Vocabulary

esteem (e stēm′) *n.*: Favorable opinion or judgment

melancholy (mel′ ən kä′l ē) *n.*: Sadness

Lady in a Black Hat, Édouard Manet, Louvre, Paris

▲ **Critical Viewing** Do you think that this nineteenth-century Frenchwoman, like Madame de Dey, was capable of great devotion? Why or why not? **[Interpret]**

instincts, she had the inexpressible joy of seeing him safely overcome the perils of childhood, and of marveling at the improvement in his health, in spite of the doctors' verdict.

Due to her constant care, this son had grown up and developed into such a charming young man that at the age of twenty he was regarded as one of the most accomplished young courtiers at Versailles. Above all, thanks to a good fortune which does not crown the efforts of every mother, she was adored by her son; they understood each other in fraternal sympathy. If they had not already been linked by the ties of nature, they would instinctively have felt for each other that mutual friendship which one meets so rarely in life. At the age of eighteen the young count had been appointed a sub-lieutenant of dragoons[4] and in

---

4. **dragoons:** Soldiers on horseback.

obedience to the code of honor of the period he had followed the princes when they emigrated.

Madame de Dey, noble, rich and the mother of an *émigré*,[5] thus could not conceal from herself the dangers of her cruel situation. As her only wish was to preserve her large fortune for her son, she had denied herself the happiness of going with him, and when she read the strict laws under which the Republic was confiscating every day the property of *émigrés* at Carentan, she congratulated herself on this act of courage. Was not watching over her son's wealth at the risk of her life? Then, when she heard of the terrible executions decreed by the Convention,[6] she slept peacefully in the knowledge that her only treasure was in safety, far from the danger of the scaffold.[7] She was happy in the belief that she had done what was best to save both her son and her fortune. To this private thought she made the concessions demanded by those unhappy times, without compromising her feminine dignity or her aristocratic convictions, but hiding her sorrows with a cold secrecy. She had understood

◆ **Literary Focus**
What conflicts does Madame de Dey experience?

the difficulties which awaited her at Carentan. To come there and occupy the first place, wasn't that a way of defying the scaffold every day? But, supported by the courage of a mother, she knew how to win the affection of the poor by relieving all kinds of distress without distinction, and made herself indispensable to the rich by ministering to their pleasures. She entertained at her house the *procureur*[8] of the commune, the mayor, the president of the district, the public prosecutor and even the judges of the revolutionary tribunal. The first four of these were unmarried and so they courted her, hoping to marry her

---

5. émigré (ā′ mē grā′): Member of the French upper class who fled the country during and after the French Revolution.
6. the Convention: The National Convention, a legislative assembly formed in 1792. As its first act, the Convention voted to abolish the French monarchy.
7. scaffold: Elevated platform on which people are executed publicly. During the Reign of Terror, many executions were ordered by the revolutionary tribunals, or courts of justice. Most of these executions were by means of the guillotine (gē′ ə tēn′), an apparatus with a large metal blade that beheads the victim.
8. procureur (prô′ kü rör′): Official elected to represent the central government on local courts and administration.

either by making her afraid of the harm they could do her or by offering her their protection. The public prosecutor, who had been *procureur* at Caen and used to look after the countess's business interests, tried to make her love him, by behaving with devotion and generosity—a dangerous form of cunning! He was the most formidable of all the suitors. As she had formerly been a client of his, he was the only one who had an intimate knowledge of the state of her considerable fortune. His passion was reinforced by all the desires of avarice and supported by an immense power, the power of life and death throughout the district. This man, who was still young, behaved with such an appearance of <u>magnanimity</u> that Madame de Dey had not yet been able to form an opinion of him. But, despising the danger which lay in vying in cunning with Normans,[9] she made use of the inventive craftiness with which Nature has endowed women to play off these rivals against each other. By gaining time, she hoped to survive safe and sound to the end of the revolutionary troubles. At that period, the royalists who had stayed in France deluded themselves each day that the next day would see the end of the Revolution, and this conviction caused the ruin of many of them.

In spite of these difficulties, the countess had very skillfully maintained her independence until the day on which, with unaccountable imprudence, she took it into her head to close her door. The interest she aroused was so deep and genuine that the people who had come to her house that evening became extremely anxious when they learned that it was impossible for her to receive them. Then, with that frank curiosity which is engrained in provincial manners, they made inquiries about the misfortune, the sorrow, or the illness which Madame de Dey must be suffering from. An old servant named Brigitte answered these questions saying that her mistress had shut herself up in her room and wouldn't see anyone, not even the members of her own household. The almost cloisterlike existence led by the inhabitants of a small town forms in them the habit of analyzing and explaining the actions of others. This habit is naturally so invincible that after pitying Madame

---

9. Normans: People from Normandy, a region in the north of France where there was considerable resistance to the Revolution.

de Dey, and without knowing whether she was really happy or sad, everyone began to look for the causes of her sudden retreat.

"If she were ill," said the first inquirer, "she would have sent for the doctor. But the doctor spent the whole day at my house playing chess. He said to me jokingly that nowadays there is only one illness . . . and that unfortunately it is incurable."

This jest was made with caution. Men and women, old men and girls then began to range over the vast field of conjectures. Each one thought he spied a secret, and this secret filled all their imaginations. The next day their suspicions had grown nastier. As life is lived in public in a small town, the women were the first to find out that Brigitte had bought more provisions than usual at the market. This fact could not be denied. Brigitte had been seen first thing in the morning in the market-square and—strange to relate—she had bought the only hare available. The whole town knew that Madame de Dey did not like game. The hare became a starting point for endless conjectures. As they took their daily walk, the old men noticed in the countess's house a kind of concentrated activity which was revealed by the very precautions taken by the servants to conceal it. The valet was beating a carpet in the garden. The previous day no one would have paid any attention to it, but this carpet became a piece of evidence in support of the fanciful tales which everyone was inventing. Each person had his own. The second day, when they heard that Madame de Dey said she was unwell, the leading inhabitants of Carentan gathered together in the evening at the mayor's brother's house. He was a retired merchant, married, honorable, generally respected, and the countess had a high regard for him. That evening all the suitors for the hand of the rich widow had a more or less probable tale to tell, and each one of them considered how to turn to his own profit the secret event which forced her to place herself in this compromising position. The public prosecutor imagined a whole drama in which Madame de Dey's son would be brought to her house at night. The mayor thought that a non-juring priest had arrived from La Vendée and sought asylum with her.[10] But the purchase of a hare on a Friday couldn't be explained by this story. The president of the district was convinced that she was hiding a chouan[11] or a Vendéen leader who was being hotly pursued. Others thought it was a noble who had escaped from the Paris prisons. In short, everyone suspected the countess of being guilty of one of those acts of generosity which the laws of the period called a crime and which could lead to the scaffold. The public prosecutor, however, whispered that they must be silent and try to save the unfortunate woman from the <u>abyss</u> towards which she was hastening.

"If you make this affair known," he added, "I shall be obliged to intervene, to search her house, and then! . . . " He said no more but everyone understood what he meant.

The countess's real friends were so alarmed for her that, on the morning of the third day, the *procureur-syndic*[12] of the commune got his wife to write her a note urging her to receive company that evening as usual. Bolder still, the retired merchant called at Madame de Dey's house during the morning. Very conscious of the service which he wanted to render her, he insisted on being allowed in to see her, and was amazed when he caught sight of her in the garden, busy cutting the last flowers from her borders to fill her vases.

"She must have given refuge to her lover," the old man said to himself, as he was overcome with pity for this charming woman. The strange expression of the countess's face confirmed his suspicion. The merchant was deeply moved by this devotion which is so natural to women, but

◆ **Build Vocabulary**

magnanimity (mag´ nə nim´ ə tē) *n*.: Generosity; high-mindedness; nobility of character

abyss (ə bis´) *n*.: An immeasurably deep pit; here, grave misfortune

10. **non-juring priest . . . asylum with her:** Priests who had not sworn allegiance to the revolutionary government often helped the inhabitants of La Vendée, in the west of France, in their uprisings against the Revolution.
11. **chouan** (sho͞o´ *a*n): *n*.: Member of a group of royalist insurgents from Western France who engaged in guerilla warfare against the Revolution. *Chouan* is a form of a local word for "screech owl" in the Brittany region of France. The *chouans* used owl-like calls to communicate with each other in the field.
12. *procureur-syndic* (prô´ kü *rör´* san dēk´): Government official.

Music in the Tuileries Gardens, Édouard Manet, National Gallery, London

▲ **Critical Viewing** This painting depicts a scene from nineteenth-century French society—a scene some years after the date of the story, 1793. However, in what ways does it help you picture Madame de Dey's world? Explain. **[Connect]**

which men always find touching because they are all flattered by the sacrifices which a woman makes for a man; he told the countess about the rumors which were all over the town, and of the danger in which she was placed. "For," he said in conclusion, "though some of our officials may be willing to forgive you for acting heroically to save a priest, nobody will pity you if they find out you are sacrificing yourself for the sake of a love affair."

At these words, Madame de Dey looked at the old man with a distraught and crazy expression which made him shudder, despite his age.

"Come with me," she said taking him by the hand and leading him into her room where, having first made sure that they were alone, she took a dirty crumpled letter from the bodice of her dress. "Read that," she cried pronouncing the words with great effort.

She collapsed into her chair, as if she were overcome. While the old merchant was looking for his glasses and cleaning them, she looked up at him, examined him for the first time with interest and said gently in a faltering voice, "I can trust you."

"Have I not come to share in your crime?" replied the worthy man simply.

She gave a start. For the first time in this little town, her soul felt sympathy with another's. The merchant understood at once both the dejection and the joy of the countess. Her son had taken part in the Granville expedition;[13] his letter to his mother was written from the depths of his prison, giving her one sad, yet joyful hope. He had no doubts about his means of escape, and he mentioned three days in the course of which he would come to her house, in disguise. The fatal letter contained heart-rending farewells in case he would not be at Carentan by the evening of the third day, and he begged his mother to give a fairly large sum of money to the messenger who, braving countless dangers, had undertaken to bring her this letter. The paper shook in the old man's hands.

"And this is the third day," cried Madame de Dey as she got up quickly, took back the letter, and paced up and down the room.

"You have acted rashly," said the merchant. "Why did you have food brought in?"

---

13. the Granville expedition: Granville is a small town, southwest of Carentan, on the other side of the Normandy's Cotentin peninsula. In 1793, the Vendéens tried unsuccessfully to capture it for the royalists.

"But he might arrive, dying with hunger, exhausted, and. . . " She said no more.

"I can count on my brother," continued the old man, "I will go and bring him over to your side."

In this situation the merchant deployed again all the subtlety which he had formerly used in business and gave the countess prudent and wise advice. After they had agreed on what they both should say and do, the old man, on cleverly invented pretexts, went to the principal houses in Carentan. There he announced that he had just seen Madame de Dey, who would receive company that evening, although she was not very well. As he was a good match for the cunning Norman minds who, in every family, cross-examined him about the nature of the countess's illness, he managed to deceive nearly everybody who was interested in this mysterious affair. His first visit worked wonders. He told a gouty[14] old lady that Madame de Dey had nearly died from an attack of stomach gout. The famous Doctor Tronchin had on a former, similar occasion advised her to lay on her chest the skin of a hare, which had been flayed alive, and to stay absolutely immobile in bed. The countess who, two days ago, had been in mortal danger, was now, after having <u>punctiliously</u> obeyed Tronchin's extraordinary instructions, well enough to receive visitors that evening. This tale had an enormous success, and the Carentan doctor, a secret royalist, added to the effect by the seriousness with which he discussed the remedy. Nevertheless, suspicions had taken root too strongly in the minds of some obstinate people, or of some doubters, to be entirely dissipated. So, that evening, Madame de Dey's visitors came eagerly, in good time, some to observe her face carefully, others out of friendship, most of them amazed at her recovery. They found the countess by the large fireplace in her drawing-room, which was almost as small as the other drawing-rooms in Carentan, for to avoid offending the narrow-minded ideas of her guests, she had denied herself the luxuries she had been used to and so had made no changes in her house. The floor of the reception room was not even polished. She left dingy old hangings on the walls, kept the local furniture, burnt tallow candles and followed the fashions of the place. She adopted provincial life, without shrinking from its most uncomfortable meannesses or its most disagreeable privations. But, as she knew that her guests would forgive her any lavishness <u>conducive</u> to their comfort, she left nothing undone which would minister to their personal pleasures. And so she always provided excellent dinners. She went as far as to feign meanness in order to please these calculating minds and she skillfully admitted to certain concessions to luxury, in order to give in gracefully. And so, about seven o'clock that evening, the best of Carentan's poor society was at Madame de Dey's house and formed a large circle around the hearth. The mistress of the house, supported in her trouble by the old merchant's sympathetic glances, endured with remarkable courage her guests' detailed questioning and their frivolous and stupid arguments. But at every knock on the door, and whenever there was a sound of footsteps in the street, she hid her violent emotion by raising questions of importance to the prosperity of the district. She started off lively discussions about the quality of the ciders and was so well supported by her confidant that the company almost forgot to spy on her, since the expression of her face was so natural and her self-possession so imperturbable. Nevertheless the public prosecutor and one of the judges of the revolutionary tribunal said little, watching carefully the least changes in her expression and, in spite of the noise, listening to every sound in the house. Every now and then they

◆ Reading Strategy
What do you predict will happen? Why?

---

14. **gouty** (gout´ ē) *adj.*: Suffering from gout, a painful inflammation.

◆ **Build Vocabulary**

punctiliously (puŋk til´ ē əs lē) *adv.*: Carefully; conscientiously

conducive (kən doo´ siv) *adj.*: Leading or contributing to

asked the countess awkward questions but she answered them with admirable presence of mind. A mother has so much courage! When Madame de Dey had arranged the card-players, and settled everyone at the tables to play boston or reversis or whist, she still lingered in quite a carefree manner to chat with some young people. She was playing her part like a consummate actress. She got someone to ask for lotto,[15] pretended to be the only person who knew where the set was, and left the room.

"I feel stifled, my dear Brigitte," she exclaimed as she wiped the tears springing from her eyes which shone with fever, grief and impatience. "He is not coming," she continued, as she went upstairs and looked round the bedroom. "Here, I can breathe and live. Yet in a few more moments he will be here! For he is alive, of that I am sure. My heart tells me so. Don't you hear anything, Brigitte? Oh! I would give the rest of my life to know whether he is in prison or walking across the countryside. I wish I could stop thinking."

She looked round the room again to see if everything was in order. A good fire was burning brightly in the grate, the shutters were tightly closed, the polished furniture was gleaming, the way the bed had been made showed that the countess had discussed the smallest details with Brigitte. Her hopes could be discerned in the fastidious care which had obviously been lavished on this room; in the scent of the flowers she had placed there could be sensed the gracious sweetness and the most chaste caresses of love. Only a mother could have anticipated a soldier's wants and made preparations which satisfied them so completely. A superb meal, choice wines, slippers, clean linen, in short everything that a weary traveler could need or desire was brought together so that he should lack for nothing, so that the delights of home should show him a mother's love.

"Brigitte," cried the countess in a heart-rending voice as she went to place a chair at the table. It was as if she wanted to make her prayers come true, as if she wanted to add strength to her illusions.

"Ah, Madame, he will come. He is not far away—I am sure that he is alive and on his way. I put a key in the Bible and I kept it on my fingers while Cottin read the Gospel of St. John. . . and, Madame, the key didn't turn."

"Is that a reliable sign?" asked the countess.

"Oh, yes! Madame, it's well known. I would stake my soul he's still alive. God cannot be wrong."

"I would love to see him, in spite of the danger he will be in when he gets here."

"Poor Monsieur Auguste," cried Brigitte, "he must be on the way, on foot."

"And there's the church clock striking eight," exclaimed the countess in terror.

She was afraid that she had stayed longer than she should have done in this room where, as everything bore witness to her son's life, she could believe that he was still alive. She went downstairs but before going into the drawing-room, she paused for a moment under the pillars of the staircase, listening to hear if any sound disturbed the silent echoes of the town. She smiled at Brigitte's husband, who kept guard like a sentinel and seemed dazed with the effort of straining to hear the sounds of the night from the village square. She saw her son in everything and everywhere. She soon went back into the room, putting on an air of gaiety, and began to play lotto with some little girls. But every now and then she complained of not feeling well and sat down in her armchair by the fireplace.

That is how people and things were in Madame de Dey's house while on the road from Paris to Cherbourg a young man wearing a brown *carmagnole*, the obligatory dress of the period, was making his way to Carentan. When the conscription of August 1793[16] first came into force, there was little or no discipline. The needs of the moment were such that the Republic could not equip its soldiers immediately, and it was not uncommon to see the roads full of conscripts still wearing their civilian clothes. These young men reached their halting places ahead of their battalions, or lagged behind, for their progress depended on their ability to

---

15. **lotto:** Game of chance that is similar to bingo.

16. **conscription of August 1793:** Decree passed by the National Convention in 1793 that called for the military service of all men between eighteen and twenty-five.

endure the fatigues of a long march. The traveler in question was some way ahead of a column of conscripts which was going to Cherbourg and which the mayor of Carentan was expecting from hour to hour, intending to billet the men on the inhabitants. The young man was marching with a heavy tread, but he was still walking steadily and his bearing suggested that he had long been familiar with the hardships of military life. Although the meadow-land around Carentan was lit up by the moon, he had noticed big white clouds threatening a snowfall over the countryside. The fear of being caught in a storm probably made him walk faster, for he was going at a pace ill-suited to his fatigue. On his back he had an almost empty rucksack, and in his hand was a boxwood stick cut from one of the high, thick hedges which this shrub forms around most of the estates of Lower Normandy. A moment after the solitary traveler had caught sight of the towers of Carentan silhouetted in the eerie moonlight, he entered the town. His step aroused the echoes of the silent, deserted streets and he had to ask a weaver who was still at work the way to the mayor's house. This official did not live far away and the conscript soon found himself in the shelter of the porch of the mayor's house. He applied for a billeting order[17] and sat down on a stone seat to wait. But he had to appear before the mayor who had sent for him and he was subjected to a scrupulous cross-examination. The soldier was a young man of good appearance who seemed to belong to a good family. His demeanor indicated that he was of noble birth and his face expressed that intelligence which comes from a good education.

"What's your name?" asked the mayor looking at him knowingly.

"Julien Jussien," replied the conscript.

"And where do you come from?" asked the official with an incredulous smile.

"From Paris."

"Your comrades must be some distance away," continued the Norman half jokingly.

"I am three miles ahead of the battalion."

"Some special feeling attracts you to Carentan, no doubt, *citoyen réquisitionnaire*,"[18] said the mayor shrewdly.

"It is all right," he added, as with a gesture he imposed silence on the young man who was about to speak. "We know where to send you. There you are," he added giving him his billeting order. "Off you go *citoyen Jussien*."

There was a tinge of irony in the official's tone as he pronounced these last two words and handed out a billet order giving the address of Madame de Dey's house. The young man read the address with an air of curiosity.

"He knows quite well that he hasn't far to go. And once he's outside he'll soon be across the square," exclaimed the mayor talking to himself as the young man went out. "He's got some nerve! May God guide him! He has an answer to everything. Yes, but if anyone but me had asked to see his papers, he would have been lost."

At this moment, the Carentan clocks had just struck half past nine. The torches were being lit in Madame de Dey's ante-chamber; the servants were helping their masters and mistresses to put on their clogs, their overcoats or their capes; the card-players had settled their accounts and they were all leaving together, according to the established custom in all little towns.

"It looks as if the prosecutor wants to stay," said a lady, who noticed that this important personage was missing when, having exhausted all the formulae of leave-taking, they separated in the square to go to their respective homes.

In fact that terrible magistrate was alone with the countess who was waiting, trembling, till he chose to go.

After a long and rather frightening silence,

---

17. billeting order: Written order to provide quarters or lodging for military personnel in the homes of citizens.

◆ **Build Vocabulary**

fastidious (fas tid´ ē əs) *adj.*: Excessively demanding in matters of taste or cleanliness

---

18. *citoyen réquisitionnaire* (sē tō yen´ rā´ kē zē´ sē ô ner´): *Citoyen*, which means "citizen," was a form of address that replaced the more formal *monsieur*, the French word for "mister," during the Revolution. This form of address was meant to capture the spirit of equality and brotherhood in which the French Revolution was conceived. *Réquisitionnaires* was the name given to the conscripts of 1793.

he said at last, "I am here to see that the laws of the Republic are obeyed . . ."

Madame de Dey shuddered.

"Have you nothing to reveal to me?" he asked.

"Nothing," she replied, amazed.

"Ah, Madame," cried the prosecutor sitting down beside her and changing his tone, "at this moment, one word could send you or me to the scaffold. I have observed your character, your feelings, your ways too closely to share the mistake into which you managed to lead your guests this evening. I have no doubt at all that you are expecting your son."

The countess made a gesture of denial, but she had grown pale and the muscles of her face had contracted under the necessity of assuming a false air of calmness.

"Well, receive him," continued the magistrate of the Revolution, "but don't let him stay under your roof after seven o'clock in the morning. At daybreak, tomorrow, I shall come to your house armed with a denunciation[19] which I shall have drawn up . . ."

She looked at him with a dazed expression which would have melted the heart of a tiger.

He went on gently, "I shall demonstrate the falsity of the denunciation by a minute search, and by the nature of my report you will be protected from all further suspicion. I shall speak of your patriotic gifts, of your civic devotion, and we shall all be saved."

Madame de Dey was afraid of a trap. She stood there motionless but her face was burning and her tongue was frozen. The sound of the door-knocker rang through the house.

"Ah," cried the terrified mother, falling on her knees. "Save him, save him!"

"Yes, let us save him!" replied the public prosecutor, looking at her passionately, "even at the cost of *our* lives."

"I am lost," she cried as the prosecutor politely helped her to rise.

---

19. **denunciation:** Formal declaration that someone is in violation of the law.

"Ah! Madame," he replied with a fine oratorical gesture, "I want to owe you to nothing . . . but yourself."

"Madame, he's—," cried Brigitte thinking her mistress was alone.

At the sight of the public prosecutor, the old servant who had been flushed with joy, became pale and motionless.

"Who is it, Brigitte?" asked the magistrate gently, with a knowing expression.

"A conscript sent by the mayor to be put up here," replied the servant showing the billet order.

"That's right," said the prosecutor after reading the order. "A battalion is due in the town tonight." And he went out.

At that moment the countess needed so much to believe in the sincerity of her former lawyer that she could not entertain the slightest doubt of it. Quickly she went upstairs, though she scarcely had the strength to stand. Then she opened her bedroom door, saw her son, and fell half-dead into his arms. "Oh, my child, my child," she cried sobbing and covering him with wild kisses.

"Madame," said the stranger.

"Oh! It's someone else," she cried. She recoiled in horror and stood in front of the conscript, gazing at him with a haggard look.

"Oh, good God, what a strong resemblance!" said Brigitte.

There was silence for a moment and even the stranger shuddered at the sight of Madame de Dey.

She leaned for support on Brigitte's husband and felt the full extent of her grief; this first blow had almost killed her. "Monsieur," she said, "I cannot bear to see you any longer; I hope you won't mind if my servants take my place and look after you."

She went down to her own room half carried by Brigitte and her old manservant.

"What, Madame!" cried the housekeeper as she helped her mistress to sit down. "Is that man going to sleep in Monsieur Auguste's bed, put on Monsieur Auguste's slippers and eat the *pâté*[20] that I made for Monsieur Auguste? If I were to be sent to the guillotine, I . . ."

"Brigitte," cried Madame de Dey.

---

20. *pâté* (pä tä´): Meat paste or spread, often made from goose livers.

Study of a Woman Weeping, Jean Baptist Carpeaux, Agnew's, London

▲ **Critical Viewing** Imagine this woman is Madame de Dey after her realization. Which details convey her feelings? Explain. **[Interpret]**

Brigitte said no more.

"Be quiet, you chatterbox," said her husband in a low voice. "You'll be the death of Madame."

At this moment, the conscript made a noise in his room as he sat down to table.

"I can't stay here," exclaimed Madame de Dey. "I shall go into the conservatory. From there I shall be able to hear better what's going on outside during the night."

She was still wavering between the fear of having lost her son and the hope of seeing him come back. The silence of the night was horrible. When the conscript battalion came into town and each man had to seek out his lodgings, it was a terrible time for the countess. Her hopes were dashed at every footstep, at every sound; then soon the awful stillness of Nature returned. Towards morning, the countess had to go back to her own room. Brigitte, who was watching her mistress's movements, did not see her come out; she went into the room and there found the countess dead.

"She must have heard the conscript finishing dressing and walking about in Monsieur Auguste's room singing their . . . *Marseillaise*,[21] as if he were in a stable," cried Brigitte. "That will have killed her!"

The countess's death was caused by a more important feeling and, very likely, by a terrible vision. At the exact moment when Madame de Dey was dying in Carentan, her son was being shot in Le Morbihan. We can add this tragic fact to all the observations that have been made of sympathies which override the laws of space. Some learned <u>recluses</u>, in their curiosity, have collected this evidence in documents which will one day serve as a foundation for a new science—a science that has hitherto failed to produce its man of genius.

---

21. ***Marseillaise*** (mȧr´ se yez´): Patriotic rallying song composed during the Revolution. It later became the national anthem of France.

Guide for Responding

◆ Literature and Your Life

Reader's Response Were you satisfied with the story's conclusion? Why or why not?

Thematic Focus Why do you think Madame de Dey is willing to risk her life for the faint hope of seeing her son for a short time?

Reader's Journal In your journal, write a letter of advice to the mother.

Questions for Research To understand Madame de Dey's position as a French aristocrat in 1793, what questions could you use for research?

☑ Check Your Comprehension

1. When and where does "The Conscript" take place?
2. What has Madame de Dey done that is so surprising?
3. In what way does the retired merchant help Madame de Dey?
4. Who is the young man that comes to Madame's house?
5. (a) What event concludes the story? (b) How does the narrator explain the event?

Guide for Responding (continued)

◆ Critical Thinking

INTERPRET
1. Why does Madame de Dey choose to live in Carentan? **[Connect]**
2. Why is it dangerous for Madame de Dey to close her home to visitors even for two days? **[Synthesize]**
3. What does the contrast between Madame's efforts and the end of the story suggest about war's disruptive power? **[Generalize]**

EVALUATE
4. Do you approve of Madame de Dey's decision to stay in France? Explain. **[Make a Judgment]**

EXTEND
5. What qualities or facets of Madame's personality might she have polished while at King Louis XVI's Court? **[Social Studies Link]**

◆ Reading Strategy

PREDICT
Participate in stories you read by **predicting,** or making educated guesses about, actions and events.
1. Based on the exposition of Madame de Dey's character, what can you predict she is doing when she closes her home to guests?
2. Whom did you expect the conscript to be? Explain your answer.
3. After the conscript's identity is made clear, do you predict that the son will still arrive? Why?

◆ Literary Focus

PLOT STRUCTURE
The **plot structure** is the sequence of the story's events. (Refer to the information on p. 621 for definitions of the parts of a plot.)
1. In the story's exposition, what do you learn about Madame de Dey's position in Carentan?
2. What inciting incident introduces the conflict?
3. What events develop the rising action?
4. Explain why Balzac may have chosen to introduce the character of Julien Jussien.
5. What event marks the climax of the story?
6. What observations does the narrator make in the story's resolution?

◆ Build Vocabulary

USING THE LATIN WORD ROOT -duc-
The Latin root -duc- means "to lead." Using this meaning, write the definition of each of the following words in your notebook.
1. conductor
2. deduction
3. abduct
4. viaduct

USING THE WORD BANK: Context
On your paper, respond to each of the numbered items using words from the Word Bank. Use each word only once.
1. Write one adjective and one adverb describing the actions of a neat, precise person.
2. Write two nouns that might characterize people with positive qualities.
3. Write a synonym for the word *hermits.*
4. Write an antonym for the word *obstructive.*
5. Identify the word you would most likely find in a story about climbing glaciers.
6. Which word could describe a depressed person?

◆ Build Grammar Skills

CORRELATIVE CONJUNCTIONS
Correlative conjunctions work in pairs to link words or phrases of equal importance within a sentence. Among the most commonly used correlative conjunctions are *both . . . and, either . . . or, neither . . . nor, not only . . . but also,* and *whether . . . or.*

Practice In each sentence, circle the correlative conjunctions, and underline the elements they connect.
1. Madame entertained all the townspeople without arousing either their hatred or their jealousy.
2. He was not only her son, but also her last surviving relative.
3. She did her best to save both her son and her fortune.
4. I would give the rest of my life to know whether he is in prison or walking across the countryside.
5. She compromised neither her feminine dignity nor her aristocratic convictions.

Writing Application Write five sentences about the story, using correlative conjunctions.

Build Your Portfolio

Idea Bank

Writing

1. **Diary Entry** As the retired merchant, write a diary entry expressing your feelings when you learn of Madame de Dey's death.

2. **Newspaper Article** Write a newspaper article reporting on events leading up to Madame's death. Include quotes from other characters in the story. **[Media Link]**

3. **Response to Criticism** The writer Henry James said that Balzac was the "final authority on human nature." Basing your response on your reading of "The Conscript," tell whether or not you agree with James. Use examples from the story to support your position.

Speaking, Listening, and Viewing

4. **Retelling** Retell the story from the conscript's point of view, as if you are sharing it with a group of fellow soldiers. Describe only the events he witnessed and experienced. **[Performing Arts Link]**

5. **Dramatic Scene** With a group, stage the evening party at Madame de Dey's house. Assign roles and rehearse before presenting your scene for the class. **[Performing Arts Link]**

Researching and Representing

6. **Map of the Story** Draw or copy a map of France. Label geographical locations that are mentioned in "The Conscript," including Carentan, Lower Normandy, Cherbourg, Granville, and Paris. Mount the map on poster board and include explanations of the role each place plays in the story. **[Social Studies Link; Art Link]**

7. **Character Chart** The author, Balzac, kept a chart of all his fictional characters. Reread the story, making notes of the characters either by name, title, or description. Create a chart identifying the characters, showing their connections with one another, and briefly describing their roles in the story.

Online Activity www.phlit.phschool.com

Guided Writing Lesson

Literary Review

A review is a critical evaluation of a work of art. When you write a literary review, you analyze a work of literature, explaining why you think it is successful or not. You evaluate the author's ideas and techniques, giving your opinions and supporting them with examples from the work. Write a review evaluating "The Conscript." Apply literary concepts to help focus your essay.

> ### Writing Skills Focus:
> ### Knowledge of Literary Concepts
>
> When writing a literary review, refer to **literary concepts**—elements that contribute to the effect of a work of literature. These elements include: plot, setting, character, style, tone, foreshadowing, and theme.

Prewriting Take notes on aspects of the story you found successful or unsuccessful. Note the literary concept that applies to each. Also, find quotations from other critics that support your ideas. Before you begin drafting, decide on the most effective and logical way to present the facts and details you have gathered.

Drafting Write your draft, weaving together the details you have collected during prewriting. In the introduction to your review, summarize your topic and your main ideas about the topic. Develop your ideas in the body of your review, noting which literary concept is involved in each case. Summarize the most important points in your conclusion. To link ideas of equal weight within sentences, use correlative conjunctions.

Revising Read your review to a small group of classmates, and invite feedback as to its effectiveness. Revise your draft with their comments in mind. Then, check your review for accuracy, and proofread it to eliminate errors in grammar, spelling, and punctuation.

Guide for Reading

Luigi Pirandello *(1867–1936)*

Luigi Pirandello is best known as a dramatist who won the Nobel Prize for Literature in 1934 for his bold innovations. He was also an accomplished fiction writer, recognized in his native Italy as the master of the short story.

Early Years Pirandello was born to an upper-class family on the island of Sicily not long after Italy was unified. His father, who was a sulfur merchant, had fought for Italy's unification. Pirandello's studies took him to Rome and eventually to Bonn, Germany. When he returned from Germany, he married the daughter of his father's business associate.

Triumphs and Tragedies In the years that followed, Pirandello met with artistic success and personal misery. The sulfur mines collapsed, and his family and his wife's family lost their fortunes. This led his wife to suffer a severe nervous breakdown that caused her to be institutionalized in 1919. By then, Pirandello had become an established literary figure, having published five novels, six collections of short stories, and more than forty plays.

A Rough Opening Night The premiere of his masterpiece, the play *Six Characters in Search of an Author,* was a fiasco. It upset the audience because it was a radical change from traditional theater. Not only was it performed on an empty stage but it was also about the creation of a play—it was a play within a play, a concept difficult for the audience to enjoy. Within a few years, however, it had been translated into more than twenty-five languages, and Pirandello had become internationally famous.

◆ Build Vocabulary

LATIN WORD ROOTS: *-litera-*

In "A Day Goes By," the main character uses the word *obliterate,* which means to "abolish" or "erase." *Obliterate* contains the Latin word root *-litera-,* which is from the Latin word *littera,* meaning "letter." The original meaning of *obliterate* was "to erase a letter."

indignation
conspicuous
obliterate
contrive
vivacious
scruple
proprietor
solicitously

WORD BANK

Preview these vocabulary words before you read.

◆ Build Grammar Skills

CORRECT USE OF *farther* AND *further*

In "A Day Goes By," the main character penetrates *farther* and *farther* into the city center, meaning he goes a greater and greater distance. *Farther* is very similar to the word *further,* and they mean nearly the same thing. Both words are comparatives of the word *far. Farther* is used to describe physical distance; *further* is used to express a greater degree of something that is not physical, like time. Look at these examples:

Every step takes me *farther* away from home.

As each day goes by, I am *further* from my goal.

A Day Goes By

◆ *Literature and Your Life*

CONNECT YOUR EXPERIENCE

Imagine what it would be like to awaken in a strange place and be unsure of your identity. This is exactly the situation in which the main character in Pirandello's story finds himself.

THEMATIC FOCUS: PERSONAL CHALLENGES

Pirandello's main character tries to meet the challenge of rediscovering his identity by looking for clues in the reactions of other characters. What would you do if you found yourself in such a situation?

Journal Writing In your journal, jot down what you think will happen in the story, based on what you know about it. When you have finished reading, review your journal entry to see how close your predictions were to the actual story.

◆ Background for Understanding

LITERATURE

Modernism is a critical term that refers to the culture of the first half of the twentieth century, a period in the history of art and literature during which artists and writers broke from traditional values, themes, and styles of art. They did this by experimenting with different forms, like abstract painting or unrhymed poetry, and new subject matter, such as the meaning and source of a person's identity.

"A Day Goes By" is considered a modernistic story because of its untraditional form (the characters and the setting are nameless and deliberately vague) and subject matter (the nature of identity).

◆ Reading Strategy

ENVISION SETTING AND ACTION

As the narrator of this story describes the events, try to picture in your mind what is happening, just as if you were participating in the action. Use the descriptive details that Pirandello provides to **envision the setting and the action.** Draw on your imagination and your own experience to fill in details that the author doesn't provide.

◆ Literary Focus

POINT OF VIEW

Point of view is the vantage point from which a story is told.

- In a **third-person point of view,** the narrator is not a character in the story and does not refer to himself at all in telling the story.
- In a **first-person point of view,** on the other hand, the narrator is a character in the story and refers to himself or herself as *I.*

A first-person point of view is the most subjective of all the types of narration. The way in which the events are presented is shaped by the thoughts, feelings, and attitudes of the narrator. In addition, the reader can only see what the narrator sees. If the narrator is unaware of his own identity, as he is in "A Day Goes By," you will not know it either. This allows you, the reader, to share the frustration and uncertainty of the narrator.

A Day Goes By

Luigi Pirandello
Translated by Frederick May

Rudely awakened from sleep—perhaps by mistake—I find myself thrown out of the train at a station along the line. It's night time. I've got nothing with me.

I can't get over my bewilderment. But what strikes me most forcibly is that nowhere on myself can I find any sign of the violence I've suffered. Not only this. I have no picture in my mind of its happening, not even the shadow of a memory.

◆ **Literary Focus**
What shows that the story is told from the first-person point of view?

I find myself on the ground, alone, in the shadowy darkness of a deserted station, and I don't know who it is I ought to ask, if I'm to find out where I am and what's happened to me.

I only got a quick glimpse of a small bull's-eye lantern which rushed forward to close the carriage-door through which I'd been ejected. The train had left immediately. And that lamp had immediately disappeared again into the inside of the station, its wobbling, flickering light struggling fruitlessly with the blackness. I was so utterly astounded by everything that it hadn't so much as passed through my mind that I might rush after it to demand an explanation and lodge my formal complaint.

But, formal complaint about *what*?

With boundless dismay I perceive that I no longer have the faintest memory of having started off on a journey by train. I haven't the slightest memory of where I started from, or where I was going to. Or if, on leaving, I really had anything with me. I had nothing, I think.

In the emptiness of this horrible uncertainty, I'm suddenly seized with terror at that spectral lantern which had immediately retreated from the scene, without paying the slightest attention to my being ejected from the train. Am I to deduce that it's the most natural thing in the world for people to get out at this station in that particular way?

In the darkness I have no luck with my attempts to decipher the name of the station. The town, however, is quite definitely one I don't know. In the first grey, feeble rays of the rising sun it looks deserted. In the vast pale square in front of the station there's a street lamp still alight. I move over to it. I stop and, not daring to raise my eyes—so terrified am I by the echo roused by my footsteps in the silence—I look at my hands, I look at the fronts, I look at the backs. I clench them, I open them again. I tap and prod myself with them, I feel myself all over. I even work out how I'm made, because I can't even be certain of this any longer—that I really exist and that all this is true.

Shortly afterwards, as I penetrate farther and farther into the city center, at every step I see things that would bring me to a standstill with utter amazement, if an even greater amazement didn't overcome me. I observe that all the other people—they all look like me, too—are moving along, weaving in and out past one another, without paying one another the slightest attention; as if, so far as they're concerned, this is the most natural and usual thing in the world for them to do. I feel as if I were being drawn along—but, here again, without getting the sensation that anyone's using violence on me. It's just that I, within myself, ignorant of everything as I am—well, it's as if I were being held somehow on every side. But I consider that, even if I don't even know how, or whence, or why I've come there, *I* must be in the wrong, and the others must quite assuredly be in the right. Not only do they seem to know this, but they also know everything that makes them sure that they never make a mistake. They're without the slightest hesitancy, so naturally convinced are they that they must do what they're doing. So I'd certainly attract their wonder, their apprehension, perhaps even their <u>indignation</u> if, either because of the way they look or because of some action or expression of theirs, I started laughing or showed how utterly astounded I was. In my acute desire to find out something, without making myself look <u>conspicuous</u>, I have continually to <u>obliterate</u> from my eyes that something akin to irritability which you quite often see fleetingly in dogs' eyes. I'm in the wrong—I'm the one who's in the wrong, if I don't understand a thing, if I still can't succeed in pulling myself together again. I must make an effort and pretend that I too am quite convinced. I must <u>contrive</u> to act like the others, however much I'm lacking in all criteria by which to appraise, and any practical notion even of those things which seem most commonplace and easy.

I don't know in which role to re-establish myself, which path to take, or what to start doing.

Is it possible, however, that I've grown as big as I have, yet remained all the time like a child, without ever having done anything? Perhaps it's only been in a dream that I've worked. I don't know how. But I certainly *have* worked. I've always worked, worked very hard, very hard indeed. It looks as if everyone knows it,

moreover, because lots and lots of people turn round and look at me, and more than one of them even goes so far as to wave to me. I don't know them, though. At first I just stand there, looking perplexed, wondering if that wave was really meant for me. I look to either side of me. I look behind me. Were they, possibly, waving to me by mistake? No, no, they really were waving to me. I struggle (in some embarrassment) with a certain vanity, which would dearly like me to deceive myself. It doesn't succeed, though. I move on as if I were suspended in mid-air, without being able to free myself from a strange sense of oppression which derives from something that is—and I recognize it as such—really quite wretched. I'm not at all sure about the suit I've got on. It seems odd that it should be mine. And now I've got a suspicion that it's this suit they're waving at and not me. And, just to make things really troublesome, I haven't got anything else with me except this suit!

I start feeling about myself again. I get a surprise. I can feel something like a small leather wallet tucked away in the breast pocket of the jacket. I fish it out, practically certain in my own mind that it doesn't belong to me but to this suit that isn't mine. It really is a small leather wallet, a faded yellow in color—with a washed-out look about it, as if it had fallen into a stream or down a well and then been fished out of the water again. I open it—or rather, I unstick two bits of it that have got stuck together—and look inside. Buried among few folded sheets of paper, which the water has rendered illegible by staining them and making the ink run, I find a small holy picture—the sort they give children in church. It's all yellowed

◆ Build Vocabulary

indignation (in´ dig nā´ shən) *n.*: Anger that is a reaction to ingratitude or injustice

conspicuous (kən spik´ yoo əs) *adj.*: Attracting attention

obliterate (ə blit´ ər āt´) *v.*: Blot out; erase

contrive (kən trīv´) *v.*: Manage; scheme

with age, and attached to it there's a photograph, almost of the same format and just as faded as it is. I detach it and study it. Oh! It's the photograph of a beautiful young woman in a bathing costume. She's almost naked. The wind is blowing strongly through her hair, and her arms are raised in a <u>vivacious</u> gesture of greeting. As I gaze at her—admiringly, yet with a certain feeling of pain (I don't know quite how to describe it, it's as if it came from far, far away)—I sense, coming from her, the impression, if not exactly the certainty, that the greeting waved by those arms is directed at me. But, no matter how hard I try, I can't recognize her. Is it even remotely possible that so lovely a woman as she can have slipped my memory? Perhaps she's been carried away by all that wind which is ruffling her hair. One thing's quite definite: in that leather wallet, which at some time in the past fell into the water, this picture, side by side with the holy picture, is in the place where you put your fiancée's photograph.

I resume my rummaging through the envelope and, more disconcerted than pleased—because I'm very doubtful about whether it belongs to me—find a huge banknote tucked away in a secret hiding-place. Heaven only knows how long ago it was put there and forgotten. It's folded in four, all worn with use and here and there on the back it's so cracked by folds that it's positively threadbare.

Unprovided as I am with anything, can I provide myself with a little help by using it? I don't know with quite what strength of conviction, but the woman portrayed in that little photograph assures me that the banknote's mine. But can you really trust a charming little head like that, so ruffled by the wind? It's already past midday. I'm dropping with weariness. I must have something to eat. I go into a restaurant.

To my amazement I find myself greeted like an honored guest. I'm obviously most welcome. I'm shown to a table that's already laid, a chair is drawn aside and I'm invited to take a seat. A <u>scruple</u> holds me back, however. I signal to the <u>proprietor</u> and, drawing him to one side, I show

▲ **Critical Viewing** Is the station in this picture like the one you envisioned in the opening scene of the story? Why or why not? **[Compare and Contrast]**

him the huge threadbare banknote. He gazes at it in utter astonishment. He examines it, filled with compassion for the condition to which it's been reduced. Then he tells me that it's undoubtedly of great value, but that it's one of a series which was withdrawn from circulation some time ago. I'm not to worry, however. If it's

The Railway Station, Georg Eisler, Private Collection, Vienna, Austria

mine, they tell me, is one of the very few of that series not yet returned to the bank. For some time now, in this part of the country, they've no longer been putting into circulation notes other than those of minute size. They give me masses and masses of them, so that I feel embarrassed, even oppressed by them. I've only got that shipwrecked leather wallet with me. But they urge me not to let myself get worried. There's a remedy for everything. I can leave that money of mine in the bank, in a current account. I pretend I've understood. I put some of the notes in my pocket, together with the passbook which they give me in return for all the rest that I'm leaving behind, and go back to the restaurant. I can't find any food there to my taste. I'm afraid of not being able to digest it. But already the rumor must have got about that, if I'm not exactly rich, I'm certainly not poor any longer. And, in fact, as I come out of the restaurant, I find a car waiting for me, accompanied by a chauffeur who raises his cap to me with one hand, while with the other he holds the door open for me to get in. I don't know where he takes me. But since I've got a motorcar, it's obvious that, without knowing it, I must have a house. Why yes, a very lovely house. It's an old house, where quite obviously lots of people have lived before me, and lots more will live after me. Is this furniture really mine? I somehow feel myself to be a stranger here, a kind of intruder. Just as this morning at dawn the city seemed deserted, now this house of mine seems deserted. I again feel frightened at hearing the echo of my footsteps, as I move through that immense silence. In winter,

presented at the bank by someone as important and respectable as myself, it will certainly be accepted and changed into notes of smaller denomination which are currently legal tender.

Saying this, the proprietor of the restaurant accompanies me to the door and out on to the pavement, where he points out the nearby building that houses the bank.

I go in, and everyone in the bank is just as happy to do me this favor. That bank note of

◆ Build Vocabulary

vivacious (vĭ vā′ shəs) *adj.*: Lively

scruple (skrōō′ pəl) *n.*: Feeling of doubt as to what is right

proprietor (prō prī′ ə tər) *n.*: Owner

A Day Goes By ◆ 639

Baptism, Antonio Donghi, Galleria d'Arte Moderna, Turin, Italy

▲ **Critical Viewing** Does this group reflect the way you picture the narrator's family at the end of the story? Why or why not **[Connect]**

would happen in a dream, when the night has passed and dawn has ushered in the morning, she's no longer there in that bed. There's no trace of her. And the bed which was so warm during the night is now, when you touch it, freezing cold, just like a tomb. And the whole house is filled with that smell which lurks in places where dust has settled, where life has been withered away by time. And there's that sensation of irritated tiredness which needs well-regulated and useful habits, simply in order to maintain itself in being. I've always had a horror of them. I want to run away. It's quite impossible that this is my house. This is a nightmare. It's quite obvious that I've dreamt one of the most absurd dreams ever dreamt. And as if seeking proof of this, I go and look at myself in a mirror that's hanging on the wall opposite, and instantly I get the terrible feeling that I'm drowning. I'm terrified, lost in a world of neverending dismay.

From what remote distance are my eyes—those eyes which, so it seems to me, I've had since I was a child—now looking wide-eyed with terror at this old man's face, without being able to convince myself of the truth of what I'm seeing? What, am I old already? So suddenly! Just like that! How is it possible?

I hear a knock at the door. My heart turns over. They tell me my children have arrived.

My *children?*

It seems utterly frightful to me that children should have been born to me. But when? I must have had them yesterday. Yesterday I was still young. It's only right and proper that I should know them, now that I'm old.

They come in, leading several small children

evening's soon upon you. I'm cold and I feel tired. I buck up my ideas, however, and start moving about. I open one of the doors, quite at random, and stand there in utter amazement, when I see that the room's ablaze with light. It's the bedroom, and there on the bed . . . There she is! The young woman in the photograph, alive, and with her two bare arms still raised in the air, but this time they're inviting me to hasten over to her so that she may welcome me and joyously clasp me in them.

Is it a dream?

Well, this much is quite certain: just as

by the hand—*their* children. They immediately rush over and tell me to lean on them. Lovingly they reprove me for having got up out of bed. Very solicitously they make me sit down, so that I shan't feel so weary. Me, weary? Why yes, they know perfectly well that I can't stand on my feet any longer and that I'm in a really bad way.

Seated there, I look at them. I listen to them. And I get the feeling that they're playing a joke on me in a dream.

Has my life already come to an end?

And while I sit there looking at them, all bent so solicitously over me, I mischievously observe—almost as if I really ought not to be noticing it—right under my very eyes, I can see, sprouting there on their heads . . . Yes, there's a considerable number of white hairs growing there. Yes, white hair's growing there on their heads.

"There, that proves it's all a joke. You've got white hair too."

And look, look at those young people who came through that door just now as tiny children. Look? All they had to do was to come up to my armchair. They've grown up. One of them—yes, that one—is already a charming young lady. She wants the rest of them to make way for her so that she can come and be admired. If her father hadn't grabbed hold of her she'd have thrown herself at me, climbed up on to my knees, put her arm round my neck, and rested her little head on my breast.

I feel the urge to leap to my feet. But I have to admit that I really can't manage it any more. And with the same childlike eyes that a little while before those children had—oh, how grown-up they are now!—I sit there, looking at my old children, standing behind these new ones, and there is great compassion in my gaze.

◆ **Build Vocabulary**

solicitously (sə lis′ ə təs lē) *adv.*: Showing care or concern

Guide for Responding

◆ *Literature and Your Life*

Reader's Response What kinds of thoughts and feelings did this story bring to mind? Why?

Thematic Focus What other personal challenges can you think of that are in some ways similar to the one faced by the narrator? Explain.

Journal Entry In a brief journal entry, describe how you would have felt and what you would have done if you had been in the situation of the story's main character.

☑ Check Your Comprehension

1. Where does the man first find himself?
2. How do the other people passing by him in the city make him feel?
3. What does he find in his jacket pocket?
4. Who treats the narrator "like an honored guest"?
5. Who comes to see him when he wakes up?

◆ Critical Thinking

INTERPRET

1. What does the large bill in the narrator's wallet tell you about him? **[Infer]**
2. How has the narrator's awareness of his identity changed by the end of the story? **[Compare and Contrast]**
3. What insights does the narrator gain as a result of his experiences? **[Analyze]**
4. What is the significance of the story's title? **[Connect]**
5. What do you think is the theme, or central message, of this story? Support your answer. **[Analyze]**

APPLY

6. Challenges to traditional values in the early 1900's created an atmosphere of alienation. How does the story reflect this atmosphere? **[Connect]**

Guide for Responding (continued)

◆ Reading Strategy

ENVISIONING SETTING AND ACTION

In "A Day Goes By" the setting of the story is vague; there are very few clues to what the city is like and where it is. Similarly, none of the characters have names. It is left up to you to "illustrate" the story in your imagination by envisioning the setting, the action, and the characters.

1. Identify some of the details that Pirandello uses that help you envision the setting.
2. What is the most fully described detail in the story? Why?
3. What do you think the narrator looks like?

◆ Build Vocabulary

LATIN WORD ROOTS: -litera-

In this story, Pirandello uses the word *obliterate*, which contains the Latin root -litera-, meaning "letter." Define each of the following words, and explain how the root -litera- contributes to their meaning.

1. literature   2. illiterate   3. literary

USING THE WORD BANK: Sentence Completions

Choose the word from the Word Bank that best fits each sentence. Write the complete sentence in your notebook.

1. In my bright orange bathing cap, I felt very ___?___ at the pool.
2. I wanted to buy some lizard food, but I could not find the ___?___ of the pet store.
3. I will ___?___ to get out of school early and meet you at the mall.
4. "How are you?" the waiter asked ___?___ .
5. When he was insulted, he could not hide his ___?___ .
6. The coach urged his players to ___?___ the other team.
7. After she was caught cheating, the others questioned whether she had a single ___?___ .
8. Because she is always full of energy, her co-workers describe her as ___?___ .

◆ Literary Focus

POINT OF VIEW

By seeing everything in the story through the eyes of the narrator in "A Day Goes By," you are able to experience what it is like to be that character; however, you cannot experience what the other characters are thinking or feeling.

1. What is the first sign that this story uses first-person point of view?
2. Why is the first-person point of view an unusual choice for a story about a person who has lost his identity?
3. What are some of the things that you know about the narrator that the other characters do not know?
4. Why do you think Pirandello uses the first-person point of view in this story?

◆ Build Grammar Skills

CORRECT USE OF *farther* AND *further*

Farther means "at a greater distance." *Further* means "to a greater extent."

Practice Copy these sentences in your notebook and use one of these two words correctly in each sentence.

1. Every step takes me ___?___ away from this delightful place.
2. New York is ___?___ from here than Boston.
3. We will need to study this strange creature ___?___ .
4. The costumes helped the actors get ___?___ into their roles.
5. The explorers did not dare to go any ___?___ into the cavern.

Writing Application In your notebook, rewrite this passage, correcting the *further/farther* usage errors. Continue the passage with two more sentences that contain *further* or *farther* or both.

> He dug farther into his pocket and found another photograph; a portrait of a handsome old man. Farther study revealed that it was a very old picture, and he wondered if it were his father. As he stood there, he began to feel lonesome, as if he were further away from home than he had ever been before.

Build Your Portfolio

 ## Idea Bank

Writing

1. **Lost-and-Found Announcement** Write an announcement for the lost-and-found section of a newspaper that describes the wallet in the story well enough so that the person who lost it would recognize it.

2. **Alternate Ending** What happened after the narrator's children and grandchildren came to visit him? Write at least three additional paragraphs that continue the story.

3. **Response to Criticism** In her book, *Understanding Luigi Pirandello,* the critic Fiora A. Bassanese wrote, "While his [typical] character is a realistic rendering in the naturalist vein, he is also a symbol for universal man in search of meaning in a chaotic [confused, unorganized], irrational world." Write a brief essay in which you explain how the critic's statement relates to "A Day Goes By."

Speaking, Listening, and Viewing

4. **Casting Decision** With a group of classmates, choose actors to play the roles in a dramatic version of this story. Present and explain your recommendations to the class. **[Media Link]**

5. **Dramatization** With a group of classmates, perform a dramatization of "A Day Goes By" using body language and dialogue to convey the characters' feelings.

Researching and Representing

6. **Map of Italy** Luigi Pirandello was born in 1867, five years before Italy became a unified country. Research this period of Italian history, and draw a map of Italy that indicates the different states that comprised the region before unification. **[Social Studies Link]**

7. **Visual Representation** In your favorite visual medium (drawing, painting, collage, for example), make a picture of a significant scene from "A Day Goes By." Use visual details from the story as the basis for your picture. **[Art Link]**

 ## Guided Writing Lesson

Narrative From Another's Point of View

Retell this story from another character's point of view. For example, you could tell it from the point of view of the proprietor of the restaurant, of the narrator's wife (the woman in the photo and at his home), or of one of his children.

Writing Skills Focus: Consistency of Point of View

Follow these three rules to make effective use of a first-person point of view:

1. Consistently use the first person pronoun *I*.
2. Write in character. This means that you are writing in your character's voice and that everything that you write is something your character would say or think.
3. Don't include any details or information that the narrator does not know.

Prewriting Get to know the character from whose point of view you will write. Ask yourself questions about the character's lifestyle, his or her feelings toward the other characters in the story, even what he or she is wearing. The more fully realized the character is in your mind, the better you will be able to capture his or her point of view.

Drafting Once you have thought about the story and the characters and made notes about how you would like to tell your story, outline it. Include the key events of the plot, along with brief sketches of the characters. Follow your outline as you write your first draft.

Revising Read your story aloud. Listen for inconsistencies in point of view, places where the language could be more precise, and points at which the dialogue seems unnatural. Mark places in your draft where you uncover weaknesses. Then, go back and make revisions at these points.

Focus on Culture

Russia and Eastern Europe

According to an early history of Russia, Prince Vladimir of Kiev wanted a new religion for his people. He sent ambassadors to learn about Islam and Judaism, as well as both the Roman and Byzantine forms of Christianity.

Vladimir's ambassadors to the Byzantine empire sent back a glowing report on its church architecture. "We knew not whether we were in heaven or on Earth," they wrote. "For on Earth there is no such splendor or beauty, and we are at a loss how to describe it. We only know that God dwells there."

In the end, Vladimir chose to adopt Byzantine Christianity. His choice, made more than 1,000 years ago, had far-reaching effects. Russia absorbed the religion and culture of Byzantine civilization, as well as its tradition of strong royal rule. As a result, Russia developed differently from Western Europe.

▲ **Critical Viewing** The Kremlin, a medieval citadel in Moscow, became the seat of the Russian government. How does its architecture reflect Byzantine influence? **[Connect]**

GEOGRAPHIC SETTING

Russia is the world's largest country, spanning two continents and covering some 6,592,800 square miles. If you rode the Trans-Siberian railroad across Russia, you would pass through eleven time zones!

Landforms The dominant landform of Russia is the huge plain that stretches from Central Asia into the middle of Europe. In Europe, it is part of the North European Plain. In Asia, it is called the West Siberian Plain.

The low-lying Ural Mountains mark the dividing line between Asia and Europe. The Urals do not form a real barrier, however. Throughout history, migrating peoples and invaders came into contact on the plain.

A Frigid Climate Most of Russia lies above 49°N latitude—the same line that marks the border between the United States and Canada. As a result, Russia has a cold continental climate, marked by long, bitterly cold winters and short, hot summers.

Eastern Europe Eastern Europe refers to the region of the North European Plain that lies between Western Europe and the eastern nations of Russia, Belarus, and Ukraine. The region includes Poland, the Czech Republic, Hungary, Yugoslavia, Romania, and the Baltic republics of Lithuania, Latvia, and Estonia.

HISTORY

The first Russian state, Kiev, arose in present day Ukraine in the late ninth century A.D. Kiev came under the influence of the Byzantine empire, which was the most powerful and advanced state in Europe at that time. As you have read, Prince Vladimir adopted Byzantine Christianity. However, in 1240, Mongol invaders destroyed Kiev.

The Czars In 1480, Prince Ivan III of Moscow— known to history as Ivan the Great— ended Mongol rule. He then built a strong government based on Byzantine traditions of absolute rule. Ivan took the title *czar* (zär), Russian for "Caesar." His grandson, Czar Ivan IV, strengthened royal autocracy. His brutal rule, enforced by secret police, earned him the nickname "Ivan the Terrible."

In the late 1600's, Peter the Great set out to close the gap between Russia and the more advanced nations of Western Europe. This energetic czar hired western technical experts and teachers to build industry, set up schools, and modernize the army and navy. He introduced western customs and ruthlessly put down nobles who resisted westernization.

By the 1900's, Russia had a long tradition of rule by all-powerful czars. Still, unrest was growing. Peasants, national minorities, middle-class liberals, and factory workers all resented inequality and repression.

Eastern Europe Meanwhile, various states developed in Eastern Europe. The Poles, a Roman Catholic Slavic people, first formed a unified state in the tenth century A.D. Through the centuries, Poland expanded and contracted as it fought invaders from the west and the east. In the 1300's, Poland built a strong empire. By 1796, however, Russia, Prussia, and Austria had partitioned Poland among themselves. An independent Polish nation did not reappear until 1919.

Further south, Prussia controlled Czech lands, including the city of Prague. Austria gained control over the once-powerful kingdom of Hungary. Like Poland, Hungary and Czechoslovakia finally regained independence in 1919.

On the Balkan Peninsula, the kingdom of Serbia fell to the Ottoman Turks in 1389. Serbs finally threw off Ottoman rule in 1912. Two years later, Serbian nationalists' efforts to form a Slav state helped trigger World War I.

Russian Revolution For Russia, World War I was a disaster. In February and March 1917, defeats on the battlefield and food shortages at home sparked riots. Czar Nicholas II was forced to abdicate. Moderate reformers drafted a constitution, but the weak new government soon lost support. The Bolsheviks, a small group of radicals led by Vladimir Ilich Lenin, seized power in November 1917 and began a civil war that lasted for three years. By 1921, Lenin and the Bolsheviks' Red Army controlled Russia.

Under Lenin, and his ruthless successor, Joseph Stalin, the Soviet Union became a communist dictatorship. The government strictly controlled the economy, education, and the media.

The Market (La Fiera) (detail), Boris Kustodiev, Tretyakov Gallery, Moscow

▲ **Critical Viewing** What impressions of Russian society do you get from this traditional market scene? **[Relate]**

World War II and the Cold War During World War II, the Soviet Union became an ally of the United States, Britain, and France. Its military and civilian casualities numbered in the millions, but with the aid of "General Winter," the Red Army was able to defeat Hitler's forces on the Eastern Front. After World War II ended in 1945, the Soviet Union and the United States engaged in a global rivalry known as the Cold War. The Soviet Union promoted communism in developing nations around the world.

The Soviet Union installed communist regimes in Eastern Europe. Soviet troops and tanks crushed uprisings or moderate reform efforts in Hungary, Czechoslovakia, and elsewhere. In 1980, when Polish shipyard workers formed an independent labor union, the Soviet Union pressured Poland to impose martial law.

In the 1980's, economic problems plagued the Soviet Union. Although a new leader, Mikhail Gorbachev (gôr bə chôf), instituted reforms, Soviet power began to unravel. In 1989, Poland held free elections and rejected communism. Other Eastern European nations followed. In 1991, the Soviet Union itself collapsed.

Since the end of the Cold War, Russia and the nations of Eastern Europe have tried to build democratic governments and capitalist economies. Still, ethnic tensions and economic hardships are ever-present obstacles.

SOCIETY AND CULTURE

Czarist Russia had a rigid class structure. Nobles owned the land. The tiny middle class had no real power. The majority of Russians were serfs: peasants who worked as near-slaves on the land.

Czarist Society Serfs were the property of the nobles who owned the land on which they were born. Nobles could buy and sell serfs or discipline them with beatings. Most peasants lived in small wooden houses, ate black bread and porridge, and never traveled more than a few miles from their own villages.

Wealthy families spent winters in Moscow or St. Petersburg, with as many as 100 serfs to serve their needs. Guests arrived almost every night for lavish meals and dancing parties.

At all levels of society, the Russian family was patriarchal. The father or oldest male headed the family, and his word was final.

Soviet Society In theory, Soviet society was "classless." In fact, the Communist Party became a privileged class. Ordinary people waited in long lines in stores whose shelves were often empty. Party leaders shopped in special stores stocked with high-quality goods. Despite severe housing shortages, the party elite lived in new apartments and vacationed in summer houses reserved for them.

Religious Life In czarist times, the Russian Orthodox Church supported the political and social order. At the same time, the Church was a source of comfort to the poor. Peasants were baptized as infants and received a priest's blessing as they lay dying. Festivals and holy days provided some joy in a wearisome life.

Russia, as well as Eastern Europe, included many Jewish communities. Laws enforced anti-semitism, or hatred of the Jews. In many cities of Eastern Europe, Jews were restricted to a single neighborhood called a *ghetto*. In Russia, the czar's government and army supported *pogroms*, organized acts of violence against Jewish communities.

After 1917, the Soviet government launched a campaign against the Russian Orthodox Church. It seized Church property and even executed some priests. Other religions also faced persecution, including Roman Catholics, Lutherans, Jews, and Muslims. Since the fall of communism, open religious worship has returned to Russia.

ARTS AND LITERATURE

Early Russian arts reflect strong Byzantine influence. Russian architects adapted features of Byzantine churches, especially their onion-shaped domes. (See the picture on p. 644.)

Art Russian artists excelled at painting icons, religious pictures of Jesus, the Virgin Mary, or the saints. Later, artists also began to focus on secular scenes of everyday life in Russia. (See the picture on p. 646.)

Under Stalin, art served the state. Soviet artists had to follow a style called Socialist Realism. Typical paintings showed heroic workers breaking the chains of capitalism or fearless soldiers carrying the Soviet flag.

Music and Dance The late 1800's were a golden age of Russian music and dance. Com-posers blended folk, religious, and western traditions. Peter Ilich Tchaikovsky (chī kôf´ skē´) helped develop a distinctly Russian school of music that expressed national pride.

Much of Tchaikovsky's finest music was composed for ballets, such as *Swan Lake* and *The Nutcracker*. Russian classical ballet set a standard that is still admired today.

Literature Nineteenth-century Russia also produced literary giants. Fyodor Dostoevsky (dôs´ tô yef skē´) and Leo Tolstoy believed that they had a duty to portray life honestly and campaign for reform. In *Anna Karenina*, Tolstoy rejects the self-indulgent manners and values of his society. (See p. 274 for Tolstoy's story "How Much Land Does a Man Need?") In *Crime and Punishment*, Dostoevsky explores good and evil in the story of a young man who commits two senseless murders. Anton Chekhov won acclaim for ironic short stories, as well as plays like *The Cherry Orchard*, which depicted the decline of the landed class. (See p. 650 for Chekhov's story "A Problem.")

Eastern Europe has produced fine modern writers. Czech writer Franz Kafka explored the anxieties of modern life. In "The Metamorphosis," he tells the story of a salesman who wakes up one day to find himself transformed into a giant insect. Like Kafka, Polish writer Bruno Schulz also combined the bleak and fantastic. (See p. 76 for Kafka's story "The Bucket Rider" and p. 486 for his parable "Before the Law"; see p. 656 for Schulz's story "Birds.")

ACTIVITY
Writing a Skit

Use Internet or library resources to find out more about the lives of either nobles, serfs, or Jews in nineteenth-century Russia. Use this information to write a skit in which a family sits down to dinner and discusses their lives. 🐾

Guide for Reading

Anton Chekhov
(1860–1904)

Anton Chekhov (än´ tōn chek´ ōf) was born in the small coastal town of Taganrog in southern Russia. After the failure of his father's grocery business, his family moved to Moscow. Chekhov continued his schooling in Taganrog, then moved to Moscow to be with his family and to enroll in the medical school.

While a medical student, he wrote comic sketches and light short stories to earn money to help support his family. Although he suffered from tuberculosis, Chekhov continued to write until he died. *The Cherry Orchard*, one of his most famous plays, was written during the last year of his life.

Although his reputation did not extend outside of Russia during his lifetime, he has come to be regarded as one of the world's great short-story writers.

Bruno Schulz   (1892–1942)

Bruno Schulz, a Polish author and painter, spent most of his life in Drohobycz, a small town in southeastern Poland. By day he taught art, and in his free time he wrote and drew. In his short stories, he wrote about his childhood and his family, mixing fantasy and personal memories.

Schulz's first book, *Cinnamon Shops*, was published in 1934. In the later American edition, it was retitled *The Street of Crocodiles*. *Sanatorium Under the Sign of the Hourglass*, published three years later, was an anthology of fiction that included Schulz's drawings.

In 1938, the Polish Academy of Literature awarded Schulz a prize for his two published works. However, his enjoyment of this literary recognition was short-lived. In 1942, during the German occupation of Poland, Schulz was killed by Nazi forces because he was Jewish.

◆ Build Vocabulary

GREEK PREFIXES: *a-* AND *an-*

The Greek prefixes *a-* and *an-* mean "without" or "not." The word *anomalies*, which appears in "Birds," combines the prefix *an-* with a word that means "alike" or "the same." The prefix negates the root it precedes, like a negative sign in front of a number. Therefore, *anomalies* means "abnormalities" or "irregularities."

WORD BANK

taciturn
rheumatic
vestibule
undulating
eccentricities
anomalies
ascetic

As you read, you will encounter the words on this list. Each word is defined on the page where it first appears. Preview this list before you read. With a partner, define any words or word parts that you already know.

◆ Build Grammar Skills

RESTRICTIVE AND NONRESTRICTIVE ADJECTIVE CLAUSES

Adjective clauses modify nouns or pronouns. An adjective clause is **restrictive** when it is necessary to the meaning of the sentence. In that case, it is not set off with a comma:

Orders were given *that no one was to be admitted.*

A **nonrestrictive clause** adds details that are not necessary to the meaning of the sentence, and it is set off with commas:

. . . and by the advice of kind-hearted Ivan Markovitch, his uncle, *who was taking his part,* he sat meekly in the hall by the door leading to the study . . .

◆ *Literature and Your Life*

CONNECT YOUR EXPERIENCE

Have you ever met a person who turned out to be different from what you had expected or whose actions and thoughts were disturbing or surprising? In "A Problem" and "Birds," you will encounter characters whose ideas and actions cause others around them worry and puzzlement.

THEMATIC FOCUS: FACING THE CONSEQUENCES

After you've read these stories, you may have a new answer to the question: Do people make choices based on the potential consequences of their actions?

Journal Writing Jot down a positive consequence of an action you took.

◆ Background for Understanding

CULTURE

People's lifestyles often reflect their culture and the time in which they lived. In early twentieth-century Europe, the class system, based on people's social status, had a lot to do with how individuals conducted themselves.

For many of the upper classes, family honor, even at the sacrifice of truthfulness, was of the utmost importance. This sense of honor pervades Chekhov's "A Problem." The characters in this story prefer to hide or ignore painful truths.

◆ Literary Focus

STATIC AND DYNAMIC CHARACTERS

Characters are the people or beings who take part in the action of a story. Characters can be classified as either static or dynamic. **Static characters** do not change during the course of a story. They remain the same no matter what happens to them. **Dynamic characters** change and usually learn something as a result of the events of the story. As you read "A Problem" and "Birds," look for examples of static and dynamic characters.

◆ Reading Strategy

DRAW CONCLUSIONS ABOUT CHARACTERS

When you meet new people, you form opinions about them based on their words and actions and, sometimes, on what others tell you about them. When you put those clues together to form an idea of a person, you **draw conclusions** about his or her personality, beliefs, or qualities.

You get to know fictional characters in a similar way. Their actions and words provide clues from which you draw conclusions. Use a graphic organizer like the one shown to draw conclusions about the characters in these stories.

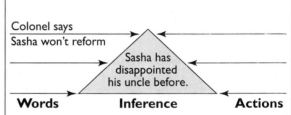

Colonel says Sasha won't reform

Sasha has disappointed his uncle before.

Words   **Inference**   **Actions**

A Problem

Anton Chekhov

Translated by Constance Garnett

The strictest measures were taken that the Uskovs' family secret might not leak out and become generally known. Half of the servants were sent off to the theater or the circus; the other half were sitting in the kitchen and not allowed to leave it. Orders were given that no one was to be admitted. The wife of the Colonel, her sister, and the governess, though they had been initiated into the secret, kept up a pretense of knowing nothing; they sat in the dining room and did not show themselves in the drawing room or the hall.

Sasha Uskov, the young man of twenty-five who was the cause of all the commotion, had arrived some time before, and by the advice of kind-hearted Ivan Markovitch, his uncle, who was taking his part, he sat meekly in the hall by the door leading to the study, and prepared himself to make an open, candid explanation.

The other side of the door, in the study, a family council was

---

▶ **Critical Viewing** If you were in Sasha's situation, would you want to go to this man for help? Why or why not? **[Connect]**

Man on a Balcony, Boulevard Haussmann, 1880, Gustave Caillebotte, Private Collection, Switzerland

being held. The subject under discussion was an exceedingly disagreeable and delicate one. Sasha Uskov had cashed at one of the banks a false promissory note,[1] and it had become due for payment three days before, and now his two paternal uncles and Ivan Markovitch, the brother of his dead mother, were deciding the question whether they should pay the money and save the family honor, or wash their hands of it and leave the case to go to trial.

To outsiders who have no personal interest in the matter such questions seem simple; for those who are so unfortunate as to have to decide them in earnest they are extremely difficult. The uncles had been talking for a long time, but the problem seemed no nearer decision.

"My friends!" said the uncle who was a colonel, and there was a note of exhaustion and bitterness in his voice. "Who says that family honor is a mere convention? I don't say that at all. I am only warning you against a false view; I am pointing out the possibility of an unpardonable mistake. How can you fail to see it? I am not speaking Chinese; I am speaking Russian!"

"My dear fellow, we do understand," Ivan Markovitch protested mildly.

"How can you understand if you say that I don't believe in family honor? I repeat once more; fa-mil-y ho-nor false-ly un-der-stood is a prejudice! Falsely understood! That's what I say: whatever may be the motives for screening a scoundrel, whoever he may be, and helping him to escape punishment, it is contrary to law and unworthy of a gentleman. It's not saving the family honor; it's civic cowardice! Take the army, for instance. . . . The honor of the army is more precious to us than any other honor, yet we don't screen our guilty members, but condemn them. And does the honor of the army suffer in consequence? Quite the opposite!"

The other paternal uncle, an official in the Treasury, a <u>taciturn</u>, dull-witted, and <u>rheumatic</u> man, sat silent, or spoke only of

the fact that the Uskovs' name would get into the newspapers if the case went for trial. His opinion was that the case ought to be hushed up from the first and not become public property; but, apart from publicity in the newspapers, he advanced no other argument in support of this opinion.

The maternal uncle, kind-hearted Ivan Markovitch, spoke smoothly, softly, and with a tremor in his voice. He began with saying that youth has its rights and its peculiar temptations. Which of us has not been young, and who has not been led astray? To say nothing of ordinary mortals, even great men have not escaped errors and mistakes in their youth. Take, for instance, the biography of great writers. Did not every one of them gamble, drink, and draw down upon himself the anger of right-thinking people in his young days? If Sasha's error bordered upon crime, they must remember that Sasha had received practically no education; he had been expelled from the high school in the fifth class; he had lost his parents in early childhood, and so had been left at the tenderest age without guidance and good, benevolent influences. He was nervous, excitable, had no firm ground under his feet, and, above all, he had been unlucky. Even if he were guilty, anyway he deserved indulgence and the sympathy of all compassionate souls. He ought, of course, to be punished, but he was punished as it was by his conscience and the agonies he was enduring now while awaiting the sentence of his relations. The comparison with the army made by the Colonel was delightful, and did credit to his lofty intelligence; his appeal to their feeling of public

> ◆ Reading Strategy
> What inferences can you make about Ivan Markovitch based on his speech?

◆ **Build Vocabulary**

taciturn (ta′ sə tərn) *adj.*: Preferring not to talk; uncommunicative; silent

rheumatic (rü ma′ tik) *adj.*: Suffering from a disease of the joints; able to move only with great pain

---

1. **promissory note:** Written promise to pay a certain sum of money on demand; an IOU.

duty spoke for the chivalry of his soul, but they must not forget that in each individual the citizen is closely linked with the Christian. . . .

"Shall we be false to civic duty," Ivan Markovitch exclaimed passionately, "if instead of punishing an erring boy we hold out to him a helping hand?"

Ivan Markovitch talked further of family honor. He had not the honor to belong to the Uskov family himself, but he knew their distinguished family went back to the thirteenth century; he did not forget for a minute, either, that his precious, beloved sister had been the wife of one of the representatives of that name. In short, the family was dear to him for many reasons, and he refused to admit the idea that, for the sake of a paltry fifteen hundred rubles,[2] a blot should be cast on the escutcheon[3] that was beyond all price. If all the motives he had brought forward were not sufficiently convincing, he, Ivan Markovitch, in conclusion, begged his listeners to ask themselves what was meant by crime? Crime is an immoral act founded upon ill-will. But is the will of man free? Philosophy has not yet given a positive answer to that question. Different views were held by the learned. The latest school of Lombroso,[4] for instance, denies the freedom of the will, and considers every crime as the product of the purely anatomical peculiarities of the individual.

"Ivan Markovitch," said the Colonel, in a voice of entreaty, "we are talking seriously about an important matter, and you bring in Lombroso, you clever fellow. Think a little, what are you saying all this for? Can you imagine that all your thunderings and rhetoric will furnish an answer to the question?"

Sasha Uskov sat at the door and listened. He felt neither terror, shame, nor depression, but only weariness and inward emptiness. It seemed to him that it made absolutely no difference to him whether they forgave him or not; he had come here to hear his sentence and to explain himself simply because kind-hearted Ivan Markovitch had begged him to do so. He was not afraid of the future. It made no difference to him where he was: here in the hall, in prison, or in Siberia.

"If Siberia, then let it be Siberia, damn it all!"

He was sick of life and found it insufferably hard. He was inextricably involved in debt; he

◆ *Literature and Your Life*
Connect this story to a time in your life when your future was in someone else's hands. What was the dominant emotion you felt?

---

2. **rubles** (rōō′ bəlz) *n.*: Russian unit of currency.
3. **escutcheon** (is kə′ chən) *n.*: Shield on which a coat of arms is displayed.
4. **Lombroso:** Cesare Lombroso (1836–1909), an Italian physician and criminologist who believed that a criminal was a distinct human type, with specific physical and mental deviations, and that a criminal tendency was the result of hereditary factors.

had not a farthing[5] in his pocket; his family had become detestable to him; he would have to part from his friends and his women sooner or later, as they had begun to be too contemptuous of his sponging on them. The future looked black.

Sasha was indifferent, and was only disturbed by one circumstance; the other side of the door they were calling him a scoundrel and a criminal. Every minute he was on the point of jumping up, bursting into the study and shouting in answer to the detestable metallic voice of the Colonel:

"You are lying!"

"Criminal" is a dreadful word—that is what

---

5. **farthing** (fär´ thing) n.: Coin of little value.

murderers, thieves, robbers are; in fact, wicked and morally hopeless people. And Sasha was very far from being all that. . . . It was true he owed a great deal and did not pay his debts. But debt is not a crime, and it is unusual for a man not to be in debt. The Colonel and Ivan Markovitch were both in debt. . . .

"What have I done wrong besides?" Sasha wondered.

He had discounted a forged note. But all the young men he knew did the same. Handrikov and Von Burst always forged IOU's from their parents or friends when their allowances were not paid at the regular time, and then when they got their money from home they redeemed them before they became due. Sasha had done the same, but had not redeemed the IOU because he had not got the money which Handrikov had promised to lend him. He was not to blame; it was the fault of circumstances. It was true that the use of another person's signature was considered reprehensible; but, still, it was not a crime but a generally accepted dodge, an ugly formality which injured no one and was quite harmless, for in forging the Colonel's signature Sasha had had no intention of causing anybody damage or loss.

"No, it doesn't mean that I am a criminal . . ." thought Sasha. "And it's not in my character to bring myself to commit a crime. I am soft, emotional. . . . When I have the money I help the poor. . . ."

Sasha was musing after this fashion while they went on talking the other side of the door.

"But, my friends, this is endless," the Colonel declared, getting excited. "Suppose we were to forgive him and pay the money. You know he would not give up leading a dissipated life, squandering money, making debts, going to our tailors and ordering suits in our names! Can you guarantee that this will be his last prank?

◀ **Critical Viewing** The ruble is the Russian monetary unit. How are these rubles similar to and different from other money, such as American dollars? **[Compare and Contrast]**

As far as I am concerned, I have no faith whatever in his reforming!"

The official of the Treasury muttered something in reply; after him Ivan Markovitch began talking blandly and suavely again. The Colonel moved his chair impatiently and drowned the other's words with his detestable metallic voice. At last the door opened and Ivan Markovitch came out of the study; there were patches of red on his cleanshaven face.

"Come along," he said, taking Sasha by the hand. "Come and speak frankly from your heart. Without pride, my dear boy, humbly and from your heart."

◆ **Literary Focus**

Explain the ways in which the Colonel and Ivan Markovitch are static characters.

Sasha went into the study. The official of the Treasury was sitting down; the Colonel was standing before the table with one hand in his pocket and one knee on a chair. It was smoky and stifling in the study. Sasha did not look at the official or the Colonel; he felt suddenly ashamed and uncomfortable. He looked uneasily at Ivan Markovitch and muttered:

"I'll pay it . . . I'll give it back. . . ."

"What did you expect when you discounted the IOU?" he heard a metallic voice.

"I . . . Handrikov promised to lend me the money before now."

Sasha could say no more. He went out of the study and sat down again on the chair near the door. He would have been glad to go away altogether at once, but he was choking with hatred and he awfully wanted to remain, to tear the Colonel to pieces, to say something rude to him. He sat trying to think of something violent and effective to say to his hated uncle, and at that moment a woman's figure, shrouded in the twilight, appeared at the drawing room door. It was the Colonel's wife. She beckoned Sasha to her, and, wringing her hands, said, weeping:

"*Alexandre*, I know you don't like me, but . . . listen to me; listen, I beg you. . . . But, my dear, how can this have happened? Why, it's awful, awful! For goodness' sake, beg them, defend yourself, entreat them."

Sasha looked at her quivering shoulders, at the big tears that were rolling down her cheeks, heard behind his back the hollow, nervous voices of worried and exhausted people, and shrugged his shoulders. He had not in the least expected that his aristocratic relations would raise such a tempest over a paltry fifteen hundred rubles! He could not understand her tears nor the quiver of their voices.

An hour later he heard that the Colonel was getting the best of it; the uncles were finally inclining to let the case go for trial.

"The matter's settled," said the Colonel, sighing. "Enough."

After this decision all the uncles, even the emphatic Colonel, became noticeably depressed. A silence followed.

"Merciful Heavens!" signed Ivan Markovitch. "My poor sister!"

And he began saying in a subdued voice that most likely his sister, Sasha's mother, was present unseen in the study at that moment. He felt in his soul how the unhappy, saintly woman was weeping, grieving, and begging for her boy. For the sake of her peace beyond the grave, they ought to spare Sasha.

The sound of a muffled sob was heard. Ivan Markovitch was weeping and muttering something which it was impossible to catch through the door. The Colonel got up and paced from corner to corner. The long conversation began over again.

But then the clock in the drawing room struck two. The family council was over. To avoid seeing the person who had moved him to such wrath, the Colonel went from the study, not into the hall, but into the vestibule. . . . Ivan Markovitch came out into the hall. . . . He was agitated and rubbing his hands joyfully. His tear-stained eyes looked good-humored and his mouth was twisted into a smile.

"Capital," he said to Sasha. "Thank God! You can go home, my dear, and sleep tranquilly. We have decided to pay the sum, but on condition that you repent and come with me tomorrow into the country and set to work."

A minute later Ivan Markovitch and Sasha in their greatcoats and caps were going down the stairs. The uncle was muttering something edifying. Sasha did not listen, but felt as though some uneasy weight were gradually slipping off his shoulders. They had forgiven him; he was free! A gust of joy sprang up within him and sent a sweet chill to his heart. He longed to breathe, to move swiftly, to live! Glancing at the street lamps and the black sky, he remembered that Von Burst was celebrating his name day[6] that evening at the "Bear," and again a rush of joy flooded his soul. . . .

"I am going!" he decided.

But then he remembered he had not a farthing, that the companions he was going to would despise him at once for his empty pockets. He must get hold of some money, come what may!

"Uncle, lend me a hundred rubles," he said to Ivan Markovitch.

His uncle, surprised, looked into his face and backed against a lamppost.

"Give it to me," said Sasha, shifting impatiently from one foot to the other and beginning

---

6. **name day:** Feast day of the saint after whom a person is named.

to pant. "Uncle, I entreat you, give me a hundred rubles."

His face worked; he trembled, and seemed on the point of attacking his uncle. . . .

"Won't you?" he kept asking, seeing that his uncle was still amazed and did not understand. "Listen. If you don't, I'll give myself up tomorrow! I won't let you pay the IOU! I'll present another false note tomorrow!"

Petrified, muttering something incoherent in his horror, Ivan Markovitch took a hundred-ruble note out of his pocketbook and gave it to Sasha. The young man took it and walked rapidly away from him. . . .

Taking a sledge,[7] Sasha grew calmer, and felt a rush of joy within him again. The "rights of youth" of which kind-hearted Ivan Markovitch had spoken at the family council woke up and asserted themselves. Sasha pictured the drinking party before him, and, among the bottles, the women, and his friends, the thought flashed through his mind:

"Now I see that I am a criminal; yes, I am a criminal."

---

7. **sledge** (slej) *n.:* Strong, heavy sled.

◆ **Build Vocabulary**

vestibule (ves´ tə byül) *n.:* Small entrance hall or room

Guide for Responding

◆ *Literature and Your Life*

Reader's Response With whom in this story do you sympathize? Why?

Thematic Focus What point about choices and consequences is demonstrated by Sasha's experiences?

☑ **Check Your Comprehension**

1. Why does Sasha need help?
2. How does Uncle Ivan convince the other uncles to help Sasha?

◆ Critical Thinking

INTERPRET

1. Why do you think most of the relatives don't want to help Sasha? **[Speculate]**
2. Why do you think Sasha wrote a note he knew he could not honor? **[Infer]**

EVALUATE

3. Do you think Uncle Ivan's attitude helps or harms Sasha? Explain. **[Make a Judgment]**

APPLY

4. What would you have done if you were one of Sasha's uncles? **[Relate]**

Birds

Bruno Schulz
Translated by Celina Wieniewska

Came the yellow days of winter, filled with boredom. The rust-colored earth was covered with a threadbare, meager table-cloth of snow full of holes. There was not enough of it for some of the roofs and so they stood there, black and brown, shingle and thatch, arks containing the sooty expanses of attics—coal-black cathedrals, bristling with ribs of rafters, beams and spars—the dark lungs of winter winds. Each dawn revealed new chimney stacks and chimney pots which had emerged during the hours of darkness, blown up by the night winds . . . The chimney-sweeps could not get rid of the crows which in the evening covered the branches of the trees around the church with living black leaves, then took off, fluttering, and came back, each clinging to its own place on its own branch, only to fly away at dawn in large flocks, like gusts of soot, flakes of dirt, <u>undulating</u> and fantastic, blackening with their insistent crowing the musty-yellow streaks of light. The days hardened with cold and boredom like last year's loaves of bread. One began to cut them with blunt knives without appetite, with a lazy indifference.

Father had stopped going out. He banked up the stoves, studied the ever elusive essence of fire, experienced the salty, metallic taste and the smoky smell of wintry flames, the cool caresses of salamanders that licked the shiny soot in the throat of the chimney. He applied himself lovingly at that time to all manner of small repairs in the upper regions of the rooms. At all hours of the day one could see him crouched on top of a ladder, working at something under the ceiling, at the cornices[1] over the tall windows, at the counterweights and chains of the hanging lamps. Following the custom of house painters, he used a pair of steps as enormous stilts and he felt perfectly happy in that bird's eye perspective close to the sky, leaves and birds painted on the ceiling. He grew more and more remote from practical affairs. When my mother, worried and unhappy about his condition, tried to draw him into a conversation about business, about the payments due at the end of the month, he listened to her absent-mindedly, anxiety showing in his abstracted look. Sometimes he stopped her with a warning gesture of the hand in order to run to a corner of the room, put his ear to a crack in the floor and, by lifting the index finger of both hands, emphasize the gravity of the inves-

◆ **Reading Strategy**
What conclusions can you draw about the mother, based on her reactions to the father's actions?

---

1. **cornices** (kôr′ nis əz) *n*.: Decorative molded features that project from the tops of some window frames.

tigation, and begin to listen intently. At that time we did not yet understand the sad origin of these <u>eccentricities</u>, the deplorable complex which had been maturing in him.

Mother had no influence over him, but he gave a lot of respectful attention to Adela. The cleaning of his room was to him a great and important ceremony, of which he always arranged to be a witness, watching all Adela's movements . . . He ascribed to all her functions a deeper, symbolic meaning. When . . . the girl pushed a . . . broom along the floor, father could hardly bear it. Tears would stream from his eyes, silent laughter transformed his face . . . He was ticklish to the point of madness. It was enough for Adela to waggle her fingers at him to imitate tickling, for him to rush through all the rooms in a wild panic, banging the doors after him, to fall at last flat on the bed in the furthest room and wriggle in convulsions of laughter, imagining the tickling which he found irresistible. Because of this, Adela's power over father was almost limitless.

◆ Build Vocabulary

undulating (un´ dyo͞o lāt iŋ) *v*.: Moving in waves

eccentricities (ek´ sen tris´ ə tēz) *n*.: Examples of slightly odd or unconventional behavior

anomalies (ə näm´ ə lēz) *n*.: Abnormalities

At that time we noticed for the first time father's passionate interest in animals. To begin with, it was the passion of the huntsman and the artist rolled into one. It was almost perhaps a deeper, biological sympathy of one creature for kindred, yet different forms of life, a kind of experimenting in the unexplored regions of existence . . .

But it all began with the hatching out of birds' eggs.

With a great outlay of effort and money, father imported from Hamburg, or Holland, or from zoological stations in Africa, birds' eggs on which he set enormous broody hens from Belgium. It was a process which fascinated me as well—this hatching out of the chicks, which were real <u>anomalies</u> of shape and color. It was difficult to anticipate in these monsters with enormous, fantastic beaks which they opened wide immediately after birth, hissing greedily to show the backs of their throats, in these lizards with frail, naked bodies of hunchbacks, the future peacocks, pheasants, grouse or condors. Placed in cotton-wool, in baskets, this dragon brood lifted blind, wall-eyed heads on thin necks, croaking voicelessly from their dumb throats. My father would walk along the shelves, dressed in a green baize apron like a gardener in a hothouse of cacti, and conjure up from nothingness these blind bubbles, pulsating with life, these impotent bellies receiving the outside world only in the form of food, these growths on the surface of life, climbing blindfold towards the light. A few weeks later when these blind buds of matter burst open, the rooms were filled with the bright chatter and scintillating chirruping of its new inhabitants. The birds perched on the curtain pelmets,[2] on the tops of wardrobes; they nestled in the tangle of tin branches and the metal scrolls of the hanging lamps.

While father pored over his large ornithological[3] textbooks and studied their colored plates, these feathery phantasms seemed to rise from the pages and fill the rooms with colors, with splashes of crimson, strips of sapphire, verdigris and silver. At feeding time they formed a motley, undulating bed on the floor, a living carpet which at the intrusion of a stranger would fall apart, scatter into fragments, flutter in the air, and finally settle high under the ceilings. I remember in particular a certain condor, an enormous bird with a featherless neck, its face wrinkled and knobbly. It was an emaciated <u>ascetic</u>, a Buddhist lama,[4] full of imperturbable dignity in its behavior, guided by the rigid ceremonial of its great species. When it sat facing my father, motionless in the monumental position of ageless Egyptian idols, its eye covered with a whitish cataract which it pulled down sideways over its pupil to shut itself

up completely in the contemplation of its dignified solitude—it seemed, with its stony profile, like an older brother of my father's. Its body and muscles seemed to be made of the same material, it had the same hard, wrinkled skin, the same desiccated bony face, the same horny deep eye sockets. Even the hands, strong in the joints, my father's long thick hands with their rounded nails, had their counterpart in the condor's claws. I could not resist the impression, when looking at the sleeping condor, that I was in the presence of a mummy—a dried out, shrunken mummy of my father. I believe that even my mother noticed this strange resemblance although we never discussed the subject. It is significant that the condor used my father's chamberpot.

♦ **Literary Focus**
Explain the ways in which the father is a dynamic character.

Not content with the hatching out of more and more new specimens, my father arranged the marriages of birds in the attic, he sent out matchmakers, he tied up eager attractive brides in the holes and crannies under the roof, and soon the roof of our house, an enormous double-ridged shingle roof, became a real birds' hostel, a Noah's ark to which all kinds of feathery creatures flew from far afield. Long after the liquidation of the birds' paradise, this tradition persisted in the avian world and during the period of spring migration our roof was besieged by whole flocks of cranes, pelicans, peacocks, and sundry other birds. However, after a short period of splendor, the whole undertaking took a sorry turn.

It soon became necessary to move my father to two rooms at the top of the house which had served as box rooms. We could hear from there, at dawn, the mixed clangor

---

2. pelmets (pel´ mits) *n*.: Horizontal ornamental features at the heads of windows, used to cover the fastenings from which curtains are hung.
3. ornithological (ôr´ nə thä lo´ ji kəl) *adj*.: Having to do with the study of birds.
4. Buddhist lama (boo͞´ dist lä´ ma): High-ranking Buddhist monk. Buddhism is a primarily Asian religion that teaches self-discipline as a way of achieving Enlightenment.

Schneehuehner, Paul Klee

▲ **Critical Viewing** Which details in this painting capture the fantastic quality of the story? Explain. **[Connect]**

of birds' voices. The wooden walls of the attic rooms, helped by the resonance of the empty space under the gables, sounded with the roar, the flutterings, the crowing, the gurgling, the mating cries. For a few weeks father was lost to view. He only rarely came down to the flat and, when he did, we noticed that he seemed to have shrunk, to have become smaller and thinner. Occasionally forgetting himself, he would rise from his chair at table, wave his arms as if they were wings, and emit a long-drawn-out bird's call while his eyes misted over. Then, rather embarrassed, he would join us in laughing it off and try to turn the whole incident into a joke.

◆ **Build Vocabulary**

ascetic (ə set′ ik) *n.*: One who lives with strict self-discipline and without the usual pleasures and comforts

One day, during spring cleaning, Adela suddenly appeared in father's birds' kingdom. Stopping in the doorway, she wrung her hands at the fetid smell that filled the room, the heaps of droppings covering the floor, the tables and the chairs. Without hesitation, she flung open a window and, with the help of a long broom, she prodded the whole mass of birds into life. A fiendish cloud of feathers and wings arose screaming and Adela, like a furious Maenad protected by the whirlwind of her thyrsus,[5] danced

the dance of destruction. My father, waving his arms in panic, tried to lift himself into the air with his feathered flock. Slowly the winged cloud thinned until at last Adela remained on the battlefield, exhausted and out of breath, along with my father who now, adopting a worried hang dog expression, was ready to accept complete defeat.

A moment later, my father came downstairs—a broken man, an exiled king who had lost his throne and his kingdom.

---

5. **like a furious Maenad** (mē´ nad) . . . **thyrsus** (thur´ səs): Like a woman under the spell of Dionysos, the Greek god of wine. According to mythology, a woman under this spell would run around in a frenzied state waving a thyrsus, a pine cone-tipped wand.

◆ **Literary Focus**
What does the term "exiled king" convey about the narrator's father? Does he prove to be a static or dynamic character?

Guide for Responding

◆ Literature and Your Life

Reader's Response If you were in the narrator's position, what would you have done about the father?

Thematic Focus Name a consequence of the father's involvement with the birds. Has he chosen this consequence?

Reader's Journal Choose a scene in "Birds" and list both the realistic and fantastic details in it.

Questions for Research Suppose you wanted a pet bird. Jot down some questions you might ask an expert in order to identify a suitable type.

☑ Check Your Comprehension

1. How does the father react when the mother tries to talk to him about business?
2. What does the father begin to pursue as a hobby?
3. Which of the father's pets does the narrator feel most closely resembles his father?
4. What does Adela, the housekeeper, do during spring cleaning that upsets the father so greatly?

◆ Critical Thinking

INTERPRET

1. Why might Schulz have chosen to begin this story in winter and end it in spring? **[Infer]**
2. What are some of the first signs of the father's detachment from reality? **[Analyze]**
3. Is the father's obsession with birds a form of escape or something more? Explain. **[Draw Conclusions]**

EVALUATE

4. Was Adela's decisive action near the story's end justifiable? Why or why not? **[Make a Judgment]**

APPLY

5. In what ways would "Birds" be different if it were told from the father's point of view? **[Modify]**

COMPARE LITERARY WORKS

6. Compare and contrast the problems created by the main characters in "A Problem" and "Birds." **[Compare and Contrast]**

Guide for Responding (continued)

◆ Reading Strategy

DRAW CONCLUSIONS ABOUT CHARACTER

You can apply logic to the evidence provided by each author to **draw conclusions** about the personalities of characters in "A Problem" and "Birds." For example, when the Colonel in "A Problem" declares about his nephew, "I have no faith whatever in his reforming," you can conclude that the nephew has disappointed his family more than once.

1. Based on the uncle's meeting, what conclusions can you draw about the importance of family at the time of "A Problem"?
2. What can you conclude about Sasha's character when he asks his uncle for money at the end of the story?
3. What conclusions about the father in "Birds" did you draw when you read his reaction to Adela's sweeping?
4. In "Birds," what might have caused Adela to sweep the birds out? What makes you think this?

◆ Build Vocabulary

USING THE GREEK PREFIXES: *a-* AND *an-*

Knowing that the Greek prefixes *a-* and *an-* mean "without or not," explain each of these phrases:

1. an *atypical* situation
2. an *asymmetrical* design
3. *atonal* music

USING THE WORD BANK: Antonyms

On your paper, write the letter of the word most nearly *opposite* in meaning to the given word.

1. taciturn : (a) loud-mouthed, (b) lightweight, (c) straightforward
2. rheumatic : (a) carefree, (b) agile, (c) cramped
3. vestibule : (a) coat, (b) dollar, (c) office
4. undulating : (a) making waves, (b) keeping silent, (c) moving steadily
5. eccentricities : (a) common features, (b) individual traits, (c) bizarre actions
6. anomalies : (a) exceptions, (b) regularities, (c) adjectives
7. ascetic : (a) monk, (b) dirt, (c) self-indulger

◆ Literary Focus

STATIC AND DYNAMIC CHARACTERS

Some characters in stories can be classified as **static characters**—characters that do not change during the course of the story. Others are **dynamic characters**—characters whose attitudes or beliefs change as a result of the story events.

In "A Problem," for example, the Colonel is a static character: He undergoes no significant change in outlook or disposition. Sasha does experience a change and is therefore dynamic.

1. (a) What realization does Sasha come to about himself? (b) What causes this new awareness and what will its effects be?
2. (a) Which characters in "Birds" are static? (b) Which, if any, are dynamic? Explain.

◆ Build Grammar Skills

RESTRICTIVE AND NONRESTRICTIVE ADJECTIVE CLAUSES

A **restrictive adjective clause** is not set off by commas because it is necessary to complete the meaning of the sentence. A **nonrestrictive adjective clause** is set off by commas. It provides additional but not necessary information.

Practice Copy the following sentences in your notebook. Underline the adjective clause in each. Then, tell whether it is restrictive or nonrestrictive.

1. "My friends!" said the uncle who was a colonel ...
2. Each dawn revealed new chimney stacks and chimney pots which had emerged during the hours of darkness. . . .
3. It soon became necessary to move my father to the rooms ... which had served as box rooms.
4. ... she wrung her hands at the fetid smell that filled the room ...

Writing Application Write the following sentences in your notebook, supplying adjective clauses where there are blank spaces.

Sasha's uncle _____?_____ said he would help. He offered to pay the notes _____?_____. Sasha wanted to go to the party _____?_____. He asked his uncle for money _____?_____. The uncle was shocked that his nephew _____?_____ would be so ungrateful.

Build Your Portfolio

 ## Idea Bank

Writing

1. **Journal Entry** Write an entry in Sasha Uskov's journal dated the day before his family met to discuss the promissory note he failed to pay.

2. **Interview Questions** Imagine you are a newspaper reporter coming to interview the father in "Birds." Write some questions that you want him to answer.

3. **Story Sequel** Write a continuation of the story for either "A Problem" or "Birds." In the course of your narrative, make at least one character dynamic.

Speaking, Listening, and Viewing

4. **Monologue** Take on the character of the narrator of "Birds" and prepare and perform a monologue in which the character describes his family to an audience. Base descriptions in the monologue on details from the story. **[Performing Arts Link]**

5. **Roundtable Discussion** With three other students, discuss how the message about choices and consequences in "A Problem" applies to modern times.

Researching and Representing

6. **Period Presentation** Find pictures in books or on the Internet that show how people dressed and lived in nineteenth-century Russia or in early twentieth-century Poland. Make a presentation of those pictures, or create your own drawings based on your research. **[Art Link; Social Studies Link; Media Link]**

7. **Multimedia Biography** Create a multimedia biography of Anton Chekhov or Bruno Schulz. Use maps to show where the author lived, and record yourself reading a passage from his writing. **[Art Link; Social Studies Link; Media Link]**

Online Activity www.phlit.phschool.com

Guided Writing Lesson

Script for a Telephone Conversation

Even though "A Problem" takes place before the telephone was invented, it is possible to imagine an updated version of the story, in which the conversations take place on a telephone. When a person talks on a telephone, the language he or she uses often reveals much about his or her personality.

Write a script for a telephone conversation between two of the characters in "A Problem." Use the kind of language contemporary people would use when talking on the phone.

Writing Skills: Realistic Dialogue

Realistic dialogue reflects the language people really use when they talk with one another. The dialogue in "A Problem" captures the way people talked in the late nineteenth century, when the story takes place. For your telephone conversation, choose and arrange words to reflect the way characters today would talk on the phone.

Prewriting Once you decide on the two characters and the attitudes they'll convey in the telephone conversation, jot down specific lines of dialogue that reveal important characteristics and the speaking style of each speaker. Then, list other words and phrases that each character might use.

Drafting Write the conversation in script format, indicating the speaker in capital letters before each line or passage of dialogue. As you draft, make the dialogue for the phone conversation as believable as you can. Use contractions, slang, and sentence fragments, where appropriate.

Revising Have two classmates read the script of the phone conversation aloud to you. Listen to make sure each speaker is responding to the other's words. If some of your dialogue does not sound realistic, revise it so that it sounds more believable.

PART 2 *Setting, Atmosphere, and Theme*

Springtime, Jean-Francois Millet, Musée d'Orsay, Paris

$\mathcal{G}$uide for Reading

Mori Ōgai *(1862–1922)*

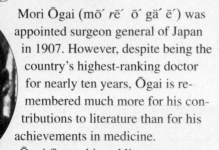

Mori Ōgai (mō´ rē´ ō´ gä´ ē´) was appointed surgeon general of Japan in 1907. However, despite being the country's highest-ranking doctor for nearly ten years, Ōgai is remembered much more for his contributions to literature than for his achievements in medicine.

Ōgai first achieved literary success in the 1890's, publishing autobiographical works of fiction based on his experiences in Germany, where he had studied medicine for several years. He later expanded his writing to include nonfiction, drama, and literary criticism.

Given the wide scope of Ōgai's contributions, some contemporary critics consider him to be the most important Japanese literary figure of the entire twentieth century.

Italo Calvino *(1923–1985)*

Italo Calvino was born in Cuba, but as a young boy, he moved with his family to Italy. He settled in Turin after fighting in the Italian Resistance during World War II. Two of his works of fiction, *The Path to the Nest of Spiders* and *Adam, One Afternoon,* were in fact inspired by his participation in the Resistance.

Calvino is best known for having edited a monumental collection of fables. According to his theory, the "fable formula," which involves a child in the woods or a knight fighting beasts, is the scheme for all human stories. One fable element that can be found in almost all of Calvino's fiction is the tension between character and environment. You will see this conflict between characters and environment in "The Garden of Stubborn Cats."

◆ Build Vocabulary

LATIN SUFFIXES: *-al*

In "The Garden of Stubborn Cats," the speaker refers to "the supernal heaven of the penthouses." *Supernal* combines the Latin root *super-*, meaning "above," with the Latin suffix *-al*, which means "of, like, or suitable for." *Supernal* therefore means "like that above; as though from the sky." By using this word, the speaker draws on the traditional association of the clouds and the sky with visions of heavenly places.

oblique
truncated
supernal
itinerary
transoms
rank
scrimmage
indigence

WORD BANK

Before you read, preview this list of words from the story. Write the words in two columns: words you know and words you need to learn.

◆ Build Grammar Skills

COMMONLY CONFUSED WORDS: *lie* AND *lay*

Because *lie* and *lay* seem similar, and because the past tense of *lie* is *lay*, these verbs are often confused. In fact, they have two different meanings and uses. *Lay* means "to put or set (something) down," and it usually takes a direct object. Its principal parts are *lay, laying, laid,* and *laid.*

dir. obj.
. . . he . . . *laid* his <u>place</u> among the packing-cases. . . .

Lie means "to recline." Its principal parts are *lie, lying, lay,* and *lain. Lie* does not take a direct object.

. . . dry leaves *lay* everywhere under the boughs. . . .

◆ Under Reconstruction ◆
The Garden of Stubborn Cats

◆ *Literature and Your Life*

CONNECT YOUR EXPERIENCE

You've exchanged hundreds of e-mails with your best friend. Suddenly, something seems to be missing—your best friend. You're starting to forget what he or she looks and sounds like because all you have to do to communicate is press "send." Situations like this call your attention to the fact that changes in the way we live have disadvantages as well as advantages.

THEMATIC FOCUS: TO THE FUTURE

These two stories highlight the need to examine the effects of moderization as we move into the future.

Journal Writing Create a chart showing the pros and cons of a technological advance in this century, such as airplanes or transatlantic communication.

◆ Background for Understanding

CULTURE

Today Japan is a highly developed nation in touch with the rest of the world. However, in the mid-nineteenth century, it was an isolated society. Only with the visit of American naval officer Matthew C. Perry in 1853 and a change in Japanese governments in the late 1860's did Japan open itself to Western influence and trade. What followed was a period of rapid transformation and modernization.

"Under Reconstruction" was written in 1910, while Japan was still in the midst of these sweeping changes. The story reflects the conflicts that these changes caused in Japanese society.

◆ Literary Focus

SETTING AND CULTURAL BACKGROUND

All stories have a **setting,** the time and place in which the story's action occurs. In some stories, the **cultural background,** what is going on in the society, is an important part of the setting. Cultural background is especially relevant when the society's beliefs and customs are undergoing a change.

In both "Under Reconstruction" and "The Garden of Stubborn Cats," the cultural background involves a clash between the forces of tradition and those of modernization. That struggle takes the form of a conflict between Japanese and Western ways in "Under Reconstruction." In "The Garden of Stubborn Cats," a city's cat population represents an older way of life that is threatened by urban development.

◆ Reading Strategy

CLARIFY

If something you read doesn't make sense, don't just ignore it and move on. To avoid misunderstandings, **clarify** any parts of the story you don't understand. The best way to do this is to read ahead for more information or read back to review what you have already learned. For example, you might want to review details of the setting, clarify the relationships among the characters, or look back at the details of a key event.

As both of these stories develop, you may come to places that are not completely clear. At these points, stop, look back or ahead, and put details together to clarify the events.

	"Under"	"Cats"
Time Details		
Place Details		
Culture Details		

Under Reconstruction

Mori Ōgai

Translated by Ivan Morris

It had just stopped raining when Councilor Watanabé got off the tram in front of the Kabuki[1] playhouse. Carefully avoiding the puddles, he hurried through the Kobiki district in the direction of the Department of Communications. Surely that restaurant was somewhere around here, he thought as he strode along the canal; he remembered having noticed the signboard on one of these corners.

The streets were fairly empty. He passed a group of young men in Western clothes. They were talking noisily and looked as if they had all just left their office. Then a girl in a kimono[2] and a gaily-colored sash hurried by, almost bumping into him. She was probably a waitress from some local teahouse, he thought. A rickshaw[3] with its hood up passed him from behind.

Finally he caught sight of a small signboard with the inscription written horizontally in the Western style: *Seiyòken Hotel*. The front of the building facing the canal was covered with scaffolding. The side entrance was on a small street. There were two oblique flights of stairs outside the restaurant, forming a sort of truncated triangle. At the head of each staircase was a glass door; after hesitating a moment, Watanabé entered the one on the left on which were written the characters for *Entrance*.

Inside he found a wide passage. By the door was a pile of little cloths for wiping one's shoes and next to these a large Western doormat. Watanabé's shoes were muddy after the rain and he carefully cleaned them with both implements. Apparently in this restaurant one was supposed to observe the Western custom and wear one's shoes indoors.

There was no sign of life in the passage, but from the distance came a great sound of hammering and sawing. The place was under reconstruction, thought Watanabé.

He waited awhile, but as no one came to receive him, he walked to the end of the passage.

Here he stopped, not knowing which way to turn. Suddenly he noticed a man with a napkin under his arm leaning against the wall a few yards away. He went up to him.

"I telephoned yesterday for a reservation."

The man sprang to attention. "Oh yes, sir. A table for two, I believe? It's on the second floor. Would you mind coming with me, sir."

The waiter followed him up another flight of stairs. The man had known immediately who he was, thought Watanabé. Customers must be few and far between with the repairs underway. As he mounted the stairs, the clatter and banging of the workmen became almost deafening.

"Quite a lively place," said Watanabé, looking back at the waiter.

"Oh no, sir. The men go home at five o'clock. You won't be disturbed while you're dining, sir."

When they reached the top of the stairs, the waiter hurried past Watanabé and opened a door to the left. It was a large room overlooking the canal. It seemed rather big for just two people. Round each of the three small tables in the room were squeezed as many chairs as could possibly be fitted. Under the window was a huge sofa and next to it a potted vine about three feet high and a dwarfed plant with large hothouse grapes.

The waiter walked across the room and opened another door. "This is your dining room, sir." Watanabé followed him. The room was small— just right, in fact, for a couple. In the middle a table was elaborately set with two covers and a large basket of azaleas and rhododendrons.

With a certain feeling of satisfaction, Watanabé returned to the large room. The waiter withdrew and Watanabé again found himself alone. Abruptly the sound of hammering stopped. He looked at his watch: yes, it was exactly five o'clock. There was still half an hour

◆ Literary Focus
In what way does the presence of the workmen connect with the story's title?

---

1. **Kabuki** (kä bōō′ kē) *n.*: A form of Japanese drama.
2. **kimono** (kə mō′ nə) *n.*: A traditional Japanese outer garment with short, wide sleeves and a sash.
3. **rickshaw** (rik′ shô) *n.*: A small, two-wheeled carriage with a hood, pulled by one or two people.

◆ **Build Vocabulary**

oblique (ə blēk′) *adj.*: Not straightforward

truncated (trun′ kāt əd) *adj.*: Cut short; with an angle cut off

till his appointment. Watanabé took a cigar from an open box on the table, pierced the end, and lit it.

Strangely enough, he did not have the slightest feeling of anticipation. It was as if it did not matter who was to join him in this room, as if he did not care in the slightest whose face it was that he would soon be seeing across that flower basket. He was surprised at his own coolness.

Puffing comfortably at his cigar, he walked over to the window and opened it. Directly below were stacked huge piles of timber. This was the main entrance. The water in the canal appeared completely stationary. On the other side he could see a row of wooden buildings. They looked like houses of assignation. Except for a woman with a child on her back, walking slowly back and forth outside one of the houses, there was no one in sight. At the far right, the massive redbrick structure of the Naval Museum imposingly blocked his view.

Watanabé sat down on the sofa and examined the room. The walls were decorated with an ill-assorted collection of pictures: nightingales on a plum tree, an illustration from a fairy tale, a hawk. The scrolls were small and narrow, and on the high walls they looked strangely short as if the bottom portions had been tucked under and concealed. Over the door was a large framed Buddhist text. And this is meant to be the land of art, thought Watanabé.

For a while he sat there smoking his cigar and simply enjoying a sensation of physical well-being. Then he heard the sound of voices in the passage and the door opened. It was she.

She wore a large Anne-Marie straw hat decorated with beads. Under her long gray coat he noticed a white embroidered batiste blouse. Her skirt was also gray. She carried a tiny umbrella with a tassel. Watanabé forced a smile to his face. Throwing his cigar in an ashtray, he got up from the sofa.

The German woman removed her veil and glanced back at the waiter, who had followed her into the room and who was now standing by the door. Then she turned her eyes to

Watanabé. They were the large, brown eyes of a brunette. They were the eyes into which he had so often gazed in the past. Yet he did not remember those mauve shadows from their days in Berlin. . . .

"I'm sorry I kept you waiting," she said abruptly in German.

She transferred her umbrella to her left hand and stiffly extended the gloved fingers of her right hand. No doubt all this was for the

Ouda (detail), Hironaga Takehiko, British Museum

▲ **Critical Viewing** In what ways might Western influences change this Japanese scene? **[Speculate]**

benefit of the waiter, thought Watanabé as he courteously took the fingers in his hand.

"You can let me know when dinner is ready," he said, glancing at the door. The waiter bowed and left the room.

"How delightful to see you," he said in German.

The woman nonchalantly threw her umbrella on a chair and sat down on the sofa with a slight gasp of exhaustion. Putting her elbows on the table, she gazed silently at Watanabé. He drew up a chair next to the table and sat down.

"It's very quiet here, isn't it?" she said after a while.

"It's under reconstruction," said Watanabé. "They were making a terrible noise when I arrived."

"Oh, that explains it. The place does give one rather an unsettled feeling. Not that I'm a particularly calm sort of person at best."

"When did you arrive in Japan?"

"The day before yesterday. And then yesterday I happened to see you on the street."

"And why did you come?"

"Well, you see, I've been in Vladivostok[4] since the end of last year."

"I suppose you've been singing in that hotel there, whatever it's called."

"Yes."

"You obviously weren't alone. Were you with a company?"

"No, I wasn't with a company. But I wasn't alone either. . . . I was with a man. In fact you know him." She hesitated a moment. "I've been with Kosinsky."

"Oh, that Pole. So I suppose you're called Kosinskaya now."

"Don't be silly! It's simply that I sing and Kosinsky accompanies me."

"Are you sure that's all?"

"You mean, do we have a good time together? Well, I can't say it never happens."

"That's hardly surprising. I suppose he's in Tokyo with you?"

"Yes, we're both at the Aikokusan Hotel."

"But he lets you come out alone."

"My dear friend, I only let him accompany me in singing, you know." She used the word *begleiten*.[5] If he accompanied her on the piano, thought Watanabé, he accompanied her in other ways too.

"I told him that I'd seen you on the Ginza," she continued, "and he's very anxious to meet you."

"Allow me to deprive myself of that pleasure."

"Don't worry. He isn't short of money or anything."

"No, but he probably will be before long if he stays here," said Watanabé with a smile. "And where do you plan to go next?"

"I'm going to America. Everyone tells me that Japan is hopeless, so I'm not going to count on getting work here."

"You're quite right. America is a good place to go after Russia. Japan is still backward. . . . It's still under reconstruction, you see."

"Good heavens! If you aren't careful, I'll tell them in America that a Japanese gentleman admitted his country was backward. In fact, I'll say it was a Japanese government official. You are a government official, aren't you?"

"Yes, I'm in the government."

"And behaving yourself very correctly, no doubt?"

"Frighteningly so! I've become a real *Fürst*,[6] you know. Tonight's the only exception."

"I'm very honored!" She slowly undid the buttons of her long gloves, took them off, and held out her right hand to Watanabé. It was a beautiful, dazzlingly white hand. He clasped it firmly, amazed at its coldness. Without removing her hand from Watanabé's grasp, she looked steadily at him. Her large, brown eyes seemed with their dark shadows to have grown to twice their former size.

"Would you like me to kiss you?" she said.

Watanabé made a wry face. "We are in Japan," he said.

Without any warning, the door was flung open and the waiter appeared. "Dinner is served, sir."

"We are in Japan," repeated Watanabé. He got up and led the woman into the little dining room. The waiter suddenly turned on the glaring overhead lights.

The woman sat down opposite Watanabé and glanced round the room. "They've given us a *chambre séparée*,"[7] she said laughing. "How exciting!" She straightened her back and looked directly at Watanabé as if to see how he would react.

"I'm sure it's quite by chance," he said calmly.

Three waiters were in constant attendance on the two of them. One poured sherry, the other served slices of melon, and the third bustled about ineffectually.

"The place is alive with waiters," said Watanabé.

◆ Literary Focus
In what way does the comment about Japan being "under reconstruction" link the title of the story, the setting, and the theme?

---

4. **Vladivostok** (vlad′ i väs′ täk): A city in Russia.
5. *begleiten* (bə glī′ tən): "Accompany" (German).
6. *Fürst* (fürst): "Duke" (German).
7. *chambre séparée* (shän′ br′ sā pà rā′): "Separate room" (French).

"Yes, and they seem to be a clumsy lot," she said, squaring her elbows as she started on her melon. "They're just as bad at my hotel."

"I expect you and Kosinsky find they get in your way. Always barging in without knocking. . . ."

"You're wrong about all that, you know. Well, the melon is good anyway."

"In America you'll be getting stacks of food to eat every morning as soon as you wake up."

The conversation drifted along lightly. Finally the waiters brought in fruit salad and poured champagne.

"Aren't you jealous—even a little?" the woman suddenly asked. All the time they had been eating and chatting away. She had remembered how they used to sit facing each other like this after the theater at the little restaurant above the Blühr Steps. Sometimes they had quarreled, but they had always made it up in the end. She had meant to sound as if she were joking; but despite herself, her voice was serious and she felt ashamed.

Watanabé lifted his champagne glass high above the flowers and said in a clear voice: "Kosinsky *soll leben!*"[8]

The woman silently raised her glass. There was a frozen smile on her face. Under the table her hand trembled uncontrollably.

It was still only half past eight when a solitary, black car drove slowly along the Ginza through an ocean of flickering lights. In the back sat a woman, her face hidden by a veil.

---

8. **soll leben** (zōl lā′ bən): "Shall live" (German).

Guide for Responding

◆ Literature and Your Life

Reader's Response How would you feel if you saw the town in which you live transforming right before your eyes? Would you welcome the change or would you miss having familiar surroundings? Explain.

Thematic Focus Technological advances have made it possible for people to communicate more easily with those in other cultures. How has this increased the need for awareness of cultural differences?

Journal Writing Write a short journal entry describing a time in your life when you experienced a conflict between tradition and progress.

☑ Check Your Comprehension

1. List three things Watanabé observes on the way to dinner that reflect the transitional state that Japan was in at that time.
2. Describe Watanabé's mental state as he awaits his dinner companion.
3. How does Watanabé describe the way the walls of the room are decorated?
4. Where does the German woman plan to go after she leaves Japan?

◆ Critical Thinking

INTERPRET

1. What evidence suggests that Watanabé and the German woman had previously been involved in a relationship? **[Support]**
2. How do you think Watanabé feels about the woman's relationship with Kosinsky? **[Analyze]**

APPLY

3. Based on the way the story ends, do you think Watanabé and the German woman will rekindle their relationship? **[Speculate]**

EXTEND

4. How does the meeting between Watanabé and the woman parallel the merging of Japanese and Western customs in early twentieth-century Japan? **[Social Studies Link]**

The Garden of Stubborn Cats

Italo Calvino   Translated by William Weaver

The city of cats and the city of men exist one inside the other, but they are not the same city. Few cats recall the time when there was no distinction: the streets and squares of men were also streets and squares of cats, and the lawns, courtyards, balconies, and fountains: you lived in a broad and various space. But for several generations now domestic felines have been prisoners of an uninhabitable city: the streets are uninterruptedly overrun by the mortal traffic of cat-crushing automobiles; in every square foot of terrain where once a garden extended or a vacant lot or the ruins of an old demolition, now condominiums loom up, welfare housing, brand-new skyscrapers; every entrance is crammed with parked cars; the courtyards, one by one, have been roofed by reinforced concrete and transformed into garages or movie houses or storerooms or workshops. And where a rolling plateau of low roofs once extended, copings,[1] terraces, water tanks, balconies, skylights, corrugated-iron sheds, now one general superstructure rises wherever structures can rise; the intermediate differences in height, between the low ground of the street and the supernal heaven of the penthouses, disappear; the cat of a recent litter seeks in vain the itinerary of its

---

1. **copings** (kō´ piŋz) *n.*: Top layers of masonry walls.

fathers, the point from which to make the soft leap from balustrade to cornice to drainpipe, or for the quick climb on the roof-tiles.

But in this vertical city, in this compressed city where all voids tend to fill up and every block of cement tends to mingle with other blocks of cement, a kind of counter-city opens, a negative city, that consists of empty slices between wall and wall, of the minimal distances ordained by the building regulations between two constructions, between the rear of one con-struction and the rear of the next; it is a city of cavities, wells, air con-duits, driveways, inner yards, accesses to base-ments, like a network of dry canals on a planet of stucco and tar, and it is through this network, grazing the walls, that the ancient cat population still scurries.

◆ **Literary Focus**
What details in this paragraph help you envision the setting?

On occasion, to pass the time, Marcovaldo would follow a cat. It was during the work-break, between noon and three, when all the personnel except Marcovaldo went home to eat, and he—who brought his lunch in his bag—laid his place among the packing-cases in the warehouse, chewed his snack, smoked a half-cigar, and wandered around, alone and idle, waiting for work to resume. In those hours, a cat that peeped in at a window was always wel-come company, and a guide for new explo-rations. He had made friends with a tabby, well fed, a blue ribbon around its neck, surely living with some well-to-do family. This tabby shared with Marcovaldo the habit of an afternoon stroll right after lunch; and naturally a friend-ship sprang up.

Following his tabby friend, Marcovaldo had started look-ing at places as if through the round eyes of a cat and even if these places were the usual environs of his firm he saw them in a different light, as set-tings for cattish stories, with connections practicable only by light, velvety paws. Though from the outside the neighborhood seemed poor in cats, every day on his rounds Marcovaldo made

the acquaintance of some new face, and a miau, a hiss, a stiffening of fur on an arched back was enough for him to sense ties and in-trigues and rivalries among them. At those mo-ments he thought he had already penetrated the secrecy of the felines' society: and then he felt himself scrutinized by pupils that became slits, under the surveillance of the antennae of taut whiskers, and all the cats around him sat impassive as sphinxes, the pink triangles of their noses convergent on the black triangles of their lips, and the only things that moved were the tips of the ears, with a vibrant jerk like radar. They reached the end of a narrow pas-sage, between squalid blank walls; and, looking around, Marcovaldo saw that the cats that had led him this far had vanished, all of them to-gether, no telling in which direction, even his tabby friend, and they had left him alone. Their realm had territories, ceremonies, customs that it was not yet granted to him to discover.

On the other hand, from the cat city there opened unsuspected peepholes onto the city of men: and one day the same tabby led him to discover the great Biarritz Restaurant.

Anyone wishing to see the Biarritz Restau-rant had only to assume the posture of a cat, that is, proceed on all fours. Cat and man, in this fashion, walked around a kind of dome, at whose foot some low, rectangular little win-dows opened. Following the tabby's example, Marcovaldo looked down.

◆ **Build Vocabulary**
supernal (sə purn´ əl) *adj.*: Celestial or divine
itinerary (ī tin´ ər er´ ē) *n.*: Route

They were <u>transoms</u> through which the luxurious hall received air and light. To the sound of gypsy violins, partridges and quails swirled by on silver dishes balanced by the white-gloved fingers of waiters in tailcoats. Or, more precisely, above the partridges and quails the dishes whirled, and above the dishes the white gloves, and poised on the waiters' patent-leather shoes, the gleaming parquet floor,[2] from which hung dwarf potted palms and tablecloths and crystal and buckets like bells with the champagne bottle for their clapper: everything was turned upside-down because Marcovaldo, for fear of being seen, wouldn't stick his head inside the window and confined himself to looking at the reversed reflection of the room in the tilted pane.

But it was not so much the windows of the dining-room as those of the kitchens that interested the cat: looking through the former you saw, distant and somehow transfigured, what in the kitchens presented itself—quite concrete and within paw's reach—as a plucked bird or a fresh fish. And it was toward the kitchens, in fact, that the tabby wanted to lead Marcovaldo, either through a gesture of altruistic friendship or else because it counted on the man's help for one of its raids. Marcovaldo, however, was reluctant to leave his belvedere[3] over the main room: first as he was fascinated by the luxury of the place, and then because something down there had riveted his attention. To such an extent that, overcoming his fear of being seen, he kept peeking in, with his head in the transom.

In the midst of the room, directly under that pane, there was a little glass fish tank, a kind of aquarium, where some fat trout were swimming. A special customer approached, a man with a shiny bald pate, black suit, black beard. An old waiter in tailcoat followed him, carrying a little net as if he were going to catch butterflies. The gentleman in black looked at the trout with a grave, intent air; then he raised one hand and with a slow, solemn gesture singled out a fish. The waiter dipped the net into the tank, pursued the appointed trout, captured it, headed for the kitchens, holding out in front of him, like a lance, the net in which the fish wriggled. The gentleman in black, solemn as a magistrate who has handed down a capital sentence, went to take his seat and wait for the return of the trout, sauteed "à la meunière."[4]

If I found a way to drop a line from up here and make one of those trout bite, Marcovaldo thought, I couldn't be accused of theft; at worst, of fishing in an unauthorized place. And ignoring the miaus that called him toward the kitchens, he went to collect his fishing tackle.

2. **parquet** (pär kā′) **floor**: Floor with inlaid woodwork in geometric forms.

Schrödinger's Cat, Elizebeth Knight, New York Academy of Sciences

▲ **Critical Viewing** What qualities of cats are captured in this picture? **[Interpret]**

3. **belvedere** (bel′ və dir′) *n.*: Open, roofed gallery in an upper story, built for giving a view of the scenery.
4. **sauteed "à la meunière"** (sô tād′ á là mə nyer′): Fish prepared by being rolled in flour, fried in butter, and sprinkled with lemon juice and chopped parsley.

Nobody in the crowded dining room of the Biarritz saw the long, fine line, armed with hook and bait, as it slowly dropped into the tank. The fish saw the bait, and flung themselves on it. In the fray one trout managed to bite the worm: and immediately it began to rise, rise, emerge from the water, a silvery flash, it darted up high, over the laid tables and the trolleys of hors d'oeuvres,[5] over the blue flames of the crêpes Suzette,[6] until it vanished into the heavens of the transom.

Marcovaldo had yanked the rod with the brisk snap of the expert fisherman, so the fish landed behind his back. The trout had barely touched the ground when the cat sprang. What little life the trout still had was lost between the tabby's teeth. Marcovaldo, who had abandoned his line at that moment to run and grab the fish, saw it snatched from under his nose, hook and all. He was quick to put one foot on the rod, but the snatch had been so strong that the rod was all the man had left, while the tabby ran off with the fish, pulling the line after it. Treacherous kitty! It had vanished.

But this time it wouldn't escape him: there was that long line trailing after him and showing the way he had taken. Though he had lost sight of the cat, Marcovaldo followed the end of the line: there it was, running along a wall; it climbed a parapet, wound through a doorway, was swallowed up by a basement . . . Marcovaldo, venturing into more and more cattish places, climbed roofs, straddled railings, always managed to catch a glimpse—perhaps only a second before it disappeared—of that moving trace that indicated a thief's path.

Now the line played out down a sidewalk, in the midst of the traffic, and Marcovaldo, running after it, almost managed to grab it. He flung himself down on his belly: there, he

◆ **Reading Strategy**
What information in this paragraph helps you clarify the title of this story?

grabbed it! He managed to seize one end of the line before it slipped between the bars of a gate.

Beyond a half-rusted gate and two bits of wall buried under climbing plants, there was a little <u>rank</u> garden, with a small, abandoned-looking building at the far end of it. A carpet of dry leaves covered the path, and dry leaves lay everywhere under the boughs of the two plane-trees, forming actually some little mounds in the yard. A layer of leaves was yellowing in the green water of a pool. Enormous buildings rose all around, skyscrapers with thousands of windows, like so many eyes trained disapprovingly on that little square patch with two trees, a few tiles, and all those yellow leaves, surviving right in the middle of an area of great traffic.

And in this garden, perched on the capitals and balustrades,[7] lying on the dry leaves of the flowerbeds, climbing on the trunks of the trees or on the drainpipes, motionless on their four paws, their tails making a question-mark, seated to wash their faces, there were tiger cats, black cats, white cats, calico cats, tabbies, angoras, Persians, house cats and stray cats, perfumed cats and mangy cats. Marcovaldo realized he had finally reached the heart of the cats' realm, their secret island. And, in his emotion, he almost forgot his fish.

It had remained, that fish, hanging by the line from the branch of a tree, out of reach of the cats' leaps; it must have dropped from its kidnapper's mouth at some clumsy movement, perhaps as it was defended from the others, or perhaps displayed as an extraordinary prize. The line had got tangled, and Marcovaldo, tug as he would, couldn't manage to yank it loose. A furious battle had meanwhile been joined among the cats, to reach that unreachable fish, or rather, to win the right to try and reach it. Each wanted to prevent the others from leaping: they hurled themselves on one another, they tangled in midair, they rolled around

---

5. **hors d'oeuvres** (ôr durvz´) *n.*: Appetizers served at the beginning of a meal.
6. **crêpes Suzette** (krāp´ soo zet´): Thin pancakes rolled or folded in a hot orange-flavored sauce and usually served in flaming brandy.

7. **capitals and balustrades** (bal´ əs trāds): Top parts of columns and railings, respectively.

◆ **Build Vocabulary**
transoms (tran´ səmz) *n.*: Small windows
rank (raŋk) *adj.*: Growing vigorously and coarsely

clutching each other, and finally a general war broke out in a whirl of dry, crackling leaves.

After many futile yanks, Marcovaldo now felt the line was free, but he took care not to pull it: the trout would have fallen right in the midst of that infuriated scrimmage of felines.

It was at this moment that, from the top of the walls of the gardens, a strange rain began to fall: fish-bones, heads, tails, even bits of lung and lights. Immediately the cats' attention was distracted from the suspended trout and they flung themselves on the new delicacies. To Marcovaldo, this seemed the right moment to pull the line and regain his fish. But, before he had time to act, from a blind of the little villa, two yellow, skinny hands darted out: one was brandishing scissors; the other, a frying pan. The hand with the scissors was raised above the trout, the hand with the frying pan was thrust under it. The scissors cut the line, the trout fell into the pan; hands, scissors and pan withdrew, the blind closed: all in the space of a second. Marcovaldo was totally bewildered.

"Are you also a cat lover?" A voice at his back made him turn round. He was surrounded by little old women, some of them ancient, wearing old-fashioned hats on their heads; others, younger, but with the look of spinsters; and all were carrying in their hands or their bags packages of leftover meat or fish, and some even had little pans of milk. "Will you help me throw this package over the fence, for those poor creatures?"

All the ladies, cat lovers, gathered at this hour around the garden of dry leaves to take the food to their protégés.[8]

"Can you tell me why they are all here, these cats?" Marcovaldo inquired.

"Where else could they go? This garden is all they have left! Cats come here from other neighborhoods, too, from miles and miles around . . ."

"And birds, as well," another lady added. "They're forced to live by the hundreds and hundreds on these few trees . . ."

"And the frogs, they're all in that pool, and at night they never stop croaking . . . You can hear them even on the eighth floor of the buildings around here."

"Who does this villa belong to anyway?" Marcovaldo asked. Now, outside the gate, there weren't just the cat-loving ladies but also other people: the man from the gas pump opposite, the apprentices from a mechanic's shop, the postman, the grocer, some passers-by. And none of them, men and women, had to be asked twice: all wanted to have their say, as always when a mysterious and controversial subject comes up.

"It belongs to a Marchesa.[9] She lives there, but you never see her . . ."

"She's been offered millions and millions, by developers, for this little patch of land, but she won't sell . . ."

"What would she do with millions, an old woman all alone in the world? She wants to hold on to her house, even if it's falling to pieces, rather than be forced to move . . ."

"It's the only undeveloped bit of land in the downtown area . . . Its value goes up every year . . . They've made her offers—"

"Offers! That's not all. Threats, intimidation, persecution . . . You don't know the half of it! Those contractors!"

"But she holds out. She's held out for years . . ."

"She's a saint. Without her, where would those poor animals go?"

"A lot she cares about the animals, the old miser! Have you ever seen her give them anything to eat?"

"How can she feed the cats when she doesn't have food for herself? She's the last descendant of a ruined family!"

"She hates cats! I've seen her chasing them and hitting them with an umbrella!"

"Because they were tearing up her flowerbeds!"

---

8. **protégés** (prōt´ ə zhāz´) n.: Those guided and helped by another.

9. **Marchesa** (mär kā´ zä): Title of an Italian noblewoman.

It might surprise you to learn that Jim Davis, creator of Garfield—one of the world's most famous and beloved cats—has no cats. His wife is allergic to the furry felines!

When Davis created Garfield in 1978, he never imagined the phenomenal success that would follow. Garfield is the most widely syndicated Sunday comic in the United States, and worldwide it has more than 220 million daily readers. In addition to the daily and Sunday comics, Davis has written dozens of Garfield books, a CBS television series, and thirteen prime-time specials.

1. What qualities does Garfield have in common with the cats in "Garden of Stubborn Cats"?
2. Compare the way Calvino and Davis portray the relationship between humans and cats.
3. Why do you think this cartoon cat is so popular?

"What flowerbeds? I've never seen anything in this garden but a great crop of weeds!"

Marcovaldo realized that with regard to the old Marchesa opinions were sharply divided: some saw her as an angelic being, others as an egoist and a miser.

"It's the same with the birds; she never gives them a crumb!"

"She gives them hospitality. Isn't that plenty?"

"Like she gives the mosquitoes, you mean. They all come from here, from that pool. In the summertime the mosquitoes eat us alive, and it's all the fault of that Marchesa!"

"And the mice? This villa is a mine of mice. Under the dead leaves they have their burrows, and at night they come out . . ."

"As far as the mice go, the cats take care of them . . ."

"Oh, you and your cats! If we had to rely on them . . ."

"Why? Have you got something to say against cats?"

Here the discussion degenerated into a general quarrel.

"The authorities should do something: confiscate the villa!" one man cried.

"What gives them the right?" another protested.

"In a modern neighborhood like ours, a mouse-nest like this . . . it should be forbidden . . ."

"Why, I picked my apartment precisely because it overlooked this little bit of green . . ."

"Green . . . ! Think of the fine skyscraper they could build here!"

Marcovaldo would have liked to add something of his own, but he couldn't get a word in. Finally, all in one breath, he exclaimed: "The Marchesa stole a trout from me!"

The unexpected news supplied fresh ammunition to the old woman's enemies, but her defenders exploited it as proof of the

◆ **Build Vocabulary**
scrimmage (skrim´ ij) *n.*: Rough-and-tumble fight

indigence to which the unfortunate noble-woman was reduced. Both sides agreed that Marcovaldo should go and knock at her door to demand an explanation.

It wasn't clear whether the gate was locked or unlocked; in any case, it opened, after a push, with a mournful creak. Marcovaldo picked his way among the leaves and cats, climbed the steps to the porch, knocked hard at the entrance.

At a window (the very one where the frying pan had appeared), the blind was raised slightly and in one corner a round, pale blue eye was seen, and a clump of hair dyed an un-definable color, and a dry skinny hand. A voice was heard, asking: "Who is it? Who's at the door?" the words accompanied by a cloud smelling of fried oil.

"It's me, Marchesa. The trout man," Marcov-aldo explained. "I don't mean to trouble you. I only wanted to tell you, in case you didn't know, that the trout was stolen from me, by that cat, and I'm the one who caught it. In fact the line . . ."

"Those cats! It's always those cats . . . " the Marchesa said, from behind the shutter, with a shrill, somewhat nasal voice. "All my troubles come from the cats! Nobody knows what I go through! Prisoner night and day of those horrid beasts! And with all the refuse people throw over the walls, to spite me!"

"But my trout . . ."

"Your trout! What am I supposed to know about your trout!" The Marchesa's voice became almost a scream, as if she wanted to drown out the sizzle of oil in the pan, which came through the win-dow along with the aroma of fried fish. "How can I make sense of anything, with all the stuff that rains into my house?"

"I understand, but did you take the trout or didn't you?"

"When I think of all the damage I suffer because of the cats! Ah, fine state of affairs! I'm not responsible for anything! I can't tell you what I've lost! Thanks to those cats, who've occupied house and garden for

years! My life at the mercy of those animals! Go and find the owners! Make them pay damages! Damages? A whole life destroyed! A prisoner here, unable to move a step!"

"Excuse me for asking: but who's forcing you to stay?"

From the crack in the blind there appeared sometimes a round, pale blue eye, sometimes a mouth with two protruding teeth; for a moment the whole face was visible, and to Marcovaldo it seemed, bewilderingly, the face of a cat.

"They keep me prisoner, they do, those cats! Oh, I'd be glad to leave! What wouldn't I give for a little apartment all my own, in a nice clean modern building! But I can't go out . . . They follow me, they block my path, they trip me up!" The voice became a whisper, as if to con-fide a secret. "They're afraid I'll sell the lot . . . They won't leave me . . . won't allow me . . . When the builders come to offer me a contract, you should see them, those cats! They get in the way, pull out their claws; they even chased a lawyer off! Once I had the contract right here, I was about to sign it, and they dived in through the window, knocked over the inkwell, tore up all the pages. . ."

All of a sudden Marcovaldo remembered the time, the shipping department, the boss. He tip-toed off over the dried leaves, as the voice contin-ued to come through the slats of the blind, enfolded in that cloud apparently from the oil of a frying pan. "They even scratched me . . . I still have the scar . . . All alone here at the mercy of these demons . . ."

Winter came. A blossoming of white flakes decked the branches and capitals and the cats' tails. Under the snow, the dry leaves dissolved into mush. The cats were rarely seen, the cat lovers even less; the packages of fish-bones were consigned only to cats who came to the door. Nobody, for quite a while, had seen anything of the March-esa. No smoke came now from the chimneypot of the villa.

One snowy day, the garden was again full of cats, who had returned as if it were spring, and they were miauing as if on a moonlight night. The neighbors realized that something had happened: they went and knocked at the Marchesa's door. She didn't answer: she was dead.

In the spring, instead of the garden, there was a huge building site that a contractor had set up. The steam shovels dug down to great depths to make room for the foundations, cement poured into the iron armatures, a very high crane passed beams to the workmen who were making the scaffoldings. But how could they get on with their work? Cats walked along all the planks, they made bricks fall and upset buckets of mortar, they fought in the midst of the piles of sand. When you started to raise an armature, you found a cat perched on top of it, hissing fiercely. More treacherous pusses climbed onto the masons' backs as if to purr, and there was no getting rid of them. And the birds continued making their nests in all the trestles,[10] the cab of the crane looked like an aviary . . . And you couldn't dip up a bucket of water that wasn't full of frogs, croaking and hopping . . .

◆ **Build Vocabulary**

indigence (in´ di jəns) *n.*: Poverty

---

10. **trestles** (tres´ əlz) *n.*: Frameworks of vertical or slanting beams and crosspieces.

Guide for Responding

◆ *Literature and Your Life*

Reader's Response What is your impression of the Marchesa's circumstances in this story? Was she trapped or not? Explain.

Thematic Focus Speculate on what will happen to street animals, such as the cats in the story, in the world of our future.

Questions for Research If you were to conduct some research about the effects of technology upon human, animal, and plant life, what questions might you hope to answer?

☑ Check Your Comprehension

1. What is the "negative city"? How is it created?
2. Why does Marcovaldo follow the cat?
3. Where does the tabby lead Marcovaldo, and what does Marcovaldo find there?
4. Describe the situation at the end of the story.

◆ **Critical Thinking**

INTERPRET

1. What do the developers represent in this story?
2. Explain why the Marchesa's supporters believe she is helping the cats and her critics think she is not. **[Infer; Compare and Contrast]**
3. What are the opposing forces in this story, and which prevails? Support your answer with evidence from the story. **[Draw Conclusions]**

EVALUATE

4. Evaluate Marcovaldo's thought, "I couldn't be accused of theft; at worst, of fishing in an unauthorized place." **[Assess]**

COMPARE LITERARY WORKS

5. Compare and contrast the views of progress and development presented in these two stories. Support your ideas with evidence from each story. **[Compare and Contrast]**

Guide for Responding (continued)

◆Reading Strategy

CLARIFY

You may have felt confused by the events that oc-curred in either of the stories until you were able to **clarify**—make clear—the reasons particular events unfolded.

1. Identify two details in "Under Reconstruction" that were unclear to you at first. Explain how you clarified these details.
2. How did Watanabé's description of the German woman help you clarify the nature of their relationship?
3. "The Garden of Stubborn Cats" opens with the statement "The city of cats and the city of men exist one inside the other, but they are not the same city." Identify three later details that helped you clarify that statement.
4. How did Marcovaldo's conversation with the Marchesa clarify the neighbors' earlier argument?

◆Build Vocabulary

USING THE LATIN SUFFIX *-al*

Knowing that the Latin suffix *-al* means "of, like, or suitable for," complete each of the following sentences with one of the words provided.

a. causal   **b.** electrical   **c.** environmental   **d.** musical

1. The lightning storm resulted in ___?___ problems all over the city.
2. The Surgeon General says there is a(n) ___?___ connection between smoking and lung cancer.
3. Some cellular phones ring in a(n) ___?___ way.
4. The oil spill was a(n) ___?___ disaster.

USING THE WORD BANK: Context

On your paper, write the word from the Word Bank suggested by each sentence.

1. You might use this word when planning a trip.
2. This word could describe a detour in the road.
3. It would be tough to squeeze through one of these to escape a burning building.
4. Ending this is a societal problem.
5. You have done this to a square if you have turned it into an octagon.
6. You'd use this word in astronomy.
7. This word describes weeds or an odor.
8. You might get hurt in this activity.

◆Literary Focus

SETTING AND CULTURAL BACKGROUND

In each these stories, the **cultural background**—what is going on in society—is an important part of the **setting,** the time and place of the story's ac-tion. For example, in "Under Reconstruction," the confusion in Japanese society between traditional and Western customs reflects and in part causes the awkwardness of the two main characters.

Calvino presents his setting of a city within a city from an unusual perspective. Marcovaldo discovers places and things he wouldn't have known if he didn't follow his feline friends.

1. In "Under Reconstruction," what objects and de-tails in the hotel suggest that the Japanese were struggling to strike a balance between their own traditions and Western methods and ideas?
2. Do you think the reunion of the two main char-acters in "Under Reconstruction" would have been less awkward if they had met in Germany rather than Japan? Explain.
3. (a) Describe the city where Marcovaldo lives. (b) Why is this a good or a bad setting for cats and other animals?
4. (a) Contrast the city with the garden Marcovaldo discovers. (b) How does this contrast reinforce the message of the story?

◆Build Grammar Skills

COMMONLY CONFUSED WORDS: *lie* AND *lay*

Lie means to "rest" or "recline." Its principal parts are *lying, lay,* and *lain. Lay* means to "set down," and its principal parts are *laying, laid,* and *laid.*

Practice Write the following sentences into your notebook, and circle the appropriate word.

1. After (lying, laying) the plate down in front of the woman, the waiter leaves the room.
2. The workers had (laid, lain) down their tools at 5:00 p.m.
3. Marcovaldo (lies, lays) the fish down.
4. When Marcovaldo arrived at the garden, cats were (lying, laying) everywhere.
5. The old woman of the house went to (lie, lay) down on her bed.

*B*uild *Y*our *P*ortfolio

 ## Idea Bank

Writing

1. **Character's Journal Entry** Write a journal entry for either Watanabé or the German woman in "Under Reconstruction." Describe how he or she felt after their encounter at dinner.
2. **Letter to the Marchesa** Imagine that you are one of the Marchesa's angry neighbors in "The Garden of Stubborn Cats." Write a letter to the Marchesa convincing her to sell her property to developers. Use details from the story to support your argument.
3. **Science-Fiction Story** "The Garden of Stubborn Cats" shows how the cats have gained control of a small section of their city. Write a continuation of the story, in which the construction workers give up and the cats gain more control.

Speaking, Listening, and Viewing

4. **Animal Dialogue** Suppose the cats in "The Garden of Stubborn Cats" could talk. What would they say about their situation? Role-play dialogue between two cats from the story.
5. **Persuasive Argument** As Marcovaldo, try to convince the Marchesa of the merits of staying in her villa and cultivating her garden. Support your argument with reasons. Present your argument to the class.

Researching and Representing

6. **Multimedia Presentation** Find out about Kabuki, a traditional form of Japanese theater mentioned in "Under Reconstruction." Using pictures, video, and music, present your findings to the class. **[Performing Arts Link]**
7. **Cat-Breed Chart** Research the traits of several different cat breeds. Then create a chart that illustrates the characteristics of each breed. **[Science Link]**

 ## Guided Writing Lesson

Location Scout's Report

Imagine that shooting is about to begin for a film based on "Under Reconstruction" or "The Garden of the Stubborn Cats." The director has asked you, the location scout, to find a suitable place to film a particular scene from the movie. She wants you to identify the place and explain why it matches the author's description of the setting for that scene.

Writing Skills: Transitions to Show Place

When describing a location, you need to use **transitions that show place**—words that help orient readers in space. Following is a list of such transitions:

above	below	nearby	under
among	beyond	opposite	
adjacent	farther	there	

Prewriting Identify the scene for which you are scouting a location. Then, find a place you know that corresponds to the setting of that scene. Jot down brief descriptions of this place and make sketches of it so you will be able to describe it in your report.

Drafting Think of your report as a set of instructions for assembling a picture in the director's mind. Make it a complete and accurate picture by using your notes and inserting transitions to show place. Also, explain how the location corresponds to the setting that the author describes.

Revising Have someone read your report and draw the scene you describe. See if the placement of objects in person's drawing matches that in the actual location. If certain areas are inconsistent, add greater detail to that part of your report.

Be sure you have used *lie* and *lay* correctly. For more on the correct use of these words, see pp. 664 and 680.

Online Activity www.phlit.phschool.com

Guide for Reading

Nadine Gordimer *(1923–   )*

Nadine Gordimer's stories and novels are almost all set in her native country of South Africa. Gordimer was a passionate opponent of apartheid, South Africa's official policy of racial segregation that ended in 1994. Documenting the society in which she lived, much of her work tackles the issue of racial injustice.

An Early Writer Born in Springs, South Africa, to immigrant parents, Nadine Gordimer grew up in a country where the white minority had very little contact with the black majority. Like most white middle-class children, she was kept separate from people of other races in private schools and segregated institutions.

By the age of thirteen, she was publishing fables in the children's section of the *Sunday Express* in Johannesburg, South Africa, and her first short story,

"Come Again Tomorrow," was published when she was fifteen. As she grew older and became more aware of the effects of apartheid, her writing came to focus on the everyday lives of white and nonwhite South Africans as they tried to cope with a segregated social structure.

Literary Success Gordimer has gone on to become one of most productive and successful writers in the world. Her many novels and collections of stories include *The Soft Voice of the Serpent* (1952), *Not for Publication* (1965), *The Conservationist* (1974), *The Essential Gesture: Writing, Politics, and Places* (1988), *Jump and Other Stories* (1991), and *The House Gun* (1998). These works have earned the recognition of fans and literary critics across the globe. Gordimer has won many awards, including the Nobel Prize for Literature in 1991.

◆ Build Vocabulary

LATIN SUFFIXES: *-tion*

The story's main character experiences a revelation. The word *revelation* ends with the Latin suffix *-tion*, which means "the act of." Knowing this suffix can help you piece together the meaning of the word *revelation:* "an act that reveals something or makes something known."

WORD BANK

enclave
secular
assent
depraved
euphemisms
furtively
revelation
phenomena

Use the definitions on the pages that follow to preview these words before you read.

◆ Build Grammar Skills

NOUN CLAUSES

A **subordinate clause** is a group of words with a subject and a verb that cannot stand by itself as a complete sentence. A **noun clause** is a subordinate clause that acts as a noun. This type of clause is often introduced by the words *that, whether, which, how,* and *why.*

The noun clause is underlined in the following sentence from "Comrades":

They're not going to be saying. . . *that* they're off on a student tour in Europe. . . .

The clause functions as a noun that is the direct object of the verb "saying."

Comrades

◆ Literature and Your Life

CONNECT YOUR EXPERIENCE

Think about what it would be like to have a group of people from a different background—maybe even a different country—in your home. Gordimer's story captures such an encounter and the discomfort it can produce.

THEMATIC FOCUS: RIGHT AND WRONG

Although they come from very different backgrounds, the characters in Gordimer's story all oppose segregation. Why is it important to have people from different backgrounds support such a cause?

Journal Writing In your journal, describe ways to help people from different backgrounds understand one another.

◆ Background for Understanding

HISTORY

This story takes place at a time when there was strong tension between nonwhite and many white South Africans. The government, controlled by the National Party, had legalized discrimination against nonwhites. At times, tension boiled over into violence. One of the bloodiest conflicts occurred in 1976 in Soweto, a segregated residential area for blacks in the capital city of Johannesburg.

The Soweto Uprising erupted out of a student-led protest over the government's decision to force all students to speak and study in Afrikaans, the language established by Dutch colonists who had become South Africa's ruling class. The police opened fire on the protestors, killing an estimated 172 people, many of whom were children. In the rioting that followed, many more people died, over a thousand were injured, and much of the township was destroyed.

◆ Literary Focus

ATMOSPHERE AND HISTORICAL BACKGROUND

A story's **setting** is the time and place of the action. One of the most important elements of setting is the **atmosphere,** or mood—the feeling created in the reader by the story's descriptive details. In "Comrades," there is an atmosphere of anxiety.

Another important element of setting is the story's **historical background.** The historical background includes the key events and circumstances occurring at the time of the story. To fully understand many stories, it is essential to know this background.

◆ Reading Strategy

IDENTIFY WITH A CHARACTER OR SITUATION

One of the keys to appreciating any story is to put yourself in the place of a character in the story and experience the events through his or her eyes. Use your imagination and your own experience to help you understand the situation and appreciate what the character must be feeling. Doing so will help you feel like you're actually a part of the story.

As you read, keep a **double-entry journal** like this one. In one column, note the feelings that Mrs. Telford has. In the other column, note how you would feel in her situation.

Mrs. Telford's Reaction	My Reaction

COMRADES

NADINE GORDIMER

As Mrs. Hattie Telford pressed the electronic gadget that deactivates the alarm device in her car a group of youngsters came up behind her. Black. But no need to be afraid; this was not a city street. This was a nonracial <u>enclave</u> of learning, a place where tended flowerbeds and trees bearing botanical identification plates civilized the wild reminder of campus guards and dogs. The youngsters, like her, were part of the crowd loosening into dispersion after a university conference on People's Education. They were the people to be educated; she was one of the committee of white and black activists (convenient generic for revolutionaries, leftists <u>secular</u> and Christian, fellow-travelers and liberals) up on the platform.

—Comrade . . .— She was settling in the driver's seat when one so slight and slim he seemed a figure in profile came up to her window. He drew courage from the friendly lift of the woman's eyebrows above blue eyes, the tilt of her freckled white face: —Comrade, are you going to town?—

No, she was going in the opposite direction, home . . . but quickly, in the spirit of the hall where these young people had been somewhere, somehow present with her (ah no, she with them) stamping and singing Freedom songs, she would take them to the bus station their spokesman named. —Climb aboard!—

The others got in the back, the spokesman beside her. She saw the nervous white of his eyes as he glanced at and away from her. She searched for talk to set them at ease. Questions, of course. Older people always start with questioning young ones. Did they come from Soweto?

They came from Harrismith, Phoneng Location.

She made the calculation: about two hundred kilometers distant. How did they get here? Who told them about the conference?

—We are Youth Congress in Phoneng.—

A delegation. They had come by bus; one of the groups and stragglers who kept arriving long after the conference had started. They had missed, then, the free lunch?

At the back, no one seemed even to be breathing. The spokesman must have had some silent communication with them, some obligation to speak for them created by the journey or by other shared experience in the mysterious bonds of the young—these young. —We are hungry.— And from the back seats was drawn an <u>assent</u> like the suction of air in a compressing silence.

She was silent in response, for the beat of a breath or two. These large gatherings both excited and left her overexposed, open and vulnerable to the rub and twitch of the mass shuffling across rows of seats and loping up the aisles,

▲ **Critical Viewing** Gordimer never directly describes a scene of protest like this one. However, in what way does this type of protest remain an important part of the story's background? **[Connect]**

babies' fudge-brown soft legs waving as their napkins are changed on mothers' laps, little girls with plaited loops on their heads listening like old crones, heavy women swaying to chants, men with fierce, unreadably black faces breaking into harmony tender and deep as they sing to God for his protection of Umkhonto weSizwe, as people on both sides have always, everywhere, claimed Divine protection for their soldiers, their wars. At the end of a day like this she wanted a drink, she wanted the <u>depraved</u> luxury of solitude and quiet in which she would be restored (enriched, oh yes! by the day) to the familiar limits of her own being.

Hungry. Not for iced whiskey and feet up. It seemed she had scarcely hesitated: —Look. I live nearby, come back to my house and have something to eat. Then I'll run you into town.—

—That will be very nice. We can be glad for that.— And at the back the tight vacuum relaxed.

They followed her in through the gate, shrinking away from the dog—she assured them he was harmless but he was large, with a fancy collar by which she held him. She trooped them in through the kitchen because that was the way she always entered her

◆ **Build Vocabulary**

enclave (en´ klāv´) *n.*: Place set apart from the surrounding region for a special purpose

secular (sek´ yə lər) *adj.*: Worldly, as distinguished from things relating to church and religion

assent (ə sent´) *n.*: Expression of agreement

depraved (dē prāv´'d´) *adj.*: Morally bad

house, something she would not have done if they had been adult, her black friends whose sophistication might lead them to believe the choice of entrance was an unthinking historical slight. As she was going to feed them, she took them not into her living-room with its sofas and flowers but into her dining-room, so that they could sit at table right away. It was a room in confident taste that could afford to be spare: bare floorboards, matching golden wooden ceiling, antique brass chandelier, reed blinds instead of stuffy curtains. An African wooden sculpture represented a lion marvelously released from its matrix in the grain of a Mukwa tree-trunk. She pulled up the chairs and left the four young men while she went back to the kitchen to make coffee and see what there was in the refrigerator for sandwiches. They had greeted the maid, in the language she and they shared, on their way through the kitchen, but when the maid and the lady of the house had finished preparing cold meat and bread, and the coffee was ready, she suddenly did not want them to see that the maid waited on her. She herself carried the heavy tray into the dining room.

◆ Literary Focus
How do the details in this description of the young men contribute to the atmosphere of the story?

They are sitting round the table, silent, and there is no impression that they stopped an undertone exchange when they heard her approaching. She doles out plates, cups. They stare at the food but their eyes seem focused on something she can't see; something that overwhelms. She urges them—Just cold meat, I'm afraid, but there's chutney[1] if you like it . . . milk everybody? . . . is the coffee too strong, I have a heavy hand, I know. Would anyone like to add some hot water?—

They eat. When she tries to talk to one of the others, he says *Ekskuus?* And she realizes he doesn't understand English, of the white man's languages knows perhaps only a little of that of the Afrikaners in the rural town he comes from. Another gives his name, as if in some delicate

---

1. **chutney** (chut′ nē) *n.*: Relish or sauce of Indian origin, typically combining sweet and sour ingredients, such as fruit and vinegar, with sugar and spices.

acknowledgement of the food. —I'm Shadrack Nsutsha.— She repeats the surname to get it right. But he does not speak again. There is an urgent exchange of eye-language, and the spokesman holds out the emptied sugarbowl to her. —Please.— She hurries to the kitchen and brings it back refilled. They need carbohydrate, they are hungry, they are young, they need it, they burn it up. She is distressed at the inadequacy of the meal and then notices the fruit bowl, her big copper fruit bowl, filled with apples and bananas and perhaps there is a peach or two under the grape leaves with which she likes to complete an edible still life. —Have some fruit. Help yourselves.—

They are stacking their plates and cups, not knowing what they are expected to do with them in this room which is a room where apparently people only eat, do not cook, do not sleep. While they finish the bananas and apples (Shadrack Nsutsha had seen the single peach and quickly got there first) she talks to the spokesman, whose name she has asked for: Dumile. —Are you still at school, Dumile?— Of course he is not at school—*they* are not at school; youngsters their age have not been at school for several years, they are the children growing into young men and women for whom school is a battleground, a place of boycotts and demonstrations, the literacy of political rhetoric, the education of revolt against having to live the life their parents live. They have pompous titles of responsibility beyond childhood: he is chairman of his branch of the Youth Congress, he was expelled two years ago—for leading a boycott? Throwing stones at the police? Maybe burning the school down? He calls it all—quietly, abstractly, doesn't know many ordinary, concrete words but knows these euphemisms— "political activity." No school for two years? No. —So what have you been able to do with yourself, all that time?—

She isn't giving him a chance to eat his apple. He swallows a large bite, shaking his head on its thin, little-boy neck.—I was inside. Detained from this June for six months.—

She looks round the others. —And you?—

Shadrack seems to nod slightly. The other two look at her. She should know, she should have known, it's a common enough answer from youths like them, their color. They're not going to be saying they've been selected for the 1st Eleven at cricket or that they're off on a student tour to Europe in the school holidays.

The spokesman, Dumile, tells her he wants to study by correspondence, "get his matric" that he was preparing for two years ago; two years ago when he was still a child, when he didn't have the hair that is now appearing on his face, making him a man, taking away the childhood. In the hesitations, the silences of the table, where there is nervously spilt coffee among plates of banana skins, there grows the certainty that he will never get the papers filled in for the correspondence college, he will never get the two years back. She looks at them all and cannot believe what she knows: that they, suddenly here in her house, will carry the AK-47s[2] they only sing about, now, miming death as they sing. They will have a career of wiring explosives to the undersides of vehicles, they will go away and come back through the bush to dig holes not to plant trees to shade home, but to plant land-mines. She can see they have been terribly harmed but cannot

___

2. **AK-47s:** Military assault rifles.

believe they could harm. They are wiping their fruit-sticky hands underlinedfurtively palm against palm.

She breaks the silence; says something, anything.

—How d'you like my lion? Isn't he beautiful? He's made by a Zimbabwean artist, I think the name's Dube.—

But the foolish interruption becomes underlinedrevelation. Dumile, in his gaze—distant, lingering, speechless this time—reveals what has overwhelmed them. In this room, the space, the expensive antique chandelier, the consciously simple choice of reed blinds, the carved lion: all are on the same level of impact, underlinedphenomena undifferentiated, undecipherable. Only the food that fed their hunger was real.

◆ Build Vocabulary

euphemisms (yōō′ fə miz′ əmz) *n.*: Words or phrases that are less expressive or direct but considered less distasteful or offensive than others

furtively (fur′ tiv lē) *adv.*: In a sneaky manner, as if to hinder observation

revelation (rev′ ə lā′ shən) *n.*: Striking disclosure of something

phenomena (fə näm′ ə nə) *n.*: Perceptible things or occurrences

Guide for Responding

◆ *Literature and Your Life*

Reader's Response What thoughts and feelings did this story evoke in you? Why?

Thematic Focus How do you think apartheid affects Mrs. Telford? How does it affect the other characters?

Reader's Journal Write a journal entry in which you explain why you think Mrs. Telford should or should not have invited the delegation back to her house for lunch.

☑ Check Your Comprehension

1. Where do the characters in the story meet?
2. Who are the group of youngsters that Mrs. Telford meets?
3. Why does Mrs. Telford take them to her house?
4. What piece of artwork is in her dining room?
5. Where had Dumile been instead of at school for six months?

Guide for Responding (continued)

◆ Critical Thinking

INTERPRET

1. How would you characterize Mrs. Telford? Support your answer. **[Analyze]**
2. How would you describe the interactions between Mrs. Telford and the students? **[Describe]**
3. (a) What are the sharp contrasts between Mrs. Telford's world and the world in which the students live? (b) What are some of the values the two parties share? **[Compare]**
4. How would you characterize the students' attitudes toward Mrs. Telford? **[Infer]**
5. What realization does Mrs. Telford come to at the end of the story? **[Interpret]**

EVALUATE

6. After Mrs. Telford carries the tray into the dining room, the narration switches from past tense to present tense. Why do you think Nadine Gordimer made this change? **[Criticize]**

EXTEND

7. What theme, or lesson about life, does this story convey? Explain your answer. **[Generalize]**

◆ Reading Strategy

IDENTIFY WITH A CHARACTER OR SITUATION

Review your double-entry journal (see p. 683). Briefly explain the key similarities and differences between how Mrs. Telford reacted to the situation and how you would have reacted. What do you think accounts for these similarities and differences?

◆ Literary Focus

ATMOSPHERE AND HISTORICAL BACKGROUND

Gordimer's story is set during the apartheid era of South Africa and uses an **atmosphere** of anxiety and social discomfort to create tension.

1. Why is the historical background an essential element of this story?
2. Why is knowing the historical background a key to understanding the story?
3. How does the atmosphere of anxiety relate to the story's theme?

◆ Build Vocabulary

USING THE LATIN SUFFIX -tion

The Latin suffix -tion means "the act of." Use your knowledge of this suffix to define each of these words.

1. competition   2. partition   3. contribution

USING THE WORD BANK: Sentence Completions

Choose the word from the Word Bank that best fits each sentence. Write the complete sentence in your notebook.

1. The pandas lived in an ___?___ within the zoo.
2. Comets, albino snakes, and 200-year-old trees are all natural ___?___.
3. If you give your ___?___, we will begin the operation.
4. "Moving on to a better place" is one of many ___?___ for dying.
5. The experience led her to a major ___?___ about the differences among people.
6. The criminal was described in the news as a ___?___ lunatic.
7. He smiled ___?___, realizing that he knew something his opponent did not.
8. Many churches considered apartheid not only a ___?___ problem but also a religious one.

◆ Build Grammar Skills

NOUN CLAUSES

A **noun clause** is a subordinate clause that acts as a noun.

Practice In your notebook, identify the noun clause in each of the following sentences.

1. Whether the mushrooms will thrive is a question I cannot answer.
2. Whoever ate my dinner is going to be sorry.
3. Everybody knew that he had been dismissed from the band.
4. He said he thought the dinner would be delicious.

Writing Application Write a brief summary of the events in the story. Include at least five noun clauses. Circle each one you use.

Build Your Portfolio

Idea Bank

Writing

1. **Journal Entry** Write a journal entry describing the events in the story from the point of view of either Mrs. Telford or one of her guests.

2. **Interview** Write a list of questions that you would like to ask the youth delegation to learn more about their backgrounds. Write answers to each of your questions.

3. **Analysis of Theme** Write an essay in which you explain what lessons about life Gordimer conveys in her story. Back up your points with details and quotations from the story.

Speaking, Listening, and Viewing

4. **Set Design** Draw or paint a picture of Mrs. Telford's dining room so that a set designer could re-create it for a dramatic version of "Comrades." Base your design on details from the story. **[Art Link; Performing Arts Link]**

5. **Dramatization** With a group of classmates, act out the scene in Mrs. Telford's dining room. Focus on capturing the awkwardness of the scene through body movements, as well as through spoken dialogue. **[Performing Arts Link]**

Researching and Representing

6. **Internet Research** Conduct research on the Internet to learn about changes in South African society since the fall of apartheid. Present your findings in a brief oral report. **[Social Studies Link; Technology Link]**

7. **Map** Conduct research to find out how colonial Africa was divided among the European nations, and create a map that illustrates these divisions. **[Social Studies Link]**

Online Activity www.phlit.phschool.com

Guided Writing Lesson

Advice Column on Creating Atmosphere

Gordimer uses descriptive details sparingly and powerfully to create atmosphere in "Comrades." Using her writing as an example, create a column for developing writers on how to create various types of atmospheres in a story. Classify details to help organize your column clearly.

Writing Skills Focus: Development by Classification

As you develop your column, classify the various types of details you mention by the type of atmosphere they create. Use the various groupings of details to help you organize your manual. For example, you may want to focus one paragraph on each type of atmosphere.

Prewriting Start by reviewing Gordimer's story and listing the details she uses to create a vivid atmosphere. Then, brainstorm to come up with other possible atmospheres a story might create. For each, list details that might be used to create it.

Drafting Begin with an introductory paragraph in which you make some generalizations about the importance of atmosphere to a short story and about the techniques a writer should use to create an atmosphere. Follow with a series of paragraphs in which you provide concrete explanations about how to create specific types of atmospheres.

Revising Share your work with a classmate. Ask the classmate to look at how effectively you have presented your main points. Ask whether you have offered enough examples of the various details that can be used to create a specific atmosphere. Use your classmate's comments as a guide when you revise.

Guide for Reading

Pär Lagerkvist *(1891–1974)*

Swedish writer Pär Lagerkvist (pär lä´ gǝr kvist´) did not achieve much public recognition until late in his career. Finally, however, when he was sixty, he won the most distinguished prize of all literary awards: the Nobel Prize.

Many Questions This Nobel Prize–winning writer was born the son of a railway worker. Unlike many of the inhabitants of his town, he received a university education, which led him to question many of his family's traditional beliefs. His resulting uncertainty marks his early work, which is notably pessimistic.

A Ray of Hope Although he continued to struggle with his beliefs, Lagerkvist's work gradually grew more optimistic. He reached a major turning point when he completed *The Triumph Over Life,* in which he expresses his growing faith in humanity.

Luisa Valenzuela *(1938–)*

Born in Buenos Aires, the capital of Argentina, Luisa Valenzuela has lived in places as diverse as New York City and Tepotzlán, Mexico, a little village with cobblestone streets where people still speak the ancient Aztec language. Married to a French sailor, she lived for a time in Normandy and Paris.

Valenzuela travels to extremes in some of her work as well. She changes spellings, creates new words, and uses many puns.

Defender of Rights Like many other Latin American writers, Valenzuela writes novels and stories with political significance. Having lived through a repressive regime herself, she is a strong defender of human rights and an active member of several international human rights organizations. "The Censors" shows one aspect of the repressions she has experienced.

◆ Build Vocabulary

LATIN WORD ROOTS: *-ultra-*

In "The Censors," a young man with an *ulterior* motive applies for a job. *Ulterior* means "undisclosed; beyond what is stated." An ulterior motive, therefore, is a reason beyond the one that you tell others.

Ulterior comes from the Latin word *ultra,* which means "further; beyond." In English, *ultra* also takes the forms *ulter* and *ulti.* Other common words with this root include *ultrasonic,* "faster than (or beyond) the speed of sound," and *ultimate,* "the farthest or last."

ardent
venerable
sordid
ulterior
staidness

WORD BANK

As you read, you will encounter the words on this list. Each word is defined on the page where it first appears. Preview the list before you read, and look for the words in the story.

◆ Build Grammar Skills

Who AND *Whom* IN ADJECTIVE CLAUSES

Adjective clauses, also known as relative clauses, modify nouns or pronouns and begin with a relative pronoun. When choosing between the relative pronouns *who* and *whom* to introduce an adjective clause, use the following rules.

Use *who* if it is the subject of the clause:

    subject
Mariana, *who* must finally feel safe there . . .

Use *whom* if it is a direct object or the object of a preposition in the clause:

                 dir. obj.
I have fought merely to win her *whom* I love, . . .

The Princess and All the Kingdom
◆ The Censors ◆

◆ *Literature and Your Life*

CONNECT YOUR EXPERIENCE

Have you ever fought for something and then found out you got more than you had bargained for? Both of these stories are about people who believe they are pursuing noble intentions but find themselves in circumstances that are very different from the results they had imagined.

Journal Writing Describe a situation in which your good intentions led to an unforeseen or even disastrous consequence.

THEMATIC FOCUS: FACING THE CONSEQUENCES

The events in these stories raise questions about how much control individuals have over the outcomes of their actions.

◆ Background for Understanding

HISTORY

Like the United States, Argentina, the setting of "The Censors," is a country with a high standard of living and a long tradition of immigration from all parts of the world. Unlike the United States, however, Argentina does not have a well-established tradition of democracy. It has suffered for many years under colonialism and military dictatorships. In the 1970's, a military regime took power and brutally hunted down suspected political foes. Luisa Valenzuela spent many of those years in self-imposed exile. Although democracy has now been restored, many Argentines are still traumatized by the events of the "Dirty War" in which thousands of people lost their lives.

◆ Literary Focus

UNIVERSAL THEMES

From Argentina to Alaska, from Zurich to Zaire, it would be difficult to find a place where fairy tales are not told. One reason that fairy tales continue to be told to generation after generation of children around the world is that they deal with **universal themes**— ideas that are relevant to people of almost any place or time, such as courage, love, and honor. "The Princess and All the Kingdom" uses a fairy-tale format to communicate a message about happiness and responsibility. The short story "The Censors" does not take the familiar fairy-tale form, but it does deal with the universal themes of power and fear.

◆ Reading Strategy

CHALLENGE THE WRITER'S MESSAGE

When you see a television commercial that implies you'll be able to jump as high as an NBA star if you just buy a particular brand of sneakers, do you go right out and buy a pair of the advertised footwear? If you're thinking critically, you'll **challenge the message** behind the advertisement. You might ask: Will a pair of sneakers really give me this ability? Are there any other reasons for buying these sneakers?

Use the same critical strategy when you're reading. Look for the writer's message. Sometimes the writer states the message openly—either through the voice of a narrator or through one of the characters. In these cases, it's easy to recognize the message.

In other stories, the message is implied—often through the actions of the main character. In stories like these, try to state the message in your own words. Then ask yourself, "Does this message prove true in real life, or am I being sold a pair of magic sneakers?"

THE PRINCESS AND ALL THE Kingdom

Pär Lagerkvist
Translated by Alan Blair

View of the Ile de la Cité, Paris, Jehan Fouquet, Bibliothèque Nationale de France, Paris

▲ **Critical Viewing** What clues does this painting give you about the style and content of the story you are about to read? **[Deduce]**

Once upon a time there was a prince, who went out to fight in order to win the princess whose beauty was greater than all others' and whom he loved above everything. He dared his life, he battled his way step by step through the country, ravaging it; nothing could stop him. He bled from his wounds but merely cast himself from one fight to the next, the most valiant nobleman to be seen and with a shield as pure as his own young features. At last he stood outside the city where the princess lived in her royal castle. It could not hold out against him and had to beg for mercy. The gates were thrown open; he rode in as conqueror.

When the princess saw how proud and handsome he was and thought of how he had dared his life for her sake, she could not withstand his power but gave him her hand. He knelt and covered it with <u>ardent</u> kisses. "Look, my bride, now I have won you!" he exclaimed, radiant with happiness. "Look, everything I have fought for, now I have won it!"

And he commanded that their wedding should take place this same day. The whole city decked itself out for the festival and the wedding was celebrated with rejoicing, pomp, and splendor.

When in the evening he went to enter the princess's bedchamber, he was met outside by the aged chancellor, a <u>venerable</u> man. Bowing his snow-white head, he tendered the keys of the kingdom and the crown of gold and precious stones to the young conqueror.

"Lord, here are the keys of the kingdom which open the treasuries where everything that now belongs to you is kept."

The prince frowned.

"What is that you say, old man? I do not want your keys. I have not fought for <u>sordid</u> gain. I have fought merely to win her whom I love, to win that which for me is the only costly thing on earth."

The old man replied, "This, too, you have won, lord. And you cannot set it aside. Now you must administer and look after it."

"Do you not understand what I say? Do you not understand that one can fight, can conquer, without asking any reward other than one's happiness—not fame and gold, not land and power on earth? Well, then, I have conquered but ask for nothing, only to live happily with what, for me, is the only thing of value in life."

"Yes, lord, you have conquered. You have fought your way forward as the bravest of the brave, you have shrunk from nothing, the land lies ravaged where you have passed by. You have won your happiness. But, lord, others have been robbed of theirs. You have conquered, and therefore everything now belongs to you. It is a big land, fertile and impoverished, mighty and laid waste, full of riches and need, full of joy and sorrow, and all is now yours. For he who has won the princess and happiness, to him also belongs this land where she was born; he shall govern and cherish it."

The prince stood there glowering and fingering the hilt of his sword uneasily.

"I am the prince of happiness, nothing else!" he burst out. "Don't want to be anything else. If you get in my way, then I have my trusty sword."

But the old man put out his hand soothingly and the young man's arm sank. He looked at him searchingly, with a wise man's calm.

"Lord, you are no longer a prince," he said gently. "You are a king."

◆ *Literature and Your Life*
Contrast the prince's situation with a time when you acquired something you wanted only to find there were unforeseen conditions attached.

And lifting the crown with his aged hands, he put it on the other's head.

When the young ruler felt it on his brow he stood silent and moved, more erect than before. And gravely, with his head crowned for power on earth, he went in to his beloved to share her bed.

◆ Build Vocabulary

ardent (är´ dənt) *adj.*: Warm or intense in feeling
venerable (ven´ ər ə bəl) *adj.*: Worthy of respect by reason of age and dignity, character, or position
sordid (sôr´ did) *adj.*: Dirty; filthy

The Censors

Luisa Valenzuela
Translated by David Unger

Poor Juan! One day they caught him with his guard down before he could even realize that what he had taken as a stroke of luck was really one of fate's dirty tricks. These things happen the minute you're careless, as one often is. Juancito let happiness—a feeling you can't trust—get the better of him when he received from a confidential source Mariana's new address in Paris and knew that she hadn't forgotten him. Without thinking twice, he sat down at his table and wrote her a letter. *The* letter that now keeps his mind off his job during the day and won't let him sleep at night (what had he scrawled, what had he put on that sheet of paper he sent to Mariana?).

Juan knows there won't be a problem with the letter's contents, that it's irreproachable, harmless. But what about the rest? He knows that they examine, sniff, feel, and read between the lines of each and every letter, and check its tiniest comma and most accidental stain. He knows that all letters pass from hand to hand and go through all sorts of tests in the huge censorship offices and that, in the end, very few continue on their way. Usually it takes months, even years, if there aren't any snags; all this time the freedom, maybe even the life, of both sender and receiver is in jeopardy. And that's why Juan's so troubled: thinking that something might happen to Mariana because of his letters. Of all people, Mariana, who must finally feel safe there where she always dreamt she'd live. But he knows that the *Censor's Secret Command* operates all over the world and cashes in on the discount in air fares; there's nothing to stop them from going as far as that hidden Paris neighborhood, kidnapping Mariana, and returning to their cozy homes, certain of having fulfilled their noble mission.

Well, you've got to beat them to the punch, do what everyone tries to do: sabotage the machinery, throw sand in its gears, get to the bottom of the problem so as to stop it.

This was Juan's sound plan when he, like many others, applied for a censor's job—not because he had a calling or needed a job: no, he applied simply to intercept his own letter, a consoling albeit unoriginal idea. He was hired immediately, for each day more and more censors were needed and no one would bother to check on his references.

Restricted Man, 1961, © Jerry Uelsmann, Collection of the Center for Creative Photography, Tucson, Arizona

▲ **Critical Viewing** In what ways does this work of art suggest fear and repression? [**Analyze**]

Ulterior motives couldn't be overlooked by the *Censorship Division,* but they needn't be too strict with those who applied. They knew how hard it would be for the poor guys to find the letter they wanted and even if they did, what's a letter or two when the new censor would snap up so many others? That's how Juan managed to join the *Post Office's Censorship Division,* with a certain goal in mind.

The building had a festive air on the outside that contrasted with its inner staidness. Little by little, Juan was absorbed by his job, and he felt at peace since he was doing everything he could to get his letter for Mariana. He didn't even worry when, in his first month, he was sent to *Section K* where envelopes are very carefully screened for explosives.

It's true that on the third day, a fellow worker had his right hand blown off by a letter, but the division chief claimed it was sheer negligence on the victim's part. Juan and the other employees were allowed to go back to their work, though feeling less secure. After work, one of them tried to organize a strike to demand higher wages for unhealthy work, but Juan didn't join in; after thinking it over, he reported the man to his superiors and thus got promoted.

> **Well, you've got to beat them to the punch, do what everyone tries to do: sabotage the machinery . . .**

You don't form a habit by doing something once, he told himself as he left his boss's office. And when he was transferred to *Section F,* where letters are carefully checked for poison dust, he felt he had climbed a rung in the ladder.

By working hard, he quickly reached *Section E* where the job became more interesting, for he could now read and analyze the letters' contents. Here he could even hope to get hold of his letter, which, judging by the time that had elapsed, had gone through the other sections and was probably floating around in this one.

Soon his work became so absorbing that his noble mission blurred in his mind. Day after day he crossed out whole paragraphs in red ink, pitilessly chucking many letters into the censored basket. These were horrible days when he was shocked by the subtle and conniving ways employed by people to pass on subversive messages; his instincts were so sharp that he found behind a simple "the weather's unsettled" or "prices continue to soar" the wavering hand of someone secretly scheming to overthrow the Government.

His zeal brought him swift promotion. We don't know if this made him happy. Very few letters reached him in *Section B*—only a handful passed the other hurdles—so he read them over and over again, passed them under a

◆ **Literary Focus**
The theme of someone's becoming so caught up in his work that he loses sight of his original mission is universal. Explain how.

◆ **Build Vocabulary**
ulterior (ul tir´ ē ər) *adj.:* Undisclosed; beyond what is openly stated
staidness (stād´ nəs) *n.:* State of being settled or resistant to change

magnifying glass, searched for microprint with an electronic microscope, and tuned his sense of smell so that he was beat by the time he made it home. He'd barely manage to warm up his soup, eat some fruit, and fall into bed, satisfied with having done his duty. Only his darling mother worried, but she couldn't get him back on the right track. She'd say, though it wasn't always true: Lola called, she's at the bar with the girls, they miss you, they're waiting for you. Or else she'd leave a bottle of red wine on the table. But Juan wouldn't overdo it: any distraction could make him lose his edge, and the

perfect censor had to be alert, keen, attentive, and sharp to nab cheats. He had a truly patriotic task, both self-denying and uplifting.

His basket for censored letters became the best fed as well as the most cunning basket in the whole *Censorship Division.* He was about to congratulate himself for having finally discovered his true mission, when his letter to Mariana reached his hands. Naturally, he censored it without regret. And just as naturally, he couldn't stop them from executing him the following morning, another victim of his devotion to his work.

Guide for Responding

◆ *Literature and Your Life*

Reader's Response Do you think the prince's prize was worth the price in "The Princess and All the Kingdom"?

Thematic Focus In both of these stories, the universal theme of power shows the great responsibilities that come with power. Find examples from both stories to illustrate this statement.

☑ Check Your Comprehension

1. In "The Princess and All the Kingdom," in addition to the princess's hand in marriage, what else does the prince receive?
2. In "The Censors," why does Juan seek a job as a censor?
3. What happens to Juan at the end of "The Censors"?

◆ Critical Thinking

INTERPRET

1. In "The Princess and All the Kingdom," why do you think the prince had to fight in order to win the princess? **[Speculate]**
2. In "The Princess and All the Kingdom," how do the attitudes of the aged chancellor and the prince contrast with each other? **[Compare and Contrast]**
3. In "The Censors," why does Juan's attitude change? **[Draw Conclusions]**
4. What is your opinion of Juan in "The Censors"? Support your opinion with examples from the story. **[Support]**

COMPARE LITERARY WORKS

5. To what types of situations in the real world do you think that the themes of these stories could be applied? **[Connect]**

Guide for Responding (continued)

◆ Reading Strategy

CHALLENGE THE WRITER'S MESSAGE

When you read critically, you **challenge the writer's message**—you test what the writer says or implies against your own experiences and opinions.

1. The prince wanted happiness without responsibility. Explain why you agree or disagree that some people approach life in a similar way.
2. Through the voice of the Chancellor, Lagerkvist states that happiness and responsibility are tied together, that every prize has a price. Explain why you agree or disagree with this idea.
3. In "The Censors," how does Juan's fast rise through the ranks of the Censorship Division relate to his downfall?
4. Did you find the changes in Juan's attitude believable or not? Explain.

◆ Literary Focus

UNIVERSAL THEMES

Though these two stories differ in style and subject matter, both have **universal themes**—timeless messages that apply to the lives of people all over the world.

1. (a) Explain how the message of "The Princess and All the Kingdom" could apply to a ruler of any country. (b) Explain how the message could apply to you and your friends.
2. What features of a fairy tale make it an effective form for communicating a theme?
3. State the theme of "The Censors" in your own words.
4. Juan sets out to beat the system of censorship that he feels is oppressive and unjust. In the end, he becomes one of the most aggressive censors. Describe another situation in which someone might become a part of a problem he or she originally tried to solve.

◆ Build Vocabulary

USING THE LATIN ROOT -*ultra*-

Many English words contain the root -*ultra*-, which means "further; beyond." On your paper, match each word with its correct definition.

1. ultraviolet   **a.** a final offer or demand
2. ultimatum   **b.** finally
3. ultimately   **c.** having wavelengths that are shorter than those of violet light

USING THE WORD BANK: Synonyms

On your paper, match each word from the Word Bank with its closest synonym.

1. ardent   **a.** filthy
2. venerable   **b.** hidden
3. sordid   **c.** revered
4. ulterior   **d.** zealous
5. staidness   **e.** stuffiness

◆ Build Grammar Skills

WHO AND WHOM IN ADJECTIVE CLAUSES

In informal speech, some people may not distinguish between *who* and *whom*. In formal writing and speaking, however, it is important to use these words correctly.

Use **who** as the subject of a clause. Use **whom** as a direct or indirect object or as an object of a preposition.

Practice Write the following sentences on your paper, choosing the correct word from the parentheses.

1. There once was a prince (who, whom) fought to win the heart of a beautiful princess.
2. The prince did not care for riches; he wanted to be with the princess (who, whom) he loved so much.
3. The chancellor, (who, whom) was a patient man, informed the prince of his new responsibilities.
4. It was Juan (who, whom) became a censor for his own letter.
5. Juan knew (who, whom) the authorities wanted.

Build Your Portfolio

Idea Bank

Writing

1. **The Censor** Choose a partner and write each other a simple postcard, such as you would write while on vacation. Then, exchange cards and pretend that you are censors in a dictatorship. Based on what you've read in "The Censors," find three suspicious details and explain why you chose them.

2. **Letter to Juan** All we know about the mysterious character Mariana in "The Censors" is that she is in Paris. Write a letter from her to Juan, explaining her reasons for leaving her country.

3. **Princess With a Point of View** Write and perform a short monologue for the princess in "The Princess and All the Kingdom," in which she expresses *her* opinions on war, victory, love and responsibility. **[Performing Arts Link]**

Speaking, Listening, and Viewing

4. **Debate** Form two groups to debate both sides of a current censorship issue.

5. **Improvised Speech** As the prince who has just become a king, give your first speech to the crowd outside the palace. Consider how your facial expressions and gestures will be viewed by your audience, and try to make them "work" for you.

Researching and Representing

6. **Music Collection** Plan a CD based on the theme of freedom versus responsibility. Collect popular songs you would include on the CD. **[Performing Arts Link]**

7. **Internet Research** Use the Internet to locate information on groups whose purpose is the advancement of human rights. Create a chart that shows your findings on at least two groups. **[Social Studies Link; Technology Link]**

Online Activity www.phlit.phschool.com

Guided Writing Lesson

Letter to an Elected Official

In "The Censors," Juan, like the author Luisa Valenzuela, has the misfortune of living under a dictatorship. In a democracy, government officials, who are often elected, must be responsive to the needs of the citizens. Conduct some research about a public issue that matters to you. Then, write a letter to an elected official about it, using the correct format.

Writing Skills Focus: Correct Format

When you write a letter to a government official, you should use the format, or style, of a standard business letter, as shown below.

> Your Address
> Date
>
> Inside Address:
> Name of Official
> Department
> Address
>
> Greeting:
>
> Body of letter
>
> Closing,
> Your Signature
> Your Typed Name

Prewriting Find the information you need to complete the inside address. Then, make notes on the points you have researched and want to discuss in your letter.

Drafting In the body of your letter, state the problem, summarize relevant information, and explain the action you want the official to take.

Revising Review your letter and eliminate any slang words or colloquial expressions. Check your spelling and grammar—especially your use of *who* and *whom*. For more on the correct use of *who* and *whom,* see pp. 690 and 698.

Writing Process Workshop

You may have noticed one character persuading another in the short stories in this section. Persuasion can take place informally or formally. A **persuasive essay** is a formal opportunity to convince an audience to think or act in a certain way.

Develop a persuasive essay in which you convince readers to accept your position on an issue that is important to you. The following skills, will help you develop your persuasive essay.

Writing Skills Focus

▶ **Consider what your audience knows.** If you write at the knowledge level of your audience, you have a better chance of persuading them to accept your position. For instance, if your topic is a road trip to another state and different state laws about driving, and your audience has little knowledge of them, make sure you let them know the facts.

▶ **Use the proper format.** A persuasive essay should first present your position, develop an argument with evidence to support that position, bring up counterarguments and then counter those arguments, and conclude with a summary or restatement.

The following excerpt from an article that recommends cycling and in-line skating at night demonstrates these skills.

① The writer mentions a possible problem with her argument and then offers reasons countering it.

② The writer backs up her original assertion with further examples.

③ The writer assumes that the audience has had experience cycling during the day but not at night, so she starts with a basic safety precaution.

MODEL

Most people automatically assume that bicycling at night is dangerous. After all, it's dark, and most decent people are safely off the streets. ① As it happens, most cars are also off the streets, which is one of the great attractions of night riding—or night in-line skating, for that matter. There are other appealing factors, too. ② You don't have to get up at 5 A.M. to get in a workout and you can enjoy the cool night air.

We are not, for obvious reasons, suggesting you go alone. Traveling with a buddy or two both increases your visibility and deters would-be harassers. . . . ③

Prewriting

Choose a Topic Think of issues that are important to you. You may want to browse through magazines and newspapers to look for ideas, or you may choose one of the following topics.

> ### Topic Ideas
> - School should be in session year-round
> - Channel One should not have advertising
> - Ticket brokers should be outlawed
> - High-school newspapers should be censored

Anticipate Readers' Questions Once you've chosen your topic, clarify the position that you will present in your essay. Then list potential objections and questions about that position. For example, if your essay presents an argument that zoos are cruel and should be closed, you might list these questions as issues that your opponents would raise and that you must address:

▶ What will happen to the animals currently in zoos?
▶ What alternatives are there to educate people about animals?
▶ What arguments are there in favor of zoos?

Gather Strong Evidence Using the questions and objections you listed as a starting point, gather evidence—facts, statistics, and reasons—to support your argument. This may require research, either in the library or on the Internet.

Drafting

Appeal to Your Audience As you write, always keep your readers in mind. Use formal, respectful language, and address each concern you think your readers may have. Also, keep your audience's level of knowledge about your subject in mind as you draft.

Present Strong Support for Your Argument Use the evidence you've gathered to support each point you make. Your argument is only as strong as the support you offer.

Use a Persuasive Tone Carefully choose your words and phrases to make readers eager to agree with your views. When criticizing zoos, for example, you might mention the "cold iron bars" and the "harsh fluorescent light" of the cages.

APPLYING LANGUAGE SKILLS: Types of Sentences

To enliven your writing, use different **types of sentences**, including simple sentences (a subject and verb), compound sentences (two independent clauses connected by a conjunction), and complex sentences (a main clause and one or more subordinate clauses).

Simple Sentence:

Seventy percent of the student body reads the school paper.

Compound Sentence:

The articles educate students on current events, <u>and</u> the columns entertain students and teachers alike.

Complex Sentence:

<u>Because some people were upset by a few recent articles</u>, they are calling for the paper to be censored.

Writing Application Make sure that your persuasive essay has a variety of sentence structures.

Writer's Solution Connection Writing Lab

To tailor your writing for a specific audience, complete the Audience Profile in the Writing Lab tutorial on Persuasion.

Applying Language Skills: Parallel Structure

Use **parallel structure**, or similar grammatical form, to express similar ideas. The similarity in form helps readers recognize the similarity in content and makes the writing easier to remember.

Not Parallel:
In the Rocky Mountains, avalanches are one threat, and you also have to watch out for flash floods.

Parallel:
In the Rocky Mountains, avalanches are one threat, while flash floods are another.

Practice On your paper, correct the faulty parallelism in the following sentence.

At Yellowstone you can take a bike ride, and hiking is fun, too.

Writing Application Review your persuasive essay, and look for places where you can use parallel structure.

Writer's Solution Connection Language Lab

For more practice with parallel structure, complete the Language Lab lesson on Varying Sentence Structure.

Revising

Hold a Peer Conference Share your draft with a classmate, and get some feedback. Use the comments as guidelines for revising your essay. Ask your peer these questions:
- ▶ Have I anticipated all my readers' questions?
- ▶ How well have I appealed to my audience?
- ▶ How persuasive is the tone in my writing?

REVISION MODEL

What advantages would a student gain by working at a job after a day of school? ① ~~One disadvantage might be that the student would not be able to keep up with his or her school work. On the other hand, the~~ *The* student may feel more independent as a result of having ~~new~~ *adult* ② responsibilities ③ *On the whole, I believe the advantages outweigh the disadvantages.* and a little extra money. ∧

① The writer deletes this line, which strays from his topic sentence.
② The writer replaces the word _new_ with the more precise _adult_.
③ This sentence completes the essay.

Publishing

- ▶ **Classroom** Invite classmates to read your persuasive essay. Encourage them to share their opinions.
- ▶ **Newspaper** Send your essay to your school or local newspaper as a letter to the editor.
- ▶ **Internet** Post your essay on a bulletin board or class Web site. See what responses you receive.

Student Success Workshop

Literary Response

Strategies for Success

You are entitled to your opinion. However, an opinion or an interpretation that is backed up with supporting information usually carries more weight. This can be especially true when you are asked to respond to or interpret something you have read. By reading carefully, you can gather information from the text to support your response or interpretation.

Use Text to Support Your Interpretation

An interpretation includes your ideas about the meaning of a literary work—whether it is a poem, short story, novel, or biography. Look to the text itself to support your interpretation. For example, in a work of fiction, you might point to specific images, passages of dialogue, or plot events to clarify your interpretation of the significance of the setting, the motivation of a character, or the author's theme. In a biography, you might note how the language used by the author indicates the tone of the work.

Use Text to Justify Your Response

When you are asked your opinion of a literary text, find support for your opinion in the text. If you think the work is superficial, point out the lack of a theme. If you find the characters appealing, state which of their traits you admire. If you find a nonfiction text confusing, describe its lack of organization. If you are entertained by an autobiography, mention a few of the details that amuse you.

Apply the Strategies

Write a few paragraphs describing your response to or interpretation of two or more of the following types of texts. Support your response with references to elements in each text.

1. short story
2. magazine article
3. poem
4. lyrics of a popular song
5. newspaper editorial

✔ Here are some situations in which using elements of text to support your interpretation or response can be helpful:
▶ Writing a book report
▶ Writing a review of a movie or play
▶ Evaluating the text of a political speech
▶ Answering a test question about a literary passage

Speaking, Listening, and Viewing Workshop

"Thumbs up," "thumbs down" . . . almost everyone understands these ratings to judge a performance. However, to be an effective critic, you need to look closely at various elements of the performance.

Recognize Interpretations Performances that are based on another work are interpretations. Poetry readings are interpretations. So are retellings of old stories. Films based on novels or plays may be the most common kind of interpretation, but other types of performances are also based on original texts. For example, the ballet "Sleeping Beauty" is based on a fairy tale, and the Greek myth of Orpheus and Eurydice has been interpreted through modern dance.

Interpret the Original Work Before you can evaluate a performance based on another work, you need to know and interpret the original work yourself. For example, if you want to know how successfully the film *Oedipus Rex* interprets Sophocles' play of the same name, you have to begin by reading the play and forming your own interpretation of it.

Evaluate Verbal and Nonverbal Techniques Various techniques may be used in a performance to convey another person's interpretation of a work. Verbal techniques include intonation and pacing in oral reading, storytelling, and dramatic performance (on stage or film). Nonverbal techniques include facial expressions, gestures, and movement in musical performances, dance, or pantomime. Particularly in plays and films, nonverbal techniques include special effects created by lighting, camera angles, sequencing, and music. For example, a tense scene from a novel might be heightened dramatically in a movie through music and special camera angles. You can evaluate the effectiveness of specific verbal or nonverbal techniques by asking yourself:

▶ How effectively does this technique convey the author's original message?
▶ How does this technique affect the viewer's understanding of the original story?

As you evaluate the effectiveness of verbal and nonverbal techniques, try to decide how well you think they communicate a valid interpretation of the original work, and why.

Apply the Strategies

Be a critic, and evaluate one of the following films as an interpretation of another work. Analyze verbal and nonverbal performance techniques, special effects, camera angles, and music. Present your critique to your class or a small group.

1. *The Hunchback of Notre Dame* (1939), based on Victor Hugo's novel of the same name.

2. *War and Peace* (1956), based on Leo Tolstoy's novel of the same name.

✔ *Tips for Evaluating Performance Techniques*
▶ Ask yourself questions about what you liked and disliked about the performance techniques.
▶ Avoid reading reviews of a performance before you see it, because they might influence your opinions of the performance techniques.

Test Preparation Workshop

Reading Comprehension

Interpret Graphic Aids; Evaluate and Make Judgments

Strategies for Success

The reading sections of national and standardized tests require you to interpret graphs, charts, diagrams, and tables. The test may also require you to evaluate and make judgments. Use the following strategies:

Interpret Information in Visual Form

Graphs, charts, diagrams, and tables are all devices for organizing and presenting information visually. To interpret graphic aids, read titles, labels, captions, and keys. Look for a caption that summarizes or explains the information shown. For example, you might be asked to interpret the information in a bar graph such as this:

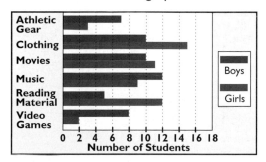

The bar graph shows the results of a poll regarding student spending habits. Thirty-one students, seventeen girls and fourteen boys, were asked which categories they spent money on in the last month. The poll shows they spent the most on clothing, movies, and music.

I In which category do the spending habits of girls and boys differ most?

A clothing   C reading material
B video games   D athletic gear

To answer, compare the endpoints of the two bars in each category. In each case, subtract the smaller number from the larger number. You'll find that **C** is correct.

Evaluate and Make Judgments After reading a passage, you may be asked to evaluate the information and make a judgment about it. Read each choice carefully, and refer to the information in the passage. The question that follows asks you to evaluate and make a judgment about the bar graph and passage about student spending habits:

2 Based on information in the bar graph and the passage, which of these statements is true?

A Girls spent the most money on clothing.
B Boys and girls spent nearly the same on movies.
C Many more boys than girls bought music.
D Most boys spent money on athletic gear.

Answer **A** is incorrect because the survey does not indicate how much students spent in each category. The difference in the music category is only three, so **C** is incorrect. **D** is incorrect because only half the boys bought athletic gear. **B** is the correct answer: About the same number of boys and girls spent money on movies.

Apply the Strategies

Refer again to the bar graph and sample passage, and answer the following questions:

I In which category are the spending habits of girls and boys most alike?

A music   C movies
B athletic gear D reading

2 The bar graph and passage offer evidence that

A more students in the class spent time reading than watching videos.

B a majority of boys in the class spent money on clothes.

C boys are more athletic than girls.

D most girls have no interest in videos.

Boy on a Wall: Rat Island, Derek Walcott, Collection of Michael and Judy Chastanet

Nonfiction in World Literature

Nonfiction introduces you to a wide variety of real people and places—some that are familiar to you and some that are far from your experience. Through the essays, biographies, and articles in this section, you can enjoy new experiences, consider new ideas, and learn new concepts.

Guide for Reading

Alexander Petrunkevitch
(1875–1964)

Zoologist, poetry translator, and political activist: Success as any one of these would be a tremendous accomplishment. Alexander Petrunkevitch (pə trōōn´ kə vich) managed to be successful as all three.

Born Into Controversy Alexander Petrunkevitch was born in the Russian town of Pliski, near Kiev. His father was an important statesman who worked hard to bring about a more democratic form of government in Russia, which was at that time still a monarchy. Petrunkevitch's father was once imprisoned for these efforts.

Alexander Petrunkevitch seems to have inherited some of his father's political spirit. While attending college in Moscow, Petrunkevitch participated in a protest against the government's treatment of students. To escape arrest for his involvement in the protest, Petrunkevitch fled to Germany to complete his education.

Gifted Scientist In 1900, Petrunkevitch received his Ph.D. from the University of Freiburg, graduating at the top of his class. He continued his scientific research at the university for several years before moving to the United States. Petrunkevitch accepted a teaching position at Yale University in 1910 and published his first important work, *The Index Catalogue of Spiders of North, Central and South America,* in the following year.

Diverse Interests As if science didn't keep him busy enough, Petrunkevitch also found time for literary pusuits. Under a pseudonym, he published a number of Russian translations of English poetry, including Lord Byron's *Manfred.* He also translated into English a number of works of Russian literature.

His diverse interests are reflected even in his scientific work. In his essay "The Spider and the Wasp," Petrunkevitch describes the interaction of two tiny creatures with a scientist's precision, a poet's sensitivity, and a philosopher's insight. In doing so, Petrunkevitch transforms an obscure occurrence in nature into a struggle of epic proportion.

◆ Build Vocabulary

RELATED WORDS: WORDS FOR THE FIVE SENSES

You can readily name the five senses: sight, hearing, smell, taste, and touch. However, the Latin-based adjectives that relate to them may not be familiar to you. In "The Spider and the Wasp," for example, Alexander Petrunkevitch uses the adjectives *tactile* and *olfactory* to refer to the senses of touch and smell, respectively.

WORD BANK

progeny
tactile
pungent
molestation
exasperated
olfactory
anesthetized

As you read this essay, you will encounter the words on this list. Each of the words is defined on the page on which it first appears. Preview this list before you read.

◆ Build Grammar Skills

COHERENCE: CONTRAST TRANSITIONS

When contrasting different items, writers create a sense of unity or **coherence** by using **contrast transitions**—words and phrases that signal a discussion of opposing things. Among the most frequently used contrast transitions are *but, however, instead, in spite of,* and *on the other hand.*

For example, the following sentence from "The Spider and the Wasp" sets up a clear contrast with the conjunction *but.*

Most tarantulas live in the tropics, *but* several species occur in the temperate zone and a few are common in the southern U.S.

Contrast transitions can also begin a sentence, making it clear that the other side of a contrast follows.

The Spider and the Wasp

◆ *Literature and Your Life*

CONNECT YOUR EXPERIENCE

As you watch a bee flying from flower to flower or examine the intricate design of a spider's web, you realize that there is another, smaller world all around us. Its inhabitants are insects and other tiny animals who, like humans, have their own ways of making sure that they have the food and shelter they need. As "The Spider and the Wasp" demonstrates, the daily challenges faced by these creatures—challenges that at first may seem trivial to us—are nothing less than a struggle for survival.

Journal Writing Write a few sentences about a time when you saw a small animal going about its business and wondered what it was doing.

THEMATIC FOCUS: IN AWE OF NATURE

"The Spider and the Wasp" depicts the interaction of two small animals that are natural enemies. As you read, ask yourself: In what ways does Petrunkevitch give this confrontation a larger-than-life quality?

◆ Background for Understanding

SCIENCE

In "The Spider and the Wasp," Alexander Petrunkevitch calls the confrontation between the spider and the wasp "a classic example of what looks like intelligence pitted against instinct." Instinct is the inborn tendency of an animal to behave in a way characteristic of its species. Intelligence is the ability to acquire and apply knowledge.

The experiment diagramed on this page was not performed by Petrunkevitch, but it proves that female digger wasps can respond intelligently to change. Its purpose was to determine whether female digger wasps use landmarks to find their nests. The experimenter placed a circle of pine cones around a nest (see diagram A), then moved the circle after the wasp had visited the nest. The biologist found that the wasp used the landmark and flew to the circle of pine cones, rather than to the nest (see diagram B).

◆ Literary Focus

EXPOSITORY ESSAY

An **expository essay** is a piece of short nonfiction writing that informs by explaining, defining, or interpreting an idea, an event, or a process. This kind of essay usually consists of a main point and evidence to support that point. Writers may develop expository essays in many ways, including analyzing, interpreting, or classifying information; giving illustrations; comparing and contrasting ideas; or presenting causes and effects.

In "The Spider and the Wasp," Alexander Petrunkevitch vividly depicts a natural phenomenon by combining colorful descriptions with an organized presentation of facts. Petrunkevitch does this while also maintaining a sense of drama. The result is an essay that is entertaining as well as informative.

Reading for Success

Strategies for Reading Nonfiction

Probably the majority of what you read is nonfiction—your textbooks, newspaper and magazine articles, information on the Internet. Reading nonfiction can open doors to new worlds, introduce you to interesting people, and help you to look at ideas and events in new ways. Because most nonfiction deals with information, concepts, or ideas, you will benefit from strategies that help you analyze it.

Recognize the writer's motivation.

Consider why the author is writing. What ideas or information does the author want to convey, or how does he or she want you to respond to this piece of writing? By being aware of the author's motivation, you can evaluate the credibility of the information you are being given, or you can be prepared to question what the writer is saying.

Identify the author's main points.

Sort out the main points the writer is making. If you're reading a textbook or news article, use the heads to help you identify the important points.

Identify support for the author's points.

Notice how the writer supports the points he or she makes. The author's reasoning and evidence should be believable and should lead you to understand and accept the points. If you find the support unsatisfactory, you may not accept the writer's ideas.

Recognize patterns of organization.

Noticing how the material is presented and developed can help you understand it. The writer may present material in a number of ways: explaining events chronologically, building up ideas in order of importance, comparing and contrasting ideas or things, showing the effects of causes, and so on.

Vary your reading rate.

You may read different kinds of nonfiction material at different rates, depending on your own purpose. When you're reading information that you need to remember, read slowly and attentively, perhaps even pausing to jot down notes. If you're looking for a fact or a single piece of information, you may want to skim very quickly, not trying to remember everything but looking only for the information you need.

As you read the following work of nonfiction by Alexander Petrunkevitch, look at the notes in the boxes. These notes demonstrate how to apply the above strategies to a piece of literature.

THE SPIDER AND THE WASP

Alexander Petrunkevitch

In the feeding and safeguarding of their progeny insects and spiders exhibit some interesting analogies to reasoning and some crass examples of blind instinct.

The author states a **main point** in the opening paragraph.

The case I propose to describe here is that of the tarantula spiders and their arch-enemy, the digger wasps of the genus Pepsis. It is a classic example of what looks like intelligence pitted against instinct—a strange situation in which the victim, though fully able to defend itself, submits unwittingly to its destruction.

Most tarantulas live in the tropics, but several species occur in the temperate zone and a few are common in the southern U.S. Some varieties are large and have powerful fangs with which they can inflict a deep wound. These formidable-looking spiders do not, however, attack man; you can hold one in your hand, if you are gentle, without being bitten. Their bite is dangerous only to insects and small mammals such as mice; for man it is no worse than a hornet's sting.

Tarantulas customarily live in deep cylindrical burrows, from which they emerge at dusk and into which they retire at dawn. Mature males wander about after dark in search of females and occasionally stray into houses. After mating, the male dies in a few weeks, but a female lives much longer and can mate several years in succession. In a Paris museum is a tropical specimen which is said to have been living in captivity for 25 years.

A fertilized female tarantula lays from 200 to 400 eggs at a time; thus it is possible for a single tarantula to produce several thousand young. She takes no care of them beyond weaving a cocoon of silk to enclose the eggs. After they hatch, the young walk away, find convenient places in which to dig their burrows and spend the rest of their lives in solitude. The eyesight of tarantulas is poor, being limited to a sensing of change in the intensity of light and to the perception of moving objects. They apparently have little

◆ **Build Vocabulary**
progeny (präj´ ə nē) *n.*: Offspring

or no sense of hearing, for a hungry tarantula will pay no attention to a loudly chirping cricket placed in its cage unless the insect happens to touch one of its legs.

But all spiders, and especially hairy ones, have an extremely delicate sense of touch. Laboratory experiments prove that tarantulas can distinguish three types of touch: pressure against the body wall, stroking of the body hair, and riffling of certain very fine hairs on the legs called trichobothria.[1] Pressure against the body, by the finger or the end of a pencil, causes the tarantula to move off slowly for a short distance. The touch excites no defensive response unless the approach is from above where the spider can see the motion, in which case it rises on its hind legs, lifts its front legs, opens its fangs and holds this threatening posture as long as the object continues to move.

The entire body of a tarantula, especially its legs, is thickly clothed with hair. Some of it is short and woolly, some long and stiff. Touching this body hair produces one of two distinct reactions. When the spider is hungry, it responds with an immediate and swift attack. At the touch of a cricket's antenna the tarantula seizes the insect so swiftly that a motion picture taken at the rate of 64 frames per second shows only the result and not the process of capture. But when the spider is not hungry, the stimulation of its hairs merely causes it to shake the touched limb. An insect can walk under its hairy belly unharmed.

The trichobothria, very fine hairs growing from disclike membranes on the legs, are sensitive only to air movement. A light breeze makes them vibrate slowly, without disturbing the common hair. When one blows gently on the trichobothria, the tarantula reacts with a quick jerk of its four front legs. If the front and hind legs are stimulated at the same time, the

---

1. **trichobothria** (trik´ ə bäth´ rē ə)

◀ **Critical Viewing** These pictures show a tarantula (left) and a wasp (right). Which do you think would get the best of the other in a conflict? Why? **[Make a Judgment]**

spider makes a sudden jump. This reaction is quite independent of the state of its appetite.

These three <u>tactile</u> responses—to pressure on the body wall, to moving of the common hair, and to flexing of the trichobothria—are so different from one another that there is no possibility of confusing them. They serve the tarantula adequately for most of its needs and enable it to avoid most annoyances and dangers. But they fail the spider completely when it meets its deadly enemy, the digger wasp Pepsis.

These solitary wasps are beautiful and formidable creatures. Most species are either a deep shiny blue all over, or deep blue with rusty wings. The largest has a wing span of about four inches. They live on nectar. When excited, they give off a <u>pungent</u> odor—a warning that they are ready to attack. The sting is much worse than that of a bee or common

wasp, and the pain and swelling last longer. In the adult stage the wasp lives only a few months. The female produces but a few eggs, one at a time at intervals of two or three days. For each egg the mother must provide one adult tarantula, alive but paralyzed. The mother wasp attaches the egg to the paralyzed spider's abdomen. Upon hatching from the egg, the larva is many hundreds of times smaller than its living but helpless victim. It eats no other food and drinks no water. By the time it has finished its single gargantuan meal[2] and become ready for wasphood, nothing remains of the tarantula but its indigestible chitinous skeleton.[3]

The mother wasp goes tarantula-hunting when the egg in her ovary is almost ready to be laid. Flying low over the ground late on a sunny

◆ **Build Vocabulary**
tactile (tak´ təl) *adj.*: Related to the sense of touch
pungent (pun´ jənt) *adj.*: Sharp and piercing

2. **gargantuan** (gär gan´ chōō ən) **meal:** Meal of gigantic size; Gargantua is a giant in a famous sixteenth-century book by the French author Rabelais, *Gargantua and Pantagruel.*
3. **chitinous** (kī´ tən əs) **skeleton:** Tough outer covering of an insect's body. Because an insect has no internal skeleton, this covering gives the insect its structure.

afternoon, the wasp looks for its victim or for the mouth of a tarantula burrow, a round hole edged by a bit of silk. The sex of the spider makes no difference, but the mother is highly discriminating as to species. Each species of Pepsis requires a certain species of tarantula, and the wasp will not attack the wrong species. In a cage with a tarantula which is not its normal prey, the wasp avoids the spider and is usually killed by it in the night.

Yet when a wasp finds the correct species, it is the other way about. To identify the species the wasp apparently must explore the spider with her antennae. The tarantula shows an amazing tolerance to this exploration. The wasp crawls under it and walks over it without evoking any hostile response. The <u>molestation</u> is so great and so persistent that the tarantula often rises on all eight legs, as if it were on stilts. It may stand this way for several minutes. Meanwhile the wasp, having satisfied itself that the victim is of the right species, moves

▲ **Critical Viewing** Does this picture of a wasp make it seem—in Petrunkevitch's words—"beautiful and formidable"? Explain. **[Connect]**

off a few inches to dig the spider's grave. Working vigorously with legs and jaws, it excavates a hole 8 to 10 inches deep with a diameter slightly larger than the spider's girth. Now and again the wasp pops out of the hole to make sure that the spider is still there.

Vary your reading rate to slow down when the writer cites specific numbers.

When the grave is finished, the wasp returns to the tarantula to complete her ghastly enterprise. First she feels it all over once more with her antennae. Then her behavior becomes more aggressive. She bends her abdomen, protruding her sting, and searches for the soft membrane

◆ **Build Vocabulary**

molestation (mō´ les tā´ shən) *n.*: Interference; attack

exasperated (eg zas´ pər āt´ id) *adj.*: Irritated; very annoyed

olfactory (äl fak´ tə rē) *adj.*: Related to the sense of smell

at the point where the spider's legs join its body—the only spot where she can penetrate the horny skeleton. From time to time, as the <u>exasperated</u> spider slowly shifts ground, the wasp turns on her back and slides along with the aid of her wings, trying to get under the tarantula for a shot at the vital spot. During all this maneuvering, which can last for several minutes, the tarantula makes no move to save itself. Finally the wasp corners it against some obstruction and grasps one of its legs in her powerful jaws. Now at last the harassed spider tries a desperate but vain defense. The two contestants roll over and over on the ground. It is a terrifying sight and the outcome is always the same. The wasp finally manages to thrust her sting into the soft spot and holds it there for a few seconds while she pumps in the poison. Almost immediately the tarantula falls paralyzed on its back. Its legs stop twitching; its heart stops beating. Yet it is not dead, as is shown by the fact that if taken from the wasp it can be restored to some sensitivity by being kept in a moist chamber for several months.

After paralyzing the tarantula, the wasp cleans herself by dragging her body along the ground and rubbing her feet, sucks the drop of blood oozing from the wound in the spider's abdomen, then grabs a leg of the flabby, helpless animal in her jaws and drags it down to the bottom of the grave. She stays there for many minutes, sometimes for several hours, and what she does all that time in the dark we do not know. Eventually she lays her egg and attaches it to the side of the spider's abdomen with a sticky secretion. Then she emerges, fills the grave with soil carried bit by bit in her jaws, and finally tramples the ground all around to hide any trace of the grave from prowlers. Then she flies away, leaving her descendant safely started in life.

In all this the behavior of the wasp evidently is qualitatively different from that of the spider. The wasp acts like an intelligent animal. This is not to say that instinct plays no part or that she reasons as man does. But her actions are to the point; they are not automatic and can be modified to fit the situation. We do not know for certain how she identifies the tarantula—probably it is by some <u>olfactory</u> or chemotactile sense[4]—but she does it purposefully and does not blindly tackle a wrong species.

On the other hand, the tarantula's behavior shows only confusion. Evidently the wasp's

This paragraph is **support** for a point that the author makes earlier—the conflict between tarantula and wasp is apparently one between "intelligence" and "instinct."

---

4. **chemotactile** (kē′ mō tak′ təl) **sense:** Ability to detect something by coming in physical contact with certain chemicals.

▼ **Critical Viewing** Petrunkevitch calls tarantulas "formidable-looking spiders." Which details in this photograph contribute to that impression? **[Analyze]**

pawing gives it no pleasure, for it tries to move away. That the wasp is not simulating sexual stimulation is certain because male and female tarantulas react in the same way to its advances. That the spider is not <u>anesthetized</u> by some odorless secretion is easily shown by blowing lightly at the tarantula and making it jump suddenly. What, then, makes the tarantula behave as stupidly as it does?

No clear, simple answer is available. Possibly the stimulation by the wasp's antennae is masked by a heavier pressure on the spider's body, so that it reacts as when prodded by a pencil. But the explanation may be much more complex. Initiative in attack is not in the nature of tarantulas; most species fight only when cornered so that escape is impossible. Their inherited patterns of behavior apparently prompt them to avoid problems rather than attack them. For example, spiders always weave their webs in three dimensions, and when a spider finds that there is insufficient space to attach certain threads in the third dimension, it leaves the place and seeks another, instead of finishing the web in a single plane. This urge to escape seems to arise under all circumstances, in all phases of life, and to take the place of reasoning. For a spider to change the pattern of its web is as impossible as for an inexperienced man to build a bridge across a chasm obstructing his way.

In a way the instinctive urge to escape is not only easier but often more efficient than reasoning. The tarantula does exactly what is most efficient in all cases except in an encounter with a ruthless and determined attacker dependent for the existence of her own species on killing as many tarantulas as she can lay eggs. Perhaps in this case the spider follows its usual pattern of trying to escape, instead of seizing and killing the wasp, because it is not aware of its danger. In any case, the survival of the tarantula species as a whole is protected by the fact that the spider is much more fertile than the wasp.

◆ **Build Vocabulary**

anesthetized (ə nes´ thə tīzd) v.: Made to lose partially or totally the sense of pain; made unconscious

Guide for Responding

◆ *Literature and Your Life*

Reader's Response For which animal did you feel more sympathy, the prey or the predator? Explain.

Thematic Focus This essay demonstrates two kinds of conflict in nature: the conflict between a predator and its prey and the conflict between instinct and intelligence. What is another type of conflict in nature?

☑ Check Your Comprehension

1. What are the three types of touch that can be sensed by tarantulas?
2. How long do the wasps described in the essay live once they have reached adulthood?
3. Why does the wasp attack the tarantula?
4. Why does the wasp begin digging a hole once she has chosen her victim?

◆ Critical Thinking

INTERPRET

1. Compare and contrast the ways in which the tarantula and the wasp lay eggs. **[Compare and Contrast]**
2. At the beginning of the essay, Petrunkevitch says that insects and spiders "exhibit some interesting analogies to reasoning." Identify an action performed by one of the animals in this essay that shows a kind of reasoning. **[Connect]**
3. Think of another title for this essay—one that states the meaning of the essay for you. Then, explain your choice. **[Interpret]**

APPLY

4. Basing your answer on what you have read in this essay, do you think that an animal using its intelligence will generally prevail over one that acts on instinct? Why or why not? **[Generalize]**

Guide for Responding (continued)

◆ Reading Strategy

STRATEGIES FOR READING NONFICTION

Review the reading strategies and notes showing how to read nonfiction. Then, apply those strategies to answer the following questions.

1. What is the author's main purpose in writing this essay?
2. (a) Which animal represents the intelligence Petrunkevitch refers to in the first paragraph? Which represents instinct? (b) Explain how Petrunkevitch supports this labeling of the spider and the wasp.
3. Why might Petrunkevitch have chosen to introduce the tarantula before the wasp?

◆ Literary Focus

EXPOSITORY ESSAY

An **expository essay** explains a concept, event, or process.

Maintaining the reader's interest is one of the most important parts of writing a successful expository essay. In describing the confrontation between the tarantula and the wasp, Petrunkevitch explains the roles that instinct and intelligence play in the interaction of different species.

In the process of providing this information, Petrunkevitch doesn't forget to keep the reader entertained. He structures his essay in a way that creates suspense, and he describes events in a vivid and dramatic way.

1. (a) What evidence in the description of the tarantula suggests that it will be able to defend itself against the wasp? (b) How does this part of the description create suspense?
2. Compare and contrast the author's description of the tarantula with that of the wasp. Which animal do you think is portrayed more favorably? Explain.
3. Basing your answer on what you have read in "The Spider and the Wasp," do you think Petrunkevitch considers intelligence the most important characteristic for the survival of a species? Why or why not?

◆ Build Vocabulary

USING WORDS FOR THE FIVE SENSES

On your paper, match each of the numbered adjectives with the sense to which it refers.

1. visual   **a.** hearing
2. auditory   **b.** taste
3. gustatory   **c.** sight
4. olfactory   **d.** touch
5. tactile   **e.** smell

USING THE WORD BANK: Sentence Completion

On your paper, write the word from the Word Bank that best completes each sentence.

1. A mother animal must find food not just for herself, but for her _____?_____, as well.
2. The cat responded negatively to all _____?_____ stimulation, even gentle petting.
3. The vinegar gave off a _____?_____ aroma.
4. Despite suffering the _____?_____ of one very persistent fly, we had a pleasant dinner outdoors.
5. The conductor became _____?_____ when the orchestra members refused to cooperate.
6. Phil has a stuffy nose, so his _____?_____ sense is not functioning properly.
7. The dentist made sure the patient was _____?_____ before he began to drill.

◆ Build Grammar Skills

CONTRAST TRANSITIONS

Alexander Petrunkevitch uses **contrast transitions** to set ideas in opposition.

Practice On your paper, underline the contrast transition in each sentence or pair of sentences.

1. Some varieties are large and have powerful fangs with which they can inflict a deep wound. These formidable-looking spiders do not, however, attack man . . .
2. After mating, the male dies in a few weeks, but a female lives much longer and can mate several years in succession.
3. The sex of the spider makes no difference, but the mother is highly discriminating as to species.
4. . . . it leaves the place and seeks another, instead of finishing the web . . .
5. In a way the instinctive urge to escape is not only easier but often more efficient than reasoning.

Build Your Portfolio

Idea Bank

Writing

1. **Contestant Introductions** Write a brief bio-graphical profile of both the tarantula and the wasp. Write the profiles as if the tarantula and the wasp are to be introduced as contestants on a game show or in some other competition.

2. **Nature Essay** Write an essay on an aspect of nature that you find interesting whether it's a spi-der's web, or a blooming flower. **[Science Link]**

3. **Poetic Interpretation** Rewrite the confronta-tion described in "The Spider and the Wasp" as an episode from an epic poem.

Speaking, Listening, and Viewing

4. **Talk by a Nature Guide** Using the informa-tion in this essay, give a talk on the relationship between the spider and the wasp as though you were a nature guide. **[Science Link; Career Link]**

5. **Dialogue** Role-play a dialogue between the tarantula and the wasp at the time they confront each other. **[Performing Arts Link]**

Researching and Representing

6. **Spiders-and-Insects Presentation** Research the relationships between other species of spi-ders and insects. Present your findings together with descriptions and pictures. **[Science Link; Art Link]**

7. **Natural Enemies** The tarantula and the wasp described in this essay are just two species who are enemies by nature. Construct a chart listing other pairs of species that are natural enemies and explaining why they battle each other. **[Science Link; Art Link]**

Online Activity www.phlit.phschool.com

Guided Writing Lesson

Proposal for a Nature Documentary

The descriptive passages in "The Spider and the Wasp" lend themselves to spectacular documentary footage! Write a proposal for a nature documentary for a television science program. Your proposal will present your plan for the documentary, summarizing the content and pointing out special features that it will include.

> **Writing Skills Focus: Transitions to Show Comparisons and Contrasts**
> As you draft your proposal, use **transitions,** words or phrases that link ideas, to show *com-parisons* (similarities) and *contrasts* (differences). Transitions such as *like, likewise,* and *similarly* indi-cate comparisons. Transitions such as *unless, de-spite,* and *on the other hand* indicate contrasts.

Prewriting Decide on a topic for your documen-tary, and then list all the elements you will capture on film, including scenery and sounds. Jot down comparisons that you will use to show the similari-ties or differences between two items.

Drafting Use vivid descriptions to make your pro-posal appealing. Include a summary of an especially exciting or beautiful scene you plan to include. Indi-cate similarities between scenes and ideas with transitions to show comparisons and contrasts.

Revising Ask a classmate to read your proposal to make sure that it is clear and engaging. Have your partner point out passages that lack clarity. Con-sider adding transitions to illustrate comparisons and contrasts more smoothly and clearly.

For more on contrasts, see pp. 708 and 717.

PART 1 *Personal Accounts, Descriptions, and Testimonies*

Memory of Oceania (Souvenir d'Océanie), Henri Matisse, Nice, summer 1952–early 1953, Gouache and crayon on cut-and-pasted paper over canvas, 9'4" x 9'4 7/8", The Museum of Modern Art, New York (Mrs. Simon Guggenheim Fund). © 2001 Succession H. Matisse, Paris/Artists Rights Society (ARS), New York

Guide for Reading

Lu Hsun (1881–1936)

The Chinese author Lu Hsun wrote stories, essays, poetry, and literary criticism. As a young man, he resolved to write literature in order to help improve the condition of the Chinese people. One of the first modern Chinese writers to write in the vernacular, using language spoken by ordinary people, he attempted to make the Chinese people aware of Western scientific, philosophical, and social advances. He wrote the reflective essay "This Too Is Life" during his final illness.

Alexander Solzhenitsyn (1918–   )

A dissident is one who departs from established opinion, and the Russian writer Alexander Solzhenitsyn (sōl′ zhə nēt′ sin) has been a dissident throughout his literary life. His first book, *One Day in the Life of Ivan Denisovitch*—the story of an inmate in a Soviet labor camp—was banned in the Soviet Union. Solzhenitsyn was tried for treason and exiled after the publication in Paris of parts of *The Gulag Archipelago*. Only since 1991 has his work been available to the people of his homeland. This excerpt from his Nobel lecture reflects on what it means to be part of a great world literature.

Elie Wiesel (1928–   )

The Romanian-born teacher, philosopher, and writer Elie Wiesel (el′ ē wi zel′) was deported to the Nazi death camp at Auschwitz at age sixteen. His parents and sister were killed, and he was forced into slave labor at Buchenwald, another Nazi death camp. After surviving the war, Wiesel studied in France and moved to the United States in 1956. In his first book, *Night,* Wiesel recounts the horrors of his experiences at the hands of the Nazis.

Elie Wiesel has been awarded the Congressional Gold Medal of Achievement and the Nobel Peace Prize. He delivered the speech "Keep Memory Alive" in 1986, in acceptance of the Nobel Peace Prize.

◆ Build Vocabulary

RELATED WORDS: FORMS OF *RECIPROCITY*

"Today," Alexander Solzhenitsyn writes, "there is an almost instant *reciprocity*" between the writers of one country and the readers and writers of another. The word *reciprocity,* which means a "mutual action or dependence," has several forms. As the adjective *reciprocal,* it means "something done in response to something else" or simply, "mutual." As the verb *reciprocate,* it means "to do in return."

WORD BANK

Before you read, preview this list of words from the selections.

relish
gainsaying
reciprocity
assimilate
inexorably
oratory
transcends

◆ Build Grammar Skills

CAPITALIZATION OF PROPER NOUNS AND ADJECTIVES

In these selections you'll see many **proper nouns and adjectives.** All proper nouns begin with capital letters. Proper nouns name specific places, people, and things.

Name of Place:	China
Name of Person:	Guangping
Name of Journal:	*Literature*
Name of Thing:	Nobel Prize

Proper adjectives are adjectives made from proper nouns. They are usually, but not always, capitalized. For instance, the following examples come from the proper nouns *China, Europe,* and *France.*

Chinese writers
European writers
french fries

This Too Is Life
◆ *from* Nobel Lecture ◆ Keep Memory Alive ◆

◆ *Literature and Your Life*

CONNECT YOUR EXPERIENCE

We all have memories, and we cherish those that are most important to us. Writers often relive their most vivid or important memories by recording them. These three works of literature are the records of three authors' recollections and reflections on important events in their lives.

THEMATIC FOCUS: FROM THE PAST

Memoirists and historic novelists, among others, reflect on the past in their writing. What do writers gain by reflecting on the past?

Journal Writing Jot down two or three memories that have stayed with you since childhood.

◆ Background for Understanding

LITERATURE

One of the highest honors a writer can receive is to be awarded the Nobel Prize for Literature. The Nobel prizes—which include awards in physics, chemistry, medicine, literature, and peace—were established by a Swede, Alfred Nobel, the inventor of dynamite. Wanting to be associated not with destruction but with peace, Nobel set up a fund to finance annual achievement and peace awards.

Both Alexander Solzhenitsyn and Elie Wiesel were awarded the Nobel Prize—Solzhenitsyn for literature and Wiesel for peace.

◆ Literary Focus

REFLECTIVE AND PERSUASIVE ESSAYS

In a **reflective essay**, an author shares his or her thoughts about an idea or a personal experience. In "This Too Is Life," Lu Hsun reflects on his illness and explains how it has affected his outlook on life.

A **persuasive essay** attempts to convince readers to adopt a particular opinion or course of action. Solzhenitsyn's and Wiesel's speeches use persuasive language and sound reasons to convince you that their ideas are worth embracing.

◆ Reading Strategy

IDENTIFY MAIN POINTS

Identifying the main points of an essay will help you understand how those main points work together to convey an author's message. The author's main points may be stated directly or implied.

The main idea of an essay is often stated in its introduction. Details that support that main idea are often found in topic sentences of the essay's paragraphs.

If the main idea is not directly stated, it will be implied. To identify implied main ideas, pause after you read a paragraph and ask yourself: What was that paragraph about? Why did the writer include these details? How can I state the main point of this paragraph in one sentence?

Writers often summarize their main points in the conclusions of their essays. Look there to identify or clarify the author's main points.

As you read these essays, pay attention to the points each author is making. You may want to create a chart like this one to keep track of the author's main points. When you have finished listing the main points, review them and identify the author's overall message.

Main Points	Author's Message

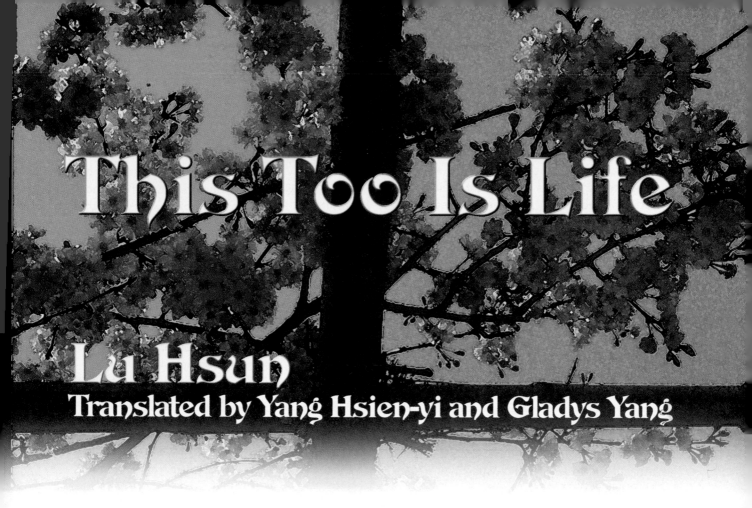

This Too Is Life

Lu Hsun
Translated by Yang Hsien-yi and Gladys Yang

This, too, happens during illness.

There are things which a healthy or a sick man ignores, either because he does not come across them or because they are too insignificant. But a man just recovering from a serious illness experiences them. In my case two good examples are the fearfulness of exhaustion and the comfort of rest. I used often to boast that I did not know what it was to be tired. In front of my desk there is a swivel-chair, and sitting there to write or read carefully was work; beside it there is a wicker reclining chair, and lying there to chat or skim through the papers was rest. I found no great difference between the two, and often boasted of the fact. Now I know my mistake. I found little difference because I was never tired, because I never did any manual labor.

A relative's son, after graduating from senior middle school, had to go to a stocking factory as an apprentice. He was very unhappy about this, and the work was so hard that he had virtually no rest the whole year round. Too proud to slack, he stuck to it for a year and more. Then one day he collapsed and told his elder brother, "I've just no energy left."

He never stood up again. He was sent home where he lay unwilling to eat or drink, to stir or speak. A Protestant doctor fetched to examine him said there was nothing organically wrong but the boy was completely worn out. Since there was no cure for this either, what followed, naturally, was a lingering death. I had two days like that, but for a different reason: whereas he was tired out by work I was tired out by illness. I had literally no desire for anything, as if nothing

▲ **Critical Viewing** Lu Hsun is shown here with his wife and son. Does the mood he projects seem similar to his mood in the essay? Why or why not? **[Connect]**

concerned me and all action would be superfluous. I did not brood over death, but neither did I feel alive. This, known as "the absence of all desire," is the first step towards death, and it made some who loved me shed secret tears. But I took a turn for the better when I wanted something to drink, and from time to time I looked at the things around me—the walls and the flies. Only then did I feel tired enough to need rest.

◆ **Literary Focus**
What evidence in this paragraph reveals that Lu Hsun is writing a reflective essay?

To lie just as one pleases, stretching one's limbs and giving a huge yawn before settling into the most comfortable position to relax in every muscle, is sheer delight. I had never enjoyed this before. I doubt if the healthy and lucky have enjoyed it either.

The year before last, I remember, after another illness I wrote "Random Talk After Sickness" in five sections and gave it to *Literature;* but since the last four sections could not be published the first was printed alone. The article started clearly with a (1) but stopped abruptly without any (2) or (3) to follow, so that anyone who thought carefully must have been puzzled; but we cannot expect this thoughtfulness from every reader, nor even from every critic. And on the basis of the first section someone passed this judgment on me: "Lu Hsun is in favor of illness." This time I may be spared, but to be on the safe side I had better announce here: "More is to follow."

Four or five days after I began to mend, waking in the night I called Guangping to wake her.

"Give me some water. And put the light on so that I can have a look round."

"What for?" She sounded rather alarmed, doubtless thinking I was raving.

"Because I want to live. Understand that? This, too, is life. I want to take a look round."

"Oh. . . ." She got up and gave me some tea, hesitated a little and quietly lay down again without putting on the light.

I knew she had not understood.

A street-lamp outside the window shed a glimmer of light in the room, and I had a quick look at the familiar walls and the angles between them, the familiar pile of books and the unbound pictures beside them, while outside night took its course, and all that infinite space, those innumerable people, were linked in some way with me. I breathed, I lived, I should live on. I began to feel more substantial and experienced an urge to action—but presently I fell asleep again.

The next morning when I looked round in the sunlight, sure enough, there were the familiar walls, the familiar piles of books . . . normally I would look at these too as a form of relaxation. But we tend to despise these things though they are one part of life, ranking them lower than drinking tea or scratching ourselves, or even counting them as nothing. We notice rare blossoms, not the branches and leaves. The biographer of a famous man generally does nothing but emphasize his peculiarities: how Li Bai wrote his poetry and became tipsy, how

Napoleon[1] fought his battles and went without sleep, not describing them when sober or asleep. In fact, a man who spends all his time getting tipsy or doing without sleep will certainly not live long. He can go without sleep or become tipsy sometimes because at other times he is sober and sleeps. Yet considering these normal events as the dregs of life, people will not spare them a glance.

So the men or happenings they see are like the elephant's leg which made the blind man groping round the elephant fancy it was shaped like a pillar. The ancient Chinese always liked to have "the whole." Even when making "black chicken pills" to cure women's disorders, they used the whole chicken, feathers, blood and all. This method may be rather ridiculous, yet the idea behind it is not a bad one.

The man who strips off the branches and leaves will never get blossoms and fruit.

Annoyed with Guangping for not putting on the light for me, I complained of her to everyone who called. By the time I was able to get about again, I looked through the magazines she had been reading. Sure enough, while I lay ill in bed quite a few distinguished journals had appeared. Though some still published "Beauty Tips," "An Old Tree Sheds Light" or "The Secrets of Nuns" in the back, the first pages had some rousingly heroic articles. Writers now have a "most vital theme": even Sai-jin-hua . . . has become canonized as a goddess in heaven to guard our realm.

Most admirable of all is the fact that the "Spring and Autumn" supplement of the *Shen Bao* which used to refer with such relish to the Empress Dowager and the Qing court,[2] has also changed completely with the times. In the

---

1. **Li Bai . . . Napoleon:** Li Bai, also known as Li Po (lē pō) (701–762), was a famous Chinese poet. Napoleon Bonaparte (bō´ nə pärt´) (1769–1821) was the military leader and self-proclaimed emperor of France between 1804 and 1815. During that time, his armies invaded much of Europe.

▲ **Critical Viewing** This photograph shows Lu Hsun in the study he describes at the beginning of the essay. Does it look like a comfortable place in which to work? Why or why not? **[Analyze]**

comments at the beginning of one number, we are even told that when eating melons we should think of our territory now carved up like a melon. Of course there is no <u>gainsaying</u> that at all times, in all places and on all occasions we should be patriotic. Still if I were to think like that while eating a melon, I doubt whether I could swallow it. Even if I made an effort and succeeded, I would probably have prolonged indigestion. And this may not be

owing to my bad nervous state after illness. To my mind, a man who uses the melon as a simile when lecturing on our national disgrace, and the next moment cheerfully eats a melon absorbing its nourishment, is rather lacking in feeling. No lecture could have any effect on such a man.

Never having joined the volunteers myself, I can only guess at their feelings. But I ask myself:

2. **Empress Dowager and the Qing** (chin) **court:** Tz'u-hsi (tzo͞o shē) (1835–1908), who ruled China through her son, the legitimate emperor, from 1861 until her death. While in power, she blocked efforts to modernize the nation.

◆ **Build Vocabulary**

relish (rel´ ish) *n.:* Pleasure; enjoyment

gainsaying (gān´ sā´ iŋ) *v.:* Contradicting; opposing

Does a soldier eating a melon make a point of eating and thinking at the same time? I doubt it. He probably just feels thirsty, wants a melon and finds it sweet, without giving a thought to any other high-sounding ideas. Eating the melon refreshes him and enables him to fight better than if he were thirsty; hence melon-eating does have something to do with resistance, but nothing to do with the rules on how to think laid down in Shanghai.[3] If we ate and drank with long faces all the time, very soon we should have no appetite at all, and then what would become of our resistance?

Still there are men who will talk in this strange way, who will not even let you eat a melon normally. Actually a soldier's daily life is not entirely heroic; but when the whole of it is bound up with heroism, you have a real soldier.

August 23, 1936

---

3. **Shanghai** (shaŋ´ hĭ´): City and seaport in eastern China. Shanghai is the country's center of scientific and technological research.

Guide for Responding

◆ *Literature and Your Life*

Reader's Response What was your reaction to Lu Hsun's feeling of complete exhaustion? Have you ever felt so thoroughly tired? Explain.

Thematic Focus How can reflecting on your past experiences help you to understand yourself and to define your values?

Reader's Journal In your journal, tell of a past event that helped you to understand yourself more fully.

Questions for Research What details of life in China does this essay highlight? How might you find out more about those details?

☑ Check Your Comprehension

1. What circumstances allow Lu Hsun to contemplate "the fearfulness of exhaustion and the comfort of rest"?
2. What happened to the relative's son who had to work in a stocking factory as an apprentice?
3. Why does Lu Hsun call in the night to wake his wife, Guangping?
4. What advice does one magazine article give about eating melons?

◆ Critical Thinking

INTERPRET

1. When he wakes up in the night and wants to look around, why does Lu Hsun tell his wife that "This, too, is life"? **[Infer]**
2. Why does Lu Hsun see "the absence of all desire" as the first step toward death? **[Connect]**
3. What is the meaning of Lu Hsun's message about melon-eating? **[Interpret]**

EVALUATE

4. Do you agree with Lu Hsun's observation that "We notice rare blossoms, not the branches and leaves"? Support your answer. **[Assess]**

APPLY

5. Why do you think Guangping is unable to fully understand Lu Hsun when he wants the light turned on? **[Speculate]**
6. In "This Too Is Life," Lu Hsun says, "[A] soldier's daily life is not entirely heroic; but when the whole of it is bound up with heroism, you have a real soldier." How would you describe a "real soldier"? **[Relate]**

from # Nobel Lecture

Alexander Solzhenitsyn

Translated by F. D. Reeve

I am, however, encouraged by a keen sense of WORLD LITERATURE as the one great heart that beats for the cares and misfortunes of our world, even though each corner sees and experiences them in a different way.

In past times, also, besides age-old national literatures there existed a concept of world literature as the link between the summits of national literatures and as the aggregate[1] of reciprocal literary influences. But there was a time lag: readers and writers came to know foreign writers only belatedly, sometimes centuries later, so that mutual influences were delayed and the network of national literary high points was visible not to contemporaries but to later generations.

Today, between writers of one country and the readers and writers of another, there is an almost instantaneous <u>reciprocity</u> as I myself know. My books, unpublished, alas, in my own country, despite hasty and often bad translations have quickly found a responsive world readership. Critical analysis of them has been undertaken by such leading Western writers as Heinrich Böll.[2] During all these recent years, when both my work and my freedom did not collapse, when against the laws of gravity they held on seemingly in thin air, seemingly ON NOTHING, on the invisible, mute surface tension of sympathetic people, with warm gratitude I learned, to my complete surprise, of the support of the world's writing fraternity. On my fiftieth birthday I was astounded to receive greetings from well-known European writers. No pressure put on me now passed unnoticed. During the dangerous weeks when I was being expelled from the Writers' Union,[3] THE PROTECTIVE WALL put forward by the prominent writers of the world saved me from worse persecution,

---

2. **Heinrich Böll** (hīn′ riH böl): German novelist (1917–1985) and winner of the Nobel Prize for Literature.
3. **the Writers Union:** Official Soviet writers' organization.

◆ **Build Vocabulary**
reciprocity (res′ ə präs′ ə tē) *n.*: Mutual action; dependence

---

1. **aggregate** (ag′ rə git) *n.*: Group of things gathered together and considered a whole.

and Norwegian writers and artists hospitably prepared shelter for me in the event that I was exiled from my country. Finally, my being nominated for a Nobel Prize was originated not in the land where I live and write but by François Mauriac[4] and his colleagues. Afterward, national writers' organizations expressed unanimous support for me.

As I have understood it and experienced it myself, world literature is no longer an abstraction or a generalized concept invented by literary critics, but a common body and common spirit, a living, heartfelt unity reflecting the growing spiritual unity of mankind. State borders still turn crimson, heated red-hot by electric fences and machine-gun fire; some ministries of internal affairs still suppose that literature is "an internal affair" of the countries under their jurisdiction; and newspaper headlines still herald, "They have no right to interfere in our internal affairs!" Meanwhile, no such thing as INTERNAL AFFAIRS remains on our crowded Earth. Mankind's salvation lies exclusively in everyone's making everything his business, in the people of the East being anything but indifferent to what is thought in the West, and in the people of the West being anything

---

4. **François Mauriac** (frän swá´ mô ryàk´): French novelist and essayist (1885–1970).

▲ **Critical Viewing** These stamps from various countries honor writers. What do they suggest about the importance of writers? [Draw Conclusions]

---

but indifferent to what happens in the East. Literature, one of the most sensitive and responsive tools of human existence, has been the first to pick up, adopt, and <u>assimilate</u> this sense of the growing unity of mankind. I therefore confidently turn to the world literature of the present, to hundreds of friends whom I have not met face to face and perhaps never will see.

My friends! Let us try to be helpful, if we are worth anything. In our own countries, torn by differences among parties, movements, castes, and groups, who for ages past has been not the dividing but the uniting force? This, essentially, is the position of writers, spokesmen of a national language, of the chief tie binding the nation, the very soil which the people inhabit, and, in fortunate circumstances, the nation's spirit too.

I think that world literature has the power in these frightening times to help mankind see itself accurately despite what is advocated by partisans[5] and by parties. It has the power to transmit the condensed experience of one region to another, so that different scales of values are combined, and so that one people accurately and concisely knows the true history of another with a power of recognition and acute awareness as if it had lived through that history itself—and could thus be spared repeating old mistakes. At the same time, perhaps we ourselves may succeed in developing our own

---

5. **partisans** (pärt´ ə zənz): Unreasoning, emotional supporters of a party or viewpoint.

WORLDWIDE VIEW, like any man, with the center of the eye seeing what is nearby but the periphery[6] of vision taking in what is happening in the rest of the world. We will make correlations[7] and maintain worldwide standards.

Who, if not writers, are to condemn their own unsuccessful governments (in some states this is the easiest way to make a living; everyone who is not too lazy does it) as well as society itself, whether for its cowardly humiliation or for its self-satisfied weakness, or the lightheaded escapades of the young, or the youthful pirates brandishing knives?

We will be told: What can literature do against the pitiless onslaught of naked violence? Let us not forget that violence does not and cannot flourish by itself; it is inevitably intertwined with LYING. Between them there is the closest, the most profound and natural bond: nothing screens violence except lies, and the only way lies can hold out is by violence. Whoever has once announced violence as his METHOD must inexorably choose lying as his PRINCIPLE. At birth, violence behaves openly and even proudly. But as soon as it becomes stronger and firmly established, it senses the thinning of the air around it and cannot go on without befogging itself in lies, coating itself with lying's sugary oratory. It does not always

or necessarily go straight for the gullet; usually it demands of its victims only allegiance to the lie, only complicity in the lie.

The simple act of an ordinary courageous man is not to take part, not to support lies! Let *that* come into the world and even reign over it, but not through me. Writers and artists can do more: they can VANQUISH LIES! In the struggle against lies, art has always won and always will. Conspicuously, incontestably for everyone. Lies can stand up against much in the world, but not against art.

Once lies have been dispelled, the repulsive nakedness of violence will be exposed—and hollow violence will collapse.

That, my friends, is why I think we can help the world in its red-hot hour: not by the nay-saying of having no armaments, not by abandoning oneself to the carefree life, but by going into battle!

In Russian, proverbs about TRUTH are favorites. They persistently express the considerable, bitter, grim experience of the people, often astonishingly:

ONE WORD OF TRUTH OUTWEIGHS THE WORLD.

On such a seemingly fantastic violation of the law of the conservation of mass and energy[8] are based both my own activities and my appeal to the writers of the whole world.

---

6. **periphery** (pə rif´ ə rē) *n.*: Boundary; perimeter.
7. **correlations** (kôr ə lā´ shənz) *n.*: Relationships; connections.

8. **the law of the conservation of mass and energy:** This law states that in any physical or chemical change, neither mass nor energy can be lost.

Guide for Responding

◆ Literature and Your Life

Reader's Response Tell how a work of literature has helped you to understand the values and traditions of different people.

Thematic Focus How can reflecting on other people's experiences help you understand yourself?

☑ Check Your Comprehension

1. To what does the "one great heart" refer?
2. What does Solzhenitsyn believe writers and artists can do?

◆ Critical Thinking

INTERPRET
1. What connection does Solzhenitsyn see between lies and violence? **[Analyze]**
2. What is the meaning of the Russian proverb that Solzhenitsyn quotes? **[Interpret]**

APPLY
3. How well do you think Solzhenitsyn supports his statement that "no such thing as INTERNAL AFFAIRS remains on our crowded Earth"? **[Judge]**
4. Explain why you agree or disagree with the statement "Lies can stand up against much in the world, but not against art." **[Assess]**

Keep *Memory* Alive
Elie Wiesel

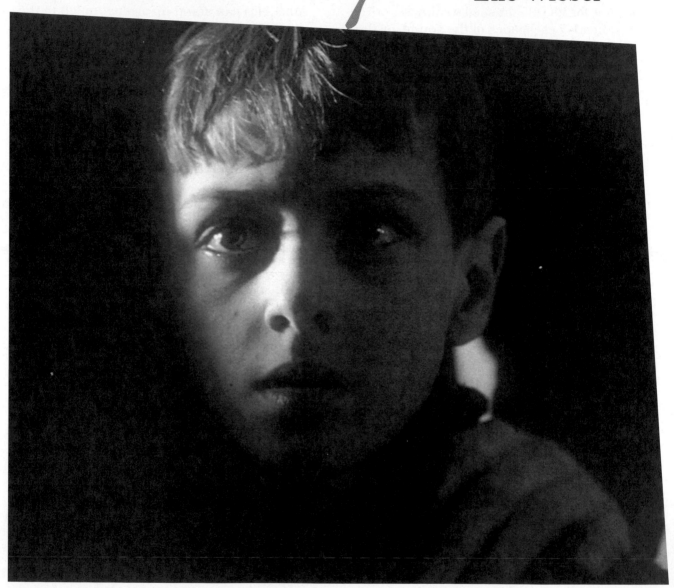

▲ **Critical Viewing** What emotion do you read on this boy's face? How does it relate to the title of this essay? [Connect]

It is with a profound sense of humility that I accept the honor you have chosen to bestow upon me. I know: your choice transcends me. This both frightens and pleases me.

It frightens me because I wonder: do I have the right to represent the multitudes who have perished? Do I have the right to accept this great honor on their behalf? I do not. That would be presumptuous. No one may speak for the dead, no one may interpret their mutilated dreams and visions.

It pleases me because I may say that this honor belongs to all the survivors and their children, and through us, to the Jewish people with whose destiny I have always identified.

I remember: it happened yesterday or eternities ago. A young Jewish boy discovered the kingdom of night. I remember his bewilderment, I remember his anguish. It all happened so fast. The ghetto. The deportation.[1] The sealed cattle car. The fiery altar upon which the history of our people and the future of mankind were meant to be sacrificed.

I remember: he asked his father: "Can this be true? This is the 20th century, not the Middle Ages. Who would allow such crimes to be committed? How could the world remain silent?"

And now the boy is turning to me: "Tell me," he asks. "What have you done with my future? What have you done with your life?"

And I tell him that I have tried. That I have tried to keep memory alive, that I have tried to fight those who would forget. Because if we forget, we are guilty, we are accomplices.

And then I explained to him how naive we were, that the world did know and remain silent. And that is why I swore never to be silent whenever and wherever human beings endure suffering and humiliation. We must always take sides. Neutrality helps the oppressor, never the victim. Silence encourages the tormentor, never the tormented.

---

1. **deportation** (dē′ pôr tā′ shən) *n.*: Expulsion from a country.

◆ **Build Vocabulary**

transcends (tran sendz′) *v.*: Surpasses; exceeds

Guide for Responding

◆ Literature and Your Life

Reader's Response Describe a situation today in which silently witnessing might do harm.

Thematic Focus Have you ever reflected on the past in order to keep a lesson in your mind? Explain.

Questions for Research Though the Holocaust was unique in many respects, it is also, sadly, not the only case of genocide in this century. Generate research questions about other cases of genocide.

☑ Check Your Comprehension

1. What right, or claim, does Wiesel question?
2. Why is the boy incredulous as he's being deported?
3. What does Wiesel call those who deliberately forget the Holocaust?

◆ Critical Thinking

INTERPRET

1. Why does Wiesel use the term "the fiery altar"? **[Interpret]**
2. What is Wiesel's purpose in having his boy self talk to his man self? **[Speculate; Synthesize]**
3. At the end of the piece, of what crime does Wiesel accuse the world, and how did this crime affect his future actions? **[Draw Conclusions]**

APPLY

4. Name two or three atrocities throughout history that were silently witnessed by some. **[Relate]**

EXTEND

5. What are some careers that might involve themselves with keeping historical memories alive? Explain your answer. **[Career Link]**

Guide for Responding (continued)

◆ Reading Strategy

IDENTIFY MAIN POINTS

Identifying a writer's main points is essential to understanding an essay. The main points of an essay may be stated in its introduction, developed and supported in the topic sentences of body paragraphs, and summarized in its conclusion.

As you read these essays, you paused to check your understanding by identifying the writer's main points and locating supporting details. Now, choose one of the essays and outline its main points. Under each main point in your outline, list supporting details or examples.

◆ Build Vocabulary

USING FORMS OF *RECIPROCITY*

Words such as *reciprocity* have other forms—nouns, adjectives, adverbs, or verbs. On your paper, complete each sentence with a form of *reciprocity*.

a. reciprocity   **c.** reciprocate
b. reciprocal   **d.** reciprocation

1. Pen pals have a _____?_____ arrangement.
2. The worldwide response to Solzhenitsyn's writing demonstrates the _____?_____ between writers and readers.
3. Although his situation did not allow him to _____?_____, he appreciated the support of other writers.
4. Now, in _____?_____, he acknowledges their help in his acceptance speech.

USING THE WORD BANK: Connotations

On your paper, write the word from the Word Bank that is suggested by each song title.

1. *All I Really Want to Do*
2. *(You Know) I Fit Right In*
3. *Give and Take*
4. *Speaking for Myself*
5. *My Love Is Higher Than the Sky*
6. *Without a Doubt (It Has to Be)*
7. *You're Always Turning Me Down*

◆ Literary Focus

REFLECTIVE AND PERSUASIVE ESSAYS

Your own ideas, experiences, and opinions affect the way you respond to Lu Hsun's thoughts in his **reflective essay** "This Too Is Life" and to the arguments in the **persuasive essays** by Solzhenitsyn and Wiesel.

1. How does Lu Hsun's recovery affect his appreciation of the "fearfulness of exhaustion" and the "comfort of rest"?
2. Identify an important realization to which Lu Hsun came during the course of his illness.
3. Analyze how well Solzhenitsyn argues his premise that world literature belongs to the world and not to a single country.
4. In your opinion, what is the most persuasive sentence in "Keep Memory Alive"? Explain your choice.

◆ Build Grammar Skills

CAPITALIZATION OF PROPER NOUNS AND ADJECTIVES

All **proper nouns** and **proper adjectives** begin with capital letters.

Practice Rewrite the following sentences, capitalizing the proper nouns and adjectives in each.
1. The chinese writer lu hsun first studied medicine in japan.
2. He then prepared himself for his literary career by learning to speak german and russian, and by studying western literature and philosophy.
3. lu hsun published many of his writings in a journal called *new life*.
4. The royal swedish academy of sciences awarded the jewish writer Elie Wiesel a nobel prize for his contributions to world peace.
5. The writer solzhenitsyn was surprised to receive greetings from european writers.

Writing Application Write a paragraph describing your achievements that would qualify you for a prize. Use at least two proper nouns and two proper adjectives.

Build Your Portfolio

Idea Bank

Writing

1. Letter Write a persuasive letter to convince a friend of the importance of remembering the Holocaust.

2. Report Write a two-page report on Communist Russia during the time Solzhenitsyn's work was being repressed, beginning in the 1940's. Emphasize the climate that resulted for writers.

3. Response to Criticism Assessing Lu Hsun's status as a leader in modern Chinese thought, Phillip Lopate observed that the "irony is that his work is irreconcilably individual . . . in feeling, tinged as it is with loneliness and sadness." Write a brief essay responding to this observation, using details from "This Too Is Life" to support your ideas.

Speaking, Listening, and Viewing

4. Persuasive Speech Choose an issue, such as whether gyms should be open at night, and give a five-minute speech persuading your audience to feel as you do. **[Performing Arts Link]**

5. Movie Review Find a copy of the movie *Shoah* and view it. Then, prepare a report for your classmates that describes the movie and offers your sense of what the film attempts. Also, tell whether you think it succeeds. **[History Link]**

Researching and Representing

6. Medical Report Lu Hsun died of tuberculosis in 1936. Research this disease—its history and how it can be cured. Present your findings to the class. **[Science Link]**

7. Writers in Prison Contact a human rights organization, or search the Internet to find out about writers who, like Solzhenitsyn, have been imprisoned as a result of what they write. **[Social Studies Link]**

Online Activity www.phlit.phschool.com

Guided Writing Lesson

Acceptance Speech

The Nobel Prize remarks of Solzhenitsyn and Wiesel have been read by people around the world. Write an acceptance speech for the award of your dreams. The achievement is up to you, but this is your chance to address yourself to the largest possible audience. Organize your speech around a strong and meaningful main point.

Writing Skills Focus: Placement for Emphasis

In a speech or persuasive essay, the **placement** of ideas can give them added emphasis. The last line of Elie Wiesel's speech—"Silence encourages the tormentor, never the tormented"—has tremendous staying power. Had he begun with this line, it might not have been as effective, because Wiesel needed to provide information to lead up to it.

Arrange your ideas in an order that is clear and logical and that emphasizes the most important points. You may, like Wiesel, choose to place your most important points at the end of your speech to make a strong final impression.

Prewriting What will be your most important point? Write a list of possible points, then cross out points that seem weaker or difficult to handle in the form of a speech.

Drafting As you draft, keep in mind the final point you plan to make. Lead up to it with examples, facts, or relevant details.

Revising Read your speech aloud to yourself. Is your key point placed effectively? Make any necessary changes to improve the effectiveness of your speech.

Check to be sure that you have capitalized all proper nouns and adjectives. For more on capitalization of proper nouns and adjectives, see pp. 720 and 732

Guide for Reading

Natalia Ginzburg *(1916–1991)*

You may think writers spend their time observing life from a distance. Often, though, history sweeps them up in its struggles. Noted for her fiction, drama, and essays, Italian author Natalia Ginzburg suffered personal tragedy in the struggle against fascism during World War II (1939–1945). Her successes after the war testify to the victory for which she and others struggled.

Dangerous Times Ginzburg was born Natalia Levi on the Italian island of Sicily. Attending the university in the mainland Italian city of Turin, Ginzburg traveled in a circle of intellectuals that included publisher Leone Ginzburg. Natalia and Leone married in 1938. Soon, however, their life together would be disrupted by larger forces.

In the 1940's, Italy, allied with Nazi Germany, was at war with the United States and its allies. Leone worked against Italy's fascist dictator, Benito Mussolini. In punishment, Leone was confined to a small village.

During the family's stay in the village, Ginzburg worked on a short novel called *The Road to the City,* published under a pen name with her husband's firm, Einaudi. In 1944, Leone returned to Rome to edit an anti-fascist newspaper while Natalia remained behind with their three small children. Arrested by the fascists, he died of torture in a prison just days before the Allies liberated Rome in 1944.

Years of Triumph After the liberation, Ginzburg worked for Leone's publishing company. In 1950, she married again and returned to Rome. Two years later, she produced one of her best-known novels, *All Our Yesterdays* (also called *A Light for Fools).* Like much of Ginzburg's writing, it scrutinizes family relationships and the roles of women in the modern world.

In 1983, Ginzburg was elected to Italy's parliament. Once victimized by her country, Ginzburg had become one of its leaders.

◆ Build Vocabulary

GREEK ROOTS: *-mim-*

In the essay, Ginzburg calls her husband "a good mimic" and later says that he *mimics* her. In Greek, a *mimus* was an actor, and the Greek root *-mim-* means "imitate." A *mimic* means "a person who imitates others"; *to mimic* is "to imitate others." You can find this same Greek root in the word *pantomime.*

palate
scorn
cadence
barren
mimic
immaculate
urbanely

WORD BANK

As you read this essay, you will encounter the words on this list. Each word is defined on the page where it first appears. Preview this list of words from the selection before you read.

◆ Build Grammar Skills

VARYING SENTENCE LENGTHS

A series of short, choppy sentences makes for very dull reading.

> He loves museums. I will go if forced. I find them unpleasant. Going is an effort and duty. He loves libraries. I hate them.

One way to achieve sentence variety is to vary the lengths of sentences. Here, for example, is a paragraph from "He and I" expressing the same ideas as those in the paragraph above. Note that it contains one rather long sentence and one short one:

> He loves museums, and I will go if I am forced to but with an unpleasant sense of effort and duty. He loves libraries and I hate them.

As you read the selection, consider how the use of different sentence lengths makes the material more interesting to read.

He and I

◆ *Literature and Your Life*

CONNECT YOUR EXPERIENCE

Someone you are close to—your best friend, for instance—can become a kind of mirror for you. You look at your friend, and you instantly see how you are similar and how you are different.

In "He and I," Natalia Ginzburg compares herself with her husband of many years.

Journal Writing Think of a married couple you know. List their similarities and differences in two columns, and then decide if they best illustrate the saying "Birds of a feather flock together" or "Opposites attract."

THEMATIC FOCUS: PEOPLE AND STYLES

As you read, ask yourself: How is Ginzburg different from her husband? How are they similar?

◆ Background for Understanding

CULTURE

The marriage Ginzburg describes in "He and I" (between herself and her second husband Gabrielle Baldini) is of a modern kind. Both she and her husband work professionally—he as a professor, she as a writer. They are largely equals.

Marriages in other periods of history assigned men and women different roles. For instance, until modern times European women had limited rights to own property. In middle-class families of the twentieth century, wives were often expected to maintain the home while men went off to work. These roles began to shift in the 1960's and 1970's.

◆ Literary Focus

PERSONAL ESSAY

An essay is a short work of nonfiction prose that usually focuses on a single subject. In a **personal essay,** the writer uses an informal, intimate style and tone to communicate and reflect on his or her experiences.

The subject of "He and I" is the author's marriage and the contrast between her and her husband's personalities. As you read the essay, consider just how personal it is. What private details does it provide about the author's life? What does it reveal about her feelings?

◆ Reading Strategy

RECOGNIZE PATTERNS OF ORGANIZATION

When you **recognize patterns of organization,** you notice the organizing principle that a writer uses to present and develop ideas. Your grasp of the pattern of organization will enable you to connect details you do not understand to details that are clear. In this way, you will gain insight into the significance of the details you do not understand.

The chart shows common patterns of organization. As you read "He and I," decide which pattern Ginzburg uses to present most or all of the material.

- **chronological order:** events in the order of occurrence
- **cause and effect:** how one event or group of events causes another
- **comparison and contrast:** similarities and differences between two things
- **order of importance:** from least to most important, or vice versa.

He And I

NATALIA GINZBURG

TRANSLATED BY DICK DAVIS

e always feels hot, I always feel cold. In the summer when it really is hot he does nothing but complain about how hot he feels. He is irritated if he sees me put a jumper¹ on in the evening.

He speaks several languages well; I do not speak any well. He manages—in his own way—to speak even the languages that he doesn't know.

He has an excellent sense of direction. I have none at all. After one day in a foreign city he can move about in it as thoughtlessly as a butterfly. I get lost in my own city; I have to ask directions so that I can get back home again. He hates asking directions; when we go by car to a town we don't know he doesn't want to ask directions and tells me to look at the map. I don't know how to read maps and I get confused by all the little red circles and he loses his temper.

He loves the theater, painting, music, especially music. I do not understand music at all, painting doesn't mean much to me and I get bored at the theater. I love and understand one thing in the world and that is poetry.

He loves museums, and I will go if I am forced to but with an unpleasant sense of effort and duty. He loves libraries and I hate them.

He loves traveling, unfamiliar foreign cities, restaurants. I would like to stay at home all the time and never move.

All the same I follow him on his many journeys. I follow him to museums, to churches, to the opera. I even follow him to concerts, where I fall asleep.

Because he knows the conductors and the singers, after the performance is over he likes to go and congratulate them. I follow him down long corridors lined with the singers' dressing-rooms and listen to him talking to people dressed as cardinals and kings.

He is not shy; I am shy. Occasionally however I have seen him be shy. With the police when they come over to the car armed with a notebook and pencil. Then he is shy, thinking he is in the wrong.

And even when he doesn't think he is in the wrong. I think he has a respect for established authority. I am afraid of established authority, but he isn't. He respects it. There is a difference. When I see a policeman coming to fine me I immediately think he is going to haul me off to prison. He doesn't think about prison; but, out of respect, he becomes shy and polite.

During the Montesi trial,² because of his respect for established authority, we had very violent arguments.

He likes tagliatelle,³ lamb, cherries, red wine. I like minestrone, bread soup, omelettes, green vegetables.

He often says I don't understand anything about food, that I am like a great strong fat friar—one of those friars who devour soup made from greens in the darkness of their monasteries; but he, oh he is refined and has a sensitive palate. In restaurants he makes long inquiries about the wines; he has them bring two or three bottles then looks at them and considers the matter, and slowly strokes his beard.

◆ **Literary Focus**
Up to this point, what evidence suggests that this is a personal essay? Explain.

There are certain restaurants in England where the waiter goes through a little ritual: he pours some wine into a glass so that the customer can test whether he likes it or not. He used to hate this ritual and always prevented the waiter from carrying it out by taking the bottle from him. I used to argue with him about this and say that you should let people carry out their prescribed tasks.

And in the same way he never lets the usherette at the cinema direct him to his seat. He immediately gives her a tip but dashes off to a completely different place from the one she shows him with her torch.

At the cinema he likes to sit very close to

---

1. **jumper:** Loose jacket or blouse.

◆ **Build Vocabulary**
palate (pal´ ət) *n.*: Sense of taste

---

2. **Montesi trial:** 1950's court case involving a murder in Rome that was believed by some to have been politically motivated.
3. **tagliatelle** (täl´ yə tel´ ē) *n.*: Pasta in the form of wide, flat noodles.

Picture From a Larger Cycle, Jan Preisler, National Gallery, Prague

the screen. If we go with friends and they look for seats a long way from the screen, as most people do, he sits by himself in the front row. I can see well whether I am close to the screen or far away from it, but when we are with friends I stay with them out of politeness; all the same it upsets me because I could be next to him two inches from the screen, and when I don't sit next to him he gets annoyed with me.

We both love the cinema, and we are ready to see almost any kind of film at almost any time of day. But he knows the history of the cinema in great detail; he remembers old directors and actors who have disappeared and been forgotten long ago, and he is ready to travel miles into the most distant suburbs in search of some ancient silent film in which an actor appears—perhaps just for a few seconds—whom he affectionately associates with memories of his early childhood. I remember one Sunday afternoon in London; somewhere in the distant suburbs on the edge of the countryside they were showing a film from the 1930s, about the French Revolution, which he had seen as a

▲ **Critical Viewing** Does this picture capture the type of relationship that the author describes? Why or why not? **[Interpret]**

child, and in which a famous actress of that time appeared for a moment or two. We set off by car in search of the street, which was a very long way off; it was raining, there was a fog, and we drove for hour after hour through identical suburbs, between rows of little gray houses, gutters and railings; I had the map on my knees and I couldn't read it and he lost his temper; at last, we found the cinema and sat in the completely deserted auditorium. But after a quarter of an hour, immediately after the brief appearance of the actress who was so important to him, he already wanted to go; I on the other hand, after seeing so many streets, wanted to see how the film finished. I don't remember whether we did what he wanted or what I wanted; probably what he wanted, so that we left after a quarter of an hour, also because it was late—though we had set off early in the afternoon it was already time for dinner. But when I begged him to tell me how the film ended I didn't get a very satisfactory answer; because, he said, the story wasn't at all important, the only thing that mattered was those few moments, that actress's curls, gestures, profile.

I never remember actors' names, and as I am not good at remembering faces it is often difficult for me to recognize even the most famous of them. This infuriates him; his scorn increases as I ask him whether it was this one or that one; "You don't mean to tell me," he says, "You don't mean to tell me that you didn't recognize William Holden!"[4]

And in fact I didn't recognize William Holden. All the same, I love the cinema too; but although I have been seeing films for years I haven't been able to provide myself with any sort of cinematic education. But he has made an education of it for himself and he does this with whatever attracts his curiosity; I don't know how to make myself an education out of anything, even those things that I love best in life; they stay with me as scattered images, nourishing my life with memories and emotions but without filling the void, the desert of my education.

He tells me I have no curiosity, but this is not true. I am curious about a few, a very few, things. And when I have got to know them I retain scattered impressions of them, or the cadence of phrase, or a word. But my world, in which these completely unrelated (unless in some secret fashion unbeknown to me) impressions and cadences rise to the surface, is a sad, barren place. His world, on the other hand, is green and populous and richly cultivated; it is a fertile, well-watered countryside in which woods, meadows, orchards and villages flourish.

Everything I do is done laboriously, with great difficulty and uncertainty. I am very lazy, and if I want to finish anything it is absolutely essential that I spend hours stretched out on the sofa. He is never idle, and is always doing something; when he goes to lie down in the afternoons he takes proofs to correct or a book full of notes; he wants us to go to the cinema, then to a reception, then to the theater—all on the same day. In one day he succeeds in doing, and in making me do, a mass of different things, and in meeting extremely diverse kinds of people. If I am alone and try to act as he does I get nothing at all done, because I get stuck all afternoon somewhere I had meant to stay for half an hour, or because I get lost and cannot find the right street, or because the most boring person and the one I least wanted to meet drags me off to the place I least wanted to go to.

If I tell him how my afternoon has turned out he says it is a completely wasted afternoon and is amused and makes fun of me and loses his temper; and he says that without him I am good for nothing.

I don't know how to manage my time; he does.

He likes receptions. He dresses casually, when everyone is dressed formally; the idea of changing his clothes in order to go to a reception never enters his head. He even goes in his old raincoat and crumpled hat; a woolen hat which he bought in London and which he wears pulled down over his eyes. He only stays for half an hour; he enjoys chatting with a glass in his hand for half an hour; he eats lots of *hors d'oeuvres*,[5] and I eat almost none because when I see him eating so many I feel that I at least must be well-mannered and show some self-control and not eat too much; after half an hour, just as I am beginning to feel at ease and to enjoy myself, he gets impatient and drags me away.

◆ **Literary Focus**
What pattern of organization does the writer use in these short paragraphs?

---

4. **William Holden** (1918–1981): American film actor who won an Oscar in 1953 for his performance in *Stalag 17*.

5. ***hors d'oeuvres*** (ôr′ dᵤrvz′) *n.*: Small appetizers usually served at the beginning of a meal.

◆ **Build Vocabulary**

scorn (skôrn) *n.*: Extreme contempt for someone or something

cadence (kād′ 'ns) *n.*: Rhythmic flow

barren (bar′ ən) *adj.*: Unproductive; lacking appeal

I don't know how to dance and he does.

I don't know how to type and he does.

I don't know how to drive. If I suggest that I should get a license, too, he disagrees. He says I would never manage it. I think he likes me to be dependent on him for some things.

I don't know how to sing and he does. He is a baritone. Perhaps he would have been a famous singer if he had studied singing.

Perhaps he would have been a conductor if he had studied music. When he listens to records he conducts the orchestra with a pencil. And he types and answers the telephone at the same time. He is a man who is able to do many things at once.

◆ Reading Strategy
In what way do statements beginning with "He . . ." and those beginning with "I . . ." organize this essay?

He is a professor and I think he is a good one.

He could have been many things. But he has no regrets about those professions he did not take up. I could only ever have followed one profession—the one I chose and which I have followed almost since childhood. And I don't have any regrets either about the professions I did not take up, but then I couldn't have succeeded at any of them.

I write stories, and for many years I have worked for a publishing house.

I don't work badly, or particularly well. All the same I am well aware of the fact that I would have been unable to work anywhere else. I get on well with my colleagues and my boss. I think that if I did not have the support of their friendship I would soon have become worn out and unable to work any longer.

For a long time I thought that one day I would be able to write screenplays for the cinema. But I never had the opportunity, or I did not know how to find it. Now I have lost all hope of writing screenplays. He wrote screenplays for a while, when he was younger. And he has worked in a publishing house. He has written stories. He has done all the things that I have done and many others too.

He is a good <u>mimic</u>, and does an old countess especially well. Perhaps he could also have been an actor.

Once, in London, he sang in a theater. He was Job.[6] He had to hire evening clothes; and there he was, in his evening clothes, in front of a kind of lectern; and he sang. He sang the words of Job; the piece called for something between speaking and singing. And I, in my box, was dying of fright. I was afraid he would get flustered, or that the trousers of his evening clothes would fall down.

He was surrounded by men in evening clothes and women in long dresses, who were the angels and devils and other characters in Job.

It was a great success, and they said that he was very good.

If I loved music I would love it passionately. But I don't understand it, and when he persuades me to go to concerts with him my mind wanders off and I think of my own affairs. Or I fall sound asleep.

I like to sing. I don't know how to sing and I sing completely out of tune; but I sing all the same—occasionally, very quietly, when I am alone. I know that I sing out of tune because others have told me so; my voice must be like the yowling of a cat. But I am not—in myself—aware of this, and singing gives me real pleasure. If he hears me he mimics me; he says that my singing is something quite separate from music, something invented by me.

When I was a child I used to yowl tunes I had made up. It was a long wailing kind of melody that brought tears to my eyes.

It doesn't matter to me that I don't understand painting or the figurative arts, but it hurts me that I don't love music, and I feel that my mind suffers from the absence of this love. But there is nothing I can do about it, I will never understand or love music. If I occasionally hear a piece of music that I like I don't know how to remember it; and how can I love something that I can't remember?

It is the words of a song that I remember. I can repeat words that I love over and over again. I repeat the tune that accompanies them too, in my own yowling fashion, and I experience a kind of happiness as I yowl.

When I am writing it seems to me that I

---

6. **Job** (jōb): A major figure in the Bible. One of the books of the Old Testament is named for him.

follow a musical cadence or rhythm. Perhaps music was very close to my world, and my world could not, for whatever reason, make contact with it.

In our house there is music all day long. He keeps the radio on all day. Or plays records. Every now and again I protest a little and ask for a little silence in which to work; but he says that such beautiful music is certainly conducive to any kind of work.

He has bought an incredible number of records. He says that he owns one of the finest collections in the world.

In the morning when he is still in his dressing gown and dripping water from his bath, he turns the radio on, sits down at the typewriter and begins his strenuous, noisy, stormy day. He is superabundant in everything; he fills the bath to overflowing, and the same with the teapot and his cup of tea. He has an enormous number of shirts and ties. On the other hand he rarely buys shoes.

His mother says that as a child he was a model of order and precision; apparently once, on a rainy day, he was wearing white boots and white clothes and had to cross some muddy streams in the country—at the end of his walk he was <u>immaculate</u> and his clothes and boots had not one spot of mud on them. There is no trace in him of that former immaculate little boy. His clothes are always covered in stains. He has become extremely untidy.

But he scrupulously keeps all the gas bills. In drawers I find old gas bills, which he refuses to throw away, from houses we left long ago.

I also find old, shriveled Tuscan cigars, and cigarette holders made from cherry wood.

I smoke a brand of king-size, filterless cigarettes called *Stop*, and he smokes his Tuscan cigars.

◆ Build Vocabulary

mimic (mim´ ik) *n.*: Someone who can imitate the speech and actions of others

immaculate (im mak´ yoo lit) *adj.*: Spotless; perfectly clean

La Primavera, Kuzma Petrov-Vodkin, Museo Statale Russo

▲ **Critical Viewing** Do the personalities of this couple contrast as strongly as those of the narrator and "He"? Explain. **[Compare and Contrast]**

I am very untidy. But as I have got older I have come to miss tidiness, and I sometimes furiously tidy up all the cupboards. I think this is because I remember my mother's tidiness. I rearrange the linen and blanket cupboards and in the summer I reline every drawer with strips of white cloth. I rarely rearrange my papers because my mother didn't write and had no papers. My tidiness and untidiness are full of complicated feelings of regret and sadness. His untidiness is triumphant. He has decided that it is proper and legitimate for a studious person like himself to have an untidy desk.

He does not help me get over my indecisiveness, or the way I hesitate before doing anything, or my sense of guilt. He tends to make fun of every tiny thing I do. If I go shopping in the market he follows me and spies on me. He makes fun of the way I shop, of the way I weigh the oranges in my hand unerringly choosing, he says, the worst in the whole market; he ridicules me for spending an hour over the shopping, buying onions at one stall, celery at another and fruit at another. Sometimes he does the shopping to show me how quickly he can do it; he unhesitatingly buys everything from one stall and then manages to get the basket delivered to the house. He doesn't buy celery because he cannot abide it.

◆ Reading Strategy
What personal revelations does the writer make in this paragraph?

And so—more than ever—I feel I do everything inadequately or mistakenly. But if I once find out that he has made a mistake I tell him so over and over again until he is exasperated. I can be very annoying at times.

His rages are unpredictable, and bubble over like the head on beer. My rages are unpredictable too, but his quickly disappear whereas mine leave a noisy nagging trail behind them which must be very annoying—like the complaining yowl of a cat.

Sometimes in the midst of his rage I start to cry, and instead of quietening him down and making him feel sorry for me this infuriates him all the more. He says my tears are just play-acting, and perhaps he is right. Because in the middle of my tears and his rage I am completely calm.

I never cry when I am really unhappy.

There was a time when I used to hurl plates and crockery on the floor during my rages. But not any more. Perhaps because I am older and my rages are less violent, and also because I dare not lay a finger on our plates now; we bought them one day in London, in the Portobello Road, and I am very fond of them.

The price of those plates, and of many other things we have bought, immediately underwent a substantial reduction in his memory. He likes to think he did not spend very much and that he got a bargain. I know the price of that dinner service—it was £16, but he says £12.[7] And it is the same with the picture of King

Lear[8] that is in our dining room, and which he also bought in the Portobello Road (and then cleaned with onions and potatoes); now he says he paid a certain sum for it, but I remember that it was much more than that.

Some years ago he bought twelve bedside mats in a department store. He bought them because they were cheap, and he thought he ought to buy them; and he bought them as an argument against me because he considered me to be incapable of buying things for the house. They were made of mud-colored matting and they quickly became very unattractive; they took on a corpse-like rigidity and were hung from a wire line on the kitchen balcony, and I hated them. I used to remind him of them, as an example of bad shopping; but he would say that they had cost very little indeed, almost nothing. It was a long time before I could bring myself to throw them out—because there were so many of them, and because just as I was about to get rid of them it occurred to me that I could use them for rags. He and I both find throwing things away difficult; it must be a kind of Jewish caution in me, and the result of my extreme indecisiveness; in him it must be a defense against his impulsiveness and open-handedness.

He buys enormous quantities of bicarbonate of soda[9] and aspirins.

Now and again he is ill with some mysterious ailment of his own; he can't explain what he feels and stays in bed for a day completely wrapped up in the sheets; nothing is visible except his beard and the tip of his red nose. Then he takes bicarbonate of soda and aspirins in doses suitable for a horse, and says that I cannot understand because I am always well, I am like those great fat strong friars who go out in the wind and in all weathers and come to no harm; he on the other hand is sensitive and delicate and suffers from mysterious ailments. Then in the evening he is better and goes into the kitchen and cooks himself tagliatelle.

When he was a young man he was slim,

7. **£16 . . . £12:** "£" is the symbol for the pound, the standard unit of currency in the United Kingdom.

8. **King Lear:** Title character of William Shakespeare's play *The Tragedy of King Lear*.
9. **bicarbonate of soda:** Another name for baking soda, which is sometimes used as an antacid.

handsome and finely built; he did not have a beard but long, soft moustaches instead, and he looked like the actor Robert Donat.[10] He was like that about twenty years ago when I first knew him, and I remember that he used to wear an elegant kind of Scottish flannel shirt. I remember that one evening he walked me back to the *pensione*[11] where I was living; we walked together along the *Via Nazionale*.[12] I already felt that I was very old and had been through a great deal and had made many mistakes, and he seemed a boy to me, light years away from me. I don't remember what we talked about on that evening walking along the *Via Nazionale*; nothing important, I suppose, and the idea that we would become husband and wife was light years away from me. Then we lost sight of each other, and when we met again he no longer looked like Robert Donat, but more like Balzac.[13] When we met again he

still wore his Scottish shirts but on him now they looked like garments for a polar expedition; now he had his beard and on his head he wore his ridiculous crumpled woolen hat; everything about him put you in mind of an imminent departure for the North Pole. Because, although he always feels hot, he has the habit of dressing as if he were surrounded by snow, ice and polar bears; or he dresses like a Brazilian coffee-planter, but he always dresses differently from everyone else.

If I remind him of that walk along the *Via Nazionale* he says he remembers it, but I know he is lying and that he remembers nothing; and I sometimes ask myself if it was us, these two people, almost twenty years ago on the *Via Nazionale*, two people who conversed so politely, so urbanely, as the sun was setting; who chatted a little about everything perhaps and about nothing; two friends talking, two young intellectuals out for a walk; so young, so educated, so uninvolved, so ready to judge one another with kind impartiality; so ready to say goodbye to one another for ever, as the sun set, at the corner of the street.

10. **Robert Donat** (1905–1958): Handsome British stage and film actor who won an Oscar in 1939 for his performance in *Goodbye, Mr. Chips.*
11. **pensione** (pen syō′ ne) *n.*: Boardinghouse.
12. **Via Nazionale** (vē′ ə nä′ tsē ə nä′ le): Well-known street in Rome.
13. **Balzac:** Honoré de Balzac (ô nô̂ rā′ də bál zàk′) (1799–1850): French novelist who had a small, roundish body shape.

◆ **Build Vocabulary**

urbanely (ur bān′ lē) *adv.*: In a smooth and polished way

Guide for Responding

◆ *Literature and Your Life*

Reader's Response Whom do you think you would rather know, the author or her husband? Why?

Thematic Focus Do the author and her husband have more in common than they seem to at first glance? How might their differences help bind them together? Explain your answer.

☑ **Check Your Comprehension**

1. Name five ways in which the author and her husband are different, according to the author.
2. Name one thing that the author feels she and her husband have in common.
3. Name two things that the author admires in her husband and two things that she criticizes.

Guide for Responding (continued)

◆ Critical Thinking

INTERPRET

1. What adjectives would you use to describe the husband? **[Synthesize]**
2. What adjectives would you use to describe the author? **[Synthesize]**
3. What do the last two paragraphs suggest about the difference between knowing a person as an acquaintance and being married to him or her? **[Interpret]**
4. Is the author's marriage a happy one? Explain why you think as you do. **[Draw Conclusions]**

APPLY

5. If you were the husband, what would you tell the author after reading this essay? **[Apply]**

EXTEND

6. Describe your own idea of an ideal marriage. Compare it to the portrait found in the essay. **[Social Studies Link]**

◆ Reading Strategy

RECOGNIZE PATTERNS OF ORGANIZATION

As you read "He and I," you probably recognized that the main **pattern of organization** was comparison-and-contrast.

1. What form of comparison-and-contrast does the author use—first one subject, then the next, or a point-by-point organization?
2. Does the author focus on the similarities or differences between her and her husband? Explain.

◆ Literary Focus

PERSONAL ESSAY

A **personal essay** uses an informal, intimate style and tone to communicate the author's experiences. In "He and I," Natalia Ginzburg provides her impressions and feelings about her husband and herself, and recalls experiences at different points in her marriage.

1. Cite three personal details about her marriage that Ginzburg provides.
2. Does the essay focus more on the author's experiences, impressions, or emotions? Support your answer with examples from the essay.

◆ Build Vocabulary

USING THE GREEK ROOT *-mim-*

Explain how the Greek root *-mim-*, meaning "imitate," figures into the meanings of these words.

1. mime   2. mimeograph   3. pantomime

USING THE WORD BANK: TRUE/FALSE

On your paper, write *T* if the statement is true and *F* if it is false.

1. Someone with a good *palate* will eat any dish with equal delight.
2. A person feeling *scorn* might sneer.
3. A musical *cadence* repeats the same note over and over.
4. Many crops grow on *barren* land.
5. A good *mimic* can reproduce the voices of others.
6. A well-kept hospital operating room is *immaculate*.
7. A person with country habits is behaving *urbanely*.

◆ Build Grammar Skills

VARYING SENTENCE LENGTHS

In the following paragraph from the selection, the **different sentence lengths** create sentence variety, preventing the writing from getting boring or choppy.

> If I loved music, I would love it passionately. But I don't understand it, and when he persuades me to go to concerts with him my mind wanders off and I think of my own affairs. Or I fall sound asleep.

Practice Rewrite this paragraph so that the sentence lengths are varied. Make your final version just five sentences long.

> Natalia Ginzburg was a famous Italian writer. She was born in Palermo, Sicily. She grew up in Turin. She went to the university there. Her first husband was a publisher. He published anti-fascist literature. The fascists arrested him. They tortured him to death. This was during World War II. After the war Ginzburg worked for a publisher. She married her second husband in 1950. He was an English professor. She describes him in the essay "He and I."

Build Your Portfolio

Idea Bank

Writing

1. **List** Write a list of at least ten tips that you would give the husband in "He and I" to make him a better, more considerate spouse. **[Career Link]**

2. **Advice Letters** Imagine that Ginzburg has written to an advice columnist to ask about ways to improve her marriage. Write the letter she might have written and the response she might have received. **[Career Link]**

3. **Character's Response** Imagine that the husband has just read "He and I." Write his response in the form of a personal essay entitled "She and I." Present essay details from the husband's viewpoint, and add other details if necessary.

Speaking, Listening, and Viewing

4. **Dramatic Scene** With a classmate, take the roles of Ginzburg and her husband in one of the incidents in "He and I" and present it to the class. **[Performing Arts Link]**

5. **Role Play** Imagine that Ginzburg and her husband have visited a marriage counselor to discuss details of their marriage and learn how to be more compatible. With two other students, role-play the scene in the counselor's office. **[Performing Arts Link]**

Researching and Representing

6. **Two Portraits** Create a dual portrait based on the details in the selection. On the left, paint or draw Ginzburg's husband; on the right, paint or draw Ginzburg herself. **[Art Link]**

7. **Musical Recordings** According to the essay, Ginzburg's husband is a music lover. Record an audiocassette of music that you think the husband would like. Share the cassette with classmates, identifying each piece and briefly explaining why you think Ginzburg's husband would like it. **[Music Link]**

Online Activity www.phlit.phschool.com

Guided Writing Lesson

Account of a Friendship

Like the husband and wife in "He and I," some friends can be very different from each other. Other friends may share many characteristics in common. Write a brief account of one of your own friendships, focusing on the similarities and differences between you and your friend. Make sure that your account has **coherence** in that the ideas are connected.

Writing Skills Focus: Use Synonyms for Coherence

Writing displays **coherence** when there is a clear connection between ideas. One way to create coherence is to use **synonyms** (words with similar meanings) to tie ideas together, as in this example, which uses the synonyms *movies* and *films*:

Model
Draft: I like the movies. He likes reading.
Revision: I like the *movies*. He likes a few *films*, but he prefers reading.

Prewriting On a two-column chart, jot down details about you (left column) and your friend (right column). Include personality traits, activities, attitudes, and details about your backgrounds and interests. Draw arrows in one color between similar details, and arrows in another color between contrasting details.

Drafting Begin your account with a general statement about your friendship. Then, describe the friendship, providing details to support broader observations. Use chronological order, comparison-and-contrast, or any other method of organization that you think works best.

Revising Be sure that your ideas are organized and coherent; if not, use synonyms and transitions to make the relationships clearer. Also, check that you have varied your sentence lengths. For more on varying sentence lengths, see pp. 734 and 744.

Guide for Reading

Isak Dinesen (1885–1962)

The vivid and mysterious works of Isak Dinesen are the products of her unusual life experiences. Combining elements of her Danish heritage with strong impressions gathered from seventeen years living in Africa, Dinesen wrote tales and scenes rich with strong imagery and highly-polished prose.

From Europe to Africa Born Karen Christence Dinesen in Rungsted, Denmark, Dinesen studied painting at the Academy of Fine Arts in Copenhagen. After marrying Baron Bror Blixen-Finecke in 1914, she moved to British East Africa (now Kenya), where she and her husband ran a coffee plantation. Although she divorced her husband in 1921, she remained in Africa for ten more years, until falling coffee prices forced her to abandon her plantation and move back to Denmark.

International Success Dinesen related her African experiences in *Out of Africa* (1937), which was published in both English and Danish and made her internationally famous. The book offers a moving picture of the African landscape and people, coupled with a poignant regret for the disappearance of many traditional customs.

Fantastic Characters *Out of Africa* was only one of many books that Dinesen produced in the years after her return to Denmark. Most of her books, including *Seven Gothic Tales* (1934), *Winter's Tales* (1942), *Last Tales* (1957), *Anecdotes of Destiny* (1958), and *Ehrengard* (1963), are collections of short stories. Generally, her stories are set in the past in romantic or mysterious places, and they often involve fantastic characters and situations.

"Some African Birds" is an essay from Dinesen's popular memoir *Out of Africa*. The essay draws fascinating comparisons between the European and African worlds that shaped Dinesen's life and writing.

◆ Build Vocabulary

LATIN SUFFIXES: *-ous*

Dinesen describes storks as "tall and ponderous birds." The Latin suffix *-ous* (spelled *-us* in Latin) means "full of." Joined with a Latin root meaning "weight," *ponderous* means "full of weight" or "heavy."

ponderous
scintillating
affectation
deportment
prudery

WORD BANK

As you read this essay, you will encounter the words on this list. Each word is defined on the page where it first appears. Preview the list before you read.

◆ Build Grammar Skills

COHERENCE: TIME TRANSITIONS

Throughout this essay, Dinesen uses **time transitions,** phrases that indicate a precise time order, to create a coherent chronology. She opens her observations with these time transitions:

"Just at the beginning of the long rains, in the last week of March, or the first week of April, I have heard the nightingale in the woods of Africa."

As you read "Some African Birds," look for other time transitions that help create coherence.

Some African Birds

◆ *Literature and Your Life*

CONNECT YOUR EXPERIENCE

When you travel, even familiar sights may seem new and different. For example, a squirrel in a city you are visiting may capture your attention, whereas a squirrel on your school grounds may not.

In this essay, Dinesen describes some birds she sees while in Africa. Some, such as the stork, she has seen often in Europe. Others, such as the greater hornbill, are unfamiliar to her.

Journal Writing In your journal, describe a sight you have seen that you find interesting.

THEMATIC FOCUS: THE NATURAL WORLD

As you read this essay, ask: What can people learn from observing the natural world around them?

◆ Background for Understanding

BACKGROUND FOR UNDERSTANDING SCIENCE

In "Some African Birds," Isak Dinesen describes birds that come to call on her plantation in Africa. Many of those birds would migrate there in springtime.

Some birds spend as much as six months a year migrating. The migration patterns of European storks have been studied by amateur and professional scientists for hundreds of years. Two distinct routes have been identified: Some storks fly east, passing through Turkey on their way to Africa. Others fly west, crossing Spain before reaching Africa. The storks then return to Europe, following different migration routes.

◆ Literary Focus

DESCRIPTIVE ESSAY

"Some African Birds" is a descriptive essay, a short, nonfiction work that contains details showing how something looks, feels, smells, sounds, or tastes. As you read, notice Dinesen's use of language that appeals to your senses, like "high shrill shrieks" and "delicate pale gray coloring." These vivid descriptions help these unusual birds travel from Africa into your imagination.

You may want to keep track of the types of descriptive details Dinesen uses by filling out a chart like this one:

◆ Reading Strategy

VARY READING RATE

As you read nonfiction, follow your instincts to vary your reading rate, or adjust your reading speed to match your purpose for reading.

When you are reading a detailed description for the first time, read slowly and attentively, pausing to build a full mental image. If you are looking for a fact or reviewing a selection to find a detail you have forgotten, you may want to skim quickly until you locate the relevant passage.

As you read "Some African Birds," you may want to slow down whenever Dinesen offers a detailed description of a type of bird she observed.

Descriptive Details				
Sight	Sound	Smell	Taste	Touch

Some African Birds

Isak Dinesen

▲ **Critical Viewing** Does this secretary bird look—in Dinesen's words—"tall and ponderous"? Why or why not? **[Make a Judgment]**

Just at the beginning of the long rains, in the last week of March, or the first week of April, I have heard the nightingale in the woods of Africa. Not the full song: a few notes only—the opening bars of the concerto,[1] a rehearsal, suddenly stopped and again begun. It was as if, in the solitude of the dripping woods, someone was, in a tree, tuning a small cello. It was, however, the same melody, and the same abundance and sweetness, as were soon to fill the forests of Europe, from Sicily to Elsinore.[2]

We had the black and white storks in Africa, the birds that build their nests upon the thatched village roofs of Northern Europe. They look less imposing in Africa than they do there, for here they had such tall and ponderous birds as the marabout and the secretary bird to be compared to. The storks have got other habits in Africa than in Europe, where they live as in married couples and are symbols of domestic happiness. Here they are seen together in big flights, as in clubs. They are called locust-birds in Africa, and follow along when the locusts come upon the land, living high on them. They fly over the plains, too, where there is a grass-fire on, circling just in front of the advancing line of small leaping flames, high up in the scintillating rainbow-colored air, and the gray smoke, on watch for the mice and snakes that run from the fire. The storks have a gay time in Africa. But their real life is not here, and when the winds of spring bring back thoughts of mating and nesting, their hearts are turned towards the North, they remember old times and places and fly off, two and two, and are shortly after wading in the cold bogs of their birthplaces.

Out on the plains, in the beginning of the rains, where the vast stretches of burnt grass begin to show fresh green sprouting, there are

---

1. **concerto** (kən cher′ tō) *n.*: Musical composition for one or more solo instruments and an orchestra, usually in three symphonic movements.
2. **from Sicily** (sis′ əl ē) **to Elsinore** (el′ sə nôr′): Sicily is an island off the southern tip of Italy. Elsinore is a city in Denmark.

many hundred plovers. The plains always have a maritime air, the open horizon recalls the sea and the long sea-sands, the wandering wind is the same, the charred grass has a saline smell, and when the grass is long it runs in waves all over the land. When the white carnation flowers on the plains you remember the chopping white-specked waves all around you as you are tacking up the Sund. Out on the plains the plovers likewise take on the appearance of sea-birds, and behave like sea-birds on a beach, legging it, on the closing grass, as fast as they can for a short time, and then rising before your horse with high shrill shrieks, so that the light sky is all alive with wings and birds' voices.

The crested cranes, which come on to the newly rolled and planted maize-land, to steal the maize out of the ground, make up for the robbery by being birds of good omen, announcing the rain; and also by dancing to us. When the tall birds are together in large numbers, it is a fine sight to see them spread their wings and dance. There is much style in the dance, and a little <u>affectation</u>, for why, when they can fly, do they jump up and down as if they were held on to the earth by magnetism? The whole ballet has a sacred look, like some ritual dance; perhaps the cranes are making an attempt to join Heaven and earth like the winged angels walking up and down Jacob's Ladder.[3] With their delicate pale grey coloring, the little black velvet skull–cap and the fan-shaped crown, the cranes have all the air of light, spirited frescoes.[4] When, after they dance, they lift and

▲ Critical Viewing Does this picture of flamingoes support Dinesen's description of them as "the most delicately colored of all African birds"? Why or why not? **[Make a Judgment]**

go away, to keep up the sacred tone of the show they give out, by the wings or the voice, a clear ringing note, as if a group of church bells had taken to the wing and were sailing off. You can hear them a long way away, even after the birds themselves have become invisible in the sky: a chime from the clouds.

◆ Literary Focus
How does Dinesen enhance her description with lively comparisons? Explain.

The greater hornbill was another visitor to the farm, and came there to eat the fruits of the cape-chestnut tree. They are very strange birds. It is an adventure or an experience to meet them, not altogether pleasant, for they look exceedingly knowing. One morning before sunrise I was woken up by a loud jabbering outside the house, and when I walked out on the terrace I saw forty-one hornbills sitting in the trees on the lawn. There they looked less like birds than like some fantastic articles of finery set on the trees here and there by a child.

◆ **Build Vocabulary**

ponderous (pän´ dər əs) *adj.*: Heavy and bulky
scintillating (sint´ 'l āt iŋ) *adj.*: Sparkling; flashing
affectation (af´ ek tā´ shən) *n.*: Artificial behavior meant to impress others

---

3. **Jacob's Ladder** In the Bible, Jacob dreamt of a ladder from Earth to Heaven.
4. **frescoes** (fres´ kōz) *n.*: Paintings of a type in which watercolors are applied to wet plaster.

Black they all were, with the sweet, noble black of Africa, deep darkness absorbed through an age, like old soot, that makes you feel that for elegance, vigor and vivacity, no color rivals black. All the hornbills were talking together in the merriest mood, but with choice deportment, like a party of inheritors after a funeral. The morning air was as clear as crystal, the somber party was bathing in freshness and purity, and, behind the trees and the birds, the sun came up, a dull red ball. You wonder what sort of a day you are to get after such an early morning.

The flamingoes are the most delicately colored of all the African birds, pink and red like a flying twig of an oleander bush. They have incredibly long legs and bizarre and recherché[5] curves of their necks and bodies, as if from some exquisite traditional prudery they were making all attitudes and movements in life as difficult as possible.

I once traveled from Port Said to Marseilles[6] in a French boat that had on board a consignment of a hundred and fifty flamingoes, which were going to the *Jardin D'Acclimatation*[7] in Marseilles. They were kept in large dirty cases with canvas sides, ten in each, standing up close to one another. The keeper, who was taking the birds over, told me that he was counting on losing twenty per cent of them on a trip. They were not made for that sort of life, in rough weather they lost their balance, their legs broke, and the other birds in the cage trampled on them. At night when the wind was high in the Mediterranean and the ship came down in the waves with a thump, at each wave I heard, in the dark, the flamingoes shriek. Every morning, I saw the keeper taking out one or two dead birds, and throwing them overboard. The noble wader of the Nile, the sister of the lotus,[8] which floats over the landscape like a stray cloud of sunset, had become a slack cluster of pink and red feathers with a pair of long, thin sticks attached to it. The dead birds floated on the water for a short time, knocking up and down in the wake of the ship before they sank.

---

8. **noble wader . . . lotus:** The flamingo wades in the Nile, the main river of Egypt, much as the lotus, a pink waterlilly, floats in the Nile.

---

5. **recherché** (rə sher´ shā) *adj.*: Refined and elegant.
6. **from Port Said** (sä ēd´) **to Marseilles** (mär sā´): Port Said is located on the north coast of Egypt. Marseilles is located on the south coast of France.
7. *Jardin D'Acclimatation* (zhàr dan´ dá´ kli mi tá´ sē ōn´): A zoo.

◆ **Build Vocabulary**

deportment (dē pôrt´ mənt) *n.*: Manner of behaving or carrying oneself

prudery (prōod´ ər ē) *n.*: Tendency to show too much modesty

Guide for Responding

◆ *Literature and Your Life*

Reader's Response Which bird's personality does Dinesen capture most effectively? Explain.

Thematic Focus What kinds of insights can a person who studies nature gather only from direct observation?

☑ Check Your Comprehension

1. What is the topic of this essay?
2. Why are crested cranes considered good omens in Africa?
3. Where was the boat from Port Said taking a consignment of flamingoes?

◆ Critical Thinking

INTERPRET

1. How are storks in Europe and in Africa similar and different? [Compare and Contrast]
2. How does Dinesen show respect for the birds she describes? [Infer]
3. What does the final image suggest about Dinesen's view of the balance between humans and nature? [Draw Conclusions]

EVALUATE

4. How well does Dinesen capture the appearance and habits of the birds she describes? Explain. [Assess]

Guide for Responding *(continued)*

◆ Reading Strategy

VARY READING RATE

Your purpose for reading should determine your **reading rate,** the speed at which you read. You might, for example, skim an essay to get an overview of its content, but you would read slowly and carefully to gain a deep understanding of what it has to say.

1. What reading rate did you choose for "Some African Birds"? Why?
2. Describe how you would read to review Dinesen's depiction of the greater hornbill.
3. Dinesen's language is rich in images and includes many poetic elements, such as metaphors and personification. How do these devices affect your reading rate?
4. What reading rate would you use to find the word "consignment" in this essay? Explain your answer.

◆ Build Vocabulary

USING THE LATIN SUFFIX -OUS

Knowing that the Latin suffix -ous means "full of," match each word with its definition.

1. generous   **a.** full of generosity
2. imperious   **b.** full of grace
3. luxurious   **c.** full of arrogance
4. gracious   **d.** full of riches

USING THE WORD BANK: Analogies

On your paper, write the word from the Word Bank that will make the relationship between the second pair of words similar to the relationship between the first pair. Use each word only once.

1. *Solemn* is to *serious* as *interesting* is to ___?___.
2. *Instruction* is to *training* as *behavior* is to ___?___.
3. *Praise* is to *censure* as *sincerity* is to ___?___.
4. *Hummingbird* is to *flighty* as *elephant* is to ___?___.
5. *Contempt* is to *admiration* as *boldness* is to ___?___.

◆ Literary Focus

DESCRIPTIVE ESSAY

A **descriptive essay** is a short, nonfiction work in which sensory details help readers envision the subject. To bring unfamiliar African birds to life for her readers, Dinesen uses many descriptive techniques, including vivid words and interesting comparisons.

1. Which of Dinesen's descriptions do you find most effective? Why?
2. Identify two similes—a comparison using the words *like* or *as*—that Dinesen uses in her essay.
3. Within the essay, find examples of language that appeals to each of the five senses.

◆ Build Grammar Skills

COHERENCE: TIME TRANSITIONS

In this essay, Dinesen uses **time transitions**—words and phrases that indicate time order. Time transitions help readers understand when various events take place. In the following passage from the essay, the time transitions are italicized:

One morning, before sunrise I was woken up by a loud jabbering outside the house, . . .

Practice In your notebook, identify the time transition(s) in each passage.

1. It was, however, the same melody, and the same abundance and sweetness, as were soon to fill the forests of Europe . . .
2. Out on the plains, in the beginning of the rains, where the vast stretches of burnt grass begin to show fresh green sprouting . . .
3. When, after they dance, they lift and go away, to keep up the sacred tone of the show they give out, by the wings or the voice, a clear ringing note . . .
4. You can hear them a long way away, even after the birds themselves have become invisible in the sky: . . .
5. Every morning, I saw the keeper taking out one or two dead birds . . .

Build Your Portfolio

Idea Bank

Writing

1. **Advertisement** Write an advertisement for the tourist board of Kenya. In your ad, emphasize the diversity of natural life there.

2. **Letter to the Author** Write a letter to the author in response to "Some African Birds." In your letter, share your response to the essay. Use details from the essay to illustrate the points you make.

3. **Fable** Choose one of the birds in Dinesen's essay, and write a fable that features that bird's unique characteristics. Keep your fable brief, and be sure that it has a moral, or lesson to teach.

Speaking, Listening, and Viewing

4. **Audio Book** Create an audio recording of "Some African Birds." Practice reading the essay aloud to determine a speaking rate that is clear and effective. Record your reading and share it with others. **[Performing Arts Link]**

5. **Interview** With a partner, prepare and present an "interview" with Isak Dinesen. During the presentation, the interviewer should ask Dinesen about living in Kenya and operating a coffee plantation. **[Performing Arts Link]**

Researching and Representing

6. **Bird Chart** Create a poster to help identify the birds described in Dinesen's essay. Choose a logical organization for your chart, such as region by region or size of bird. Post your chart in the classroom. **[Science Link]**

7. **Multimedia Presentation** Learn more about the African country Kenya. For example, research its location, natural resources, music, and topography. Then, share your findings with the class in the form of a multimedia presentation. **[Social Studies Link]**

Online Activity www.phlit.phschool.com

Guided Writing Lesson

Observation

In "Some African Birds," Dinesen shares her observations of birds. An observation is a firsthand, factual account of an event or experience. Like Dinesen, write your own observation of an aspect of nature. You might, for example, decide to describe a bird, an ant, or a stray dog. Alternatively, you might choose to describe a plant or even a weather condition.

Writing Skills Focus: Outlining

After conducting your observation, organize your thoughts. An **outline** such as this one will help you plan an effective, coherent organization. The following outline reflects the opening elements of "Some African Birds."

Essay Outline

I. Introduction
II. Storks
    A. What storks are like in Europe
    B. What storks are like in Africa
III. Plovers
    A. Plains are like oceans
    B. Plovers move about like sea-birds

Prewriting Conduct your observation of the subject you chose. Take careful notes during and after your viewing, and organize your ideas into an outline.

Drafting Use your outline to guide your first draft. If, while drafting, you think of a new idea, write it down and then use your outline to help you get back on track. As you write, choose descriptive words that are precise and vivid.

Revising Read your observation aloud to a partner, and ask for feedback. Rearrange stray details to better fit the organization you have chosen. Then, proofread your observation carefully to correct grammar, spelling, and punctuation errors.

Check to see that you have used time transitions to make your observation more coherent. For more on such transitions, see pp. 746 and 751.

PART 2 *A Variety of Essays*

The Totonaca Civilization-The Great Pyramid of Tajin, Diego Rivera, National Palace, Mexico City

Guide for Reading

Vincent Canby *(1924–2000)*

If you were looking for all the news fit to print about movies between 1969 and 1993, you would have, no doubt, read the film reviews written by the lead film critic of *The New York Times*, Vincent Canby. In addition to theater and film reviews, he also wrote the play *After All* (1981) and the novel *Unnatural Scenery* (1979). For many years he produced movie reviews as the Sunday drama critic for *The New York Times*.

Roger Ebert *(1942–)*

Thumbs up, thumbs down. These symbols for movies worth seeing or avoiding were made popular by the duo of Roger Ebert and the late Gene Siskel, Chicago-based movie reviewers and co-hosts of their own television program. Roger Ebert's reviews appear in the *Chicago Sun-Times* and two hundred other newspapers around the country. He has won two Pulitzer Prizes for his work. About movie viewing he has said: "The audience: In the dark, lined up facing the screen. The light comes from behind their heads—from back there where dreams come true."

◆ Build Vocabulary

CONNOTATIONS

In his review of the re-released 1997 version of *Star Wars*, Roger Ebert describes Han Solo, the character portrayed by Harrison Ford, as "laconic." The denotation, or dictionary definition, of *laconic* is "using few words to express thoughts." In this case, *laconic* has a connotation as well. A connotation is what a word suggests or implies. A *laconic* character is a person who not only uses few words, but usually does so almost impolitely because he or she understands the uselessness of idle chatter.

apotheosis
eclectic
facetiousness
adroit
piously
condescension
watershed
synthesis
fastidious
effete
laconic

WORD BANK

As you read these reviews, you will encounter the words in this list. Each word is defined on the page where it first appears. Preview the list before you read, and look for each word as it appears in the reviews.

◆ Build Grammar Skills

PARENTHETICAL INTERRUPTERS

As if they are having an informal conversation about a movie, reviewers add side remarks that interrupt the main flow of a sentence. These remarks are **parenthetical interrupters**—expressions that comment on or give additional information about the main part of a sentence. Because they interrupt the main idea, they are set off from the rest of the sentence with commas.

Look at these sentences from the movie reviews of *Star Wars* by Vincent Canby and Roger Ebert. The parenthetical interrupters are italicized:

All of these works, *of course,* had earlier left their marks . . .

Those who analyze its philosophy do so, *I imagine,* with a smile in their minds.

As you read these reviews, notice how such remarks make you feel that the reviewers are engaged in a conversation with you.

Star Wars: A Trip to a Far Galaxy That's Fun and Funny . . .
◆ Star Wars: Breakthrough Film Still Has the Force ◆

◆ *Literature and Your Life*

CONNECT YOUR EXPERIENCE

You're sitting in a crowded movie theater. The houselights dim. The audience, once chattering away, falls silent. As the projector cackles and the screen in front of you bursts into sight and sound, you feel a tinge of excitement and anticipation.

Sometimes a film is so bad that you feel that you've wasted both your time and money. Other times, you're pleasantly surprised. Occasionally, a film comes along that completely surpasses any expectations you may have had and redefines the movie-going experience for you. For millions of people, *Star Wars* was just such a film.

THEMATIC FOCUS: TO THE FUTURE

What movie have you seen recently that you think will still be popular twenty years from now? Why?

Journal Writing Imagine that a Hollywood studio has given you an unlimited budget to produce and direct a film. What kind of film would you make, and why?

◆ Background for Understanding

CULTURE

If you travel down a long road, certain landmarks—say, a mountain, gorge, or building—will at once jump out at you and remain in your memory long after the trip has ended. These landmarks help define the road and put it in perspective. In a similar way, movies and other art forms become cultural landmarks for entire generations. From the moment in 1977 when *Star Wars* first opened, it became a landmark in the lives of people who were old enough to go see it at the movie theater. These reviews will help you understand why *Star Wars* is considered a landmark in cinema.

◆ Literary Focus

CRITICAL REVIEW

If you see a terrific movie, you might try to persuade a friend to go see it. Film critics provide this service for millions of newspaper readers every day. Reviewers, using evidence to support any claims, aim to convince you to follow their recommendation. They write **critical reviews** in which they discuss the various elements of a film and recommend that you see it—or not see it. Critical reviews tend to be persuasive.

◆ Reading Strategy

IDENTIFY EVIDENCE

When you read a piece that is intended to persuade you, it is important that you identify the evidence the writer uses to support his or her claims. **Evidence** may be facts, statistics, observations, examples, and statements from authorities that support the writer's opinion.

Look to identify evidence that supports the claims each reviewer makes. You might use a chart like the one below. Then determine whether or not there is enough evidence to support the claim.

Claim	Evidence
	✓
	✓
	✓
	✓
	✓
	✓
	✓
	✓
	✓

STAR WARS

—A TRIP TO A FAR GALAXY THAT'S FUN AND FUNNY ...

Vincent Canby
from *The New York Times*, May 26, 1977

"Star Wars," George Lucas's first film since his terrifically successful "American Graffiti," is the movie that the teen-agers in "American Graffiti" would have broken their necks to see. It's also the movie that's going to entertain a lot of contemporary folk who have a soft spot for the virtually ritualized manners of comic-book adventure.

"Star Wars," which opened yesterday[1] at the Astor Plaza, Orpheum and other theaters, is the most elaborate, most expensive, most beautiful movie serial ever made. It's both an apotheosis of "Flash Gordon" serials and a witty critique that makes associations with a variety of literature that is nothing if not eclectic: "Quo Vadis?", "Buck Rogers," "Ivanhoe," "Superman," "The Wizard of Oz," "The Gospel According to St. Matthew," the legend of King Arthur and the knights of the Round Table.

All of these works, of course, had earlier left their marks on the kind of science-fiction comic strips that Mr. Lucas, the writer as well as director of "Star Wars," here remembers with affection of such cheerfulness that he avoids facetiousness. The way definitely not to approach "Star Wars," though, is to expect a film of cosmic implications or to footnote it with so many references that one anticipates it as if it were a literary duty. It's fun and funny.

The time, according to the opening credit card, is "a long time ago" and the setting "a galaxy far far away," which gives Mr. Lucas and his associates total freedom to come up with their own landscapes, housing, vehicles, weapons, religion, politics—all of which are variations on the familiar.

When the film opens, dark times have fallen upon the galactal empire once ruled, we are given to believe, from a kind of space-age Camelot. Against these evil tyrants there is, in progress, a rebellion led by a certain Princess Leia Organa, a pretty round-faced young woman of old-fashioned pluck who, before you can catch your breath, has been captured by the guardians of the empire. Their object is to retrieve some secret plans that can be the empire's undoing.

That's about all the plot that anyone of voting age should be required to keep track of. The story of "Star Wars" could be written on the head of a pin and still leave room for the Bible. It is, rather, a breathless succession of escapes, pursuits, dangerous missions, unexpected encounters, with each one ending in some kind of defeat until the final one.

◆ **Reading Strategy**
What evidence does Canby give to support his claim that the film is "fun and funny"?

These adventures involve, among others, an ever-optimistic young man named Luke Skywalker (Mark Hamill), who is innocent without being naive; Han Solo (Harrison Ford), a free-booting freelance, space-ship captain who goes where he can make the most money, and an old mystic named Ben Kenobi (Alec Guinness), one of the last of the Old Guard, a fellow in possession of what's called "the force," a mixture of what appears to be ESP and early Christian faith.

Accompanying these three as they set out to liberate the princess and restore justice to the empire are a pair of Laurel-and-Hardyish robots. The thin one, who looks like a sort of brass woodman, talks in the polished phrases of a valet ("I'm adroit but I'm not very knowledgeable"), while the squat one, shaped like a portable washing machine, who is the one with the knowledge, simply squeaks and blinks his

---

1. **which opened yesterday:** Wednesday, May 25, 1977.

◀ **Critical Viewing** In what ways do R2-D2 and C-3PO remind you of Laurel and Hardy? [Compare]

◆ **Build Vocabulary**
apotheosis (ə päth´ ē ō´ sis) *n.*: Glorification of a person or thing; raising of something to the status of a god
eclectic (ek lek´ tik) *adj.*: Composed of material from various sources
facetiousness (fə sē´ shəs nəs) *n.*: Act of making jokes at an inappropriate time
adroit (ə droit´) *adj.*: Clever

lights. They are the year's best new comedy team.

In opposition to these good guys are the imperial forces led by someone called the Grand Moff Tarkin (Peter Cushing) and his executive assistant, Lord Darth Vader (David Prowse), a former student of Ben Kenobi who elected to leave heaven sometime before to join the evil ones.

The true stars of "Star Wars" are John Barry, who was responsible for the production design, and the people who were responsible for the incredible special effects—space ships, explosions of stars, space battles, hand-to-hand combat with what appear to be lethal neon swords. I have a particular fondness for the look of the interior of a gigantic satellite called the Death Star, a place full of the kind of waste space one finds today only in old Fifth Avenue mansions and public libraries.

There's also a very funny sequence in a low-life bar on a remote planet, a frontierlike establishment where they serve customers who look like turtles, apes, pythons and various amalgams of same, but draw the line at robots. Says the bartender piously: "We don't serve *their* kind here."

It's difficult to judge the performances in a film like this. I suspect that much of the time the actors had to perform with special effects that were later added in the laboratory. Yet everyone treats his material with the proper combination of solemnity and good humor that avoids condescension. One of Mr. Lucas's particular achievements is the manner in which he is able to recall the tackiness of the old comic strips and serials he loves without making a movie that is, itself, tacky. "Star Wars" is good enough to convince the most skeptical 8-year-old sci-fi buff, who is the toughest critic.

◆ Build Vocabulary

piously (pī' əs lē) *adv.*: With actual or pretended religious devotion

condescension (kän' di sen' shən) *n.*: Looking down upon; regarding as below one's dignity

Guide for Responding

◆ *Literature and Your Life*

Reader's Response Do you think you would enjoy this movie based on Canby's review?
Thematic Focus How does *Star Wars* combine the past and the future?

☑ Check Your Comprehension

1. What are two sources that inspired *Star Wars*?
2. Summarize the plot elements of *Star Wars* that Canby identifies as all you "should be required to keep track of."
3. According to Canby, who are the "true stars" of *Star Wars*?

◆ Critical Thinking

INTERPRET

1. Why do you think Canby considers an "8-year-old sci-fi buff" the toughest critic of *Star Wars*? **[Speculate]**
2. Did Canby enjoy watching *Star Wars*? Explain. **[Infer]**
3. Explain how each of these elements affects Canby's evaluation of the film: acting, plot, special effects. **[Evaluate]**

EXTEND

4. What three skills do you think are important for a movie reviewer to have to judge movies well and to write interesting reviews? **[Career Link]**

Star Wars

Breakthrough Film Still Has the Force

Roger Ebert
Of the *Chicago Sun-Times*

**from *The Oakland Press*,
Friday, January 31, 1997**

To see "Star Wars" again after 20 years is to revisit a place in the mind. George Lucas' space epic has colonized our imaginations, and it is hard to stand back and see it simply as a motion picture because it has so completely become part of our memories. It's as goofy as a children's tale, as shallow as an old Saturday afternoon serial, as corny as Kansas in August—and a masterpiece. Those who analyze its philosophy do so, I imagine, with a smile in their minds. May the Force be with them.

Like "Birth of a Nation" and "Citizen Kane," "Star Wars" was a technical <u>watershed</u> that influenced many of the movies that came after. These films have little in common, except for the way they came along at a crucial moment in cinema history, when new methods were ripe for <u>synthesis</u>. "Birth of a Nation" brought together the developing language and shots and editing. "Citizen Kane" married special effects, advanced sound, a new photographic style and a freedom from linear storytelling. "Star Wars" combined a new generation of special effects with the high-energy action picture; it linked space opera and soap opera, fairy tales and legend, and

◆ Build Vocabulary

watershed (wô´ tər shed) *n.*: Moment or event after which nothing is the same

synthesis (sin´ thə sis) *n.*: Whole made up of separate elements put together

packaged them as a wild visual ride.

"Star Wars" effectively brought to an end the golden era of early-1970's personal filmmaking and focused the industry on big-budget special effects blockbusters, blasting off a trend we are still living through. But you can't blame it for what it did; you can only observe how well it did it. In one way or another all the big studios have been trying to make another "Star Wars" ever since (pictures like "Raiders of the Lost Ark," "Jurassic Park" and "Independence Day" are its heirs). It located Hollywood's center of gravity at the intellectual and emotional level of a bright teenager.

It's possible, however, that as we grow older, we retain within the tastes of our earlier selves. How else to explain how much fun "Star Wars" is, even for those who think they don't care for science fiction? It's a good-hearted film in every single frame, and shining through is the gift of a man who knew how to link state-of-the-art technology with a deceptively simple, really very powerful, story. It was not by accident that George Lucas worked with Joseph Campbell, an expert on the world's basic myths, in fashioning a screenplay that owes much to man's oldest stories.

By now the ritual of classic film revival is well established: an older classic is brought out from the studio vaults, restored frame by frame, re-released in the best theaters, and then re-launched on home video. With this "special edition" of the "Star Wars" trilogy (which includes new versions of "Return of the Jedi" and "The Empire Strikes Back"), Lucas has gone one step beyond. His special effects were so advanced in 1977 that they spun off an industry, including his own Industrial Light & Magic Co., the computer wizards who do many of today's best special effects.

Now Lucas has put IL&M to work touching up the effects, including some that his limited 1977 budget left him unsatisfied with. Most of

◆ *Literature and Your Life*

How does *Star Wars* compare and contrast with the types of films you enjoy?

the changes are subtle: you'd need a side-by-side comparison to see that a new shot is a little better. There's about five minutes of new material, including a meeting between Han Solo and Jabba the Hut that was shot for the first version but not used. (We learn that Jabba is not immobile, but sloshes along in a kind of spongy undulation.) There's also an improved look to the city of Mos Eisley ("A wretched hive of scum and villainry," says Obi-Wan Kenobi). And the climactic battle scene against the Death Star has been rehabbed.[1]

The improvements are well done, but they point up how well the effects were done to begin with: If the changes are not obvious,

---

1. **rehabbed** (rē´ habˊd) v.: Rehabilitated.

▲ **Critical Viewing** This scene between Han Solo and Jabba the Hut was added to the new version of *Star Wars*. What can you learn about these characters from this picture? **[Analyze]**

---

that's because "Star Wars" got the look of the film so right in the first place. The obvious comparison is with Kubrick's "2001: A Space Odyssey," made 10 years earlier, in 1967, which also holds up perfectly well today. (One difference is that Kubrick went for realism, trying to imagine how his future world would really look, while Lucas cheerfully plundered the past; Han Solo's Millennium Falcon has a gun turret with a hand-operated weapon that would be at

home on a World War II bomber, but too slow to hit anything at space velocities.)

Two Lucas inspirations started the story with a tease: He set the action not in the future but "long ago," and jumped into the middle of it with "Chapter 4: A New Hope." These seemingly innocent touches were actually rather powerful; they gave the saga the aura of an ancient tale, and an ongoing one.

As if those two shocks were not enough for the movie's first moments, I learn from a review by Mark R. Leeper that this was the first film to pan the camera across a star field: "Space scenes had always been done with a fixed camera, and for a very good reason. It was more economical not to create a background of stars large enough to pan through." As the camera tilts up, a vast spaceship appears from the top of the screen and moves overhead, an effect reinforced by the surround sound. It is such a dramatic opening that it's no wonder Lucas paid a fine and resigned from the Directors' Guild rather than obey its demand that he begin with conventional opening credits.

The film has simple, well-defined characters, beginning with the robots R2D2 (childlike, easily hurt) and C3PO (fastidious, a

◆ **Build Vocabulary**

fastidious (fas tid′ ē əs) *adj*.: Not easy to please; discriminating

▲ **Critical Viewing** Which traits of the characters of *Star Wars* do you think helped to make them popular with viewers? **[Speculate]**

little <u>effete</u>). The evil Empire has all but triumphed in the galaxy, but rebel forces are preparing an assault on the Death Star. Princess Leia (pert, sassy Carrie Fisher) has information pinpointing the star's vulnerable point, and feeds it into R2D2's computer; when her ship is captured, the robots escape from the Death Star and find themselves on Luke Skywalker's planet, where soon Luke (Mark Hamill as an idealistic youngster) meets the wise, old, mysterious Ben Kenobi (Alec Guinness) and they hire the freelance space jockey Han Solo (Harrison Ford, already <u>laconic</u>) to carry them to Leia's rescue.

The story is advanced with spectacularly effective art design, set decoration and effects. Although the scene in the intergalactic bar is famous for the menagerie of alien drunks, there is another scene, when the two robots are thrown into a hold with other used droids, which equally fills the scene with fascinating throwaway details. And a scene in the Death Star's garbage bin (inhabited by a snake with head curiously shaped like E.T.'s) is also well done.

Many of the planetscapes are startlingly beautiful, and owe something to Chesley Bonestell's imaginary drawings of other worlds. The final assault on the Death Star, when the fighter rockets speed between parallel walls, is a nod in the direction of "2001," with its light trip into another dimension: Kubrick showed, and Lucas learned, how to make the audience feel it is hurtling headlong through space.

Lucas fills his screen with loving touches.

◆ **Literary Focus**
What words and phrases does Ebert use to advance his notion that *Star Wars* is a modern-day film classic?

There are little alien rats hopping around the desert, and a chess game played with living creatures. Luke's weather-worn "Speeder" vehicle, which hovers over the sand, reminds me uncannily of a 1965 Mustang. And consider the details creating the presence, look and sound of Darth Vader, whose fanged face mask, black cape and hollow breathing are the setting for James Earl Jones's cold voice of doom.

Seeing the film the first time, I was swept away, and have remained swept ever since. Seeing this restored version, I tried to be more objective, and noted that the gun battles on board the space ships go on a bit too long; it is remarkable that the empire marksmen never hit anyone important; and the fighter raid on the enemy ship now plays like the computer games it predicted. I wonder, too, if Lucas could have come up with a more challenging philosophy behind the Force. As Kenobi explains it, it's basically just going with the flow. What if Lucas had pushed a little further to include elements of nonviolence or ideas about

intergalactic conservation? (It's a great waste of resources to blow up star systems.)

The film philosophies that will live forever are the simplest-seeming ones. They may have profound depths, but their surfaces are as clear to an audience as a beloved old story. The way I know this is because the stories that seem immortal—the "Odyssey," the "Tale of Genji," "Don Quixote," "David Copperfield," "Huckleberry Finn"—are all the same: a brave but flawed hero, a quest, colorful people and places, sidekicks, the discovery of life's underlying truths. If I were asked to say with certainty which movies will still be widely known a century or two from now, I would list "2001," and "The Wizard of Oz," and Keaton and Chaplin, and Astaire and Rogers, and probably "Casablanca" . . . and "Star Wars," for sure.

◆ **Build Vocabulary**

effete (e fēt´) *adj.*: Lacking vigor; overrefined
laconic (lə kän´ ik) *adj.*: Terse; using few words

Guide for Responding

◆ *Literature and Your Life*

Reader's Response What aspect of *Star Wars* did you find most interesting or surprising in either review?

Thematic Focus What are some ways in which Roger Ebert thinks of *Star Wars* as a film legacy for future movie viewers?

☑ **Check Your Comprehension**

1. According to Ebert, what quality does *Star Wars* as a film have in common with *Birth of a Nation* and *Citizen Kane*?
2. Give two examples of aspects of the newer version of the film that differ from the original.

◆ **Critical Thinking**

INTERPRET

1. The title of Ebert's review is "Breakthrough Film Still Has the Force." What makes *Star Wars* a breakthrough, original film? **[Analyze]**
2. In what ways does *Star Wars* fit Ebert's statement that "The films that will live forever are the simplest-seeming ones"?

EVALUATE

3. What movies do you think will be widely known a century or two from now? Explain why. **[Make a Judgment]**
4. Compare and contrast the two essays in terms of their purpose and tone. **[Compare and Contrast]**

Guide for Responding (continued)

◆ Reading Strategy

IDENTIFY EVIDENCE

As a conscientious and critical reader, you **identify the evidence** writers provide to support their opinions. The evidence may be facts, observations, examples, statements from authorities, or statistics.

When Roger Ebert praises the changes in special effects in the 1997 re-release of *Star Wars*, he cites examples of some of those changes, such as "an improved look to the city of Mos Eisley."

1. How does Vincent Canby support his claim that "The way definitely not to approach 'Star Wars,' though, is to expect a film of cosmic implications . . . It's fun and funny"?
2. What evidence does Roger Ebert give to support his claim that *Star Wars* presents a "deceptively simple, really very powerful, story"?
3. How does Roger Ebert support his claim that "the film has simple, well-defined characters"?

◆ Build Vocabulary

USING CONNOTATIONS

The connotation of a word is the thing or idea that the word suggests. The following pairs of words have similar meanings. On your paper, explain how the connotations of the words make them slightly different.

1. facetiousness, sarcasm   2. adroit, cunning

USING THE WORD BANK: Antonyms

On your paper, write the letter of the word that is the best antonym, or opposite, of the first word.

1. condescension: (a) criticism, (b) praise, (c)pride
2. eclectic: (a) varied, (b) boring, (c) consistent
3. apotheosis: (a) scorn, (b) acclaim, (c) flattery
4. laconic: (a) talkative, (b) quiet, (c) reticent
5. effete: (a) soft, (b) weak, (c) strong
6. fastidious: (a) finicky, (b) critical, (c) obliging
7. synthesis: (a) unification, (b) separation, (c) fusion
8. watershed: (a) trifle, (b) breakthrough, (c) river
9. piously: (a) religiously, (b) carelessly, (c) jokingly
10. adroit: (a) skillful, (b) clumsy, (c) practiced
11. facetiousness: (a) solemnity, (b) humor, (c) playfulness

◆ Literary Focus

CRITICAL REVIEW

In a **critical review**, the writer makes a recommendation and tries to persuade you to accept that recommendation.

Critical reviews, which frequently appear in newspapers or magazines, are a type of persuasive essay that helps people make informed choices about the movies on which to spend their entertainment dollars.

1. What are the main points that Roger Ebert uses to back up his assertion that *Star Wars* was a breakthrough film?
2. What is it about Vincent Canby's review that persuades you most—either positively or negatively—about *Star Wars*?

◆ Build Grammar Skills

PARENTHETICAL INTERRUPTERS

Parenthetical interrupters make Ebert's and Canby's reviews sound more conversational. Because parenthetical interrupters are not essential to the sentence, they are set off with commas.

Practice Rewrite each sentence, adding the parenthetical interrupter in parentheses. Remember to include commas.

1. This film will survive technical innovations over the next decade. (*I am sure*)
2. *Star Wars* is a classic movie. (*in my opinion*)
3. The talents of the special effects crew are admirable. (*everyone can agree*)
4. Many people are familiar with characters from *Star Wars*. (*of course*)
5. *Star Wars* was the first film to pan the camera across a star field. (*interestingly*)

Writing Application Write sentences using each of the following parenthetical interrupters.

1. after all
2. by the way
3. incidentally
4. I believe
5. in fact

Build Your Portfolio

 ## Idea Bank

Writing

1. **Press Release** Imagine that your school is going to have a special showing of *Star Wars*. Write a press release about the movie that explains why the film is worth seeing.

2. **Speech** Write a brief speech a person on the special effects crew of *Star Wars* might give upon winning an award for his or her work.

3. **Interview** Imagine that you could talk to Roger Ebert or Vincent Canby about reviewing movies. Write the interview questions and responses from that imaginary conversation.

Speaking, Listening, and Viewing

4. ***Star Wars* Recording** Play an excerpt from the *Star Wars* theme by composer John Williams. Then, give an explanation to your class about how the music enhances the mood of specific scenes from the movie.

5. **Skit** With a partner, improvise a skit in which two people come out of a theater after seeing the re-release of *Star Wars* and share their initial impressions. **[Performing Arts Link]**

Researching and Representing

6. **Movie Collage** Create a collage of quotations, images, and advertisements showing the types of movies you enjoy. Explain your collage to the class. **[Art Link]**

7. **Science-Fiction Exhibit** Design a *Star Wars* exhibit for a science-fiction museum. Create your own illustrations or use *Star Wars* souvenirs you might already have. Write display tags that explain or describe the items. Then organize them to exhibit for the class. **[Art Link]**

Online Activity www.phlit.phschool.com

 ## Guided Writing Lesson

Movie Review

A **movie review** influences people's opinions and choices of movies to see. The title of a review and the first paragraph should hook the reader and promote the reviewer's point of view. The body of the review supports the opinion with summaries of the movie, facts, examples, and observations. The last paragraph repeats the initial opinions in a new and interesting way. Choose a movie you have recently seen and write a review to persuade a reader to see it—or not to see it.

Writing Skills Focus: Use Specific Examples

Include **specific examples** so that your readers will be able to picture aspects of the movie in their mind's eye. For each statement or claim you make about a movie, refer to a specific detail or scene to support your opinion. For instance, if you say, "This movie is guaranteed to make you cry," give an example of what happens in a sad scene or discuss background music that evokes a feeling of sorrow.

Prewriting Create an idea web to organize your ideas and find specific examples for your review. Start with your overall opinion. Then create branches for aspects of the movie that support that opinion. Cite specific examples for each aspect.

Drafting State your opinion at the beginning of the review, then support it with specific examples. You might include parenthetical interrupters to keep your tone conversational.

Revising Have a partner read your review for specific examples to back up your opinion. If necessary, you might include more examples or details to back up your opinion. Then check to see that your last paragraph interestingly restates your opinion.

CONNECTIONS TO TODAY'S WORLD

The Stars Wars movies have captured the imaginations and devotion of millions of people from around the world. Movie fans, young and old, rich and poor, have seen these movies countless times—in movie theaters, in their homes, and on television. Fan clubs hold lively debates about what will come in future episodes.

In recent years, another entertainment phenomenon has taken hold of fans worldwide: Japanese animation, which is called *anime* (ä´ nē mā). Forms of *anime* can be seen in movie theaters, on television, and on videocassettes. Devotees of *anime* have created numerous Web sites and fan clubs dedicated to the discussion of various *anime* products.

from Samurai From Outer Space
by Antonia Levi

The Rising Popularity of *Anime*

Generation X calls it *anime* . . . The Japanese took the word from the French to describe all animated films. Then, the Americans took it from the Japanese to describe the unique type of animation that comes from Japan . . .

Anime's popularity with young Americans is probably one of the biggest surprises of the nineties. For all the complaints about Generation X's "sound byte mentality," and all the cracks about the "dumbing of America," this generation has chosen a form of entertainment that is uniquely difficult to appreciate. It's not just the language barrier. Subtitles and dubbing take care of that. Culturally, *anime* comes without an operator's manual.

Anime author-artists tend to assume that they are creating for the Japanese domestic market exclusively. The fact that their product is now being seen by non-Japanese comes

as a surprise and sometimes a source of confusion. Rumiko Takahashi, Japan's First Lady of *anime,* expressed it best in a 1989 interview with *Amazing Heroes.* When informed of the phenomenal popularity of her translated [comics] in the United States, she replied:

> If it's true, then I'm truly happy. But I must confess to being rather puzzled as to why my work should be so well received. It's my intention to be putting in a lot of Japanese refer-

ences, Japanese lifestyle and feelings . . . I really have to wonder if foreign readers can understand all this, and if so, how?

Ms. Takahashi's point is well taken. The truth is, many *anime* fans enjoy the product without worrying about its Japanese nature. There's nothing wrong with that. One of the things that makes art such an excellent medium for intercultural exchange is the fact that it allows for individual interpretations beyond what the artist intended. . . .

A New Art Form From the Old

What [fans of *anime*] are really talking about when they praise the high tech look of *anime* is the fact that Japanese animators are getting powerful dramatic effects with only a fraction of the financial and technological effort [of American studios].

To some degree, this is a matter of necessity. *Anime* studios simply do not have the kind of budgets [American] animators take for granted. However, it is also a matter of choice. Unlike the West, Japan's artistic and

theatrical traditions have never aimed at realism. Instead, both in art and drama the Japanese have emphasized techniques that capture the essence of the subject in a way that assumes some participation by the audience. *Anime* sets the stage, but the viewer's imagination must fill in the gaps. *Anime*'s most powerful scenes never appear on the screen at all.

. . . Such interactive art is a longstanding tradition in Japan. Japanese artists, particularly the woodblock printers of the sixteenth to nineteenth centuries whose influence on *anime* is as clear as the picture on the screen, special-

ized in deceiving their viewers into believing they had seen more than they had. . . .

Woodblock prints also seem more realistic than they are. This is because the artists strategically apply detailing and elaborate shading in areas where they know the eye will focus, thus deceiving their viewers into assuming that everything in the picture is equally meticulous. It isn't. And it isn't in *anime* either. In fact, *anime*, with its bright, primary colors (although not quite the same primary colors American studios use) and . . . special effects, is really an extension of the traditional art of woodblock printing. Only now, this traditional Japanese art form moves, talks, and sings.

1. What does Antonia Levi mean when she says that "Culturally, *anime* comes without an operator's manual"?
2. According to Rumiko Takahashi, why might Americans find her work hard to understand?
3. What two reasons does Levi give for *anime's* unique quality?
4. In *Samurai From Outer Space*, Levi shows how *anime* sprang from an ancient art form. What other art form today has its roots in past times? Explain.

Guide for Reading

Michel Butor (1926–)

French author Michel Butor (mi shəl´ boo tôr´) emphasizes the essential role of writing plays in his life when he says that he wants to "capture in writing the most important things that I see, hear, read, and think." His experimental novels and insightful essays reflect his desire to unify the different arts.

After receiving a degree in philosophy, Butor taught in France, Egypt, England, Greece, Switzerland, and the United States. He was named "professor *extraordinaire*" (French for "extraordinary") at the University of Geneva in 1975.

Playful Novelist In his novels, Butor creates unconventional works that abandon traditional plot and characters. His best-known novel, *La Modification* (1957), is told in the second-person plural. On a train journey from Paris to Rome, the narrator talks to himself, eventually deciding to write a book that turns out to be *La Modification* itself.

In *Portrait of the Artist as a Young Ape* (1967), Butor creates a unique autobiography in which a young man is transformed into an ape. The reader is plunged into Butor's perplexing world, where the line between fantasy and reality blurs.

Insightful Essayist Butor also writes essays on a wide variety of subjects from literature and music to art and architecture. He views all forms of creativity as unified, pointing out that "writing, music, and painting are three faces of the same enterprise."

This essay, "Claude Monet or The World Upside Down," shows how he applies careful scrutiny of art to reveal deep insights into both the artist's work and Butor's own response to it.

◆ Build Vocabulary

LATIN WORD ROOTS: -cap-

Butor calls one painting a "recapitulation" of Monet's entire career as an artist. The Latin word root -cap- refers to "the headings or divisions of a book." The word *chapter* comes from the same root. Adding the prefix *re-*, which means "again," recapitulation means "to state the ideas of a work again." A recapitulation is usually "a brief summary."

WORD BANK

fidelity
crux
paradoxical
inflection
intervene
luminous
recapitulation
inversion

As you read this essay, you will encounter the words on this list. Each word is defined on the page where it first appears. Preview the list before you read.

◆ Build Grammar Skills

CORRECT USE OF SEMICOLONS AND COLONS

The translators of Butor's essay use punctuation carefully. They know that a **colon** serves as a signal to the reader to expect something. It appears before a list or introduces a quotation.

Nineteenth-century realist landscape would tell us: "Here is nature not as painters ordinarily represent it but as you yourselves see it."

The translators use a **semicolon** between two closely related main clauses in a compound sentence.

The vision I offer you is superior to the one we put up with; my painting will change reality for you.

Because the main clauses can stand by themselves, the semicolon takes the place of a coordinating conjunction, such as *and* or *for*.

from Claude Monet or The World Upside Down

◆ *Literature and Your Life*

CONNECT YOUR EXPERIENCE

What artworks have grabbed your attention and held it? You might have been drawn to a painting in a museum by a powerful first impression. Then, you kept looking and found more and more layers of meaning.

In this essay, Michel Butor shares his well-developed thoughts about Monet's art. He applies both his feelings and his knowledge of the artist to present a complete analysis.

Journal Writing Briefly describe a favorite painting, photograph, or poster. Note why this artwork appeals to you.

THEMATIC FOCUS: EXPANDING HORIZONS

Preview the art included with this selection. Then, as you read, ask yourself: How does the essay alter my perceptions of the art?

◆ Background for Understanding

CULTURE

Claude Monet (mō nā´) (1840–1926) was the leader of an artistic movement known as Impressionism, whose name comes from the title of Monet's 1872 work *Impression: Sunrise.* As that title suggests, Impressionists attempted to reproduce quickly changing, temporary aspects of nature.

Their work was very different from that of realists like Gustave Courbet (koor be´) (1819–1877), who aimed to depict scenes in an objecive way. Impressionists like Monet, Alfred Sisley (sēs lā´) (1839–1899), and Édouard Manet (mä nā´) (1832–1883) reacted against the literal qualities of realism to create highly personal works that sought to capture a fleeting moment.

◆ Literary Focus

ESSAY ON ART

An **essay on art** is a nonfiction work in which the author shares his or her response to an artist's work. Writers use descriptive imagery and careful analysis to explain the meaning or impact of an artwork.

In "Claude Monet," Butor applies his knowledge of Monet's technical skills as well as key incidents in the artist's life. Butor's goal is to open your mind by sharing his own responses. He hopes that you will return to the artworks he describes and see them with fresh eyes.

◆ Reading Strategy

RELATE PICTURES TO TEXT

When reading an illustrated essay like this one, take time to **relate pictures to text,** comparing the written descriptions with the images themselves. You might begin by previewing the illustrations to form your own opinions. Also, read the captions to identify the artist and title of the work.

As you read "Claude Monet," pause when Butor mentions an artist or a painting. See whether the illustrations include works by the artist mentioned. For example, as Butor analyzes *L'Inondation de Port-Marly,* refer to the reproduction on p. 772. Compare Butor's reflections xwith the painting itself. Then, decide whether or not you agree with the author's analysis.

from

Claude Monet
or
The World Upside Down

Michel Butor
Translated by Joan Templeton and Richard Howard

The Waterlily Pond—Green Harmony, Claude Monet, Musée d'Orsay, Paris

▲ **Critical Viewing** How does this picture of Monet's reflect an impression of a scene? **[Analyze]**

FLEETING

Fidelity to nature is the crux of Impressionist strategy against the Salon or the Academy,[1] but consider Monet's paradoxical inflection of it. When Courbet or the early Manet tell us they paint objects or people as they are, they are implying we can verify what they have done; for them the model must have a certain stability, must hold still so that the painter can compare it point by point with the representation of it he has just made, and the spectator after him: so a calm scene is required, a quiet landscape, a still life, a ceremony, a moment of leisure. Painting out of doors or with a palette knife[2] alters nothing in these fundamental données;[3] we may now verify the exactitude of the nuance, as we once did that of the detail. But Monet, with his insistence on the fleeting, explores the old notion of fidelity. Traditional verification becomes impossible—denied not only to the spectator but to the painter himself. Already the colors he has put on the canvas no longer correspond to those he sees. The design of the reflection has obviously changed.

So not Cézanne's famous "What an eye!" should be said about Monet, but "What a memory!" If what he painted for us really corresponds to a fleeting moment, we must conclude he painted it without having it before his eyes. His construction is as "grand" as that of the Franche-Comté[4] landscapes Courbet was reconstituting in his studio: but while Courbet's reconstitutions, like Cézanne's later on, are attached to something permanent, something available to the spectator, Monet's are attached to an object which, by definition, has disappeared forever. The only verification still available to us is the encounter in nature, say on a walk, with an *effect* of the same kind, differing in the same way from habitual vision. Monet's instantaneity, far from being passivity, requires on the contrary an extraordinary power of generalization, of abstraction.

Nineteenth-century *realist* landscape would tell us: "Here is nature not as painters ordinarily represent it but as you yourselves see it." Neither Courbet nor Corot asked us to look at things differently, but Monet announces: "Here is nature as you don't usually see it, as I myself don't usually see it, but as you can see it—not necessarily this particular effect but, in my wake, others which resemble it. The vision I offer you is superior to the one we put up with; my painting will change reality for you."

So he must discover subjects in which there is an obvious instability, subjects whose dynamic enables them to intervene in the spectator's vision.

Compare his landscapes to Sisley's. The latter adopts everything in the early Monet which can be taken as a continuation of Corot, but the instability I have just alluded to remains foreign to Sisley, in whose art everything is calm. In the dark apartments of Paris and London, he opens windows onto a countryside, or a suburb, peaceful, airy, luminous, where time keeps flowing, spreading. . . . We feel nothing has moved between the moment Sisley set up his easel and the moment he finished the painting. In *l'Inondation de Port-Marly*[5] he spreads before our eyes the surface of dead-calm water which reflects the light, heightens the colors: the reflections playing upon it are

---

5. *l'Inondation* (lē´ nōn dá´ sē ōn´ də) *de Port-Marly*: Flood at Port-Marly.

---

1. **Impressionist strategy . . . Academy:** The Salon and the Royal Academy of Painting and Sculpture in Paris, which tended to uphold tradition in art, initially opposed the Impressionist movement and its attempt to capture fleeting glimpses of nature.
2. **palette knife:** Knife with a very flexible steel blade and no cutting edge, normally used by painters to mix colors or spread paint.
3. *données* (dô nāz´) *n.*: Premises or assumptions.
4. **Franche-Comté** (fränsh kōn tā´): Eastern region of France near the Swiss border.

◆ Build Vocabulary

fidelity (fə del´ ə tē) *n.*: Faithfulness; trueness

crux (kruks) *n.*: Essential point

paradoxical (par´ ə daks´ i kəl) *adj.*: Contradictory

inflection (in flek´ shən) *n.*: Special interpretation of something

intervene (in´ tər vēn´) *v.*: To influence

luminous (loo´ mə nəs) *adj.*: Shining; bright

The Flood at Port Marley, Alfred Sisley, Musée des Beaux-Arts, Rouen, France

▲ **Critical Viewing** Does this picture of Sisley's support Butor's observations that Sisley's art is "calm" and that Sisley is not especially interested in the reflections in water? Why or why not? **[Analyze]**

there only to make us feel that the substance represented is water; in themselves they are of no interest. Conversely, in Monet, the reflection, with its ceaselessly evanescent design, will often be the center of the composition. . . .

LES NYMPHÉAS *(Orangerie, Paris)*

It is to an intention of this kind that *Les Nymphéas*[6] corresponds, that monument to peace created in the midst of war. Far from capturing a chance effect met with on some walk or *hunt*, Monet deliberately altered the course of the Epte[7] to form a small pond.

Work *"sur le motif"*[8] is still very apparent in the first paintings of the series, those of 1898, but there is no longer a trace of it in the decoration of the Orangerie.

At the time, Monet was going almost blind, suffering from a double cataract and from difficulties in the perception of color. In several astonishing canvases painted just before his operation, the tints were entirely *invented*. Even after recovering the use of his eyes, he could no longer trust them; working at times with numbered tubes, he was to rely more on what he knew of the pigments than on his *impressions*.

---

6. *Les Nymphéas:* Waterlillies.
7. **Epte** (ept): River outside Paris.

8. *"sur le motif"* (sür lə mō tēf´): "On the visual theme"— in this case, the pond.

Water Lilies and Willows, Claude Monet, Musée de l'Orangerie, Paris, France

▲ **Critical Viewing** Is there evidence in this picture by Monet that, as Butor suggests, "the real pond is no longer there as a model"? Why or why not? **[Interpret]**

The Orangerie's *Nymphéas* is an altogether constructed work; the real pond is no longer there as a model (or as an alibi), but as a *master.* Listen to the painter:

If I remained insensitive to the subtleties and modulations of color seen at close range, nonetheless my eyes did not deceive me when I stepped back and considered the subject in large masses, and this was my point of departure for new compositions. A modest point of departure, to tell the truth, for I mistrusted myself and wanted to leave nothing to chance. Slowly I tested my powers in countless rough sketches which at first convinced me that the study of natural light was permanently forbidden, but reassured me, too, by proving that if my color-diversions and landscapes were no longer my specialty, I still saw as clearly as ever when it came to bright tones isolated in a mass of dark ones.

◆ **Reading Strategy**
Is Monet's phrase—"bright tones isolated in a mass of dark ones"—an accurate desciption of the picture on this page? Explain.

How could I turn this to good advantage?

Gradually my intentions took shape. Since the age of sixty I had always meant to devote myself to a sort of "synthesis" in each of the categories of subjects which in turn had attracted me; I planned to return in one painting or on some occasions in two to my earlier impressions and sensations. Now I had given this up, for I would have had to travel far and wide, review one by one all the stages of my life as a painter and examine my emotions of long ago. I decided while I was doing my rough sketches that a series of general impressions, recorded at the time when my eyesight had the best chance of being exact, would have an interest. I waited until the idea had taken flesh, and the arrangement and composition of the subjects had of their own accord gradually etched themselves in my brain, and on the day when I felt I had enough trumps in my hand to try my chances with real hope of success I resolved to act, and I did.

from *Claude Monet or the World Upside Down* ◆ 773

Etretat After the Storm, Gustave Courbet, Louvre, Paris

▲ **Critical Viewing** In what way does this picture show Courbet's determination to—in Butor's words—"paint objects or people as they are"? **[Interpret]**

Cosa Mentale.[9]

It does not occur to Monet to stand in front of his pond in order to reproduce his already conceived composition—he calls in a contractor to build him a new studio:

blind walls with no opening except the door; glass panes in two-thirds of the roof . . .

The war halts the construction of this cell, but the painter achieves its equivalent in his old studio by having wheeled easels made which allow him to surround himself entirely with his work-in-progress.

The water of the *Nymphéas* will save his sight. However remote he had been, all his life, from classical Fable, he was to rediscover it here in his title, spelled out hundreds of times over by the flowers; they are the divinities of the springs to whom he prays.

No longer able to trust himself sufficiently with color, he marks out the different elements of the canvas by a whole vocabulary of brush strokes. In this respect, the *Nymphéas* is indeed a recapitulation of his entire *oeuvre,*[10] but on a monumental scale. He works with calculated contrasts of tones whose properties he has already tested, all the details which might

---

9. ***Cosa Mentale*** (kō′ sä men tä′lē): Italian for "a thing of the mind."

10. ***oeuvre*** (ë′ vr) *n.*: All the works of a particular artist.

escape him now having to function as *fleeting effects* subordinated to the general composition.

Great hairy filaments of reeds and waterside rushes, woolly verticals of tree trunks in the second room; tiny vertical filaments of willow branches; surfaces clogged with inverted clouds, longer or shorter, more or less animated horizontals of the water's surface; great enveloping flourishes for the lily pads with brilliant splotches for their flowers.

The raising of the horizon, already so marked in the past, is now absolute—the sky or the distance appear only in their <u>inversion</u>, and the surface of the water tips up toward the vertical all around us, inspiring dreams of flying or diving.

The trees in the second room repel us by the obvious unreality of their woolly substance—they are said to be painted "like a stage set," that is, like something which should be viewed from far away, from farther away than is possible here—while the water's surface imperturbably advances toward us from a distance

impossible to specify, the perspective groupings occurring among the flowers remaining unstable, if only because of the curve of the wall; and balancing this repulsion is the enveloping welcome of the entire elliptical liquid extent, gathering us in on all sides, making those trees shift behind us in an incessant movement.

So we fall gently into the sky, and the waters of the sky stream over us.

Monet has kept only a few indications of ordinary landscape; the waters take them, stir them to life, discover in them thousands of properties, but all this can happen only because there is already something which defines the canvas as a voluminous mirror, germinating and blossoming, because there are the water lilies, starting from which everything becomes legible.

In the real pond at Giverny,[11] the world's aspect would be reflected even if the flowers had not been there; but in the work, the figuration appears only by means of the presence. They are the nymphs of the springs which come into the city's very heart to make us turn upside down.

◆ Build Vocabulary

recapitulation (rē kə pich´ ə lā shən) *n.*: Summary of brief restatement

inversion (in vər´ zhən) *n.*: A turning upside down

---

11. **real pond at Giverny** (zhi ver nē´): Actual pond that Monet depicted in Les Nymphéas; it was located in the town of Giverny, not far from Paris.

Guide for Responding

◆ *Literature and Your Life*

Reader's Response Which painting in this illustrated essay do you think best captures an instant of nature? Why?

Thematic Focus How did reading this essay expand your response to Monet's paintings?

☑ Check Your Comprehension

1. What is the subject of *Les Nymphéas*?
2. What physical challenge did Monet face as he grew older?
3. What building project does Monet begin in order to reproduce his earlier painting?
4. What is unique about the horizon line in the painting *Water Lilies and Willows*?

◆ Critical Thinking

INTERPRET

1. What are the differences in the ways Monet and Courbet approach their art? **[Compare and Contrast]**
2. Butor asserts that "Not Cezanne's famous 'What an eye!' should be said about Monet, but 'What a memory!'" Why does Butor claim Monet has a remarkable memory? **[Interpret]**
3. What does Butor admire about Monet's "world upside down"? Why does he think this achievement is so important? **[Draw Conclusions]**

APPLY

4. Do you think that Monet would agree with Butor's analysis of his works? Why or why not? **[Hypothesize]**

Guide for Responding (continued)

◆ Reading Strategy

RELATE PICTURES TO TEXT

When you **relate pictures to text,** you compare the writer's comments with the accompanying illustrations. You can follow an author point by point, taking time to view the art and draw your own conclusions. For example, as you read Butor's description of *Les Nymphéas,* pause to see whether his portrayal matches what you see.

1. How does Courbet's *Etretat After the Storm* reflect Butor's assertion that a realist painter usually chooses a subject with "a certain stability"?
2. (a) Does Butor claim that Sisley paints more like Courbet or Monet? (b) Do the paintings selected support his view?
3. Which of Monet's paintings best illustrates the theme of "the world turned upside down"? Why?
4. In an interview, Butor once said that "painting is also a process toward organized composition, like music. It is a matter of imagining a structure within which colors and shapes can form an artistic whole." Which reproduction do you think best supports this view of artistic creation? Why?

◆ Build Vocabulary

USING THE LATIN WORD ROOT *-cap-*

Knowing that the Latin word root *-cap-* refers to "the headings of a book, or the head itself," match each word with its definition.

1. recap   **a.** remove the head
2. decapitate   **b.** retell the main ideas
3. capitulate   **c.** bow the head; surrender

USING THE WORD BANK: Synonyms

In your notebook, write the synonym for each word from the Word Bank.

1. crux: (a) essence, (b) cruelty, (c) reward
2. fidelity: (a) permanence, (b) age, (c) faithfulness
3. inflection: (a) condition, (b) interpretation, (c) mirror
4. intervene: (a) influence, (b) obsess, (c) combine
5. inversion: (a) contentment, (b) retelling, (c) reversal
6. luminous: (a) radiant, (b) wealthy, (c) bulky
7. paradoxical: (a) complex, (b) contradictory (c) glorious
8. recapitulation: (a) survey, (b) summary, (c) surprise

◆ Literary Focus

ESSAY ON ART

Michel Butor's illustrated commentary is an **essay on art,** a nonfiction work in which the author shares his or her response to an artist's work. He presents a series of insights about Monet's work by comparing him with other artists and producing a detailed analysis of individual paintings.

1. Why does Butor include references to paintings by Courbet and Sisley in an essay on Monet?
2. Why do you think Butor chooses to include a long passage from Monet's own writing?
3. Do you think this essay would have the same impact without the accompanying illustrations? Why or why not?
4. What are some of the difficulties facing any essayist writing about art? Explain.

◆ Build Grammar Skills

CORRECT USE OF SEMICOLONS AND COLONS

A **colon** serves as a signal to the reader to expect something. Use colons to introduce a list of items or to cite long quotations. Use a **semicolon** to form a compound sentence when the two closely related ideas being joined are not joined by a conjunction.

Practice Copy the sentences on your paper. Complete each sentence with a colon or semicolon.

1. Courbet was a Realist _____?_____ Monet was an Impressionist.
2. *Les Nymphéas* includes these dominant colors _____?_____ blue, green, white, and pink.
3. The experience of viewing Monet's painting is personal _____?_____ every viewer will have a unique perspective.
4. Monet's strengths are many _____?_____ he was a superb colorist, a practiced draftsman, and a master of composition.
5. The painting, of course, is motionless _____?_____ Monet freezes light as it shimmers.

Build Your Portfolio

Idea Bank

Writing

1. **Letter to a Friend** As Monet, write a letter to a friend after you have just completed one of the paintings accompanying this selection.

2. **Art Analysis** Choose a painting and write an essay in which you analyze the artist's central imagery and theme.

3. **Respond to Commentary** Michel Butor has commented: "When I quote someone in my books, it is a form of collaboration since the citation, placed in a new context, becomes an integral part of my text." Write an essay describing how Butor collaborates with Monet in this selection.

Speaking, Listening, and Viewing

4. **Audio Tour** Record an audio tour for the paintings in the selection or for other paintings of your choice. **[Performing Arts Link]**

5. **Art Out Loud** Describe a painting to a partner without revealing the artwork. After completing your description, show the painting and ask your partner whether or not the work matches his or her expectations. **[Art Link]**

Researching and Representing

6. **Impressionist Painters** Present a multimedia report about an Impressionist painter. Explain how the painter's work reflects the primary goals of Impressionism. **[Art Link]**

7. **Reproduction Analysis** Choose two reproductions and find out the dimensions of the original paintings. Calculate the percentage by which the reproductions were reduced. Evaluate whether or not the larger image is more satisfying to view. **[Mathematics Link]**

Online Activity **www.phlit.phschool.com**

Guided Writing Lesson

Captions for an Exhibit

This essay is like a small exhibit of Monet's work. Create your own exhibit by choosing several reproductions related to a topic. Write a caption for each painting that includes the artist's name, the title of the work, and information to help viewers interpret the work.

Writing Skills Focus: Relate Text to Pictures

Your captions should **relate** directly to the work being discussed, referring to it and giving information about it. In a brief note, you do not have time for lengthy explanations. You can, however, add specific points of interest that viewers might not know. Each caption should also tie the work to the organizing theme of your exhibit.

Prewriting Choose the topic or theme of your exhibit and select the artworks you will include. Write a separate note card—like the one below—for each artwork, including details and thoughts from your research.

Title	
Artist	
Thematic Relevance	
Other Details	

Drafting Organize your note cards in a logical order, the order in which you would like viewers to see the art. Then, use your note cards to write captions one at a time.

Revising Review your captions from the point of view of someone who has never seen these works before. Make sure you have provided enough information. Also, review the spelling and punctuation of names and titles. Finally, check your use of colons and semicolons. For more on using these punctuation marks, see pp. 768 and 776.

Focus on Culture

Latin America

Before dawn on September 16, 1810, church bells woke the Indian peasants of Dolores, a small town in Mexico. Hurrying to church, they found their priest, Miguel Hidalgo. "My children, will you be free?" Father Hidalgo asked. "Will you make the effort to recover from the hated Spaniards the lands stolen from your forefathers 300 years ago?"

Hidalgo's words—known as the *grito de Dolores,* or "cry of Dolores"—sparked a long, difficult struggle for independence. Within a year, Father Hidalgo was executed by a firing squad. Yet, in the end, Mexico did shake off Spanish rule. Today, Mexicans celebrate September 16 as their Independence Day.

▲ **Critical Viewing** The Incan city of Macchu Picchu (mä´ chŌŌ pēk´ chŌŌ) was built to withstand earthquakes. How does this picture reflect the geography of the Incan empire? [**Analyze**]

GEOGRAPHIC SETTING

Latin America stretches for about 5,500 miles, from the Rio Grande to Cape Horn at the tip of South America. It is a vast cultural region largely made up of former Spanish and Portuguese colonies. Its two main subregions are Middle America and South America.

Regions Middle America lies in the Northern Hemisphere. It includes Mexico, the seven nations of Central America, and the Caribbean.

Most of South America lies in the Southern Hemisphere. It includes twelve independent nations and two foreign-ruled territories. Brazil alone covers half the land area and has half the population of the entire continent.

Landforms A backbone of high mountains, known as La Cordillera (kôr´ dil yer´ ə), runs the length of Latin America. These mountains actually begin in the Canadian Rockies before splitting into the two Sierra Madre ranges of Mexico.

Western South America is dominated by the snowcapped Andes Mountains. Second only to the great ranges of Asia, the Andes have dozens of peaks that rise more than 20,000 feet above sea level. Nested in the Andes is Lake Titicaca, the largest lake in South America and the highest navigable lake in the world.

The largest lowland area is the Amazon Basin, which occupies 40 percent of South America. (The Amazon is the world's second longest river.) The Amazon Basin is also home to the world's largest tropical rain forest.

HISTORY

Between A.D. 300 and 900, Mayan city-states flourished from Mexico's Yucatan Peninsula through much of Central America. Temple-pyramids and artifacts in the jungles of Central America testify to the artistic and technological skills of the Mayas.

Powerful Empires After the 1200's, the Aztecs dominated the Central Plateau of Mexico. The Aztecs built an advanced civilization and a magnificent capital city, Tenochtitlán (tä nôch tē tlän´). They also conquered neighboring lands, sacrificing countless prisoners of war to the Aztec gods.

Far to the south of the Aztec empire, the Incas built a powerful empire in the Andes. (See the picture on p. 778.) To rule their vast territories, the Incas built an extensive system of roads and bridges.

Conquest and Colonization In 1492, Christopher Columbus reached the Caribbean. Spanish conquistadors (kän kwis´ tə dôrz), or conquerors, soon followed. In the 1520's, Hernando Cortés (kôr´ tez) defeated the Aztec empire. The Spanish destroyed the city of Tenochtitlán. In the 1530's, the Incan empire fell to the brutal conquistador Francisco Pizarro.

Spain colonized almost all of Middle and South America. Gold and silver from the Americas enriched Spain. (See p. 792 for the essay "Temptation of America.") The Spanish also set up plantations to grow cash crops such as

▲ **Critical Viewing** This is a sculpture from a Mayan temple. What does it suggest about the artistic skills of the Mayas? [**Infer**]

fruit, coffee, and sugar. Labor was supplied by slaves, first Native Americans, then West Africans. At the same time, missionaries spread Roman Catholicism throughout the colonies.

A rigid social structure emerged. At the top stood the peninsulares, officials sent from Spain to govern the colonies. Next came creoles, American-born descendants of Spanish settlers.

Far below them were the mestizos, people of mixed Indian and European descent. Occupying the bottom rungs of society were Native Americans, free blacks, and slaves.

Independence By the late 1700's, many groups sought to end Spanish rule. Creoles felt that they, rather than royal officials, deserved to govern. Mestizos and Indians also resented Spanish rule, while slaves saw independence as a step toward freedom.

The first Latin American nation to achieve independence was a French colony, Haiti, in

1804. As you have read, Mexico's drive for freedom began in 1810 with the *grito de Dolores*. Mexico finally became independent in 1821.

In South America, Simón Bolívar (sē môn´ bô lē´ vär) won the title "the Liberator" for his role in the wars for independence. A wealthy creole, Bolívar defeated Spanish armies in Venezuela and Colombia. He then joined forces with the Argentinian patriot José de San Martín (hô se´ de sän´ mär tēn´) to liberate Ecuador and Peru. By 1825, all of South America had thrown off Spanish rule.

Struggles of the New Nations Bolívar had hoped to forge a strong, united republic. However, his efforts failed. By the 1830's, Latin America was divided into eighteen separate nations.

Latin American leaders ended slavery and wrote constitutions modeled on that of the United States. Yet the new constitutions did not ensure democracy. Military leaders often seized power and ruled as dictators.

The new nations remained economically dependent on Europe. In time, the United States also invested heavily in Latin America. Financial interests led the United States to intervene in nations such as Cuba, Nicaragua, and the Dominican Republic. Such incidents fed resentment against the "colossus of the north."

Slow Progress Social inequality, military rule, economic dependence, foreign influence—such challenges continued into the twentieth century. Still, some nations made progress.

In 1910, the Mexican Revolution began. After nearly eleven years of violence, the nation emerged with a new democratic constitution. Since then, Mexico has worked to fulfill the promises of democracy. It has also developed its agriculture and industry.

During the Cold War, leftist revolutionaries clashed with right-wing governments. In 1959, Fidel Castro ousted Cuba's dictator and later set up a communist regime. In 1973, General

Nazca Jar With Bridge Spout,
Peru, British Museum, London

▲ **Critical Viewing** This jar was produced in the 700's by the Nazca people of southern Peru. Why do you think such traditional styles of pottery are still popular? **[Speculate]**

Augusto Pinochet (pē nō shā') overthrew Chile's elected socialist president. By 2000, however, Castro was the only major nonelected ruler in Latin America.

SOCIETY AND CULTURE

After independence, the rigid colonial class system remained in place. Today, a wide gap still separates rich and poor.

Country and City In very poor countries, such as Bolivia and Guatemala, the majority of people still live in rural areas. Landless peasants often work on large estates as tenant farmers. Many tenant farmers remain permanently in debt to large landowners.

Millions of rural villagers have sought work in booming urban centers like Mexico City or São Paolo, Brazil. Sprawling slums have sprung up around every city.

Family Life Across Latin America, family ties remain strong. In rural areas, an extended family—grandparents, aunts, uncles, cousins—usually lives nearby, ready to help in times of need. Today, as in the past, the man dominates the family. Still, if men leave the village to find work, women assume their responsibilities.

The Church In Latin America, about 90 percent of the people are Roman Catholic. The Church has dominated many aspects of life, including education, hospitals, and services for the poor. Dozens of solemn or joyous festivals dot the Church year.

ARTS AND LITERATURE

Latin American art and literature often reflect a blend of traditions. Europeans, Native Americans, and Africans have all contributed to a rich cultural heritage.

Music The blend of cultures is perhaps best seen in Latin American music. Some musicians have created unique sounds by using a mix of Native American bamboo flutes, African percussion instruments, and European guitars.

Art Pre-Columbian civilizations perfected skills in architecture and sculpture. Today, Native Americans still practice traditional crafts, producing colorful pottery or weaving patterned cloth. (See the picture on p. 780.)

The Mexican Revolution gave rise to a bold school of painters. The murals of Diego Rivera and José Clemente Orozco (ô rôs' kô) depicted the struggles and triumphs of the Mexican people. Rivera's wife, Frieda Kahlo, blended realism and fantasy in vibrant self-portraits.

Literature Modern writers also blended fantasy, fact, and humor in a style called magical realism. *One Hundred Years of Solitude*, by the Colombian Gabriel García Márquez, recounts the history of an imaginary town. The novel is full of miracles, flying carpets, and odd dreams. Yet it captures basic human experiences. (See García Márquez's essay "Uses and Abuses of the Umbrella" on p. 784.)

Many writers explored political themes. Miguel Angel Asturias of Guatemala described living under a dictatorship. (His essay "Lake Titicaca," on p. 794, also has a political dimension.) Chilean poet Pablo Neruda expressed anger at foreign influence in Latin America. (See his poem "Cristobal Miranda," on p. 204, which expresses his solidarity with workers.) Neruda, Asturias, and García Márquez were among several Latin American writers to receive the Nobel Prize for Literature. The first Latin American writer to receive the prize was Gabriela Mistral. (See her poem "Fear" on p. 202.)

Finally, nearly every famous Latin American author has written essays. You will read some of these on the following pages.

ACTIVITY

Making a Timeline for Art and Literature Choose one Latin American nation. Use Internet or library resources to find out more about the history and culture of that nation. Then, create a timeline showing important literary and artistic events in that nation's history.

Guide for Reading

Gabriel García Márquez
(1928–)

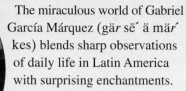

The miraculous world of Gabriel García Márquez (gär sē´ ä mär´ kes) blends sharp observations of daily life in Latin America with surprising enchantments.

García Márquez was born in Aracataca, a small town in northern Colombia. His gifts as a storyteller were obvious even as a child. He told one interviewer, "I started telling about things, stories and so on, almost ever since I was born."

His novel *One Hundred Years of Solitude* (1967) is often called one of the greatest books written in Spanish. After winning the Nobel Prize for Literature in 1982, he wrote many other best-selling novels.

As an essayist, García Márquez has focused on a wide range of topics. An example from his early journalistic career, "Uses and Abuses of the Umbrella" was published in 1955 in a Colombian newspaper.

Jorge Ibargüengoitia (1928–1983)

Born in Mexico City, Mexico, Jorge Ibargüengoitia (ē´ ber gōō en goi tē´ ə) pursued a variety of writing styles throughout his life. From novels and short stories to criticism and newspaper columns, Ibargüengoitia focused on urban themes.

Ibargüengoitia studied dramatic art at college. When his first play was poorly received, he shifted his focus and began to work as a theater critic. He also turned away from playwriting to develop several novels, including *The Dead Girls* (1977) and *Two Crimes* (1979).

He wrote a column for the Mexican newspaper *Excélsior* (Excelsior) and later for Octavio Paz's monthly magazine. "Solve This Case for Me" was first published as a newspaper obituary for the well-known British mystery writer Agatha Christie.

◆ Build Vocabulary

LATIN WORD ROOTS: *-pel-*

García Márquez imagines a man forced to devise a new invention simply because he faces a "compelling concept." The verb *compel* includes the Latin root *-pel-*, which means "drive" or "push." Something that is *compelling* is forceful or demanding; the Latin root *-pel-* helps you remember that something compelling demands attention, as a pushy idea might.

WORD BANK

compelling
intuition
mundane
contemptuous
cadavers

As you read these essays, you will encounter the words on this list. Each word is defined on the page where it first appears. Preview the list before you read.

◆ Build Grammar Skills

THE SUBJUNCTIVE MOOD

The **subjunctive mood** is a verb form indicating possibility, supposition, or desire. Writers use this form in two ways. The subjunctive often expresses a condition that is contrary to fact:

If one *were* to research the history of the umbrella . . .

In this situation, the verb form is always *were*. Writers also use the subjunctive in clauses beginning with *that* to indirectly express a demand, recommendation, suggestion, or statement of necessity.

Three people suggested that Ibargüengoitia *write* an article about Agatha Christie.

Here, the verb is always the base form. It does not change, regardless of the subject.

Uses and Abuses of the Umbrella
◆ Solve This Case for Me ◆

◆ *Literature and Your Life*

CONNECT YOUR EXPERIENCE

Even the most familiar things in your life can seem strange or amazing when you view them from a new perspective. You may have seen the same tree outside your window every day, but hadn't noticed its structure until it was covered with lights.

By noticing unusual features of common things, you are following the trail of García Márquez and Ibargüengoitia. These writers discover comic insights by turning everyday perceptions upside down.

Journal Writing Create a quick word sketch of something you see every day. Try to uncover a new aspect that you've never noticed.

THEMATIC FOCUS: OVERCOMING OBSTACLES

Life is not guaranteed to be interesting. Making life vital and engaging is up to each person. As you read, ask yourself: How do García Márquez and Ibargüengoitia conquer the obstacle of everyday dullness?

◆ Background for Understanding

LITERATURE

Although readers are most familiar with the magical fiction of Latin America, the essay holds a prominent position in the region's literature. Almost every major Latin American writer has contributed essays to newspapers, journals, or magazines.

Writers such as Gabriel García Márquez, Octavio Paz, Carlos Fuentes, and Jorge Luís Borges use the essay to discuss political and social topics, as well as to entertain. Critic Ilan Stavans feels that Latin American essays are a mirror in which readers can view a true picture of the region's people, problems, and possibilities.

◆ Literary Focus

HUMOROUS ESSAY

A **humorous essay** is a nonfiction composition that presents the author's thoughts on a subject in an amusing way. The author's goal is to amuse the reader, often by pointing out universal truths in a lighthearted or unexpected way.

Plunging into the absurd is one route to humor. García Márquez and Ibargüengoitia use preposterous logic and peculiar points of view to create comic and surprising portraits of umbrellas, silverware, and other everyday items.

◆ Reading Strategy

IDENTIFY TONE

When an essay makes you laugh, you are connecting with the writer's sense of humor. In literary terms, you are sharing and enjoying the writer's **tone**—the attitude he or she takes toward the subject. A writer's attitude can be humorous, sad, angry, sly, or a great many other things.

In speech, you convey attitude through your tone of voice as well as your words. Writers, who are speechless on the page, have only style and word choice to convey their attitudes. However, you can read passages of these essays aloud to turn them back into speech. Your own voice may naturally find the appropriate attitude. For example, you might discover that a formal but sly tone captures the mock-seriousness of this García Márquez sentence:

> The umbrella, though we are led to believe otherwise, was not made for the rain.

▲ **Critical Viewing** García Márquez's essay uses absurd humor. Which elements in this picture reflect a similar type of humor? Explain. **[Analyze]**

Punting for Business, Liz Wright, Private Collection

Uses and Abuses of the Umbrella

Gabriel García Márquez   Translated by Mark Schafer

If one were to produce a careful statistical tabulation of the men who use umbrellas, one would determine that when the rains begin the umbrellas disappear. It's only natural: the umbrella is too fine, too delicate and lovely an article for water to be allowed to ruin it.

The umbrella, though we are led to believe otherwise, was not made for the rain. It was made to be carried on the arm like an enormous ornamental bat and to allow one the opportunity to put on British airs[1] as the atmospheric conditions demanded. If one were to research the history of the umbrella, one would discover that

---

1. put on British airs: Assume the affected, superior manners and graces associated with some upper-class inhabitants of Great Britain.

it was created with a purpose far different from that which formal umbrellists wish to attribute to it—those gentlemen who mistakenly take their umbrellas to the street when it looks like rain, unaware that they are exposing their precious devices to a washing that never figured into their plan.

Cork hats and newspapers of more than eight pages were invented for the rain. Furthermore, before the cork hat and the newspaper of more than eight pages, rain had been invented for just this purpose: to fall on the happy pedestrian who has no reason in the world not to enjoy a shower of pure water from the heavens, still the best prevention against baldness ever invented.

The reduction in umbrellas during the rainy season demonstrates that there are still a goodly number of gentlemen who know what that black, molded tree with metal branches is for, a device invented by someone who grew desperate in the face of the <u>compelling</u> concept of being unable to fold up a bush and take it for a stroll, dangling from his arm. An intelligent woman once said: "The umbrella is an article proper to the desk." And so it is, and it is well that it is so, for it presumes that next to every desk there ought to be a coat rack and, hanging on the coat rack, an umbrella. A dry one, however. For a wet umbrella is an accident, a barbarism, a spelling mistake that must be spread open in a corner until it is fully corrected and has become a true umbrella once again. An item to be carried in the street, to be used to startle friends and—in the worst of cases—to fend off one's creditors.

◆ **Build Vocabulary**

compelling (kəm pel´ iŋ) *adj.*: Captivating; keenly interesting

Guide for Responding

◆ Literature and Your Life

Reader's Response How did this essay affect the way you feel about umbrellas?

Thematic Focus How do you think Márquez would suggest people overcome the obstacle of rain?

Reader's Journal Briefly note humorous directions for using an everyday item or gadget. For example, you might exaggerate the difficulty of using a can opener and write complicated instructions for opening a can with it.

Questions for Research Write three questions you would like to answer if you were to conduct research on the life or work of Gabriel García Márquez.

☑ Check Your Comprehension

1. What are "umbrellists"?
2. Name three uses that García Márquez recommends for umbrellas.
3. For García Márquez, how does one make a wet umbrella "a true umbrella once again"?

◆ Critical Thinking

INTERPRET

1. Give three examples that show how García Márquez turns traditional logic upside down. **[Analyze]**
2. Why do you think García Márquez uses absurd logic in this essay? **[Draw Conclusions]**

APPLY

3. Instead of umbrellas, García Márquez might have written about teapots or paper clips. Name one alternative object and describe how the essay would be different with this topic. **[Modify]**

EXTEND

4. A syllogism presents one or more statements, and then draws a logical conclusion. For example: All umbrellas are tools. Some umbrellas can fold. Therefore, some tools can fold. García Márquez plays with logic to make his humorous point. Construct a faulty or illogical syllogism based on the topic of his essay. Explain why your syllogism is inaccurate. **[Mathematics Link]**

Solve This Case For Me

Jorge Ibargüengoitia

Translated by Fernanda Soicher

In the last few weeks three different people have asked why didn't I write an article about Agatha Christie[1] under the pretext of her death. I told all three the same thing: that to me the lady's books seem unreadable, because the ones I have read or tried to read have caused me one of two experiences: I have found out on page 40 who the murderer was because of my own <u>intuition</u>, for which she isn't to blame (for instance, I think that if a gentleman's only characteristic is that he winds all the clocks in the house every day, he must be the criminal), or, on the contrary, I finish the novel not knowing which way is up and I can't understand the explanation Poirot[2] gives at the end.

But this <u>mundane</u> and <u>contemptuous</u> attitude is, on second thought, false. I think what actually happens to me with Agatha Christie and with any detective story is that I'm hopeless at solving mysteries.

When I examine my past, the opposite of what happens to Hercule Poirot happens to me:

I see in the shadow of the past a forest of unanswered cases.

Not that I have found <u>cadavers</u> when entering the dining room, nor shoes by the swimming pool, nor received a letter signed with little drops of blood. The cases that I have tried to solve are of another nature. If I may, they are small mysteries but no less needling. Above all, no easier to solve.

One of the most unsolvable: Who took the nutcrackers?

In my house there were two identical nutcrackers that had been in my family's possession for at least seventy years. They were old but not so very old (my mother would classify them as old rubbish), not well designed (their form resembled instruments of torture from the Middle Ages), nor were they of precious metal (they were heavy with a peeling silver coating).

This is the *corpus delicti*.[3] The suspects are the ten of us who ate at the house one Sunday in August 1967. Among the fruits there were figs and nuts, and since that day, in my house,

---

1. **Agatha Christie** (1890–1976): English writer of detective stories.
2. **Poirot** Hercule Poirot (er kyəl′ pwä rō′): The detective and protagonist in many of Agatha Christie's stories.

3. ***corpus delicti*** (kôr′ pəs də lik′ tē): "Body of the crime" in Latin; in other words, the facts constituting or proving a crime.

there is only one nutcracker. I have gone over that scene many times in my mind, and I always get wrapped up in its complexity. Of the ten of us who were sitting there, no one has a criminal record, nor has gotten money illegally, nor do we know of anyone who blacks out before a metallic shine. All, I'm sure, have nutcrackers in their respective homes. And I'm also sure that a nutcracker identical to the one I now hold would not have seemed endowed with irresistible beauty to anyone. Nevertheless, there is but one nutcracker.

Another disquieting possibility is that the nutcracker was thrown into the trash, with the nut shells and the fig peel. Who would dare discard this alternative?

Another unsolvable mystery that haunts me is represented by a fork with a different design from the rest that are to be found in my house. It appeared in the silverware drawer in 1950. If I am not mistaken this fork was the property of the Herrasti family. I am the guilty party in that crime. This is clear. The mystery is the circumstance that led me to commit it.

There is another mystery that I think is solved. I'm going to explain it because I believe its solution represents a triumph, not of logic but of parabolic deduction.[4]

I'll start at the end. A few months ago we had a fairly large group of people over for dinner. When the guests left, my wife discovered a very long platinum blonde hair tangled in the bristles of her brush. Later on she noticed that the pot we mix the mustard in had disappeared. In one instant we solved the mystery: at the party there was only one woman with platinum blonde hair. We imagined her using the brush and then putting the mustard pot in her handbag.

But this deduction led me to an even more important conclusion: that woman had been present on another occasion many years before, the night that half a chicken pie disappeared. The triple crime was solved.

---

4. **parabolic deduction:** Using known facts to narrow down several possibilities to a single conclusion.

◆ **Build Vocabulary**

intuition (in tōō ish´ ən) *n.*: Knowing something without conscious use of reason

mundane (mun dān´) *adj.*: Everyday; ordinary

contemptuous (kən temp´ chōō əs) *adj.*: Scornful

cadavers (kə dav´ ərz) *n.*: Dead bodies

Guide for Responding

◆ *Literature and Your Life*

Reader's Response What everyday mysteries remain unsolved in your home or school?

Thematic Focus Do you think that the author's "mysteries" represent obstacles in his life? Why or why not?

Reader's Journal List four or five questions you would ask Ibargüengoitia to help him solve his mysteries.

☑ **Check Your Comprehension**

1. Why does Ibargüengoitia find it difficult to read Agatha Christie's books?
2. What four mysteries does the author try to solve?

◆ **Critical Thinking**

INTERPRET

1. What does the author mean when he says that when he examines his past, "the opposite of what happens to Hercule Poirot happens to me"? **[Interpret]**
2. How does this essay reflect twisted or inverted logic? **[Deduce]**
3. What point does Ibargüengoitia's reasoning make about real-life mysteries? **[Draw Conclusions]**

COMPARE LITERARY WORKS

4. Compare how García Márquez and Ibargüengoitia use common household items as key elements in their essays. **[Compare and Contrast]**

Guide for Responding (continued)

◆ Reading Strategy

IDENTIFY TONE

Your response to an essay depends on under-standing the author's **tone**—the attitude the writer takes toward the subject and the audience. For example, as you begin to read "Uses and Abuses of the Umbrella," you will notice that García Márquez uses a formal tone to address his readers.

Soon, however, you recognize that the tone is almost too formal. The author signals his tone with bluntly emphatic statements and phrases like "though we are led to believe otherwise." After you identify his tone as slyly satirical, you can begin to interpret his meaning.

1. Would you describe García Márquez's attitude as confident or uncertain? Explain your answer.
2. If you were going to make an audio recording of García Márquez's essay, what tips would you give the reader to make sure the tone is correct?
3. How would you describe the tone of "Solve This Case for Me"?
4. Do you think that García Márquez or Ibargüen-goitia treats his audience with greater respect? Why?

◆ Literary Focus

HUMOROUS ESSAY

In these **humorous essays,** García Márquez and Ibargüengoitia transform everyday objects and events into amusing topics, partly by exaggerating their importance. For example, Ibargüengoitia's careful analysis of the disappearance of a nutcracker is amusing because so much attention is given to such a trivial event.

Authors also create humor by contradicting a reader's expectations. Surprising twists can be funny because they are so unexpected or absurd.

1. How does García Márquez use exaggeration to create humor in "Uses and Abuses of the Umbrella"?
2. Explain why Ibargüengoitia's mysteries are comic rather than serious.
3. What do you expect an obituary to include? How does Ibargüengoitia avoid these expectations?
4. Which essay do you think is funnier? Why?

◆ Build Vocabulary

USING THE LATIN ROOT -pel-

Knowing that the Latin root -pel- means "to drive" or "to push," match each word with its definition.

1. expel   **a.** push forward
2. impel   **b.** push away
3. repel   **c.** drive out

USING THE WORD BANK: Synonyms

In your notebook, write the synonym for each word from the Word Bank.

1. contemptuous: (a) modern, (b) scornful, (c) attractive
2. cadavers: (a) adventures, (b) corpses, (c) scoundrels
3. mundane: (a) daily, (b) normal, (c) hypocritical
4. compelling: (a) marginal, (b) repulsive, (c) forceful
5. intuition: (a) instruction, (b) payment, (c) insight

◆ Build Grammar Skills

SUBJUNCTIVE

The use of the **subjunctive mood** in contrary-to-fact statements always requires the past-tense form were.

> If one *were* to count all of the umbrellas in the world.

In sentences that indirectly state a demand or re-quest, the subjunctive form, used with third-person singular subjects, is the form of the verb without s.

> García Márquez suggested that the observer consider the umbrella.

Practice In your notebook, write each sentence using the correct verb from those in parentheses.

1. The flapping umbrella looks as though it (was, were) alive.
2. It is important that the reader (pay, pays) close attention.
3. If umbrellas (was, were) meant to get wet, they would be waterproof.
4. The author insisted that his guest (find, finds) the missing silverware.
5. Ibargüengoitia writes as though he (was, were) a detective of the absurd.

Build Your Portfolio

 Idea Bank

Writing

1. **Real-Life Mystery** Write a detailed description of an unsolved mystery from your own life.

2. **Satirical Essay** Choose a social custom, such as carrying an umbrella pretentiously, and write an essay in which you satirize this common habit.

3. **Response to Criticism** Translator Miguel Arisa has commented that "the Latin American essay is often a funhouse vision of the real world." Write an essay in which you explain how these essays support or refute Arisa's statement.

Speaking, Listening, and Viewing

4. **Book on Tape** Record one of these essays on audiotape. Rehearse reading the essay in order to achieve an appropriate tone. Consider using background music or special effects to enhance your recording. **[Media Link]**

5. **Photo Research** Find a photograph or drawing that you would choose to illustrate the García Márquez or Ibargüengoitia essay. Write a caption in which you explain how this artwork is related to the essay. **[Art Link]**

Researching and Representing

6. **Social Survey** García Márquez parodies the ways in which people use umbrellas. Conduct an observational survey of students in your school to identify common behaviors. For example, you might evaluate student use of backpacks. Share your findings in a report to the class. **[Social Studies Link]**

7. **Latin American Bibliography** Create an annotated bibliography describing works of Latin American fiction and nonfiction. Use a variety of reference sources, from books and magazines to the Internet and CD-ROMs, to gather information about well-known authors and works. **[Social Studies Link]**

Online Activity www.phlit.phschool.com

 Guided Writing Lesson

Humorous Anecdote

Essayists often find humor in retelling events in a way that emphasizes their funny aspects. Write a humorous anecdote—a brief account of a comic event—about a true-life experience. Choose something that happened to you or a true story with which you are familiar.

Writing Skills Focus: Clear Beginning, Development, and Conclusion

A successful anecdote tells a complete story. Although the form is brief, your anecdote should still have a clear **beginning**, a very thorough **development**, and a satisfying **conclusion**. Remember that your audience is not familiar with this story, so they need enough information to understand it fully.

Prewriting Brainstorm for ideas by thinking about real-life events that have made you laugh. After choosing a topic, use an outline or flowchart to help you identify the essential elements that will make up the beginning, development, and conclusion of your anecdote.

Drafting Keep a humorous or light tone in mind while your draft. Look for opportunities to exaggerate and to use absurd or unexpected language that will contribute to the humor of your writing.

Revising Have a partner read your anecdote. Discuss whether or not your anecdote feels complete. Check that your opening clearly introduces your anecdote and that your conclusion is satisfying.

Review the verb tenses in your writing. If you have used the subjunctive mood, circle the verb and make sure its form is correct. For more on the subjunctive mood, see pp. 782 and 788.

Guide for Reading

Eduardo Galeano *(1940–)*

Living in Montevideo, Uruguay, Eduardo Galeano (ed wär´ dō gä lē ä´ nō) reflects on essential aspects of Latin American life as experienced by everyone from workers and children to politicians and celebrities.

Galeano's trilogy, *Memories of Fire* (1985–1988), provides a sweeping history of Latin America and the New World by assembling anecdotes and tales, newspaper clippings, and surprising statistics. The second volume, *Faces and Masks,* includes "Temptation of America."

Miguel Angel Asturias *(1899–1974)*

Winner of the Nobel Prize for Literature in 1967, Miguel Angel Asturias (mi gel´ än hel´ as tōōr´ ē əs) wrote many books that explore the cultures, histories, and abuses of the native peoples of Latin America.

As a student, Asturias became fascinated with Mayan culture. He translated *Popol Vuh,* a sacred Mayan text, into Spanish. The influence of these ancient mystical tales can be felt in many of his other works.

"Lake Titicaca," from an essay collection published in 1972, demonstrates Asturias's use of inventive poetic imagery to create an intense description.

Ernesto Ruelas Inzunza *(1968–)*

Author of "Work That Counts," Ernesto Ruelas Inzunza is the executive director of Pronatura-Vera Cruz, a conservation organization in Vera Cruz, Mexico. Pronatura is raising money to meet a challenge grant from the National Fish and Wildlife Foundation and the Agency of International Development. The money will be used to build a nature center and bird observatory in Cardel, one of the monitoring stations mentioned in Inzunza's article. Contributors to this effort are dubbed "Friends of River of Raptors."

◆ Build Vocabulary

LATIN SUFFIXES: *-mony*

Watching a woman weaving ceaselessly, Asturias wonders, "From what old hegemony does that sorrow come?" *Hegemony* contains the Latin suffix *-mony,* which means "a resulting condition, state, or thing." The word part *hege-* comes from the Greek word for "leader." *Hegemony* is "the condition resulting from being under the influence of a leader." It is often used to refer to the influence of one nation over another.

WORD BANK

| undulating |
| foundry |
| palpable |
| avian |
| hegemony |
| myriad |
| topography |

As you read these essays, you will encounter the words on this list. Each word is defined on the page where it first appears. Preview the list before you read.

◆ Build Grammar Skills

VARIED SENTENCE BEGINNINGS: ADVERB PHRASES

Good writing exhibits variety in sentence structure. To create variety and interest, writers sometimes begin their sentences with **adverb phrases**—prepositional phrases that modify a verb, adjective, or an adverb:

In laboratories and in factories, technicians can now create conditions . . .

In this example, two introductory prepositional phrases modify the verb *create. In laboratories* and *in factories* answer the question, Where can technicians create conditions?

Temptation of America
◆ Lake Titicaca ◆ Work That Counts ◆

◆ *Literature and Your Life*

CONNECT YOUR EXPERIENCE

Think of a place that you have never seen, but would like to visit. What images or ideas have made you curious about this place? You might have read articles, viewed photographs, or seen films set there. A variety of sources have combined to create your impression.

These essayists all describe places to create impressions for their readers.

THEMATIC FOCUS: THE NATURAL WORLD

As you read these essays, ask yourself: What techniques do these writers use to increase your appreciation of the natural world or of legendary places?

Journal Writing Jot down a list of preparations you would make before visiting an unfamiliar place.

◆ Background for Understanding

SOCIAL STUDIES

Eduardo Galeano reflects on the legend of El Dorado that Spanish conquerors brought home from Latin America in the sixteenth century. This legend built a small kernel of truth into a tale of fabulous riches. "El Dorado"—"The Golden Man"— was first a story of a community that was so rich with gold that the king wore this precious metal as a costume.

Latin America's spectacular geography helped encourage the exaggerations linked to El Dorado. Although its waters are not made of gold, Lake Titicaca is one of the continent's great spectacles. The subject of Asturias's dreamlike essay, this lake perches high in the Andes mountains and spreads an awesome 145 miles across.

◆ Literary Focus

THEME

The **theme** of a work is its central meaning—the main idea that an author is trying to communicate. In an essay, the theme can be stated directly in a thesis statement, or implied, through the author's selection of details, facts, and opinions.

For example, "Work That Counts" implies the idea that animal migrations are an important pattern in our world. By relating each part of his essay to this implied theme, Inzunza creates strong support for it and emphasizes the need to understand this fascinating natural behavior.

◆ Reading Strategy

RECOGNIZE THE WRITER'S MOTIVATION

As you read, consider the **writer's motivation**—the reasons or causes—for presenting a theme in a certain form and style. Here are some questions you might ask yourself to uncover an author's motivation:

- What ideas or information does the author want to convey?
- How does the author want me to respond?
- What inspired the writer to choose this topic?
- Why did the writer choose this writing style?

For example, as you read "Temptation of America," you will notice that Galeano describes El Dorado through the eyes of a European geographer. You might ask why Galeano uses this perspective. You may conclude that Galeano's motivation is to create an vivid historical portrait that illustrates the European view of Latin America.

TEMPTATION OF AMERICA

Eduardo Galeano
Translated by Cedric Belfrage

In his study in Paris, a learned geographer scratches his head. Guillaume Delisle[1] draws exact maps of the earth and the heavens. Should he include El Dorado[2] on the map of America? Should he paint in the mysterious lake, as has become the custom, somewhere in the upper Orinoco?[3] Delisle asks himself whether the golden waters, described by Walter Raleigh[4] as the size of the Caspian Sea, really exist. And those princes who plunge in and swim by the light of torches, undulating golden fish: are they or were they ever flesh and bone?

The lake, sometimes named El Dorado, sometimes Paríma, figures on all maps drawn up to now. But what Delisle has heard and read makes him doubt. Seeking El Dorado, many soldiers of fortune have

1. **Guillaume Delisle** (gē ōm´ də lēl´): French scientist (1675–1726) and one of the founders of modern geography. His highly scientific approach to cartography made his maps amazingly accurate for their time.
2. **El Dorado:** Legendary country in South America, supposed to be rich in gold and precious stones and sought by early Spanish explorers.
3. **Orinoco** (ôr´ ə nō´ kō): River in Venezuela, flowing from the Brazil border into the Atlantic.
4. **Walter Raleigh:** English statesman, explorer, and poet (c. 1552–1618). He founded one of the earliest English colonies in the New World.

penetrated the remote new world, over there where the four winds meet and all colors and pains mingle, and have found nothing. Spaniards, Portuguese, Englishmen, Frenchmen, and Germans have spanned abysses that the American gods dug with nails and teeth; have violated forests warmed by tobacco smoke puffed by the gods; have navigated rivers born of giant trees the gods tore out by the roots; have tortured and killed Indians the gods created out of saliva, breath, or dream. But that fugitive gold has vanished and always vanishes into the air, the lake disappearing before anyone can reach it. El Dorado seems to be the name of a grave without coffin or shroud.

♦ **Build Vocabulary**

undulating (un´ dyo͞o lāt´ iŋ) *adj.*: Moving in waves

In the two centuries that have passed since the world grew and became round, pursuers of hallucinations have continued heading for the lands of America from every wharf. Protected by a god of navigation and conquest, squeezed into their ships, they cross the immense ocean. Along with shepherds and farmhands whom Europe has not killed by war, plague, or hunger, go captains and merchants and rogues and mystics and adventurers. All seek the miracle. Beyond the ocean, magical ocean that cleanses blood and transfigures destinies, the great promise of all the ages lies open. There, beggars will be avenged. There, nobodies will turn into marquises, scoundrels into saints, gibbet-fodder[5] into founders . . .

---

5. **gibbet-fodder** (jib´ it fä´ dər): A gibbet is a structure on which criminals are executed publicly by hanging. Metaphorically, criminals are fodder, or food, for gibbets.

Guide for Responding

♦ Literature and Your Life

Reader's Response Which image from this essay do you find most memorable? Why?

Thematic Focus How does Galeano use larger-than-life qualities to describe the Latin American landscape?

Questions for Research Write three questions you would like to answer in a research report about El Dorado. Tell four sources you would use to find the information.

✓ **Check Your Comprehension**

1. What is Guillaume Delisle's job?
2. What decision is he trying to make?

♦ Critical Thinking

INTERPRET

1. What does Galeano feel motivates Europeans to come to "the lands of America"? **[Infer]**
2. How does Galeano's description of this migration reflect his attitude toward it? **[Deduce]**

APPLY

3. Does Galeano encourage his readers to be trusting? **[Generalize]**

EXTEND

4. How did travelers' tales encourage the expansion of the United States as well as the exploration of the Americas? **[Social Studies Link]**

◀ **Critical Viewing**
What feeling does this photograph of Lake Titicaca call up in you? Why?
[Respond]

Lake Titicaca

Miguel Angel Asturias   Translated by Jesse H. Lytle

The wind blows, making calls. We listen to it pass. Gusts. And we are still distant. Two, three condor flights. We know we must keep our eyes. Not let our eyes be stolen by the altiplano[1] that emerges and submerges in every direction. They grow. They grow. The hills, the highlands, the mountains grow. Waves. Waves of a gigantic, seamless mass from the Cretaceous[2] that become, at the height of the American world, the fairest crown of water: Titicaca.

Mineral water. Other American lakes have vegetable waters. The sun knows it. And it is not a heavenly body, but a foundry in the west. Water with the cold and shimmer of precious stone. Its sweetness surprises. Water in which the armor of the Incan empire's conquistadors[3] has not rusted. And it has been entombed already for centuries in its profound vase.

Now close your history books. I saw, as the sun was setting, the conquistadors' steel shadows sink in search of the city of gold, hidden by the waters of this Andean[4] sweet-lake sea. They accompanied me from the high solitudes, and we discerned, not burning, but set ablaze by the sun, boats that looked more like the braided tresses of women, basaltic reflections of

---

1. **altiplano** (al´ ti plä´ nō) *n.*: High plateau, or plain.
2. **Cretaceous** (kri tā´ shəs) *n.*: The Cretaceous Period in geological history, between approximately 65 and 136 million years ago.

3. **Incan empire's conquistador's** (kän kwis´ tə dôrz´): Spanish explorers who, in the sixteenth century, conquered the Incas, a native South American civilization.
4. **Andean** (an´ dē ən) *adj.*: Of the Andes Mountains, which span the length of western South America. Lake Titicaca is located within this mountain range.

pick-cut rocks; the reflection here is palpable, bulrushes[5] shaking with every sight of the advancing night, solemn, with all its stars lying in wait, through the Puerta del Tiahuanaco,[6] and the island on which man and woman, the first ones, created by the dying star, went crazy and broke their golden canes.

You're not going to cut my hand off . . . ! I heard the voice of the Indian whose wrist I had just taken unexpectedly, in a no-man's-land of waters and silences, to raise the hollow of that fingered conch[7] to my ear, like an aquatic snail, with curdled lines of cabalistic marks, tiny fingernails of yellowish mother-of-pearl, gnawed by an avian beak, and the skin of labor.

I heard, I discovered the origin of man, in the hollowed hand of that Indian, who belonged to the oldest race on the planet, the lone example who spoke a language like water falling from his lips, and then I wrote these verses:

The Indian knows full well what this means,
it is to be from here, whence America comes.

When I released his hand, he told me of his riches, and I understood that he spoke of the great lake of ears of corn that all of us Indians have in our heart and from which we get tiny drops of moonlight to adorn the liquid, nocturnal gods, whose faces mimic the dark sky with eyes.

Other tributaries[8] of the great lake join us as we walk. They travel with their llamas. They see me,

knitting their cheeks to contemplate me with tiny eyes. Do I not deserve to be seen by their big eyes? They play with bulrush roots with their magnificent teeth. The path narrows, weaves through the hills; it will elude us if we do not follow it closely. Another grove of craggy heights and deep, sleeping waters. We approach the shore. Dizzily, we descend. The wind. The waves unfolding upon the sand. Someone. The stranger's feet are not dragging, but they seem to drag, the blistered skirt is so low. From the hat, one would say a man. But it is a woman, by her tresses and her clothing. Her hands do not rest. She weaves with black thread. From what old hegemony does that sorrow come? Other Indians accompany her. But far behind. And others farther. The space does not separate them, but unites them.

The great emptiness and the immense silence. The scarce vegetation. Perspectives persist in angles that open and close, and the innocence of the transparent air, through which some bird of prey crosses, while the clouds quilt the sky, and we have time to turn around to see Lake Titicaca from an even higher footing.

---

8. **tributaries:** People who are proceeding to the lake as though bearing gifts to a king.

---

5. **bulrushes** (boͦl′ rush′ əz) *n.*: Marsh plants having slender, solid stems tipped with brown spikelets of tiny flowers.
6. **Puerta del Tiahuanaco** (pwer′ tə del tē′ hwä nä′ kō): Port located on Lake Titicaca that was once inhabited by a great pre-Incan civilization.
7. **conch** (känch) *n.*: Shell of a large marine snail.

◆ **Build Vocabulary**

foundry (foun′ drē) *n.*: Place where metal is cast
palpable (pal′ pə bəl) *adj.*: Capable of being touched or felt
avian (ā′ vē ən) *adj.*: Of a bird; having to do with birds
hegemony (hi jem′ ə nē) *n.*: Condition of being under a leader's influence

Guide for Responding

◆ Literature and Your Life

Reader's Response Did this essay make you want to visit Lake Titicaca? Why or why not?

☑ **Check Your Comprehension**

1. Where is the narrator of the essay going?
2. Who is with him?

◆ Critical Thinking

INTERPRET

1. What emotional insight does the narrator reach by listening to the Indian's hand? **[Infer]**
2. How does Asturias try to share his emotional response to the lake with his readers? **[Analyze]**

Work That Counts
Ernesto Ruelas Inzunza

After sunset, I finally have time to sit peacefully and tell my friend Jeros, who is new to hawk watching, the story of the discovery of the River of Raptors.

It is the end of a long day of watching and counting birds of prey in the small town of Chichicaxtle in the state of Veracruz, Mexico. At eight this morning, as Jeros and I climbed the observation tower, about forty-five Swainson's hawks were just taking off from the nearby canyon where they had spent the night. Shortly afterward, we saw hundreds of them turning circles in the thermal columns of hot air, effortlessly gaining altitude. By eleven, the Swainson's had joined smaller numbers of broad-winged hawks and turkey vultures, forming long streams of migrants. Such large flocks, totaling more than 20,000 birds at times, can take up to thirty minutes to pass overhead. Resembling myriad moving organisms in a plankton sample, the raptors filled our binoculars' field of view. We watched the avian river continue north until it disappeared.

Each spring and fall, the spectacle of raptor

◆ **Build Vocabulary**

myriad (mir´ ē əd) *adj.*: Huge number; seemingly countless

topography (tə päg´ rə fē) *n.*: Surface features of a place, such as rivers, lakes, mountains, and so on

migration fills the skies of Veracruz in eastern Mexico as the birds funnel through a narrow geographic corridor and above our monitoring stations at Chichicaxtle and Cardel. This bottle-neck is formed where the Mexican central volcanic belt reaches the Gulf of Mexico and almost cuts the lowlands of the coastal plain in two. The topography and atmospheric conditions of the lowlands provide birds of prey and many other migrants with the conditions needed for migrating with the least expenditure of energy: tail winds and warm thermal updrafts.

Among the migrating raptors are turkey vultures; ospreys; swallow-tailed, Mississippi, and plumbeous kites; northern harriers; sharp-shinned, Cooper's, Harris's, red-shouldered, broad-winged, Swainson's, zone-tailed, and red-tailed hawks; and falcons, including kestrels, merlins, and peregrines. The migrations of a few other species—hook-billed kites, golden eagles and ferruginous hawks—are less well documented in Veracruz and are currently being studied. Five species of swallows, scissor-tailed flycatchers, white-winged and mourning doves, wood storks, white pelicans, cormorants, and white-faced and white ibises are also among the list of more than 220

species of migratory birds recorded at Veracruz. In fall, the count totals range between 2.5 million and 4 million birds, the highest count anywhere in the world, as birds journeying from eastern, central, and western North America converge here in Veracruz.

After five in the evening, when the temperature dropped down to 82° F and the thermals ceased to form, the pace slowed. Now I can respond in more detail to Jeros's question about the discovery of the River of Raptors. I read him a paragraph written in the spring of 1897 by ornithologist Frank M. Chapman, of the American Museum of Natural History: "On April 6 and 16, flights of hawks—I was unable to determine the species—were observed passing northward, exceeding in number any migration of these birds I have before seen." Almost a hundred years passed before bird counts were organized at Veracruz and Chapman's statements were borne out. Yet as long as these lowlands have been inhabited, the migration must have been seen and accepted by the local inhabitants as an autumn phenomenon. I conclude by telling my friend that perhaps the River of Raptors has always been known. And, he adds, admired.

Guide for Responding

◆ *Literature and Your Life*

Reader's Response Describe any bird migrations that you've observed. Where were you? What formation did the birds fly in? Could you identify the species?

Thematic Focus What observations have you made about the effect of natural forces, such as storms and droughts, upon birds?

☑ Check Your Comprehension

1. What is Inzunza's work as described in this essay?
2. What conditions allow birds to migrate with the least expenditure of energy?
3. (a) Who discovered the River of Raptors? (b) Why was it unique at the time?

◆ Critical Thinking

INTERPRET
1. What geographic conditions contribute to the phenomenon called the River of Raptors? **[Analyze Cause and Effect]**
2. What does Inzunza suggest with the double meaning of his title? **[Infer]**

APPLY
3. Imagine that you are raising funds for Pronatura-Vera Cruz, the organization for which Inzunza collects data. What arguments might you use to attract donations to monitor and protect the River of Raptors? **[Defend]**

EXTEND
4. Birds of prey are carnivorous, or flesh eating. Name some other creatures that are carnivorous. Explain. **[Science Link]**

Guide for Responding (continued)

◆ Reading Strategy

RECOGNIZE THE WRITER'S MOTIVATION

Evaluating a **writer's motivation**—why he or she wrote a particular text—helps you understand both the writing and the writer's process. As you reflect on your reading, put yourself in the writer's place. Consider why the author chose a particular topic and how he or she wants the reader to react.

For example, after reading "Work That Counts," you might decide that Inzunza's motivation is to share his enthusiasm for birds with a wide audience.

1. Why do you think Galeano describes the American landscape as having been created by gods?
2. What does Galeano's depiction of Latin American geography indicate about his motivation?
3. How do you think Asturias would like his readers to feel about Lake Titicaca?
4. (a) Which of the three authors do you think was primarily motivated by a desire to share concrete facts? (b) Which author was more interested in sharing an emotional response?

◆ Literary Focus

THEME

The **theme** of a work is its central meaning—the main idea the writer wants to share. In most essays, the theme is implied, through an accumulation of details and insights.

For example, Galeano describes the fictional El Dorado to analyze the reasons that Europeans were drawn to Latin America. These strands combine to highlight the theme of how unrealistic expectations led Europeans to invade and oppress Latin America.

1. How does the title of Galeano's essay point to his theme?
2. In your own words, state the theme of "Lake Titicaca."
3. Asturias breaks from prose to include this verse: "The Indian knows full well what this means, /it is to be from here, whence America comes." Does this verse directly state the theme of Asturias's essay? Why or why not?

◆ Build Vocabulary

USING THE LATIN SUFFIX -mony

Knowing that the Latin suffix -*mony*, which appears in *hegemony*, means "a resulting condition, state, or thing," match each word with its definition.

1. matrimony   **a.** state of affected piety
2. patrimony   **b.** condition of being stingy
3. parsimony   **c.** condition of marriage
4. sanctimony   **d.** condition in which something is inherited from one's father

USING THE WORD BANK: Analogies

Complete these sentences with the best word from the Word Bank. Write the words in your notebook, and use each word only once.

1. The lake appeared to be a mirage of soft currents and ___?___ waves.
2. The ___?___ of the European conquerors has oppressed many native peoples.
3. He studied the relationship between ___?___ migration patterns and insect populations.
4. The researcher was surprised that the wind from the soaring flock was ___?___ on land.
5. Dark smoke emerged from the iron ___?___.

◆ Build Grammar Skills

ADVERB PHRASES

Adverb phrases are prepositional phrases that modify a verb, adjective, or another adverb. Placing an adverb phrase at the beginning of a sentence is one way to achieve sentence variety.

Practice On your paper, write the adverb phrase in each sentence and tell what it modifies.

1. In dreams and in legends, El Dorado exerts a strong pull.
2. Upon their return to Spain, the men told inspirational, and implausible, tales of America.
3. On a clear night, the water of Lake Titicaca sparkles like ice.
4. In the Andes, water is an essential natural resource.
5. With its wide expanse and breathtaking setting, the lake retains an almost legendary quality.

Build Your Portfolio

 ## Idea Bank

Writing

1. **Persuasive Letter** As Ernesto Ruelas Inzunza, write a fund-raising letter describing the importance of studying and protecting birds.

2. **Verse Response** Create a poem that responds to Galeano's portrait of El Dorado or Asturias's impressions of Lake Titicaca.

3. **Political Analysis** The essay is often a political form, even when the topic is not obviously about governments or politicians. Choose one of the essays and analyze the social or political commentary or criticism implied by the author. **[Social Studies Link]**

Speaking, Listening, and Viewing

4. **Audio Tour** Prepare an audio tour of a natural site in your area. Use narration, sound effects, music, and silence to create a strong impression. Consider taping your tour on location. **[Career Link; Performing Arts Link]**

5. **Bird Shapes** Create your own poster that would help a novice ornithologist identify several kinds of raptors. **[Science Link]**

Researching and Representing

6. **Conservation Update** Using pictures and research material from books or the Internet, prepare an update on efforts to preserve the status of endangered birds worldwide. **[Science Link]**

7. **Itinerary** Use maps, schedules, and other resources to plan the itinerary for a geographic tour of Latin America. Describe your itinerary in a class report. **[Social Studies Link]**

Online Activity www.phlit.phschool.com

 ## Guided Writing Lesson

Reflective Essay

Galeano, Asturias, and Inzunza were each inspired to write an essay to share specific thoughts with their readers. In a reflective essay, an author shares his or her thoughts about an idea or personal experience. Choose an event or place you have experienced firsthand, and write an essay in which you share your feelings and insights about this topic.

Writing Skills Focus: Main Impression

As you develop your reflective essay, consider the **main impression,** or "big picture," you want to leave with your readers. All of the elements in a unified and effective essay will contribute to this main impression.

For example, Miguel Asturias uses fragmented images and highly poetic language to create the impression of Lake Titicaca as a sacred and magical place.

Prewriting Brainstorm for a list of adjectives that describe the main impression you want to create. Select two or three adjectives that help you focus your selection of details

Drafting As you draft, refer to the adjectives you selected to help you choose language that will contribute to your main impression. Remember that you are writing for a reader who may not share your experiences.

Revising Read your essay aloud to a partner. Ask your listener to summarize the "big picture" your essay creates. Have you reached your reader as you intended? If not, add further details to support this impression.

Check that you have included an interesting variety of sentences. To create additional variety, introduce several sentences with adverb phrases.

For more on adverb phrases, see pp. 790 and 798.

Writing Process Workshop

In this unit, you've met some interesting characters—both fictional and real—from dashing Pepe Gonzalez to the famous Anthony Quinn. Choose someone you know, and write a **firsthand biography** of him or her. A firsthand biography is a narrative about a person—the subject—with whom you have had direct experience. A firsthand biography can be about the entire life of the subject or it may focus on an important episode or period in the subject's life. Your relationship with your subject should give you insights not found in biographies based solely on research.

The following skills will help you write an interesting firsthand biography.

Writing Skills Focus

▶ **Grab your reader's attention** at the beginning with a startling quotation or interesting anecdote.

▶ Like other stories, a biography should have a **beginning, middle,** and **end.**

▶ **Choose words with appropriate connotations**. For example, when describing a person, the word *skinny* has a different connotation from the word *lean*.

The following excerpt from Truman Capote's *A Christmas Memory* illustrates these skills.

MODEL FROM LITERATURE

from *A Christmas Memory* by Truman Capote

① The connotation of the phrase *pitifully hunched* creates sympathy by conjuring up the image of a frail, old woman.

② When the writer says that "We are each other's best friend," he grabs the reader's attention, since the ages of the two are so far apart.

She is wearing tennis shoes and a shapeless gray sweater over a summery calico dress. She is small and sprightly, like a bantam hen; but due to a long youthful illness her shoulders are pitifully hunched ①. Her face is remarkable—not unlike Lincoln's, craggy like that, and tinted by the sun and wind; but it is delicate too, finely boned, and her eyes are sherry-colored and timid. "Oh my," she exclaims, her breath smoking the windowpane, "it's fruitcake weather!"

The person to whom she is speaking is myself. I am seven; she is sixty-something. We are each other's best friend. ②

Prewriting

Choose a Topic Think about a person whom you admire. It might be a close friend, a student or teacher you admire, a favorite relative, or someone who has done something interesting. Make a list of several possibilities, and then consider which one you know best. Choose that person as the subject of your firsthand biography.

Consider Your Audience Before you begin to write, think about the people for whom you are writing. Consider your audience's interests and background, and make sure your details and language are appropriate for such an audience. The following checklist will help you define your audience:

▶ Who are your readers—classmates, relatives, or a teacher?

▶ How much does your audience know about your subject?

▶ Is your audience familiar with words or phrases that your subject may use or has used?

▶ If you wish to convey a message, how do you think your readers will feel about it?

Drafting

Reveal Your Subject You can reveal important aspects of your subject's personality or life either directly or indirectly. When you reveal the character of your subject directly, you openly state the personality traits of the subject. To reveal your subject's character indirectly, present his or her own thoughts, words, or actions. Use direct quotations and vivid verbs to reveal your character's personality more effectively. Look at the following two examples:

Direct

Tom is a very competitive person. He always wants to have the highest score. He is rude to anyone who scores higher than he does.

Indirect

Last week I ran into Tom at the mall. My smile of greeting froze on my face when he said, "Hey Brad! What's the big idea? Since when did you become the brilliant math student? How did you get a better score than I did?" I had expected Tom to be upset. He's been known to sulk for days if he doesn't get the highest score on an exam.

APPLYING LANGUAGE SKILLS: Quotation Marks

You'll probably want to use **quotations** in your firsthand biography. Make sure that you punctuate all of your direct quotations correctly.

• Use quotation marks to set off the exact words of a speaker.

• Place commas and periods inside final quotation marks.

• Start a new paragraph when the speaker changes.

Practice On your paper, punctuate the following dialogue correctly.

I can't believe Mike isn't here yet said Frank. Me neither, replied Bob. He was supposed to be here an hour ago. Where could he be? You got me, answered Frank.

Writing Application Include direct quotations in your firsthand biography. Punctuate them correctly.

Writer's Solution Connection
Language Lab

For more practice with quotation marks, complete the Language Lab lesson on Quotation Marks, Colons, and Semicolons.

Applying Language Skills: Vivid Verbs

Good writers use **vivid verbs** to make their writing clear and precise. A vivid verb describes an action in a strong, exact manner.

Vague Verbs:
Rows of books and trophies are on John's shelves. Posters are on his wall. On his desk is a small totem-pole.

Vivid Verbs:
Rows of books and trophies clutter John's shelves. Posters decorate his wall. On his desk stands a small totem pole.

Practice On your paper, replace the vague verbs in the following sentence with vivid ones.

The weather was hot last week. The morning sun was bright as John came up to my house on his bike.

Writing Application Review your firsthand biography and replace vague, weak verbs with vivid ones.

Writer's Solution Connection
Writing Lab

To see more ideas for publishing your firsthand biography, refer to Publishing and Presenting in the Writing Lab tutorial on Narration.

Revising

Read Your Firsthand Biography Aloud A good revising technique is to read your work aloud. If you find parts difficult to read aloud, chances are a reader will also have trouble reading and understanding it. Work on making those areas smooth and clear.

Proofreading

Use a Proofreading Checklist Use the following checklist to make sure your draft is free of errors in grammar, spelling, and punctuation:

▶ Have you punctuated all dialogue correctly?
▶ Does each sentence end with the appropriate punctuation?
▶ Have you spelled all words correctly, including homophones such as *your* and *you're*?
▶ If you're using a computer, did you check that you didn't accidentally substitute one small word for another, such as *and* for *an* or *of* for *or*?

REVISION MODEL

① *"Belay on! Climb when ready!"* ② *those words,* ③ *stared*
When I heard Lynn shout¸I took a big gulp,¸looked up at

③ *stepped*
the rope snaking into the distance above me, and¸moved

out onto the blank rock face.

① The writer adds this direct quotation to make the situation more lifelike.
② This addition is needed to clarify the connection to the direct quotation.
③ The writer replaces these vague verbs with vivid ones.

Publishing

Publish On-line On-line magazines, Usenet news groups, and electronic bulletin boards are just a few of the options for publishing your writing on the World Wide Web. For more information, consult Prentice Hall on the Web at **http://www.phschool.com**.

Student Success Workshop

Real-World Reading Skills

Evaluating the Credibility of Information Sources

Strategies for Success

These days, thanks to the availability of research tools such as the Internet, it is possible to locate all kinds of information sources, on nearly any topic. But not all information sources are equally credible—that is, believable or accurate. Before you accept any piece of information as being true or factual, it is often wise to evaluate the credibility of the person or publication that is its source. For example, before you believe what a pamphlet says about what quantities of vitamins and minerals to take, you should know whether the author is medically qualified to give this advice. Do some research to check the credibility of your information sources.

Read Critically In order to evaluate the credibility of an information source, it helps to read critically:

▶ **Analyze "Facts" and Supporting "Evidence"** Any book, newspaper article, Web site, or magazine that intends to present "facts" about a topic must provide convincing supporting evidence in order to be considered believable. If the author has failed to do this, it may be worth taking time to analyze what he or she has presented. You can do some research. If you've read an account of UFO sightings, you can evaluate the credibility of the writer's "facts" and supporting "evidence" in the light of statistics gathered by scientific researchers. Consider all sides of an issue, rather than accepting one writer's version of the truth.

▶ **Evaluate the Author's Motivation** An important question to ask yourself when reading any article is whether the author is being objective, or unbiased—or whether he or she might be biased or trying to promote a certain point of view. For example, someone who works as a speechwriter or consultant for a political candidate might not be motivated to provide an unbiased or full report on the policies of that candidate's political opponent. Likewise, a writer hired to write an advertisement for a fast-food company is likely to downplay the health risks associated with high-fat foods.

Apply the Strategies

Locate and read two sources of information that present different viewpoints on the same topic. For example, you might read two magazine articles expressing opposite points of view on responsible forest management. Compare how credibly each side of the controversy—perhaps a timber company and a group of concerned forest rangers—presents its facts and supporting evidence. Make a list of the facts and supporting evidence each writer offers, and evaluate his or her motivation. Write several paragraphs evaluating the credibility of each information source.

✔ Here are some situations in which to evaluate the credibility of an information source:

▶ Reviewing sales information about a new product or service
▶ Reading a review of a particular work of art, such as a book, film, painting, or performance
▶ Evaluating an account of a controversial incident
▶ Reading an article about a new medical procedure

Speaking, Listening, and Viewing Workshop

One of the quickest ways to find out about current events is to turn on a television set. However, don't be in a hurry to accept all you see. Think of a media presentation as a product; analyze and critique it for quality before accepting it. Consider all the elements that contribute to the way information is presented.

Recognize the Genre Identify the type of media presentation you are viewing. Be aware that each genre has its own style, and adjust your response to its message accordingly.

Straightforward news reports, such as the nightly news, are meant to recount information factually and objectively—that is, without stating the newscaster's or the station's opinion. For example, a report on a political campaign would present the results of popularity polls, but not the reporters' opinions about the candidates.

Documentaries offer an in-depth, factual exploration of a topic and may or may not reveal the personal slant of the filmmaker. They often include visual and sound techniques, such as special editing effects, camera angles, music, and sequencing, which convey additional messages to the viewer.

Television newsmagazines offer in-depth exploration of a topic, often with a less objective slant. In either genre, a focus on overcrowding in homeless shelters might include interviews with homeless people or a tour of a shelter, as well as facts and statistics.

Editorials offer an opinion, often persuasively and usually on a controversial topic. They are usually accompanied by an announcement that the views presented are the opinions of one individual. An editorial that proposes raising the speed limit might offer personal opinions supported by facts and statistics.

Recognize Persuasive Techniques Be on the lookout for any visual symbols in a media message. Listen closely to the language used.

Broad generalizations, statements that may not be completely logical, and emotional words may be intended to persuade you to think a certain way or change your point of view. Notice how different word choices can completely change the effect of a news report:

> A wild grizzly terrorized a group of unsuspecting Boy Scouts camping in the wilderness.

> A group of Boy Scouts were surprised by an unexpected visitor to their campsite—a grizzly!

Apply the Strategies

Choose one or more of these activities. Apply the strategies for critically viewing media presentations.

1. Watch a media presentation on television. Identify the genre of the presentation. Explain its basic message. Then critique the presentation. Note and evaluate any persuasive techniques that influence your response.

2. Watch a documentary or newsmagazine on television. Critique and evaluate how its use of visual and sound techniques conveys messages.

3. Compare and contrast the media coverage of the same event on television, in a newspaper, and on the Internet.

Tips for Analyzing Media Presentations

▶ Identify the type of report you are seeing.

▶ Separate the main idea of the media message from any persuasive techniques.

▶ Pay attention to language and word choice that might cause you to react in a certain way.

Test Preparation Workshop

Critical Reading

Strategies for Success

The reading sections of certain standardized tests require you to read a passage to recognize forms of propaganda. The tests also require you to distinguish between facts and nonfacts in a passage. Use the following strategies to help you answer test questions on these skills:

Recognize Propaganda Propaganda is information that may or may not be factual or accurate but which aims to persuade the public that it is. It may appear in speeches, brochures, advertisements, or editorials. As you read, try to determine what the writer hopes you will believe, what the writer's motives may be, and whether or not the information is factual or misleading.

For example, you might be asked to recognize propaganda in a passage such as the following:

> The mayor blames our factory for polluting the river. His new program will force us to report on how we are working to prevent industrial emissions from contaminating the air, ground, and water. If we don't comply, our company will face steep fines. The result? Predictably, workers will be laid off. The city can't afford to take this risk! We should all protest the mayor's plan.

1 You can tell from this that the author will
   A work personally to reduce pollution.
   B present the mayor's plan in a positive way.
   C persuade readers not to support the mayor's program, despite its potential benefits to the environment.
   D expose other businesses that are polluters.

The author does not speak of his or her own personal plans, so **A** is incorrect. **B** is incorrect, since the author does not praise the mayor's program. **D** is incorrect, since the author mentions no other businesses. The correct answer is **C**.

Distinguish Between Fact and Nonfact

Facts can be proved or checked. Nonfacts, or opinions, cannot be proved.

2 Which of these statements about the mayor's plan is an opinion?
   A The mayor blames our factory for polluting the river.
   B The program will force us to report.
   C The city can't afford to take this risk!
   D If we don't comply, our company will face steep fines.

Answers **A, B,** and **D** are all facts that can be proven or checked. **C** is an opinion that cannot be proven and is the correct answer.

Apply the Strategies

Read the following passage from a political speech, and answer the questions.

> We are all aware of our schools' budget deficits. Yet the majority of taxpayers do not support a tax increase to help fund the schools. Many school programs have been eliminated or cut back over the last two years. I ask you to think about what our students' future will be if we don't help them today. A tax increase is the only answer. Please give our students hope for the future.

1 You can tell that the speaker
   A is not telling the whole truth.
   B is only trying to discredit an opponent.
   C hopes to persuade the audience to take action.
   D wants to convince the audience to vote.
2 Which of these is a fact stated in the passage?
   A School programs have been cut back.
   B Most taxpayers support a tax increase.
   C A tax increase is the only answer.
   D We are all aware of our schools' budget deficits.

Drama in World Literature

Drama is one of our earliest literary forms. Ancient people would act out great triumphs, deep fears, or heartfelt wishes in religious rites. Since then, drama has evolved into its modern forms, which range from lively musicals to realistic prose dramas. It is the doing or acting quality that makes drama unique in literature. As you read the dramas in this unit, see and hear the action being performed on the stage in your mind.

Commedia dell'arte, Andre Rouillard

Reading for Success

Strategies for Reading Drama

While plays share many elements with prose, fiction, and poetry, the greatest difference is that a drama is designed to be acted out on a stage before an audience. The story is told mostly through dialogue and action. Stage directions indicate when and how the actors move and sometimes suggest sound and lighting effects. When you read a play, you are reading a script; you must always keep in mind that it was written to be performed.

The following strategies will help you interact with the text of a drama and imagine the action and characters in performance.

Envision the action.

Reading a play without envisioning the action is like watching a movie with your eyes shut. Use the stage directions and other details to create the scene in your mind. How and where do the actors move? What do they sound like? What goes on between the characters?

Predict.

As the action develops, make predictions about what you think will happen. Look for hints in the dialogue or action that seem to suggest a certain outcome. As you read on, you will see whether your predictions are correct.

Question.

Note the questions that come to mind as you read. For example, why do the characters act as they do? What causes events to happen? Why does the author include certain information? Look for answers to your questions as you read.

Connect the play to its historical context.

When does the action of the drama occur? What conditions exist during the times? If the drama takes place in a historical or foreign setting, you may have to consider that customs and accepted conduct may differ from that to which you are accustomed.

Summarize.

Dramas are often broken into acts or scenes. These natural breaks give you an opportunity to review the action. What is the conflict? What happens to move it toward its resolution? Put the characters' actions and words together as you summarize.

When you read the plays in this unit, use these general strategies, as well as those specifically suggested with each drama. They will help you understand the conflict and resolution of the dramas and gain insight into the themes.

PART 1 *Dramatic Beginnings*

Theatre of Herodes Atticus, Acropolis, Odeon, Athens, Greece

THE GREEK THEATER

Theater was a celebration in ancient Greece. The Athenians of the fifth century B.C. held festivals to honor Dionysos (dī´ ə nī´ səs), their god of wine. During these holidays, citizens gathered to watch competitions between playwrights, who presented plays derived from well-known myths. These plays depicted events that exposed arrogance and that emphasized reverence for the gods.

Thousands of Athenians saw the plays. In an outdoor theater like the one shown on page 811, seats rose away in a semicircle from a level orchestral area. The plays performed in these theaters had limited numbers of characters, and scenes were interspersed with songs. There were no curtains to allow for changes of scenery between acts. No violence or irreverence was depicted on stage, although such matters were central to the plots of many plays. Such events occurred offstage and were reported in dialogue.

THE PRESENTATION OF THE PLAYS

Ancient Greek playwrights used a consistent format for most of their productions. Plays opened with a prologue, or exposition, which presented the background to situate the conflict. The entering chorus then sang a parados (par´ əd əs), or opening song. This was followed by the first scene. The chorus's song, called an ode, divided scenes, thus serving the same purpose as a curtain does in modern theater.

The Chorus. The role of the chorus was central to the production and important in interpreting the meaning of the plays. During the odes, a leader called the choragos (kō rā´ gəs) might exchange thoughts with the group in a dialogue. During that recital, the group rotated first from right to left, singing the strophe (strō´ fē). Then the chorus members moved in the opposite direction during the antistrophe. An epode was included in some odes as a sort of final stanza. At the conclusion, there was a paean (pē´ ən) of thanksgiving to Dionysos and an exodos (ek´ sə dəs), or final exiting scene. Clearly, the chorus played an essential part in any play's success.

THE OEDIPUS MYTH

Sophocles wrote three tragedies about the royal family of Thebes, a city in northeastern Greece. Called the Theban plays, these tragedies were *Oedipus the King*, *Oedipus at Colonus*, and *Antigone*. The stories of these plays were as familiar to the audience as the story of Noah and the Ark or Jonah and the Whale is to many people today.

Abandoned at Birth. Oedipus (ed´ ə pəs) was abandoned at birth by his parents, the Theban king Laios (lā´ yəs) and his wife, Iocaste (yō kas´ tə). A fortuneteller proclaimed in an oracle that the infant would kill his father and marry his mother. Wishing to avoid that fate, the couple had Oedipus taken off to be abandoned on a mountaintop by a servant who was to ensure the baby's death. The parents assumed that this mission was completed. In fact, however, the servant pitied the newborn and gave him to a childless couple in a distant city who raised the boy without ever mentioning his adoption.

A Famous Riddle. When Oedipus left that city to start his adult life, he still did not know that his real father was Laios and that his mother was Iocaste. His travels took him toward Thebes, where he killed a man without knowing it was Laios. Oedipus' fame grew

▲ **Critical Viewing** What might be some advantages and disadvantages to watching a performance in a theater like this one? [**Assess**]

after he confronted the Sphinx, a monster that killed those unable to answer its riddle. The riddle was this: What creature walks on four legs at dawn, two legs at noon, and three legs in the evening? Oedipus answered that the creature was man, a being who crawls as an infant on all fours, walks erect in midlife, and uses a third leg in the form of a cane during old age. The Sphinx leaped into the sea after Oedipus gave the correct answer, and Oedipus was received in the city as a hero.

A Royal Marriage. Iocaste, now a widow, agreed to marry the unknown champion. The couple lived happily for years and raised four children of their own. Then a plague befell the city. The priests claimed the plague was punishment for some unknown sin. During an investigation of his own background, Oedipus learned the facts of his birth. In horror at this revelation, Iocaste committed suicide and Oedipus blinded himself. Iocaste's brother, Creon (krē´ än), took control of the city and allowed one of Oedipus' children, Antigone (an tig´ ə nē), to lead Oedipus into exile where he died.

A Daughter Mourns. After her return to Thebes, Antigone was deeply troubled by her experience. Her sister, Ismene (is mē´ nē), and brothers, Eteocles (ē tē´ ə klēz) and Polyneices (päl´ ə nī´ sēz), were also burdened by their family background. They were haunted by the curse that caused their father to fulfill his own prophecy and condemned his sons to kill each other for the control of Thebes.

Order Restored. By the time *Antigone* opens, Creon has restored some order to Thebes. The civil war between the brothers has just ended. Eteocles and Polyneices have killed each other in combat. Eteocles had supported Creon's established order and was buried with honors. Polyneices had rebelled with the forces of Argos against Thebes, and Creon ordered that his corpse be left to rot. Antigone's decision to disobey that command is central to the play.

Guide for Reading

Sophocles (c. 496–406 B.C.)

The ancient Greek dramatist Sophocles (säf´ ə klēz) wrote one hundred twenty-three plays, but only seven remain in existence. His most famous are the three dealing with Oedipus and his children: *Oedipus Rex* (Oedipus the King), *Oedipus at Colonus*, and *Antigone*. This trilogy was written over a span of forty years.

Born in Kolonos, near Athens, Sophocles was one of the most respected Greek dramatists of his time. He was admired not only for his poetic and dramatic skills but also for his good looks and musical talent. Sophocles frequently won first place in the competitions of plays performed in the Dionysian festivals. With his first tragedy, written at age twenty-seven, he defeated the highly respected Aeschylus (es´ kə ləs). Sophocles made some changes to the traditions of Greek theater. He may have increased the size of the chorus, and he introduced a third actor. Previous playwrights used just two actors and a chorus.

In his dramas, Sophocles was mainly concerned with the search for truth and self-understanding—even when the search leads to tragedy. His ability to see current values in old myths thrilled his contemporaries. Audiences since have continued to appreciate the freshness and vitality of his world view.

In *Antigone*, King Creon reaches an understanding of his own faults only after paying a very high price.

◆ Build Vocabulary

LATIN PREFIXES: *trans-*

In Act I of *Antigone,* the chorus asks, "What mortal arrogance *transcends* the wrath of Zeus?" The Latin prefix *trans-*, which means "through," "across," or "over," will help you to define *transcends* as "to go above or beyond limits." As you read *Antigone,* you will be *transported* to another time and place.

WORD BANK

As you read this drama, you will encounter the words on this list. Each word is defined on the page where it first appears. Preview the list before you read. Though you may not know the words, you may still be able to identify the part of speech of each word, which will give you a clue to the word's use. In your notebook, write the words and their parts of speech.

sated
anarchists
sententiously
sultry
transcends

◆ Build Grammar Skills

COORDINATING CONJUNCTIONS

A **coordinating conjunction** links two or more words or groups of words of equal importance. Many sentences in *Antigone* consist of two clauses of equal rank joined by a coordinating conjunction. The conjunction not only joins the clauses but shows the relationship between the ideas in the clauses. Look at these examples from *Antigone*.

The conjunction *and* shows addition:
Our temples shall be sweet with hymns of praise,
And the long night shall echo with our chorus.

The conjunctions *but* and *yet* show contrast or exception:
No one values friendship more highly than I; *but* we must remember . . .

The conjunction *or* shows alternatives:
Find that man, bring him here to me, *or* your death / Will be the least of your problems. . . .

Antigone

◆ *Literature and Your Life*

CONNECT YOUR EXPERIENCE

History is full of instances where political situations create family conflicts. In American history, the Civil War is often noted for pitting brother against brother. In this play, a young woman must decide whether to act on loyalty to her family or to follow the law of the land.

THEMATIC FOCUS: CHOICES AND CONSEQUENCES

Not every conflict has a clear winner and loser. Notice the ways in which Creon and Antigone, the main characters in this play, experience both victory and defeat.

Journal Entry Jot down a list of issues on which you would be willing to take a stand. Next to each issue, write down under what circumstances, if any, you might choose *not* to take a stand.

◆ Background for Understanding

LITERATURE

The chorus is an essential element of Greek drama. This group comments on and may explain the action of the play. Sometimes the chorus speaks in a single voice as a group, sometimes in dialogue between two sections of the group.

In an opening song—the *parados* (par´ əd əs)—the chorus explains the central conflict of the play. Between scenes, the chorus recites an *ode*. During the ode, the group moves from right to left, singing the *strophe* (strō´ fē). Then the chorus members move in the opposite direction during the *antistrophe*.

◆ Literary Focus

PROTAGONIST AND ANTAGONIST

When you describe a movie to a friend, you probably relate the story in terms of the main character and what happens to him or her. A movie is usually written so that you side with one of the characters more than the others and hope that he or she succeeds. In a literary work, the main character is called the **protagonist.** The protagonist is the main character, the one at the center of the action. The **antagonist** is the character or force in conflict with the protagonist.

In this play, Antigone is the protagonist; she is in conflict with the antagonist, her uncle—Creon the king.

◆ Reading Strategy

QUESTION THE CHARACTERS' MOTIVES

When you decide to do something, what causes you to act? The inner drive or impulse that makes you act is called your motive. When you read about a character like Antigone, you wonder why she acts the way she does and makes the decisions she does. To understand the conflict and resolution in any play, **question the characters' motives.**

At the beginning of the play, Antigone says to her sister, Ismene:

And now you can prove
  what you are:
A true sister, or a traitor to
  your family.

What do you think is Antigone's motive in confronting her sister so harshly? Is Antigone a strong, ethical character testing her sister's strength or is she too proud, too willful, too full of her own self-worth? Your questioning of her motives and the motives of the king, Creon, will help you better understand and appreciate the forces at work in the play.

ANTIGONE

PROLOGUE THROUGH SCENE 2

Sophocles

Translated by Dudley Fitts
and Robert Fitzgerald

Scene. *Before the palace of* CREON, *King of Thebes. A central double door, and two lateral doors. A platform extends the length of the facade, and from this platform three steps lead down into the "orchestra," or chorus-ground.*

Time. *Dawn of the day after the repulse of the Argive[1] army from the assault on Thebes.*

Prologue

[ANTIGONE *and* ISMENE *enter from the central door of the Palace.*]

ANTIGONE. Ismene, dear sister.
You would think that we had already suffered enough
For the curse on Oedipus:[2]

---

1. Argive (är´ gīv): From Argos, the capital of a section of ancient Greece.
2. curse on Oedipus: This curse refers to the fate of Oedipus, who was doomed by a decree of the gods to kill his father and marry his mother while ignorant of their true identities.

PERSONS REPRESENTED

ANTIGONE (an tig´ ə nē´), daughter of Oedipus, former King of Thebes

ISMENE (is mē´ nē), another daughter of Oedipus

EURYDICE (yoo rid´ ə sē´), wife of Creon

CREON (krē´ än), King of Thebes, uncle of Antigone and Ismene

HAIMON (hī´ mən), Creon's son, engaged to Antigone

TEIRESIAS (tī rē´ sē əs), a blind prophet

A SENTRY

A MESSENGER

CHORUS

CHORAGOS (kō rā´ gəs), leader of the chorus

A BOY, who leads Teiresias

GUARDS

SERVANTS

▲ **Critical Viewing** What does this temple, dedicated to Poseidon, the god of the sea, suggest about the importance of the gods in Greek life? **[Draw Conclusions]**

I cannot imagine any grief
That you and I have not gone through.
5   And now—
Have they told you of the new decree of
    our King Creon?

ISMENE. I have heard nothing: I know
That two sisters lost two brothers, a
    double death
In a single hour; and I know that the Argive
    army
10 Fled in the night; but beyond this, nothing.

ANTIGONE. I thought so. And that is why I
    wanted you
To come out here with me. There is
    something we must do.

ISMENE. Why do you speak so strangely?

ANTIGONE. Listen, Ismene:
15 Creon buried our brother Eteocles
With military honors, gave him a soldier's
    funeral,
And it was right that he should;
    but Polyneices,
Who fought as bravely
    and died as miserably,—
        They say that Creon has
            sworn
No one shall bury him,
            no one mourn for him,
20 But his body must lie in
        the fields, a
            sweet treasure

For carrion birds[3] to find as they search
    for food.
That is what they say, and our good Creon
    is coming here
To announce it publicly; and the
    penalty—
Stoning to death in the public square!
25   There it is,
And now you can prove what you are:
A true sister, or a traitor to your family.

ISMENE. Antigone, you are mad! What could
    I possibly do?

ANTIGONE. You must decide whether you will
    help me or not.

ISMENE. I do not understand you. Help you
30 in what?

ANTIGONE. Ismene, I am going to bury him.
    Will you come?

ISMENE. Bury him! You have just said the
    new law forbids it.

ANTIGONE. He is my brother. And he is your
    brother, too.

ISMENE. But think of the danger! Think what
    Creon will do!

ANTIGONE. Creon is not strong enough to
35 stand in my way.

ISMENE. Ah sister!
Oedipus died, everyone hating him

◆ **Literary Focus**
What qualities does
Antigone show here
20 that help you
identify her as the
protagonist?

---

3. **carrion** (kar´ ē ən) **birds:** Scavenger birds, such as
vultures, that eat the decaying leftovers of another
animal's kill.

For what his own search brought to light, his eyes
Ripped out by his own hand; and Iocaste died,
His mother and wife at once: she twisted
40   the cords
That strangled her life; and our two brothers died,
Each killed by the other's sword. And we are left:
But oh, Antigone,
Think how much more terrible than these
Our own death would be if we should go
45   against Creon
And do what he has forbidden! We are only women,
We cannot fight with men, Antigone!
The law is strong, we must give in to the law
In this thing, and in worse. I beg the Dead
To forgive me, but I am helpless: I must
50   yield
To those in authority. And I think it is dangerous business
To be always meddling.

ANTIGONE.   If that is what you think,
I should not want you, even if you asked to come.
You have made your choice and you can be what you want to be.
55 But I will bury him; and if I must die,
I say that this crime is holy: I shall lie down
With him in death, and I

◆ Reading Strategy
What is Antigone's motive for wanting to bury her brother?

shall be as dear
To him as he to me.
      It is the dead,
Not the living, who make the longest demands:
We die for ever . . .
60   You may do as you like,
Since apparently the laws of the gods mean nothing to you.

ISMENE. They mean a great deal to me; but I have no strength
To break laws that were made for the public good.

ANTIGONE. That must be your excuse, I

suppose. But as for me,
I will bury the brother I love.

65 ISMENE.   Antigone,
I am so afraid for you!

ANTIGONE.   You need not be:
You have yourself to consider, after all.

ISMENE. But no one must hear of this, you must tell no one!
I will keep it a secret, I promise!

ANTIGONE.   Oh tell it! Tell everyone!
Think how they'll hate you when it all comes out
70   comes out
If they learn that you knew about it all the time!

ISMENE. So fiery! You should be cold with fear.

ANTIGONE. Perhaps. But I am doing only what I must.

ISMENE. But can you do it? I say that you cannot.

ANTIGONE. Very well: when my strength
75   gives out, I shall do no more.

ISMENE. Impossible things should not be tried at all.

ANTIGONE. Go away, Ismene:
I shall be hating you soon, and the dead will too,
For your words are hateful. Leave me my foolish plan:
I am not afraid of the danger; if it means
80   death,
It will not be the worst of deaths—death without honor.

ISMENE. Go then, if you feel that you must.
You are unwise.
But a loyal friend indeed to those who love you.

[*Exit into the Palace.* ANTIGONE *goes off, left.
Enter the* CHORUS.]

Parodos

CHORUS.   [STROPHE 1]

Now the long blade of the sun, lying

Level east to west, touches with glory
Thebes of the Seven Gates.[4] Open,
  unlidded
Eye of golden day! O marching light
Across the eddy and rush of Dirce's
5   stream,[5]
Striking the white shields of the enemy
Thrown headlong backward from the blaze
  of morning!

CHORAGOS. Polyneices their commander
Roused them with windy phrases,
10 He the wild eagle screaming
Insults above our land,
His wings their shields of snow,
His crest their marshalled helms.

CHORUS.   [ANTISTROPHE 1]
Against our seven gates in a yawning ring
The famished spears came onward in the
15   night;
But before his jaws were <u>sated</u> with our
  blood,
Or pinefire took the garland of our towers,
He was thrown back; and as he turned,
  great Thebes—
No tender victim for his noisy power—
Rose like a dragon behind him, shouting
20   war.

CHORAGOS. For God hates utterly
The bray of bragging tongues;
And when he beheld their smiling,
Their swagger of golden helms,
25 The frown of his thunder blasted
Their first man from our walls.

CHORUS.   [STROPHE 2]
We heard his shout of triumph high in the
  air
Turn to a scream; far out in a flaming arc
He fell with his windy torch, and the earth
  struck him.
And others storming in fury no less than
30 his
Found shock of death in the dusty joy of
  battle.

---

4. **Seven Gates:** The city of Thebes was defended by
walls containing seven entrances.
5. **Dirce's** (dʉr´ sēz) **stream:** Small river near Thebes
into which the body of Dirce, one of the city's early
queens, was thrown after her murder.

CHORAGOS. Seven captains at seven gates
Yielded their clanging arms to the god
That bends the battle-line and breaks it.
35 These two only, brothers in blood,
Face to face in matchless rage,
Mirroring each the other's death,
Clashed in long combat.

CHORUS.   [ANTISTROPHE 2]
But now in the beautiful morning of
  victory
Let Thebes of the many chariots sing for
40   joy!
With hearts for dancing we'll take leave of
  war:
Our temples shall be sweet with hymns of
  praise,
And the long night shall echo with our
  chorus.

Scene 1

CHORAGOS. But now at last our new King is
  coming:
Creon of Thebes, Menoikeus'[6] son.
In this auspicious dawn of his reign
What are the new complexities
5 That shifting Fate has woven for him?
What is his counsel? Why has he
  summoned
The old men to hear him?

[*Enter* CREON *from the Palace, center. He
addresses the* CHORUS *from the top step.*]

CREON. Gentlemen: I have the honor to inform
  you that our Ship of State, which
10   recent storms have threatened to destroy,
has come safely to harbor at last, guided
by the merciful wisdom of Heaven. I have
summoned you here this morning because
I know that I can depend upon you: your
15   devotion to King Laïos was absolute; you
never hesitated in your duty to our late
ruler Oedipus; and when Oedipus died,
your loyalty was transferred to his children.
Unfortunately, as you know, his two sons,

---

6. **Menoikeus** (me noi´ kē əs)

◆ **Build Vocabulary**

sated (sāt´ əd): Satisfied or pleased

20 the princes Eteocles and Polyneices,
    have killed each other in battle;
    and I, as the next in blood, have succeeded
    to the full power of the throne.
        I am aware, of course, that no Ruler can
25 expect complete loyalty from his subjects
    until he has been tested in office. Never-
    theless, I say to you at the very outset that
    I have nothing but contempt for the kind
    of Governor who is afraid, for whatever
30 reason, to follow the course that he knows
    is best for the State; and as for the man
    who sets private friendship above the pub-
    lic welfare—I have no use for him,
    either. I call God to witness that if I saw
35 my country headed for ruin, I should not
    be afraid to speak out plainly; and I need
    hardly remind you that I would never have
    any dealings with an enemy of the people.
    No one values friendship more highly than
40 I; but we must remember that friends
    made at the risk of wrecking our Ship are
    not real friends at all.
        These are my principles, at any rate, and that
    is why I have made the following
45 decision concerning the sons of Oedipus:
    Eteocles, who died as a man should die,
    fighting for his country, is to be buried
    with full military honors, with all the
    ceremony that is usual when the greatest
50 heroes die; but his brother Polyneices, who
    broke his exile to come back with fire and
    sword against his native city and the
    shrines of his fathers' gods, whose one
    idea was to spill the blood of his blood and
55 sell his own people into slavery—Polynei-
    ces, I say, is to have no burial:
    no man is to touch him or say the least
    prayer for him; he shall lie on the plain,
    unburied; and the birds and the scaveng-
60   ing dogs can do with
        him whatever they like.
    This is my command
        and you can see the
        wisdom behind it. As
        long as I am King, no
    traitor is going to be honored with the loyal
65 man. But whoever shows by word and
    deed that he is on the side of the State—he

◆ **Literary Focus**
How do Creon's
words reveal him
as the **antagonist**
in this play?

shall have my respect while he is living,
and my reverence when he is dead.

CHORAGOS. If that is your will, Creon son of
    Menoikeus,
You have the right to enforce it: we are
70 yours.

CREON. That is my will. Take care that you
    do your part.

CHORAGOS. We are old men: let the younger
    ones carry it out.

CREON. I do not mean that: the sentries
    have been appointed.

CHORAGOS. Then what is it that you would
    have us do?

CREON. You will give no support to whoever
75 breaks this law.

CHORAGOS. Only a crazy man is in love with
    death!

CREON. And death it is; yet money talks,
    and the wisest
Have sometimes been known to count a
    few coins too many.

[*Enter* SENTRY *from left.*]

SENTRY. I'll not say that I'm out of breath from
80 running, King, because every time I
    stopped to think about what I have to tell
    you, I felt like going back. And all the time
    a voice kept saying, "You fool, don't you
    know you're walking straight into trouble?";
85 and then another voice: "Yes, but if you let
    somebody else get the news to Creon first,
    it will be even worse than that for you!" But
    good sense won out, at least I hope it was
    good sense, and here I am with a story that
90 makes no sense at all; but I'll tell it any-
    how, because, as they say, what's going to
    happen's going to happen, and—

CREON. Come to the point. What have you to
    say?

SENTRY. I did not do it. I did not see who did
95 it. You must not punish me for what
    someone else has done.

CREON. A comprehensive defense! More

effective, perhaps,
If I knew its purpose. Come: what is it?

SENTRY. A dreadful thing . . . I don't know how to put it—

CREON. Out with it!

100 **SENTRY.**   Well, then;
The dead man—

                    Polyneices—

[*Pause. The* SENTRY *is overcome, fumbles for words.* CREON *waits impassively.*]

                                        out there—
                                someone,—

New dust on the slimy flesh!

[*Pause. No sign from* CREON.]

Someone has given it burial that way, and
105 Gone . . .

[*Long pause.* CREON *finally speaks with deadly control.*]

CREON. And the man who dared do this?

SENTRY.   I swear I
Do not know! You must believe me!

                                Listen:
The ground was dry, not a sign of digging, no,
Not a wheeltrack in the dust, no trace of anyone.
It was when they relieved us this morning:
110   and one of them,
The corporal, pointed to it.

                        There it was,
The strangest—
                Look:
The body, just mounded over with light dust: you see?
Not buried really, but as if they'd covered it
Just enough for the ghost's peace. And no
115   sign
Of dogs or any wild animal that had been there.
And then what a scene there was! Every man of us
Accusing the other: we all proved the other man did it,
We all had proof that we could not have done it.

120 We were ready to take hot iron in our hands,
Walk through fire, swear by all the gods,
It was not I!
I do not know who it was, but it was not I!

[CREON's *rage has been mounting steadily, but the* SENTRY *is too intent upon his story to notice it.*]

And then, when this came to nothing, someone said
125 A thing that silenced us and made us stare
Down at the ground: you had to be told the news,
And one of us had to do it! We threw the dice,
And the bad luck fell to me. So here I am,
No happier to be here than you are to have me:
Nobody likes the man who brings bad
130   news.

CHORAGOS. I have been wondering, King:
can it be that the gods have done this?

CREON. [*Furiously*] Stop!
Must you doddering wrecks
Go out of your heads entirely? "The gods!"
135 Intolerable!
The gods favor this corpse? Why? How had he served them?
Tried to loot their temples, burn their images,
Yes, and the whole State, and its laws with it!
Is it your senile opinion that the gods love to honor bad men?
A pious thought!—
140   No, from the very beginning
There have been those who have whispered together,

◆ **Build Vocabulary**

anarchists (an´ ər kists) *n.*: Those who disrespect laws or rules

sententiously (sen ten´ shəs lē) *adv.*: Using proverbs and sayings in a pompous way

Stiff-necked <u>anarchists</u>, putting their heads together,
Scheming against me in alleys. These are the men,
And they have bribed my own guard to do this thing.

145 Money!   [*Sententiously*]
There's nothing in the world so demoralizing as money.
Down go your cities,
Homes gone, men gone, honest hearts corrupted,
Crookedness of all kinds, and all for money!

[*To* SENTRY]

                                 But you—!

150 I swear by God and by the throne of God,
The man who has done this thing shall pay for it!
Find that man, bring him here to me, or your death
Will be the least of your problems: I'll string you up
Alive, and there will be certain ways to make you

155 Discover your employer before you die;
And the process may teach you a lesson you seem to have missed:

The dearest profit is sometimes all too dear:
That depends on the source. Do you understand me?
A fortune won is often misfortune.

SENTRY. King, may I speak?

160 **CREON.**   Your very voice distresses me.

SENTRY. Are you sure that it is my voice, and not your conscience?

CREON. By God, he wants to analyze me now!

SENTRY. It is not what I say, but what has been done, that hurts you.

CREON. You talk too much.

SENTRY.   Maybe; but I've done nothing.

CREON. Sold your soul for some silver: that's
165   all you've done.

SENTRY. How dreadful it is when the right judge judges wrong!

CREON. Your figures of speech
May entertain you now; but unless you bring me the man,
You will get little profit from them in the end.

[*Exit* CREON *into the Palace.*]

170 **SENTRY.** "Bring me the man"—!
I'd like nothing better than bringing him the man!
But bring him or not, you have seen the last of me here.
At any rate, I am safe!

[*Exit* SENTRY.]

Ode 1

CHORUS.   [STROPHE 1]
Numberless are the world's wonders, but none
More wonderful than man; the stormgray sea
Yields to his prows, the huge crests bear him high;
Earth, holy and inexhaustible, is graven
With shining furrows where his plows
5   have gone

Year after year, the timeless labor of
stallions.

[ANTISTROPHE 1]
The lightboned birds and beasts that cling
to cover,
The lithe fish lighting their reaches of
dim water,
All are taken, tamed in the net of his
mind;
The lion on the hill, the wild horse
10   windy-maned,
Resign to him; and his blunt yoke has
broken
The sultry shoulders of the mountain bull.

[STROPHE 2]
Words also, and thought as rapid as air,
He fashions to his good use; statecraft is his,
And his the skill that deflects the arrows
15   of snow,
The spears of winter rain: from every wind
He has made himself secure—from all but
one:
In the late wind of death he cannot stand.

[ANTISTROPHE 2]
O clear intelligence, force beyond all measure!
20 O fate of man, working both good and evil!
When the laws are kept, how proudly his
city stands!
When the laws are broken, what of his city
then?
Never may the anarchic man find rest at
my hearth,
Never be it said that my thoughts are his
thoughts.

Scene 2

[Re-enter SENTRY leading ANTIGONE.]

CHORAGOS. What does this mean? Surely
this captive woman
Is the Princess, Antigone. Why should she
be taken?

SENTRY. Here is the one who did it! We
caught her
In the very act of burying him.—Where is
Creon?

CHORAGOS. Just coming from the house.

[Enter CREON, center.]

5 CREON.   What has happened?

Why have you come back so soon?

SENTRY. [Expansively]   O King,
A man should never be too sure of anything:
I would have sworn
That you'd not see me here again: your
anger
Frightened me so, and the things you
10   threatened me with;
But how could I tell then
That I'd be able to solve the case so soon?
No dice-throwing this time: I was only too
glad to come!

Here is this woman. She is the guilty one:
15 We found her trying to bury him.
Take her, then; question her; judge her as
you will.
I am through with the whole thing now,
and glad of it.

CREON. But this is Antigone! Why have you
brought her here?

SENTRY. She was burying him, I tell you!

20 CREON. [Severely]   Is this the truth?

SENTRY. I saw her with my own eyes. Can I
say more?

CREON. The details: come, tell me quickly!

SENTRY.   It was like this:
After those terrible threats of yours, King,
We went back and brushed the dust away
from the body.
25 The flesh was soft by now, and stinking,
So we sat on a hill to windward and kept
guard.
No napping this time! We kept each other
awake.
But nothing happened until the white
round sun
Whirled in the center of the round sky over
us:
30 Then, suddenly,
A storm of dust roared up from the earth,
and the sky
Went out, the plain vanished with all its trees

◆ Build Vocabulary

sultry (sul′ trē) adj.: Oppressively hot or moist;
inflamed

In the stinging dark. We closed our eyes
and endured it.
The whirlwind lasted a long time, but it
passed;
And then we looked, and there was
35   Antigone!
I have seen
A mother bird come back to a stripped
nest, heard
Her crying bitterly a broken note or two
For the young ones stolen. Just so, when
this girl
Found the bare corpse, and all her love's
40   work wasted,
She wept, and cried on heaven to damn
the hands
That had done this thing.
   And then she brought more dust
And sprinkled wine three times for her
brother's ghost.
We ran and took her at once. She was not
afraid,
Not even when we charged her with what
45   she had done.
She denied nothing.
         And this was a comfort to me,
And some uneasiness: for it is a good thing
To escape from death, but it is no great
pleasure
To bring death to a friend.
                  Yet I always say
There is nothing so comfortable as your
50   own safe skin!

CREON. [*Slowly, dangerously*] And you,
Antigone,
You with your head hanging,—do you
confess this thing?

ANTIGONE. I do. I deny nothing.

CREON. [*To* SENTRY]   You may go.

[*Exit* SENTRY.]

[*To* ANTIGONE] Tell me, tell me briefly:
Had you heard my proclamation touching
55   this matter?

ANTIGONE. It was public. Could I help
hearing it?

CREON. And yet you dared defy the law.

ANTIGONE.   I dared.
It was not God's proclamation. That final
Justice
That rules the world below makes no such
laws.

60 Your edict, King, was strong,
But all your strength is weakness itself
against
The immortal unrecorded laws of God.
They are not merely now: they were, and
shall be,
Operative forever, beyond man utterly.

I knew I must die, even without your
65   decree:
I am only mortal. And if I must die
Now, before it is my time to die,
Surely this is no hardship: can anyone
Living, as I live, with evil all about me,
Think Death less than a friend? This death
70   of mine
Is of no importance; but if I had left my
brother
Lying in death unburied, I should have
suffered.
Now I do not.
         You smile at me. Ah Creon,
Think me a fool, if you like; but it may well
be
75 That a fool convicts me of folly.

CHORAGOS. Like father, like daughter: both
headstrong, deaf to reason!
She has never learned to yield.

CREON.   She has much to learn.
The inflexible heart breaks first, the
toughest iron
Cracks first, and the wildest horses bend
their necks.
At the pull of the smallest curb.
80   Pride? In a slave?
This girl is guilty of a double insolence,
Breaking the given laws and boasting of it.
Who is the man here,
She or I, if this crime goes unpunished?
85 Sister's child, or more than sister's child,
Or closer yet in blood—she and her sister
Win bitter death for this!

[*To* SERVANTS]   Go some of you,

Arrest Ismene. I accuse her equally.
Bring her: you will find her sniffling in the
   house there.

90 Her mind's a traitor: crimes kept in the dark
Cry for light, and the guardian brain
   shudders;
But how much worse than this
Is brazen boasting of barefaced anarchy!

ANTIGONE. Creon, what more do you want
   than my death?

CREON.   Nothing.
That gives me everything.

95 ANTIGONE.   Then I beg you: kill me.
This talking is a great weariness: your
   words
Are distasteful to me, and I am sure that
   mine
Seem so to you. And yet they should not
   seem so:
I should have praise and honor for what I
   have done.
100 All these men here would praise me
Were their lips not frozen shut with fear of
   you.

[Bitterly]
Ah the good fortune of kings,
Licensed to say and do whatever they
   please!

CREON. You are alone here in that opinion.

ANTIGONE. No, they are with me. But they
105   keep their tongues in leash.

CREON. Maybe. But you are guilty, and they
   are not.

ANTIGONE. There is no guilt in reverence for
   the dead.

CREON. But Eteocles—was he not your
   brother too?

ANTIGONE. My brother too.

CREON.   And you insult his memory?

ANTIGONE. [Softly] The dead man would not
110   say that I insult it.

CREON. He would: for you honor a traitor as
   much as him.

ANTIGONE. His own brother, traitor or not,
   and equal in blood.

CREON. He made war on his country.
   Eteocles defended it.

ANTIGONE. Nevertheless, there are honors
   due all the dead.

CREON. But not the same for the wicked as
115   for the just.

ANTIGONE. Ah Creon, Creon,
Which of us can say what the gods hold
   wicked?

CREON. An enemy is an enemy, even dead.

ANTIGONE. It is my nature to join in love, not
   hate.

CREON. [Finally losing patience] Go join
120   them, then; if you must have your love,
Find it in hell!

CHORAGOS. But see, Ismene comes:

[Enter ISMENE, guarded.]

Those tears are sisterly, the cloud
That shadows her eyes rains down gentle
  sorrow.

CREON. You too, Ismene,
Snake in my ordered house, sucking my
125 blood
Stealthily—and all the time I never knew
That these two sisters were aiming at my
  throne!
            Ismene,
Do you confess your share in this crime, or
  deny it?
Answer me.

ISMENE. Yes, if she will let me say so. I am
130 guilty.

ANTIGONE. [Coldly] No, Ismene. You have no
  right to say so.
You would not help me, and I will not have
  you help me.

ISMENE. But now I know what you meant;
  and I am here
To join you, to take my share of punishment.

ANTIGONE. The dead man and the gods who
135 rule the dead
Know whose act this was. Words are not
  friends.

ISMENE. Do you refuse me, Antigone? I want
  to die with you:
I too have a duty that I must discharge to
  the dead.

ANTIGONE. You shall not lessen my death by
  sharing it.

ISMENE. What do I care for life when you are
140 dead?

ANTIGONE. Ask Creon. You're always hanging
  on his opinions.

ISMENE. You are laughing at me. Why,
  Antigone?

ANTIGONE. It's a joyless laughter, Ismene.

ISMENE.   But can I do nothing?

ANTIGONE. Yes. Save yourself. I shall not
  envy you.
There are those who will praise you; I shall
145 have honor, too.

ISMENE. But we are equally guilty!

ANTIGONE.   No more, Ismene.
You are alive, but I belong to Death.

CREON. [To the CHORUS] Gentlemen, I beg
  you to observe these girls:
One has just now lost her mind; the other,
150 It seems, has never had a mind at all.

ISMENE. Grief teaches the steadiest minds to
  waver, King.

CREON. Yours certainly did, when you
  assumed guilt with the guilty!

ISMENE. But how could I go on living
  without her?

CREON.   You are.
She is already dead.

ISMENE.   But your own son's bride!

CREON. There are places enough for him to
155 push his plow.
I want no wicked women for my sons!

ISMENE. O dearest Haimon, how your father
  wrongs you!

CREON. I've had enough of your childish
  talk of marriage!

CHORAGOS. Do you really intend to steal this
  girl from your son?

CREON. No; Death will do that for me.

160 CHORAGOS.   Then she must die?

CREON. [Ironically] You dazzle me.
              —But enough of this talk!

[To GUARDS] You, there, take them away and
  guard them well:
For they are but women, and even brave
  men run
When they see Death coming.

[Exit ISMENE, ANTIGONE, and GUARDS.]

Ode II

CHORUS.   [STROPHE 1]

Fortunate is the man who has never tasted
   God's vengeance!
Where once the anger of heaven has struck,
   that house is shaken
Forever: damnation rises behind each child
Like a wave cresting out of the black
   northeast,
5 When the long darkness undersea roars up
And bursts drumming death upon the
   windwhipped sand.

                      [ANTISTROPHE 1]

I have seen this gathering sorrow from time
   long past
Loom upon Oedipus' children: generation
   from generation
Takes the compulsive rage of the enemy
   god.
10 So lately this last flower of Oedipus' line
Drank the sunlight! but now a passionate
   word
And a handful of dust have closed up all its
   beauty.

◆ Build Vocabulary

transcends (tran sendz´) v.: Goes above or
beyond limits; exceeds

                              [STROPHE 2]

What mortal arrogance
<u>Transcends</u> the wrath of Zeus?[7]
Sleep cannot lull him, nor the effortless
15   long months
Of the timeless gods: but he is young
   forever,
And his house is the shining day of high
   Olympos.[8]
   All that is and shall be,
   And all the past, is his.
No pride on earth is free of the curse of
20   heaven.

                      [ANTISTROPHE 2]

The straying dreams of men
   May bring them ghosts of joy:
But as they drowse, the waking embers
   burn them;
Or they walk with fixed eyes, as blind men
   walk.
But the ancient wisdom speaks for our
25   own time:
   Fate works most for woe
   With Folly's fairest show.
Man's little pleasure is the spring of sorrow.

---

7. **Zeus** (zoos): King of all Greek gods, he was
believed to throw lightning bolts when angry.
8. **Olympos** (ō lim´ pəs): Mountain in Greece, also
known as Olympus, where the gods were believed to
live in ease and splendor.

Guide for Responding

◆ Literature and Your Life

Reader's Response Antigone and Ismene disagree over the burial of Polyneices. With whom do you agree?

Thematic Focus Antigone chooses to do what she thinks is right, rather than give in to Creon's law. What consequences do you think she will face as a result of her choices?

☑ Check Your Comprehension

1. Why does Antigone feel that her brother should get a proper burial?
2. How does Creon react to the news of Polyneices' burial?

◆ Critical Thinking

INTERPRET

1. Explain what Ismene means when she says, "We are only women,/We cannot fight with men, Antigone!" **[Interpret]**
2. How might Ismene's advice to her sister seem cowardly to some readers? **[Analyze]**
3. In his argument with Antigone, Creon declares "An enemy is an enemy, even dead." What does he mean? Do you agree? **[Interpret]**

EXTEND

4. Compare and contrast the government of Creon in Thebes with a modern-day government. **[Social Studies Link]**

Guide for Responding (continued)

◆ Reading Strategy

QUESTION THE CHARACTERS' MOTIVES
To fully understand the action of the play, **question the characters' motives.**

1. What was Ismene's motive for not going along with Antigone at first?
2. What is Antigone's motive for burying Polyneices?
3. What is Creon's motive for insisting on Antigone's death?

◆ Literary Focus

PROTAGONIST AND ANTAGONIST
A **protagonist** is the main character of a literary work, and an **antagonist** is a character or force in conflict with the main character.

1. Describe the conflict between Antigone and Creon.
2. What qualities of each character contribute to the conflict?
3. Give examples of actions and feelings that show that Antigone is the protagonist and Creon is the antagonist.

◆ Build Vocabulary

USING THE LATIN PREFIX *trans-*
Knowing that the Latin prefix *trans-* means "through," "above," or "across" will help you define other words that contain *trans-*. On your paper, match each word with its appropriate definition.

1. transparent   **a.** send through the air
2. transmit   **b.** lift up and move
3. transplant   **c.** pierce through
4. transfix   **d.** lets light shine through

USING THE WORD BANK: Definitions
Copy the words from Column A into your notebook. Next to each word, write the letter of its definition from Column B.

Column A	Column B
1. sated	a. pompously
2. anarchists	b. oppressively hot or moist
3. sententiously	c. go above or beyond the limit
4. sultry	d. satisfied or pleased
5. transcend	e. those who disrespect rules

◆ Build Grammar Skills

COORDINATING CONJUNCTIONS
A **coordinating conjunction** links two words or grammatical structures of equal importance.

Practice Rewrite each pair of sentences as one sentence, with the coordinating conjunction *but, for, or,* or *and.* Choose the conjunction based on the way ideas are linked.

1. Antigone wants to bury her brother. Ismene is afraid to break the law that Creon decreed.
2. Oedipus learned the truth of what he had done. Antigone accompanied her father into exile.
3. Both Antigone and Ismene grieved. Their brothers killed each other during battle.
4. Ismene could choose to stand up to Creon. She could accept scorn from her sister, Antigone.

Writing Application Write a summary of *Antigone* from the Prologue through Scene 2. Combine clauses using each of the following coordinating conjunctions at least once: *yet, for, and,* and *but.*

Idea Bank

Writing

1. **Newspaper Article** Write a brief newspaper article with a headline that would have appeared in a Thebes newspaper (if newspapers existed then) the day after Polyneices was buried. Answer the questions *who? what? where? when?* and *why?* in your article.

2. **Letter** Imagine that you are Ismene. Write a letter to your sister, Antigone, before her arrest by the sentry. What would you tell her about her plans to bury Polyneices? How would you present this delicate situation?

Speaking, Listening, and Viewing

3. **Readers Theatre** With a small group, rehearse and present a scene from *Antigone* in a Readers Theatre performance for your class. Have a group of students perform as the chorus and assign individuals for the other roles. **[Performing Arts Link]**

Guide for Reading

◆ Review and Anticipate

In Scenes 1 and 2, Antigone decides to give her brother Polyneices a proper burial, defying the orders of her uncle Creon, the ruler of Thebes. When Creon finds out, he orders her put to death, claiming that he cannot allow her to disobey him just because she is his niece. Both Creon and Antigone seem locked in a course of action by circumstances and their beliefs. As Scene 2 ends, the Chorus sings, "*Fate works most for woe / With Folly's fairest show. / Man's little pleasure is the spring of sorrow.*" Notice how the events in the remainder of the play carry out the statement that Fate works most for woe.

◆ Literary Focus

TRAGIC CHARACTER

In this play, two strong-willed people, Creon and Antigone, can both be seen as tragic. A **tragic character** is a significant person who experiences a reversal of fortune as a result of fate or a flaw or weakness in his or her character. Critics debate who the tragic hero is in *Antigone*. Some claim Creon fits the definition better, although Antigone's name has been used in the title. The exchanges between Creon and Antigone lead to an irreversible point from which Creon's pride will not allow him to retreat. His actions bring about the tragic events that follow. Others see the flaw in Antigone. To them, her determination is a form of pride, which makes her unyielding and leads to her doom.

◆ Build Grammar Skills

PRONOUN CASE IN INCOMPLETE CLAUSES

In certain kinds of English constructions, some words are omitted because they are understood. When a pronoun occurs in an **incomplete clause,** its case is what it would be if the construction were complete. Clauses beginning with *than* or *as* are often incomplete. Look at this line from Scene 3:

> Let's lose to a man, at least! Is a woman stronger than we?

The understood word in this line is *are*. The completed clause therefore would be "Is a woman stronger than *we are*?" When you complete the clause, you can see that *we* is the correct pronoun; you would not say, "Is a woman stronger than *us are*?"

◆ Reading Strategy

IDENTIFY WITH A CHARACTER

When you **identify with a character**, you put yourself in the character's place. Because you take on his or her feelings or issues, and you experience what he or she does, you sympathize with that character. You may even feel as if you *are* that character. For example, you may suffer with Antigone as she struggles to do what she thinks is right, or you may feel Ismene's fear of punishment. Putting yourself in a character's place can give you greater insight into that character's motives and the events of the play.

◆ Build Vocabulary

GREEK ROOTS: *-chor-*

An important feature of Greek tragedy is the chorus; a member of the chorus is called a *chorister*. The root of *chorister* and *chorus* is *-chor-*, which comes from Terpsichore (terp sik´ ə rē), the Greek Muse of dance and song.

WORD BANK

Before you read, preview this list of words from the play.

deference
vile
piety
blasphemy
lamentation
chorister

ANTIGONE

SCENES 3 THROUGH 5

Sophocles

*Translated by Dudley Fitts
and Robert Fitzgerald*

Scene 3

CHORAGOS. But here is Haimon, King, the
last of all your sons.
Is it grief for Antigone that brings him here,
And bitterness at being robbed of his bride?

[*Enter* HAIMON.]

CREON. We shall soon see, and no need of
diviners.[1]
          —Son,
You have heard my final judgment on that
5   girl:
Have you come here hating me, or have you
come
With <u>deference</u> and with love, whatever I
do?

HAIMON. I am your son, father. You are my
guide.
You make things clear for me, and I obey
you.
No marriage means more to me than your
10   continuing wisdom.

CREON. Good. That is the way to behave:
subordinate
Everything else, my son, to your father's
will.

This is what a man prays for, that he may
get
Sons attentive and dutiful in his house,
15 Each one hating his father's enemies,
Honoring his father's friends. But if his
sons
Fail him, if they turn out unprofitably,
What has he fathered but trouble for
himself
And amusement for the malicious?
                       So you are right
20 Not to lose your head over this woman.
Your pleasure with her would soon grow
cold, Haimon,
And then you'd have a hellcat in bed and
elsewhere.
Let her find her husband in Hell!
Of all the people in this city, only she
25 Has had contempt for my law and broken it.

Do you want me to show myself weak before
the people?
Or to break my sworn word? No, and I will
not.
The woman dies.
I suppose she'll plead "family ties." Well,
let her.

---

1. **diviners** (də vīn′ ərz): Those who forecast the
future.

◆ **Build Vocabulary**

deference (def′ ər əns) *n.*: Yielding in thought

If I permit my own family to rebel,
How shall I earn the world's obedience?
Show me the man who keeps his house in
    hand,
He's fit for public authority.
                            I'll have no dealings
With lawbreakers, critics of the
    government:
Whoever is chosen to govern should be
35   obeyed—
Must be obeyed, in all things, great and
    small,
Just and unjust! O Haimon,
The man who knows how to obey, and that
    man only,
Knows how to give commands when the
    time comes.
40 You can depend on him, no matter how fast
The spears come: he's a good soldier, he'll
    stick it out.

Anarchy, anarchy! Show me a greater evil!
This is why cities tumble and the great
    houses rain down,
This is what scatters armies!

No, no: good lives are made so by
45   discipline.
We keep the laws then, and the lawmakers,
And no woman shall seduce us. If we must
    lose,
Let's lose to a man, at least! Is a woman
    stronger than we?

CHORAGOS. Unless time has rusted my wits,
What you say, King, is said with point and
50   dignity.

HAIMON. [*Boyishly earnest*] Father:
Reason is God's crowning gift to man, and
    you are right
To warn me against losing mine. I cannot
    say—
I hope that I shall never want to
    say!—that you
Have reasoned badly. Yet there are other
55   men
Who can reason, too; and their opinions
    might be helpful.
You are not in a position to know everything
That people say or do, or what they feel:
Your temper terrifies them—everyone

Will tell you only what
60   you like to hear.
But I, at any rate, can
    listen; and I have
    heard them
Muttering and whis-
    pering in the dark
    about this girl.
They say no woman has ever, so
    unreasonably,
Died so shameful a death for a generous
    act:
"She covered her brother's body. Is this
65   indecent?
She kept him from dogs and vultures. Is
    this a crime?
Death?—She should have all the honor
    that we can give her!"

This is the way they talk out there in the
    city.

You must believe me:
Nothing is closer to me than your
70   happiness.
What could be closer? Must not any son
Value his father's fortune as his father
    does his?
I beg you, do not be unchangeable:
Do not believe that you alone can be right.
75 The man who thinks that,
The man who maintains that only he has
    the power
To reason correctly, the gift to speak, the
    soul—
A man like that, when you know him,
    turns out empty.

It is not reason never to yield to reason!

In flood time you can see how some trees
80   bend,
And because they bend, even their twigs
    are safe,
While stubborn trees are torn up, roots
    and all.
And the same thing happens in sailing:
Make your sheet fast, never slacken—and

◆ **Build Vocabulary**
vile (vīl) *adj.*: Extremely disgusting

over you go,
Head over heels and under: and there's
85 your voyage.
Forget you are angry! Let yourself be
moved!
I know I am young; but please let me say
this:
The ideal condition
Would be, I admit, that men should be
right by instinct;
90 But since we are all too likely to go astray,
The reasonable thing is to learn from those
who can teach.

CHORAGOS. You will do well to listen to him,
King,
If what he says is sensible. And you,
Haimon,
Must listen to your father.—Both speak
well.

CREON. You consider it right for a man of
95 my years and experience
To go to school to a boy?

HAIMON.   It is not right
If I am wrong. But if I am young, and right,
What does my age matter?

CREON. You think it right to stand up for an
anarchist?

HAIMON. Not at all. I pay no respect to
100 criminals.

CREON. Then she is not a criminal?

HAIMON. The City would deny it, to a man.

CREON. And the City proposes to teach me
how to rule?

HAIMON. Ah. Who is it that's talking like a
boy now?

CREON. My voice is the one voice giving
105 orders in this City!

HAIMON. It is no City if it takes orders from
one voice.

CREON. The State is the King!

HAIMON.   Yes, if the State is a desert.

[*Pause*]

CREON. This boy, it seems, has sold out to a
woman.

HAIMON. If you are a woman: my concern is
only for you.

CREON. So? Your "concern"! In a public
110 brawl with your father!

HAIMON. How about you, in a public brawl
with justice?

CREON. With justice, when all that I do is
within my rights?

HAIMON. You have no right to trample on
God's right.

CREON. [*Completely out of control*] Fool,
adolescent fool! Taken in by a woman!

HAIMON. You'll never see me taken in by
115 anything <u>vile</u>.

CREON. Every word you say is for her!

HAIMON. [*quietly, darkly*]   And for you.
And for me. And for the gods under the
earth.

CREON. You'll never marry her while she
lives.

HAIMON. Then she must die.—But her death
will cause another.

120 **CREON.** Another?
Have you lost your senses? Is this an open
threat?

HAIMON. There is no threat in speaking to
emptiness.

CREON. I swear you'll regret this superior
tone of yours!
You are the empty one!

HAIMON.   If you were not my
father,
125 I'd say you were perverse.

CREON. You girlstruck
fool, don't play at
words with me!

HAIMON. I am sorry.
You prefer silence.

◆ **Reading Strategy**
In what ways can you
identify with Haimon
in this scene?

CREON.   Now, by God—!
I swear, by all the gods in heaven above us,
You'll watch it, I swear you shall!

[*To the* SERVANTS]   Bring her out!
Bring the woman out! Let her die before
130   his eyes!
Here, this instant, with her bridegroom
     beside her!

HAIMON. Not here, no; she will not die here,
     King.
And you will never see my face again.
Go on raving as long as you've a friend to
     endure you.

[*Exit* HAIMON.]

135 **CHORAGOS.** Gone, gone.
Creon, a young man in a rage is dangerous!

CREON. Let him do, or dream to do, more
     than a man can.
He shall not save these girls from death.

CHORAGOS.   These girls?
You have sentenced them both?

CREON.   No, you are right.
I will not kill the one whose hands are
140   clean.

CHORAGOS. But Antigone?

CREON. [*Somberly*] I will carry her far away
Out there in the wilderness, and lock her
Living in a vault of stone. She shall have
     food,
As the custom is, to absolve the State of her
     death.
145 And there let her pray to the gods of hell:

They are her only gods:
Perhaps they will show her an escape from
     death,
Or she may learn,
                    though late,
That piety shown the dead is pity in vain.

[*Exit* CREON.]

Ode III

CHORUS.   [STROPHE]
Love, unconquerable
Waster of rich men, keeper
Of warm lights and all-night vigil
In the soft face of a girl:
5 Sea-wanderer, forest-visitor!
Even the pure Immortals cannot escape
     you,
And mortal man, in his one day's dusk,
Trembles before your glory.
                         [ANTISTROPHE]

Surely you swerve upon ruin
10 The just man's consenting heart,
As here you have made bright anger
Strike between father and son—
And none has conquered but Love!
A girl's glance working the will of heaven:
15 Pleasure to her alone who mocks us,
Merciless Aphrodite.[2]

---

2. **Aphrodite** (af rə dīt′ ē): Goddess of beauty and love, who is sometimes vengeful in her retaliation for offenses.

◆ Build Vocabulary

piety (pī′ ə tē) *n*.: Holiness; respect for the divine
blasphemy (blas′ fə mē) *n*.: Disrespectful action or speech against a deity

Scene 4

CHORAGOS. [As ANTIGONE *enters guarded*] But
    I can no longer stand in awe of this,
Nor, seeing what I see, keep back my tears.
Here is Antigone, passing to that chamber
Where all find sleep at last.

ANTIGONE.   [STROPHE 1]
5 Look upon me, friends, and pity me
Turning back at the night's edge to say
Good-by to the sun that shines for me no
    longer;
Now sleepy Death
Summons me down to Acheron,³ that cold
    shore:
10 There is no bridesong there, nor any music.

CHORUS. Yet not unpraised, not without a
    kind of honor,
You walk at last into the underworld;
Untouched by sickness, broken by no
    sword.
What woman has ever found your way to
    death?

ANTIGONE.   [ANTISTROPHE 1]
15 How often I have heard the story of Niobe,⁴
Tantalos'⁵ wretched daughter, how the
    stone
Clung fast about her, ivy-close: and they
    say
The rain falls endlessly
And sifting soft snow; her tears are never
    done.
20 I feel the loneliness of her death in mine.

CHORUS. But she was born of heaven, and
    you

---

3. **Acheron** (ak´ ər än´): River in the underworld over which the dead are ferried.
4. **Niobe** (nī ə bē´): A queen of Thebes who was turned to stone while weeping for her slain children. Her seven sons and seven daughters were killed by Artemis and Apollo, the divine twins of Leto. These gods ruined Niobe after Leto complained that Niobe insulted her by bragging of maternal superiority. It was Zeus who turned the bereaved Niobe to stone, but her lament continued and her tears created a stream.
5. **Tantalos** (tan´ tə ləs): Niobe's father, who was condemned to eternal frustration in the underworld because he revealed the secrets of the gods. Tantalos was tormented by being kept just out of reach of the water and food that was near him but which he could never reach to enjoy.

Are woman, woman-born. If her death is
    yours,
A mortal woman's, is this not for you
Glory in our world and in the world
    beyond?

ANTIGONE.   [STROPHE 2]
25 You laugh at me. Ah, friends, friends,
Can you not wait until I am dead? O
    Thebes,
O men many-charioted, in love with
    Fortune,
Dear springs of Dirce, sacred Theban
    grove,
Be witnesses for me, denied all pity,
30 Unjustly judged! and think a word of love
For her whose path turns
Under dark earth, where there are no more
    tears.

CHORUS. You have passed beyond human
    daring and come at last
Into a place of stone where Justice sits.
35 I cannot tell
What shape of your father's guilt appears
    in this.

ANTIGONE.   [ANTISTROPHE 2]
You have touched it at last: that bridal bed
Unspeakable, horror of son and mother
    mingling:
Their crime, infection of all our family!
40 O Oedipus, father and brother!
Your marriage strikes from the grave to
    murder mine.
I have been a stranger here in my own land:
All my life
The blasphemy of my birth has followed me.

45 CHORUS. Reverence is a
    virtue, but strength
Lives in established
    law: that must prevail.
You have made your
    choice,
Your death is the doing of your conscious
    hand.

> ◆ **Literary Focus**
> What flaw in Antigone does the chorus point out?

ANTIGONE.   [EPODE]
Then let me go, since all your words are
    bitter,
50 And the very light of the sun is cold to me.

Etruscan Amphora, black-figured, Pontic original (6th BC), fighting soldiers, a white dove on the shield, Muzeum Naradowe, Warsaw, Poland

▲ **Critical Viewing** What does the art on this vessel indicate about the significance of warfare in ancient Greece? **[Infer]**

Lead me to my vigil, where I must have
Neither love nor <u>lamentation</u>; no song, but silence.

[CREON *interrupts impatiently.*]

CREON. If dirges and planned lamentations could put off death,
Men would be singing forever.

[*To the* SERVANTS]   Take her, go!
55 You know your orders: take her to the vault
And leave her alone there. And if she lives or dies,
That's her affair, not ours: our hands are clean.

♦ **Build Vocabulary**

lamentation (lam´ ən tā´ shən) *n.*: An expression of grief; weeping

ANTIGONE. O tomb, vaulted bride-bed in eternal rock,
Soon I shall be with my own again
Where Persephone[6] welcomes the thin
60   ghosts underground:
And I shall see my father again, and you, mother,
And dearest Polyneices—

                dearest indeed
To me, since it was my hand
That washed him clean and poured the ritual wine:
65 And my reward is death before my time!

And yet, as men's hearts know, I have done no wrong,
I have not sinned before God. Or if I have,
I shall know the truth in death. But if the guilt
Lies upon Creon who judged me, then, I pray,
May his punishment equal my own.

70 **CHORAGOS.**   O passionate heart,
Unyielding, tormented still by the same winds!

CREON. Her guards shall have good cause to regret their delaying.

ANTIGONE. Ah! That voice is like the voice of death!

CREON. I can give you no reason to think you are mistaken.

ANTIGONE. Thebes, and you my fathers'
75   gods,
And rulers of Thebes, you see me now, the last
Unhappy daughter of a line of kings,
Your kings, led away to death. You will remember
What things I suffer, and at what men's hands,
Because I would not transgress the laws of
80   heaven.

[*To the* GUARDS, *simply*]

Come: let us wait no longer.

[*Exit* ANTIGONE, *left, guarded.*]

6. **Persephone** (pər sef´ ə nē): Queen of the underworld.

Ode IV

CHORUS. [STROPHE 1]

All Danae's beauty[7] was locked away
In a brazen cell where the sunlight could
   not come:
A small room, still as any grave, enclosed
   her.
Yet she was a princess too,
And Zeus in a rain of gold poured love
5   upon her.
O child, child,
No power in wealth or war
Or tough sea-blackened ships
Can prevail against untiring Destiny!

[ANTISTROPHE 1]

10 And Dryas' son[8] also, that furious king,
Bore the god's prisoning anger for his pride:
Sealed up by Dionysos[9] in deaf stone,
His madness died among echoes.
So at the last he learned what dreadful
   power
15 His tongue had mocked:
For he had profaned the revels,
And fired the wrath of the nine
Implacable Sisters[10] that love the sound of
   the flute.

[STROPHE 2]

And old men tell a half-remembered tale
Of horror done where a dark ledge splits
20   the sea

And a double surf beats on the gray shores:
How a king's new woman, sick
With hatred for the queen he had
   imprisoned,
Ripped out his two sons' eyes with her
   bloody hands
While grinning Ares[11] watched the shuttle
25   plunge
Four times: four blind wounds crying for
   revenge,

[ANTISTROPHE 2]

Crying, tears and blood mingled.
   —Piteously born,
Those sons whose mother was of heavenly
   birth!
Her father was the god of the North Wind
30 And she was cradled by gales,
She raced with young colts on the
   glittering hills
And walked untrammeled in the open light:
But in her marriage deathless Fate found
   means
To build a tomb like yours for all her joy.

Scene 5

[*Enter blind* TEIRESIAS, *led by a boy. The opening speeches of* TEIRESIAS *should be in singsong
contrast to the realistic lines of* CREON.]

TEIRESIAS. This is the way the blind man
   comes, Princes, Princes,
Lock-step, two heads lit by the eyes of one.

CREON. What new thing have you to tell us,
   old Teiresias?

TEIRESIAS. I have much to tell you: listen to
   the prophet, Creon.

CREON. I am not aware that I have ever
5   failed to listen.

TEIRESIAS. Then you have done wisely, King,
   and ruled well.

CREON. I admit my debt to you.[12] But what
   have you to say?

---

  7. Danae's (dan′ ā ēz′) **beauty:** Danae was imprisoned in a brazen, dark tower when it was foretold that she would mother a son who would kill her father. Her beauty attracted Zeus, who visited her in the form of a shower of gold. Perseus was born of the union, and Danae was exiled with the child over stormy seas from which Zeus saved them. Years later, as prophesied, the boy did kill the man he failed to recognize as his grandfather.

  8. Dryas' (drī′ əs) **son:** Lycorgos (lī kʉr′ gəs), whose opposition to the worship of Dionysos was severely punished by the gods. He drove the followers of the god from Thrace and was driven insane for having done so. Lycorgos recovered from his madness while imprisoned in a cave, but he was later blinded by Zeus as additional punishment for his offense.

  9. Dionysos (dī ə nī′ səs): God of wine, in whose honor the Greek plays were performed.

  10. nine Implacable Sisters: Nine muses, or goddesses, of science and literature. They are the daughters of Zeus and Mnemosyne (ne mas′ ə ne′)—Memory—who inspired invention and influenced the production of art. They are called implacable (im plak′ ə bəl) because they were unforgiving and denied inspiration to anyone who offended them.

  11. Ares (er′ ēz): God of war.

  12. my debt to you: Creon is here admitting that he would not have acquired the throne if Teiresias had not moved the former king, Oedipus, to an investigation of his own background that led eventually to his downfall. The news of his personal history, uncovered with help from Teiresias, forced Oedipus into exile.

TEIRESIAS. This, Creon: you stand once
   more on the edge of fate.

CREON. What do you mean? Your words are
   a kind of dread.

10 **TEIRESIAS.** Listen, Creon:
   I was sitting in my chair of augury,[13] at the
      place
   Where the birds gather about me. They
      were all a-chatter,
   As is their habit, when suddenly I heard
   A strange note in their jangling, a scream, a
   Whirring fury; I knew that they were
15   fighting,
   Tearing each other, dying
   In a whirlwind of wings clashing. And I
      was afraid.
   I began the rites of burnt-offering at the
      altar,
   But Hephaistos[14] failed me: instead of
      bright flame,
   There was only the sputtering slime of the
20   fat thigh-flesh
   Melting: the entrails dissolved in gray
      smoke,
   The bare bone burst from the welter. And
      no blaze!

   This was a sign from heaven. My boy
      described it,
   Seeing for me as I see for others.

25 I tell you, Creon, you yourself have brought
   This new calamity upon us. Our hearths
      and altars
   Are stained with the corruption of dogs
      and carrion birds
   That glut themselves on the corpse of
      Oedipus' son.
   The gods are deaf when we pray to them,
      their fire
   Recoils from our offering, their birds of
30   omen
   Have no cry of comfort, for they are gorged

With the thick blood of the dead.
                              O my son,
These are no trifles! Think: all men make
   mistakes,
But a good man yields when he knows his
   course is wrong,
35 And repairs the evil. The only crime is pride.

Give in to the dead man, then: do not fight
   with a corpse—
What glory is it to kill a man who is dead?
Think, I beg you:
It is for your own good that I speak as I do.
You should be able to yield for your own
40   good.

CREON. It seems that prophets have made
   me their especial province.
All my life long
I have been a kind of butt for the dull
   arrows
Of doddering
   fortunetellers!
      No, Teiresias:

If your birds—if the great eagles of God
45   himself
Should carry him stinking bit by bit to
   heaven,
I would not yield. I am not afraid of pollution:

---

13. chair of augury: The seat near the temple from
which Teiresias would deliver his predictions about the
future. Augury was the skill of telling such fortunes from a
consideration of omens, like the flight of birds or the position of stars.
14. Hephaistos (he fes′ təs): God of fire and the forge.
He would be invoked, as he is here by Teiresias, for aid in
the starting of ceremonial fires.

No man can defile the gods.

Do what you will,
Go into business, make money, speculate
In India gold or that synthetic gold from
50   Sardis,[15]
Get rich otherwise than by my consent to
   bury him.
Teiresias, it is a sorry thing when a wise man
Sells his wisdom, lets out his words for
   hire!

TEIRESIAS. Ah Creon! Is there no man left in
   the world—

CREON. To do what?—Come, let's have the
55   aphorism![16]

TEIRESIAS. No man who knows that wisdom
   outweighs any wealth?

CREON. As surely as bribes are baser than
   any baseness.

TEIRESIAS. You are sick, Creon! You are
   deathly sick!

CREON. As you say: it is not my place to
   challenge a prophet.

TEIRESIAS. Yet you have said my prophecy is
60   for sale.

CREON. The generation of prophets has
   always loved gold.

TEIRESIAS. The generation of kings has
   always loved brass.

CREON. You forget yourself! You are
   speaking to your King.

TEIRESIAS. I know it. You are a king because
   of me.

CREON. You have a certain skill; but you
65   have sold out.

TEIRESIAS. King, you will drive me to words
   that—

CREON.   Say them, say them!
Only remember: I will not pay you for them.

---

15. **Sardis** (sär′ dis): Capital of ancient Lydia, which produced the first coins made from an alloy of gold and silver.
16. **aphorism** (af′ ə riz′ əm): Brief, insightful saying.
Creon is taunting the prophet and suggesting that the old
man is capable only of relying on trite, meaningless
expressions instead of any original thinking.

TEIRESIAS. No, you will find them too costly.

CREON.   No doubt. Speak:
Whatever you say, you will not change my
   will.

TEIRESIAS. Then take this, and take it to
70   heart!
The time is not far off when you shall pay
   back
Corpse for corpse, flesh of your own flesh.
You have thrust the child of this world into
   living night,
You have kept from the gods below the
   child that is theirs:
The one in a grave before her death, the
75   other,
Dead, denied the grave. This is your crime:
And the Furies[17] and the dark gods of Hell
Are swift with terrible punishment for you.

Do you want to buy me now, Creon?

     Not many days,
And your house will be full of men and
80   women weeping,
And curses will be hurled at you from far
Cities grieving for sons unburied, left to rot
Before the walls of Thebes.

These are my arrows, Creon: they are all
   for you.

85 But come, child: lead me home.   [*To* BOY]
Let him waste his fine anger upon younger
   men.
Maybe he will learn at last
To control a wiser tongue in a better head.

[*Exit* TEIRESIAS.]

CHORAGOS. The old man has gone, King, but
   his words
90 Remain to plague us. I am old, too,
But I cannot remember
that he was ever false.

CREON. That is true. . . . It
troubles me.
Oh it is hard to give in! but
   it is worse

◆ **Reading Strategy**
What details help
you identify with
Creon's refusal to
yield?

---

17. **Furies** (fyoor′ ēz): Goddesses of vengence, who
made insane those whose crimes were unpunished, especially those who had sinned against their own families.

To risk everything for stubborn pride.

CHORAGOS. Creon: take my advice.

95 **CREON.**   What shall I do?

CHORAGOS. Go quickly: free Antigone from
    her vault
And build a tomb for the body of Polyneices.

CREON. You would have me do this?

CHORAGOS.   Creon, yes!
And it must be done at once: God moves
100 Swiftly to cancel the folly of stubborn men.

CREON. It is hard to deny the heart! But I
Will do it: I will not fight with destiny.

CHORAGOS. You must go yourself, you
    cannot leave it to others.

CREON. I will go.
                —Bring axes, servants:
105 Come with me to the tomb. I buried her, I
Will set her free.
            Oh quickly!
My mind misgives—
The laws of the gods are mighty, and a
    man must serve them
To the last day of his life!

[*Exit* CREON.]

Pæan

CHORAGOS.   [STROPHE 1]
God of many names

CHORUS.   O Iacchos[18]
                                  son
of Kadmeian Semele[19]
                    O born of the Thunder!
Guardian of the West
                Regent
of Eleusis' plain[20]

---

18. **Iacchos** (ē´ ə kəs): One of several alternate
names for Dionysos.
19. **Kadmeian Semele** (sem´ ə lē´): Semele was a
mortal and the mother of Dionysos. She was the
daughter of Thebes' founder, Kadmos.
20. **Eleusis'** (i l\overline{oo}´ sis) **plain:** Located north of
Athens, this plain was a site of worship for Dionysos
and Demeter, gods who protected the harvests of
grapes and corn, respectively.

O Prince of maenad Thebes[21]
and the Dragon Field by rippling
5   Ismenos:[22]

CHORAGOS.   [ANTISTROPHE 1]
God of many names

CHORUS.   the flame of torches
flares on our hills
                        the nymphs of Iacchos
dance at the spring of Castalia:[23]

from the vine-close mountain
                    come ah come in ivy:
Evohe evohe![24] sings through the streets of
10   Thebes

CHORAGOS.   [STROPHE 2]
    God of many names

CHORUS.   Iacchos of Thebes
    heavenly Child
        of Semele bride of the Thunderer!
The shadow of plague is upon us:
15   come
with clement feet[25]
                oh come from Parnasos[26]
down the long slopes
                across the lamenting water

CHORAGOS.   [ANTISTROPHE 2]
Io[27] Fire! Chorister of the throbbing stars!

---

21. **maenad** (mē´ nad) **Thebes:** The city is here compared
to a maenad, one of Dionysos' female worshipers. Such a
follower would be thought of as uncontrolled or disturbed,
much as Thebes was while being upset by the civil war.
22. **Dragon Field . . . Ismenos** (is mē´ nas): The Dragon
Field was located by the banks of Ismenos, a river sacred to
Apollo that flows near Thebes. The Dragon Field was where
Kadmos miraculously created warriors by sowing the teeth
of the dragon he killed there. Those men helped him establish the city.
23. **Castalia** (kas tā´ lē ə): Location of a site sacred to Apollo,
where his followers would worship.
24. **Evohe** (ē vō´ ē): Triumphant shout of affirmation (like
"Amen") used at ceremonies dedicated to Dionysos.
25. **clement feet:** *Clement* means "kind" or "favorable." The
chorus is here asking Dionysos to step gently into the troubled
path and to intervene in a healing manner.
26. **Parnasos** (pär nas´ əs): Mountain that was sacred to both
Dionysos and Apollo, located in central Greece.
27. **Io** (ē´ ō): Greek word for "Behold" or "Hail."

◆ **Build Vocabulary**

chorister (kôr´ is tər) *n.*: Member of a chorus

20 O purest among the voices of the night!
Thou son of God, blaze for us!

CHORUS. Come with choric rapture of
  circling Maenads
Who cry *Io Iacche!*[28]

                    God of many names!

Exodus

[*Enter* MESSENGER, *left.*]

MESSENGER. Men of the line of Kadmos,[29]
  you who live
Near Amphion's citadel:[30]
                    I cannot say
Of any condition of human life "This is
  fixed,
This is clearly good, or bad." Fate raises up,
And Fate casts down the happy and
5   unhappy alike:
No man can foretell his Fate.
                    Take the case of Creon:
Creon was happy once, as I count
  happiness:
Victorious in battle, sole governor of the
  land,
Fortunate father of children nobly born.
And now it has all gone from him! Who
10   can say
That a man is still alive when his life's joy
  fails?
He is a walking dead man. Grant him rich,
Let him live like a king in his great house:
If his pleasure is gone, I would not give
So much as the shadow of smoke for all he
15   owns.

CHORAGOS. Your words hint at sorrow: what
  is your news for us?

MESSENGER. They are dead. The living are
  guilty of their death.

CHORAGOS. Who is guilty? Who is dead?
  Speak!

---

28. *Io Iacche* (ē ō ē′ ə ke): Cry of celebration used
by Dionysian worshipers.
29. **Kadmos** (kad′ məs): Founder of the city of Thebes,
whose daughter, Semele, gave birth to Dionysos.
30. **Amphion's** (am fī′ ənz) **citadel:** Amphion was a king
of Thebes credited with erecting the walls of the fortress, or
citadel, by using his lyre so magically that its music caused
the stones to move themselves into proper place.

MESSENGER. Haimon.
Haimon is dead; and the hand that killed
  him
Is his own hand.

20 **CHORAGOS.**   His father's? or his own?

MESSENGER. His own, driven mad by the
  murder his father had done.

CHORAGOS. Teiresias, Teiresias, how clearly
  you saw it all!

MESSENGER. This is my news: you must
  draw what conclusions you can from it.

CHORAGOS. But look: Eurydice, our Queen:
25 Has she overheard us?

[*Enter* EURYDICE *from the Palace, center.*]

EURYDICE. I have heard something, friends:
As I was unlocking the gate of Pallas'[31]
  shrine,
For I needed her help today, I heard a voice
Telling of some new sorrow. And I fainted
There at the temple with all my maidens
30   about me.
But speak again: whatever it is, I can bear
  it:
Grief and I are no strangers.

MESSENGER.   Dearest Lady,
I will tell you plainly all that I have seen.
I shall not try to comfort you: what is the use,
Since comfort could lie only in what is not
35   true?
The truth is always best.
                    I went with Creon
To the outer plain where Polyneices was
  lying,
No friend to pity him, his body shredded by
  dogs.
We made our prayers in that place to
  Hecate[32]
And Pluto,[33] that they would be merciful.
40   And we bathed
The corpse with holy water, and we brought
Fresh-broken branches to burn what was

---

31. **Pallas** (pal′ əs): Pallas Athena, the goddess of
wisdom.
32. **Hecate** (hek′ ə tē): Goddess of the underworld.
33. **Pluto** (plo͞o′ ō): God of the underworld who managed the souls of the departed.

left of it,
And upon the urn we heaped up a towering
barrow
Of the earth of his own land.
When we were done, we ran
To the vault where Antigone lay on her
45   couch of stone.
One of the servants had gone ahead,
And while he was yet far off he heard a
voice
Grieving within the chamber, and he came
back
And told Creon. And as the King went
closer,
50 The air was full of wailing, the words lost,
And he begged us to make all haste. "Am I a
prophet?"
He said, weeping, "And must I walk this
road,
The saddest of all that I have gone before?
My son's voice calls me on. Oh quickly,
quickly!
55 Look through the crevice there, and tell me
If it is Haimon, or some deception of the
gods!"

We obeyed; and in the cavern's farthest
corner
We saw her lying:
She had made a noose of her fine linen veil
60 And hanged herself. Haimon lay beside her,
His arms about her waist, lamenting her,
His love lost underground, crying out
That his father had stolen her away from
him.

When Creon saw him the tears rushed to
his eyes
And he called to him: "What have you
65   done, child? Speak to me.
What are you thinking that makes your
eyes so strange?
O my son, my son, I come to you on my
knees!"
But Haimon spat in his face. He said not a
word,
Staring—
And suddenly drew his sword

And lunged. Creon shrank back, the blade
70   missed; and the boy,
Desperate against himself, drove it half its
length
Into his own side, and fell. And as he died
He gathered Antigone close in his arms
again,
Choking, his blood bright red on her white
cheek.
And now he lies dead with the dead, and
75   she is his
At last, his bride in the houses of the dead.

[*Exit* EURYDICE *into the Palace.*]

CHORAGOS. She has left us without a word.
What can this mean?

MESSENGER. It troubles me, too; yet she
knows what is best,
Her grief is too great for public lamentation,
And doubtless she has gone to her
80   chamber to weep
For her dead son, leading her maidens in
his dirge.

CHORAGOS. It may be so: but I fear this deep
silence.

[*Pause*]

MESSENGER. I will see what she is doing. I
will go in.

[*Exit* MESSENGER *into the Palace.*]

[*Enter* CREON *with attendants, bearing*
HAIMON'S *body.*]

CHORAGOS. But here is the King himself: oh
look at him,
85 Bearing his own damnation in his arms.

CREON. Nothing you say can touch me any
more.
My own blind heart has brought me
From darkness to final darkness. Here you
see
The father murdering, the murdered son—
90 And all my civic wisdom!

Haimon my son, so young, so young to die,
I was the fool, not you; and you died for me.

CHORAGOS. That is the truth; but you were late in learning it.

CREON. This truth is hard to bear. Surely a god
Has crushed me beneath the hugest weight
95   of heaven,
And driven me headlong a barbaric way
To trample out the thing I held most dear.

The pains that men will take to come to pain!

[*Enter* MESSENGER *from the Palace.*]

MESSENGER. The burden you carry in your hands is heavy,
But it is not all: you will find more in your
100   house.

CREON. What burden worse than this shall I find there?

MESSENGER. The Queen is dead.

CREON. O port of death, deaf world,
Is there no pity for me? And you, Angel of evil,
105 I was dead, and your words are death again.
Is it true, boy? Can it be true?
Is my wife dead? Has death bred death?

MESSENGER. You can see for yourself.

[*The doors are opened, and the body of*
EURYDICE *is disclosed within.*]

CREON. Oh pity!
110 All true, all true, and more than I can bear!

O my wife, my son!

MESSENGER. She stood before the altar, and her heart
Welcomed the knife her own hand guided,
And a great cry burst from her lips for Megareus[34] dead,
And for Haimon dead, her sons; and her
115   last breath
Was a curse for their father, the murderer of her sons.
And she fell, and the dark flowed in through her closing eyes.

CREON. O God, I am sick with fear.
Are there no swords here? Has no one a blow for me?

MESSENGER. Her curse is upon you for the
120   deaths of both.

CREON. It is right that it should be. I alone am guilty.
I know it, and I say it. Lead me in,
Quickly, friends.
I have neither life nor substance. Lead me in.

CHORAGOS. You are right, if there can be
125   right in so much wrong.
The briefest way is best in a world of sorrow.

---

34. Megareus (mə ga′ rē əs): Oldest son of Creon and Eurydice, who was killed in the civil war by Argive forces invading Thebes.

CREON. Let it come,
Let death come quickly, and be kind to me.
I would not ever see the sun again.

CHORAGOS. All that will come when it will;
but we, meanwhile,
130 Have much to do. Leave the future to itself.

CREON. All my heart was in that prayer!

CHORAGOS. Then do not pray any more: the
sky is deaf.

CREON. Lead me away. I have been rash and
foolish.
135 I have killed my son and my wife.

I look for comfort; my comfort lies here dead.
Whatever my hands have touched has
come to nothing.
Fate has brought all my pride to a thought
of dust.

[As CREON *is being led into the house, the*
CHORAGOS *advances and speaks directly to
the audience.*]

CHORAGOS. There is no happiness where
there is no wisdom;
140 No wisdom but in submission to the gods.
Big words are always punished,
And proud men in old age learn to be wise.

Guide for Responding

◆ *Literature and Your Life*

Reader's Response In Scene 3, Creon and Haimon express sharply different points of view. With which character do you most agree? Why?

Thematic Focus What choices do Creon and Antigone make that lead to their downfall?

Journal Activity List the reasons you think Creon should or should not have changed his mind. Explain which reason you feel is most compelling.

☑ Check Your Comprehension

1. Why do Creon and Haimon argue?
2. According to Teiresias, what terrible punishment awaits Creon?
3. What action does Creon take after Teiresias's prophecy?
4. What does the Messenger tell Eurydice before she leaves the stage during the Exodus?
5. What finally happens to Antigone? Haimon? Eurydice?

◆ Critical Thinking

INTERPRET
1. Explain the conflicts that drive Haimon to take extreme measures. Does he seem more concerned with divine law, to which Antigone turns for her justification, or with human law? Support your answer. **[Analyze]**
2. Why does Creon say "I have neither life nor substance" in the Exodus? **[Infer]**
3. How great a role do you think fate plays in dictating the outcome of the story? **[Support]**

EVALUATE
4. Both Antigone and Creon are unwilling to appear weak. How could this trait influence a person's outlook on life? **[Evaluate]**

APPLY
5. Explain how this play demonstrates the tension that sometimes exists between individual conscience and designated authority. **[Analyze]**
6. Near the end of the play, Creon says, "The pains that men will take to come to pain!" How do his words apply to contemporary society? **[Relate]**

Guide for Responding (continued)

◆ Literary Focus

TRAGIC CHARACTER

A **tragic character** is one who suffers a downfall. This character is marked with a tragic flaw that contributes to his or her doom.

1. (a) In your opinion, who is brought down most completely at the conclusion of the action?
   (b) Give evidence to support your answer.
2. (a) What is this character's tragic flaw? (b) How does this flaw lead to the character's downfall?
3. What role, if any, does fate play in leading to the downfall?

◆ Reading Strategy

IDENTIFY WITH A CHARACTER

When you **identify with a character** in a drama, you sympathize with his or her struggles or experiences.

1. With which character did you most identify? Why?
2. Which actions, events, or lines in the play led you to identify with that character?
3. How did your identification with a character draw you into the action of the play?

Beyond Literature

Cultural Connection

Burial Customs Different societies and cultures have different "burial" customs, some of which are not burials at all! Antigone "buries" her brother by sprinkling his corpse with wine and dust. The Vikings placed kings and great warriors on barges and then set them on fire. Some Aborigines in Australia leave bodies in trees. In Tibet a sky burial returns the body to nature by exposing it to birds and the elements on a high mountain.
Activity Find out more about a burial custom and write a brief explanation of how it reflects the needs and beliefs of a culture.

◆ Build Grammar Skills

PRONOUN CASE IN INCOMPLETE CLAUSES

In **incomplete clauses** introduced by *than* or *as*, a pronoun takes the case that it would have if the understood words were present.

Practice On your paper, write the correct pronoun to complete each sentence. Then write the words that are needed to complete each sentence.

1. The Chorus members see all; no one sees more than (*they/them*) ____?____.
2. When Haimon heard of Antigone's sentence, no one was more enraged than (*he/him*) ____?____.
3. The rest of the group was as certain as (*I/me*) ____?____ about the outcome of the play.
4. Though Ismene avoids her sister's fate, most people believe that Antigone is a much stronger character than (*she/her*) ____?____.
5. Although the details of her problems are different, Antigone faces some of the same issues as ____?____. (*we/us*)

◆ Build Vocabulary

USING THE GREEK ROOT -*chor*-

The Greek root -*chor*- comes from Terpsichore, the Muse of dance and song. Match each of the words in Column A with its definition in Column B.

Column A	Column B
1. choral	a. creating dance
2. choir	b. group of singers
3. choreography	c. sung or performed by a chorus

USING THE WORD BANK: Synonyms

On your paper, write the letter of the word that is the best synonym of the first word.

1. deference: (a) indignity, (b) respect, (c) irony
2. vile: (a) corrupt, (b) honorable, (c) edible
3. piety: (a) atheism, (b) reverence, (c) solitude
4. blasphemy: (a) violence, (b) vandalism, (c) disrespect
5. lamentation: (a) mourning, (b) cheer, (c) glee
6. chorister: (a) warden, (b) singer, (c) lawgiver

Build Your Portfolio

Idea Bank

Writing

1. Introduction Imagine that you are the director of a student theater group in your school. Write a brief introduction to present to an audience before they see a performance of *Antigone*.

2. Final Speech Create a brief final speech in which the messenger has one last chance to comment on the action. You might begin with the line "I shall go now over the world's paths to tell the sad story of . . ."

3. Editorial Imagine that you are an editor for a Thebes newspaper. Write an editorial on whether Creon's response to Antigone's action was appropriate. **[Career Link]**

Speaking, Listening, and Viewing

4. Mock Trial Hold a mock trial in which both sides of Antigone's case are argued before the class. Have the class act as a jury to determine which argument is more convincing.

5. Film Response If possible, see a video version of a few scenes of *Antigone*. With other classmates, compare and contrast your ideas about the characters from reading the play with the interpretations on the video.

Researching and Representing

6. Multimedia Presentation Create a multimedia presentation on ancient Greek theater. Include illustrations or labeled diagrams, tape recordings of excerpts from *Antigone*, historical maps, timelines, and other items. **[Social Studies Link; Media Link]**

Online Activity www.phlit.phschool.com

Guided Writing Lesson

Scene of Conflict

In Scene 2, as the Sentry hands over to Creon the person arrested for burying Polyneices, Creon exclaims: "But this is Antigone! Why have you brought her here?" That moment captures the major conflict in the play. Think of a conflict from a story, play, or novel that would make a gripping scene for a movie. Who are the characters? What is the reason for their confrontation? Focus on this moment and use it to write a **scene of conflict** for a screenplay.

Writing Skills Focus: Format

The **format** for a screenplay is similar to that of other kinds of drama. The characters' words are set in blocks following the characters' names and special directions are printed in italics, often enclosed in parentheses. Use the format for *Antigone* as a model. Your directions will include information about lights, sound, and camera angles, which are obviously not a part of this ancient Greek script.

Prewriting Draw a picture to get a sense of the setting of the scene for which you will give directions. Indicate where the characters will be seen, and jot down notes about how they might move or what kind of background music to play.

Drafting Write out what the characters say and do as they act out their conflict. Include directions about character movement, camera shots, and background sounds or music within parentheses, separate from the dialogue.

Revising Ask a partner to read your scene and tell you whether your conflict conveys suspense or tension. Your partner may help you sharpen the characters' lines or clarify and expand descriptions that help the reader envision the background.

PART 2 *Modern Drama*

La Loge, Pierre Auguste Renoir,
Courtauld Institute Galleries, London

Focus on Culture

Nineteenth-Century Europe

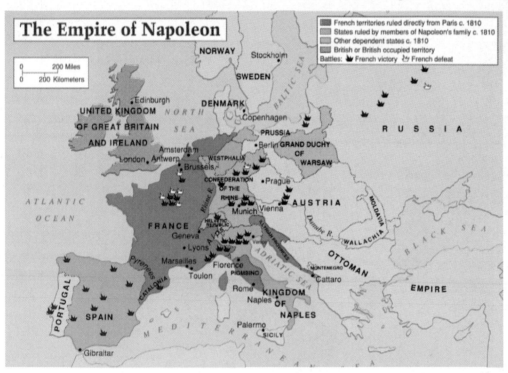

The Empire of Napoleon

French territories ruled directly from Paris c. 1810
States ruled by members of Napoleon's family c. 1810
Other dependent states c. 1810
British or British occupied territory
Battles: ✹ French victory ✹ French defeat

◀ **Critical Viewing**
Which parts of
Europe remained
beyond Napoleon's
control? **[Analyze]**

"*H*ave you ever been employed in a factory?"

"Yes."

"At what age did you first go to work in one?"

"Eight."

"How long did you continue in that occupation?"

"Four years."

"Will you state the hours of labor at the period when you first went to the factory, in ordinary times?"

"From six in the morning to eight at night."

This testimony was part of an investigation conducted by the English Parliament in 1832. Evidence on child labor and harsh factory conditions shocked many people. It also revealed the tremendous impact that the rise of industry had on nineteenth-century Europe.

GEOGRAPHIC SETTING

In land area, Europe is second smallest of the seven continents. Despite its size, however, Europe has had a huge impact on the modern world.

Europe occupies the western end of Eurasia, the giant landmass that stretches from Portugal to China. Its varied regions include Scandinavia, the large northern peninsula that includes Sweden, Denmark, and Norway. (Playwright Henrik Ibsen, whose work you will read next, was born in Norway.)

Importance of the Seas Europe includes several other major peninsulas that jut out into the surrounding waters. It also has a long coastline with countless natural harbors. For centuries, the seas around Europe have served as highways to the rest of the world.

In the nineteenth century, Western Europe came to dominate much of the world. Sea power played a major role in this expansion, which we call imperialism. Nations such as Britain, France, and Germany controlled much of the world's trade. They also seized and colonized much of Africa, Asia, and the Pacific.

Natural Resources Natural resources also played a role in European expansion. At the start of the century, Europe had abundant mineral supplies. In particular, iron and coal helped fuel the rise of industry, allowing Europeans to build and power factories, trains, and steamships. (See the picture on page 848.)

Still, such resources were not unlimited. Europe used up much of its precious coal supplies. Industrialists also needed resources that were not available locally, such as rubber and palm oil. The need for resources was another motive for imperialism.

HISTORY

As the nineteenth century began, Europe was in the midst of two revolutions. One was a violent political upheaval. The other was a more gradual, but even more turbulent, revolution in technology.

Political Upheavals In 1789, revolution broke out in France. The battle cry of "Liberty, Equality, Fraternity" echoed from France across the continent and many European leaders felt threatened by the French Revolution, especially after the king and queen were beheaded. Between 1792 and 1815, France was almost constantly at war with other European nations.

In 1804, an ambitious young general, Napoleon Bonaparte, made himself emperor of France. Although in many ways a dictator, Napoleon did institute some democratic reforms in France. He also conquered much of Europe. (See the map on page 846).

After Napoleon was defeated in 1815, conservative leaders tried to "turn back the clock." They restored older monarchies and repressed democratic movements. Yet the principles of the French Revolution lived on. Although a series of uprisings in 1848 failed, democratic ideals continued to gain force throughout the century.

The Industrial Revolution Like the French Revolution, the Industrial Revolution took shape in the 1700's. In the British textile industry, inventors produced new machines that reduced the time needed to spin and weave cloth. The new machines led to the growth of the factory system, which brought workers and machinery together in one place to manufacture goods.

Industry got a further boost with the invention of the steam engine. By the 1850's, steam was the main source of power, not only in factories, but also in new means of transportation such as the railroad and the steamship.

By the end of the century, scientists and inventors had developed countless new products, including the first automobiles. Electricity became an important new source of power. The Industrial Revolution had transformed Europe's entire way of life.

SOCIETY AND CULTURE

The Industrial Revolution brought many benefits. It created millions of new jobs and produced a variety of goods more cheaply than ever before. At the same time, the rise of industry brought new problems.

Industrial Hardships Early industrial workers often faced great hardships. Pay was low. As you have read, children labored in factories and coal mines. Working conditions were often dangerous, and those who were injured received no compensation. As people moved from the countryside to the growing industrial cities, they crowded into unhealthy urban slums.

Claude Monet, *Gare Saint-Lazare*, Burstein Collection © CORBIS

▲ **Critical Viewing** How does this picture indicate the influence of the Industrial Revolution? **[Connect]**

By the end of the century, reformers were at work to raise wages, outlaw child labor, and win better conditions in factories and slums. Gradually, the standard of living for workers and their families improved.

Middle-Class Values Industry and the growth of cities sparked the rise of a new middle class. At its top stood business owners, as well as professionals, such as doctors and lawyers. The lower middle class included office workers, teachers, and shopkeepers.

The values of the new middle class came to dominate society. These values included duty, thrift, honesty, hard work, and, above all, respectability. A strict code of morality and etiquette governed social behavior. Rules dictated how to dress, how long to mourn for a dead relative, and how to make social calls.

At the center of middle-class life was the home and family. Parents strictly supervised their children. The ideal home was seen as one in which the father went to work while the mother remained at home to oversee the household and servants. Most people, rich or poor, accepted these traditional values. "Home, sweet home" was the center of an orderly, prosperous society.

Changing Lives of Women
By the middle of the century, some reformers had begun to protest restrictions on women. Even in the most democratic nations, such as Britain, women could not vote. Women were banned from most schools and married women could not legally control their own property.

In response, some reformers called for women to receive suffrage, or the right to vote. Although the women's suffrage movement met with little success before 1900, a few women did begin to attend universities or move into some professions such as law, medicine, and even the ministry.

ARTS AND LITERATURE

The Industrial Revolution had a deep impact on European literature and arts. Two artistic movements in particular, Romanticism and realism, represented differing responses to the new industrial society.

Romanticism Since the eighteenth century, many European thinkers had emphasized notions of reason and scientific progress. A new group of writers, artists, and musicians rejected such ideas. Instead, these romantics valued feelings and emotion over reason. In Britain, poets such as William Wordsworth and landscape painters such as J.M.W. Turner glorified the beauty and power of nature. The turbulent, passionate music of German composer Ludwig van Beethoven also reflected the values of Romanticism.

Romantics often portrayed the pre-industrial past as a heroic age. The German poet Heinrich

Heine called for a "revival of medievalism in art, letters, and life." The Middle Ages provided the setting for novels such as Sir Walter Scott's *Ivanhoe* and Victor Hugo's *The Hunchback of Notre Dame*.

Realism Another group of artists and writers, called realists, took a different approach. They sought to describe life as it really was. Instead of turning away from the grimness of industrial life, many realists took it as their subject. In *Oliver Twist* and *Hard Times*, English novelist Charles Dickens looked at such social problems as urban crime, factory conditions, and the mistreatment of children. Painters, too, took up the banner of realism. "I cannot paint an angel," said French artist Gustave Courbet, "because I have never seen one." Instead, Courbet often portrayed simple working people, such as women washing clothes or men breaking rocks along a roadside.

The Norwegian dramatist Henrik Ibsen was a champion of realism. He was one of the first writers to make drama a vehicle for social criticism, often exploring topics that were considered daring or socially unacceptable. Against a realistic background of middle-class family life, Ibsen's play *A Doll's House* focused on the social rules and restrictions affecting women (see page 852).

New Directions in the Visual Arts
By the 1840's, a new technology—photography—was transforming the visual arts. Some artists argued that it was pointless to try for realism when a photograph could record actual events faster and more easily. Instead, a group of painters known as impressionists tried to capture fleeting visual "impressions" made by light and shadow. By placing bright, glowing colors side by side, French painters such as

Claude Monet created shimmering effects to capture the viewer's eye.

Other artists also moved away from precise realism. A group of painters known as expressionists, for example, used distortion and exaggeration to reproduce extreme psychological states, such as anxiety or even madness. Important early expressionists included the Norwegian artist Edvard Munch. (See the painting below.)

ACTIVITY
Writing an Etiquette Book

Use library or Internet resources to find out about middle-class manners in the nineteenth century. Then, use your research to compile an etiquette book listing at least ten rules for social behavior or home life. If you prefer, you may choose instead to draw a poster illustrating some of these *"dos"* and *"don'ts."* 🌑

Edvard Munch, *Workers Returning Home*

▲ **Critical Viewing** This painting, *Workers Returning Home*, is by the Norwegian artist Edvard Munch. Which details make this an expressionistic painting? Why? **[Assess]**

Guide for Reading

Henrik Ibsen (1828–1906)

If you visit the grave of dramatist Henrik Ibsen (hen´ rik ib´ sən) in Norway, you will see the picture of an arm holding a hammer on his tomb.

Ibsen had an arm and hammer placed on his tomb to symbolize the way in which his plays shattered illusions.

Poverty and Humiliation A hard early life prepared him for his role as a teller of hard truths. Ibsen was raised in a small Norwegian town, an out-of-the-way place for an aspiring literary talent. His father, a merchant, went bankrupt and moved the family to an isolated farm.

Ibsen suffered the bitter humiliation of his father's financial failure. At age fifteen, he became a druggist's apprentice and wrote his first poems as he worked at a job that he hated.

In 1850, hoping to attend the university, he moved to the capital city of Christiania (now Oslo), but he failed the entrance examination. Turning to the theater, he worked as a playwright and manager until 1862, when his theater went bankrupt. After twelve years of practical experience, Ibsen knew how the theater worked, but was no nearer to his goal of artistic fame.

The Turning Point In 1864 came the move that made the difference. He left Norway to live for twenty-seven years of self-imposed exile in Italy and in Germany. During this period, Ibsen wrote many of the great plays of his maturity.

These prose plays, including *A Doll's House* (1879), *Ghosts* (1881), and *The Wild Duck* (1884), were translated into different languages and performed on stages all over Europe. Ibsen's revolutionary ideas—about morality, social pressures, and the importance of individual choice—were talked about everywhere.

He came home in triumph as the inventor of modern drama and Norway's greatest writer.

◆ Build Vocabulary

LATIN PREFIXES: *sub-*

In Act I of *A Doll's House,* a character speaks of keeping his "subordinate position in the bank." Knowing that the Latin prefix *sub-* means "under, beneath, below" will help you define *subordinate* as an adjective meaning "inferior, ranking under or below." The word can also function as a noun. One who works under someone else's direction can be referred to as a *subordinate*.

Many common words use the Latin prefix *sub-,* including *subway* and *submarine*.

WORD BANK

As you read Act I of *A Doll's House,* you will encounter the words on this list. Preview the list before you read.

> spendthrift
> squandering
> prodigal
> indiscreet
> frivolous
> contraband
> subordinate

◆ Build Grammar Skills

PARALLELISM

Parallelism is the placement of equal ideas in words, phrases, or clauses of similar types. In Act I, the translator of *A Doll's House* uses all three of these types of parallelism:

Parallel Words: Yes, at odd jobs—*needlework, crocheting, embroidery* . . .

Parallel Phrases: This secret—*my joy* and *my pride* . . .

Parallel Clauses: *I begged* and *I cried* . . .

Look for these and other examples of parallelism in *A Doll's House*. Also, learn to use parallelism in your own writing.

A Doll's House

◆ *Literature and Your Life*

CONNECT YOUR EXPERIENCE

As you know, some nicknames express affection and approval. Others may offend people to whom they are applied, creating a false idea of who they are.

In Act I of *A Doll's House*, Helmer has many pet names for his wife, Nora, including *squirrel, lark,* and *sweet tooth.* Ibsen wants you to decide how much these names express affection and how much they give a false impression of Nora.

Journal Writing Jot down some positive functions that nicknames can serve and provide a few examples.

THEMATIC FOCUS: TURNING POINTS

What moments of decision in the past lives of the characters do you learn about in Act I?

◆ Background for Understanding

CULTURE

A Doll's House shocked its original audience because it addressed a controversial issue: the status of women. In 1879, when the play was written, it was unthinkable in Europe and America that a middle-class wife would imagine herself as an independent person.

Few such women were highly educated or had careers of their own. Women in Norway could not even vote until 1913—in the United States and Britain, women did not win full voting rights until 1920 and 1928, respectively. In addition, most women could not even borrow money without their husband's permission.

◆ Literary Focus

MODERN PROSE DRAMA

In order to examine social beliefs and customs, Ibsen invented the **modern prose drama,** a type of play that:
- is written in prose, not verse
- reflects the way people actually talk
- depicts characters and situations as they really are
- addresses controversial issues
- often questions society's assumptions

Ibsen's *A Doll's House,* written in 1879, was the first great modern prose drama. Its characters, ordinary men and women, deal with the problems that confronted middle-class Europeans in the late nineteenth century. In particular, the play focuses on the role and status of women.

◆ Reading Strategy

FORM MENTAL IMAGES

By **forming mental images,** watching an imagined performance in your mind, you will get more from reading a play. You, the reader, can direct this performance by:

- using stage directions to visualize the setting
- hearing voice and tone as you read dialogue
- using directions to picture characters' gestures
- finding clues in the dialogue to characters' movements

Look for clues in *A Doll's House* that will help you see your own private performance. Then, enter those clues in a chart like this one and use them to create mental images

Detail from Play	Mental Image
• Helmer's nicknames for his wife, Nora: *squirrel* or *skylark*	• She should move as if she were a small animal, skipping and twittering.
•	•

A Doll's House

Henrik Ibsen   Translated by Rolf Fjelde

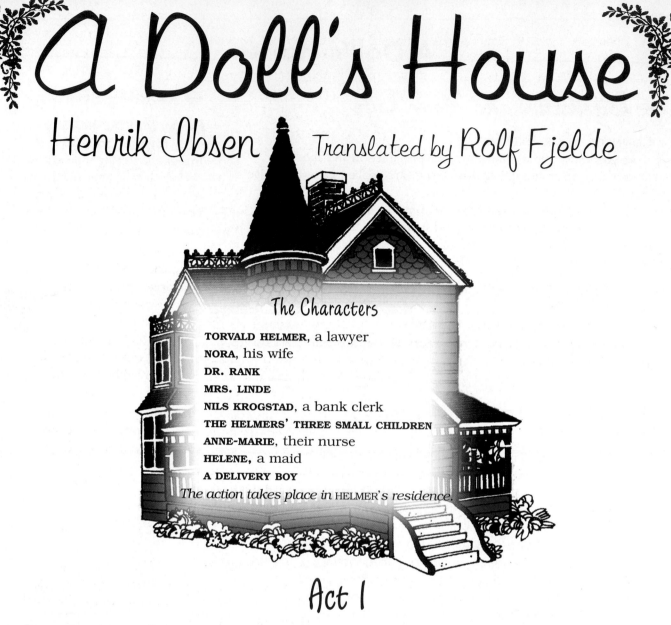

The Characters

TORVALD HELMER, a lawyer
NORA, his wife
DR. RANK
MRS. LINDE
NILS KROGSTAD, a bank clerk
THE HELMERS' THREE SMALL CHILDREN
ANNE-MARIE, their nurse
HELENE, a maid
A DELIVERY BOY

The action takes place in HELMER's *residence.*

Act 1

[*A comfortable room, tastefully but not expensively furnished. A door to the right in the back wall leads to the entryway; another to the left leads to* HELMER's *study. Between these doors, a piano. Midway in the left-hand wall a door, and farther back a window. Near the window a round table with an armchair and a small sofa. In the right-hand wall, toward the rear, a door, and nearer the foreground a porcelain stove with two armchairs and a rocking chair beside it. Between the stove and the side door, a small table. Engravings on the walls. An étagère[1] with china* figures and other small art objects; a small bookcase with richly bound books; the floor carpeted; a fire burning in the stove. It is a winter day.

A bell rings in the entryway; shortly after we hear the door being unlocked. NORA *comes into the room humming happily to herself; she is wearing street clothes and carries an armload of packages, which she puts down on the table to the right. She has left the hall door open; and through it a* DELIVERY BOY *is seen, holding a Christmas tree and a basket, which he gives to the* MAID *who let them in.*]

---

1. étagère (ā tà zher'): *n.*: A stand with open shelves for displaying small art objects and ornaments.

NORA. Hide the tree well, Helene. The children mustn't get a glimpse of it till this evening, after it's trimmed. [*To the* DELIVERY BOY, *taking out her purse*] How much?

DELIVERY BOY. Fifty, ma'am.

NORA. There's a crown.[2] No, keep the change. [*The* BOY *thanks her and leaves.* NORA *shuts the door. She laughs softly to herself while taking off her street things. Drawing a bag of macaroons from her pocket, she eats a couple, then steals over and listens at her husband's study door.*] Yes, he's home. [*Hums again as she moves to the table right*]

HELMER. [*From the study*] Is that my little lark twittering out there?

NORA. [*Busy opening some packages*] Yes, it is.

HELMER. Is that my squirrel rummaging around?

NORA. Yes!

HELMER. When did my squirrel get in?

NORA. Just now. [*Putting the macaroon bag in her pocket and wiping her mouth*] Do come in, Torvald, and see what I've bought.

HELMER. Can't be disturbed. [*After a moment he opens the door and peers in, pen in hand.*] Bought, you say? All that there? Has the little spendthrift been out throwing money around again?

NORA. Oh, but Torvald, this year we really should let ourselves go a bit. It's the first Christmas we haven't had to economize.

HELMER. But you know we can't go squandering.

NORA. Oh yes, Torvald, we can squander a little now. Can't we? Just a tiny, wee bit. Now that you've got a big salary and are going to make piles and piles of money.

HELMER. Yes—starting New Year's. But then it's a full three months till the raise comes through.

NORA. Pooh! We can borrow that long.

HELMER. Nora! [*Goes over and playfully takes her by the ear*] Are your scatterbrains off again? What if today I borrowed a thousand crowns,

and you squandered them over Christmas week, and then on New Year's Eve a roof tile fell on my head, and I lay there—

NORA. [*Putting her hand on his mouth*] Oh! don't say such things!

HELMER. Yes, but what if it happened—then what?

NORA. If anything so awful happened, then it just wouldn't matter if I had debts or not.

HELMER. Well, but the people I'd borrowed from?

NORA. Them? Who cared about them! They're strangers.

HELMER. Nora, Nora, how like a woman! No, but seriously, Nora, you know what I think about that. No debts! Never borrow! Something of freedom's lost—and something of beauty, too—from a home that's founded on borrowing and debt. We've made a brave stand up to now, the two of us; and we'll go right on like that the little while we have to.

NORA. [*Going toward the stove*] Yes, whatever you say, Torvald.

HELMER. [*Following her*] Now, now, the little lark's wings mustn't droop. Come on, don't be a sulky squirrel. [*Taking out his wallet*] Nora, guess what I have here.

NORA. [*Turning quickly*] Money!

HELMER. There, see. [*Hands her some notes*] Good grief, I know how costs go up in a house at Christmastime.

NORA. Ten—twenty—thirty—forty. Oh, thank you, Torvald; I can manage no end on this.

HELMER. You really will have to.

NORA. Oh yes, I promise I will! But come here so I can show you everything I bought. And so cheap! Look, new clothes for Ivar here—and a sword. Here a horse and a trumpet for Bob.

> ◆ **Literary Focus**
> What elements of modern prose drama have you seen so far in the play?

◆ **Build Vocabulary**

spendthrift (spend′ thrift′) *n.*: Person who spends money carelessly

squandering (skwän′ dər iŋ) *v.*: Spending money wastefully

---

2. **crown:** The crown, or krone, is the monetary unit of Denmark and Norway.

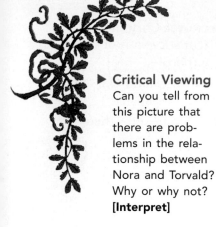

▶ **Critical Viewing**
Can you tell from this picture that there are problems in the relationship between Nora and Torvald? Why or why not?
[Interpret]

And a doll and a doll's bed here for Emmy; they're nothing much, but she'll tear them to bits in no time anyway. And here I have dress material and handkerchiefs for the maids. Old Anne-Marie really deserves something more.

HELMER. And what's in that package there?

NORA. [*With a cry*] Torvald, no! You can't see that till tonight!

HELMER. I see. But tell me now, you little <u>prodigal</u>, what have you thought of for yourself?

NORA. For myself? Oh, I don't want anything at all.

HELMER. Of course you do. Tell me just what—within reason—you'd most like to have.

NORA. I honestly don't know. Oh, listen, Torvald—

HELMER. Well?

NORA. [*Fumbling at his coat buttons, without looking at him*] If you want to give me something, then maybe you could—you could—

HELMER. Come on, out with it.

NORA. [*Hurriedly*] You could give me money, Torvald. No more than you think you can spare; then one of these days I'll buy something with it.

HELMER. But Nora—

NORA. Oh, please, Torvald darling, do that! I beg you, please. Then I could hang the bills in pretty gilt paper on the Christmas tree. Wouldn't that be fun?

HELMER. What are those little birds called that always fly through their fortunes?

NORA. Oh yes, spendthrifts; I know all that. But let's do as I say, Torvald; then I'll have time to decide what I really need most. That's very sensible, isn't it?

HELMER. [*Smiling*] Yes, very—that is, if you actually hung onto the money I give you, and you actually used it to buy yourself something. But it goes for the house and for all sorts of foolish things, and then I only have to lay out some more.

NORA. Oh, but Torvald—

HELMER. Don't deny it, my dear little Nora. [*Putting his arm around her waist*] Spendthrifts are sweet, but they use up a frightful amount of money. It's incredible what it costs a man to feed such birds.

NORA. Oh, how can you say that! Really, I save everything I can.

HELMER. [Laughing] Yes, that's the truth. Everything you can. But that's nothing at all.

NORA. [Humming, with a smile of quiet satisfaction] Hm, if you only knew what expenses we larks and squirrels have, Torvald.

HELMER. You're an odd little one. Exactly the way your father was. You're never at a loss for scaring up money; but the moment you have it, it runs right out through your fingers; you never know what you've done with it. Well, one takes you as you are. It's deep in your blood. Yes, these things are hereditary, Nora.

NORA. Ah, I could wish I'd inherited many of Papa's qualities.

HELMER. And I couldn't wish you anything but just what you are, my sweet little lark. But wait; it seems to me you have a very—what should I call it?—a very suspicious look today—

NORA. I do?

HELMER. You certainly do. Look me straight in the eye.

NORA. [Looking at him] Well?

HELMER. [Shaking an admonitory³ finger] Surely my sweet tooth hasn't been running riot in town today, has she?

NORA. No. Why do you imagine that?

HELMER. My sweet tooth really didn't make a little detour through the confectioner's?

NORA. No, I assure you, Torvald—

HELMER. Hasn't nibbled some pastry?

NORA. No, not at all.

HELMER. Not even munched a macaroon or two?

NORA. No, Torvald, I assure you, really—

HELMER. There, there now. Of course I'm only joking.

NORA. [Going to the table, right] You know I could never think of going against you.

HELMER. No, I understand that; and you *have* given me your word. [Going over to her] Well, you keep your little Christmas secrets to yourself, Nora darling. I expect they'll come to light this evening, when the tree is lit.

NORA. Did you remember to ask Dr. Rank?

HELMER. No. But there's no need for that; it's assumed he'll be dining with us. All the same. I'll ask him when he stops by here this morning. I've ordered some fine wine. Nora, you can't imagine how I'm looking forward to this evening.

NORA. So am I. And what fun for the children, Torvald!

HELMER. Ah, it's so gratifying to know that one's gotten a safe, secure job, and with a comfortable salary. It's a great satisfaction, isn't it?

NORA. Oh, it's wonderful!

HELMER. Remember last Christmas? Three whole weeks before, you shut yourself in every evening till long after midnight, making flowers for the Christmas tree, and all the other decorations to surprise us. Ugh, that was the dullest time I've ever lived through.

NORA. It wasn't at all dull for me.

HELMER. [Smiling] But the outcome *was* pretty sorry, Nora.

NORA. Oh, don't tease me with that again. How could I help it that the cat came in and tore everything to shreds.

HELMER. No, poor thing, you certainly couldn't. You wanted so much to please us all, and that's what counts. But it's just as well that the hard times are past.

NORA. Yes, it's really wonderful.

HELMER. Now I don't have to sit here alone, boring myself, and you don't have to tire your precious eyes and your fair little delicate hands—

NORA. [Clapping her hands] No, is it really true, Torvald, I don't have to? Oh, how wonderfully lovely to hear! [Taking his arm] Now I'll tell you just how I've thought we should plan things. Right after Christmas—[The doorbell rings.] Oh,

---

3. **admonitory** (əd män′ ə tôr′ ē) *adj.*: Warning.

the bell. [*Straightening the room up a bit*] Somebody would have to come. What a bore!

HELMER. I'm not at home to visitors, don't forget.

MAID. [*From the hall doorway*] Ma'am, a lady to see you—

NORA. All right, let her come in.

MAID. [*To* HELMER] And the doctor's just come too.

HELMER. Did he go right to my study?

MAID. Yes, he did. [HELMER *goes into his room. The* MAID *shows in* MRS. LINDE, *dressed in traveling clothes, and shuts the door after her.*]

MRS. LINDE. [*In a dispirited and somewhat hesitant voice*] Hello, Nora.

NORA. [*Uncertain*] Hello—

MRS. LINDE. You don't recognize me.

NORA. No, I don't know—but wait, I think—[*Exclaiming*] What! Kristine! Is it really you?

MRS. LINDE. Yes, it's me.

NORA. Kristine! To think I didn't recognize you. But then, how could I? [*More quietly*] How you've changed, Kristine!

MRS. LINDE. Yes, no doubt I have, in nine—ten long years.

NORA. Is it so long since we met! Yes, it's all of that. Oh, these last eight years have been a happy time, believe me. And so now you've come in to town, too. Made the long trip in the winter. That took courage.

MRS. LINDE. I just got here by ship this morning.

NORA. To enjoy yourself over Christmas, of course. Oh, how lovely! Yes, enjoy ourselves, we'll do that. But take your coat off. You're not still cold? [*Helping her*] There now, let's get cozy here by the stove. No, the easy chair there! I'll take the rocker here. [*Seizing her hands*] Yes, now you have your old look again; it was only in that first moment. You're a bit more pale, Kristine—and maybe a bit thinner.

MRS. LINDE. And much, much older, Nora.

NORA. Yes, perhaps a bit older; a tiny, tiny bit; not much at all. [*Stopping short; suddenly serious*] Oh, but thoughtless me, to sit here, chattering away. Sweet, good Kristine, can you forgive me?

MRS. LINDE. What do you mean Nora?

NORA. [*Softly*] Poor Kristine, you've become a widow.

MRS. LINDE. Yes, three years ago.

NORA. Oh, I knew it, of course; I read it in the papers. Oh, Kristine, you must believe me; I often thought of writing you then, but I kept postponing it, and something always interfered.

MRS. LINDE. Nora dear, I understand completely.

NORA. No, it was awful of me, Kristine. You poor thing, how much you must have gone through. And he left you nothing?

MRS. LINDE. No.

NORA. And no children?

MRS. LINDE. No.

NORA. Nothing at all, then?

MRS. LINDE. Not even a sense of loss to feed on.

NORA. [*Looking incredulously at her*] But Kristine, how could that be?

MRS. LINDE. [*Smiling wearily and smoothing her hair*] Oh, sometimes it happens, Nora.

NORA. So completely alone. How terribly hard that must be for you. I have three lovely children. You can't see them now; they're out with the maid. But now you must tell me everything—

MRS. LINDE. No, no, no, tell me about yourself.

NORA. No, you begin. Today I don't want to be selfish. I want to think only of you today. But there is something I must tell you. Did you hear of the wonderful luck we had recently?

MRS. LINDE. No, what's that?

NORA. My husband's been made manager in the bank, just think!

MRS. LINDE. Your husband? How marvelous!

NORA. Isn't it? Being a lawyer is such an uncertain living, you know, especially if one won't touch any cases that aren't clean and decent. And of course Torvald would never do that, and I'm with him completely there. Oh, we're simply delighted, believe me! He'll join the bank right after New Year's and start getting a huge salary

◀ **Critical Viewing**
Does this picture
indicate that Mrs.
Linde and Nora
are enjoying each
other's company?
Explain. **[Interpret]**

◆ **Reading Strategy**
Is your mental image
of the scene like the
picture on this page?
Why or why not?

and lots of commissions. From now on we can live quite differently—just as we want. Oh, Kristine, I feel so light and happy! Won't it be lovely to have stacks of money and not a care in the world?

MRS. LINDE. Well, anyway, it would be lovely to have enough for necessities.

NORA. No, not just for necessities, but stacks and stacks of money!

MRS. LINDE. [*Smiling*] Nora, Nora, aren't you sensible yet? Back in school you were such a free spender.

NORA. [*With a quiet laugh*] Yes, that's what Torvald still says. [*Shaking her finger*] But "Nora, Nora" isn't as silly as you all think. Really, we've been in no position for me to go squandering. We've had to work, both of us.

MRS. LINDE. You too?

NORA. Yes, at odd jobs—needlework, crocheting, embroidery, and such—[*Casually*] and other things too. You remember that Torvald left the department when we were married? There was no chance of promotion in his office, and of course he needed to earn more money. But that first year he drove himself terribly.

He took on all kinds of extra work that kept him going morning and night. It wore him down, and then he fell deathly ill. The doctors said it was essential for him to travel south.

MRS. LINDE. Yes, didn't you spend the whole year in Italy?

NORA. That's right. It wasn't easy to get away, you know. Ivar had just been born. But of course we had to go. Oh, that was a beautiful trip, and it saved Torvald's life. But it cost a frightful sum, Kristine.

MRS. LINDE. I can well imagine.

NORA. Four thousand, eight hundred crowns it cost. That's really a lot of money.

MRS. LINDE. But it's lucky you had it when you needed it.

NORA. Well, as it was, we got it from Papa.

MRS. LINDE. I see. It was just about the time your father died.

NORA. Yes, just about then. And, you know, I couldn't make that trip out to nurse him. I had to stay here, expecting Ivar any moment, and with my poor sick Torvald to care for. Dearest Papa, I never saw him again, Kristine. Oh, that was the worst time I've known in all my marriage.

MRS. LINDE. I know how you loved him. And then you went off to Italy?

NORA. Yes. We had the means now, and the doctors urged us. So we left a month after.

MRS. LINDE. And your husband came back completely cured?

NORA. Sound as a drum!

MRS. LINDE. But—the doctor?

NORA. Who?

MRS. LINDE. I thought the maid said he was a doctor, the man who came in with me.

NORA. Yes, that was Dr. Rank—but he's not making a sick call. He's our closest friend, and he stops by at least once a day. No, Torvald hasn't had a sick moment since, and the children are fit and strong, and I am, too. [*Jumping up and clapping her hands*] Oh, dear God, Kristine, what a lovely thing to live and be happy! But how disgusting of me—I'm talking of nothing but my own affairs. [*Sits on a stool close by* KRISTINE, *arms resting across her knees*] Oh, don't be angry with me! Tell me, is it really true that you weren't in love with your husband? Why did you marry him, then?

MRS. LINDE. My mother was still alive, but bedridden and helpless—and I had my two younger brothers to look after. In all conscience, I didn't think I could turn him down.

NORA. No, you were right there. But was he rich at the time?

MRS. LINDE. He was very well off, I'd say. But the business was shaky, Nora. When he died, it all fell apart, and nothing was left.

NORA. And then—?

MRS. LINDE. Yes, so I had to scrape up a living with a little shop and a little teaching and whatever else I could find. The last three years have been like one endless workday without a rest for me. Now it's over, Nora. My poor mother doesn't need me, for she's passed on. Nor the boys, either; they're working now and can take care of themselves.

NORA. How free you must feel—

MRS. LINDE. No—only unspeakably empty. Nothing to live for now. [*Standing up anxiously*] That's why I couldn't take it any longer out in that desolate hole. Maybe here it'll be easier to find something to do and keep my mind occupied. If I could only be lucky enough to get a steady job, some office work—

NORA. Oh, but Kristine, that's so dreadfully tiring, and you already look so tired. It would be much better for you if you could go off to a bathing resort.

MRS. LINDE. [*Going toward the window*] I have no father to give me travel money, Nora.

NORA. [*Rising*] Oh, don't be angry with me.

MRS. LINDE. [*Going to her*] Nora dear, don't you be angry with me. The worst of my kind of situation is all the bitterness that's stored away. No one to work for, and yet you're always having to snap up your opportunities. You have to live; and so you grow selfish. When you told me the happy change in your lot, do you know I was delighted less for your sakes than for mine?

NORA. How so? Oh, I see. You think maybe Torvald could do something for you.

MRS. LINDE. Yes, that's what I thought.

NORA. And he will, Kristine! Just leave it to me; I'll bring it up so delicately—find something attractive to humor him with. Oh, I'm so eager to help you.

MRS. LINDE. How very kind of you, Nora, to be so concerned over me—double kind, considering you really know so little of life's burdens yourself.

NORA. I—? I know so little—?

MRS. LINDE. [*Smiling*] Well, my heavens—a little needlework and such—Nora, you're just a child.

NORA. [*Tossing her head and pacing the floor*] You don't have to act so superior.

MRS. LINDE. Oh?

NORA. You're just like the others. You all think I'm incapable of anything serious.

MRS. LINDE. Come now—

NORA. That I've never had to face the raw world.

MRS. LINDE. Nora dear, you've just been telling me all your troubles.

NORA. Hm! Trivia! [*Quietly*] I haven't told you a big thing.

MRS. LINDE. Big thing? What do you mean?

NORA. You look down on me so, Kristine, but you shouldn't. You're proud that you worked so long and hard for your mother.

MRS. LINDE. I don't look down on a soul. But it is true: I'm proud—and happy, too—to think it was given to me to make my mother's last days almost free of care.

NORA. And you're also proud thinking of what you've done for your brothers.

MRS. LINDE. I feel I've a right to be.

NORA. I agree. But listen to this, Kristine—I've also got something to be proud and happy for.

MRS. LINDE. I don't doubt it. But whatever do you mean?

NORA. Not so loud. What if Torvald heard! He mustn't, not for anything in the world. Nobody must know, Kristine. No one but you.

MRS. LINDE. But what is it, then?

NORA. Come here. [*Drawing her down beside her on the sofa*] It's true—I've also got something to be proud and happy for. I'm the one who saved Torvald's life.

MRS. LINDE. Saved—? Saved how?

NORA. I told you about the trip to Italy. Torvald never would have lived if he hadn't gone south—

MRS. LINDE. Of course; your father gave you the means—

NORA. [*Smiling*] That's what Torvald and all the rest think, but—

MRS. LINDE. But—?

NORA. Papa didn't give us a pin. I was the one who raised the money.

MRS. LINDE. You? That whole amount?

NORA. Four thousand, eight hundred crowns.

◆ Build Vocabulary

indiscreet (in´ di skrēt´) *adj.*: Unwise or not careful

What do you say to that?

MRS. LINDE. But Nora, how was it possible? Did you win the lottery?

NORA. [*Disdainfully*] The lottery? Pooh! No art to that.

MRS. LINDE. But where did you get it from then?

NORA. [*Humming, with a mysterious smile*] Hmm, tra-la-la-la.

MRS. LINDE. Because you couldn't have borrowed it.

NORA. No? Why not?

MRS. LINDE. A wife can't borrow without her husband's consent.

NORA. [*Tossing her head*] Oh, but a wife with a little business sense, a wife who knows how to manage—

MRS. LINDE. Nora, I simply don't understand—

NORA. You don't have to. Whoever said I *borrowed* the money? I could have gotten it other ways. [*Throwing herself back on the sofa*] I could have gotten it from some admirer or other. After all, a girl with my ravishing appeal—

MRS. LINDE. You lunatic.

NORA. I'll bet you're eaten up with curiosity, Kristine.

MRS. LINDE. Now listen here, Nora—you haven't done something indiscreet?

NORA. [*Sitting up again*] Is it indiscreet to save your husband's life?

MRS. LINDE. I think it's indiscreet that without his knowledge you—

NORA. But that's the point: he mustn't know! My Lord, can't you understand? He mustn't ever know the close call he had. It was to *me* the doctors came to say his life was in danger—that nothing could save him but a stay in the south. Didn't I try strategy then! I began talking about how lovely it would be for me to travel abroad like other young wives; I begged and I cried; I told him please to remember my condition, to be kind and indulge me; and then I dropped a hint that he could easily take out a loan. But at that Kristine, he nearly exploded.

He said I was <u>frivolous</u>, and it was his duty as man of the house not to indulge me in whims and fancies—as I think he called them. Aha, I thought, now you'll just have to be saved—and that's when I saw my chance.

MRS. LINDE. And your father never told Torvald the money wasn't from him?

NORA. No, never. Papa died right about then. I'd considered bringing him into my secret and begging him never to tell. But he was too sick at the time—and then, sadly, it didn't matter.

MRS. LINDE. And you've never confided in your husband since?

NORA. For heaven's sake, no! Are you serious? He's so strict on that subject. Besides—Torvald, with all his masculine pride—how painfully humiliating for him if he ever found out he was in debt to me. That would just ruin our relationship. Our beautiful, happy home would never be the same.

MRS. LINDE. Won't you ever tell him?

NORA. [*Thoughtfully, half smiling*] Yes—maybe sometime, years from now, when I'm no longer so attractive. Don't laugh! I only mean when Torvald loves me less than now, when he stops enjoying my dancing and dressing up and reciting for him. Then it might be wise to have something in reserve—[*Breaking off*] How ridiculous! That'll never happen—Well, Kristine, what do you think of my big secret? I'm capable of something too, hm? You can imagine, of course, how this thing hangs over me. It really hasn't been easy meeting the payments on time. In the business world there's what they call quarterly interest and what they call amortization,[4] and these are always so terribly hard to manage. I've had to skimp a little here and there, wherever I could, you know. I could hardly spare anything from my house allowance, because Torvald has to live well. I couldn't let the children go poorly dressed; whatever I got for them, I felt I had to use up completely—the darlings!

MRS. LINDE. Poor Nora, so it had to come out of your own budget, then?

NORA. Yes, of course. But I was the one most responsible, too. Every time Torvald gave me money for new clothes and such, I never used more than half; always bought the simplest, cheapest outfits. It was a godsend that everything looks so well on me that Torvald never noticed. But it did weigh me down at times, Kristine. It is such a joy to wear fine things. You understand.

MRS. LINDE. Oh, of course.

NORA. And then I found other ways of making money. Last winter I was lucky enough to get a lot of copying to do. I locked myself in and sat writing every evening till late in the night. Ah, I was tired so often, dead tired. But still it was wonderful fun, sitting and working like that, earning money. It was almost like being a man.

MRS. LINDE. But how much have you paid off this way so far?

NORA. That's hard to say, exactly. These accounts, you know, aren't easy to figure. I only know that I've paid out all I could scrape together. Time and again I haven't known where to turn. [*Smiling*] Then I'd sit here dreaming of a rich old gentleman who had fallen in love with me—

MRS. LINDE. What! Who is he?

NORA. Oh, really! And that he'd died, and when his will was opened, there in big letters it said, "All my fortune shall be paid over in cash, immediately, to that enchanting Mrs. Nora Helmer."

MRS. LINDE. But Nora dear—who *was* this gentleman?

NORA. Good grief, can't you understand? The old man never existed; that was only something I'd dream up time and again whenever I was at my wits' end for money. But it makes no difference now; the old fossil can go where he pleases for all I care; I don't need him or his will—because now I'm free. [*Jumping up*] Oh, how lovely to think of that, Kristine! Carefree! To know you're carefree, utterly carefree; to be able to romp and play with the children, and to

---

4. **amortization** (am′ ər ti zā′ shən) *n.*: The putting aside of money at intervals, for gradual payment.

keep up a beautiful, charming home—everything just the way Torvald likes it! And think, spring is coming, with big blue skies. Maybe we can travel a little then. Maybe I'll see the ocean again. Oh yes, it *is* so marvelous to live and be happy! [*The front doorbell rings.*]

MRS. LINDE. [*Rising*] There's the bell. It's probably best that I go.

NORA. No, stay. No one's expected. It must be for Torvald.

MAID. [*From the hall doorway*] Excuse me, ma'am—there's a gentleman here to see Mr. Helmer, but I didn't know—since the doctor's with him—

NORA. Who is the gentleman?

KROGSTAD. [*From the doorway*] It's me, Mrs. Helmer. [MRS. LINDE *starts and turns away toward the window.*]

NORA. [*Stepping toward him, tense, her voice a whisper*] You? What is it? Why do you want to speak to my husband?

KROGSTAD. Bank business—after a fashion. I have a small job in the investment bank, and I hear now your husband is going to be our chief—

NORA. In other words, it's—

KROGSTAD. Just dry business, Mrs. Helmer. Nothing but that.

NORA. Yes, then please be good enough to step into the study. [*She nods indifferently as she sees him out by the hall door, then returns and begins stirring up the stove.*]

MRS. LINDE. Nora—who was that man?

♦ Literary Focus
Does this dialogue reflect the way people really speak? Why or why not?

NORA. That was a Mr. Krogstad—a lawyer.

MRS. LINDE. Then it really was him.

NORA. Do you know that person?

MRS. LINDE. I did once—many years ago. For a time he was a law clerk in our town.

♦ Build Vocabulary

frivolous (friv´ ə ləs) *adj.*: Silly and light-minded; not sensible

NORA. Yes, he's been that.

MRS. LINDE. How he's changed.

NORA. I understand he had a very unhappy marriage.

MRS. LINDE. He's a widower now.

NORA. With a number of children. There now, it's burning. [*She closes the stove door and moves the rocker a bit to one side.*]

MRS. LINDE. They say he has a hand in all kinds of business.

NORA. Oh? That may be true; I wouldn't know. But let's not think about business. It's so dull. [DR. RANK *enters from* HELMER's *study.*]

RANK. [*Still in the doorway*] No, no, really—I don't want to intrude, I'd just as soon talk a little while with your wife. [*Shuts the door, then notices* MRS. LINDE.] Oh, beg pardon. I'm intruding here too.

NORA. No, not at all. [*Introducing him*] Dr. Rank, Mrs. Linde.

RANK. Well now, that's a name much heard in this house. I believe I passed the lady on the stairs as I came.

MRS. LINDE. Yes, I take the stairs very slowly. They're rather hard on me.

RANK. Uh-hm, some touch of internal weakness?

MRS. LINDE. More overexertion, I'd say.

RANK. Nothing else? Then you're probably here in town to rest up in a round of parties?

MRS. LINDE. I'm here to look for work.

RANK. Is that the best cure for overexertion?

MRS. LINDE. One has to live, Doctor.

RANK. Yes, there's a common prejudice to that effect.

NORA. Oh, come on, Dr. Rank—you really do want to live yourself.

RANK. Yes, I really do. Wretched as I am, I'll gladly prolong my torment indefinitely. All my patients feel like that. And it's quite the same, too, with the morally sick. Right at this moment there's one of those moral invalids in there with Helmer—

MRS. LINDE. [*Softly*] Ah!

NORA. Who do you mean?

RANK. Oh, it's a lawyer, Krogstad, a type you wouldn't know. His character is rotten to the root—but even he began chattering all-importantly about how he had to *live.*

NORA. Oh? What did he want to talk to Torvald about?

RANK. I really don't know. I only heard something about the bank.

NORA. I didn't know that Krog—that this man Krogstad had anything to do with the bank.

RANK. Yes, he's gotten some kind of berth down there. [*To* MRS. LINDE] I don't know if you also have, in your neck of the woods, a type of person who scuttles about breathlessly, sniffing out hints of moral corruption, and then maneuvers his victim into some sort of key position where he can keep an eye on him. It's the healthy these days that are out in the cold.

MRS. LINDE. All the same, it's the sick who most need to be taken in.

RANK. [*With a shrug*] Yes, there we have it. That's the concept that's turning society into a sanatorium. [NORA, *lost in her thoughts, breaks out into quiet laughter and claps her hands.*]

RANK. Why do you laugh at that? Do you have any real idea of what society is?

NORA. What do I care about dreary old society? I was laughing at something quite different— something terribly funny. Tell me, Doctor—is everyone who works in the bank dependent now on Torvald?

RANK. Is that what you find so terribly funny?

NORA. [*Smiling and humming*] Never mind, never mind! [*Pacing the floor*] Yes, that's really immensely amusing: that we—that Torvald has so much power now over all those people. [*Taking the bag out of her pocket*] Dr. Rank, a little macaroon on that?

RANK. See here, macaroons! I thought they were <u>contraband</u> here.

NORA. Yes, but these are some that Kristine gave me.

▶ **Critical Viewing**
What does this picture reveal about the economic status of the Helmers? **[Interpret]**

MRS. LINDE. What? I—?

NORA. Now, now, don't be afraid. You couldn't possibly know that Torvald had forbidden them. You see, he's worried they'll ruin my teeth. But hmp! Just this once! Isn't that so, Dr. Rank? Help yourself. [*Puts a macaroon in his mouth*] And you too, Kristine. And I'll also have one, only a little one—or two, at the most. [*Walking about again*] Now I'm really tremendously happy. Now there's just one last thing in the world that I have an enormous desire to do.

RANK. Well! And what's that?

NORA. It's something I have such a consuming desire to say so Torvald could hear.

RANK. And why can't you say it?

NORA. I don't dare. It's quite shocking.

MRS. LINDE. Shocking?

RANK. Well, then it isn't advisable. But in front of us you certainly can. What do you have such a desire to say so Torvald could hear?

NORA. I have such a huge desire to say—to hell and be damned!

RANK. Are you crazy?

MRS. LINDE. My goodness, Nora!

RANK. Go on, say it. Here he is.

NORA. [*Hiding the macaroon bag*] Shh, shh, shh! [HELMER *comes in from his study, hat in hand, overcoat over his arm.*]

NORA. [*Going toward him*] Well, Torvald dear, are you through with him?

HELMER. Yes, he just left.

NORA. Let me introduce you—this is Kristine, who's arrived here in town.

HELMER. Kristine—? I'm sorry, but I don't know—

NORA. Mrs. Linde, Torvald dear. Mrs. Kristine Linde.

HELMER. Of course. A childhood friend of my wife's, no doubt?

MRS. LINDE. Yes, we knew each other in those days.

NORA. And just think, she made the long trip down here in order to talk with you.

HELMER. What's this?

MRS. LINDE. Well, not exactly—

NORA. You see, Kristine is remarkably clever in office work, and so she's terribly eager to come under a capable man's supervision and add more to what she already knows—

HELMER. Very wise, Mrs. Linde.

NORA. And then when she heard that you'd become a bank manager—the story was wired out to the papers—then she came in as fast as she could and—Really, Torvald, for my sake you can do a little something for Kristine, can't you?

HELMER. Yes, it's not at all impossible. Mrs. Linde, I suppose you're a widow?

MRS. LINDE. Yes.

HELMER. Any experience in office work?

MRS. LINDE. Yes, a good deal.

HELMER. Well, it's quite likely that I can make an opening for you—

NORA. [*Clapping her hands*] You see, you see!

HELMER. You've come at a lucky moment, Mrs. Linde.

MRS. LINDE. Oh, how can I thank you?

HELMER. Not necessary. [*Putting his overcoat on*] But today you'll have to excuse me—

RANK. Wait, I'll go with you. [*He fetches his coat from the hall and warms it at the stove.*]

NORA. Don't stay out long, dear.

HELMER. An hour; no more.

NORA. Are you going too, Kristine?

MRS. LINDE. [*Putting on her winter garments*] Yes, I have to see about a room now.

HELMER. Then perhaps we can all walk together.

NORA. [*Helping her*] What a shame we're so cramped here, but it's quite impossible for us to—

◆ Build Vocabulary

contraband (kän´ trə band´) *n*.: Unlawful or forbidden goods

► **Critical Viewing**
What does this
picture suggest
about the relation-
ship between Nora
and her children?
[Interpret]

MRS. LINDE. Oh, don't even think of it! Good-
bye, Nora dear, and thanks for everything.

NORA. Good-bye for now. Of course you'll be
back this evening. And you too, Dr. Rank.
What? If you're well enough? Oh, you've got to
be! Wrap up tight now. [*In
a ripple of small talk the
company moves out into
the hall; children's voices
are heard outside on the
steps.*]

◆ **Reading Strategy**
What mental picture
do you form after
reading the stage
directions?

NORA. There they are! There they are! [*She runs
to open the door. The children come in with their
nurse,* ANNE-MARIE.] Come in, come in! [*Bends
down and kisses them*] Oh, you darlings—!
Look at them, Kristine. Aren't they lovely!

RANK. No loitering in the draft here.

HELMER. Come, Mrs. Linde—this place is unbear-
able now for anyone but mothers. [DR. RANK,
HELMER, *and* MRS. LINDE *go down the stairs.* ANNE-
MARIE *goes into the living room with the children.*
NORA *follows, after closing the hall door.*]

NORA. How fresh and strong you look. Oh, such
red cheeks you have! Like apples and roses. [*The
children interrupt her throughout the following.*]
And it was so much fun? That's wonderful.
Really? You pulled both Emmy and Bob on the
sled? Imagine, all together! Yes, you're a clever
boy, Ivar. Oh, let me hold her a bit, Anne-Marie.
My sweet little doll baby! [*Takes the smallest
from the nurse and dances with her*] Yes, yes,
Mama will dance with Bob as well. What? Did
you throw snowballs? Oh, if I'd only been there!
No, don't bother, Anne-Marie—I'll undress them
myself. Oh yes, let me. It's such fun. Go in and
rest; you look half frozen. There's hot coffee
waiting for you on the stove. [*The nurse goes
into the room to the left.* NORA *takes the children's
winter things off throwing them about, while the
children talk to her all at once.*] Is that so? A big
dog chased you? But it didn't bite? No, dogs
never bite little, lovely doll babies. Don't peek
in the packages, Ivar! What is it? Yes, wouldn't
you like to know. No, no, it's an ugly something.
Well? Shall we play? What shall we play? Hide-
and-seek? Yes, let's play hide-and-seek. Bob
must hide first. I must? Yes, let me hide first.
[*Laughing and shouting, she and the children play
in and out of the living room and the adjoining*

room to the right. *At last* NORA *hides under the table. The children come storming in, search, but cannot find her, then hear her muffled laughter, dash over to the table, lift the cloth up and find her. Wild shouting. She creeps forward as if to scare them. More shouts. Meanwhile, a knock at the hall door; no one has noticed it. Now the door half opens, and* KROGSTAD *appears. He waits a moment; the game goes on.*]

KROGSTAD. Beg pardon, Mrs. Helmer—

NORA. [*With a strangled cry, turning and scrambling to her knees*] Oh! What do you want?

KROGSTAD. Excuse me. The outer door was ajar; it must be someone forgot to shut it—

NORA. [*Rising*] My husband isn't home, Mr. Krogstad.

KROGSTAD. I know that.

NORA. Yes—then what do you want here?

KROGSTAD. A word with you.

NORA. With—? [*To the children, quietly*] Go in to Anne-Marie. What? No, the strange man won't hurt Mama. When he's gone, we'll play some more. [*She leads the children into the room to the left and shuts the door after them. Then, tense and nervous*] You want to speak to me?

KROGSTAD. Yes, I want to.

NORA. Today? But it's not yet the first of the month—

KROGSTAD. No, it's Christmas Eve. It's going to be up to you how merry a Christmas you have.

NORA. What is it you want? Today I absolutely can't—

KROGSTAD. We won't talk about that till later. This is something else. You do have a moment to spare, I suppose?

NORA. Oh, yes, of course—I do, except—

KROGSTAD. Good. I was sitting over at Olsen's Restaurant when I saw your husband go down the street—

NORA. Yes?

KROGSTAD. With a lady.

NORA. Yes. So?

KROGSTAD. If you'll pardon my asking: wasn't that lady a Mrs. Linde?

NORA. Yes.

KROGSTAD. Just now come into town?

NORA. Yes, today.

KROGSTAD. She's a good friend of yours?

NORA. Yes, she is. But I don't see—

KROGSTAD. I also knew her once.

NORA. I'm aware of that.

KROGSTAD. Oh? You know all about it. I thought so. Well, then let me ask you short and sweet: is Mrs. Linde getting a job in the bank?

NORA. What makes you think you can cross-examine me, Mr. Krogstad—you, one of my husband's employees? But since you ask, you might as well know—yes, Mrs. Linde's going to be taken on at the bank. And I'm the one who spoke for her, Mr. Krogstad. Now you know.

KROGSTAD. So I guessed right.

NORA. [*Pacing up and down*] Oh, one does have a tiny bit of influence, I should hope. Just because I am a woman, don't think it means that—When one has a <u>subordinate</u> position, Mr. Krogstad, one really ought to be careful about pushing somebody who—hm—

KROGSTAD. Who has influence?

NORA. That's right.

KROGSTAD. [*In a different tone*] Mrs. Helmer, would you be good enough to use your influence on my behalf?

NORA. What? What do you mean?

KROGSTAD. Would you please make sure that I keep my subordinate position in the bank.

NORA. What does that mean? Who's thinking of taking away your position?

KROGSTAD. Oh, don't play the innocent with me. I'm quite aware that your friend would hardly relish the chance of running into me again; and I'm also aware now whom I can thank for being turned out.

NORA. But I promise you—

♦ **Build Vocabulary**

subordinate (sə bôrd´'n it) *adj.*: Inferior; ranking under or below

KROGSTAD. Yes, yes, yes, to the point: there's still time, and I'm advising you to use your influence to prevent it.

NORA. But Mr. Krogstad, I have absolutely no influence.

KROGSTAD. You haven't? I thought you were just saying—

NORA. You shouldn't take me so literally. I! How can you believe that I have any such influence over my husband?

KROGSTAD. Oh, I've known your husband from our student days. I don't think the great bank manager's more steadfast than any other married man.

NORA. You speak insolently about my husband, and I'll show you the door.

KROGSTAD. The lady has spirit.

NORA. I'm not afraid of you any longer. After New Year's, I'll soon be done with the whole business.

KROGSTAD. [*Restraining himself*] Now listen to me, Mrs. Helmer. If necessary, I'll fight for my little job in the bank as if it were life itself.

NORA. Yes, so it seems.

KROGSTAD. It's not just a matter of income; that's the least of it. It's something else—All right, out with it! Look, this is the thing. You know, just like all the others, of course, that once, a good many years ago, I did something rather rash.

NORA. I've heard rumors to that effect.

KROGSTAD. The case never got into court; but all the same, every door was closed in my face from then on. So I took up those various activities you know about. I had to grab hold somewhere; and I dare say I haven't been among the worst. But now I want to drop all that. My boys are growing up. For their sakes, I'll have to win back as much respect as possible here in town. That job in the bank was like the first rung in my ladder And now your husband wants to kick me right back down in the mud again.

NORA. But for heaven's sake, Mr. Krogstad, it's simply not in my power to help you.

KROGSTAD. That's because you haven't the will to—but I have the means to make you.

NORA. You certainly won't tell my husband that I owe you money?

KROGSTAD. Hm—what if I told him that?

NORA. That would be shameful of you. [*Nearly in tears*] This secret—my joy and my pride—that he should learn it in such a crude and disgusting way—learn it from you. You'd expose me to the most horrible unpleasantness—

KROGSTAD. Only unpleasantness?

NORA. [*Vehemently*] But go on and try. It'll turn out the worse for you, because then my husband will really see what a crook you are, and then you'll never be able to hold your job.

KROGSTAD. I asked if it was just domestic unpleasantness you were afraid of?

NORA. If my husband finds out, then of course he'll pay what I owe at once, and then we'd be through with you for good.

KROGSTAD. [*A step closer*] Listen, Mrs. Helmer— you've either got a very bad memory, or else no head at all for business. I'd better put you a little more in touch with the facts.

NORA. What do you mean?

KROGSTAD. When your husband was sick, you came to me for a loan of four thousand, eight hundred crowns.

NORA. Where else could I go?

KROGSTAD. I promised to get you that sum—

NORA. And you got it.

KROGSTAD. I promised to get you that sum, on certain conditions. You were so involved in your husband's illness, and so eager to finance your trip, that I guess you didn't think out all the details. It might just be a good idea to remind you. I promised you the money on the strength of a note I drew up.

NORA. Yes, and that I signed.

KROGSTAD. Right. But at the bottom I added some lines for your father to guarantee the loan. He was supposed to sign down there.

NORA. Supposed to? He did sign.

KROGSTAD. I left the date blank. In other words, your father would have dated his signature himself. Do you remember that?

NORA. Yes, I think—

KROGSTAD. Then I gave you the note for you to mail to your father. Isn't that so?

NORA. Yes.

KROGSTAD. And naturally you sent it at once—because only some five, six days later you brought me the note, properly signed. And with that, the money was yours.

NORA. Well, then; I've made my payments regularly, haven't I?

KROGSTAD. More or less. But—getting back to the point—those were hard times for you then, Mrs. Helmer.

NORA. Yes, they were.

KROGSTAD. Your father was very ill, I believe.

NORA. He was near the end.

KROGSTAD. He died soon after?

NORA. Yes.

KROGSTAD. Tell me, Mrs. Helmer, do you happen to recall the date of your father's death? The day of the month, I mean.

NORA. Papa died the twenty-ninth of September.

KROGSTAD. That's quite correct; I've already looked into that. And now we come to a curious thing— [*Taking out a paper*] which I simply cannot comprehend.

NORA. Curious thing? I don't know—

KROGSTAD. This is the curious thing: that your father co-signed the note for your loan three days after his death.

NORA. How—? I don't understand.

KROGSTAD. Your father died the twenty-ninth of September. But look. Here your father dated his signature October second. Isn't that curious, Mrs. Helmer? [NORA *is silent.*] Can you explain it to me? [NORA *remains silent.*] It's also remarkable that the words "October second" and the year aren't written in your father's hand, but rather in one that I think I know. Well, it's easy to understand. Your father forgot perhaps to date his signature, and then someone or other added it, a bit sloppily, before anyone knew of his death. There's nothing wrong in that. It all comes down to the signature. And

there's no question about that, Mrs. Helmer. It really *was* your father who signed his own name here, wasn't it?

NORA. [*After a short silence, throwing her head back and looking squarely at him*] No, it wasn't. *I* signed Papa's name.

KROGSTAD. Wait, now—are you fully aware that this is a dangerous confession?

NORA. Why? You'll soon get your money.

KROGSTAD. Let me ask you a question—why didn't you send the paper to your father?

NORA. That was impossible. Papa was so sick. If I'd asked him for his signature, I also would have had to tell him what the money was for. But I couldn't tell him, sick as he was, that my husband's life was in danger. That was just impossible.

KROGSTAD. Then it would have been better if you'd given up the trip abroad.

NORA. I couldn't possibly. The trip was to save my husband's life. I couldn't give that up.

KROGSTAD. But didn't you ever consider that this was a fraud against me?

NORA. I couldn't let myself be bothered by that. You weren't any concern of mine. I couldn't stand you, with all those cold complications you made, even though you knew how badly off my husband was.

KROGSTAD. Mrs. Helmer, obviously you haven't the vaguest idea of what you've involved yourself in. But I can tell you this: it was nothing more and nothing worse that I once did—and it wrecked my whole reputation.

NORA. You? Do you expect me to believe that you ever acted bravely to save your wife's life?

KROGSTAD. Laws don't inquire into motives.

NORA. Then they must be very poor laws.

KROGSTAD. Poor or not—if I introduce this paper in court, you'll be judged according to law.

NORA. This I refuse to believe. A daughter hasn't a right to protect her dying father from anxiety and care? A wife hasn't a right to save her husband's life? I don't know much about laws, but I'm sure that somewhere in the books these things are allowed. And you don't know anything about it—you who practice the law? You must be an awful lawyer, Mr. Krogstad.

KROGSTAD. Could be. But business—the kind of business we two are mixed up in—don't you think I know about that? All right. Do what you want now. But I'm telling you *this:* if I get shoved down a second time, you're going to keep me company. [*He bows and goes out through the hall.*]

NORA. [*Pensive[5] for a moment, then tossing her head*] Oh, really! Trying to frighten me! I'm not so silly as all that. [*Begins gathering up the children's clothes, but soon stops*] But—? No, but that's impossible! I did it out of love.

THE CHILDREN. [*In the doorway, left*] Mama, that strange man's gone out the door.

NORA. Yes, yes, I know it. But don't tell anyone about the strange man. Do you hear? Not even Papa!

THE CHILDREN. No, Mama. But now will you play again?

NORA. No, not now.

THE CHILDREN. Oh, but Mama, you promised.

NORA. Yes, but I can't now. Go inside; I have too much to do. Go in, go in, my sweet darlings. [*She herds them gently back in the room and shuts the door after them. Settling on the sofa, she takes up a piece of embroidery and makes some stitches, but soon stops abruptly.*] No! [*Throws the work aside, rises, goes to the hall door and calls out*] Helene! Let me have the tree in here. [*Goes to the table, left, opens the table drawer, and stops again*] No, but that's utterly impossible!

MAID. [*With the Christmas tree*] Where should I put it, ma'am?

NORA. There. The middle of the floor.

MAID. Should I bring anything else?

NORA. No, thanks. I have what I need. [*The* MAID, *who has set the tree down, goes out.*]

NORA. [*Absorbed in trimming the tree*] Candles here—and flowers here. That terrible creature! Talk, talk, talk! There's nothing to it at all. The tree's going to be lovely. I'll do anything to please you, Torvald. I'll sing for you, dance for you— [HELMER *comes in from the hall, with a sheaf of papers under his arm.*]

NORA. Oh! You're back so soon?

HELMER. Yes. Has anyone been here?

NORA. Here? No.

HELMER. That's odd. I saw Krogstad leaving the front door.

NORA. So? Oh yes, that's true. Krogstad was here a moment.

HELMER. Nora, I can see by your face that he's been here, begging you to put in a good word for him.

NORA. Yes.

HELMER. And it was supposed to seem like your own idea? You were to hide it from me that he'd been here. He asked you that, too, didn't he?

NORA. Yes, Torvald, but—

HELMER. Nora, Nora, and you could fall for that? Talk with that sort of person and promise him anything? And then in the bargain, tell me an untruth.

NORA. An untruth—?

HELMER. Didn't you say that no one had been here? [*Wagging his finger*] My little songbird must never do that again. A songbird needs a clean beak to warble with. No false notes. [*Putting his arm about her waist*] That's the way it should be, isn't it? Yes, I'm sure of it. [*Releasing her*] And so, enough of that. [*Sitting by the stove*] Ah, how snug and cozy it is here. [*Leafing among his papers*]

NORA. [*Busy with the tree, after a short pause*] Torvald!

HELMER. Yes.

NORA. I'm so much looking forward to the Stenborgs' costume party, day after tomorrow.

---

5. **pensive** (pen′ siv) *adj*.: Thinking deeply or seriously, often of sad or melancholy things.

HELMER. And I can't wait to see what you'll surprise me with.

NORA. Oh, that stupid business!

HELMER. What?

NORA. I can't find anything that's right. Everything seems so ridiculous, so inane.[6]

HELMER. So my little Nora's come to *that* recognition?

NORA. [*Going behind his chair, her arms resting on his back*] Are you very busy, Torvald?

HELMER. Oh—

NORA. What papers are those?

HELMER. Bank matters.

NORA. Already?

HELMER. I've gotten full authority from the retiring management to make all necessary changes in personnel and procedure. I'll need Christmas week for that. I want to have everything in order by New Year's.

NORA. So that was the reason this poor Krogstad—

HELMER. Hm.

NORA. [*Still leaning on the chair and slowly stroking the nape of his neck*] If you weren't so very busy, I would have asked you an enormous favor, Torvald.

HELMER. Let's hear. What is it?

NORA. You know, there isn't anyone who has your good taste—and I want so much to look well at the costume party. Torvald, couldn't you take over and decide what I should be and plan my costume?

HELMER. Ah, is my stubborn little creature calling for a lifeguard?

NORA. Yes, Torvald, I can't get anywhere without your help.

HELMER. All right—I'll think it over. We'll hit on something.

NORA. Oh, how sweet of you. [*Goes to the tree again. Pause*] Aren't the red flowers pretty—? But tell me, was it really such a crime that this Krogstad committed?

HELMER. Forgery. Do you have any idea what that means?

NORA. Couldn't he have done it out of need?

HELMER. Yes, or thoughtlessness, like so many others. I'm not so heartless that I'd condemn a man categorically for just one mistake.

NORA. No, of course not, Torvald!

HELMER. Plenty of men have redeemed themselves by openly confessing their crimes and taking their punishment.

NORA. Punishment—?

HELMER. But now Krogstad didn't go that way. He got himself out by sharp practices, and that's the real cause of his moral breakdown.

NORA. Do you really think that would—?

HELMER. Just imagine how a man with that sort of guilt in him has to lie and cheat and deceive on all sides, has to wear a mask even with the nearest and dearest he has, even with his own wife and children. And with the children, Nora —that's where it's most horrible.

NORA. Why?

HELMER. Because that kind of atmosphere of lies infects the whole life of a home. Every breath the children take in is filled with the germs of something degenerate.

NORA. [*Coming closer behind him*] Are you sure of that?

HELMER. Oh, I've seen it often enough as a lawyer. Almost everyone who goes bad early in life has a mother who's a chronic liar.

NORA. Why just—the mother?

HELMER. It's usually the mother's influence that's dominant, but the father's works in the same way, of course. Every lawyer is quite familiar with it. And still this Krogstad's been going home year in, year out, poisoning his own children with lies and pretense; that's why I call him morally lost. [*Reaching his hands out toward her*] So my sweet little Nora must promise me never to plead his cause. Your hand on it. Come, come, what's this? Give me your hand. There, now. All settled. I can tell you it'd be impossible

---

6. **inane** (in ān′) *adj.*: Foolish; silly.

for me to work alongside of him. I literally feel physically revolted when I'm anywhere near such a person.

NORA. [*Withdraws her hand and goes to the other side of the Christmas tree*] How hot it is here! And I've got so much to do.

HELMER. [*Getting up and gathering his papers*] Yes, and I have to think about getting some of these read through before dinner. I'll think about your costume, too. And something to hang on the tree in gilt paper, I may even see about that. [*Putting his hand on her head*] Oh you, my darling little songbird. [*He goes into his study and closes the door after him.*]

NORA. [*Softly, after a silence*] Oh, really! It isn't so. It's impossible. It must be impossible.

ANNE-MARIE. [*In the doorway, left*] The children are begging so hard to come in to Mama.

NORA. No, no, no, don't let them in to me! You stay with them, Anne-Marie.

ANNE-MARIE. Of course, ma'am. [*Closes the door*]

NORA. [*Pale with terror*] Hurt my children—? Poison my home? [*A moment's pause; then she tosses her head.*] That's not true. Never in all the world.

Guide for Responding

◆ *Literature and Your Life*

Reader's Response Do you feel more sympathy for Helmer or for Nora? Explain.

Thematic Focus In what way did Krogstad and Nora face a similar moment of decision in the past?

Reader's Journal Jot down three adjectives to describe the Helmers' marriage, and briefly explain your choices.

Questions for Research Formulate three questions that would help you research the status of women in nineteenth-century Europe.

☑ Check Your Comprehension

1. In what season of the year does the play begin?
2. What recent good news are the Helmers celebrating?
3. Which characters did Mrs. Linde know in the past?
4. What favor did Krogstad once do for Nora, and what favor does he now ask in return?
5. What act of Nora's gives Krogstad a hold on her?

◆ Critical Thinking

INTERPRET

1. What does Helmer's use of pet names for his wife suggest about his attitude toward her? **[Infer]**
2. What does Nora's behavior toward Helmer reveal about her attitude toward him? **[Infer]**
3. In what ways is the side that Nora presents to Helmer different from the side she presents to Mrs. Linde? **[Compare and Contrast]**
4. What developments in Act I suggest that Nora is in trouble? Explain. **[Draw Conclusions]**

EVALUATE

5. How well does the title of the play characterize the Helmers' relationship? Explain. **[Make a Judgment]**

EXTEND

6. What advice might a marriage counselor have to offer Nora and Helmer? **[Career Link]**

Guide for Responding (continued)

◆ Reading Strategy

FORM MENTAL IMAGES

If you **form mental images** while reading a drama, you can see in your mind the characters and the actions behind the words. In *A Doll's House*, Act I, stage directions and hints in the dialogue can help you create an imaginary performance.

1. When Mrs. Linde enters and says, "You don't recognize me," Nora looks at her and says, "No, I don't know—but wait, I think—[*Exclaiming.*] What! Kristine! Is it really you?" (See p. 856.) Describe the facial expressions and gestures that would accompany Nora's speech.
2. When Krogstad questions Nora about her father's death, he takes out a piece of paper. (See p. 867.) What might he do with it as he talks about the signature?

◆ Build Vocabulary

USING THE LATIN PREFIX *sub-*

The Latin prefix *sub-*, meaning "under, beneath, below," appears in many English words. On your paper, write the *sub-* words matching the following definitions.

1. less than human in development
2. the layer of dirt or soil lying below the topsoil
3. not supersonic; less than the speed of sound
4. a group of animals not as differentiated as a species.
5. a title that appears below the main title

USING THE WORD BANK

On your paper, write the word from the Word Bank described by each item. Use each word only once.

1. This might be seized by customs officers as illegal.
2. This is the opposite of a thrifty person or a miser.
3. This kind of position involves low-level work.
4. This type of behavior will make you seem silly.
5. One should not be doing this with one's money.
6. Being this leads to poor decisions.
7. This is a good synonym for *spendthrift*.

◆ Literary Focus

MODERN PROSE DRAMA

A Doll's House is a **modern prose drama** because it uses prose and realistic dialogue to depict real life, and it challenges accepted ideas.

1. Find a passage of realistic dialogue. Explain how it resembles a real-life conversation.
2. How does Mrs. Linde's situation challenge the accepted ideas of the time about women?

◆ Build Grammar Skills

PARALLELISM

Parallelism is the placement of equal ideas in words, phrases, or clauses of similar types.

Practice On your paper, identify the parallel words, phrases, or clauses in each sentence.

1. Helmer calls Nora a lark, a squirrel, and a spendthrift.
2. Secret knowledge and quiet satisfaction cause Nora to hum.
3. Nora wants to be carefree and to keep a home.
4. Thinking of Torvald, Nora says, "I'll sing for you, and I'll dance for you."
5. For Torvald, Krogstad is dishonest and shifty.

Idea Bank

Writing

1. **Letter of Appeal** Suppose that Mrs. Linde could not come to see Nora in person. Write the letter that she might have written instead of visiting, appealing for Nora's help.
2. **Dramatic Scene** Write the dialogue that takes place in Act I between Krogstad and Helmer off-stage in Helmer's study. Include stage directions to help readers picture the setting and action.

Researching and Representing

3. **Report on Women's Status** Research the status of women in Norway in the late 1870's, when Ibsen wrote his play. Focus on employment, education, and politics. **[Social Studies Link]**

Guide for Reading

◆ Review and Anticipate

Years ago Nora secretly borrowed money from Krogstad to help her husband travel and recover from illness. Desperate for a signature to guarantee the loan but reluctant to disturb her dying father, she forged her father's name on the document.

Nora shares the secret of her forgery with Mrs. Linde, her childhood friend, now widowed and penniless, for whom she hopes to get a position at the bank. Helmer agrees to hire Mrs. Linde, but Nora learns from Krogstad that Helmer has fired him to make room for Mrs. Linde. Now Krogstad threatens to make her secret public if she does not urge her husband to keep him employed at the bank. Helmer, not knowing what is at stake, refuses to rehire Krogstad.

Act II opens with Krogstad's threat of public disgrace still hanging over Nora's head and Nora in a state of near panic.

◆ Literary Focus

CHARACTERIZATION IN DRAMA

Characterization in drama is the dramatist's process of developing a character. In the verse dramas written before Ibsen's time, dramatists had characters reveal their innermost thoughts in speeches called *soliloquies*. However, realistic prose dramas rarely contain soliloquies. Modern dramatists must therefore develop characters indirectly through their dialogue and actions.

For example, in Act I of *A Doll's House,* Nora's game of hide-and-seek with her children shows her vigor and vitality. Helmer's refusal to relate to the children shows his inability to break free of his own stuffy self-image as the adult, male authority figure of the house.

◆ Build Grammar Skills

COMPOUND PREDICATES

Compound predicates are two or more verbs or verb phrases with the same subject in the same sentence. Compound predicates permit a writer to pack a lot of action into one sentence without having to repeat the subject.

In this example drawn from Act II, the two verb phrases are connected using the conjunction *and*.

I'll *go to the inner office* and *shut both doors* . . .

◆ Reading Strategy

QUESTION

When you **question** as you read, you do not simply absorb information, but you ask yourself about the meaning of events, choices, and details.

In reading *A Doll's House,* ask yourself why characters act as they do. For example, Helmer forbids Nora to eat macaroons. Why? Helmer claims that they will harm her teeth. However, he also may want to treat his wife as if she were an irresponsible child.

◆ Build Vocabulary

LATIN PREFIXES: *dis-*

In Act II, Dr. Rank speaks about his *disease.* This word employs a common Latin prefix, *dis-*. Combined with an adjective or a noun, *dis-* usually means "not," "opposite of," or "lack of (something)."

A *disease* or illness is literally a "lack of ease."

WORD BANK

Preview the list before you read.

proclaiming
intolerable
impulsive
tactless
excruciating
retribution
disreputable

A Doll's House

Act II

[*Same room. Beside the piano the Christmas tree now stands stripped of ornaments, burned-down candle stubs on its ragged branches.* NORA*'s street clothes lie on the sofa.* NORA, *alone in the room, moves restlessly about; at last she stops at the sofa and picks up her coat.*]

NORA. [*Dropping the coat again*] Someone's coming! [*Goes toward the door, listens*] No—there's no one. Of course—nobody's coming today, Christmas Day—or tomorrow, either. But maybe— [*Opens the door and looks out*] No, nothing in the mailbox. Quite empty. [*Coming forward*] What nonsense! He won't do anything serious. Nothing terrible could happen. It's impossible. Why, I have three small children.

[ANNE-MARIE, *with a large carton, comes in from the room to the left.*]

ANNE-MARIE. Well, at last I found the box with the masquerade clothes.

NORA. Thanks. Put it on the table.

ANNE-MARIE. [*Does so*] But they're all pretty much of a mess.

NORA. Ahh! I'd love to rip them in a million pieces!

ANNE-MARIE. Oh, mercy, they can be fixed right up. Just a little patience.

NORA. Yes, I'll go get Mrs. Linde to help me.

ANNE-MARIE. Out again now? In this nasty weather? Miss Nora will catch cold—get sick.

NORA. Oh, worse things could happen—How are the children?

ANNE-MARIE. The poor mites are playing with their Christmas presents, but—

NORA. Do they ask for me much?

ANNE-MARIE. They're so used to having Mama around, you know.

NORA. Yes. But Anne-Marie, I *can't* be together with them as much as I was.

ANNE-MARIE. Well, small children get used to anything.

NORA. You think so? Do you think they'd forget their mother if she was gone for good?

◆ **Reading Strategy**
Why do you think Nora uses the phrase "gone for good"?

ANNE-MARIE. Oh, mercy—gone for good!

NORA. Wait, tell me, Anne-Marie—I've wondered so often—how could you ever have the heart to give your child over to strangers?

ANNE-MARIE. But I had to, you know, to become little Nora's nurse.

NORA. Yes, but how could you *do* it?

ANNE-MARIE. When I could get such a good place? A girl who's poor and who's gotten in trouble is glad enough for that. Because that slippery fish, he didn't do a thing for me, you know.

NORA. But your daughter's surely forgotten you.

ANNE-MARIE. Oh, she certainly has not. She's written to me, both when she was confirmed and when she was married.

NORA. [*Clasping her about the neck*] You old Anne-Marie, you were a good mother for me when I was little.

ANNE-MARIE. Poor little Nora, with no other mother but me.

NORA. And if the babies

didn't have one, then I know that you'd—What silly talk! [*Opening the carton*] Go in to them. Now I'll have to—Tomorrow you can see how lovely I'll look.

ANNE-MARIE. Oh, there won't be anyone at the party as lovely as Miss Nora. [*She goes off into the room, left.*]

NORA. [*Begins unpacking the box, but soon throws it aside*] Oh, if I dared to go out. If only nobody would come. If only nothing would happen here while I'm out. What craziness—nobody's coming. Just don't think. This muff—needs a brushing. Beautiful gloves, beautiful gloves. Let it go. Let it go! One, two, three, four, five, six—[*With a cry*] Oh, there they are! [*Poises to move toward the door, but remains irresolutely standing.* MRS. LINDE *enters from the hall where she has removed her street clothes.*]

NORA. Oh, it's you, Kristine. There's no one else out there? How good that you've come.

MRS. LINDE. I hear you were up asking for me.

NORA. Yes, I just stopped by. There's something you really can help me with. Let's get settled on the sofa. Look, there's going to be a costume party tomorrow evening at the Stenborgs' right above us, and now Torvald wants me to go as a Neapolitan[1] peasant girl and dance the tarantella that I learned in Capri.[2]

MRS. LINDE. Really, are you giving a whole performance?

NORA. Torvald says yes, I should. See, here's the dress. Torvald had it made for me down there; but now it's all so tattered that I just don't know—

MRS. LINDE. Oh, we'll fix that up in no time. It's nothing more than the trimmings—they're a bit loose here and there. Needle and thread? Good, now we have what we need.

NORA. Oh, how sweet of you!

MRS. LINDE. [*Sewing*] So you'll be in disguise tomorrow, Nora. You know what? I'll stop by then

for a moment and have a look at you all dressed up. But listen, I've absolutely forgotten to thank you for that pleasant evening yesterday.

NORA. [*Getting up and walking about*] I don't think it was as pleasant as usual yesterday. You should have come to town a bit sooner, Kristine—Yes, Torvald really knows how to give a home elegance and charm.

MRS. LINDE. And you do, too, if you ask me. You're not your father's daughter for nothing. But tell me, is Dr. Rank always so down in the mouth as yesterday?

NORA. No, that was quite an exception. But he goes around critically ill all the time—tuberculosis of the spine, poor man. You know, his father was a disgusting thing who kept mistresses and so on—and that's why the son's been sickly from birth.

MRS. LINDE. [*Lets her sewing fall to her lap*] But my dearest Nora, how do you know about such things?

NORA. [*Walking more jauntily*] Hmp! When you've had three children, then you've had a few visits from—from women who know something of medicine, and they tell you this and that.

MRS. LINDE. [*Resumes sewing; a short pause*] Does Dr. Rank come here every day?

NORA. Every blessed day. He's Torvald's best friend from childhood, and *my* good friend, too. Dr. Rank almost belongs to this house.

MRS. LINDE. But tell me—is he quite sincere? I mean, doesn't he rather enjoy flattering people?

NORA. Just the opposite. Why do you think that?

MRS. LINDE. When you introduced us yesterday, he was proclaiming that he'd often heard my name in this house; but later I noticed that your husband hadn't the slightest idea who I really was. So how could Dr. Rank—?

NORA. But it's all true, Kristine. You see, Torvald loves me beyond words, and, as he puts it, he'd like to keep me all to himself. For a long time he'd almost be jealous if I even mentioned any of my old friends back home. So of course I dropped that. But with Dr. Rank I talk a lot

---

1. Neapolitan (nē̆ ə päl′ ə t'n): Of Naples, a seaport in southern Italy.
2. Capri (ka prē′): An island near the entrance to the Bay of Naples.

about such things, because he likes hearing about them.

MRS. LINDE. Now listen, Nora; in many ways you're still like a child. I'm a good deal older than you, with a little more experience. I'll tell you something: you ought to put an end to all this with Dr. Rank.

NORA. What should I put an end to?

MRS. LINDE. Both parts of it, I think. Yesterday you said something about a rich admirer who'd provide you with money—

NORA. Yes, one who doesn't exist—worse luck. So?

MRS. LINDE. Is Dr. Rank well off?

NORA. Yes, he is.

MRS. LINDE. With no dependents?

NORA. No, no one. But—?

MRS. LINDE. And he's over here every day?

NORA. Yes, I told you that.

MRS. LINDE. How can a man of such refinement be so grasping?

NORA. I don't follow you at all.

MRS. LINDE. Now don't try to hide it, Nora. You think I can't guess who loaned you the forty-eight hundred crowns?

NORA. Are you out of your mind? How could you think such a thing! A friend of ours, who comes here every single day. What an <u>intolerable</u> situation that would have been!

MRS. LINDE. Then it really wasn't him.

NORA. No, absolutely not. It never even crossed my mind for a moment—And he had nothing to lend in those days; his inheritance came later.

MRS. LINDE. Well, I think that was a stroke of luck for you, Nora dear.

NORA. No, it never would have occurred to me to ask Dr. Rank—Still, I'm quite sure that if I had asked him—

MRS. LINDE. Which you won't, of course.

NORA. No, of course not. I can't see that I'd ever need to. But I'm quite positive that if I talked to Dr. Rank—

MRS. LINDE. Behind your husband's back?

NORA. I've got to clear up this other thing; *that's* also behind his back. I've *got* to clear it all up.

MRS. LINDE. Yes, I was saying that yesterday, but—

NORA. [*Pacing up and down*] A man handles these problems so much better than a woman—

MRS. LINDE. One's husband does, yes.

NORA. Nonsense. [*Stopping*] When you pay everything you owe, then you get your note back, right?

MRS. LINDE. Yes, naturally.

NORA. And can rip it into a million pieces and burn it up—that filthy scrap of paper!

MRS. LINDE. [*Looking hard at her, laying her sewing aside, and rising slowly*] Nora, you're hiding something from me.

NORA. You can see it in my face?

MRS. LINDE. Something's happened to you since yesterday morning. Nora, what is it?

NORA. [*Hurrying toward her*] Kristine! [*Listening*] Shh! Torvald's home. Look, go in with the children a while. Torvald can't bear all this snipping and stitching. Let Anne-Marie help you.

MRS. LINDE. [*Gathering up some of the things*] All right, but I'm not leaving here until we've talked this out. [*She disappears into the room, left, as* TORVALD *enters from the hall.*]

NORA. Oh, how I've been waiting for you, Torvald dear.

HELMER. Was that the dressmaker?

NORA. No, that was Kristine. She's helping me fix up my costume. You know, it's going to be quite attractive.

HELMER. Yes, wasn't that a bright idea I had?

NORA. Brilliant! But then wasn't I good as well to give in to you?

HELMER. Good—because you give in to your

◆ **Build Vocabulary**

proclaiming (prō klām´ iŋ) *v*.: Announcing publicly and loudly

intolerable (in täl´ ər ə bəl) *adj*.: Unbearable; painful; cruel

husband's judgment? All right, you little goose, I know you didn't mean it like that. But I won't disturb you. You'll want to have a fitting, I suppose.

NORA. And you'll be working?

HELMER. Yes. [*Indicating a bundle of papers*] See. I've been down to the bank. [*Starts toward his study*]

NORA. Torvald.

HELMER. [*Stops*] Yes.

NORA. If your little squirrel begged you, with all her heart and soul, for something—?

HELMER. What's that?

NORA. Then would you do it?

HELMER. First, naturally, I'd have to know what it was.

NORA. Your squirrel would scamper about and do tricks, if you'd only be sweet and give in.

HELMER. Out with it.

NORA. Your lark would be singing high and low in every room—

HELMER. Come on, she does that anyway.

NORA. I'd be a wood nymph and dance for you in the moonlight.

HELMER. Nora—don't tell me it's that same business from this morning?

NORA. [*Coming closer*] Yes, Torvald, I beg you, please!

HELMER. And you actually have the nerve to drag that up again?

NORA. Yes, yes, you've got to give in to me; you *have* to let Krogstad keep his job in the bank.

HELMER. My dear Nora, I've slated his job for Mrs. Linde.

NORA. That's awfully kind of you. But you could just fire another clerk instead of Krogstad.

HELMER. This is the most incredible stubbornness! Because you go and give an <u>impulsive</u> promise to speak up for him, I'm expected to—

NORA. That's not the reason, Torvald. It's for your own sake. That man does writing for the worst papers; you said it yourself. He could do

you any amount of harm. I'm scared to death of him—

HELMER. Ah, I understand. It's the old memories haunting you.

NORA. What do you mean by that?

HELMER. Of course, you're thinking about your father.

NORA. Yes, all right. Just remember how those nasty gossips wrote in the papers about Papa and slandered him so cruelly. I think they'd have had him dismissed if the department hadn't sent you up to investigate, and if you hadn't been so kind and open-minded toward him.

HELMER. My dear Nora, there's a notable difference between your father and me. Your father's official career was hardly above reproach. But mine is; and I hope it'll stay that way as long as I hold my position.

NORA. Oh, who can ever tell what vicious minds can invent? We could be so snug and happy in our quiet, carefree home—you and I and the children, Torvald! That's why I'm pleading with you so—

HELMER. And just by pleading for him you make it impossible for me to keep him on. It's already known at the bank that I'm firing Krogstad. What if it's rumored around now that the new bank manager was vetoed by his wife—

NORA. Yes, what then—?

HELMER. Oh yes—as long as our little bundle of stubbornness gets her way—! I should go and make myself ridiculous in front of the whole office—give people the idea I can be swayed by all kinds of outside pressure. Oh, you can bet I'd feel the effects of that soon enough! Besides—there's something that rules Krogstad right out at the bank as long as I'm the manager.

NORA. What's that?

HELMER. His moral failings I could maybe overlook if I had to—

NORA. Yes, Torvald, why not?

HELMER. And I hear he's quite efficient on the job. But he was a crony of mine back in my teens—one of those rash friendships that crop up again and again to embarrass you later in

◀ **Critical Viewing**
This picture suggests that Nora has faith in her husband. Which details contribute to this impression? **[Analyze]**

life. Well, I might as well say it straight out: we're on a first-name basis. And that <u>tactless</u> fool makes no effort at all to hide it in front of others. Quite the contrary—he thinks that entitles him to take a familiar air around me, and so every other second he comes booming out with his "Yes, Torvald!" and "Sure thing, Torvald!" I tell you, it's been <u>excruciating</u> for me. He's out to make my place in the bank unbearable.

NORA. Torvald, you can't be serious about all this.

HELMER. Oh no? Why not?

NORA. Because these are such petty considerations.

HELMER. What are you saying? Petty? You think I'm petty!

◆ **Build Vocabulary**

impulsive (im pul′ siv) *adj*.: Sudden and unthinking

tactless (takt′ ləs) *adj*.: Without skill in dealing with people

excruciating (eks kroo′ shē āt′ iŋ) *adj*.: Causing intense mental or bodily pain

NORA. No, just the opposite, Torvald dear. That's exactly why—

HELMER. Never mind. You call my motives petty; then I might as well be just that. Petty! All right! We'll put a stop to this for good. [*Goes to the hall door and calls*] Helene!

NORA. What do you want?

HELMER. [*Searching among his papers*] A decision. [*The* MAID *comes in.*] Look here; take this letter; go out with it at once. Get hold of a messenger and have him deliver it. Quick now. It's already addressed. Wait, here's some money.

MAID. Yes, sir. [*She leaves with the letter.*]

HELMER. [*Straightening his papers*] There, now, little Miss Willful.

NORA. [*Breathlessly*] Torvald, what was that letter?

HELMER. Krogstad's notice.

NORA. Call it back, Torvald! There's still time. Oh, Torvald, call it back! Do it for my sake—for your sake, for the children's sake! Do you hear,

A Doll's House, Act II ◆ 877

Torvald; do it! You don't know how this can harm us.

HELMER. Too late.

NORA. Yes, too late.

HELMER. Nora dear, I can forgive you this panic, even though basically you're insulting me. Yes, you are! Or isn't it an insult to think that *I* should be afraid of a courtroom hack's revenge? But I forgive you anyway, because this shows so beautifully how much you love me. [*Takes her in his arms*] This is the way it should be, my darling Nora. Whatever comes, you'll see: when it really counts, I have strength and courage enough as a man to take on the whole weight myself.

NORA. [*Terrified*] What do you mean by that?

HELMER. The whole weight, I said.

NORA. [*Resolutely*] No, never in all the world.

HELMER. Good. So we'll share it, Nora, as man and wife. That's as it should be. [*Fondling her*] Are you happy now? There, there, there—not these frightened dove's eyes. It's nothing at all but empty fantasies—Now you should run through your tarantella and practice your tambourine. I'll go to the inner office and shut both doors, so I won't hear a thing; you can make all the noise you like. [*Turning in the doorway*] And when Rank comes, just tell him where he can find me. [*He nods to her and goes with his papers into the study, closing the door.*]

NORA. [*Standing as though rooted, dazed with fright, in a whisper*] He really could do it. He will do it. He'll do it in spite of everything. No, not that, never, never! Anything but that! Escape! A way out—[*The doorbell rings.*] Dr. Rank! Anything but that! *Anything*, whatever it is! [*Her hands pass over her face, smoothing it; she pulls herself together, goes over and opens the hall door.* DR. RANK *stands outside, hanging his fur coat up. During the following scene, it begins getting dark.*]

NORA. Hello, Dr. Rank. I recognized your ring. But you mustn't go in to Torvald yet; I believe he's working.

RANK. And you?

NORA. For you, I always have an hour to spare—you know that. [*He has entered, and she shuts the door after him.*]

RANK. Many thanks. I'll make use of these hours while I can.

NORA. What do you mean by that? While you can?

RANK. Does that disturb you?

NORA. Well, it's such an odd phrase. Is anything going to happen?

RANK. What's going to happen is what I've been expecting so long—but I honestly didn't think it would come so soon.

NORA. [*Gripping his arm*] What is it you've found out? Dr. Rank, you have to tell me!

RANK. [*Sitting by the stove*] It's all over with me. There's nothing to be done about it.

NORA. [*Breathing easier*] Is it you—then—?

RANK. Who else? There's no point in lying to one's self. I'm the most miserable of all my patients, Mrs. Helmer. These past few days I've been auditing my internal accounts. Bankrupt! Within a month I'll probably be laid out and rotting in the churchyard.

NORA. Oh, what a horrible thing to say.

RANK. The thing itself is horrible. But the worst of it is all the other horror before it's over. There's only one final examination left; when I'm finished with that, I'll know about when my disintegration will begin. There's something I want to say. Helmer with his sensitivity has such a sharp distaste for anything ugly. I don't want him near my sickroom.

NORA. Oh, but Dr. Rank—

RANK. I won't have him in there. Under no condition. I'll lock my door to him—As soon as I'm completely sure of the worst, I'll send you my calling card marked with a black cross, and you'll know then the wreck has started to come apart.

◆ **Literary Focus**
What does Nora's dramatic reponse to what Rank says reveal about her?

◆ **Build Vocabulary**
retribution (re´ trə byoo´ shən) *n*.: Punishment; revenge

NORA. No, today you're completely unreasonable. And I wanted you so much to be in a really good humor.

RANK. With death up my sleeve? And then to suffer this way for somebody else's sins. Is there any justice in that? And in every single family, in some way or another, this inevitable retribution of nature goes on—

NORA. [*Her hands pressed over her ears*] Oh, stuff! Cheer up! Please—be gay!

RANK. Yes, I'd just as soon laugh at it all. My poor, innocent spine, serving time for my father's gay army days.

NORA. [*By the table, left*] He was so infatuated with asparagus tips and *pâté de foie gras*,[3] wasn't that it?

RANK. Yes—and with truffles.

NORA. Truffles, yes. And then with oysters, I suppose?

RANK. Yes, tons of oysters, naturally.

NORA. And then the port and champagne to go with it. It's so sad that all these delectable things have to strike at our bones.

RANK. Especially when they strike at the unhappy bones that never shared in the fun.

NORA. Ah, that's the saddest of all.

RANK. [*Looks searchingly at her*] Hm.

NORA. [*After a moment*] Why did you smile?

RANK. No, it was you who laughed.

NORA. No, it was you who smiled, Dr. Rank!

RANK. [*Getting up*] You're even a bigger tease than I'd thought.

NORA. I'm full of wild ideas today.

RANK. That's obvious.

NORA. [*Putting both hands on his shoulders*] Dear, dear Dr. Rank, you'll never die for Torvald and me.

RANK. Oh, that loss you'll easily get over. Those who go away are soon forgotten.

NORA. [*Looks fearfully at him*] You believe that?

RANK. One makes new connections, and then—

NORA. Who makes new connections?

RANK. Both you and Torvald will when I'm gone. I'd say you're well under way already. What was that Mrs. Linde doing here last evening?

NORA. Oh, come—you can't be jealous of poor Kristine?

RANK. Oh yes, I am. She'll be my successor here in the house. When I'm down under, that woman will probably—

NORA. Shh! Not so loud. She's right in there.

RANK. Today as well. So you see.

NORA. Only to sew on my dress. Good gracious, how unreasonable you are. [*Sitting on the sofa*] Be nice now, Dr. Rank. Tomorrow you'll see how beautifully I'll dance; and you can imagine then that I'm dancing only for you—yes, and of course for Torvald, too—that's understood. [*Takes various items out of the carton*] Dr. Rank, sit over here and I'll show you something.

RANK. [*Sitting*] What's that?

NORA. Look here. Look.

RANK. Silk stockings.

NORA. Flesh-colored. Aren't they lovely? Now it's so dark here, but tomorrow—No, no, no, just look at the feet. Oh well, you might as well look at the rest.

RANK. Hm—

NORA. Why do you look so critical? Don't you believe they'll fit?

RANK. I've never had any chance to form an opinion on that.

NORA. [*Glancing at him a moment*] Shame on you. [*Hits him lightly on the ear with the stockings*] That's for you. [*Puts them away again*]

RANK. And what other splendors am I going to see now?

NORA. Not the least bit more, because you've been naughty. [*She hums a little and rummages among her things.*]

RANK. [*After a short silence*] When I sit here together with you like this, completely easy and

---

3. *pâté de foie gras* (pä tā′ də fwä grä): A paste made of goose livers.

open, then I don't know—I simply can't imagine—whatever would have become of me if I'd never come into this house.

NORA. [Smiling] Yes, I really think you feel completely at ease with us.

RANK. [More quietly, staring straight ahead] And then to have to go away from it all—

NORA. Nonsense, you're not going away.

RANK. [His voice unchanged]—and not even be able to leave some poor show of gratitude behind, scarcely a fleeting regret—no more than a vacant place that anyone can fill.

NORA. And if I asked you now for—? No—

RANK. For what?

NORA. For a great proof of your friendship—

RANK. Yes, yes?

NORA. No, I mean—for an exceptionally big favor—

RANK. Would you really, for once, make me so happy?

NORA. Oh, you haven't the vaguest idea what it is.

RANK. All right, then tell me.

NORA. No, but I can't, Dr. Rank—it's all out of reason. It's advice and help, too—and a favor—

RANK. So much the better. I can't fathom what you're hinting at. Just speak out. Don't you trust me?

NORA. Of course. More than anyone else. You're my best and truest friend, I'm sure. That's why I want to talk to you. All right, then, Dr. Rank: there's something you can help me prevent. You know how deeply, how inexpressibly dearly Torvald loves me; he'd never hesitate a second to give up his life for me.

RANK. [Leaning close to her] Nora—do you think he's the only one—

NORA. [With a slight start] Who—?

RANK. Who'd gladly give up his life for you.

NORA. [Heavily] I see.

RANK. I swore to myself you should know this before I'm gone. I'll never find a better chance. Yes, Nora, now you know. And also you know now that you can trust me beyond anyone else.

NORA. [Rising, natural and calm] Let me by.

RANK. [Making room for her, but still sitting] Nora—

NORA. [In the hall doorway] Helene, bring the lamp in. [Goes over to the stove] Ah, dear Dr. Rank, that was really mean of you.

RANK. [Getting up] That I've loved you just as deeply as somebody else? Was that mean?

NORA. No, but that you came out and told me. That was quite unnecessary—

RANK. What do you mean? Have you known—? [The MAID comes in with the lamp, sets it on the table, and goes out again.]

RANK. Nora—Mrs. Helmer—I'm asking you: have you known about it?

NORA. Oh, how can I tell what I know or don't know? Really, I don't know what to say—Why did you have to be so clumsy, Dr. Rank! Everything was so good.

RANK. Well, in any case, you now have the knowledge that my body and soul are at your command. So won't you speak out?

NORA. [Looking at him] After that?

RANK. Please, just let me know what it is.

NORA. You can't know anything now.

RANK. I have to. You mustn't punish me like this. Give me the chance to do whatever is humanly possible for you.

NORA. Now there's nothing you can do for me. Besides, actually, I don't need any help. You'll see—it's only my fantasies. That's what it is. Of course! [Sits in the rocker, looks at him, and smiles] What a nice one you are, Dr. Rank. Aren't you a little bit ashamed, now that the lamp is here?

RANK. No, not exactly. But perhaps I'd better go—for good?

NORA. No, you certainly can't do that. You must come here just as you always have. You know Torvald can't do without you.

RANK. Yes, but you?

NORA. You know how much I enjoy it when you're here.

RANK. That's precisely what threw me off. You're a mystery to me. So many times I've felt you'd almost rather be with me than with Helmer.

NORA. Yes—you see, there are some people that one loves most and other people that one would almost prefer being with.

RANK. Yes, there's something to that.

NORA. When I was back home, of course I loved Papa most. But I always thought it was so much fun when I could sneak down to the maids' quarters, because they never tried to improve me, and it was always so amusing, the way they talked to each other.

RANK. Aha, so it's *their* place that I've filled.

NORA. [*Jumping up and going to him*] Oh, dear, sweet Dr. Rank, that's not what I meant at all. But you can understand that with Torvald it's just the same as with Papa—[*The* MAID *enters from the hall.*]

MAID. Ma'am—please! [*She whispers to* NORA *and hands her a calling card.*]

NORA. [*Glancing at the card*] Ah! [*Slips it into her pocket*]

RANK. Anything wrong?

NORA. No, no, not at all. It's only some—it's my new dress—

RANK. Really? But—there's your dress.

NORA. Oh, that. But this is another one—I ordered it—Torvald mustn't know—

RANK. Ah, now we have the big secret.

NORA. That's right. Just go in with him—he's back in the inner study. Keep him there as long as—

RANK. Don't worry. He won't get away. [*Goes into the study*]

NORA. [*To the* MAID] And he's standing waiting in the kitchen?

MAID. Yes, he came up by the back stairs.

NORA. But didn't you tell him somebody was here?

MAID. Yes, but that didn't do any good.

NORA. He won't leave?

MAID. No, he won't go till he's talked with you, ma'am.

NORA. Let him come in, then—but quietly. Helene, don't breathe a word about this. It's a surprise for my husband.

MAID. Yes, yes, I understand—[*Goes out*]

NORA. This horror—it's going to happen. No, no, no, it can't happen, it mustn't. [*She goes and bolts* HELMER's *door. The* MAID *opens the hall door for* KROGSTAD *and shuts it behind him. He is dressed for travel in a fur coat, boots, and a fur cap.*]

NORA. [*Going toward him*] Talk softly. My husband's home.

KROGSTAD. Well, good for him.

NORA. What do you want?

KROGSTAD. Some information.

NORA. Hurry up, then. What is it?

KROGSTAD. You know, of course, that I got my notice.

NORA. I couldn't prevent it, Mr. Krogstad. I fought for you to the bitter end, but nothing worked.

KROGSTAD. Does your husband's love for you run so thin? He knows everything I can expose you to, and all the same he dares to—

NORA. How can you imagine he knows anything about this?

KROGSTAD. Ah, no—I can't imagine it either, now. It's not at all like my fine Torvald Helmer to have so much guts—

NORA. Mr. Krogstad, I demand respect for my husband!

KROGSTAD. Why, of course—all due respect. But since the lady's keeping it so carefully hidden, may I presume to ask if you're also a bit better informed than yesterday about what you've actually done?

NORA. More than you ever could teach me.

KROGSTAD. Yes, I *am* such an awful lawyer.

NORA. What is it you want from me?

KROGSTAD. Just a glimpse of how you are, Mrs.

Helmer. I've been thinking about you all day long. A cashier, a night-court scribbler, a—well, a type like me also has a little of what they call a heart, you know.

NORA. Then show it. Think of my children.

KROGSTAD. Did you or your husband ever think of mine? But never mind. I simply wanted to tell you that you don't need to take this thing too seriously. For the present, I'm not proceeding with any action.

NORA. Oh no, really! Well—I knew that.

KROGSTAD. Everything can be settled in a friendly spirit. It doesn't have to get around town at all; it can stay just among us three.

NORA. My husband must never know anything of this.

KROGSTAD. How can you manage that? Perhaps you can pay me the balance?

NORA. No, not right now.

KROGSTAD. Or you know some way of raising the money in a day or two?

NORA. No way that I'm willing to use.

KROGSTAD. Well, it wouldn't have done you any good, anyway. If you stood in front of me with a fistful of bills, you still couldn't buy your signature back.

NORA. Then tell me what you're going to do with it.

KROGSTAD. I'll just hold onto it—keep it on file. There's no outsider who'll even get wind of it. So if you've been thinking of taking some desperate step—

NORA. I have.

KROGSTAD. Been thinking of running away from home—

NORA. I have!

KROGSTAD. Or even of something worse—

NORA. How could you guess that?

KROGSTAD. You can drop those thoughts.

NORA. How could you guess I was thinking of that?

KROGSTAD. Most of us think about that at first. I thought about it too, but I discovered I hadn't the courage—

NORA. [*Lifelessly*] I don't either.

KROGSTAD. [*Relieved*] That's true, you haven't the courage? You too?

NORA. I don't have it—I don't have it.

KROGSTAD. It would be terribly stupid, anyway. After that first storm at home blows out, why, then—I have here in my pocket a letter for your husband—

NORA. Telling everything?

KROGSTAD. As charitably as possible.

NORA. [*Quickly*] He mustn't ever get that letter. Tear it up. I'll find some way to get money.

KROGSTAD. Beg pardon, Mrs. Helmer, but I think I just told you—

NORA. Oh, I don't mean the money I owe you. Let me know how much you want from my husband, and I'll manage it.

KROGSTAD. I don't want any money from your husband.

NORA. What do you want, then?

KROGSTAD. I'll tell you what. I want to recoup, Mrs. Helmer; I want to get on in the world—and there's where your husband can help me. For a year and a half I've kept myself clean of anything disreputable—all that time struggling with the worst conditions; but I was satisfied, working my way up step by step. Now I've been written right off, and I'm just not in the mood to come crawling back. I tell you, I want to move on. I want to get back in the bank—in a better position. Your husband can set up a job for me—

NORA. He'll never do that!

KROGSTAD. He'll do it. I know him. He won't dare breathe a word of protest. And once I'm in there together with him, you just wait and see! Inside of a year, I'll be the manager's right-hand man. It'll be Nils Krogstad, not Torvald Helmer, who runs the bank.

NORA. You'll never see the day!

KROGSTAD. Maybe you think you can—

NORA. I have the courage now—for *that*.

KROGSTAD. Oh, you don't scare me. A smart, spoiled lady like you—

► Critical Viewing
In what ways does this picture capture the tension between Nora and Krogstad? [Interpret]

NORA. You'll see; you'll see!

KROGSTAD. Under the ice, maybe? Down in the freezing, coal-black water? There, till you float up in the spring, ugly, unrecognizable, with your hair falling out—

NORA. You don't frighten me.

KROGSTAD. Nor do you frighten me. One doesn't do these things, Mrs. Helmer. Besides, what good would it be? I'd still have him safe in my pocket.

NORA. Afterwards? When I'm no longer—?

KROGSTAD. Are you forgetting that *I'll* be in control then over your final reputation? [NORA *stands speechless, staring at him.*] Good; now I've warned you. Don't do anything stupid. When Helmer's read my letter, I'll be waiting for his reply. And bear in mind that it's your husband himself who's forced me back to my old ways. I'll never forgive him for that. Good-bye, Mrs. Helmer. [*He goes out through the hall.*]

NORA. [*Goes to the hall door, opens it a crack, and listens*] He's gone. Didn't leave the letter. Oh no, no, that's impossible too! [*Opening the door more and more*] What's that? He's standing outside—not going downstairs. He's thinking it over? Maybe he'll—? [*A letter falls in the mailbox; then* KROGSTAD*'s footsteps are heard, dying away down a flight of stairs.* NORA *gives a muffled cry and runs over toward the sofa table. A short pause.*] In the mailbox. [*Slips warily over to the hall door*] It's lying there. Torvald, Torvald—now we're lost!

MRS. LINDE. [*Entering with the costume from the room, left*] There now, I can't see anything else to mend. Perhaps you'd like to try—

NORA. [*In a hoarse whisper*] Kristine, come here.

MRS. LINDE. [*Tossing the dress on the sofa*] What's wrong? You look upset.

NORA. Come here. See that letter? *There!* Look— through the glass in the mailbox.

MRS. LINDE. Yes, yes, I see it.

NORA. That letter's from Krogstad—

MRS. LINDE. Nora—it's Krogstad who loaned you

♦ **Build Vocabulary**
disreputable (dis rep´ yoo tə bəl) *adj.*: Not fit to be seen or approved

the money!

NORA. Yes, and now Torvald will find out everything.

MRS. LINDE. Believe me, Nora, it's best for both of you.

NORA. There's more you don't know. I forged a name.

MRS. LINDE. But for heaven's sake—?

NORA. I only want to tell you that, Kristine, so that you can be my witness.

MRS. LINDE. Witness? Why should I—?

NORA. If I should go out of my mind—it could easily happen—

MRS. LINDE. Nora!

NORA. Or anything else occurred—so I couldn't be present here—

MRS. LINDE. Nora, Nora, you aren't yourself at all!

NORA. And someone should try to take on the whole weight, all of the guilt, you follow me—

MRS. LINDE. Yes, of course, but why do you think—?

NORA. Then you're my witness that it isn't true, Kristine. I'm very much myself; my mind right now is perfectly clear; and I'm telling you: nobody else has known about this; I alone did everything. Remember that.

MRS. LINDE. I will. But I don't understand all this.

NORA. Oh, how could you ever understand it? It's the miracle now that's going to take place.

MRS. LINDE. The miracle?

NORA. Yes, the miracle. But it's so awful, Kristine. It mustn't take place, not for anything in the world.

MRS. LINDE. I'm going right over and talk with Krogstad.

NORA. Don't go near him; he'll do you some terrible harm!

MRS. LINDE. There was a time once when he'd gladly have done anything for me.

NORA. He?

MRS. LINDE. Where does he live?

NORA. Oh, how do I know? Yes. [*Searches in her pocket*] Here's his card. But the letter, the letter—!

HELMER. [*From the study, knocking on the door*] Nora!

NORA. [*With a cry of fear*] Oh! What is it? What do you want?

HELMER. Now, now, don't be so frightened. We're not coming in. You locked the door—are you trying on the dress?

NORA. Yes, I'm trying it. I'll look just beautiful, Torvald.

MRS. LINDE. [*Who has read the card*] He's living right around the corner.

NORA. Yes, but what's the use? We're lost. The letter's in the box.

MRS. LINDE. And your husband has the key?

NORA. Yes, always.

MRS. LINDE. Krogstad can ask for his letter back unread; he can find some excuse—

NORA. But it's just this time that Torvald usually—

MRS. LINDE. Stall him. Keep him in there. I'll be back as quick as I can. [*She hurries out through the hall entrance.*]

NORA. [*Goes to* HELMER's *door, opens it, and peers in*] Torvald!

HELMER. [*From the inner study*] Well—does one dare set foot in one's own living room at last? Come on, Rank, now we'll get a look—[*In the doorway*] But what's this?

NORA. What, Torvald dear?

HELMER. Rank had me expecting some grand masquerade.

RANK. [*In the doorway*] That was my impression, but I must have been wrong.

NORA. No one can admire me in my splendor—not till tomorrow.

HELMER. But Nora, dear, you look so exhausted. Have you practiced too hard?

NORA. No, I haven't practiced at all yet.

HELMER. You know, it's necessary—

NORA. Oh, it's absolutely necessary, Torvald. But I can't get anywhere without your help. I've forgotten the whole thing completely.

HELMER. Ah, we'll soon take care of that.

NORA. Yes, take care of me, Torvald, please! Promise me that? Oh, I'm so nervous. That big party—You must give up everything this evening for me. No business—don't even touch your pen. Yes? Dear Torvald, promise?

HELMER. It's a promise. Tonight I'm totally at your service—you little helpless thing. Hm—but first there's one thing I want to—[*Goes toward the hall door*]

NORA. What are you looking for?

HELMER. Just to see if there's any mail.

NORA. No, no, don't do that, Torvald!

HELMER. Now what?

NORA. Torvald, please. There isn't any.

HELMER. Let me look, though. [*Starts out.* NORA, *at the piano, strikes the first notes of the tarantella.* HELMER, *at the door, stops.*] Aha!

NORA. I can't dance tomorrow if I don't practice with you.

HELMER. [*Going over to her*] Nora dear, are you really so frightened?

NORA. Yes, so terribly frightened. Let me practice right now; there's still time before dinner. Oh, sit down and play for me, Torvald. Direct me. Teach me, the way you always have.

HELMER. Gladly, if it's what you want. [*Sits at the piano*]

NORA. [*Snatches the tambourine up from the box, then a long, varicolored shawl, which she throws around herself, whereupon she springs forward and cries out*] Play for me now! Now I'll dance! [HELMER *plays and* NORA *dances.* RANK *stands behind* HELMER *at the piano and looks on.*]

HELMER. [*As he plays*] Slower. Slow down.

NORA. Can't change it.

HELMER. Not so violent, Nora!

NORA. Has to be just like this.

HELMER. [*Stopping*] No, no, that won't do at all.

NORA. [*Laughing and swinging her tambourine*] Isn't that what I told you?

RANK. Let me play for her.

HELMER. [*Getting up*] Yes, go on. I can teach her more easily then. [RANK *sits at the piano and plays;* NORA *dances more and more wildly.* HELMER *has stationed himself by the stove and repeatedly gives her directions; she seems not to hear them; her hair loosens and falls over her shoulders; she does not notice, but goes on dancing.* MRS. LINDE *enters.*]

MRS. LINDE. [*Standing dumbfounded at the door*] Ah—!

NORA. [*Still dancing*] See what fun, Kristine!

HELMER. But Nora darling, you dance as if your life were at stake.

NORA. And it is.

HELMER. Rank, stop! This is pure madness. Stop it, I say! [RANK *breaks off playing, and* NORA *halts abruptly.*]

HELMER. [*Going over to her*] I never would have believed it. You've forgotten everything I taught you.

NORA. [*Throwing away the tambourine*] You see for yourself.

HELMER. Well, there's certainly room for instruction here.

NORA. Yes, you see how important it is. You've got to teach me to the very last minute. Promise me that, Torvald?

HELMER. You can bet on it.

NORA. You mustn't, either today or tomorrow, think about anything else but me; you mustn't open any letters—or the mailbox—

HELMER. Ah, it's still the fear of that man—

NORA. Oh yes, yes, that too.

HELMER. Nora, it's written all over you—there's already a letter from him out there.

NORA. I don't know. I guess so. But you mustn't read such things now; there mustn't be anything ugly between us before it's all over.

RANK. [*Quietly to* HELMER] You shouldn't deny her.

HELMER. [*Putting his arm around her*] The child can have her way. But tomorrow night, after you've danced—

NORA. Then you'll be free.

MAID. [*In the doorway, right*] Ma'am, dinner is served.

NORA. We'll be wanting champagne, Helene.

MAID. Very good, ma'am. [*Goes out*]

HELMER. So—a regular banquet, hm?

NORA. Yes, a banquet—champagne till daybreak! [*Calling out*] And some macaroons, Helene. Heaps of them—just this once.

HELMER. [*Taking her hands*] Now, now, now—no hysterics. Be my own little lark again.

NORA. Oh, I will soon enough. But go on in—and you, Dr. Rank. Kristine, help me put up my hair.

RANK. [*Whispering, as they go*] There's nothing wrong—really wrong, is there?

HELMER. Oh, of course not. It's nothing more than this childish anxiety I was telling you about. [*They go out, right.*]

NORA. Well?

MRS. LINDE. Left town.

NORA. I could see by your face.

MRS. LINDE. He'll be home tomorrow evening. I wrote him a note.

NORA. You shouldn't have. Don't try to stop anything now. After all, it's a wonderful joy, this waiting here for the miracle.

MRS. LINDE. What is it you're waiting for?

NORA. Oh, you can't understand that. Go in to them; I'll be along in a moment. [MRS. LINDE *goes into the dining room.* NORA *stands a short while as if composing herself; then she looks at her watch.*]

NORA. Five. Seven hours to midnight. Twenty-four hours to the midnight after, and then the tarantella's done. Seven and twenty-four? Thirty-one hours to live.

HELMER. [*In the doorway, right*] What's become of the little lark?

NORA. [*Going toward him with open arms*] Here's your lark!

Guide for Responding

◆ Literature and Your Life

Reader's Response What would you advise Nora to do about her dilemma? Why?

Thematic Focus In what way has Nora reached a turning point in her life with Torvald?

Reader's Journal Elaborating on the stage directions on page 885, write your own description of Nora's dance.

☑ Check Your Comprehension

1. (a) From whom does Mrs. Linde first think Nora borrowed the money? (b) From whom did she actually borrow it?
2. What is Helmer's real reason for dismissing Krogstad at the bank?
3. How does Dr. Rank disappoint Nora?
4. Having received his dismissal, what does Krogstad do and why?
5. How does Nora manage to distract Helmer from reading his mail at the end of Act II?

◆ Critical Thinking

INTERPRET

1. What do Dr. Rank and Anne-Marie offer Nora that Torvald does not? **[Analyze]**
2. What opinion of Torvald does Krogstad seem to have? **[Infer]**
3. What might be the "miracle" that Nora says must never take place? Explain. **[Interpret]**
4. Compare and contrast the situations of Dr. Rank, Krogstad, Torvald, and Nora as Act II ends. **[Compare and Contrast]**

EVALUATE

5. Is Mrs. Linde a loyal friend to Nora? Why or why not? **[Make a Judgment]**

APPLY

6. What favor do you think Nora might have asked of Dr. Rank if he had not told her he loved her? Why do you think she changes her mind? **[Speculate]**

Guide for Responding (continued)

◆ Reading Strategy

QUESTION

A good reader **questions** while reading, posing, and answering questions about the meaning of events, choices, and details.

Explore the meaning of each of these actions by asking and answering a question about it.

1. Dr. Rank's telling Nora that he is in love with her
2. Nora's dancing as if her "life were at stake"

◆ Literary Focus

CHARACTERIZATION IN DRAMA

Characterization in drama is the process by which dramatists develop characters. In *A Doll's House,* Ibsen uses the characters' dialogue and actions to reveal their personalities.

What does each statement reveal about the character who makes it?

1. **HELMER.** Nora dear, I can forgive you this panic, even though basically you're insulting me. (p. 878)
2. **RANK.** Those who go away are soon forgotten. (p. 879)

◆ Build Vocabulary

USING THE LATIN PREFIX *dis-*

Combined with an adjective or a noun, the Latin prefix *dis-* means "not," "opposite of," or "lack of." Add *dis-* to the following words to change their meaning. Then, on your paper, complete the sentences with one of the words you created.

orderly   honest   comfort

1. Nora feels _____ when Dr. Rank says he loves her.
2. Both Nora and Krogstad have done something _____.
3. Act II closes with Nora's wild, _____ tarantella.

USING THE WORD BANK: Synonyms and Antonyms

On your paper, write *S* if the two words in each pair are synonyms and *A* if they are antonyms.

1. impulsive, cautious
2. retribution, revenge
3. proclaiming, announcing
4. disreputable, respectable
5. intolerable, endurable
6. tactless, offensive
7. excruciating, mild

◆ Build Grammar Skills

COMPOUND PREDICATES

A **compound predicate** is two or more verbs or verb phrases that have the same subject and are usually connected by a conjunction.

Practice Copy the following sentences from Act II in your notebook. In each, underline and label the subject *S*, the first verb *V1*, the second verb *V2*, and the third verb (if there is one) *V3*.

1. At last she stops at the sofa and picks up her coat.
2. Rank sits at the piano and plays. . . .
3. Her hair loosens and falls over her shoulders. . . .
4. She hums a little and rummages among her things.
5. Nora goes to the hall door, opens it a crack, and listens.

Writing Application On your paper, rewrite the following pairs of sentences, combining them by using compound predicates.

1. Ibsen left Norway. Ibsen lived in Italy.
2. Ibsen wrote plays. Ibsen became famous for it.

Idea Bank

Writing

1. **Direct Characterization** Write a paragraph characterizing Krogstad, Rank, or Mrs. Linde as if you were the narrator of a story about one of them. Support your points with at least three details.

2. **Krogstad's Letter** Write the letter to Helmer that Krogstad leaves in the Helmers' mailbox, demanding his job and revealing what Nora did.

Speaking, Listening, and Viewing

3. **Film Review** Rent and view the 1969 or the 1973 film version of *A Doll's House.* Then, give an oral review of the film for your classmates. Consider the directing, the acting, and the camera work. **[Media Link; Performing Arts Link]**

Guide for Reading

◆ Review and Anticipate

When Nora defies Helmer, begging him not to fire Krogstad, Helmer abruptly sends off his dismissal. Not even the dying Dr. Rank can be trusted to save her after he reveals his love for her.

Krogstad, having received his dismissal, comes with a letter to Helmer that reveals everything. He plans to blackmail Helmer into giving him back his job at the bank. He puts the letter in the locked mailbox.

To delay the catastrophe, Nora pretends to have forgotten everything Helmer taught her about the tarantella. Certain now that the secret will come out, she is determined to prevent Helmer from taking the blame, as she thinks he will. Her wild dancing expresses the chaos of her emotions.

Act III opens as one marriage comes together and another breaks apart.

◆ Literary Focus

THEME IN DRAMA

A drama's **theme** is its central message, idea, or insight—a generalization about people or about life for which the work provides a specific example. The dramatist can have one or more characters state this theme directly or can suggest it by means of dialogue and actions.

A complex play like *A Doll's House* may have several themes, depending on readers' interpretations. A reader concerned with women's rights may interpret *A Doll's House* as a plea for women to escape the restrictions of society. Ibsen agreed, but insisted that the play was also about a larger idea: The right of each of us, male or female, to become an individual.

◆ Build Grammar Skills

COMMONLY CONFUSED WORDS: *to, two, too*

Three words are commonly confused:

- **To,** a preposition, begins a prepositional phrase or an infinitive verb.
- **Two** refers to a number.
- **Too,** an adverb meaning "also, as well, or in excess," modifies adjectives and other adverbs.

◆ Reading Strategy

PREDICT

As a plot develops, an attentive reader can **predict**—make educated guesses about—what will happen. Besides adding to your fun, predicting what will happen or what a character will do is the best way to read for comprehension. Predicting helps you to pay close attention to details and relate them to your developing sense of the play's meaning.

For example, after hearing Krogstad described as an unprincipled man in Act I, you might have predicted that he would try to blackmail Helmer in Act II. Now, as you read Act III, see if you can predict some of the surprises that will occur.

◆ Build Vocabulary

LATIN AND GREEK SUFFIXES: *-ic*

In Act III, Mrs. Linde says, "I've learned to be realistic." Added to the noun *realist* ("someone concerned with actual things") the suffix *-ic* ("having to do with") creates a word meaning "having to do with realities, not with dreams."

WORD BANK

As you read Act III, you will encounter the words on this list. Each word is defined on the page where it first appears. Preview the list before you read.

calculating
evasions
naturalistic
proprieties
bewildered
hypocrite
grafter

A Doll's House

Act III

[*Same scene. The table, with chairs around it, has been moved to the center of the room. A lamp on the table is lit. The hall door stands open. Dance music drifts down from the floor above.* MRS. LINDE *sits at the table, absently paging through a book, trying to read, but apparently unable to focus her thoughts. Once or twice she pauses, tensely listening for a sound at the outer entrance.*]

MRS. LINDE. [*Glancing at her watch*] Not yet— and there's hardly any time left. If only he's not—[*Listening again*] Ah, there he is. [*She goes out in the hall and cautiously opens the outer door. Quiet footsteps are heard on the stairs. She whispers*] Come in. Nobody's here.

KROGSTAD. [*In the doorway*] I found a note from you at home. What's back of all this?

MRS. LINDE. I just *had* to talk to you.

KROGSTAD. Oh? And it just *had* to be here in this house?

MRS. LINDE. At my place it was impossible; my room hasn't a private entrance. Come in; we're all alone. The maid's asleep, and the Helmers are at the dance upstairs.

KROGSTAD. [*Entering the room*] Well, well, the Helmers are dancing tonight? Really?

MRS. LINDE. Why not?

KROGSTAD. How true—why not?

MRS. LINDE. All right, Krogstad, let's talk.

◆ **Build Vocabulary**

calculating (kalʹ kyo͞o lāt iŋ) *adj.*: Shrewd or cunning

KROGSTAD. Do we two have anything more to talk about?

MRS. LINDE. We have a great deal to talk about.

KROGSTAD. I wouldn't have thought so.

MRS. LINDE. No, because you've never understood me, really.

KROGSTAD. Was there anything more to understand—except what's all too common in life? A calculating woman throws over a man the moment a better catch comes by.

MRS. LINDE. You think I'm so thoroughly calculating? You think I broke it off lightly?

KROGSTAD. Didn't you?

MRS. LINDE. Nils—is that what you really thought?

KROGSTAD. If you cared, then why did you write me the way you did?

MRS. LINDE. What else could I do? If I had to break off with you, then it was my job as well to root out everything you felt for me.

KROGSTAD. [*Wringing his hands*] So that was it. And this—all this, simply for money!

MRS. LINDE. Don't forget I had a helpless mother and two small brothers. We couldn't wait for you, Nils; you had such a long road ahead of you then.

KROGSTAD. That may be; but you still hadn't the right to abandon me for somebody else's sake.

MRS. LINDE. Yes—I don't know. So many, many times I've asked myself if I did have that right.

KROGSTAD. [*More softly*] When I lost you, it was

as if all the solid ground dissolved from under my feet. Look at me; I'm a half-drowned man now, hanging onto a wreck.

MRS. LINDE. Help may be near.

KROGSTAD. It was near—but then you came and blocked it off.

MRS. LINDE. Without my knowing it, Nils. Today for the first time I learned that it's you I'm replacing at the bank.

KROGSTAD. All right—I believe you. But now that you know, will you step aside?

MRS. LINDE. No, because that wouldn't benefit you in the slightest.

KROGSTAD. Not "benefit" me, hm! I'd step aside anyway.

MRS. LINDE. I've learned to be realistic. Life and hard, bitter necessity have taught me that.

KROGSTAD. And life's taught me never to trust fine phrases.

MRS. LINDE. Then life's taught you a very sound thing. But you do have to trust in actions, don't you?

KROGSTAD. What does that mean?

MRS. LINDE. You said you were hanging on like a half-drowned man to a wreck.

KROGSTAD. I've good reason to say that.

MRS. LINDE. I'm also like a half-drowned woman on a wreck. No one to suffer with; no one to care for.

KROGSTAD. You made your choice.

MRS. LINDE. There wasn't any choice then.

KROGSTAD. So—what of it?

MRS. LINDE. Nils, if only we two shipwrecked people could reach across to each other.

KROGSTAD. What are you saying?

MRS. LINDE. Two on one wreck are at least better off than each on his own.

KROGSTAD. Kristine!

MRS. LINDE. Why do you think I came into town?

KROGSTAD. Did you really have some thought of me?

MRS. LINDE. I have to work to go on living. All my born days, as long as I can remember, I've worked, and it's been my best and my only joy. But now I'm completely alone in the world; it frightens me to be so empty and lost. To work for yourself—there's no joy in that. Nils, give me something—someone to work for.

KROGSTAD. I don't believe all this. It's just some hysterical feminine urge to go out and make a noble sacrifice.

MRS. LINDE. Have you ever found me to be hysterical?

KROGSTAD. Can you honestly mean this? Tell me—do you know everything about my past?

MRS. LINDE. Yes.

KROGSTAD. And you know what they think I'm worth around here.

MRS. LINDE. From what you were saying before, it would seem that with me you could have been another person.

KROGSTAD. I'm positive of that.

MRS. LINDE. Couldn't it happen still?

KROGSTAD. Kristine—you're saying this in all seriousness? Yes, you are! I can see it in you. And do you really have the courage, then—?

MRS. LINDE. I need to have someone to care for; and your children need a mother. We both need each other. Nils, I have faith that you're good at heart—I'll risk everything together with you.

KROGSTAD. [Gripping her hands] Kristine, thank you, thank you—Now I know I can win back a place in their eyes. Yes—but I forgot—

MRS. LINDE. [Listening] Shh! The tarantella. Go now! Go on!

KROGSTAD. Why? What is it?

MRS. LINDE. Hear the dance up there? When that's over, they'll be coming down.

KROGSTAD. Oh, then I'll go. But—it's all pointless. Of course, you don't know the move I made against the Helmers.

MRS. LINDE. Yes, Nils, I know.

KROGSTAD. And all the same, you have the courage to—?

MRS. LINDE. I know how far despair can drive a man like you.

◀ **Critical Viewing**
What do you think is on Nora's mind? Explain. **[Interpret]**

KROGSTAD. Oh, if I only could take it all back.

MRS. LINDE. You easily could—your letter's still lying in the mailbox.

KROGSTAD. Are you sure of that?

MRS. LINDE. Positive. But—

KROGSTAD. [*Looks at her searchingly*] Is that the meaning of it, then? You'll save your friend at any price. Tell me straight out. Is that it?

MRS. LINDE. Nils—anyone who's sold herself for somebody else once isn't going to do it again.

KROGSTAD. I'll demand my letter back.

MRS. LINDE. No, no.

KROGSTAD. Yes, of course. I'll stay here till Helmer comes down; I'll tell him to give me my letter again—that it only involves my dismissal—that he shouldn't read it—

MRS. LINDE. No, Nils, don't call the letter back.

KROGSTAD. But wasn't that exactly why you wrote me to come here?

MRS. LINDE. Yes, in that first panic. But it's been a whole day and night since then, and in that time I've seen such incredible things in this house. Helmer's got to learn everything; this dreadful secret has to be aired; those two have to come to a full understanding; all these lies and <u>evasions</u> can't go on.

◆ **Build Vocabulary**

evasions (ē vā′ zhenz) *n.*: Attempts to avoid duties or questions

KROGSTAD. Well, then, if you want to chance it. But at least there's one thing I can do, and do right away—

MRS. LINDE. [*Listening*] Go now, quick! The dance is over. We're not safe another second.

KROGSTAD. I'll wait for you downstairs.

MRS. LINDE. Yes, please do; take me home.

KROGSTAD. I can't believe it; I've never been so happy. [*He leaves by way of the outer door; the door between the room and the hall stays open.*]

MRS. LINDE. [*Straightening up a bit and getting together her street clothes*] How different now! How different! Someone to work for, to live for—a home to build. Well, it is worth the try! Oh, if they'd only come! [*Listening*] Ah, there they are. Bundle up. [*She picks up her hat and coat* NORA'S *and* HELMER'S *voices can be heard outside; a key turns in the lock, and* HELMER *brings* NORA *into the hall almost by force. She is wearing the Italian costume with a large black shawl about her; he has on evening dress, with a black domino open over it.*]

NORA. [*Struggling in the doorway*] No, no, no, not inside! I'm going up again. I don't want to leave so soon.

HELMER. But Nora dear—

NORA. Oh, I beg you, please, Torvald. From the bottom of my heart, *please*—only an hour more!

HELMER. Not a single minute, Nora darling. You know our agreement. Come on, in we go; you'll catch cold out here. [*In spite of her resistance, he gently draws her into the room.*]

MRS. LINDE. Good evening.

NORA. Kristine!

HELMER. Why, Mrs. Linde—are you here so late?

MRS. LINDE. Yes, I'm sorry, but I did want to see Nora in costume.

NORA. Have you been sitting here, waiting for me?

MRS. LINDE. Yes. I didn't come early enough; you were all upstairs; and then I thought I really

couldn't leave without seeing you.

HELMER. [*Removing* NORA's *shawl*] Yes, take a good look. She's worth looking at, I can tell you that, Mrs. Linde. Isn't she lovely?

MRS. LINDE. Yes, I should say—

HELMER. A dream of loveliness, isn't she? That's what everyone thought at the party, too. But she's horribly stubborn—this sweet little thing. What's to be done with her? Can you imagine, I almost had to use force to pry her away.

NORA. Oh, Torvald, you're going to regret you didn't indulge me, even for just a half hour more.

HELMER. There, you see. She danced her taran-tella and got a tumultuous[1] hand—which was well earned, although the performance may have been a bit too <u>naturalistic</u>—I mean it rather overstepped the <u>proprieties</u> of art. But never mind—what's important is, she made a success, an overwhelming success. You think I could let her stay on after that and spoil the effect? Oh no; I took my lovely little Capri girl—my capricious[2] little Capri girl, I should say—took her under my arm; one quick tour of the ballroom, a curtsy to every side, and then—as they say in novels—the beautiful vision disappeared. An exit should always be effective, Mrs. Linde, but that's what I can't get Nora to grasp. Phew, its hot in here. [*Flings the domino on a chair and opens the door to his room*] Why's it dark in here? Oh, yes, of course. Excuse me. [*He goes in and lights a couple of candles.*]

NORA. [*In a sharp, breathless whisper*] So?

MRS. LINDE. [*Quietly*] I talked with him.

NORA. And—?

MRS. LINDE. Nora—you must tell your husband everything.

NORA. [*Dully*] I knew it.

MRS. LINDE. You've got nothing to fear from Krogstad, but you have to speak out.

NORA. I won't tell.

MRS. LINDE. Then the letter will.

NORA. Thanks, Kristine. I know now what's to be done. Shh!

---

1. **tumultuous** (tŏ̅o mult′ chŏo wəs) *adj.*: Wild and noisy.
2. **capricious** (kə prish′ əs) *adj.*: Erratic; flighty.

▲ **Critical Viewing** Do you think the mood in this picture will last until the end of the play? Why or why not? **[Speculate]**

HELMER. [*Reentering*] Well, then, Mrs. Linde—have you admired her?

MRS. LINDE. Yes, and now I'll say good night.

HELMER. Oh, come, so soon? Is this yours, this knitting?

MRS. LINDE. Yes, thanks. I nearly forgot it.

HELMER. Do you knit, then?

MRS. LINDE. Oh yes.

HELMER. You know what? You should embroider instead.

MRS. LINDE. Really? Why?

HELMER. Yes, because it's a lot prettier. See here, one holds the embroidery so, in the left hand, and then one guides the needle with the right—so—in an easy, sweeping curve—right?

MRS. LINDE. Yes, I guess that's—

HELMER. But, on the other hand, knitting—it

can never be anything but ugly. Look, see here, the arms tucked in, the knitting needles going up and down, there's something Chinese about it. Ah, that was really a glorious champagne they served.

MRS. LINDE. Yes, goodnight, Nora, and don't be stubborn anymore.

HELMER. Well put, Mrs. Linde!

MRS. LINDE. Good night, Mr. Helmer.

HELMER. [*Accompanying her to the door*] Good night, good night. I hope you get home all right.

◆ **Build Vocabulary**

naturalistic (nach´ ər ə lis´ tik) *adj.*: Faithful to nature, to the extent of not avoiding what is low or improper

proprieties (prə prī´ ə tēz) *n.*: Whatever is considered fitting, suitable, or proper; rules of conduct or expression

▲ **Critical Viewing** Which qualities of Dr. Rank does this picture capture? **[Explain]**

I'd be very happy to—but you don't have far to go. Good night, good night. [*She leaves. He shuts the door after her and returns.*] There, now, at last we got her out the door. She's a deadly bore, that creature.

NORA. Aren't you pretty tired, Torvald?

HELMER. No, not a bit.

NORA. You're not sleepy?

HELMER. Not at all. On the contrary, I'm feeling quite exhilarated. But you? Yes, you really look tired and sleepy.

NORA. Yes, I'm very tired. Soon now I'll sleep.

HELMER. See! You see! I was right all along that we shouldn't stay longer.

NORA. Whatever you do is always right.

HELMER. [*Kissing her brow*] Now my little lark talks sense. Say, did you notice what a time Rank was having tonight?

NORA. Oh, was he? I didn't get to speak with him.

HELMER. I scarcely did either, but it's a long time since I've seen him in such high spirits. [*Gazes at her a moment, then comes nearer her*] Hm—it's marvelous, though, to be back home again—to be completely alone with you. Oh, you bewitchingly lovely young woman.

NORA. Torvald, don't look at me like that!

HELMER. Can't I look at my richest treasure? At all that beauty that's mine, mine alone—completely and utterly.

NORA. [*Moving around to the other side of the table*] You mustn't talk to me that way tonight.

HELMER. [*Following her*] The tarantella is still in your blood, I can see—and it makes you even more enticing. Listen. The guests are beginning to go. [*Dropping his voice*] Nora—it'll soon be quiet through this whole house.

NORA. Yes, I hope so.

HELMER. You do, don't you, my love? Do you realize—when I'm out at a party like this with you—do you know why I talk to you so little, and keep such a distance away; just send you a stolen look now and then—you know why I do it? It's because I'm imagining then that you're my secret darling, my secret young bride-to-be, and that no one suspects there's anything between us.

NORA. Yes, yes; oh, yes, I know you're always thinking of me.

HELMER. And then when we leave and I place the shawl over those fine young rounded shoulders—over that wonderful curving neck—then I pretend that you're my young bride, that we're just coming from the wedding, that for the first time I'm bringing you into my house—that for the first time I'm alone with you—completely alone with you, your trembling young beauty! All this evening I've longed for nothing but you. When I saw you turn and sway in the tarantella—my blood was pounding till I couldn't stand it—that's why I brought you down here so early—

NORA. Go away, Torvald! Leave me alone. I don't want all this.

HELMER. What do you mean? Nora, you're teasing me. You will, won't you? Aren't I your husband—? [*A knock at the outside door*]

NORA. [*Startled*] What's that?

HELMER. [*Going toward the hall*] Who is it?

RANK. [*Outside*] It's me. May I come in a moment?

HELMER. [*With quiet irritation*] Oh, what does he want now? [*Aloud*] Hold on. [*Goes and opens the door*] Oh, how nice that you didn't just pass us by!

RANK. I thought I heard your voice, and then I wanted so badly to have a look in. [*Lightly glancing about*] Ah, me, these old familiar haunts. You have it snug and cozy in here, you two.

HELMER. You seemed to be having it pretty cozy upstairs, too.

RANK. Absolutely. Why shouldn't I? Why not take in everything in life? As much as you can, anyway, and as long as you can. The wine was superb—

HELMER. The champagne especially.

RANK. You noticed that too? It's amazing how much I could guzzle down.

NORA. Torvald also drank a lot of champagne this evening.

RANK. Oh?

NORA. Yes, and that always makes him so entertaining.

RANK. Well, why shouldn't one have a pleasant evening after a well-spent day?

HELMER. Well spent? I'm afraid I can't claim that.

RANK. [*Slapping him on the back*] But I can, you see!

NORA. Dr. Rank, you must have done some scientific research today.

RANK. Quite so.

HELMER. Come now—little Nora talking about scientific research!

NORA. And can I congratulate you on the results?

RANK. Indeed you may.

NORA. Then they were good?

RANK. The best possible for both doctor and patient—certainty.

NORA. [*Quickly and searchingly*] Certainty?

RANK. Complete certainty. So don't I owe myself a gay evening afterwards?

NORA. Yes, you're right, Dr. Rank.

HELMER. I'm with you—just so long as you don't have to suffer for it in the morning.

RANK. Well, one never gets something for nothing in life.

NORA. Dr. Rank—are you very fond of masquerade parties?

RANK. Yes, if there's a good array of odd disguises—

NORA. Tell me, what should we two go as at the next masquerade?

HELMER. You little featherhead—already thinking of the next!

RANK. We two? I'll tell you what: you must go as Charmed Life—

HELMER. Yes, but find a costume for *that!*

RANK. Your wife can appear just as she looks every day.

HELMER. That was nicely put. But don't you know what you're going to be?

RANK. Yes, Helmer, I've made up my mind.

HELMER. Well?

RANK. At the next masquerade I'm going to be invisible.

HELMER. That's a funny idea.

RANK. They say there's a hat—black, huge—have you never heard of the hat that makes you invisible? You put it on, and then no one on earth can see you.

HELMER. [*Suppressing a smile*] Ah, of course.

RANK. But I'm quite forgetting what I came for.

Helmer, give me a cigar, one of the dark Havanas.

HELMER. With the greatest pleasure. [*Holds out his case*]

RANK. Thanks. [*Takes one and cuts off the tip*]

NORA. [*Striking a match*] Let me give you a light.

RANK. Thank you. [*She holds the match for him; he lights the cigar.*] And now good-bye.

HELMER. Good-bye, good-bye, old friend.

NORA. Sleep well, Doctor.

RANK. Thanks for that wish.

NORA. Wish me the same.

RANK. You? All right, if you like—Sleep well. And thanks for the light. [*He nods to them both and leaves.*]

HELMER. [*His voice subdued*] He's been drinking heavily.

NORA. [*Absently*] Could be. [HELMER *takes his keys from his pocket and goes out in the hall.*] Torvald—what are you after?

HELMER. Got to empty the mailbox; it's nearly full. There won't be room for the morning papers.

NORA. Are you working tonight?

HELMER. You know I'm not. Why—what's this? Someone's been at the lock.

NORA. At the lock—?

HELMER. Yes, I'm positive. What do you suppose—? I can't imagine one of the maids—? Here's a broken hairpin. Nora, it's yours—

NORA. [*Quickly*] Then it must be the children.

HELMER. You'd better break them of that. Hm, hm—well, opened it after all. [*Takes the contents out and calls into the kitchen*] Helene! Helene, would you put out the lamp in the hall? [*He returns to the room, shutting the hall door, then displays the handful of mail.*] Look how it's piled up. [*Sorting through them*] Now what's this?

NORA. [*At the window*] The letter! Oh, Torvald, no!

HELMER. Two calling cards—from Rank.

NORA. From Dr. Rank?

HELMER. [*Examining them*] "Dr. Rank, Consulting Physician." They were on top. He must have dropped them in as he left.

NORA. Is there anything on them?

HELMER. There's a black cross over the name. See? That's a gruesome notion. He could almost be announcing his own death.

NORA. That's just what he's doing.

HELMER. What! You've heard something? Something he's told you?

NORA. Yes. That when those cards came, he'd be taking his leave of us. He'll shut himself in now and die.

HELMER. Ah, my poor friend! Of course I knew he wouldn't be here much longer. But so soon—And then to hide himself away like a wounded animal.

NORA. If it has to happen, then it's best it happens in silence—don't you think so, Torvald?

HELMER. [*Pacing up and down*] He'd grown right into our lives. I simply can't imagine him gone. He with his suffering and loneliness—like a dark cloud setting off our sunlit happiness. Well, maybe it's best this way. For him, at least. [*Standing still*] And maybe for us too, Nora. Now we're thrown back on each other completely. [*Embracing her*] Oh you, my darling wife, how can I hold you close enough? You know what, Nora—time and again I've wished you were in some terrible danger, just so I could stake my life and soul and everything for your sake.

NORA. [*Tearing herself away, her voice firm and decisive*] Now you must read your mail, Torvald.

HELMER. No, no, not tonight. I want to stay with you, dearest.

NORA. With a dying friend on your mind?

HELMER. You're right. We've both had a shock. There's ugliness between us—these thoughts of death and corruption. We'll have to get free of them first. Until then—we'll stay apart.

NORA. [*Clinging about his neck*] Torvald—good night! Good night!

HELMER. [*Kissing her on the cheek*] Good night, little songbird. Sleep well, Nora. I'll be reading my mail now. [*He takes the letters into his room and shuts the door after him.*]

NORA. [*With bewildered glances, groping about, seizing* HELMER's *domino, throwing it around her, and speaking in short, hoarse, broken whispers*] Never see him again. Never, never. [*Putting her shawl over her head*] Never see the children either—them, too. Never, never. Oh, the freezing black water! The depths—down—Oh, I wish it were over—He has it now; he's reading it—now. Oh no, no, not yet. Torvald, good-bye, you and the children—[*She starts for the hall; as she does,* HELMER *throws open his door and stands with an open letter in his hand.*]

HELMER. Nora!

NORA. [*Screams*] Oh—!

HELMER. What is this? You know what's in this letter?

NORA. Yes, I know. Let me go! Let me out!

HELMER. [*Holding her back*] Where are you going?

NORA. [*Struggling to break loose*] You can't save me, Torvald!

HELMER. [*Slumping back*] True! Then it's true what he writes? How horrible! No, no it's impossible—it can't be true.

NORA. It *is* true. I've loved you more than all this world.

HELMER. Ah, none of your slippery tricks.

NORA. [*Taking one step toward him*] Torvald—!

HELMER. What *is* this you've blundered into!

NORA. Just let me loose. You're not going to suffer for my sake. You're not going to take on my guilt.

HELMER. No more playacting. [*Locks the hall door*] You stay right here and give me a reckoning. You understand what you've done? Answer! You understand?

NORA. [*Looking squarely at him, her face hardening*] Yes. I'm beginning to understand everything now.

HELMER. [*Striding about*] Oh, what an awful awakening! In all these eight years—she who was my pride and joy—a hypocrite, a liar—worse, worse—a criminal! How infinitely disgusting it all is! The shame! [NORA *says nothing and goes on looking straight at him. He stops in front of her.*] I should have suspected something of the kind. I should have known. All your father's flimsy values—Be still! All your father's flimsy values have come out in you. No religion, no morals, no sense of duty—Oh, how I'm punished for letting him off! I did it for your sake, and you repay me like this.

NORA. Yes, like this.

HELMER. Now you've wrecked all my happiness—ruined my whole future. Oh, it's awful to think of. I'm in a cheap little grafter's hands; he can do anything he wants with me, ask for anything, play with me like a puppet—and I can't breathe a word. I'll be swept down miserably into the depths on account of a featherbrained woman.

NORA. When I'm gone from this world, you'll be free.

HELMER. Oh, quit posing. Your father had a mess of those speeches too. What good would that ever do me if you were gone from this world, as you say? Not the slightest. He can still make the whole thing known; and if he does, I could be falsely suspected as your accomplice. They might even think that I was behind it—that I put you up to it. And all that I can thank you for—you that I've coddled the whole of our marriage. Can you see now what you've done to me?

NORA. [*Icily calm*] Yes.

HELMER. It's so incredible, I just can't grasp it. But we'll have to patch up whatever we can. Take off the shawl. I said, take it off! I've got to appease him somehow or other. The thing has to be hushed up at any cost. And as for you and me, it's got to seem like everything between us is just as it was—to the outside world, that is. You'll go right on living in this house, of course. But you can't be allowed to bring up the children; I don't dare trust you with them—Oh, to have to say this to someone I've loved so much! Well,

---

◆ Build Vocabulary

bewildered (bi wil′ dərd) *adj.*: Puzzled, confused

hypocrite (hip′ ə krit) *n.*: Person who pretends to be what he or she is not

grafter (graft′ ər) *n.*: Someone who takes advantage of his or her position to gain money or property dishonestly

▲ **Critical Viewing** In what way does this picture reflect a change in the relationship between Torvald and Nora? **[Interpret]**

that's done with. From now on happiness doesn't matter; all that matters is saving the bits and pieces, the appearance—[*The doorbell rings.* HELMER *starts.*] What's that? And so late. Maybe the worst—? You think he'd—? Hide, Nora! Say you're sick. [NORA *remains standing motionless.* HELMER *goes and opens the door.*]

MAID. [*Half dressed, in the hall*] A letter for Mrs. Helmer.

HELMER. I'll take it. [*Snatches the letter and shuts the door*] Yes, it's from him. You don't get it; I'm reading it myself.

NORA. Then read it.

HELMER. [*By the lamp*] I hardly dare. We may be ruined, you and I. But—I've got to know. [*Rips open the letter, skims through a few lines, glances at an enclosure, then cries out joyfully.*] Nora! [NORA *looks inquiringly at him.*] Nora!

Wait!—better check it again—Yes, yes, it's true. I'm saved. Nora, I'm saved!

NORA. And I?

HELMER. You too, of course. We're both saved, both of us. Look. He's sent back your note. He says he's sorry and ashamed—that a happy development in his life—oh, who cares what he says! Nora, we're saved! No one can hurt you. Oh, Nora, Nora—but first, this ugliness all has to go. Let me see—[*Takes a look at the note*] No, I don't want to see it; I want the whole thing to fade like a dream. [*Tears the note and both letters to pieces, throws them into the stove and watches them burn*] There—now there's nothing left—He wrote that since Christmas Eve you—Oh, they must have been three terrible days for you, Nora.

NORA. I fought a hard fight.

HELMER. And suffered pain and saw no escape but—No, we're not going to dwell on anything unpleasant. We'll just be grateful and keep on repeating: it's over now, it's over! You hear me, Nora? You don't seem to realize—it's over. What's it mean—that frozen look? Oh, poor little Nora, I understand. You can't believe I've forgiven you. But I have Nora; I swear I have. I know that what you did, you did out of love for me.

NORA. That's true.

HELMER. You loved me the way a wife ought to love her husband. It's simply the means that you couldn't judge. But you think I love you any the less for not knowing how to handle your affairs? No, no—just lean on me; I'll guide you and teach you. I wouldn't be a man if this feminine helplessness didn't make you twice as attractive to me. You mustn't mind those sharp words I said—that was all in the first confusion of thinking my world had collapsed. I've forgiven you, Nora; I swear I've forgiven you.

NORA. My thanks for your forgiveness. [*She goes out through the door, right.*]

HELMER. No, wait—[*Peers in*] What are you doing in there?

NORA. [*Inside*] Getting out of my costume.

HELMER. [*By the open door*] Yes, do that. Try to calm yourself and collect your thoughts again, my frightened little songbird. You can rest easy now; I've got wide wings to shelter you with. [*Walking about close by the door*] How snug and nice our home is, Nora. You're safe here; I'll keep you like a hunted dove I've rescued out of a hawk's claws. I'll bring peace to your poor, shuddering heart. Gradually it'll happen, Nora; you'll see. Tomorrow all this will look different to you; then everything will be as it was. I won't have to go on repeating I forgive you; you'll feel it for yourself. How can you imagine I'd ever conceivably want to disown you—or even blame you in any way? Ah, you don't know a man's heart, Nora. For a man there's something indescribably sweet and satisfying in knowing he's forgiven his wife—and forgiven her out of a full and open heart. It's as if she belongs to him in two ways now: in a sense he's given her fresh into the world again, and she's become his wife and his child as

well. From now on that's what you'll be to me—you little, bewildered, helpless thing. Don't be afraid of anything, Nora; just open your heart to me, and I'll be conscience and will to you both—[NORA *enters in her regular clothes.*] What's this? Not in bed? You've changed your dress?

NORA. Yes, Torvald, I've changed my dress.

HELMER. But why now, so late?

NORA. Tonight I'm not sleeping.

HELMER. But Nora dear—

NORA. [*Looking at her watch*] It's still not so very late. Sit down, Torvald; we have a lot to talk over. [*She sits at one side of the table.*]

HELMER. Nora—what is this? That hard expression—

NORA. Sit down. This'll take some time. I have a lot to say.

HELMER. [*Sitting at the table directly opposite her*] You worry me, Nora. And I don't understand you.

NORA. No, that's exactly it. You don't understand me. And I've never understood you either—until tonight. No, don't interrupt. You can just listen to what I say. We're closing out accounts, Torvald.

HELMER. How do you mean that?

NORA. [*After a short pause*] Doesn't anything strike you about our sitting here like this?

HELMER. What's that?

NORA. We've been married now eight years. Doesn't it occur to you that this is the first time we two, you and I, man and wife, have ever talked seriously together?

HELMER. What do you mean—seriously?

NORA. In eight whole years—longer even—right from our first acquaintance, we've never exchanged a serious word on any serious thing.

HELMER. You mean I should constantly go and involve you in problems you couldn't possibly help me with?

◆ Reading Strategy
What do you think Nora's change of dress indicates about her intentions?

NORA. I'm not talking of problems. I'm saying that we've never sat down seriously together and tried to get to the bottom of anything.

HELMER. But dearest, what good would that ever do you?

NORA. That's the point right there: you've never understood me. I've been wronged greatly, Torvald—first by Papa, and then by you.

HELMER. What! By us—the two people who've loved you more than anyone else?

NORA. [*Shaking her head*] You never loved me. You've thought it fun to be in love with me, that's all.

HELMER. Nora, what a thing to say!

NORA. Yes, it's true now, Torvald. When I lived at home with Papa, he told me all his opinions, so I had the same ones too; or if they were different I hid them, since he wouldn't have cared for that. He used to call me his doll-child, and he played with me the way I played with my dolls. Then I came into your house—

HELMER. How can you speak of our marriage like that?

NORA. [*Unperturbed*] I mean, then I went from Papa's hands into yours. You arranged everything to your own taste, and so I got the same taste as you—or I pretended to; I can't remember. I guess a little of both, first one, then the other. Now when I look back, it seems as if I'd lived here like a beggar—just from hand to mouth. I've lived by doing tricks for you, Torvald. But that's the way you wanted it. It's a great sin what you and Papa did to me. You're to blame that nothing's become of me.

HELMER. Nora, how unfair and ungrateful you are! Haven't you been happy here?

NORA. No, never. I thought so—but I never have.

HELMER. Not—not happy!

NORA. No, only lighthearted. And you've always been so kind to me. But our home's been nothing but a playpen. I've been your doll-wife here, just as at home I was Papa's doll-child. And in turn the children have been my dolls. I thought it was fun when you played with me, just as

they thought it fun when I played with them. That's been our marriage, Torvald.

HELMER. There's some truth in what you're saying—under all the raving exaggeration. But it'll all be different after this. Playtime's over; now for the schooling.

NORA. Whose schooling—mine or the children's?

HELMER. Both yours and the children's, dearest.

NORA. Oh, Torvald, you're not the man to teach me to be a good wife to you.

HELMER. And you can say that?

NORA. And I—how am I equipped to bring up children?

HELMER. Nora!

NORA. Didn't you say a moment ago that that was no job to trust me with?

HELMER. In a flare of temper! Why fasten on that?

NORA. Yes, but you were so very right. I'm not up to the job. There's another job I have to do first. I have to try to educate myself. You can't help me with that. I've got to do it alone. And that's why I'm leaving you now.

HELMER. [*Jumping up*] What's that?

NORA. I have to stand completely alone, if I'm ever going to discover myself and the world out there. So I can't go on living with you.

HELMER. Nora, Nora!

NORA. I want to leave right away. Kristine should put me up for the night—

HELMER. You're insane! You've no right! I forbid you!

NORA. From here on, there's no use forbidding me anything. I'll take with me whatever is mine. I don't want a thing from you, either now or later.

HELMER. What kind of madness is this?

NORA. Tomorrow I'm going home—I mean, home where I came from. It'll be easier up there to find something to do.

HELMER. Oh, you blind, incompetent child!

NORA. I must learn to be competent, Torvald.

HELMER. Abandon your home, your husband, your children! And you're not even thinking what people will say.

NORA. I can't be concerned about that. I only know how essential this is.

HELMER. Oh, it's outrageous. So you'll run out like this on your most sacred vows.

NORA. What do you think are my most sacred vows?

HELMER. And I have to tell you that! Aren't they your duties to your husband and children?

NORA. I have other duties equally sacred.

HELMER. That isn't true. What duties are they?

NORA. Duties to myself.

HELMER. Before all else, you're a wife and a mother.

NORA. I don't believe in that anymore. I believe that, before all else, I'm a human being, no less than you—or anyway, I ought to try to become one. I know the majority thinks you're right, Torvald, and plenty of books agree with you, too. But I can't go on believing what the majority says, or what's written in books. I have to think over these things myself and try to understand them.

♦ **Literary Focus**
Do you think Nora is stating the play's theme in this speech? Why or why not?

HELMER. Why can't you understand your place in your own home? On a point like that, isn't there one everlasting guide you can turn to? Where's your religion?

NORA. Oh, Torvald, I'm really not sure what religion is.

HELMER. What—?

NORA. I only know what the minister said when I was confirmed. He told me religion was this thing and that. When I get clear and away by myself, I'll go into that problem too. I'll see if what the minister said was right, or, in any case, if it's right for me.

HELMER. A young woman your age shouldn't talk like that. If religion can't move you, I can try to rouse your conscience. You do have some moral feeling? Or, tell me—has that gone too?

NORA. It's not easy to answer that, Torvald. I simply don't know. I'm all confused about these things. I just know I see them so differently from you. I find out, for one thing, that the law's not at all what I'd thought—but I can't get it through my head that the law is fair. A woman hasn't a right to protect her dying father or save her husband's life! I can't believe that.

HELMER. You talk like a child. You don't know anything of the world you live in.

NORA. No, I don't. But now I'll begin to learn for myself. I'll try to discover who's right, the world or I.

HELMER. Nora, you're sick; you've got a fever. I almost think you're out of your head.

NORA. I've never felt more clearheaded and sure in my life.

HELMER. And—clearheaded and sure—you're leaving your husband and children?

NORA. Yes.

HELMER. Then there's only one possible reason.

NORA. What?

HELMER. You no longer love me.

NORA. No. That's exactly it.

HELMER. Nora! You can't be serious!

NORA. Oh, this is so hard, Torvald—you've been so kind to me always. But I can't help it. I don't love you anymore.

HELMER. [*Struggling for composure*] Are you also clearheaded and sure about that?

NORA. Yes, completely. That's why I can't go on staying here.

HELMER. Can you tell me what I did to lose your love?

NORA. Yes, I can tell you. It was this evening when the miraculous thing didn't come—then I knew you weren't the man I'd imagined.

HELMER. Be more explicit; I don't follow you.

NORA. I've waited now so patiently eight long years—for, my Lord, I know miracles don't come every day. Then this crisis broke over me, and such a certainty filled me: *now* the miraculous event would occur. While Krogstad's letter was lying out there, I never for an instant dreamed that you could give in to his terms. I was so utterly sure you'd say to him: go on, tell your tale to the whole wide world. And when he'd done that—

HELMER. Yes, what then? When I'd delivered my own wife into shame and disgrace—!

NORA. When he'd done that, I was so utterly sure that you'd step forward, take the blame on yourself and say: I am the guilty one.

HELMER. Nora—!

NORA. You're thinking I'd never accept such a sacrifice from you? No, of course not. But what good would my protests be against you? That was the miracle I was waiting for, in terror and hope. And to stave that off, I would have taken my life.

HELMER. I'd gladly work for you day and night, Nora—and take on pain and deprivation. But there's no one who gives up honor for love.

NORA. Millions of women have done just that.

HELMER. Oh, you think and talk like a silly child.

NORA. Perhaps. But you neither think nor talk like the man I could join myself to. When your big fright was over—and it wasn't from any threat against me, only for what might damage you—when all the danger was past, for you it was just as if nothing had happened. I was exactly the same, your little lark, your doll, that you'd have to handle with double care now that I'd turned out so brittle and frail. [*Gets up*] Torvald—in that instant it dawned on me that for eight years I've been living here with a stranger, and that I'd even conceived three children—oh, I can't stand the thought of it! I could tear myself to bits.

HELMER. [*Heavily*] I see. There's a gulf that's opened between us—that's clear. Oh, but Nora, can't we bridge it somehow?

NORA. The way I am now, I'm no wife for you.

HELMER. I have the strength to make myself over.

NORA. Maybe—if your doll gets taken away.

HELMER. But to part! To part from you! No, Nora, no—I can't imagine it.

NORA. [*Going out, right*] All the more reason why it has to be. [*She reenters with her coat and a small overnight bag, which she puts on a chair by the table.*]

HELMER. Nora, Nora, not now! Wait till tomorrow.

NORA. I can't spend the night in a strange man's room.

HELMER. But couldn't we live here like brother and sister—

NORA. You know very well how long that would last. [*Throws her shawl about her*] Good-bye, Torvald. I won't look in on the children. I know they're in better hands than mine. The way I am now, I'm no use to them.

HELMER. But someday, Nora—someday—?

NORA. How can I tell? I haven't the least idea what'll become of me.

HELMER. But you're my wife, now and wherever you go.

NORA. Listen, Torvald—I've heard that when a wife deserts her husband's house just as I'm doing, then the law frees him from all responsibility. In any case, I'm freeing you from being responsible. Don't feel yourself bound, any more than I will. There has to be absolute freedom for us both. Here, take your ring back. Give me mine.

HELMER. That too?

NORA. That too.

HELMER. There it is.

NORA. Good. Well, now it's all over, I'm putting the keys here. The maids know all about keeping up the house—better than I do. Tomorrow, after I've left town, Kristine will stop by to pack up everything that's mine from home. I'd like those things shipped up to me.

HELMER. Over! All over! Nora, won't you ever think about me?

NORA. I'm sure I'll think of you often, and about the children and the house here.

HELMER. May I write you?

NORA. No—never. You're not to do that.

HELMER. Oh, but let me send you—

NORA. Nothing. Nothing.

HELMER. Or help you if you need it.

NORA. No. I accept nothing from strangers.

HELMER. Nora—can I never be more than a stranger to you?

NORA. [*Picking up the overnight bag*] Ah, Torvald— it would take the greatest miracle of all—

HELMER. Tell me the greatest miracle!

NORA. You and I both would have to transform ourselves to the point that—Oh, Torvald, I've stopped believing in miracles.

HELMER. But I'll believe. Tell me! Transform ourselves to the point that—?

NORA. That our living together could be a true marriage. [*She goes out down the hall.*]

HELMER. [*Sinks down on a chair by the door, face buried in his hands*] Nora! Nora! [*Looking about and rising*] Empty. She's gone. [*A sudden hope leaps in him.*] The greatest miracle—? [*From below, the sound of a door slamming shut.*]

Guide for Responding

◆ *Literature and Your Life*

Reader's Response How do you feel about Nora's decision to leave her husband and children? Explain.

Thematic Focus Explain what you think Helmer could have done differently to prevent Nora from leaving.

Reader's Journal Write a paragraph in your journal about whether or not anything in Act III surprised you.

Questions for Research What questions would you keep in mind—and try to answer—while viewing the 1969 and 1973 film versions of *A Doll's House?*

☑ Check Your Comprehension

1. What does Mrs. Linde want from Krogstad?
2. What is the meaning of the black cross inked above the name on Dr. Rank's calling card?
3. Where is Nora headed as Helmer bursts out of his study after reading Krogstad's letter?
4. Why is Helmer relieved after reading Krogstad's second letter?
5. Summarize the ways in which Nora surprises Helmer after Krogstad's second letter is received.

◆ Critical Thinking

INTERPRET

1. How does Mrs. Linde manage to solve several problems at once by marrying Krogstad? **[Analyze]**
2. How would you contrast the marriage of Nora and Helmer with the partnership of Mrs. Linde and Krogstad? **[Compare and Contrast]**
3. What does Nora discover about Helmer when the crisis comes? **[Draw Conclusions]**
4. In what way does the play's title relate to Nora's discoveries about Helmer and to her decision to leave him? **[Synthesize]**

EVALUATE

5. Do you think Torvald truly understands Nora's reasons for leaving? Why or why not? **[Make a Judgment]**

APPLY

6. How likely is it that the transformation Nora speaks of will come about and the Helmers have a true marriage? **[Speculate]**

COMPARE LITERARY WORKS

7. Compare and contrast Nora with Sophocles' tragic character Antigone. **[Compare and Contrast]**

Guide for Responding (continued)

◆ Reading Strategy

PREDICT

As you read *A Doll's House,* you can participate in the action by **predicting**—making educated guesses about—what will happen.

For example, certain earlier details in the play might lead you to predict that Mrs. Linde would propose marriage to Krogstad. In Act I, Mrs. Linde says she feels "unspeakably empty," so you might assume that she would welcome a relationship. Also, in Act II, Mrs. Linde indicates that she once had a very close relationship to Krogstad: "There was a time once when he'd gladly have done anything for me."

1. What earlier information suggests that Mrs. Linde would ask Krogstad not to remove his letter from the Helmers' mailbox? Explain.
2. Do any earlier events in the play suggest that Nora might leave Torvald? Why or why not?

◆ Literary Focus

THEME IN DRAMA

The **theme** of *A Doll's House* is its central message, idea, or insight about life. Your interpretation of the play's theme will depend on how you interpret the final scene between Torvald and Nora.

For example, the connection Nora makes between her father's treatment of her and Torvald's treatment suggests that women should be treated as adults, not as pretty dolls: "I've been your doll-wife here, just as at home I was Papa's doll-child."

1. Find additional evidence in the play's final scene to support this theme.
2. Find evidence in the final scene to support the theme that everyone, men and women alike, must have the right to develop as an individual.

◆ Build Vocabulary

USING THE LATIN AND GREEK SUFFIX -ic

Use the suffix *-ic*, which means "having to do with or like" something, to make an adjective that completes each of these sentences.

1. Believing in romance makes you _____.
2. Thinking like an artist makes you _____.
3. Having the qualities of an angel makes you _____.

USING THE WORD BANK: Sentence Completion

On your paper, complete the following sentences using words from the Word Bank. Use each word once.

1. A shrewd, _____ person may employ _____ to avoid facing the truth.
2. A(n) _____ observes the _____ but only on the surface.
3. A(n) _____ victim may be left _____ by the person who has taken advantage of him or her.
4. Lacking the orderliness of art, Nora's dance looked too _____ to Helmer.

◆ Build Grammar Skills

COMMONLY CONFUSED WORDS: *to, two, too*

Be sure you correctly use three words that sound alike but have different meanings: the preposition *to,* the number *two,* and the adverb *too.*

Practice Some of the following sentences from Act III contain confusions of *to, two,* and *too.* On your paper, indicate which sentences are correct and revise the incorrect sentences.

1. Do we two have anything more to talk about?
2. Or, tell me—has that gone two?
3. But too part! Too part from you!
4. To calling cards—from Rank.
5. Nils, if only we two shipwrecked people could reach across to each other.

Writing Application On your paper, briefly summarize Act III of *A Doll's House,* using *to, two,* and *too* correctly.

Build Your Portfolio

 ## Idea Bank

Writing

1. **Helmer's Letter** As Helmer, write a letter to Nora the next morning, asking her to come home. Give her convincing reasons for thinking that she should return.
2. **Definition** As Henrik Ibsen, write a definition of a good marriage. Use examples from *A Doll's House* to illustrate your definition.
3. **Dramatic Scene** Write the scene that will take place between Nora and Mrs. Linde when Nora arrives at her friend's room to spend the night.

Speaking, Listening, and Viewing

4. **Debate** With a group of classmates, participate in a debate on this resolution: Nora was right to leave Torvald. **[Performing Arts Link]**
5. **Dramatic Interpretation** With a partner, choose an interesting passage from the final scene of the play. After rehearsing it, perform it for the class, using gestures and expressions to capture the emotions of the characters. **[Performing Arts Link]**

Researching and Representing

6. **Casting Report** As a casting director for a movie version of *A Doll's House,* choose actors for the parts of Nora, Torvald, Krogstad, Mrs. Linde, and Dr. Rank. Give reasons for your choices. **[Media Link; Performing Arts Link]**
7. **Report on Women's Rights** Using the Internet, encyclopedias, books, and magazine articles, prepare a report on one of the major breakthroughs in women's rights. Focus on Europe in the late nineteenth or early twentieth century. **[Social Studies Link]**

Online Activity www.phlit.phschool.com

 ## Guided Writing Lesson

Literary Analysis

Write an analysis of Nora's transformation in *A Doll's House.* This analysis should include an examination of the *why* and *how* of Nora's change, together with an evaluation of how believable it is. To support your analysis, use examples of dialogue and action from all three acts of the play.

Writing Skills Focus: Use Sufficient Details

As support, use **sufficient details,** examples of dialogue and action that directly relate to and illustrate the points you are making. Avoid insufficient details—mere lists of examples or repetitious summaries of the play's action.

Prewriting Brainstorm to gather details of Nora's behavior. For example, from Act I, you might include details of childlike behavior *and* evidence of what she has done for her husband.

Drafting Begin by formulating a thesis statement in which you argue that Nora does or does not experience a believable transformation. Then support your statement with sufficient details from the play, including passages of dialogue or descriptions of action.

Revising Be sure your analysis begins with a thesis statement. Then, evaluate your supporting details to determine whether or not they are sufficient. Eliminate repetitious summaries of the play's action and lists of examples that do not relate to a point you are making.

Also, be sure that you have used parallelism, stating equal ideas in words, phrases, or clauses of a similar type. For more on parallelism, see pages 850 and 871.

CONNECTIONS TO TODAY'S WORLD

The slamming of the door at the end of *A Doll's House* was a sound that echoed around the world. Like a pistol-shot, it symbolized Nora's explosive assertion of her freedom and independence. That fierce noise was not only a direct challenge to Torvald's authority, but also a challenge to society's beliefs about the role and place of women.

In the late-nineteenth century, the notion that a middle-class woman could leave her husband and children to live independently was shocking to many. Women did not enjoy the same rights and privileges as men. Few women received a quality education, and most had severely limited career opportunities. Women were expected to marry and to devote their lives to serving their husbands and raising children.

The story was somewhat different for working-class women, whose opportunities were even more limited. They had to take low-paying, menial jobs to help support their families and could not afford the relative luxury of staying home all day to care for children. In other words, they did not find outside work to fulfill themselves, but merely to keep their families' bellies filled.

Ibsen's play did not sweep away overnight the obstacles that women faced. However, the door that Nora slammed shut actually opened the minds of some theater goers, causing them to reconsider the role of women in society. The play also inspired those who struggled to give women greater freedom.

Over the last century, the status of women has steadily improved—for women, the twentieth century has been a time of opening doors. Some highlights of the enormous changes in women's status are as follows:

- In almost all Western countries, women have gained the right to vote. In Europe, Finland (in 1906) and Norway (in 1913) were the first European countries to grant women the right to vote.

- Women have been awarded Nobel prizes in the arts, humanities, and sciences throughout the twentieth century.

- Many women are now involved in politics, and in a number of countries, including Great Britain, Pakistan, Israel, and the Philippines, women have been elected to the highest-ranking government post.

A Doll's House continues to interest present-day audiences. It has been produced for film and stage throughout the twentieth century.

Portrayals of Nora in some recent productions have reflected women's growing self-confidence. As a result, Nora has seemed stronger and more defiant from the start of the play than Ibsen may have intended.

In 1997, however, the British actress Janet McTeer gave a performance that was more in keeping with Ibsen's original intentions. Critics found this performance impressive, as indicated in this excerpt from one highly favorable review:

Drama Review:
A Doll's House
David Sheward

What makes the new British imported production of Ibsen's immortal work thrilling is that Janet McTeer plays the climactic scene as if she doesn't know the ending. She is living it moment by moment. We actually see her get the idea that she must leave, and it scares . . . her. Her eyes reveal the fear of the unknown world outside the safety of her cozy home, . . . but the steel in her voice shows it's a move she must make.

Usually the actress playing Nora rises up in righteous feminist anger at her chauvinist husband, Torvald, and vanquishes him. This Nora is not viewed from a 1997 perspective, but enacted as if she really were in 1879 with no prospects if she walks out. The entire performance is filled with similar visceral impulses and telling details such as the childish tossing about of coats, surreptitious gobbling of macaroons, and the breathless, desperate dancing of the tarantella. McTeer's is the definitive interpretation of the role.

---

1. Why do you think *A Doll's House* continues to be produced today?
2. Why is the reviewer David Sheward so impressed with an interpretation of Nora's role that assumes the social developments of the past century had not occurred?
3. Explain why Nora's actions at the end of *A Doll's House* would or would not be considered acceptable in contemporary American society.

Writing Process Workshop

When you're deciding whether or not to see a new movie, you may look at television or newspaper reviews of the movie to see what the critics think. A movie review is one type of critical evaluation—a written or spoken examination of what is and is not effective in a literary work, television program, or movie. Most often, a critical evaluation includes a brief summary of the work, comments upon its merits or weaknesses, and recommendations to readers or viewers.

Write a critical evaluation of *A Doll's House* or another literary work you've read. The following skills will help you.

Writing Skills Focus

▶ **Choose words with appropriate connotations.** Choosing words that have strong connotations—feelings and ideas associated with them—will give your evaluation more punch.

▶ **Provide examples** from the text for support. For example, if you say that Nora seems to be a charming, irresponsible child at the beginning of *A Doll's House*, follow that with a sentence such as, "She childishly sneaks some macaroons and then hides the bag when Torvald enters."

The following is an excerpt from Ben Okri's critical evaluation of *Clear Light of Day*, a novel by Anita Desai.

① The writer offers an opinion about the effect of silence in Desai's novel.

② The writer gives an indication of the mood of the book.

③ The writer uses a word with connotations that create an image in readers' minds.

MODEL FROM LITERATURE

① Silence is clarity and white heat in Anita Desai's *Clear Light of Day*, a novel about a family reunion, its unease, and the ② disturbing remembrances that accompany it. Tara, now married to a diplomat, revisits her childhood home in Old Delhi and finds that, on the ③ shabby surface, nothing has changed.

Prewriting

Choose a Topic To which selection in this book have you had the strongest reaction? That selection will make the best subject for a critical evaluation. Scan the table of contents, or flip through the book to spark your memory.

Clarify Your Opinions Once you've chosen your selection, collect your thoughts about it. Create a chart like this one, listing what you liked about the selection and what you didn't like about it.

What I Liked	What I Didn't Like

Identify Your Purpose Review your list of likes and dislikes. Decide whether you will or will not recommend the work to other readers.

Summarize Your Opinions Begin by jotting down a brief summary of the selection. Then list your opinions about various aspects of the work, as well as the work as a whole. Next, jot down details from the story that will help support each opinion.

Drafting

Follow a Format Using the details you've gathered, draft your evaluation. Start with a paragraph that reveals your general opinion of the selection. Follow with a brief summary of the key details. Then elaborate on your opinion of the work, providing examples and details for support. End with a recommendation to readers.

Use Evaluative Modifiers Present your opinions forcefully and clearly by using precise adjectives to either praise or criticize the work. Look at these examples:

Precise Adjectives			
Mild Praise	**High Praise**	**Mild Disapproval**	**Strong Disapproval**
readable	imaginative	dull	awful
expressive	hilarious	unfocused	tactless
solid	inspired	vague	tedious
mildly amusing	stimulating	inconsistent	painfully boring
informative	original	melodramatic	useless

APPLYING LANGUAGE SKILLS: Quotation Marks and Underlining

Place quotation marks around any examples that you quote directly from the text. If you are evaluating a poem or short story, place its title in quotation marks. If you are evaluating a novel or play, underline the title (if you are writing by hand) or enter it in italics (if you are working on a computer).

Plays and Novels:
A Doll's House
Things Fall Apart

Poems and Short Stories:
"A Pace Like That"
"House Taken Over"

Practice On your paper, write the following passage, placing quotation marks or underlining where necessary.

In Shakespeare's play Hamlet, the famous lines "To be or not to be" show Prince Hamlet's classic moment of indecision.

Writer's Solution Connection Language Lab

For more practice with quotation marks, complete the Language Lab lesson on Semicolons, Colons, and Quotation Marks.

APPLYING LANGUAGE SKILLS:
Capitalization

Observe the following rules of capitalization of sentence beginnings:

1. Capitalize the first word of a direct quotation that can stand alone as a sentence:

The soothsayer says to Caesar, "Beware the ides of March."

2. Capitalize the first word of a sentence in parentheses if that sentence stands alone:

Caesar made a show of refusing the crown. (In fact, he had arranged with Brutus to offer it to him.)

3. Capitalize the first word of a sentence after a colon:

Brutus has a quality that makes Antony admire him: He is honest.

Practice In your notebook, capitalize the proper words in the following sentence.

> In the end, perhaps, it is Caesar's belief in his own immortality that proves to be his downfall: just before he dies, he tells the senators, "but I am constant as the northern star."

Writer's Solution Connection
Writing Lab

For more help using quotations in your literary analysis, see Using Quotations in the Writing Lab tutorial on Response to Literature.

Offer Precise Details It's not enough to simply say that you found a story humorous; you must back up your opinions. Explain *why* you found the story humorous, and cite specific examples of details that contributed to the humor.

Revising

Use a Checklist Use this checklist to guide your revision.

▶ Have you summarized the selection in a way that will enable readers to follow what you're saying?

▶ Have you clearly expressed your opinion of the work?

▶ Do your evaluative modifiers express the appropriate degree of praise or disappointment?

▶ What can you do to strengthen your support for your opinion?

Use a Model Look at the revisions made in this paragraph from a review of Shakespeare's poem *The Tragedy of Julius Caesar*.

REVISION MODEL

In the ①"Tragedy of Julius Caesar," ②Cassius is one of the conspirators against Caesar. Cassius believes that the gods do not interest themselves in human affairs. ②*and that omens are merely superstitions* Now he credits his fate to bad omens. He thinks that when eagles follow their armies to Philippi, it is a good sign. However, when the eagles are replaced by ravens and crows, this foreshadows death to him. ③*"Their shadows seem a canopy most fatal," says Cassius.*

① The writer changes the quotation marks to underscore because a play is a full-length work.

② The writer adds information that clarifies her point.

③ This quotation from the text supports the writer's point.

Publishing

▶ **Create a Class Publication** With some classmates, create a class magazine of critical reviews.

▶ **Create a Book Group on the Internet** Post your critical evaluation on a bulletin board. Invite other readers to share their responses to your evaluation and to share evaluations of books they have enjoyed.

Student Success Workshop

Research Skills | Conducting a Research Project

Strategies for Success

Research assignments require you to use various strategies to locate and categorize information. Text organizers—such as overviews, headings, and graphic features—can guide you in your search. You can gather your information in various ways: by taking notes, by creating an outline, or by writing up a summary. As you write your report, keep your audience in mind and direct your final report to that audience. In your report, state your conclusions clearly, supporting them with facts.

Use Text Organizers The first challenge every researcher faces is figuring out where to find helpful information. Fortunately, many texts include organizing features—such as a table of contents, section titles, and chapter titles—that can point you in the right direction. For instance, a biography of Henrik Ibsen might be divided by sections and chapters that allow you to locate and categorize information about his life, poems, and plays.

Report to Your Audience The tone and style in which you report the findings of your research should be appropriate for your audience. Think about arranging and presenting your research findings in a way that is most engaging to that particular audience. For example, a report to middle-grade students about Sophocles' play *Antigone* might rely heavily on illustrations and other graphic features to convey information. A report on the same subject presented to college students might include quotations from the play and from research sources, plus maps and a timeline.

Draw Conclusions Conducting research is a lot like piecing together a puzzle or solving a mystery. As you gather more and more information about your topic, a clearer picture emerges. Finally, you are able to draw some conclusions based on the information you've gathered. Your research into the life and work of Henrik Ibsen, for example, might lead you to draw conclusions about why he wrote about what he did and how audiences of his time may have responded to his work. When you present your conclusions, support them with evidence from your research.

Apply the Strategies

Choose one of the topics listed below, and research it fully using the strategies you've learned.

1. Compare the status of women in the late nineteenth century with the details presented in Ibsen's play.

2. Find out what life was like for an actor in Ibsen's day.

3. Write a biographical portrait of another playwright who wrote during the time of Ibsen.

4. Report on the reception of a modern-day production of *A Doll's House*.

✔ *Here are some situations in which you need to know how to conduct research:*
- ▶ *Writing a term paper*
- ▶ *Comparing opinions on a controversial topic*
- ▶ *Presenting a review of competing products or services*
- ▶ *Writing a newspaper or magazine article*

Speaking, Listening, and Viewing Workshop

Any dramatic performance—a play, a satirical skit, or an improvisation—involves exciting challenges of self-expression. Most dramatic performances, especially those based on literary works, involve interpretation.

Get Into It Your first step in a dramatic performance based on a literary work is to become familiar with the text itself. Read the original work several times; talking it over with friends can help you decide how you'll interpret it. If you are portraying a specific character, get to know who you are. Think about your character's mood, motivation, and personality.

Know Your Audience You need to know your audience, too. Will you be performing for your entire class or for a small group? As you prepare, keep in mind where your audience will be. You will need to keep your body turned toward them.

Use Your Voice Your voice and how you use it will determine how effective your performance will be. Practice ways of using the pitch and intonation of your voice to convey your interpretation of your character's mood and personality. Think about timing: Your pauses can be as important as your words. Remember to project your voice at a level that everyone can hear—even if your character seems to be whispering or saying something quietly.

Use Body Language Don't forget to use nonverbal strategies. Your facial expressions, gestures, and posture all work to communicate your interpretation of the character you are portraying. When deciding how to use body language, consider your character's age, background, and gender.

Apply the Strategies

Choose one or two of the following activities, and apply the strategies for performing a dramatic scene.

1. Prepare a parody of a scene from *A Doll's House* for your class.
2. In a small group, choose a scene from *A Doll's House* and produce a modern adaptation of it for your class.
3. Prepare an original dramatic work based on a myth, true story, fable, fairy tale, or poem, and present it to your friends and family members.

Tips on Learning Your Lines

✔ *Use these tricks for memorizing your lines:*

▶ Audiotape your performance, and listen to the recording again and again.

▶ Repeat your lines while you're doing other things, like cleaning your room.

▶ Become familiar with other characters' lines, so you will recognize your cues to speak.

Test Preparation Workshop

Reading Comprehension

Strategies for Success

The reading sections of standardized tests require you to compare and contrast aspects—such as themes, conflicts, and allusions—of two texts. The tests may also require you to analyze the literary language.

Compare and Contrast Aspects of Texts

To compare and contrast, read each passage carefully and analyze the literary elements. If a test asks you to compare and contrast the themes of two passages, think about the similarities or differences between the main ideas or messages of the texts. Look at the following example:

Read the passages, and answer the question:

Passage A:

The first settlers in the Western Hemisphere were faced with a world that was strange and unknown to them. They encountered unfamiliar lands, animals, and weather conditions. They had to learn to survive in a climate that could turn deadly in an instant.

Passage B:

The members of the Concordia space station had entered an uncharted universe. All of their most technically advanced equipment was useless to them. Alien life forces surrounded their ship. Intelligence experts on board raced to figure out who these forces were and what they wanted.

I What theme is shared by both passages?

  A Space travel   **C** Entering unknown worlds

  B Frontier life   **D** Fighting off enemies

Only one passage deals with space travel, so **A** is wrong. Only one deals with frontier life, so **B** is wrong. Although there are dangers in both, **D** is not correct. The theme of both passages, although presented differently, is **C**.

Analyze Melodies of Literary Language

Writers often create "melodies" in the language of their work with evocative words, rhyme, repeated sounds, or rhythms. On a reading test, "listen" to the sound effects and think about what they express. Read the passage that follows, and answer the questions.

> Let others cheer the winning man,
> There's one I hold worthwhile;
> 'Tis he who does the best he can,
> Then loses with a smile.
> Beaten he is, but not to stay
> Down with rank and file;
> That man will win some other day,
> Who loses with a smile.

2 How are evocative words and rhythms used to create a kind of melody in the poem?

  A Evocative words express happiness.

  B No melody is present in the poem.

  C The poem's regular rhythm and rhyme create an upbeat kind of melody.

  D The poem's words and rhythms sing a song of a man shamed by defeat.

The correct answer is **C**.

Apply the Strategies

Reread the poetry, and answer the questions:

I What is the theme of the poem?

  A Winning is everything.

  B It's hard to smile when you lose.

  C The real winner can smile in defeat.

  D Don't ever accept defeat.

2 In what way is the word "smile" an example of evocative literary language?

  A It conveys the idea that competition is fun.

  B It conveys a spirit of joy.

  C It conveys two different emotions in the lines where it is used: first, good sportsmanship; second, the happiness of victory.

  D It is used here sarcastically.

Summer Night, Maruyama Okyo, Cleveland Museum of Art

UNIT

9

Poetry in World Literature

There are almost as many definitions of poetry as there are poets. Poetry can appear in neat stanzas, or it can look almost like prose on a page. Sometimes, the visual pattern of the words even forms a picture of the poem's subject. A poem can tell a story, express an idea, define a character, convey an emotion, describe a setting, or examine a situation. The poems in this unit come from many different cultures and times. Together, these poems will give you a sense of the wide range of literature that we call poetry.

Guide for Reading

Sappho (c. 630 B.C.–570 B.C.)

Sappho (saf´ō) was known to the Greek world as "the Poetess," much as Homer was known as "the Poet." Whereas Homer wrote of war, Sappho wrote of love.

Although Sappho was one of the most famous poets of antiquity, only a handful of complete or nearly complete poems by her have survived, along with hundreds of verse fragments.

Family Background No one knows for sure when Sappho was born or when she died—only that she was active in the late seventh and early sixth centuries B.C. Of the little that scholars know about Sappho's life, this much has become clear: She and her brother were born to a wealthy family. She married, had a daughter, and, at one point in her life, fled to Sicily to escape political persecution.

A Woman of Mystery Ancient traditions represent Sappho in various ways—as a priestess of Aphrodite, as a devoted schoolmistress, and as a lovesick poetess who hurled herself from a cliff after being rejected by the man she loved. There is much untruth in these biographies, but they all insist on the preoccupation of Sappho's poetry with love—its symptoms, its nature, its causes, and its effects.

The Poet's Work Sappho wrote nine books of poems on various subjects, for a variety of occasions. They were performed to the accompaniment of a stringed instrument called the lyre. Sappho also wrote wedding songs and hymns to goddesses (Athene, Aphrodite, and Hera) that may have been performed on festival days by choruses.

A Unique Voice Sappho made a revolutionary contribution to literature by giving voice to the experiences of girls and women. Much of her poetry speaks of the qualities of love and friendship. Whether describing a glimpse of beauty or simply remembering an absent friend, Sappho's poetry displays a vivid intensity of emotion that was not rivaled in the ancient world.

◆ Build Vocabulary

LATIN PREFIXES: *pre-*

In "You Know the Place: Then," the speaker talks of "precincts" sacred to the listener. *Precincts* contains the prefix *pre-*, which means "before" or "in front of," combined with a word meaning "to encircle." The resulting word has come to mean "an area surrounding a church or other building."

WORD BANK

awed
splendor
precincts
sleek

In reading the poems by Sappho, you will encounter these words. Each word is defined on the page where it first appears. Preview the list before you read.

◆ Build Grammar Skills

DIRECT ADDRESS

When a speaker in a poem speaks directly to a particular listener, using his or her name or other identifier, it is called **direct address.** Lyric poets often use words of direct address to emphasize or focus attention on the particular person, place, or thing about which they are writing.

Words of direct address are set off with commas, and occasionally, an exclamation mark. These lines from "You Know the Place: Then" contain two examples of direct address:

. . . *Queen! Cyprian!*
Fill our gold cups with love
stirred in clear nectar

Although They Are ◆ And Their Feet Move ◆ Awed by Her Splendor ◆ You Know the Place: Then

◆ Literature and Your Life

CONNECT YOUR EXPERIENCE

Sometimes, an ordinary sight, sound, or smell can trigger a vivid memory of a time past. The ripples on a pond, for example, may remind you of skipping stones with a friend, or a balloon caught in a tree may remind you of a bygone holiday celebration.

Sappho often recaptured in her work important or vivid times that had passed.

Journal Writing Jot down a description of a time in which your natural surroundings vividly reminded you of the past.

THEMATIC FOCUS: HUMANS AND NATURE

As you read these poems, look for examples in which nature mirrors the human experience.

◆ Background for Understanding

CULTURE

Sappho wrote her poems for a group of female students who came to her, the famed poetess, to learn the graceful arts of music, dance, and poetry. The school's patron deity was Aphrodite, the goddess of love. Ancient Greeks believed that under Aphrodite's influence, the world thrived, flowered, and blossomed.

In her poems, Sappho often calls upon Aphrodite to serve as an ally in love's campaigns.

Woman with Lyre, Greek vase painting, Olympia Museum, Greece

◆ Literary Focus

ORIGINS OF LYRIC POETRY

Sappho is famous for her **lyric poetry**, which expresses her personal thoughts and feelings. This poetry was so named because it was recited, chanted, or sung to the accompaniment of the lyre. The lyre was a stringed musical instrument, an ancestor of the guitar. Devices such as rhythm and repetition of sounds (alliteration and rhyme) enhanced the musical quality of the lyrics.

Today, we tend to think that lyric poetry, though no longer accompanied by music, is the only or at least the main kind of poem. However, Sappho lived at a time when poetry was commonly associated with long epics like the *Iliad*. She practically invented the lyric, or at least she was one of the earliest and best writers of lyric poems.

Guide for Reading ◆ 917

Reading for Success

Strategies for Reading Poetry

Poetry is a very distinctive kind of writing. It differs from other forms of writing in its appearance, its use of language, and its sound. Poets' imaginative use of language can sometimes make a poem seem complex or hard to understand. Here are strategies to help you read poetry successfully and enjoy it, as well.

Identify the speaker.

When you read a poem, you are hearing the voice of the poem's speaker. The speaker is not necessarily the poet, although it can be, or it can be a part of the poet's personality. The speaker may be a character created by the poet. Determine who you think is "telling" the poem, and try to determine his or her perspective on the situation in the poem. Recognizing the speaker and his or her perspective will give you an insight into the meaning of the poem.

Envision images and figures of speech.

Use your senses to experience the pleasures of a poem. For instance, see the dancers in Sappho's "And Their Feet Move," and feel the "smooth flowering grass."

Read according to punctuation.

Keep in mind that even if a poem is shaped to fit a particular rhythm and rhyme, a poem's words are put together and punctuated as sentences. For example, when you read Sappho's "Although They Are," notice that the poem is a complete sentence, expressing a complete thought. When you read a poem, don't stop at the end of each line unless a punctuation mark (period, comma, colon, semicolon, or dash) stops you.

Listen to the poem.

One of the things that distinguishes poetry from prose is its sound. Poetry is meant to be read aloud; only by doing so will you hear the music of the poet's words.

Paraphrase.

Restate the speaker's experiences and feelings in your own words. Restating the lines or stanzas will help you clarify their meaning.

Respond to what you read.

Think about what the speaker has said. How do the images in the poem affect you? What does the poem say to you?

As you read Sappho's poems, look at the notes in the boxes. The notes demonstrate how to apply these strategies to a poem.

Although They Are
Sappho
Translated by Mary Barnard

Although they are

Only breath, words
which I command
are immortal

> This poem is a single sentence. Read it **according to punctuation**, pausing for the comma but not automatically stopping at the ends of lines without punctuation.

And Their Feet Move
Sappho
Translated by Mary Barnard

◆ **Build Vocabulary**

awed (ôd) *adj.*: Affected by a feeling of reverence, fear, and wonder

splendor (splen′ dər) *n.*: Great brightness

And their feet move

Rhythmically as tender
feet of Cretan girls[1]
danced once around an

altar of love, crushing
a circle in the soft
smooth flowering grass

> **Envision** the scene Sappho describes in "And Their Feet Move."

---

1. **Cretan** (krēt′ 'n) **girls**: Girls from Crete, an island in the eastern Mediterranean Sea.

Awed by Her Splendor
Sappho
Translated by Mary Barnard

Awed by her splendor

Stars near the lovely
moon cover their own
bright faces
        when she
is roundest and lights
earth with her silver

> **Paraphrase** "Awed by Her Splendor" by restating it in your own words.

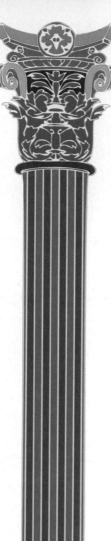

You Know the Place: Then
Sappho
Translated by Mary Barnard

You know the place: then

Leave Crete and come to us
waiting where the grove is
pleasantest, by <u>precincts</u>

5 sacred to you; incense
smokes on the altar, cold
streams murmur through the

apple branches, a young
rose thicket shades the ground
10 and quivering leaves pour

down deep sleep; in meadows
where horses have grown <u>sleek</u>
among spring flowers, dill

scents the air. Queen! Cyprian![1]
15 Fill our gold cups with love
stirred into our clear nectar

---

1. **Cyprian** (si′ prē ən) *n.*: Name Sappho uses
to address the goddess Aphrodite.

◆ **Build Vocabulary**

precincts (prē′ siŋkts) *n.*: Special places or areas

sleek (slēk) *adj.*: Smooth and shiny

Sappho, detail of a Greek vase painting, c. 440 B.C.

▲ **Critical Viewing** Which details in this
Greek vase painting identify Sappho as
a poet? **[Interpret]**

Guide for Responding

◆ Literature and Your Life

Reader's Response What contemporary singer
reminds you most of Sappho? Why?

Thematic Focus Might Sappho have enjoyed
walking in the rain or planting flowers in a garden?
What makes you think as you do?

Reader's Journal Jot down what you might say
if you, like the speaker in "Although They Are," had
command of immortal words.

☑ Check Your Comprehension

1. In "Awed by Her Splendor," what do the stars
do?

2. What does the speaker in "Although They Are"
describe as immortal?

3. What takes place in "And Their Feet Move"?

4. (a) What two requests does the speaker in "You
Know the Place: Then" make of Aphrodite?
(b) What are the speaker's expectations?

Guide for Responding (continued)

◆ Critical Thinking

INTERPRET

1. In "Awed by Her Splendor," what sort of moon "is roundest and lights earth with her silver"? **[Interpret]**
2. Which details in the description of "You Know the Place: Then" suggest a place well suited for the enjoyments of friendship? Explain. **[Interpret]**
3. (a) Why does the speaker of "Although They Are" claim that her words are immortal? (b) What does her claim suggest about the effects of poetry?

EVALUATE

4. Are words "only breath," as the speaker in "Although They Are" states? Explain. **[Assess]**

◆ Reading for Success

STRATEGIES FOR READING POETRY

Review the reading strategies and the notes showing how to read poetry. Then, apply the strategies to the following.

1. (a) Who is the speaker in "Although They Are?" (b) How would you describe the speaker's personality? Explain.
2. To which senses does Sappho appeal in "You Know the Place: Then"?
3. Paraphrase "And Their Feet Move."

◆ Literary Focus

ORIGINS OF LYRIC POETRY

Sappho was one of the earliest **lyric poets;** she wrote about her personal thoughts and feelings. In contrast, Homer, who lived about a century and a half earlier, wrote about the deeds of heroes. Sappho's poems were accompanied by lyre music, and they often capture a moment in time or convey a single, dominant message.

1. What is the dominant message in "Although They Are"?
2. Which poem appeals most to your senses? Explain.
3. What mood might music have created during a reading of "You Know the Place: Then"? Explain.

◆ Build Vocabulary

USING THE PREFIX: *pre-*

The prefix *pre-* means "before" or "in advance." Use that knowledge to define each of the following words.

1. preview
2. precondition
3. precaution
4. prevent

USING THE WORD BANK: Synonyms

In your notebook, write the letter of the word that is the best synonym of, or is closest in meaning to, the Word Bank word.

1. awed: (a) terrified, (b) drilled, (c) pleased
2. splendor: (a) love, (b) brilliance, (c) gloom
3. precincts: (a) medicines, (b) surroundings, (c) advantages
4. sleek: (a) dull, (b) storm, (c) smooth

◆ Build Grammar Skills

WORDS OF DIRECT ADDRESS

When the speaker in a poems talks directly to a particular listener using identifying words or names, the speaker is using **direct address.** Words of direct address are followed by a comma or exclamation mark, and they appear often in invocations, in which the poet or poem's speaker calls upon an absent god, person, or place for help.

Examples: O *majestic mountain,* lift my spirits . . .

Send me inspiration, *divine muse,* to guide my pen . . .

Practice On your paper, identify the words of direct address.

1. Cypris and Nereids, may my brother come home unharmed . . .
2. Evening Star, you bring back all that radiant dawn has scattered . . .
3. Sing to me, Muse, the man of many guises and deceits.
4. Who is it, Sappho, that hurt you?
5. I entreat you not with griefs and bitternesses to break my spirit, O goddess;

Build Your Portfolio

Idea Bank

Writing

1. **Letter to Sappho** Write a letter to Sappho explaining why you want to attend her famous school, what you expect to learn, and why you are particularly qualified.

2. **Lyric Poem** Write an original lyric poem inviting Aphrodite to your favorite place. Choose words that help create an enticing image of the place you are describing.

3. **Analysis** Write an essay in which you analyze Sappho's use of imagery in "You Know the Place: Then." Use specific details from the poem to support your ideas.

Speaking, Listening, and Viewing

4. **Recitation** Memorize a Sappho poem. Then, rehearse speaking the poem aloud, adjusting the pitch of your voice and your rate of speaking to best suit your interpretation. Present your recitation to classmates. **[Performing Arts Link]**

5. **Song and Dance** Working with classmates, choose, or compose, music suited to one of Sappho's poems, and choreograph a dance to go with it. **[Performing Arts Link]**

Researching and Representing

6. **History of the Lyre** Research the history of the lyre, the stringed instrument that accompanied lyric poetry, and write a paper explaining your findings. **[Music Link]**

7. **Diorama of a Greek School** Research what schools were like in ancient Greece. Then, bring one to life by making a diorama—a three-dimensional representation of it. **[Art Link; Social Studies Link]**

Online Activity www.phlit.phschool.com

Guided Writing Lesson

Literary Interpretation

In the poems of Sappho, love is represented as an irresistible force that acts on all creatures and things. In other words, love conquers all. Write a literary interpretation discussing the nature of love—or a single aspect of love—as you understand it from your reading of Sappho's poems. As you write, make your points clear by using transitions.

Writing Skills Focus: Transitions to Show Repetition

In a literary interpretation, it is helpful to summarize your main points or to repeat key ideas. **Transitions,** connecting words, that indicate repetition include *all of this means*, *in brief*, and *in other words*. Use of such transitions alerts readers that you are restating crucial concepts.

Prewriting Review Sappho's poems to gather details about the nature of love. For example, you may find the description of the moon's silvery beauty in "Awed by Her Splendor" to mean that beauty is a requirement for love.

Drafting Once you have gathered details, weave them together into an essay that is logically and effectively organized. You may, for example, decide to devote one paragraph to each aspect of love as revealed in Sappho's poems. As you draft, use transitions to connect your ideas.

Revising Reread your draft critically. Where support is lacking, add details from the poem or from other sources. Delete any details that stray from your main points. Add transitions to show repetition, wherever necessary.

Proofread your essay, fixing errors in grammar, spelling, and punctuation.

PART **1** *Meaning and Sound*

Untitled, Shinichi Eguchi

Guide for Reading

John McCrae (1872–1918)

A Canadian physician working as a medical officer in France during World War I, McCrae witnessed and wrote about the tragedy and nobility of the wartime experience. "In Flanders Fields" was published by the British magazine *Punch* in 1915. The poem was reprinted in the United States to boost the morale of soldiers and to encourage civilians to join the armed forces.

Petrarch (1304–1374)

Francesco Petrarca, whom the English called Petrarch (pē´ trärk´), was among the greatest Italian poets of the fourteenth century. As a writer, he was equally at home in Italian and Latin, and his self-centered reflections set a pattern for love poetry over the next three centuries.

The earliest lyrics in Petrarch's collection of Italian poems, the *Canzoniere* (kän tsô nyer´ ē), were written in the 1320's. Petrarch continued to revise these poems throughout his life. Most of the 366 poems concern the poet's unrequited love for Laura.

Who was this Laura who inspired Petrarch to write some of the world's greatest love poetry? She may have been Laura de Noves. Petrarch himself creates a picture of her as golden-haired, beautiful, and rich. Whoever she was, her beauty inspired Petrarch to a love that lasted *his* whole life—even though she died in the Great Plague of 1348.

Petrarch, Anonymous, Uffizi, Florence, Italy

Guillaume Apollinaire (1880–1918)

Guillaume Apollinaire (gē yōm´ à pô lē ner´) was a French poet of the early twentieth century who experimented with new forms and ideas. His experiments helped modernize French poetry while preserving its traditional beauty and music.

The poem "Mirabeau Bridge," noted for its rhythms and deep personal feelings, appeared in a book he published in 1913.

Apollinaire was a soldier in World War I and died of complications from a wound in November of 1918, just two days before the war ended.

◆ **Build Vocabulary**

LATIN WORD ROOTS: -journ-
Petrarch creates a lyrical image of death by referring to Laura's death as "her heavenly sojourn." *Sojourn,* which means "visit," contains the Latin word root *-journ-*, meaning "day." The prefix *so-* means "under or during." A sojourn is therefore "a temporary visit," lasting a day or not much more.

WORD BANK
As you read these poems, you will encounter the words on this list. Each word is defined on the page where it first appears. Preview the list before you read.

> radiant
> unearthly
> dreary
> sated
> exults
> sojourn
> gracious

◆ **Build Grammar Skills**

CONCRETE AND ABSTRACT NOUNS
As you read these poems, you will notice that McCrae, Petrarch, and Apollinaire explore psychological and emotional truths by describing the physical world. To achieve this goal, they use two different types of nouns.

A **concrete noun** names something physical that can be directly perceived by one of the five senses. An **abstract noun** names an idea, belief, quality, or concept—something that cannot be seen, heard, smelled, tasted, or touched.

"In Flanders Fields" refers to *poppies,* a concrete noun referring to something you can see, touch, and smell. The poem also contains the word *faith,* an abstract noun that refers to something you cannot directly perceive.

In Flanders Fields ◆ *from* Canzoniere ◆ Mirabeau Bridge ◆

◆ *Literature and Your Life*

CONNECT YOUR EXPERIENCE

A story read aloud, a moving speech, a dramatic proclamation: When you hear any of these, you may have the impression that you are hearing music. Similarly, when you read poetry, your inner voice can turn the lines into a song in your head.

Think about the songs you like, and what it is about them that appeals to you. Then, as you read these poems, try to hear them as songs.

Journal Writing Write down the lyrics to one of your favorite songs, and read them aloud without music. Do the words themselves suggest music? Why or why not?

THEMATIC FOCUS: FROM THE PAST

As you read these poems, ask yourself: Do my favorite songs and poems relate in structure and subject matter to these poems from the past?

◆ Background for Understanding

HISTORY

Many factors led to World War I (1914–1918), the backdrop of John McCrae's poem "In Flanders Fields." Principal among them were the territorial and economic rivalries between Russia, France, and Great Britain on one side and Germany and Austria-Hungary on the other. These conflicts had been brewing since the late nineteenth century. Flanders, a region in northern France and western Belgium, was a chief battlefield of the war. Many towns were destroyed, and once-productive farmland was blighted with miles of bomb craters, trenches—and bodies.

◆ Reading Strategy

LISTEN

Listening is an important skill for appreciating all literature, but especially for poetry, which is created for the ear as well as for the eye. To appreciate the sound of a poem, listen to it as it is read aloud. Hear the rhythm of the lines and listen for rhymes and other repeated sounds.

Often, the rhythms and sounds of a poem suggest a mood or reflect an idea. "In Flanders Fields," for example, has a regular beat, suggesting the evenly-spaced rows of grave markers repeating and repeating. Notice the effect when the regular rhythm is broken, and note how the broken rhythm calls attention to certain lines.

◆ Literary Focus

MUSICAL DEVICES

Musical devices are tools of language that make a poem sound more like a song.

Alliteration is the repetition of the first consonant sound or any vowel sounds in closely associated syllables, especially stressed syllables. In McCrae's poem, the repetition of *l* sounds in "*L*oved and were *l*oved, and now we *l*ie" adds to the music.

Onomatopoeia (än´ ō mat´ ō pē´ ə) is the use of words to imitate actual sounds—*bang* and *thump* are examples.

Assonance is the repetition of the same or similar vowel sounds in syllables that end with different consonant sounds. In the final lines of "Spring," translator Morris Bishop uses words with the *ow* sound to create assonance: *loud, flowering, prowl.*

Consonance is the repetition of similar consonant sounds at the end of accented syllables when these sounds are preceded by different vowels. In "The White Doe," the translator rhymes "sun" and "gone."

Meter is the formal organization of rhythms in a poem. You can hear the pattern of alternating unstressed and stressed syllables in the first two lines of "In Flanders Fields": in FLANders FIELDS the POPpies BLOW . . ."

Repetition and **rhyme** also give a poem the sound of a song.

In Flanders Fields

John McCrae

In Flanders fields the poppies blow
Between the crosses, row on row,
    That mark our place; and in the sky
    The larks, still bravely singing, fly
5 Scarce heard amid the guns below.

We are the Dead. Short days ago
We lived, felt dawn, saw sunset glow,
    Loved and were loved, and now we lie
    In Flanders fields.

10 Take up our quarrel with the foe:
To you from failing hands we throw
    The torch; be yours to hold it high.
    If ye break faith with us who die
We shall not sleep, though poppies grow
    In Flanders fields.

▲ **Critical Viewing** How do you think the poet would feel about this simple marker? **[Speculate]**

from Canzoniere
Petrarch

Laura
Translated by Morris Bishop

She used to let her golden hair fly free
    For the wind to toy and tangle and molest;
    Her eyes were brighter than the <u>radiant</u> west.
(Seldom they shine so now.) I used to see
5 Pity look out of those deep eyes on me.
    ("It was false pity," you would now protest.)
    I had love's tinder[1] heaped within my breast;
    What wonder that the flame burned furiously?

She did not walk in any mortal way,
10   But with angelic progress; when she spoke,
    <u>Unearthly</u> voices sang in unison.
She seemed divine among the <u>dreary</u> folk
    Of earth. You say she is not so today?
    Well, though the bow's unbent,[2] the wound
        bleeds on.

---

1. tinder (tin´ dər) *n.*: Dry, easily flammable material used for starting a fire.
2. though the bow's unbent: Though she is older and does not have her original beauty; the bow referred to is Cupid's.

◆ **Build Vocabulary**
radiant (rā´ dē ənt) *adj.*: Shining brightly
unearthly (un ʉrth´ lē) *adj.*: As if not of this world; strange and mysterious
dreary (drir´ ē) *adj.*: Cheerless and dull

The White Doe

Translated by Anna Maria Armi

▲ **Critical Viewing** Does this painting of
Laura correspond to your image of her?
Explain. **[Relate]**

A pure-white doe in an emerald glade
Appeared to me, with two antlers of gold,
Between two streams, under a laurel's shade,
At sunrise, in the season's bitter cold.

5   Her sight was so suavely¹ merciless
That I left work to follow her at leisure,
Like the miser who looking for his treasure
Sweetens with that delight his bitterness.

Around her lovely neck "Do not touch me"
10 Was written with topaz² and diamond stone,
"My Caesar's will has been to make me free."

Already toward noon had climbed the sun,
My weary eyes were not <u>sated</u> to see,
When I fell in the stream and she was gone.

---

1. suavely (swäv´ lē): In a smoothly gracious manner.
2. topaz (tō´ paz´): A yellow gem.

Spring

Translated by Morris Bishop

Zephyr[1] returns, and scatters everywhere
    New flowers and grass, and company does bring,
    Procne and Philomel,[2] in sweet despair,
    And all the tender colors of the Spring.
5 Never were fields so glad, nor skies so fair;
    And Jove <u>exults</u> in Venus'[3] prospering.
    Love is in all the water, earth, and air,
    And love possesses every living thing.
But to me only heavy sighs return
10 For her who carried in her little hand
    My heart's key to her heavenly <u>sojourn</u>.
The birds sing loud above the flowering land;
    Ladies are <u>gracious</u> now.—Where deserts burn
    The beasts still prowl on the ungreening sand.

---

1. **Zephyr** (zef´ ər): The west wind.
2. **Procne** (präk´ nē) **and Philomel** (fil´ ō mel´): In Greek mythology, Philomel was a princess of Athens raped by Tereus, husband of her sister Procne. The gods changed Philomel into a nightingale, Procne into a swallow, and Tereus into a hawk.
3. **Jove . . . Venus':** Jove was the chief god in Roman mythology, and Venus was the goddess of love.

♦ **Build Vocabulary**

sated (sāt´ əd) *adj.*: Completely satisfied

exults (eg zults´) *v.*: Rejoices greatly

sojourn (sō´ jɵrn) *n.*: Brief or temporary stay; visit

gracious (grā´ shəs) *adj.*: Showing kindness, courtesy, and charm

Mirabeau Bridge

Guillaume Apollinaire

Translated by William Meredith

Under Mirabeau Bridge flows the Seine.[1]
    Why must I be reminded again
       Of our love?
Doesn't happiness issue from pain?

5   Bring on the night, ring out the hour.
      The days wear on but I endure.

      Face to face, hand in hand, so
        That beneath
           The bridge our arms make, the slow
10 Wave of our looking can flow.

      Then call the night, bell the day.
      Time runs off, I must stay.

And love runs down like this
      Water, love runs down.
15   How slow life is,
How violent hope is.

      Come night, strike hour.
      Days go, I endure.

Nor days nor any time detain.
20   Time past or love
        Can not come again.
Under Mirabeau Bridge flows the Seine.

      Bring on the night, ring out the hour.
      Days wear away, I endure.

---

1. **Under Mirabeau** (mir′ ə bō′) **Bridge . . . Seine** (sen):
Mirabeau Bridge in Paris is a bridge over the Seine River.

Guide for Responding

◆ Literature and Your Life

Reader's Response Does "In Flanders Fields" reflect how you feel when you visit a cemetery? Why or why not? What do you imagine Petrarch's Laura was actually like? Does Apollinaire's poem remind you of any songs you know? Why or why not?

Thematic Focus Do Petrarch's poems make you think that life in the fourteenth century was very similar to life today, or very different from it? Why?

Reader's Journal What advice would you give to a friend who felt the way the speaker in "Mirabeau Bridge" feels? Jot down some guidance you would offer.

Questions for Research How could you find out about influential poets of World War I other than John McCrae? Name three sources, and tell how you would use each one to find out more about this topic.

☑ Check Your Comprehension

1. What physical details of Flanders fields does McCrae's poem describe?
2. In what line of "In Flanders Fields" do the multiple speakers announce who they are?
3. What do the speakers in the poem "In Flanders Fields" ask the reader to do?
4. Name four details about Laura that the speaker recalls in "Laura."
5. Describe the animal that the speaker sees in "The White Doe."
6. In "The White Doe," what does the sign around the animal's neck say?
7. What happens to the speaker at the end of "The White Doe"?
8. Name three details that characterize the new season in "Spring."
9. What words does the speaker in "Spring" use to describe his mood?
10. In "Mirabeau Bridge," what is the speaker reminded of by the water flowing under the bridge?
11. What different kind of bridge does the speaker describe in "Mirabeau Bridge"?

◆ Critical Thinking

INTERPRET

1. What are two pairs of images that contrast life and death in the poem "In Flanders Fields"? **[Support]**
2. The speakers in the poem "In Flanders Fields" deliver an urgent message. What is this message? **[Interpret]**
3. How does the speaker in "Laura" contrast the past and the present? Describe what has changed and what has remained the same. **[Interpret]**
4. How are the speaker and the doe contrasted in "The White Doe"? **[Infer]**
5. In "Spring," what essential contrast does the speaker draw? How is this contrast different from the one in "Laura"? **[Compare and Contrast]**
6. In "Mirabeau Bridge," what mood does the speaker convey? Explain. **[Analyze]**
7. The speaker in "Mirabeau Bridge" asks two questions in the opening stanza. How does the rest of the poem answer these questions? **[Draw Conclusions]**

EVALUATE

8. After World War I ended, "In Flanders Fields" was sometimes published without the final stanza. Why do you think editors made this decision? Was it an appropriate choice? **[Assess]**
9. Do you think the speaker in Petrarch's poems is self-aware or self-absorbed? Explain. **[Make a Judgment]**

APPLY

10. If you were making a film about Petrarch and Laura, would you update the story or set it in the fourteenth century? Why? **[Make a Decision]**

EXTEND

11. What, if anything, does "In Flanders Fields" reveal about World War I? Explain. **[Social Studies Link]**

COMPARE LITERARY WORKS

12. How are the speakers in Petrarch's poems similar to the speaker in "Mirabeau Bridge"? **[Compare and Contrast]**

Guide for Responding (continued)

◆ Reading Strategy

LISTEN

Listening to the sounds and rhythms of these poems is part of the poetic experience. The sound of a poem gives you insight into the poem's meaning.

For example, "Mirabeau Bridge" opens with two questions that the rest of the poem answers. This pattern of question-and-answer plays out in the sound of the poem as well. As is often the case in English, the questions end on a higher pitch, and the answers "resolve" them with a lower pitch.

1. Identify the lines where the rhythm of "In Flanders Fields" is broken, and explain the effect of these lines.
2. How do the parenthetical remarks in "Laura" affect the way you read the poem aloud?
3. How do the rhythms of the alternating stanzas of "Mirabeau Bridge" differ?

◆ Literary Focus

MUSICAL DEVICES

Just as composers of music must know harmony and melody in order to create the effects they desire, poets use language tools called **musical devices** to create effects in their poems. For example, McCrae chose an alliterative title for "In Flanders Fields" (the repeated *f* sounds) to establish immediately the strong rhythm of the poem.

1. Describe the rhyme pattern of "In Flanders Fields." How does this pattern affect the musical quality of the poem?
2. Find two examples of assonance and one of consonance in "Mirabeau Bridge," and describe how they contribute to the sound of the poem.
3. "Mirabeau Bridge" also contains internal rhymes—exact rhymes that do not fall at the ends of lines. Find two examples of internal rhymes.
4. The poems by Petrarch and Apollinaire were translated from Italian and French, respectively. What challenges do translators face when trying to reproduce the musical quality of the original poem?

◆ Build Vocabulary

USING THE LATIN ROOT *-journ-*

The Latin word root *-journ-* means "day," and many familiar words contain this root. For example, *journey* once meant "a day's travel" but now means "any trip." On your paper, match each numbered *-journ-* word with its lettered definition.

1. adjourn   **a.** a daily record
2. journalism   **b.** to stop for the day
3. journalist   **c.** one who gathers daily news
4. journal   **d.** the gathering of daily news

USING THE WORD BANK: Synonyms

On your paper, write the word whose meaning is closest to that of the first word.

1. sated: (a) implied, (b) rationed, (c) satisfied
2. radiant: (a) glowing, (b) wide, (c) tremendous
3. sojourn: (a) wit, (b) diary, (c) visit
4. dreary: (a) unreal, (b) gloomy, (c) vague
5. gracious: (a) sly, (b) precious, (c) courteous
6. unearthly: (a) coarse, (b) supernatural, (c) rude
7. exults: (a) leaves, (b) rejoices, (c) begs

◆ Build Grammar Skills

CONCRETE AND ABSTRACT NOUNS

Concrete nouns name specific things that can be perceived by the senses. **Abstract nouns** name ideas or concepts that cannot be seen, heard, felt, tasted, or smelled.

The word *bell* from "Mirabeau Bridge" is a concrete noun because it names something you can see, feel, and hear. *Happiness,* on the other hand, is a concept that cannot be directly perceived by the senses.

Practice On your paper, label each noun as *concrete* or *abstract.*

1. poppies   5. wound   9. colors
2. sky   6. sunrise   10. bridge
3. wind   7. despair   11. pain
4. pity   8. love   12. hope

Writing Application On your paper, write an enthusiastic criticism of these poems. Use at least four of these abstract and concrete nouns: *fields, faith, conflict, passion, doe, poem, heart, face, anguish, water, sadness, music, regret.* Underline the concrete nouns, and circle the abstract nouns.

Build Your Portfolio

Idea Bank

Writing

1. **Letter to the Editor** It is 1915 and World War I is raging. You have just read "In Flanders Fields." Write a letter to the editor saying why you do or do not agree with the message of this poem.

2. **Poetic Response** Write a poem that responds to "Laura" from Laura's point of view or that responds to "Mirabeau Bridge" from the point of view of the speaker's beloved.

3. **Comparison and Contrast** Compare and contrast two of these poems in terms of the musical devices used in them.

Speaking, Listening, and Viewing

4. **Poetry Reading** Organize a class poetry reading, including readings of the poems in this group. Encourage participants to rehearse with a tape recorder and to emphasize the musical qualities of the poems they read. **[Performing Arts Link]**

5. **Audio Presentation** Imagine that you are going to set one of the poems in this group to music. Decide what style of music would be most appropriate, and play examples of it for the class. **[Music Link]**

Researching and Representing

6. **Statistical Analysis** For one of the poems in this group, answer questions like the following in a statistical report: What percentage of vowel sounds are long rather than short? Which long or short vowel sounds are dominant? **[Mathematics Link]**

7. **World War I Poetry** Both John McCrae and Guillaume Apollinaire served in World War I. Compile an annotated bibliography of works by other poets who served in this war. **[Social Studies Link]**

Online Activity www.phlit.phschool.com

Guided Writing Lesson

Proposal for a Poetry Anthology

Brief poems are well suited to **anthologies**—collections of works with something in common. Write a proposal for a poetry anthology that you would like to create. Include the common theme or poetic form that unites the poems, your reasons for choosing your method of organization, and a sample of the poems you would use.

Writing Skills Focus: Specific Examples

Once you have decided on the common element that will link the poems, support your method of organization with **specific examples**—samples of poems you will include.

For example, if you plan to organize your anthology by musical devices, show examples of alliteration, consonance, and assonance in the poems you suggest.

Prewriting Consider how you will arrange your poems. For example, if you are going to use musical devices as an organizing feature, you might make a chart like this one:

Musical Device	Title	Example
• Alliteration	"In Flanders Fields"	the title
•		

Drafting Begin by explaining your concept of organization. Then, introduce some of the specific poems you have selected and explain why you chose each one.

Revising Ask several classmates to review your proposal. Do they understand your method of organization? Is it clear to them why you want to include each poem?

Consider different titles for your anthology, some with abstract nouns and others with concrete nouns. For more on concrete and abstract nouns, see pp. 924 and 932.

Guide for Reading

Pak Tu-jin *(1916–1998)*

Before World War II, Korea had been dominated politically and culturally by China and Japan. After 1945, though, a distinctive group of Korean writers emerged, among them Pak Tu-jin (päk too´ jin). Influenced by the French Symbolists, Pak writes poetry that mingles sound, symbol, and nature imagery to create beauty.

Yehuda Amichai *(1924–2000)*

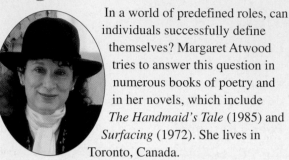

Poet Yehuda Amichai (yə hoo´ də ä´ mi khī) intertwines timeless themes with the contemporary history of his country, Israel. Born in Germany, he migrated with his family to Palestine, the region where Israel was created in 1948. Serving as a soldier in the Israeli defense forces, he fought in several wars. Amichai wrote in Hebrew, the ancient language that is now Israel's official tongue.

Margaret Atwood *(1939–   )*

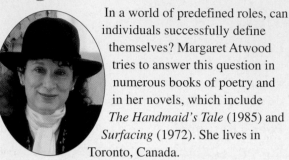

In a world of predefined roles, can individuals successfully define themselves? Margaret Atwood tries to answer this question in numerous books of poetry and in her novels, which include *The Handmaid's Tale* (1985) and *Surfacing* (1972). She lives in Toronto, Canada.

Nazim Hikmet *(1902–1963)*

After studying economics and political science at the University of Moscow, Nazim Hikmet returned to his native Turkey in 1924 to spread his radical political vision. As punishment for his political activities, the Turkish government sentenced him to many years in jail. In 1951, he left Turkey forever to live in the Soviet Union and Eastern Europe. His work, initially censored in Turkey, was published and widely read there after his death.

◆ Build Vocabulary

LATIN WORD ROOTS: *-trad-*

In "August River," you will encounter an unusual river—one that can remember betrayals. *Betrayals* and related words come from the Latin word *tradere,* which means "hand over." *Betrayals* means "acts in which one hands over something or someone to the enemy." Related words include *treason, traitor,* and *tradition* ("that which is handed over to younger generations").

WORD BANK

embers
wrath
betrayals

Preview this list of words from the selection before you read. Each word is defined on the page where it first appears.

◆ Build Grammar Skills

ELLIPTICAL CLAUSES

In an **elliptical clause,** one or more words are omitted: They are assumed to be understood by the reader. Often, in adjective clauses, the relative pronoun *that* is not written or spoken. In the following example, the complete clause is *that I planted,* but the word *that* is understood and so is omitted.

> I'm looking at the lemon tree [*that*] I planted.

Elliptical clauses in which the relative pronoun is not stated have an informal, conversational tone.

Mushrooms ◆ The Cucumber
A Pace Like That ◆ August River

◆ Literature and Your Life

CONNECT YOUR EXPERIENCE
Sometimes, all it takes to end your bad mood is a sunrise, glitters reminding you that life is larger than yourself. By inviting you into this larger life, natural beauty releases you from yourself, as these poems show.

THEMATIC FOCUS: A LARGER WORLD
As you read, notice how the poets use natural beauty to take you beyond yourself and give you perspective.

Journal Writing Write a paragraph describing a favorite scene from nature and the feelings it evokes.

◆ Background for Understanding

CULTURE
In "A Pace Like That," Amichai makes a comparison to a Torah scroll, which is a long roll of parchment (a kind of paper made of animal skin). On this parchment, the first five books of the Bible—Genesis, Exodus, Leviticus, Numbers, and Deuteronomy—are written in Hebrew. In Jewish tradition, readings from the Torah are assigned to each day; the entire cycle of readings takes a year to complete.

◆ Literary Focus

FIGURATIVE LANGUAGE
Figurative language is writing or speech that plays with the ordinary use of words. By using various types of figurative language, writers create beauty and help readers see things in new ways. Figurative language includes:

- **Similes**, which compare dissimilar things using the word *like* or *as*. In "Mushrooms," Atwood uses a simile when she says the mushrooms "ooze up through the earth . . . like bubbles."
- **Metaphors**, which compare dissimilar things *without* using *like* or *as*. To make a metaphor, a poet refers to one thing as if it were another. In "The Cucumber," Hikmet refers to a cucumber as "a green sun."
- **Personifications**, which describe an object, animal, or idea as if it were human. In "August River," Pak Tu-jin says the river "claps its hands."

◆ Reading Strategy

PARAPHRASE
Poets use concise language, squeezing a wealth of meaning into just a few words. To unpack this meaning, pause occasionally as you read, and **paraphrase** the poem, restating in your own words what each line says. For example, after you read the first four lines of Amichai's poem "A Pace Like That," you might paraphrase them like this:

> I realized when I was looking at the lemon tree I planted last year that I'd like to slow down. I'd like to take the time to appreciate things like the growth of the tree I planted.

Keep a chart on which you paraphrase passages from the poems.

Poet's Words	Paraphrase

Mushrooms

Margaret Atwood

i

In this moist season,
mist on the lake and thunder
afternoons in the distance

they ooze up through the earth
5   during the night,
like bubbles, like tiny
bright red balloons
filling with water;
a sound below sound, the thumbs of rubber
10   gloves turned softly inside out.

In the mornings, there is the leaf mold
starred with nipples,
with cool white fishgills,
leathery purple brains,
15   fist-sized suns dulled to the color of <u>embers</u>,
poisonous moons, pale yellow.

ii

Where do they come from?

For each thunderstorm that travels
overhead there's another storm
20   that moves parallel in the ground.
Struck lightning is where they meet.

Underfoot there's a cloud of rootlets,
shed hairs or a bundle of loose threads
blown slowly through the midsoil.
25   These are their flowers, these fingers
reaching through darkness to the sky,
these eyeblinks
that burst and powder the air with spores.

◆ **Build Vocabulary**

embers (em′ bərz) *n.*: Glowing remains of a fire; coals, pieces of wood, and so on, that no longer are in flames but still glowing

Mushrooms, 1940, William Nicholson, Tate Gallery, London

◀ **Critical Viewing** What figure of speech for mushrooms does this picture inspire you to invent? Explain. **[Connect]**

iii

       They feed in shade, on halfleaves
30   as they return to water,
       on slowly melting logs,
       deadwood. They glow
       in the dark sometimes. They taste
       of rotten meat or cloves[1]
35   or cooking steak or bruised
       lips or new snow.

iv

       It isn't only
       for food I hunt them
       but for the hunt and because
40   they smell of death and the waxy
       skins of the newborn,
       flesh into earth into flesh.

       Here is the handful
       of shadow I have brought back to you:
45   this decay, this hope, this mouth-
       ful of dirt, this poetry.

1. cloves (klōvs) *n.*: Spice with a hot and sharp taste

The Cucumber

Nazim Hikmet

Translated by Randy Blasing and Mutlu Konut

The snow is knee-deep in the courtyard
and still coming down hard:
it hasn't let up all morning.
We're in the kitchen.
5   On the table, on the oilcloth,[1] spring—
on the table there's a very tender young cucumber,
                pebbly and fresh as a daisy.
We're sitting around the table staring at it.
It softly lights up our faces,
10   and the very air smells fresh.
We're sitting around the table staring at it,
amazed
          thoughtful
                 optimistic.
We're as if in a dream.
On the table, on the oilcloth, hope—
15   on the table, beautiful days,
a cloud seeded with a green sun,
an emerald crowd impatient and on its way,
loves blooming openly—
on the table, there on the oilcloth, a very tender young
20   cucumber,
            pebbly and fresh as a daisy.
The snow is knee-deep in the courtyard
and coming down hard.
It hasn't let up all morning.

---

1. **oilcloth:** Cloth, made waterproof with oil, used to cover tables.

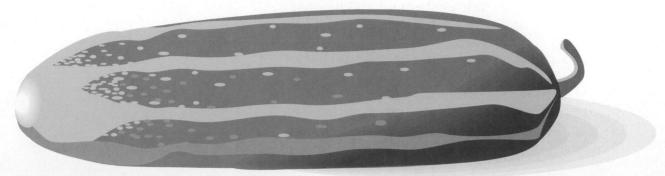

A Pace Like That

Yehuda Amichai

Translated by Chana Bloch

I'm looking at the lemon tree I planted.
A year ago. I'd need a different pace, a slower one,
to observe the growth of its branches, its leaves as they open.
I want a pace like that.
5   Not like reading a newspaper
but the way a child learns to read,
or the way you quietly decipher the inscription
on an ancient tombstone.

And what a Torah scroll takes an entire year to do
10   as it rolls its way from Genesis to the death of Moses,
I do each day in haste
or in sleepless nights, rolling over from side to side.

The longer you live, the more people there are
who comment on your actions. Like a worker
15   in a manhole: at the opening above him
people stand around giving free advice
and yelling instructions,
but he's all alone down there in his depths.

August River

Pak Tu-jin Translated by Peter H. Lee

The August river claps its hands,
The August river writhes,[1]
The August river agonizes,
The river hides its brilliance.

5 The river remembers yesterday's sighs, tears,
    spilling of blood, and deaths,
Remembers the forked tongues and bloodied
    teeth of snakes and wolves
That harbor[2] the <u>wrath</u>, supplications,[3]
    and <u>betrayals</u> of yesterday.

Remembers the remote idea of the Milky Way,[4] the
    brilliant solar system
And its golden sublimation.[5]

10 For the sake of victory, attainment, fulfillment for all
It commits yesterday to today, today to tomorrow.

The river, the river of August is long and bright.
Full of spirit, slapping its hands, flying its flags,
It moves on, on to the vast sea.

---

1. **writhes** (rīth̠z) v.: Contorts itself in agony.
2. **harbor** (här´ bər) v.: Shelter; conceal.
3. **supplications** (sup´ lə kā´ shənz) n.: Humble requests; prayers.
4. **the Milky Way:** The spiral galaxy in which our sun is found.
5. **sublimation** (sub´ lə mā´ shən) n.: Purification; refinement.

◆ **Build Vocabulary**

wrath (rath) n.: Intense anger, rage

betrayals (bə trā´ yəlz) n.: Acts that help an enemy or break
faith with people

Mountain Landscape in Moonlight, Kim Ki-Chang, Brooklyn Museum of Art

▲ **Critical Viewing** In what way does the mood of
this painting correspond to the mood of "August
River"? **[Connect]**

Guide for Responding

◆ Literature and Your Life

Reader's Response Do you feel that life flows like a river "Full of spirit, slapping its hands, flying its flags" ("August River," l. 13)?

Thematic Focus Which of the images from nature in these poems did you find most memorable? Why?

Reader's Journal In your journal, write words and images from the poems that appeal to each of the five senses.

Questions for Research "August River" refers to a past full of "betrayals." Write one or more questions for research to learn more about the history behind this reference.

☑ Check Your Comprehension

1. Name three concrete items to which the speaker compares mushrooms in "Mushrooms."
2. In "Mushrooms," what reasons does the speaker give for hunting mushrooms?
3. To what does the speaker compare mushrooms in the final line of "Mushrooms"?
4. In "Cucumber," where are the people gathered and what are they doing?
5. What effect does the cucumber have on the people in the room?
6. Name three things to which the speaker compares the cucumber.
7. In "A Pace Like That," what does the speaker remember doing a year ago?
8. What will a slower pace enable the speaker to appreciate?
9. In "A Pace Like That," what does the speaker say happens more, the more you live?
10. Name three things the river does at the opening of "August River."
11. What images from yesterday does the river remember?
12. For the sake of what does the river commit "yesterday to today, today to tomorrow"?
13. Where is the river going in "August River"?

◆ Critical Thinking

INTERPRET

1. Each image in Section iii of "Mushrooms" shows mushrooms to be "halfway" between two qualities or things. Explain, using examples. **[Support]**
2. Explain how in Section iv of "Mushrooms" the speaker links images of life and of death. **[Analyze]**
3. What view of life does the poet suggest in ll. 43–46 of "Mushrooms"? **[Draw Conclusions]**
4. In ll. 8–9 of "Cucumber," how does the speaker suggest the power of the cucumber? **[Analyze]**
5. Why might the speaker in "Cucumber" call the cucumber "hope" in l. 15? **[Interpret]**
6. In ll. 15–19 of "Cucumber," the speaker repeats the phrase "on the table." Explain how this repetition, combined with the figures of speech, creates a sense of wonder. **[Support]**
7. In "A Pace Like That," why might the speaker want a slower pace for his life? **[Infer]**
8. What connection is there between the pace at which one reads a graveyard inscription and the respect one feels for the dead? **[Connect]**
9. Using images from "A Pace Like That," explain what, besides a slower speed, is required for the right "pace." **[Synthesize]**
10. Why does Pak Tu-jin name this river "August River"? **[Infer]**
11. What is the meaning of the following line in "August River": "It commits yesterday to today, today to tomorrow"?
12. What attitude toward life and the passage of time do the last five lines of "August River" reveal? **[Draw Conclusions]**

EVALUATE

13. In "Mushrooms," does Atwood effectively describe mushrooms? Why or why not? **[Criticize]**

APPLY

14. Keeping "August River" in mind, identify a body of water that you would use to symbolize a happy time in your life. Then, explain your choice. **[Relate]**

Guide for Responding (continued)

◆ Reading Strategy

PARAPHRASE

Paraphrasing—restating in your own words—is one way to clarify the meaning of complex or abstract sections of a poem. For instance, you might paraphrase l. 5 of "August River" as follows: "The river remembers the unhappiness and bloodshed of the past."

1. Paraphrase the second stanza of "August River."
2. (a) Choose words that describe the speed of each event or activity in the first two stanzas of "A Pace Like That." (b) Use these words to paraphrase what Amichai says about the kind of pace he wants to achieve.
3. "Mushrooms" is divided into four sections. Paraphrase one of those sections.
4. (a) Identify three words Hikmet uses to describe the people in the kitchen, and give a synonym for each. (b) Paraphrase the events of the poem using the synonyms you have chosen.

◆ Build Vocabulary

USING THE LATIN ROOT -trad-

Betrayal and related words come from a Latin word, *tradere*, which means "to hand over." Use this information and your knowledge of prefixes and suffixes to complete the following sentences. Choose from these words:

traditional   traitorous   treason

1. Benedict Arnold performed ____?____ acts.
2. He has his own ideas, and rejects ____?____ ways of doing things.
3. The act of ____?____ is a capital offense.

USING THE WORD BANK: Analogies

Note the relationship between the first pair of words in each numbered item. In your notebook, fill in the blanks with Word Bank words to form a second pair of words with a similar relationship.

1. *Remember* is to *recall* as ____?____ is to *anger*.
2. *Property* is to *thefts* as *truth* is to ____?____ .
3. *Bathtub* is to *water* as *fireplace* is to ____?____ .

◆ Literary Focus

FIGURATIVE LANGUAGE

Figurative language is speech or writing that plays with, or departs from, ordinary speech. Specific types of figurative language are called *figures of speech*. Common figures of speech are **similes** (comparisons of dissimilar things using *like* or *as*), **metaphors** (comparisons of dissimilar things made by referring to one thing as if it were another), and **personifications** (the attribution of human traits to a nonhuman thing). Writers use figurative language to create vivid word pictures, to concentrate meaning and feeling, and to offer new insights into things.

1. Using examples, explain which of the four poems uses the most vivid personification.
2. (a) What simile does Amichai use in "A Pace Like That" to describe the irrelevance of people's comments on his actions? (b) Explain how this comparison makes his meaning clear.
3. Identify two metaphors in "Mushrooms." Explain what qualities of a mushroom each captures.
4. Compare a metaphor from the beginning of "Mushrooms" to one in the fourth section. Explain how the idea of a mushroom deepens in significance from the beginning to the end.
5. (a) What does the cucumber embody in "The Cucumber"? (b) What does the poet imply about the truth of metaphors in lines such as "on the table, beautiful days" (l. 15)?

◆ Build Grammar Skills

ELLIPTICAL CLAUSES

In an **elliptical clause**, words that are understood or implied are omitted.

Practice Copy the following sentences in your notebook. Underline the elliptical clause in each; then, list the omitted word or words.

1. Have you seen the river he described?
2. I don't understand the way you decipher the inscription.
3. The poem she wrote is about mushrooms.
4. The cucumber you gave me is very beautiful.

Build Your Portfolio

Idea Bank

Writing

1. **A Slower Pace** Imagine that you could slow down your pace. Write a schedule of your ideal slow day, and explain why it is ideal.

2. **Description** Write a descriptive paragraph using figurative language about a vegetable or fruit you find exceptionally beautiful or interesting.

3. **Metaphor Poem** Pak Tu-jin uses the metaphor of a river to make a political statement. Write a brief poem in which you use one central metaphor to make a comment on a political or social situation.

Speaking, Listening, and Viewing

4. **Interview** With a classmate, prepare and act out an interview with the speaker in "A Pace Like That." **[Performing Arts Link]**

5. **Dialogue** Perform a dialogue that the speakers in "A Pace Like That" and "The Cucumber" might have while stuck in a blizzard on their way to an important meeting. **[Performing Arts Link]**

Researching and Representing

6. **Mushrooms** Do some research on mushrooms. Find out about the main varieties, their structures, their means of acquiring nutrients and of reproducing, and their uses to humans. Present your findings to the class using illustrations and diagrams. **[Science Link]**

7. **Multimedia Presentation** *Cooperative Learning* Present a report on the history and literature of Korea, Israel, Canada, or Turkey. Divide the following tasks: researching the nation's history; researching the nation's literature; and acquiring audiovisual material, such as maps, charts, and music, for the report. **[Social Studies Link; Art Link]**

Online Activity www.phlit.phschool.com

Guided Writing Lesson

Character Creation

In "August River," Pak Tu-jin brings the river to life with personification. Use techniques similar to Pak Tu-jin's to create a character from an object (such as a computer), a plant (such as a tree outside your window), or a weather condition (such as rain). Write a description of how this character acts and sounds, giving the subject of your description human qualities.

Writing Focus: Consistent Focus

In describing your character, be sure to keep a **consistent focus**. For instance, if you begin by characterizing an object as an energetic three-year-old child, use comparisons that suggest this image throughout your description. To help keep your focus, draw a two-column chart. As you prewrite, list various aspects of the object you are describing (its size, its color, typical actions and events, and so on) in one column. List matching characteristics for the person to whom you are comparing the object in the second column.

Prewriting Create a chart like the one described above. Begin by listing the qualities of the object you are describing. Ask yourself questions about how it acts, moves, looks, and sounds. Based on these details, determine the type of person your subject is.

Drafting Organize your description around a specific moment. You might describe a moment when a tree is scratching on your window, or your computer is "waking up." As you draft, elaborate on your chosen focus with vivid descriptive details.

Revising Ask a classmate to read your description and tell you the general impression he or she gets from it. Together, look for any details that do not contribute to the general impression or central focus. Revise to create a more unified picture of your subject.

PART 2 *Structure*

Helicon Desk, Cathleen Toelke

$\mathcal{G}$uide for Reading

Origin of the Epic

According to some, French literature begins with the *Song of Roland (Chanson de Roland)*. This historical poem about a medieval knight is by far the best known and most studied of all medieval epic poems. Despite its popularity, scholars are hard pressed to say just when the *Song of Roland* was written or who its author was. The manuscript on view at Oxford University, England, dates from the decades after A.D. 1100 and is written in the Norman dialect of Old French.

An Early Version Scholars do agree, however, that the original poem must be dated much earlier, because the story of Roland seems to have become part of the tradition of French ballads by the ninth century. At the battle of Hastings, in 1066, a minstrel named Taillefer is said to have sung an early version of the story.

An Unknown Author *The Song of Roland*'s author remains as much a mystery as the date when it was written. The poem concludes with these lines in Old French: *Ci falt la geste que Turoldus declinet* ("Thus concludes the deeds of which Turold ___"). Just what *did* Turold do? The last word is left untranslated because scholars are not certain what *declinet* means in this context. It could mean "translate" or "compose" or "recite." These three tasks, however, are very different, and Turold's relationship to the *Song of Roland* clearly depends on how you translate this word.

Numerous Authors It is interesting to note that authorship in the Middle Ages was either undetermined or unimportant. Most stories and ballads sprang from the oral tradition: They were passed down through generations by word of mouth. In fact, you could say that each singer of the *Song of Roland* helped to contribute to its authorship.

◆ Build Vocabulary

WORD GROUPS: WORDS LINKED WITH FEUDALISM

Feudalism was a medieval system of rule in which powerful lords divided large land-holdings among lesser lords. The feudal system had its own vocabulary of specialized terms. One such word, which you will encounter in the *Song of Roland,* is *fief.* A *fief* is "land that is given by a lord to a *vassal,* or tenant, in return for services, such as military duty." The land would be worked by *serfs,* servants who could not leave the land and who could be sold along with the land.

redeeming
blustering
girds
brocaded
brandished
fief
palfrey

WORD BANK
Preview this list of words before you read.

◆ Build Grammar Skills

PARALLELISM

Parallelism is the use of similar grammatical forms to express similar ideas. The use of parallelism helps writers to emphasize certain points or to make certain ideas more memorable. The following lines from the *Song of Roland* contain parallel structure.

> The Emperor *held his head,* bowed down with this, and *stroked his beard,* and *smoothed his mustache* down.

The three actions that the Emperor performs are described using parallel structure. Each consists of a verb and an object (in two cases, an additional modifying phrase or word follows the verb and object).

from the Song of Roland

◆ *Literature and Your Life*

CONNECT YOUR EXPERIENCE

Suppose you were an avid fan of a local baseball team, but your best friend strongly supported another team. Would you have a friendly rivalry, or would you have to find another way to work out your differences?

In the *Song of Roland*, the epic's hero and his stepfather have clashing loyalties that lead to treachery and war.

THEMATIC FOCUS: FATEFUL MOMENTS

The conflict between two nations in the *Song of Roland* divides friends and families. As you read, look for decisions the characters make that prove fateful.

Journal Writing Identify a fateful moment from sports, literature, movies, or real life. Explain the ways in which the moment was an important one.

◆ Background for Understanding

HISTORY

The *Song of Roland* is based on the following historical facts, although it takes liberties with these facts.

Charlemagne, or Charles the Great, was king of the Franks from 768–814 and emperor of the Holy Roman Empire from 800–814. In 778, Charlemagne intervened in a dispute in Spain between two rival Moorish rulers. The Moors were Muslims from northwest Africa who invaded Spain in the eighth century. Charlemagne's troops had to return to France because of a Saxon uprising, and his rear guard, captained by his nephew Roland, was attacked and decimated by a band of Basques while crossing the Pyrenees.

◆ Literary Focus

THE ORAL TRADITION

The structure of the Song of Roland reveals that it springs from the **oral tradition**—it was passed down through the ages by word of mouth before it was written. The stanzas are of unequal length, allowing the storyteller to pause and improvise. Unlike most medieval poetry, this poem does not rhyme. Instead, the poet makes use of **assonance,** the same or similar vowel sounds in stressed syllables that end in different consonants: Charles the King, our Emperor, the Great / has been in Spain for seven full years, . . .

The poet also uses **epithets,** repeated descriptive phrases for the characters to help listeners identify them.

◆ Reading Strategy

RESPOND

When you read poetry, think about what it means and **respond** to it. You may, for example, respond to its imagery, its speaker, its message, or its structure. There are no right and wrong responses to poetry, as long as your responses are thoughtful reactions to your reading.

For example, when you read Roland's words "Every man knows that threats don't worry me," you might respond by admiring Roland or by thinking he is foolish. Either response is acceptable, because it stems from your own ideas or experiences. Keep track of your responses by filling in a two-column chart like this one:

Event	Your Response

▲ **Critical Viewing** Do you think
this portrayal of medieval warfare
is realistic? Why or why not?
[Make a Judgment]

from the

Song of Roland

Translated by Frederick Goldin

1

Charles the King, our Emperor, the Great,
has been in Spain for seven full years,
has conquered the high land down to the sea.
There is no castle that stands against him now,
5 no wall, no citadel left to break down—
except Saragossa, high on a mountain.
King Marsilion holds it, who does not love God,
who serves Mahumet and prays to Apollin.[1]
He cannot save himself: his ruin will find him there. AOI.[2]

13

10 "Barons, my lords," said Charles the Emperor,
"King Marsilion has sent me messengers,
wants to give me a great mass of his wealth,
bears and lions and hunting dogs on chains,
seven hundred camels, a thousand molting[3] hawks,
15 four hundred mules packed with gold of Araby,
and with all that, more than fifty great carts;
but also asks that I go back to France:
he'll follow me to Aix,[4] my residence,
and take our faith, the one <u>redeeming</u> faith,
20 become a Christian, hold his march lands[5] from me.
But what lies in his heart? I do not know."
And the French say: "We must be on our guard!" AOI.

14

The Emperor has told them what was proposed.
Roland the Count will never assent to that,
25 gets to his feet, comes forth to speak against it;
says to the King: "Trust Marsilion—and suffer!
We came to Spain seven long years ago,
I won Noples for you, I won Commibles,
I took Valterne and all the land of Pine,
30 and Balaguer and Tudela and Seville.
And then this king, Marsilion, played the traitor:
he sent you men, fifteen of his pagans—
and sure enough, each held an olive branch;
and they recited just these same words to you.
35 You took counsel with all your men of France;
they counseled you to a bit of madness:
you sent two Counts across to the Pagans,
one was Basan, the other was Basile.
On the hills below Haltille, he took their heads.
40 They were your men. Fight the war you came to fight!
Lead the army you summoned on to Saragossa!
Lay siege to it all the rest of your life!
Avenge the men that this criminal murdered!" AOI.

1. **Mahumet . . . Apollin:** The prophet Mohammed (A.D. 570–632), the founder of Islam, and a god whose name, Apollin, derives from the Greek god Apollo. The point is that, from the perspective of the author, Marsilion does not follow the true Christian faith. He and his men are referred to as pagans or Saracens.
2. **AOI:** These three mysterious letters appear at certain moments throughout the text, 180 times in all. No one has ever adequately explained them, though every reader feels their effect.

3. **molting:** Shedding their feathers.

4. **Aix** (eks): A city in southeastern France.
5. **march lands:** A frontier province or territory.

◆ **Build Vocabulary**
redeeming (ri dēm′ iŋ) *adj.*: Recovering; paying back

from the *Song of Roland* ◆ 949

15

45 The Emperor held his head bowed down with this,
and stroked his beard, and smoothed his mustache down,
and speaks no word, good or bad, to his nephew.
The French keep still, all except Ganelon:
he gets to his feet and comes before King Charles,
how fierce he is as he begins his speech;
50 said to the King: "Believe a fool—me or
another—and suffer! Protect your interest!
When Marsilion the King sends you his word,
that he will join his hands and be your man,[6]
and hold all Spain as a gift from your hands
55 and then receive the faith that we uphold—
whoever urges that we refuse this peace,
that man does not care, Lord, what death we die.
That wild man's counsel must not win the day here—
let us leave fools, let us hold with wise men!" AOI.

20

60 "My noble knights," said the Emperor Charles,
choose me one man: a baron from my march,[7]
to bring my message to King Marsilion."
And Roland said: "Ganelon, my stepfather."
The French respond: "Why, that's the very man!
65 Pass this man by and you won't send a wiser."
And hearing this Count Ganelon began to choke,
pulls from his neck the great furs of marten
and stands there now, in his silken tunic,
eyes full of lights, the look on him of fury,
70 he has the body, the great chest of a lord;
stood there so fair, all his peers gazed on him;
said to Roland: "Madman, what makes you rave?
Every man knows I am your stepfather,
yet you named me to go to Marsilion.
75 Now if God grants that I come back from there,
you will have trouble: I'll start a feud with you,
it will go on till the end of your life."
Roland replies: "What wild words—all that blustering!
Every man knows that threats don't worry me.
80 But we need a wise man to bring the message:
if the King wills, I'll gladly go in your place."

21

Ganelon answers: "You will not go for me. AOI.
You're not my man, and I am not your lord.
Charles commands me to perform this service:
85 I'll go to Marsilion in Saragossa.

6. he will join his hands . . . man: Part of the gesture by which a vassal swore allegiance to a lord; the lord enclosed the joined hands of his vassal with his own hands.

7. a baron . . . march: Charlemagne wants them to choose a baron from an outlying region and not one of the Twelve Peers, the circle of his dearest men.

◆ **Build Vocabulary**

blustering (blus´ tər in) *n.*: Noisy bullying

girds (gurdz) *v.*: Fastens on with a belt

And I tell you, I'll play a few wild tricks
before I cool the anger in me now."
When he heard that, Roland began to laugh. AOI.

27

Count Ganelon goes away to his camp.
90　He chooses, with great care, his battle-gear,
picks the most precious arms that he can find.
The spurs he fastened on were golden spurs;
he girds his sword, Murgleis, upon his side;
he has mounted Tachebrun, his battle horse,
95　his uncle, Guinemer, held the stirrup.
And there you would have seen brave men in tears,
his men, who say: "Baron, what bad luck for you!
All your long years in the court of the King,
always proclaimed a great and noble vassal!
100　Whoever it was doomed you to go down there—
Charlemagne himself will not protect that man.
Roland the Count should not have thought of this—
and you the living issue of a mighty line!"
And then they say: "Lord, take us there with you!"
105　Ganelon answers: "May the Lord God forbid!
It is better that I alone should die
　　　than so many good men and noble knights.
You will be going back, Lords, to sweet France:
go to my wife and greet her in my name,
and Pinabel, my dear friend and peer,
110　and Baldewin, my son, whom you all know:
give him your aid, and hold him as your lord."
And he starts down the road; he is on his way. AOI.

28

Ganelon rides to a tall olive tree,
there he has joined the pagan messengers.
115　And here is Blancandrin,[8] who slows down for him:
with what great art they speak to one another.
Said Blancandrin: "An amazing man, Charles!
conquered Apulia, conquered all of Calabria,[9]
crossed the salt sea on his way into England,
120　won its tribute, got Peter's pence[10] for Rome:
what does he want from us here in our march?"
Ganelon answers: "That is the heart in him.
There'll never be a man the like of him." AOI.

30

Said Blancandrin: "A wild man, this Roland!
125　wants to make every nation beg for his mercy
and claims a right to every land on earth!

8. **Blancandrin:** An envoy from King Marsilion.
9. **Apulia** (ə pyo͞ol′ yə) . . . **Calabria** (kə lā′ brē ə): Regions in southeastern Italy.
10. **Peter's pence:** A tribute of one penny per house "for the use of Saint Peter," that is, for the Pope in Rome.

But what men support him, if that is his aim?"
Ganelon answers: "Why, Lord, the men of France.
They love him so, they will never fail him.
130 He gives them gifts, masses of gold and silver,
mules, battle horses, <u>brocaded</u> silks, supplies.
And it is all as the Emperor desires:
he'll win the lands from here to the Orient." AOI.

31

Ganelon and Blancandrin rode on until
135 each pledged his faith to the other and swore
they'd find a way to have Count Roland killed.
They rode along the paths and ways until,
in Saragossa, they dismount beneath a yew.
There was a throne in the shade of a pine,
140 covered with silk from Alexandria.
There sat the king who held the land of Spain,
and around him twenty thousand Saracens.
There is no man who speaks or breathes a word,
poised for the news that all would like to hear.
145 Now here they are: Ganelon and Blancandrin.

36

Now Ganelon drew closer to the King
and said to him: "You are wrong to get angry,
for Charles, who rules all France, sends you this word:
you are to take the Christian people's faith;
150 he will give you one half of Spain in fief,[11]
the other half goes to his nephew: Roland—
quite a partner you will be getting there!
If you refuse, if you reject this peace,
he will come and lay siege to Saragossa;
155 you will he taken by force, put into chains,
and brought straight on to Aix, the capital.
No saddle horse, no war horse for you then,
no he-mule, no she-mule for you to ride:
you will be thrown on some miserable dray;
160 you will be tried, and you will lose your head.
Our Emperor sends you this letter."
He put the letter in the pagan's right fist.

11. in fief (fēf): Held from a lord in return for service.

37

Marsilion turned white; he was enraged;
he breaks the seal he's knocked away the wax
165 runs through the letter sees what is written there:
"Charles sends me word, this king who rules in France:
I'm to think of his anger and his grief—
he means Basan and his brother Basile,
I took their heads in the hills below Haltille;

◆ Build Vocabulary

brocaded (brō kād' id) *adj.*: Adorned with a rich fabric, usually of gold or silver

brandished (bran' disht) *v.*: Waved; flourished

952 ◆ *Poetry in World Literature*

Death of Roland (detail), Vincent de Beauvais, Musée Condé, Chantilly, France

170   if I want to redeem the life of my body,
         I must send him my uncle: the Algalife.[12]
         And otherwise he'll have no love for me."
         Then his son came and spoke to Marsilion,
         said to the King: "Ganelon has spoken madness.
175   He crossed the line he has no right to live.
         Give him to me, I will do justice on him."
         When he heard that, Ganelon <u>brandished</u> his sword;
         he runs to the pine, set his back against the trunk.

▲ **Critical Viewing** This picture shows the death of Roland. What does it reveal about medieval warfare? **[Infer]**

12. **Algalife:** Caliph, an Islamic leader.

38

     King Marsilion went forth into the orchard,
180   he takes with him the greatest of his men:
     Blancandrin came, that gray-haired counselor,
     and Jurfaleu, Marsilion's son and heir,
     the Algalife, uncle and faithful friend.
     Said Blancandrin: "Lord, call the Frenchman back.
185   He swore to me to keep faith with our cause."
     And the King said: "Go, bring him back here, then."
     He took Ganelon's right hand by the fingers,
     leads him into the orchard before the King.
     And there they plotted that criminal treason. AOI.

39

190   Said Marsilion: "My dear Lord Ganelon,
     that was foolish, what I just did to you,
     I showed my anger, even tried to strike you.
     Here's a pledge of good faith, these sable furs,
     the gold alone worth over five hundred pounds:
195   I'll make it all up before tomorrow night."
     Ganelon answers: "I will not refuse it.
     May it please God to reward you for it." AOI.

42

     Said the pagan: "Truly, how I must marvel
     at Charlemagne who is so gray and white—
200   over two hundred years, from what I hear;
     gone through so many lands a conqueror,
     and borne so many blows from strong sharp spears,
     killed and conquered so many mighty kings:
     when will he lose the heart for making war?"
205   "Never," said Ganelon, "while one man lives: Roland!
     no man like him from here to the Orient!
     There's his companion, Oliver, a brave man.
     And the Twelve Peers, whom Charles holds very dear,
     form the vanguard, with twenty thousand Franks.
210   Charles is secure he fears no man alive." AOI.

44

     "Dear Lord Ganelon," said Marsilion the King,
     "What must I do to kill Roland the Count?"
     Ganelon answers: "Now I can tell you that.
     The King will be at Cize,[13] in the great passes,
215   he will have placed his rear-guard at his back:
     there'll be his nephew, Count Roland, that great man,
     and Oliver, in whom he puts such faith,
     and twenty thousand Franks in their company.
     Now send one hundred thousand of your pagans
220   against the French—let them give the first battle.

13. Cize: A pass through the Pyrenees mountains.

The French army will be hit hard and shaken.
I must tell you: your men will be martyred.
Give them a second battle, then, like the first.
One will get him, Roland will not escape.
225   Then you'll have done a deed, a noble deed,
and no more war for the rest of your life!" AOI.

52

Marsilion took Ganelon by the shoulder
and said to him: "You're a brave man, a wise man.
Now by that faith you think will save your soul,
230   take care you do not turn your heart from us.
I will give you a great mass of my wealth,
ten mules weighed down with fine Arabian gold;
and come each year, I'll do the same again.
Now you take these, the keys to this vast city:
235   present King Charles with all of its great treasure;
then get me Roland picked for the rear-guard.
Let me find him in some defile or pass,
I will fight him, a battle to the death."
Ganelon answers: "It's high time that I go."
240   Now he is mounted, and he is on his way. AOI.

54

The Emperor rose early in the morning,
the King of France, and has heard mass and matins.[14]
On the green grass he stood before his tent.
Roland was there, and Oliver, brave man,
245   Naimon the Duke, and many other knights.
Ganelon came, the traitor, the foresworn.
With what great cunning he commences his speech;
said to the King: "May the Lord God save you!
Here I bring you the keys to Saragossa.
250   And I bring you great treasure from that city,
and twenty hostages, have them well guarded,
And good King Marsilion sends you this word:
Do not blame him concerning the Algalife:
I saw it all myself, with my own eyes:
      four hundred thousand men, and all in arms,
255   their hauberks on, some with their helms[15] laced on.
swords on their belts, the hilts enameled gold.
who went with him to the edge of the sea.
They are in flight: it is the Christian faith—
they do not want it, they will not keep its law.
260   They had not sailed four full leagues[16] out to sea
when a high wind, a tempest swept them up.
They were all drowned; you will never see them;
if he were still alive, I'd have brought him.
As for the pagan King, Lord, believe this:

14. matins (mat'ins): Morning prayers.

15. hauberks (hô' bərks) . . . **helms:** Chain mail armor and helmets, respectively.

16. four full leagues: About twelve miles.

265 before you see one month from this day pass,
he'll follow you to the Kingdom of France
and take the faith—he will take your faith, Lord,
and join his hands and become your vassal.
He will hold Spain as a _fief_ from your hand."
270 Then the King said: "May God be thanked for this.
You have done well, you will be well rewarded."
Throughout the host they sound a thousand trumpets.
The French break camp, strap their gear on their pack-horses.
They take the road to the sweet land of France. AOI.

56

275 The day goes by; now the darkness of night.
Charlemagne sleeps, the mighty Emperor.
He dreamt he was at Cize, in the great passes,
and in his fists held his great ashen lance.
Count Ganelon tore it away from him
280 and brandished it, shook it with such fury
the splinters of the shaft fly up toward heaven.
Charlemagne sleeps, his dream does not wake him.

58

The day goes by, and the bright dawn arises.
Throughout that host. . . .[17]
285 The Emperor rides forth with such fierce pride.
"Barons, my lords," said the Emperor Charles,
"look at those passes, at those narrow defiles—
pick me a man to command the rear-guard."
Ganelon answers: "Roland, here my stepson.
290 You have no baron as great and brave as Roland."
When he hears that, the King stares at him in fury;
and said to him: "You are the living devil,
a mad dog—the murderous rage in you!
And who will precede me in the vanguard?"
295 Ganelon answers. "Why, Ogier of Denmark,[18]
you have no baron who could lead it so well."

59

Roland the Count, when he heard himself named,
knew what to say, and spoke as a knight must speak:
"Lord Stepfather, I have to cherish you!
300 You have had the rear-guard assigned to me.
Charles will not lose, this great King who rules France,
I swear it now, one _palfrey_, one war horse—
while I'm alive and know what's happening—
one he-mule, one she-mule that he might ride,
Charles will not lose one sumpter,[19] not one pack horse
305 that has not first been bought and paid for with swords."
Ganelon answers: "You speak the truth, I know." AOI.

17. host . . . : The second part of the line is unintelligible in the manuscript.

18. Ogier (ō´ ji er) **of Denmark:** One of Charlemagne's best-known knights.

19. sumpter (sump´ tər): A pack animal.

King Charles the Great cannot keep from weeping.
A hundred thousand Franks feel pity for him;
and for Roland, an amazing fear.
310 Ganelon the criminal has betrayed him;
got gifts for it from the pagan king,
gold and silver, cloths of silk, gold brocade,
mules and horses and camels and lions.
315 Marsilion sends for the barons of Spain,
counts and viscounts and dukes and almaçurs,
and the emirs,[20] and the sons of great lords:
four hundred thousand assembled in three days.
In Saragossa he has them beat the drums,
they raise Mahumet upon the highest tower:
320 no pagan now who does not worship him
and adore him. Then they ride, racing each other,
search through the land, the valleys, the mountains;
and then they saw the banners of the French.
The rear-guard of the Twelve Companions
325 will not fail now, they'll give the pagans battle.

20. **almaçurs** (ál mə sʉrz´) . . . **emirs** (e mirz´): Titles

◆ **Build Vocabulary**

fief (fēf) *n.*: Under feudalism, land given in return for service

palfrey (pôl´ frē) *n.*: Saddle horse

Guide for Responding

◆ Literature and Your Life

Reader's Response If you could speak to Roland as he takes command of the rear guard, what advice would you give him?

Thematic Focus What, for you, is the most fateful moment for Roland in this epic poem? Why?

Reader's Journal List the reasons you think Charlemagne should or should not have put Roland in charge of the rear guard.

Questions for Research List three questions about history that the *Song of Roland* raises in your mind. How would you find the answers to those questions?

☑ Check Your Comprehension

1. (a) What message has Marsilion sent to Charlemagne? (b) What is Charlemagne's immediate reaction to the message?
2. (a) What advice does Roland give to Charlemagne regarding the message from Marsilion? (b) What advice does Ganelon give to Charlemagne?
3. What message does Charlemagne want Ganelon to bring to Marsilion?
4. What do Marsilion and Ganelon plan together?
5. As this section ends, what is Roland hoping to do for Charlemagne?

Guide for Responding (continued)

◆ Critical Thinking

INTERPRET

1. In stanza 14, what personality traits does Roland reveal? **[Infer]**
2. Analyze Roland and Ganelon's exchange in stanzas 20 and 21. (a) Why is Ganelon so angry? (b) What does Roland's response suggest about his attitude toward Ganelon? **[Analyze]**
3. Based on what you know of Roland's character, what do you think will happen when he meets Marsilion's men in battle? **[Draw Conclusions]**

EVALUATE

4. What character traits has Roland demonstrated that might lead to problems for him? **[Assess]**

APPLY

5. Imagine telling this story from the Saracen point of view. (a) How would it be different? (b) How would it be the same? **[Modify]**

◆ Literary Focus

THE ORAL TRADITION

The structure and sound devices in the *Song of Roland* are suited to its origins as part of the **oral tradition.** For example, the use of **epithets,** descriptive phrases, for the characters would help listeners identify them.

1. (a) Identify the epithets used for Charles. (b) Explain why epithets are especially suitable for a story in which there are "good guys" and "bad guys."
2. Would the *Song of Roland* have been more effective if it had end rhymes? Why or why not?

◆ Reading Strategy

RESPOND

Your **response** to the *Song of Roland* arises from your reactions to the characters and events in the poem. For example, you may find Ganelon's actions baffling, or you may be annoyed by Roland's overconfidence. Your reactions are unique and usually stem from your experiences or knowledge of human nature.

1. What is your response to Ganelon's threat and Roland's laughter in lines 86–88 (stanza 21)?
2. (a) Do you find Marsilion's reaction to the letter from Charlemagne understandable? (b) What would you have done in Marsilion's place?

◆ Build Vocabulary

WORD GROUPS: WORDS LINKED WITH FEUDALISM

Use what you know about the feudal system to complete the following sentence. On your paper, write the word that belongs in each blank. Choose from these words: *fief, vassal, overlord, serfs.*

To reward his loyal (1) _____, the (2) _____ granted him a large (3) _____, complete with the (4) _____ who would work the land.

USING THE WORD BANK: Synonyms

On your paper, write the letter of the word or phrase closest in meaning to that of the Word Bank selection.

1. redeeming: (a) leaving (b) saving (c) hoping
2. blustering: (a) noisy talk (b) quiet nap (c) long cry
3. girds: (a) patterns (b) decorates (c) binds
4. brocaded: (a) richly adorned (b) very shabby (c) very big
5. brandished: (a) hid (b) stole (c) waved
6. fief: (a) pipe (b) land (c) thief
7. palfrey: (a) tiger (b) camel (c) horse

◆ Build Grammar Skills

PARALLELISM

Parallelism—the use of similar grammatical forms to express similar ideas—helps create emphasis and make passages more memorable.

Practice Identify the parallel structures in each of the following passages.

1. We came to Spain seven long years ago, / I won Noples for you, I won Commibles, / I took Valterne and all the land of Pine, ...
2. ... you sent two counts across to the Pagans, / one was Basan, the other was Basile.
3. "That wild man's counsel must not win the day here— / let us leave fools, let us hold with wise men!"
4. No saddle horse, no war horse for you then, / no he-mule, no she-mule, for you to ride: ...
5. Marsilion sends for the barons of Spain / counts and viscounts and dukes and almaçurs ...

Build Your Portfolio

 ## Idea Bank

Writing

1. **Character Description** Write a character description of Roland. Use evidence from the poem to help you.

2. **Newspaper Article** Write a news article about Ganelon's actions. In the article, tell *who, what, when, where,* and *why.* **[Media Link]**

3. **Comparison-and-Contrast Essay** In an essay, discuss the similarities and differences between Ganelon and Roland. Cite details from the poem to support your points.

Speaking, Listening, and Viewing

4. **Dramatic Scene** Write a dramatic scene based on an episode in this poem. Cast the scene, rehearse it, and present it for classmates. **[Media Link; Performing Arts Link]**

5. **Press Conference** In a small group, appoint one member to role-play the character of Charlemagne, who is holding a press conference. The rest of the group members should take on the role of reporters, who ask Charlemagne for information about recent developments in his military campaign. **[Media Link]**

Researching and Representing

6. **Movie-Title Poll** Develop a list of five possible titles for a movie based on the *Song of Roland.* Use the list as a class survey, and record the results in a bar graph or pie chart. **[Math Link]**

7. **Poster of Medieval Dress** Research medieval clothing and military dress. Then, create a poster illustrating what you find. Include on your poster the uniforms Roland and his men might have worn in battle. Display your poster in the classroom. **[Social Studies Link; Art Link]**

Online Activity www.phlit.phschool.com

 ## Guided Writing Lesson

Critique of Values

In the *Song of Roland,* Ganelon and Roland held different values—each had different ideas about loyalty and honesty. Write a critique of values, in which you identify the values, and then interpret them, analyze them, and evaluate or assess them. As you critique Roland's and Ganelon's values, develop them by defining them.

Writing Skills Focus: Develop by Definition

As you discuss the values held by Roland and Ganelon, be sure that you **develop them by defining them:** State what the values are, compare and contrast them, and give examples from the poem that help explain or illustrate them.

Prewriting Begin by rereading the *Song of Roland,* finding evidence of the values held by the characters. Jot down specific quotations that reveal these values. You may record this information in the form of a chart, a list, or an outline.

Drafting Write a critique of the values you have listed, using your prewriting notes as a starting point. Begin by defining the values, and then develop your critique by interpreting, analyzing, and evaluating them.

Revising Reread your draft, and add details where necessary, to support your ideas. Delete details that stray from your topic. Also check to be sure your critique is logical.

Review your critique, looking for places where you have not expressed similar ideas with parallel structures. Correct these examples of faulty parallelism.

For more on parallelism, see pp. 946 and 958.

Guide for Reading

Federico García Lorca *(1898–1936)*

Federico García Lorca wrote many of his poems shortly after World War I, a culturally vibrant time in his homeland of rural Andalusia, Spain. Although García Lorca didn't intend his work to be political, Nationalist forces found it offensive, and they assassinated him at the beginning of the Spanish Civil War.

Ishigaki Rin *(1920–   )*

Japanese poet Ishigaki Rin began working at age fourteen in a bank. She pursued her interest in writing, however, and began publishing stories and poems about the importance of women's roles.

Wole Soyinka *(1934–   )*

In 1986, the Nigerian writer Wole Soyinka (wō´ lā shô yiŋ´ kə) became the first black African to receive the Nobel Prize in Literature. A total commitment both to African culture and to human rights lies behind all of Soyinka's work.

Tu Fu *(712–770)*

Chinese poet Tu Fu was little known during his lifetime. Today, however, he is regarded as a supreme craftsman. His poems celebrate nature, condemn the senselessness of war, and, as in "Jade Flower Palace," lament the passage of time.

Li Po *(701–762)*

A major Chinese classical poet of the T'ang dynasty, Li Po was a romantic who wrote about the joys of nature, love, friendship, and solitude. Although he was influenced by Taoist thought, he did not embrace the simple lifestyle this philosophy encouraged.

Rosellen Brown *(1939–   )*

In addition to being a poet, Rosellen Brown is an accomplished novelist and short-story writer. Her novel *Tender Mercies* was a national bestseller and became a major motion picture.

Wisława Szymborska *(1923–   )*

The author of a number of poetry books, Wisława Szymborska of Poland has said, "No questions are of such significance as those that are naive." Her poetry asks direct questions about the meaning of life and death. Upon granting her the 1996 Nobel Prize for Literature, the Swedish Academy called her the "Mozart of poetry."

◆ Build Vocabulary

GREEK ROOTS: *-path-*

In "Jade Flower Palace," the "pathos" of the scene overcomes the poet. *Pathos* contains the Greek root *-path-*, which means "feelings" or "suffering." *Pathos* itself describes the quality in an object or situation that evokes strong feelings of sorrow, compassion, or sym*path*y.

WORD BANK

Before you read, preview this list of words from the poems.

monotonously
unflagging
aggravate
pathos
wistful

◆ Build Grammar Skills

ADJECTIVAL MODIFIERS

Several types of structures act as adjectives. Among the structures that may be **adjectival modifiers** are prepositional phrases, participial phrases, and adjectival clauses.

Prepositional Phrase

Now begins the cry / *Of the guitar*

The prepositional phrase *of the guitar* modifies *cry*.

Participial Phrase

the heat of the fire *inherited from time immemorial*—

The participial phrase *inherited from time immemorial* modifies *fire*.

Adjectival Clause

And of those tonight in the upper chambers / *Who toss and sigh and cannot rest.*

The adjectival clause *Who toss and sigh and cannot rest* modifies the noun *those*.

The Guitar ◆ The Pan, the Pot . . . ◆ Civilian and Soldier ◆ Jade Flower Palace ◆ The Moon at the Fortified Pass ◆ What Are Friends For ◆ Some Like Poetry

◆ *Literature and Your Life*

CONNECT YOUR EXPERIENCE

If you've ever reflected upon the meaning of friendship, beauty, war, or death, you already have something in common with these poets. Questioning issues such as these is often where poetry begins.

Look for important themes in these poems, and compare the poets' reflections with your own.

Journal Writing Jot down several themes that you might want to explore in a poem. Note several of your reflections on each theme.

THEMATIC FOCUS: TO THE FUTURE

The poems in this group span the time from the eighth through the twentieth centuries. Because the poets' thoughts are timeless, people of future generations can read the poems and reflect on them, just as you are doing.

◆ Background for Understanding

CULTURE

The poets whose works follow are from different times and different places. All these poets, however, have sought to understand the world around them. As you read their poems, look for ways in which they reveal truths about life.

◆ Literary Focus

LYRIC POETRY

Lyric poetry is poetry expressing the observations and feelings of a single speaker. It was originally written to be accompanied by music; its musicality is one of its distinctive features.

A lyric poem may follow a traditional form, such as a sonnet, or it may be written in *free verse*—verse not written in a formal rhythmical pattern. "The Pan, the Pot, the Fire I Have Before Me," "Civilian and Soldier," and "What Are Friends For" are written in free verse.

While reading, you'll notice that a lyric poem, unlike a narrative poem, never tells a full story. Rather, it zeros in on an experience or creates and explores a single effect. Use an organizer like the one shown to explore how the details in each poem contribute to its main effect.

◆ Reading Strategy

READ IN SENTENCES

One way that poetry is different from prose is that poetry is written in lines and stanzas, while prose is written in sentences and paragraphs. Yet poetry, like prose, achieves its meaning through sentences. In poetry, a sentence may extend over several lines, or it may even end in the middle of a line.

To get the literal meaning of a poem, **read** it **according to its sentences,** not its lines. Don't stop at the end of a line unless there is a period, comma, colon, semicolon, or dash. Notice where the stops are in the following lines from Federico García Lorca's "The Guitar":

> Now begins the cry
> Of the guitar,
> Breaking down the vaults
> Of dawn.
> Now begins the cry
> Of the guitar.

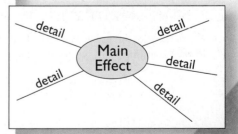

The Guitar
Federico García Lorca
Translated by Elizabeth du Gué Trapier

The Old Guitarist, 1903, Pablo Picasso, Art Institute of Chicago

▲ **Critical Viewing** What kind of song do you think the man in this painting is playing? Explain your answer. **[Infer]**

Now begins the cry
Of the guitar,
Breaking the vaults
Of dawn.
5   Now begins the cry
Of the guitar.
Useless
To still it.
Impossible
10 To still it.
It weeps <u>monotonously</u>
As weeps the water,
As weeps the wind
Over snow.
15 Impossible
To still it.
It weeps
For distant things,
Warm southern sands
20 Desiring white camellias.[1]
It mourns the arrow without a
          target,
The evening without morning.
And the first bird dead
Upon a branch.
25 O guitar!
A wounded heart,
Wounded by five swords.

---

1. **camellias** (kə mēl´ yəz): Flowers of the camellia, a type of evergreen tree and shrub that grows mainly in the Far East.

◆ **Build Vocabulary**

monotonously (mə nät´ən əs lē) *adv.*: Going on and on without variation

CONNECTIONS TO TODAY'S WORLD

In the past thirty years, few guitarists have had as great an impact on rock music as has Carlos Santana. He electrified the audience at the historic Woodstock festival in 1969, and he continues to thrill audiences today. His recent Grammy-winning CD *Supernatural* has raised his popularity to new heights and proven that Santana is still a vital force in contemporary music.

The following is *Rolling Stone* magazine's review of his 1992 CD *Milagro*.

Review of Milagro by John Swenson

After releasing his first twenty-six recordings on CBS/Sony, Carlos Santana begins a new phase of his career with *Milagro*, one of the finest sessions he's done. The album reaffirms Santana's position as the standard-bearer for fusion music.

Santana is the most successful practitioner of fusion because he understands the style not as a souped-up rock-jazz hybrid but as an embrace of musical pantheism. Elements of salsa, pop, blues, jazz, R&B, rock, world music and reggae work their way in and out of the arrangements on *Milagro*, due in no small part to the smarts of coproducer Chester Thompson, whose virtuoso keyboard work shares the soloing spotlight with Santana's guitar.

Santana's vision of fusion grew out of the same creative upheavals responsible for the social and political ferment of the Sixties and early Seventies. The difference between Santana and other guitarists, such as Alvin Lee, who first came to prominence as a result of the Woodstock documentary, is that Santana never stopped considering his music an outgrowth of deeply held spiritual values. . . .

1. Why do you think Santana has remained popular for so long?
2. The reviewer says Santana considers his music "an outgrowth of deeply held spiritual values." Do you think the music described in Lorca's poem "The Guitar" (see p. 962) is also an outgrowth of deeply held spiritual values? Why or why not?

Guide for Responding

◆ *Literature and Your Life*

Reader's Response What single image in "The Guitar" did you find most striking? Why?

Thematic Focus Would you include this poem in a time capsule? Why?

☑ Check Your Comprehension

1. For what is the guitar weeping?
2. To what does García Lorca compare the weeping of the guitar?

◆ Critical Thinking

INTERPRET
1. What emotions does García Lorca describe the guitar as having? **[Connect]**
2. What are the "five swords" that wound the heart? **[Interpret]**
3. Why is it impossible to still the guitar's weeping? **[Synthesize]**

EVALUATE
4. Do you find the imagery in this poem effective? Why or why not? **[Criticize]**

EXTEND
5. What musical instrument seems most like a person to you? Why? **[Music Link]**

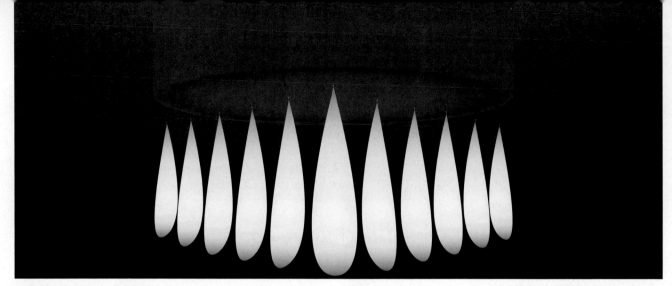

THE PAN, THE POT, THE FIRE
I HAVE BEFORE ME

Ishigaki Rin Translated by Hiroaki Sato

For a long time
these things have always been placed
before us women:
the pan of a reasonable size
5 suited to the user's strength,
the pot in which it's convenient for rice
to begin to swell and shine, grain by grain,
the heat of the fire inherited from time
    immemorial—
before these there have always been
10 mothers, grandmothers, and their mothers.

What measures of love and sincerity
these persons must have poured
into these utensils—
now red carrots,
15 now black seaweed,
now crushed fish

in the kitchen, always accurately
for morning, noon, and evening,
    preparations have been made
and before the preparations, in a row, there
    have always been
20 some pairs of warm knees and hands.

Ah without those persons waiting
how could women have gone on

cooking so happily?
their unflagging care,
25 so daily a service they became unconscious
    of it.
Cooking was mysteriously assigned
to women, as a role,
but I don't think that was unfortunate;
because of that, their knowledge and
    positions in society
30 may have lagged behind the times
but it isn't too late:
the things we have before us,

the pan and the pot, and the burning fire,
before these familiar things,
35 let us study government, economy,
    literature
as sincerely
as we cook potatoes and meat.

not for vanity and promotion
but so everyone
40 may serve all
so everyone may work for love.

◆ **Build Vocabulary**

unflagging (un flag´ iŋ) *adj.*: Without losing strength

aggravate (ag´ rə vāt´) *v.*: To make worse

Civilian and Soldier

Wole Soyinka

My apparition[1] rose from the fall of lead,
Declared, "I'm a civilian." It only served
To <u>aggravate</u> your fright. For how could I
Have risen, a being of this world, in that hour
5 Of impartial death! And I thought also: nor is
Your quarrel of this world.

                    You stood still
For both eternities, and oh I heard the lesson
Of your training sessions, cautioning—
Scorch earth behind you, do not leave
10 A dubious[2] neutral to the rear. Reiteration
Of my civilian quandary,[3] burrowing earth
From the lead festival of your more eager friends
Worked the worse on your confusion, and when
You brought the gun to bear on me, and death
15 Twitched me gently in the eye, your plight
And all of you came clear to me.

                    I hope some day
Intent upon my trade of living, to be checked
In stride by *your* apparition in a trench,
Signaling, I am a soldier. No hesitation then
20 But I shall shoot you clean and fair
With meat and bread, a gourd of wine
A bunch of breasts from either arm, and that
Lone question—do you friend, even now, know
What it is all about?

---

1. **apparition** (ap´ ə rish´ ən) *n.*: A strange, suddenly appearing figure, thought to be a ghost.
2. **dubious** (do͞o´ bē əs) *adj.*: Causing suspicion.
3. **quandary** (kwän´ də rē) *n.*: Dilemma.

Guide for Responding

◆ Literature and Your Life

Reader's Response With which poem's speaker do you identify more? Why?
Thematic Focus Explain the ways in which both poems deal with the future.

☑ Check Your Comprehension

1. In "The Pan, the Pot, the Fire I Have Before Me," what role does the speaker say was "mysteriously assigned to women"?
2. In "Civilian and Soldier," what happens to the poem's speaker in the opening line of the poem?
3. What does the civilian in Soyinka's poem say he would do if he met the soldier?

◆ Critical Thinking

INTERPRET
1. How does the speaker in "The Pan, the Pot, the Fire I Have Before Me" regard the role of cooking? Explain. **[Infer]**
2. How does the speaker envision women's roles in the future? **[Analyze]**
3. Why does the speaker's declaration of being a civilian increase the soldier's fright in "Civilian and Soldier"? **[Infer]**
4. The civilian thinks of the soldier's quarrel as "not being of this world."
   (a) With what is the soldier's quarrel?
   (b) Why is it not of this world? **[Analyze]**
5. Why would the speaker ask the soldier if he "knows what it is all about"? **[Interpret]**

APPLY
6. What does "Civilian and Soldier" have to say about the judgments many people make about strangers? **[Apply]**

EXTEND
7. Which terms in "Civilian and Soldier" are military jargon? How do you know? **[Social Studies Link]**

Jade Flower Palace

Tu Fu

Translated by
Kenneth Rexroth

The stream swirls. The wind moans in
The pines. Gray rats scurry over
Broken tiles. What prince, long ago,
Built this palace, standing in
5   Ruins beside the cliffs? There are
Green ghost fires in the black rooms.
The shattered pavements are all
Washed away. Ten thousand organ
Pipes whistle and roar. The storm
10 Scatters the red autumn leaves.
His dancing girls are yellow dust.
Their painted cheeks have crumbled
Away. His gold chariots
And courtiers are gone. Only

15 A stone horse is left of his
Glory. I sit on the grass and
Start a poem, but the <u>pathos</u> of
It overcomes me. The future
Slips imperceptibly away.
20 Who can say what the years will bring?

◆ Build Vocabulary

pathos (pā´ thäs) *n.*: Quality in something
experienced or observed that arouses feelings
of pity, sorrow, sympathy, or compassion

wistful (wist´ fəl) *adj.*: Expressing longing

The Moon
at the Fortified Pass

Li Po
Translated by
Lin Yutang

The bright moon lifts from the Mountain of Heaven
In an infinite haze of cloud and sea,
And the wind, that has come a thousand miles,
Beats at the Jade Pass[1] battlements. . . .
5   China marches its men down Po-teng Road
While Tartar[2] troops peer across blue waters of the
        bay. . . .
And since not one battle famous in history
Sent all its fighters back again,
The soldiers turn round, looking toward the border,
10 And think of home, with <u>wistful</u> eyes,
And of those tonight in the upper chambers
Who toss and sigh and cannot rest.

---

1. **Jade Pass:** Gap in the Great Wall in northeastern China.
2. **Tartar** (tär´ tər): Tartars were nomadic tribes who originally
lived in Mongolia, Manchuria, and Siberia. From A.D. 200
through 400, the Tartars were almost constantly at war with
the Chinese. A thousand years later, under the leadership
of Genghis Khan, the Tartars conquered China as well as a
number of European and Asian countries.

◄ **Critical Viewing** Imagine this picture as a setting
for "The Moon at the Fortified Pass." What might
make the soldiers "wistful"? **[Analyze]**

from Cora Fry

What Are Friends For

Rosellen Brown

Best Friends, Craig Nelson/Bernstein & Andriulli, Inc.

What are friends for, my mother asks.
A duty undone, visit missed,
casserole unbaked for sick Jane.
Someone has just made her bitter.

5   Nothing. They are for nothing, friends,
I think. All they do in the end—
they *touch* you. They fill you like music.

▲ **Critical Viewing** What qualities of friendship has the artist captured? **[Analyze]**

Some Like Poetry

Wisława Szymborska
Translated by Joanna Trzeciak

Some—
that means not all.
Not even the majority of all but the minority.
Not counting school, where one must,
5   and poets themselves,
there will be perhaps two in a thousand.

Like—
but one also likes chicken-noodle soup,
one likes compliments and the color blue,
10   one likes an old scarf,
one likes to prove one's point,
one likes to pet a dog.

Poetry—
but what sort of thing is poetry?
15   More than one shaky answer
has been given to this question.
But I do not know and do not know and clutch on to it,
as to a saving bannister.

Guide for Responding

◆ Literature and Your Life

Reader's Response With which speaker would you most like to have a conversation? Why?

Thematic Focus What do these poems draw from the past?

☑ Check Your Comprehension

1. Where does the speaker of "Jade Flower Palace" sit, and what does he do?
2. Identify the event on which Li Po focuses in "The Moon at the Fortified Pass."
3. What answer is given by the speaker to the title question "What Are Friends For"?
4. Identify two examples in "Some Like Poetry" of different meanings of the word *like*.

◆ Critical Thinking

INTERPRET

1. Explain the statement in "Jade Flower Palace," "The future/slips imperceptibly away." **[Draw Conclusions]**
2. In "The Moon ..." how does Li Po feel toward the soldiers going into battle? **[Interpret]**
3. In "What Are Friends For," how do the speaker's feelings contrast with her mother's? **[Contrast]**
4. What is the speaker's point in "Some Like Poetry"? **[Interpret]**

COMPARE LITERARY WORKS

5. Compare and contrast the attitudes toward soldiers and war in "Civilian and Soldier" and "The Moon ..." **[Compare and Contrast]**

Guide for Responding (continued)

◆ Reading Strategy

READ IN SENTENCES

Reading poetry in sentences, not necessarily by line, can guide you through a poem's structure and help you understand its meaning.

1. The second sentence in "The Guitar" is a repetition of part of the first sentence. Explain how the punctuation leads you to read the two sentences differently.
2. Contrast the sentences in "Jade Flower Palace" and "The Moon at the Fortified Pass," based on the use of commas and periods.
3. "Some Like Poetry" interrupts one short sentence with elaboration about each word. What is the brief sentence "hidden" in Szymborska's poem?

◆ Literary Focus

LYRIC POETRY

A **lyric poem** takes a sharp-eyed and concentrated look at a single incident or experience, and in doing so, reveals the feelings of the poem's speaker. Some of these lyric poems suggest a story beneath the surface, but they don't actually tell that story.

1. What would you say is the central emotion conveyed in "The Guitar"?
2. (a) On what single subject does "Some Like Poetry" focus? (b) What is the speaker's personal feeling about the subject?

Beyond Literature

Cultural Connection

Poetry and Politics Federico García Lorca was assassinated by Nationalist forces during the Spanish Civil War. In assassinating a poet, the Nationalists signified the power of the poet. Many governments, too, have noted this power and either sought to silence poets or to cultivate relations with them.

Activity Research the role of America's poet laureate. How does the office bring the power of the poet into service of the nation today?

◆ Build Vocabulary

USING THE GREEK ROOT -path-

The Greek root -path- means "feeling; suffering." On your paper, write the word you would most closely associate with the person or thing in each numbered item.

1. A very sad movie: (a) pathology, (b) pathos, (c) antipathy
2. A medical researcher: (a) pathos, (b) sympathy, (c) pathology
3. An enemy: (a) sympathy, (b) antipathy, (c) empathy
4. A suffering animal: (a) empathy, (b) sympathy, (c) pathos
5. A very close friend: (a) antipathy, (b) pathology, (c) empathy

Using the Word Bank: Word Choice

On your paper, write the word from the Word Bank suggested by each book title. Use each word only once.

1. *A Film Critic's Guide to the 100 Saddest Movies of All Time*
2. *Endlessly Devoted: An Enthusiast's Life Story*
3. *Memories of Eden: The Disappearance of Childhood*
4. *The Story Remains the Same, Part XIV*
5. *Making a Bad Situation Worse*

◆ Build Grammar Skills

ADJECTIVAL MODIFIERS

These poems use several different types of word groups as **adjectival modifiers** to describe or limit the meaning of nouns or pronouns.

Practice Copy each of the following items in your notebook. Underline the modifier in each, and draw a line to the word that it modifies.

1. It mourns the arrow without a target.
2. The soldiers turn round, looking toward the border.
3. And the wind, that has come a thousand miles . . .
4. . . . While Tartar troops peer across blue waters of the bay.
5. . . . Warm southern sands/Desiring white camellias.

Build Your Portfolio

 ## Idea Bank

Writing

1. Diary Entry In "Civilian and Soldier," the speaker reveals his thoughts as a civilian. In a diary entry, reveal the thoughts of the soldier.

2. Statement Poem Each section of "Some Like Poetry" elaborates on one of the three words in the poem's title. Write a simple three- or four-word statement, and create a poem around the words, using Szymborska's poem as a model.

3. Story Write a short story using the mother and speaker of "What Are Friends For" as your main characters. Create a plot, conflict, and resolution.

Speaking, Listening, and Viewing

4. Reading to Music Find and play for the class a recording of classical Spanish guitar music. Play the recording a second time, softly, as you read "The Guitar." Explain why you chose the music you did. **[Performing Arts Link]**

5. Visual Presentation What would the Jade Flower Palace have looked like? Research Chinese architecture, and collect images of palaces from Tu Fu's era to present to your class, along with a brief explanation of the subject. **[Art Link]**

Researching and Representing

6. Painting/Drawing Imagine that the speaker of "Jade Flower Palace" sits on the grass to paint rather than to write. In your favorite medium, draw or paint what the speaker sees. **[Art Link]**

7. Women in Japan Research women's lives and roles in twentieth-century Japan. Find out about their legal rights, their educational opportunities, and the career paths open to them. Share your findings in a report. **[Social Studies Link]**

Online Activity www.phlit.phschool.com

 ## Guided Writing Lesson

Lyric Poem

Think about an experience or moment in time that left a particularly strong impression on you. Watching the ocean during a storm, the first time you heard the song that became your favorite, the sight of a shooting star streaking across the night sky—the possibilities are limitless. Write a **lyric poem** in which you enable your readers to experience the moment as you did.

Writing Skills Focus: Setting and Mood

A poem's **setting,** the time and place in which the experience occurred, and its **mood,** the feeling you get while reading, are often closely related. In "Jade Flower Palace," the setting of the forsaken and decrepit palace creates a desolate mood. Focus on a setting that will create a distinct mood.

Prewriting Where did your memorable moment occur? What did the place look like, and what feelings did it give you? Before you write, use a chart like this to organize your information:

Place	Descriptive Words	Feelings I Got
Lake at night	Clear, cool, mysterious	Calm, awe, delight

Drafting Write your impressions and feelings using vivid descriptive language to capture the mood of the setting. Although you may use partial sentences or break sentences over several lines, use punctuation to indicate pauses and stops.

Revising It is useful to read a poem aloud to yourself when you are revising it. Trust your ear to pick up any awkward rhythms or clunky word choices, and then revise to correct these problems.

Add adjectival modifiers where more detail is needed to describe the setting or create a mood. For more on these modifiers, see pp. 960 and 970.

Guide for Reading

Pierre de Ronsard (1524–1585)

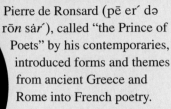

Pierre de Ronsard (pē er´ də rōn sàr´), called "the Prince of Poets" by his contemporaries, introduced forms and themes from ancient Greece and Rome into French poetry.

Ronsard was a younger son in a family of minor French nobility. From an early age he prepared for a diplomatic career and served as an attendant in the royal household. When he was a young man, however, an illness left him partly deaf and ruined his chances to become a diplomat.

Consequently, Ronsard devoted himself to poetry. In 1544, he joined a group called the *Pléiade* (plā yàd´), whose name is the Greek term for a constellation of seven stars. The literary "stars" of this group used their knowledge of ancient Greek and Roman authors to remake French poetry.

During his later years, Ronsard continually revised his poems. He prepared a seventh and final edition of his work just before his death in 1585.

Charles Baudelaire (1821–1867)

Frenchman Charles Baudelaire (shàrl´ bōd ler´) was one of the most inventive poets of his time. A Romantic in his taste for what was faraway and mysterious, he went beyond Romanticism in his accurate portrayal of the modern city. Also, he pioneered a new type of writing called *Symbolism*—viewing things in the visible world as symbols of a greater spiritual reality. He was influenced in his theories by the work of Edgar Allan Poe, much of which he translated into French.

Baudelaire was as rebellious in his life as he was in his writing. Often at odds with his stepfather (his father died when he was a boy), he was expelled from school in 1839. Living an artist's life in Paris, he often lacked money and had to flee from bill collectors. Then, in 1857, his defiant work caused a book of his to be temporarily banned by the courts. He died in 1867, the victim of a serious illness he had contracted years before.

◆ Build Vocabulary

LATIN WORD ROOTS: *-fide-*

In the poem "When You Are Old," you will encounter the word *fidelities*. This word contains the Latin word root *-fide-*, meaning "faith, trust, or confidence." You can see the influence of that root in the meaning of *fidelities*: "acts of faith or devotion."

fidelities
disdain
oppressive
languishing
luster
proffering
swells
ply

WORD BANK

As you read these poems, you will encounter the words on this list. Each word is defined on the page where it first appears. Preview the list before you read.

◆ Build Grammar Skills

SENTENCE VARIETY: SENTENCE LENGTHS

Good writers keep readers interested by **varying the lengths of their sentences.** For example, in "Invitation to the Voyage," Baudelaire's translator balances the long sentences of the elaborate stanzas with the relatively short sentence of the refrain, shown below:

> There, there is nothing else but grace and
>   measure,
> Richness, quietness, and pleasure.

Each time it appears, this brief sentence provides a satisfying sense of completion for the longer descriptive sentence that precedes it.

When You Are Old ◆ Roses
Invitation to the Voyage

◆ *Literature and Your Life*

CONNECT YOUR EXPERIENCE

In blues songs, the singer may say that a loved one will be sorry for mistreating the singer. In love ballads, the singer may invite a special someone to escape to a special place.

Like a blues song, Ronsard's "When You Are Old" is a warning to his lover. Like a romantic ballad, Baudelaire's "Invitation to the Voyage" is an offer to a loved one: Let's get away from it all.

Journal Writing Jot down the titles of some of your favorite songs that are either warnings, invitations, or both.

THEMATIC FOCUS: CHOICES AND CONSEQUENCES

As you read these poems, ask yourself: What choices are the speakers asking a loved one to make?

◆ Background for Understanding

LITERATURE

Renaissance poets like Ronsard often viewed themselves dramatically, comparing the world to a stage on which people play many different parts. Ronsard's sonnets "When You Are Old" and "Roses" serve as little stages that give him the opportunity to play the parts of rejected lover and mourner, respectively.

Baudelaire's "Invitation to the Voyage" was one of a group of poems written for a young actress named Marie Daubrun. The paradise to which he invites her combines details from an imaginary Holland with those from a faraway Dutch colony like Java. Also, his description of this ideal place contains items that seem to come from Dutch paintings—for example, "Mirrors deep as the sea."

◆ Reading Strategy

IDENTIFY THE SPEAKER IN A POEM

By **identifying the speaker** in a poem—figuring out who says the poem's words—you will better understand the dramatic situation that gives rise to the poem.

In Ronsard's "When You Are Old," the poet is speaking with his own voice—he refers to himself as "Ronsard." He is addressing a female because he says she will be a "crone," a shriveled old woman, in years to come. The words "my love" and "your proud disdain" are clues to his feelings for this woman and the message he is sending her.

Identify that message, and determine the speaker and the situation in Ronsard's "Roses" and Baudelaire's "Invitation to the Voyage."

◆ Literary Focus

POETIC FORMS: SONNET, STANZA, REFRAIN

Poets often use traditional forms to send their warnings or invitations:

- **sonnet** — a poem that is almost always fourteen lines and uses one of several rhyme schemes.
- **stanza** — a repeated grouping of two or more verse lines with a set pattern of lengths, rhythms, and (frequently) rhymes.
- **refrain** — a phrase, a line, or lines repeated regularly in a poem, often at the end of a stanza.

Ronsard's poems are sonnets, each with a slightly different rhyme scheme. However, notice how in the translations of both poems, the first eight lines work together as a unit, as do the final six lines.

The translation of Baudelaire's poem has three twelve-line stanzas, each followed by a two-line refrain. Determine whether the stanzas follow the same pattern with regard to number of lines, lengths of lines, rhythms, and rhyme.

Rembrandt's Mother Reading, Rembrandt van Rijn, Wilton House, Wiltshire, Salisbury, England

▶ **Critical Viewing**
With what emotion or emotions is this woman reading?
[Speculate]

When You Are Old

Pierre de Ronsard
Translated by Humbert Wolfe

When you are old, at evening candle-lit
beside the fire bending to your wool,
read out my verse and murmur, "Ronsard writ
this praise for me when I was beautiful."
5 And not a maid but, at the sound of it,
though nodding at the stitch on broidered stool,
will start awake, and bless love's benefit
whose long <u>fidelities</u> bring Time to school.
I shall be thin and ghost beneath the earth
10 by myrtle shade in quiet after pain,
but you, a crone, will crouch beside the hearth
mourning my love and all your proud <u>disdain</u>.
And since what comes tomorrow who can say?
Live, pluck the roses of the world today.

◆ **Build Vocabulary**
fidelities (fə del′ ə tēz′) *n.*: Faithful devotions to a loved one
disdain (dis dān′) *n.*: Scorn

Roses

Pierre de Ronsard
Translated by Vernon Watkins

As one sees on the branch in the month of May the rose
In her beautiful youth, in the dawn of her flower,
When the break of day softens her life with the shower,
Make jealous the sky of the damask[1] bloom she shows:
5 Grace lingers in her leaf and love sleeping glows
Enchanting with fragrance the trees of her bower,
But, broken by the rain or the sun's <u>oppressive</u> power,
<u>Languishing</u> she dies, and all her petals throws.
Thus in thy first youth, in thy awakening fair
10 When thy beauty was honored by lips of Earth and Air,
Atropos[2] has killed thee and dust thy form reposes.
O take, take for obsequies[3] my tears, these poor showers,
This vase filled with milk, this basket strewn with flowers,
That in death as in life thy body may be roses.

1. **damask** (dam´ əsk): Deep pink or rose.
2. **Atropos** (a´ trə päs´): In Greek and Roman mythology, the goddess who cuts the thread of life.
3. **obsequies** (äb´ si kwēz´): Funeral rites or ceremonies.

◆ **Build Vocabulary**

oppressive (ə pres´ iv) *adj.*: Hard to put up with; causing great discomfort

languishing (laŋ´ gwish iŋ) *v.*: Becoming weak; failing in vitality or health

Guide for Responding

◆ Literature and Your Life

Reader's Response How do you think the woman to whom "When You Are Old" was addressed responded to the poem? Explain.

Thematic Focus What choice made by Ronsard's beloved may have prompted him to write "When You Are Old"?

☑ Check Your Comprehension

1. Briefly describe the scene that Ronsard summons up in ll. 1–8 of "When You Are Old."
2. Paraphrase the message in ll. 13–14 of "When You Are Old."
3. What has happened to the person Ronsard addresses in "Roses"?
4. To what does he compare this person?

◆ Critical Thinking

INTERPRET

1. In "When You Are Old," what is the poet's attitude toward the changes that time brings? **[Infer]**
2. How is the poet's attitude toward time in "When You Are Old" a key to the poem's message? **[Draw Conclusions]**
3. In "Roses," what is the effect of not explaining the situation behind the poem immediately? **[Analyze]**
4. Which words and phrases in "Roses" convey the speaker's feelings about the person addressed? Explain. **[Interpret]**

EVALUATE

5. Does Ronsard convey his message persuasively in "When You Are Old"? Why or why not? **[Criticize]**

▶ Critical Viewing
On what voyage might this boat be going? [Connect]

Fishing Boats on the Beach at Saintes-Maries de la Mer, 1888, Vincent Van Gogh, Amsterdam, Van Gogh Museum (Vincent Van Gogh Foundation)

Invitation to the Voyage
Charles Baudelaire   Translated by Richard Wilbur

      My child, my sister, dream
      How sweet all things would seem
Were we in that kind land to live together
      And there love slow and long,
5   There love and die among
Those scenes that image you, that sumptuous[1] weather.
      Drowned suns that glimmer there
      Through cloud-disheveled[2] air
Move me with such a mystery as appears
10   Within those other skies
      Of your treacherous eyes
When I behold them shining through their tears.

There, there is nothing else but grace and measure,
Richness, quietness, and pleasure.

1. **sumptuous** (sump´ chŏŏ wəs) *adj.*: Magnificent or splendid.

2. **disheveled** (di shev´ 'ld) *adj.*: Disarranged and untidy.

◆ **Build Vocabulary**
luster (lus´ tər) *n.*: Shine; radiance
proffering (präf´ ər iŋ) *v.*: offering
swells (swelz) *n.*: Large waves that move steadily without breaking
ply (plī) *v.*: Sail regularly back and forth across

15   Furniture that wears
        The <u>luster</u> of the years
     Softly would glow within our glowing
        chamber,
     Flowers of rarest bloom
        <u>Proffering</u> their perfume
20   Mixed with the vague fragrances of
        amber;
        Gold ceilings would there be,
        Mirrors deep as the sea,
     The walls all in an Eastern splendor
        hung—
     Nothing but should address
25   The soul's loneliness,
     Speaking her sweet and secret native
        tongue.

     There, there is nothing else but grace
        and measure,
     Richness, quietness, and pleasure.

        See, sheltered from the <u>swells</u>
30   There in the still canals
     Those drowsy ships that dream of sail-
        ing forth;
        It is to satisfy
        Your least desire, they <u>ply</u>
     Hither through all the waters of the
        earth.
35   The sun at close of day
        Clothes the fields of hay,
     Then the canals, at last the town
        entire
        In hyacinth and gold:
        Slowly the land is rolled
40   Sleepward under a sea of gentle fire.

     There, there is nothing else but grace
        and measure,
     Richness, quietness, and pleasure.

Guide for Responding

◆ Literature and Your Life

Reader's Response Is Baudelaire's "invitation" a tempting one? Why or why not?

Reader's Journal Jot down some of the qualities that your ideal place would have.

Questions for Research If you wanted to find other translations of "Invitation to the Voyage," where might you look? Why?

☑ Check Your Comprehension

1. Using details from the poem, briefly describe the place to which Baudelaire invites his beloved in "Invitation to the Voyage."
2. What qualities of this place does Baudelaire emphasize in the two lines that follow each stanza?

◆ Critical Thinking

INTERPRET

1. (a) What overall impression does Baudelaire convey of the "kind land" he describes? (b) Which words and phrases contribute most to this impression? Explain. **[Analyze]**
2. Is Baudelaire's strategy in this poem to frighten his beloved into accepting his invitation or to soothe her into it? Explain. **[Support]**

EXTEND

3. Which details from the description in "Invitation" probably came from paintings? Why? **[Art Link]**

COMPARE LITERARY WORKS

4. Which poem, "When You Are Old" or "Invitation to the Voyage," works best as an invitation? Why? **[Compare and Contrast]**

Guide for Responding (continued)

◆ Reading Strategy

IDENTIFY THE SPEAKER IN A POEM

By **identifying the speaker** in a poem, the invented character who says the poem's words, you will better understand the meaning of those words.

The speaker in "When You Are Old" says at the poem's end: "Live, pluck the roses of the world today." Without identifying the speaker, you might assume that he is giving a general piece of advice: Enjoy yourself while you can. Knowing that the speaker has been rejected by the woman he is addressing—he refers to her "proud disdain"—you know that the last line means the following: Accept my offer now, or you'll be sorry later!

1. In "Roses," what relationship do you think the speaker had to the woman who died? Explain.
2. Find passages in "Invitation to the Voyage" that suggest the speaker's identity and his or her relationship to the person addressed in the poem.

◆ Literary Focus

POETIC FORMS: STANZA, REFRAIN, SONNET

In these poems, the poet shapes the speaker's message by using such forms as the **sonnet**, with its fourteen lines and traditional rhyme schemes; the **stanza**, a regularly repeated group of verse lines with a pattern of lengths, rhythms, and possibly rhymes; and the **refrain**, a phrase, a line, or lines repeated regularly in a poem, usually after a stanza.

The different rhyme schemes of Ronsard's sonnets suit their different messages. For example, "When You Are Old" has the following pattern of rhymes: ababababcdcdee. The rhyming of the final two lines gives his last words a memorable emphasis: "And since what comes tomorrow who can say? / Live, pluck the roses of the world today."

1. (a) Identify the rhyme scheme of "Roses." (b) Explain how the rhymes in the last four lines link the woman's death and the poet's offering.
2. (a) Identify the pattern of Baudelaire's stanzas. (b) How does the alternation of stanza and refrain convey the idea of a paradise that is both elaborately beautiful and beautifully simple?

◆ Build Vocabulary

USING THE LATIN WORD ROOT *-fide-*

Knowing that the Latin word root *-fide-* means "faith, trust, or confidence," explain the following (use a dictionary, if necessary):

1. why a bank would call itself Fidelity Trust
2. why many dogs used to be called Fido
3. why friends confide in one another
4. why the motto of the marines is *semper fidelis*

WORD BANK: Antonyms

On your paper, match each numbered word with the lettered word that is opposite in meaning.

1. fidelities   a. strengthening
2. disdain   b. dullness
3. oppressive   c. withdrawing
4. languishing   d. respect
5. luster   e. breakers
6. proferring   f. betrayals
7. swells   g. idle
8. ply   h. comfortable

◆ Build Grammar Skills

SENTENCE VARIETY: SENTENCE LENGTHS

Ronsard and Baudelaire **vary sentence lengths,** combining long sentences with brief ones, to create dramatic effects.

For example, Ronsard begins "Roses" with an elaborate eight-line sentence describing the life and death of a "rose." Then, with a briefer three-line sentence, he shifts the focus to the death of a young woman. The brevity of this sentence in itself dramatizes the cutting short of the woman's life.

Practice Explain how the following combinations of a long sentence followed by one or two brief ones add drama to these poems.

1. "When You Are Old": ll. 9–12, followed by l. 13 and l. 14
2. "Invitation to the Voyage": ll. 15–26, followed by ll. 27–28

Build Your Portfolio

Idea Bank

Writing

1. **Poetic Invitation** In the spirit of Baudelaire's "Invitation to the Voyage," write a poem for a card inviting friends to a party. Use regular stanzas.

2. **Song** Write a verse and a refrain of a song that is an invitation or a warning. Vary sentence lengths to create dramatic effects.

3. **Response to Criticism** Baudelaire's biographer Enid Starkie says "Invitation to the Voyage" reflects the poet's wish for "a settled life of calm" with Marie Daubrun. Using details from the poem, support or refute this comment.

Speaking, Listening, and Viewing

4. **Oral Interpretation** Read one of these poems aloud for classmates. First, practice conveying the speaker's personality and goals by varying your pace and stressing key words. **[Performing Arts Link]**

5. **Monologue** As one of the women addressed by these poets, perform a monologue responding to the poem's message. **[Performing Arts Link]**

Researching and Representing

6. **Art and Poetry** Use biographies of Baudelaire and art books to research the Dutch paintings that this poet would have known. Then, bring in reproductions of these paintings and show how they might have influenced his poem. **[Art Link]**

7. **Report on Humanism** Use the Internet, encyclopedias, and books on the Renaissance to research Humanism. Report on your findings to the class, showing how Ronsard was influenced by this cultural movement. **[Social Studies Link]**

Online Activity www.phlit.phschool.com

Guided Writing Lesson

Description of a Poem's Speaker

The words of these and many other poems are spoken by an imaginary character—the speaker. Choose a poem with a speaker and, using clues from the poem itself, give a full description of this invented person. (The speaker is "invented" even when he or she bears the poet's name.) Consider such details as dress, behavior, background, and way of talking.

Writing Skills Focus: Appropriate Details

Your description will be more convincing if you use **appropriate details**—details that are directly suggested by the poem or in keeping with evidence from it.

Prewriting Choose a poem. Then, use a chart like the one below to fill in appropriate details as you review the poem.

Poem: Baudelaire's "Invitation to the Voyage"

Aspects	Description	Evidence
Personality	loves rare and beautiful sights, sounds, odors	ll. 6–8, 18–20, 25–26
Behavior		
Background		

Drafting Referring to your chart, create a full description of the speaker. Devote a paragraph to each of the speaker's aspects: personality, dress, and so forth. When the poem does not provide specific details, make up appropriate details.

Revising Have several classmates who know the poem review your description. If they think that some of the details are inappropriate, consider deleting them or replacing them with appropriate details.

Vary the lengths of your sentences to avoid monotony and create dramatic effects. For more on this subject, see pp. 972 and 978.

Focus on Culture

Japan

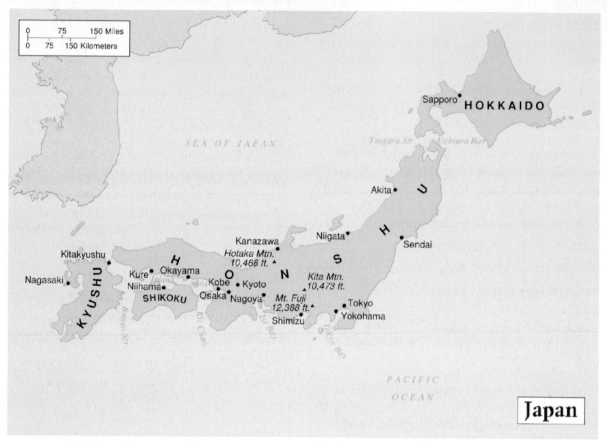

0   75   150 Miles
0   75   150 Kilometers

HOKKAIDO
Sapporo•

SEA OF JAPAN

Tsugaru Str. *Uchiura Bay*

Akita•

Niigata•

Sendai•

Kanazawa•
Hotaka Mtn.
10,466 ft. ▲

Kita Mtn.
10,473 ft. ▲

Kitakyushu•

H   O   N   S   H   U

Nagasaki•

Kure• Okayama•
Niihama•   Kobe• Kyoto•
SHIKOKU Osaka• Nagoya•   *Mt. Fuji*
                            12,388 ft. ▲   Tokyo•
                            Shimizu•   Yokohama•

KYUSHU

Bungo Str.

PACIFIC
OCEAN

Japan

▲ **Critical Viewing** This map shows the four main islands of Japan. Which island would you expect to be the most isolated? Explain. **[Analyze]**

*T*ucked away in a garden off a busy street sits a traditional Japanese tea hut. The doorway is so low that guests must enter humbly, on their hands and knees.

Inside, the tea master and a few guests sit on the floor of a small, bare room. The aroma of incense fills the air. The master prepares the tea according to elaborate, age-old rules. As the guests slowly sip their tea, they praise the beauty of the only decorations in the room—a flower arrangement and a scroll painting.

Even in the rush of modern city life, the tea ceremony is popular. Today, as in the past, traditional values such as humility, simplicity, and love of beauty help to mold Japanese life.

GEOGRAPHIC SETTING

Japan is an archipelago (är´kə pel´ ə gō´), or chain of islands, about 100 miles off the coast of East Asia. It consists of four main islands and more than 3,000 tiny ones. (See the map above.)

The Seas The Sea of Japan and Korea Strait separate Japan from the mainland. In the past, the stormy seas isolated and protected Japan. Yet, when they chose, the Japanese crossed the seas to make contact with other societies.

Within Japan, the sheltered Inland Sea has served as a major highway between islands.

Japan's isolated island setting helped shape its society and view of the world. From earliest times, the Japanese had a strong sense of their own separate, special identity.

Resources More than 80 percent of Japan is mountainous. As a result, the Japanese found ways to use every available piece of soil. They carved terraces into steep hillsides and drained marshes, swamps, and deltas. A favorable climate helps the Japanese make the most of their limited farmland. The major crop is rice.

Fish is Japan's major source of protein. Coastal waters provide plentiful catches of sardines, tuna, herring, salmon, and cod. The Japanese also raise fish in flooded rice paddies and harvest shellfish and seaweed in inlets.

On the other hand, Japan has few mineral resources. In early times, this scarcity had little effect. As Japan industrialized, however, it needed to import such vital resources as coal, copper, iron, and oil.

HISTORY

By A.D. 400, the Yamato clan united much of Japan. In time, they set up Japan's first and only ruling dynasty. The present emperor traces his descent directly to the Yamato clan.

Early History In the 500's, Japan began its cultural borrowing from China. The Japanese modeled their government on that of China. The ideas of the Chinese sage Confucius—respect for elders and the importance of doing right—became popular. The wealthy adopted Chinese music, dancing, and food. Yet the Japanese maintained their own identity.

In 794, the emperor moved his court to Heian (hā än´), present-day Kyoto. Courtiers lived a refined life devoted to elaborate ceremonies and festivals. Outside the palace walls, however, the emperor's power was in decline.

Feudalism During the 1100's, turmoil rocked Japan. Samurai, or warrior knights, battled for power. Out of the struggles, a feudal system emerged. Local lords ruled the land, but they were bound to higher lords and the emperor by ties of loyalty.

In theory, the *shogun* (shō´ gun), or most powerful samurai, commanded the loyalty of his lords. In fact, samurai lords and their followers battled the shogun and one another. By the 1400's, Japan was in a state of constant warfare.

Strong military leaders pushed to reunite Japan. In the 1600's, the Tokugawas (tō´ kōō gä´ wäz) claimed the right to be shoguns. The Tokugawa shoguns created a peaceful, orderly society. They left feudal classes in place but strengthened the central government. They also built a new capital at Edo (Tokyo).

Isolation and Reopening The Tokugawas felt threatened by the arrival of European traders and missionaries. The government began persecuting foreign missionaries and Japanese Christians. Finally, in 1639, the shogun closed Japan to the world. Foreigners were expelled, though the Dutch were allowed to keep a tiny trading post at Nagasaki.

Japan enforced its policy of isolation for 200 years. Then, in 1853, the United States sent a fleet to open Japan to trade. Japanese leaders realized that their weapons were no match for American cannon and steamships. They signed a treaty granting limited trading rights to Americans. Before long, the United States and other western nations won additional rights.

In 1868, rebellious samurai forced the last Tokugawa shogun to step down. They then restored the emperor to power. The emperor called his reign *Meiji* (mā jē´), or "enlightened rule." During the Meiji restoration, reformers sent hundreds of Japanese to Europe and the United States to study western forms of government, industry, and military organization.

▲ **Critical Viewing** Zen monasteries like this one were places of retreat for samurai lords. Why would the natural setting be important? **[Speculate]**

SOCIETY AND CULTURE

Modern Japanese society is largely secular. However, two religious traditions, Shinto and Buddhism, helped shape Japanese culture.

Religion Shinto is based on the belief that spirits, or *kami,* live in all things, from animals and plants to mountains, rocks, and streams. To win favor of the kami, who also control natural forces, the Japanese make offerings.

Shinto did not answer questions about life after death, morality, or human suffering. Therefore, many Japanese also embraced Buddhism. Missionaries from China and Korea first brought Buddhism to Japan in the 500's.

During the feudal age, Zen Buddhism took root. Unlike other Buddhist sects, Zen taught that tranquility could be achieved in this world through meditation, physical discipline, and devotion to duty. Both the rituals of the tea ceremony and the rigors of samurai training reflect Zen values. (See the picture above.)

Becoming a World Power By 1900, Japan had become a modern industrial nation. It then set out to gain an overseas empire. By expanding, Japan sought equal standing with western imperialist powers. It also gained raw materials for its growing industries.

In 1905, Japan defeated Russia in the Russo-Japanese War and won control of Korea. In the 1930's, extreme nationalists and militarists gained power in Japan. They pushed for further expansion. In a brutal invasion, Japan seized the Chinese province of Manchuria.

Japanese expansion in Asia helped spark World War II. The war ended in disaster for Japan. In 1945, after the United States dropped atomic bombs on Hiroshima and Nagasaki, Japan surrendered. For the first time in history, Japan was occupied by a foreign power. Japan had to disarm and give up its overseas empire.

In the postwar years, Japan adopted a democratic constitution. It then embarked on decades of astounding economic growth. Despite setbacks in the 1990's, Japan is today one of the world's economic superpowers.

Family Life Confucian traditions guided traditional Japanese family life. Family members owed complete obedience to the head of the household. He, in turn, had a duty to provide for the family, arrange suitable marriages, and protect the family honor.

In modern Japan, the head of a household no longer has legal authority over other family members. Arranged marriages are rare. Despite such changes, family loyalty remains central to Japanese life.

Women In early Japan, women enjoyed certain rights. As Confucian ideas spread, though, the status of women gradually declined. Confucian thinkers saw women as inferior to men. Feudalism, with its emphasis on warfare, also tended to devalue women.

In 1947, Japan's new constitution gave men and women the same rights. Still, traditional attitudes remained strong. Women had a harder time getting into universities and were paid less than men in the work force. Despite such obstacles, almost half the workers in Japan today are women. In 1993, Japan's legislature elected its first woman speaker.

ARTS AND LITERATURE

Japan has a long heritage of music, dance, and drama. Many traditional forms of theater are still popular with audiences today.

Theater The oldest surviving form of Japanese theater is No drama. Most No plays reflect Shinto or Buddhist themes. Wearing traditional masks and costumes, the actors slowly move about a nearly bare stage, using highly stylized movements and gestures.

A livelier form of drama, kabuki, emerged in the 1500's. Kabuki plays are melodramatic, colorful spectacles. Unlike No, kabuki requires elaborate stage sets. Dancing, acrobatics, and swordplay add to the excitement. (See the picture on this page.)

Visual Arts During Japan's feudal period, the visual arts reflected Zen values of self-discipline, simplicity, and closeness to nature. Painters learned to suggest an idea or feeling with a minimum of detail. A few bold lines might be enough to convey an impression of a mountain. Zen also influenced such crafts as landscape gardening and flower arranging.

In the Tokugawa period, new art styles reflected the tastes of a growing middle class. Among the best-known works of this period are

The Actor Ichimura Mitsuzo as a Samurai, Torii Kiyomasu II, Metropolitan Museum of Art

▲ **Critical Viewing** This print shows a popular kabuki actor portraying a samurai. Why would plays about samurai be popular? **[Connect]**

brilliantly colored woodblock prints of city life called *ukiyoe* (oō´kē ō). In the late 1800's, ukiyoe influenced art styles in Europe.

Literature At the Heian court, aristocrats competed to write elegant poetry. Many of the greatest Heian writers were women. Around 1008, Lady Murasaki Shikibu wrote *The Tale of Genji*. Considered the world's first novel, it gives a vivid picture of the ceremonies and manners of the Heian court.

Sei Shōnagon, another woman writer, gave a detailed portrait of upper-class life during the Heian age in her *Pillow Book*. It contains character descriptions, anecdotes, and witty insights. (See p. 23.)

Traditional Japanese poetry follows precise forms. Most early poetry was written in a form called *tanka*, consisting of five lines of five, seven, five, seven, and seven syllables. (See p. 986.)

By the 1700's, the *haiku* (hī´koō´) form had become popular. A haiku is a short poem—just 17 syllables long in Japanese—that seeks to convey a single vivid emotion by means of images from nature. Skilled poets like Matsuo Bashō or Kobayashi Issa could express a wide range of feelings in just a few words. (See p. 987.)

ACTIVITY
Preparing an Oral Report

Use Internet or library resources to research Japanese kabuki theater. Then, prepare an oral report on some aspect of kabuki. You may wish to accompany your report with pictures, video, or sound clips, if available on the Web.

*G*uide for Reading

Ki no Tsurayuki
(872–945)

Ki no Tsurayuki (kē nō tsoo rä yoo kē) was the chief aide to Emperor Daigo and one of the leading poets, critics, and diarists of his time. He helped assemble a major anthology of Japanese poetry from the previous 1,100 years. In his insightful preface, Tsurayuki explored the character and purpose of Japanese poetry, explaining that the poet "strives to find words to express the impression left on his heart by sight and sound."

Priest Jakuren
(c. 1139–1202)

Jakuren (jä koo rən) was a Buddhist priest and a prominent tanka poet whose poems are filled with beautiful yet melancholy imagery. After entering the priesthood at the age of twenty-three, he spent his time traveling the countryside, writing poetry, and seeking spiritual fulfillment. He also participated in many poetry contests.

Matsuo Bashō
(1644–1694)

Generally regarded as the greatest Japanese haiku poet, Matsuo Bashō (mä tsoo ō bä shō) lived the life of a hermit, supporting himself by teaching and judging poetry contests.

Bashō carried with him only the barest essentials as he traveled through central and northern Japan. He recorded his observations and insights in both poems and thoughtful travel diaries.

Kobayashi Issa
(1763–1828)

Banished from his rural home as a teenager, Kobayashi Issa (kō bä yä shē ē sä) lived his life in urban poverty and struggled to overcome the loneliness and pain resulting from the deaths of loved ones. His difficult circumstances contributed to his appreciation for the fleeting lives of small creatures. This appreciation is reflected in his haiku "A gentle spring rain."

◆ Build Vocabulary

WORD ORIGINS: WORDS FROM NAMES

Some people's names have become English words for surprising reasons. Consider the word *camellia*, which you will encounter in Bashō's haiku.

This name was given to the plant by Swedish botanist Carl Linnaeus, who named the camellia in 1735. He wanted to honor Georg Josef Kamel, a Jesuit missionary who studied the native plants of the Philippines. The tribute lives on in English, even though Kamel probably never saw a camellia.

WORD BANK

As you read these poems, you will encounter the words on this list. Each word is defined on the page where it first appears. Preview the list before you read.

| camellia |
| lapping |

◆ Build Grammar Skills

STYLISTIC USE OF SENTENCE FRAGMENTS

Poets sometimes stretch or break the rules of grammar for precise stylistic reasons. Due to the condensed form of Japanese tanka and haiku, translators sometimes use **sentence fragments**—groups of words that do not express a complete thought—to create individual images.

Many sentence fragments in translations of Japanese poetry include only a noun and descriptive adjectives. The verb or action is omitted. For example, a tanka by Priest Jakuren ends

On the cypress-mountain,
Autumn evening.

By responding to this fragment, you can add meaning to it. After envisioning the cypress-covered mountain on an autumn evening, you can think about how this image relates to the idea of loneliness.

◆ Literature and Your Life

CONNECT YOUR EXPERIENCE

When you participate in a sport or play a game, you agree to follow certain rules. The rules exist, in part, to create a challenge—to test a player's skill. In the same way, the rules governing certain forms of poetry challenge the poets' skills. When poets choose to write a tanka or a haiku, they accept the challenge of using a concentrated, precise form to express a unique and effective insight.

THEMATIC FOCUS: HUMANS AND NATURE

Each of these poems, like countless others, includes specific references to nature. As you read the poems, ask yourself: Why do you think poets frequently focus on nature?

Journal Writing Jot down an image from nature that you might use as the basis for a poem.

◆ Background for Understanding

CULTURE

Haiku grew out of a collaborative form of poetry known as *renga*. At festive poetry contests, groups of writers would gather to create interlocking groups of renga verses. The results were judged and evaluated by a poetry master. Listeners who attended the contests developed a love for the simple yet profound poetic forms.

In his book *The Essential Haiku*, American poet Robert Hass compares this kind of artistic collaboration to "the American jazz band of the 1920's." He sees the following similarities between composing renga and improvising jazz: "a popular medium, reverence for masters, styles, soloists of the past, rival styles in the same city, different traditions in different cities . . ."

◆ Literary Focus

POETIC FORMS

The **tanka** is the most prevalent verse form in traditional Japanese literature. Each short poem consists of five lines of five, seven, five, seven, and seven syllables. Most tanka include at least one **caesura** (si zyoor′ ə), or pause, often indicated by punctuation in English translations.

The **haiku** consists of three lines of five, seven, and five syllables. Almost all haiku include a *kigo,* or seasonal word, such as "snow" or "cherry blossoms," that indicates the time of year being described. Most haiku present an explicit or implicit comparison between two images, actions, or states of being.

◆ Reading Strategy

ENVISION IMAGERY

To appreciate the images that the poets use, create a mental picture. When you **envision** such a picture, you use your memory and imagination to see, feel, hear, smell, and taste what the poets describe.

For example, when you read Tsurayuki's image of a winter night, feel the bitter wind blowing off the river and hear the birds' mournful calls pierce the icy air. Use associations to help you. For example, although you may never have heard a plover cry, you have probably heard some bird that makes a sad sound.

Use a graphic organizer like the one shown to help you envision the imagery in these poems.

Image	Association
Spring rain	Freshness Renewal

Tanka

Translated by
Geoffrey Bownas

Ki no Tsurayuki

When I went to visit
The girl I love so much,
That winter night
The river blew so cold
That the plovers[1] were crying.

---

1. plovers (pluv´ ərz) *n.*: Wading shore
birds with short tails, long, pointed
wings, and short, stout beaks.

Priest Jakuren

One cannot ask loneliness
How or where it starts.
On the cypress-mountain,[1]
Autumn evening.

---

1. cypress-mountain: Cypress trees are
cone-bearing evergreen trees, native to
North America, Europe, and Asia.

◀ **Critical Viewing** Compare the mood of this painting
with the mood or feelings evoked in these tankas.
[Compare and Contrast]

◆ **Build Vocabulary**

camellia (kə mēl´ yə) *n.*: Waxy, roselike flower
of an Asiatic evergreen shrub

lapping (lap´ iŋ) *v.*: Dipping a liquid up with
the tongue, as a dog might

Haiku
Translated by
Daniel C. Buchanan

落お
ち
ざ
ま
に
水みづ
こ
ぼ
し
け
り
花はな
椿つばき

Bashō

Falling upon earth,
Pure water spills from the cup
Of the <u>camellia</u>.

Issa

A gentle spring rain.
Look, a rat is <u>lapping</u>
Sumida River.

春はる
雨さめ
や
鼠ねずみ
の
な
め
る
隅すみ
田だ
川がわ

Beyond Literature

Cultural Connection

Haiku Competitions You may not think of poetry as a national pastime, but for many people in Japan, haiku is as popular as baseball or football is here. Japanese children learn to compose the 5-7-5 poems in elementary school. Many of them develop a love for the simple yet profound form. Every year, at New Year's Day, a poetry competition called the *utakai* is held. Thousands of people, including the emperor, submit poems that are then read before a national television audience.

Guide for Responding

◆ *Literature and Your Life*

Reader's Response Which poem created the strongest mental images for you? Why?

Thematic Focus Do you think that haiku or tanka could describe urban environments as effectively as natural settings? Why or why not?

Reader's Journal On your paper, copy two or three of the most effective words from each poem.

Questions for Research How old is the haiku, and who were its earliest practitioners? Generate research questions about the origins and development of haiku.

☑ Check Your Comprehension

1. What event does Tsurayuki describe in his tanka?
2. What does the word *it* refer to in the line by Priest Jakuren: "How or where it starts"?
3. In your own words, restate the scene Bashō describes in his haiku.
4. What creature is the subject of Issa's haiku?

◆ Critical Thinking

INTERPRET
1. How does the natural world in Tsurayuki's tanka seem to reflect human emotions? **[Analyze]**
2. What is the connection between loneliness and the cypress-mountain in the tanka by Priest Jakuren? **[Connect]**
3. How do the contrasting images in Issa's haiku complement one another? **[Compare and Contrast]**

APPLY
4. Choose one of the poems and change one word to alter the overall impact of the poem. Explain how your change affects the poem's imagery and meaning. **[Modify]**

COMPARE LITERARY WORKS
5. Imagine that you were judging a poetry contest and these four poems <u>were the finalists</u>. Which poem would you award the grand prize? Why? **[Evaluate]**

Guide for Responding (continued)

◆ Reading Strategy

ENVISION IMAGERY

In these poems, the language that appeals to the senses helps you **envision the imagery**—create a mental picture. Experiencing the imagery, in turn, helps you understand the poet's message. For example, in Issa's haiku, the images of a gentle spring rain and a rat lapping at Sumida River combine to convey a message of natural balance, with the fresh rainwater feeding the river from which a common animal softly drinks.

1. What images in Tsurayuki's tanka emphasize the speaker's love for the girl?
2. Does the opening sentence of Jakuren's tanka create a strong image? Why or why not?
3. Does Bashō's haiku feel more like a close-up photograph or distant view? Why?
4. If you were going to paint a picture to illustrate one of these poems, which one would you select? What would your painting show?

◆ Literary Focus

POETIC FORMS

In the Japanese language, these poems follow precise structural rules. A **tanka** consists of five lines of five, seven, five, seven, and seven syllables. A **haiku** consists of three lines of five, seven, and five syllables. Almost all haiku include a *kigo,* or seasonal word, that indicates the time of year being described.

Because a Japanese word may have a different number of syllables in English, translations of these forms do not always contain the required number of syllables. However, translators do preserve other essential aspects of the forms. For example, when translating Tsurayuki's tanka, Geoffrey Bownas ends the second line with a comma to indicate a brief pause. He also uses short, sharply concise language that reflects the original Japanese.

1. Why do you think the translation of Jakuren's tanka has four lines instead of five?
2. What is the *kigo* in each haiku and what time of year does it suggest?
3. How does the *kigo* in a haiku support the idea that nature has certain rhythms and cycles?
4. (a) How are tanka and haiku different? (b) How are they similar?

◆ Build Vocabulary

USING WORDS FROM NAMES

English contains some words that derive from the name of a person, as camellia derives from a botanist named Kamel. On your paper, match the following words with the definition and description of the person from whose name they derive.

1. draconian
2. boycott
3. maverick

   a. a nonconformist; from a Texas rancher who refused to brand his cattle
   b. severe; from a harsh Athenian lawgiver
   c. to protest by refusing to use an item; from a nineteenth-century Irish land agent who refused to lower his rents

USING THE WORD BANK: Analogies

Notice the relationship between the first pair of words in each numbered item. In your notebook, complete the second pair of words by supplying a word that indicates a similar relationship.

1. *Heron* is to *bird* as *camellia* is to ___?___.
2. *Lapping* is to *drink* as *chewing* is to ___?___.
3. *Camellia* is to *earth* as *fish* is to ___?___.
4. *Falling* is to *dropping* as ___?___ is to *lapping*.

◆ Build Grammar Skills

STYLISTIC USE OF SENTENCE FRAGMENTS

A **sentence fragment** is a group of words that does not express a complete thought. Learning to recognize sentence fragments can help you identify when poets break grammatical rules to create special effects. For example, Issa's translator opens his haiku with a fragment that lacks a verb: "A gentle spring rain." By leaving out the verb, the translator conveys the happening-right-now quality of the rain.

Practice In your notebook, tell whether each item below is a *sentence* or a *sentence fragment*

1. When I went to visit the girl I love so much.
2. The river blew so cold that the plovers were crying.
3. Falling upon earth, pure water.
4. How or where it starts.
5. One cannot ask loneliness how or where it starts.

Build Your Portfolio

 ## Idea Bank

Writing

1. **Haiku** Choose a theme or scene from nature and write a haiku. Follow the 5-7-5 syllable pattern of haiku.

2. **Collaborative Poem** Work with a group of three or four classmates and write a collaborative poem. Choose a topic and theme and take turns adding lines. Before you begin, you might choose a syllable pattern for your poem, such as alternating lines of 5 and 7 syllables.

3. **Response to Criticism** American poet Robert Hass says that haiku have "unusual wakefulness and clarity." Using the haiku by Bashō and Issa as examples, support or refute his statement.

Speaking, Listening, and Viewing

4. **Listener Survey** Choose one of the poems in this group and read it aloud to five or more people, one at a time. Discuss each listener's reaction, and summarize all the responses in a class report.

5. **Documentary Script** Create a storyboard for a short documentary introducing tanka or haiku to students. Write the narration and use sketches to show the images you would use in your video film. **[Performing Arts Link]**

Researching and Representing

6. **Author Poster** Choose one of the authors in this group and find out more about his life and poetry. Then, create a poster celebrating the poet's life and works, including additional examples of his poems. **[Art Link]**

7. **Japanese Poetry Timeline** Create an annotated timeline that includes events in the history of Japanese poetry. **[Social Studies Link]**

Online Activity www.phlit.phschool.com

 ## Guided Writing Lesson

Public Service Announcement

In Japan, writing haiku seems to be very popular. In the United States, a public service announcement might help to stimulate a similar interest in writing poetry. A public service announcement is a message broadcast to gain public support or provide important information. You might think of them as advertisements for good causes. For example, you can create a public service announcement that will spark student interest in poetry. Your radio message could be broadcast over the school intercom or on a local station.

Writing Skills: Grab Listeners' Attention

Like advertising, a public service announcement needs to capture and keep people listening. Use lively language and intriguing ideas to **grab listeners' attention.** Start with a boldly engaging statement or question. This "teaser" can make your listeners stop what they are doing and pay attention. Consider how these openings might capture an audience's attention:

Can poetry really save your life?
A poem a day keeps boredom away.
Haiku—infinity in about seventeen words.

Prewriting Brainstorm for a list of benefits that readers gain from reading poetry. These are the selling points you will want to emphasize in your public service announcement. Next, consider the strategies you will use to persuade your audience.

Drafting Use strong and engaging language as you write an announcement that will appeal to listeners. Your writing will be spoken, so you may want to practice reading it aloud as you draft.

Revising Read your announcement to a partner, using a persuasive tone. Does your introduction grab your partner's attention? Is the rest of your announcement effective and clear? Consider your partner's suggestions, and make the necessary revisions.

Writing Process Workshop

One of the poems in this section is a narrative poem. A **narrative poem** tells a story; it is usually longer than other types of poems. Like a story, a narrative poem has one or more characters, a conflict, and a series of events that come to a conclusion. Most narrative poems are divided into stanzas, or groups of lines that have the same rhyme pattern.

Write a narrative poem. The following skills will help you write a narrative poem.

Writing Skills Focus

▶ **Grab the reader's attention.** Begin your poem with a dramatic statement or scene. Next, introduce a conflict. Build up that conflict to a **climax,** and then end the poem with the resolution of the climax.

▶ **Use musical devices** such as alliteration, onomatopoeia, and consonance to give your narrative poem a musical quality.

▶ **Pay attention to setting and mood.** Establish a setting that lets your reader envision the action. Use vivid verbs, adjectives, adverbs, and exact nouns to set the proper mood.

The following stanzas from John Keats's narrative poem show these skills at work.

La Belle Dame sans Merci, John W. Waterhouse, Hessiches Landes Museum, Darmstadt

---

MODEL FROM LITERATURE

from "La Belle Dame sans Merci" by John Keats

O what can ail thee, knight-at-arms,
    Alone and palely loitering? ①
The sedge has withered from the lake,
    And no birds sing. ②
         * * *
I met a lady in the meads,
    Full beautiful—a faery's child,
Her hair was long, her foot was light,
    And her eyes were wild.
         * * *
She took me to her elfin grot,
   ③ And there she wept, and sighed full sore,
And there I shut her wild wild eyes
    With kisses four. . . .

① The poet grabs the reader's attention with a mysterious question.

② The poet creates a somber mood with these images.

③ The poet uses alliteration in this stanza, repeating the s and sh sounds with She . . . she . . . sighed . . . sore . . . shut.

Prewriting

Choose a Topic A narrative poem tells a story. Think of a story that will be the basis for your poem. You can use your imagination or you can write about a real-life event or experience. Use the following suggestions to help you come up with a story for your narrative poem:

▶ **Examine photos, newspapers, or magazines.** Most pictures and articles have a story behind them. Look for those that will stimulate your imagination.

▶ **Create a Conflict Word Bin.** Create two lists, like the ones below. The first should have main characters; the second, a person, group, force, or problem that the main character must face. Mix and match the two columns until you find a suitable combination for your narrative poem.

Conflict Word Bin	
Character	*Conflict*
A knight	searching for an answer
A teenager	struggling with a decision
A detective	preparing for a challenge
An athlete	searching for a criminal

▶ **Use sensory images**—words that appeal to the senses of sight, sound, smell, taste, and touch—to make your narrative poem more vivid. Before drafting, make a list of words relevant to your narrative that appeal to each of these senses. Refer to this list as you write.

▶ **Think of a climax and resolution.** The plot of your narrative poem must eventually lead to a climax, the high point of the action. After the conflict, the action falls and a resolution is reached, in which the conflict is settled and loose ends are tied up.

Drafting

Use Musical Devices In poetry, sound is often as important as meaning. Use one or all of the following musical devices to enhance the mood and meaning of your poem:

Rhyme is the most commonly used sound device:

This darksome burn, horseback brown,
His rollrock highroad roaring down . . .

**Writer's Solution Connection
Writing Lab**

To help you with your story line, refer to the Story Line Diagram in the Writing Lab tutorial on Creative Writing.

APPLYING LANGUAGE SKILLS: Problems With Modifiers

Avoid the following **problems with modifiers** as you draft your poem:

Double Negative:
There <u>weren't no</u> stars out.

Double Comparison:
Bullet was a <u>more faster</u> horse.

Improper Use of *Here*:
This <u>here</u> car is my favorite.

Confusing Adjective and Adverb:
That cat moves <u>slow</u>.
(correct: <u>slowly</u>)

Practice On your paper, correct the problems with modifiers in the following poem.

> And as I stared
> The most greatest beast
> Leaped quick to my side
> "Don't fear nothing!"
> I said to myself . . .

Writing Application Review your narrative poem and correct any problems with modifiers.

Writer's Solution Connection Language Lab

For more practice with modifiers, complete the Language Lab lesson on Problems With Modifiers.

Rhythm and Meter Rhythm is the pattern of accented and unaccented syllables in a line of poetry. Meter is the number of beats per line. Experiment with different rhythms and meters to create different moods.

Alliteration is the repetition of consonant sounds at the beginning of words:

> The *l*ong *l*ight shakes across the *l*akes . . .

Onomatopoeia is the use of words that imitate the sounds they name. Examples include *whirr*, *buzz*, and *bang*.

Revising

Have a Peer Check Your Work Use the following checklist with a peer to help you revise your narrative poem.

▶ Is the story easy to follow? How can the writer clarify what happens?
▶ Are the images striking and vivid? How might the images be made more effective?
▶ Does the author use musical devices?

REVISION MODEL

As I recall, the night was clear,

And scarcely a whisper could I ① hear ~~discern,~~

From the people on the street below,
② *Shuffling about*
~~Walking around~~ in the evening snow.

① *The writer changes this word to preserve the rhyme and meter.*
② *Shuffling is more descriptive and onomatopoetic than walking.*

Publishing

▶ **Give a Dramatic Reading** With a group of classmates, arrange to have a reading of your narrative poems. You might wish to have another student serve as host of the reading and introduce each poet. When you present your poem, speak clearly and with emotion.

▶ **Perform Your Poem** Stage a performance of your narrative poem. Act as the director, and use classmates as actors.

Student Success Workshop

Real-World Reading Skills

Strategies for Success

Many things you read are made up of one type of writing and cover just one topic. For instance, a biography is nonfiction writing about one person's life, and a novel tells a story about fictional characters. A newspaper, on the other hand, contains various topics and types of writing. In some newspapers, you can read articles about everything from sports to computers. You can get information from news and feature articles, classified ads, calendars of events, and the weather report. You can get opinions from editorials, interpretations from news analyses, and entertainment from comics and crossword puzzles. Here are some strategies for making the most of your newspaper reading:

Learn the Paper's Contents If a newspaper contains so much information, how can you know where to begin reading it? Start by learning how the newspaper is organized and what subject matter it contains.

▶ Read the index to find page numbers for specific sections and articles.
▶ Skim sections to see what they contain.
▶ Pull out the sections that interest you.
▶ Read the headlines. Then, read the articles or other types of text that interest you.

Know What You Want Few people read the whole paper. Most people read a few articles and locate information they need. Knowing what you're looking for can help you use a newspaper effectively. Are you looking for information about a national or an international event? Try the front page. Do you want to know about a fire that occurred in town last night? Try the front page of the city (or "Metro") section. Do you want to find out who won a game? Look in the Sports section.

Apply the Strategies

Try out your newspaper-reading skills with one or more of these exercises:

1. Read an editorial. Write a letter to the editor responding to it.
2. Read a front-page story. In a paragraph, summarize its main ideas.
3. Choose a local news story. Use it as a model for writing one of your own.
4. After reading a sports article, explain why you do or don't consider it well written.
5. Read an article about a new business. Then, write a paragraph describing what you've learned about it.

INDEX

World/Nation, **A**	Broadway Revisited, **D6**
Space Station Scare, **A9**	Travel, **E**
Metro, **B**	Leisure Spurs: Vacations on
Local Taxes Rebuild Schools, **B5**	Horseback, **E3**
Business, **C**	Real Estate, **F**
Virtual Merger: Internet Giant Grows, **C12**	Local House Bargains, **F2**
Arts and Entertainment, **D**	Classified Ads, **G**
	Help Wanted, **G3**

✔ Here are some reasons for reading a newspaper:

▶ Learning about recent scientific discoveries
▶ Finding the weather forecast
▶ Hunting for a job in the classified ads
▶ Reading different points of view about current events

Speaking, Listening, and Viewing Workshop

Moviegoers roared with laughter while watching Charlie Chaplin perform, though he never said a word! The work of actors in silent films, such as Chaplin, Mary Pickford, and Buster Keaton, has endured over time. Pantomime, dance, and instrumental music are all creative means of expressing ideas nonverbally. When interpreting a literary work, you may choose nonverbal techniques—and prove that actions can speak louder than words.

Think About It When selecting a work to interpret, consider your own interests. Your audience won't feel excited about your performance if you aren't. Once you've chosen a text, you will need to decide exactly what you have to say about it. Your nonverbal performance should express your own unique interpretation of the entire work or a specific aspect of it. Will you focus on the theme of the play, the moral of the story, the plot of the epic, or the feelings of the poem's speaker? Remember that your interpretation should be valid—in other words, you should be able to defend it by pointing to the text.

Plan Your Performance Don't forget who your audience will be. Your performance for an audience of young children should differ from a performance before your classmates. Your classmates may instantly associate the action of a mime raising a hand with the action of a student offering to answer a teacher's question, but a group of preschool children might not. Consider also how some nonverbal actions may be universally understood, while others might "speak" only to specific groups.

Experiment Your body movements, gestures, and facial expressions are your tools: Find out what effects you can get. Remember that timing is another of your tools—and one of the most important. Based on what you want to

communicate, try varying the speed of your movements. Short pauses and prolonged stillness "speak," too. Classic pantomime artists, like Marcel Marceau, often seem to move in slow motion, so don't rush through your performance unless your interpretation demands it.

Rehearse Again and Again Nonverbal performances take time to perfect. Practicing in front of a mirror will help you see what's working. Ask friends and family members to give you feedback. If you can, videotape a rehearsal. Make sure your performance communicates your ideas as obviously as possible. Rehearse until you feel comfortable and confident.

Apply the Strategies

Alone or with a partner, choose a poem from this unit to pantomime for your class. Use the strategies presented here, and plan your performance as a nonverbal interpretation of the text. Afterwards, invite questions from your audience. Explain why you selected your nonverbal performance techniques, based on your analysis and interpretation of the poem.

Tips for Performing Nonverbally

✔ When planning a nonverbal performance of a literary text, use these techniques:

▶ Practice in front of a mirror to see what your expressions, body language, and gestures are "saying." As you evaluate what you see, pretend you're an audience member.

▶ Experiment with using actions in different "sizes." Does exaggerating a movement change your message?

Test Preparation Workshop

Reading Comprehension

Strategies for Success

The reading sections of standardized tests often require you to analyze the characteristics of clear texts, including patterns of organization and word choice. Use the following strategies to help you answer test questions on these skills:

Identify Patterns of Organization The organization of information within a text affects the meaning of the text. Writers may organize information to compare or contrast things, to establish chronological order, or to show a cause-and-effect relationship. As you read, identify these patterns of organization. Read the following sample passage, and write your answer to the question on a separate piece of paper.

> The use of automobiles has increased around the world. Twenty years ago, you could travel to many places without encountering a noisy, exhaust-spewing car. As global trade and world economies have expanded, more people have purchased cars. Environmentalists contend that this increase is not a healthy trend. In parts of China today, it is nearly impossible to breathe because of the glut of unnecessary cars on the roads. Twenty years ago, those same roads were filled with nonpolluting bicycles.

What patterns of organization are used in this passage? Support your answer.

Sample answer: Chronology is used in speaking of the number of cars twenty years ago and today. Comparison is used in comparing these two time periods. Cause and effect is used in mentioning the effects of expanded trade and the polluting effects of cars.

Notice Word Choice The words that a writer chooses help to establish the writer's point of view or opinion. On a separate sheet of paper, write an answer to the following question:

> Explain how key words in the previous passage on the use of automobiles express the writer's point of view. Support your answer.

Sample answer: The writer has a negative opinion of cars: The words "noisy, exhaust-spewing" and "unnecessary" show that the writer doesn't favor cars.

Apply the Strategies

Read the following passage, and write short answers to the questions.

> At the end of World War II, the United States and the Soviet Union distrusted each other. The two superpowers competed to influence other nations. The Soviet Union supported a brutal system called communism. The United States embraced democracy for its freedom-loving people. Tensions mounted as each country built nuclear weapons. As a result, each side stockpiled enough weapons to destroy each other—and the world. Then, the two countries began to reduce their arms. By the 1980's, the reduction of nuclear weapons had resulted in decreased world tensions.

1 Explain how the writer has used patterns of organization. Support your answer.

2 Explain how the writer's choice of certain words reveals his or her point of view. Support your answer.

Suleyman Battling the Christians, Bibliotheque de l'Arsenal, Paris

Epics and Legends in World Literature

Great legends develop in every culture, reflecting the history and beliefs of the people who create them. These stories serve two purposes: They explain important events in the history of a people, and they shape these events into a heroic and memorable form. The various tales of different cultures have become identifying marks of these cultures; other people can read these stories and sense how the culture was shaped and what figures and issues are central to its history.

Within each of these stories, the customs, folklore, and history of a particular culture are revealed, sometimes in an entertaining manner.

Reading for Success

Strategies for Reading Epics and Legends

Every culture has its epics and legends—stories of heroes who embody the values, strengths, and traditions of that culture. While the legends may differ from culture to culture, the feature they have in common is a hero who achieves fame through great deeds. Because the legendary stories in this unit come from widely different time periods and cultures, you need to be open to differences in style and structure. The following strategies will help you read epics and legends effectively.

Reread or read ahead.

If you don't understand a passage, reread it, looking for connections among the words or sentences. It might also help you to read ahead, because a word or idea may be clarified further on. Try to follow the plot line.

Summarize.

As you read, pause periodically to restate in your own words what you have read. By doing this in your mind, you can check your understanding of the key events and their significance.

Be aware of the historical and cultural context.

The heroic tales in this unit took place long ago and far away. Customs and attitudes are very different from those that you know, and places may be unfamiliar. It's important to be open to these differences and not to impose preset expectations. Before you begin the following selections, familiarize yourself with the names of the characters.

Look for the writer's purpose and attitude.

Most epics and legends were passed on from generation to generation to preserve the history and values of a culture. The stories you will read here have other purposes as well. For instance, the purpose of *Don Quixote* is to poke fun at the values of the culture in which Cervantes lived.

You will read heroic tales more effectively if you actively use these strategies. You will be better able to follow the plot and apply your understanding to your own world.

PART 1 *European Traditions*

The Hunt of the Unicorn VII, "The Unicorn in Captivity,"
From the Chateau of Verteuil, Metropolitan Museum of Art, N.Y.

Guide for Reading

Miguel de Cervantes
(1547–1616)

As the creative genius behind *Don Quixote*, Miguel de Cervantes (mē gel *the the*r vän´ tes) is counted among the world's greatest writers. His masterpiece *Don Quixote* has been translated into more than sixty languages and continues to be studied, critiqued, and debated even today. A poet and playwright as well as a novelist, Cervantes was born in a small town outside Madrid, Spain. Little is known about the author's early life—except the misfortunes he experienced.

A Life Full of Adventure As a young soldier in a battle fought with the Turkish fleet, Cervantes was wounded and permanently lost the use of his left arm and hand. Sailing home from the war, he was captured and enslaved by pirates. They took him to Algiers, where he was held prisoner for five years. Finally, he was freed when the Trinitarian friars paid a five-hundred-ducat ransom for him.

Settling Down Back in Spain, Cervantes married and took a job as a purchasing agent for the navy. His misfortunes continued, however; problems with work and finances resulted in fines and imprisonment. His luck finally turned when he published the first part of *Don Quixote*. He settled in Madrid and devoted his last years to writing. Wildly popular when it was first published, *Don Quixote* later became the model for a new type of fiction: that of the hero who does not conform to his times.

◆ Build Vocabulary

LATIN WORD ROOTS: -son-

In this selection, Don Quixote decides to name his horse Rocinante because he believes it is a "lofty, sonorous name." *Sonorous* has the Latin root *-son-,* which comes from the Latin *sonorus,* meaning "a sound." Knowing this root helps you to see that *sonorous* means "having a powerful, rich sound." You can also see this root in words such as *sonic,* which means "having to do with sound."

WORD BANK

As you read this story, you will encounter the words in this list. Each word is defined on the page where it first appears. Preview the list before you read.

lucidity
adulation
interminable
affable
sallying
requisite
sonorous
veracious
vanquish
extolled

◆ Build Grammar Skills

GERUNDS AND GERUND PHRASES

As you read *Don Quixote,* look for examples of gerunds and gerund phrases. A **gerund** is a verb form ending in *-ing* that acts as a noun. A **gerund phrase** includes all the words that go with a gerund. Like nouns, gerunds and gerund phrases can perform all the roles of a noun in a sentence: subject, direct or indirect object, object of a preposition, and appositive. In this example, the gerund *hunting* is used as the object of the preposition *of:*

Don Quixote was an early riser and fond of *hunting.*

In the following example, the gerund phrase *reading books of chivalry* acts as the object of the preposition *to:*

... the above named gentleman devoted his leisure ... to *reading books of chivalry* ...

from Don Quixote

◆ *Literature and Your Life*

CONNECT YOUR EXPERIENCE

You're reading the latest suspense or adventure novel and have encountered a devious villain. As the conflict intensifies, you find yourself silently shouting at the pages. You know they're just words on the page, but in the excitement of the tale you get a little carried away. The main character in *Don Quixote* gets carried away by the excitement of the romantic stories he reads about knights and battles. His overactive imagination creates some humorous scenes and situations.

Journal Writing Briefly describe the last book, movie, or video game that "carried you away."

THEMATIC FOCUS: OVERCOMING OBSTACLES

Don Quixote's imagination is a powerful force. You may wonder, as you follow his adventures, whether his imagination helps him or hurts him.

◆ Background for Understanding

CULTURE

Cervantes was born at the peak of Spain's Golden Age, a time when Spanish power and influence in Europe and the Western Hemisphere were greater than ever before or since. By the time Cervantes wrote *Don Quixote,* however, Spain's fortunes were fast declining because of a series of disastrous wars, bad economic policies, and the stunning defeat of the Spanish Armada by the British Navy in 1588. This last event signaled the end of Spain's rule of the seas and the beginning of England's. To some extent, Spain's transition from great confidence to deep despair is echoed in the novel, as Don Quixote takes refuge in chivalry from the realities of an unfriendly world.

◆ Literary Focus

PARODY

A **parody** is a comical piece of writing that mocks the characteristics of a specific literary form. By exaggerating or humorously imitating the ideas, language, tone, or action in a work of literature, a parody calls attention to the ridiculous qualities of its subject. A parody works best when the object of its ridicule is a usually serious topic. *Don Quixote* is a parody that ridicules knights and the literature of chivalry. By exaggerating Don Quixote's behavior, Cervantes entertains his audience while making fun of the traditional "knight in shining armor."

◆ Reading Strategy

COMPARE AND CONTRAST

Much of the humor in *Don Quixote* comes from the sharp difference between the ideal knight and Don Quixote's version of a knight. **Comparing and contrasting** the two versions will highlight the humor of Don Quixote, a mock "knight in shining armor." To help you identify the similarities and differences between Don Quixote and an "ideal knight," make a chart with three columns. In the first column, list the qualities or things that you associate with real knights—a war horse, armor, a squire, a lady love, bold adventures, and so on. Label the second column "Ideal Knight," and list details about the ideal knight's horse, armor, and so on. Label the third column Don Quixote. Then, as you read the selection, jot down details that compare and contrast Don Quixote's knightly attributes and possessions with the ideal.

Qualities or Things	Ideal Knight	Don Quixote
armor		
squire		
war horse		
adventures		
opponents		
motivation		

The First Part of The Ingenious Gentleman Don Quixote of La Mancha[1]

from Don Quixote

Miguel de Cervantes
Translated by John Ormsby

Don Quixote on Horseback, Honoré Daumier, Neue Pinakothek, Munich

▲ **Critical Viewing** What heroic qualities of Don Quixote are captured in this picture? What ridiculous qualities? **[Evaluate]**

CHAPTER I
Which Treats of the Character and Pursuits of the Famous Gentleman Don Quixote of La Mancha

In a village of La Mancha, which I prefer to leave unnamed, there lived not long ago one of those gentlemen that keep a lance in the lance-rack, an old shield, a lean hack, and a greyhound for hunting. A stew of rather more beef than mutton, hash on most nights, bacon and eggs on Saturdays, lentils on Fridays, and a pigeon or so extra on Sundays consumed three quarters of his income. The rest went for a coat of fine cloth and velvet breeches and shoes to match for holidays, while on week-days he cut a fine figure in his best home-spun. He had in his house a housekeeper past forty, a niece under twenty, and a lad for the field and marketplace, who saddled the hack as well as handled the pruning knife. The age of this gentleman of ours was bordering on fifty. He was of a hardy constitution, spare, gaunt-featured, a very early riser, and fond of hunting. Some say that his surname was Quixada or Quesada (for there is no unanimity among those who write on the subject), although reasonable conjectures tend to show that he was called Quexana. But this scarcely affects our story; it will be enough not to stray a hair's breadth from the truth in telling it.

---

1. **La Mancha:** Province in south central Spain.

You must know that the above-named gentleman devoted his leisure (which was mostly all the year round) to reading books of chivalry—and with such ardor and avidity that he almost entirely abandoned the chase and even the management of his property. To such a pitch did his eagerness and infatuation go that he sold many an acre of tillage land to buy books of chivalry to read, bringing home all he could find.

But there were none he liked so well as those written by the famous Feliciano de Silva, for their lucidity of style and complicated conceits[2] were as pearls in his sight, particularly when in his reading he came upon outpourings of adulation and courtly challenges. There he often found passages like *"the reason of the un-reason with which my reason is afflicted so weakens my reason that with reason I complain of your beauty"*; or again, *"the high heavens, that of your divinity divinely fortify you with the stars, render you deserving of the desert your greatness deserves."*

Over this sort of folderol[3] the poor gentleman lost his wits, and he used to lie awake striving to understand it and worm out its meaning; though Aristotle[4] himself could have made out or extracted nothing, had he come back to life for that special purpose. He was rather uneasy about the wounds which Don Belianís gave and received, because it seemed to him that, however skilled the surgeons who had cured him, he must have had his face and body covered all over with seams and scars. He commended, however, the author's way of ending his book, with a promise to go on with that interminable adventure, and many a time he felt the urge to take up his pen and finish it just as its author had promised. He would no doubt have done so, and succeeded with it too, had he not been occupied with greater and more absorbing thoughts.

Many an argument did he have with the priest of his village (a learned man, and a graduate of Sigüenza[5]) as to which had been the better knight, Palmerín of England or Amadís of Gaul. Master Nicolás, the village barber, however, used to say that neither of them came up to the Knight of Phœbus, and that if there was any that could compare with *him* it was Don Galaor, the brother of Amadís of Gaul, because he had a spirit equal to every occasion, and was no wishy-washy knight or a crybaby like his brother, while in valor he was not a whit behind him.

In short, he became so absorbed in his books that he spent his nights from sunset to sunrise, and his days from dawn to dark, poring over them; and what with little sleep and much reading his brain shriveled up and he lost his wits. His imagination was stuffed with all he read in his books about enchantments, quarrels, battles, challenges, wounds, wooings, loves, agonies, and all sorts of impossible nonsense. It became so firmly planted in his mind that the whole fabric of invention and fancy he read about was true, that to him no history in the world was better substantiated. He used to say the Cid Ruy Díaz[6] was a very good knight but that he was not to be compared with the Knight of the Burning Sword who with one backstroke cut in half two fierce and monstrous giants. He thought more of Bernardo del Carpio because at Roncesvalles he slew Roland in spite of enchantments, availing himself of Hercules' trick when he strangled Antæus the son of Terra in his arms. He approved highly of the giant Morgante, because, although of the giant breed which is always arrogant and

---

2. **conceits** (kən sētsʹ) *n*.: Elaborate comparisons or metaphors.
3. **folderol** (fälʹ də rälʹ) *n*.: Mere nonsense.
4. **Aristotle** (arʹ is tätʹəl): Ancient Greek philosopher.

---

5. **Sigüenza** (sē gwānʹ sä): One of a group of "minor universities" granting degrees that were often laughed at by Spanish humorists.
6. **Cid Ruy Díaz** (sēd ro͞oʹē dēʹ äs): Famous Spanish soldier Ruy Diaz de Vivar: called the Cid, a derivation of the Arabic word for lord.

◆ **Build Vocabulary**

lucidity (lo͞o sidʹ ə tē) *n*.: Clarity; ability to be understood

adulation (aʹ jo͞o lāʹ shən) *n*.: Excessive praise or admiration

interminable (in turʹ mi nə bəl) *adj*.: Lasting, or seeming to last forever

ill-mannered, he alone was <u>affable</u> and well-bred. But above all he admired Reinaldos of Montalbán, especially when he saw him <u>sallying</u> forth from his castle and robbing everyone he met, and when beyond the seas he stole that image of Mohammed which, as his history says, was entirely of gold. To have a bout of kicking at that traitor of a Ganelon he would have given his housekeeper, and his niece into the bargain.

In a word, his wits being quite gone, he hit upon the strangest notion that ever madman in this world hit upon. He fancied it was right and <u>requisite</u>, no less for his own greater renown than in the service of his country, that he should make a knight-errant of himself, roaming the world over in full armor and on horseback in quest of adventures. He would put into practice all that he had read of as being the usual practices of knights-errant: righting every kind of wrong, and exposing himself to peril and danger from which he would emerge to reap eternal fame and glory. Already the poor man saw himself crowned by the might of his arm Emperor of Trebizond[7] at least. And so, carried away by the intense enjoyment he found in these pleasant fancies, he began at once to put his scheme into execution.

The first thing he did was to clean up some armor that had belonged to his ancestors and had for ages been lying forgotten in a corner, covered with rust and mildew. He scoured and polished it as best he could, but the one great defect he saw in it was that it had no closed helmet, nothing but a simple morion.[8] This deficiency, however, his ingenuity made good, for he contrived a kind of half-helmet of pasteboard which, fitted on to the morion, looked like a whole one. It is true that, in order to see if it was strong and fit to withstand a cut, he drew his sword and gave it a couple of slashes, the first of which undid in an instant what had taken him a week to do. The

ease with which he had knocked it to pieces disconcerted him somewhat, and to guard against the danger he set to work again, fixing bars of iron on the inside until he was satisfied with its strength. Then, not caring to try any more experiments with it, he accepted and commissioned it as a helmet of the most perfect construction.

He next proceeded to inspect his nag, which, with its cracked hoofs and more blemishes than the steed of Gonela, that "*tantum pellis et ossa fuit,*"[9] surpassed in his eyes the Bucephalus of Alexander or the Babieca of the Cid.[10] Four days were spent in thinking what name to give him, because (as he said to himself) it was not right that a horse belonging to a knight so famous, and one with such merits of its own, should be without some distinctive name. He strove to find something that would indicate what it had been before belonging to a knight-errant, and what it had now become. It was only reasonable that it should be given a new name to match the new career adopted by its master, and that the name should be a distinguished and full-sounding one, befitting the new order and calling it was about to follow. And so, after having composed, struck out, rejected, added to, unmade, and remade a multitude of names out of his memory and fancy, he decided upon calling it Rocinante. To his thinking this was a lofty, <u>sonorous</u> name that nevertheless indicated what the hack's[11]

9. **"tantum pellis et ossa fuit"** (tän´ tum pel´ is et äs´ ə froo´ it): "It was nothing but skin and bones" (Latin).
10. **Bucephalus** (byoo sef´ ə ləs) **of Alexander or the Babieca** (bäb ē ā´ kä) **of the Cid:** Bucephalus was Alexander the Great's war horse; Babieca was the Cid's war horse.
11. **hack's:** Horse's.

7. **Trebizond** (treb´ i zänd´): In medieval times, a Greek empire off the southeast coast of the Black Sea.
8. **morion** (mōr´ ē än´) *n.*: Old-fashioned soldier's helmet with a brim, covering the top part of the head.

status had been before it became what now it was, the first and foremost of all the hacks in the world.

Having got a name for his horse so much to his taste, he was anxious to get one for himself, and he spent eight days more pondering over this point. At last he made up his mind to call himself Don Quixote—which, as stated above, led the authors of this <u>veracious</u> history to infer that his name quite assuredly must have been Quixada, and not Quesada as others would have it. It occurred to him, however, that the valiant Amadís was not content to call himself Amadís and nothing more but added the name of his kingdom and country to make it famous and called himself Amadís of Gaul. So he, like a good knight, resolved to add on the name of his own region and style himself Don Quixote of La Mancha. He believed that this accurately described his origin and country, and that he did it honor by taking its name for his own.

So then, his armor being furbished, his morion turned into a helmet, his hack christened, and he himself confirmed, he came to the conclusion that nothing more was needed now but to look for a lady to be in love with, for a knight-errant without love was like a tree without leaves or fruit, or a body without a soul.

"If, for my sins, or by my good fortune," he said to himself, "I come across some giant hereabouts, a common occurrence with knights-errant, and knock him to the ground in one onslaught, or cleave him asunder at the waist, or, in short, <u>vanquish</u> and subdue him, will it not be well to have someone I may send him to as a present, that he may come in and fall on his knees before my sweet lady, and in a humble, submissive voice say, 'I am the giant Caraculiambro, lord of the island of Malindrania, vanquished in single combat by the never sufficiently <u>extolled</u> knight Don Quixote of La Mancha, who has commanded me to present myself before your grace, that your highness may dispose of me at your pleasure'?"

Oh, how our good gentleman enjoyed the delivery of this speech, especially when he had thought of someone to call his lady! There was, so the story goes, in a village near his own a very good-looking farm-girl with whom he had been at one time in love, though, so far as is

Don Quixote and the Windmill, c.1900, Francisco J. Torrome

▲ **Critical Viewing** How does this picture illustrate the effects of the "shriveled brain" of the hero? **[Connect]**

from *Don Quixote* ◆ 1005

known, she never knew it nor gave a thought to the matter. Her name was Aldonza Lorenzo, and upon her he thought fit to confer the title of Lady of his Thoughts. Searching for a name not too remote from her own, yet which would aim at and bring to mind that of a princess and great lady, he decided upon calling her Dulcinea del Toboso, since she was a native of El Toboso. To his way of thinking, the name was musical, uncommon, and significant, like all those he had bestowed upon himself and his belongings.

CHAPTER VIII

Of the Good Fortune Which the Valiant Don Quixote Had in the Terrible and Undreamed-of Adventure of the Windmills, With Other Occurrences Worthy to Be Fitly Recorded

At this point they came in sight of thirty or forty windmills that are on that plain.

"Fortune," said Don Quixote to his squire, as soon as he had seen them, "is arranging matters for us better than we could have hoped. Look there, friend Sancho Panza,[12] where thirty or more monstrous giants rise up, all of whom I mean to engage in battle and slay, and with whose spoils we shall begin to make our fortunes. For this is righteous warfare, and it is God's good service to sweep so evil a breed from off the face of the earth."

"What giants?" said Sancho Panza.

"Those you see there," answered his master, "with the long arms, and some have them nearly two leagues[13] long."

"Look, your worship," said Sancho. "What we see there are not giants but windmills, and what seem to be their arms are the vanes that turned by the wind make the millstone go."

"It is easy to see," replied Don Quixote,

"that you are not used to this business of adventures. Those are giants, and if you are afraid, away with you out of here and betake yourself to prayer, while I engage them in fierce and unequal combat."

So saying, he gave the spur to his steed Rocinante, heedless of the cries his squire Sancho sent after him, warning him that most certainly they were windmills and not giants he was going to attack. He, however, was so positive they were giants that he neither heard the cries of Sancho, nor perceived, near as he was, what they were.

"Fly not, cowards and vile beings," he shouted, "for a single knight attacks you."

A slight breeze at this moment sprang up, and the great vanes began to move.

"Though ye flourish more arms than the giant Briareus, ye have to reckon with me!" exclaimed Don Quixote, when he saw this.

So saying, he commended himself with all his heart to his lady Dulcinea, imploring her to support him in such a peril. With lance braced and covered by his shield, he charged at Rocinante's fullest gallop and attacked the first mill that stood in front of him. But as he drove his lance-point into the sail, the wind whirled it around with such force that it shivered the lance to pieces. It swept away with it horse and rider, and they were sent rolling over the plain, in sad condition indeed.

Sancho hastened to his assistance as fast as the animal could go. When he came up he found Don Quixote unable to move, with such an impact had Rocinante fallen with him.

"God bless me!" said Sancho. "Did I not tell your worship to watch what you were doing, because they were only windmills? No one could have made any mistake about it unless he had something of the same kind in his head."

"Silence, friend Sancho," replied Don Quixote. "The fortunes of war more than any other are liable to frequent fluctuations. Moreover I think, and it is the truth, that that same sage Frestón who carried off my study and books, has turned these giants into mills in order to rob me of the glory of vanquishing them, such is the enmity he bears me. But in the end his wicked arts will avail but little against my good sword."

---

12. **Sancho Panza:** A simple country man whom Don Quixote takes as his squire. In contrast to Don Quixote, Panza is practical and has common sense.

13. **leagues:** A league is about three miles.

"God's will be done," said Sancho Panza, and helping him to rise got him up again on Rocinante, whose shoulder was half dislocated. Then, discussing the adventure, they followed the road to Puerto Lápice, for there, said Don Quixote, they could not fail to find adventures in abundance and variety, as it was a well-traveled thoroughfare. For all that, he was much grieved at the loss of his lance, and said so to his squire.

"I remember having read," he added, "how a Spanish knight, Diego Pérez de Vargas by name, having broken his sword in battle, tore from an oak a ponderous bough or branch. With it he did such things that day, and pounded so many Moors, that he got the surname of Machuca, and he and his descendants from that day forth were called Vargas y Machuca. I mention this because from the first oak I see I mean to tear such a branch, large and stout. I am determined and resolved to do such deeds with it that you may deem yourself very fortunate in being found worthy to see them and be an eyewitness of things that will scarcely be believed."

"Be that as God wills," said Sancho, "I believe it all as your worship says it. But straighten yourself a little, for you seem to be leaning to one side, maybe from the shaking you got when you fell."

◆ **Literature and Your Life**

How has Don Quixote let his books "go to his head"? Can you relate to his feelings?

"That is the truth," said Don Quixote, "and if I make no complaint of the pain it is because knights-errant are not permitted to complain of any wound, even though their bowels be coming out through it."

"If so," said Sancho, "I have nothing to say. But God knows I would rather your worship complained when anything ailed you. For my part, I confess I must complain however small the ache may be, unless this rule about not complaining applies to the squires of knights-errant also."

Don Quixote could not help laughing at his squire's simplicity, and assured him he might complain whenever and however he chose, just as he liked. So far he had never read of anything to the contrary in the order of knighthood.

Sancho reminded him it was dinner time, to which his master answered that he wanted nothing himself just then, but that Sancho might eat when he had a mind. With this permission Sancho settled himself as comfortably as he could on his beast, and taking out of the saddlebags what he had stowed away in them, he jogged along behind his master munching slowly. From time to time he took a pull at the wineskin with all the enjoyment that the thirstiest tavernkeeper in Málaga might have envied. And while he went on in this way, between gulps, he never gave a thought to any of the promises his master had made him, nor did he rate it as hardship but rather as recreation going in quest of adventures, however dangerous they might be.

Guide for Responding

◆ **Literature and Your Life**

Reader's Response Which aspect of Don Quixote's appearance or behavior do you think is most ridiculous? Why?

Thematic Focus How does Don Quixote's imagination both create obstacles and help him overcome them?

✓ **Check Your Comprehension**

1. What sorts of books does Don Quixote read?
2. What unusual decision does Don Quixote make as a result of his reading?
3. What sent Don Quixote and his horse rolling across the plain?

Guide for Responding (continued)

◆ Critical Thinking

INTERPRET

1. How has reading books about chivalry affected Don Quixote's mind? **[Analyze]**
2. Why does Don Quixote like to use special names for people and things? **[Infer]**
3. What makes Don Quixote see the windmills as giant monsters? **[Speculate]**
4. Why is Sancho Panza a particularly helpful squire to Don Quixote? **[Deduce]**

EVALUATE

5. Don Quixote makes the world fit his illusions. What are the advantages and dangers of such an approach to life? **[Evaluate]**

EXTEND

6. Don Quixote tries to learn about being a knight from reading romantic, fictional accounts. What sources would you use to find out about a career that interested you? **[Career Link]**

◆ Reading Strategy

COMPARE AND CONTRAST

To see the humor of *Don Quixote*, **compare and contrast** the elements of the parody with the original. Look for similarities and differences between Don Quixote and the "ideal knight."

1. In what ways is Don Quixote, at least in his own mind, similar to the knights of old?
2. In what general ways does Don Quixote contrast with his idealized image of a knight?
3. What does this contrast tell us about Cervantes's view of chivalry?

◆ Literary Focus

PARODY

Cervantes creates a **parody** of the literature of chivalry by ridiculing the behavior of knights and suggesting that chivalrous ideals are pure illusion.

1. How does Cervantes poke fun at the way knights dressed?
2. How is the incident with the windmills an example of parody?
3. What specific aspects of chivalry does Cervantes parody? Give examples.

◆ Build Vocabulary

USING THE LATIN ROOT -son-

Knowing that the Latin root -son- means "hearing or sound," match each word with its definition. On your paper, write the correct definition next to each numbered word.

1. sonic   a. unity of sound
2. consonance   b. not in harmony
3. dissonant   c. having to do with sound
4. unison   d. harmony of musical tones

USING THE WORD BANK: Synonyms

On your paper, write the word from the Word Bank whose meaning is closest to that of the words below.

1. necessary   6. unending
2. dashing forth   7. honest
3. friendly   8. conquer
4. resonant   9. clearness
5. praised   10. excessive praise

◆ Build Grammar Skills

GERUNDS AND GERUND PHRASES

A **gerund** is a verb form ending in -ing used as a noun. A **gerund phrase** includes all the words that go with the gerund. Gerunds and gerund phrases perform all the same roles in a sentence that a noun does: subject, direct or indirect object, object of preposition, and appositive.

Practice Copy the following sentences in your notebook. Underline the gerunds or gerund phrases. Identify the function of each gerund or gerund phrase in the sentence.

1. It will be enough not to stray from the truth in telling it.
2. He commends the author's way of ending his books.
3. He follows the usual practice of knights: righting wrongs and exposing himself to all kinds of danger.
4. On his journey, Don Quixote tries attacking windmills.
5. Eating is one of Sancho's greatest pleasures.

Build Your Portfolio

Idea Bank

Writing

1. **Definition of a Hero** Write a definition of a modern hero. Include the qualities that you think people of today admire. Give examples from movies, sports, or entertainment to illustrate your points.

2. **Don Quixote in America** Suppose Don Quixote were to wander into your community for his next adventure. Write one or two paragraphs describing problems he might encounter.

3. **Create a Scene** In another scene from the novel, Don Quixote decides a flock of sheep is an enemy army and charges! Write the dialogue Don Quixote and Sancho might have had before or after the charge.

Speaking, Listening, and Viewing

4. **Role Play** Role-play the scene in which Sancho tries to talk Don Quixote out of attacking the windmills. **[Performing Arts Link]**

5. **Musical Drama** The musical *Man of La Mancha* is based on the character Don Quixote. Watch a video performance, noting how the story's theme is portrayed visually. Then discuss what the songs reveal about the hero's infatuation with romantic ideals. Share your conclusions with the class. **[Music Link]**

Researching and Representing

6. **Cartoon** Reread the description of Don Quixote's armor and horse. Then draw a cartoon of the forlorn-looking knight astride Rocinante as they joust the windmill. **[Art Link]**

7. **Visual Essay** Create a visual essay on the theme of heroes. Use photos from magazines and newspapers. Write captions that illustrate how your examples and opinions relate to a central message about heroes. **[Social Studies Link]**

Online Activity www.phlit.phschool.com

Guided Writing Lesson

Sketch of a Comic Hero

The typical hero of a work of literature—whether warrior, political leader, great athlete, or something else—usually has one defining characteristic: He or she is very serious. The quest or challenge that the hero undertakes is also one of the gravest import. Cervantes, however, turned the entire genre of the heroic tale on its head when he created his comic hero Don Quixote. In the spirit of Cervantes, create a comic hero and write a **sketch** of that hero. Describe your hero's character traits and achievements.

Writing Skills Focus: Clear and Logical Organization

To present your hero in a sketch, you'll need a **clear and logical organization.** For instance, you might want to describe the hero's life and exploits chronologically. Or you may discuss your hero's attributes in order of importance, starting from the least important and moving to the most. Whatever method you choose, use it consistently for the entire sketch.

Prewriting Start by creating a character chart like the one below, using it to categorize the various character traits of your hero. Underneath each trait, give an example that you can use in your draft.

Trait:	Example:
Nearsighted	Attempts to slay windmills
Absorbed in heroic books	Thinks of himself as a great Hero

Drafting Begin your profile with a catchy introduction, such as a quotation, question, or anecdote that illustrates a humorous quality of your hero. Then discuss qualities of your hero and give examples of each.

Revising Ask a peer whether your sketch conveys the comic qualities of your hero. If not, add further details to show those qualities.

Focus on Culture

Medieval Europe

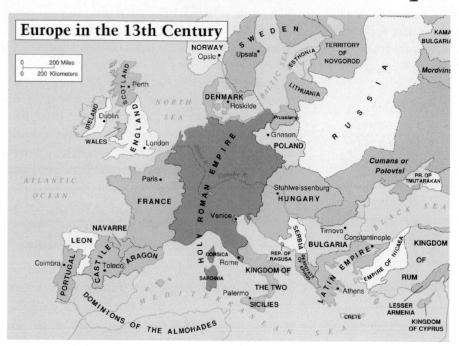

Europe in the 13th Century

0 200 Miles
0 200 Kilometers

◀ **Critical Viewing** Compare this map to a map of modern Europe. Which thirteenth-century lands became present-day Spain? Germany? Italy? **[Compare and Contrast]**

From out of the mists the terror appeared: fleets of ships with huge, square-rigged sails and prows carved to look like fierce dragons. Rough men with reddish hair came ashore, ready to kill and plunder. On shore, the people cried, "From the fury of the Northmen, O Lord, protect us!"

Beginning in the 800's, the Northmen, or Vikings, sailed out of Scandinavia to wreak havoc on Western Europe. One French chronicler described how the Vikings "laid waste the whole kingdom with fire and sword. . . . They destroyed houses, and razed monasteries and churches to the ground."

The Vikings were among several groups who invaded Western Europe during the Middle Ages, or Medieval (mē´ dē ē´ vəl) period. Out of the chaos, though, rose a new social system and a new European civilization.

GEOGRAPHIC SETTING

The historical period we now call the Middle Ages began around A.D. 500, after the collapse of the Roman empire. Rome had been a Mediterranean power, centered on the Italian peninsula that juts out from southern Europe. By contrast, medieval civilization largely developed in northern Europe. (See the map above.)

North European Plain One quarter of Western Europe consists of lowland plains located along seacoasts and in river valleys. The largest and most important is the North European Plain, which stretches more than 1,000 miles from Britain through France and Germany and into Eastern Europe.

From about 500 to 1000, this region was a frontier land, sparsely populated and relatively undeveloped. Much of the region was covered with dense forests or mosquito-ridden marshes.

By the late Middle Ages, Europeans began to develop the technology to drain the marshlands and open up rich new land for farming. Today, the North European Plain still contains some of the world's most productive farmland, as well as a number of major cities.

Lack of Natural Barriers Many navigable rivers flow through Europe's plains. In addition, the plains have few natural barriers. For centuries, the lowlands served as routes for migration and trade. At the same time, the absence of natural barriers has contributed to warfare. Rival groups and nations could invade neighboring lands with relative ease.

HISTORY

In the fourth century A.D., Rome was master of most of Europe. Yet the powerful empire had begun a gradual decline. One factor was pressure from Germanic tribes on the empire's northern border. Tribes such as the Vandals, the Goths, and the Visigoths migrated into, and sometimes invaded, Roman lands in Western Europe.

Early Middle Ages By the early Middle Ages, the unified Roman Empire was gone. In its place stood many small Germanic kingdoms. The most successful was the kingdom of the Franks. The Franks converted to Christianity in the 400's, forging an important alliance with the Church in Rome.

Around 800, Western Europe enjoyed a brief period of order under the Frankish king Charlemagne (shär´ lə män´). A skillful general, Charlemagne reunited much of the Western Roman Empire. He set up an efficient government, encouraged a revival of learning and the arts, and sent Christian missionaries throughout northern Europe.

Charlemagne's empire broke up soon after his death. For the next 200 years, Western Europe was battered by invasions. Magyars swept in from the east. Muslim forces from North

The Sleep of Arthur in Avalon, (detail), Sir Edward Burne-Jones, The Museo de Arte de Ponce, The Luis A. Ferré Foundation, Inc. Ponce, Puerto Rico

▲ **Critical Viewing** This nineteenth-century British painting shows the death of King Arthur. How can you tell that Arthur was considered a Christian hero? **[Infer]**

Africa controlled Spain and threatened Italy. However, the attacks by Viking raiders from the north were the most devastating of all.

The Feudal Period In response to these invasions, a feudal system evolved. Under feudalism, a king granted fiefs (fēfs), or estates, to powerful lords, who owed him loyalty and military service in exchange. (In practice, feudal kings had little power outside their own estates.) The lords, in turn, divided their own fiefs among vassals, or lesser lords. Vassals further divided their fiefs among noble knights, or mounted warriors.

At the bottom of feudal society were the common people. Mostly peasants, commoners made up the majority of the population.

After the age of Charlemagne, warfare was constant as feudal lords battled for power. To protect their lands, they built fortified castles. In the later Middle Ages, knights adopted a

The Month of October, Sowing, Limbourg Brothers, from Très riches heures du duc de Berry, Chateau du Louvre, Musée Condé, France

▲ **Critical Viewing** This painting shows activities on a medieval manor in October. Do you think this painting represents a realistic or idealistic view? Explain. [**Assess**]

code of behavior known as chivalry (shiv´ əl rē). Chivalry required knights to be brave and loyal, fight fairly, and protect women.

Revival and Growth By the 1100's, important changes were expanding people's horizons beyond the narrow world of the early Middle Ages. The population was growing. New technologies increased food production. Warfare declined as kings began to exercise more power over rival feudal lords.

The decline in feudal warfare encouraged the revival of trade and travel. Some kings and feudal lords repaired roads and bridges. Coined money, which had largely gone out of use, reappeared. At annual trade fairs, merchants and traders from all over Western Europe gathered. Increased trade led to the growth of towns.

The Crusades and the Black Death In 1095, Pope Urban II called for a crusade to take the Holy Land—the lands near Jerusalem where Jesus Christ had lived—away from the Muslims who lived there. For the next 200 years, armies of Christians left their homes in Europe to fight for lands in the Middle East.

In the end, the Crusades failed in their goal. Yet renewed contact with the Middle East did benefit Europe. Returning crusaders brought back a taste for goods such as sugar, spices, and silks. This new demand increased European trade across the Mediterranean. The Crusades also sparked the desire of Europeans to learn more about the outside world.

In 1348, ships returning to Europe from the eastern Mediterranean brought back the bubonic plague. Carried by flea-infested rats, the dreaded "Black Death" spread quickly. In all, the plague killed an estimated 25 million people—more than one third of the population of Europe. The epidemic also brought despair, economic collapse, and social unrest. Europe would not fully recover from the effects of the Black Death for more than 100 years.

SOCIETY AND CULTURE

The feudal economic system was based on the manor. A manor included a village and the surrounding lands administered by a lord. (See the picture above.)

Peasants and the Manor Peasants living on the manor owed service to the lord in exchange for his protection. Most peasants were serfs, tied to the lord's land. Although they were not slaves, serfs were not free to leave the land.

Each manor was a self-sufficient community, where people produced almost everything they needed to survive. Peasants raised sheep for wool and spun the wool into cloth. They raised cattle and grew grain and vegetables. Each manor also had its own mill and blacksmith shop, as well as its own church.

The Role of the Church The Church played a major role in all areas of medieval life. For peasants and nobles alike, the Church offered a chance of salvation and eternal life. Village priests taught the gospels, comforted people in times of need, and administered the sacraments, the seven sacred rites that were seen as paths to salvation.

The Church also played a central role in politics. Because they were educated, Church officials served as advisors to kings and nobles. At the top of the Church, the pope in Rome exercised supreme spiritual and supreme political authority. By the late Middle Ages, the pope's claim of supremacy over kings was being challenged as the kings grew in power. This led to clashes between popes and rulers.

Many Christians joined religious orders. As monks and nuns, they dedicated their lives to serving God. Some religious orders founded hospitals and furnished other services for the sick and poor. In monasteries, scholarly monks preserved the learning of the ancient world by copying Greek and Roman manuscripts.

Revival of Learning The clergy set up schools in cathedrals to train young men for service in the Church. In the late Middle Ages, as interest in learning grew, some cathedral schools evolved into universities. Medieval scholars such as Thomas Aquinas studied the works of ancient Greek philosophers, as well as Muslim and Jewish scholars. Aquinas found new ways to harmonize faith and reason.

ARTS AND LITERATURE

During the later Middle Ages, the Church became the chief patron of the arts. Medieval churches were decorated with statues, paintings, and stained-glass windows. These artworks not only beautified the churches, but also helped teach Bible stories.

The Gothic Cathedral Cities competed to build the tallest and most beautiful churches.

In the 1100's, architects developed a style now called Gothic. Gothic cathedrals, such as Notre Dame in Paris, were more elaborate than earlier styles. They had higher ceilings and larger windows, which created a sense of airiness. Soaring spires carried the eye toward heaven, reminding worshipers of the power of God.

Literature Medieval writers produced fine literature in many genres. In the courts of nobles, wandering poets called *troubadours* (trōō´ bə dôrz´) praised the perfection, beauty, and wit of women throughout the ages. The songs of the troubadours helped shape modern ideas of romantic love.

Other works told of the heroic deeds of knights. The *Song of Roland* from France (see page 948) and the *Song of the Cid* from Spain were long epics featuring Christian heroes who fought against the Muslims in Spain. In France and Britain, popular tales featured the legendary King Arthur and his Knights of the Round Table. (See the picture on page 1011.) Arthurian legend inspired the romance *Perceval* by the French writer Chrétien de Troyes (krà tya*n* də t*r*wȧ´). (See the excerpts from *Perceval* on p. 1016.)

Perhaps the greatest medieval writers were Dante Alighieri of Italy and Geoffrey Chaucer of Britain. In *The Divine Comedy*, Dante described an imaginary journey through hell, purgatory, and heaven. (See the excerpt from this poem on p. 30.) Chaucer's *Canterbury Tales* offer a series of tales that provide a cross-section of late medieval society.

ACTIVITY
Giving a Presentation

Use library or Internet resources to research one medieval art form, such as stained glass, tapestry, illuminated manuscript, metalwork, or sculpture. Then, prepare a five-minute presentation featuring one work of art. Include an explanation of how it was made and what purpose it served. 🌐

$\mathscr{G}$uide for Reading

Chrétien de Troyes
(fl. 1165–1180)

Although very little is known about Chrétien de Troyes (krā tya*n* də t*r*wá´), the influence of his writings has lasted for more than eight centuries. He did more than any other writer to introduce tales of King Arthur's knights to literature.

Romances Chrétien lived in France at a time when learning and literature were expanding. Members of the nobility hired writers and storytellers to entertain their guests. Chrétien, who spent time at aristocratic courts in northern France, wrote popular narratives called romances. His romances included fantastic events and adventures, as well as details about the life at nobles' castles.

Legends of King Arthur Chrétien was one of the first writers to make use of the legends of King Arthur. The legends were told originally by the Celts

(selts), who lived in Great Britain, especially in Wales, and in Brittany in northwestern France. The stories described Arthur's court at Camelot, where he gathered the Knights of the Round Table, including Lancelot, Galahad, Gawain, and Perceval.

Chrétien de Troyes' three major works, *Yvain*, *Lancelot*, and *Perceval*, are all tales of knights of King Arthur's Round Table. *Yvain* and *Lancelot* explore the conflict between love and the knight's chivalric duty to seek out new adventures and to bring greater glory to himself and to his lord. Lancelot sacrifices his honor for love. Yvain abandons the woman he loves in favor of a quest for knightly glory, only to learn of the foolishness of his choice. *Perceval*, on the other hand, focuses on a knight's spiritual quest (see the Background for Understanding, p. 1015).

◆ Build Vocabulary

LATIN WORD ROOTS: *-naviga-*

In line 27 of this selection from *Perceval*, the men in the boat *navigated*. The Latin word root *-naviga-* means "to sail a ship." In the poem, *navigated* means "steered the boat." The root is also found in the adjective *navigable,* which means "deep and wide enough for boats or ships to travel on."

sovereign
navigated
elated
serene
ebony
tonic
nimble

WORD BANK

As you read, you will encounter the words on this list. Each word is defined on the page where it first appears. Preview the list before you read.

◆ Build Grammar Skills

COHERENCE THROUGH REPETITION

Writers achieve **coherence through repetition** when they repeat words as a way of holding ideas together in a passage. Look at the beginning of the selection, lines 3–6:

> He did not meet one living soul:
> no creature from the wide earth's span,
> no Christian woman, Christian man
> who could direct him on his way.

To emphasize the loneliness of Perceval's journey, the poet describes the loneliness in several ways:
- he did not meet one living soul
- no creature from the wide earth's span
- no Christian woman, Christian man

from Perceval

◆ *Literature and Your Life*

CONNECT YOUR EXPERIENCE

You've probably had dreams in which strange things happen. You may fly over the rooftops or step out of your door and find yourself in a neighborhood that you moved away from long ago.

The adventures in *Perceval*, like the adventures in many legends and folk tales, can seem as strange as the incidents in a dream. You'll read about a castle that appears out of nowhere and a magical lance from which drops of blood flow.

THEMATIC FOCUS: TURNING POINTS

Characters in an adventurous tale usually experience many turning points. What turning points does Perceval experience?

◆ Background for Understanding

LITERATURE

Perceval tells of the adventures of one of King Arthur's knights, Perceval, on his quest to find the Holy Grail—the cup from which Jesus drank at the Last Supper. According to medieval legend, this cup was hidden in a magical castle. Only an innocent person, free of sin, could find the Grail and, in finding it, have a vision of heaven. Perceval is one of the few knights virtuous enough to see the Grail.

◆ Literary Focus

MEDIEVAL QUEST

In stories about knights, the **quest** is a series of adventures each knight must undertake to become a worthy person. He may have to rescue a maiden, defeat evil men or monsters, or restore health to a land by seeking a holy object like the Grail.

The knight returns from the quest a better man. He may have greater knowledge or understanding. He may be more mature and ready to lead his people. Luke Skywalker in the *Star Wars* movies is a modern example of a young hero who matures on his quest.

In this section of *Perceval*, the young knight is in the middle of his quest to become a knight.

◆ Reading Strategy

SUMMARIZE

To **summarize** is to write a shortened version of events in your own words. A good summary can help you to remember facts as you read, to write about a literary work, or to study for a test. A summary can be in sentence form or in a chart or other graphic organizer.

There are many places in *Perceval* where the details may seem overwhelming. You can remember them if you organize them in a web. The following web summarizes the details about the lance in lines 216–236.

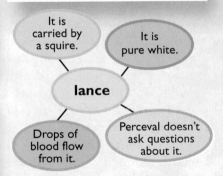

from Perceval, the grail

Chrétien de Troyes

Translated by Ruth Harwood Cline

The youth began his journey from
the castle, and the daytime whole
he did not meet one living soul:
no creature from the wide earth's span,
5 no Christian woman, Christian man
who could direct him on his way.
The young man did not cease to pray
the <u>sovereign</u> father, God, Our Lord,
if He were willing, to accord
10 that he would find his mother still
alive and well. He reached a hill
and saw a river at its base.
So rapid was the current's pace,
so deep the water, that he dared
15 not enter it, and he declared,
"Oh God Almighty! It would seem,
if I could get across this stream,
I'd find my mother, if she's living."
He rode the bank with some misgiving
20 and reached a cliff, but at that place
the water met the cliff's sheer face
and kept the youth from going through.
A little boat came into view;
it headed down the river, floating
25 and carrying two men out boating.
The young knight halted there and waited.
He watched the way they <u>navigated</u>
and thought that they would pass the place

he waited by the cliff's sheer face.
30 They stayed in mid-stream, where they
    stopped
and took the anchor, which they dropped.
The man afore,[1] a fisher, took
a fish to bait his line and hook;
in size the little fish he chose
35 was larger than a minnow grows.
The knight, completely at a loss,
not knowing how to get across,
first greeted them, then asked the pair,
"Please, gentlemen, nearby is there
40 a bridge to reach the other side?"
To which the fisherman replied,
"No, brother, for besides this boat,
the one in which we are afloat,
which can't bear five men's weight as charge,
45 there is no other boat as large
for twenty miles each way and more, and
you can't cross on horseback, for
there is no ferry, bridge, nor ford."
"Tell me," he answered, "by Our Lord,
50 where I may find a place to stay."
The fisherman said, "I should say
you'll need a roof tonight and more,
so I will lodge you at my door.
First find the place this rock is breached
55 and ride uphill, until you've reached
the summit of the cliff," he said.
"Between the wood and river bed
you'll see, down in the valley wide,
the manor house where I reside."
60 The knight rode up the cliff until

---

1. **afore** (ə fôr'): Before.

◆ Build Vocabulary

sovereign (säv´rən) *adj.*: Above or superior to all others

navigated (nav´ə gāt´ id) *v.*: Steered or directed a ship

elated (ē lāt´ id) *adj.*: Filled with joy

he reached the summit of the hill.
He looked around him from that stand
but saw no more than sky and land.
He cried, "What have I come to see?
65 Stupidity and trickery!
May God dishonor and disgrace
the man who sent me to this place!
He had the long way round in mind,
when he told me that I would find
70 a manor when I reached the peak.
Oh, fisherman, why did you speak?
For if you said it out of spite,
you tricked me badly!" He caught sight
of a tower starting to appear
75 down in a valley he was near,
and as the tower came into view,
if people were to search, he knew,
as far as Beirut,[2] they would not
find any finer tower or spot.
80 The tower was dark gray stone, and square,
and flanked by lesser towers, a pair.
Before the tower the hall was laid;
before the hall was the arcade.[3]
On toward the tower the young man rode
85 in haste and called the man who showed
the way to him a worthy guide.
No longer saying he had lied,
he praised the fisherman, _elated_
to find his lodgings as he stated.
90 The youth went toward the gate and found
the drawbridge lowered to the ground.
He rode across the drawbridge span.
Four squires awaited the young man.
Two squires came up to help him doff
95 his arms and took his armor off.
The third squire led his horse away
to give him fodder, oats, and hay.
The fourth brought a silk cloak, new-made,
and led him to the hall's arcade,
100 which was so fine, you may be sure
you'd not find, even if you were
to search as far as Limoges,[4] one
as splendid in comparison.

The young man paused in the arcade,
105 until the castle's master made
two squires escort him to the hall.
The young man entered with them all
and found the hall was square inside:
it was as long as it was wide;
110 and in the center of its span
he saw a handsome nobleman
with grayed hair, sitting on a bed.
The nobleman wore on his head
a mulberry-black sable cap
115 and wore a dark silk robe and wrap.
He leaned back in his weakened state
and let his elbow take his weight.
Between four columns, burning bright,
a fire of dry logs cast its light.
120 In order to enjoy its heat,
four hundred men could find a seat
around the outsized fire, and not
one man would take a chilly spot.
The solid fireplace columns could
125 support the massive chimney hood,
which was of bronze, built high and wide.
The squires, one squire on either side,
appeared before their lord foremost
and brought the youth before his host.
130 He saw the young man, whom he greeted.
"My friend," the nobleman entreated,
"don't think me rude not to arise;
I hope that you will realize
that I cannot do so with ease."
135 "Don't even mention it, sir, please,
I do not mind," replied the boy,
"may Heaven give me health and joy."
The lord rose higher on the bed,
as best he could, with pain, and said,
140 "My friend, come nearer, do not be
embarrassed or disturbed by me,
for I command you to come near.
Come to my side and sit down here."
The nobleman began to say,
145 "From where, sir, did you come today?"
He said, "This morning, sir, I came
from Belrepeire, for that's its name."
"So help me God," the lord replied,
"you must have had a long day's ride:
150 to start before the light of morn

2. **Beirut** (bā ro͞ot'): The capital of Lebanon and a seaport
on the Mediterranean.
3. **arcade** (är kād') n.: A passage with an arched roof or
any covered passageway.
4. **Limoges** (lē mōzh'): A city in west central France.

before the watchman blew his horn."
"Sir, I assure you, by that time
the morning bells had rung for prime,"[5]
the young man made the observation.
155 While they were still in conversation,
a squire entered through the door
and carried in a sword he wore
hung from his neck and which thereto
he gave the rich man, who withdrew
160 the sword halfway and checked the blade
to see where it was forged and made, which
had been written on the sword. The blade
was wrought, observed the lord,
of such fine steel, it would not break
165 save with its bearer's life at stake
on one occasion, one alone,
a peril that was only known
to him who forged and tempered it.
The squire said, "Sir, if you permit,
170 your lovely blonde niece sent this gift,
and you will never see or lift
a sword that's lighter for its strength,
considering its breadth and length.
Please give the sword to whom you choose,
175 but if it goes to one who'll use
the sword that he is given well,
you'll greatly please the demoiselle.
The forger of the sword you see
has never made more swords than three,
180 and he is going to die before
he ever forges any more.
No sword will be quite like this sword."
Immediately the noble lord
bestowed it on the newcomer,
185 who realized that its hangings were
a treasure and of worth untold.
The pommel[6] of the sword was gold,
the best Arabian or Grecian;
the sheath's embroidery gold Venetian.
190 Upon the youth the castle's lord
bestowed the richly mounted sword
and said to him, "This sword, dear brother,
was destined for you and none other.
I wish it to be yours henceforth.

195 Gird on the sword and draw it forth."
He thanked the lord, and then the knight
made sure the belt was not too tight,
and girded on the sword, and took
the bare blade out for a brief look.
200 Then in the sheath it was replaced:
it looked well hanging at his waist
and even better in his fist.
It seemed as if it would assist
the youth in any time of need
205 to do a brave and knightly deed.
Beside the brightly burning fire
the youth turned round and saw a squire,
who had his armor in his care,
among the squires standing there.
210 He told this squire to hold the sword
and took his seat beside the lord,
who honored him as best he might.
The candles cast as bright a light
as could be found in any manor.
215 They chatted in a casual manner.
Out of a room a squire came, clasping
a lance of purest white: while grasping
the center of the lance, the squire
walked through the hall between the fire
220 and two men sitting on the bed.
All saw him bear, with measured tread,
the pure white lance. From its white tip
a drop of crimson blood would drip
and run along the white shaft and
225 drip down upon the squire's hand,
and then another drop would flow.
The knight who came not long ago
beheld this marvel, but preferred
not to inquire why it occurred,
230 for he recalled the admonition
the lord made part of his tuition,[7]
since he had taken pains to stress
the dangers of loquaciousness.[8]
The young man thought his questions might
235 make people think him impolite,

---

7. **the admonition . . . tuition:** The warning that the lord made part of his teaching.
8. **loquaciousness** (lō kwā´ shəs nis) n.: Talkativeness.

---

5. **prime:** The first hour of daylight, usually 6 A.M.
6. **pommel** (pum´ əl) n.: The knob on the end of the hilt of a sword or dagger.

◆ **Build Vocabulary**

serene (sə rēn´) adj.: Calm; not disturbed or troubled

The Damsel of Sanct Grael, Dante Gabriel Rossetti, Tate Gallery, London

▲ **Critical Viewing** How is the Grail in this picture similar to and different from the Grail described in lines 255–264? **[Compare and Contrast]**

and that's why he did not inquire.
Two more squires entered, and each squire
held candelabra, wrought of fine
pure gold with niello work design.[9]
240 The squires with candelabra fair
were an extremely handsome pair.
At least ten lighted candles blazed
in every holder that they raised.
The squires were followed by a maiden
245 who bore a grail, with both hands laden.
The bearer was of noble mien,[10]
well dressed, and lovely, and <u>serene</u>,
and when she entered with the grail,
the candles suddenly grew pale,
250 the grail cast such a brilliant light,
as stars grow dimmer in the night
when sun or moonrise makes them fade.
A maiden after her conveyed
a silver platter past the bed.
255 The grail, which had been borne ahead,
was made of purest, finest gold
and set with gems; a manifold
display of jewels of every kind,
the costliest that one could find
260 in any place on land or sea,
the rarest jewels there could be,
let not the slightest doubt be cast.
The jewels in the grail surpassed
all other gems in radiance.
265 They went the same way as the lance:
they passed before the lord's bedside
to another room and went inside.
The young man saw the maids' procession
and did not dare to ask a question
270 about the grail or whom they served;
the wise lord's warning he observed,
for he had taken it to heart.
I fear he was not very smart;
I have heard warnings people give:
275 that one can be too talkative,
but also one can be too still.
But whether it was good or ill,
I do not know, he did not ask.

---

9. niello (nē el´ ō) **work design:** Deep black inlaid work used to decorate metal.

10. grail (grāl) **. . . mien** (mēn): The grail is the legendary cup or platter used by Jesus at the Last Supper and by Joseph of Arimathea to collect drops of Jesus' blood at the crucifixion. *Mien* signifies "appearance."

from *Perceval* ◆ 1019

The squires who were assigned the task
280 of bringing in the water and
the cloths obeyed the lord's command.
The men who usually were assigned
performed these tasks before they dined.
They washed their hands in water, warmed,
285 and then two squires, so I'm informed,
brought in the ivory tabletop,
made of one piece: they had to stop
and hold it for a while before
the lord and youth, until two more
290 squires entered, each one with a trestle.[11]
The trestles had two very special,
rare properties, which they contained
since they were built, and which remained
in them forever: they were wrought
295 of ebony, a wood that's thought
to have two virtues: it will not
ignite and burn and will not rot;
these dangers cause no harm nor loss.
They laid the tabletop across
300 the trestles, and the cloth above.
What shall I say? To tell you of
the cloth is far beyond my scope.
No legate, cardinal, or pope
has eaten from a whiter one.
305 The first course was of venison,
a peppered haunch, cooked in its fat,
accompanied by a clear wine that
was served in golden cups, a pleasant,
delicious drink. While they were present
310 a squire carved up the venison.
He set the peppered haunch upon
a silver platter, carved the meat,
and served the slices they would eat
by placing them on hunks of bread.
315 Again the grail passed by the bed,
and still the youth remained reserved

about the grail and whom they served.
he did not ask, because he had
been told so kindly it was bad
320 to talk too much, and he had taken
these words to heart. He was mistaken;
though he remembered, he was still
much longer than was suitable.
At every course, and in plain sight,
325 the grail was carried past the knight,
who did not ask whom they were serving,
although he wished to know, observing
in silence that he ought to learn
about it prior to his return.
330 So he would ask: before he spoke
he'd wait until the morning broke,
and he would ask a squire to tell,
once he had told the lord farewell
and all the others in his train.
335 He put the matter off again
and turned his thoughts toward drink and
        food.
They brought, and in no stingy mood,
the foods and different types of wine,
which were delicious, rich and fine.
340 The squires were able to provide
the lord and young knight at his side
with every course a count, king, queen,
and emperor eat by routine.
At dinner's end, the two men stayed
345 awake and talked, while squires made
the beds and brought them fruit: they ate
the rarest fruits: the nutmeg, date,
fig, clove, and pomegranate red.
With Alexandrian gingerbread,
350 electuaries[12] at the end,
restoratives, a tonic blend,
and pliris archonticum
for settling his stomachum.
Then various liqueurs were poured
355 for them to sample afterward:
straight piment, which did not contain
sweet honey or a single grain
of pepper, wine of mulberries,
clear syrups, other delicacies.

---

11. **trestle** (tres´ əl) *n.*: A frame consisting of a horizontal beam fastened to two pairs of spreading legs.

◆ **Build Vocabulary**

ebony (eb´ə nē) *n.*: Hard, heavy, dark wood
tonic (tän´ ik) *adj.*: Health-giving; strengthening
nimble (nim´ bəl) *adj.*: Moving quickly and lightly

---

12. **electuaries** (ē lek´ chōō er´ ēz): Medicines made by
mixing drugs with honey or syrup to form a paste. Pliris
archonticum, mentioned two lines later, is such a medicine.

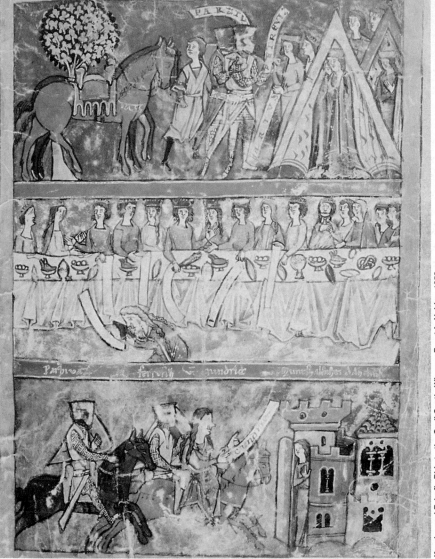

Kundry and Feirefiz Ride to the Grail Castle Where a Feast Is Held, c. 1250, German manuscript of *Perceval,* Bayerische Staatsbibliothek Munchen

◀ **Critical Viewing** The bottom band of this illustrated manuscript page shows Perceval and others approaching the Grail Castle. Is the mood of this scene similar to or different from the mood created by the poem? Explain. **[Compare and Contrast]**

360 The youth's astonishment persisted;
    he did not know such things existed.
    "Now, my dear friend," the great lord said,
    "the time has come to go to bed.
    I'll seek my room—don't think it queer—
365 and you will have your bed out here
    and may lie down at any hour.
    I do not have the slightest power
    over my body anymore
    and must be carried to my door."
370 Four <u>nimble</u> servants, strongly set,
    came in and seized the coverlet
    by its four corners (it was spread
    beneath the lord, who lay in bed)
    and carried him away to rest.

375 The others helped the youthful guest.
    As he required, and when he chose,
    they took his clothing off, and hose,
    and put him in a bed with white,
    smooth linen sheets; he slept all night
380 at peace until the morning broke.
    But when the youthful knight awoke,
    He was the last to rise and found
    that there was no one else around.
    Exasperated and alone,
385 he had to get up on his own.
    He made the best of it, arose,
    and awkwardly drew on his hose
    without a bit of help or aid.
    He saw his armor had been laid

390 at night against the dais' head
a little distance from his bed.
When he had armed himself at last,
he walked around the great hall past
the rooms and knocked at every door
395 which opened wide the night before,
but it was useless: juxtaposed,[13]
the doors were tightly locked and closed.
He shouted, called, and knocked outside,
but no one opened or replied.
400 At last the young man ceased to call,
walked to the doorway of the hall,
which opened up, and passed through there,
and went on down the castle stair.
His horse was saddled in advance.
405 The young man saw his shield and lance
were leaned against the castle wall
upon the side that faced the hall.
He mounted, searched the castle whole,
but did not find one living soul,
410 one servant, or one squire around.
He hurried toward the gate and found
the men had let the drawbridge down,
so that the knight could leave the town
at any hour he wished to go.
415 His hosts had dropped the drawbridge so
the youth could cross it undeterred.

---

13. **juxtaposed** (juks´ tə pōzd) *adj.*: Put side by side or close together.

The squires were sent, the youth inferred,
out to the wood, where they were set
to checking every trap and net.
420 The drawbridge lay across the stream.
He would not wait and formed a scheme
of searching through the woods as well
to see if anyone could tell
about the lance, why it was bleeding,
425 about the grail, whom they were feeding,
and where they carried it in state.
The youth rode through the castle gate
and out upon the drawbridge plank.
Before he reached the other bank,
430 the young man started realizing
the forefeet of his horse were rising.
His horse made one great leap indeed.
Had he not jumped well, man and steed
would have been hurt. His rider swerved
435 to see what happened and observed
the drawbridge had been lifted high.
He shouted, hearing no reply,
"Whoever raised the bridge," said he,
"where are you? Come and talk to me!
440 Say something to me; come in view.
There's something I would ask of you,
some things I wanted to inquire,
some information I desire."
His words were wasted, vain and fond;
445 no one was willing to respond.

Guide for Responding

◆ Literature and Your Life

Reader's Response Would you enjoy being on an adventure or quest like Perceval? Why or why not?

Thematic Focus Identify a turning point that Perceval experiences.

☑ Check Your Comprehension

1. Who directs Perceval to the castle?
2. What is the condition of Perceval's host?
3. Why doesn't Perceval ask about the Grail?
4. Why is Perceval unable to find out about the lance and the Grail the next morning?

◆ Critical Thinking

INTERPRET

1. Why does Perceval not hesitate to approach the castle that appears in the valley? **[Speculate]**
2. In lines 360–361, we learn that Perceval "did not know such things existed." What does this show about his life up to this point? **[Interpret]**
3. From the events in the selection, what kind of person does Perceval seem to be? **[Draw Conclusions]**

EVALUATE

4. Was Perceval right to follow his host's instructions to be quiet? **[Make a Judgment]**

Guide for Responding (continued)

◆ Reading Strategy

SUMMARIZE

To **summarize** events or details is to put them into your own words in a shortened form. You can use a chart or web to organize the information, or you can write sentences that condense the information in paragraph form.

There are many objects and incidents in this selection that could require summarizing in order to organize and recall the details.

1. Summarize the ways in which Perceval discovered that the castle was deserted in the morning.
2. On your paper, draw a web like the one on p. 1019. Fill in details about the sword that the host gives to Perceval.

◆ Build Vocabulary

USING WORDS WITH THE LATIN ROOT *-naviga-*

The root *-naviga-* means "to steer a ship." Words from boating and sailing are also used when speaking of airplanes or driving. Fill in each blank with a word that contains the root *-naviga-*.

1. The flight pattern had to be changed by the __?__ because of the storm.
2. After it was dredged, the river was _____?_____ by the company's barges.
3. If you give me the roadmap, I'll try to _____?_____ our way to the concert.

USING THE WORD BANK: SYNONYMS

On your paper, write the word whose meaning is closest to that of the first word.

1. navigated: (a) reached an agreement, (b) became sick, (c) steered a boat
2. sovereign: (a) highest, (b) lowest, (c) wealthiest
3. elated: (a) tardy, (b) raised, (c) joyful
4. serene: (a) boastful, (b) beautiful, (c) calm
5. ebony: (a) a measure of strength, (b) a kind of wood, (c) careful work
6. tonic: (a) healthful, (b) thirsty, (c) musical
7. nimble: (a) cloudy, (b) careless, (c) agile

◆ Literary Focus

MEDIEVAL QUEST

Like other knights in romances, Perceval is engaged in a **quest** to prove his worthiness as a knight—an adventure or series of adventures that involve:

- a purpose
- encounters with other knights, nobles, or monsters
- a result, such as finding a sacred object, freeing an individual or the people of a region, or achieving some kind of wisdom.

1. At the beginning of the selection, what is the purpose of Perceval's traveling?
2. At the end of the selection, what knowledge is Perceval searching for?
3. What is the result of Perceval's quest in this selection?

◆ Build Grammar Skills

COHERENCE THROUGH REPETITION

When you give your writing **coherence through repetition,** you bring unity and clarity to your writing by repeating a word or phrase.

Practice Sometimes repetition of a word or phrase can be dull. Other times, repetition of a word or phrase can clarify a meaning. Rewrite the following sentences in your notebook, using repetition for greater coherence and clarity.

1. Perceval spoke to a man in a boat, and he told him where to find lodging.
2. Perceval saw a tower while riding up the hill on his horse. It was gray.
3. A squire brought Perceval a silk cloak, while his horse was led away by another.
4. Two maidens carried a Grail and a silver platter. The candles seemed pale, because it cast a stronger light than they did.
5. As Perceval rode his horse onto the drawbridge, someone lifted it up.

Build Your Portfolio

Idea Bank

Writing

1. **Letter** Write a letter from Perceval to his mother, in which he summarizes what he has seen at the castle.

2. **Modern Quest** Write a brief tale of a modern-day adventurer on a quest. You can base your tale on Perceval's travels.

3. **Narrative Poem** Write a short narrative poem in the same kind of rhymed couplets used in *Perceval*. Or, if you prefer, write your narrative in free verse.

Speaking, Listening, and Viewing

4. **Oral Interpretation** Read *Perceval* aloud for an audience, pausing for punctuation but not stopping automatically at the ends of lines. **[Performing Arts Link]**

5. **Music and Arthur** Find recordings of music based on the tales of King Arthur and his knights. One example is the musical *Camelot;* another is the opera *Parsifal.* As you listen to the music, identify references to the legends in the words or musical themes. **[Music Link]**

Researching and Representing

6. **Map of the Celts** Draw a map of France and the British Isles, showing where Celtic culture prevailed before and during the Middle Ages. Include the names of the Celtic groups in the regions where they lived. **[Social Studies Link]**

7. **Illustrate the Text** Artists have often drawn or painted characters, incidents, and scenes from the King Arthur legends. Do your own illustration of a character or incident from *Perceval* or another King Arthur story. **[Art Link]**

Online Activity www.phlit.phschool.com

Guided Writing Lesson

Interpreting a Symbol

A **symbol** in literature is an object that stands for something else, usually for an abstract quality or an idea. For example, when Perceval reaches the river at the beginning of the selection, he finds that there is no way for him to cross it. At this point in the poem, the river is a symbol of all the difficulties he faces in his journey home to see his mother.

Choose a symbol in *Perceval* or another literary work, and write a brief essay on the meaning and importance of the symbol in the work.

> ### Writing Skills Focus:
> ### Relatedness of Supporting Details
>
> Use **supporting details** that relate to the point you are making in your interpretation. The details can be direct quotations from the literary work, or they can be paraphrased statements that you write yourself. Introduce each of the details in a way that makes clear how it is related to the point that you are trying to make.

Prewriting Select a poem or story you have read in which you can identify an important symbol. Think about what it means. Then, jot down a number of ideas about its meaning within the story or poem.

Drafting Describe the symbol and then explain what it means (a) literally, and (b) as something larger than itself in the meaning of the story or poem.

Revising Read your draft to a small group of students. Ask if your meaning is clear. Do you explain the importance of the symbol to the literary work? Do the details you use support your ideas?

Are there places where repetition of a word or phrase will clarify your meaning? For more on coherence through repetition, see pp. 1014 and 1023.

Part 2 *World Heroes*

Rama and Lakshman Confer with the Animal Armies. From *the Ramayana of Valmiki,* Freer Gallery of Art, Smithsonian Institution, Washington, DC

Dipankara Buddha, 17th Century A.D., Nepal, Asian Art Museum of San Francisco, The Avery Brundage Collection

Guide for Reading

About the *Ramayana*

The great Indian epic, the *Ramayana,* written by the poet Valmiki, consists of twenty-four thousand couplets. It probably dates from after 300 B.C.

The epic tells how Prince Rama wins his bride, Sita, by proving his strength. Just as he is about to inherit the throne, evil plots result in his banishment from the kingdom. For fourteen years, he wanders in exile with his wife, Sita, and his brother, Lakshmana. Sita is kidnapped, and Rama rescues her with the help of Hanuman, the monkey god. After the rescue, Rama is welcomed back to the kingdom.

The excerpt you are about to read tells of adventures from Rama's childhood, before his banishment. Even as boys, Rama and his brother Lakshmana show extraordinary strength and ability.

R. K. Narayan (1906–)

For the writer R. K. Narayan (nə rī´ en), the *Ramayana* and *Mahabharata* played a significant role in fostering a love for literature. He often cites the importance of oral literature in traditional Indian society: "The storyteller who has studied the epics, the *Ramayana* and the *Mahabharata,* may take up any of the thousand episodes in them, create a narrative with his individual stamp on it, and hold the attention of an audience, numbering thousands, for hours."

Born into the Hindu Brahmin caste, Narayan spoke Tamil at home, used English at school, and was taught traditional Indian melodies and prayers in Sanskrit, India's ancient classical language. In addition to his contemporary versions of Indian epics, R. K. Narayan has published dozens of novels and short story collections.

◆ Build Vocabulary

LATIN WORD ROOTS: -min-

The character Agasthya in this episode from the *Ramayana* is referred to as *diminutive.* The Latin root *-min-* in *diminutive* comes from the Latin *minutus,* meaning "small." Therefore, when Agasthya is described as being *diminutive,* it means he is tiny in size.

austerities
decrepitude
sublime
august
secular
obeisance
exuberance
diminutive
esoteric

WORD BANK

As you read "Rama's Initiation" from the *Ramayana*, you will encounter the words on this list. Each word will be defined on the page where it first appears. Before you read, list in your notebook any words or word parts that you think you recognize. Then, as you read, check whether the words mean what you thought they did.

◆ Build Grammar Skills

RESTRICTIVE AND NONRESTRICTIVE APPOSITIVES

An appositive is a noun or pronoun placed next to another noun or pronoun to identify, rename, or explain it. An appositive phrase is a noun or pronoun with modifiers, placed next to a noun or pronoun to add information or details. An appositive is **restrictive** when it is necessary to clarify or identify the noun to which it refers. Commas are not used with restrictive appositives.

Restrictive: Send your son *Rama* with me.

Since the king has more than one son, the appositive *Rama* is necessary to identify which son.

An appositive is **nonrestrictive** if it provides additional, but not necessary, information. Nonrestrictive appositives are set off with commas.

Nonrestrictive: This Thataka is more dreadful than Yama, *the god of death,* who takes a life only when the time is ripe.

Since there is only one Yama, the appositive phrase adds information, but it is not necessary.

Rama's Initiation *from the* Ramayana

◆ *Literature and Your Life*

CONNECT YOUR EXPERIENCE

What qualities do you think a hero possesses? As you read this episode from the *Ramayana,* you might be surprised to note that ancient heroes have much in common with contemporary superheroes; heroes have always combated evil, and as you'll see in the *Ramayana,* they have respected the land that nurtures all people.

Journal Writing All over the world, young people prove their mental, spiritual, and physical strength to themselves, to their peers, and to adults. Choose a young person who you believe has heroic qualities. In your journal, jot down some notes upon which you could base an epic focusing on this person.

THEMATIC FOCUS: FROM THE PAST

The *Ramayana* has influenced nearly every aspect of Indian culture—from children's bedtime stories to religious studies. Ask yourself what Rama's adventures reveal about Indian culture.

◆ Background for Understanding

CULTURE

Hinduism, one of the oldest living religions in the world, is the major religion of India. While it has no single book that outlines all its doctrines and beliefs, there are many sacred writings. These include the *Vedas,* which contain prayers, hymns, explanations, and philosophy; the *Puranas,* which tell the tales of Hindu gods and goddesses; the Hindu epics, the *Mahabharata* and the *Ramayana;* and the *Manu-smitri,* a code of religious and social law. The *Ramayana* tells of Prince Rama, believed by many to be another incarnation of the Hindu god Krishna.

◆ Literary Focus

THE EPIC HERO

The **epic hero** possesses certain qualities—bravery, great strength, and a desire to achieve immortality through heroic deeds. The hero is based on a legendary or historic person who travels on a long and challenging journey, during which he proves his heroic qualities: He fights evil, falls in love, protects his honor, and rescues people in distress.

This episode from the *Ramayana* puts Rama in a situation in which he must prove some of his heroic qualities.

◆ Reading Strategy

DRAW INFERENCES ABOUT CULTURE

You can use information revealed in sources such as epics to **draw inferences about a culture.** Chances are, you don't know a great deal about life in India 2,000 years ago. However, if you combine the details in the *Ramayana* with your own experiences, you can draw some strong inferences about this ancient culture. In particular, the experiences of the hero Rama will reveal the customs and values of his culture.

To help you draw inferences about a culture, use a chart like the one below to jot down cultural details from the epic, details from your own background and experience, and the resulting cultural inferences.

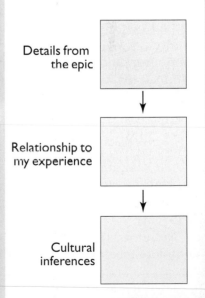

Details from the epic

↓

Relationship to my experience

↓

Cultural inferences

Rama's Initiation

from the Ramayana

R. K. Narayan

The new assembly hall, Dasaratha's[1] latest pride, was crowded all day with visiting dignitaries, royal emissaries, and citizens coming in with representations or appeals for justice. The King was always accessible, and fulfilled his duties as the ruler of Kosala without grudging the hours spent in public service.

On a certain afternoon, messengers at the gate came running in to announce, "Sage Viswamithra."[2] When the message was relayed to the King, he got up and hurried forward to receive the visitor. Viswamithra, once a king, a conqueror, and a dreaded name until he renounced his kingly role and chose to become a sage (which he accomplished through severe <u>austerities</u>), combined in himself the sage's eminence and the king's authority and was quick tempered and positive. Dasaratha led him to a proper seat and said, "This is a day of glory for us; your gracious presence is most welcome. You must have come from afar. Would you first rest?"

"No need," the sage replied simply. He had complete mastery over his bodily needs

Persian translation of the Ramayana of Valmiki (detail), Mughal, School of Akbar, Freer Gallery of Art, Smithsonian Institution, Washington, DC

▲ Critical Viewing What do you think the topic of this public meeting is? **[Speculate]**

through inner discipline and austerities, and was above the effects of heat, cold, hunger, fatigue, and even <u>decrepitude</u>. The King later asked politely, "Is there anything I can do?" Viswamithra looked steadily at the King and answered, "Yes. I am here to ask of you a favor.

---

1. **Dasaratha's** (dä sä rä´ täz)
2. **Viswamithra** (vish wä´ mē trä): Teacher of Rama, the main character of the Ramayana.

I wish to perform, before the next full moon, a yagna[3] at Sidhasrama.[4] Doubtless you know where it is?"

"I have passed that sacred ground beyond the Ganges[5] many times."

The sage interrupted. "But there are creatures hovering about waiting to disturb every holy undertaking there, who must be overcome in the same manner as one has to conquer the five-fold evils[6] within before one can realize holiness. Those evil creatures are endowed with immeasurable powers of destruction. But it is our duty to pursue our aims undeterred. The yagna I propose to perform will strengthen the beneficial forces of this world, and please the gods above."

"It is my duty to protect your sublime effort. Tell me when, and I will be there."

The sage said, "No need to disturb your august self. Send your son Rama with me, and he will help me. He can."

"Rama!" cried the King, surprised, "When I am here to serve you."

Viswamithra's temper was already stirring. "I know your greatness," he said, cutting the King short. "But I want Rama to go with me. If you are not willing, you may say so."

The air became suddenly tense. The assembly, the ministers and officials, watched in solemn silence. The King looked miserable. "Rama is still a child, still learning the arts and practicing the use of arms." His sentences never seemed to conclude, but trailed away as he tried to explain. "He is a boy, a child, he is too young and tender to contend with demons."

"But I know Rama," was all that Viswamithra said in reply.

"I can send you an army, or myself lead an army to guard your performance. What can a stripling[7] like Rama do against those terrible forces . . .? I will help you just as I helped Indra[8] once when he was harassed and deprived of his kingdom."

Viswamithra ignored his speech and rose to leave. "If you cannot send Rama, I need none else." He started to move down the passage.

The King was too stricken to move. When Viswamithra had gone half way, he realized that the visitor was leaving unceremoniously and was not even shown the courtesy of being escorted to the door. Vasishtha,[9] the King's priest and guide, whispered to Dasaratha, "Follow him and call him back," and hurried forward even before the King could grasp what he was saying. He almost ran as Viswamithra had reached the end of the hall and, blocking his way, said, "The King is coming; please don't go. He did not mean . . ."

A wry smile played on Viswamithra's face as he said without any trace of bitterness, "Why are you or anyone agitated? I came here for a purpose; it has failed: no reason to prolong my stay."

"Oh, eminent one, you were yourself a king once."

"What has that to do with us now?" asked Viswamithra, rather irked, since he hated all

---

3. **yagna** (yäg nä´) *n.*: Sacrifice.
4. **Sidhasrama** (sēd häs rä´ mä)
5. **Ganges** (gan´ jēz): River in northern India.
6. **five-fold evils:** Lust, anger, miserliness, egoism, and envy.

7. **stripling** (strip´ liŋ) *n.*: Young boy passing into manhood.
8. **Indra** (in´ drə): Hindu god associated with rain and thunderclouds.
9. **Vasishtha** (vä sē´ sh tä): King's priest and guide.

◆ Build Vocabulary

austerities (ô ster´ ə tēz) *n.*: Self-denials

decrepitude (dē krep´ ə tood) *n.*: State of being worn out by old age or illness

sublime (sə blīm´) *adj.*: Noble; admirable

august (ô gust´) *adj.*: Worthy of respect because of age and dignity

reference to his <u>secular</u> past and wanted always to be known as a Brahma Rishi.[10]

Vasishtha answered mildly, "Only to remind you of an ordinary man's feelings, especially a man like Dasaratha who had been childless and had to pray hard for an issue . . ."

"Well, it may be so, great one; I still say that I came on a mission and wish to leave, since it has failed."

"It has not failed," said Vasishtha, and just then the King came up to join them in the passage; the assembly was on its feet.

Dasaratha made a deep <u>obeisance</u> and said, "Come back to your seat, Your Holiness."

"For what purpose, Your Majesty?" Viswamithra asked.

"Easier to talk seated . . ."

"I don't believe in any talk," said Viswamithra; but Vasishtha pleaded with him until he returned to his seat.

When they were all seated again, Vasishtha addressed the King: "There must be a divine purpose working through this seer, who may know but will not explain. It is a privilege that Rama's help should be sought. Do not bar his way. Let him go with the sage."

◆ **Literary Focus**
Explain how this speech of Vasishtha relates to Rama's status as an epic hero.

"When, oh when?" the King asked anxiously.

"Now," said Viswamithra.

The King looked woebegone and desperate, and the sage relented enough to utter a word of comfort. "You cannot count on the physical proximity of someone you love, all the time. A seed that sprouts at the foot of its parent tree remains stunted until it is transplanted. Rama will be in my care, and he will be quite well. But ultimately, he will leave me too. Every human being, when the time comes, has to depart and seek his fulfillment in his own way."

"Sidhasrama is far away . . .?" began the King.

"I'll ease his path for him, no need for a chariot to take us there," said Viswamithra reading his mind.

"Rama has never been separated from his brother Lakshmana.[11] May he also go with him?" pleaded the King, and he looked relieved when he heard Viswamithra say, "Yes, I will look after both, though their mission will be to look after me. Let them get ready to follow me; let them select their favorite weapons and prepare to leave."

Dasaratha, with the look of one delivering hostages into the hand of an enemy, turned to his minister and said, "Fetch my sons."

Following the footsteps of their master like his shadows, Rama and Lakshmana went past the limits of the city and reached the Sarayu River, which bounded the capital on the north. When night fell, they rested at a wooded grove and at dawn crossed the river. When the sun came over the mountain peak, they reached a pleasant grove over which hung, like a canopy, fragrant smoke from numerous sacrificial fires. Viswamithra explained to Rama, "This is where God Shiva[12] meditated once upon a time and reduced to ashes the god of love when he attempted to spoil his meditation. From time immemorial saints praying to Shiva come here to perform their sacrifices, and the pall of smoke you notice is from their sacrificial fires."

A group of hermits emerged from their seclusion, received Viswamithra, and invited him and his two disciples to stay with them for the night. Viswamithra resumed his journey at dawn and reached a desert region at midday. The mere expression "desert" hardly conveys the absolute aridity of this land. Under a relentless sun, all vegetation had dried and turned to dust, stone and rock crumbled into powdery sand, which lay in vast dunes, stretching away to the horizon. Here every inch was scorched and dry and hot

---

10. **Brahma Rishi** (brä´ mä ri´ shē): Enlightened sage.

11. **Lakshmana** (läks mä´ nä)
12. **God Shiva** (shē´ və): Hindu god of destruction.

beyond imagination. The ground was cracked and split, exposing enormous fissures everywhere. The distinction between dawn, noon, and evening did not exist here, as the sun seemed to stay overhead and burn the earth without moving. Bleached bones lay where animals had perished, including those of monstrous serpents with jaws open in deadly thirst; into these enormous jaws had rushed (says the poet) elephants desperately seeking shade, all dead and fossilized, the serpent and the elephant alike. Heat haze rose and singed the very heavens. While traversing this ground, Viswamithra noticed the bewilderment and distress on the faces of the young men, and transmitted to them mentally two *mantras*[13] (called "Bala" and "Adi-Bala"). When they meditated on and recited these incantations, the arid atmosphere was transformed for the rest of their passage and they felt as if they were wading through a cool stream with a southern summer breeze blowing in their faces. Rama, ever curious to know the country he was passing through, asked, "Why is this land so terrible? Why does it seem accursed?"

◆ Reading Strategy
What inferences can you make about the role of meditation and incantations in Indian culture and religion?

"You will learn the answer if you listen to this story—of a woman fierce, ruthless, eating and digesting all living creatures, possessing the strength of a thousand mad elephants."

---

13. *mantras* (män´träz): Sacred syllables.

◆ **Build Vocabulary**

secular (sek´ yə lər) *adj.*: Not sacred or religious

obeisance (ō bā´ səns) *n.*: Gesture of respect

exuberance (eg zoo´ bər əns) *n.*: State of high spirits and good health

diminutive (də min´ yoo tiv) *adj.*: Smaller than average

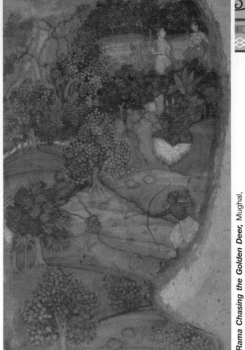

Rama Chasing the Golden Deer, Mughal, National Museum of India, New Delhi

▲ **Critical Viewing** What details in this painting support inferences you've made from reading this epic? [**Connect; Support**]

Thataka's Story

The woman I speak of was the daughter of Suketha[14] a *yaksha,* a demigod of great valor, might, and purity. She was beautiful and full of wild energy. When she grew up she was married to a chieftain named Sunda. Two sons were born to them—Mareecha and Subahu[15]—who were endowed with enormous supernatural powers in addition to physical strength; and in their conceit and <u>exuberance</u> they laid waste their surroundings. Their father, delighted at their pranks and infected by their mood, joined in their activities. He pulled out ancient trees by their roots and flung them about, and he slaughtered all creatures that came his way. This depredation came to the notice of the great savant Agasthya[16] (the <u>diminutive</u> saint

---

14. **Suketha** (soo kā´ tä)
15. **Mareecha** (mä´ rē chä) **and Subahu** (sä bä´ hoo)
16. **savant** (sə vänt´) **Agasthya** (ä gus tē yä´): Learned man named Agasthya.

Rama Chases a Demon Disguised as a Golden Deer, Fazl, Freer Gallery of Art, Smithsonian Institution, Washington, D.C.

▲ **Critical Viewing** What details in this painting indicate Rama's importance? **[Analyze]**

who once, when certain demoniac beings hid themselves at the bottom of the sea and Indra appealed for his help to track them, had sipped off the waters of the ocean). Agasthya had his hermitage in this forest, and when he noticed the destruction around, he cursed the perpetrator of this deed and Sunda fell dead. When his wife learned of his death, she and her sons stormed in, roaring revenge on the saint. He met their challenge by cursing them. "Since you are destroyers of life, may you become *asuras*[17] and dwell in the nether worlds." (Till now they had been demigods. Now they were degraded to demonhood.) The three at once underwent a transformation; their features and stature became forbidding, and their natures changed to

match. The sons left to seek the company of superdemons. The mother was left alone and lives on here, breathing fire and wishing everything ill. Nothing flourishes here; only heat and sand remain. She is a scorcher. She carries a trident with spikes; a cobra entwined on her arm is her armlet. The name of this fearsome creature is Thataka.[18] Just as the presence of a little *loba* (meanness) dries up and disfigures a whole human personality, so does the presence of this monster turn into desert a region which was once fertile. In her restlessness she constantly harasses the hermits at their prayers; she gobbles up anything that moves and sends it down her entrails.

Touching the bow slung on his shoulder, Rama asked. "Where is she to be found?"

Before Viswamithra could answer, she arrived, the ground rocking under her feet and a storm preceding her. She loomed over them with her eyes spitting fire, her fangs bared, her lips parted revealing a cavernous mouth; and her brows twitching in rage. She raised her trident and roared, "In this my kingdom, I have crushed out the minutest womb of life and you have been sent down so that I may not remain hungry."

Rama hesitated; for all her evil, she was still a woman. How could he kill her? Reading his thoughts, Viswamithra said, "You shall not consider her a woman at all. Such a monster must receive no consideration. Her strength, ruthlessness, appearance, rule her out of that category. Formerly God Vishnu himself killed Kyathi, the wife of Brigu,[19] who harbored the

---

17. **asuras** (ä sŏŏ´ räz)

18. **Thataka** (tä tä´ kä)
19. **Vishnu** (vēsh´ nŏŏ) . . . **Kyathi** (kyä´ tē) . . . **Brigu** (brĕ´gŏŏ)

◆ **Build Vocabulary**

esoteric (es´ ə ter´ ik) *adj.*: Beyond the understanding of most people

asuras fleeing his wrath, when she refused to yield them. Mandorai,[20] a woman bent upon destroying all the worlds, was vanquished by Indra and he earned the gratitude of humanity. These are but two instances. A woman of demoniac tendencies loses all consideration to be treated as a woman. This Thataka is more dreadful than Yama, the god of death, who takes a life only when the time is ripe. But this monster, at the very scent of a living creature, craves to kill and eat. Do not picture her as a woman at all. You must rid this world of her. It is your duty."

Rama said, "I will carry out your wish."

Thataka threw her three-pronged spear at Rama. As it came flaming, Rama strung his bow and sent an arrow which broke it into fragments. Next she raised a hail of stones under which to crush her adversaries. Rama sent up his arrows, which shielded them from the attack. Finally Rama's arrow pierced her throat and ended her career; thereby also inaugurating Rama's life's mission of destroying evil and demonry in this world. The gods assembled in the sky and expressed their joy and relief and enjoined Viswamithra, "Oh, adept and master of weapons, impart without any reserve all your knowledge and powers to this lad. He is a savior." Viswamithra obeyed this injunction and taught Rama all the <u>esoteric</u> techniques in weaponry. Thereafter the presiding deities of various weapons, *asthras*,[21] appeared before Rama submissively and declared, "Now we are yours: command us night or day."

> ◆ *Literature and Your Life*
> How does Rama compare to most contemporary superheros?

---

20. **Mandorai** (mänd rä´ ē)

21. *asthras* (äs´ träz)

Guide for Responding

◆ *Literature and Your Life*

Reader's Response Do you think Viswamithra did the right thing by persuading Rama to overcome his hesitation about killing Thataka? Why or why not?

Thematic Focus At the time Viswamithra asked for Rama, Dasaratha was still trying to pass down to his son the qualities that would equip him to be a hero. If you had been in Dasaratha's place, would you have let Rama go? Explain your answer.

Questions for Research The *Ramayana* has a long, glorious history, but is it still central to Hindu culture? Generate research questions about the place of the *Ramayana* in current Indian society.

☑ Check Your Comprehension

1. Why does the sage Viswamithra want Rama to accompany him to Sidhasrama?
2. Why is King Dasaratha at first reluctant to grant the sage's request?
3. Why is the region through which Rama, Lakshmana, and Viswamithra pass so inhospitable?
4. (a) Why is Rama reluctant to fight Thataka at first? (b) How does Viswamithra persuade him to fight?
5. What are the outcomes of Rama's first battle?

Guide for Responding (continued)

◆ Critical Thinking

INTERPRET

1. Explain why Viswamithra chose the young and inexperienced Rama to help him perform such a dangerous task. **[Infer]**
2. Why do you think Viswamithra dislikes all references to his nonreligious past? **[Interpret]**
3. Why do you think Thataka and her two sons undergo a physical transformation as one result of Agasthya's curse? **[Draw Conclusions]**
4. Explain why Viswamithra is a worthy teacher to Rama in his quest to be a hero. **[Interpret]**

APPLY

5. Explain how Viswamithra's comparison of a child to a seed could apply in any time period. **[Relate]**

EXTEND

6. Compare and contrast Rama with a popular superhero in a story, book, or film with which you are familiar. **[Literature Link]**

◆ Literary Focus

THE EPIC HERO

The **epic hero** is the central character of an epic. In his adventures, the hero demonstrates extraordinary skills and special qualities.

1. How does Rama begin the passage from childhood to adulthood?
2. How does Rama show his heroic powers?
3. How do the events that follow Rama's battle with Thataka indicate that Rama is an epic hero?

◆ Reading Strategy

DRAW INFERENCES ABOUT CULTURE

The *Ramayana* presents a picture of Indian culture 2,000 years ago. From the stories told and the details given, you can **infer** beliefs, values, and customs of the period.

1. How does the *Ramayana* show the importance of the sage in Indian culture?
2. What does the *Ramayana* reveal about the relationship between kings and sages in ancient India?
3. Rama hesitates before killing Thataka because she is a woman. What can you infer from this about Indian culture and society?

◆ Build Vocabulary

USING THE LATIN ROOT -*min*-

The Latin root -*min*- means "small." Use this knowledge to help you define each of the following words:

1. minimum 2. minority 3. minute 4. diminish

USING THE WORD BANK: Synonyms

On your paper, write the word whose meaning is closest to that of the first word.

1. austerities: (a) savings, (b) deprivations, (c) blows
2. decrepitude: (a) weariness, (b) unconcern, (c) fear
3. sublime: (a) pleasant, (b) tragic, (c) noble
4. august: (a) overheated, (b) dignified, (c) confused
5. secular: (a) nonreligious, (b) expansive, (c) serious
6. obeisance: (a) anger, (b) shallowness, (c) respect
7. exuberance: (a) excitement, (b) gloom, (c) conceit
8. diminutive: (a) foolish, (b) little, (c) showy
9. esoteric: (a) mysterious, (b) accessible, (c) haughty

◆ Build Grammar Skills

RESTRICTIVE AND NONRESTRICTIVE APPOSITIVES

Restrictive appositives and appositive phrases are essential to the meaning of the sentence; they are not set off by commas. **Nonrestrictive** appositives are not essential to the sentence's meaning; these are set off with commas.

Practice In your notebook, write the following sentences. Underline the appositive or appositive phrase in each. If the appositive is nonrestrictive, set it off with commas.

1. Viswamithra a sage of great understanding entered the king's assembly hall.
2. King Dasaratha the father of two young sons greeted the sage warmly.
3. "Send your son Rama with me, and he will help me," said the sage.
4. Vasishtha the king's priest and guide urged Dasaratha to agree to the sage's demand.
5. In the end, the brothers Rama and Lakshmana accompanied the holy man on his quest.

*B*uild *Y*our *P*ortfolio

 ## Idea Bank

Writing

I. Letter As Viswamithra, write a letter to Dasaratha asking permission for Rama to accompany you on a dangerous mission. Explain why the mission will be a growth experience.

2. Personal Narrative Rama's initiation into adulthood was characteristic for an epic hero. What experience has helped prepare you for adulthood? Write a brief personal narrative relating this experience and its impact on you.

3. Opening Argument You are a lawyer called upon to defend Thataka. Write an opening argument in which you detail how you will prove that Thataka was grossly misjudged. Your objective is to restore Thataka to her status as a demigod.

Speaking, Listening, and Viewing

4. Oral Tales Prepare a version of this episode for an audience of young children. Make an audiotape to give to young relatives or friends. **[Performing Arts Link]**

5. Poster Rama is believed to be just one of the *avatars,* or incarnations, of the Hindu god Vishnu. Create a poster that shows Vishnu in some of his other forms, using classical Hindu imagery. Include text that explains any symbolism present in the image.

Researching and Representing

6. Painting Reread the description of the devouring creature Thataka and the desert domain she inhabited. Create a painting that expresses the terrifying mood of this scene. **[Art Link]**

7. Dance With a group of classmates, reenact the heroic journey and battle of Rama as a dance. Incorporate classical Indian music into your performance. **[Performing Arts Link]**

Online Activity www.phlit.phschool.com

 ## Guided Writing Lesson

Script Treatment Proposal

The *Ramayana* has all the ingredients for a summer blockbuster—exotic settings, a fearless superhero, an old sage with magical powers. Think what a special effects artist could do with an evil creature like Thataka! Write a **script treatment** outlining how you propose to tell the story, cast the film, and use special effects and music to create a box-office success.

Writing Skills Focus: Appropriate Language for Your Purpose

Your script treatment has to show its readers that you're onto a great film idea. To do this, you'll have to make every word count. Use vivid words and phrases to express the excitement and suspense of key scenes. Also, use **language** that appeals to the emotions, such as a *stirring* scene, and *sympathetic* and *inspiring* characters.

Prewriting Before you begin writing, envision your film in your mind. To help you plan your script treatment, make an outline with headings such as story events, cast, special effects, and music. For each heading, list ideas and suggestions that you think will keep the attention of a large audience.

Events	Cast	Special Effects	Music

Drafting As you draft your treatment, draw on the information in your outline. Add to it as you envision new and better scene ideas. Use vivid and precise terms and language that will appeal to your readers' emotions.

Revising Reread your draft. Ask: Have I left out any information the backers of the film will want to know? Is my persuasive language convincing and emotional? Is it *too* emotional? Revise accordingly.

Guide for Reading

Sundiata

Although the original author is not known, the story of Sundiata has been told  by the storytellers, or griots (grē´ ōz), of Mali— an African republic—for many centuries. Many African ethnic groups rely on the memories of their griots, rather than on written accounts, to preserve a record of the past.

Griots are both storytellers and historians. They call themselves the memory of the people, and they travel from village to village, teaching the history and legends of their ancestors to the new generations. Thus, the griots preserve their history and culture orally.

D. T. Niane

After listening to the stories told by Mamadou Kouyate (mä´ mä dōō kōō ya´ te), a griot of the Keita clan, Djibril Tamsir Niane (dyē´ bril täm´ sēr nī´ yan) wrote *Sundiata: An Epic of Old Mali* in his Malinke language. Niane's work was translated into English and other languages, and now people all over the world profit from the griot's wisdom.

Niane's own ancestors were griots. In addition to *Sundiata,* D. T. Niane has collected and retold many other ancient legends of Mali. His translations of the ancient oral histories is one way he affirms their value. A noted historian, his specific area of interest is medieval African empires. This expertise has helped him to create the background for *Sundiata* and other works.

◆ Build Vocabulary

LATIN WORD ROOTS: -firm-

The hero in this selection, Mari Djata, is said to have an *infirmity.* The root *-firm-* is derived from the Latin word *firmare,* "to strengthen." By combining this meaning with the meaning of the prefix *in-,* "lacking" or "without," you can figure out that *infirmity* means "without strength" or "physical weakness."

WORD BANK

fathom
taciturn
malicious
infirmity
innuendo
diabolical
estranged
affront

As you read this selection from *Sundiata,* you will encounter the words on this list. Each word is defined on the page where it first appears.

With a partner, read the words aloud. Share the meaning of any of the words you already know.

◆ Build Grammar Skills

SENTENCE VARIETY

Writers use **sentence variety** to create an interesting rhythm in their writing. They vary their sentences in several ways. D. T. Niane uses a mix of sentence lengths and structures. He also varies his sentence types, using declarative, interrogative, and exclamatory sentences:

Declarative: *Malicious tongues began to blab.*

Interrogative: *What three-year-old has not yet taken his first steps?*

Exclamatory: *How impatient man is!*

Using different sentence beginnings also adds variety:

Begins With an Adverb: *Now* he was resting on nothing ...

Begins With a Prepositional Phrase: *At the age of three* he still crawled along on all-fours ...

Begins With a Participial Phrase: *Having become all-powerful,* Sassouma Bérété persecuted Sogolon ...

As you read from *Sundiata,* notice the effect of the sentence variety.

from Sundiata: An Epic of Old Mali

◆ *Literature and Your Life*

CONNECT YOUR EXPERIENCE

If you've ever been ridiculed—even over something as trivial as a bad haircut or a botched basketball shot—you know that the temptation to strike back can be strong. While it may not always be appropriate to strike back, often there are other ways to put a stop to ridicule. In this episode, the much-belittled Mari Djata finds a noble way to not only stop the ridicule, but also to become a hero.

Journal Writing Write about a time when, like Mari Djata in this story, you were unfairly compared with another. Describe the situation and how you felt.

THEMATIC FOCUS: FROM THE PAST

Ideally, the legacy handed down from king to king encompasses wisdom, prudence, courage, and great strength. What are the results when one of these qualities is absent? How do people respond? Think about these questions as you read this selection.

◆ Background for Understanding

HISTORY

Almost 1,000 years ago, the area of west Africa that includes present-day Ghana and Mali was highly unstable. Rival kings fought for control of the salt and gold caravan trade that passed through their territory. Eventually, Sumanguru, a warrior king, gained control of the region and cruelly oppressed the Mandingo people of Mali. Although weak and scattered, the Mandingo rebelled against Sumanguru. Just when Mali needed a leader most, against all odds, the hero Sogolon-Djata rose to power. (In rapidly spoken Mandingo, "Sogolon-Djata" became "Sundiata.") A member of the Keita clan which had ruled Mali for centuries, Sundiata united his people, fought off Sumanguru, and ushered in a glorious period of peace and prosperity.

◆ Literary Focus

EPIC CONFLICT

At the heart of any epic is an **epic conflict**—a situation in which the hero struggles against an obstacle or set of obstacles. Part of an epic conflict may be a difficult situation in childhood. In the traditional epic, the hero surmounts difficulties, conquers enemies, and finally emerges triumphant. Through these struggles, the hero passes from childhood to adulthood, proving his wisdom, bravery, and power.

As you read from the folk epic *Sundiata*, take note of the obstacles that confront Mari Djata, blocking his path on the way to achieving heroism.

◆ Reading Strategy

STORYTELLER'S PURPOSE

Griots have a **purpose,** or reason for relating their stories. The griots who told and retold the story of Sundiata for centuries had several purposes. First, they wanted to inform their people about important historical events. In addition, they intended to entertain their listeners with an exciting account of a hero's adventures. Further, by recounting the positive and negative results of various actions, the griots instructed the people in appropriate or expected behavior. Thinking about these different purposes will give you greater insight into the epic *Sundiata*.

To help you keep track of the storyteller's purposes, make a chart like the one shown. As you read the selection, list events, passages, or other aspects of the epic that illustrate each of the purposes.

Inform	Entertain	Persuade

from SUNDIATA:
An Epic of Old Mali
D. T. Niane

Senegalese glass painting, Collection of Professor Donal Cruise-O'Brien

CHARACTERS IN *SUNDIATA*

Balla Fasséké (bä´ lä fä sə´ kä): Griot and counselor of Sundiata.

Boukari (bo͞o kä´ rē): Son of the king and Namandjé, one of his wives; also called Manding (män´ diŋ) Boukari.

Dankaran Touman (dän´ kä rän to͞o´ män): Son of the king and his first wife, Sassouma, who is also called Sassouma Bérété.

Djamarou (jä mä´ ro͞o): Daughter of Sogolon and the king; sister of Sundiata and Kolonkan.

Farakourou (fä rä ko͞o´ ro͞o): Master of the forges.

Gnankouman Doua (nän ko͞o´ män do͞o´ ə) The king's griot; also called simply, Doua.

Kolonkan (kō lōn´ kən): Sundiata's eldest sister.

Namandjé (nä män´ jā): One of the king's wives.

Naré Maghan (nä´ rä mäg´ hän): Sundiata's father.

Nounfaïri (no͞on´ fä ē´ rē): Soothsayer and smith; father of Farakourou.

Sassouma Bérété (sä so͞o´ mä be re´ tä): The king's first wife.

Sogolon (sô gô lōn´): Sundiata's mother; also called Sogolon Kedjou (kä´ jo͞o).

Sundiata (so͞on dyä´ tä): Legendary king of Mali; referred to as Djata (dyä´ tä) and Sogolon Djata, which means "son of Sogolon." Sundiata is also called Mari (mä´ rē) Djata.

CHILDHOOD

God has his mysteries which none can fathom. You, perhaps, will be a king. You can do nothing about it. You, on the other hand, will be unlucky, but you can do nothing about that either. Each man finds his way already marked out for him and he can change nothing of it.

Sogolon's son had a slow and difficult childhood. At the age of three he still crawled along on all-fours while children of the same age were already walking. He had nothing of the great beauty of his father Naré Maghan. He had a head so big that he seemed unable to support it; he also had large eyes which would open wide whenever anyone entered his mother's house. He was taciturn and used to spend the whole day just sitting in the middle of the house. Whenever his mother went out he would crawl on all-fours to rummage about in the calabashes[1] in search of food, for he was very greedy.

Malicious tongues began to blab. What three-year-old has not yet taken his first steps? What three-year-old is not the despair of his parents through his whims and shifts of mood? What three-year-old is not the joy of his circle through his backwardness in talking? Sogolon Djata (for it was thus that they called him, prefixing his mother's name to his), Sogolon Djata, then, was very different from others of his own

age. He spoke little and his severe face never relaxed into a smile. You would have thought that he was already thinking, and what amused children of his age bored him. Often Sogolon would make some of them come to him to keep him company. These children were already walking and she hoped that Djata, seeing his companions walking, would be tempted to do likewise. But nothing came of it. Besides, Sogolon Djata would brain the poor little things with his already strong arms and none of them would come near him any more.

The king's first wife was the first to rejoice at Sogolon Djata's infirmity. Her own son, Dankaran Touman, was already eleven. He was a fine and lively boy, who spent the day running about the village with those of his own age. He had even begun his initiation in the bush.[2] The king had had a bow made for him and he used to go behind the town to practice archery with his companions. Sassouma was quite happy and snapped her fingers at Sogolon, whose child was still crawling on the ground. Whenever the latter happened to pass by her house, she would say, "Come, my son, walk, jump, leap about. The jinn[3] didn't promise you anything out of the ordinary, but I prefer a son who walks on his two legs to a lion that crawls on the ground." She spoke thus whenever Sogolon went by her door. The innuendo would go straight home and then she would burst into laughter, that diabolical laughter which a jealous woman knows how to use so well.

Her son's infirmity weighed heavily upon Sogolon Kedjou; she had resorted to all her talent as a sorceress to give strength to her son's legs, but the rarest herbs had been useless. The king himself lost hope.

How impatient man is! Naré Maghan became imperceptibly estranged but Gnankouman

---

1. **calabashes** (kal´ ə bash´ iz) n.: Dried, hollow shells of gourds, used as bowls.

◀ **Critical Viewing** How does the artist show which is the most important character in this painting? **[Analyze]**

◆ Build Vocabulary

fathom (faṯẖ´ əm) v.: Understand thoroughly

taciturn (tas´ ə tʉrn) adj.: Uncommunicative

malicious (mə lish´ əs) adj.: Intentionally harmful

infirmity (in fʉr´ mə tē) n.: Physical weakness

innuendo (in´ yo͞o en´ dō) n.: Insinuation

diabolical (dī ə bäl´ ik əl) adj.: Wicked; cruel

estranged (e strānjd´) adv.: Removed from; at a distance

---

2. **initiation in the bush:** Education in tribal lore given to twelve-year-old West African boys so they can become full members of the tribe.
3. **jinn** (jin) n.: Supernatural beings that influence human affairs. Their promise was that the son of Sogolon would make Mali a great empire.

Doua never ceased reminding him of the hunter's words. Sogolon became pregnant again. The king hoped for a son, but it was a daughter called Kolonkan. She resembled her mother and had nothing of her father's beauty. The disheartened king debarred Sogolon from his house and she lived in semi-disgrace for a while. Naré Maghan married the daughter of one of his allies, the king of the Kamaras. She was called Namandjé and her beauty was legendary. A year later she brought a boy into the world. When the king consulted soothsayers[4] on the destiny of this son, he received the reply that Namandjé's child would be the right hand of some mighty king. The king gave the newly-born the name of Boukari. He was to be called Manding Boukari or Manding Bory later on.

Naré Maghan was very perplexed. Could it be that the stiff jointed son of Sogolon was the one the hunter soothsayer had foretold?

"The Almighty has his mysteries," Gnankouman Doua would say and, taking up the hunter's words, added, "The silk cotton tree emerges from a tiny seed."

One day Naré Maghan came along to the house of Nounfaïri, the blacksmith seer of Niani. He was an old, blind man. He received the king in the anteroom which served as his workshop. To the king's question he replied, "When the seed germinates growth is not always easy; great trees grow slowly but they plunge their roots deep into the ground."

"But has the seed really germinated?" said the king.

"Of course," replied the blind seer. "Only the growth is not as quick as you would like it; how impatient man is."

This interview and Doua's confidence gave the king some assurance. To the great displeasure of Sassouma Bérété the king restored Sogolon to favor and soon another daughter was born to her. She was given the name of Djamarou.

However, all Niani talked of nothing else but the stiff-legged son of Sogolon. He was now seven and he still crawled to get about. In spite of all the king's affection, Sogolon was in despair. Naré Maghan aged and he felt his time coming to an end. Dankaran Touman, the son of Sassouma Bérété, was now a fine youth.

One day Naré Maghan made Mari Djata come to him and he spoke to the child as one speaks to an adult. "Mari Djata, I am growing old and soon I shall be no more among you, but before death takes me off I am going to give you the present each king gives his successor. In Mali every prince has his own griot. Doua's father was my father's griot, Doua is mine and the son of Doua, Balla Fasséké here, will be your griot. Be inseparable friends from this day forward. From his mouth you will hear the history of your ancestors, you will learn the art of governing Mali according to the principles which our ancestors have bequeathed to us. I have served my term and done my duty too. I have done everything which a king of Mali ought to do. I am handing an enlarged kingdom over to you and I leave you sure allies. May your destiny be accomplished, but never forget that Niani is your capital and Mali the cradle of your ancestors."

The child, as if he had understood the whole meaning of the king's words, beckoned Balla Fasséké to approach. He made room for him on the hide he was sitting on and then said, "Balla, you will be my griot."

"Yes, son of Sogolon, if it pleases God," replied Balla Fasséké.

The king and Doua exchanged glances that radiated confidence.

The Lion's Awakening

A short while after this interview between Naré Maghan and his son the king died. Sogolon's son was no more than seven years old. The council of elders met in the king's palace. It was no use Doua's defending the king's will which reserved the throne for Mari Djata, for the council took no account of Naré Maghan's wish. With the help of Sassouma Bérété's intrigues, Dankaran Touman was proclaimed king and a regency council was formed in which the queen mother was all-powerful. A

---

4. **soothsayers** (sō̅ōth′ sā′ ərz) n.: People who can foretell the future.

short time after, Doua died.

As men have short memories, Sogolon's son was spoken of with nothing but irony and scorn. People had seen one-eyed kings, one-armed kings, and lame kings, but a stiff-legged king had never been heard tell of. No matter how great the destiny promised for Mari Djata might be, the throne could not be given to someone who had no power in his legs; if the jinn loved him, let them begin by giving him the use of his legs. Such were the remarks that Sogolon heard every day. The queen mother, Sassouma Bérété, was the source of all this gossip.

Having become all-powerful, Sassouma Bérété persecuted Sogolon because the late Naré Maghan had preferred her. She banished Sogolon and her son to a back yard of the palace. Mari Djata's mother now occupied an old hut which had served as a lumber-room of Sassouma's.

The wicked queen mother allowed free passage to all those inquisitive people who wanted to see the child that still crawled at the age of seven. Nearly all the inhabitants of Niani filed into the palace and the poor Sogolon wept to see herself thus given over to public ridicule. Mari Djata took on a ferocious look in front of the crowd of sightseers. Sogolon found a little consolation only in the love of her eldest daughter, Kolonkan. She was four and she could walk. She seemed to understand all her mother's miseries and already she helped her with the housework. Sometimes, when Sogolon was attending to the chores, it was she who stayed beside her sister Djamarou, quite small as yet.

Sogolon Kedjou and her children lived on the queen mother's leftovers, but she kept a little garden in the open ground behind the village. It was there that she passed her brightest moments looking after her onions and gnougous.[5] One day she happened to be short of condiments

◆ **Literature and Your Life**
Why do you think people ridicule others even when they know the pain and hurt it causes?

and went to the queen mother to beg a little baobab leaf.[6]

"Look you," said the malicious Sassouma, "I have a calabash full. Help yourself, you poor woman. As for me, my son knew how to walk at seven and it was he who went and picked these baobab leaves. Take them then, since your son is unequal to mine." Then she laughed derisively with that fierce laughter which cuts through your flesh and penetrates right to the bone.

Sogolon Kedjou was dumbfounded. She had never imagined that hate could be so strong in a human being. With a lump in her throat she left Sassouma's. Outside her hut Mari Djata, sitting on his useless legs, was blandly eating out of a calabash. Unable to contain herself any longer, Sogolon burst into sobs and seizing a piece of wood, hit her son.

---

6. **baobab** (bā′ ō bab′) **leaf** *n.*: Baobab is a thick-trunked tree; its leaves are used to flavor foods.

▲ **Critical Viewing** What skills might be needed to gather leaves from these baobab trees? **[Infer]**

---

5. **gnougous** (nōō′ gōōz′) *n.*: Root vegetables.

"Oh son of misfortune, will you never walk? Through your fault I have just suffered the greatest <u>affront</u> of my life! What have I done, God, for you to punish me in this way?"

Mari Djata seized the piece of wood and, looking at his mother, said, "Mother, what's the matter?"

"Shut up, nothing can ever wash me clean of this insult."

"But what then?"

"Sassouma has just humiliated me over a matter of a baobab leaf. At your age her own son could walk and used to bring his mother baobab leaves."

"Cheer up, Mother, cheer up."

"No. It's too much. I can't."

"Very well then, I am going to walk today," said Mari Djata. "Go and tell my father's smiths to make me the heaviest possible iron rod. Mother, do you want just the leaves of the baobab or would you rather I brought you the whole tree?"

◆ **Literary Focus**
In what way does this event contribute to the epic conflict?

"Ah, my son, to wipe out this insult I want the tree and its roots at my feet outside my hut."

Balla Fasséké, who was present, ran to the master smith, Farakourou, to order an iron rod.

Sogolon had sat down in front of her hut. She was weeping softly and holding her head between her two hands. Mari Djata went calmly back to his calabash of rice and began eating again as if nothing had happened. From time to time he looked up discreetly at his mother, who was murmuring in a low voice, "I want the whole tree, in front of my hut, the whole tree."

All of a sudden a voice burst into laughter behind the hut. It was the wicked Sassouma telling one of her serving women about the scene of humiliation and she was laughing loudly so that Sogolon could hear. Sogolon fled into the hut and hid her face under the blankets so as not to have before her eyes this heedless boy, who was more preoccupied with eating than with anything else. With her head buried in the bedclothes Sogolon wept and her body shook violently. Her daughter, Sogolon Djamarou, had come and sat down beside her and she said, "Mother, Mother, don't cry. Why are you crying?"

Mari Djata had finished eating and, dragging himself along on his legs, he came and sat under the wall of the hut for the sun was scorching. What was he thinking about? He alone knew.

The royal forges were situated outside the walls and over a hundred smiths worked there. The bows, spears, arrows and shields of Niani's warriors came from there. When Balla Fasséké came to order the iron rod, Farakourou said to him, "The great day has arrived then?"

"Yes. Today is a day like any other, but it will see what no other day has seen."

The master of the forges, Farakourou, was the son of the old Nounfaïri, and he was a soothsayer like his father. In his workshops there was an enormous iron bar wrought by his father, Nounfaïri. Everybody wondered what this bar was destined to be used for. Farakourou called six of his apprentices and told them to carry the iron bar to Sogolon's house.

When the smiths put the gigantic iron bar down in front of the hut the noise was so frightening that Sogolon, who was lying down, jumped up with a start. Then Balla Fasséké, son of Gnankouman Doua, spoke.

"Here is the great day, Mari Djata. I am speaking to you, Maghan, son of Sogolon. The waters of the Niger can efface the stain from the body, but they cannot wipe out an insult. Arise, young lion, roar, and may the bush know that from henceforth it has a master."

The apprentice smiths were still there, Sogolon had come out, and everyone was watching Mari Djata. He crept on all-fours and came to the iron bar. Supporting himself on his knees and one hand, with the other hand he picked up the iron bar without any effort and stood it up vertically. Now he was resting on nothing but his knees and held the bar with both his hands. A deathly silence had gripped all those present. Sogolon Djata closed his eyes, held tight, the muscles in his arms tensed. With a violent jerk he threw his weight on to it and his knees left the ground. Sogolon Kedjou was all eyes and watched her son's legs, which were trembling as though from an electric shock. Djata was sweating and the sweat ran from his brow. In a great effort he straightened up and was on his feet at one go—but the great bar of iron was twisted and had taken the form of a bow!

Then Balla Fasséké sang out the "Hymn to the Bow," striking up with his powerful voice:

"Take your bow, Simbon.
Take your bow and let us go.
Take your bow, Sogolon Djata."

When Sogolon saw her son standing she stood dumb for a moment, then suddenly she sang these words of thanks to God, who had given her son the use of his legs:

"Oh day, what a beautiful day,
Oh day, day of joy;
Allah[7] Almighty, you never created a finer day.
So my son is going to walk!"

Standing in the position of a soldier at ease, Sogolon Djata, supported by his enormous rod, was sweating great beads of sweat.

---

7. **Allah** (al´ ə): Muslim name for God.

Balla Fasséké's song had alerted the whole palace and people came running from all over to see what had happened, and each stood bewildered before Sogolon's son. The queen mother had rushed there and when she saw Mari Djata standing up she trembled from head to foot. After recovering his breath Sogolon's son dropped the bar and the crowd stood to one side. His first steps were those of a giant. Balla Fasséké fell into step and pointing his finger at Djata, he cried:

"Room, room, make room!
The lion has walked;
Hide antelopes,
Get out of his way."

Behind Niani there was a young baobab tree and it was there that the children of the town came to pick leaves for their mothers. With all his might the son of Sogolon tore up the tree and put it on his shoulders and went back to his mother. He threw the tree in front of the hut and said, "Mother, here are some baobab leaves for you. From henceforth it will be outside your hut that the women of Niani will come to stock up."

◆ **Build Vocabulary**

affront (ə frunt´) n.: Intentional insult

Guide for Responding

◆ Literature and Your Life

Reader's Response Were you surprised when Sogolon struck Mari Djata toward the end of the epic? Explain why you were or were not surprised.

Thematic Focus As part of his legacy, King Naré Maghan passed down to Mari Djata "an enlarged kingdom" and "sure allies." Do you think Mari Djata is qualified to build upon that legacy? Explain.

Group Discussion Discuss the qualities that make a hero. Does Mari Djata possess those qualities? Why or why not?

☑ Check Your Comprehension

1. What is the attitude of Sassouma Bérété and other people in the kingdom toward Mari Djata?
2. What prediction does the soothsayer make about the king's son?
3. What happens to Sogolon and her son after the king dies?
4. What surprising announcement does Mari Djata make after Sassouma Bérété insults his mother?
5. What extraordinary feat does seven-year-old Mari Djata accomplish?

Guide for Responding (continued)

◆ Critical Thinking

INTERPRET

1. What does the soothsayer mean when he tells the king, "great trees grow slowly"? **[Interpret]**
2. Why doesn't Mari Djata respond to the crowds who torment and tease him? **[Infer]**
3. In what specific ways does this epic illustrate the importance of honor? **[Support]**

COMPARE LITERARY WORKS

4. In "Rama's Initiation," you learn that Viswamithra became an important sage through "great austerities." Is there any parallel in Sundiata's rise to greatness? Explain. **[Connect]**

◆ Reading Strategy

STORYTELLER'S PURPOSE

The griots of ancient Mali had different purposes in mind as they retold the story of Sundiata.

1. What do you think was the storyteller's main purpose for telling this epic? Explain.
2. Why do you think the storyteller includes praises to Allah at the end of the epic?

◆ Literary Focus

EPIC CONFLICT

Mari Djata's confrontation of his physical disability creates the **epic conflict** in this tale.

1. How does Mari Djata respond to the way people react to his disability?
2. In what specific ways does Mari Djata's disability contribute to his effectiveness as a leader?

Beyond Literature

Community Connection

Preserving History Through Stories

Most cultures owe a great deal of their preserved history to storytellers. The *griots* of Mali preserved the epic tale of Sundiata. Celtic history was passed on by the *bards;* their Anglo-Saxon counterparts were called *scops.* Storytellers captured attitudes and customs of a time and preserved the names of important historical figures. Find out more about the function of storytellers in a culture that interests you. Share what you learn with your class.

◆ Build Vocabulary

USING THE LATIN ROOT *-firm-*

The Latin root *-firm-* means "to strengthen." Incorporate the meaning of "strengthen" in the definitions of each of the following words:

1. confirm   2. affirm   3. firmament

USING THE WORD BANK: Synonyms

On your paper, write the word whose meaning is closest to that of the first word.

1. fathom: (a) confuse, (b) understand, (c) remove
2. taciturn: (a) angry, (b) gracious, (c) tight-lipped
3. malicious: (a) mournful, (b) harmful, (c) changeable
4. infirmity: (a) sadness, (b) illness, (c) fear
5. innuendo: (a) style, (b) hint, (c) allowance
6. diabolical: (a) evil, (b) passionate, (c) extreme
7. estranged: (a) removed, (b) indecent, (c) plentiful
8. affront: (a) coverup, (b) accident, (c) insult

◆ Build Grammar Skills

SENTENCE VARIETY

It's important to vary the structure and kinds of sentences you use. **Sentence variety** means more than using sentences of different length. Beginning sentences with different constructions is also an effective way to achieve sentence variety.

Practice In your notebook, rewrite the following sentences so that each begins with either an adverb, prepositional phrase, participial phrase (Verb form, acting as an adjective, along with the words that complete it), or subordinate clause (A group of words, containing a subject and a verb, that cannot stand alone as a sentence).

1. Sogolon tried in vain to heal her son using potions and herbs.
2. The stiff-legged son of Sogolon still crawled about although he was now seven.
3. The young prince slowly straightened up and was on his feet in one go.
4. Mari Djata tore up the tree with all his might and went back to his hut.
5. Sogolon wept with her head buried in the bedclothes, and her body shook violently.

Build Your Portfolio

Idea Bank

Writing

1. **News Article** You are an eyewitness to Mari Djata's extraordinary feat. Write an account of this event for a newspaper. Answer the questions *who? what? when? where? why?* and *how?*

2. **Writing in the Heroic Tradition** Write a brief episode in the later life of Mari Djata. Show how he fulfills the heroic tradition. Include cultural details revealed in *Sundiata*.

3. **Critical Evaluation** In an essay, evaluate the central conflict in *Sundiata*. Keeping in mind the characteristics of an epic, is the conflict believable and engaging? Support your points with examples from the epic.

Speaking, Listening, and Viewing

4. **Oral Tales** Many families keep their histories alive in the same way that Mali villages do. Share a family story that focuses on your family's origins or on a milestone, such as a birth, death, or a special achievement. **[Social Studies Link]**

5. **Role Play** Imagine that Sogolon and Sassouma Bérété meet each other right after Sundiata tears up the baobab tree. Role-play a conversation between them. **[Performing Arts Link]**

Researching and Representing

6. **Documentary** Do research to learn about the arts in the country of Mali. Present your findings to the class in the form of a mini-documentary. **[Art Link; Social Studies Link]**

7. **Herb Research** Sogolon used the rarest herbs in an effort to cure her son. Write a research report on the different ways herbs have been used as healing agents in ancient and current times. **[Science Link; Social Studies Link]**

Online Activity www.phlit.phschool.com

Guided Writing Lesson

Storytelling Notes

Although the griots of ancient Mali presented epics from memory, a modern storyteller might want to work from a good set of notes. Combine the old and the new to write the outline for a storytelling of the *Sundiata* epic today. The following tip will help you write effective notes.

Writing Skills Focus: Audience Knowledge

Considering your **audience's knowledge** is an important part of storytelling. You can't assume, for example, that your listeners know where Mali is. They may not know what a baobab, a calabash, or even a soothsayer is either. In your notes, be sure to identify and define the terms with which a general audience may be unfamiliar.

Prewriting Make a chart that lists the characters and events you will include. Under each heading, jot down ideas for what might best enrich your telling of the story. Remember, you don't have to develop a finished piece of writing, only notes.

Drafting In your draft, elaborate on the thoughts and notes you compiled in prewriting. Account for all the parts of a story: an introduction to characters and setting, a conflict, a climax, and a resolution. Also, make sure you consider the knowledge level of your audience. For example, for a general audience of any age, define unfamiliar terms. You might also want to compare ancient practices with contemporary ones.

Revising Read through your notes to be sure they will serve you well when you go to tell your story. Ask: Did I account for all parts of the story? Did I provide enough background information to keep my audience informed?

The epics in this section reflect the values and traditions of the cultures from which they come. In "Star Wars: An Epic for Today," Eric Nash explores the ways in which the *Star Wars* trilogy brings together elements of contemporary American society with references to epics of the world.

George Lucas's science-fiction *Star Wars* trilogy includes *Star Wars* (1977), *The Empire Strikes Back* (1980), and *Return of the Jedi* (1983). These films were so popular that upon re-release in 1996, they drew larger crowds than any other films released at the same time.

Star Wars is widely viewed as a modern epic. It contains many of the elements of a classic epic: It chronicles the adventures of a hero; it vividly describes battles between good and evil; and it reflects the values of a culture.

Star Wars: An Epic for Today

Eric P. Nash

Twenty years ago, the film maker George Lucas expanded everybody's notion of how fast a movie could really move with the first installment of his "Star Wars" trilogy. A new generation of moviegoers will be introduced to "Star Wars" on Friday, when the film returns to the big screen with a digitally remastered soundtrack, new scenes (including a meeting between Han Solo and the gelatinous Jabba the Hutt) and some visually enhanced effects. Part of what makes the "Star Wars" universe such fun is that the characters seem to emerge from their own complex cultures. Then there is the ear-tickling felicity of the names. It's hard to resist saying Boba Fett, Bounty Hunter, out loud just to try it on the lips. Just where did George Lucas come up with all these weird names?

"Basically, I developed the names for the characters phonetically," Mr. Lucas

▲ **Critical Viewing** What details make the subject of this picture look like a legendary hero? **[Analyze]**

said. "I obviously wanted to telegraph a bit of the character in the name. The names needed to sound unusual but not spacey. I wanted to stay away from the kind of science fiction names like Zenon and Zorba. They had to sound indigenous and have consistency between their names and their culture."

Much has been made of the director's use of world myths from Joseph Campbell's "Hero With a Thousand Faces," but "Star Wars" is also a synthesis of the treasure trove of American pop culture—everything from comic strips, pulp fiction and films ranging from John Ford's "Searchers" to Victor Fleming's "Wizard of Oz" to Akira Kurosawa's "Hidden Fortress."

"Star Wars" in turn has spawned a galaxy of sub-industries—more than two dozen novels, trading cards, action figures, role-playing games, scores of websites and guides specializing in intergalactic arcana—many of which

▲ Critical Viewing What other mythical creatures does this Wookiee bring to mind? [Relate]

have been consulted in preparing this interstellar who's who.

Darth Vader: Mr. Lucas went back to the Dutch root for father to arrive at a name that approximates "Dark Father." Vader's original name is Anakin Skywalker. Anakin is a variation on a race of giants in Genesis, and Skywalker is an appellation for Loki, the Norse god of fire and mischief. The inspiration for Vader's face mask was in all likelihood the grille of a '56 Chevy.

Luke Skywalker: The name of the character played by Mark Hamill derives from the Greek leukos, or light, an interesting contrast to Darth Vader. Luke of the Gospels was a gentile who converted to Christianity, an appropriate name for a boy who discovers the power of the Force.

Tatooine is the name of Luke's home planet, derived from the town of Tataouine in Tunisia, the country where the desert scenes in "Star Wars" were filmed. An early draft of the script was called "The Adventures of Luke Starkiller." It's easy to read Luke S. as a stand-in for Lucas.

Princess Leia Organa (Carrie Fisher) has braids that resemble dinner rolls, but her name evokes the lovely Dejah Thoris in the

John Carter of Mars tales by Edgar Rice Burroughs, as well as Lady Galadriel of Lothlorien in J. R. Tolkien's "Lord of the Rings." The surname Organa reflects the conflict of nature and technology seen in the forest-dwelling heroes pitted against the machines of the Empire, according to Lucas's biographer, Dale Pollock.

The name **Han Solo** (Harrison Ford) capitalizes on the archaic sound of Han, a variation of John, to set us in a mythical world. The name Solo addresses his key character issue. Solo is a lone gun who must learn to trust others and identify with a greater cause. The swashbuckler's name also recalls one of the great pop culture adventurers, Napoleon Solo, "The Man from U.N.C.L.E." Napoleon Solo, by the way, first appeared as a minor hood in the James Bond novel "Goldfinger."

R2-D2 According to Mr. Lucas, the robot who resembles a whistling Hoover vacuum cleaner got his name from a sound editor's shorthand for "Reel Two, Dialogue Two" during the making of his earlier hit, "American Graffiti."

Chewbacca, the towering Wookiee, was a name inspired by Indiana, Mr. Lucas's rambunctious malamute. (The dog also lent his name to the hero of the film maker's Indiana Jones series.) Wookiee comes from an ad lib in "THX 1138," the film maker's first feature film: "I think I ran over a Wookiee back there."

Jedi, the name of the ancient knighthood, is a tip of the hat to Burroughs's Barsoom, where lords bear the title of Jed or Jeddak.

Obi-Wan Kenobi (Alec Guinness), also known as old Ben Kenobi, is revealed to us as a Jedi knight and introduces Luke to the power of the Force. Obi is the Japanese word for the sash used to tie a kimono; it may connote the Jedi knight's status as a martial arts master. Similarly, Wan sounds like the Japanese honorific suffix san. "OB" is also short for Old Ben, but there is chatter on the Internet that his name is really OB-1, a cryptic reference to Mr. Lucas's much anticipated history of the Clone Wars in future "Star Wars" installments.

Ewoks, those almost unbearably cute, highly marketable teddy-bear characters who saved the day in "The Return of the Jedi" inhabit the forest moon of Endor (the witch in the Book of Samuel hailed from a similarly named locale). Their name may sound like a variant of Wookiee, but it is taken from Miwok, the Indian tribe indigenous to San Rafael, California, the location of Mr. Lucas's Skywalker ranch.

Boba Fett, at least according to one fan on the World Wide Web, is a sly reference to another hotshot jockey, Bob Falfa, the drag racer played by none other than Mr. Ford in "American Graffiti."

Banthas, the shaggy, screw-horned mounts of the honking **Sand People,** are a variation on banth, a beast found on Barsoom. The Sand People bear similarities to nomadic tribes in the science fiction writer Frank Herbert's desert classic "Dune." The diminutive **Jawas,** who chatter like the cartoon chipmunks Chip 'n Dale, call to mind Indonesian Islam. Their name is perhaps echoic of Moroccan Gnawa trance music.

1. Why do you think George Lucas looked to world myths, literature, and popular culture for the characters' names for *Star Wars*?
2. Name three sources Lucas used for names and explain how the names and their sources are significant in terms of world cultures.
3. What does *Star Wars* reveal about contemporary American culture?
4. In what ways is the *Star Wars* trilogy a modern-day epic?

Writing Process Workshop

When you present factual information on a topic you've researched—such as the Arthurian legends—you're writing a **research paper.** A research paper usually includes an introduction that states the main idea, a body that develops and elaborates on the main idea, and a conclusion that summarizes the points you have made. When you refer to information you've found through your research, you need to give credit to the source in a footnote or parenthetical citation. At the end of the paper, include a bibliography that lists all the sources you used.

Write a research paper on a topic that interests you. The following skills will help.

Writing Skills Focus

▶ **Use clear and logical organization** for your paper. Whether you choose order of importance, chronological, or compare-and-contrast, stick with that method of organization for the body of your research paper.

▶ **Have a clear, consistent purpose** for your research paper. State your purpose in your opening paragraph, and develop it in the body of the paper.

The following introduction from a paper on the effect of CDs on the music industry shows these skills at work.

WRITING MODEL

① The purpose of this report is to describe the influence of CDs on the music industry. The writer sticks to this point in his introduction.

② The writer uses point-by-point organization: He makes an observation or comment about CDs and then backs it up with an example.

① CDs have had a dramatic impact on the music industry. Although music has always been big business, CDs have made it even more so.

Since the 1983 introduction of CD technology, the music industry has increased sales by $100 million annually. The new technology created consumer demand in nearly every category. From pop to jazz to rock to rap, the instant popularity of CDs created a revolution in how music is delivered. ②

Prewriting

Choose a Topic To choose a topic for your research paper, ask a question that is interesting, relevant, and for which there is plenty of information available. If you can't think of a topic, consider one of the topic ideas listed here.

Topic Ideas

- A famous writer
- An endangered animal or plant
- A recent invention or discovery
- The source of a famous myth or legend

Find Appropriate Sources In a library, locate the resources that will help you. These may include history books, newspapers, magazines, databases, and the Internet. Use the most up-to-date resources, because they may contain information not included in older materials.

Take Accurate Notes Use note cards and source cards to record your information. Here are some tips:

Note Cards

- Enter only one piece of information on each card.
- Include the page number from which you obtained the information.
- Write a head at the top of each card telling on which aspect of your topic the note focuses.

Source Cards

- Create one source card for each source you use.
- List all the information you will need for crediting the source: author, title, publisher, date, and so on.

Drafting

Organize Your Ideas Write a thesis statement, which indicates the main point you want to make about your topic. All of the information in your paper should support your thesis statement. Include your thesis statement in your introduction. Follow with a series of body paragraphs, each focusing on a single subpoint and providing supporting details. End with a conclusion that drives home your main idea.

Work With Your Notes Use your note cards as you draft your research paper. Work the information from your notes into your draft. Copy facts and page references accurately, but draw your own conclusions from that information.

APPLYING LANGUAGE SKILLS: Topic Sentence and Support

Each of your paragraphs has a main idea that is stated in a **topic sentence.** The **supporting sentences** further develop the main idea with details, explanations, and examples. Notice the topic sentence (the first sentence) and supporting sentences in the following paragraph:

A medieval feast was designed to appeal to the senses. The dishes were colorful, such as green eel stew, and highly spiced, such as rabbit seasoned with ginger and nutmeg. Regarding flavor, most dishes were a bit sour and salty.

Practice On your paper, add a topic sentence to the following paragraph.

One of the ways in which fiber-rich foods help is by reducing the risk of heart disease. Another is by cleansing the digestive system of infection.

Writer's Solution Connection Language Lab

For more help writing effective topic sentences, complete the Language Lab lesson on Topic Sentence and Support.

APPLYING LANGUAGE SKILLS: Citing Sources

When you quote a passage directly and when you paraphrase an idea from a source, **cite the source** in a parenthetical citation or in a footnote. A parenthetical citation immediately follows the quoted information. A footnote appears at the bottom of the page.

Parenthetical Citation:

Astronomers suspected that supernovas "might serve as stellar forges." (Murdin 119)

Footnote:

1. Paul Murdin, *Supernovae* (Cambridge: Cambridge University Press, 1985), 119.

Writing Application Add quotations to your research paper. Then document those quotations.

Writer's Solution Connection
Writing Lab

For additional help in crediting sources, use the Citing and Crediting Sources section of the Writing Lab tutorial on Research Writing.

Document Your Sources You are required to document, or give credit to, your sources in the following situations:
- When you use another person's exact words
- When you use another person's idea, even if you rephrase it in your own words

Failure to do so is called plagiarism—presenting someone else's ideas as your own. Plagiarism is a serious offense.

Quote Your Sources Accurately At some points in your paper, you will wish to quote a source directly. Be sure that you record those passages word for word.

Revising

Use a Checklist The following checklist will help you revise.

▶ Do all the body paragraphs support my thesis statement?
As you revise, make sure that you've actually made a point about your topic in each paragraph, rather than just restating information you've gathered. For example, if you're writing a paper about Peter the Great, you wouldn't simply state the facts of his life, you'd want to draw some conclusions about why he was a great leader.

▶ Is my information accurate?
Invite a peer to read your draft. If the reader questions the accuracy of any information, go back to your notes and check them.

▶ Have I accurately cited my sources of information?
Make sure that every source that you rephrase and every passage that you quote directly are marked with a footnote or a parenthetical citation. If you have omitted one, use your note cards to identify the source. Then add a citation.

▶ Is my paper clearly organized?
Read through your paper from start to finish, looking for any places where it seems to jump around or where one idea doesn't seem to flow logically from the previous one. Rearrange your ideas to make the organization clear, and add transitions to make connections from one idea to the next.

Publishing

▶ **Classroom** Share your research paper by presenting it to classmates as a special news report.
▶ **Audio Corner** Make a recording of your report. Create a classroom corner where classmates can listen to your recording.

Student Success Workshop

Study Skills — Using Study Strategies

Strategies for Success

Certain study strategies can enhance your comprehension and retention of assigned reading:

Skim and Scan To start reading a text, you can begin by skimming or scanning it. To skim, rapidly glance through the pages without reading every word. To scan, look through the pages in a broad, searching way to get a feel for the work's tone, subject matter, or purpose. Notice unfamiliar ideas, uses of language, or vocabulary.

Take Notes As you read, take notes. Write down the main ideas and any questions that come to mind. Jot down those unfamiliar words or ideas. Notes can help you clarify what you don't understand. Suppose, for example, an article refers to "flight pioneer Amelia Earhart." You might better understand the entire passage if you know more about Amelia Earhart. After making a note of her name, you can conduct some research.

Outline One way to make complex reading understandable is to create an outline that breaks down the text into topics and subtopics—or headings and subheadings. If you were reading an article about the artist Pablo Picasso, one topic heading might be "His Painting Career." Subheadings listed below might include: "Training," "First Exhibits," and "Cubist Style." By creating an outline, you can organize information so that it is easier to follow.

Use Study-Guide Questions Most textbooks include study-guide questions that can help you understand the text more fully. Study-guide questions for a science text might help you review the facts. Study-guide questions for a fictional story might help you concentrate on the author's point of view or on the development of a certain character.

Apply the Strategies

Look at the following passage, and apply the study strategies that follow.

Visiting a foreign country had always been one of Lori Benson's dreams. As a girl growing up in the working-class neighborhoods of Pittsburgh, Lori seldom traveled any farther than the Maryland coast. When given the opportunity to travel abroad for six months with her classmates, it appeared that Lori's dream might come true. If only she could convince her parents to allow her to go on the trip. Working after school and on weekends, Lori had saved enough money to pay for the trip, but she knew she still needed her parents' permission. Ever since her brother Bobby had been injured in a car accident, Lori's parents were cautious about letting her travel. Lori knew she faced an uphill battle.

1. First, skim the text. Then, take notes. Are the ideas and details you recorded in your notes different from the ideas you got from skimming? Explain.

2. Create an outline of the passage. What are the main ideas in the text?

3. Write a set of study-guide questions that might help another reader to understand the text.

✔ Here are some reading situations in which to use study strategies:
  ▶ Reading an article about a complex science topic
  ▶ Gathering research information for a term paper
  ▶ Writing a review of a novel or a play

The story of Cinderella has been told and retold in countries and cultures around the world, with each storyteller interpreting and retelling the tale in his or her own way. Legends, fairy tales, tall tales, and epics all have their origins in ancient oral literary traditions. Yet each time an old story is told, it becomes new again, as each storyteller brings a unique perspective to familiar fictional details.

Find a Tale to Tell When you are going to tell a story, it is important to choose one that you especially like. When considering what tale to tell, ask yourself these questions:

▶ Who will my audience be? What kind of tale will this particular audience enjoy?

▶ Where will I be telling the story?

▶ How much time will I have?

Learn It You can't tell a story well if you forget an important event in the middle! Learn the story, and be comfortable with its plot elements, including the rising action, climax, and resolution. Give special attention to the ending and how you will tell it: From your interpretation of the story, what do you want your audience to feel, understand, or go away thinking?

Make It Yours Experiment with different ways to tell the story. A powerful character should have a strong voice, while a weak one might speak softly or hesitantly. Make each character's voice unique and appropriate. Use a dialect only if it is necessary and only if you can perform it convincingly—otherwise, it will be a distraction to your audience. Consider creative ways of using your voice to suggest sounds and details of setting, such as a howling wind or an echo in a canyon. Remember that the way you use your body—through movement and gestures—is often as important as the way you use your voice. It's your interpretation, so make the story your own.

Add Some Extras You might consider using some simple props or costume parts in your storytelling. If they are significant in the story, these kinds of visual elements can strengthen your performance. Using percussion instruments or objects to create more sounds (of a door opening, footsteps descending a staircase, hooves galloping away) can be effective, too.

Try It Out Rehearsing the storytelling for an audience is the best way to find out how you're doing. Tell the story to a few friends or family members first. Ask them for comments and suggestions, and consider their feedback carefully. Be sure to find out what they especially liked about the story or the way you told it.

Apply the Strategies

Choose a legend, myth, or epic tale to retell to a small group or the whole class. Plan, prepare, and practice your performance. Afterwards, invite your audience to evaluate and ask questions about your performance. Defend your storytelling on the basis of your interpretation of the legend, myth, or epic.

Storytelling Tips

✔ When retelling a story, these tips can help:

▶ Experiment to find the most effective ways to get the story's point across to the audience.

▶ Vary the sounds of your voice to indicate changes—of characters, moods, and scenes.

▶ Practice telling the story while you're doing other things, like cleaning your room.

Test Preparation Workshop

Writing Skills
Strategy, Organization, and Style

Strategies for Success

Some standardized tests ask you to demonstrate your knowledge of writing skills. The test questions often ask about organization or sequence of sentences, the choice of words, and the overall style and tone of a passage. Some questions may ask you to evaluate the author's strategy.

Strategy Questions Strategy questions ask whether a given revision in the passage is appropriate in the context of the essay. For example:

> Many lake areas now have signs placed by the Environmental Protection Agency warning against doing harm to wetlands.

1 Suppose that the writer wanted to say more about the warnings to protect wetlands. Which of these additions is most suitable?
   A Violations could result in a serious fine.
   B Many people like to tramp through wetlands.
   C People have developed organizations aimed at saving wetlands.
   D Wetlands are threatened by development.

   While **B**, **C**, and **D** provide additional information about wetlands and the people who protect or abuse them, only **A** provides additional information about the warnings. **A** is correct.

Organization Questions These questions ask you to choose the most logical sequence of ideas or to decide whether a sentence should be added, deleted, or moved. For example:

> (1) Drivers are compelled to wear seat belts or be in violation of the law. (2) As more people have worn seat belts, the number of automobile deaths has dropped. (3) Many states now have seat-belt laws. (4) More states should consider enacting seat-belt laws as a way of saving lives. (5) Drivers who violate the law are given hefty fines.

2 Choose the sequence of sentence numbers that will make the structure most logical:
   A 1, 4, 2, 3, 5   C 3, 1, 5, 2, 4
   B 5, 4, 3, 1, 2   D Correct as is

   The correct answer is **C**. Any arrangement of sentences provides information, but the one in **C** makes the passage most logical.

Style Questions These questions focus on conveying the writer's point of view and the use of appropriate and effective language for the intended audience. Reread the passage about seat belts, and answer the question that follows.

3 The tone may best be described as:
   A persuasive.   C matter-of-fact.
   B emotional.   D whimsical.

   The correct answer is **A**. Reread sentence 4. Any time a sentence tells you what "should" be done, the writer is using persuasion.

Apply the Strategies

Read this passage, and answer the questions.

> (1) It's time for all cities to realize that these laws make sense. (2) Several cities have enacted laws prohibiting bicycle riding on sidewalks. (3) When will people realize that bicycles should not be allowed on sidewalks? (4) Such laws have prevented injuries to pedestrians. (5) Many city sidewalks are clogged with cyclists competing for space with pedestrians.

1 Choose the sequence that will make the paragraph's structure most logical:
   A 3, 5, 2, 4, 1   C 5, 3, 1, 2, 4
   B 1, 2, 3, 5, 4   D 4, 2, 1, 3, 5

2 The tone of this passage may best be described as:
   A emotional.   C funny.
   B persuasive.   D gloomy.

Analyzing Real-World Texts

About the Author

Like other Jews, **Anne Frank** (1929–1945) and her family faced persecution in Nazi-ruled Germany. They fled to Holland in 1933, but in 1942 the Nazis invaded their new homeland. The Franks hid but were eventually arrested. Anne died in a concentration camp in 1945.

◆Reading Strategy

Establish a Purpose for Reading To guide you through a text, **establish a purpose for reading.**

You might read Anne's *Diary* to learn about the fate of European Jews. In that case, you will spend time with her list of anti-Jewish laws. If instead you are reading for insight into her character, you will muse over her self-descriptions. You might also read to appreciate the writer's craft, to be entertained, or to find models for your writing.

Use a graphic organizer like the one below to list details from the *Diary* that fit your purpose in reading.

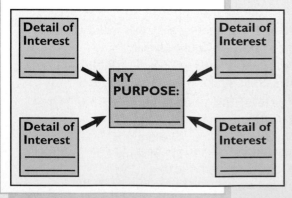

from The Diary of Anne Frank

Anne Frank

20 June, 1942

I haven't written for a few days, because I wanted first of all to think about my diary. It's an odd idea for someone like me to keep a diary; not only because I have never done so before, but because it seems to me that neither I—nor for that matter anyone else—will be interested in the [confessions] of a thirteen-year-old schoolgirl. Still, what does that matter? I want to write, but more than that, I want to bring out all kinds of things that lie buried deep in my heart.

There is a saying that "paper is more patient than man"; it came back to me on one of my slightly melancholy days, while I sat chin in hand, feeling too bored and limp even to make up my mind whether to go out or stay at home. Yes, there is no doubt that paper is patient and as I don't intend to show this cardboard-covered notebook, bearing the proud name of "diary," to anyone, unless I find a real friend, boy or girl, probably nobody cares. And now I come to the root of the matter, the reason for my starting a diary: it is that I have no such real friend.

Let me put it more clearly, since no one will believe that a girl of thirteen feels herself quite alone in the world, nor is it so. I have darling parents and a sister of sixteen. I know about thirty people whom one might call friends—I have strings of boy friends, anxious to catch a glimpse of me and who, failing that, peep at me through mirrors in class. I have relations, aunts and uncles, who are darlings too, a good home, no—I don't seem to lack anything, [save "the" friend]. But it's the same with all my friends, just fun and joking, nothing more. I can never bring myself to talk of anything outside the common round. We don't seem to be able to get any closer, that is the root of the trouble. Perhaps I lack confidence, but anyway, there it is, a stubborn fact and I don't seem to be able to do anything about it.

Hence, this diary. In order to enhance in my mind's

eye the picture of the friend for whom I have waited so long, I don't want to set down a series of bald facts in a diary like most people do, but I want this diary itself to be my friend, and I shall call my friend Kitty. No one will grasp what I'm talking about if I begin my letters to Kitty just out of the blue, so, albeit unwillingly, I will start by sketching in brief the story of my life.

My father was thirty-six when he married my mother, who was then twenty-five. My sister Margot was born in 1926 in Frankfort-on-Main, I followed on June 12, 1929, and, as we are Jewish, we emigrated to Holland in 1933,[1] where my father was appointed Managing Director of Travies N.V. This firm is in close relationship with the firm of Kolen & Co. in the same building, of which my father is a partner.

The rest of our family, however, felt the full impact of Hitler's anti-Jewish laws, so life was filled with anxiety. In 1938 after the pogroms,[2] my two uncles (my mother's brothers) escaped to the U.S.A. My old grandmother came to us, she was then seventy-three. After May 1940 good times rapidly fled: first the war, then the capitulation,[3] followed by the arrival of the Germans, which is when the sufferings of us Jews really began. Anti-Jewish decrees followed each other in quick succession. Jews must wear a yellow star, Jews must hand in their bicycles, Jews are banned from trams and are forbidden to drive, Jews are only allowed to do their shopping between three and five o'clock and then only in shops which bear the placard "Jewish shop." Jews must be indoors by eight o'clock and cannot even sit in their own gardens after that hour. Jews are forbidden to visit theaters, cinemas, and other places of entertainment. Jews may not take part in public sports. Swimming baths, tennis courts, hockey fields, and other sports grounds are all prohibited to them. Jews may not visit Christians. Jews must go to Jewish schools, and many more restrictions of a similar kind.

So we could not do this and were forbidden to do that. But life went on in spite of it all. Jopie used to say to me, "You're scared to do anything, because it may be forbidden." Our freedom was strictly limited. Yet things were still bearable.

Granny died in January 1942; no one will ever know how much she is present in my thoughts and how much I love her still.

In 1934 I went to school at the Montessori Kindergarten[4] and continued there. It was at the end of the school year, I was in form 6B, when I had to say good-by to Mrs. K. We both wept, it was very sad. In 1941 I went, with my sister Margot, to the Jewish Secondary School, she into the fourth form and I into the first.

So far everything is all right with the four of us and here I come to the present day.

---

1. **1933:** The year the Nazis came to power in Germany.
2. **pogroms** (pō grämz´) *n.*: Organized massacres.
3. **the capitulation** (kə pich´ yoo lā´ shən): The Netherlands surrendered to the invading Germans in May 1940.

---

4. **Montessori Kindergarten:** School founded on the liberal educational ideas of Maria Montessori (1870–1952).

◆ Apply the Reading Strategy

1. Cite three details in Anne's diary entry on which you would focus if your purpose were to learn more about the history of Jews in Nazi-occupied Europe.
2. Cite three details from the entry of special interest if your purpose were to learn more about Anne's character.
3. Which of these two purposes does the diary entry better serve? Explain.

◆ Compare Literary Forms

1. Read or review Guy de Maupassant's short story "Two Friends," page 210. Citing details from this story and from Anne Frank's diary, explain ways in which war can dramatize the importance of friendship.
2. The friends in "Two Friends" barely say anything to each other; Anne wants to tell her "friend" everything. What conclusions about friendship can you draw from this contrast?

Analyzing Real-World Texts

Background
Cambridge University, the host of this Web site, was founded around 1209 in the city of Cambridge, near London, England. It is one of the world's oldest universities.

◆ Reading Strategy
Use Reference Material
You may occasionally meet unfamiliar words, phrases, or concepts. To answer questions you may have, use reference material, such as encyclopedias and Internet resources.

For instance, you can find information about the study of ancient Egypt through this Egyptology Web page. As with many Web pages, the main links offered by the site are laid out in a sidebar. Scan the sidebar to determine where to find information. Be aware that many sites offer a "Search" feature and site index to help you locate information quickly.

In a graphic organizer like the one below, list each link, and note the kind of information you expect to find through it.

Link	Information I Expect to Find
News & Gossip	Information about recent discoveries, as well as professional news that only archaeologists would be interested in

Egyptology Web

Popular local items
News & Gossip
Announcements
Bulletin Board
Email addresses
Commercial stuff
Tomb of Senneferi (TT99)
Beinlich Wordlist
Wilbour Library Acquisitions

Main pages
Local resources
Essential resources elsewhere
Institutions
Museums

This page is set up with the kind assistance of the Newton Institute in the University of Cambridge to provide a World Wide Web resource for Egyptological information. The pages are not a publication of the Newton Institute, and all matters concerning them (e.g. comments, criticisms, and suggestions for items to include) should be sent to Nigel Strudwick.

Click here for guidelines on the format of material.

HISTORY: Egyptology Resources was set up in 1994 and was the first web page set up specifically for the benefit of those interested in Egyptology, whether laymen or professionals. The links you can go to from here are grouped into hopefully helpful divisions, with those which have their homes on this site separated at the top.

◆ Apply the Reading Strategy

1. Where can users click to learn more about the people who put together the site?
2. What link should users click to find a good Egyptian exhibit near them?

◆ Compare Literary Forms

Read or review the ancient Egyptian poems on pages 292–294. Compare what you learn about ancient Egypt from these poems with what you learn about it from this site.

Background

The following article gives would-be travelers advice for traveling in India, the world's seventh-largest country in land mass—and a country of diverse geographic regions, including the Himalayas, a mountain range in the northern part of the country. Each summer, from June through September, India is drenched by rains that form as moist air masses and move in from the Indian Ocean. These rain-bearing winds are known as tropical monsoons.

◆ Reading Strategy

Use Formatting Clues to Locate Information

When you read guide books or articles, it is not usually necessary to read every word or every section of the book. This type of writing is meant to be used for reference—to answer specific questions a reader might have. As you read guide books and similar types of writing, **look for formatting clues** that indicate or call out what type of information you'll find in each section.

Look for the following types of formatting as you read this article on travel:

FORMATTING CLUES
Titles and Heads
Read heads or titles to find out what kind of information is contained within chapters or sections.
Bulleted Lists
These lists usually call out items or tips, sometimes in order of importance.
Numbered Lists
These lists show steps of a process that should be followed in a certain order.
Parentheses
Information contained in parentheses is usually not necessary to the understanding of the text. Often, text within parentheses gives extra or more detailed information.
Features Boxes
Interesting, related, or critical information is often set by itself in a features box. These boxes are often colorful and eye-catching.

from Indian Himalaya

Bradley Mayhew *et al.*

What to Bring

The usual traveler's rule applies—bring as little as possible. It's much better to have to buy something you've left behind than find you have too much and need to get rid of it.

Clothes In the Himalayan regions, it can be quite cool in the evenings, even in summer, and farther north it will get down to freezing at night, so you will need at least some cold-weather gear whatever time of year you plan to go. If you are traveling between October and March you will probably need a fleece and a down jacket, especially if you are headed for higher altitudes. For colder climates, the "layers theory" is your best bet.

If you're traveling to Ladakh or Spiti, be prepared for dramatic temperature changes and for the extreme burning power of the sun in the thin air. A cloud across the sun can change the air temperature from T-shirt to sweater level in seconds.

A reasonable clothes list might include:

- one pair of cotton trousers (for summer and lower elevations)
- one pair of warmer and more durable trousers (for winter and higher elevations)
- one long cotton skirt (women)
- a few T-shirts or short-sleeved cotton shirts
- one fleece, thick sweater or woolen shirt (for high elevations and cold nights)
- one pair of sneakers or shoes, plus socks; good, comfortable walking boots with ankle support if you're planning to trek

Analyzing Real-World Texts

- sandals or thongs (flipflops; handy when showering in common bathrooms)
- lightweight jacket or raincoat (during the monsoon) or a more heavyweight jacket of high-quality fabric . . . (for higher elevations)
- gloves and balaclava[1] for winter (both items can be purchased locally; a balaclava is particularly important at higher elevations, as considerable body heat is lost through the head)
- sun hat or cap
- set of "dress-up" clothes (for dining in Raj-era hotels!)

Bedding A sleeping bag can be a hassle to carry, but can serve as something to sleep in (and avoid unsavory-looking hotel bedding), a cushion on hard train seats, a pillow on long bus journeys or a bed-top cover (since cheap hotels rarely give you one). They are particularly useful in places like Ladakh and Spiti, where the nights can get very cold. Visiting many of the remote gompas[2] by public transport will require an overnight stop, often in basic guesthouses. If you're trekking then a sleeping bag will be an absolute necessity. . . .

Toiletries Western brands of soap, toothpaste, and other toiletries are readily available (often in hand sachets so you don't have to carry around a whole bottle of the stuff). Hair conditioner usually comes in the "shampoo and conditioner in one" format, so if you don't use

this, bring your own. Astringent is useful for cleaning away the grime at the end of the day—bring cotton balls for application.

Men can safely leave their shaving gear at home. One of the pleasures of Indian travel is a shave in a barber shop every few days. For around Rs 10[3] you'll get the full treatment—lathering, followed by a shave, then the process is repeated, and finally there's the hot, damp towel and buckets of cheap cologne. If you're not quick you'll find that before you know it you're also in for a scalp massage.

Always keep an emergency stash of toilet paper with you in case of emergencies. Bring your own deodorant. See the Health section later in this chapter for details about medical supplies.

Monsoon Essentials

If you're planning to travel to the Himalayan region during the monsoon, don't underestimate its ability to turn your trip into a waterlogged misery, if you're not properly prepared. Monsoon essentials include:

- sturdy umbrella (available just about everywhere)
- raincoat
- full set of wet-weather gear, including over-pants with elasticized ankles
- waterproofing spray for boots and packs
- plastic cover for your pack
- gumboots/Wellingtons (readily available in the hill stations, but if you have large feet, you'll need to bring a pair with you) . . .

---

1. **balaclava** (bäl´ ə klä´ və): Knitted head covering.
2. **gompas**: Hermitages; retreats.
3. **Rs 10:** The rupee is the basic monetary unit of India. *Rs 10* is the notation for ten rupees.

◆ Apply the Reading Strategy

1. (a) What type of formatting is used to list travel essentials? (b) Do you find this format effective? Why or why not?
2. Where in the article would you look to learn about the types of clothing to pack? Why?
3. Why might the authors have decided to put information about the monsoon essentials in a feature box?

◆ Compare Literary Forms

Read or review Rabindranath Tagore's "The Cabuliwallah" on page 378. (a) What aspects of life in India does the story capture that the travel guide does not? (b) Which book, the travel guide or the short story, would you rather take with you on a trip to Calcutta? Why?

Two Old Men, Many Young Lives

[*New York Times* Editorial, June 5, 1989]

Deng Xiaoping Defiles His Legacy With Blood

Mao Zedong taught Chinese Communists that political power grows out of the barrel of a gun. Deng Xiaoping[1] believes it. Now 84 years old, and said to be in failing health, he is neither too old nor too ill to order the army massacre of hundreds of unarmed, idealistic Chinese students in Beijing's central square. Tiananmen, it is called: the Gate of Heavenly Peace. America's conscience cries out.

The challenge for the Bush Administration is to distinguish between China and its present bloodstained regime. It would unconscionably contort America's principles to continue business as usual with an unstable leadership which has so discredited and disabled itself. Further, trying to preserve links with the regime for strategic reasons could ultimately backfire, associating America, in the eyes of the next generation of Chinese leaders, with Mr. Deng's crimes.

President Bush,[2] who has not hesitated to rebuke the Soviet Union and Nicaragua for lesser crimes, has so far failed adequately to express the revulsion Americans now feel.

But conditions in China are too fluid to support impulsive policy lurches. The most prudent course is to suspend official cooperation until the political situation sorts out.

• • •

The weekend events will likely prove to be monumental folly as well as monumental tragedy. This was the first time in the 40-year history of the People's Republic that the field army was used against the people in the capital. The regime's remaining legitimacy seems virtually destroyed. Even in the wake of overwhelming firepower and ruthlessness, resistance, in one form or another, seems certain to

---

1. **Deng Xiaoping** (duŋ shou´ piŋ) **(1904–1997):** Former Chinese Communist leader.
2. **George Herbert Walker Bush (1924–   ):** President of the United States, 1989–1993.

Analyzing Real-World Texts

continue. Mr. Deng and his narrow group rule only by force and fear.

Poland's recent history shows what that means: isolation, stagnation and instability. China's unity, its economic development and its relations with the rest of the world are all now imperiled. It is inconceivable that the small group of hard-line politicians can long impose its will on hundreds of millions of restive Chinese, even with full command over the People's Liberation Army and the Communist Party apparatus.

For all their stern savagery, the hard-liners' mastery of army and party cadres[3] nationwide is anything but assured. During the last month, there has been ample evidence of strong opposition to the use of military force by many ranking figures. And even if centralized party control holds, new reports of Mr. Deng's ebbing vitality make clear that the struggle to succeed him will continue.

Mr. Deng and his protégé, Prime Minister Li Peng, are now surely the most hated men in China. Mr. Li is shown to have lied to his people when he promised that troops would not be used against the peaceful student demonstrators. And Mr. Deng has defiled his reputation and 10 years of leading the way to an educated, modernized China.

It's a familiar, poignant, ironic story: the old leader's insistence on wielding power to the end, poisoning the legacy and destroying any hope of orderly succession.

Deng Xiaoping, more than anyone, rescued China from the near-anarchy of the Cultural Revolution. Deng Xiaoping, more than anyone, ushered in a decade of transforming prosperity. Economic opening brought increased contact with the outside world and nurtured yearnings for democratic reforms as well. And it enhanced the importance of a new student generation, no longer the destructive Red Guard zealots but now the intellectual pioneers of national progress.

Deng Xiaoping has never accepted the necessary political corollary of his economic plans. How has he now responded to the students, fired by the visions he ignited? By gunning them down in the streets. Americans join Chinese in their mourning.

---

3. cadres (ka´ drēz´): Midlevel members of the Communist government or party.

◆ Apply the Reading Strategy

1. In paragraph 2 of the editorial, locate three examples of loaded language. Explain why you chose each as an example.
2. (a) Find two instances of parallel structure—repeated words or phrases—within this editorial. (b) Why might the writer have used parallelism in those places?
3. What effect might the rhetorical question in the final paragraph have on readers? Explain.
4. Do you find the editorial effective, even after identifying the persuasive techniques used within it? Why or why not?

◆ Compare Literary Forms

Read or review Bei Dao's "The Homecoming Stranger," beginning on page 468.
1. Which piece, the story or the editorial, do you find a more convincing argument against the government of Communist China? Explain.
2. What persuasive techniques, if any, can you find in "The Homecoming Stranger"? Explain.

◆ Reading Strategy

Analyze Text Structures: Cause and Effect **Cause and effect** is a structure that shows the connection between events. A cause is an event or force that brings about another event (its effect). The effect of one event can also be the cause of another event.

In "Lightning and Thunder," the writer explains how the attraction between charges in a cloud and charges in the ground causes an effect—the flow of negative charges from the cloud to the earth below. This event is one in the series that causes lightning.

Use a graphic organizer like the one below to list three causes and their effects as described in the article.

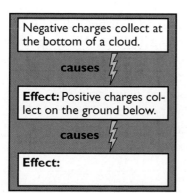

Negative charges collect at the bottom of a cloud.

causes

Effect: Positive charges collect on the ground below.

causes

Effect:

Lightning and Thunder

Science text from *The Nature Company Guides: Weather*

Eleanor Vallier-Talbot

Lightning is the result of a build-up of opposite electrical charges within a cumulonimbus cloud.[1] Exactly how this happens is not yet clear, but it seems that ice crystals, which form in the upper part of the cloud, are generally positively charged while water droplets, which tend to sink to the bottom of the cloud, are normally negatively charged. It may be that updrafts carry the positive charges up and downdrafts[2] drag the negative charges down.

As this build-up occurs, a positive charge also forms near the ground under the cloud and moves with the cloud.

Opposites Attract

The opposing electrical charges are strongly attracted to each other. Eventually, the insulating[3] layer of air between the charges cannot keep them apart any longer and a discharge takes place. Negative charges move toward positive charges in an invisible, jagged, zigzag pattern, called a stepped leader. When the negative charge meets the positive charge, a massive electrical current—the lightning bolt—is created and then sustained[4] by a return positive charge back to the cloud. This positive charge travels extremely quickly—about 60,000 miles per second (96,000 kps).

All of this can be repeated rapidly in the same lightning bolt, which gives the lightning its flickering appearance. The process continues until all the charges in the cloud have dissipated.[5]

Most discharges take place within a cloud, between clouds, or between a cloud and the air if there is sufficient

---

1. **cumulonimbus** (kyo͞o′ myo͞o lō nim′ bəs) **cloud:** Dense, puffy cloud stretching for a considerable vertical distance.
2. **updrafts . . . downdrafts:** Air currents blowing up and down, respectively.
3. **insulating** (in′ sə lāt′ iŋ) *adj.*: Not allowing the passage of electric current.
4. **sustained** (sə stānd′) *v.*: Kept in existence.
5. **dissipated** (dis′ ə pāt′ id) *v.*: Disappeared; became scattered.

Analyzing Real-World Texts

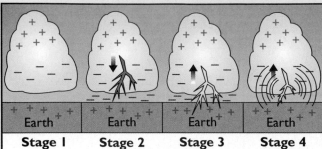

Stage 1	Stage 2	Stage 3	Stage 4
Induction*	Stepped Leader	Lightning	Thunder

*Positive charges collect on the ground underneath the negatively charged cloud.

air around it is superheated, which causes the air to expand then contract rapidly. This creates sound waves that we hear as thunder. Because light waves travel much faster than sound waves, we see the lightning before hearing the thunder. It takes about 5 seconds for thunder to travel 1 mile (3 seconds/km), so it's possible to calculate how far away a storm is by counting the seconds between seeing the lightning flash and hearing the thunder, and dividing by five, for miles (or three, for km). Generally, thunder is inaudible farther than 20 miles (32 km) away.

charge in the air. Only about one in four lightning bolts strikes the ground. When this happens, the descending leader attracts ground-level positive charges upward, usually from an elevated object such as a tree or building. A lightning bolt that travels all the way from the top of a cloud to negatively charged ground outside the area beneath the cloud is known as a positive flash.

All forms of lightning may appear as forked, sheet, or streaked lightning, depending on how far the observer is from the charge.

The Sound and the Fury

The temperature of a lightning bolt exceeds 40,000° F (22,000° C). When a bolt forms, the

Sparks May Fly

There are two other types of atmospheric electricity. A rare form, known as ball lightning, occurs when some of the charge from a cloud-to-ground strike forms a small, round ball. This ball of light may roll along the ground or climb objects until it either explodes or dissipates.

Sometimes, when the build-up of opposite charges is insufficient for a lightning bolt to form, a mass of sparks appears high above the ground in the vicinity of the thunderstorm. This phenomenon was first noted at the top of ships' masts and was subsequently named St. Elmo's fire, after the patron saint of sailors.

◆ Apply the Reading Strategy

1. Cite three cause-and-effect relationships described in the article.
2. Outline each step leading to the creation of a normal lightning flash between cloud and earth.
3. What factor causes the difference between forked and sheet lightning?

◆ Compare Literary Forms

1. Read or review Alexander Solzhenitsyn's "A Storm in the Mountains," p. 594. What aspect of a thunderstorm does his description capture that this article does not? What does this article show that Solzhenitsyn's piece does not?
2. Which do you think presents a deeper truth: a scientific explanation of lightning or a poetic description of a storm? Explain your response.

◆ Reading Strategy

Connect Literature to Historical Context By connecting a work to its **historical context**—the beliefs, trends, and events that shaped people's lives at the time—you can better understand it. Your knowledge of Nelson Mandela will help answer questions you may have about his prison letters. For example, knowing that prison authorities routinely read his mail helps you understand why he does not ask his wife Winnie for political news.

Read "About the Author." Then, as you read the letters, list each sign of the historical context that you find, using a graphic organizer like the one below.

Fact About Historical Context	How Reflected in Letters
Mandela was an enemy of the former white South African government. His mail was screened by authorities.	He writes about his feelings, memories, and the visits he has received—not about politics.

Letters From Nelson Mandela

Written from prison to his wife

26 October 1976

I have been fairly successful in putting on a mask behind which I have pined for the family, alone, never rushing for the post when it comes until somebody calls out my name. I also never linger after visits although sometimes the urge to do so becomes quite terrible. I am struggling to suppress my emotions as I write this letter.

I have received only one letter since you were detained, that one dated 22 August. I do not know anything about family affairs, such as payment of rent, telephone bills, care of children and their expenses, whether you will get a job when released. As long as I don't hear from you, I will remain worried and dry like a desert.

I recall the Karoo I crossed on several occasions. I saw the desert again in Botswana on my way to and from Africa—endless pits of sand and not a drop of water. I have not had a letter from you. I feel dry like a desert.

Letters from you and the family are like the arrival of summer rains and spring that liven my life and make it enjoyable.

Whenever I write you, I feel that inside physical warmth, that makes me forget all my problems. I become full of love.

26 May 1978

I feel sad that I write letters to you and you never receive them.

◆ Apply the Reading Strategy

(a) Cite three facts or feelings that reflect the historical circumstances in which Mandela was writing. (b) For each, explain how it reflects the circumstances.

◆ Compare Literary Forms

Read or review Nadine Gordimer's "Comrades," page 684. Compare Mandela, as he reveals himself in this letter, with the young men in Gordimer's story.

Analyzing Real-World Texts

Background

Entries in a bird handbook give information about different species of birds, including common and scientific names, physical measurements, geographical location or distribution, a brief description of habits, and a picture or drawing. These two entries from the handbook *Birds of the World,* provide such information for two African birds.

◆ Reading Strategy

Make Inferences By **making inferences,** or educated guesses, based on what you read, you can use information in a handbook for your own purposes. For example, readers of bird handbooks often want to observe the birds about which they read. The authors of *Birds of the World* do not say directly what you must do to observe the red-crested turaco. However, you can infer from their description of the bird where you should be and what you should do to observe this bird in action.

As you read the entries for these birds, use a chart like the one below to record key details in the entry and what you can infer from them about observing the bird.

from Birds of the World

Colin Harrison and Alan Greensmith

Family MUSOPHAGIDAE	Species *Turaco erythrolophus*	Length 16 in (40 cm)

RED-CRESTED TURACO

Despite its bright, distinctive crest, this slender turaco is unobtrusive as it feeds among forest trees. The fine, almost hairlike texture of its head and breast feathers are typical of turacos. The red flight feathers flash as the bird takes off and flies from tree to tree, flapping at first, and then swooping into the cover of the foliage. The species lives in open forest and bands of forest along rivers, feeding on fruit.

- **NEST** Unknown, but related species nest on a platform of sticks placed high in a tree.
- **DISTRIBUTION** W. Angola.

dense crest of fine feathers

WING PATTERN

decorative eye ring

reversed outer toe

DISTRIBUTION

broad, glossy tail

Plumage Sexes alike	Habitat	Migration Non-migrant

Detail	Inference Based on Detail

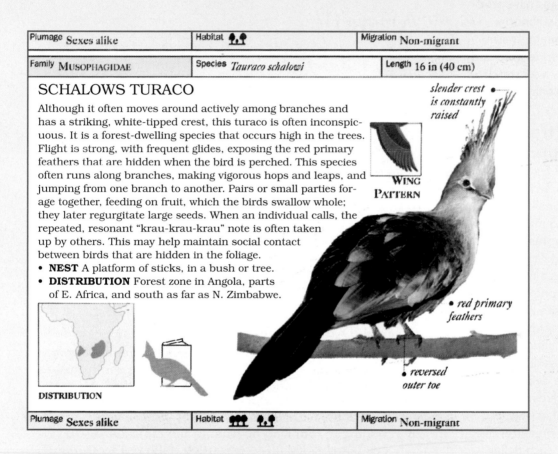

Plumage Sexes alike	Habitat 🌳👥	Migration Non-migrant
Family MUSOPHAGIDAE	Species *Tauraco schalowi*	Length 16 in (40 cm)

SCHALOWS TURACO

slender crest is constantly raised

Although it often moves around actively among branches and has a striking, white-tipped crest, this turaco is often inconspicuous. It is a forest-dwelling species that occurs high in the trees. Flight is strong, with frequent glides, exposing the red primary feathers that are hidden when the bird is perched. This species often runs along branches, making vigorous hops and leaps, and jumping from one branch to another. Pairs or small parties forage together, feeding on fruit, which the birds swallow whole; they later regurgitate large seeds. When an individual calls, the repeated, resonant "krau-krau-krau" note is often taken up by others. This may help maintain social contact between birds that are hidden in the foliage.

WING PATTERN

- **NEST** A platform of sticks, in a bush or tree.
- **DISTRIBUTION** Forest zone in Angola, parts of E. Africa, and south as far as N. Zimbabwe.

red primary feathers

reversed outer toe

DISTRIBUTION

Plumage Sexes alike	Habitat 🌳 👥🌳	Migration Non-migrant

◆ Apply the Reading Strategy

1. What country or countries should you visit to observe Schalow's turaco in the wild?
2. What inferences can you make from the description of this bird about the best way to observe it? Explain.

◆ Compare Literary Forms

Read or review Isak Dinesen's "Some African Birds," page 748. Then, compare and contrast her descriptions of birds with those in the bird handbook.

◆Reading Strategy

Analyze Text Structures: Definitions and Examples

To capture an idea, writers move between **definitions**—statements that apply to many cases—and **examples**—cases that illustrate the definition.

Aristotle defines a reversal as "a change from one state of affairs to its opposite, one which conforms . . . to probability or necessity." This definition applies to a number of tragedies. He next illustrates the definition with examples, including the messenger's arrival in *Oedipus*.

Using a graphic organizer like the one below, list each definition and example in this piece.

Term Defined	Definition	Examples
Reversal	"A change from one state of affairs to its opposite, one which conforms . . . to probability or necessity"	I. In *Oedipus*, the arrival of the messenger, who thinks he brings good news but actually brings disaster 2.

On Tragedy (from *The Poetics*)

Aristotle

Critical commentary

A Description of Tragedy

. . .

Tragedy . . . is a representation of an action that is worth serious attention, complete in itself, and of some amplitude;[1] in language enriched by a variety of artistic devices appropriate to the several parts of the play; presented in the form of action, not narration; by means of pity and fear bringing about the purgation[2] of such emotions. By language that is enriched I refer to language possessing rhythm, and music or song; and by artistic devices appropriate to the several parts I mean that some are produced by the medium of verse alone, and others again with the help of song.

. . .

Reversal, Discovery, and Calamity

As has already been noted, a reversal is a change from one state of affairs to its opposite, one which conforms, as I have said, to probability or necessity. In *Oedipus*,[3] for example, the Messenger who came to cheer Oedipus and relieve him of his fear about his mother did the very opposite by revealing to him who he was. In the *Lynceus*, again, Lynceus is being led off to execution, followed by Danaus[4] who is to kill him, when, as a result of events that occurred earlier, it comes about that he is saved and it is Danaus who is put to death.

As the word itself indicates, a discovery is a change from ignorance to knowledge, and it leads either to love

---

1. **amplitude** (am´ plə to͞od´) *n*.: Fullness; scope.
2. **purgation** (pər gā´ shən) *n*.: Cleansing.
3. ***Oedipus*** (ed´ i pəs) *n*.: *Oedipus Rex,* a tragedy by Sophocles (säf´ ə klēz´) (c. 496–406). Oedipus, king of Thebes, mistakenly kills his father and marries his mother, learning of his crime years later.
4. ***Lynceus*** (link´ ā əs) . . . **Danaus** (dan´ ā əs): In Greek mythology, Danaus, King of Argos, instructed his daughters, the Danaïds, to kill their husbands; only Lynceus survived. *Lynceus* is a lost play.

or to hatred between persons destined for good or ill fortune. The most effective form of discovery is that which is accompanied by reversals, like the one in *Oedipus*. There are of course other forms of discovery, for what I have described may happen in relation to inanimate and trifling objects, and moreover it is possible to discover whether a person has done something or not. But the form of discovery most essentially related to the plot and action of the play is the one described above, for a discovery of this kind in combination with a reversal will carry with it either pity or fear, and it is such actions as these that, according to my definition, tragedy represents; and further, such a combination is likely to lead to a happy or an unhappy ending.

As it is persons who are involved in the discovery, it may be that only one person's identity is revealed to another, that of the second being already known. Sometimes, however, a natural recognition of two parties is necessary, as for example, when the identity of Iphigenia was made known to Orestes[5] by the sending of the letter, and a second discovery was required to make him known to Iphigenia.

Two elements of plot, then, reversal and discovery, turn upon such incidents as these. A third is suffering, or calamity. Of these three, reversal and discovery have already been defined. A calamity is an action of a destructive or painful nature, such as death openly represented, excessive suffering, wounding, and the like.

Tragic Action

. . .

We saw that the structure of tragedy at its best should be complex, not simple, and that it should represent actions capable of awakening fear and pity—for this is a characteristic function of representations of this type. It follows in the first place that good men should not be shown passing from prosperity to misery, for this does not inspire fear or pity, it merely disgusts us. Nor should evil men be shown progressing from misery to prosperity. This is the most untragic of all plots, for it has none of the requisites of tragedy; it does not appeal to our humanity, or awaken pity or fear in us. Nor again should an utterly worthless man be seen falling from prosperity into misery. Such a course might indeed play upon our humane feelings, but it would not arouse either pity or fear; for our pity is awakened by undeserved misfortune, and our fear by that of someone just like ourselves—pity for the undeserving sufferer and fear for the man like ourselves—so that the situation in question would have nothing in it either pitiful or fearful.

There remains a mean between these extremes. This is the sort of man who is not conspicuous for virtue and justice, and whose fall into misery is not due to vice and depravity, but rather to some error, a man who enjoys prosperity and a high reputation, like Oedipus and Thyestes[6] and other famous members of families like theirs.

---

5. **Iphigenia** (if ə jə nē´ ə) . . . **Orestes** (ôr es´ tēz´): Daughter and son of King Agamemnon and Clytemnestra. In *Iphigenia Among the Taurians,* by Euripides (yoō rip´ i dēz´) (c. 484–406 B.C.), Orestes is captured and sent to Iphigenia to be sacrificed; she recognizes him and they escape.

6. **Thyestes** (thī es´ tēz´): In Greek mythology, ruler of Mycenae (mī sē´ nē); he, his brother Atreus (ā´ trē əs), and Atreus' descendants (the House of Atreus), committed terrible crimes and met terrible ends.

◆ Apply the Reading Strategy

1. Cite four definitions Aristotle makes. Also cite the example, if any, that illustrates each.
2. Explain the way in which Aristotle uses his definition of tragedy to support a judgment about good tragic plots.

◆ Compare Literary Forms

1. Read or review Sophocles' play *Antigone,* page 814. Explain whether it contains a reversal, discovery, or calamity as Aristotle defines the terms.
2. Compare your response to the play with Aristotle's definition of the effect of tragedy on viewers.

About the Author

Thomas A. Hill (1954–   ) has pursued a variety of occupations—farming, magazine writing, cabinetmaking. He has also played the guitar on tour as a folk singer.

◆ Reading Strategy

Analyze Characteristics of Texts: Patterns of Organization Writers can organize information in a variety of ways. **Patterns of organization** include chronological order, spatial order, order of importance, and point-by-point comparisons.

In "The History of the Guitar," the author orders much of his information chronologically, starting with the guitar's earliest ancestors and then moving to later instruments. He also compares instruments point by point.

Using a graphic organizer like the one below, note an example of items that are ordered chronologically (one example has been provided). Complete the example of a point-by-point comparison. Then, find another example of this pattern.

Pattern of Organization	Examples
Chronological Order	*Topic 1.* Greeks had stringed instruments with sound boxes. *Topic 2.* These instruments influenced English gitterns and Spanish vihuelas.
Point-by-Point Comparison	*Topic 1.* Gittern and vihuela *versus* guitar: body shape *Topic 2.* _____

The History of the Guitar

Thomas A. Hill

Historical essay

. . .

When we attempt to pinpoint the origins of deliberately produced, carefully designed instruments, we run into problems, because the very first instrument makers were not very concerned with posterity. They did not leave written records. One approach we might try, in an effort to find out where the guitar came from, would be an examination of languages.

The ancient Assyrians,[1] four thousand years ago, had an instrument that they called a *chetarah.* We know little more about it other than that it was a stringed instrument with a sound-box, but the name is intriguing. The ancient Hebrews had their *kinnura,* the Chaldeans[2] their *qitra,* and the Greeks their *cithara* and *citharis*—which Greek writers of the day were careful to emphasize were *not* the same instrument. It is with the Greeks, in fact, that the first clear history of the evolution of an instrument begins; some of this history can again be traced with purely linguistic devices. The cithara and citharis were members of a family of musical instruments called *fides*—a word that is ancient Greek for "strings." From the *fides* family it is easy to draw lines to the medieval French *vielle,* the German *fiedel,* the English *fithele* or *fiddle,* and the *vihuela,* national instrument of medieval Spain. Significantly, much of the music for the vihuela (of which a great deal survives to the present day) can easily be transcribed[3] for the guitar.

In England, the influences of the cithara and citharis led to the evolution of such instruments as the *cither, zither, cittern,* and *gittern,* with which instrument the linguistic parallel we seek is fairly easy to draw.

---

1. Assyrians (ə sir´ ē ənz): Founders of an ancient empire in the Middle East, flourishing in the seventh century B.C.
2. Chaldeans (kal dē´ ənz): A people that rose to power in Babylon, an ancient empire of the Middle East, during the sixth century B.C.
3. transcribed (tran skrībd´) *v.*: Adapted a piece of music for an instrument other than the one for which it was written.

Gitterns dating back to 1330 can be seen in the British Museum. In Spain, there is music for the vihuela that dates back at least that far.

What did these instruments look like? Superficially, they bore a substantial resemblance to the guitar as we know it today, although the sides seldom curved in as far as do the sides of the modern guitar. They were usually strung with *pairs* of strings, or *courses,* much like a modern twelve-string guitar. The two strings of each course were tuned either in unison or an octave[4] apart. For a while, there seemed to be no standard for the number of courses an instrument should have; there are both vihuelas and gitterns with as few as four courses and as many as seven. By the fifteenth century, the vihuela seems to have settled on six as the standard number of courses. . . . In England, the gittern settled down to four courses. . . . Historians of this period do note the existence in Spain of an instrument called the *guitarra.* . . . But no music was being written for this instrument, and nobody seems to have been paying much attention to it.

Meanwhile, in Africa, the Arabs had been playing an instrument that they called *al-ud,* or "the wood," for centuries. When the Moors crossed the Straits of Gibraltar[5] in the twelfth century to conquer Spain, they brought this instrument with them. It quickly became popular, and by the time anybody who spoke English was talking about it, al-ud had become *lute.* The lute's main contribution to the evolution of the guitar as we know it today seems to have been the fret, a metal bar on the fingerboard. Until the arrival of the lute, the European forerunners of the guitar had no frets at all. Since the fret made it a little easier to play the same tune the same way more than once, and helped to standardize tunings, it was a resounding success. The first Arabic lutes in Europe had movable frets, tied to the neck, usually about eight in number. Consequently, the first vihuelas to which frets were added also had movable ones.

The lute—or rather the people who brought it to Europe—made another important contribution. The Moorish artistic influence, blowing the cobwebs away from stodgy Spanish art and society, created an artistic climate that encouraged music to flourish. And so the instruments on which the music was played flourished as well, and continued to evolve and improve. This is a contribution that cannot be overestimated.

If any general lines can be drawn, perhaps it can be said that descendants of the original al-ud, crossing the Straits of Gibraltar, collided in Spain with the descendants of the Greek cithara and citharis. Sprinkled with a little bit of gittern influence from England, the result led ultimately to what we know today as the guitar.

---

4. **unison** (yoon´ ə sən) . . . **octave** (äk´ tiv): A unison consists of two tones of the same pitch. An octave consists of two tones that are eight notes apart in the scale. The pitches in an octave sound "the same" and are named by the same note.
5. **Moors** (moorz) . . . **Gibraltar** (ji brôl´ tər): Groups of Moors, an Arab people of north Africa, invaded Spain at various times, starting in the eighth century A.D. The Straits of Gibraltar are waters dividing Spain from Africa.

◆ Apply the Reading Strategy

1. What pattern of organization does Hill use when he discusses the Assyrians before he discusses Greek instruments?
2. What pattern of organization leads Hill to discuss the Arabian al-ud after describing the English gittern and Spanish vihuela?

◆ Compare Literary Forms

Read or review Federico García Lorca's poem "The Guitar," page 962. Explain whether Hill's essay helps you to understand the special place of the guitar in the heart of a Spaniard such as Lorca.

Analyzing Real-World Texts

Background

The maps in an atlas show physical features of the world, such as cities, mountains, rivers, and roads. They may also provide information on climate, population, and political systems. The Dorling Kindersley atlas combines the two kinds of information in one visual display.

◆ Reading Strategy

Skimming and Scanning

By **skimming** a text, you can get an idea of the organization and scope of a work before reading it. Read quickly, taking in groups of words. Stop for headings and other set-off text, such as bold, italicized, or oversized.

By **scanning,** you can locate specific information fast. Let your eyes move quickly over the page. Look for words related to the information you are seeking. Stop and read the sections where they are found.

Skim this entry from an atlas. Use a graphic organizer such as the one below to record each kind of information you can find.

Subjects Covered	How I Know
Politics of Mali	Heading
Languages spoken in Mali	Icon of person with dialogue balloon

Mali

Adapted from the Dorling Kindersley *World Reference Atlas*

MALI

Official Name: Republic of Mali
Capital: Bamako
Population: 10.8 million
Currency: CFA franc
Official Language: French

Mali is landlocked in the heart of West Africa. Its mostly flat terrain comprises virtually uninhabited Saharan plains in the north and more fertile savanna land in the south, where most of the population live. The River Niger irrigates the central and southwestern regions of the country. Following independence in 1960, Mali experienced a long period of largely single-party rule. It became a multiparty democracy in 1992.

CLIMATE

In the south, intensely hot, dry weather precedes the westerly rains. Mali's northern half is almost rainless.

TRANSPORTATION

 Bamako-Senou Has no fleet

Mali is linked by rail with the port of Dakar in Senegal, and by good roads to the port of Abidjan in Ivory Coast.

TOURISM

 16,000 visitors Down 33% in 1994

Tourism is largely safari-oriented, although the historic cities of Djénné, Gao, and Mopti, lying on the banks of the River Niger, also attract visitors. A national domestic airline began operating in 1990.

PEOPLE

 Bambara, Fulani, Senufo, Soninke, French   24 people per sq. mile

Mali's most significant ethnic group, the Bambara, is also politically dominant. The Bambara speak the *lingua franca* of the River Niger, which is shared with other groups including the Malinke. The relationship between the Bambara–Malinke majority and the Tuareg nomads of the Saharan north is often tense and sometimes violent. As with elsewhere in Africa, the extended family, often based around the village, is a vital social security system and a link between the urban and rural poor. There are a few powerful women in Mali but, in general, women have little status.

POLITICS

The successful transition to multi-party politics in 1992 followed the overthrow in the previous year of Moussa Traoré, Mali's dictator for 23 years. The army's role was crucial in leading the coup, while Colonel Touré, who acted as interim president, was responsible for the swift return to civilian rule in less than a year. The change marks Mali's first experience of multipartyism. Maintaining good relations with the Tuaregs, after a peace agreement in 1991, is a key issue. However, the main challenge facing President Alpha Oumar Konaré's government is to alleviate poverty while placating the opposition, which feels that the luxury of multipartyism is something that Mali cannot afford. As Konaré's austerity measures have begun to take effect, opposition to his policies has increased.

MALI

Total Land Area : 1 220 190 sq. km
(471 115 sq. miles)

POPULATION

over100 000	◎
over 50 000	○
over 10 000	●
under 10 000	·

LAND HEIGHT

500m/1640ft
200m/656ft
over 100m/328ft

◆ Apply the Reading Strategy

1. Name three different kinds of information you can find in this entry. For each, explain whether you discovered it by skimming or by scanning.
2. Referring to this entry, explain an important change to the political system of Mali in the 1990's. How did you find this information?
3. Scan the map to locate the capital of Mali. Explain how you found it.

◆ Compare Literary Forms

Scan the introductory material to the *Sundiata*, an epic of Old Mali, pp. 1036–1037. Then, refer to this atlas to determine whether the ethnic group that told the story of Sundiata is the most dominant group in Mali.

The Art of Translation

This section contains literary works that were written in Spanish, and it shows the Spanish originals together with English translations. Even if you do not read Spanish, the use of both languages will give you a greater awareness of literature written in Spanish and a greater appreciation for the work that translators do.

The Spanish Literary Tradition Spanish has a rich literary tradition, both in Spain and in the Americas. That tradition is well represented here, with works by writers from Mexico, El Salvador, Chile, Peru, and the United States.

Translation Seeing the original and its translation together will remind you that a translator worked hard to create a faithful English version of the Spanish text. Translation *is* hard work because no language corresponds exactly to another. Translators must therefore make many choices as they create a version of the original in another language, and qualified translators can disagree about these choices. That is why translation is an art, not a science.

About the Authors

Octavio Paz [ôk tä′ vyô päs] (1914–1998) traveled around the world as a diplomat for his native Mexico. In addition to his imaginative poetry, he wrote literary criticism and essays. Paz was awarded the Nobel Prize for Literature in 1990.

Gabriela Mistral [gà b͞rē e′ là mē stràl′] (1889–1957) grew up in northern Chile and had a many-sided career as an educator, cultural minister, diplomat, and poet. In 1945, she became the first Latin American woman to win the Nobel Prize for Literature.

Literary Note

Each of these poets explores the theme of personal identity—*who am I?*— in a different way. Paz experiments with summarizing the whole meaning of his life in a few words ("Epitaph for No Stone"). Mistral reenacts the way in which we lose the world and ourselves every night ("Night").

Epitaph for No Stone

Octavio Paz
Translated by Eliot Weinberger

Mixcoac was my village: three nocturnal
   syllables,
a half-mask of shadow across a face of
   sun.
Our Lady, Mother Dustcloud, came,
came and ate it. I went out in the world.
5   My words were my house, air my tomb.

Epitafio sobre ninguna piedra

Octavio Paz

Mixcoac fue mi pueblo: tres sílabas
   nocturnas,
un antifaz de sombra sobre un rostro
   solar.
Vino Nuestra Señora, la Tolvanera Madre.
Vino y se lo comió. Yo andaba por
   el mundo.
5   Mi casa fueron mis palabras, mi tumba
   el aire.

Night

Gabriela Mistral
Translated by Doris Dana

Mountain ranges dissolve,
cattle wander astray,
the sun returns to its forge,
all the world slips away.

5   Orchard and garden are fading,
the farmhouse already immersed.
My mountains submerge their crests
and their living cry.

All creatures are sliding aslant
10   down toward forgetfulness and sleep.
You and I, also, my baby,
tumble down toward night's keep.

Noche

Gabriela Mistral

Las montañas se deshacen,
el ganado se ha perdido;
el sol regresa a su fragua:
todo el mundo se va huido.

5   Se va borrando la huerta,
la granja se ha sumergido
y mi cordillera sume
su cumbre y su grito vivo.

Las criaturas resbalan
10   de soslayo hacia el olvido,
y también los dos rodamos
hacia la noche, mi niño.

Critical Thinking

1. What do you think Paz means in "Epitaph for No Stone" when he says that "Mother Dustcloud...ate" his village? **[Interpret]**

2. In "Epitaph for No Stone," how could "words" have been Paz's "house"? **[Interpret]**

3. What feeling does "Night" convey about the loss of identity in "forgetfulness and sleep"? Explain. **[Analyze]**

4. Sum up who you are in a brief paragraph for your school yearbook. **[Relate]**

Compare English and Spanish Texts

5. Compare the first lines of the Spanish original and the English translation of "Epitaph for No Stone." What are the Spanish counterparts for the English words *village*, *three*, *nocturnal*, and *syllables*? **[Compare and Contrast]**

6. Look at the final words in each line of the Spanish and English texts of "Night." Does the English translation exactly reproduce the rhyme scheme of the Spanish original? Explain. **[Compare and Contrast]**

About the Authors

César Vallejo [sā′ zär və yā′ hō] (1892–1938), from a small town in northern Peru, is now recognized as one of the greatest poets of the twentieth century. Among his important books are *Trilce* and *Human Poems*. Robert Bly wrote that Vallejo "had a tremendous feeling for . . . his family."

Tino Villanueva [tē′ nō vi yä nwā′ və] (1941–   ), who comes from San Marcos, Texas, teaches Spanish at Boston University. His book of poems *Scene from the Movie "Giant,"* one of four books of poetry he has written, won a 1994 American Book Award.

To My Brother Miguel
in memoriam

César Vallejo
Translated by John Knoepfle
and James Wright

Brother, today I sit on the brick bench
   outside the house,
where you make a bottomless emptiness.
I remember we used to play at this hour
   of the day, and mama
would calm us: "There now, boys . . ."

5 Now I go hide
as before, from all these evening
prayers, and I hope that you will not
   find me.
In the parlor, the entrance hall, the
   corridors.
Later, you hide, and I do not find you.
10 I remember we made each other cry,
brother, in that game.

Miguel, you hid yourself
one night in August, nearly at daybreak,
but instead of laughing when you hid,
   you were sad.
15 And your other heart of those dead
   afternoons
is tired of looking and not finding you.
   And now
shadows fall on the soul.

Listen, brother, don't be too late
coming out. All right? Mama might worry.

A mi hermano Miguel
in memoriam

César Vallejo

Hermano, hoy estoy en el poyo de la casa,
donde nos haces una falta sin fondo!
Me acuerdo que jugábamos esta hora, y
   que mamá
nos acariciaba: "Pero, hijos . . ."

5 Ahora yo me escondo,
como antes, todas estas oraciones
vespertinas, y espero que tú no des
   conmigo.
Por la sala, el zaguán, los corredores.
Después, te ocultas tú, y yo no doy contigo.
10 Me acuerdo que nos hacíamos llorar,
hermano, en aquel juego.

Miguel, tú te escondiste
una noche de agosto, al alborear;
pero, en vez de ocultarte riendo, estabas
   triste.
15 Y tu gemelo corazón de esas tardes
extintas se ha aburrido de no
   encontrarte. Y ya
cae sombra en el alma.

Oye hermano, no tardes
en salir. ¿Bueno? Puede inquietarse
   mamá.

I Only Know That Now

Tino Villanueva
Translated by James Hoggard

In memory,
that moving wind,
I'm the muted places
where I've been,
5 I'm the suns
that stunned me,
the fatigue I felt as a child
and the diminishment that came with it.
And maybe
10 this solidarity of words
is inadequate
to tell all that
and, as is true in understanding time,
it's not enough
15 to understand
how soul measures past.
I only know
that now that I see myself
in the path I've made
20 I'm at home with myself and all that
     means,
I recognize
how much of all I've been
waits in memory.
And I could never walk away from
25 anything behind this story.

Sólo sé que ahora

Tino Villanueva

En el viento móvil
del recuerdo
soy los lugares apagados
donde he estado,
5 los soles
que me dejaron azonzado,
los cansancios infantiles
y su negación acorde.
Y pienso que quizás esta
10 solidaridad de palabras
no sea suficiente
para contar
tal y como entiendo el tiempo,
no sea suficiente
15 para entender
cómo el alma mide el tiempo atrás.
Sólo sé
que ahora que me veo
en la vereda que he formado
20 estoy conmigo y con mi todo,
reconozco
que todo cuanto he sido
espera en la memoria.
Las razones de esta historia
25 jamás podré abdicar.

Critical Thinking

1. In "To My Brother Miguel," why do you think the brothers "made each other cry" in the game of hide-and-seek? **[Infer]**
2. In what way is Miguel "hiding" as Vallejo writes the poem? **[Interpret]**
3. What specific passages in "To My Brother Miguel" suggest Vallejo's love for his brother? Explain. **[Support]**
4. In "I Only Know That Now," does Villanueva suggest positive or negative experiences in talking about his past? Explain. **[Classify]**
5. What passage in "I Only Know That Now" indicates that Villanueva has accepted everything that has happened to him? Explain. **[Support]**
6. In what way would human life be different if memory extended back only a single year? **[Hypothesize]**

Compare English and Spanish Texts

7. Using the English translation of "To My Brother Miguel," identify the Spanish word for *brother* and find where it appears in the Spanish original. **[Compare and Contrast]**

About the Authors

Federico García Lorca [fe de *rē´* kô gä*r* *thē´* ä lô*r´* kä] (1898–1936) drew inspiration for his poetry from the diverse cultures of his native Andalusia [an´ da lōō´ zha] in southern Spain. He was especially influenced by the songs and dances of gypsies.

Pablo Neruda [pä´ blô ne *rōō´ thä*] (1904–1973) was a Chilean poet and Nobel Prize-winner who had a deep feeling for his country and its people. In 1948, he had to flee from the secret police of the Chilean dictator González Videla. Neruda wrote "It Was the Grape's Autumn" to honor one of the men who helped save his life by hiding him.

Cultural Note

The Aztec were the dominant Native American group when the Spanish arrived in what is now Mexico. As the Aztec myth "The Sun and the Moon" indicates, the Aztec believed that the gods had to sacrifice themselves to create the universe.

Literary Note

The selections in this group show that poetry and legend help readers look at the natural world with fresh eyes. The poets help readers appreciate the hypnotic beauty of the Moon ("The Moon Rising") and a way of life in touch with the Earth ("It Was the Grape's Autumn"). The Mexican legend gives an imaginative explanation for the origin of the sun and the moon.

The Moon Rising

Federico García Lorca
Translated by Lysander Kemp

When the moon rises,
the bells hang silent,
and impenetrable footpaths
appear.

5   When the moon rises,
the sea covers the land,
and the heart feels
like an island in infinity.

Nobody eats oranges
10 under the full moon.
One must eat fruit
that is green and cold.

When the moon rises,
moon of a hundred equal faces,
15 the silver coinage
sobs in the pocket.

La luna asoma

Federico García Lorca

Cuando sale la luna
se pierden las campanas
y aparecen las sendas
impenetrables.

5   Cuando sale la luna,
el mar cubre la tierra
y el corazón se siente
isla en el infinito.

Nadie come naranjas
10 bajo la luna llena.
Es preciso comer
fruta verde y helada.

Cuando sale la luna
de cien rostros iguales,
15 la moneda de plata
solloza en el bolsillo.

"It Was the Grape's Autumn"

Pablo Neruda
Translated by James Wright
and Robert Bly

It was the grape's autumn.
The dense vinefield shivered.
The white clusters, half-hidden,
found their mild fingers cold,
5   and the black grapes were filling
their tiny stout udders
from a round and secret river.
The man of the house, an artisan
with a hawk's face, read to me
10 the pale earth book
about the darkening days.
His kindliness saw deep into the fruit,
the trunk of the vine, and the work
of the pruning knife, which lets the tree
        keep
15 its simple goblet shape.
He talked to his horses
as if to immense boys: behind him
the five cats trailed,
and the dogs of that household,
20 some arched and slow moving,
others running crazily
under the cold peach trees.
He knew each branch,
each scar on his trees,
25 and his ancient voice taught me
while it was stroking his horses.

"Era el otoño de las uvas"

Pablo Neruda

Era el otoño de las uvas.
Temblaba el parral numeroso.
Los racimos blancos, velados,
escarchaban sus dulces dedos,
5   y las negras uvas llenaban
sus pequeñas ubres repletas
de un secreto río redondo.
El dueño de casa, artesano
de magro rostro, me leía
10 el pálido libro terrestre
de los días crepusculares.
Su bondad conocía el fruto,
la rama troncal y el trabajo
de la poda que deja al árbol
15 su desnuda forma de copa.
A los caballos conversaba
como a inmensos niños: seguían
detrás de él los cinco gatos
y los perros de aquella casa,
20 unos enarcados y lentos,
otros corriendo locamente
bajo los fríos durazneros.
Él conocía cada rama,
cada cicatriz de los árboles,
25 y su antigua voz me enseñaba
acariciando a los caballos.

The Sun and the Moon

Retold by Genevieve Barlow and William N. Stivers

Before there was light in the world, the gods of Teotihuacan [tā ō tē wä kän´, city of the gods near Mexico City] were talking among themselves, trying to decide who was going to give light to the world. All the gods were in a large room in one of the many temples. They asked, "Who among us are willing to give light to the world?" All of them knew that to give light to the world was not an easy task. It was going to cost the lives of those who decided to do it, for they would have to throw themselves into a great fire.

No one answered at first. Then, one of the youngest of the gods, Tecuciztecatl, spoke and said in a loud voice, "I am willing to throw myself into the fire." Everyone said together, "The god Tecuciztecatl is a great god! We all congratulate him."

But there had to be two gods and there was no one else among them brave enough to accompany Tecuciztecatl. He made fun of the others saying, "Where is there a god as brave as I in the whole region? Isn't there anyone willing to sacrifice his life to give light to the world?"

No one answered. All of them kept silent for a few minutes and then they began to talk among themselves. During this discussion, there was so much noise and such moving about that no one noticed that a very old god got up slowly and stood in front of them all.

The old god was poor and humble. His clothing was not elegant. All the others wanted to know why he had stood up.

"What does he want?" some said.

"Who does he think he is?" others commented.

El sol y la luna

Narración: Genevieve Barlow y William N. Stivers

Antes de que hubiera luz en el mundo, los dioses de Teotihuacán hablaron entre sí para decidir quiénes iban a dar luz al mundo. Todos los dioses estaban en un salón grande de uno de los muchos templos. Preguntaron:

—¿Quiénes de nosotros van a dar luz al mundo?

Todos sabían que dar luz al mundo no era una tarea fácil. Iba a costar la vida de los que decidieran hacerlo, pues tenían que echarse en una gran hoguera.

Nadie contestó al principio. Luego uno de los más jóvenes de los dioses, Tecuciztécatl, habló y dijo en voz alta:

—Yo estoy dispuesto a echarme al fuego.

Todos a una voz dijeron: —¡El dios Tecuciztécatl es un gran dios! Todos te felicitamos.

Pero necesitaban dos dioses y no había otro dios lo suficientemente valiente para acompañar a Tecuciztécatl. Él se burló de los otros diciendo:

—¿Dónde hay un dios tan valiente como yo en toda la región? ¿Nadie se atreve a ofrecer su vida para dar luz al mundo?

Nadie contestó. Todos guardaron silencio por unos minutos y luego comenzaron a discutir entre sí. Durante la discusión el ruido era tan grande y el movimiento tanto que no se dieron cuenta de que un dios viejito se levantó lentamente y se puso delante de todos ellos.

El viejito era pobre y humilde. Su ropa no era elegante. Los otros quisieron saber por qué él se había levantado.

—¿Qué quiere él? —dijeron algunos.

—¿Quién cree él que es? —dijeron otros.

Traducción de literatura
Lecturas en pareja en español y en inglés

English

"We do not have time for the old now," the younger gods said.

"He is not brave enough," some of the gods shouted.

"How can an old god want to give up his life?" the chiefs of the gods said.

But the old god, raising his hand, asked for silence and said, "I am Nanoatzin, and I am old indeed, but I am willing to give my life. The world needs light. And, since there are no other volunteers, I want to offer what is left of my life to give light to the world."

After a moment of silence they all shouted, "Great is Nanoatzin!" If the congratulations given to Tecuciztecatl were many, those given to Nanoatzin were even more.

Then, they all began to make the necessary garments for the ceremony. They were truly beautiful, made of very fine cotton, with gold, silver, and bird feathers of every color.

For a whole week no one ate anything. All of them meditated, because giving the world light was very important.

When the day arrived, a great fire was lit in the center of the room. The light illuminated everything.

Tecuciztecatl was the first to approach the fire, but the heat was so intense that he moved back. Four times he tried to enter, but he was never brave enough.

Then Nanoatzin, the old god, got up and walked toward the fire. He entered the fire and lay down calmly.

"Oh!" everyone said reverently. And everyone repeated in a whisper, "Great is Nanoatzin!"

Then it was Tecuciztecatl's turn. He was ashamed. The old god was not afraid, but he was. So he threw himself into the fire too.

All the gods waited and when there was no longer any fire, all of them got up and left the room to wait for the light.

Español

—No tenemos tiempo para los viejitos ahora—dijeron los más jóvenes.

—Él no es lo suficientemente valiente—gritaron unos de los dioses.

—¿Cómo puede querer un viejito dar su vida?—dijeron los principales de entre los dioses.

Pero el viejito, levantando la mano, pidiendo silencio, dijo:

—Y soy Nanoatzín, viejo sí, pero dispuesto a dar mi vida. El mundo necesita luz. Como no hay otros voluntarios, quiero ofrecer lo que queda de mi vida para dar luz al mundo.

Después de un momento de silencio, —Grande es Nanoatzín—gritaron todos. Si las felicitaciones dadas a Tecuciztécatl fueron muchas, las dadas a Nanoatzín fueron mayores.

Luego todos se pusieron a hacer la ropa necesaria para la ceremonia. Era muy bonita, de algodón muy fino, con oro, plata y plumas de aves de todos colores.

Durante toda una semana nadie comió. Todos estaban en estado de meditación porque dar luz al mundo era muy importante.

Cuando llegó el día, encendieron una gran hoguera en el centro del salón. La luz iluminó todo.

Tecuciztécatl fue el primero que se acercó al fuego, pero el calor era tanto que él se retiró. Cuatro veces trató de entrar, pero él no se atrevía.

Luego Nanoatzín, el viejito, se levantó y caminó hacia la hoguera. Él entró en el fuego y se acostó tranquilamente.

—¡Ay!—dijeron todos con mucha reverencia. Y en voz baja todos repitieron: ¡Grande es Nanoatzín!

Después le tocó a Tecuciztécatl. Él tenía vergüenza. El viejito no tenía miedo y él sí. Así que él se echó al fuego también.

Todos los dioses esperaron y, cuando ya no había fuego, todos se levantaron y salieron del salón para esperar las luces.

Literature in Translation
Paired Readings in English and Spanish

English

They did not know from which direction the light would appear, nor how it would appear. Suddenly, a ray of sun appeared in the east, then the full sun. It was very brilliant and everyone knew that it was Nanoatzin because he had entered the fire first.

Then, after some time, another light appeared. It was the moon, and it was as brilliant as the sun.

One of the gods then said, "We should not have two lights that are the same. Nanoatzin entered first. He should have the brighter light. We should darken the second light a little."

Then, another god took a rabbit and threw it into the sky, hitting the moon.

To this day, the sun is brighter than the moon and if one looks carefully at the moon, one can see the tracks of the rabbit.

Español

No sabían de qué dirección ni cómo iba a llegar la luz. De repente, un rayo de sol apareció en el este; luego, el sol entero. Era muy brillante y todos sabían que era Nanoatzín porque él entró en el fuego primero.

Después de algún tiempo, salió también otra luz. Era la luna, y era tan brillante como el sol.

Uno de los dioses luego dijo:

—No debemos tener dos luces iguales. Nanoatzín entró primero. Él debe tener la luz más fuerte. Debemos oscurecer un poco la segunda luz.

Y otro de los dioses agarró un conejo y lo arrojó al cielo, pegándole a la luna.

Hasta el día de hoy, el sol es más brillante que la luna; y si uno se fija bien en la luna, puede ver las huellas del conejo.

Critical Thinking

1. Explain three ways in which "The Moon Rising" suggests the mystery of the moon. **[Support]**

2. What instrument or instruments would provide the best accompaniment for a song based on "The Moon Rising"? Why? **[Music Link]**

3. Find three passages in "It Was the Grape's Autumn" that show the closeness of the "man of the house" and the natural world, and explain your choices. **[Support]**

4. Explain how, in "The Sun and the Moon," the life of the gods is not simply one of pleasure and ease. **[Analyze]**

Compare English and Spanish Texts

5. Compare the first stanzas of the Spanish original and the translation of Federico García Lorca's "The Moon Rising." How does the position of the verb in the sentence differ in the Spanish original and in the English translation? (Hint: Does it go before or after the noun?) **[Compare and Contrast]**

6. (a) By comparing the Spanish and English texts of "It Was the Grape's Autumn," identify the Spanish words for *horses, cats,* and *dogs.* (b) Which Spanish word is most closely related to its English counterpart? **[Compare and Contrast]**

Suggestions for Sustained Reading

Sustained Reading and Its Benefits

Novels, plays, short-story collections, and full-length nonfiction works all provide a great opportunity for sustained reading—reading that takes place over an extended period of time. Through any of these types of writing, you can travel to new and distant worlds, follow a character's life from birth through adulthood, and experience events unlike anything that happens in your everyday life.

The Keys to Successful Sustained Reading

Reading longer works can be more challenging than reading brief pieces because longer works usually involve more characters and plot events and because it is unlikely that you will read a longer work in a single sitting. Following are a few of the keys to successful sustained reading:

- **Set aside extended periods of time.** It is very hard to follow a longer work if you read it in short intervals of a few minutes at a time. Read in periods of a half hour or more. Do not allow yourself to be distracted by the television set or the telephone.
- **Make yourself comfortable.** You'll concentrate better if you make yourself comfortable each time you sit down to read. Choose a comfortable chair in a place you like.
- **Take notes as you read.** Jot down details of the settings, note information about the characters, and record important events.

- **Hold book-circle discussions.** Get together with classmates who are reading the same work. Share your reactions. Discuss what you learn about the characters, and try to analyze the message the writer is trying to convey.

The Prentice Hall Literature Library

The Prentice Hall Literature Library includes many longer works that fit in well with the literature included in this book. Your teacher can provide you with access to many of these titles. In addition, you can find an unlimited array of other extended reading possibilities in bookstores and in your local libraries.

Suggested Works and Connections to Unit Themes

Following are some suggestions for longer works that will give you the opportunity to experience the fun of sustained reading. Each of the suggestions further explores one of the themes in this book. Many of the titles are included in the Prentice Hall Literature Library.

Suggested Titles Related to Thematic Units

Introductory Unit

Candide
Voltaire

In this fast-moving story, Voltaire uses his hero—a naïve young man named Candide—to satirize the intolerance and cruelty of humans. Candide experiences these horrors first-hand, but nevertheless finds it hard to give up the ridiculous optimism of his teacher, Pangloss. The accelerated pace and sheer ridiculousness of the story enable Voltaire to make serious points while keeping readers entertained.

Literature From Around the World
Prentice Hall Collection

A collection of short stories, poems, and essays, this anthology includes the most respected writers of the twentieth century and the past. Works of authors from around the world deal with the universal themes of success, personal challenges, and overcoming obstacles. The book features works from all regions, including Europe, Asia, Africa, South America, and the Middle East.

Unit 1

The Odyssey
Homer

This great epic poem was written down about 3,000 years ago (it was originally part of the oral tradition.) However, it deals with themes that are timeless: fighting temptations and battling threats in order to return home

and claim one's rightful place. It tells about the crafty Greek warrior Odysseus and his long return voyage from the Trojan War in Asia Minor to his own Greek island of Ithaca. It also contains a fascinating cast of characters, from the one-eyed giant Polyphemus to the beautiful young princess Nausicaa.

Night
Elie Wiesel

This novel, which is closely based on the author's experience, tells about a teenage Romanian Jew who loses his family and almost loses his life in Hitler's concentration camps. It is a frightening story, perhaps all the more so because the author tells it simply, clearly, and with close attention to detail. However, the narrator's determination to survive and the writer's determination to bear witness are testimonies to the strength of the human spirit.

The Diary of Anne Frank
Anne Frank

This diary by a teenage girl has become one of the most famous books ever written. It documents the daily life of a Jewish girl living in Holland as her family attempts to hide from the Nazis. At the same time, it describes a teenager's ordinary experience of growing up under the most extraordinary circumstances. Finally, it contains a message of hope from someone who became a victim of a regime that set out to destroy the Jews of Europe.

Unit 2

Siddhartha
Herman Hesse

This novel will whisk you away to an exotic, faraway land. In sixth century B.C. India, you will be introduced to Siddhartha, a bright, handsome young prince who is admired by everyone. You will learn, however, that despite his popularity, Siddhartha feels restless, unsettled, and even unhappy. Driven by an unquenchable thirst for wisdom, he embarks on a search for greater spiritual understandng.

Great Short Works of Leo Tolstoy
Leo Tolstoy

This book contains short fiction by one of Russia's greatest authors. Among the stories is one that just might be the best piece of short fiction ever written, "The Death of Ivan Ilych." It tells the story of an apparently contented civil servant who, after becoming ill, discovers that everything he believed about the world was wrong. It is only after his misfortunes begin that he learns what is truly worth valuing. Tolstoy's writing is so powerful and psychologically accurate that readers feel they are making a spiritual journey together with Ivan Ilych.

Unit 3

Cry, the Beloved Country
Alan Paton

This story, considered the greatest novel ever to come

Suggested Titles Related to Thematic Units

out of South Africa, concerns the unlikely relationship that develops between two men. A black pastor from a rural village, who journeys to the city of Johannesburg to find his sister and son, and a cold-hearted white man find themselves on the opposite sides of a tragic event. The two men discover their races and families have more in common than they ever could have imagined.

The Man Eater of Malgudi
R. K. Narayan

Like many of Narayan's stories, this tale takes place in the fictional Indian town of Malgudi. Nataraj, the main character, owns a small printing press in the town and has never had any enemies. Things change abruptly when an unruly taxidermist named Vasu moves into his attic, bringing with him a jungle's worth of stuffed animals. In the end, Nataraj dares to confront his intimidating tenant. Share the suspense as Nataraj waits to see the results of his daring decision.

All Quiet on the Western Front
Erich Maria Remarque

This novel about a young German soldier fighting in World War I was inspired by the author's own experiences of trench warfare on the Western Front. The book's vivid portrayal of such warfare delivers a strong antiwar message. In fact, when the Nazis came to power in Germany, they strongly denounced the book.

The Nazis also denounced the fine 1930 film—one of the first sound films—that was based on the novel.

Unit 4

Cyrano de Bergerac
Edmond Rostand

This play is about Cyrano de Bergerac, a formidable swordsman whose face is disfigured by a large nose but whose heart is pure and brave. You will cheer him on as his expert swordplay enables him to overcome almost impossible odds. You will also feel his sorrow as he woos the woman he loves—but for the sake of another, handsomer man. You will be amazed by all the exploits of this larger-than-life character.

Don Quixote
Miguel de Cervantes

The eccentric nobleman Don Quixote, believing he is a great knight, sallies forth to battle with ogres, giants, and evil knights. However, he and his more realistic squire Sancho get into countless scrapes with mule-drivers, innkeepers, thieves, shepherds, students, and peasants. This novel is filled with comic scenes, but it also deals with serious themes, such as the relationship between reality and fantasy.

Unit 5

Things Fall Apart
Chinua Achebe

This story by one of Africa's most famous and respected novelists tells of Okonkwo, a wealthy and powerful man from a rural Nigerian village named Umofia. From the first sentence of the novel, Achebe envelops readers in the sights and sounds of a traditional African village. Achebe's voice is both loving and critical of the traditional culture—a culture that starts to fall apart when it runs headlong into European colonialism.

The Brothers Karamazov
Fyodor Dostoevsky

As you read this great novel by one of Russia's most famous authors you will plunge into the complex and sometimes nightmarish lives of the Karamazovs as they become embroiled in a bitter family dispute. You will absorb the teachings of a renowned holy man and will follow the Karamazov brothers on their quests for truth and understanding. After learning of a murder, you will take part in the trial of the man accused of commiting this crime.

Tartuffe
Molière

In this comedy, a hypocrite fools a man who is extreme in his beliefs. *Tartuffe* is a social comedy, a form that French playwrights of the seventeenth century used to analyze aspects of contemporary society. Molière is a master of French social comedy and is credited with establishing it as an enduring type of drama. He is most popular for his comic, critical insight into various character types.

Test Practice Bank

Reading Comprehension

Using Context Clues to Determine Word Meanings

Read the passage, and then answer the questions that follow. Mark the letter of your answer on a bubble sheet if your teacher provides one; otherwise, number from 1 to 6 on a separate sheet of paper, and write the letter of the correct answer next to each number.

> In February 1999, President William Clinton gave a posthumous pardon to Henry O. Flipper, a West Point graduate who died in 1940. Flipper, the first African American graduate of the army military academy, was court-martialed in 1881 on apparently fabricated charges. Flipper commanded the "Buffalo Soldier" unit of the 10th Cavalry. While in charge of funds at Fort Davis, Texas, he was charged with stealing $2,500. He was acquitted of the theft, but he was found guilty of conduct unbecoming an officer. Historical research revealed that other soldiers stole the money and blamed Flipper out of racial animosity.
>
> Flipper is revered in army history. The annual Henry Flipper award is presented to a West Point cadet who overcomes adversity.

1 The word posthumous in this passage means—
  A before death
  B after death
  C during service
  D after birth

2 The word fabricated in this passage means—
  A invented
  B truthful
  C extravagant
  D sincere

3 In this passage, the word acquitted means—
  A blamed for other crimes
  B discharged from duty
  C found to be guilty
  D found to be not guilty

4 The word animosity in this passage means—
  A distrust
  B indifference
  C hatred
  D warmth

5 In this passage, the word revered means—
  A forgotten
  B respected
  C belittled
  D forgiven

6 The word adversity in this passage means—
  A difficulties
  B gossip
  C poverty
  D wrongdoing

See the Test Preparation Workshop on page 347 for tips on answering questions about using context clues.

Test Practice Bank

Reading Comprehension

Recognize Facts, Details, and Sequence

Read the passage, and then answer the questions that follow. Mark the letter of your answer on a bubble sheet if your teacher provides one; otherwise, number from 1 to 6 on a separate sheet of paper, and write the letter of the correct answer next to each number.

> During the Civil War, many Texans wanted to secede from the United States. However, the state's governor fought hard to keep Texas in the Union and to sidestep a bloody war. After the Secession Convention voted to withdraw from the Union in 1861, Governor Sam Houston put the question before a statewide vote, but Texas voters also chose secession. Houston then sought a compromise, arguing that Texas could become a republic—as it had been before joining the United States—and thus avoid being drawn into the war; this measure also failed.
>
> To prevent Union sympathizers from holding power, the Secession Convention declared that elected officials must swear allegiance to the Confederacy. Houston refused. Although President Abraham Lincoln offered to keep Houston in power with federal troops, the governor feared such action would cause a war among Texans. Instead of accepting Lincoln's support, he resigned from office.

1 Which of the following was an obstacle to Texas's secession?
  A Governor Sam Houston
  B Secession Convention
  C Texas voters
  D troops sent by Lincoln

2 When did Sam Houston put secession to a statewide vote?
  A after hearing the Secession Convention's decision
  B after refusing Lincoln's offer
  C before attempting compromise
  D after resigning from office

3 Sam Houston refused President Lincoln's offer because he—
  A feared for his life
  B respected the voters' decision
  C wanted to avoid a Texas civil war
  D approved of the Secession Convention's decision

4 Why did the Secession Convention demand that all elected officials swear an oath of allegiance?
  A to promote Union ideals
  B to remove Union sympathizers
  C to identify Confederate officers
  D to protect Governor Houston

5 Why did President Lincoln offer to send federal troops to Texas?
  A to begin the Civil War
  B to form a republic
  C to keep Texas in the Union
  D to keep Houston in office

6 Why did Governor Houston resign?
  A to avoid compromise
  B to avoid swearing allegiance to the Confederacy
  C to join the Union army
  D to seek another office

See the Test Preparation Workshop on page 431 for tips on answering questions about facts, details, and sequence.

Test Practice Bank

Reading Comprehension

Stated and Implied Main Ideas

Read the passage, and then answer the questions that follow. Mark the letter of your answer on a bubble sheet if your teacher provides one; otherwise, number from 1 to 6 on a separate sheet of paper, and write the letter of the correct answer next to each number.

> Up to one half of a city's water supply might be used on residential landscapes in the summer. A lawn of St. Augustine grass can demand 50 inches of rain per year, which is more than the average rainfall of many dry areas. A typical yard of tropical grass can use an extravagant 10,000 gallons of water in a year.
>
> Increasingly, people in dry areas are using native, drought-tolerant plants in their landscaping. For example, buffalo grass requires only 20 inches of rain yearly. Hardy trees such as mountain laurel and redbud require little water and are beautiful as well. As municipal water demand grows and aquifers are depleted, more people are turning to native plants to conserve water.

1 What is the stated main idea of the first paragraph?
   A Some people waste water.
   B St. Augustine grass is beautiful.
   C People should not water lawns.
   D Landscaping uses much water.

2 What is the implied main idea of the first paragraph?
   A Lawns should be abolished.
   B Cities need more water.
   C Water should be conserved.
   D City water should be rationed.

3 What is the stated main idea of the second paragraph?
   A People should buy buffalo grass.
   B Redbud trees are hardy.
   C Use of native plants is increasing.
   D Tropical grasses use much water.

4 What is the implied main idea of the second paragraph?
   A Water is expensive.
   B Mountain laurels will be popular.
   C Buffalo grass is attractive.
   D Water is a limited resource.

5 In the second paragraph, the author implies that
   A growing cities will use more water.
   B most areas receive 20 inches of annual rain.
   C summer water use is high.
   D aquifers are not being depleted.

6 What is the implied main idea of the passage?
   A People should conserve water by using more native plants.
   B Cities charge too much for water.
   C More buffalo grass is needed.
   D Native plants are attractive.

See the Test Preparation Workshop on page 509 for tips on answering questions about main ideas.

Reading Comprehension

Recognizing Cause and Effect; Predicting Outcomes

Read the passage, and then answer the questions that follow. Mark the letter of your answer on a bubble sheet if your teacher provides one; otherwise, number from 1 to 6 on a separate sheet of paper, and write the letter of the correct answer next to each number.

Joyce's trip to the airport was a disaster. She had planned to pick up her friend from Ohio. However, Hal's flight was delayed because of bad weather, and he missed his final connection. He was too busy to call Joyce and tell her his schedule had changed; he was trying to make sure his checked bags would be transferred correctly. Besides, he told himself, Joyce was such an experienced traveler, she would certainly confirm his schedule and discover the delay.

When Joyce arrived at the airport, she discovered that Hal's plane wouldn't land for two hours. She knew she should have checked on the status of his flight, but she had assumed that the flight would be on time. As a result, she had to wait and was annoyed with herself for her carelessness. Eventually, though, her impatience vanished as she looked forward to seeing her friend. Although the delay wasn't Hal's fault, he worried that Joyce would be inconvenienced. He didn't want to waste his good friend's time.

1 How did the weather affect Hal's trip?
   A He lost his luggage.
   B His flight was canceled.
   C He was two hours late.
   D Joyce was angry with him.

2 Why did Joyce have to wait at the airport?
   A She thought Hal would call her.
   B She had not checked the flight's schedule.
   C Hal was always late.
   D She drove through bad weather.

3 Why didn't Hal call Joyce to tell her he would arrive late?
   A He forgot to call her.
   B She was already at the airport.
   C He was busy taking care of his luggage.
   D He lost her phone number.

4 How might Hal react to Joyce when the plane finally arrives?
   A He will ask her to carry his luggage.
   B He will be angry with her.
   C He will laugh at her mistake.
   D He will apologize for the delay.

5 How might Joyce respond when Hal steps off the plane?
   A She might be annoyed.
   B She might be relieved.
   C She will be happy to see him.
   D She will probably be angry.

6 What can you predict about Joyce's next trip to the airport?
   A She will ask Hal to pick her up.
   B She will check the flight's status.
   C She will expect a long wait.
   D She will not check her bags.

See the Test Preparation Workshop on page 605 for tips on answering questions about recognizing cause and effect and predicting outcomes.

Test Practice Bank

Reading Comprehension

Interpret Graphic Aids; Evaluate and Make Judgments

Look at the graph, read the passage, and then answer the questions that follow. Mark the letter of your answer on a bubble sheet if your teacher provides one; otherwise, number from 1 to 6 on a separate sheet of paper, and write the letter of the correct answer next to each number.

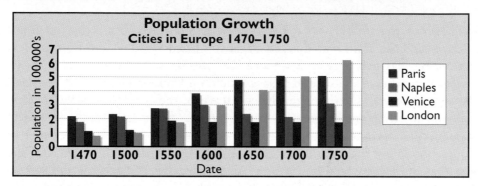

Population Growth
Cities in Europe 1470–1750

The bar graph shows the growth of four cities in Europe from 1470 to 1750.

1 During which years was the population of Venice greater than the population of London?
A 1470–1550
B 1550–1600
C 1650–1750
D 1700–1750

2 In the year 1550, the population of—
A London declined from the previous measurement.
B Paris and Naples were the same.
C Venice doubled from the previous measurement.
D Paris was greater than Naples.

3 From 1600 to 1750, the population of what city remained unchanged?
A Paris
B Naples
C Venice
D London

4 Based on information in the bar graph, which of these statements is true?
A Paris was Europe's largest city.
B London grew larger than Paris.
C Naples grew steadily in size.
D Venice's population declined.

5 During which years did Naples's population decline from the previous measurement?
A 1500 and 1550
B 1550 and 1600
C 1600 and 1650
D 1650 and 1700

6 What was the last year in which Paris was larger than London?
A 1600
B 1650
C 1700
D 1750

See the Test Preparation Workshop on page 705 for tips on answering questions about interpreting graphic aids and evaluating and making judgments.

Test Practice Bank

Critical Reading

Recognize Forms of Propaganda; Distinguish Between Fact and Nonfact

Read the passage, and then answer the questions that follow. Mark the letter of your answer on a bubble sheet if your teacher provides one; otherwise, number from 1 to 6 on a separate sheet of paper, and write the letter of the correct answer next to each number.

Austin, Texas, city officials have stated that neighborhood swimming pools must close by August 31. In Texas, however, the temperature can remain in the 90's until almost October! The city declares that it does not have the money to staff all neighborhood pools and that people who wish to swim can go to the main municipal pool. The main municipal pool is not convenient for children, and it could not accommodate all the people who now use neighborhood pools.

Neighborhood pools contribute greatly to our community. They keep children busy and out of trouble. In hot weather, they are a necessity! Help Neighborhood Pools (HNP) urges you to contact your city council members, circulate petitions, and help us raise the money necessary to keep pools open for another five weeks. Our children and our neighborhood deserve to have access to this valuable resource.

---

1 You can tell from this passage that the author intends to—
A go to the main municipal pool
B stop swimming on August 31
C persuade readers to support neighborhood pools
D give children swimming lessons

2 Which of these statements about neighborhood pools is an opinion?
A Pools help the community.
B Extended staffing for pools will cost extra money.
C Pools must close by August 31.
D Children often use pools in hot weather.

3 You can tell that the speaker is—
A supporting HNP
B exaggerating the situation
C trying to discredit city officials
D attempting to win readers' votes

4 Which of these statements about neighborhood pools is a fact?
A They are a necessity.
B They keep children out of trouble.
C The main pool is not convenient.
D Fall weather in Texas can be hot.

5 You can tell from the passage that city officials—
A oppose neighborhood pools
B need money to extend pool hours
C favor the main municipal pool
D dislike neighborhood groups

6 The author indicates that the best way to extend pool hours is to—
A make demands of the mayor
B contact city council members
C write letters to the newspaper
D volunteer to staff the pool

See the Test Preparation Workshop on page 805 for tips on answering questions about forms of propaganda and fact and nonfact.

Test Practice Bank

Reading Comprehension

Comparing and Contrasting Texts; Analyzing Literary Language

Read the passages, and then answer the questions that follow. Mark the letter of your answer on a bubble sheet if your teacher provides one; otherwise, number from 1 to 5 on a separate sheet of paper, and write the letter of the correct answer next to each number.

Passage A:

The British adventurer T. E. Lawrence worked as an archaeologist in the Middle East. He used his knowledge of Arabic language and culture to advise Arab leaders in an uprising against the Ottoman Empire in 1917 and 1918. His participation in the Arab revolt made him the romantic hero known as "Lawrence of Arabia."

Passage B:

In the movie "Raiders of the Lost Ark," an American archaeologist named Indiana Jones has a series of adventures while searching for an ancient treasure. His search is complicated by both romance and run-ins with enemy soldiers. The character Indiana Jones performs courageous deeds in a romantic desert setting.

1 What theme is shared by both passages?
A Love
B Adventure
C Hardship
D Literature

2 What is the biggest difference between the subjects of the passages?
A Jones was in the desert.
B Lawrence was in Arabia.
C Jones was a fictional character.
D Lawrence was an archaeologist.

A single flow'r he sent me, since we met.
　　All tenderly his messenger he chose.
Deep-hearted, pure, with scented dew still wet—
　　One perfect rose.
I knew the language of the floweret;
　　"My fragile leaves," it said, "his heart enclose."
Love long has taken for his amulet
　　One perfect rose.

Why is it no one ever sent me yet
　　One perfect limousine, do you suppose?
Ah no, it's always just my luck to get
　　One perfect rose.

3 What feelings do the words "tenderly" and "fragile" evoke?
A romance
B betrayal
C humor
D suspicion

4 What kind of mood is set by the poem's rhythm and language?
A abrupt
B harsh
C upbeat and happy
D soothing and romantic

5 What change occurs in the poem's last stanza?
A The poet's love abandons her.
B The language changes for comic effect.
C The poet ends with a lovely image.
D The poet receives an unusual present.

See the Test Preparation Workshop on page 913 for tips on questions about comparing and contrasting texts and analyzing literary language.

Test Practice Bank

Reading Comprehension

Characteristics of Text

Writers may organize information to compare or contrast things, to establish chronological order, or to show cause-and-effect relationships. As you read, identify these patterns of organization. Read the following passage, and then answer the questions that follow. Write your answers to the questions on a separate sheet of paper.

The kingdom of Great Britain is changing in ways that would leave Americans dizzy. Since the sixteenth century, England, Scotland, and Wales have been ruled together. Now, both Scotland and Wales have voted for self-government. Imagine the states of Texas and Florida becoming independent from the United States! British currency may change from the British pound to the euro of the European Union. Can you think of buying lunch with anything but dollars and cents? Even the flag is changing—from the blue and red British union jack to the simple red and white St. George's Cross of England. Would a flag other than the United States stars and stripes seem odd to you?

In some countries, all these changes might seem like a frightening, revolutionary upheaval. Yet the English seem to be focusing on the idea of change rather than on a sense of loss. Their adaptability seems to echo the words of the writer George Orwell, who hoped that there would always be an England with "the power to change out of recognition and yet remain the same."

---

1 What patterns of organization are used in this passage? Support your answer.

2 The words that a writer chooses help to establish the writer's point of view or opinion. On a separate sheet of paper, write an answer to the following question: Explain how key words in the passage on Great Britain express the writer's point of view. Support your answer.

See the Test Preparation Workshop on page 995 for tips on answering questions about characteristics of text.

Test Practice Bank

Reading Comprehension

Analyzing an Author's Meaning and Style

Read the passage, and then answer the questions that follow. Mark the letter of your answer on a bubble sheet if your teacher provides one; otherwise, number from 1 to 6 on a separate sheet of paper, and write the letter of the correct answer next to each number.

> Ski resorts once depended upon nature to provide adequate snow. However, skiing is a business, and resort operators cannot trust their investments to chance. Instead, they have made snowmaking a science. Machines can provide trails with almost-perfect snow in all types of weather. The trick is to atomize water with compressed air, sending it out to freeze into tiny ice pellets.
>
> This snow science, which now calculates snowflakes with computers, requires a great deal of skill to produce perfect snow in imperfect conditions. The water pipes in snow machines are inclined to freeze. Magnificent snow will melt when it comes into contact with barely frozen ground. Variations in temperature and humidity must be taken into account or a machine will produce soggy sludge or flyaway snow that is useless for skiing.

1 In this passage, the phrase "soggy sludge or flyaway snow" means—
 A snow that is dirty
 B snow that is blown away
 C snow that is perfect for skiing
 D snow that is too wet or too dry

2 With which of the following statements might the author agree?
 A Snow machines always produce perfect snow in all conditions.
 B Snow machines help increase the skiing business.
 C Computers are essential for perfect skiing.
 D Resort operators should depend on natural snow.

3 The phrase "cannot trust their investments to chance" means—
 A resorts can't depend on weather
 B natural snow is inferior

 C resorts ignore weather reports
 D skiers demand adequate snow

4 The phrase "calculates snowflakes with computers" means computers—
 A measure snowfall
 B design snowflakes
 C help produce artificial snow
 D cannot produce perfect snow

5 The author might agree that—
 A it is difficult to manufacture snow
 B anyone can make perfect snow
 C weather is unimportant
 D wet snow is somewhat useful

6 The passage implies that—
 A artificial snow is beautiful
 B artificial snow is big business
 C artificial snow is not a challenge
 D artificial snow melts quickly

See the Test Preparation Workshop on page 1055 for tips on answering questions about an author's meaning and style.

Combined Skills

Reading Comprehension and Critical Reading

Read the passage, and then answer the questions that follow. Mark the letter of your answer on a bubble sheet if your teacher provides one; otherwise, number from 1 to 9 on a separate sheet of paper, and write the letter of the correct answer next to each number.

In 1973, a young Italian student went to the South Pacific to implement a life-long dream. After preparing himself by reading all the available materials, Giancarlo Scoditti set out for the island of Kitawa. This tiny island north of New Guinea became his life's work, and, as he wrote down details of the inhabitants' culture, the anthropologist became known as "the man who remembers."

Kitawa islanders are famous for their canoes, which are decorated with beautifully carved boards on the prow, the front of the boat. Yet, until Scoditti arrived, even the most complete accounts of the canoes were secondhand. During his many visits, Scoditti studied with artisans, learning the techniques and engineering required for creating the traditional canoes. A master craftsman named Towitara, a wise, aged <u>repository</u> of tradition and lore, taught him the symbolism of the carvings and even shared with him the chant recited during the carver's initiation ceremony. Scoditti translated the chant, which reads in part:

My mind, enveloped, creates images,
Lost in dreams will create images—
Images for our companions.
You are transformed into me.
You are transformed into me, Towitara.

After living on the island for about a year, Scoditti was included in a ritual called the Kula Ring. In this social ritual, men travel by canoe to other islands—traveling east in the spring and west in the fall—to exchange ceremonial gifts. The ceremony is a test of skill and endurance that proves the men can recognize ocean currents and navigate by the stars.

Although the Kitawa islanders possess no written language, they have passed along details about their religion and legends for hundreds of years. However, as modern society encroaches on the island, many of the traditional stories and methods are in danger of being lost. As children go away to school, they return with Western values and desires. Many young people now refuse to participate in traditional dances or village gatherings.

Ironically, "the man who remembers" may know more about some aspects of Kitawa culture than many of the islanders. After all, he has been writing down his observations, recording conversations, and filming traditional dances for more than twenty-five years. Even his teacher, the master carver, encouraged Scoditti to return to his home and record his observations about this South Pacific island people.

1 In the passage, the word <u>repository</u> means
  A reference book
  B storehouse
  C lost work
  D deposit

2 Which of the following did Scoditti do first?
  A He filmed traditional dances.
  B He studied with artisans.
  C He traveled to Kitawa in 1973.
  D He read about Kitawa.

3 What is the implied main idea of the fourth paragraph?
  A Scoditti should teach children how to carve canoe prows.
  B Children should stay on the island of Kitawa.
  C The Kitawa have no written language.
  D Contact with Western ideas can change traditional cultures.

4 How might the master carver respond to Scoditti's twenty-five-year study of Kitawa?
  A He would be pleased that the island's culture was so carefully recorded.
  B He would be curious as to why fewer people learned to carve prow boards.
  C He would be proud that young people had learned more about Western ideas.
  D He would be angry at Scoditti's interference.

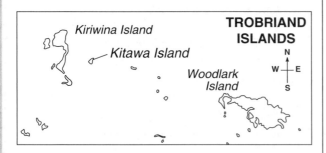

5 Refer to the map and to the sample passage. Then answer the following question: In the fall, Kitawa islanders participating in the Kula Ring would likely travel first to what island?
  A Woodlark Island
  B the Trobriand islands
  C Kiriwina Island
  D New Guinea

6 Which of the following statements about Kitawa Island is an opinion?
  A The canoes made on the island are beautiful.
  B Scoditti began visiting the island in 1973.
  C Some Kitawa children now travel to other islands to go to school.
  D Kitawa has no written language.

7 How are evocative words and rhythms in the carver's initiation chant used to create a kind of melody in the poem?
  A There are no rhyming words or melodies in the chant.
  B The repetition of the word "images" and of the last two lines give the chant a regular rhythm.
  C The chant is abrupt and irregular.
  D The poet details what he will carve into the prow of a canoe.

8 The phrase "proves the men can recognize ocean currents and navigate by the stars" means—
  A travel by canoe is no longer valued
  B Kitawa men once knew how to travel by the ocean's currents
  C ocean travel is a necessary skill for the people of Kitawa
  D navigation must be taught to children on other islands

9 On a separate sheet of paper, explain the patterns of organization used in this passage. Support your answer.

Test Practice Bank

Writing Skills

Strategy, Organization, and Style

Read the passages, and then answer the questions that follow. Mark the letter of your answer on a bubble sheet if your teacher provides one; otherwise, number from 1 to 4 on a separate sheet of paper, and write the letter of the correct answer next to each number.

As the U.S. population ages, more people are moving to retirement communities. Now, though, retirement communities are being advertised not just as places to pass the time as you watch yourself grow older. Retirement was once thought of as a sedentary time. Now, advertisements for retirement resorts describe retirement as an action-packed time of personal growth, exploration, and, most of all, enjoyment.

1 Suppose the writer wanted to say more about the aging of the U.S. population. Which of the following additions is most suitable?
A The U.S. population is choosing to ignore that it is growing older.
B Baby boomers are, by their sheer numbers, affecting retirement.
C Because of economics, more people are delaying retirement.
D Many baby boomers are still caring for their aging parents.

2 Suppose the writer wanted to say more about the growth of retirement resorts. Which of the following additions is most suitable?
A Retirement communities provide a useful service for aging adults.
B Retirement communities have outstanding golf courses.
C It is in the best interests of retirement communities to make the "golden years" look good.

D With more people retiring, many jobs should be opening up for younger people.

(1) In the mid-nineteenth century, three million people in Ireland subsisted almost entirely on potatoes and buttermilk. (2) More than one million people perished from starvation and disease; another million and a half people emigrated. (3) When potatoes were imported from America, they became a necessary food source. (4) The potato blight, which raged between 1845 and 1851, turned this vital source of food into rotting slime. (5) The famine also took its toll on Irish culture: With the population decimated, the Irish language declined as well.

3 Choose the sequence of sentence numbers that will make the paragraph's structure most logical:
A NO CHANGE
B 5, 4, 3, 2, 1
C 4, 3, 1, 2, 5
D 3, 1, 4, 2, 5

4 The tone of this passage may best be described as—
A persuasive
B emotional
C matter-of-fact
D whimsical

See the Test Preparation Workshop on page 1055 for tips on answering questions about strategy, organization, and style.

Test Practice Bank

Writing Skills

Punctuation; Grammar and Usage; Sentence Structure

Read the passage, and then answer the questions that follow. Mark the letter of your answer on a bubble sheet if your teacher provides one; otherwise, number from 1 to 5 on a separate sheet of paper, and write the letter of the correct answer next to each number.

---

(1) The cookbook recipe appears to be extremely fussy about it's requirements for a basic loaf of bread. (2) Henry complains, "The author makes a combination of water flour, salt, and yeast seem too complicated." (3) Only one of his friends <u>spends</u> enough time in the kitchen to tackle such a recipe. (4) An enthusiastic amateur baker, he <u>think</u> that everyone should enjoy making fresh bread. (5) He says, "Complicated instructions are a <u>mistake. Discouraging</u> everyone."

---

1 Which of the following corrections is correct for sentence 1?
A NO CHANGE
B The cookbook recipe appears to be extremely fussy about it's requirements, for a basic loaf of bread.
C The cookbooks' recipe appears to be extremely fussy about it's requirements for a basic loaf of bread.
D The cookbook recipe appears to be extremely fussy about its requirements for a basic loaf of bread.

2 Which of the following selections is correct for sentence 2?
A NO CHANGE
B Henry complains, "The author makes a combination of water flour, salt, and yeast, seem too complicated."
C Henry complains, "The author makes a combination of water, flour, salt, and yeast seem too complicated."

D Henry complains "The author makes a combination of water flour, salt, and yeast seem too complicated."

3 Correct the underlined word in sentence 3:
A NO CHANGE
B spend
C are spending
D were spending

4 Correct the underlined word in sentence 4:
A NO CHANGE
B thinks
C thought
D were thinking

5 Correct the underlined words in sentence 5:
A NO CHANGE
B mistake; discouraging
C mistake. They discourage
D mistake, they discourage

Writing Skills

Spelling, Capitalization, and Punctuation

Read the passage, and decide which type of error, if any, appears in each underlined section. Mark the letter of your answer on a bubble sheet if your teacher provides one; otherwise, number from 1 to 6 on a separate sheet of paper, and write the letter of the correct answer next to each number.

The History Club will be showing a special film <u>in honor of veterans day.</u>
(1)

Because we <u>have been studying World War II</u> in our history class, we will watch
(2)

a classic movie <u>about veterans' who return from that war.</u> The film is called *The*
(3)

Best Years of Our <u>*Lives* and it won several</u> Academy Awards when it was released.
(4)

The film, which follows the lives of several <u>soldiers, shows the difficultys of</u>
(5)

<u>returning to</u> civilian life. Our teacher, Ms. Cornwell, <u>said, The scene that shows</u>
(6)

dozens of scrapped, rusting airplanes illustrates how useless many of the

returning veterans felt."

---

1   **A** Spelling error
    B Capitalization error
    C Punctuation error
    D No error

2   **A** Spelling error
    B Capitalization error
    C Punctuation error
    D No error

3   **A** Spelling error
    B Capitalization error
    C Punctuation error
    D No error

4   **A** Spelling error
    B Capitalization error
    C Punctuation error
    D No error

5   **A** Spelling error
    B Capitalization error
    C Punctuation error
    D No error

6   **A** Spelling error
    B Capitalization error
    C Punctuation error
    D No error

Test Practice Bank

Writing Skills

Construction, Usage, and Editing Skills

Read the passage. Some sections are underlined. The underlined sections may be one of the following: incomplete sentences, run-on sentences, correctly written sentences that should be combined, correctly written sentences that do not need to be rewritten. Mark the letter of your answer on a bubble sheet if your teacher provides one; otherwise, number from 1 to 3 on a separate sheet of paper, and write the letter of the correct answer next to each number.

A small town just south of here has not yet been swallowed up by the big city, it still
(1)
stands on its own. It's not hip, or restored, or historically significant. Perhaps its charm
(2)
is that it remains decidedly uncool. For example, dinner at the volunteer fire department.

Few establishments are brave enough to put cheese on Chinese entrees. The cooks,
(3)
must figure you didn't come for elegant cuisine. Don't insult you with pretend sophistication.

1 **A** A small town just south of here has not yet been swallowed up by the big city; it still stands on its own.
   B A small town just south of here has not yet been swallowed up by the big city, but it still stands on its own.
   C A small town just south of here has not yet been swallowed up by the big city, however, it still stands on its own.
   D Correct as is

2 **A** Perhaps its charm is that it remains decidedly uncool. Dinner at the volunteer fire department.
   B Perhaps its charm is that it remains decidedly uncool, for example. In offering dinner at the volunteer fire department.

   C Perhaps its charm is that it remains decidedly uncool. For example, dinner is served at the volunteer fire department.
   D Correct as is

3 **A** The cooks, they must figure. You didn't come for elegant cuisine, and they don't insult you with pretend sophistication.
   B The cooks must figure you didn't come for elegant cuisine, and they don't insult you with pretend sophistication.
   C The cooks must figure you didn't come for elegant cuisine, they don't insult you with pretend sophistication.
   D Correct as is

Test Practice Bank

Writing Skills

Usage

Read the passage and choose the word or group of words that belongs in each space. Mark the letter of your answer on a bubble sheet if your teacher provides one; otherwise, number from 1 to 6 on a separate sheet of paper, and write the letter of the correct answer next to each number.

I think that the new apartment building being planned in New York City __(1)__ ! To begin with, the edifice will be __(2)__ than all the buildings around it. It will loom over all of __(3)__ . The city zoning officials have interpreted city codes much too __(4)__ . People __(5)__ time to protest the building permit. When people become more aware of the building proposal, they certainly __(6)__ their objections known.

1   **A** had been dreadful
    B will be dreadful
    C has been dreadful
    D should have been dreadful

2   **A** much taller
    B tallest
    C more taller
    D most tallest

3   **A** it
    B those
    C them
    D they

4   **A** losing
    B lose
    C loose
    D loosely

5   **A** haven't had no
    B haven't had
    C ain't had any
    D hadn't no

6   **A** will make
    B will have made
    C made
    D will have been making

Writing Prompts: Persuasive Letters

Some people believe that students should be required to participate in volunteer work before being allowed to graduate from high school. What is your position on this issue? Write a letter to your local school board stating your position and supporting it with convincing reasons. Be sure to explain your reasons in detail.

Imagine that you could have a safety feature on your computer that would protect your personal data, such as your social security number and financial information, from being misused. However, the safety feature also would allow people to record your use of the Internet. Would you give up some of your privacy in exchange for this safety feature? Write a letter to the editor of your local newspaper stating your position and supporting it with convincing reasons.

Test Practice Bank

Writing Skills

Revising and Editing

Read the passage, and then answer the questions that follow. Mark the letter of your answer on a bubble sheet if your teacher provides one; otherwise, number from 1 to 4 on a separate sheet of paper, and write the letter of the correct answer next to each number.

1 One of the best used-book stores around is emerging in an out-of-the
2 way place. This out-of-the-way place is a small town in North Texas. Larry
3 McMurtry, the author of <u>Lonesome Dove</u>, an epic novel about a Texas
4 cattle drive, and <u>The Last Picture Show</u>, a novel about modern life in the
5 Texas Panhandle is bringing used books to Archer City. A lot of them. He
6 plans for his store, called Booked Up, eventually to have a million books.
7   Closed-up buildings in Archer City have provided ample room for housing
8 McMurtrys collection, which now fills up four storefronts. A former car
9 dealership provides the most space. Poetry fiction, and literature in trans-
10 lation are spread out over three stores across the street. Some of the
11 store's treasures could be expected—loads of mysteries, children's books,
12 and biographies. Others are a charming surprise.

1 What is the **BEST** way to combine the two sentences in lines 1–2? (*"One of . . . North Texas."*)

A In a small town in North Texas, one of the best used-book stores around is emerging in an out-of-the way place.

B One of the best used-book stores around is emerging in an out-of-the way place, a small town in North Texas.

C One of the best used-book stores around is emerging, and it is emerging in an out-of-the way place—a small town in North Texas.

D One of the best used-book stores around is emerging in an out-of-the way place, but this out-of-the-way place is a small town in North Texas.

2 What is the **BEST** change, if any, to make in the sentence in lines 2–5? (*"Larry McMurtry . . . Archer City."*)

A change **The Last Picture Show** to **"The Last Picture Show"**

B Delete the comma after **drive**

C Insert a comma after **Panhandle**

D Make no change

3 What is the **BEST** change to make in the sentence in lines 7–8 (*"Closed-up . . . four storefronts."*)

A Delete the comma after **collection**

B Change **fills** to **fill**

C Change **housing** to **houses**

D Change **McMurtrys** to **McMurtry's**

4 What is the **BEST** change to make in the sentence in lines 9–10 (*"Poetry fiction . . .the street."*)

A Insert a comma after **Poetry**

B Insert a comma after **literature**

C Change **translation** to **translate**

D Make no change

Reading Comprehension and Writing Tasks

Read the passage, and then answer the questions that follow. Mark the letter of your answer on a bubble sheet if your teacher provides one; otherwise, number from 1 to 9 on a separate sheet of paper, and write the letter of the correct answer next to each number.

Wheat Field With Kayak

1 If one must be present for an act of severe weather, I recommend the relatively well-mannered type of flood I once witnessed. Floods can be violent, dangerous, and destructive. They trap people in houses, forcing them onto roofs and into rescue boats. They whisk people out of their cars, leaving them clinging to the tops of trees. My flood wasn't like that. It was destructive, yes, but leisurely enough to allow time for reflection.

2 When I went to bed that evening, no one appeared at all worried about the creek that ran past our farm. It had been raining all day, and raining upstream even harder, but Turkey Creek hadn't flooded in years. Well, it occasionally came out of its banks and plopped mud on the alfalfa field, but that didn't hurt much. When I woke up in the middle of the night, I hadn't a clue why there were so many people around. The neighbors had come to help move machinery to higher ground and to move furniture out of the basement. They advised us that a soggy mattress weighs several hundred pounds and that we really wanted to move beds while they were dry.

3 Rearranging furniture at midnight was a novelty, and I cheerfully contributed my part. Still, the preparations for our flood seemed rather casual. No, we didn't need to move all the equipment, my father said. Surely the water won't get that high. The neighbors took their leave and went home to their houses on the hill. After a time, my mother suggested that we should leave, too. I said I couldn't possibly go without ironing my clothes for school the next day. In the time it took for my parents to get the car from the garage, a wall of water rolled across the driveway. As we watched from the porch, the water over the road became too high to drive through even in the pickup. Sixth grade would have to wait.

4 Even at this point, our flood remained interesting rather than threatening. (The prospect of missing school was interesting, indeed.) At some point, the electricity went out, and we used the emergency kerosene lamps that were stored in the kitchen cabinet. I watched them glow in the bedroom mirror as I listened to the sound of water pouring in the basement window and lapping against the walls. My father was listening, too, and at some point he cleared the stairs to the attic, just in case.

5 He could have saved himself the trouble. The water crested at the end of the sidewalk, just at the bottom of our front porch stairs. It kindly left our house dry, but when we rose the next morning, we saw how it had transformed our farm. My father stood on the front porch, looking at the muddy brown water flowing over our yard, and he recited his version of a line from Whittier's "Snowbound": "I looked out on a world unknown/A world I could not call my own."

1 The narrator's family prepares for a flood by—
   A moving furniture and equipment
   B moving livestock
   C leaving for higher ground
   D repairing kayaks

2 The problem shown in Paragraph 2 is that—
   A water has entered the narrator's house
   B cattle are stranded
   C rain has been falling all day
   D furniture has been destroyed

3 The family's neighbors arrive to—
   A take them to safety
   B help them move property
   C take shelter from the flood
   D discuss the change in weather

4 The main idea of Paragraph 3 is that the family—
   A managed to save all their belongings
   B scoffed at their neighbors' warnings
   C were panicked by the rushing water
   D waited too long to leave their home

5 From Paragraph 3, the reader can tell that the narrator's father is NOT easily—
   A embarrassed
   B worried
   C angered
   D pleased

6 From Paragraph 4, the reader can tell that the narrator is treating the events of the flood as—
   A a tragedy
   B a comedy
   C an adventure
   D a catastrophe

7 The actions of the narrator's father in Paragraph 4 show that he is—
   A lackadaisical concerning the flood
   B vigilant about preparing for the flood
   C nervous about his valuable property
   D prepared to move his family to safety

8 In Paragraph 5, the narrator's father uses figurative language to describe
   A the foolhardiness of human beings
   B nature's power
   C the gift of friendship
   D the wisdom of animals

9 Which of these is a theme for this essay?
   A Nature's power can be fascinating when viewed from a safe distance.
   B Nature's power can be cruel and brutal.
   C Nature's power can be random and unpredictable.
   D Nature's power can be gentle and beautiful.

Test Practice Bank

Writing Tasks

The following activity is designed to assess your writing ability. The prompts will ask you to explain something. You may think of your audience as being any reader other than yourself.

Explain how the actions of the narrator's father give you insight into his character. Support your answer with evidence from the essay.

The author states that the flood "was destructive, yes, but leisurely enough to allow time for reflection." Write a short essay discussing the ways in which the author supports this statement.

How does a potential crisis, such as the flood in this essay, tend to bring out the best in people? Find instances in the essay of people being good-natured. Then write your own essay, using real or made-up examples, describing how people come together in a time of need.

In "Wheat Field With Kayak," the narrator witnesses a potentially devastating flood that causes her to reflect on forces beyond her control and her own family's good fortune.

Write an essay explaining how high-school students deal with forces beyond their control. You may use examples from real life, the selection you just read, books, movies, music, or television shows.

GLOSSARY

abject (ab´ jekt') *adj.*: Of the worst kind; miserable, wretched

abstract (ab strakt') *n.*: That which concerns general qualities, considered apart from particular things; things that cannot be perceived by the senses

abysmal (ə biz´ m'l) *adj.*: Immeasurably bad

abyss (ə bis') *n.*: An immeasurably deep pit; here grave misfortune

acute (ə kyo͞ot') *adj.*: Sharp

adjured (a joord') *v.*: Commanded; ordered

adroit (ə droit') *adj.*: Clever

adulation (a´ jo͞o lā´ shən) *n.*: Excessive praise or admiration

affable (af´ ə bəl) *adj.*: Pleasant; friendly

affectation (af´ ek tā´ shən) *n.*: Artificial behavior meant to impress others

affront (ə frunt') *n.*: Intentional insult

aggrieved (ə grēvd') *v.*: Wronged

agog (ə gäg') *adj.*: In a state of eager anticipation

ambit (am´ bit) *n.*: Limits or range of a phenomenon

amenable (ə mē´ nə bəl) *adj.*: Responsive; open

amiably (ā´ mē ə blē) *adv.*: In a cheerful, friendly way

anarchists (an´ ər kists) *n.*: Those who disrespect laws or rules

anesthetized (ə nes´ thə tīzd) *v.*: Made to lose partially or totally the sense of pain; made unconscious

anguished (aŋ´ gwisht) *adj.*: Showing worry, grief, or pain

annals (an´ əlz) *n.*: Historical records or chronicles; history

anoint (ə noint') *v.*: To put oil or some other substance on in a ceremony of blessing

anomalies (ə näm´ ə lēz) *n.*: Abnormalities

antiquity (an tik wə tē) *n.*: The early period of history

aplomb (ə pläm´) *n.*: Poise; self-assurance

apprehension (ap´rē hen´shən) *n.*: Nervous fear; anxiety

apprenticed (ə pren´ tist) *v.*: Assigned to work a specified length of time in a craft or trade in return for instruction

apotheosis (ə päth´ ē ō´ sis) *n.*: Glorification of a person or thing; raising of something to the status of a god

arable (ar´ ə bəl) *adj.*: Suitable for growing crops

arbitrary (är´ bə trer´ ē) *adj.*: Random; not based on a system or rules

ardent (är´ dənt) *adj.*: Warm or intense in feeling

ascetic (ə set´ ik) *n.*: One who lives with strict self-discipline and without the usual pleasures and comforts

assent (ə sent´) *n.*: Expression of agreement

assimilate (ə sim´ ə lāt´) *v.*: To absorb into a greater body

audaciously (ô dā´ shəs lē) *adv.*: In a bold manner

audibly (ô´ də blē) *adv.*: Loudly enough to be heard

august (ô gust´) *adj.*: Worthy of respect because of age and dignity

austerities (ô ster´ ə tēz) *n.*: Self-denials

avail (ə vā´) *n.*: Benefit; use

avarice (av´ ə ris) *n.*: Greed

avenger (ə ven´ jər) *n.*: One who takes revenge, especially on behalf of another

avian (ā´ vē ən) *adj.*: Of a bird; having to do with birds

awe (ô) *n.*: Feelings of reverence, fear, and wonder caused by something impressive

awed (ôd) *adj.*: Affected by a feeling of reverence, fear, or wonder

babel (bā´ bəl) *n.*: Confusion of voices or sounds

ballast (bal´ əst) *n.*: Anything heavy carried in a ship to make it more stable

bangle (baŋ´ gəl) *n.*: A decorative bracelet

baptizing (bap´ tīz´ iŋ) *n.*: Immersion of an individual in water or sprinkling of an individual with water as a sign of admission into Christianity or a specific Christian church

barren (bar´ ən) *adj.*: Unproductive; lacking appeal

basking (bas´ kiŋ) *v.*: Enjoying a pleasant warmth

beguilement (bē gīl´ mənt) *n.*: Trickery; deceit

belay (bi lā´) *n.*: Rope support

benevolent (bə nev´ ə lənt) *adj.*: Doing good; kindly

beseeching (bē sēch´ iŋ) *adj.*: Pleading

besieging (bē sēj´ iŋ) *v.*: Surrounding with attacking forces; crowding in on

bewildered (bi wil´ dərd) *adj.*: Puzzled, confused

bile (bīl) *n.*: Bodily fluid associated with bitterness or anger

blasphemous (blas´fə məs) *adj.*: Showing lack of respect for a deity or religious teachings

blasphemy (blas´ fə mē) *n.*: Disrespectful action or speech against a deity

blustering (blus´ tər iŋ) *n.*: Noisy bullying

brandished (bran´ disht) *v.*: Waved; flourished

bristle (bris´ əl) *v.*: Become stiff, like bristles

brocaded (brō kād´ id) *adj.*: Adorned with a rich fabric, usually of gold or silver

brusquely (brusk´ lē) *adv.*: In an abrupt manner

cadavers (kə dav´ ərz) *n.*: Dead bodies

cadence (kād´ 'ns) *n.*: Rhythmic flow

calamity (kə lam´ ə tē) *n.*: Deep trouble

calculating (kal´ kyoo lāt iŋ) *adj.*: Shrewd or cunning

candid (kan´ did) *adj.*: Honest; fair

cardinal (kärd´ nəl) *adj.*: Principal; chief; of main importance

celestial (sə les´ chəl) *adj.*: Of heaven; divine

chastised (chas´ tīzed´) *v.*: Punished severely

chastisements (chas tīz´ mintz) *n.*: Punishments

chorister (kôr´ is tər) *n.*: Member of a chorus

cognitive (käg´ nit iv) *adj.*: Related to knowing, memory, and judgment

commiserate (kə miz´ ər āt´) *v.*: Sympathize; share suffering

compelling (kəm pel´ iŋ) *adj.*: Captivating; keenly interesting

compunction (kəm puŋk´shən) *n.*: Sense of guilt or regret

concrete (kän krēt´) *n.*: That which is specific, particular, or material; things that can perceived by the senses

condescension (kän´ di sen´ shən) *n.*: Looking down upon; regarding as below one's dignity

conducive (kən dōō´ siv) *adj.*: Leading or contributing to

conflagration (kän flə grā shən) *n.*: A large fire

congealed (kən jēl'd´) *adj.*: Grew more solid, as by cooling; thickened

conjecture (kən jek´ chər) *n.*: Prediction based on guesswork

connoisseur (kän´ ə sʉr´) *n.*: An expert in matters of art, taste, or beauty

conspicuous (kən spik´ yoo əs) *adj.*: Attracting attention

contemplation (kän´ təm plā´ shən) *n.*: Thoughtful inspection or study

contemptuous (kən temp´ choo əs) *adj.*: Scornful

contemptuously (kən temp´ choo əs lē) *adv.*: In a rude or dismissive manner; scornfully; disrespectfully

contention (kən ten´ shən) *n.*: Disputing; quarreling

contraband (kän´ trə band´) *n.*: Unlawful or forbidden goods

contrition (kən trish´ ən) *n.*: Feeling of remorse for having done something wrong

contrive (kən trīv´) *v.*: Manage; scheme

convalescent (kän´ və les´ ənt) *n.*: Someone who is recovering his or her health

convulsive (kən vul´ siv) *adj.*: Marked by an involuntary muscular contraction

corrosive (kə rōs´ iv) *adj.*: Eating or wearing away, by rust or chemical action

countenance (koun´ tə nəns) *n.*: Facial expression

crone (krōn) *n.*: Withered old woman

crux (kruks) *n.*: Essential point

cryptic (krip´ tik) *adj.*: Secret and mysterious

decipher (dē sī´ fər) *v.*: Translate; make out the meaning

decrepitude (dē krep´ ə tōōd) *n.*: State of being worn out by old age or illness

deference (def´ ər əns) *n.*: Yielding in thought

deliverance (di liv´ ər əns) *n.*: Rescue; release

demarcation (dē mär kā shən) *n.*: Boundary

denounce (dē nouns´) *v.*: Accuse publicly; tell the authorities about someone's wrongdoing

deportees (de´por te´z) *n.*: People who are officially ordered to leave a place

deportment (dē pôrt´ mənt) *n.*: Manner of behaving or carrying oneself

depraved (dē prāv´d´) *adj.*: Morally bad

desolation (des´ ə lā´ shən) *n.*: Characterized by loneliness, emptiness, and destruction

despotism (des´ pət iz´ əm) *n.*: Tyranny; rule or domination by a person with unlimited authority

destitute (des´ tə tōōt) *adj.*: Not having; lacking; poor

dexterity (deks ter´ ə tē) *n.*: Skillfulness in the use of one's hands

diabolical (dī ə bäl´ ik əl) *adj.*: Wicked; cruel

diminutive (də min´ yōō tiv) *adj.*: Smaller than average

discernible (di zʉrn´ i bəl) *adj.*: Recognizable; noticeable

disconcerted (dis´ kən sʉrt´ id) *adj.*: Upset, embarrassed, or confused

disdain (dis dān´) *n.*: Scorn

disparaged (di spar´ ijd) *v.*: Spoke slightly of; belittled

disreputable (dis rep´ yōō tə bəl) *adj.*: Not fit to be seen or approved

dissipation (dis´ ə pa´ shən) *n.*: Wasteful or immoral behavior; overindulgence

dissonances (dis´ ə nəns´ iz) *n.*: Sounds that are not harmonious; discords

distracted (dis trakt´ əd) *adj.*: Having one's attention diverted

dregs (dregz) *n.*: Particles of solid matter that settle at the bottom of a liquid

earnest (ʉr´ nist) *adj.*: Serious; not joking

ebony (eb´ə nē) *n.*: Hard, heavy, dark wood

eccentricities (ek´ sen tris´ ə tēz) *n.*: Examples of slightly odd or unconventional behavior

eclectic (ek lek´ tik) *adj.*: Composed of material from various sources

ecstatic (ek stat´ tik) *adj.*: Overpowered by emotion, usually joy

edification (ed´ ifi kā´ shən) *n.*: Instruction; enlightenment

edifice (ed´ i fis) *n.*: Building

effete (e fēt´) adj.: Lacking vigor; over-refined

elaborated (ē lab´ ə rāt əd) v.: Changed into usable substances by an organism

elated (ē lāt´ id) adj.: Filled with joy

elusive (ē lōō´ siv) adj.: Hard to grasp mentally; puzzling

emaciated (ē mā´ shē āt´ əd) v.: Made abnormally lean, as by starvation or disease

embers (em´ bərz) n.: Glowing remains of a fire; coals, pieces of wood, and so on, that no longer are in flames but still glowing

enclave (en´ klāv´) n.: Place set apart from the surrounding region for a special purpose

encroaching (en krōch´ iŋ) v.: Trespassing or intruding

engrossed (en grōst) adj. Completely involved

enjoined (en joind´) v.: Forced by law, custom, or circumstance; imposed

enmity (en´ mə tē) n.: Hostility, the bitter attitude of an enemy

enraptured (en rap´ chʉrd) adj.: Filled with great delight; enchanted

entrails (en´ trālz) n.: Intestines; guts

entropy (en´ trə pē) n.: A state of affairs that has the least order

esoteric (es´ ə ter´ ik) adj.: Beyond the understanding of most people

essence (es´ əns) n.: The crucial element or basis

esteem (e stēm´) n.: Favorable opinion or judgment

estranged (e strānjd´) adv.: Removed from; at a distance

estrangement (e stranj´mənt) n.: The act or process of becoming hostile or indifferent

eternity (ē tʉr´ nə tē) n.: Time without end; the endless time after death

euphemism (yōō´ fə miz´ əm) n.: Word or phrase substituted for a more offensive word or phrase

evasions (ē vā´ zhenz) n.: Attempts to avoid duties or questions

ewe (yōō) n.: Female sheep

exasperated (eg zas´ pər āt´ id) adj.: Irritated; very annoyed

excruciating (eks krōō´ shē āt´ iŋ) adj.: Causing intense mental or bodily pain

explicit (eks plis´ it) adj: Outspoken; saying what is meant, without disguise

expound (eks pound´) v.: Explain in detail

extensively (ek sten´ siv lē) adv.: Widely

extolled (eks tōld´) adj.: Praised

exuberance (eg zōō´ bər əns) n.: State of high spirits and good health

facetiousness (fə sē´ shəs nəs) n.: Act of making jokes at an inappropriate time

fallow (fal´ ō) adj.: Plowed, but not planted

fastidious (fas tid´ ē əs) adj.: Excessively demanding in matters of taste or cleanliness

fathom (fa*th*´ əm) v.: Understand thoroughly

fettered (fet´ ərd) adj.: Shackled; tied; chained

fidelities (fə del´ ə tēz) n.: Faithful devotions to a loved one

fidelity (fə del´ ə tē) n.: Faithfulness; trueness

fief (fēf) n.: Under feudalism, land given in return for service

flounders (floun´ dərz) v.: Struggles awkwardly when moving, as if stumbling

foreboding (fôr bōd´ iŋ) n.: Feeling that something bad will happen

forbore (fôr bôr´) v.: Refrained from

foretaste (fôr´ tāst´) n.: Slight experience or hint of something that is still to come

formidable (fôr´ mə də bəl) adj.: Inspiring awe; impressive; imposing

fossilized (fäs´ ə līz'd´) adj.: Turned into a fossil, the hardened imprint left behind by once-living things

foundry (foun´ drē) n.: Place where metal is cast

frivolous (friv´ ə ləs) adj.: Silly and light-minded; not sensible

frond (fränd) n.: Leaflike shoot of seaweed

fruitful (frōōt´ fəl) adj.: Producing much, productive

furtive (fʉr´ tiv) adj.: Done in a secret or sneaky way

furtively (fʉr´ tiv lē) adv.: In a sneaky manner, as if to hinder observation

gainsaying (gān´ sā´ iŋ) v.: Contradicting; opposing

garrulous (gar´ ə ləs) adj.: Talkative

gaudy (gôd´ ē) adj.: Cheaply bright and showy

gaunt (gônt) adj.: Thin and haggard, as if from great hunger

genocide (jen´ ə sīd) n.: Systematic killing of a whole national or ethnic group

gentry (jen´ trē) n.: Well-born landowning families ranked just below the nobility; gentlemen and gentlewomen

girds (gʉrdz) v.: Fastens on with a belt

gout (gout) n.: Spurt; splash; glob

grafter (graft´ ər) n.: Someone who takes advantage of his or her position to gain money or property dishonestly

grotesque (grō tesk´) adj.: Strangely distorted, absurdly ridiculous

guileless (gīl´ lis) adj.: Candid; frank

hastened (hās´ ənd) v.: Hurried; moved swiftly

hegemony (hi jem´ ə nē) n.: Condition of being under a leader's influence

hindrance (hin´drəns) n.: An obstacle

honing (hōn´ iŋ) v.: Perfecting a skill as one would sharpen a blade

hubbub (hu´ bub) n.: Noise; commotion

hypocrite (hip´ ə krit) n.: Person who pretends to be what he or she is not

immaculate (im mak´ yōō lit) adj.: Spotless; perfectly clean

immobile (im mō´ bəl) adj.: Motionless; unmoving

immolation (im´ ə lā´ shən) n.: Offering of a victim as a sacrifice to the gods

impediments (im pēd´ ə məntz) n.: Something standing in the way of something else

impending (im pen´ diŋ) adj.: About to happen

impenetrable (im pen´ i trə bəl) adj.: Impossible to get through

imperious (im pir´ ē əs) adj.: Commanding; powerful

imperiously (im pir´ ē əs lē) adv.: Arrogantly

impertinences (im pʉrt'n əns əs) n.: Examples of insolence or lack of respect

impetuous (im pech´ōō əs) adj.: Deciding and acting quickly: impulsive

implore (im plôr´) v.: To ask or beg someone to do something

imploring (im plôr´ iŋ) v.: Asking or begging

importunity (im´ pôr tōōn´ i tē) n.: Persistence in requesting or demanding

impulsive (im pul´ siv) adj.: Sudden and unthinking

incessantly (in ses´ ənt lē) adv.: Endlessly; constantly

incredulity (in´ krə dyōō´ lə tē) n.: Disbelief; astonishment

indefatigable (in´ di fat´ i gə bəl) adj.: Untiring; not giving in to fatigue

indigence (in´ di jəns) n.: Poverty

indignantly (in dig´ nənt lē) adv.: Insulted or angry because someone has not shown respect

indignation (in´ dig nā´ shən) n.: Anger that is a reaction to ingratitude or injustice

indiscreet (in´ di skrēt´) adj.: Unwise or not careful

indispensable (in´ di spen´ sə bəl) adj.: Absolutely necessary or required

indomitable (in däm´ it ə bəl) adj.: Not easily defeated

ineffable (in ef´ ə b'l) adj.: Inexpressible

inestimable (in es´ tə mə bəl) adj.: Priceless; beyond measure

inexorably (in eks´ ə rə blē) adv.: Certainly

infirmity (in fʉr´ mə tē) n.: Physical weakness

inflection (in flek´ shən) n.: Special interpretation of something

ingratiating (in grā´ shē āt´ iŋ) adj.: Bringing into favor

innuendo (in´ yōō en´ dō) n.: Insinuation

innumerable (in nōō´ mer ə bəl) adj.: Too many to be counted

insatiable (in sā´ shə bəl) adj.: Cannot be satisfied; constantly wanting more

interminable (in tʉr´ mi nə bəl) adj.: Lasting, or seeming to last forever

intervene (in´ tər vēn´) v.: To influence

intimacy (in´ tə mə sē) n.: Familiarity; closeness

intricate (in´ tri kit) adj.: Complicated; elaborate

intrigue (in trēg´) v.: Plot or scheme secretly

intolerable (in täl´ ər ə bəl) adj.: Unbearable; painful; cruel

intuition (in tōō ish´ ən) n.: Knowing something without conscious use of reason

inversion (in vər´ zhən) n.: A turning upside down

inverted (in vʉrt´ id) adj.: Upside down

iridescent (ir´i des´ ənt) adj.: Showing shifting changes in color; rainbowlike

irrefutably (ir ref´ yōō tə blē) adv.: In a way that cannot be disproved

itinerary (ī tin′ ər er′ ē) *n.*: Route

jauntiness (jȯnt′ ē nis) *n.*: Carefree attitude

judicious (jo͞o dish′ əs) *adj.*: Exhibiting sound judgment or common sense

knead (nēd) *v.*: Mix and work into a pliable mass by folding over, pressing, and squeezing, usually with the hands, as a baker does with dough

laborious (lə bôr′ ē əs) *adj.*: Involving or calling for much hard work; difficult

laconic (lə kän′ ik) *adj.*: Terse; using few words

lamentation (lam′ ən tā′ shən) *n.*: An expression of grief; weeping

languishing (laŋ′ gwish lŋ) *v.*: Becoming weak; failing in vitality or health

limpid (lim′ pid) *adj.*: Perfectly clear; transparent

liquidated (lik′ wi dat′ id) *adj.*: Disposed of; killed

lithe (līth) *adj.*: Bending easily; supple; limber

livid (liv′ id) *adj.*: Bruised; grayish blue or pale

loathsome (lōth′ səm) *adj.*: Disgusting; detestable

loomed (lo͞omd) *v.*: Appeared in a large or threatening form

lucidity (lo͞o sid′ ə tē) *n.*: Clarity; ability to be understood

lumbering (lum′bər iŋ) *adj.*: Moving heavily and clumsily

luminous (lo͞o′ mə nəs) *adj.*: Giving off light

luster (lus′ tər) *n.*: Shine; radiance

magnanimity (mag′ nə nim′ ə tē) *n.*: Generosity; high-mindedness; nobility of character

magnanimous (mag nan′ ə məs) *adj.*: Noble in mind; generous in spirit

malicious (mə lish′ əs) *adj.*: Intentionally harmful

manifest (man′ ə fest) *v.*: To make evident or plain

manifestations (man′ ə fes tā′ shənz) *n.*: Forms in which something is shown or experienced

manifold (man′ ə fold′) *adj.*: Having many forms

mannequins (man′ i kinz) *n.*: Models of the human body, used by tailors and dressmakers

meditation (med′ ə tā′ shən) *n.*: Deep, continued thought

melancholy (mel′ ən käl′ ē) *n.*: Sadness

memento (mə men′ tō) *n.*: Something serving as a reminder or warning

mimic (mim′ ik) *n.*: Someone who can imitate the speech and actions of others

mode (mōd) *n.*: Method; the manner in which one does something

molestation (mō′ les tā′ shən) *n.*: Interference; attack

monotonously (mə nät′ ən əs lē) *adv.*: Going on and on without variation

mottled (mät′ 'ld) *adj.*: Marked with spots of differenct shades

multifarious (mul′ tə far′ ē əs) *adj.*: Of great variety; diverse

mundane (mun dān′) *adj.*: Everyday; ordinary

munificence (myo͞o nif′ ə səns) *n.*: Generosity

myriad (mir′ ē əd) *adj.*: Huge number; seemingly countless

naturalistic (nach′ ər ə lis′ tik) *adj.*: Faithful to nature, to the extent of not avoiding what is low or improper

navigated (nav′ ə gāt′ id) *v.*: Steering or directed a ship

nimble (nim′ bəl) *adj.*: Moving quickly and lightly

nimbleness (nim′ bəl nes) *n.*: The quality of being quick and agile

nonchalantly (nän′ shə länt′ lē) *adv.*: Casually; indifferently

obeisance (ō bā′ səns) *n.*: Gesture of respect, such as a bow or curtsy

objectively (äb′ jek′ tiv lē) *adv.*: Impartially

oblique (ə blēk′) *adj.*: Not straightforward

obliquely (ə blēk′ lē) *adv.*: At an angle; indirectly

obliterate (ə blit′ ər āt′) *v.*: Blot out; erase

obsolete (äb′ sə lēt′) *adj.*: out of date; no longer in fashion

officious (ə fish′ əs) *adj.*: Overly ready to serve

olfactory (äl fak′ tə rē) *adj.*: Related to the sense of smell

ominous (äm′ ə nəs) *adj.*: Hinting at bad things to come

oppressive (ə pres′ iv) *adj.*: Hard to put up with; causing great discomfort

oracles (ȯr′ ə kəlz) *n.*: Messages or signs from the gods that reveal special instructions or predict the future

oratory (ȯr′ ə tôr′ ē) *n.*: Skill in public speaking

ostentatious (äs′ tən tā′ shəs) *adj.*: Done as a showy display

palate (pal′ ət) *n.*: Sense of taste

palfrey (pôl′ frē) *n.*: Saddle horse

palpable (pal′ pə bəl) *adj.*: Capable of being touched or felt

paradoxical inflection (par′ ə daks′ i kəl) *adj.*: Contracdictory

parameters (pə ram′ ə tərz) *n.*: Factors; characteristics

paternalistic (pə tur′ nə lis′ tik) *adj.*: Treating people as a father would treat children

pathos (pā′ thäs) *n.*: Quality in something experienced or observed that arouses feelings of pity, sorrow, sympathy, or compassion

paucity (pô′ sə tē) *n.*: Scarcity; fewness

perfidy (pur′ fə dē) *n.*: Betrayal of trust; treachery

perished (per′ isht) *v.*: Died a violent or untimely death

pervaded (pər vād′ id) *v.*: Spread throughout; filled

phenomena (fə näm′ ə nə) *n.*: Perceptible things or occurrences

piety (pī′ ə tē) *n.*: Holiness; respect for the divine

pilfering (pil′fə r iŋ) *n.*: The theft of a small sum or of items of little value

piously (pī′ əs lē) *adv.*: With actual or pretended religious devotion

piqued (pēkt) *v.*: Offended

pitiable (pit′ ē ə bəl) *adj.*: Being weak or foolish and therefore inspiring sorrow mixed with contempt or scorn

plaintive (plān′ tiv) *adj.*: Sad; mournful

plaiting (plāt′ iŋ) *v.*: Braiding or interweaving

plateau (pla tō′) *n.*: Elevated tract of relatively level land

plausibility (plô′ zə bil′ ə tē) *n.*: Believability

ply (plī) *v.*: Sail regularly back and forth across

ponderous (pän′ dər əs) *adj.*: Heavy and bulky

portentously (pôr ten′ təs lē) *adv.*: Ominously; scarily

postulated (päs′ chə lāt′ id) *v.*: Assumed without proof to be true or necessary

pungent (pun′ jənt) *adj.*: Sharp and piercing

precarious (prē ker′ ē əs) *adj.*: Dangerously lacking in security or stability

precincts (prē′ siŋkts) *n.*: Special places or areas

precipitous (prē sip′ ə təs) *adj.*: Steep

prerequisite (pri rek′ wə zit) *n.*: Something required before something else can happen

presumed (prē zo͞omd′) *v.*: Taken for granted

procession (prō sesh′ ən) *n.*: Number of persons or things moving forward in an orderly or formal way

proclaiming (prō klām′ iŋ) *v.*: Announcing publicly and loudly

prodigal (präd′ i gəl) *n.*: Person who spends money wastefully

prodigal (präd′ i gəl) *adj.*: Extremely generous; lavish

prodigy (präd′ ə jē) *n.*: A child of highly unusual talent or genius

proffered (präf′ ərd) *v.*: Offered

proffering (präf′ ər iŋ) *v.*: Offering

proficiency (prō fish′ ən sē) *n.*: Expertise

progeny (präj′ ə nē) *n.*: Offspring

proliferated (prō lif′ ər āt′ id) *v.*: Grew rapidly

promontories (präm′ ən tôr′ ēz) *n.*: High places extending out over a body of water

proprieties (prə prī′ ə tēz) *n.*: Whatever is considered fitting, suitable, or proper; rules of conduct or expression

proprietor (prō prī′ ə tər) *n.*: Owner

protagonist (prō tag′ ə nist′) *n.*: Main character; person who plays a leading part

providential (präv′ ə den′ shəl) *adj.*: As if decreed by God

prudence (pro͞od′ 'ns) *n.*: Practical, sound judgment

prudery (pro͞od′ ər ē) *n.*: Tendency to show too much modesty

punctiliously (puŋk til′ ē əs lē) *adv.*: Carefully; conscientiously

raked (rākd) *v.*: Scratched or scraped, as with a rake

ramshackle (ram′ shak′ əl) *adj.*: Of poor construction; flimsy and shaky

rank (raŋk) *adj.*: Growing vigorously and coarsely

recapitulation (rē kə pich′ ə lā shən) *n.*: Summary or brief restatement

recess (rē′ ses) *n.*: Space set back in a wall.

reciprocity (res′ ə präs′ ə tē) *n.*: Mutual action; dependence

recluses (rek′ loo siz) *n.*: People who live apart from society

redeeming (ri dēm′ iŋ) *adj.*: Recovering; paying back

rehabilitation (rē′ hə bil′ ə tā′ shən) *n.*: Restoration of rank, privileges, and property

relinquish (ri liŋ′ kwish) *v.*: Give up; abandon

relish (rel′ ish) *n.*: Pleasure; enjoyment

replenish (ri plen′ ish) *v.*: Make full or complete again

replete (ri plēt′) *adj.*: Well-filled; stocked

reproach (ri prōch′) *n.*: An expression of blame

requisite (rek′ wə zit) *adj.*: Required by circumstances

resolutely (rez′ ə loot′ lē) *adv.*: In a determined manner; without hesitation

restraint (ri strānt′) *n.*: Self-control in matters of emotion and behavior

retinue (ret′n yoo′) *n.*: A train of followers

retribution (re′ trə byoo′ shən) *n.*: Punishment; revenge

revelation (rev′ ə lā′ shən) *n.*: Striking disclosure of something

rheumatic (rü ma′ tik) *adj.*: Suffering from a disease of the joints; able to move only with great pain

rime (rīm) *n.*: Icy crystals that form on a freezing surface as moist air contacts it; frost

sallying (sal′ ē iŋ) *v.*: Rushing forth suddenly

sated (sāt′ əd): Satisfied or pleased

scintillating (sint′ 'l āt iŋ) *adj.*: Sparkling; flashing

scorn (skôrn) *n.*: Extreme contempt for someone or something

scrimmage (skrim′ ij) *n.*: Rough-and-tumble fight

scruple (skroo′ pəl) *n.*: Feeling of doubt as to what is right

scrupulously (skroo′ pyə ləs lē) *adv.*: Acting with care to do the right or proper thing

scrutinized (skroot′ ən īzd′) *v.*: Looked at carefully; examined closely

secular (sek′ yə lər) *adj.*: Not sacred or religious

seductive (si duk′ tiv) *adj.*: Tempting; enticing

sententiously (sen ten′ shəs lē) *adv.*: Using proverbs and sayings in a pompous way

serene (sə rēn′) *adj.*: Calm; not disturbed or troubled

sheaf (shēf) *n.*: Bundle of grain

shirked (shûrkt) *v.*: Neglected or avoided

shriveled (shriv′ əld) *adj.*: Shrunken and made wrinkled and withered

sleek (slēk) *adj.*: Smooth and shiny

slovenliness (sluv′ ən lē nes) *n.*: Lack of care for one's appearance; untidiness

solicitously (sə lis′ ə təs lē) *adv.*: Showing care or concern

somber (säm′ bər) *adj.*: Dark; gloomy

sonorous (sə nôr′ əs) *adj.*: Having a powerful, impressive sound

sordid (sôr′ did) *adj.*: Dirty; filthy

sovereign (säv′rən) *adj.*: Above or superior to all others

spasm (spaz′ əm) *n.*: Sudden, involuntary muscular contraction

spasmodically (spaz mad′ ik lē) *adv.*: In spasms; intermittently; irregularly

spendthrift (spend′ thrift′) *n.*: Person who spends money carelessly

spite (spīt) *n.*: Mean or evil feeling toward another

splendor (splen′ dər) *n.*: Great brightness

spores (spôrz) *n.*: Seeds

squandering (skwän′ dər iŋ) *v.*: Spending money wastefully

staidness (stād′ nəs) *n.*: State of being settled or resistant to change

stealthily (stel′ thə lē) *adv.*: In a sneaky manner; sercretly

stupefied (stoo′ pə fīd′) *adj.*: Dazed; stunned

stupor (stoo′ per) *n.*: Mental dullness, as if drugged

subdue (səb doo′) *v.*: Conquer or master

sublime (sə blīm′) *adj.*: Noble; admirable

submissive (sub mis′ iv) *adj.*: Yielding; giving in

subordinate (sə bôrd′n it) *adj.*: Inferior; ranking under or below

subsided (səb sīd′ əd) *v.*: Became less intense or sank to a lower level

subtleties (sut′ 'l tēz) *n.*: Complex and fine distinctions

succor (suk′ ər) *n.*: Aid or help in time of distress

sultry (sul′ trē) *adj.*: Oppressively hot and moist; sweltering

supernal (sə pʉrn′ əl) *adj.*: Celestial or divine

supple (sup′ əl) *adj.*: Able to bend and move easily; flexible; agile

supplication (sup′ lə kā′ shən) *n.*: The act of asking humbly and earnestly

swells (swelz) *n.*: Large waves that move steadily without breaking

syndrome (sin′ drōm) *n.*: Group of signs that occur together and may form a pattern

synthesis (sin′ thə sis) *n.*: Whole made up of separate elements put together

taciturn (ta′ sə tʉrn) *adj.*: Preferring not to talk; uncommunicative; silent

tactile (tak′ təl) *adj.*: Related to the sense of touch

tactless (takt′ ləs) *adj.*: Without skill in dealing with people

talisman (tal′ is mən) *n.*: A charm or token; a lucky object

teemed (tēmd) *v.*: Produced a great many people

tempering (tem′ pə riŋ) *adj.*: Modifying or adjusting

terminal tk *adj.*: Final or fatal

terra firma (ter′ ə fur′ mə): Latin for "solid earth"

terrestrial (tə res′ trē əl) *adj.*: Of this world; earthly

testimony (tes′ tə mō′ nē) *n.*: Statement, word, or declaration

throngs (thrônz) *n.*: Crowds

timidity (tə mid′ ə tē) *n.*: Quality of being shy and easily frightened

timorous (tim′ ər es) *adj.*: Full of fear; timid

tonic (tän′ ik) *adj.*: Health-giving; strengthening

topography (tə päg′ rə fē) *n.*: Surface features of a place, such as rivers, lakes, mountains, and so on

torsos (tôr′ sōz) *n.*: Main parts of body structures. In humans, the body excluding the head and limbs

transcends (tran sendz′) *v.*: Goes above or beyond limits; exceeds; surpasses

transgressor (trans gres′ sər) *n.*: Person who breaks a law or commandment

transoms (tran′ səmz) *n.*: Small windows

treacherous (trech′ ər əs) *adj.*: Untrustworthy

tremulous (trem′ yoo ləs) *adj.*: Trembling; fearful or timid

troop *v.*: To gather or go together in a group; to walk or go

truncated (truŋ′ kāt əd) *adj.*: Cut short; with an angle cut off

tumult (too′ mult) *n.*: Noisy commotion

ulterior (ul tir′ ē ər) *adj.*: Undisclosed; beyond what is openly stated

undulating (un′ dyoo lāt′ iŋ) *adj.*: Moving in waves

undulations (un′ dyoo lā′ shənz) *n.*: Waves

unflagging (un flag′ iŋ) *adj.*: Without losing strength

unhampered (un ham pərd) *v.*: Not hindered or impeded; free of burdens or other constraints

unmarred (un märd′) *adj.*: Unspoiled; unimpaired

unpretentious (un′ prē ten′ shəs) *adj.*: Simple and modest

unremittingly (un′ ri mit′ iŋ lē) *adv.*: Persistently

unscrupulous (un skroo′ pyə ləs) *adj.*: Not acting according to what is right or correct

urbanely (ʉr bān′ lē) *adv.*: In a smooth and polished way

vanquish (vaŋ′ kwish) *v.*: Conquer; force into submission

venerable (ven′ ər ə bəl) *adj.*: Worthy of respect by reason of age and dignity, character, or position

veracious (və rā′ shəs) *adj.*: Truthful; accurate

vernal (vʉrn′ əl) *adj.*: Springlike

vestibule (ves′ tə byül) *n.*: Small entrance hall or room

vociferous (vō sif′ ər əs) *adj.*: Loud; noisy

void (void) *adj.*: Vacant or empty

vile (vīl) *adj.*: Extremely disgusting

vivacious (vī vā′ shəs) *adj.*: Lively

watershed (wô′ tər shed) *n.*: Moment or event after which nothing is the same

wistful (wist′ fəl) *adj.*: Expressing longing

writhes (rīthz) *v.*: Twists and turns the body, as in agony

zeal (zēl) *n.*: Fervor, intense enthusiasm

LITERARY TERMS HANDBOOK

ACT *See Drama.*

ALLITERATION *Alliteration* is the repetition of initial consonant sounds. Writers use alliteration to give emphasis to words, to imitate sounds, and to create musical effects. Notice, in the following lines from Jean Toomer's "Reapers," how the s sounds suggest the sound of the blades sliding against stones to be sharpened.

> Black reapers with the sound of steel on
> stones/Are sharpening scythes . . .

See also Assonance, Consonance, *and* Rhyme.

ALLUSION An *allusion* is a reference to a well-known person, place, event, literary work, or work of art. Writers often make allusions to famous works such as the Bible or William Shakespeare's plays. They also make allusions to mythology, politics, or current events. For example, the title of Stephen Vincent Benét's story "By the Waters of Babylon" is an allusion to Psalm 137 in the Bible.

ANECDOTE An *anecdote* is a brief story about an interesting, amusing, or strange event. Anecdotes are told to entertain or to make a point. James Thurber, for example, fills "The Dog That Bit People" with humorous anecdotes about his family and their dog, Muggs.

See also Narrative.

ANTAGONIST The *antagonist* of a work is the character who opposes the protagonist (the character whom readers want to see succeed). Creon is the antagonist in the play *Antigone*, p. 814.

See also Character *and* Protagonist.

ANTICLIMAX Like a climax, an *anticlimax* is the turning point in a story. However, an anticlimax is always a letdown. It's the point at which you learn that the story will not turn out the way you'd expected.

APHORISM An *aphorism* is a brief, memorable saying that expresses a basic truth. Many cultures pass on wisdom in the form of aphorisms, such as the aphorisms from Confucius' *The Analects*, p. 336.

ASIDE An *aside* is a short speech delivered by an actor in a play, expressing the character's thoughts. Traditionally, the aside is directed to the audience and is

In his autobiography, *Rare Air: Michael on Michael*, Michael Jordan shares his experiences through words and photographs.

presumed to be inaudible to the other actors.

ASSONANCE *Assonance* is the repetition of vowel sounds followed by different consonants in two or more stressed syllables. In "The Kraken," Tennyson repeats the long e sound in the following lines:

> Below the thunders of the upper *deep*;
> Far, far beneath in the abysmal *sea*,
> His ancient, dreamless, uninvaded *sleep*
> The Kraken sleepeth: faintest sunlights *flee*

See also Consonance.

ATMOSPHERE *Atmosphere*, or *mood*, is the feeling created in a reader by a literary work or passage. The atmosphere is often suggested by descriptive details. The following lines from "The Stolen Child," by William Butler Yeats, create a mysterious, mystical atmosphere:

> Where the wave of moonlight glosses
> The dim grey sands with light

AUTOBIOGRAPHY An *autobiography* is a form of nonfiction in which a person tells his or her own life story. An autobiography may tell about the person's whole life or only a part of it. "A Child's Christmas in Wales" is an autobiographical incident from the life of writer Dylan Thomas.

See also Biography *and* Nonfiction.

BIOGRAPHY A *biography* is a form of nonfiction in which a writer tells the life story of another person.

Biographies have been written about many famous people, historical and contemporary, but they can also be written about "ordinary" people. "Marian Anderson: Famous Concert Singer" is a brief biography by Langston Hughes.

See *also* Autobiography and Nonfiction.

BLANK VERSE *Blank verse* is poetry written in unrhymed iambic pentameter lines. This verse form was widely used by Elizabethan dramatists like William Shakespeare. *The Tragedy of Julius Caesar* is written mostly in blank verse.

See *also* Meter.

CHARACTER A *character* is a person or an animal who takes part in the action of a literary work. The *main character,* or *protagonist,* is the most important character in a story. This character often changes in some important way as a result of the story's events.

The *antagonist* opposes the main character. Characters are sometimes classified as round or flat, dynamic or static. A round character shows many different traits—faults as well as virtues. Annie John's mother in *A Walk to the Jetty* by Jamaica Kincaid is an example of a round character. At times, she is kind and loving to Annie; at other times, she is stern and overbearing. Annie's father is a flat character. We see him only as a quiet, nonconfrontational man. A dynamic character develops and grows during the course of the story, as does Sasha Uskov in Anton Chekhov's "A Problem," on p. 650. A static character does not change. The Colonel in the same story by Chekhov is a static character.

See *also* Antagonist, Characterization, Motivation, *and* Protagonist.

CHARACTERIZATION *Characterization* is the act of creating and developing a character. In *direct characterization,* the author directly states a character's traits. For example, in Guy de Maupassant's "Two Friends," on p. 210, Maupassant says of M. Morissot and M. Sauvage, "they had similar tastes and responded to their surroundings in exactly the same way." A writer uses *indirect characterization* when showing a character's personality through his or her actions, thoughts, feelings, words, and appearance or through another character's observations and reactions. In the same story, Maupassant presents the Prussian officer through indirect characterization. Instead of directly saying that he is brutal, he lets readers infer his brutality by witnessing his treatment of the two Frenchmen.

See *also* Character.

CLIMAX The *climax* of a story, novel, or play is the high point of interest or suspense. The events that make up the rising action lead up to the climax. The events that make up the falling action follow the climax. The climax of "Damon and Pythias," p. 224, occurs when the deadline has been reached and Pythias has not yet returned.

See *also* Conflict, Plot, *and* Anticlimax.

CONFLICT A *conflict* is a struggle between opposing forces. Characters in conflict form the basis of stories, novels, epics, and plays.

There are two kinds of conflict: external and internal. In an *external conflict,* the main character struggles against an outside force, as in Homer's *Iliad,* p. 228, in which Achilleus struggles against Hektor. The outside force may be nature itself, in a person-against-nature conflict. Edmund Hillary and Tenzing Norgay face such a conflict in "The Final Assault" on p. 142.

An *internal conflict* involves a character in conflict with himself or herself. For example, in Doris Lessing's "Through the Tunnel," p. 353, Jerry faces a struggle between his desire to swim through the tunnel and his fear of the danger involved.

A story may have more than one conflict. In addition to his internal conflict, Jerry also faces external conflicts—the tunnel's length and the oppressive water pressure.

See *also* Plot.

CONNOTATION The *connotation* of a word is the set of ideas associated with it in addition to its explicit meaning. For example, the title "The Bean Eaters" refers literally to people who eat beans. The phrase connotes simplicity and poverty.

The connotation of a word can be personal, based on individual experiences, but more often, cultural connotations—those recognizable by most people in a group—determine a writer's word choices.

See *also* Denotation.

CONSONANCE *Consonance* is the repetition of similar consonant sounds at the end of accented syllables. In "Meeting at Night," the repeated *t* and *ch* sounds in "the spurt of a lighted match" create consonance. Consonance is used to create musical effects, to link ideas, and to emphasize particular words.

See *also* Assonance.

COUPLET A *couplet* is a pair of rhyming lines, usually of the same length and meter. A couplet generally expresses a single idea. Shakespeare's Sonnet 18 ends with the following couplet:

> So long as men can breathe, or eyes can see
> So long lives this, and this gives life to thee.

See *also* Stanza.

CRITICAL REVIEW A *critical review* offers one person's judgment of a movie, play, or other performance. In the review, the reviewer discusses the various elements of the performance and makes a recommendation. Critical reviews tend to be persuasive.

See *also* Persuasion.

DENOTATION The *denotation* of a word is its dictionary meaning, independent of other associations that the word may have. The denotation of the word *lake*, for example, is an inland body of water.

See *also* Connotation.

DENOUEMENT See Plot.

DESCRIPTION A *description* is a portrait in words of a person, place, or object. Descriptive writing uses sensory details—those that appeal to the senses: sight, hearing, taste, smell, and touch. Description can be found in all types of writing. Isak Dinesen's essay "Some African Birds," on p. 748, contains descriptive passages.

DEVELOPMENT See Plot.

DIALECT *Dialect* is the form of language spoken by people in a particular region or group. Pronunciation, vocabulary, and sentence structure are affected by dialect. Writers use dialect to make their characters sound realistic and to create local color. In Chinua Achebe's "Civil Peace," on p. 550, some of the characters speak in a Nigerian dialect of English.

DIALOGUE A *dialogue* is a conversation between characters. Writers use dialogue to reveal character, to present events, to add variety to a narrative, and to interest readers.

DICTION *Diction* is word choice. To discuss a writer's diction is to consider the vocabulary used, the appropriateness of the words, and the vividness of the language. Both the *denotation*, or literal meaning, and the *connotation*, or associations, of words contribute to the overall effect. Diction can be formal, as in this excerpt from Edgar Allan Poe's "The Masque of the Red Death":

> It was a voluptuous scene, that masquerade.

> But first let me tell of the rooms in which it was held. There were seven—an imperial suite.

Diction can also be informal and conversational, as in these lines from "Flood" by Annie Dillard:

> Women are bringing coffee in mugs to the road crew . . . Some kid starts doing tricks on a skateboard; I head home.

See *also* Connotation *and* Denotation.

DIRECT CHARACTERIZATION
See Characterization.

DRAMA A *drama* is a story written to be performed by actors. The script of a drama is made up of dialogue—the words the actors say—and stage directions, which are comments on how and where action occurs.

The drama's setting is the place where the action occurs. It is indicated by one or more sets that suggest interior or exterior scenes. Props are objects, such as a sword or a cup of tea, that are used onstage.

At the beginning of most plays, a brief exposition gives the audience some background information about the characters and the situation. Just as in a story or novel, the plot of a drama is built around characters in conflict.

Dramas are divided into large units called *acts* and into smaller units called *scenes*. A long play may include many sets that change with the scenes or it may indicate a change of scene with lighting.

See *also* Genre, Stage Directions, *and* Tragedy.

DRAMATIC IRONY See Irony.

DRAMATIC POETRY *Dramatic poetry* is poetry that uses the techniques of drama. A dramatic poem is a verse that presents the speech of one or more characters. Dramatic poems are like little plays and usually involve many narrative elements, such as setting, conflict, and plot. Such elements may be found in Rudyard Kipling's "Danny Deever."

EPIC An *epic* is a long narrative or narrative poem about the deeds of gods or heroes. Because of its length and its loftiness of theme, an epic usually presents a telling portrait of the culture in which it was produced. The ancient *folk epics* like the *Ramayana* and *Sundiata* were recited aloud as entertainment at feasts and were not written down until long after they were composed.

See *also* Narrative Poem.

ESSAY An *essay* is a short nonfiction work about a particular subject. In an *analytical essay*, the author breaks down a large idea into parts. By explaining how the parts of a concept or an object fit together, the essay helps readers understand the whole idea or thing.

A *descriptive* essay seeks to convey an impression about a person, animal, place, or object. In "Some African Birds," p. 748, Isak Dinesen describes birds she observed.

An e*xpository* essay gives information, discusses ideas, or explains a process. In Alexander Petrunkevitch's "The Spider and the Wasp," p. 711, the author presents examples and facts about the battle between these two creatures in an entertaining way.

A *humorous essay* presents the author's thoughts on a subject in an amusing way that is intended to make readers laugh. Gabriel García Márquez's "Uses and Abuses of the Umbrella," p. 784, is a humorous essay.

A *narrative essay* tells a true story. In the narrative essay from "Speak, Memory," on p. 437, Nabokov tells a true story from his childhood.

In a *reflective essay*, a writer shares his or her thoughts about and impressions of an idea or experience. In "This Too Is Life," p. 722, Lu Hsun reflects on his illness.

A *persuasive essay* attempts to convince readers to adopt a particular opinion or course of action. The excerpt from Solzhenitsyn's Nobel lecture, p. 727, and "Keep Memory Alive," p. 730, are persuasive essays.

A *visual essay* presents information or makes a point about a subject through photographs and other visual forms as well as through text. A visual essay in this book is "Claude Monet, or The World Upside Down," p. 770.

This classification of essays is loose at best. Most essays contain passages that could be classified differently from the essay as a whole. For example, a descriptive passage may be found in a narrative essay, or a factual, expository section may be used to support a persuasive argument.

See *also* Description, Exposition, Genre, Narration, Nonfiction, *and* Persuasion.

EXPOSITION *Exposition* is writing or speech that explains a process or presents information. In the plot of a story or drama, the exposition is the part of the work that introduces the characters, the setting, and the basic situation.

EXTENDED METAPHOR In an *extended metaphor,* as in a regular metaphor, a subject is spoken or written of as though it were something else. However, an extended metaphor differs from a regular metaphor in that several comparisons are made. All extended metaphors sustain the comparison for several lines or for an entire poem. Eve Merriam uses an extended metaphor in her poem "Metaphor," on p. 836, to compare morning to "a new sheet of paper."

See *also* Figurative Language *and* Metaphor.

FALLING ACTION See Plot.

FANTASY A *fantasy* is highly imaginative writing that contains elements not found in real life. Examples of fantasy include stories that involve supernatural elements, stories that resemble fairy tales, and stories that deal with imaginary places and creatures. Many science-fiction stories, such as Ray Bradbury's "There Will Come Soft Rains," contain elements of fantasy.

See *also* Science Fiction.

FICTION *Fiction* is prose writing that tells about imaginary characters and events. The term is usually used for novels and short stories, but it also applies to dramas and narrative poetry. Some writers rely on their imaginations alone to create their works of fiction. Others base their fiction on actual events and people, to which they add invented characters, dialogue, and plot situations.

See *also* Genre, Narrative, *and* Nonfiction.

FIGURATIVE LANGUAGE *Figurative language* is writing or speech not meant to be interpreted literally.

Figurative language is often used to create vivid impressions by setting up comparisons between dissimilar things.

Look, for example, at this description from Emily Dickinson's "The Wind tapped like a tired Man":

> His Countenance—a Billow—
> His Fingers, as He passed
> Let go a music—as of tunes
> Blown tremulous in Glass—

Some frequently used figures of speech are *metaphors, similes,* and *personification*.

See *also* Literal Language, Metaphors, Personification, *and* Similes.

FOOT See Meter.

FORESHADOWING *Foreshadowing* is the use in a literary work of clues that suggest events that have yet to occur. Use of this technique helps to create suspense, keeping readers wondering and speculating about what will happen next. There are many instances of foreshadowing in Julio Cortázar's "House Taken Over," p. 164. For example, the narrator hears something mysterious "in the library or the dining room." This noise foreshadows the invasion of the house by unknown forces or beings.

See *also* Suspense.

FREE VERSE *Free verse* is poetry not written in a regular rhythmical pattern, or meter. Free verse seeks to capture the rhythms of speech. It is the dominant form of contemporary poetry. "What Are Friends For" by Rosellen Brown, p. 968, and "Civilian and Soldier," by Wole Soyinka, p. 965, are examples of free verse.

See also Meter.

GENRE A *genre* is a category or type of literature. Literature is commonly divided into three major genres: poetry, prose, and drama. Each major genre is in turn divided into smaller genres, as follows:

1. Poetry: Lyric Poetry, Concrete Poetry, Dramatic Poetry, Narrative Poetry, and Epic Poetry
2. Prose: Fiction (Novels and Short Stories) and Nonfiction (Biography, Autobiography, Letters, Essays, and Reports)
3. Drama: Serious Drama and Tragedy, Comic Drama, Melodrama, and Farce

See also Drama, Poetry, and Prose.

HAIKU The *haiku* is a three-line verse form. The first and third lines of a haiku each have five syllables. The second line has seven syllables. A haiku seeks to convey a single vivid emotion by means of images from nature. The poems on p. 987 are haiku.

Translators of Japanese haiku try to maintain the syllabic requirements. Western writers, however, sometimes use the form more loosely.

IAMB See Meter.

IMAGE An *image* is a word or phrase that appeals to one or more of the five senses—sight, hearing, touch, taste, or smell. Writers use images to re-create sensory experiences in words.

See also Description.

IMAGERY *Imagery* is the descriptive or figurative language used in literature to create word pictures for the reader. These pictures, or images, are created by details of sight, sound, taste, touch, smell, or movement.

INDIRECT CHARACTERIZATION See Characterization.

IRONY *Irony* is the general term for literary techniques that portray differences between appearance and reality, expectation and result, or meaning and intention. In *verbal irony*, words are used to suggest the opposite of what is meant. In *dramatic irony*, there is a contradiction between what a character thinks and what the reader or audience knows to be true. In *irony*

of situation, an event occurs that directly contradicts the expectations of the characters, the reader, or the audience.

During the funeral in William Shakespeare's *The Tragedy of Julius Caesar,* Antony calls Brutus "an honorable man" when, in fact, he wants the people to think just the opposite. This is an example of verbal irony.

In the same play, dramatic irony occurs when the audience, knowing that Caesar will be assassinated, watches him set out on the ides of March.

In W. W. Jacobs's "The Monkey's Paw," the Whites expect the paw to bring them happiness; instead, it brings them nothing but grief. This is an example of irony of situation.

LEGEND A *legend* is a widely told story about the past that may or may not have a foundation in fact. One example, retold in many versions, is the legend of King Arthur. A legend often reflects a people's identity or cultural values. It generally has more historical truth and less emphasis on the supernatural than does a myth.

See also Myth.

LITERAL LANGUAGE *Literal language* uses words in their ordinary senses. It is the opposite of *figurative language.* If you tell someone standing on a diving board to jump in, you are speaking literally. If you tell someone standing on a street corner to jump in a lake, you are speaking figuratively.

See also Figurative Language.

LYRIC POEM A *lyric poem* is a highly musical verse that expresses the observations and feelings of a single speaker. In ancient times, lyric poems were sung to the accompaniment of the lyre, a type of stringed instrument. Modern lyric poems are not usually sung. However, they still have a musical quality that is achieved through rhythm and such other devices as alliteration and rhyme. Federico García Lorca's "The Guitar," on p. 962, is a lyric poem expressing the wailing and crying sound of a guitar.

METAPHOR A *metaphor* is a figure of speech in which one thing is spoken of as though it were something else. Unlike a simile, which compares two things using *like* or *as,* a metaphor implies a comparison between them. In "Making a Fist," Naomi Shihab Nye uses this metaphor:

My stomach was a melon
split wide inside my skin.

See also Extended Metaphor and Figurative Language.

Mark Antony's "Friends, Romans, countrymen . . ." monologue from *The Tragedy of Julius Caesar* is one of the most famous dramatic speeches in literature.

METER   The *meter* of a poem is its rhythmical pattern. This pattern is determined by the number and types of stresses, or beats, in each line. To describe the meter of a poem, you must scan its lines. *Scanning* involves marking the stressed and unstressed syllables. Each strong stress is marked with a slanted accent mark (´) and each unstressed syllable with a curved accent mark (˘). The stressed and unstressed syllables are then divided by vertical lines (|) into groups called *feet*. The following types of feet are common in English poetry:

1. *Iamb:* a foot with one unstressed syllable followed by a stressed syllable, as in the word "again"

2. *Trochee:* a foot with a stressed syllable followed by an unstressed syllable, as in the word "wonder"

3. *Anapest:* a foot with two unstressed syllables followed by one strong stress, as in the phrase "on the beach"

4. *Dactyl:* a foot with one strong stress followed by two unstressed syllables, as in the word "wonderful"

5. *Spondee:* a foot with two strong stresses, as in the word "spacewalk"

Depending on the type of foot that is most common in them, lines of poetry are described as *iambic, trochaic, anapestic,* and so forth.

Lines are also described in terms of the number of feet that occur in them, as follows:

1. *Monometer:* one foot
   Ăll thíngs
   Áre ă
   Bĕcómíng.

2. *Dimeter:*
   Ă búyĕr | fŏr thém
   Ă hándsŏme | yŏung man
   —"The Bridegroom," p. 170

3. *Trimeter:*
   Sŭcceśs iš | cóuntĕd | sẃeetĕst
   Bў thóse| whŏ ne´er | sŭcceéd.
   —"Success is counted sweetest"

4. *Tetrameter:* verse written in four-foot lines

5. *Pentameter:* verse written in five-foot lines

6. *Hexameter:* verse written in six-foot lines

7. *Heptameter:* verse written in seven-foot lines

Blank verse is poetry written in unrhymed iambic pentameter. Poetry that does not have a regular meter is called *free verse.*

MONOLOGUE   A *monologue* is a speech by one character in a play, story, or poem. A monologue may be addressed to another character or to the audience, or it may be a *soliloquy*—a speech that presents the character's thoughts as though the character were overheard when alone. In Act II, Scene i, of *The Tragedy of Julius Caesar,* Brutus delivers an impassioned monologue citing reasons to assassinate Caesar.

See also Drama *and* Soliloquy.

MOOD   See Atmosphere.

MORAL   A *moral* is a lesson taught by a literary work. A fable usually ends with a moral that is directly stated.

MOTIVATION   *Motivation* is a reason that explains or partially explains why a character thinks, feels, acts, or behaves in a certain way. Motivation results from a combination of the character's personality and the situation that confronts the character.

See also Character *and* Characterization.

MYTH   A *myth* is a fictional tale that explains the actions of gods or the causes of natural phenomena. Unlike legends, myths have little historical truth and involve supernatural elements. Every culture has its collection of myths. Among the most familiar are the myths of the ancient Greeks and Romans. "Damon and Pythias," on p. 224, is a classic Greek myth about the unbreakable bond of friendship.

See also Oral Tradition.

NARRATION *Narration* is writing that tells a story. The act of telling a story in speech is also called narration. Novels and short stories are fictional narratives. Nonfiction works such as news stories, biographies, and autobiographies are also narratives. A narrative poem tells a story in verse.

See also Anecdote, Essay, Narrative Poem, Nonfiction, Novel, *and* Short Story.

NARRATIVE A *narrative* is a story told in fiction, nonfiction, poetry, or drama.

See also Narration.

NARRATIVE POEM A *narrative poem* is one that tells a story. "La Belle Dame sans Merci," on p. 842, is an example of a narrative poem. It tells the story of a knight driven to despair because he loves a pitiless woman.

See also Dramatic Poetry, Epic, *and* Narration.

NARRATOR A *narrator* is a speaker or character who tells a story. The narrator may be either a character in the story or an outside observer. The writer's choice of narrator determines the story's *point of view,* which in turn determines the type and amount of information the writer can reveal.

See also Speaker *and* Point of View.

NONFICTION *Nonfiction* is prose writing that presents and explains ideas or that tells about real people, places, objects, or events. Nonfiction narratives are about actual people, places, and events, unlike fictional narratives, which present imaginary characters and events. To be classed as nonfiction, a work must be true.

Among nonfiction forms are essays, newspaper and magazine articles, journals, travelogues, biographies, and autobiographies. Historical, scientific, technical, political, and philosophical writings are also nonfiction.

See also Autobiography, Biography, *and* Essay.

NOVEL A *novel* is a long work of fiction. Like a short story, a novel has a plot that explores characters in conflict. However, a novel is much longer than a short story and may have one or more subplots, or minor stories, and several themes.

OCTAVE See Stanza.

ONOMATOPOEIA *Onomatopoeia* is the use of words that imitate sounds. *Whirr, thud, sizzle,* and *hiss* are typical examples. Writers can deliberately choose words that contribute to a desired sound effect.

ORAL TRADITION The *oral tradition* is the passing of songs, stories, and poems from generation to generation by word of mouth. Many folk songs, ballads, fairy tales, legends, and myths originated in the oral tradition.

See also Myth.

PARABLE A *parable* is a simple, brief narrative that teaches a lesson by using characters and events to stand for abstract ideas. The parable "How Much Land Does a Man Need?" p. 130, teaches a lesson about greed.

PARODY A *parody* is a comical piece of writing that mocks the characteristics of a specific literary form. Through exaggeration of the types of ideas, language, tone, or action in a type of literature or a specific work, a parody calls attention to the ridiculous aspects of its subject. The excerpt from *Don Quixote,* p. 1002, is a parody of the romantic literature that was popular in the late sixteenth century.

PENTAMETER See Meter.

PERSONIFICATION *Personification* is a type of figurative language in which a nonhuman subject is given human characteristics. Pak tu-jin personifies a river when he says it "claps its hands" in "August River" p. 940.

See also Figurative Language.

PERSUASION *Persuasion* is writing or speech that attempts to convince the reader to adopt a particular opinion or course of action. A newspaper editorial that says a city council decision was wrong is an example of persuasive writing attempting to mold opinion. Critical reviews, such as the reviews of the movie *Star Wars,* pp. 756 and 759, are a form of persuasive writing.

See also Critical Review *and* Essay.

PLOT *Plot* is the sequence of events in a literary work. In most novels, dramas, short stories, and narrative poems, the plot involves both characters and a central conflict. The plot usually begins with an *exposition* that introduces the setting, the characters, and the basic situation. This is followed by the *inciting incident,* which introduces the central conflict. The conflict then increases during the *development* until it reaches a high point of interest or suspense, the *climax.* All the events leading up to the climax make up the *rising action.* The climax is followed by the *falling action,* which leads to the *resolution,* or end, of the central conflict. Any events that occur after the resolution make up the *denouement.*

POETRY *Poetry* is one of the three major types of literature; the others are prose and drama. Most poems make use of highly concise, musical, and emotionally charged language. Many also make use of imagery, figurative language, and special devices of sound such as rhyme. Poems are often divided into lines and stanzas and often employ regular rhythmical patterns, or meters. However, some poems are written out just like prose, and some poems are written in free verse.

See *also* Free Verse, Genre, Meter, Rhyme, *and* Rhythm.

POINT OF VIEW The *point of view* is the perspective, or vantage point, from which the story is told. If the narrator is part of the action, the story is told from the *first-person* point of view. We see and know only what the character telling the story knows. "A Day Goes By," p. 636, is told from the first-person point of view. In a story told by a *third person,* the narrator is someone outside the action. An *omniscient third-person* narrator is all-knowing; the narrator knows more about the characters and events than any one character can know. The third-person omniscient narrator of "The Street of the Cañon," on p. 584, reveals the thoughts and feelings of several characters. A *limited third-person* narrator tells only the thoughts and feelings of one character. "The Glass of Milk," p. 611, is told by a third-person limited narrator.

See *also* Narrator.

PROSE *Prose* is the ordinary form of written language. Most writing that is not poetry, drama, or song is considered prose. Prose, one of the major genres of literature, occurs in two forms: fiction and nonfiction.

See *also* Fiction, Genre, *and* Nonfiction.

PROTAGONIST The main character in a work of fiction—the character readers would like to see succeed—is the *protagonist.* Antigone is the protagonist of the play *Antigone.*

See *also* Antagonist *and* Character.

REPETITION *Repetition* is the use of any element of language—a sound, a word, a phrase, a clause, or a sentence—more than once. In "Prayer of First Dancers" from *The Night Chant,* the words "in the house made" are repeated eight times, each time in connection with a different image.

Poets use many kinds of repetition. Alliteration, assonance, rhyme, and rhythm are repetitions of certain sounds and sound patterns.

A refrain is a repeated line or group of lines. In both prose and poetry, repetition is used for musical effects and for emphasis.

See *also* Alliteration, Assonance, Consonance, Rhyme, *and* Rhythm.

RESOLUTION See Plot.

RHYME *Rhyme* is the repetition of sounds at the ends of words. *End rhyme* occurs when the rhyming words come at the ends of lines, as in "The Kraken," by Alfred, Lord Tennyson:

Below the thunders of the upper *deep;*
Far, far beneath in the abysmal **sea,**
His ancient, dreamless, uninvaded *sleep*
The Kraken sleepeth: faintest sunlights **flee**

Internal rhyme occurs when the rhyming words fall within a line.

See *also* Repetition *and* Rhyme Scheme.

RHYME SCHEME A *rhyme scheme* is a regular pattern of rhyming words in a poem. The rhyme scheme of a poem is indicated by using different letters of the alphabet for each new rhyme. In an *aabb* stanza, for example, line 1 rhymes with line 2 and line 3 rhymes with line 4.

Many poems use the same pattern of rhymes, though not the same rhymes, in each stanza.

See *also* Rhyme.

RHYTHM *Rhythm* is the pattern of *beats,* or stresses, in spoken or written language. Some poems have a very specific pattern, or meter, whereas prose and free verse use the natural rhythms of everyday speech.

See *also* Meter.

RISING ACTION See Plot.

SCENE See Drama.

SCIENCE FICTION *Science fiction* is writing that tells about imaginary events that involve science or technology. Many science-fiction stories are set in the future. The setting can be on Earth, in space, on other planets, or in a totally imaginary place. Ray Bradbury's "There Will Come Soft Rains" is an example of science fiction.

See *also* Fantasy.

SENSORY LANGUAGE Sensory language is writing or speech that appeals to one or more of the senses.

See *also* Image.

SESTET See Stanza.

SETTING The *setting* of a literary work is the time and place of the action. Time can include not only the historical period—past, present, or future—but also a specific year, season, or time of day. Place may involve not only the geographical place—a region, country, state, or town—but also the social, economic, or cultural environment.

In some stories, setting serves merely as a backdrop for action, a context in which the characters move and speak. In others, however, setting is a crucial element. The setting functions in a symbolic way in Albert Camus's "The Guest," p. 84.

Description of the setting often helps establish the mood of a story. For example, in Edgar Allan Poe's "The Masque of the Red Death," the setting contributes to the growing horror.

See also Mood.

SHORT STORY A *short story* is a brief work of fiction. The short story resembles the longer novel but generally has a simpler plot and setting. In addition, the short story tends to reveal character at a crucial moment rather than to develop it through many incidents. For example, Doris Lessing's "Through the Tunnel," p. 353, concentrates on what happens as Jerry learns to swim through the tunnel.

See also Fiction, Genre, and Novel.

SIMILE A *simile* is a figure of speech in which *like* or *as* is used to make a comparison between two basically unlike ideas. "Alexandra is as bright as Jason" is a comparison, not a simile. "Alexandra is as bright as a bulb" is a simile.

Poets often use similes. The following example from Yehoda Amichai's "A Pace Like That," p. 939, compares a person growing older to a worker in a manhole:

The longer you live, the more people there are who comment on your actions. Like a worker in a manhole: at the opening above him people stand around giving free advice

By drawing together different elements, effective similes make vivid and meaningful comparisons that enrich what the writer has to say.

See also Figurative Language.

SOLILOQUY A *soliloquy* is a long speech expressing the thoughts of a character alone on stage. In William Shakespeare's *The Tragedy of Julius Caesar*, Brutus begins a soliloquy while he is alone in his orchard. This soliloquy reveals Brutus' fears about how Caesar might change were he crowned king.

See also Monologue.

SONNET A *sonnet* is a fourteen-line lyric poem, usually written in rhymed iambic pentameter. The *English*, or *Shakespearean*, sonnet consists of three quatrains (four-line stanzas) and a couplet (two lines), usually rhyming *abab cdcd efef gg*.

The couplet usually comments on the ideas contained in the preceding twelve lines. The sonnet is usually not printed with the stanzas divided, but a reader can see distinct ideas in each.

The *Italian*, or *Petrarchan*, sonnet consists of an octave (eight-line stanza) and a sestet (six-line stanza). Often the octave rhymes *abbaabba* and the sestet rhymes *cdecde*. The octave states a theme or asks a question. The sestet comments on or answers the question. See Petrarch's sonnets on pp. 927–929.

The Petrarchan sonnet took its name from Petrarch, a fourteenth-century Italian poet. Once the form was introduced in England, it underwent changes. The Shakespearean sonnet is, of course, named after William Shakespeare.

See also Lyric Poem, Meter, and Stanza.

SPEAKER The *speaker* is the imaginary voice assumed by the writer of a poem. In many poems, the speaker is not identified by name. When reading a poem, remember that the speaker within the poem may be a person, an animal, a thing, or an abstraction. The speaker in Gabriela Mistral's "Fear," on p. 202, is a woman who fears for her daughter's future.

STAGE DIRECTIONS *Stage directions* are notes included in a drama to describe how the work is to be performed or staged. These instructions are printed in italics and are not spoken aloud. They are used to describe sets, lighting, sound effects, and the appearance, personalities, and movements of characters.

See also Drama.

STANZA A *stanza* is a formal division of lines in a poem, considered as a unit. Often the stanzas in a poem are separated by spaces.

Stanzas are sometimes named according to the number of lines found in them. A *couplet*, for example, is a two-line stanza. A *tercet* is a stanza with three lines. Other types of stanzas include the following:

1. *Quatrain*: four-line stanza
2. *Cinquain*: five-line stanza
3. *Sestet*: six-line stanza
4. *Heptastich*: seven-line stanza
5. *Octave*: eight-line stanza

Sonnets, limericks, and haiku all have distinct stanza forms. A *sonnet* is a fourteen-line poem that is made up either of three quatrains and a couplet or of an octave followed by a sestet. A *limerick* consists of a single five-line stanza with a particular pattern of rhymes. A *haiku* is made up of a single three-line stanza.

See also Haiku *and* Sonnet.

SURPRISE ENDING A *surprise ending* is a conclusion that violates the expectations of the reader but in a way that is both logical and believable. Barbara Kimenye's "The Winner," on p. 562, has a surprise ending.

SUSPENSE *Suspense* is a feeling of curiosity or uncertainty about the outcome of events in a literary work. Writers create suspense by raising questions in the minds of their readers.

SYMBOL A *symbol* is anything that stands for or represents something else. An object that serves as a symbol has its own meaning, but it also represents abstract ideas. Marks on paper can symbolize spoken words. A flag symbolizes a country. A flashy car may symbolize wealth. Writers sometimes use such conventional symbols in their work, but sometimes they also create symbols of their own through emphasis or repetition.

In Edgar Allan Poe's "The Masque of the Red Death," the masked figure symbolizes death and the clock symbolizes the passage of time.

TANKA A tanka consists of five unrhymed lines with a pattern of five, seven, five, seven, seven syllables. Tankas appear on p. 986.

TECHNICAL ARTICLE A *technical article* is a type of expository writing that explains a procedure, provides instructions, or represents specialized information. Often, specialized vocabulary is used. Sometimes, diagrams or charts illustrate complicated structures or steps.

TETRAMETER See Meter.

THEME A *theme* is a central message or insight into life revealed through a literary work. The theme is not a condensed summary of the plot. Instead, it is a generalization about people or about life that is communicated through the literary work.

The theme of a literary work may be stated directly or implied. In "The Princess and All the Kingdom," on p. 692, the moral is clearly and simply stated by the old chancellor, who explains to the prince that his conquests have brought him new responsibilities. In "The

Censors," on p. 694, a powerful message is also delivered, but no one states exactly what it is. The theme of Valenzuela's short story is not stated—it's implied.

When the theme of a work is *implied,* readers think about what the work seems to say about the nature of people or about life. The story or poem can be viewed as a specific example of the generalization the writer is trying to communicate.

Note that there is usually no single correct statement of a work's theme, though there can be incorrect ones. Also, a long work, like a novel or a full-length play, may have several themes. Finally, not all literary works have themes. A work meant only to entertain may have no theme at all.

TONE The *tone* of a literary work is the writer's attitude toward his or her audience and subject. The tone can often be described by a single adjective, such as *formal* or *informal, serious* or *playful, bitter* or *ironic.* Rachel Carson's awed and respectful tone in "The Marginal World" expresses her intensity as she seeks the meaning behind the beauty of the natural world.

TRAGEDY A *tragedy* is a work of literature, especially a play, that results in a catastrophe for the main character. In ancient Greek drama, the main character was always a significant person, a king or a hero, and the cause of the tragedy was a tragic flaw, or weakness, in his or her character. In modern drama, the main character can be an ordinary person and the cause of the tragedy can be some evil in society itself. The purpose of tragedy is not only to arouse fear and pity in the audience, but also, in some cases, to convey a sense of the grandeur and nobility of the human spirit.

Shakespeare's *The Tragedy of Julius Caesar* is a tragedy. Brutus is a brave and noble figure whose tragic flaw is assuming that honorable ends justify dishonorable means.

See also Drama.

TRIMETER See Meter.

VERBAL IRONY See Irony.

VILLANELLE A *villanelle* is a lyric poem written in three-line stanzas, ending with a four-line stanza. It has two refrain lines that appear initially in the first and third lines of the first stanza; then they appear alternately as the third line of subsequent stanzas, and finally, as the last two lines of the poem. Theodore Roethke's "The Waking" is an example of a villanelle.

THE WRITING PROCESS

A polished piece of writing can seem to have been effortlessly created, but most good writing is the result of a process of writing, rethinking, and rewriting. The process can roughly be divided into a series of stages: prewriting, drafting, revising, editing, proofreading, and publishing.

It's important to remember that the writing process is one that moves backward as well as forward. Even while you are moving forward in the creation of your composition, you may still return to a previous stage— to rethink or rewrite.

Following are stages of the writing process, with key points to address during each stage.

Prewriting

In this stage, you plan out the work to be done. You prepare to write by exploring ideas, gathering information, and working out an organization. Following are the key steps to take at this stage.

Step 1: Analyze the writing situation. Start by clarifying your assignment, so that you know exactly what you are supposed to do.

- *Focus your topic.* If necessary, narrow the topic—the subject you are writing about—so that you can write about it fully in the space you have.
- *Know your purpose.* What is your goal for this paper? What do you want to accomplish? Your purpose will determine what you include in it.
- *Know your audience.* Who will read your paper influences what you say and how you say it.

Step 2: Gather ideas and information. You can do this in a number of ways:

- *Brainstorm.* When you brainstorm, either alone or with others, you come up with possible ideas to use in your paper. Not all of your brainstormed ideas will be useful or suitable. You'll need to evaluate them later.
- *Consult other people about your subject.* Speaking informally with others may suggest an idea or approach you did not see at first.
- *Make a list of questions about your topic.* When your list is complete, find the answers to your questions.

- *Do research.* Your topic may require information that you don't have, so you will need to go to other sources to find information. There are numerous ways to find information on a topic. See the Research Handbook on p. 1029 for suggestions.

The ideas and information you gather will become the content of your paper. Not all of the information you gather will be needed. As you develop and revise your paper, you will make further decisions about what to include and what to leave out.

Step 3: Organize. First, make a rough plan for the way you want to present your information. Sort your ideas and notes; decide what goes with what and which points are the most important. You can make an outline to show the order of ideas, or you can use some other organizing plan that works for you.

There are many ways in which you can organize and develop your material. Use a method that works for your topic. Following are common methods of organizing information in the development of a paper:

- *Chronological Order* In this method, events are presented in the order in which they occurred. This organization works best for presenting narrative material or explaining in a "how to."
- *Spatial Order* In spatial order, details are presented as seen in space; for example, from left to right or from foreground to background. This order is good for descriptive writing.
- *Order of Importance* This order helps readers see the relative importance of ideas. You present ideas from most to least important or from least to most important.
- *Main Idea and Details* This logical organization works well to support an idea or opinion.

Drafting

When you draft, you put down your ideas on paper in rough form. Working from your prewriting notes and your outline or plan, you develop and present your ideas in sentences and paragraphs.

Don't worry about getting everything perfect at the drafting stage. Concentrate on getting your ideas down.

Draft in a way that works for you. Some writers work best by writing a quick draft—putting down all their ideas without stopping to evaluate them. Other writers prefer to develop each paragraph carefully and thoughtfully, making sure that each main idea is supported by details.

As you are developing a draft, keep in mind your purpose and your audience. These determine what you say and how you say it.

Don't be afraid to change your original plans during drafting. Some of the best ideas are those that were not planned at the beginning. Write as many drafts as you like. You can draft over and over until you've got it the way you like.

Most papers, regardless of the topic, are developed with an introduction, a body, and a conclusion. Here are tips for developing these parts:

Introduction In the introduction to a paper, you want to engage your readers' attention and let them know the purpose of your paper. You may use the following strategies in your introduction:

- State your main idea.
- Take a stand.
- Use an anecdote.
- Quote someone.
- Startle your readers.

Body of the paper In the body of your paper, you present your information and make your points. Your **organization** is an important factor in leading readers through your ideas. Your elaboration on your main ideas is also important. **Elaboration** is the development of ideas to make your written work precise and complete. You can use the following kinds of details to elaborate your main ideas:

- Facts and statistics
- Anecdotes
- Sensory details
- Examples
- Explanation and definition
- Quotations

Conclusion The ending of your paper is the final impression you leave with your readers. Your conclusion should give readers the sense that you have pulled everything together. Following are some effective ways to end your paper:

- Summarize and restate.
- Ask a question.
- State an opinion.
- Tell an anecdote.
- Call for action.

Revising

Once you have a draft, you can look at it critically or have others review it. This is the time to make changes—on many levels. Revising is the process of reworking what you have written to make it as good as it can be. You may change some details so that your ideas flow smoothly and are clearly supported. You may discover that some details don't work, and you'll need to discard them. Two strategies may help you start the revising process:

1. Read your work aloud. This is an excellent way to catch any ideas or details that have been left out and to notice errors in logic.
2. Ask someone else to read your work. Choose someone who can point out its strengths and suggest how to improve it.

How do you know what to look for and what to change? Here is a checklist of major writing issues. If the answer to any of these questions is no, then that is an area that needs revision.

1. Does the writing achieve your purpose?
2. Does the paper have unity? That is, does it have a single focus, with all details and information contributing to that focus?
3. Is the arrangement of information clear and logical?
4. Have you elaborated enough to give your audience adequate information?

Editing

When you edit, you look more closely at the language you have used, so that the way you express your ideas is most effective.

- Replace dull language with vivid, precise words.
- Cut or change redundant expressions (unnecessary repetition).
- Cut empty words and phrases—those that do not add anything to the writing.
- Check passive voice. Usually active voice is more effective.
- Replace wordy expressions with shorter, more precise ones.

Proofreading

After you finish your final draft, the last step is to proofread the draft to make it ready for a reader. You may do this on your own or with the help of a partner.

It's useful to have both a dictionary and a usage handbook to help you check for correctness. Here are the tasks in proofreading:

- Correct errors in grammar and usage.
- Correct errors in punctuation and capitalization.
- Correct errors in spelling.

THE MODES OF WRITING

Description

Description is writing that creates a vivid picture for readers, draws readers into a scene, and makes readers feel as if they are meeting a character or experiencing an event firsthand. A description may stand on its own or be part of a longer work, such as a short story.

When you write a description, bring it to life with sensory details, which tell how your subject looks, smells, sounds, tastes, or feels. You'll want to choose your details carefully so that you create a single main impression of your subject. Avoid language and details that don't contribute to this main impression. Keep these guidelines in mind whenever you are assigned one of the following types of description:

Observation In an observation, you describe an event that you have witnessed firsthand, often over an extended period of time. You may focus on an aspect of daily life or on a scientific phenomenon, such as a storm or an eclipse.

Remembrance When you write a remembrance, you use vivid, descriptive details to bring to life memorable people, places, or events from your past.

Description of a Place Often used to set the scene in a story or drama, your description of a place should convey the physical look and atmosphere of a scene—either interior or exterior.

Character Profile In a character profile, you capture a person's appearance and personality traits and reveal information about his or her life. Your subject may be a real person or a fictional character.

Narration

Whenever writers tell any type of story, they are using **narration.** While there are many kinds of narration, most narratives share certain elements—characters, a setting, a sequence of events (or plot, in fiction), and, often, a theme. You might be asked to try your hand at one of these types of narration:

Anecdote An anecdote, which may be oral or written, is a brief and often humorous narrative that is true or based on the truth. You may use an anecdote both to entertain and to make a general point about life.

Personal Narrative A personal narrative is a true story about a memorable experience or period in your life. In a personal narrative, your feelings about events shape the way you tell the story—even the way you describe people and places.

Firsthand Biography A firsthand biography tells about the life (or a period in the life) of a person whom you know personally. You can use your close relationship with the person to help you include personal insights not found in biographies based solely on research.

Short Story Short stories are short fictional, or made-up, narratives in which a main character faces a conflict that is resolved by the end of the story. In planning a short story, you focus on developing the plot, the setting, and the characters. You must also decide on a point of view: Will your story be told by a character who participates in the action or by someone who describes the action as an outside observer?

Exposition

Exposition is writing that informs or explains. The information you include in expository writing is factual or (when you're expressing an opinion) based on fact.

Your expository writing should reflect a well-thought-out organization—one that includes a clear introduction, body, and conclusion and is appropriate for the type of exposition you are writing. Here are some types of exposition you may be asked to write:

Cause-and-Effect Essay In a cause-and-effect essay, you consider the reasons something did happen or might happen. You may examine several causes of a single effect or several effects of a single cause.

Comparison-and-Contrast Essay When you write a comparison-and-contrast essay, you consider the similarities and differences between two or more subjects. You may organize your essay point by point—discussing each aspect of your subject in turn—or subject by subject—discussing all the qualities of one subject first and then the qualities of the next subject.

Problem-and-Solution Essay In a problem-and-solution essay, you identify a conflict or problem and offer a resolution. Begin with a clear statement of the problem and follow with a reasoned path to a solution.

Summary To write a summary or synopsis of an event or a literary work, you include only the details that your readers will need in order to understand the key features of the event or the literary work. Omit any personal opinions; include only factual details.

How-to Instructions You use how-to instruc

to explain the steps involved in doing a particular task. In writing instructions, it is also important to anticipate and answer questions the reader may have about why a particular procedure is being recommended.

Persuasion

Persuasion is writing or speaking that attempts to convince people to agree with a position or to take a desired action. When used effectively, persuasive writing has the power to change people's lives. As a reader and a writer, you will find yourself engaged in many forms of persuasion. Here are a few of them:

Persuasive Essay In writing a persuasive essay, you build an argument, supporting your opinions with a variety of evidence: facts, statistics, examples, statements from experts. You also anticipate and develop counter-arguments to opposing opinions.

Advertisement When you write an advertisement, you present information in an appealing way to make the product or service seem desirable.

Position Paper In a position paper, you try to persuade readers to accept your views on a controversial issue. Most often, your audience will consist of people who have some power to shape policy related to the issue. Your views in a position paper should be supported with evidence.

Persuasive Speech A persuasive speech is a piece of persuasion that you present orally instead of in writing. As a persuasive speaker, you use a variety of techniques, such as repetition of key points, to capture your audience's interest and to add force to your argument.

Letter to the Editor When you write a letter to the editor, you may be responding to an article or an editorial published earlier or you may be writing to express concern on an issue of importance to the community. Your letter should describe the issue briefly, present your views supported with evidence, and state any action you think should be taken.

Research Writing

Writers often use outside research to gather information and explore subjects of interest. The product of this research is called **research writing.** In connection with your reading, you may occasionally be asked one of the following types of research writing:

Biographical Report In a biographical report, you examine a person's life and achievements. You

include the dates and details of the main events in the person's life and, at times, make educated guesses about the reasons behind those events. For your biographical report, you may need to research not only the life of an individual but also the times in which he or she lived.

Research Paper A research paper uses information gathered from a variety of outside sources to explore a topic. In your research paper, you will usually include an introduction, in which your thesis, or main point, is stated; a body, in which you present support for the thesis; and a conclusion that summarizes, or restates, your main points. You should credit the sources of information, using footnotes or other types of citation, and include a bibliography, or general list of sources, at the end.

Multimedia Presentation In preparing a multimedia presentation, you will gather and organize information in a variety of media, or means of communication. You may use written materials, slides, videos, audiocassettes, sound effects, art, photographs, models, charts, and diagrams.

Creative Writing

Creative writing blends imagination, ideas, and emotions and allows you to present your own unique view of the world. Poems, plays, short stories, dramas, and even some cartoons are examples of creative writing. All are represented in this anthology and may provide inspiration for you to produce your own creative works, such as the following:

Lyric Poem In a lyric poem, you use sensory images, figurative language, and sound devices to express deep thoughts and feelings about a subject. To give your lyric poem a musical quality, employ sound devices, such as rhyme, rhythm, alliteration, and onomatopoeia.

Narrative Poem Writing a narrative poem is similar to writing a short story, with a plot, characters, and a theme. However, your narrative poem, unlike a story, will be divided into stanzas (groups of lines that form a unit) usually composed of rhyming lines that have a definite rhythm, or beat.

Song Lyrics In writing lyrics, or words, for a song, you use many elements of poetry—rhyme, rhythm, repetition, and imagery. In addition, your song lyrics should convey emotions, as well as interesting ideas.

Drama When you write a drama or a dramatic scene, you are writing a story that is intended to be performed. Since a drama consists almost entirely of the words and actions of the characters, be sure to write dialogue that clearly shows the characters' personalities, thoughts, and emotions, and stage directions that convey your ideas about sets, props, sound effects, and the speaking style and movements of the characters.

Response to Literature

In a **response to literature,** you express your thoughts and feelings about a work and often, in so doing, gain a better understanding of what the work is all about. Your response to literature can take many forms—oral or written, formal or informal. During the course of your reading, you may be asked to respond to a work of literature in one of these forms:

Literary Analysis In a literary analysis, you take a critical look at various important elements in the work. You then attempt to explain how the author has used those elements and how they work together to convey the author's message.

Retelling of a Fairy Tale Most fairy tales—stories about good and evil characters, giants, and magic deeds—have been handed down from generation to generation, and often the original authors are unknown. When you retell a fairy tale in your own way, you can add to the original or change it. For example, you might set it in another place or time period or write it as a poem or a drama.

Reader's Response Journal Entry Your reader's response journal is a record of your thoughts and feelings about works you have read. Use it to remind yourself of writers and works that you particularly liked or disliked or to provide a source of writing ideas.

Letter to an Author People sometimes respond to a work of literature by writing a letter to the author. You can praise the work, ask questions, or offer constructive criticism.

Critical Review In a critical review of a literary work, you discuss various elements in the work and offer opinions about them. You may also give a summary of the work and a recommendation to readers.

Practical and Technical Writing

Practical writing is fact-based writing that people do in the workplace or in their day-to-day lives. Business letters, memos, school forms, and job applications are examples of practical writing. **Technical writing,** which is also based on facts, explains procedures, provides instructions, or presents specialized information. You encounter technical writing every time you read a manual or a set of instructions.

In the following descriptions, you'll find tips for tackling several types of practical and technical writing:

Letter Requesting Information In a letter requesting information, you state the information you're searching for and ask any specific questions you have. In your letter, include your name and address so that you can receive a response. Include the date, which can help you or the recipient keep track of correspondence. It is also customary to include the address of the party to whom you are writing. Use a formal greeting followed by a colon. Keep the body of the letter as brief and clear as possible. Use a polite closing, and remember to sign as well as type or print your name.

News Release News releases announce factual information about upcoming events. Also called press releases, they are usually sent to local newspapers, local radio stations, and other media. When you write a news release, use this format: Position your name and phone number in the upper right corner. Then capture your main point in a centered headline, which will allow the recipient to see at a glance what the news release is about. In the body, present factual information in a concise way. You may begin with an opening location tag that tells in which town or city the news release originated. The numeral 30 or number signs (###) customarily indicate the end of the news release.

Guidelines When you write guidelines, you give information about how people should act or you provide tips on how to do something. List guidelines one by one, using somewhat formal language. Your guidelines may or may not be numbered. In addition to factual information, which should be complete and accurate, guidelines may contain your opinions.

Process Explanation In a process explanation, you offer a step-by-step explanation of how to do something. Your explanation should be specific, using headings, labels, or numbers to make the process clear. You may also include diagrams or other illustrations to further clarify the process.

GRAMMAR AND MECHANICS HANDBOOK

Nouns A **noun** is the name of a person, place, or thing. A **common noun** names any one of a class of people, places, or things. A **proper noun** names a specific person, place, or thing.

Common Noun	Proper Noun
city	Washington, D.C.

Pronouns A **pronoun** is a word that stands for a noun or for a word that takes the place of a noun.

A **personal pronoun** refers to (1) the person speaking, (2) the person spoken to, or (3) the person, place, or thing spoken about.

	Singular	Plural
First Person	I, me, my, mine	we, us, our, ours
Second Person	you, your, yours	you, your, yours
Third Person	he, him, his, she, her, hers, it, its	they, them, their, theirs

A **reflexive pronoun** ends in *-self* or *-selves* and adds information to a sentence by pointing back to a noun or a pronoun earlier in the sentence.

> I was saying to *myself*, "Ed, my boy, this is Everest— you've got to push it a bit harder!"
>
> —"The Final Assault," Edmund Hillary

An **intensive pronoun** ends in *-self* or *-selves* and simply adds emphasis to a noun or a pronoun in the same sentence.

> After a time, I *myself* was allowed to go into the dead houses and search for metal.
>
> —"By the Waters of Babylon," Stephen Vincent Benét

A **demonstrative pronoun** directs attention to a specific person, place, or thing.

> this these that those
>
> *These* are the juiciest pears I've ever tasted.

A **relative pronoun** begins a subordinate (relative) clause and connects it to another idea in the sentence.

> The poet *who* wrote "Fear" is Gabriela Mistral.

An **indefinite pronoun** refers to a person, place, or thing, often without specifying which one.

> And then, for a moment, *all* is still, ...
>
> —"The Masque of the Red Death," Edgar Allan Poe

Verbs A **verb** is a word that expresses time while showing an action, a condition, or the fact that something exists.

An **action verb** indicates the action of someone or something.

An action verb is **transitive** if it directs action toward someone or something named in the same sentence.

> He *dusted* his hands, muttering.
>
> —"Contents of the Dead Man's Pocket," Jack Finney

An action verb is **intransitive** if it does not direct action toward something or someone named in the same sentence.

> I *waved* and *shouted*, then as suddenly *stopped* as I realized my foolishness.
>
> —"The Final Assault," Edmund Hillary

A **linking verb** is a verb that connects the subject of a sentence with a noun or pronoun that renames or describes the subject. All linking verbs are intransitive.

> Romance at short notice *was* her specialty.
>
> —"The Open Window," Saki

A **helping verb** is a verb that can be added to another verb to make a verb phrase.

> Nor *did* I suspect that these experiences could be part of a novel's meaning.

Adjectives An **adjective** describes a noun or a pronoun or gives a noun or a pronoun a more specific meaning. Adjectives answer these questions:

What kind?	*blue* lamp, *large* tree
Which one?	*this* table, *those* books
How many?	*five* stars, *several* buses
How much?	*less* money, *enough* votes

The articles *the*, *a*, and *an* are adjectives. *An* is used before a word beginning with a vowel sound.

A noun may sometimes be used as an adjective.

> *diamond* necklace   *summer* vacation

Adverbs An **adverb** modifies a verb, an adjective, or another adverb. Adverbs answer the questions *where*, *when*, *in what way*, or *to what extent*.

> He could stand *there*. (modifies verb *stand*)
>
> He was *blissfully* happy. (modifies adjective *happy*)
>
> It ended *too* soon. (modifies adverb *soon*)

Prepositions A preposition relates a noun or a pronoun that appears with it to another word in the sentence.

before the end   *near* me   *inside* our fence

Conjunctions A conjunction connects other words or groups of words.

A **coordinating conjunction** connects similar kinds or groups of words.

mother *and* father   simple *yet* stylish

Correlative conjunctions are used in pairs to connect similar words or groups of words.

both Sue *and* Meg   *neither* he *nor* I

A **subordinating conjunction** connects two complete ideas by placing one idea below the other in rank or importance.

You would know him *if* you saw him.

Sentences A sentence is a group of words with a subject and a predicate. Together, these parts express a complete thought.

A **fragment** is a group of words that does not express a complete thought.

Subject and Verb Agreement To make a subject and verb agree, make sure that both are singular or both are plural.

Many *storms are* the cause of beach erosion.
Either the *cats* or the *dog is* hungry.
Neither *Angie* nor her *sisters were* present.
The *conductor,* as well as the soloists, *was applauded.*

Phrase A phrase is a group of words, without a subject and a verb, that functions in a sentence as one part of speech.

A **prepositional phrase** is a group of words that includes a preposition and a noun or a pronoun that is the object of the preposition.

outside my window   below the counter

An **adjective phrase** is a prepositional phrase that modifies a noun or a pronoun by telling *what kind* or *which one.*

The wooden gates *of that lane* stood open.

An **adverb phrase** is a prepositional phrase that modifies a verb, an adjective, or an adverb by pointing out *where, when, in what way,* or *to what extent.*

On a sudden impulse, he got to his feet.
—"Contents of the Dead Man's Pocket,"
Jack Finney

An **appositive phrase** is a noun or a pronoun with modifiers, placed next to a noun or a pronoun to identify it or add information and details.

M. Morissot, *watchmaker by trade but local militiaman for the time being,* stopped short . . .
—"Two Friends," Guy de Maupassant

A **participial phrase** is a participle with its modifiers or complements. The entire phrase acts as an adjective.

Choosing such a tide, I hoped for a glimpse of the pool.
—"The Marginal World," Rachel Carson

A **gerund phrase** is a gerund with modifiers or a complement, all acting together as a noun.

. . . moving along the ledge was quite as easy as he thought it would be.
—"Contents of the Dead Man's Pocket,"
Jack Finney

An **infinitive phrase** is an infinitive with modifiers, complements, or a subject, all acting together as a single part of speech.

To be alive to hear this song is a victory . . .
—"Old Song," Traditional

Clauses A clause is a group of words with a subject and a verb.

An **independent clause** has a subject and a verb and can stand by itself as a complete sentence.

A **subordinate clause** has a subject and a verb but cannot stand by itself as a complete sentence; it can only be part of a sentence.

An **adjective clause** is a subordinate clause that modifies a noun or a pronoun by telling *what kind* or *which one.*

For country people, *who only knew the dismantled tilting ground of Sir Ector's castle,* the scene which met their eyes was ravishing.
—"Arthur Becomes King of Britain,"
T. H. White

An **adverb clause** modifies a verb, an adjective, an adverb, or a verbal by telling *where, when, in what way, to what extent, under what condition,* or *why.*

She took up that magazine *when her daughter-in-law came in* . . .
—"The Good Deed," Pearl S. Buck

A **noun clause** is a subordinate clause that acts as a noun.

> *That you have wronged me* doth appear in this.
>
> —*The Tragedy of Julius Caesar,*
> William Shakespeare

Summary of Capitalization and Punctuation

CAPITALIZATION

Capitalize the first word of a sentence and also the first word in a quotation if the quotation is a complete sentence.

> "Mummy," he said, "I can stay under water for two minutes—..."
>
> —"Through the Tunnel," Doris Lessing

Capitalize all proper nouns and adjectives.

> W. W. Jacobs   Flanders Fields   African writers

Capitalize a person's title when it is followed by the person's name or when it is used in direct address.

> Reverend Tallboys   Mrs. Prothero   Major Moberly

Capitalize titles showing family relationships when they refer to a specific person, unless they are preceded by a possessive noun or pronoun.

> Grandmother   his father

Capitalize the first word and all other key words in the titles of books, periodicals, poems, stories, plays, paintings, and other works of art.

> *The Way to Rainy Mountain*   "Spring and All"

PUNCTUATION

End Marks Use a **period** to end a declarative sentence, an imperative sentence, an indirect question, and most abbreviations.

> She broke off with a little shudder.
>
> —"The Open Window," Saki

Use a **question mark** to end a direct question, an incomplete question, or a statement that is intended as a question.

> "Monkey's paw?" said Mrs. White curiously.
>
> —"The Monkey's Paw," W. W. Jacobs

Use an **exclamation mark** after a statement showing strong emotion, an urgent imperative sentence, or an interjection expressing strong emotion.

> "Bring him in! Bring him in now!"
>
> —"The Dog That Bit People,"
> James Thurber

Commas Use a **comma** before the coordinating conjunction to separate two independent clauses in a compound sentence.

> His arms had begun to tremble from the steady strain of clinging to his narrow perch, and he did not know what to do now ...
>
> —"Contents of the Dead Man's Pocket,"
> Jack Finney

Use commas to separate three or more words, phrases, or clauses in a series.

> Animals took shape: yellow giraffes, blue lions, pink antelopes, lilac panthers cavorting in crystal substance.
>
> —"There Will Come Soft Rains,"
> Ray Bradbury

Use commas to separate adjectives of equal rank. Do not use commas to separate adjectives that must stay in a specific order.

> I was immediately transported to the foot of mountains, with narrow defiles twisting in and out amongst their *towering, arid* peaks.
>
> —"The Cabuliwallah,"
> Rabindranath Tagore

Use a comma after an introductory word, phrase, or clause.

> When Marian Anderson again returned to America, she was a seasoned artist.
>
> —"Marian Anderson: Famous Concert Singer,"
> Langston Hughes

Use commas to set off parenthetical and nonessential expressions.

> All of these works, *of course,* had earlier left their marks ...
>
> —"Star Wars: A Trip to a Galaxy ...,"
> Vincent Canby

Use commas with places, dates, and titles.

> Poe was raised in Richmond, Virginia.
> August 4, 2026
> Alfred, Lord Tennyson

Use a comma to indicate words left out of an elliptical sentence, to set off a direct quotation, and to prevent a sentence from being misunderstood.

> Vincent Canby writes for *The New York Times;* Roger Ebert, for the *Chicago Sun Times.*

Semicolons Use a **semicolon** to join independent clauses that are not already joined by a conjunction.

> They could find no buffalo; *they had to hang an old hide from the sacred tree.*
>
> —*The Way to Rainy Mountain,*
> N. Scott Momaday

Use a semicolon to join independent clauses separated by either a conjunctive adverb or a transitional expression.

> James Thurber wrote many books; moreover, he was a cartoonist and a journalist.

Use semicolons to avoid confusion when independent clauses or items in a series already contain commas.

> There were the Useful Presents: engulfing mufflers of the old coach days, and mittens made for giant sloths; zebra scarfs of a substance like silky gum that could be tug-o'-warred down to the galoshes; . . .
>
> —"A Child's Christmas in Wales,"
> Dylan Thomas

Colons Use a **colon** in order to introduce a list of items following an independent clause.

> The authors we are reading include a number of poets: Robert Frost, Octavio Paz, and Emily Dickinson.

Use a colon to introduce a formal quotation.

> The next day Howard Taubman wrote enthusiastically in *The New York Times:*
> Marian Anderson has returned to her native land one of the great singers of our time . . .
>
> —"Marian Anderson: Famous Concert Singer,"
> Langston Hughes

Quotation Marks A **direct quotation** represents a person's exact speech or thoughts and is enclosed in quotation marks.

> "Clara, my mind is made up."
>
> —"With All Flags Flying," Anne Tyler

An **indirect quotation** reports only the general meaning of what a person said or thought and does not require quotation marks.

> She rattled on cheerfully about the shooting and the scarcity of birds, . . .
>
> —"The Open Window," Saki

Always place a comma or a period inside the final quotation mark.

> "There are ceremonies going on," I said, "and I am busy."
>
> —"The Cabuliwallah,"
> Rabindranath Tagore

Place a question mark or an exclamation mark inside the final quotation mark if the end mark is part of the quotation; if it is not part of the quotation, place it outside the final quotation mark.

> "If you only cleared the house, you'd be quite happy, wouldn't you?"
>
> —"The Monkey's Paw," W. W. Jacobs
>
> Have you ever read the poem "Africa"?

Use single quotation marks for a quotation within a quotation.

Use quotation marks around the titles of short written works, episodes in a series, songs, and titles of works mentioned as parts of a collection.

> "Making a Fist"   "These Are Days"

Underline or italicize titles of longer works, such as plays, movies, or novels.

Dashes Use **dashes** to indicate an abrupt change of thought, a dramatic interrupting idea, or a summary statement.

> It made her so mad to see Muggs lying there, oblivious of the mice—they came running up to her—that she slapped him and he slashed at her, but he didn't make it.
>
> —"The Dog That Bit People,"
> James Thurber

Parentheses Use **parentheses** to set off asides and explanations only when the material is not essential or when it consists of one or more sentences.

> Automatically I looked at our pressure gauges—just over 2,900 pounds (2,900 pounds was just over 700 liters; 180 into 700 was about 4). . .
>
> —"The Final Assault," Edmund Hillary

Hyphens Use a **hyphen** with certain numbers, after certain prefixes, with two or more words used as one word, and with a compound modifier coming before a noun.

fifty-two   greenish-blue water

Apostrophes Add an **apostrophe** and -s to show the possessive case of most singular nouns.

Prospero's castle   the playwright's craft

Add an apostrophe to show the possessive case of plural nouns ending in -s and -es.

the sailors' ships   the babies' mothers

Add an apostrophe and -s to show the possessive case of plural nouns that do not end in -s or -es.

the children's games   the people's friend

Use an apostrophe in a contraction to indicate the position of the missing letter or letters.

I *didn't* love any one of you more than the other.

—"A Visit to Grandmother," William Melvin Kelley

GLOSSARY OF COMMON USAGE

among, between

Among is usually used with three or more items. *Between* is generally used with only two items.

Among the poems we read this year, Eve Merriam's "Metaphor" was my favorite.

"Like the Sun" tells of one man's conflict *between* telling the truth and telling white lies.

amount, number

Amount refers to a mass or a unit, whereas *number* refers to individual items that can be counted. Therefore, *amount* generally appears with a singular noun, and *number* appears with a plural noun.

Being able to climb Mount Everest requires a huge *amount* of training.

In his story "The Masque of the Red Death," Poe uses a *number* of intriguing symbols.

any, all

Any should not be used in place of *any other* or *all*.

Rajika liked Anne Tyler's "With All Flags Flying" better

than *any other* short story.

Of *all* W. W. Jacobs's short stories, "The Monkey's Paw" is the most famous.

around

In formal writing, *around* should not be used to mean *approximately* or *about*. These usages are allowable, however, in informal writing or in colloquial dialogue.

Shakespeare's *Romeo and Juliet* had its first performance in *approximately* 1595.

Shakespeare was *about* thirty when he wrote this play.

as, because, like, as to

The word *as* has several meanings and can function as several parts of speech. To avoid confusion, use *because* rather than *as* when you want to indicate cause and effect.

Because Cyril was interested in the history of African American poetry, he decided to write his report on Langston Hughes.

Do not use the preposition *like* to introduce a clause that requires the conjunction *as*.

James Thurber conversed *as* he wrote—wittily.

The use of *as to* for *about* is awkward and should be avoided.

Rosa has an interesting theory *about* Edgar Allan Poe's choice of subject matter.

bad, badly

Use the predicate adjective *bad* after linking verbs such as *feel, look*, and *seem*. Use *badly* whenever an adverb is required.

Sara Teasdale's poem "There Will Come Soft Rains" shows clearly that the author felt *bad* about the destruction of the war.

In "Through the Tunnel," Jerry *badly* wants to be able to swim the length of the tunnel.

because of, due to

Use *due to* if it can logically replace the phrase *caused by*. In introductory phrases, however, *because of* is better usage than *due to*.

The popularity of the mystery is largely *due to* the works of Edgar Allan Poe.

Because of lack of oxygen, Edmund Hillary and

Tenzing Norgay moved more and more lethargically as they made their way up Everest.

being as, being that

Avoid these expressions. Use *because* or *since* instead.

> *Because* the protagonist of Anton Chekhov's "A Problem" is a static character, he changes little in the course of the story.

> *Since* there was a question about who reached the summit of Everest first, Tenzing Norgay decided to answer that question once and for all in his biography.

beside, besides

Beside is a preposition meaning "at the side of" or "close to." Do not confuse *beside* with *besides*, which means "in addition to." *Besides* can be a preposition or an adverb.

> As the three men cross the lawn and approach the open window, a brown spaniel trots *beside* them.

> There are many other Indian oral epics *besides* the *Ramayana.*

can, may

The verb *can* generally refers to the ability to do something. The verb *may* generally refers to permission to do something.

> Dylan Thomas describes his childhood Christmases so vividly that most readers *can* visualize the scene.

> Creon's edict states that no one *may* bury Polyneices.

different from, different than

The preferred usage is *different from*.

> The structure and rhyme scheme of a Shakespearean sonnet are *different from* the organization of a Petrarchan sonnet.

farther, further

Use *farther* when you refer to distance. Use *further* when you mean "to a greater degree" or "additional."

> The *farther* the ants travel, the more ominous and destructive they seem.

> The storm at the end of Act I of *The Tragedy of Julius Caesar further* hints at the ominous deeds to come.

fewer, less

Use *fewer* for things that can be counted. Use *less* for amounts or quantities that cannot be counted.

> Poetry often uses *fewer* words than prose to convey ideas and images.

> It takes *less* time to perform a Greek tragedy than to perform a Shakespearean play.

good, well

Use the adjective *good* after linking verbs such as *feel, look, smell, taste,* and *seem.* Use *well* whenever you need an adverb or as an adjective describing health.

> Caesar remarks that Cassius does not look *good*; on the contrary, his appearance is "lean" and "hungry."

> Twain wrote especially *well* when he described eccentric characters.

hopefully

You should not attach this adverb to a sentence loosely, as in "*Hopefully*, the rain will stop by noon." Rewrite the sentence so that *hopefully* modifies a specific verb. Other possible ways of revising such sentences include using the adjective *hopeful* or a phrase such as *everyone hopes that.*

> Dr. Martin Luther King, Jr., wrote and spoke *hopefully* about his dream of racial harmony.

> Mr. White was *hopeful* that the monkey's paw would bring him good fortune.

> Everyone *hopes* that the class production of *Antigone* will be a big success.

its, it's

Do not confuse the possessive pronoun *its* with the contraction *it's*, used in place of "it is" or "it has."

> In *its* very first lines, "The Stolen Child" establishes an eerie mood.

> In "The Street of the Cañon," Pepe knows that *it's* dangerous to attend Don Roméo's party.

just, only

When you use *just* as an adverb meaning "no more than," be sure you place it directly before the word it logically modifies. Likewise, be sure you place *only* before the word it logically modifies.

> *Just* one wish changed the Whites' lives forever.

> A short story can usually develop *only* a few characters, whereas a novel can include many.

kind of, sort of

In formal writing, you should not use these colloquial expressions. Instead, use a word such as *rather* or *somewhat*.

> Poe portrays Prince Prospero as *rather* arrogant.

> The tone of Tenzig Norgay's biography is *somewhat* defensive.

lay, lie

Do not confuse these verbs. *Lay* is a transitive verb meaning "to set or put something down." Its principal parts are *lay, laying, laid, laid. Lie* is an intransitive verb meaning "to recline." Its principal parts are *lie, lying, lay, lain.*

> The monkey's paw *lay* on the table in the living room for a while before anyone dared to pick it up.

> La belle dame sans merci enchants the knight as he *lies* in her "elfin grot."

leave, let

Be careful not to confuse these verbs. *Leave* means "to go away" or "to allow to remain." *Let* means "to permit."

> Threatening *Antigone* not to disobey his orders, Creon angrily *leaves* the stage.

> At first Mr. Carpenter's family does not want to *let* him enter the retirement home.

raise, rise

Raise is a transitive verb that usually takes a direct object. *Rise* is an intransitive verb and never takes a direct object.

> In his speech, Antony unexpectedly *raises* the subject of Caesar's will.

> When the Cabuliwallah comes to call, Mini *rises* from her chair and runs to greet him.

set, sit

Do not confuse these verbs. *Set* is a transitive verb meaning "to put (something) in a certain place." Its principal parts are *set, setting, set, set. Sit* is an intransitive verb meaning "to be seated." Its principal parts are *sit, sitting, sat, sat.*

> Antigone's conduct *sets* a high standard for all those who believe that conscience must be our ultimate guide.

> Jerry's mother *sits* in her beach chair while Jerry swims in the ocean.

so, so that

Be careful not to use the coordinating conjunction *so* when your context requires *so that. So* means "accordingly" or "therefore" and expresses a cause-and-effect relationship. *So that* expresses purpose.

> He wanted to do well on the test, *so* he read *The Tragedy of Julius Caesar* again.

> Antony uses eloquent rhetoric to stir up the people *so that* they will turn against the conspirators.

than, then

The conjunction *than* is used to connect the two parts of a comparison. Do not confuse *than* with the adverb *then*, which usually refers to time.

> I enjoyed "The Marginal World" more *than* "The Flood."

> Marian Anderson gave a triumphant singing recital in New York that evening, and she *then* embarked on a coast-to-coast American tour.

that, which, who

Use the relative pronoun *that* to refer to things or people. Use *which* only for things and *who* only for people.

> The poem *that* Cheryl liked the most was "The street."

> Haiku, *which* consists of only seventeen syllables, is often built around one or two vivid images.

> The assassin *who* strikes Caesar first is Casca.

unique

Because *unique* means "one of a kind," you should not use it carelessly to mean "interesting" or "unusual." Avoid such illogical expressions as "most unique," "very unique," and "extremely unique."

> Emily Dickinson's unconventional themes and bold experiments with form make her *unique* in the history of nineteenth-century American poetry.

when, where

Do not directly follow a linking verb with *when* or *where*. Be careful not to use *where* when your context requires *that.*

> **Faulty:** The exposition is *when* an author provides the reader with important background information.

> **Revised:** In the exposition, an author provides the reader with important background information.

> **Faulty:** Madras, India, is *where* R. K. Narayan was born.

> **Revised:** R. K. Narayan was born in Madras, India.

Speaking, Listening, and Viewing Handbook

Language—such as the literature in this book—is often written down. But even more often, it is communicated orally or visually. Oral and visual forms of communication involve speaking, listening, and viewing.

Having strong speaking, listening, and viewing skills will benefit you both in and out of school. Many of the assignments accompanying the literature in this textbook involve speaking, listening, and viewing skills. The terms in this handbook will give you a better understanding of the many elements that are part of oral and visual communication.

Oral and Visual Communication

You use oral and visual forms of communication in many types of situations every day. You use them in conversations as well as in class discussions, speeches, interviews, debates, performances, and media presentations. When you communicate face to face or before an audience, you may use more than spoken words to get your message across. When you speak on the phone, you rely on numerous verbal and listening skills.

The following terms will give you a better understanding of the many elements that are part of oral and visual communication:

ARTICULATION is the process of forming sounds into words by using the tongue, teeth, lower jaw, and soft palate to produce speech sounds.

BODY LANGUAGE refers to the use of facial expressions, eye contact, gestures, posture, and movement to communicate a feeling or an idea.

CONNOTATION is the set of associations a word calls to mind. The connotations of the words you choose influence the message you send. For example, most people respond more favorably to being described as "slim" rather than as "skinny." The connotation of *slim* is more appealing than that of *skinny*.

EYE CONTACT is direct visual contact with another person's eyes.

FEEDBACK is the set of verbal and nonverbal reactions that indicate to a speaker that a message has been received and understood.

GESTURES are the movements made with arms, hands, face, and fingers to communicate.

INFLECTION refers to the rise and fall in the pitch of the voice in speaking; it is also called **intonation.**

LISTENING is understanding and interpreting sound in a meaningful way. You listen differently for different purposes.

Listening for key information: For example, when a teacher gives an assignment, or when someone gives you directions to a place, you listen for key information.

Listening for main points: In a classroom exchange of ideas or information, or while watching a television documentary, you listen for main points.

Listening critically: When you evaluate a performance, song, or a persuasive or political speech, you listen critically, questioning and judging the speaker's message.

NONVERBAL COMMUNICATION is communication without the use of words. People communicate nonverbally through gestures, facial expressions, posture, and body movements. Sign language is an entire language based on nonverbal communication.

PROJECTION is speaking in such a way that the voice carries clearly to an audience. It's important to project your voice when speaking in a large space like a classroom or an auditorium.

VOCAL DELIVERY is the way in which you present a message. Your vocal delivery involves all of the following elements:

Volume: the loudness or quietness of your voice
Pitch: the high or low quality of your voice
Rate: the speed at which you speak; also called pace
Stress: the amount of emphasis placed on different syllables in a word or on different words in a sentence

All of these elements, individually and together, contribute to the meaning of a spoken message.

Speaking, Listening, and Viewing

The following terms apply to speaking, listening, and viewing presentations and productions:

AUDIENCE Your audience in any situation is the person or people to whom you direct your message. An audience can be a group of people sitting in a classroom or an auditorium observing a performance or just one person to whom you address a question or a comment. When preparing for any speaking situation, it's useful to analyze your audience, learning what you can about their background, interests, and attitudes so that you can tailor your message to them.

DEBATE A debate is a formal public-speaking situation in which participants prepare and present arguments on opposing sides of a question, stated as a **proposition.** The proposition must be controversial: It must concern an issue that may be solved in two different, valid ways.

The two sides in a debate are the *affirmative* (pro) and the *negative* (con). The affirmative side argues in favor of the proposition, while the negative side argues against it. The affirmative side begins the debate, since it is seeking a change in a belief or policy. The opposing sides take turns presenting their arguments, and each side has an opportunity for *rebuttal,* in which they may challenge or question the other side's argument.

DOCUMENTARY A documentary is a film that presents in-depth, factual information on a given topic. The topic may be about people, places, or events. Through visual and sound techniques, the documentary may communicate the filmmaker's analysis of the topic.

INTERVIEW An interview is a form of interaction in which one person, the interviewer, asks questions of another person, the interviewee. Interviews may take place for many purposes: to obtain information, to discover a person's suitability for a job or a college, or to inform the public of a notable person's opinions.

MEDIA PRESENTATION Media presentations convey information to viewers and listeners by means of radio, TV, films, videos, still photography, Internet Web pages, newspapers, magazines, animation, and other forms of visual art.

NEWSMAGAZINE refers to a television program that offers news about current topics. The newsmagazine is usually less objective, or strictly factual, than a **news report,** because it may include interviews, opinions, and viewer responses.

ORAL INTERPRETATION is the reading or speaking of a work of literature aloud for an audience. Oral interpretation involves explaining the ideas, meaning, or structure of a work of literature. The speaker interprets the work through his or her vocal delivery. **Poetry reading** and **storytelling,** in which a speaker reads a poem or tells a story expressively, are forms of oral interpretation.

PANEL DISCUSSION is a group discussion on a topic of interest common to all members of a panel and to a listening audience. A panel is usually composed of four to six experts on a particular topic who are brought together to share information and opinions.

PANTOMIME is a form of nonverbal communication in which an idea or a story is communicated completely through the use of gestures, body language, and facial expressions, without any words at all.

READERS THEATRE is a dramatic reading of a work of literature in which participants take parts from a story or play and read them aloud in expressive voices. Unlike a play, however, sets and costumes are not part of the performance, and the participants remain seated or standing as they deliver their lines.

ROLE PLAY To role-play is to take the role of a person or character and, as that character, act out a given situation, speaking, acting, and responding in the manner of the character.

SPECIAL EFFECTS are used in media presentations to communicate various types of things to viewers and listeners. They include artificial sounds and images. Special **visual and sound techniques,** often used to communicate in films, include unusual camera angles, reaction shots, sequencing, and music.

SPEECH A speech is a talk or an address given to an audience. A speech may be **impromptu**—delivered on the spur of the moment with no preparation—or formally prepared and delivered for a specific purpose or occasion.

- *Purposes:* The most common purposes of speeches are to persuade (for example, political speeches), to entertain, to explain, and to inform.
- *Occasions:* Different occasions call for different types of speeches. Speeches given on these occasions could be persuasive, entertaining, or informative, as appropriate. The following are common occasions for speeches.
  Introduction: Introducing a speaker or presenter at a meeting or assembly
  Presentation: Giving an award or acknowledging the contributions of someone
  Acceptance: Accepting an award or a tribute
  Keynote: Giving an inspirational address at a large meeting or convention
  Commencement: Honoring the graduates of a school or university

VISUAL REPRESENTATION Visual representations include informative texts, entertaining texts, and advertisements. They use elements of design—such as shape, line, color, and texture—to communicate.

*R*ESEARCH *H*ANDBOOK

Many of the assignments and activities in this literature book require you to find out more about your topic. Whenever you need ideas, details, or information, you must conduct research. You can find information by using library resources and computer resources, as well as by interviewing experts in a field.

Before you begin, create a research plan that lists the questions you want answered about your topic. Then decide which sources will best provide answers to those questions. When gathering information, it is important to use a variety of sources and not to rely on one main source of information. It is also important to document where you find different pieces of information you use so that you can cite those sources in your work.

The suggestions that follow can help you locate your sources.

Library Resources

Libraries contain many sources of information in both print and electronic form. You'll save time if you plan your research before actually going to the library. Make a list of the information you think you will need, and for each item list possible sources for the information. Here are some sources to consider:

NONFICTION BOOKS An excellent starting point for researching your topic, nonfiction books can provide either broad coverage or specific details, depending on the book. To find appropriate nonfiction books, use the library catalog, which may be in card files or in electronic form on computers. In either case, you can search by author, title, or subject; in a computer catalog, you can also search by key word. When you find the listing for a book you want, print it out or copy down the title, author, and call number. The call number, which also appears on the book's spine, will help you locate the book in the library.

NEWSPAPERS AND MAGAZINES Books are often not the best places for finding up-to-the-minute information. Instead, you might try newspapers and magazines. To find information about an event that occurred on a specific date, go directly to newspapers and magazines for that date. To find articles on a particular topic, use indexes like the *Readers' Guide to Periodical Literature*, which lists magazine articles under subject headings. For each article that you want, jot down the title, author (if given), page number or numbers, and the name and date of the magazine in which the article appears. If your library does not have the magazine you need, either as a separate issue or on microfilm, you may still be able to obtain photocopies of the article through an interlibrary loan.

REFERENCE WORKS The following important reference materials can also help you with your research.

- *General encyclopedias* have articles on thousands of topics and are a good starting point for your research, although they shouldn't be used as primary sources.
- *Specialized encyclopedias* contain articles in particular subject areas, such as science, music, or art.
- *Biographical dictionaries and indexes* contain brief articles on people and often suggest where to find more information.
- *Almanacs* provide statistics and data on current events and act as a calendar for the upcoming year.
- *Atlases*, or books of maps, usually include geographical facts and may also include information like population and weather statistics.
- *Indexes and bibliographies*, such as the *Readers' Guide to Periodical Literature*, tell you in what publications you can find specific information, articles, or shorter works (such as poems or essays).
- *Vertical files* (drawers in file cabinets) hold pamphlets, booklets, and government publications that often provide current information.

Computer Research

The Internet Use the Internet to get up-to-the-minute information on virtually any topic. The Internet provides access to a multitude of resource-rich sources such as news media, museums, colleges and universities, and government institutions. There are a number of indexes and directories organized by subject to help you locate information on the Internet, including Yahoo!, the World Wide Web Virtual Library, the Kids Web, and the Webcrawler. These indexes and directories will help you find direct links to information related to your topic.

Internet Sources and Addresses

- *Yahoo! Directory* allows you to do word searches or link directly to your topic by clicking on such subjects as the arts, computers, entertainment, or government.
  http://www.yahoo.com
- *World Wide Web Virtual Library* is a comprehensive and easy-to-use subject catalog that provides direct links to academic subjects in alphabetical order.
  http://celtic.stanford.edu/vlib/Overview.html
- *Kids Web* supplies links to reference materials, such as dictionaries, *Bartlett's Familiar Quotations*, a thesaurus, and a world fact book.
  http://www.npac.syr.edu/textbook/kidsweb/
- *Webcrawler* helps you to find links to information about your topic that are available on the Internet when you type in a concise term or key word.
  http://www.webcrawler.com

CD-ROM References

Other sources that you can access using a computer are available on CD-ROM. The Wilson Disk, Newsquest, the *Readers' Guide to Periodical Literature,* and many other useful indexes are available on CD-ROM, as are encyclopedias, almanacs, atlases, and other reference works. Check your library to see which are available.

Interviews as Research Sources

People who are experts in their field or who have experience or knowledge relevant to your topic are excellent sources for your research. If such people are available to you, the way to obtain information from them is through an interview. Follow these guidelines to make your interview successful and productive:

- Make an appointment at a time convenient to the person you want to interview, and arrange to meet in a place where he or she will feel comfortable talking freely.
- If necessary, do research in advance to help you prepare the questions you will ask.
- Before the interview, list the questions you will ask, wording them so that they encourage specific answers. Avoid questions that can be answered simply with *yes* or *no.*
- Make an audiotape or videotape of the interview, if possible. If not, write down the answers as accurately as you can.

- Include the date of the interview at the top of your notes or on the tape.
- Follow up with a thank-you note or phone call to the person you interviewed.

Sources for a Multimedia Presentation

When preparing a multimedia presentation, keep in mind that you'll need to use some of your research findings to illustrate or support your main ideas when you actually give the presentation. Do research to find media support, such as visuals, CDs, and so on—in addition to those media you might create yourself. Here are some media that may be useful as both sources and illustrations:

- Musical recordings on audiocassette or compact disk (CD), often available at libraries
- Videos that you prepare yourself
- Fine art reproductions, often available at libraries and museums
- Photographs that you or others have taken
- Computer presentations using slide shows, graphics, and so on
- Video- or audiocassette recordings of interviews that you conduct

INDEX OF AUTHORS AND TITLES

Page numbers in *italics* refer to biographical information.

INDEX OF SKILLS

CRITICAL THINKING AND VIEWING

WRITING

Writing Opportunities

Eulogy, 199
Evaluation, 417
Everyday epic, 243
Extended definition of friendship, 217
Extended definition of paradise, 72
Eyewitness account, 253
Fable update, 375
Fable, 752
Fairy tale, 394
Fan magazine interview, 535
Film treatment, 16, 503, 733, 789, 633, 643, 989, 979
Final speech, 844
Firsthand biography, 387, 800
Five morals, 375
Guide for reading, 138
Guidelines, 394
Haiku, 27, 989
Hall-of-fame placards, 161
Helmer's letter, 905
Hero, 243
How-to manual for new students, 186
Human interest article, 559
Humorous anecdote, 789
Imagery, 489
Instruction manual, 81
Interpreting a symbol, 1024
Interview questions, 304
Interview, 765, 662, 689
Introduction, 844
Inventory, 581
Journal entry, 27, 425, 662, 689
Justification, 407
Krogstad's letter, 887
Land advertisement, 289
Legend, 591
Letter, 119, 138, 199, 317, 362, 417, 481, 503, 733, 827, 1024, 1035
Letter of introduction, 186
Letter to a friend, 425, 777
Letter to a local leader, 138
Letter to a poet, 207, 297
Letter to an author, 341
Letter to an elected official, 699
Letter to Juan, 699
Letter to Sappho, 922
Letter to the author, 752
Letter to the editor, 489, 524, 933
letter to the embassy, 387
Letter to the Marchesa, 681
Letter writing, 270
Life poem, 341
List, 745
Literary analysis of a persona, 304
Literary analysis, 175, 329, 503, 581, 905
Literary interpretation, 81, 922
Literary review, 633
Location scout's report, 681
Lost-and-found announcement, 643
Lyric poem, 922, 971
Memory of a milestone, 442
Metaphor poem, 944
Modern quest, 1024
Monologue spoken by a plant or an animal, 599

Mountain's eye view, 161
Movie review, 765
Museum plaque, 59
Narrative about reaching a goal, 317
Narrative from another point of view, 643
Narrative poem, 990, 1024
Nature essay, 718
News article, 1045
News commentary, 464
News interview, 559
Newspaper article, 289, 633, 827, 959
Newspaper headlines, 175
Newspaper story, 425, 570
Observation, 362, 752
On-line message, 442
Opening argument, 1035
Parable, 289, 489
Personal credo, 317
Personal narrative, 1035
Persuasive essay, 700
Persuasive letter, 799
Poem about a turning point, 464
Poem, 207, 304, 503, 535, 559, 599
Poetic interpretation, 718
Poetic invitation, 979
Poetic response, 933
Police report, 97, 375
Political analysis, 799
Position paper, 426
Postcard, 42, 591
Prediction, 97
Press release, 765
Princess with a point of view, 699
Problem-and-solution essay, 342
Problem-solution letter, 111
Proposal for a nature documentary, 718
Proposal for a poetry anthology, 933
Prose poem, 489
Public service announcement, 989
Radio advertisement, 329
Real-life mystery, 789
Reflective essay, 799
Report of the Prussian officer, 217
Report, 733
Research paper, 1050
Respond to commentary, 777
Responding to literature on an essay test, 600
Response to criticism, 16, 42, 59, 81, 97, 633
Retelling from another point of view, 570
Review of a song, 394
Review of a story, 481
Review, 27
Satirical essay, 789
Scene of conflict, 844
School records, 417
Science-fiction story, 681
Script for a telephone conversation, 662
Script treatment proposal, 1035
Short story based on a poem, 207
Sketch of a comic hero, 1009
Song for a moment in the story, 591

Song, 119, 979
Speech, 765
Sports article, 407
Statement poem, 971
Story continuation, 175
Story from a different point of view, 618
Story outline, 407
Story sequel, 481, 662
Story, 971
Storytelling notes, 1045
Study notes: summary, 618
Summaries, 464
Surrealistic description, 270
Telegrams, 570
Timed-test essay, 120
Travel brochure, 97, 362
Travel feature, 42
Verse response, 799
Video script, 289
Water-safety rules, 362
Writing from another perspective, 455
Writing in the heroic tradition, 1045
Yearbook prediction, 175
Yearbook profiles, 217

Writing Skills
Accurate cultural details, 27
Appropriate details, 979
Appropriate language for your purpose, 1035
Audience knowledge, 1045
Balancing realistic and surrealistic details, 270
Be accurate, 426
Be brief and clear, 120
Brevity and clarity, 341, 559
Cause-and-effect relationships, 207
Choose a logical method of organization, 254
Choose words with appropriate connotations, 800, 908
Classification, 243
    development by, 42
Clear and logical organization, 1009, 1050
Clear beginning, development, and conclusion, 789
Clear explanation of procedures, 186, 289
Clear purpose and moral, 375
Concrete examples, 217
Concrete examples, 253
Connotation, 591
Consider what your audience knows, 700
Consistency of perspective, 455
Consistency of point of view, 643
Consistent focus, 944
Correct format, 699
Definition,
    development by, 959
Development by classification, 689
Effective dialogue, 317
Elaborate to make writing personal, 481, 489

SPEAKING, LISTENING, AND VIEWING

LIFE AND WORK SKILLS

ACKNOWLEDGMENTS (CONTINUED)

BPI Communications, Inc. "A Doll's House" (Belasco Theater, New York) theater review by David Sheward, from *Back Stage*, April 18, 1997, v38 n16 p60(1). Copyright © 1997 BPI Communications, Inc. Used by permission.

Carcanet Press Limited "He and I" by Natalia Ginzburg, translated by Dick Davis from *The Little Virtues*. Copyright © 1962 by Giulio Einaudi editore s.p.a. Translation copyright © 1985 by Dick Davis. Reprinted by permission.

Cartouche, Inc. "My Darling, You Are the Glow in My Eyes" by Ahmed Shatta, translated by Tahseen Alkoudsi from *Habibi Ya Nour El Ain* (My Darling, You Are the Glow in My Eyes)–www.shira.net. Copyright © Tahseen Alkoudsi.

CNN.com Excerpt from "Mars Pathfinder enlisted in search of lost Polar Lander" from CNN.com, January 25, 2000.

Toby Cole for the Pirandello Estate "A Day Goes By" from *Luigi Pirandello: Short Stories by Luigi Pirandello*, translated by Frederick May. Copyright © 1965 by The Pirandello Estate. Used by permission of the Pirandello Estate and Toby Cole, Agent.

Columbia University Press and Oxford University Press UK "In Spring It Is the Dawn" and "The Cat Who Lived in the Palace" from *The Pillow Book of Sei Shonagon* by Sei Shonagon, translated and edited by Ivan Morris. Used by permission.

Crown Publishers, a division of Random House, Inc. "Damon and Pythias" from *Classic Myths to Read Aloud* by William F. Russell, Ed.D. Copyright © 1988 by William F. Russell. Reprinted by permission of Crown Publishers, a division of Random House, Inc.

Darhansoff and Verrill Literary Agency "I Am Not One of Those Who Left the Land . . ." from *Poems of Akhmatova* by Anna Akhmatova, selected, translated, and introduced by Stanley Kunitz and Max Hayward. Copyright © 1973.

Dorling Kindersley Publishing, Inc. From *Birds of the World* (pg. 187) by Colin Harrison and Alan Greensmith. Text copyright © 1993 by Colin Harrison and Alan Greensmith. Photo copyright for Schalow's Turaco © R. Van Nostrand. Photo copyright for Red-crested Turaco © Dorling Kindersley.

Doubleday, a division of Random House, Inc. From *An Introduction to Haiku* by Harold G. Henderson, copyright © 1958 by Harold G. Henderson. "The Bridge" by Leopold Staff from *Postwar Polish Poetry* by Czeslaw Milosz, copyright 1965 by Czeslaw Milosz. "Half a Day" from *The Time and Place and Other Stories* by Naguib Mahfouz, copyright © 1991 by the American University in Cairo Press. From *The Diary of Anne Frank: The Critical Edition* by Anne Frank, translated by Arnold J. Pomerans & B. M. Mooyaart-Doubleday from *The Diary of Anne Frank: The Critical Edition*. Copyright © 1986 by Anne Frank-Fonds, Basle/Switzerland, for all texts of Anne Frank. Used by permission of Doubleday, a division of Random House, Inc.

Doubleday, a division of Random House, Inc. and Harold Ober Associates, Inc. "Civil Peace" from *Girls at War and Other Stories* by Chinua Achebe, copyright © 1972, 1973 by Chinua Achebe. Used by permission.

Dutton Signet, a division of Penguin Putnam Inc. "A Doll House" from *The Complete Major Prose Plays of Henrik Ibsen* by Henrik Ibsen, translated by Rolf Fjelde. Copyright © 1965, 1970, 1978 by Rolf Fjelde. Used by permission of Dutton Signet, a division of Penguin Putnam Inc.

Eastern Washington University Press "Small White Clothes"("Ropitas Blancas"), from *Poemas de Las Madres*, by Gabriela Mistral. © Gabriela Mistral, 1992, © Doris Dana, 1996. *The Mothers' Poems*, translation by Christiane Jacox Kyle. © Christiane Jacox Kyle, 1996 (by permission of Doris Dana). Published by Eastern Washington University Press, MS-1, 705 W. 1st Avenue, Spokane, Washington, 1-800-508-9095. Used by permission.

Roger Ebert "'Star Wars' Breakthrough Film Still Has the Force" by Roger Ebert from *Chicago Sun Times*, January 1997. Copyright © 1977 The Ebert Co., Ltd. Used by permission of Roger Ebert.

Farrar, Straus & Giroux, LLC. "Comrades" from *Jump and Other Stories* by Nadine Gordimer. Copyright © 1991 by Felix Licensing B.V. All rights reserved. Excerpt from "A Walk to the Jetty" from *Annie John* by Jamaica Kincaid. © 1985 by Jamaica Kincaid. Excerpt from "Canto I" from *The Inferno of Dante, A New Verse Translation*, translated by Robert Pinsky. Copyright © 1994 by Farrar, Straus & Giroux. English translation copyright © 1994 by Robert Pinsky. From *Cora Fry's Pillow Book* by Rosellen Brown. Copyright © 1994 by Rosellen Brown. Excerpt from *Nobel Lecture* by Alexander Solzhenitsyn, translated by F.D. Reeve. Copyright © 1972 by the Nobel Foundation. Translation copyright © 1972 by Farrar, Straus & Giroux. "A Storm in the Mountains" from *Stories and Prose Poems* by Alexander Solzhenitsyn, translated by Michael Glenny. Translation copyright © 1971 by Michael Glenny. "The Bracelet" from *The Collected Stories of Colette* edited by Robert Phelps, and translated by Matthew Ward. Translation copyright © 1983 by Farrar, Straus & Giroux, LLC.

Foreign Languages Press "This Too Is Life" from *Selected Works of Lu Hsun* and "My Old Home" from *Selected Stories of Lu Hsun*, translated by Yang Hsien-yi and Gladys Yang. Published and copyrighted by Foreign Languages Press, Beijing, China, 1960. Reproduced by permission of the publisher.

Jennifer Gosse for the Estate of Sir Edmund Gosse "In the Orchard" from *An Anthology of World Poetry* by Henrik Ibsen, translated by Edmund Gosse. Reprinted by permission.

Grove/Atlantic Inc. "I Built My House Near Where Others Dwell" by T'ao Ch'ien from *Anthology of Chinese Literature* edited by Cyril Birch. Copyright © 1965 by Grove Press, Inc. Used by permission of Grove/Atlantic Inc.

Harcourt, Inc. "Antigone" from *Sophocles, the Oedipus Cycle: An English Version* by Dudley Fitts and Robert Fitzgerald, copyright © 1939 by Harcourt, Inc. and renewed 1967 by Dudley Fitts and Robert Fitzgerald. CAUTION: All rights, including professional, amateur, motion picture, recitation, lecturing, performance, public reading, radio broadcasting, and television are strictly reserved. Inquiries on all rights should be addressed to Harcourt, Inc., Permissions Department, Orlando, FL 32887-6777. "How to React to Familiar Faces" from *How to Travel with a Salmon and Other Essays* by Umberto Eco, copyright © Gruppo Editoriale Fabbri, Bompiani, Sonzogno, Etas S.p.A., English translation by William Weaver copyright © 1994 by Harcourt, Inc. "Charles Baudelaire: L'invitation au Voyage" from *Things of This World*, copyright © 1956 and renewed 1984 by Richard Wilbur. "The Garden of Stubborn Cats" from *Marcovaldo or the Seasons in the City* by Italo Calvino, copyright © 1963 by Giulio Einaudi editore s.p.a., Torino, English translation by William Weaver copyright © 1983 by Harcourt, Inc. and Martin Secker & Warburg, Ltd. Reprinted by permission of the publisher.

HarperCollins Publishers, Inc. "A Very Old Man With Enormous Wings" from *Leaf Storm and Other Stories* by Gabriel García Márquez. Copyright © 1971 by Gabriel García Márquez. Reprinted by permission of HarperCollins Publishers, Inc.

1971 by Schocken Books. Reprinted by permission of Schocken Books, a division of Random House, Inc.

Scientific American "The Spider and the Wasp" by Alexander Petrunkevitch, from *Scientific American,* August 1952. Copyright 1952 by Scientific American, Inc. All rights reserved. Reprinted with permission.

Scribner, a division of Simon & Schuster, Inc. "Ha'penny" from *Tales from a Troubled Land* by Alan Paton. Copyright © 1961 Alan Paton, renewed 1989 by Anne Paton. From *Kaffir Boy* by Mark Mathabane. Copyright © 1986 by Mark Mathabane. Reprinted by permission of Scribner, a division of Simon & Schuster.

La Societe Nouvelle Presence Africaine "Childhood" and "The Lion's Awakening" from *Sundiata: An Epic of Old Mali* by D.T. Niane, translated by G.D. Pickett. Copyright © Presence Africaine, 1960 (original French version: *Soundjata, ou L'Epopee Mandingue*). © Longman Group Ltd. (English). "Africa" from *Coup de Pilon* by David Diop. © 1956 Presence Africaine, Paris.

Sony ATV Music Publishing "Yesterday" by John Lennon and Paul McCartney. Copyright © 1965 Sony/ATV Songs LLC. (Renewed) All rights administered by Song/ATV Music Publishing, 8 Music Square West, Nashville, TN 37203. All Rights Reserved. Used by permission.

Rosalie Torres-Rioseco "The Glass of Milk" by Manuel Rojas, translated by Zoila Nelken from *Short Stories of Latin America* edited by Arturo Torres-Rioseco, translated by Zoila Nelken and Rosalie Torres-Rioseco. Copyright © 1963 by Las Americas Publishing Company. Reprinted by permission.

Joanna Trzeciak "Some Like Poetry" by Wislawa Szymborska, translated by Joanna Trzeciak from *The New Yorker,* October 1996. Copyright © 1996 by Wislawa Szymborska. All rights reserved. Reprinted by permission.

Charles E. Tuttle Co., Inc, of Boston, Massachusetts, and Tokyo, Japan "The Story of Princess Amaradevi" from *Cambodian Folk Stories from the Gatiloke* retold by Muriel Paskin Carrison from a translation by The Venerable Kong Chhean. Copyright © 1987 by Charles E. Tuttle Co. "Under Reconstruction" by Mori Orgai from *Modern Japanese Stories.* Copyright in Japan, 1962 by Charles E. Tuttle Co. All rights reserved. Used by permission.

David Unger "The Censors" from *Short Stories* by Luisa Valenzuela. Copyright © 1976 by Luisa Valenzuela, renewed 1988. Translation copyright © 1982 by David Unger, first published in *Short Stories,* ed. Howe, David Godine. Used by permission of the translator.

University of California Press "A Pace Like That" from *The Selected Poetry of Yehuda Amichai* by Yehuda Amichai, translated by Chana Bloch. Copyright © 1996 The Regents of the University of California. "Although They Are," "And Their Feet Move," "You Know the Place: Then" and "Awed by Her Splendor" from *Sappho: A New Translation* by Mary Bernard. Copyright © 1958 The Regents of the University of California; © renewed 1986 by Mary Bernard. Reprinted by permission of the University of California Press.

University of Chicago Press "The Brahman, the Thief, and the Ghost" and "The Mice That Set Elephants Free" from *The Panchatantra* translated by Arthur W. Ryder. Copyright 1952 by The University of Chicago; copyright renewed 1953 by Mary E. Ryder and Winifred Ryder. All rights reserved. Book XXII, "The Death of Hector" from *Iliad of Homer,* translated by Richmond Lattimore. Copyright 1951, The University of Chicago. Reprinted by permission.

University of Georgia Press "The Grail" from *Perceval* or *The Story of the Grail* by Chretien de Troyes, translated by Ruth Harwood Cline. Copyright © 1983 by Ruth Harwood Cline. Reproduced by permission of University of Georgia Press.

University of Massachusetts Press "Can You?" translated by Robert Marquez, reprinted from *Man-Making Words: Selected Poems of Nicolas Guillen,* transl., annot., with an introduction by Robert Marquez and David Arthur McMurray (Amherst: The University of Massachusetts Press, 1972), copyright © 1972 by Robert Marquez and David Arthur McMurray. Used by permission.

University of North Carolina Press "The Street of the Canon" from *Mexican Village* by Josefina Niggli. Copyright © 1945 by the University of North Carolina Press, renewed 1972 by Josefina Niggli. Used by permission of the publisher.

University of Texas Press "I love a girl, but she lives over there," p. 21; "I think I'll go home and lie very still," p. 72; "My heart remembers how I once loved you," p. 112 from *Love Songs of the New Kingdom,* translated from the Ancient Egyptian by John L. Foster and illustrated with hieroglyphics drawn by John L. Foster. Copyright © 1969, 1970, 1971, 1972, 1973, 1974 by John L. Foster. Reproduced by permission of the University of Texas Press.

Viking Penguin, a division of Penguin Putnam Inc. "Under the Banyan Tree" (pp. 187–92), copyright © 1969 by R.K. Narayan, from *Under the Banyan Tree* by R.K. Narayan. Used by permission of Viking Penguin, a division of Penguin Putnam Inc.

Tino Villanueva and James Hoggard "I Only Know That Now/Solo se que ahora" from *Cronica de mis años peores* by Tino Villanueva, translated into English by James Hoggard. Copyright 1987 by Tino Villanueva. Translation copyright by James Hoggard. Used by permission.

Villard Books, a division of Random House, Inc. Excerpts from *Into Thin Air* by Jon Krakauer. Copyright © 1997 by Jon Krakauer. Reprinted by permission of Villard Books, a division of Random House, Inc.

Vintage Books, a division of Random House, Inc. From *Speak, Memory* by Vladimir Nabokov. Copyright © 1960, 1966 by Vladimir Nabokov. Reprinted by permission of Vintage Books, a division of Random House, Inc.

Visva-Bharati University "The Cabuliwallah" from *The Tagore Reader* by Rabindranath Tagore. Copyright © 1945 Rabindranath Tagore. Used by permission.

Wake Forest University Press "The Butterfly" from *Francis Ponge: Selected Poems* translated by C.K. Williams. Copyright © C.K. Williams, John Montague, and Margaret Guiron and Wake Forest University Press. Used by permission.

Walker Publishing Company "Birds" from *The Complete Fiction of Bruno Schulz* by Bruno Schulz, translated by Celina Wieniewska. Copyright © 1989 by Ella Podstolski-Schulz. Reprinted by permission of Walker Publishing Company.

Wallace Literary Agency "Rama's Initiation" from *The Ramayana* by R.K. Narayan. Published by Penguin Books. Copyright © 1972 by R.K. Narayan. Used by permission.

A.M. Watkins for the Estate of Vernon Watkins "Roses" ("Comme on voit sur la branche") by Pierre Ronsard, translated by Vernon Watkins from *Poems from France.* Copyright © A.M. Watkins. Used by permission.

A P Watt Ltd. "A Problem" by Anton Chekhov, translated by Constance Garnett. Reproduced by permission of A P Watt Ltd. on behalf of the Executor of the Estate of Constance Garnett.

Weldon Owen Publishing, Australia "Lightning and Thunder" extract by Eleanor Vallier-Talbot from *The Nature Company Guides: Weather* © Weldon Owen Pty Ltd. Reprinted by permission.

Euphemia Ann Wolfe "When You Are Old" by Pierre de Ronsard, translated by Humbert Wolfe from *Poems of France.*

NOTE: Every effort has been made to locate the copyright owner of material reprinted in this book. Omissions brought to our attention will be corrected in subsequent printings.

ART CREDITS

Cover and Title Page: Corel Professional Photos CD-ROM™; **v:** *The Forest, Inferno I* (detail). New York Public Library Special Collections, *L'Enfer de Dante Alighieri avec dessins de Gustave Dore,* 1862; **vi:** *Amphora,* Greece, Attica, Athens, about 480 B.C.; The Dutuit Painter. *Hephaestus Making Armor for Achilles* (detail). Ceramic, Red Figure; H: 34.2 cm. (13 ¹/₂ in.) Francis Bartlett Fund, 13.188. Courtesy, Museum of Fine Arts, Boston. Reproduced with permission.©1999 Museum of Fine Arts, Boston. All Rights Reserved; **vii:** (bl) ©Neil Rabinowitz/ CORBIS; (br) *Ladies offering a lemon and a mandragora root to another lady during a banquet.* Detail of a wall painting in the tomb of Nakht, scribe and priest under Pharaoh Thutmosis IV (18th Dynasty), in the cemetery of Sheikh Abd al-Qurnah. Photo ©Erich Lessing/Art Resource, NY; **viii:** (bl) *Akbar inspecting the wild elephant captured from the herd near Malwa, from the 'Akbarnama'* (detail), Mughal, c. 1590, (illustrated text). Victoria and Albert Museum, London, UK/ Bridgeman Art Library; (br) Kandinsky, Wassily (1866-1944), *Cossacks, 1910-11.* ©2001 Artists Rights Society (ARS), New York/ADAGP, Paris. Tate Gallery, London/Art Resource, NY; **ix:** Sun Jingbo, *Dawei* (detail), 1982. Photography by Joan Lebold Cohen; **x:** ©Marc & Evelyn Bernheim/Woodfin Camp & Associates; **xi:** (bl) Gustave Caillebotte (1848-1894). *Man on a Balcony, Boulevard Haussmann, 1880.* Oil on canvas, 117 x 90 cm. Private Collection, Switzerland. Photo ©Erich Lessing/Art Resource, NY; (br) Joan Slatkin/Omni-Photo Communications, Inc.; **xii:** ©Kevin Schafer/ Corbis; **xiii:** Paramount Pictures and Elkins Productions of Canada Ltd. The Kobal Collection, New York; **xiv:** Kim Ki-chang, born 1914. *Mountain Landscape in Moonlight,* 1975. Ink and color on silk, 19 ³/₄ x 21 ³/₄ in. (overall: 24 x 26 in.). Brooklyn Museum of Art, Gift of Dr. and Mrs. Peter Reimann. 81.124. **xv:** Pablo Picasso, Spanish, 1881-1973, *The Old Guitarist,* oil on panel, 1903/04, 122.9 x 82.6 cm. Helen Birch Bartlett Memorial Collection, 1926.253. Photograph ©1998 courtesy of The Art Institute of Chicago. All Rights Reserved, ©2001 Estate of Pablo Picasso/Artists Rights Society (ARS), New York; **xvi:** Photofest; **xxx–1:** *Walking Lions in relief* (detail). One of a pair. Wall of the processional street, Babylon. Mesopotamian, Babylonian. Ceramics. Period of Nebuchadnezzar II (605–562 B.C.). Tin-enameled earthenware, molded and glazed in colors. H. 3 ft. 2-¹/₄ in., L. 7 ft. 5-¹/₂ in. The Metropolitan Museum of Art, Fletcher Fund, 1931. (31.13.1) Photograph © 1993 The Metropolitan Museum of Art; **2:** (clockwise from top left) NASA; © Copyright 2001 PhotoDisc, Inc.; NASA; © Copyright 2001 PhotoDisc, Inc.; Gerry Gay/The Image Bank; Tony Stone Images; Tony Stone Images; **3:** (l) NASA; (c) © Copyright 2001 PhotoDisc, Inc.; (r) Gerry Gay/The Image Bank; **4:** (l) NASA; (c) © Copyright 2001 PhotoDisc, Inc.; (r) NASA; **5:** (l) NASA; (c) © Copyright 2001 PhotoDisc, Inc.; (r) Gerry Gay/The Image Bank; **6:** © Corbis/Bettmann Archive; **11:** Giraudon/Art Resource, NY; **17:** *Wall painting of a bird in a garden,* Pompeii, 1st century A.D. (fresco). Private Collection/Bridgeman Art Library; **18:** (t) T'ao Ch'ien, Collection of the National Palace Museum, Taipei, Taiwan, Republic of China; (c) Heibonsha/Pacific Press Service; (b) The Granger Collection, New York; **20:** Wang Chien, *White Clouds Over Xiao and Xiang,* Courtesy of the Freer Gallery of Art, Smithsonian Institution, Washington, DC. F1956.27; **20–21:** (background) Corel Professional Photos CD-ROM™; **22:** Christie's, New York; **24:** Shunsho, *Triptych of Snow, Moon, and Flower* (center panel, detail depicting Lady Murasaki at her desk), Museum of Art, Atami, Japan; **28:** Scala/Art Resource, NY; **32, 37:** New York Public Library Special Collections, *L'Enfer de Dante Alighieri avec dessins de Gustave Dore,* 1862; **45:** *Group of votive statuettes, Tell Asmar (ancient Ashnunak).* Square Temple of the god Abu—carved in the style of the Diyala River Valley region; materials include limestone, alabaster and gypsum; probably Early Dynastic I–II Period, ca. 2900–2600 B.C.; excavated by the Iraq Expedition of The Oriental Institute of the University of Chicago, February 13, 1935. Courtesy of The Oriental Institute of the University of Chicago. Photographed by Victor J. Boswell, 1982; **46:** *Ziggurat at Ur, 2250–2233 B.C.,* Hirmer Verlag München; **47:** *Babylonian globe, c. 500 B.C.* British Museum, London/ Bridgeman Art Library; **48 (profile), 51 (front view):** Bagdad Museo, Scala/Art Resource, NY; **52:** *Front of lyre from tomb of Queen Pu-abi,* Early Dynastic period, c. 2685–2290 B.C. ©Copyright The British Museum; **55:** New York Public Library, Astor, Lenox, and Tilden Foundations; **56:** *Transporting Timber by Sea* (Alabaster Relief from the Palace of King Sargon II at Khorsabad), 721–705 B.C. Louvre, Paris ©Photo RMN; **60:** Guido Reni, *Moses with the Tablets of the Law* (detail). Galleria Borghese, Rome, Italy. Scala/Art Resource, NY; **64–5:** Scala/Art Resource, NY; **67:** *David Composing the Psalms,* Illustrated Paris Psalter, 10th century. Bibliothéque nationale de France photographic plate; **68:** *Il Buon Pastore (The Good Shepherd),* Early Christian, 4th century. Vatican Museum. Scala/Art Resource, NY; **70:** *King James Bible, New Testament title page.* By Permission of the Folger Shakespeare Library, Washington, DC. (STC 2216); **73:** *Mechanical Elements,* 1918–23 (oil on canvas) by Fernand Leger (1881–1955). Kunstmuseum, Basle, Switzerland ©2001 Artists Rights Society (ARS), New York/ ADAGP, Paris. Peter Willi/Bridgeman Art Library; **74:** (l) The Granger Collection, Ltd.; (r) UPI/Corbis/Bettmann; **77:** Georg Baselitz, *Untitled, 1983.* Charcoal and gouache on paper, 24x17 in. (61x43.2 cm). Signed and dated (lower right): G. Baselitz VI, 1983. The Metropolitan Museum of Art, Purchase, Anna-Maria and Stephen Kellen Foundation Gift. 1990. (1990.14) Photograph ©1990/Metropolitan Museum of Art; **82:** ©Bettmann/CORBIS; **85:** Giraudon/Art Resource, NY; **86:** Eugene Delacroix, *Arab at the Door of His House,* Rijksmuseum; **89:** Giraudon/ Art Resource, NY; **90:** *Arabe assis de face, les mains croisees (Seated Arab),* (detail), Eugene Delacroix (1798–1863), 1832, watercolor. Louvre, Paris ©Photo RMN – J. G. Berizzi; **94–5:** Sylvain Grandadam/Photo Researchers, Inc.; **98:** Photograph courtesy Gail E. Mathabane; **101:** James P. Blair/NGS Image Collection; **102:** ©Christine Pemberton/ Omni-Photo Communications, Inc.; **107:** M. Courtney Clarke/ Photo Researchers, Inc.; **108:** Richard Lord; **112:** Photo ©Miriam Berkley; **114:** Corel Professional Photos CD-ROM™; **115:** ©Bruna Stude/ Omni-Photo Communications, Inc.; **116:** ©Wolfgang Kaehler 2001 www.wkaehlerphoto.com; **120:** Ken Karp Photography; **123:** Corel Professional Photos CD-ROM™; **126–7:** Biblioteca Riccardiana, Firenze, Italy; **128:** John Johnson Ltd., London, UK; **131:** Photo ©2000 by Stan Schnier; **134–5:** ©Russell Thompson/Omni-Photo Communications, Inc.; **139:** Rene Magritte (1898–1967), *Le Modele Vivant.* ©2001 C. Herscovici, Brussels/Artists Rights Society (ARS), New York. Christie's Images/ SuperStock, Inc.; **140:** (l) ©Bettmann/CORBIS; (r) AP/Wide World Photos; **142–3:** ©Fotopic/Omni-Photo Communications, Inc.; **146–7:** Paul Keel/ Photo Researchers, Inc.; **149:** Corbis/ Bettmann-UPI; **150:** ©Fotopic/Omni-Photo Communications, Inc.; **154:** The Granger Collection, New York; **155:** Guido Alberto Rossi/The Image Bank; **156:** Paul Keel/Photo Researchers, Inc.; **158:** ©Fotopic/ Omni-Photo Communications, Inc.; **162:** (l) Magnum Photos, Inc. ©Susan Meiselas; (r) Orest Adamovich Kiprensky (1782-1836), *Portrait of the poet Pushkin,* Tretyakov Gallery, Moscow, Russia. Scala/Art Resource, NY; **164:** Rene Magritte (1898–1967), *La Nuit (Night).* Private Collection. ©2001 C. Herscovici, Brussels/Artists Rights Society (ARS), New York. Art Resource, NY; **166:** George Tooker, *Door,* 1972, egg tempera on gesso panel, 24" x 24." New Britain Museum of American Art, Connecticut. Gift of Olga H. Knoepke; **171:** Marc Chagall, *The Lights of Marriage* (detail). Kunsthaus, Zurich ©2001 Artists Rights Society (ARS), New York/ADAGP, Paris; **176:** Photo by Sigrid Estrada; **179:** José Antonio Velásquez, *San Antonio De Oriente* (detail), 1957. Oil on canvas. 26 x 37 Inches. Art Museum of the Americas, OAS, Washington, DC; **181:** Lois Mailou Jones, *Port de la Saline, Haiti;* **185:** *Fragment of an Indian Animal Carpet,* Unknown artist, third quarter of the 16th century, The Textile Museum, Washington, DC, R63.00.20A; **187:** Photo: John Lei/Omni-Photo Communications, Inc.; **188:** AP Photo/File; **191:** Pfc. G.A. Haynia ©CORBIS; **192:** UPI/Corbis; **196:** Sgt. Robert Holliway ©CORBIS; **197:** Todd Gipstein ©CORBIS; **200:** (t) UPI/Corbis/ Bettmann; (c) AP Photo/ Mary Kent; (b) Magnum Photos, Inc. ©Sergio Larrain; **202:** Pablo Picasso (1881–1973). *Woman with Child.* Museo Picasso, Barcelona, Spain ©2001 Estate of Pablo Picasso/Artists Rights Society (ARS), New York. Scala/Art Resource, NY; **205:** Hamilton Wright/AP Photo; **208:** ©Corbis-Bettmann; **211:** Georges Seurat

(1859–1891). *The Anglers,* study for *La Grand Jatte.* Oil on wood panel, 1883. 6 1/4 x 9 7/8 in. (16 x 25 cm). Musee Nat. d'Art Moderne, Troyes, France. Giraudon/Art Resource, NY; **212:** Scala/Art Resource, NY; **218:** Scala/Art Resource, NY; **220:** Blaine Harrington III/Stock Market; **225:** Culver Pictures, Inc.; **230:** Giraudon/Art Resource, NY; **234:** *Andromache and Priam Urging Hector Not to Go to War.* From a series of tapestries: The Story of the Trojan War. Probably produced through Pasquier Grenier of Tournai, about 1472–1474. Wool and silk. H. 15 feet 10 in. W. 8 feet 8 in. (4.83 m x 2.64 m). Probably made for Charles the Bold. Textiles-Tapestries. Netherlandish, South. Late 15th Century, 1470–90. The Metropolitan Museum of Art, Fletcher Fund, 1939. (39.74) Photograph © 1992 The Metropolitan Museum of Art; **239:** Amphora, Greece, Attica, Athens, about 480 B.C.; The Dutuit Painter. *Hephaestus Making Armor for Achilles.* Ceramic, Red Figure; H: 34.2 cm. (13 1/2 in.) Courtesy Museum of Fine Arts, Boston, Francis Bartlett Fund, 13.188. Reproduced with permission. ©1999 Museum of Fine Arts, Boston. All Rights Reserved; **244:** ©Corbis-Bettmann; **246:** Giraudon/Art Resource, NY; **254:** (t) Lisa Quinones/Black Star/PictureQuest; (b) Hiroyuki Matsumoto/Black Star/PictureQuest; **258:** Ken Karp Photography; **260:** The Granger Collection, New York; **262:** Magnum Photos, Inc. ©1989 Chris Steele-Perkins; **263:** ©Will & Deni McIntyre/Tony Stone Images; **265, 267:** ©Wolfgang Kaehler 2001 www.wkaehlerphoto.com; **271:** Shraga Weil, *Pilgrimage,* serigraph. Courtesy of Pucker Gallery, Inc., Boston, Massachusetts; **272:** Tretyakov Gallery, Moscow, Russia. TASS/Sovfoto; **274:** Scala/Art Resource, NY; **274–87: (background)** Corel Professional Photos CD-ROM™; **279:** Art Resource, NY; **281:** Scala/Art Resource, NY; **284:** ©David Brookover/Photonica; **290, 292:** Photo ©Erich Lessing/Art Resource, NY; **293:** *Lid of a canopic jar, representing a royal woman of the Amarna period.* Egyptian. Funerary Customs–Canopic jars. Dynasty 18, reign of Amenhotep IV/Akhenaten, ca. 1353–1336 B.C. from western Thebes, tomb 55 in the Valley of the Kings. Alabaster, with stone and glass inlay. H. 7 in. (17.8 cm.) The Metropolitan Museum of Art, Theodore M. Davis Collection, Bequest of Theodore M. Davis, 1915. (30.8.54). Photograph by Bruce White ©1996 The Metropolitan Museum of Art; **298:** Sophie Bassouls/Corbis Sygma; **301:** Josef Albers, (1888–1976), *Homage to the Square,* 1958. Galleria Naziona d'Arte Moderna, Rome ©2001 The Josef and Anni Albers Foundation/ Artists Rights Society (ARS), New York; **305:** *Three Jumping Carp,* Yi Dynasty, 19th century, The Brooklyn Museum of Art, Gift of Mr. and Mrs. Burton Krouner, 82.79; **306:** Photo Valerie Wilmer. From *African Writers Talking,* edited by Dennis Duerden and Cosmo Pieterse, Africana Publishing Corporation, New York, 1972. Copyright ©1972 by Dennis Duerden and Cosmo Pieterse. Reprinted by permission of the publisher; **309:** ©SEF/Art Resource, NY; **310:** ©Neil Rabinowitz/CORBIS; **311:** ©Adam Woolfitt/ CORBIS; **314:** Lois Mailou Jones, *Ubi Girl from Tai Region.* The Hayden Collection, Courtesy, Museum of Fine Arts, Boston. Reproduced with permission. ©1999 Museum of Fine Arts, Boston. All Rights Reserved; **318:** UPI/Corbis-Bettmann; **321:** Gustav Klimt, *The Old Burgtheater, 1888–1889.* Historisches Museum der Stadt Wien, Vienna; **325:** *At the Theatre (La Premiere Sortie)* (detail), 1876–1877 (oil on canvas) by Pierre Auguste Renoir (1841–1919). National Gallery, London, UK/ Bridgeman Art Library; **332:** Hokusai, *The Poet Li Po Admiring a Waterfall,* c.1830. Honolulu Academy of Arts. Gift of James A. Michener 1969 (21.892); **334:** (t) AP/Wide World Photos; (c), (b) Photo ©Dorothy Alexander; **336:** AP/Wide World Photos; **338:** Wen Zhengming (1470?1559), *Old Trees by a Cold Waterfall,* Ming dynasty, 1531. 86 1/2 x 17 1/8 inches (209.55 x 43.50 cm); Roller width 20 1/2 in. (52.07 cm), hanging scroll, ink and color on paper. Los Angeles County Museum of Art. The Ernest Larsen Blanck Memorial Collection. 55.67.1 Photograph ©2000 Museum Associates/LACMA; **342:** ©Kee Van den Berg/Photo Researchers, Inc.; **346:** Bob Daemmrich/ Stock Boston/PictureQuest; **348–9:** New York Public Library, Astor, Lenox and Tilden Foundations; **350:** Thomas Victor/Harriet Spurlin; **353:** ©1995 Yukimasa Hirota/Photonica; **354–5:** Suzanne Nagler, *The Beach Treat* (detail), Photograph ©Stephen Tucker, Collection of Mr. and Mrs. X. Daniel Kafcas; **357:** Dennis Angel, *The Diver,* oil on panel, 40" x 32"; **359:** Childe Hassam (1859–1935), *Coast Scene, Isles of Shoals.* Oil on canvas. H: 24-7/8; W: 30-1/8 inches (63.2 x 76.5 cm.). The Metropolitan Museum of Art,

Gift of George A. Hearn, 1909 (09.72.6) Copyright ©2001 by The Metropolitan Museum of Art; **363:** Art Resource, NY; **365:** The Granger Collection, New York; **367:** Scala/Art Resource, NY; **371:** *Akbar inspecting the wild elephant captured from the herd near Malwa,* from the 'Akbarnama,' Mughal, c. 1590, (illustrated text). Victoria and Albert Museum, London, UK/ Bridgeman Art Library; **376:** The Granger Collection, New York; **378–9:** Peter & Georgina Bowater/The Image Bank; **383:** Corel Professional Photos CD-ROM™; **388:** AP/Wide World Photos; **390–1:** Stock Illustration Source, Inc.; **395:** Giorgio de Chirico, *The Torment of the Poet,* 1914. Yale University Art Gallery, Bequest of Kay Sage Tanguy. (1963.43.2). ©2001 Artists Rights Society (ARS), New York/SIAE, Rome; **398:** Edmund Dulac, *Illustration from 'Arabian Nights'* for the story "The Fisherman and the Jinnie." NY, Scribner's & Sons: 1907, Photo courtesy of the New York Public Library, Astor, Lenox and Tilden Foundations; **403:** Photo by John Lei/Omni-Photo Communications, Inc.; **408:** ©CORBIS; **410:** Photo by John Lei/Omni-Photo Communications, Inc.; **412:** James Blair/NGS Image Collection; **413:** Georg Gerster/Photo Researchers, Inc.; **414:** *Port Elizabeth, Old Town,* 1940 (oil on hard board) by Robert Broadley (1908–89). South African National Gallery, Cape Town, South Africa/Bridgeman Art Library; **418:** ©Hulton Getty/Liaison Agency; **420–1:** Kandinsky, Wassily (1866–1944), *Cossacks, 1910–11.* Tate Gallery, London ©2001 Artists Rights Society (ARS), New York/ ADAGP, Paris. Art Resource, NY; **426:** Corel Professional Photos CD-ROM™; **429:** Kopstein/Monkmeyer; **430:** Ken Karp Photography; **432:** Pham Luan (b. 1954), *Spring Returns to the Streets,* 1998. Oil on canvas, H: 52 inches W: 60 inches. Photograph courtesy of Judith Hughes Day, Fine Contemporary Vietnamese Art; **434:** From collection of Rene Guerra. Photo V. Velikzhanin, ITAR-TASS/Sovfoto; **435:** Family archives, the Estate of Vladimir Nabokov. Smith Skolnik; **438:** ©Tina Merandon/ Photonica; **443:** Photo ©Erich Lessing/Art Resource, NY; **444:** Magnum Photos, Inc. ©1999 Susan Meiselas; **446–447:** Salvador Dali, *Landscape of Port Lligat,* (1950) Oil on canvas, 23 x 31 inches, Collection of the Salvador Dali Museum, St. Petersburg, Florida. Copyright 2000 Salvador Dali Museum, Inc.; **449:** Odilon Redon (1840–1916), *Vieillard aile barbu (Old Man with Wings and Beard),* 1895. Louvre, D.A.G. (fonds Orsay) ©Photo RMN - Arnaudet; **450:** Odilon Redon, *The Accused,* 1886. Charcoal on paper, 21" x 14 5/8" (53.3 x 37.1 cm). Acquired through the Lillie P. Bliss Bequest. Photograph ©2000 The Museum of Modern Art, New York; **452:** Odilon Redon, *Rodolphe Bresdin,* 1865. Charcoal and black chalk; 31 x 24.2 cm. Louvre, D.A.G. (fonds Orsay). ©Photo RMN - M. Bellot; **456:** (t), (c) The Granger Collection, New York; (b) ©Archive Photos; **459:** Corel Professional Photos CD-ROM™; **460:** Art Zamur/Liaison Agency; **461:** ©Archive Photos; **465:** *They Did Not Expect Him,* 1884, by Ilya Efimovich Repin (1844-1930). Tretyakov Gallery, Moscow, Russia/Bridgeman Art Library; **466:** Courtesy of New Directions; **469:** James McMullan, *Untitled (People Arrested During the Cultural Revolution).* James McMullan, Inc.; **472:** Sun Jingbo, *Dawei,* 1982, Photography by Joan Lebold Cohen; **477:** *Rise with Force and Spirit* by James Bama ©1989, The Greenwich Workshop, Inc. All artwork by James Bama has been reproduced with the permission of The Greenwich Workshop, Inc. For information on limited edition fine art prints contact The Greenwich Workshop, Inc., One Greenwich Place, Shelton, CT 06484 USA; **482:** (t) Agence France-Presse; (b) The Granger Collection, Ltd.; **484:** ©G. R. Roberts/ Omni-Photo Communications, Inc.; **486:** Giorgio de Chirico (1888–1978). *Enigma of the Hour,* 1912. Coll. Mattloll, Mllan, Italy ©2001 Artists Rights Society (ARS), New York/SIAE, Rome; **490:** ©Wolfgang Kaehler 2000 www.wkaehlerphoto.com; **492:** *Jewelled elephant from Thailand,* 20th century. Private Collection/Bridgeman Art Library; **496–7:** Tran Nguyen Dan, *Peacefulness,* Indochina Arts Project; **499:** ©Wolfgang Kaehler 2000 www.wkaehlerphoto.com; **504:** Corel Professional Photos CD-ROM™; **508:** Ken Karp Photography; **510–11:** Photo William Campbell/TIME Magazine; **512:** China Photo Service/ Eastfoto; **518:** Photo courtesy of Joan Lebold Cohen; **525:** SuperStock, Inc.; **526:** J. P. Gauthier/Globe Photos; **527:** Gifford/Liaison International; **528:** ©Grace Davies/Omni-Photo Communications, Inc.; **530:** (l) ©Farrel Grehan/Photo Researchers, Inc.; (c) ©Jack Fields/Photo Researchers, Inc.; (r) ©Grace Davies/Omni-Photo Communications, Inc.; **532:** Gifford/Liaison International; **536:** Photo ©Miriam Berkley;